The International Handbook of Suicide and Attempted Suicide

The International Handbook of Suicide and Attempted Suicide

Edited by
Keith Hawton
Department of Psychiatry, Oxford University, UK
and
Kees van Heeringen
Department of Psychiatry, University of Gent, Belgium

JOHN WILEY & SONS, LTD
Chichester · New York · Weinheim · Brisbane · Singapore · Toronto

National 01243 779777
International (+44) 1243 779777
e-mail (for orders and customer service enquiries): cs-books@wiley.co.uk
Visit our Home Page on http://www.wiley.co.uk
or http://www.wiley.com

Reprinted November 2000

Published in Paperback May 2002

Other Wiley Editorial Offices

John Wiley & Sons, Inc., 605 Third Avenue,
New York, NY 10158-0012, USA

WILEY-VCH GmbH, Pappelallee 3,
D-69469 Weinheim, Germany

Jacaranda Wiley Ltd, 33 Park Road, Milton,
Queensland 4064, Australia

John Wiley & Sons (Asia) Pte Ltd, 2 Clementi Loop #02-01,
Jin Xing Distripark, Singapore 129809

John Wiley & Sons (Canada) Ltd, 22 Worcester Road,
Rexdale, Ontario M9W 1L1, Canada

Library of Congress Cataloging-in-Publication Data

The international handbook of suicide and attempted suicide / edited by Keith Hawton and Kees van Heeringen.
p. cm.
Includes bibliographical references and index.
ISBN 0-471-98367-5 (cased)
1. Suicide. 2. Suicidal behavior. I. Hawton, Keith, 1942– II. Heeringen, Kees van.
HV6545.I59 2000
362.28—dc21 99-059519

British Library Cataloguing in Publication Data

A catalogue record for this book is available from the British Library

ISBN 0-471-98367-5 (hbk)
0 470 84959 2 (pbk)

Typeset in 10/12pt Times by SNP Best-set Typesetter Ltd., Hong Kong
Printed and bound in Great Britain by TJ International Ltd, Padstow, Cornwall
This book is printed on acid-free paper responsibly manufactured from sustainable forestry, in which at least two trees are planted for each one used for paper production.

Contents

About the Editors

Keith Hawton is Professor of Psychiatry at Oxford University and Consultant Psychiatrist to Oxford Mental Healthcare Trust at the Warneford Hospital in Oxford. He is Director of the Centre for Suicide Research at Oxford University Department of Psychiatry, where he is responsible for a broad programme of interdisciplinary research concerning the causes, treatment and prevention of suicidal behaviour. The work of Professor Hawton and his research team has particularly focused on suicidal behaviour in young people, the epidemiology of attempted suicide, specific occupations and other groups at risk of suicide, media influences on suicidal behaviour, and the development and evaluation of treatments for suicide attempters. He is a member of the International Academy for Suicide Research, the International Association for Suicide Prevention, the American Academy of Suicidology and the American Foundation for Suicide Prevention. In 1995 the International Association for Suicide Prevention presented him with the Stengel Research Award for his research on suicide prevention.

Kees van Heeringen is Professor of Psychiatry at the University of Gent, Chef de Clinique at the Department of Psychiatry of the University Hospital of Gent, and Director of the Unit for Suicide Research at the University of Gent, Belgium. He has carried out research on suicidal behaviour for many years in local, national and international projects and acts as a consultant for the development of national and international suicide prevention programmes. His research interests are the epidemiology of suicidal behaviour and the study of the relationship between psychological and biological characteristics in the development of suicidal behaviour.

List of Contributors

Christer Allgulander, *Karolinska Institute, Neurotec, Department of Clinical Neuroscience, Division of Psychiatry, M57, Huddinge University Hospital, S-141 86 Huddinge, Sweden*

Louis Appleby, *School of Psychiatry and Behavioural Sciences, Withington Hospital, West Didsbury, Manchester M20 8LR, UK*

Alan Apter, *Department of Child and Adolescent Psychiatry, Sackler School of Medicine, Tel Aviv University, Geha Hospital, PO Box 102, Petach Tikva 49100, Israel*

Simon Armson, *The Samaritans, 10 The Grove, Slough, Berkshire SL1 1QP, UK*

Unni Bille-Brahe, *Unit for Suicidological Research, Tietgens Allé 108, 5230 Odense M, Denmark*

Christopher H. Cantor, *Australian Institute for Suicide Research and Prevention, Griffith University, Nathan, Queensland 4111, Australia*

Jose Catalan, *Imperial College of Science, Technology and Medicine, University of London, Psychological Medicine Unit, Chelsea and Westminster Hospital, 369 Fulham Road, London SW10, UK*

Andrew T. A. Cheng, *Division of Epidemiology and Public Health, Institute of Biomedical Sciences, Academia Sinica, Taipei 11529, Taiwan*

Sheila E. Clark, *Department of General Practice, University of Adelaide, Adelaide 5005, South Australia*

John Connolly, *St Mary's Hospital, Castlebar, Ireland*

Philip J. Cowen, *Psychopharmacology Research Unit, University of Oxford, Warneford Hospital, Oxford OX3 7JX, UK*

Marc De Hert, *University Centre St Jozef, Leuvensesteenweg 517, B-3070 Kortenberg, Belgium*

Diego De Leo, *Australian Institute for Suicide Research and Prevention, Griffith University, Nathan, Brisbane, Queensland 4111, Australia*

Erik Jan de Wilde, *Faculty of Social and Behavioural Sciences, Department of Clinical and Health Psychology, Leiden University, Pieter de la Court Building, Wassenaarseweg 52, PO Box 9555, 2300 RB Leiden, The Netherlands*

Marlene EchoHawk, *Alcoholism and Substance Abuse Program, Indian Health Service, Headquarters West, 5300 Homestead Road, Albuquerque, NM 87110, USA*

Ornit Freudenstein, *Department of Child and Adolescent Psychiatry, Sackler School of Medicine, Tel Aviv University, Geha Psychiatric Hospital, PO Box 120, Petach Tikva 49100, Israel*

Danute Gailiene, *University of Vilnius, Traidenio 27, 2004 Vilnius, Lithuania*

Robert D. Goldney, *The Adelaide Clinic, 33 Park Terrace, Gilberton, South Australia 5081, and Department of Psychiatry, University of Adelaide, Adelaide, South Australia 5005, Australia*

Madelyn Gould, *Columbia University College of Physicians and Surgeons and School of Public Health, and New York State Psychiatric Institute, PI Annex, 722 West 168th Street, New York, NY 10032, USA*

Daniel Harwood, *Section of Old Age Psychiatry, University Department of Psychiatry, Warneford Hospital, Oxford OX3 7JX, UK*

Keith Hawton, *Centre for Suicide Research, University Department of Psychiatry, Warneford Hospital, Oxford OX3 7JX, UK*

Philip Hazell, *Discipline of Psychiatry, Faculty of Medicine and Health Sciences, University of Newcastle, Callaghan, New South Wales 2308, Australia*

Zhao Xiong He, *Guangxi Academy of Social Sciences, Nanning, Guangxi, People's Republic of China*

Heidi L. Heard, *Department of Psychology, University of Washington, Seattle, WA 98195, USA*

Robin Jacoby, *Section of Old Age Psychiatry, University Department of Psychiatry, Warneford Hospital, Oxford OX3 7JX, UK*

Rachel Jenkins, *WHO Collaborating Centre, Institute of Psychiatry, De Crespigny Park, Denmark Hill, London SE5 8AF, UK*

Ad J.F.M. Kerkhof, *Department of Clinical Psychology, Vrije Universiteit, De Boelelaan 1109, 1081 HV Amsterdam, The Netherlands*

Natalia Kokorina, *Kemorovo State Medical Academy, N. Ostrovosky Street 23-33, 99 Kemerovo 650099, Russia*

Chau-Shoun Lee, *Department of Psychiatry, Lotung Poa-Ai Hospital, Lotung, Ilan, Taiwan*

Antoon Leenaars, *University of Leiden, The Netherlands, and 880 Ouellette Avenue, Suite 7-806, Windsor, Ontario, Canada N9A 1C7*

David Lester, *Center for the Study of Suicide, RR41, 5 Stonegate Road, Blackwood, NJ 08012, USA*

Marsha M. Linehan, *Behavioral Research and Therapy Clinics, Department of Psychology, University of Washington, Seattle, WA 98195-1525, USA*

Jouko K. Lönnqvist, *Department of Mental Health and Alcohol Research, National Public Health Institute, Mannerheimintie 166, SF-00300 Helsinki, Finland*

Andrew A. Lopatin, *Kemorovo State Medical Academy, N. Ostrovosky Street 23-33, 99 Kemerovo 650099, Russia*

J. John Mann, *Department of Neuroscience, New York State Psychiatric Institute, Columbia University, 1051 Riverside Drive, Box 42, New York, NY 10032, USA*

Peter M. Marzuk, *Joan and Sanford I. Weill Medical College of Cornell University, New York, NY 10021, USA*

Konrad Michel, *Psychiatrische Poliklinik, Universitätsspital, Mürtenstrasse 21, CH-3010 Bern, Switzerland*

George E. Murphy, *Washington University, 4940 Children's Place, St. Louis, MO 63110-1093, USA*

R. Srinivasa Murthy, *Department of Psychiatry, National Institute of Mental Health and Neurosciences, PO Box 2900, Bangalore 56 029, India*

David Nielsen, *Labaratory of Neurogenetics, National Institute of Alcohol Abuse and Alcoholism, Bethesda, MD, USA*

Matthew K. Nock, *Department of Psychology, Yale University, Box 208205, New Haven, CT 06520, USA*

Benjamin Page, *University of Colorado, Boulder, CO 80309, USA*

Jozef Peuskens, *University Center St Jozef, Leuvensesteenweg 517, 3070 Kortenberg, Belgium*

Cynthia R. Pfeffer, *New York Presbyterian Hospital, Westchester Division, 21 Bloomingdale Road, White Plains, New York 10605, USA*

Stephen Platt, *Research Unit in Health and Behavioural Change, University of Edinburgh Medical School, Teviot Place, Edinburgh EH8 9AG, UK*

Leslie R. Pollock, *Institute of Medical and Social Care Research, University of Wales, Wheldon Building, Bangor LL57 2UW, UK*

Mario Rodriguez, *Calle 5ta, nr 29404 entre 294Y 296, Santa Fe Plaza, Ciudad Habana, Codigo Postal 19100, Cuba*

Alec Roy, *Department of Veterans Affairs, New Jersey Health Care Systems, Psychiatry Service, Medical Center, 385 Tremont Avenue, East Orange, NJ 07018, USA*

Gunnar Rylander, *Department of Psychiatry, Karolinska Institute, 17177 Stockholm, Sweden*

Shireen L. Rizvi, *Behavioral Research and Therapy Clinics, Department of Psychology, Box 351525, University of Washington, Seattle, WA 98195-1525, USA*

Isaac Sakinofsky, *High Risk Consultation Clinic and Suicide Studies Programme, Centre for Addiction and Mental Health, Clarke Institute of Psychiatry, University of Toronto, 250 College Street, Toronto, Ontario, Canada M5T 1R8*

Marco Sarchiapone, *Department of Psychiatry, Catholic University, Rome, Italy*

Sylvia Schaller, *Universitäts-Nervenklinik, Fuchsleinstrasse 15, D-97080 Würzburg, Germany*

Lourens Schlebusch, *Faculty of Medicine, University of Natal, 719 Umbilo Road, Durban, South Africa*

Armin Schmidtke, *Universitäts-Nervenklinik, Füchsleinstrasse 15, D-97080 Würzburg, Germany*

Paolo Scocco, *Department of Mental Health, ULSS no. 12 Veneziana, Mestre Venice, Italy*

Vanda Scott, *La Barade, 32330 Gondrin, Le Gers, France; formerly Director General, Befrienders International, London, UK*

David Shaffer, *Columbia University College of Physicians and Surgeons, and New York State Psychiatric Institute, Division of Child and Adolescent Psychiatry, PI Annex, 722 West 168th Street, New York, NY 10032, USA*

Stacy Shaw Welch, *Behavioral Research and Therapy Clinics, Department of Psychology, University of Washington, Seattle, WA 98195-1525, USA*

Bruce Singh, *Department of Psychiatry, Faculty of Medicine, Dentistry and Health Science, University of Melbourne 3052, Australia*

Elsebeth Nylev Stenager, *Department of Social Medicine, Odense Municipality, Tolderlundsvej 2, 5, DK-5000, Odense C, and Institute of Public Health, Odense University, Odense, Denmark*

Egon Stenager, *Esbjerg Centralsygehus, Esbjerg, and The Danish Multiple Sclerosis Registry, Rigshospitalet, Copenhagen, Denmark*

Yoshitomo Takahashi, *Tokyo Institute of Psychiatry, 124-21 Akebono, Tachikawa-shi, Tokyo 190, Japan*

Lil Träskman-Bendz, *Department of Psychiatry, University Hospital, S-221 85 Lund, Sweden*

Kees van Heeringen, *Unit for Suicide Research, Department of Psychiatry, University Hospital, De Pintelaan 185, B-9000 Gent, Belgium*

Robbert J. Verkes, *333 Department of Psychiatry, University Hospital Nijmegen, PO Box 9101, 6500 HB Nijmegen, The Netherlands*

Lakshmi Vijayakumar, *21 Ranjith Road, Kotturpuram, Madras 600085, India*

J. Mark G. Williams, *Institute of Medical and Social Care Research, University of Wales, Wheldon Building, Bangor LL57 2UW, UK*

Manfred Wolfersdorf, *Bezirkskrankenhaus Bayreuth, Klinik für Psychiatrie und Psychotherapie, Nordring 2, 95445 Bayreuth, Germany*

Preface

The field of suicide and attempted suicide has attracted considerably increased attention in recent years. Several governments around the world have established suicide prevention programmes. A major reason for this has been the very large increase in suicide in young people, especially males, seen in many countries. Another is the increase in the numbers of people that are attempting suicide, again particularly among the young. Some of these non-fatal acts are intended to result in death, others are acts involving a suicidal message to communicate needs or achieve other ends, and many involve a mixture of motivational reasons. There is also increasing interest in suicidal behaviour in the elderly. Attention to this age group, which in most countries continues to have the highest rates of suicide, probably reflects greater recognition of the importance of depression in older people and the extent to which it can be treated successfully.

The increased attention to suicide and attempted suicide has resulted in a massive expansion in research, which has occurred on all fronts, including psychiatry, psychology, social sciences, biology and genetics. There has been a greater focus on risk in specific subgroups, defined according to demographic and diagnostic categories. More recently, with the recognition that risk factors for suicidal behaviour are often multi-dimensional, classical diagnostic boundaries have been crossed in order to describe more precisely the characteristics of individuals at increased risk. There has also been more attention to development and evaluation of the effectiveness of psychological and pharmacological treatments for suicide attempters and to the complex and difficult challenges inherent in trying to evaluate the effectiveness of preventive strategies and initiatives.

The major stimulus to our preparing this Handbook has been the need to bring together, in an easily accessible form, the burgeoning amount of knowledge from research and experience about the causes of suicidal behaviour, and its treatment and prevention. We thought it essential that the book should cover the diverse range of important topics in the field. We also wanted the book to reflect the international nature of the problem of suicide and attempted suicide and therefore invited contributors from many countries of the world. The fact that most are from countries in the Western World reflects the particular attention that is being paid to this problem in these countries. Now, however, there is increasing awareness that suicidal behaviour is a problem in many developing countries, as will become evident from the chapters focusing on the situation in Asia and the Far East. The contributors are leaders in the field, especially in research and/or development of prevention strategies. Each was asked to prepare chapters that included the main areas of knowledge in their assigned topics, to present information where possible for which there is a research evidence base, and also to take a broad approach that would reflect different viewpoints and models. We have taken a very active approach to our editorial responsibilities with the aim of producing what we hope is a comprehensive and integrated volume. We thank our contributors for their patience and for responding so positively to our suggestions.

Our ultimate aim has been to produce a Handbook that, as we enter the new millennium, will serve as an invaluable source of information for researchers, clinicians and scholars from a wide range of disciplines, including psychiatry, psychology and the social sciences. We believe it will be an invaluable source for people starting out in this field of study as well as to experienced researchers. We hope that clinicians will find in it much of value and that policy makers will use it as an authoritative source of information relevant to formulation of local and national prevention strategies. Volunteers and counsellors will find much in the book to improve their knowledge base and skills. It will be an important reference text for trainees in psychiatry, psychology, social work, psychiatric nursing and allied disciplines. Finally, we believe that, for people who have themselves been afflicted by suicidal inclinations and those who have experienced suicidal behaviour in people close to them, the book may provide understanding of the issues that lead to suicidal behaviour and the factors that can prevent it. We hope that the overall impact of this book will be to ensure that knowledge about suicide and attempted suicide is easily accessible, with consequent benefits for the advancement of thinking about research and prevention in this most important of fields concerning the quality and value of human life.

We wish to acknowledge the considerable support we have received in the preparation of this book from a range of individuals. These include Michael Coombs and Lesley Valerio at Wiley, who initially encouraged our interest in this project and supported us throughout. We also thank our families, who have had to endure our regular absences for editorial meetings in a range of locations, our secretaries, Members of the Advisory Board and our other colleagues in the field, who have encouraged us at times when our enthusiasm was on the wane. Lastly, but most importantly, we thank the contributors, who have put so much work into helping to bring this project to fruition.

Keith Hawton
Kees van Heeringen
January, 2000

Introduction

Keith Hawton
Department of Psychiatry, Oxford University, Oxford, UK
and
Kees van Heeringen
Department of Psychiatry, University Hospital, Gent, Belgium

It is estimated that worldwide between 500,000 and 1.2 million people die by suicide each year (United Nations, 1996). Non-fatal acts of deliberate self-poisoning or self-injury are many times more frequent, especially in young people. Suicidal behaviour is, therefore, an extremely important health and social issue throughout the world. This was a major reason for producing a comprehensive book with an international focus.

This Handbook is about the causes, treatment and prevention of suicidal behaviour. However, the question of the extent to which suicidal behaviour actually can be treated and/or prevented has justifiably and repeatedly been posed. Strikingly different answers to this question emerge from reviews of the literature. Reviews of treatments and interventions aiming at reducing the occurrence of suicidal behaviour have led to rather disappointing conclusions, although methodological and ethical limitations of studies in this field need to be taken into account when interpreting the results of studies of the effectiveness of interventions (Gunnell and Frankel, 1994; Wilkinson, 1994; Hawton et al, 1998). In view of such limitations, and given the fact that the effects of interventions, such as the elimination of means to commit suicide, cannot be assessed by means of conventional research methods, the use of alternative and innovative approaches at individual high-risk and population levels has been advocated. The results of a review of such approaches suggest more optimistic conclusions (Goldney, 1998).

Whether based on conventional research methodologies (such as randomized controlled trials) or on innovative methodologies, all approaches to the treatment of suicidal individuals and to the prevention of suicidal behaviour should be based on a thorough knowledge of causes and risk factors. A major contribution to this knowledge comes from epidemiological studies, in which the distribution of the occurrence of suicidal behaviour across the general population and the factors that influence this distribution are investigated. Substantial methodolog-

The International Handbook of Suicide and Attempted Suicide. Edited by K. Hawton and K. van Heeringen.

ical controversies emerge in reviewing epidemiological studies in this field, including those associated with nomenclature and ascertainment procedures.

With regard to the issue of nomenclature, the terms "suicide" and "attempted suicide", as used in the title of this book, refer to behaviours that share intentional or deliberate self-harming characteristics but differ with regard to the outcome, that is, whether or not they result in death. However, the use of the term "attempted suicide" has been criticized because of the fact that a vast majority of suicide attempts are not characterized by suicidal intent (i.e. a wish to die), and that attempts may vary widely with regard to other relevant characteristics, such as medical seriousness or the lethality of methods used to attempt suicide. We therefore need to stress that the term "attempted suicide" is used in this book to describe any self-injurious behaviour with a non-fatal outcome, irrespective of whether death was intended (see Chapter 3 for a further discussion of this issue). We are aware of the fact that this approach is partially in conflict with a recently proposed nomenclature for suicidology, in which the term "attempted suicide" is used to describe self-inflicted behaviours for which there is evidence that the person intended "at some level" to kill him/herself (O'Carroll et al, 1998). Our use of the term "attempted suicide" reflects a pragmatic approach, which is partly based on the fact that any motives or intent involved in self-injurious behaviours may be ambivalent and difficult to assess in an unequivocal way. Throughout the book the term "attempted suicide" will be used interchangeably with the term "deliberate self-harm", referring to "deliberate self-poisoning" or "deliberate self-injury", depending on the method used to attempt suicide. As such, an initial distinction should be made between "attempted suicide" and behaviours that have been called self-injurious and risk-taking behaviours with immediate (e.g. skydiving) or remote (e.g. smoking) risk (O'Carroll et al, 1998). Secondly, the term "attempted suicide" does not refer to self-injurious behaviours that may share characteristics of the so-called "deliberate self-harm syndrome" (Pattison and Kahan, 1983). This usually has an onset in late adolescence, involves multiple recurrent episodes of self-cutting or other similar damaging acts of low lethality, and the behaviour often continues for many years. It has, however, been suggested since the 1970s that persons suffering from the deliberate self-harm syndrome may be at increased risk of committing suicide after many years of self-injurious behaviour (Morgan, 1979). Also, as will be discussed further in Chapters 14 and 21, more recent epidemiological research indeed indicates that many forms of self-harming behaviour may, in fact, occur along a continuum ranging from suicidal ideation to completed suicide.

The second issue to be considered when interpreting results from epidemiological research concerns the effect of differences in procedures of ascertainment of suicide between countries. The range of official ascertainment procedures is very wide. For example, in some countries possible suicides are investigated by the police, in others by medical practitioners, and in yet others by coroners or their equivalents. Each approach is likely to be limited by biases of one kind or another, most of which result in an underestimate of suicide rates, because there is a general tendency towards not reaching a verdict of suicide rather than the reverse. This may reflect, first, a wish to avoid upset to families; second, national religious and cultural values; and third, ignorance of the extent and heterogeneity of suicidal acts. Crude rank order comparison of national suicide rates does, however, appear to reflect real differences (Sainsbury, 1983), although the absolute levels may be misleading. If influences on ascertainment procedures change, this can result in spurious changing trends in suicidal behaviour. This appears to have been the case to some extent in Ireland (see Chapter 1), although the rising recent suicide rate there also appears to reflect a real underlying trend. Interpretation and study of cross-national suicide rates would be greatly aided if there were more consistency in ascertainment procedures. The WHO/EU Multicentre Study on Parasuicide (see Chapter 3) represents a recent encouraging effort to achieve this for non-fatal suicidal behaviour, in which ascertainment is possibly even more hazardous because of definition issues and problems of case identification.

Part I of this Handbook begins with three chapters in which the epidemiology of suicide and attempted suicide in countries throughout the world is examined in detail. These are followed by overviews of models that have been developed to understand suicidal behaviour. Individual chapters are devoted to each of the three "classical" approaches, that is the psychological, biological and sociological. There is a further chapter in which an ethological perspective on the link between early psychodynamic hypotheses and biological formulations of suicidal behaviour is described. Findings from genetic and, more recently, molecular biological research, add to these models the possibility of a genetically defined predisposition to suicidal behaviour, which may run across the boundaries between psychiatric disorders. As demonstrated in Chapters 7 to 11, in which the occurrence of suicide and attempted suicide in people suffering from depressive disorders, schizophrenia, personality disorders, anxiety and substance abuse disorders are examined, longitudinal investigations and psychological autopsy studies have indeed indicated that suicidal behaviour may occur within the context of diverse psychiatric disorders. In the concluding chapter of Part I an attempt is made to integrate the findings from epidemiological, biological, psychological, ethological, psychopathological and sociological investigations. This shows how early hypotheses have evolved into cognitive psychological and biological models that may serve as a robust basis for the treatment of suicidal behaviour and further research in this field.

Part II of this book is dedicated to the description of populations and circumstances in which suicidal behaviour may occur, or which may be affected by the occurrence of suicidal behaviour. The detailed description of these populations and circumstances can further help us in understanding suicidal behaviour, and point to issues that require specific attention. As was shown in Part I, there is an urgent need for specific attention to young people, as rates of suicidal behaviour among them are strongly increasing in most parts of the globe. The initial chapters in Part II are dedicated to the description of developmental pathways and psychopathological characteristics of suicidal behaviour among children and adolescents. From the studies that are reviewed it is clear that the characteristics of suicidal youngsters in the general population closely resemble those of suicidal young people in treatment settings. This suggests that many adolescents in the general population may be in need of help, the more so as almost any diagnosable psychiatric disorder is a major risk factor for youth suicide. There follows a chapter focused on the other end of the age span, in which risk factors for suicidal behaviour among the elderly are described. Specific populations and circumstances associated with suicidal behaviour are discussed in other individual chapters in this part of the book. A chapter on sexuality and the reproductive cycle examines the risk of suicidal behaviour in homosexual populations, during pregnancy and following childbirth or stillbirth, and in individuals with deviant sexual behaviour. Suicide and attempted suicide rates vary with employment status and occupation, and these associations are examined in a chapter on suicidal behaviour and the labour market. It has long been recognized that physical illness is linked to risk of suicidal behaviour, and this is described in detail in the next chapter. Risk of suicide is a major reason for admission to psychiatric inpatient care. This means that in psychiatric units there is a high concentration of people at risk. In spite of intensive preventive efforts, suicides do occur in this setting and a chapter is devoted to examination of the extent and nature of suicidal behaviour in psychiatric units. The impact of suicide on relatives and friends is usually highly traumatic. A chapter is therefore focused on the specific experiences of people who suffer such a loss and ways in which they can be helped. One of the most important features of suicidal behaviour is that it is often repeated, not infrequently with a fatal outcome. In the subsequent chapter, the problem of repetition of suicidal behaviour and factors associated with it are, therefore, examined in depth. A host of important legal and ethical issues surround suicide and attempted suicide. As these differ between countries a chapter is devoted to their examination from an international perspective. There are strong links between suicidal behaviours and both aggression and violence. These associations, including suicide associated with homicide, suicide pacts, and suicidal behaviour in prisons, are explored fully in the subsequent chapter. The findings from the studies reviewed in these chapters further refine the description of the social, biological and psychological characteristics that are associated with suicidal behaviour, and constitute the fundamentals of the approaches to treatment and prevention as described in Parts III and IV of this Handbook.

Perhaps the most difficult area in suicidological research concerns the study of the effectiveness of interventions to reduce the occurrence of suicidal behaviour. The fact that the results of such studies have, in general, been rather disappointing may reflect our limited knowledge of pathogenic mechanisms underlying suicidal behaviour, but may also be attributable to methodological issues, such as small sample sizes and patient selection. While conventional treatment strategies focus on categorically defined psychiatric disorders, such as depressive disorders, and thus may contribute to the prevention of suicidal behaviour, it is suggested that the effectiveness of interventions may benefit further from addressing the specific psychological, biological and behavioural characteristics of the patient population. This should include attention to the problems of poor compliance and engagement with treatment that many of these patients show. There have been recent promising findings from studies of psychopharmacological and psychotherapeutic approaches, using selective serotonin reuptake inhibitors and dialectical behaviour therapy, respectively. Two chapters in this part of the Handbook focus on service issues, particularly management of patients in the general hospital following presentation for deliberate self-poisoning or self-injury, and the assessment and treatment of attempted suicide patients by staff from a range of professional backgrounds, including nurses, social workers and general physicians. Two further chapters in Part III review in detail studies that have evaluated the efficacy of the treatment of suicidal ideation and behaviour in adolescents and the elderly. The final two chapters in Part III.

Part IV of the Handbook is dedicated to the prevention of suicide and attempted suicide. With regard to prevention approaches, a general distinction has to be made between high-risk and population strategies (Lewis et al, 1997). The first chapter provides an overview of the currently available knowledge about the prediction of suicidal behaviour, indicating that our limited ability to predict suicidal behaviour among the many who are suicidal should be taken into account as a limiting factor in the former approach. In view of the demonstrated association between suicidal behaviour and psychiatric disorders, as described in Part I, psychiatric patients can be regarded as constituting a high-risk group, usually based, however, within the general population. The effective prevention of suicide in these patients may, therefore, require a combination of high-risk and population approaches. Components of such general population strategies are described in two chapters by means of discussion of initiatives which have been developed in the Western world and in Asia and the Far East, respectively. While such programmes in different parts of the world can probably include common strategies, it is also emphasized that characteristics related to local culture and the organization of mental health care have to be taken into account. In a further chapter, school-based suicide prevention programmes and their evaluation are described. One chapter addressess an important component in a population-based strategy, but which includes a high-risk element, namely improving general practitioners' detection and management of psychiatric disorders, especially depression, that are associated with suicide risk. Another chapter examines the contribution of media portrayal of suicidal acts to the spread of suicidal behaviour in the population, with suggestions about how media approaches might be modified to reduce the risk of imitative behaviour. There follows a chapter which explores the important role of volunteer organizations in prevention of suicidal behaviour. In the concluding chapter of the Handbook, future perspectives regarding potentially fruitful developments in research, clinical practice and prevention are outlined.

REFERENCES

Goldney, R.D. (1998) Suicide prevention is possible: a review of recent studies. Archives of Suicide Research, 4: 329–339.

Gunnell, D. and Frankel, S. (1994) Prevention of suicide: aspirations and evidence. British Medical Journal, 308: 1227–1233.
Hawton, K., Arensman, E., Townsend, E., Bremner, S., Feldman, E., Goldney, R., Gunnell, D., Hazell, P., van Heeringen, K., House, A., Owens, D., Sakinofsky, I. and Träskman-Bendz, L. (1998) Deliberate self-harm: a systematic review of the efficacy of psychosocial and pharmacological treatments in preventing repetition. British Medical Journal, 317: 441–447.
Lewis, G., Hawton, K. and Jones, P. (1997) Strategies for preventing suicide. British Journal of Psychiatry, 171: 351–354.
Morgan, H. (1979) Death Wishes? The Understanding and Management of Deliberate Self-harm. Chichester: Wiley.
O'Carroll, P.W., Berman, A.L., Maris, R., Moscicki, E., Tanney, B. and Silverman, M. (1998) Beyond the Tower of Babel: a nomenclature for suicidology. In R.J. Kosky, H.S. Eshkevari, R.D. Goldney and R. Hassan (Eds), Suicide Prevention: the Global Context, pp. 23–39. New York: Plenum.
Pattison, E.M. and Kahan, J. (1983) The deliberate self-harm syndrome. American Journal of Psychiatry, 140: 867–872.
Sainsbury, P. (1983) Validity and reliability of trends in suicide statistics. World Health Statistics Quarterly, 36: 339–348.
United Nations (1996) Prevention of Suicide: Guidelines for the Formulation and Implementation of National Strategies. New York: United Nations.
Wilkinson, G. (1994) Can suicide be prevented? British Medical Journal, 309: 860–862.

Part I

Understanding Suicidal Behaviour

Chapter 1

Suicide in the Western World

Christopher H. Cantor
Australian Institute for Suicide Research and Prevention, Griffith University, Brisbane, Australia

Abstract

International perspectives on suicide have tended to compare diverse nations with little consideration of whether the comparisons were worthwhile. This chapter narrows the international focus by comparing suicide rates in the Western World, with only passing mention of other countries. New data on Western suicide rates are presented with consideration of the cultural and geographical similarities and dissimilarities. The most significant recent trends have been increased suicide rates in young males in many countries, especially those in the New World and in several countries in Western Europe. Trends in methods of suicide seem to have reflected changes in both their availability and acceptability. Substantial progress with respect to studies of methods of suicide is also summarized. Marital status, parenthood and suicide is presented, as these issues have been relatively neglected. Examination of the associations of seasons and weather with suicidal behaviour is also included. The chapter concludes with more general speculation about reasons for secular trends and suggestions for future research.

INTRODUCTION

Epidemiology is concerned with distributions of disease and factors that influence distribution. Suicide is a behaviour—not a disease. Nevertheless, epidemiological approaches are of value to the understanding of suicide. While disease patterns may be influenced by cultural factors, including alcohol consumption, cigarette smoking and sanitation, behaviours like suicide are more open to cultural influences, including, for example, modelling of suicide via the mass media (see Chapter 39) and inhibition of suicide by religious influences.

The reliability of international suicide data is highly variable. Nevertheless, a World Health Organization (WHO, 1982) working group and others (Sainsbury

The International Handbook of Suicide and Attempted Suicide. Edited by K. Hawton and K. van Heeringen.

and Barraclough, 1968) expressed confidence in the use of international suicide statistics. Within the Western world, Schmidtke (1997) has commented on the different European death registration practices—for example, the Coroner-based system of the UK contrasts with that of Germany, which permits general practitioner certification. In Australia there are eight different systems, corresponding to the six states and two territories. International comparisons are valuable but must consider the influences of varying data collection systems.

HISTORY AND CULTURE

The history of suicide was until recently dominated by the determination of intent, which was important for consideration of punishment of an individual or his/her family for such acts. Persecution of families bereaved by suicide was officially sanctioned, even in progressive European countries, until it was outlawed as late as the eighteenth Century (Colt, 1987). In most Western countries suicide attempts were decriminalized only in the 1960s and 1970s. Cultural attitudes have changed from those of persecution to more diverse orientations that are still in states of flux. While suicide in most countries is no longer illegal, certain religious influences act as deterrents. Islamic and Catholic religions strongly disapprove of suicide and suicide rates in countries adhering to orthodox teachings tend to be low. Conversely, certain aspects of modern youth culture, for example heavy metal music, tend to portray suicide in positive terms. Lay people tend to overestimate the extent of rational suicide and underestimate the consequences of suicide on loved ones. Morality is a topic mental health professionals rightly are reserved about. Nevertheless, moral attitudes are of relevance to the epidemiology of suicide. Ideally, moral attitudes might differentiate and understand diverse motivations for suicide, including mental illness, rational self-euthanasia and the desire to hurt others.

INTERNATIONAL COMPARISONS

Epidemiological reviews have often presented suicide rates from diverse nations selected on the basis of data availability. Diversity may obscure observations that might be evident if more homogenous nations were studied. There is no reason to expect that suicide rates in a thriving developed nation would conform with those of a culturally different developing nation. Consequently, former Eastern bloc nations that might be considered "Western" are not included in the comparisons that follow, as their social environments are still quite different from the West and are undergoing rapid change which in itself might influence suicide rates. Generally, Eastern European suicide rates are substantially higher than those of Western Europe and have risen in recent years (Sartorius, 1996). Between 1987 and 1991–1992 suicide rates in Eastern European countries increased, in contrast to decreases in other European countries. Also, the male:

female suicide ratio widened more in Eastern Europe. However, suicide rates in those over 75 years in Eastern Europe declined (Sartorius, 1996).

While exploration of diverse nations may yield information about gross or universal suicide trends, exploration of more similar nations may ultimately be more productive. Cantor and colleagues (1996) studied suicide rates of eight predominantly English-speaking nations with shared characteristics, finding relatively similar suicide patterns between 1960 and 1989. They subdivided the nations into two groups of four—"Old World" nations, comprising England and Wales, Scotland, Northern Ireland and Ireland; and "New World" nations, comprising the USA, Canada, Australia and New Zealand. New World nations had briefer histories, pioneering masculine-orientated heritages, large distances between communities, indigenous populations, high firearm ownership, climatic extremes and other similarities. The data supported their hypotheses, that suicide rates and trends would be similar across the eight nations and more so in the subgroups. Furthermore, New World rates, while relatively uniform overall, formed two clusters—USA and Canada as one and Australia and New Zealand as another. Minor trends in one nation may become more credible when observed in similar nations.

Subsequently, Lester and colleagues (1997) explored data in the UK and Ireland for 1960–1990. They noted that while Ireland, Northern Ireland and Scotland experienced a rise in overall suicide rates, England and Wales experienced a decline. These works suggest that valuable similarities and dissimilarities may emerge in the data when studying similar nations. Historical data collated by Diekstra (1995) further supports this suggestion. Suicide rates from 1881 to 1988 for 16 European nations were presented. The rank order of national suicide rates remained relatively constant. Similarly, Makinen and Wasserman (1997) found that rankings of European countries by suicide rates were even more stable than the rates themselves. These findings suggest that suicide rates are determined by persisting cross-national differences, including traditions, customs, religions, social attitudes and climate.

In line with this reasoning, this approach will now be extended to include three further groups of Western nations: Southern Europe, comprising Greece, Italy, Portugal and Spain; Western Europe, comprising Austria, Belgium, France, Germany, The Netherlands and Switzerland; and Scandinavia, comprising Denmark, Finland, Norway and Sweden. These sub-groups have been selected intuitively but are supported by Diekstra's (1995) data, with Western European and Scandinavian rates being consistently greater than those of Southern Europe and the UK and Ireland. Nevertheless, this sub-grouping is open to anthropological challenge. For example, Finland has cultural similarities with Hungary, and both nations have high suicide rates, yet in the following analysis Finland is classified as Scandinavian. Debate over the validity of this classification may yield valuable insights, but in the interests of brevity will have to occur elsewhere. The data were sourced with gratitude from Lester and Yang (1998) and the World Health Organization (1996). The findings are presented with a particular focus on 15–24 year-old males, as this is the subgroup which has generated most inter-

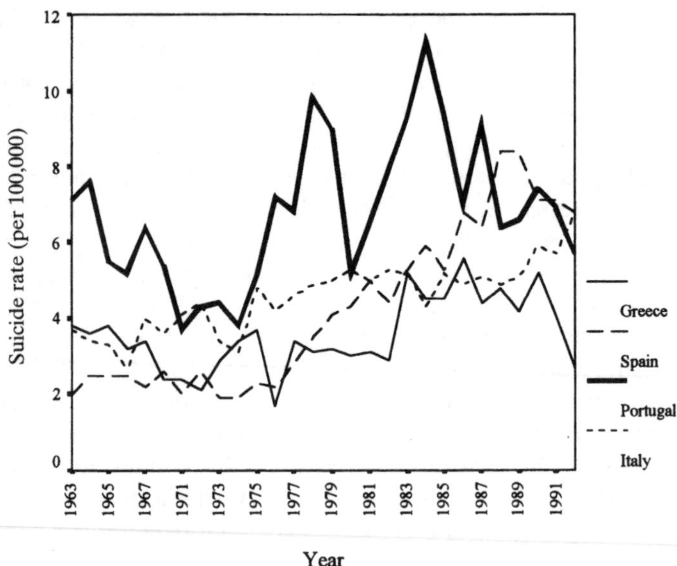

Figure 1.1 Suicide rates for Southern Europe, males 15–24 years

national concern and because of the rapid changes in rates that have occurred in some countries.

Southern Europe (Greece, Italy, Portugal and Spain)

Southern European rates were uniformly low. Portugal had the highest rates of the four countries and Greece the lowest. Nevertheless, suicide rates of males aged 35–74 years showed significant decreases in Portugal that were not evident in the other Southern European countries. Trends for 15–24 year-old males were variable and modest, with only Spain and Italy showing convincing rises (Figure 1.1). Modest increases in females 65–75+ years old in Spain and Italy were observed.

Western Europe (Austria, Belgium, France, Germany, West Germany, The Netherlands and Switzerland)

Western European suicide rates were uniformly high, with the exception of The Netherlands, where rates in males were low but moderate in females. Suicide rates in The Netherlands have historically been consistently much lower than other Western European rates, more in keeping with Britain and Ireland. Suicide rates in Switzerland and Austria, which are geographically, economically and cul-

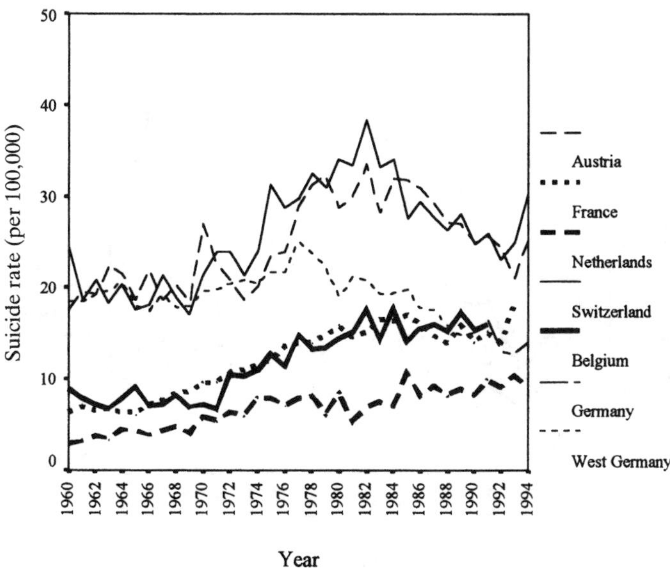

Figure 1.2 Suicide rates for Western Europe, males 15–24 years

turally closely related, were remarkably similar in most age groups. Suicide rates in West Germany also showed distinct similarities, not only with Western European nations in general, but more particularly with Austria and Switzerland. However, West Germany's suicide rates in a number of age groups showed a greater decline in rates from 1979 to 1994 compared with Austria and Switzerland. Figure 1.2 shows Western European suicide rates for 15–24 year-old males. Trends for Austria, Switzerland and Germany in the 1960s and 1980s were remarkably uniform, but in the 1970s West German rates diverged from those of Austria and Switzerland. As a result, West German rates for young males were no higher at the end of the period than before. In France, Belgium and The Netherlands, however, the suicide rates in young males showed a steady increase during this period. Knowledge of why these different trends have occurred might yield valuable clues for prevention. The other interesting feature is the peaking of suicide rates in the third quarter of the period, with subsequent declines—most marked in Austria, Switzerland and Germany, less so in Belgium and France and absent in The Netherlands. However, for both sexes and all ages, except 75+ years, suicide rates were declining in the later stages of this period, suggesting influences other than simply youth.

Scandinavia (Denmark, Finland, Norway and Sweden)

Overall, Scandinavian suicide rates were on average moderately high but lower than in Western Europe, with the exception of Finland, where the male rates were

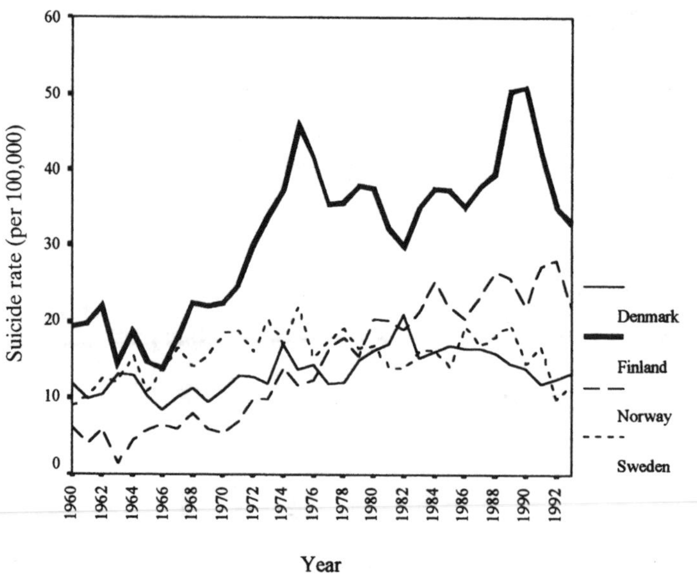

Figure 1.3 Suicide rates for Scandanavia, males 15–24 years

particularly high. It has been suggested that the Finnish cultural tendency that men should be tough and resilient may relate to these high rates (Retterstol, 1992). Finnish female suicide rates across all ages were similar to other Scandinavian rates and those of Western Europe, with the exception of Denmark where the rates were strikingly high. Greenland is not presented here. However, Greenland has the highest suicide rates in Scandinavia, especially among young males. Greenland's primitive hunting and fishing society has changed to a modern industrialized society within a short time, with increases in alcoholism, promiscuity, venereal disease, violence and hopelessness (Retterstol, 1992). In the Faroe Islands, suicide rates are more modest, with farming and fishing, religious, language and cultural traditions remaining more intact.

The most unfavourable developments over this period occurred in Norway, where the rates for 15–24 year-old males rose four-fold, elevating its position from fourth to second for these nations (Figure 1.3). Norwegian trends for females aged 15–44 years were also upwards. To a lesser extent, most other Norwegian age and sex group rates rose over this period.

UK and Ireland

Generally, UK and Irish suicide rates lay between the low rates of Southern Europe and the higher rates of Western Europe and Scandinavia. Irish suicide rates increased across all ages. Several authors have suggested that in earlier

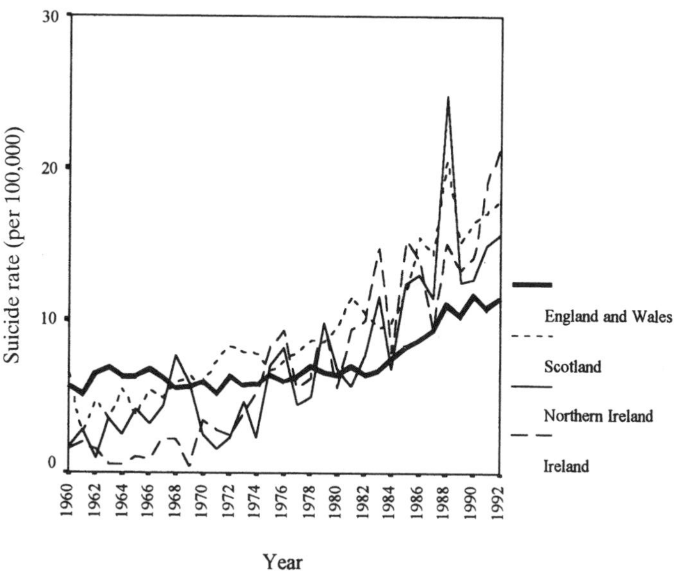

Figure 1.4 Suicide rates for the UK and Ireland, males 15–24 years

times the Irish method of registration of suicide contributed to under-reporting (e.g. Barraclough, 1978).

England and Wales showed strikingly favourable trends, which were evident in all female age groups except 15–24 years and in the older male ages from 55 years upwards. Scotland showed the most unfavourable changes in rates for the UK. The most concerning trends were in males aged 15–24 years, whose rates continued upwards at 1992—even in England and Wales (Figure 1.4). However, trends were also upward, although progressively diminishing with age, for males in the 25–34 and 35–44 year age groups, suggesting the problem is most severe in youth but not confined to it. There has been a small but encouraging reduction in rates in 15–24 year-olds in more recent years (Kelly and Bunting, 1998).

New World (Australia, Canada, New Zealand and USA)

Although showing similarities to the UK, rates in the New World were generally close to double those of the UK in males of all ages, although more similar for older females. The New World countries, along with the UK and Ireland, showed disturbing trends in males 15–24 years of age, with lesser rises in 25–34 year-old males. However, a distinct plateau of suicide rates for the 15–24 age group occurred in both the USA and Canada throughout the 1980s (Figure 1.5). In contrast, suicide rates in Australia and New Zealand continued to rise, although

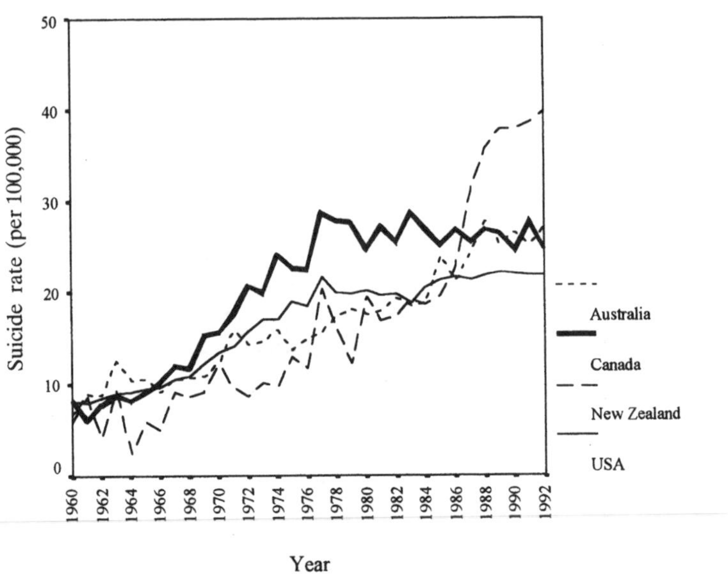

Figure 1.5 Suicide rates for New World males, 15–24 years

Australian rates have plateaued out since 1989. This plateau coincides with the above-mentioned decline in rates in Western Europe. In contrast, suicide rates in New Zealand for 15–24 year-old males rose alarmingly from 1986 to 1992, from around 20 to 40 per 100,000. This may partly relate to the small population base, contributing to marked fluctuations in rates. There were favourable declines in suicide rates in 35–74 year-old New World females, including in New Zealand.

GENDER

Suicide rates consistently involve greater mortality in males (see Table 1.1). This contrasts with hospital admission rates for suicide attempts, in which females predominate (see Chapter 3). Among suicide attempters presenting to hospitals, drug overdoses (the major method of female suicide) and self-cutting are far more common than among suicides. These methods provide more opportunity for rescue and resuscitation than more lethal male methods, such as firearms.

In the 22 Western nations surveyed, the greatest male:female suicide differentials in rank order were in Ireland, USA, Australia, Canada, New Zealand, Finland, Greece, England and Wales, Northern Ireland and Portugal. With the exception of Finland, these gender differentials were driven more by relatively low female rates than by high male rates.

Brent and Moritz (1996) have suggested six potential explanations for male predominance in suicide. First, males tend to choose more lethal methods.

Table 1.1 Suicide rates and ratios for Western countries reporting to the World Health Organization (most recent year)

Country	All ages		
	Male	Female	Male : female ratio
Southern European			
Greece (1994)	5.5	1.4	3.9 : 1
Italy (1992)	12.1	4.1	3.0 : 1
Portugal (1994)	12.3	3.4	3.6 : 1
Spain (1992)	11.0	3.4	3.2 : 1
Western European			
Austria (1994)	33.0	11.9	2.8 : 1
Belgium (1991)	32.0	13.8	2.3 : 1
France (1993)	31.6	11.5	2.7 : 1
Germany (1994)	22.9	8.6	2.7 : 1
The Netherlands (1994)	14.3	6.4	2.2 : 1
Switzerland (1994)	30.9	12.2	2.5 : 1
Scandinavian			
Denmark (1993)	29.3	15.6	1.9 : 1
Finland (1994)	43.6	11.8	3.7 : 1
Norway (1993)	21.1	6.5	3.2 : 1
Sweden (1993)	22.2	9.5	2.3 : 1
Old World			
England and Wales (1994)	11.1	3.0	3.7 : 1
Ireland (1992)	16.8	3.3	5.1 : 1
Northern Ireland (1994)	13.3	3.7	3.6 : 1
Scotland (1994)	18.6	6.1	3.0 : 1
New World			
Australia (1993)	18.7	4.5	4.2 : 1
Canada (1993)	21.0	5.4	3.9 : 1
New Zealand (1993)	20.5	5.4	3.8 : 1
USA (1992)	19.6	4.6	4.3 : 1

Second, they have a greater propensity to impulsive violence. Third, males are more inclined to substance abuse. Fourth, some studies (e.g. Rich et al, 1988) have suggested that co-morbid affective and substance abuse disorders are more common in males. Fifth, males tend to be more reluctant to seek help. Sixth, males may be more brittle with respect to the consequences of relationship breakdown and other stresses. While these points may be important, they do not explain the relatively low female suicide rates of some of these nations.

Conversely, Western nations with lower male : female differentials include Denmark, The Netherlands, Belgium, Sweden and Switzerland. Of these, only in The Netherlands is this ratio driven by a relatively low male rate. The others have moderate or high male suicide rates but with accompanying female rates that are at the upper end of world rankings. Denmark has witnessed an increase in female suicide rates of 124% since 1922, while the male rate increased by 26%, resulting in the male:female ratio declining from 3.16:1 to 1.79:1 (Bille-Brahe, 1987). Social integration in middle-aged Danish women is said to be relatively poor.

AGE

Traditionally, suicide has increased with age and this generally remains the case. In all five groups of nations, rises occurred in suicide rates for 15–24 year-old males but with significant variations. Rises in this group in the UK and Ireland were marked, remarkably uniform and ongoing at the end of the study period (although, as noted above, the rate in the UK has declined somewhat in the past few years). To a lesser extent, rises were evident in 25–34 year-old UK and Irish males, suggesting that this is a problem of young adulthood, albeit adolescents have shown the most marked rises. The New World also experienced marked rises in 15–24 year-old males. Pritchard (1992) suggested that Australia and New Zealand have in recent years been unusual in having higher suicide rates in males aged 15–24 than in most older age groups. Rates in Western European 15–24 year-old males rose until around 1980, thereafter declining, with the exception of The Netherlands, France and Belgium, where the rates continued to rise. Scandinavian rates in 15–24 year-old males also rose, although less markedly than the UK and Ireland and the New World. The situation in Southern Europe was variable, with Greece and Portugal showing minimal rises. Suicide rates by age for 22 western countries for the period 1960–1992 are shown in Table 1.2.

Changes in suicide rates of populations aged 35 years and over were mostly sporadic and modest. The New World nations witnessed significant declines in suicide rates of females 25–74 years old in the second half of the time period. New World male rates for ages 55–74 years also showed modest declines. Rates in England and Wales for these and other ages (males over 55 years and females 25 years and upwards) also declined, but more markedly. Portuguese rates for 34–74 year-old males also showed marked declines. Suicide rates in late life (75+ years) were the highest for most nations. These rates rose further over this period in Western European males and in Scandinavians, especially females. Rates in the elderly rose significantly in other individual nations, such as Italy and Spain.

Important questions emerge from these observations. What are the characteristics of the UK and Ireland and the New World that are associated with their major rises among young males? Are these the same as have fuelled rises in other countries? Are the cultural similarities of the UK and Ireland and the New World relevant to the mutually witnessed rises, or are they just coincidental? Is the North American plateau for this age group from the 1980s onwards related to the same phenomena as account for the levelling and declining rates of most of the Western European rates? What differences were there in Britain and Ireland compared with Western Europe in the latter period that accounted for the divergence of trends? Do the marked differences between the rates in The Netherlands and other Western European nations trends tell us anything? Why are suicide rates in Western Europe and Scandinavia high? Why have

Table 1.2 Suicide rates by age (per 100,000) for 22 Western countries, 1960–1992

Country	Gender	15–24 years		25–34 years		35–44 years		45–54 years		55–64 years		65–74 years		75+ years	
		1960	1992	1960	1992	1960	1992	1960	1992	1960	1992	1960	1992	1960	1992
Southern European															
Greece	m	3.2	2.7	5.1	4.9	4.1	5.6	9.4	7.4	9.6	7.5	17.6	11.4	15.4	16.1
	f	6.4	0.6	2.9	1.3	2.2	1.5	2.6	1.3	4.0	2.3	2.0	2.6	3.6	3.1
Italy	m	4.1	6.8	5.0	11.0	8.2	11.1	17.1	13.9	22.0	17.5	23.1	22.4	31.0	40.7
	f	3.7	1.8	3.1	2.5	3.0	4.0	5.6	5.0	7.2	6.9	8.8	7.8	6.2	8.7
Portugal	m	8.0	5.7	6.8	13.1	13.7	10.8	30.8	14.2	37.9	21.0	44.5	29.0	72.8	63.4
	f	4.9	2.1	2.6	4.6	5.1	4.2	6.3	5.7	6.0	8.7	7.6	7.0	8.5	11.9
Spain*	m	2.0	6.8	5.7	10.7	8.4	9.0	14.1	12.5	17.9	17.0	24.6	21.2	29.2	48.0
	f	1.4	1.3	2.0	2.1	2.6	3.5	3.4	3.1	5.3	5.4	8.6	7.9	6.3	10.5
Western European															
Austria	m	17.6	24.4	32.3	30.0	36.6	34.6	56.0	44.2	58.0	49.0	60.8	64.1	79.6	109.5
	f	8.1	6.1	13.9	7.6	15.0	13.5	23.5	18.0	23.2	17.4	27.7	14.8	22.0	27.4
Belgium**	m	8.9	16.0	10.8	34.6	13.7	36.9	32.7	41.4	47.7	43.5	55.3	56.6	89.1	103.4
	f	3.8	4.8	4.4	13.2	5.8	14.4	12.1	21.4	16.5	20.3	17.1	25.0	21.9	26.8
France	m	6.3	14.0	15.3	32.4	23.9	40.4	41.9	40.3	55.8	38.8	57.0	46.1	94.7	103.3
	f	3.7	4.3	4.8	8.9	7.7	12.6	11.5	16.4	16.8	16.9	18.1	17.4	20.6	24.3
The Netherlands	m	2.8	9.1	5.9	15.8	9.8	18.1	14.4	17.3	21.2	17.7	22.8	23.7	36.6	37.2
	f	1.7	3.8	3.7	6.7	4.5	10.0	11.2	10.8	11.6	10.1	15.9	10.1	13.1	12.3
Switzerland	m	24.5	23.1	27.0	35.6	30.5	31.8	40.7	39.1	52.8	43.8	56.5	47.2	62.8	83.4
	f	7.3	6.3	10.9	7.0	11.2	13.0	18.9	14.0	21.4	16.5	15.2	18.3	17.7	21.8
West Germany***	m	18.4	15.0	24.4	21.3	27.5	22.2	42.9	28.2	48.2	31.0	46.0	34.6	55.1	72.2
	f	7.1	4.5	9.6	6.9	13.8	7.6	21.8	11.4	23.2	12.8	20.2	17.1	19.6	23.7

continued overleaf

Table 1.2 *(continued)*

Country	Gender	15–24 years		25–34 years		35–44 years		45–54 years		55–64 years		65–74 years		75+ years	
		1960	1992	1960	1992	1960	1992	1960	1992	1960	1992	1960	1992	1960	1992
Scandinavian															
Denmark	m	12.1	12.6	32.1	24.6	33.5	34.0	50.8	47.9	53.4	39.4	44.8	43.0	56.0	81.4
	f	4.2	3.4	12.6	8.5	19.4	14.6	25.1	26.0	24.7	28.4	23.6	27.6	27.5	28.7
Finland	m	19.3	35.2	41.8	65.9	54.9	68.3	69.1	68.8	72.5	59.7	57.2	41.6	48.2	64.3
	f	3.9	8.3	12.1	12.5	14.0	15.7	18.1	21.0	17.1	17.0	16.1	10.8	6.1	9.5
Norway	m	6.3	28.2	12.2	23.3	15.0	22.7	18.1	27.6	21.8	24.2	13.2	30.6	11.4	31.8
	f	0.9	5.2	2.8	6.6	1.2	12.6	7.2	12.2	6.0	9.0	3.0	12.3	1.2	9.2
Sweden	m	9.1	10.0	22.6	23.0	32.0	27.7	46.1	32.2	51.3	27.7	48.4	31.1	50.7	52.2
	f	5.3	6.7	9.5	8.4	9.0	10.4	15.0	14.8	15.1	13.6	14.7	15.9	9.4	13.3
Old World															
England and Wales	m	5.7	11.5	11.4	15.9	13.9	18.9	20.1	17.0	30.7	13.6	33.0	12.9	38.5	15.6
	f	2.6	2.1	5.6	3.7	8.6	3.8	14.7	5.1	18.0	4.5	18.6	5.7	11.9	5.6
Ireland	m	1.5	21.5	2.7	30.4	6.6	22.0	7.0	20.9	12.0	23.8	10.5	20.0	3.7	13.9
	f	0.0	2.0	2.0	5.2	2.3	2.5	3.7	5.7	3.7	7.1	4.9	6.1	3.7	5.0
Northern Ireland	m	1.7	15.7	3.7	19.1	9.9	11.0	8.6	15.3	15.8	15.0	13.2	15.2	10.4	14.0
	f	0.0	1.6	3.3	3.3	4.5	3.0	2.3	3.4	5.5	2.7	16.1	3.0	3.4	1.8
Scotland	m	6.5	18.0	9.1	25.0	12.0	28.2	18.2	21.0	25.4	18.1	21.0	11.8	18.1	17.8
	f	1.6	4.5	4.9	9.1	7.9	8.1	11.1	8.2	8.4	7.5	12.3	6.0	2.5	4.1
New World															
Australia	m	6.7	27.3	18.2	28.7	22.4	24.7	27.0	24.9	29.1	23.8	38.2	26.6	32.8	29.1
	f	2.0	5.6	5.5	6.8	9.5	6.3	12.8	6.3	16.5	7.4	11.0	7.4	9.0	9.1
Canada	m	8.3	24.7	15.3	28.8	16.5	27.3	24.2	24.7	29.4	26.2	25.8	20.5	26.3	27.2
	f	1.7	6.0	4.1	6.2	3.9	7.9	6.6	9.1	7.7	6.6	6.9	5.9	4.0	4.2
New Zealand	m	5.8	39.9	15.3	36.9	24.7	24.2	29.3	22.8	28.9	32.3	29.3	20.6	32.9	25.5
	f	2.4	6.2	2.7	5.4	9.4	5.6	10.0	11.4	17.8	11.5	15.5	4.9	4.6	6.0
USA	m	8.1	21.9	14.7	24.0	21.1	23.7	31.5	22.4	37.9	24.1	40.4	29.9	55.5	52.3
	f	2.2	3.7	5.5	5.0	7.7	6.6	10.1	7.3	10.1	6.5	8.5	5.9	8.6	6.2

*1963 was the nearest available year.
**1991 was the nearest available year.
***1990 was the nearest available year.

overall trends in England and Wales been so favourable compared with the rest of Britain, Ireland and elsewhere? Specific answers for these questions have yet to be found.

MARITAL AND PARENTAL STATUS

Bearing in mind the importance of interpersonal problems and attachment theory in the understanding of suicidal behaviour, relatively little attention has been paid to researching this area. Positive associations between divorced status and suicide rates have been reported from the USA (Lester, 1993), Canada (Leenaars et al, 1993), Norway (Rossow, 1993), Japan (Motohashi, 1991) and Taiwan (Yang et al, 1992). These studies do not permit causal attribution. Nevertheless, psychological autopsy studies have reported the increased occurrence of stressful life events—especially separation—and family discord in the 3 months prior to suicide in Finland (Heikkinen et al, 1992). Younger men appear especially vulnerable to separation.

Most marital status research has used legal classifications of status that place separated persons in the married category. Married status for both genders is associated with the lowest suicide rates (Bucca et al, 1994; Hulten and Wasserman, 1992; Kreitman, 1988; Lester, 1987; Smith et al, 1988) and therefore this policy confounds both the married and separated groups. Using a suicide register comprising 1375 cases and a complex methodology, Cantor and Slater (1995) provided a conservative estimate of the risk associated with separated status in an Australian population. Using standardized mortality ratios (SMRs) for males (and females) the SMRs were married 1 (1), single 2 (1.5), divorced 2.8 (3.2), widowed 3.3 (2.5) and separated 6.2 (1.6). Separated males had a more than six-fold increased rate of suicide compared with married males (three-fold compared with single and two-fold compared with both divorced and widowed), while separated females had a SMR only slightly greater than the married. This suggests a differential impact of separation, with males showing greater impact. Further research is needed to confirm this association and whether a causal relationship exists.

This work begs the question of why the impact in females of separated status on suicide rates was relatively modest during such a distressing stage of life? Attachment theory (Adam, 1990) and Linehan and colleagues' (1983) work on reasons for living suggest that parenthood is protective against suicide. Furthermore, an association between child-abusing mothers and maternal suicide attempts has been found, implying that attachment problems may be risk factors for suicidal behaviour (Hawton et al, 1985).

More often than not, females become the principal custodians of offspring following separation. A prospective study of almost one million females in Finland in 1970–1985 generating 1,190 suicides found a strong linear decrease in suicide in females with increasing numbers of children, independent of social class (Hoyer and Lund, 1993). Large numbers of children were only associated with vulnerability if children were born to parents of particularly young or old age. Cantor and Slater's (1995) work also found lower suicide rates in mothers with increasing numbers of children. One problem with this reasoning is that religions associated with stronger suicide taboos—for example Catholicism and Islam—may also restrict contraception.

METHODS

It can be argued that the most dramatic reductions in suicide rates to date have occurred not as a result of improvements in well-being but through reductions in availability of certain lethal methods of suicide. In the UK around 1960, close to 50% of all suicides were by domestic gas (Clarke and Lester, 1989). During the 1960s the carbon monoxide content of domestic gas declined nationally as safer natural gas was substituted for the older coal gas for economic reasons. While there were 2,499 suicides by domestic gas in 1960, by 1977 the figure had declined to 8. The near total elimination of a method that had previously accounted for a large proportion of suicides made estimation of impact possible. Following detoxification, not only did male and female rates of domestic gas suicide decline from around 6 and 4 per 100,000, respectively, to near zero for both, but also overall suicide rates declined from 14 to 10 per 100,000 in males and from 9 to 6.5 per 100,000 in females (Kreitman, 1976). In a detailed analysis, Clarke and Lester (1989) concluded that little displacement to other methods occurred.

A negative result from The Netherlands (WHO, 1982) is often cited as challenging this UK result. This challenge can be rebutted on three grounds. First, domestic gas suicides in The Netherlands had previously been modest in proportion, limiting detection of significant effects on overall rates. Second, during the 6-year changeover period, overall suicide rates remained steady whereas subsequently overall rates rose steeply, suggesting that during the changeover period overall rates might well have risen as a result of independent factors, had it not been for detoxification (Clarke and Lester, 1989). Third, what might work under one set of cultural and environmental conditions might not work under another. Kreitman (1976) concluded that, "it may be that the scenario of suicide specifies the use of a particular method, and that if this is not available, actual suicide is then less likely. Virtually nothing is known about such questions".

Clarke and Lester (1989) have described 20 "choice-structuring properties" representing some of the key factors influencing method choice. Availability was but one of the 20. The others related more to acceptability and can be subdivided into opportunities, costs (deterrants) and other issues. Opportunities include familiarity with the method, technical skills and planning needed; for example, farmers tend to own firearms and know how to use them. Factors acting as possible deterrants include anticipated pain, consequences of failure, disfigurement after death, danger or inconvenience to others, messiness or bloodiness, who might discover the body, and scope for concealing suicide. Other issues include certainty of death, time taken to die while conscious, scope for second thoughts, chances of intervention, symbolism, masculine or feminine associations and dramatic impact.

Methods used for suicide vary both between countries and within them. The New World nations described above, especially the USA, have high firearm suicide rates, where they account for approximately 60% of suicides (Moscicki, 1997). Males tend to use more disfiguring and more lethal methods than females, which in part accounts for their higher suicide rates.

Marzuk and colleagues (1992) compared five counties in New York. The populations of these counties had similar access to some methods (e.g. hanging, suffocation, laceration and burns) but different levels of access to other methods (e.g. jumping from heights, exhaust gassing and drowning). Age- and sex-adjusted results showed that counties had similar suicide rates for those methods similarly accessible to the populations, but different rates for methods that were differentially accessible. Counties with more tall buildings had more suicides by jumping and those with more private garages had more suicides by motor vehicle exhaust gas.

Drug overdoses are common in most countries. Hawton and colleagues (1996) have described relatively high rates of paracetamol poisonings in the UK, attributing this to its availability over the counter. Curiously, in Australia, with similar over-the-counter availability of paracetamol, it is not as commonly implicated, illustrating that both availability and acceptability play roles, although which of these factors is most important has yet to be demonstrated.

Much has been written regarding the different toxicity levels of antidepressant drugs, with the older tricyclic antidepressants associated with greater overdose fatality rates (Cassidy and Henry, 1987). This problem should recede as newer, safer antidepressants become increasingly used. From a medical negligence perspective there need to be compelling reasons for prescribing more lethal medications, such as the older antidepressants, to high-risk populations now that safer alternatives are available, although more expensive at the prescription cost level (Beerworth and Tiller, 1998).

Motor vehicle exhaust gas suicides are a relatively modern phenomenon, with still rising rates in some countries. Lester (1989) found that US car emission controls introduced in 1968 were associated with an initial fall in exhaust suicide rates, followed by an upward trend in the 1980s. Lester (1994) found that national exhaust suicide rates of 28 countries were proportional to per capita car ownership rates. It seems likely that the rise in rates more recently may be related to major increases in car ownership.

Pounder (1993) and McClure (1994) in the UK and Cantor and Baume (1998) in Australia have reported recent rising suicide rates by hanging. Opportunity and availability for hanging has remained unaltered, hence changing acceptability must be the answer. The abolition of capital punishment in the UK may have removed the criminal association of hanging in that country (Pounder, 1993). In

Australia, an Inquiry into Deaths in Custody, most of which were by hanging, was followed by a four-fold rise in hangings in males and females 15–24 years of age. It is possible that the considerable public sympathy for these deaths, many of which occurred in alienated indigenous Australians, may have been a factor. These suggestions are speculative, as minimal attention has been paid to this in the research literature. Hanging may be a fertile area of research into the changing fashions of suicide methods.

SEASONS AND WEATHER

While seasonal and climatic factors affect suicide rates, intuitive notions are misleading. In Finland, with its proximity to the pole, winter days are gloomy, with only a few hours of daylight. While high winter suicide rates might be expected, the reverse has been found, with the lowest rates in December to February and the peak in May (Kunz and Kunz, 1997). Studies reviewed by Lester (1992) suggest that weather variables are not associated with altered suicide rates when studied on a day-to-day as opposed to a seasonal basis.

Chew and McCleary (1995) analysed data from the 1960s to 1980s from 28 nations, confirming a nearly universal spring peak. Bi-seasonal spring (primary) and autumn (secondary) peaks have been reported from the USA (Lester, 1992), UK 1958–1974 (Meares et al, 1981), Italy 1969–1981 (Micciolo et al, 1989), Finland 1961–1976 (Nayha, 1982) and Australia 1971–1976 (Parker and Walter, 1982). However, studies of suicide rates from South Africa 1980–1989 (Fisher et al, 1997), Hong Kong and Taiwan 1981–1993 (Ho et al, 1997) and Australia and New Zealand 1981–1993 (Yip et al, 1998) found single spring seasonal peaks for both sexes. The more recent study periods of these negative reports and the mostly different nations studied might account for the differences.

Explanations for seasonal variations in suicide have included both the sociological and biological. Durkheim's nineteenth century theories linked the spring peak with increased social activity, which may bring increased relationship conflict and consumption of alcohol, both being risk factors for suicide. The spring peak has been found to be greater in agricultural workforces (Chew and McLeary, 1995).

It has also been suggested that seasonal variations in suicide may relate to biorhythms associated with seasonal affective disorders. It is hypothesized that the increase in daylight in spring stimulates the pineal gland in such a way that affective disorders result (Parker and Walter, 1982).

A third hypothesis is that during winter, depressed persons might externalize their misery to the weather. With the advent of spring their distress becomes internalized, with obvious implications for suicidal behaviour. This theory is supported by the finding that tropical nations (with less climatic variation) showed less seasonality of suicide than temperate nations (Chew and McLeary, 1995). However, this pattern is also consistent with the social activity and biorhythms theories.

CONCLUSIONS

International suicide rates have shown consistent patterns over time (Diekstra, 1995). Striking variations between countries are evident, with low suicide rates in Southern Europe and high rates in Western Europe and Scandinavia. The most concerning trends in recent times have been the rises in suicide rates in 15–24 year-olds, especially males. This has been most evident in the English-speaking nations, whose suicide rates generally lie between the above extremes.

The explanations for these observations remain mostly inadequate. In young people in recent decades there have been marked increases in rates of depression (Klerman, 1988; Fombonne, 1995) and alcohol consumption (Smith and Rutter, 1995), both of which are major risk factors for suicide. However, the factors fuelling the rises in both depression and alcohol abuse remain unclear.

Future international studies should consider the relevance of the nations being compared and include testable hypotheses. This chapter has chosen to compare relatively homogeneous nations and in the author's opinion there is much to be learned from this approach. Suicide epidemiology also needs to include an expanded interdisciplinary perspective. Mental health epidemiology may become increasingly relevant as it comes of age. The psychosocial *patterns* of transitions from adolescence to adulthood have greatly altered in recent times, as reflected by sexual development commencing earlier but independence being reached later (Rutter and Smith, 1995; Diekstra et al, 1995). It seems likely that these issues may relate to rising rates of depression and alcohol abuse. This may also be a fertile area for suicide research. Greater familiarity with the sociological and anthropological literature is also likely to be instructive.

REFERENCES

Adam, K.S. (1990) Environmental, psychosocial, and psychoanalytic aspects of suicidal behavior. In S.J. Blumenthal and D.J. Kupfer (Eds), Suicide over the Life Cycle: Risk Factors, Assessment, and Treatment of Suicidal Patients, pp. 39–97. Washington, DC: American Psychiatric Press.

Barraclough, B.M. (1978) The different incidence of suicide in Eire and in England and Wales. British Journal of Psychiatry, 132: 36–38.

Beerworth, E.E. and Tiller, J.W.G. (1998) Liability in prescribing choice: the example of the antidepressants. Australian and New Zealand Journal of Psychiatry, 32: 560–566.

Bille-Brahe, U. (1987) A pilot study of the level of integration in Norway and Denmark. Acta Psychiatrica Scandinavica, 76: 45–62.

Brent, D.A. and Mortiz, G. (1996) Developmental pathways to adolescent suicide. In D. Cichetti and S. Toth (Eds), Adolescents: Opportunities and Challenges. Rochester, NY: University of Rochester Press.

Bucca, M., Ceppi, M., Peloso, P., Arcellaschi, M. and Fele, P. (1994) Social variables and suicide in the population of Genoa, Italy. Comprehensive Psychiatry, 35: 64–69.

Cantor, C.H. and Baume, P.J.M. (1998) Changing methods of suicide by young Australians, 1974–1994. Archives of Suicide Research, 4: 41–50.

Cantor, C.H. and Slater, P.J. (1995) Marital breakdown, parenthood and suicide. Journal of Family Studies, 1: 91–102.

Cantor, C.H., Leenaars, A.A., Lester, D., Slater, P.J., Wolanowski, A.M. and O'Toole, B. (1996) Suicide trends in eight predominantly English-speaking countries, 1960–1989. Social Psychiatry and Psychiatric Epidemiology, 31: 364–373.

Cassidy S. and Henry, J. (1987) Fatal toxicity of antidepressant drugs in overdose. British Medical Journal, 245: 1021–1024.

Chew, K.S.Y. and McLeary, R. (1995) The spring peak in suicides: a cross-national analysis. Social Science and Medicine, 40: 223–230.

Clarke, R.V. and Lester, D. (1989) Suicide: Closing the Exits. New York: Springer-Verlag.

Colt, T.H. (1987) The history of the suicide survivor: the mark of Cain. In E.J. Dunne, J.L. McIntosh and K. Dunne-Maxim (Eds), Suicide and Its Aftermath. New York: W.W. Norton.

Diekstra, R.F.W. (1995) The epidemiology of suicide and parasuicide. In R.F.W. Diekstra, W. Gulbinat, I. Kienhorst and D. De Leo (Eds), Preventive Strategies on Suicide. World Health Organization and Leiden: E.J. Brill.

Diekstra, R.F.W., Kienhorst, C.W.M. and de Wilde, E.J. (1995) Suicide and suicidal behaviour among adolescents. In: M. Rutter and D.J. Smith (Eds), Psychosocial Disorders in Young People: Time Trends and Their Causes. Chichester: Wiley.

Fisher, A.J., Parry, C.D.H., Bradshaw, D. and Juritz, J.M. (1997) Seasonal variation of suicide in South Africa. Psychiatry Research, 66: 13–22.

Fombonne, E. (1995) Depressive disorders: time trends and possible explanatory mechanisms. In M. Rutter and D.J. Smith (Eds), Psychosocial Disorders in Young People: Time Trends and Their Causes. Chichester: Wiley.

Hawton, K., Roberts, J. and Goodwin, G. (1985) The risk of child abuse among mothers who attempt suicide. British Journal of Psychiatry, 146: 486–489.

Hawton, K., Ware, C., Mistry, H., Hewitt, J., Kingsbury, S., Roberts, D. and Weitzel, H. (1996) Paracetamol self-poisoning: characteristics, prevention and harm reduction. British Journal of Psychiatry, 168: 43–48.

Heikkinen, M., Aro, H. and Lonnqvist, J. (1992) Recent life events and their role in suicide as seen by the spouses. Acta Psychiatrica Scandinavica, 86: 489–494.

Ho, T.P., Chao, A. and Yip, P.S.F. (1997) Seasonal variation in suicides re-examined: no sex difference in Hong Kong and Taiwan. Acta Psychiatrica Scandinavica, 95: 25–31.

Hoyer, G. and Lund, E. (1993) Suicide among women related to the number of children in marriage. Archives of General Psychiatry, 50: 134–137.

Hulten, A. and Wasserman, D. (1992) Suicide among young people aged 10–29 in Sweden. Scandinavian Journal of Social Medicine, 2: 65–72.

Kelly, S. and Bunting, J. (1998) Trends in suicide in England and Wales, 1982–96. Population Trends, 92: 29–41.

Klerman, G.L. (1988) The current age of youthful melancholia: evidence for increase in depression in adolescents and young adults. British Journal of Psychiatry, 152: 4–14.

Kreitman, N. (1976) The coal gas story. British Journal of Preventative and Social Medicine, 30: 86–93.

Kreitman, N. (1988) Suicide, age and marital status. Psychological Medicine, 18: 121–128.

Kunz, P.R. and Kunz, J. (1997) Depression and suicide in the dark months. Perceptual and Motor Skills, 84: 537–538.

Leenaars, A.A., Yang, B. and Lester, D. (1993) The effect of domestic and economic stress on suicide rates in Canada and the United States. Journal of Clinical Psychology, 49: 918–921.

Lester, D. (1987) Benefits of marriage for reducing risk of violent death from suicide and homicide for white and non-white persons: generalizing Gove's findings. Psychological Reports, 61: 198.

Lester, D. (1989) Changing rates of suicide by car exhaust in men and women in the United States after car exhaust was detoxified. Crisis, 10: 164–168.

Lester, D. (1992) Why People Kill Themselves: A 1990s Summary of Research Findings on Suicidal Behavior. Springfield, IL: Charles C. Thomas.

Lester, D. (1993) Marital integration, suicide and homicide. Psychological Reports, 73: 1354.

Lester, D. (1994) Car ownership and suicide by car exhaust in nations of the world. Perceptual and Motor Skills, 79: 898.

Lester, D., Cantor, C.H. and Leenaars, A.A. (1997) Suicide in the United Kingdom and Ireland. European Psychiatry, 12: 300–304.

Lester, D. and Yang, B. (1998) Suicide and Homicide in the Twentieth Century: Changes over Time. Commack, NY: Nova Science.

Linehan, M.M., Goodstein, J.L., Nielsen, S.L. and Chiles, J.A. (1983) Reasons for staying alive when you are thinking of killing yourself. The reasons for living inventory. Journal of Consulting and Clinical Psychology, 51: 276–286.

McClure, G.M.G. (1994) Suicide in children and adolescents in England and Wales 1960–1990. British Journal of Psychiatry, 165: 510–514.

Makinen, I.H. and Wasserman, D. (1997) Suicide prevention and cultural resistance: stability in European countries' suicide ranking, 1970–1988. Italian Journal of Suicidology, 7: 73–85.

Marzuk, P.M., Leon A.C., Tardiff, K., Morgan, E.B., Stajic, M. and Mann, J.J. (1992) The effect of access to lethal methods of injury on suicide rates. Archives of General Psychiatry, 49: 451–458.

Meares, R., Mendelson, F.A.O. and Milgrom-Friedman, J. (1981) A sex difference in the seasonal variation of suicide rates. British Journal of Psychiatry, 138: 321–325.

Micciolo, R., Zimmerman-Tansella, C., Williams, P. and Tansella, M. (1989) Seasonal variation in suicide. Psychological Medicine, 19: 199–203.

Moscicki, E.K. (1997) Identification of suicide risk factors using epidemiologic studies. Psychiatric Clinics of North America, 20: 499–517.

Motahashi, Y. (1991) Effects of socioeconomic factors on secular trends in suicide in Japan, 1953–86. Journal of Biosocial Science, 23: 221–227.

Nayha, S. (1982) Autumn incidence of suicide re-examined: data from Finland by sex, age and occupation. British Journal of Psychiatry, 141: 512–517.

Parker, G. and Walter, S. (1982) Seasonal variation in depressive and suicidal deaths in New South Wales. British Journal of Psychiatry, 140: 626–632.

Pounder, D.J. (1993) Why are the British hanging themselves? American Journal of Forensic Medicine and Pathology, 14: 135–140.

Pritchard, C. (1992) Youth suicide and gender in Australia and New Zealand compared with countries of the Western world, 1973–1987. Australian and New Zealand Journal of Psychiatry, 26: 609–617.

Retterstol, N. (1992) Suicide in the Nordic countries. Psychopathology, 25: 254–265.

Rich, C., Ricketts, J., Fowler, R.C. and Young, D. (1988) Some differences between men and women who commit suicide. American Journal of Psychiatry, 145: 718–722.

Rossow, I. (1993) Suicide, alcohol and divorce: aspects of gender and family integration. Addiction, 88: 1659–1665.

Rutter, M. and Smith, D.J. (1995) Towards causal explanations of time trends in psychosocial disorders in youth. In M. Rutter and D.J. Smith (Eds), Psychosocial Disorders in Young People: Time Trends and Their Causes, pp. 782–809. Chichester: Wiley.

Sainsbury, P. and Barraclough, B.M. (1968) Differences between suicide rates. Nature, 220: 1252.

Sartorius, N. (1996) Recent changes in suicide rates in selected Eastern European and other European countries. In J.L. Pearson and Y. Conwell (Eds), Suicide and Aging. New York: Springer.

Schmidtke, A. (1997) Perspective: suicide in Europe. Suicide and Life-Threatening Behavior, 27: 127–136.

Smith, J.C., Mercy, J.A. and Conn, J.M. (1988) Marital status and the risk of suicide. American Journal of Public Health, 78: 78–80.

Smith, D.J. and Rutter, M. (1995) Time trends in psychosocial disorders of youth. In M. Rutter and D.J. Smith (Eds), Psychosocial Disorders in Young People: Time Trends and Their Causes, pp. 763–782. Chichester: Wiley.
World Health Organization (1982) Changing patterns in suicidal behaviour. European Reports and Studies, No 74. Copenhagen: WHO.
World Health Organization (1996) World Health Statistics Annual, 1995. Geneva: WHO.
Yang, B., Lester, D. and Yang, C.H. (1992) Sociological and economic theories of suicide: a comparison of the USA and Taiwan. Social Science and Medicine, 34: 333–334.
Yip, P.S.F., Chao, A. and Ho, T.P. (1998) A re-examination of seasonal variation in suicides in Australia and New Zealand. Journal of Affective Disorders, 47: 141–150.

Chapter 2

Suicide in Asia and the Far East

Andrew T. A. Cheng
Institute of Biomedical Science, Academia Sinica, Taipei, Taiwan,
and
Chau-Shoun Lee
Department of Psychiatry, Lotung Poh-Ai Hospital, Ilan, Taiwan

Abstract

The incidence, patterns and trends of suicide differ considerably between Asian and Western countries. They also differ between Asian countries and regions. Suicide rates are very low in Islamic countries and very high in Sri Lanka, and rates have tended to increase over time in south-east Asia but to decrease in the Far East. In most Asian countries, rates increase with age in men and women but with a smaller male preponderance compared to their Western counterparts. In China, however, more women than men kill themselves, particularly amongst the young in rural areas. The evidence tends to suggest that the psychiatric antecedents of suicide, notably depressive illness and alcoholism, are the same in the East and the West. A higher risk of suicide appears to be associated with political reversion, low social status, migration, and a higher level of social integration. Firearms-related suicides, commonly seen in certain Western countries, are rare in Asian nations. The common methods of suicide in Asia are society-dependent. Apart from traditional methods of hanging and drowning, Asian people living in urban areas (notably Hong Kong and Singapore) commonly use jumping, whereas those living in rural areas (notably China, Taiwan, Sri Lanka and India) tend to use self-poisoning (pesticides). There are some culture-related suicides in Asian regions associated mainly with one gender. These include dowry suicide among young married women and Suttee (from the Sanskrit *Sati*, a type of self-cremation) among widows in India; hara-kiri in men and shinju in women in Japan; and juramentado in Islamic men. The problem in the ascertainment of suicide has never been well-investigated in Asian countries. Well-designed and well-conducted research on the demographic, biological, psychiatric and social factors of suicide and suicide prevention in Asian regions, with East–West comparison, is urgently required.

The International Handbook of Suicide and Attempted Suicide. Edited by K. Hawton and K. van Heeringen.

INTRODUCTION

In this chapter, some facts about the epidemiology and trends in suicide among societies in Asia and the Far East are examined and compared, and possible explanations for their similarities and differences critically reviewed. The regions include those in the Far East, such as Japan, China, Taiwan, Singapore, Hong Kong and Korea; those in south and south-east Asia, including Thailand, India and Sri Lanka; and those in the Middle East, including Israel and Jordan. With an emphasis on recent work, the areas covered in this chapter include (a) basic patterns and trends in suicide; (b) psychiatric risk factors; (c) social risk factors; and (d) culture-specific types of suicide. The review will mainly be concerned with studies of completed suicide, since the literature on non-fatal suicidal behaviour is not sufficiently comprehensive and detailed to permit comparisons across nations and regions.

BASIC PATTERNS AND TRENDS

The suicide rates for analysis of patterns and trends in suicide are basically derived from official vital statistics (La Vecchia et al, 1994; Lester, 1997; Marecek, 1998; Yip, 1996). The standard of data collection and the verdict of suicide death may vary considerably between different regions. Therefore, changes in suicide rates over time and international variations should be interpreted with caution. This issue is particularly relevant to non-Western regions, where no vigorous examination of error in suicide ascertainment has ever been conducted, and many developing nations still lack standard demographic and vital statistics.

Cross-national Variations

There are considerable international variations in suicide rates among Asian countries. Of the countries reporting suicide statistics to the World Health Organization (WHO, 1987–1998) and of the literature published in the 1980s and 1990s, the range in rates spans from below 1.0 per 100,000 in countries like Iran, Syria, Kuwait and The Philippines, to the remarkably high rate of 47.3 per 100,000 in Sri Lanka in 1995. The overall suicide rates are relatively low (5–15 per 100,000) in Taiwan, Japan, Singapore, Hong Kong, China, South Korea, Thailand, Israel and India (see Table 2.1). This rank order has not changed much over the past decades. This is true in spite of the changes in suicide rates in individual nations during this period. Moreover, it is quite tempting to speculate that geographic location may have some effect on suicide, i.e. people living in a cold climate (high latitude) may have a greater tendency to commit suicide than those living in a hot climate (near the equator), Singapore and Sri Lanka, however, being the exceptions.

Table 2.1 Age-standardized suicide rates per 100,000 in 1987 and 1994 by sex in selected Asian regions*

Country/Region	Male		Female		Total	
	1987	1994	1987	1994	1987	1994
Japan	20.8	17.3	10.0	7.2	15.3	12.2
Singapore	13.9	13.1	9.5	8.5	11.4	10.7
Hong Kong**	11.9	11.4	9.5	9.1	10.8	10.3
China	24.4	24.1	31.3	27.8	27.7	25.8
Korea	12.0	12.6	4.2	5.5	7.9	8.8
Thailand		5.4		2.3		3.8
Kuwait	1.4	1.2	0.3	1.4	1.0	1.2
Israel	9.1	11.1	3.2	3.6	6.0	7.2
Bahrain	0.9		1.1		1.0	
Sri Lanka***	49.0	64.6	17.5	22.9	33.6	43.4

Sources: *WHO, World Health Statistics Annual, 1987–98; **(1987 data) Dr P. Yip, Hong Kong; ***(1994 data) Dr R. Ratnayeke, Sri Lanka.

The picture with regard to temporal changes in suicide rates in Asian countries is complicated, with relatively larger increases for the south-east and smaller changes or appreciable decreases for the Far East. For example, Thailand has experienced a steady upward trend in suicide, with a 66% increase between 1960 and 1985 (3.5 per 100,000 in 1960 and 5.8 per 100,000 in 1985) (Diekstra, 1989). Sri Lanka has witnessed a nearly eight-fold increase in the incidence of suicide over the past 50 years (6.5 per 100,000 in 1950). In some regions of Sri Lanka the death toll has climbed to 118 per 100,000. The increase in suicide rates was particularly marked between 1975 (20.0 per 100,000) and 1985 (39.5 per 100,000) (Marecek, 1998).

In the Far East, Japan had very high suicide rates in the late 1950s (30.9 per 100,000 in men and 19.4 per 100,000 in women), the highest rates worldwide at that time, but these declined steadily in both sexes to 20.3 per 100,000 in men and 9.9 per 100,000 in women in the later 1980s. However, from the later 1970s onward, a reversal of this trend was observed in middle-aged Japanese men, whose rate had almost doubled by the late 1980s (36.7 per 100,000) as compared with the figures three decades earlier. This phenomenon draws attention to the life development of the particular cohort, who had unique social experiences. This cohort generation includes infants born around the years 1930–1935; i.e. children growing up in war-time, teenagers experiencing the post-war crisis, and adults working very hard during the nation's reconstruction periods (La Vecchia et al, 1994; Yoshimatsu, 1992). This cohort showed an increase in suicide in those 20–30 years of age (40.4 per 100,000 in 1955–1959) followed by a decrease, then another peak in the 50–60 age group (42.7 per 100,000 in 1980–1989). Interestingly, these two peaks were close to the early and late onset ages for major depression, suggesting a link between a higher prevalence of major depression in this cohort and their specific age trend for suicide. A peak in young suicides was also observed in post-war Taiwan in 1955–1959 (around 30 per 100,000 in men), but not in 1980–1989. Such a difference deserves further enquiry.

Yip (1996) examined suicide trends from 1981 to 1994 in Hong Kong, Taiwan and Beijing. In Taiwan (from 1981) and Beijing (from 1987), suicide rates declined significantly over this period, but Hong Kong experienced a slight increase. The populations of these three areas are all ethnically Chinese and share some common cultural characteristics, but they have very different sociopolitical environments. In the past decade, Taiwan has experienced greater economic prosperity and a remarkable liberalization of social and political restraints. In Beijing, people have also witnessed remarkable economic growth and the political situation there seems to be more stable than before. Hong Kong has enjoyed economic prosperity, but people have been under considerable anxiety related to the changes of sovereignty and problems associated with it. The difference in suicide trends between these three places seems to suggest that the sociopolitical and economic environments are equally important in suicide. However, suicide rates in Taiwan gradually increased in the 1990s (6.2–7.2 per 100,000 between 1990 and 1994, and 7.6–10.0 between 1995 and 1997). The reasons for changes in suicide rates over time still remain obscure and need further investigation.

Relationships of Sex and Age to Suicide

In most nations of the world, suicide rates in men increase with age (Lester, 1982). For females, the age distribution of suicide rates varies with the level of economic development of nations. For the wealthiest nations, female suicide rates tend to peak in middle age. For poorer nations the peak is shifted to elderly women, whereas for the poorest nations the peak is in younger adult women. Many countries have had a considerable to very marked increase in the frequency of suicide in the 15–29 years group over the past decade.

In most Asian countries, the certified suicide data confirm the general observation that suicide rates increase with age, but the recent increase in young suicides has not been observed (Figures 2.1–2.4). In many Asian countries, adolescent suicide rates are lower than adult ones, and have even been falling. In Taiwan, for instance, there has been a decline in adolescent suicide rates from 20 per 100,000 in 1964 to just under 5 per 100,000 in 1988 (Chong and Cheng, 1995). The corresponding rate was even lower in Hong Kong (1.8 per 100,000 in 1982–1986) (Lo, 1992) and in Singapore (3.3 per 100,000 in 1986) (Peng and Choo, 1992). This could reflect a general trend towards improvement in economic conditions, or it could mean that adolescents in countries like Hong Kong and Singapore are less attracted to resorting to suicidal behaviour as a means of coping with stress.

The suicide problem among the aged in Asia is more serious than among their Western counterparts. The rates among the elderly in some Asian areas, such as

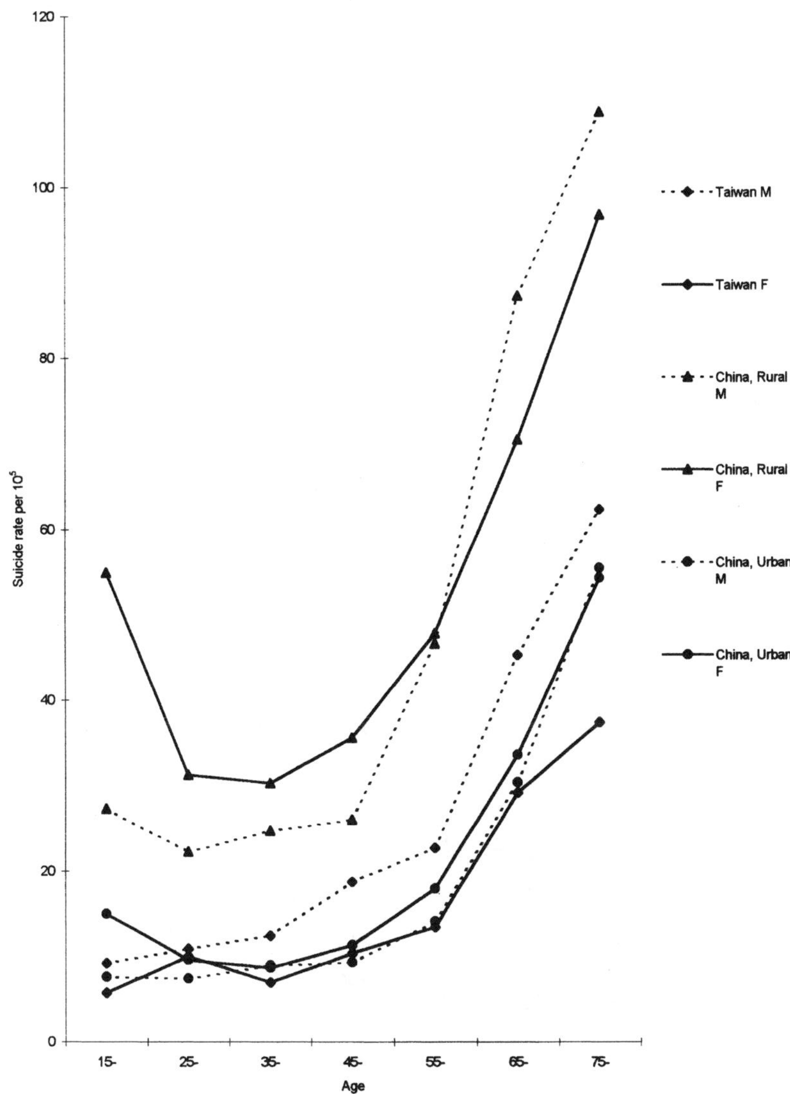

Figure 2.1 Age trend of suicides by sex in China and Taiwan in 1987. From World Health Organization Statistics (1988)

Hong Kong, Taiwan and Beijing, are four to five times the average in Western countries. This may be explained by better welfare systems in the West. In Asian countries, social support for the aged normally falls to their adult children. The increase in migration and the tendency not to live with parents in Hong Kong and Taiwan leave more elderly people on their own, with limited government support, particularly for sickness and physical handicaps (Yip, 1996).

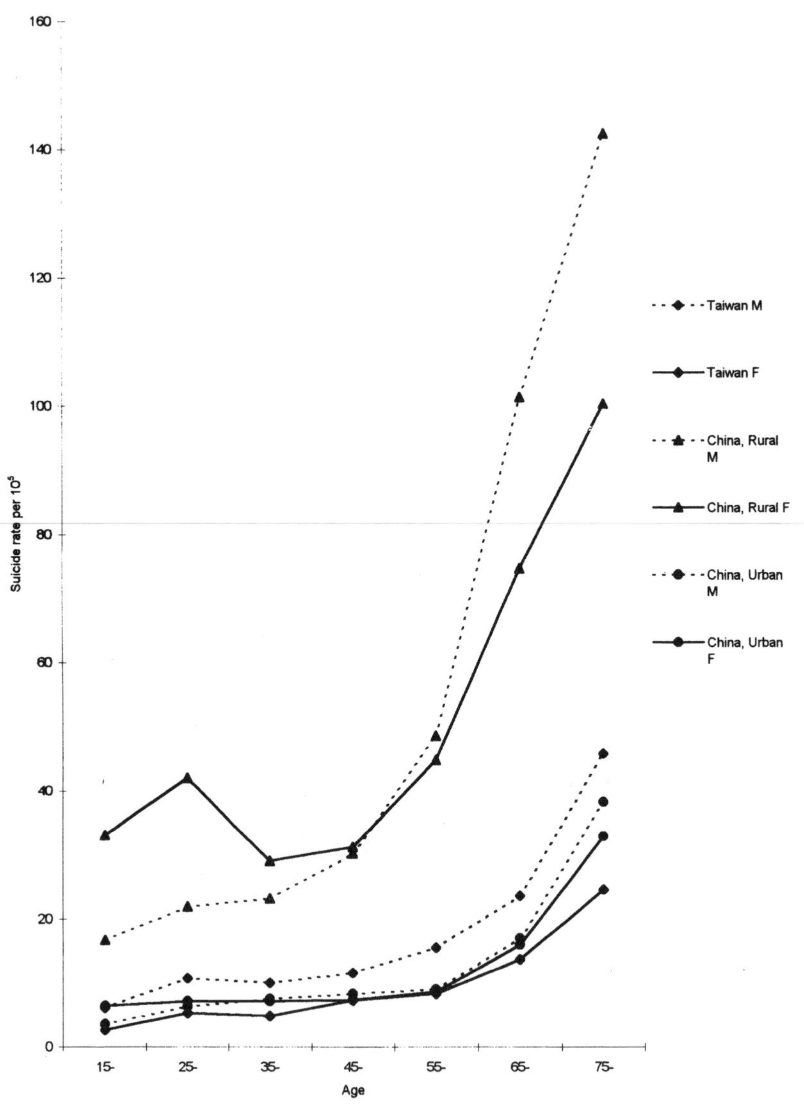

Figure 2.2 Age trend of suicides by sex in China and Taiwan in 1994. From World Health Organization Statistics (1995)

However, the pattern for suicide rates to be higher among the elderly is violated in countries like Sri Lanka, Thailand and Jordan. In Sri Lanka, the 15–29 year-old age group is the cohort at the highest risk of suicide (see Figure 2.3). This has been true since at least the late 1960s and much of the overall increase in suicide deaths over the past 50 years can be attributed to an increase in this age group. In Jordan, between 1980 and 1985, the average annual male suicide

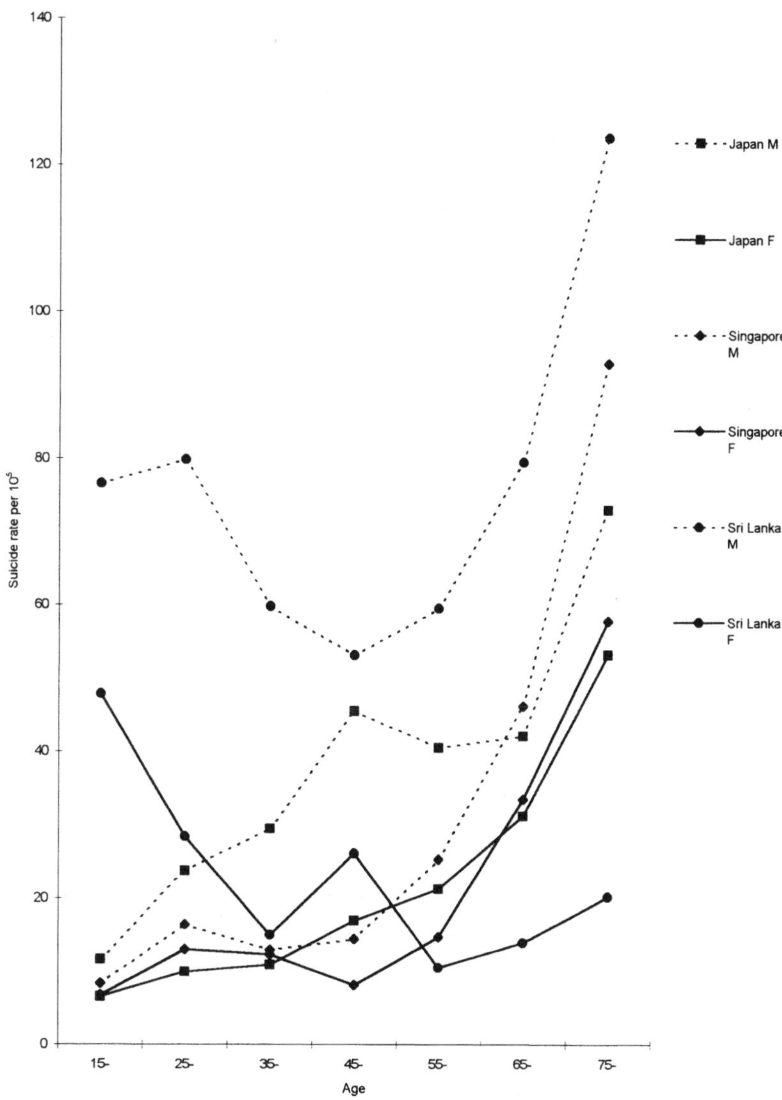

Figure 2.3 Age trend of suicides by sex in selected Asian regions in 1987. From World Health Organization Statistics (1988)

rate was 2.55 per 100,000 and the highest rates were in the 15–24 (3.35) and 25–34 (3.73) year-old age groups. The averaged annual female suicide rate was 1.65 per 100,000, and the highest rates were also among the same age groups (3.38 and 2.53, respectively). There are two possible explanations for such findings in Jordan. First, the majority of the mentally ill who committed suicide (accounting for 63% of the total suicides) were in the younger age group. Secondly, young

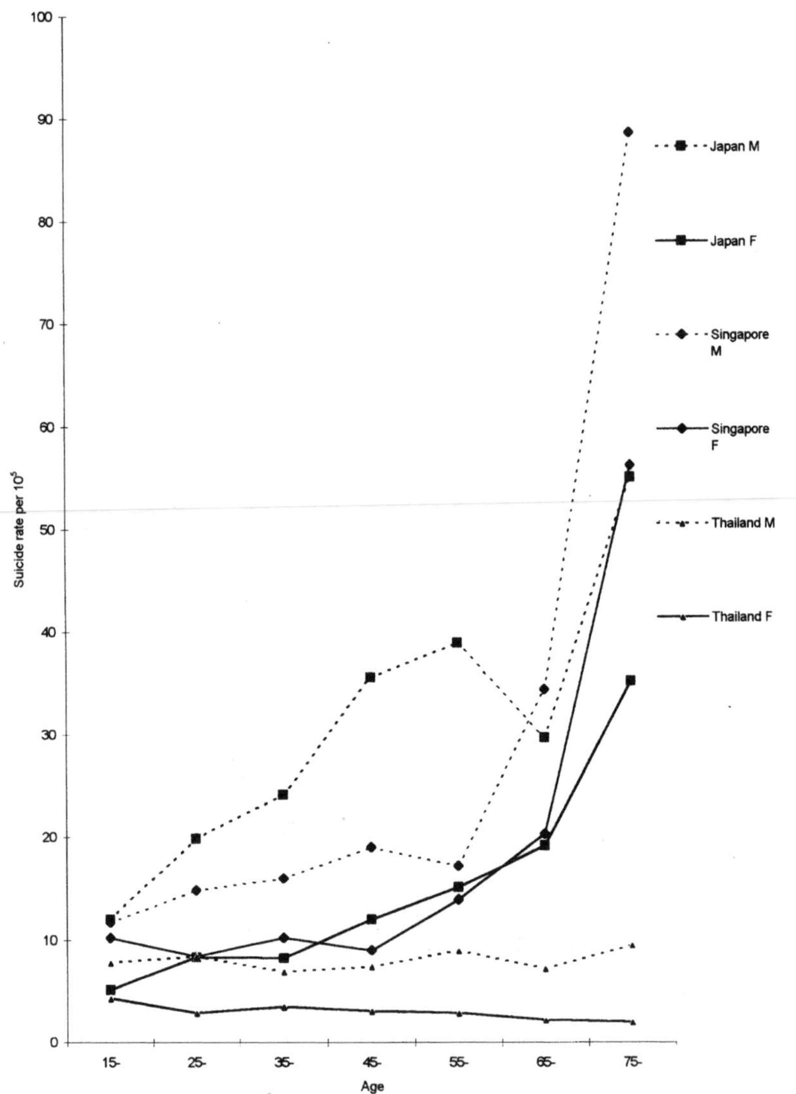

Figure 2.4 Age trend of suicides by sex in selected Asian regions in 1994. From World Health Organization Statistics (1995)

adults are thought to be less religious Muslims than the elderly, thus making them more vulnerable to stress (Daradkeh, 1989).

In Thailand, age-specific suicide rates in men show peaks at the ages of 20–24 years (13.8 per 100,000 in 1984), 50–54 years (14.7 per 100,000) and over 74 years (13.2 per 100,000), showing a W-shape curve compared to the U-shaped one in Sri Lanka (Choprapawon and Visalyaputra, 1992).

Regarding the gender ratio among suicides, the suicide rate is higher in men than in women in Asian nations, although the difference is lower than that elsewhere. The striking exception is China. Pritchard (1996) conducted an analysis of suicide in The People's Republic of China and found that the profile was the opposite to that reported in the rest of the world. In China, more female than male subjects killed themselves, particularly in the younger age groups. As compared to other Asian countries, the male: female suicide ratio was 0.77 in China, 1.3 in India (1988), 1.42 in Singapore, 1.51 in Hong Kong, 1.91 in Japan, 2.19 in Sri Lanka, and 2.30 in the Republic of Korea. The suicide data in China support a cultural explanation of lower social status and self-esteem in Chinese women. However, Desjarlais and colleagues (1995) quoted two field studies in India, which computed male: female ratios of 0.3 and 0.8, respectively. These results are more likely to indicate an actual pattern rather than an artifact of suicide recording, as field research in developing countries provides more reliable data.

BIOLOGICAL FACTORS

One possible explanation for differences in suicide rates across nations is that people from different nationalities might differ in their brain concentrations of the neurotransmitters responsible for depression, such as serotonin. As yet there are few data from Asia to test this possibility. Lester (1991) found that the estimated B_{max} level of 3H-imipramine platelet binding sites in members of eight nations (Japan as the only Asian country) were significantly associated with the suicide rates of these nations. However, the discrepant data from Japan suggested the need for further studies of B_{max} values in other oriental nations.

Seasonal variations in suicide rates have long been recognized (Lester, 1971). Recently, it has been suggested that annual rhythms in peripheral and central serotonergic turnover are related to the annual rhythm in suicide. Variations in serotonergic turnover may underline a changing susceptibility to various stressors that are known to be causally related to suicide (such as depression), psychological stresses (such as negative life events), socio-economic problems, or the presence of physical illness (Maes et al, 1994). Using harmonic analysis, Ho and colleagues (1997) examined the seasonal variation in suicides in Hong Kong and Taiwan during the period 1981–1993. A single cycle per year, with the lowest incidence in the winter months, was found in both locations and for both sexes. No biseasonal distribution of female suicides was observed, which was contrary to that reported in many Western countries (Meares et al, 1981).

PSYCHIATRIC FACTORS

Previous studies in Western societies have reported high rates of mental illness before suicide, ranging from 82% to 100% (Cheng, 1995). The two leading mental disorders prior to suicide have consistently been found to be depressive illness and alcoholism. However, mental illness has rarely or infrequently been reported as a cause of suicide in Asian populations. Some authors have speculated that a relative lack of psychological sophistication among families and investigating agencies, greater social stigma attached to mental illness, and limited psychosocial treatment resources, may have led to an underestimation of psychiatric disorders among suicides in Asia (Patel and Gaw, 1996). However, the only matched case-control biographical study of suicide in Asia, recently conducted among 116 consecutive suicides in East Taiwan, found that a high proportion of suicides suffered from mental illness (98%) and ICD-10 personality disorders (62%) before committing suicide (Cheng, 1995; Cheng et al, 1997). The two most prevalent psychiatric disorders were major depression (87%) and alcohol use disorders (44%), and these two disorders formed the most common co-morbid condition (40%). Of all suicides, 51% had consulted medical professionals in the month before death. The authors therefore concluded that despite the widely different rates of depressive illness and alcoholism in different cultures previously reported, the psychiatric antecedents of suicide are the same in the East and the West.

One biographical case study was conducted among 50 consecutive suicides from South African Indian immigrants (Gangat et al, 1987), in which major depression (54%) and alcoholism (30%) were also found to be very common. Depression and alcohol abuse occurred together in 36% of the suicides, a figure comparable to that in the Taiwan study.

Follow-up studies of psychiatric patients or suicide attempters can reduce any possible bias in diagnosing psychiatric illness or in determining previous suicidal behaviour after a suicide. However, it is likely that suicide is more readily acknowledged in people with such a history than in those without. In Singapore, Chia (1983) conducted the first prospective study of suicide in a total of 1,873 patients registered and treated by him between 1968 and 1976. Twenty-five (1.3%) were found to have committed suicide, among whom 14 suffered from schizophrenia and 11 from depressive illness.

SOCIAL FACTORS

Studies of social risk factors for suicide have employed ecological, correlational, case-control or cohort studies. Few studies of sound quality have been conducted in Asian countries. In the East Taiwan case-control study, the previously mentioned socio-environmental factors, including unemployment, marital disruption, living alone and stressful life events, were found to be significantly associated with the risk of suicide (unpublished data).

Islamic Religion and Suicide

Using factor analysis, Conklin and Simpson (1987) identified two clusters of social variables that were associated with national suicide rates. One cluster had the highest loading from the Islamic religion and the second cluster seemed to assess economic development. In a study of suicide in Jordan, where 95% of the population is Muslim, there was a total of only 219 suicides between 1980 and 1985, with an annual suicide rate of 2.1 per 100,000, which is below most of the rates reported elsewhere in the world (Daradkeh, 1989). A comparison of suicide rates among different religious groups in Israel revealed that rates were much higher for Jews than for Muslim Arabs, with a rate ratio of 4.2 for men and 2.4 for women. The two groups differed in several socio-demographic characteristics that were found to be correlated with suicide risk: (a) divorce rates were lower among Muslim Arabs; (b) there was a lower proportion of single males among Muslim Arabs; (c) there were four times fewer Muslims aged 15 years and over living in single households; and (d) there was a higher mean number of Muslims living in a household with persons aged 65 years and over (Levav and Aisenberg, 1989). Another suicide study comparing Indians, Chinese and Malays (Islamic group) in Singapore also found the lowest suicide rate in Malays (Peng and Choo, 1992). The low suicide rates in the Islamic group could be associated with the Islamic religion, which poses strong sanctions against suicide as it is viewed as a form of homicide, forbids alcohol consumption, and teaches a problem-solving method for times of acute stress by the recitation of sayings from the *Koran*, thus reducing impulsive suicide acts.

Political Environment and Reversion Anxiety

The differences in suicide rates between Hong Kong, Beijing, and Taiwan might be associated with changes in socio-political and socio-economic environments in these regions. In a comparison of longitudinal changes in youth suicide in Okinawa and mainland Japan, Kageyama and Naka (1996) found that the increasing trend in teenage suicide in Okinawa during the 1970s and 1980s might be associated with a "reversion anxiety". Okinawa, the most southern prefecture of Japan, was occupied by the USA for 27 years, from the end of World War II to 1972. Youth suicide rates in Okinawa were very low in 1960, 1965 and 1970, as compared to the corresponding figures in mainland Japan. The figures sharply increased, however, during the 1970s and 1980s, especially for males. This trend in Okinawa parallels the increase and decrease of the so-called "reversion anxiety" prevalent in Okinawa before and after its reversion to Japan in 1972. This type of social anxiety includes anxiety about national identity, further participation in war, loss of autonomy, loss of civil rights after reversion, loss of jobs for those occupied by the US military, and the abolition of support for students studying in Japan with funding by the Japanese government.

Sri Lanka as an Area with the Highest Suicide Rate in Asia

Most suicide rates in less developed areas of the world have been comparatively low and there is generally no evidence of significant rises. The only major exception is Sri Lanka, where suicide rates have risen from a modest level to one of the highest in the world. The rates of years of potential life lost through suicide in Sri Lanka were very high, being 1447.9 per 100,000 for men, and 761.8 per 100,000 for women in 1983. The corresponding figures were 1071.4 and 388.3 in Hungary and 424.6 and 191.9 in Japan in 1988 (WHO yearly statistics, World Health Organization, 1987–1998). There is still no clear explanation for such huge differences. Neither ethnic violence, nor impoverishment, nor rigid status hierarchies suffice to explain this suicide trend. Marecek (1998) tried to investigate some material and institutional dimensions of the Sri Lankan society that may have implications for suicidal behaviour.

Sri Lanka is a multi-ethnic, multilingual, and multicultural country, where people identify themselves as members of one or another so-called "ethnic" group—Sinhala, Tamil, Muslim and Burgher being the most prominent. Roughly 74% of the inhabitants in Sri Lanka are Sinhala, most with Buddhism as their religion. The estimated rates of suicide death for 1995 in Sri Lanka show a slight over-representation of Sinhala people and slight under-representations of Tamil and Muslim people. In the early 1980s, guerrilla activity led by discontented Tamils erupted into a civil war. Many civilians living in the war zone were forced to enter refugee camps. Although most people (78%) were rural cultivators, labour migration has become an important strategy for economic survival among impoverished families in the past 20 years. Most Sri Lankan migrant workers were married women who went to the Middle East alone. There is no evidence that suicide acts occur more frequently among the children or partners of migrant women, or among the women themselves, but suicide prevention workers frequently voiced elaborate claims of such a connection.

Suicide rates in Sri Lanka present a striking contrast to the relatively low corresponding rates in neighbouring countries, such as India (9.9 per 100,000). India and Sri Lanka share many cultural, religious, linguistic and social traditions. Furthermore, with respect to public health, literacy, women's rights and material well-being, Sri Lanka appears to be better off than many parts of the Indian subcontinent. Thus, it is hard to explain why the suicide rate in Sri Lanka is nearly five times that in India. We might guess that Buddhism holds a key to suicide in Sri Lanka. However, the high suicide rate in Sri Lanka is also in striking contrast to the relatively lower incidence of suicide in Myanmar (former Burma) and Thailand, which are also predominantly Buddhist countries.

Hence, the question of whether suicide rates may vary among different ethnic groups is subject to much speculation in Sri Lanka. Claims about a preponderance of death in one group or another are often used to counter claims of ethnic discrimination. One possible explanation might be the high availability of a common fatal suicide method in Sri Lanka, namely self-poisoning with agricultural chemicals. There is a high mortality rate (90%) with this method in rural areas, where the lack of transport and telephones, along with long distance to hospitals and poor roads, have prevented speedy treatment. In addition, medical management of acute self-poisoning is poor and, in a recent study, 12.7% of admitted cases died, compared to 1–2% in the UK (Eddleston et al, 1998). A similar picture has been observed among the aboriginal suicides in Taiwan (Cheng, 1997).

Female Social Status in China

A recent study in China suggested a greater cultural influence on suicide rates than had previously been realized (Pritchard, 1996). There are four important findings in this study. First, rural women had the highest female suicide rates (32.3 per 100,000 in 1987 and 30.5 in 1994) in the world. Second, whilst the suicide rate in young men was not especially high compared to other countries, a striking gender difference was observed in this age group. Third, while the lowest suicide rate was found in young women in many countries, the figure in rural Chinese young women (54.9 per 100,000 in 1987) was only exceeded by men and women over the age of 65 years in rural China. Finally, suicide occurred far more often in rural than in urban China. Rural men had a 2.7-fold (1987) to 3.6-fold (1994) higher suicide rate than their urban counterparts, and rural women had a 5.0-fold (1987) to 4.4-fold (1994) higher suicide rate than their urban counterparts. Such high suicide rates in Chinese women may reflect the enormous stresses accompanying social, cultural and economic changes that China has been undergoing, which are prevalent to a greater extent in rural areas. Possible factors may include suicide as a traditional coping and revenge strategy for women in Chinese society, with a much lower social status in the family, the one-child policy, and the lack of women's control over their own lives. The risk of suicide in rural regions might be further increased because of the fewer psychiatric services available.

To a lesser extent, the impact of rapid urbanization leading to an increased suicide rate was also observed in Taiwan in the early 1960s, with a peak of 19 per 100,000. However, a male excess in suicide rate was found during that period, suggesting less psychosocial stress for women in Taiwan than in China.

Migration and Suicide

It has been suggested that the relationship between migration and suicide rates may be explained by subsequent poor levels of social integration (Monk, 1987). Earlier studies have revealed significantly higher suicide rates among various immigrant groups than those in the respective countries of origin. In a recent suicide study including all immigrant groups in Sweden, Asian immigrants were also found to have higher suicide rates than people in the respective countries of origin (Ferrada-Noli, 1997). However, the ascertainment of suicide might be different between Asian immigrants in developed nations and their counterparts in their original countries.

The differential suicide rates between immigrants and the people in their original countries have been correlated with specific demographic factors. Suicide rates of young female immigrants from the Indian subcontinent (India, Pakistan,

Bangladesh and Sri Lanka) were consistently higher than their counterparts in the original countries (Patel and Gaw, 1996). On the other hand, suicide rates among older men in this immigrant group have been reported to be low. However, a study of completed suicide in the city of San Francisco, California, between 1987 and 1994, found that Asian elderly emigrants were at relatively high risk of suicide, especially women over the age of 85 years (Shiang et al, 1997).

Social Integration and Suicide

Previous work has shown that societies with lower levels of social integration have higher suicide rates (e.g. Sainsbury, 1986). However, a recent study in Japan (Chandler and Tsai, 1993) found that suicide rates in Japanese women were associated with a higher level of social integration. Rates were higher in prefectures where marriage was more common and divorce was less common, and where migration rates were lower. Male suicide rates were, on the whole, not related to these measures of social integration. A time-series study of suicide rates in men and women in Taiwan from 1959 to 1987 also indicated that suicide rates were higher when measures of social integration were higher, suggesting that suicide in Taiwan may be more fatalistic or altruistic (related to a high level of social regulation or integration) rather than anomic or egoistic in nature (Lester and Yang, 1995; see also Chapter 12).

METHODS OF SUICIDE

Although the risk of suicide has been found to be strongly associated with mental illness and social factors, all these features are dwarfed by the fact that men generally kill themselves more often than their female counterparts, who have an excess of depressive illness, irrespective of age and ethnicity. This male preponderance appears to be at least partly linked to the lethality of suicide methods employed, i.e. men tend to choose more aggressive methods, even in suicides which are related to psychiatric disorders. The availability of particular methods of suicide as an important contributing factor to suicide completion has received considerable recent attention.

In fact, apart from personal preference, the availability of suicide methods is largely society-dependent. Therefore, firearms are the most frequently used means for homicide and suicide in certain Western countries like the USA, but not in Asian nations. In the USA, 61% of suicides are firearms-related, whereas this is rare in Asian countries (only 0.03–1.78%) (Krug et al, 1998).

The pattern of suicide methods has changed in Asian countries. In Hong Kong, hanging accounted for 46% of the total suicides in 1981, whereas jumping showed a marked increase from 39% in 1981 to 59% in 1994. Suicides by poisoning and drowning were much less common than jumping and hanging in Hong Kong (Yip, 1996) as well as in Singapore, where about 80% of the population live in high-rise accomodation (Peng and Choo, 1992). Young people preferred jumping and the elderly used the more traditional method of hanging. There was no gender difference in the methods used to commit suicide. In Taiwan, poisoning by pesticides and hanging were the most frequently used methods, accounting for about 80% of all suicides in 1994, and jumping from a high place accounted for only 3% of the suicides (Cheng, unpublished data). It is interesting to note that for most Asian migrants in San Francisco, hanging is still the preferred method of suicide.

In Jordan, 60% of males and 45% of females committing suicide used violent methods, such as shooting, burning and hanging. Insecticides were also used by 26% of the males and 37% of the females.

Some cultures give different meaning to certain types of suicide methods. Self-immolation or self-sacrifice that involves giving up one's life for another person or a particular cause has been observed in suicidal behaviour. Burning oneself, consuming poison, fasting and drowning are some of the better known methods of self-sacrifice. In the contemporary literature, setting oneself on fire is considered to be self-immolation. In recent times, self-immolation was frequently employed as a means of protest by Buddhist monks in South Vietnam and Sri Lanka. Singh and colleagues (1998) examined the relationship between self-immolation and psychosocial variables in 22 young people in India, and found that all except one were free from manifest psychopathology. The absence of psychopathology may set this group apart from cases of deliberate self-harm arising in the context of psychiatric morbidity. It was speculated that thwarted ambitions, a sense of alienation and intropunitive hostility may lead to protest that at times becomes altruistic and results in self-immolation. However, the thoroughness of psychiatric assessment in such cases, including examination of personality characteristics, might be an interesting issue to be investigated further.

CULTURE-RELATED TYPES OF SUICIDE

Some kinds of culture-related suicide are associated more with one gender than with another. In India, dowry death by suicide occurs when a young married women or her parents are pressured after a marriage to continue to pay a dowry that exceeds the family financial capacity. Dowry suicide usually occurs by burning. The number of dowry-related deaths in India more than doubled between 1988 and 1990, which could in part have reflected an increased awareness of this problem. Suttee, which has a mythological status, refers to a type of self-cremation of a widow on her husband's pyre. It was symbolically the sign of the superiority of the feminine principle in the cosmos. This self-immolation of the widow is therefore an acceptable suicide, one in which the woman elects to remain connected with her husband instead of surviving as an outcast and a person without identity. This revered sacrifice had three kinds of advantages: a blessed existence for husband and wife in paradise and throughout their subsequent rebirth, prestige for both the husband's and the wife's kin, and blessings for all those who attended the cremation. Although many Indians pay a high respect to the mythical figure of the Suttee widow, they would prefer the custom to be discontinued (Tousignant et al, 1998).

Japan is often regarded as a country in which suicide is permissible to some extent. It is reported that the Japanese regard suicide as an honourable way to take responsibility, similar to seppuku (hara-kiri, self-disembowelment), the traditional form of suicide committed by warriors in the feudal era (Andriolo, 1998). Hara-kiri was in some cases a self-imposed demonstration of loyalty, indignation or atonement, and in other cases a self-execution ordered by authority on account of improper conduct. Suicide by disembowelment is very painful and death is not immediate. This form of suicide symbolizes the value of self-control and of exerting some sense of power over one's death. As late as 1945, several hundred army officers committed suicide through hara-kiri after the defeat of Japan. The Japanese word "shinju" literally means "oneness of mind" (Takahashi, 1997). It was originally used to mean a lovers' suicide pact based on a mutual agreement, but now it has been used more widely to mean a murder–suicide complex, in that a mother, usually in her 20s or 30s, kills her small children and then commits suicide. In Japan, the border between the mother and her children is very obscure. Even a delusional symbolic bond is sometimes observed. Society is largely sympathetic to such a mother who has been unable to find any other way of solving her problems, and does not criticize her behaviour. Conversely, society may be distinctly unsympathetic towards a mother who kills only herself and leaves her children alive and alone.

Another example of culture-related suicide, juramentado, comes from the Moros of The Philippines, who professed Islam as their common religion (Andriolo, 1998). The Moros considered Christians as evil. Although Islam condemns self-killing, death at the hands of Christians qualifies as a martyr's death and therefore a sure pathway into paradise. A man who wished to end his life because he had been shamed, or had marital or other difficulties, would swear an oath that he would go to a place frequented by Christians and would kill as many as possible in the always realistic hope that he would be killed. Some of these suicides were self-punishments, performed by persons who had committed a serious religious crime. This ritual suicide in its traditional form is no longer practised, although all of the basic beliefs are still accepted.

IMITATIVE SUICIDE

A considerable amount of research has focused on the impact of the media on suicide (Phillips, 1989; see Chapter 39). Stack (1996) analysed the effect of the media on suicide in Japan between 1955 and 1985 and found that the imitative effect is restricted to stories concerning Japanese victims (differential identification). The increase is similar in magnitude to that reported in the American cultural context. The less critical attitude to suicide among the Japanese might multiply imitative effects, but the effect was offset by a lower divorce rate, less of an emphasis on the importance of the couple, and a high level of extended family support in Japanese society.

PROBLEMS IN THE ASCERTAINMENT OF SUICIDE

A pervasive issue in suicide research is the problem of accurate ascertainment of suicide as the cause of death. Suicide tends to be under-reported, and ascertainment may depend in part on the background and training of the persons responsible for certifying the cause of death. A death is more likely to be reported as a suicide if preceded by mental illness or suicide threats, and the kind of method used to commit suicide may influence its classification. Indeed, it has been argued that research on suicide using official certifications or statistics is perhaps intellectually dishonest. Precise knowledge of whether a given death is a suicide would require careful study of a person's behaviour over a long period and access to his/her thoughts and values over that time. The psychological autopsy has been suggested as one way in which causes of death could be better classified. Such studies are time-consuming and expensive and therefore are not likely to be frequently used. In fact, Cheng's (1995) study using psychological autopsy among suicides in East Taiwan resulted in different findings from that using hospital records, which showed a much lower prevalence of mental illness (10%) among suicides in Taiwan (Rin, 1983). Furthermore, the age-standardized suicide rate in Cheng's study was more than twice that from official statistics.

Doubts are frequently cast on the validity of the official suicide data in Asian countries and, therefore, on whether rates from different nations can be compared. The ascertainment of suicide in Hong Kong under the British system should be as accurate as that in Western nations. The number of undetermined deaths due to injuries and accidents in Hong Kong has decreased significantly in recent years (Yip, 1996). However, the misclassification of causes of death, particularly between suicide, accidental death and undetermined death, may be a problem in other Asian countries. For example, suicide cannot be compensated by insurance and failed suicides cannot be legally confined in a hospital in Taiwan. Very often, therefore, suicides have been treated as accidental deaths (Chong and Cheng, 1995). Accurate suicide figures for mainland China are even more difficult to obtain because of the large population and differences in reporting systems. The stigma surrounding mental illness and suicide appears to be strong in Chinese populations, which may mean greater loss of face for men than for women when suicide occurs, and therefore may lead to a great reluctance to record male deaths as suicide (Pritchard, 1996).

Even when suicide rates are examined in a multiracial society such as Israel, where there is a common system of data collection and processing of mortality statistics, the differential risk for suicide is somewhat changed once possible artifacts are considered. For example, whereas the ratio between deaths by suicide and by undetermined external causes among Jews was 2.9 (average over the 10-year period 1976–1985), the respective rate among non-Jews was 0.8 for the same period (Levav and Aisenberg, 1989). Hence, a more conservative comparison is achieved by grouping together both types of deaths. Using such a procedure, the differential risk for Jews compared to non-Jews is reduced by almost a half.

CONCLUSIONS

There are differences in patterns and trends of suicide between Asian and Western countries. The sex ratio for suicide in Asia is smaller than that in the West, especially in China, where a female excess in suicide is evident for the last decade. The occurrence of suicide in Asia tends to increase with age, and the young population has not, as in Western societies, shown any increase in the past two decades. There is new evidence suggesting that mental illness, especially depressive illness and alcoholism, is a strong risk factor for suicide in both the East and the West. More research into biological factors in depressive and in suicidal persons is important and needed in Asia. The sociopolitical environment might be a stronger correlate of suicide in some Asian countries. Very low suicide rates are found in Islamic societies. The common methods of suicide seen in Asia indicate that they are considerably society-dependent. A number of culture-specific types of suicide, such as burning or self-immolation, or self-disembowelment, are reported in Asia.

From this review it is clear that studies of the demographic, biological, psychiatric and social causes of suicide and of suicide prevention in Asian regions are very limited. Furthermore, very few well-designed studies have so far simultaneously examined the individual and combined effects of socio-environmental and psychiatric factors on the risk of suicide (Gould et al, 1996). Future comparative studies between East and West can be expected to provide more insight into the causes and possible measures for the prevention of suicide.

REFERENCES

Andriolo, K.R. (1998) Gender and the culture construction of good and bad suicides. Suicide and Life-Threatening Behavior, 28: 37–49.

Chandler, C.R. and Tsai, Y.M. (1993) Suicide in Japan and in the West. International Journal of Comparative Sociology, 34: 244–259.

Cheng, A.T.A. (1995) Mental illness and suicide: a case-control study in East Taiwan. Archives of General Psychiatry, 52: 594–603.

Cheng, A.T.A., Mann, A.H. and Chan, K.A. (1997) Personality disorder and suicide. British Journal of Psychiatry, 170: 441–446.

Cheng, A.T.A. (1997) Suicide among two Aboriginal groups in Taiwan. Paper presented at XIX Congress of the International Association for Suicide Prevention, Adelaide.

Chia, B.H. (1983) Suicide in Singapore. In L.A. Headley (Ed.), Suicide in Asia and Near East, pp. 101–141. Berkeley, CA: University of California Press.

Chong, M.Y. and Cheng, T.A. (1995) Suicidal behavior observed in Taiwan: trend over four decades. In T.Y. Lin, E.K. Yeh and W.S. Tseng (Eds), Chinese Societies and Mental Health, pp. 209–218. Hong Kong: Oxford University Press.

Choprapawon, C. and Visalyaputra, S. (1992) Suicidal behaviour in Thailand. In K.L. Peng and W.S. Tseng (Eds), Suicidal Behaviour in the Asia–Pacific Region, pp. 127–143. Singapore: Singapore University Press.

Conklin, G. and Simpson, M.E. (1987) The family, socioeconomic development and suicide. Journal of Comparative Family Studies, 18: 99–111.

Daradkeh, T.K. (1989) Suicide in Jordan, 1980–1985. Acta Psychiatrica Scandinavica, 79: 241–244.

Desjarlais, R., Eisenberg, L., Good, B. and Kleinman, A. (1995) World Mental Health: Problems and Priorities in Low-income Countries. New York: Oxford University Press.

Diekstra, R.F.W. (1989) Suicide and the attempted suicide: an international perspective. Acta Psychiatrica Scandinavica, 80 (Suppl. 354): 1–24.

Eddleston, M., Sheriff, M.H.R. and Hawton, K. (1998) Deliberate self-harm in Sri Lanka: an overlooked tragedy in the developing world. British Medical Journal, 317: 133–135.

Ferrada-Noli, M. (1997) A cross-cultural breakdown of Swedish suicide. Acta Psychiatrica Scandinavica, 96: 108–116.

Gangat, A.E., Naidoo, L.R. and Wessels, W.H. (1987) Suicide in South African Indians. South African Medical Journal, 71: 169–171.

Gould, M.S., Fisher, P., Parides, M., Flory, M. and Shaffer, D. (1996) Psychosocial risk factors of child and adolescent completed suicides. Archives of General Psychiatry, 53: 1155–1162.

Ho, T.P., Chao, A. and Yip, P. (1997) Seasonal variation in suicides re-examined: no sex difference in Hong Kong and Taiwan. Acta Psychiatrica Scandinavica, 95: 26–31.

Kageyama, T. and Naka, K. (1996) Longitudinal change in youth suicide mortality in Okinawa after World War II: a comparative study with mainland Japan. Psychiatry and Clinical Neurosciences, 50: 239–242.

Krug, E.G., Powell, K.E. and Dahlberg, L.L. (1998) Firearm-related deaths in the United States and 35 other high- and upper-middle-income countries. International Journal of Epidemiology, 27: 214–221.

La Vecchia, C., Lucchini, F. and Levi, F. (1994) Worldwide trends in suicide mortality, 1955–1989. Acta Psychiatrica Scandinavica, 90: 53–64.

Lester, D. (1971) Seasonal variation in suicide deaths. British Journal of Psychiatry, 118: 627–628.

Lester, D. (1982) The distribution of sex and age among completed suicides. International Journal of Social Psychiatry, 28: 256–260.

Lester, D. (1991) The association between platelet imipramine binding sites and suicide. Pharmacopsychiatry, 24: 232.

Lester, D. (1997) Suicide in an international perspective. Suicide and Life-Threatening Behavior, 27: 104–111.

Lester, D. and Yang, B. (1995) Do Chinese women commit fatalistic suicide? Chinese Journal of Mental Health, 8: 23–26.

Levav, I. and Aisenberg, E. (1989) Suicide in Israel: cross-national comparisons. Acta Psychiatrica Scandinavica, 79: 468–473.

Lo, W.H. (1992) Suicidal behaviour in Hong Kong. In K.L. Peng and W.S. Tseng (Eds), Suicidal Behaviour in the Asia–Pacific Region, pp. 83–111. Singapore: Singapore University Press.

Maes, M., De Meyer, F. and Thompson, P. (1994) Synchronized annual rhythm in violent suicide rate, ambient temperature and light–dark span. Acta Psychiatrica Scandinavica, 90: 191–196.

Marecek, J. (1998) Culture, gender, and suicidal behavior in Sri Lanka. Suicide and Life-Threatening Behavior, 28: 69–81.

Meares, R., Mendelson, F.A.O. and Milgrom-Friedman, J. (1981) A sex difference in the seasonal variation in suicide rate: a single cycle for men, and two cycles for women. British Journal of Psychiatry, 138: 321–325.

Patel, S.P. and Gaw, A.C. (1996) Suicide among immigrants from the Indian subcontinent: a review. Psychiatric Services, 47: 517–521.

Monk, M. (1987) Epidemiology of suicide. Epidemiologic Review, 9: 51–69.

Peng, K.L. and Choo, A.S. (1992) Suicide in Singapore, 1986. Australian and New Zealand Journal of Psychiatry, 26: 599–608.

Phillips, D.P. (1989) Recent advances in suicidology: the study of imitative suicide. In R. Diekstra (Ed.), Suicide and Its Prevention, pp. 299–312. New York: E.J. Brill.

Pritchard, C. (1996) Suicide in the People's Republic of China categorized by age and gender: evidence of the influence of culture on suicide. Acta Psychiatrica Scandinavica, 93: 362–367.

Rin, H. (1983) Suicide in Taiwan. In L.A. Headley (Ed.), Suicide in Asia and Near East, pp. 60–86. Berkeley, CA: University of California Press.

Sainsbury, P. (1986) The epidemiology of suicide. In A. Roy (Ed.), Suicide, pp. 17–40. Baltimore, MD: Williams & Wilkins.

Shiang, J., Blinn, R., Bongar, B., Stephens, B., Allison, D. and Schatzberg, A. (1997) Suicide in San Francisco, CA: a comparison of Caucasian and Asian groups, 1987–1994. Suicide and Life-Threatening Behavior, 27: 80–91.

Singh, S.P., Santosh, P.J., Avasthi, A. and Kulhara, P. (1998) A psychosocial study of "self-immolation" in India. Acta Psychiatrica Scandinavica, 97: 71–75.

Stack, S. (1996) The effect of the media on suicide: evidence from Japan, 1955–1985. Suicide and Life-Threatening Behavior, 26: 132–142.

Takahashi, Y. (1997) Culture and suicide: from a Japanese psychiatrist's perspective. Suicide and Life-Threatening Behavior, 27: 137–145.

Tousignant, M., Seshadri, S. and Raj, A. (1998) Gender and Suicide in India: a multiperspective approach. Suicide and Life-Threatening Behavior, 28: 50–61.

Yip, P.S.F. (1996) Suicides in Hong Kong, Taiwan and Beijing. British Journal of Psychiatry, 169: 495–500.

Yoshimatsu, K. (1992) Suicidal behaviour in Japan. In K.L. Peng and W.S. Tseng (Eds), Suicidal Behaviour in the Asia-Pacific Region, pp. 15–40, Singapore: Singapore University Press.

World Health Organization (1987–1998) World Health Statistics Annual. Geneva: WHO.

Chapter 3

Attempted Suicide: Patterns and Trends

Ad J.F.M. Kerkhof
Department of Clinical Psychology, Vrije Universiteit, Amsterdam, The Netherlands

Abstract

In this chapter an overview of empirical findings on the size of the problem of attempted suicide, social and demographic characteristics, risk factors and risk moments, and patterns and trends for separate countries is presented. There was a sharp increase in attempted suicide rates in the Western European countries, Australia and the USA in the 1960s and 1970s. Attempted suicide is more prevalent everywhere among females than males, except in Finland. In particular, young women of 15–24 years of age are over-represented. In Europe, high suicide attempt rates are found in northern regions and low rates in Mediterranean regions. Single and divorced people are over-represented among suicide attempters, as well as people with low education, unemployment and histories of psychiatric treatment. Socio-economic deprivation is a well-established determinant of psychiatric morbidity and attempted suicide. Those likely to repeat are characterized by higher levels of depression, hopelessness, powerlessness, substance abuse, personality disorders, unstable living conditions, criminal records, psychiatric treatment and a history of traumatic life events, including broken homes and family violence. Seasonal and weather conditions and major public holidays have small but significant effects on attempted suicide referrals. No empirical support has been found in the past for the existence of a modelling effect, although this has recently been challenged. Cultural factors are important in understanding attempted suicide. In some Asian countries attempted suicide may be influenced by dowry problems and problems with in-laws. The methods used in Asian countries reflect the importance of the accessibility of means, such as organophosphate pesticides and other household poisons. There are substantial differences between communities in the prevalence of attempted suicide. This suggests that some communities meet the needs of their underprivileged youngsters better than others. There is a need for

The International Handbook of Suicide and Attempted Suicide. Edited by K. Hawton and K. van Heeringen.

improved health promotion policies and effective socio-economic empowerment strategies for underprivileged youngsters.

INTRODUCTION

Attempted suicide probably has a high prevalence in many countries. Exact figures are lacking, however, because epidemiological research into attempted suicide has only recently used standardized procedures. In this chapter an overview of empirical findings on the size of the problem, social and demographic characteristics, risk factors and risk periods, and patterns and trends for separate countries is presented. Results are summarized from individual epidemiological studies, collaborative studies, and survey studies of self-reported suicide attempts. As far as international studies allow, comparisons between nations will be presented along with associations with social indicators. The conclusion is that we need better national registration of attempted suicide in order to enhance our knowledge of the problem (Bille-Brahe, 1998). To facilitate understanding of the phenomenon we start with a description and definition of attempted suicide.

DESCRIPTION AND DEFINITION

The term "attempted suicide" is an umbrella term that covers a number of different behaviours. Common to these behaviours is that people inflict acute harm upon themselves, poison or injure themselves, or try to do so, with non-fatal outcome. Also common to these behaviours is that they occur in conditions of emotional turmoil. Suicide attempts are undertaken with a view to, and expectation of, acute self-harm or unconsciousness as a means of realizing changes through the actual or intended consequences.

In many ways, however, non-fatal suicidal behaviours differ enormously. Some attempts are aimed at dying, many are aimed at mobilizing help, and others are ambiguously aimed to a certain extent at both. Some attempts are well-prepared, others are carried out impulsively. Attempts may result in very different physical consequences, depending upon intention, preparation, knowledge of the lethality of the chosen method and purely coincidental factors.

It is often difficult to establish the meaning of attempted suicide based on overt characteristics of the behaviour or on a person's self-report. Because of fear for consequences (admission to a psychiatric hospital, stigmatization) or because of psychological defence mechanisms, people sometimes deny or conceal their intentions (dissimulation tendencies). Furthermore, sometimes people who perform potentially lethal self-destructive behaviour do not in fact have any wish to die, but impulsively act out a wish to change their circumstances. Or people who present at a general hospital with minor self-injury or minor self-poisoning, may have had strong intentions to die, but had insufficient knowledge of the lethality of the method. All this caused Kreitman and colleagues in 1969 to state that . . . "the term 'attempted suicide' is highly unsatisfactorily, for the excellent reason that the great majority of patients so designated are not in fact attempting suicide" (pp. 746–7). Other terms, such as deliberate self-poisoning, harm or self-injury have disadvantages as well because they ". . . neglect the very real association that exists between attempted suicide and completed suicide (not only repetition, but also the coincidental actions of others which may influence the outcome)". Therefore, they proposed the term "parasuicide", designating "an act which is like suicide, yet is something other than suicide". This proposal has received support from researchers, but clinicians never got used to the term. In clinical practice, the term "parasuicide" can only be explained with reference to the term "attempted suicide". The term "parasuicide" suffers a similar drawback: it implies suicidal intention which in fact may be absent (Hawton and Catalan, 1987). In modern studies and in this chapter the two terms are therefore used as synonyms. For convenience, the terms "parasuicide" or "attempted suicide" (and even "deliberate self-harm"), can each be conceived as the sum of "deliberate self-injury" plus "deliberate self-poisoning" (Hawton et al, 1997a).

A definition was developed for the World Health Organization/European Study on Parasuicide (see below). The terms "attempted suicide" and "parasuicide" are used as equivalents and are defined as follows (Platt et al, 1992):

> An act with non-fatal outcome, in which an individual deliberately initiates a non-habitual behaviour that, without intervention from others, will cause self-harm, or deliberately ingests a substance in excess of the prescribed or generally recognized therapeutic dosage, and which is aimed at realizing changes which the subject desired via the actual or expected physical consequences.

Attempted suicides in some cases may be conceived as failed suicides. In most cases, however, attempted suicides should not be viewed as failed suicides, because the dynamics are often very different. This difference is reflected in the characteristics of the actors: completed suicides more often concern males who are relatively old, attempted suicides more often concern young women.

EPIDEMIOLOGY

In Europe, the USA and Australia during the 1960s and 1970s there was a sharp increase in the numbers of people treated in hospitals because of intentional overdoses or self-injury (Weissman, 1974; Hawton and Catalan, 1987). In the 1980s several studies showed a stabilization in rates (Hawton and Fagg, 1992; Platt et al, 1988). In the early 1990s these numbers increased further in some catchment areas (Hawton et al, 1997a). The number of persons treated for attempted suicide in general hospitals does not, however, adequately reflect the size of the problem. These numbers should be calculated against the size and the characteristics of the population in the area that is being served by the hospital. Furthermore, in some countries suicide attempters are treated by general practitioners when there is no need for hospital admission. In many instances simple emergency attendance for overdosing is not even registered. There are no national registrations that reliably monitor trends in attempted suicide seen in general hospitals. Furthermore, differences in the definition of non-fatal suicidal behaviour make it difficult to compare the results of epidemiological studies. Also, of course, there are probably many attempted suicides that do not come to the attention of medical professionals. Furthermore, studies on attempted suicide have mainly been from the USA, Canada, Western Europe and Australia. Few studies originate from other parts of the world.

Until recently, there has been continuous monitoring of attempted suicide over a long period of time, where characteristics of persons attempting suicide have been related to the catchment area population, in only a very few places. In Oxford and Edinburgh in the UK, for instance, trends in attempted suicide rates have been documented reliably (Kreitman, 1977; Platt et al, 1988; Hawton et al, 1997a). After a period of stabilization in the 1980s, a marked increase could be observed. Between 1985 and 1995 the rates of deliberate self-harm in Oxford increased by 62% in males and 42% in females (but with a slight decrease between 1989 and 1992). The increase in deliberate self-harm has been especially marked among young males. This appeared to be related to considerable excess of substance misuse in males. A strong increase in rates of deliberate self-harm among young males has also been described recently in Gent (van Heeringen and De Volder, in press).

THE WHO/EURO MULTICENTRE STUDY ON PARASUICIDE

So far only one international multicentre study into attempted suicide has been conducted, taking into consideration the methodological pitfalls outlined above. The World Health Organization Regional Office for Europe in Copenhagen initiated a collaborative multicentre study in 16 catchment areas in Europe, using the same methodology, definition and case-finding criteria in each centre (Platt et al, 1992; Kerkhof et al, 1994). The findings were related to the size and characteristics of the catchment areas in order to study rates, trends, risk factors and social indicators (Tables 3.1 and 3.2). Most of the epidemiological data presented in this section have been drawn from that study for the 1989–1992 period (Schmidtke et al, 1996). The design was that in each centre standardized monitoring forms were filled out by medical personnel on all consecutive suicide attempts that were medically treated in general hospitals, in other medical facilities and by general practitioners in a well-defined catchment area of at least

Table 3.1 Female person-based attempted suicide rates per 100,000 population aged 15 years and over, 1989–1992, in 16 centres of the WHO/EU Multicentre Study on Parasuicide

Centre	Country	1989	1990	1991	1992	Mean 1989–1992	Age-standardized mean
Cergy-Pontoise	France	509	570	546	*	542	462
Oxford	UK	384	363	364	362	368	323
Bordaux	France	248	***	***	***	248	***
Helsinki	Finland	237	266	247	238	247	246
Stockholm	Sweden	314	227	192	195	232	229
Szeged	Hungary	222	208	218	167	204	213
Odense	Denmark	233	199	173	175	194	195
Sor Trondelag	Norway	210	210	177	169	192	191
Bern	Switzerland	178	119	**	**	149	152
Umea	Sweden	148	145	143	144	145	150
Leiden	The Netherlands	148	144	129	134	139	132
Innsbruck	Austria	141	95	101	97	108	107
Emilia-Romagna	Italy	98	114	110	101	106	112
Wurzburg	Germany	99	84	105	108	99	102
Padova	Italy	117	90	93	94	98	103
Guipuzcoa	Spain	85	69	62	*	72	69
Mean	Europe	211	193	190	165	193	186

Reproduced by permission from Schmidtke et al (1996).
Standard population: European population according to 1992 World Population Prospects (United Nations, 1993a,b).
*** 1989 Data only.
** 1989–1990 Data.
* 1989–1991 Data.

250,000 inhabitants. The catchment areas were clearly defined, both geographically and administratively, to allow for comparison of information on the population of attempted suicides with official statistics for the total population of that area.

Differences between Catchment Areas and Countries

Obviously there are enormous differences between areas in Europe in rates of attempted suicide. For females the rates varied between 542 per 100,000 (age 15 years and over) in Cergy-Pontoise, France, and 72 in Guipuzcoa (San Sebastian, Spain), a seven-fold difference. Oxford ranked second with 368, followed by Bordeaux with 248, Helsinki with 247, and Stockholm with 232 per 100,000. Low rates were found in the Italian and Spanish centres, and in Würzburg, Germany and Innsbruck, Austria. The average female suicide attempt rate for all centres combined was 193 per 100,000 females of 15 years and older. Even within a single

Table 3.2 Male person-based attempted suicide rates per 100,000 population aged 15 years and over, 1989–1992, in 16 centres of the WHO/EU Multicentre Study on Parasuicide

Centre	Country	1989	1990	1991	1992	Mean 1989–1992	Age-standardized mean
Helsinki	Finland	330	340	323	314	327	314
Oxford	UK	277	272	271	239	264	251
Cergy-Pontoise	France	248	263	246	*	252	223
Szeged	Hungary	190	188	203	157	184	186
Odense	Denmark	188	175	152	159	169	172
Stockholm	Sweden	179	176	115	148	154	153
Sor Trondelag	Norway	147	145	151	142	146	147
Bordaux	France	129	***	***	***	129	***
Bern	Switzerland	130	99	**	**	115	115
Umea	Sweden	94	104	92	77	92	96
Leiden	The Netherlands	81	102	82	78	86	82
Innsbruck	Austria	94	78	75	85	83	81
Wurzburg	Germany	72	66	68	55	65	66
Padova	Italy	70	55	55	63	61	61
Emilia-Romagna	Italy	58	48	54	42	50	53
Guipuzcoa	Spain	65	53	20	*	46	45
Mean	Europe	147	144	136	130	140	136

Reproduced by permission from Schmidtke et al (1996).
Standard population: European population according to 1992 World Population Prospects (United Nations, 1993a,b).
*** 1989 data only.
** 1989–1990 data.
* 1989–1991 data.

country there appear to be differences between catchment areas. In Sweden, the urban catchment area of Stockholm had a rate of 232, whereas the much less urbanized catchment area of Umea had a rate of 145. The two Italian centres had similar rates for females.

For males the rates varied between 327 per 100,000 in Helsinki and 46 in Guipuzcoa, again a seven-fold difference. Oxford again ranked second with 264, followed by Cergy-Pontoise with 252. Low rates were found in the Italian and Spanish centres and in Würzburg, Germany. The male average suicide attempt rate for all centres combined was 140 per 100,000 males of 15 years and older. Within Sweden the difference in rates between Stockholm (154) and Umea (92) is remarkable.

In general it appears that high rates of attempted suicide are found in northern European regions, and low rates in Mediterranean regions, a pattern similar to suicide rates (see Chapter 1).

Differences between catchment areas in suicide attempt rates have been studied in relation to socio-economic characteristics of these areas by Bille-Brahe and colleagues (1996). No correlation was found with many social and economical factors supposedly related to suicide attempt rates (population density, urban/rural distribution, proportion working in agriculture forestry or fishery, sex ratio, percentage aged 40 and over, number of people per household, percentage of people living alone, percentage of single-parent families, per capita income, unemployment rate, life expectancy, mortality rate, infant mortality, crimes per year per 1,000 and per capita alcohol consumption). Only two characteristics of the catchment areas seemed to be related to suicide attempt rates: the percentage of divorced people in the area (Spearman's rank correlations, 0.87 for males, $p < 0.001$, and 0.76 for females, $p < 0.01$; $n = 15$ regions on which data complete) and the percentage receiving public assistance (0.81 for males, $p < 0.01$, and 0.68 for females, $p < 0.05$; $n = 11$ regions). Family stability, and the percentage of the population relying on welfare, both seem to be related to the frequency of attempted suicide, but the interpretation of these findings is difficult since one would expect the other related social indicators of societal cohesion to co-vary as well (see Chapter 12).

It is important, however, to realize that the characteristics mentioned above relate to regions or countries, and do not relate to individuals. At the individual level, characteristics such as unemployment do play an important role, but that does not mean that at a sociological level unemployment rates explain high attempted suicide rates in a region (Platt, 1984; Platt and Dyer, 1987). This relationship holds only for some regions and not for others, as has been documented repeatedly (Adam, 1990).

Trends

In the WHO/EURO Study on Parasuicide during the period 1989–1992, the male suicide attempt rates decreased on average by 17%, and the female rates by 14% (Schmidtke et al, 1996). The largest average decreases were found in the 35–44 years age group for both males and females (both 19%), in females of 45–54 years (18%), and young males aged 15–24 years (18%). Only in the age group of 55 years and older was an increase found (males by 11%, females by 9%). The trends in suicide attempt rates over the 4 years of monitoring were different for each centre. In most centres there were also years with increases in rates. The decreasing overall trend was therefore not attributable to a decline in the completeness of the monitoring system in the various centres.

Sex and Age

In all but one centre, namely Helsinki, the female attempted suicide rates were higher than the male suicide attempt rates. On average, the rates for females were

1.5 times higher then those for men. Highest average rates were found for young females aged 15–24 years (283), followed by 25–34 years (262), and 35–44 years (235). High rates for 15–24 year-olds were found in Cergy-Pontoise (766 per 100,000) and Oxford (629 per 100,000). For males, the highest average rates were found in 25–34 year-olds (199), followed by 35–44 year-olds (169) and young males of 15–24 years (168). The male rate was particularly high among 25–44 year-olds in Helsinki (459/460 per 100,000). High rates among young males of 15–24 years were found in Helsinki (372), Cergy-Pontoise (337), and Oxford (314 per 100,000). In most but not all centres, the ratio of females to males in suicide attempt rates appear to be declining.

Other Sociodemographic Characteristics

Single and divorced people were over-represented among suicide attempters in the WHO/EURO Study (Schmidtke et al, 1996). In the Dutch part of this study the rates for divorced women (248 per 100,000) and men (191 per 100,000) were highest, and rates were lowest for the widowed (39 per 100,000 for women, 16 per 100,000 for men; Arensman et al, 1995). Compared with the general population, those with low levels of education and the unemployed or disabled were significantly over-represented among suicide attempters. An average of 20% of all male and 12% of all female suicide attempters in the various catchment areas were unemployed. About 57% had a low level of formal education and the majority had no vocational training. In the Dutch part of the study there were much higher rates (expressed in rates per 100,000) in the unemployed (322 for males, 455 for females) and the disabled (113 for males, 205 for females) than in the employed (27 for males, 31 for females). Those with only primary education had rates of 160 per 100,000 compared to 27 per 100,000 for those with higher vocational training or university education (Arensman et al, 1995). These results support many findings in the UK and elsewhere, where low social class and unemployment repeatedly appear as characteristics of the attempted suicide population (see also Chapter 20; Hawton and Catalan, 1987; Hawton et al, 1994; van Heeringen, 1994).

These findings may be partly related to underlying common causes, such as the presence of psychiatric disorders. But these findings also suggest the influence of sociological factors impacting on a relatively economically deprived group in society with a greater share of adversity (Adam, 1990). Socio-economic deprivation is now a well-established determinant of psychiatric morbidity and attempted suicide (Gunnell et al, 1995; Congdon, 1996). In contrast to completed suicide, where the presence of psychiatric disorders is well documented (up to 95% of suicides may have suffered from a psychiatric disorder), the presence of psychiatric disorders is much less documented among attempted suicide patients. Among first-evers (those who engage in suicidal behaviour for the first time in their lives), the prevalence of psychiatric disorders may be rather low, whereas among repeaters psychiatric morbidity is common (Arensman and Kerkhof, 1996).

Method

Methods used in suicide attempts are mostly "non-violent". In the WHO/EU Multicentre Study, 64% of males and 80% of females used self-poisoning. Cutting, mostly wrist-cutting, was employed in 17% of male cases and 9% of female cases. There are some differences between countries in the use of particular methods. In Szeged, Hungary, for example, 19% of males and 15% of females used poisoning with pesticides, herbicides or other toxic agricultural chemicals. In Sor Trondelag (Norway), relatively high percentages of individuals attempted suicide by deliberate alcohol overdosage (6% of males, and 5% of females). In general, somewhat more older men used the method of jumping or lying before a moving vehicle. In the Oxford studies during 1985–1995, 88% of all episodes involved self-poisoning, 8% involved self-injury, and 4% involved both. There was an increase in the use of paracetamol from 31% of poisoning cases in 1985 to 50% in 1995 (Hawton et al, 1997b). There was also an increase in antidepressant overdoses, and a decrease in overdoses of minor tranquillizers and sedatives. The differences in methods between countries may be related to differences in the accessibility of certain methods. Until recently, paracetamol was available in large quantities in the UK, which is different from most other European countries (Gunnell et al, 1997). The ingestion of alcohol during or before the act can sometimes be considered to be a part of the actual method of attempted suicide (when used to bring about unconsciousness, or to increase the risk of a fatal outcome), as part of the preparation (to lower the threshold for engaging in an attempt because of disinhibition), or as a long-term risk factor. Hawton and colleagues (1997/1998) found that 22–26% of attempted suicide patients had consumed alcohol at the time of the attempt (males more frequently than females) and that 44–50% had consumed alcohol during the 6 hours before the episodes, this again being more common in males than in females. About 28% of attempted suicide patients in Oxford could be labelled substance misusers (alcohol and drugs).

REPETITION

Repetition is one of the core characteristics of suicidal behaviour. Among those who commit suicide, up to 40% have attempted suicide previously. Among suicide attempters, "repeaters" are probably more common than "first-evers". On the basis of several studies it appears that 30–60% of suicide attempters have made previous attempts, and 15–25% have done so within the year before an episode (Kreitman and Casey, 1988; Platt et al, 1988, 1992; Hawton and Fagg, 1995).

Prospectively, suicide attempters have a high risk of committing suicide. Between 10% and 15% may eventually die because of suicide (Maris, 1992), although the figure varies greatly between different countries (see Chapter 21). Mortality by suicide is higher among suicide attempters who have made previous attempts (Hawton and Catalan, 1981; Hawton and Fagg, 1988). Risk of repeated suicidal behaviour is highest during the first year after a suicide attempt, and especially within the first 3–6 months (Goldacre and Hawton, 1985; Hawton and Fagg, 1988, 1995). In the WHO/EURO Multicentre Study on Parasuicide it was found that at least 54% of attempters had attempted before, 30% at least twice, and that 30% of suicide attempters made another attempt during a 1 year follow-up (Kerkhof et al, 1998; Arensman et al, 1999). The problem of repetition of attempted suicide is discussed in more detail in Chapter 21.

All this points to the obvious interest in knowing how to prevent repetition. It is hoped that knowledge of antecedents or risk factors may foster early identification of persons at risk and better treatment. Many studies have tried to identify risk factors or antecedents and some of these are now well known. Sociodemographic risk factors associated with repetition are age group 25–49 years, being divorced, unemployed and from a lower social class. Psychiatric and psychosocial characteristics of repeaters are substance abuse, depression, hopelessness, powerlessness, personality disorders, unstable living conditions or living alone, criminal records, previous psychiatric treatment, and a history of stressful traumatic life events, including broken homes and family violence. Prospectively, a history of attempts predicts future non-fatal suicide attempts (Buglass and Horton, 1974; Van Egmond and Diekstra, 1989; Kreitman and Foster, 1991; Arensman and Kerkhof, 1996; Sakinofsky et al, 1990).

SELF-REPORTED ATTEMPTED SUICIDE

A number of surveys have been conducted to estimate the prevalence of attempted suicide (see also Chapter 16). Some of these surveys have concerned adolescents and were administered anonymously. Most questionnaire studies revealed that 1–4% of respondents have attempted suicide at some point in time (Paykell et al, 1974; Kienhorst et al, 1991; Dressen et al, 1998), but some studies have reported figures as high as 20% (Rubinstein et al, 1989). The validity of these findings is, however, questionable: the life-time prevalence of attempted suicide among non-respondents is not known, the influence of social desirability is not known, and the wording of the questions is rather important. The simple question, "Did you ever attempt suicide?" is inappropriate because it implies suicidal intent that may have been absent. The question, "Did you ever take too many pills when you were in crisis?" is inappropriate because it does not in any way refer to suicidal intention that may have been present. Furthermore, a person taking three sleeping tablets for a good sleep might answer affirmatively. Estimates of the lifetime prevalence of attempted suicide in adolescents or in the general population based upon these kinds of questions may have resulted in overestimation. Based upon the rates from the WHO/EURO study, the lifetime prevalence of medically treated suicide attempts probably is around 3% for females and 2% for males. Suicide attempts that do not lead to attendance at a hospital or contact with a general practitioner are very difficult to study because of the unreliability of self-report when it comes to the difference between self-destructive gestures and attempted suicide. The problem of self-reported suicidal behaviour is discussed in more detail in Chapter 16.

TEMPORAL FACTORS

Most attempted suicides are seen in hospital in the afternoon and evening. They occur more frequently on Saturdays, Sundays, Mondays and Wednesdays. More cases happen in the months of March and July (Kerkhof, 1985; Leiden, The Netherlands), or May and June (Barker et al, 1994; Oxford, UK), with a definite dip in winter (Masterton, 1991). Attempted suicide is somewhat less frequent immediately before and more frequent immediately after major holidays, especially Christmas and Easter (Cullum et al, 1993; Jessen et al, 1999). Major holidays may bring periods of stress related to changed sleep rhythms, alcohol use, family conflicts, financial burdens, and may bring disappointments due to (unrealistic) elevated expectations of joy and harmony (Jessen et al, 1999). Gabbenesh (1988) called this the "broken-promise effect", stating that springtime, weekends and holidays are usually affective positive events that at times may promise more positive things than actually occur (Jessen et al, 1999). Even elections may affect suicidal behaviour (Masterton and Platt, 1989), possibly influencing vulnerability in people with low tolerance for frustrated expectations. Weather conditions and seasonal cycling may have a small influence on attempted suicide rates, particularly in females (Masterton, 1991; Barker et al, 1994). On warmer, wetter days with little wind, somewhat more hospital referrals for female suicide attempters have been observed, possibly explained by the gender difference in thermoregulation (Barker et al, 1994).

MODELLING

Many authors have suggested that imitation or copycat behaviour has a role in attempted suicide. However, few studies have used adequate control groups to demonstrate this effect. In a study using matched controls from general practitioners in the same catchment area as the attempted suicide group, Platt (1993) found no empirical support for the existence of a modelling effect, neither was it possible to find evidence for a modelling effect of attempted suicide portrayed in a televized soap opera (*East Enders*) by Platt (1989), but further examination of the data from this study and more recent work has challenged this finding (see Chapter 39).

CULTURAL VARIATION

In Canada the rate of attempted suicide was estimated to be 304 per 100,000 (Sakinofsky, 1996). In the US National Institute of Mental Health Epidemiological Catchment Area Study (1980–1985) it was found that 2.9% of the respondents had made a suicide attempt at some point in time (Moscicki, 1988). Cultural variation in attempted suicide has been documented from India (Latha et al, 1996), Sri Lanka (Eddleston et al, 1998) and Pakistan (Khan et al, 1996), and from ethnic groups within Western societies, such as the Inuit in Canada (Kirmayer et al, 1996). Neeleman and colleagues (1996) studied ethnic differences in attempted suicide in Camberwell, London, and found considerable differences between the attempted suicide rates for whites, UK-born Indian females and Afro-Caribbeans. Indian females had a particularly high rate, 7.8 times that of UK-born white females. Marital problems seem to be related to attempted suicide in Asian countries like India, Pakistan, Sri Lanka and China. Young married women may have serious difficulties after moving in with their husbands and their extended families. Dowry problems and problems with in-laws are thought to be precipitants of attempted suicide among young married women. In Asian countries the methods used in attempted suicide reflect differences in accessibility. Self-poisoning with organophosphate pesticides and other household poisons are prevalent. As in the Western world, attempted suicide appears to reflect feelings of hopelessness and helplessness in adverse living conditions with no prospect of improvement. Women especially tend to be more powerless to bring about changes in their living conditions. In Sri Lanka the continuous warfare, poverty and lack of opportunities at home and abroad frustrates the young who are relatively well-educated (Eddleston et al, 1998).

CONCLUSIONS

Attempted suicide is a major problem in many contemporary societies. Attempted suicide seems to reflect the degree of powerlessness and hopelessness of young people with low education, low income, unemployment and difficulties in coping with life stresses. As such, attempted suicide should be a major concern for politicians. There are substantial differences between communities in the prevalence of attempted suicide. This suggests that some communities meet the needs of their underprivileged youngsters better than others. We still barely understand the relevant differences between communities and nations. Preventive action is therefore difficult to design. There is a need for better nationwide continuous registration of attempted suicide and related socio-economic conditions. There is also a need for better mental health care management of suicide attempters, and for further experimental studies on the prevention of repetition. Although we know that persons who attempt suicide are at high risk for future fatal and non-fatal suicidal behaviour, we still lack effective socio-economic empowerment strategies or general health promotion policies for preventing suicidal careers.

REFERENCES

Adam, K.S. (1990) Environmental, psychosocial and psychoanalytic aspects of suicidal behavior. In S.J. Blumenthal and D.J. Kupfer (Eds), Suicide Over the Life Cycle. Washington, DC: American Psychiatric Press.

Arensman, E., Kerkhof, A.J.F.M., Hengeveld, M. and Mulder, J. (1995) Medically treated suicide attempts: a four year monitoring study of the epidemiology in The Netherlands. Journal of Epidemiology and Commmunity Health, 49: 285–289.

Arensman, E. and Kerkhof, A.J.F.M. (1996) Classification of attempted suicide: a review of empirical studies, 1963–1993. Suicide and Life-Threatening Behavior, 26: 46–67.

Arensman, E., Kerkhof, A., Dirkzwager, A., Verduin, C., Bille-Brahe, U., Crepet, P., De Leo, D., Hawton, K., Hjelmeland, H., Lonnqvist, J., Michel, K., Querejeta, I., Salander-Renberg, E., Schmidtke, A., Temesvary, B. and Wasserman, D. (1999) Prevalence and risk factors for repeated suicidal behaviour: results from the WHO/EURO Multicentre Study on Parasuicide, 1989–1992 (submitted for publication).

Barker, A., Hawton, K., Fagg, J. and Jennison, C. (1994) Seasonal and weather factors in parasuicide. British Journal of Psychiatry, 165: 375–380.

Bille-Brahe, U., Andersen, K., Wasserman, D., Schmidtke, A., Bjerke, T., Crepet, P., De Leo, D., Haring, C., Hawton, K., Kerkhof, A., Lonnqvist, J., Michel, K., Philippe, A., Querejeta, I., Salander-Renberg, E. and Temesvary, B. (1996) The WHO/EURO Multicentre Study: risk of parasuicide and the comparability of the areas under study. Crisis: The Journal of Crisis Intervention and Suicide Prevention, 17/1: 32–42.

Bille-Brahe, U. (1998) Suicidal Behaviour in Europe: The Situation in the 1990s. Copenhagen: World Health Organization. (EUR/ICP/HPSA 01 0403).

Buglass, D. and Horton, J. (1974) A scale for predicting subsequent suicidal behaviour. British Journal of Psychiatry, 124: 573–578.

Congdon, P. (1996) Suicide and parasuicide in London: a small area study. Urban Studies, 1: 137–158.

Cullum, S.J., Catalan, J., Berelowitz, K., O'Brien, S., Millington, H.T. and Preston, D. (1993) Deliberate self-harm and public holidays: is there a link? Crisis: The Journal of Crisis Intervention and Suicide Prevention, 14/1: 39–42.

Dressen, C., Janvrin, M.P. and Arènes, J. (1998) Idées suicidaires et tentatives de suicide. Premieres résultats issus de l'enquête Baromètre santé jeunes 1997. In M. Debout (Ed.), Deuxième Journée Nationale pour la Prevention du Suicide, pp. 37–40. Paris: Groupement d'Études et de Prévention du Suicide.

Eddleston, M., Rezvi Sheriff, M.H. and Hawton, K. (1998) Deliberate self harm in Sri Lanka: an overlooked tragedy in the developing world. British Medical Journal, 317: 133–135.

Gabbennesh, H. (1988) When promises fail: a theory of temporal fluctuations in suicide. Social Forces, 76: 129–145.

Goldacre, M. and Hawton, K. (1985) Repetition of self-poisoning and subsequent death in adolescents who take overdoses. British Journal of Psychiatry, 146: 395–398.

Gunnell, D.J., Peters, T.J., Kammerling, R.M. and Brooks, J. (1995) Relation between parasuicide, suicide, psychiatric admissions and socioeconomic deprivation. British Medical Journal, 311: 226–230.

Gunnell, D., Hawton, K., Murray, V., Garnier, R., Bismuth, C., Fagg, J. and Simkin, S. (1997) Use of paracetamol for suicide and non-fatal poisoning in the UK and France: are

restrictions on availability justified? Journal of Epidemiology and Community Health, 51: 175–179.
Hawton, K. and Catalan, J. (1981) Psychiatric management of attempted suicide patients. British Journal of Hospital Medicine, 26: 365–368.
Hawton, K. and Catalan, J. (1987) Attempted Suicide. A Practical Guide to its Nature and Management, 2nd edn. Oxford: Oxford University Press.
Hawton, K. and Fagg, J. (1988) Suicide and other causes of death, following attempted suicide. British Journal of Psychiatry, 152: 359–366.
Hawton, K. and Fagg, J. (1992) Trends in deliberate self-poisoning and self-injury in Oxford, 1976–1990. British Medical Journal, 304: 1409–1411.
Hawton, K. and Fagg, J. (1995) Repetition of attempted suicide: the performance of the Edinburgh predictive scales in patients in Oxford. Archives of Suicide Research, 1: 261–272.
Hawton, K., Fagg, J., Simkin, S. and Mills, J. (1994) The epidemiology of attempted suicide in the Oxford area, England (1989–1992). Crisis: The Journal of Crisis Intervention and Suicide Prevention, 15/3: 123–135.
Hawton, K., Fagg, J., Simkin, S., Bale, E. and Bond, A. (1997a) Trends in deliberate self-harm in Oxford, 1985–1995. British Journal of Psychiatry, 171: 556–560.
Hawton, K., Fagg, J., Simkin, S., Harris, L., Bale, E. and Bond, A. (1997/1998) Deliberate self-harm in Oxford, 1996, 1997. Reports from the Oxford Monitoring System for Attempted Suicide. Oxford: University Department of Psychiatry (unpublished).
Hawton, K., Simkin, S. and Fagg, J. (1997b) Deliberate self-harm in alcohol and drug misusers: patient characteristics and patterns of clinical care. Drug and Alcohol Review, 16: 123–129.
Jessen, G., Jensen, B.F., Arensman, E., Bille-Brahe, U., Crepet, P., De Leo, D., Hawton, K., Haring, C., Hjelmeland, H., Michel, K., Ostamo, A., Salander-Renberg, E., Schmidtke, A., Temesvary, B. and Wasserman, D. (1999) Attempted suicide and major public holidays in Europe (submitted for publication).
Kerkhof, A.J.F.M. (1985) Suicide en de Geestelijke Gezondheidszorg. Lisse: Swets and Zeitlinger.
Kerkhof, A.J.J.M., Schmidtke, A., Bille Brahe, U., De Leo, D. and Lönnqvist, J. (1994) Attempted Suicide in Europe. Leiden/Copenhagen: DSWO-Press/World Health Organization.
Kerkhof, A.J.F.M., Arensman, E., Bille-Brahe, U. et al (1998) Repetition of attempted suicide: results from the WHO/EU Multicentre Study on Parasuicide. Lecture presented at the 7th European Symposium on Suicide and Suicidal Behaviour, Gent, Belgium.
Khan, M.M., Islam, S. and Kundi, A.K. (1996) Parasuicide in Pakistan: experience at a university hospital. Acta Psychiatrica Scandinavica, 94: 264–267.
Kienhorst, C.W.M., de Wilde, E.J., Diekstra, R.F.W. and Wolters, W.H.G. (1991) Construction of an index for predicting suicide attempts in depressed adolescents. British Journal of Psychiatry, 159: 676–682.
Kirmayer, L.J., Malus, M. and Boothroyd, L.J. (1996) Suicide attempts among Inuit youth: a community survey of prevalence and risk factors. Acta Psychiatrica Scandinavica, 94: 8–17.
Kreitman, N., Philip, A.E., Greer, S. and Bagley, C.R. (1969) Parasuicide. British Journal of Psychiatry, 115: 746–747.
Kreitman, N. (1977) Parasuicide. London: Wiley.
Kreitman, N. and Casey, P. (1988) Repetition of parasuicide: an epidemiological and clinical study. British Journal of Psychiatry, 153: 792–800.
Kreitman, N. and Foster, J. (1991) Construction and selection of predictive scales, with special reference to parasuicide. British Journal of Psychiatry, 159: 185–192.
Latha, K.S., Bhat, S.M. and D'Souza, P. (1996) Suicide attempters in a general hospital

unit in India: their socio-demographic and clinical profile—emphasis on cross-cultural aspects. Acta Psychiatrica Scandinavica, 94: 26–30.

Maris, R.W. (1992) The relationship of non-fatal suicide attempts to completed suicide. In R.W. Maris, A.L. Berman, J.T. Maltsberger and R.I. Yufit (Eds), Assessment and Prediction of Suicide. New York: Guilford.

Masterton, G. (1991) Monthly and seasonal variation in parasuicide. A sex difference. British Journal of Psychiatry, 158: 155–157.

Masterton, G. and Platt, S. (1989) Parasuicide and general elections. British Medical Journal, 298: 803–804.

Moscicki, E.K., O'Carroll, P., Rae, D.S., Locke, B.Z., Roy, A. and Regier, D.A. (1988) Suicide attempts in the Epidemiologic Catchment Area Study. Yale Journal of Biology and Medicine, 61: 259–268.

Neeleman, J., Jones, P., Van Os, J. and Murray, R.M. (1996) Parasuicide in Camberwell: ethnic differences. Social Psychiatry and Epidemiology, 31: 284–287.

Paykel, E.S., Myers, J.K., Lindentall, J.J. and Tanner, J. (1974) Suicidal feelings in the general population: a prevalence study. British Journal of Psychiatry, 124: 460–469.

Platt, S. (1984) Unemployment and suicidal behaviour: a review of the literature. Social Science and Medicine, 19: 1993–115.

Platt, S. and Dyer, J. (1987) Psychological correlates of unemployment among male parasuicides in Edinburgh. British Journal of Psychiatry, 151: 27–32.

Platt, S. (1989) The consequences of a televised soap opera drug overdose. In R.F.W. Diekstra, R. Maris, S. Platt, A. Schmidtke and G. Sonneck (Eds), Suicide and Its Prevention: The Role of Attitude and Imitation. Leiden: Brill.

Platt, S., Bille-Brahe, U., Kerkhof, A., Schmidtke, A., Bjerke, T., Crepet, P., De Leo, D., Haring, C., Lonnqvist, J., Michel, K., Philippe, A., Pommereau, X., Querejeta, I., Salander-Renberg, E., Temesvary, B., Wasserman, D. and Sampaio Faria, J. (1992) Parasuicide in Europe: the WHO/EURO Multicentre Study on Parasuicide. I. Introduction and preliminary analysis for 1989. Acta Psychiatrica Scandinavica, 85: 97–104.

Platt, S., Hawton, K., Kreitman, N., Fagg, J. and Foster, J. (1988) Recent clinical and epidemiological trends in parasuicide in Edinburgh and Oxford: a tale of two cities. Psychological Medicine, 18: 405–418.

Platt, S. (1993) The social transmission of parasuicide: is there a modeling effect? Crisis: The Journal of Crisis Intervention and Suicide Prevention, 14/1: 23–31.

Rubinstein J.L., Heeren, T., Housman, D., Rubin, C. and Stechler, G. (1989) Suicidal behavior in "normal" adolescents: risk and protective factors. American Journal of Orthopsychiatry, 59: 59–71.

Sakinofsky, I., Roberts, R.S., Brown, Y., Cumming, C. and James, P. (1990) Problem resolution and repetition of parasuicide: a prospective study. British Journal of Psychiatry, 156: 395–399.

Sakinofsky, I. (1996) The epidemiology of suicide in Canada. In A. Leenaars et al (Eds), Suicide in Canada. Toronto: University of Toronto Press.

Schmidtke, A., Bille Brahe, U., De Leo, D., Kerkhof, A., Bjerke, T., Crepet, P., Haring, C., Hawton, K., Lonnqvist, J., Michel, K., Pommereau, X., Querejeta, I., Philippe, A., Salander-Renberg, E., Temesvary, B., Wasserman, D., Fricke, S., Weinacker, B. and Sampaio Faria, J. (1996) Attempted suicide in Europe: rates, trends and sociodemographic characteristics of suicide attempters during the period 1989–1992. Results of the WHO/EURO Multicentre Study on Parasuicide. Acta Psychiatrica Scandinavica, 93: 327–338.

United Nations (Eds) (1993a) The Sex and Age Distribution of the World Populations, 1992 Revision. New York: United Nations, Department of Economic and Social Information and Policy Analysis.

United Nations (Eds) (1993b) World Population Prospects, 1992 Revision. New York:

United Nations, Department of Economic and Social Information and Policy Analysis.

van Egmond, M. and Diekstra, R.F.W. (1989) The predictability of suicidal behaviour: the results of a meta-analysis of published studies. In R.F.W. Diekstra, R. Maris, S. Platt, A. Schmidtke and G. Sonneck (Eds), Suicide and Its Prevention, pp.37–61. Leiden: Brill.

van Heeringen, C. (1994) Epidemiological aspects of attemped suicide. A case control study in Gent, Belgium. Crisis: The Journal of Crisis Intervention and Suicide Prevention, 15/3: 116–122.

van Heeringen, C. and De Volder, V. (in press) Trends in attempted suicide in adolescents and young adults in Gent, 1986–1995. Archives of Suicide Research.

Weissman, M.M. (1974) The epidemiology of suicide attempts. Archives of General Psychiatry, 30: 737–746.

Chapter 4

Biological Aspects of Suicidal Behaviour

Lil Träskman-Bendz
Department of Psychiatry, University Hospital, Lund, Sweden,
and
J. John Mann
Department of Neuroscience, New York State Psychiatric Institute, Department of Psychiatry, Columbia University, New York, USA

Abstract

There are three major lines of evidence for an association between biology and suicidal behaviour. These are: evidence of a correlation between altered serotonergic activity and suicide attempts; altered serotonergic activity and suicide; and a genetic contribution to the risk of suicide, independently of the genetic predisposition to psychiatric disorders associated with greater suicide risk. Abnormalities in the serotonergic (5-hydroxytryptamine, 5-HT) system in suicide attempters and suicide victims have been one of the most consistent neurobiological findings in psychiatry. Less extensive data suggest abnormalities in other neurotransmitter systems, such as the noradrenergic, dopaminergic, GABAergic and glutamatergic systems. Hyperactivity of the hypothalamic–pituitary–adrenal axis has also been reported by several, but not all, studies. Recently, low concentrations of cholesterol have been linked with suicidal behaviour. After the original biological observations were made in suicidal individuals, the roles of serotonin and cholesterol in impulsivity, violence and aggression have been studied extensively, in both humans and other primates. Impaired serotonergic function is a correlate of serious suicidal acts and of impulsive aggression towards others or property. This suggests that a common biological substrate underlies the propensity for aggression and suicide. Furthermore, it has become apparent that these behavioural and biological relationships hold true across psychiatric diagnoses, indicating that there is a more general explanatory model of suicidal behaviour, as well as of aggression.

The International Handbook of Suicide and Attempted Suicide. Edited by K. Hawton and K. van Heeringen.

INTRODUCTION

It is a common misconception that suicide is a complication of depressive syndromes, and rarely occurs in the context of other psychiatric disorders. This is also apparent in diagnostic classification systems and rating scales. This view is not correct. Individuals who present with severe deliberate self-harm form a heterogeneous group. Suicidal acts occur in association with many psychiatric diagnoses, temperaments and biological states or traits. Thus, risk factors or biological correlates of suicidal behaviour may be common to many psychiatric disorders or specific to only some psychiatric disorders.

DISTINGUISHING THE BIOLOGY OF MOOD AND OTHER PSYCHIATRIC DISORDERS FROM BIOLOGICAL CORRELATES OF SUICIDAL BEHAVIOUR

Some studies of cerebrospinal fluid and neuroendocrine studies of the prolactin response to serotonin release have indicated a relationship between impaired serotonergic function and major depression (Mann et al, 1995). A deficiency in serotonergic function is reported to correlate with suicidal behaviour. What is the distinction between the serotonergic abnormality of major depression and that associated with suicide risk? Given the diversity of symptoms associated with major depression (mood, sleep, appetite, cognition, libido, etc.), a diffuse deficiency of serotonergic function is likely. Post-mortem brain studies suggest that the serotonergic abnormalities associated with suicide are concentrated in the ventral prefrontal cortex. This area of the brain is abnormal on PET scanning in criminals such as remanded murderers. Lesions of the ventral prefrontal cortex result in behavioural disinhibition. Serotonin input to this brain region may contribute to behavioural inhibition, and impairment may increase suicide risk.

Rates of life-time aggression and impulsivity are higher in suicide attempters compared to psychiatrically matched non-attempters. We and others have postulated that impulsivity contributes to the risk for both self-directed (suicidal) and outwardly directed aggression. Such a model implies a common biological factor. Indeed, low serotonergic activity is a correlate of both externally directed aggression, such as homicide, infanticide and arson, and of suicide and suicide attempts. Thus, low serotonergic function may underlie an impairment of behavioural inhibition of self-control at times of intense suicidal ideation or anger.

Serotonergic dysfunction may be a biological trait, as suggested by its prediction of future suicide or suicide attempts, and its prediction of recidivism in murderers being released from prison. Studies in non-human primates indicate that serotonergic function can be partly inherited and is quite stable in the long term. Thus, it is a biochemical trait with behavioural correlates.

High levels of cortisol may affect mood in patients with Cushing's disease. Exogenous adrenocorticotropic hormone alters mood. Patients with major depression often have elevated cortisol levels, and hypothalamic–pituitary–adrenal (HPA) axis challenges with dexamethasone reveal high rates of non-suppression of cortisol levels (Carroll et al, 1981). Thus, this major stress response system is in overdrive in many patients with more severe forms of depression.

Cholesterol, the precursor of steroid synthesis, has also been related to mood changes, but more so to violence, impulsivity and suicidality in a variety of studies (Muldoon et al, 1990; Kaplan et al, 1994).

The results of these biological studies indicate that it is crucial to distinguish between the biological correlates of major depression and the correlates of suicidal behaviour. This has generally been achieved by having a control group of patients who have major depression but have never made a suicide attempt. It is a problem in most post-mortem brain studies because in almost all such studies to date, there is no psychiatric control group.

THE SEROTONIN SYSTEM AND METHODS OF STUDY

Serotonin was first purified from blood and named in 1948 by Rapport et al (1948). The distribution of this monoamine was first visualized in brain by Swedish researchers, who developed histochemical techniques in which serotonin reacted to form fluorescent derivatives (Dahlström and Fuxe, 1964). Serotonin-containing cell bodies are found in the brainstem raphe nuclei. These nuclei are phylogenetically very old, which means that they subserve fundamental functions that are necessary for survival. Neuroendocrine rhythms, mood, sleep, appetite and cognition are modulated by the midbrain raphe 5-HT system. Serotonin neurones project to areas as diverse as the spinal cord, throughout the cortex, the limbic system, hippocampus and hypothalamus. Among multiple 5-HT receptors known today, the presynaptic serotonin transporter, and the 5-HT_{1A} and postsynaptic 5-HT_{2A} receptors have been the object of the greatest research in mood disorders and suicidality. Genes have been coded for the transporter and both these receptors. Mutations in these genes are the subject of association studies in psychiatric disorders.

A number of approaches are available for studying the serotonergic system *in vivo* and post-mortem samples *in vitro* (Arango et al, 1997). Administration of 5-HT or 5-HT agonists to brain slices or platelets allow measurements of 5-HT_{2A} receptor-mediated signal transduction. Members of a family consisting of at least five different phosphoinositide-specific phospholipases C are activated. These enzymes hydrolyse phosphatidylinositol 4,5-biphosphate (PIP2), an action which leads to the formation of inositol 1,4,5-triphosphate (IP3) and diacylglycerol

(DAG). IP3 and DAG are second messengers that regulate important cellular functions. G protein studies further illuminate the postreceptor signalling system. The interplay between 5-HT_{1A} receptors and corticosteroids in the hippocampus seems to be of importance for mood and cognition (Meijer and De Kloet, 1998). This highlights the importance of considering other transmitter systems and the interaction of neurotransmitter systems.

Neuroendocrine challenge tests have informed us about the overall responsiveness of systems. For example, administration of 5-HT agonists, such as tryptophan, 5-hydroxytryptrophan and fenfluramine, activate the serotonergic input into the hypothalamus, resulting in corticosteroid and prolactin release into plasma (Murphy et al, 1996). The platelet utilizes serotonin in mediating its role in aggression and creation of a platelet plug to block perforations in blood vessels. It is readily available as an index of function of some serotonin-related proteins. Clearly, platelet studies are a poor index of function of such serotonin-related proteins in neurones, because the local neuronal inputs and regulatory effects are all missing. Cerebrospinal fluid (CSF) levels of monoamine metabolites, such 5-hydroxyindoleacetic acid (5-HIAA) for serotonin, are an index of monoamine release and turnover.

CSF 5-HIAA

One of the original observations regarding a relationship between the serotonin system and serious suicidal behaviour stems from studies of the serotonin metabolite 5-HIAA in lumbar CSF in psychiatric inpatients mainly suffering from melancholia (Åsberg et al, 1976). Later, these findings were replicated in patients with other psychiatric disorders, including schizophrenia and personality disorders. The only exception appears to be in patients with bipolar mood disorders, where there are fewer studies and the results are mostly negative; however, not all the studies are in agreement. A meta-analysis of 20 CSF studies reveals that patients with a history of attempted suicides, by and large, have lower CSF 5-HIAA than psychiatric controls (Lester, 1995).

A few studies have reported that low CSF 5-HIAA is predictive of future suicide attempts. Low CSF 5-HIAA has also been found in impulsive violent offenders and alcoholics, and can predict future violence (Virkkunen et al, 1989, 1994). Therefore, it has been suggested that these low levels of CSF 5-HIAA are also related to aggression and/or impulsivity. Non-human primate and rodent studies all confirm a relationship between low serotonergic activity, as indicated by 5-HIAA, and aggression.

Early studies suggested that the low CSF 5-HIAA concentrations were more commonly found in patients who had used violent methods of suicide attempt. Recently, studies by Mann and co-workers (1992) were able to relate these low concentrations to high suicidal intent and to the medical severity of the suicide attempts.

It has been demonstrated that the 5-HIAA measured in lumbar CSF correlates with levels in the prefrontal cortex (Stanley et al, 1985). This validates the CSF measures as an index of brain function.

Neuroendocrine Studies of the Serotonergic System

Fenfluramine-stimulated prolactin release appears blunted in patients with major depression and a history of serious suicidal behaviour. Analogous to CSF 5-HIAA, the prolactin response to fenfluramine is more blunted when the suicidal acts are more serious. Coccaro and colleagues (1989) showed blunted prolactin-levels in suicidal depressed patients and/or patients with personality disorders. This finding was confirmed by Mann and colleagues (Mann et al, 1992; Mann and Malone, 1997), who also reported an association between blunted prolactin response and medical lethality of the suicide attempt. It is also blunted in relation to a history of impulsive aggression. Thus, this is a second index of serotonergic dysfunction that is related to both a history of suicidal behaviour in proportion to its seriousness and to impulsive aggression. The convergence of findings by these two methods increases the confidence of the conclusion. Too few studies have been carried out with other challenge agents to draw firm conclusions.

Platelet 5-HT_2 Receptor Binding

Studies of the 5-HT_{2A} receptor in suicidal patients have been performed in platelets, which are looked upon as peripheral models of neurones, but of course lack the circuitory environment of neurones in the brain. Irrespective of ligands chosen, higher platelet 5-HT_{2A} binding has been related to depressive disorder, but above all to suicidality (Pandey, 1997). In contrast, most studies find that 5-HT_{2A} signal transduction is blunted in suicide attempters (Mann et al, 1992), although one study found significantly higher PIP2 hydrolysis after 5-HT challenge of platelets (Simonsson et al, 1991).

Molecular Genetic Studies

Details of the genetic aspects of suicidal behaviour are provided in Chapter 13. The gene coding for the rate-limiting enzyme, tryptophan-hydroxylase (TPH), in the synthesis of serotonin, has been investigated in suicidal and non-suicidal populations. One of the alleles, denoted L, seems to be more common in impulsive, alcoholic criminals (Nielsen et al, 1998; New et al, 1998; Furlong et al, 1998). Others have shown an association of the U allele with suicidality in major depression (Mann et al, 1997; Buresi et al, 1997), low serotonergic function in normals (Jönsson et al, 1997; Manuck et al, 1999) and aggressive, impulsive traits in normals (Manuck et al, 1999).

THE HPA AXIS

There are several key peptides and steroids acting within the HPA axis. In man, the main ones are corticotrophin-releasing hormone (CRH), ACTH and cortisol. Lately, the interplay between the hypothalamus, hippocampus and amygdala in major depression has been discussed. It has been suggested that chronic stress, which results in high levels of cortisol, could cause changes in cells in the hippocampus and thus lead to a breakdown in glucocorticoid feedback, cognitive disturbances and mood changes.

Studies on glucocorticoids (cortisol) date back to the 1960s, and since then many studies have reported HPA overactivity in severe depressive illness, which has been related to suicidality. From a study showing high diurnal plasma cortisol levels, Sachar and Louisgurs (1976) suggested that depressed individuals suffer from "an inner turmoil". Bearing this is mind, individuals experiencing severe depression will have more difficulties in coping with stressful life events, and experience more severe and repeated stress-related situations. Whether this is correct and contributes to suicidal impulses remains to be determined. Regardless, there is no agreement among studies that the rate of increased HPA activity, or non-suppression on the dexamethasone suppression test, is any higher in suicidal patients.

Serotonin agonists cause the release of ACTH and cortisol. Meltzer and co-workers (1984) showed that the serotonin precursor 5-hydroxytryptophan (5-HTP) caused enhanced increase of cortisol in depressed suicidal patients. They explained their finding as reflecting increased 5-HT_{2A} receptor-mediated responses. Another possibility is that the adrenal gland's capacity for cortisol release is increased, as reflected by the presence of adrenal hypertrophy reported in some patients with major depression and in suicide victims.

CHOLESTEROL

There are indications, from epidemiological studies and studies of cholesterol-lowering therapies, that increased rates of violent deaths, including suicide, are found to be associated with low cholesterol (Muldoon et al, 1990; Fawcett et al, 1997; Kunugi et al, 1997; Golomb, 1998). Total cholesterol is found in various fat particles in the blood. Very low density (VLD) lipoproteins are released from the liver and are metabolized by lipases in the capillaries. Low-density lipoproteins (LDL) contain about 70% cholesterol, while high-density lipoproteins (HDL) contain about 30% cholesterol. Concentrations of cholesterol are determined, for example, by elimination into cells, the number of receptors, unsaturated fat, the amount of HDL and the activity of lipases. Hypothalamic peptides regulate the ingestion and metabolism of fat. These include galanin (GAL), opioid peptides and the mineralocorticoid aldosterone. Dopamine may serve to attenuate the effect of GAL and the opiates on fat intake (Leibowitz, 1992). Cholesterol acyltransferase (LCAT) is secreted by the liver and reacts with free cholesterol of the HDL particles. This esterification protects membranes from being damaged by free cholesterol. A recent study showed that depressives and their relatives had lower amounts of esterified cholesterol than normal controls. Another investigation showed that serum HDL levels were significantly lower in depressed men who had a history of serious suicide attempts (Maes et al, 1994, 1997). This latter finding is of particular interest, as HDL correlated positively with both 5-HIAA and the dopamine metabolite homovanillic acid (HVA) in the CSF in a study of suicide attempters (Engström et al, 1995). There are several studies of man and monkey populations showing a significant interplay between cholesterol, aggression and serotonin (Kaplan et al, 1994).

Studies of the association between cholesterol and suicidality in adult psychiatric patients indicate a link between low cholesterol and suicide attempts/suicide (Sullivan et al, 1994; Modai et al, 1994; Gallerani et al, 1995; Kunugi et al, 1997; Fawcett et al, 1997; Papassotiropoulos et al, 1999). In two studies, findings in females were, however, negative (Golier et al, 1995; Maes et al, 1997).

AUTOPSY STUDIES OF SUICIDE

Another approach to understanding the neurobiological substrate for suicide behaviour is through the post-mortem examination of the brain from suicide victims. By examining coronal sections through the prefrontal cortex of the human brain, we can observe the anatomical distribution of serotonin receptors, (Arango et al, 1995). Serotonin transporter sites are densest in ventral regions, and least dense in dorsal and dorsolateral regions, of the prefrontal cortex. Serotonin transporter binding is one index of serotonin nerve terminal input into, or innervation of, cortical areas (Zhou et al, 1995). Comparison of suicide victims with controls who have died from other causes, regardless of the diagnosis, reveals a reduction in binding to the serotonin transporter sites in certain locations in the brain (Arango et al, 1995). This reduction is most pronounced in the ventral prefrontal cortex and not detectable in the dorsal prefrontal cortex (Hrdina et al, 1993; Arango et al, 1995).

One of the most studied postsynaptic serotonin receptors is the 5-HT_{1A} receptor. The 5-HT_{1A} receptor is uniformly distributed across prefrontal cortical areas (Arango et al, 1995), but across cortical layers it is mainly localized to layer 2. A comparison of suicide victims and controls indicates that there is an increase in the number of these postsynaptic receptors in suicide victims (Yates and Ferrier, 1990; Matsubara et al, 1991; Joyce et al, 1993; Arango et al, 1995). The increase in 5-HT_{1A} receptor binding is also mainly in ventral cortical areas. In fact, there is an inverse relationship between the number of 5-HT_{1A} receptors and the number of serotonin transporter sites, which suggests reciprocity in the way the two systems are regulated. A lack of neurotransmitter is often associated with a compensatory increase in the postsynaptic cortical area of suicide victims, as indicated by fewer transporter sites. Therefore, the increase in 5-HT_{1A} receptor binding may be secondary to reduced serotonergic innervation. Thus, although serotonin neurones project all over the brain, the specific projection to the ventral prefrontal cortex may be deficient. Of note, these studies demonstrate a biochemical finding that is independent of psychiatric diagnosis. It is present in suicide victims with major depression as well as in those with other psychiatric conditions (Joyce et al, 1993; Sumiyoshi et al, 1996).

These studies of serotonin receptors raise the question of the function of the ventral prefrontal cortex. Some information is available from examining regional glucose metabolism with positron emission tomography (PET) in murderers compared to non-murderers (Raine et al, 1997). These studies found a significant reduction in the resting glucose metabolism in the prefrontal cortical areas of murderers, highlighting the potential importance of this brain region in regulating behaviour. In addition, there is considerable neuropsychiatric literature on the role of the ventral prefrontal cortex and the executive function of behavioural or cognitive inhibition. A breakdown in this inhibitory role may result in a greater potential for acting on powerful feelings or impulses, such as suicidal ideation or anger. In other words, the ventral prefrontal cortex may act as a restraint system, relaxation of this leading to more impulsive behaviours.

OTHER NEUROTRANSMITTERS

Stressful external conditions and psychological stress initiate the secretion of several hormones, including catecholamines. If this stress is long-lasting, a chronic activation of the norepinephrine-specific nucleus in the brain, the locus coeruleus, will result in a decreased number of neurones, high levels of the degradating enzyme tyrosine hydroxylase and increased binding of α-2 receptors. Such findings have been reported in suicide victims (Arango et al, 1997; Ordway, 1997).

Already in the 1950s there were findings of high urinary norepinephrine: epinephrine ratios in aggressive/hostile individuals, while depressed/suicidal persons had low ratios. Accordingly, the "anger-out and anger-in" catecholamine hypothesis was formulated. Later studies of suicide attempters have replicated these original findings of low urinary norepinephrine to epinephrine, and especially in those who made violent suicide attempts (Ostroff et al, 1982; Prasad, 1985).

High tonic levels of sympathetic arousal, low sedation thresholds and diminished habituation to novel stimuli are usually seen in anxious and inhibited individuals. Suicide attempters and violent offenders seem to have several personality characteristics in common, such as high trait anxiety, low socialization, impulsiveness, rebelliousness and suspiciousness (Engström et al, 1999; Plutchik, 1995). One study showed that verbalized anger and hostility was more common in violent offenders, while guilt, intrapunitively expressed anger and hostility was more often noticed in suicide attempters (Maiuro et al, 1989). These similarities and differences probably reflect personality disorders included in the "dramatic-emotional" cluster (B) described in the DSM system and/or the mood disorders often diagnosed in suicide attempters. When temperament ratings were compared between healthy individuals and major depressed patients with and without suicide attempts, trait-anxiety appeared to be the most prominent temperament dimension in suicide attempters (Pendse et al, 1999).

In patients with mood disorders, the most consistent findings in studies of CSF monoamine metabolites are low CSF concentrations of the dopamine.metabolite homovanillic acid (HVA). In studies of suicide attempters, CSF HVA was lower than normal, regardless of the method of the suicide attempt (Träskman et al, 1981; Roy et al, 1986; Jones et al, 1990; Engström et al, 1999). This HVA reduction has been interpreted as reflecting mood disturbances rather than suicidality. Dopamine, glutamate and γ-aminobutytic acid (GABA) are interconnected in the brain, and cholesystokinin (CCK) is co-localized with parts of GABA or glutamate cortical interneurones. An increase in CCK mRNA levels in the prefronal cortex of suicide victims has recently been reported (Bachus et al, 1997). CCK has also been studied in the CSF of depressed subjects, where suicide attempters tended to have higher concentrations than non-attempters (Löfberg et al, 1998).

CONCLUSION

Suicidal behaviour occurs in vulnerable individuals with a psychiatric disorder. Amongst the factors that distinguish this vulnerable subgroup are genetic factors and abnormalities involving the serotonergic system. It is postulated that at least part of the genetically determined risk for suicidal behaviour is mediated via the serotonergic system. Therefore, it would be a challenge to perform controlled studies of drugs acting on the serotonergic system, such as lithium or SSRIs. Recently, one such placebo-controlled SSRI-study was successful in decreasing suicidal behaviour in individuals not suffering from major depression (see Chapter 27; Verkes et al, 1998).

REFERENCES

Åsberg, M., Träskman, L. and Thorén, P. (1976) 5-HIAA in the cerebrospinal fluid. A biochemical suicide predictor? Archives of General Psychiatry, 33: 1193–1197.

Arango, V., Underwood, M.D., Gubbi, A.V. and Mann, J.J. (1995) Localized alterations in pre- and postsynaptic serotonin binding sites in the ventrolateral prefrontal cortex of suicide victims. Brain Research, 688: 121–133.

Arango, V., Underwood, M.D. and Mann, J.J. (1997) Postmortem findings in suicide victims: Implications for *in vivo* imaging studies. Annals of the New York Academy of Sciences, 836: 269–287.

Bachus, S.E., Hyde, T.M., Herman, M.M., Egan, M.F. and Kleinman, J.E. (1997) Abnormal cholecystokinin mRNA levels in entorhinal cortex of schizophrenics. Journal of Psychiatric Research, 31: 233–256.

Buresi, C., Courtet, Ph., Leboyer, M., Feingold, J. and Malafosse, A. (1997) Association between suicide attempt and the trytophane hydroxylase (TPH) gene. Abstracts of the American Association of Human Genetics, p. A270.

Carroll, B.J., Feinberg, M., Greden, J.F., Tarika, J., Albala, A.A., Haskett, R.F., James, N.M., Kronfol, Z., Lohr, N., Steiner, M., de Vinge, J.P. and Young, E. (1981) A specific laboratory test for the diagnosis of melancholia. Standardization, validation, and clinical utility. Archives of General Psychiatry, 38: 15–22.

Coccaro, E.F., Siever, L.J., Klar, H.M., Maurer, G., Cochrane, K., Cooper, T.B., Mohs, R.C. and Davis, K.L. (1989) Serotonergic studies in patients with affective and personality disorders. Archives of General Psychiatry, 46: 587–599.

Dahlström, A. and Fuxe, K. (1964) Evidence for the existence of monoamine-containing neurons in the central nervous system. I. Demonstration of monoamines in the cell bodies of brain stem neurons. Acta Physiologica Scandinavica, 62: 1–55.

Engström, G., Alsén, M., Regnéll, G. and Träskman-Bendz, L. (1995) Research note. Serum lipids in suicide attempters. Suicide and Life-Threatening Behavior, 25: 393–400.

Engström, G., Alling, C., Blennow, K., Regnéll, G. and Träskman-Bendz, L. (1999) Reduced HVA concentrations and HVA/5-HIAA ratios in suicide attempters. Monoamine metabolites in 120 suicide attempters and 47 controls. European Neuropsychopharmacology, 9: 399–405.

Fawcett, J., Busch, K.A., Jacobs, D., Kravitz, H.M. and Fogg, L. (1997) Suicide: a four-pathway clinical–biochemical model. Annals of the New York Academy of Sciences, 836: 288–301.

Furlong, R.A., Ho, L., Rubinstein, J.S., Walsh, C., Paykel, E.S. and Rubinstein, D.C. (1998) No association of the tryptophan hydroxylase gene with bipolar affective disorder, unipolar affective disorder, or suicidal behaviour in major affective disorder. American Journal of Medical Genetics (Neuropsychiatric Genetics), 81: 245–247.

Gallerani, M., Manfredini, R., Caracciolo, S., Scapoli, C., Molinari, S. and Fersini, C. (1995) Serum cholesterol concentrations in parasuicide. British Medical Journal, 310: 1632–1636.

Golier, J.A., Marzuk, P.M., Leon, A.C., Weiner, C. and Tardiff, K. (1995) Low serum cholesterol level and attempted suicide. American Journal of Psychiatry, 152: 419–423.

Golomb, B.A. (1998) Cholesterol and violence: is there a connection? Annals of Internal Medicine, 128: 478–487.

Hrdina, P.D., Demeter, E., Vu, T.B., Sótónyi, P. and Palkovits, M. (1993) 5-HT uptake sites and 5-HT_2 receptors in brain of antidepressant-free suicide victims/depressives: Increase in 5-HT_2 sites in cortex and amygdala. Brain Research, 614: 37–44.

Jönsson, E.G., Goldman, D., Spurlock, G., Gustavsson, J.P., Nielsen, D.A., Linnoila, M., Owen, M.J. and Sedvall, G.C. (1997) Tryptophan hydroxylase and catechol-O-methyltransferase gene polymorphisms: relationships to monoamine metabolite concentrations in CSF of healthy volunteers. European Archives of Psychiatry and Clinical Neuroscience, 247: 297–302.

Jones, J.S., Stanley, B., Mann, J.J., Frances, A.J., Guido, J.R., Träskman-Bendz, L., Winchel, R., Brown, R.P. and Stanley, M. (1990) CSF 5-HIAA and HVA concentrations in elderly depressed patients who attempted suicide. American Journal of Psychiatry, 147: 1225–1227.

Joyce, J.N., Shane, A., Lexow, N., Winokur, A., Casanova, M.F. and Kleinman, J.E. (1993) Serotonin uptake sites and serotonin receptors are altered in the limbic system of schizophrenics. Neuropsychopharmacology, 8: 315–336.

Kaplan, J.R., Shively, C.A., Fontenot, M.B., Morgan, T.M., Howell, S.M., Manuck, S.B., Muldoon, M.F. and Mann, J.J. (1994) Demonstration of an association among dietary cholesterol, central serotonergic activity, and social behavior in monkeys. Psychosomatic Medicine, 56: 479–484.

Kunugi, H., Takei, N., Aoki, H. and Nanko, S. (1997) Low serum cholesterol in suicide attempters. Biological Psychiatry, 41: 196–200.

Leibowitz, S.F. (1992) Neurochemical–neuroendocrine systems in the brain controlling macronutrient intake and metabolism. Trends in Neurosciences, 15: 491–497.

Lester, D. (1995) The concentration of neurotransmitter metabolites in the cerebrospinal fluid of suicidal individuals: a meta-analysis. Pharmacopsychiatry, 28: 77–79.

Löfberg, C., Ågren, H., Harro, J. and Oreland, L. (1998) Cholecystokinin in CSF from depressed patients: possible relations to serverity of depression and suicidal behaviour. European Neuropsychopharmacology, 8: 153–157.

Maes, M., Delanghe, J., Meltzer, H.Y., Scharpé, S., Dhondt, P.D. and Cosyns, P. (1994) Lower degree of esterification of serum cholesterol in depression: relevance for depression and suicide research. Acta Psychiatrica Scandinavica, 90: 252–258.

Maes, M., Smith, R., Christophe, A., Vandoolaeghe, E., Van Gastel, V., Neels, H., Demedts, P., Wauters, A. and Meltzer, H.Y. (1997) Lower serum high-density lipoprotein cholesterol (HDL-C) in major depression and in depressed men with serious suicidal attempts: relationship with immune-inflammatory marker. Acta Psychiatrica Scandinavica, 95: 212–221.

Mann, J.J. and Malone, K.M. (1997) Cerebrospinal fluid amines and higher lethality suicide attempts in depressed inpatients. Biological Psychiatry, 41: 162–171.

Mann, J.J., Malone, K.M., Nielsen, D.A., Goldman, D., Erdos, J. and Gelernter, J. (1997) Possible association of a polymorphism of the tryptophan hydroxylase gene with suicidal behavior in depressed patients. American Journal of Psychiatry, 154: 1451–1453.

Mann, J.J., McBride, P.A., Brown, R.P., Linnoila, M., Leon, A.C., DeMeo, M., Mieczkowski, T., Myers, J.E. and Stanley, M. (1992) Relationship between central and peripheral serotonin indexes in depressed and suicidal psychiatric inpatients. Archives of General Psychiatry, 49: 442–446.

Mann, J.J., McBride, P.A., Malone, K.M., DeMeo, M.D. and Keilp, J. (1995) Blunted serotonergic responsivity in depressed patients. Neuropsychopharmacology, 13: 53–64.

Manuck, S.B., Flory, J.D., Ferrell, R.E., Dent, K., Mann, J.J. and Muldoon, M.F. (1999) Aggression and anger-related traits associated with a polymorphism of the tryptophan hydroxylase gene. Biological Psychiatry, 45: 603–614.

Matsubara, S., Arora, R.C. and Meltzer, H.Y. (1991) Serotonergic measures in suicide brain: 5-HT_{1A} binding sites in frontal cortex of suicide victims. Journal of Neural Transmission, 85: 181–194.

Maiuro, R.D., O'Sullivan, M.J., Michael, M.C. and Vitaliano, P.P. (1989) Anger, hostility, and depression in assaultive vs. suicide-attempting males. Journal of Clinical Psychology, 45: 531–541.

Meijer, O.C. and De Kloet, E.R. (1998) Corticosterone and serotonergic neurotransmission in the hippocampus: functional implications of central corticosteriod receptor diversity. Critical Reviews in Neurobiology, 12: 1–20.

Meltzer, H.Y., Perline, R., Tricou, B.J., Lowy, M. and Robertson, A. (1984) Effect of 5-hydroxytryptophan on serum cortisol levels in major affective disorders. II. Relation to suicide, psychosis and depressive symptoms. Archives of General Psychiatry, 41: 379–387.

Modai, I., Valevski, A., Dror, S. and Weizman, A. (1994) Serum cholesterol and suicidal tendencies in psychiatric inpatients. Journal of Clinical Psychiatry, 55: 252–254.

Muldoon, M.F., Manuck, S.B. and Matthews, K.A. (1990) Lowering cholesterol concentrations and mortality: a quantitative review of primary prevention trials. British Medical Journal, 301: 309–314.

Murphy, D.L., Aulakh, C., Mazzola-Pomietto, P. and Briggs, N.C. (1996) Neuroendocrine responses to serotonergic agonists as indices of the functional status of central serotonin neurotransmission in humans: a preliminary comparative analysis of neuroendocrine endpoints vs. other endpoint measures. Behavioural Brain Research, 73: 209–214.

New, A.S., Gelernter, J., Yovell, Y., Trestman, R.L., Nielsen, D.A., Silverman, J., Mitropoulou, V. and Siever, L.J. (1998) Trytophan hydroxylase genotype is associated with impulsive-aggression measures: a preliminary study. American Journal of Medical Genetics (Neuropsychiatric Genetics), 81: 13–17.

Nielsen, D.A., Virkkunen, M., Lappalainen, J., Eggert, M., Brown, G.L., Long, J.C., Goldman, D. and Linnoila, M. (1998) A tryptophan hydroxylase gene marker for suicidality and alcoholism. Archives of General Psychiatry, 55: 593–602.

Ordway, G.A. (1997) Pathophysiology of the locus coeruleus in suicide. Annals of the New York Academy of Sciences, 836: 233–252.

Ostroff, R., Giller, E., Bonese, K., Ebersole, E., Harkness, L. and Mason, J. (1982) Neuroendocrine risk factors of suicidal behavior. American Journal of Psychiatry, 139: 1323–1325.

Pandey, G.N. (1997) Altered serotonin function in suicide. Evidence from platelet and neuroendocrine studies. Annals of the New York Academy of Sciences, 836: 182–183.

Papassotiropoulos, A., Hawellek, B., Frahnert, C., Rao, G. and Rao, M.L. (1999) The risk of acute suicidality in psychiatric patients increases with low plasma cholesterol. Pharmacopsychiatry, 32: 1–4.

Pendse, B., Westrin, Å. and Engström, G. (1999) Temperament traits in seasonal affective disorder, suicide attempters with non-seasonal major depression and healthy controls. Journal of Affective Disorders, 54: 55–56.

Plutchik, R. (1995) Outward and inward directed aggressiveness: the interaction between violence and suicidality. Pharmacopsychiatry, 28 (Suppl.): 47–57.

Prasad, A. (1985) Neuroendocrine differences between violent and non-violent parasuicides. Neuropsychobiology, 13: 157–159.

Raine, A., Buchsbaum, M. and LaCasse, L. (1997) Brain abnormalities in murderers indicated by positron emission tomography. Biological Psychiatry, 42: 495–508.

Rapport, M.M., Green, A.A. and Page, I.H. (1948) Crystalline serotonin. Science, 108: 329–330.

Roy, A., Ågren, H., Pickar, D., Linnoila, M., Doran, A.R., Cutler, N.R. and Paul, S.M. (1986) Reduced CSF concentrations of HVA and HVA to 5-HIAA ratios in depressed patients: relationships to suicidal behavior and dexamethasone non-suppression. American Journal of Psychiatry, 143: 1539–1545.

Sachar, E.J., Roffwarg, H.P., Gruen, P.H., Altman, N. and Sassin, J. (1976) Neuroendocrine studies of depressive illness. Pharmacopsychiatry, 9: 11–17.

Simonsson, P., Träskman-Bendz, L., Alling, C., Oreland, L., Regnéll, G. and Öhman, R. (1991) Peripheral serotonergic markers in patients with suicidal behavior. European Neuropsychopharmacology, 1: 503–510.

Stanley, M., Träskman-Bendz, L. and Dorovini-Zis, K. (1985) Correlations between aminergic metabolites simultaneously obtained from human CSF and brain. Life Sciences, 37: 1279–1286.

Sullivan, P.F., Joyce, P.R., Bulik, C.M., Mulder, R.T. and Oakley-Browne, M. (1994) Total cholesterol and suicidality in depression. Biological Psychiatry, 36: 472–477.

Sumiyoshi, T., Stockmeier, C.A., Overholser, J.C., Dilley, G.E. and Meltzer, H.Y. (1996) Serotonin$_{1A}$ receptors are increased in post-mortem prefrontal cortex in schizophrenia. Brain Research, 708: 209–214.

Träskman, L., Åsberg, M., Bertilsson, L. and Sjöstrand, L. (1981) Monoamine metabolites in CSF and suicidal behavior. Archives of General Psychiatry, 38: 631–636.

Verkes, R.J., Van der Mast, R.C., Hengeveld, M.W., Tuyl, J.P., Zwinderman, A.H. and Van Kempen, G.M. (1998) Reduction by paroxetine of suicidal behavior in patients with repeated suicide attempts but not major depression. American Journal of Psychiatry, 155: 543–547.

Virkkunen, M., De Jong, J., Bartko, J., Goodwin, F.K. and Linnoila, M. (1989) Relationship of psychobiological variables to recidivism in violent offenders and impulsive fire setters. A follow-up study. Archives of General Psychiatry, 46: 600–603.

Virkkunen, M., Rawlings, R., Tokola, R., Poland, R.E., Guidotti, A., Nemeroff, C.B., Bissette, G., Kalogeras, K., Karonen, S.L. and Linnoila, M. (1994) CSF biochemistries, glucose metabolism, and diurnal activity rhythms in alcoholic, violent offenders, fire setters, and healthy volunteers. Archives of General Psychiatry, 51: 20–27.

Yates, M. and Ferrier, I.N. (1990) 5-HT_{1A} receptors in major depression. Journal of Psychopharmacology, 4: 69–74.

Zhou, F.C., Lumeng, L. and Li, T.-K. (1995) Quantitative immunocytochemical evaluation of serotonergic innervation in alcoholic rat brain. Neurochemistry International, 26: 135–143.

Chapter 5

The Psychology of Suicidal Behaviour

J. Mark G. Williams
Institute of Medical and Social Care Research, University of Wales, Bangor, UK,
and
Leslie R. Pollock*
Institute of Medical and Social Care Research, University of Wales, Bangor, UK

Abstract

This chapter briefly reviews different psychological approaches to suicidal behaviour. It begins with psychodynamic models and shows how early researchers developed and elaborated the intrapsychic concepts of suicidal behaviour proposed by Freud, to include external environmental factors. Personality variables that have been associated with suicidal behaviour are then examined, focusing particularly on impulsivity, which has been found to be associated with suicidal behaviour in both research and clinical settings. We review the work on dichotomous thinking and cognitive rigidity and show how these factors influence problem solving in suicidal individuals. Recent research has investigated the psychological processes underlying problem solving and how this is related to suicidal behaviour. We discuss this work and show how memory biases and a sense of hopelessness can have an impact on the way interpersonal problem situations are approached. Drawing together the threads of this contemporary research leads us to describe a recent model of suicidal behaviour. The "cry of pain" model sees suicidal behaviour as an attempt to escape from a feeling of entrapment. These individuals believe they cannot escape from an external situation or from their own inner turmoil, and that there is no prospect of rescue. This model provides us with a framework for understanding the psychological research and shows how psychology can create a bridge between research on social and biological factors.

* Also at Powys Healthcare NHS Trust, Powys, Wales, UK.

The International Handbook of Suicide and Attempted Suicide. Edited by K. Hawton and K. van Heeringen.

INTRODUCTION

This chapter will review the research on the psychological mechanisms that contribute to the triggering of suicidal crises, bringing the research together into the "cry of pain" model. This model seeks to identify the setting conditions for suicidal behaviour, rather than focusing on its consequences. On the basis of our review of psychodynamic models, personality variables and cognitive factors that have been associated with suicidal behaviour, we suggest that the particular stress events that precede suicidal behaviour are those that signal "defeat"; the particular psychological processes that increase vulnerability are those that signal that there is "no escape" (by, for example, problem-solving and autobiographical memory deficits); and the particular psychological processes that turn a crisis into a suicidal crisis are those that signal "no rescue", increasing hopelessness through, for example, biased judgements of the future.

PSYCHOANALYTICAL PERSPECTIVES ON SUICIDE

Freud is regarded as the father of psychological explanations of suicide, although he never wrote a paper specifically about suicide. Much of his early thinking is contained in the influential 1917 paper, *Mourning and Melancholia*, in which he explored the psychodynamics of depression. In particular, he was concerned with comparing severe depression with the normal experience of mourning following loss (see Adams, 1991). Freud proposed that most individuals cope with the loss of a loved person through the experience of mourning. However, he believed that there are other certain vulnerable individuals for whom the loss experience is unbearable and generates enormous anger. The individual feels ambivalence but preserves the mental image of the loved person by internalization and it becomes part of the ego. Feelings of anger towards the lost object are not possible to express and so they are transformed into self-censure and the wish to harm oneself. When these feelings reach a critical pitch, they lead to the urge to destroy the self.

This was not Freud's last statement on suicide and in later writings, as his ideas developed, he addressed this topic again. Stillion and McDowell (1996) have highlighted the relevant issues in Freud's writing. They point out how Freud envisaged individuals as being closed energy systems with a limited amount of psychic energy at any one time (libido). He proposed the presence of two major forces which are in constant dynamic balance—Eros and Thanatos. Eros is the life force, driving us towards survival, and Thanatos, the death instinct, propels us towards a state of non-existence. There is a constant interplay between these forces during an individual's life. Freud believed that threatening thoughts or experiences are repressed in the unconscious, using libidinal energy. As a result of the energy being used in this way, the individual system may experience disequilibrium, with less energy available for growth and development. In this situation the person risks the life force being overwhelmed by the death force. Essentially, Freud saw suicide as the outcome of this intrapsychic struggle.

Zilboorg (1937) was critical of the view that the death instinct explained suicide. He developed Freud's ideas by arguing that revenge, fear, spite and fantasies of escape are often the psychological triggers for suicide. He also suggested that most suicides are impulsive acts. His work expanded the focus on internal mechanisms to include external factors. Menninger (1938) suggested that suicides had three psychological components; the wish to kill, the wish to be killed and the wish to die. Litman (1967) agreed that the dynamics underlying suicidal behaviour involved more than hostility. He suggested that feelings of abandonment, helplessness and hopelessness are noteworthy, as well as the emotional states of guilt, rage, anxiety and dependency. Many of the themes in psychodynamic theory have recurred in later empirical studies, and it is to these studies that we now turn.

PERSONALITY VARIABLES

Impulsivity

The search for personality variables that are associated with suicidal behaviour has a somewhat chequered history. Eyman and Eyman (1992) reviewed three personality assessment methods—the Rorschach, the Thematic Apperception Test, and the Minnesota Multiphasic Personality Inventory (MMPI). In each case, studies in the 1950s and 1960s that appeared to show some promise could not be replicated.

Later studies have used Eysenck's personality tests (Lolas et al, 1991; Nordstrom et al, 1995; Pallis and Jenkins, 1977) and these have found that suicide attempters produce higher scores than controls on neuroticism and psychoticism. In addition, an association between repeat attempts and neuroticism has been noted for both sexes, while for males there was an association between low intent to die and impulsivity.

From a clinician's point of view, impulsivity is one of the personality attributes that gives most cause for concern in preventing self-destructive behaviour. First, non-fatal suicidal behaviour tends to be impulsive, with over 50% saying later that they did not think of it for more than 1 hour beforehand (Williams, 1997). Second, neurobiological research has studied the connection between the personality dimensions of aggression and impulsiveness in suicidal and violent individuals. Results of this research point towards violent impulsivity as being biologically mediated by the serotonin system (see Chapter 4) and an important component of highly lethal suicide attempts.

Several psychological studies have focused on impulsivity (Apter et al, 1993; Evans et al, 1996), together with anger and hostility (Maiuro et al, 1989). These studies confirm that impulsivity is associated with suicide risk and that the manner in which suicidal people manifest their anger and hostility is generally more intropunitive and covert, with high levels of guilt and depression. Consistent with these findings, the two personality disorders particularly associated with suicidal behaviour, antisocial personality disorder and borderline personality disorder (see Chapter 10), are associated with symptoms of affective instability and impulsive behaviour, involving anger, hostility, low frustration tolerance and lack of planning. Some studies have suggested that suicidal individuals tend to be controlled by external events rather than moderated by internal stimuli (Arffa, 1983).

Much of the research on impulsivity has concentrated on adolescents, in whom it is a particularly common feature. For example, it appears that most adolescent suicides are unplanned (Hawton et al, 1982). Indeed, some studies have shown that only 25% of completed suicides by adolescents show evidence of planning; most are impulsive acts (Shaffer et al, 1988; Hoberman and Garfinkel, 1988). Maris (1981) also found that adolescents who had completed suicide had shown higher levels of impulsivity, together with more aggressive feelings, more intense emotions and dissatisfaction with their lives than older completed suicides.

In a study of adolescent suicides, Shaffer (1974) found that associated personality features were impulsivity, perfectionism, the tendency to withdraw and aloofness. Studying a community sample, Pfeffer and colleagues (1988) found that adolescents with a tendency towards explosive and aggressive behaviour are at greater risk for repetition of their suicidal behaviour. Schafii and Schafii (1982) noted that the risk of suicidal behaviour was significantly increased when there was impulsivity or a lack of concern for danger in the histories of suicidal children and adolescents.

In summary, of all personality features, impulsivity is the one that has been found to be associated with suicidal behaviour in both research studies and the clinical setting. The availability of a means of suicide may be enough to trigger an attempt by an impulsive person who feels defeated, that there is no escape, and hopeless about the future. Impulsivity helps to explain the probability and intensity of any behaviour. It does not, however, explain the choice of that particular behaviour (e.g. suicide or attempted suicide) over other behaviours. For that we turn to research on cognitive variables.

Dichotomous Thinking

Dichotomous thinking refers to the tendency to think in all-or-nothing (black and white) terms (Beck et al, 1979). An example might be, "If I can't have my boyfriend back, then there's no point in living". Much of the work in this area was conducted by Neuringer (1961, 1967, 1968). He used the semantic differential test with groups of suicide attempters, psychosomatic patients and control patients and found, in two separate studies, that suicide attempters were substantially more dichotomous in their thinking than were the other two groups. The results were even more extreme when only suicide attempters who carried out highly serious acts were compared with the other two groups. He concluded that these individuals displayed a distinct form of cognitive style which he labelled "extremeness". Results of a later study (Neuringer and Lettieri, 1971), in which the researchers recorded daily measures of dichotomous thinking from high-risk, medium-risk and zero-risk individuals over a 3-week period following a suicidal crisis, showed that this effect persisted over time, thus supporting the notion of extremeness as a long-term cognitive style.

Neuringer (1976) concluded that suicidal individuals are more rigid and extreme in their thinking than non-suicidal persons, regardless of their psychiatric status. He pointed out that most people have the capacity to moderate or ignore dichotomies, but suicidal people lack this flexibility, and so if they are dissatisfied with something in their lives, they find it difficult or impossible to modulate their expectancies or to imagine compromise. In this way, when faced with a problematical situation, suicidal individuals will experience their environment as offering few opportunities for relief or change. This tendency is clearly relevant to the "cry of pain" model in outlining one important contributor to the perception of there being no escape and no rescue (see later).

Cognitive Rigidity

Dichotomous thinking is closely related to another cognitive variable studied by Neuringer over several years—that of cognitive rigidity. Neuringer (1964) conducted a study to evaluate the presence and extent of such rigidity in a suicidal group, a non-suicidal psychosomatic group and a control group made up of individuals hospitalized for minor transient medical conditions. First, they completed a 29-item questionnaire designed to assess the tendency to think in rigid categories. Second, they traced the shortest route from one point to another on a series of street maps, identical except for the street names. The results showed that on both tasks the suicidal subjects were more rigid in their thinking than the other two groups. Levenson and Neuringer (1971) extended this work by examining the relationship between problem-solving ability and self-destructive behaviour. Their results confirmed that suicidal individuals were more rigid and inflexible and less able to change their problem-solving strategies. Other studies have found similar results, showing that young suicide attempters were more field-dependent (that is, their decisions are more influenced by their environment), but not more cognitively impulsive (measured by decision latency) than psychiatric controls (Levenson, 1974; Patsiokas et al, 1979).

These early studies of cognitive rigidity were based on impersonal problem-solving tasks, such as word association, map reading and arithmetic. More recent work has focused on interpersonal problem solving, as several researchers have argued that these processes may be inherently different (Schotte and Clum,1982; Arffa, 1983; Linehan et al, 1986). If we are looking for evidence that suicidal behaviour is associated with the feeling that there is no escape from present circumstances, then impairment in ability to solve current problems is likely to be a critical factor.

Problem-solving

D'Zurilla and Nezu (1990) highlight five components in the problem-solving process: problem orientation; generation of alternative solutions; decision making; solution implementation; and solution verification. Pollock and Williams (1998) have reviewed this area, and point out that these stages are not necessarily based on how healthy individuals approach problem solving, but are an attempt to understand which steps in the process might break down.

Several studies comparing suicidal individuals and controls have found important qualitative differences in problem solving. One study examined the relationship between depressive symptoms and problem-solving appraisal in a group of undergraduate college students. It was found that students who were more depressed also saw themselves as less confident in their problem-solving skills, less systematic and active in their problem-solving attempts and felt less in control in problem situations when compared with students with low levels of depression (Nezu, 1986). Another study which investigated problem solving among inpatient suicide attempters, suicidal ideators and non-suicidal psychiatric inpatients, found that the inpatient suicide attempters were more passive and less active in their problem solving than the other two groups, i.e. they tended to let problems solve themselves or they relied on others for solutions (Linehan et al, 1987). Similarly, Orbach and colleagues (1990) found that patients who had harmed themselves were more passive (tending to depend more on others), as well as being less versatile and less relevant in the solutions they supplied. Their solutions also made less reference to the future than the solutions of non-suicidal patients.

How can the differences in problem-solving performance between suicidal people and other groups be explained? There are several possibilities. First, as a group, suicidal people may be less effective or more passive in solving problems in general. Second, there may be a sub-set of people for whom specific problem-solving deficits are a trait feature. Third, there may be a highly sensitive sub-group who do not display deficits between suicidal episodes but react to small mood changes with dramatic problem-solving failures. Current research findings cannot distinguish between these possibilities.

In particular, it is surprising that so little research has addressed the question of whether difficulties in interpersonal problem solving arise as a result of state or trait factors. There is evidence to show that mood states are related to changes in personal and social judgements, alterations in spatial judgements and impairment of recall (Seibert and Ellis, 1991). A number of studies also show how mood determines the way in which events are encoded and that this context may affect the ease with which memories are retrieved (see Williams et al, 1997, for review). It would be surprising if mood did not, therefore, play an important part in problem-solving deficits. Mitchell and Madigan (1984) showed that participants under experimentally-induced depressed mood functioned poorly on interpersonal problem-solving tasks. However, it is not clear whether mood impairs access to relevant memories or makes some people generally pessimistic about trying to solve their problems. Current research focuses almost exclusively on solving real or hypothetical problems in relationships with other people, yet one of the major issues for suicidal patients is how they can solve the problem of how to gain control over their feelings. Clinicians know that affective regulation is a major problem for their patients, but researchers have not yet risen to the challenge of how best to understand it. We suggest that many patients attempt to control their emotions by telling themselves to "grow up" or "pull themselves together". Such "invalidating" strategies (Linehan, 1993) are known to be unsuccessful, and Linehan has suggested that mindfulness training is a useful component of treatment to allow patients to learn more skilful means. This is an area of important future research.

Recently, researchers have begun to focus on the psychological processes underlying problem solving and how this is linked to suicidal behaviour. Several researchers have suggested that cognitive deficits make it difficult for a depressed individual to generate new or alternative solutions to the problems that face them (Goddard et al, 1996). It is well known that an increase of negative life events in combination with reduced problem-solving ability may place an individual at risk for suicidal behaviour (Schotte and Clum, 1987). Further, there is increasing evidence that the way a person remembers his/her past can be an important contributing factor.

Autobiographical Memory

Levenson and Neuringer (1971) and Wilson and colleagues (1995) have pointed out the important connection between life experiences, as resources to draw on in solving problems, and self-destructive behaviour. The link between problem-solving deficits and memory for personal events has been investigated by Williams and his colleagues.

Williams has looked, in particular, at the quality of autobiographical memories that are retrieved, how these are affected by mood and their relationship to suicidal behaviour. A number of studies has shown that depressed and attempted suicide patients perform poorly when required to produce a specific memory in response to a cue word. Instead, these individuals tend to remember events in a summarized and over-general way (see Williams, 1996 for review). For example, when asked to think of a specific event associated with the word "happy", a suicidal patient may respond with, "when I used to go for long walks by myself". To the cue word "sorry", they may reply, "when I lie to my mum". In these cases, the patient has responded with a memory that summarizes a number of events, an "over-general" memory, rather than singling out one event to respond with (an example of a specific memory to "happy" might be, "when I walked through Leighton forest with my grandad last Saturday afternoon"; and to "sorry", "how I felt after the argument I had with my mum when I came home late"). There is increasing evidence to suggest that this tendency is associated with a history of negative events (Williams, 1996), but the important aspect of this research for our present purposes is the effect that such over-general memory has on problem solving.

Evans and colleagues (1992) examined the effectiveness of solutions produced on the Means–Ends Problem Solving Test and the level of over-general memory in patients who had taken overdoses, and found a strong correlation between the two. Sidley and colleagues (1997) carried out a replication of this study, with the same result: a correlation between increased over-generality of autobiographical memory and ineffectiveness of problem-solving. Further work has found that the deficit in remembering the past is correlated with inability to imagine the future in a specific way (Williams et al, 1996). Interestingly, the evidence to date suggests that the tendency to retrieve events from the past in an over-general way is a trait, not a state, factor. Williams and Dritschel (1988) compared patients who had just taken overdoses and a group of individuals who had taken an overdose between 3 and 14 months earlier. Both groups were found to be significantly more over-general in their memories than normal controls. However, the fact that over-general retrieval is a cognitive style does not mean that it cannot be changed, and there is now preliminary evidence that a mindfulness-based cognitive therapy can change it, allowing a person to retrieve more specific memories from his/her past (Williams et al, in press).

Williams and colleagues propose that successful problem solving depends largely on the quality of the type of memories individuals are able to retrieve. Depressed and suicidal patients are poor at problem solving because they are unable to access specific memories successfully. Specific memories are very useful as a resource in solving problems, as they are detailed and offer a large number of cues from which to generate a range of potential solutions (Williams, 1996; Goddard et al, 1996). For example, in a problem situation, individuals might try and think of what they did the last time they were in similar situations. In this way they might recall specific strategies that worked and possibly generate a range of other potential solutions to try.

Autobiographical memory research offers a potentially important strategy for investigating the psychological mechanisms that underlie the process whereby a life event leads to a catastrophic failure to cope. If, under these circumstances, individuals can only retrieve generic memories, memories that give few cues on how to cope with the current crisis, this is an important contributor to the feeling that there is no escape. Once this feeling is generalized into the future, hopelessness is likely to increase and the possibility of future "rescue" diminishes.

Hopelessness

If a person feels defeated, and there is little chance of escape, then he/she becomes very vulnerable. But we suggest that the element that turns such a situation into a suicidal crisis is the absence of any rescue factors: the prediction that nothing will change in the future. It has been known for some time that hopelessness is one of the main factors mediating the relationship between depression and suicidal intent (Rudd et al, 1994; Dixon et al, 1991; Minkoff et al, 1973). Earlier work suggested that cognitive rigidity, dichotomous thinking and problem-solving deficits played a role in the development of hopelessness (Neuringer, 1967; Levenson and Neuringer, 1971; Patsiokas et al, 1979). Yet, more recently, when McLeavey and colleagues (1987) examined the role of interpersonal problem-solving deficits in self-poisoning patients, they found they were independent—there was little correlation between hopelessness and performance on problem-solving measures. In another study, Schotte and Clum (1987) controlled for the level of depression and found that hopelessness remained a good predictor of the level of suicidal intent. Although they also found non-significant correlations between the degree of hopelessness and the measures of problem-solving skill, suicidal patients tended to focus more on the negative side-effects of implementation than a non-suicidal control group, which they took to be an indication of a general maladaptive orientation toward problems.

Rudd and colleagues (1994) have suggested that similar processes may be at work in the tendency of suicidal ideators to focus on the potentially negative consequences of implementing alternative solutions, and negative problem-solving appraisal. Dixon and colleagues (1994) have extended this work by examining problem-solving appraisal. They concluded that hopelessness mediates the relationship between problem-solving appraisal and suicidal ideation, and argued that hopelessness was useful in predicting suicidal ideation. Another recent study by Wilson and colleagues (1995) supports these conclusions and suggests that the relationship between self-appraisal of problem-solving ability and hopelessness may be important and needs to be examined in more detail in future research.

The research clearly suggests that in treatment it may be of value to focus on hopelessness and problem-solving appraisal (Dixon et al, 1994). Psychological treatments for suicidal behaviour (see Chapter 28) do indeed focus on such variables, but it is important for our purposes to ask what the psychological mechanisms are that underlie hopelessness, so that if therapy becomes difficult, therapist and patient may have a "map" to guide their way in treatment.

Processes Underlying Hopelessness: the Role of Future Thinking

Until fairly recently there was a paucity of research focusing specifically on the concept of hopelessness. Abramson and colleagues (1989) formulated a theory of hopelessness in which they discuss hopelessness in terms of an expectancy that positive consequences will not occur, or that negative consequences will occur. Melges and Bowlby (1969), more narrowly, suggest that it is the reduced expectancy of success that most characterizes hopelessness. Is hopelessness an increased ability to think of negative things in the future, or a decreased ability to think of positive things, or both?

MacLeod and colleagues (1993) conducted a study to examine future-directed thinking in suicidal subjects. They adapted the verbal fluency paradigm to study the degree to which suicidal individuals, hospital controls and normal controls were able to think of future positive and future negative events. The task for the participants was to generate as many things in the future that they were looking forward to, or not looking forward to, in the 30-second time period allowed. They were asked to do this for a number of different future time periods. The researchers then measured the fluency with which participants produced their answers. They found that, relative to controls, participants who had recently taken an overdose showed an inability to think of positive things that might happen in the future, but no increased anticipation of future negative events. This effect was present for both the immediate and longer-term future.

How do these tendencies affect probability judgements? In another study, Macleod and Tarbuck (1994) presented patients who had taken overdoses with nine future, negative, self-relevant events on which they had to make subjective probability judgements, i.e. how likely it was that these events would or would not occur. They found that the suicide attempters judged negative events more likely to occur than positive events. It appears that this comes about because of the same deficit in fluency of generating positive things. When asked to judge whether a negative event will occur, there follows, as it were, a "race" between the negative "reasons why it will happen" and positive "reasons why it will not". Macleod and Tarbuck (1994) found that suicidal patients found it more difficult to think of why the negative events might not happen, but were no different from controls in thinking of reasons why the unpleasant event would happen. In other words, when presented with negative events, suicidal people judge them as likely to occur because they are unable to think of positive aspects of themselves or their circumstances that would prevent the events taking place. These issues highlight the importance of therapeutic strategies directed at improving this specific aspect of a patient's problem-solving ability.

But are these tendencies simply due to the co-occurrence of depression? Macleod and colleagues (1997) investigated whether the lack of anticipation of positive future events would be found in suicidal people who were not depressed. Again they found that suicidal patients generated fewer positive experiences than controls, but did not anticipate more negative experiences. Their results showed no differences between the depressed and non-depressed suicidal patients. From a clinical standpoint, lack of positive expectancies is an important factor in suicidal behaviour and should be taken into account more explicitly in assessments and interventions.

SUICIDAL BEHAVIOUR AS A CRY OF PAIN

For many years it was supposed that completed suicide and non-fatal deliberate self-harm (DSH) required different explanatory models. After all, as well as differences in outcome, there were differences in age and sex distribution, and in terms of the rise and fall of rates over time. In the 1960s, when suicide rates were falling, non-fatal DSH (i.e. attempted suicide) rates were rising. It is now clear that differences between completed suicide and deliberate self-harm have been overstated. For example, differences in age and sex distribution do not imply that different explanations are required. In the UK over the past 20 years, the male suicide rate has been rising while the female suicide rate has been falling. Over the same period, younger male suicide rates have been rising, whereas (apart from the very old) older male rates have remained steady or fallen. Given that one may observe differences in the falling and rising of rates *within* the suicide statistics, one cannot assume that such differences between suicide and DSH give any indication that the two behaviours require different explanations.

Williams (1997) suggests that we conceive of suicidal behaviour (whether the outcome is life or death) as a "cry of pain". Suicidal behaviour is seen as an attempt to escape from a trap ("arrested flight" in sociobiological terms), a feeling of being both "defeated" and "closed in". This feeling of being defeated can arise from external circumstances (e.g. poor relationships, unemployment, job stress) or from uncontrollable inner turmoil. The important aspect of such stress is that it signals to the individual that he/she is *defeated* in some important aspect of his/her life. Such defeats activate primitive (evolutionarily old) psychobiological mechanisms (see Gilbert, 1989). However, to trigger a full-blown "defeat response", in which the person will tend to give up, there also needs to be a sense of being trapped in the situation: the person expects that there is nothing that he/she will be able to do to escape from the things that are most disturbing. Further, the person believes that there is little likelihood that he/she will be "rescued" from the situation by other people or circumstances. Thus, suicidal behaviour is seen as the "cry of pain" that is elicited by a combination of circumstances in which the person perceives him/herself to have been defeated, where there appears to be no possibility of escape or rescue, and where the means by which a person may harm him/herself is available.

How does this model account both for non-lethal self-harm and for more lethal suicidal behaviour and suicide itself? According to the theory, a person is sensitive to the degree to which there is "escape potential" from any stressful situation (i.e. potential to escape from external stress or a person's own symptoms). Where one's escape is (or appears to be) blocked, then a range of responses are observed, of which suicidal behaviour is one element. Early in the sequence, where escape potential is threatened but not yet eliminated, escape attempts will be characterized by high levels of activity, anger and "protest". This is closely analogous to the early response to threatened loss observed in animals and humans (Bowlby, 1969, 1973, 1980).

Thus, less "serious" suicidal behaviour is an attempt to re-establish escape routes following defeat or rejection, representing the earlier "protest" or "reactance" phase of the psychobiological script that follows defeat and threatened helplessness. Lethal suicide attempts and completed suicide represent the "cry of pain" from a person who feels completely defeated, with no escape routes and no possibility of rescue at all. People who have perfectionistic standards may, for reasons that are not completely understood, move directly to this "despair" phase of the sequence. Their first attempt on their lives may be very dangerous and result in death.

The "cry of pain" model emphasizes the "reactive" element of suicidal behaviour (the way it is elicited by a certain combination of circumstances), rather than its "communicative" element (the way it is seen by some as a cry for help, for example). Like an animal caught in a trap that cries in pain, the cry is *elicited* by the situation of being trapped and in pain. Only secondarily is the cry an attempt to bring help, although this may be an important incidental consequence, but the behaviour is not motivated by, or dependent on, its consequences. In learning theory terms, it is not an "operant". Of course, it is possible that in some cases of repeated suicidal behaviour, the response comes to function as an operant. But even here, it is likely to be more useful to focus on which aspects of the person's mood and cognition, and which aspect of his/her environment, precede and elicit such behaviour.

CONCLUDING REMARKS

A number of psychological variables have been found associated with suicidal behaviour: impulsivity, dichotomous thinking, cognitive constriction, hopelessness, problem-solving deficits, over-general autobiographical memory and biases in future judgement. We have suggested that the important aspect of these variables is the role they play in increasing the likelihood that events will be reacted to in catastrophic ways. That is, they help us understand, first, which elements of life experience are most likely to trigger such behaviour (we suggested that life events that signal defeat are important here); second, what mechanisms contribute to the feeling that there is no escape from the consequences of such defeat (memory deficits preventing access to useful specific cues from the past); and third, the mechanisms underlying the belief that there will be no possibility of rescue in the future (dysfluency in generating future positive events).

The "cry of pain" model emphasizes the aspects of the person and his/her circumstances that elicit the behaviour in question (the "triggering conditions"), and explicitly de-emphasizes the communicative "cry for help" element that sees such behaviour as determined by its consequences. The "cry of pain" may be shown first in its "protest" aspect, as a person becomes aware that escape potential is reducing and seeks to reassert control. But some individuals may rapidly move into the latter "despair" phase in which the psychobiological "defeat script" is triggered by the perception of uncontrollable rejection or loss, in which escape or rescue is thought to be impossible. Under these circumstances, lack of social support and the availability of lethal means makes extreme self-damaging behaviour likely. The intensity of the behaviour at all phases is dependent not only on the severity of the events that triggered them, and the temperament (e.g. affective instability) and learning history of the individual, but also on the lability of the biological substrates of impulsive and destructive behaviour. Against this background, we can see how understanding the psychological mechanisms can create a vital bridge between research on social and biological factors to help us towards a more comprehensive understanding of suicidal behaviour.

REFERENCES

Adams, K.S. (1991) Environmental, psychosocial and psychoanalytic aspects of suicidal behavior. In S.J. Blumenthal and D.J. Kupfer (Eds), Suicide Over the Life Cycle, pp. 39–96, Washington, DC: American Psychiatric Press.

Apter, A., Plutchick, R. and Van Praag, H.M. (1993) Anxiety, impulsivity and depressed mood in relation to suicidal and violent behavior. Acta Psychiatrica Scandinavica, 87: 1–5.

Arffa, S. (1983) Cognition and suicide: a methodological review. Suicide and Life-Threatening Behavior, 13: 109–122.

Abramson, L.Y., Metalsky, G.I. and Alloy, L.B. (1989) Hopelessness depression: a theory-based subtype of depression. Psychological Review, 96: 358–372.

Beck, A.T., Rush, A.J., Shaw, B.F. and Emery, G. (1979) Cognitive Therapy of Depression. New York: Guilford.

Bowlby, J. (1969) Attachment. Attachment and Loss, Vol. 1. London: Hogarth.

Bowlby, J. (1973) Separation, Anxiety and Anger. Attachment and Loss, Vol. 2. London: Hogarth.

Bowlby, J. (1980) Loss: Sadness and Depression. Attachment and Loss, Vol. 3. London: Hogarth.

Dixon, W.A., Heppener, P.P. and Anderson, W.P. (1991) Problem-solving appraisal, stress, hopelessness and suicide ideation in a college population. Journal of Counseling Psychology, 38: 51–56.

Dixon, W.A., Heppener, P.P. and Rudd, M.D. (1994) Problem solving appraisal, hopelessness and suicidal ideation: evidence for a mediational model. Journal of Counseling Psychology, 41: 91–98.

D'Zurilla, T.J. and Nezu, A.M. (1990) Development and preliminary evaluation of the Social Problem-Solving Inventory (SPSI). Psychological Assessment: A Journal of Consulting and Clinical Psychology, 2: 156–163.

Evans, J., Platts, H. and Liebenau, A. (1996) Impulsiveness and deliberate self-harm: a comparison of "first-timers" and "repeaters". Acta Psychiatrica Scandinavica, 93: 378–380.

Evans, J., Williams, J.M.G., O'Loughlin, S. and Howells, K. (1992) Autobiographical memory and problem-solving strategies of parasuicide patients. Psychological Medicine, 22: 399–405.

Eyman, J.R. and Eyman, S.K. (1992) Personality assessment in suicide prediction. In R.W. Maris, A.L. Berman, J.T. Maltsberger and R.I. Yufit (Eds), Assessment and Prediction of Suicide, pp. 183–201. New York: Guilford.

Freud, S. (1917) Mourning and Melancholia, Standard Edition, Vol. 14. London: Hogarth.

Gilbert, P. (1989) Human Nature and Suffering. Hove and London: Erlbaum.

Goddard, L., Dritschel, B. and Burton, A. (1996) Role of autobiographical memory in social problem solving and depression. Journal of Abnormal Psychology, 105: 609–616.

Hawton, K., O'Grady, J., Osborn, M. and Cole, D. (1982) Adolescents who take overdoses: their characteristics, problems, and contacts with helping agencies. British Journal of Psychiatry, 140: 118–123.

Hoberman, H.M. and Garfinkel, B.D. (1988) Completed suicide in children and adolescents. Journal of the American Academy of Child and Adolescent Psychiatry, 27: 689–695.

Levenson, M. (1974) Cognitive correlates of suicide risk. In C. Neuringer (Ed.), Psychological Assessment of Suicidal Risk. Chicago, IL: Charles E. Thomas.

Levenson, M. and Neuringer, C. (1971) Problem-solving behavior in suicidal adolescents. Journal of Consulting and Clinical Psychology, 37: 433–436.

Linehan, M.M. (1993) Cognitive Behavioural Treatment for Borderline Personality Disorder. New York: Guilford.

Linehan, M.M., Camper, P., Chiles, J.A., Strohsahl, K. and Shearin, E. (1987) Interpersonal problem solving and parasuicide. Cognitive Therapy and Research, 11: 1–12.
Linehan, M.M., Chiles, J.A., Devine, R.H., Luffaw, J.A. and Egan, K.A. (1986) Presenting problems of parasuicides versus suicide ideators and non-suicidal psychiatric patients. Journal of Consulting and Clinical Psychology, 54: 880–881.
Litman, R.E. (1967) Sigmund Freud on suicide. In E. Schneidman (Ed.), Essays in Self-Destruction. New York: Science House.
Lolas, F., Gomez, A. and Suarez, L. (1991) EPQ-R and suicide attempt: the relevance of psychoticism. Personality and Individual Differences: 12: 899–902.
MacLeod, A.K., Rose, G.S. and Williams, J.M.G. (1993) Components of hopelessness about the future in parasuicide. Cognitive Therapy and Research, 17: 441–455.
MacLeod, A.K. and Tarbuck, A.F. (1994) Explaining why negative events will happen to oneself: parasuicides are pessimistic because they can't see any reason not to be. British Journal of Clinical Psychology, 33: 317–326.
MacLeod, A.K., Pankhania, B., Lee, M. and Mitchell, D. (1997) Parasuicide, depression and the anticipation of positive and negative future experiences. Psychological Medicine, 27: 973–977.
Maiuro, R.D., O'Sullivan, M.J., Michael, M.C. and Vitaliano, P.P. (1989) Anger, hostility and depression in assaultive vs. suicide-attempting males. Journal of Clinical Psychology, 45: 532–541.
Maris, R. (1981) Pathways to Suicide. Baltimore, MD: Johns Hopkins University Press.
McLeavey, B.C., Daly, R.J., Murray, C.M., O'Riordan, J. and Taylor, M. (1987) Interpersonal problem-solving deficits in self-poisoning patients. Suicide and Life-Threatening Behavior, 17: 33–49.
Melges, F.T. and Bowlby, J. (1969) Types of hopelessness in psychopathological process. Archives of General Psychiatry, 20: 690–699.
Menninger, K. (1938) Man Against Himself. New York: Harcourt, Brace and World.
Minkoff, K., Bergman, E., Beck, A.T. and Beck, R. (1973) Hopelessness, depression and attempted suicide. American Journal of Psychiatry, 130: 455–459.
Mitchell, J.E. and Madigan, R.J. (1984) The effects of induced elation and depression on interpersonal problem solving. Cognitive Therapy and Research, 8: 277–285.
Neuringer, C. (1961) Dichotomous evaluations in suicidal individuals. Journal of Consulting Psychology, 25: 445–449.
Neuringer, C. (1964) Rigid thinking in suicidal individuals. Journal of Consulting Psychology, 28: 54–58.
Neuringer, C. (1967) The cognitive organisation of meaning in suicidal individuals. Journal of General Psychology, 76: 91–100.
Neuringer, C. (1968) Divergences between attitudes toward life and death among suicidal, psychosomatic and normal hospitalized patients. Journal of Consulting and Clinical Psychology, 32: 59–63.
Neuringer, C. (1976) Current developments in the study of suicidal thinking. In E.S. Schneidman (Ed.), Suicidology: Contemporary Developments. New York: Grune and Stratton.
Neuringer, C. and Lettieri, D.J. (1971) Affect, attitude and cognition in suicidal persons. Journal of Life-Threatening Behaviors, 1: 106–124.
Nezu, A.M. (1986) Cognitive appraisal of problem-solving effectiveness: relation to depression and depressive symptoms. Journal of Clinical Psychology, 42: 42–48.
Nordstrom, P., Schalling, M. and Asberg, M. (1995) Temperamental vulnerability in attempted suicide. Acta Psychiatrica Scandinavica, 92: 155–160.
Orbach, I., Bar-Joseph, H. and Dror, N. (1990) Styles of problem solving in suicidal individuals. Suicide and Life-Threatening Behavior, 20: 56–64.
Pallis, D.J. and Jenkins, J.S. (1977) Extraversion, neuroticism and intent in attempted suicides. Psychological Reports, 41: 19–22.

Patsiokas, A.T., Clum, G. and Luscomb, R.L. (1979) Cognitive characteristics of suicide attempters. Journal of Consulting and Clinical Psychology, 47: 478–484.
Pfeffer, C.R., Newcorn, J., Kaplan, G., Misruchi,M.S. and Plutchik, R. (1988) Subtypes of suicidal and assaultive behaviors in adolescent psychiatric in-patients: a research note. Journal of Child Psychology and Psychiatry, 30: 151–163.
Pollock, L.R. and Williams, J.M.G. (1998) Problem solving and suicidal behavior. Suicide and Life-Threatening Behavior, 28: 375–387.
Rudd, M.D., Rajab, M.H. and Dahm, P.F. (1994) Problem solving appraisal in suicide ideators and attempters. American Journal of Orthopsychiatry, 64: 136–149.
Schafii, M. and Schafii, S.L. (1982) Pathways of Human Development, pp. 164–180. New York: Thieme and Stratton.
Schotte, D.E. and Clum, G.A. (1982) Suicide ideation in a college population. A test of a model. Journal of Consulting and Clinical Psychology, 50: 690–696.
Schotte, D.E. and Clum, G.A. (1987) Problem-solving skills in suicidal psychiatric patients. Journal of Consulting and Clinical Psychology, 55: 49–54.
Seibert, P.S. and Ellis, H.C. (1991) Irrelevant thoughts, emotional mood states and cognitive task performance. Memory and Cognition, 19: 507–513.
Shaffer, D. (1974) Suicide in childhood and early adolescence. Journal of Child Psychology and Psychiatry, 15: 275–291.
Shaffer, D., Garland, A., Gould, M., Fisher, P. and Trautman, P. (1988) Preventing teenage suicide: a critical review. Journal of the American Academy of Child and Adolescent Psychiatry, 27: 675–687.
Sidley, G.L., Whitaker, K., Calam, R.M. and Wells, A. (1997) The relationship between problem-solving and autobiographical memory in parasuicide patients. Behavioural and Cognitive Psychotherapy, 25: 195–202.
Stillion, J.M. and McDowell, E.E. (1996) Suicide Across the Life Span. Washington, DC: Taylor and Francis.
Williams, J.M.G. (1996) Depression and the specificity of autobiographical memory. In D.C. Rubin (Ed.), Remembering Our Past—Studies in Autobiographical Memory. Cambridge: Cambridge University Press.
Williams, J.M.G. (1997) Cry of Pain: Understanding Suicide and Self-harm. Harmondsworth: Penguin.
Williams, J.M.G. and Dritschel, B.H. (1988) Emotional disturbance and the specificity of autobiographical memory. Cognition and Emotion, 2: 221–234.
Williams, J.M.G., Ellis, N., Tyers, C., Healy, H., Rose, G. and Macleod, A.K. (1996) The specificity of autobiographical memory and imageability of the future. Memory & Cognition, 24: 116–125.
Williams, J.M.G., Teasdale, J.D., Segal, Z.V. and Soulsby, J. (in press) Mindfulness-based Cognitive Therapy reduces overgeneral autobiographical memory in formerly depressed patients. *Journal of Abnormal Psychology*.
Williams, J.M.G., Watts, F.N., Macleod, C. and Mathews, A. (1997) Cognitive Psychology and Emotional Disorders, 2nd Edn. Chichester: Wiley.
Wilson, K.G., Stelzer, J., Bergman, J.N., Kral, M.J., Inayatullah, M. and Elliott, C.A. (1995) Problem solving, stress and coping in adolescent suicide attempts. Suicide and Life-Threatening Behavior, 25: 241–252.
Zilboorg, G. (1937) Considerations on suicide, with particular reference to that of the young. American Journal of Orthopsychiatry, 7: 15–31.

Chapter 6

Ethology and Suicidal Behaviour

Robert D. Goldney
Department of Psychiatry, University of Adelaide, South Australia, Australia

Abstract

It is over 40 years since initial reference to ethology was made in regard to suicidal behaviour. In the 1950s, tentative analogies were drawn from the then new principles of ethology, following which there were several theoretical formulations based on general clinical observations of suicidal subjects. However, only in the last 20 years has experimental work on animal behaviour provided an ethological perspective on what is, in essence, the link between early psychodynamic hypotheses and biological formulations of suicidal behaviour, hypotheses which had at times been regarded as mutually exclusive. This chapter traces the development of ethological hypotheses and then refers to recent biological observations, the experimental manipulation of behaviour in animals and also findings from naturalistic longitudinal cohort studies, each of which may contribute to a better understanding of the enigma of suicide.

INTRODUCTION

Ethology is the biological study of behaviour in natural settings. It was developed by Karl von Frisch, Konrad Lorenz and Nikko Tinbergen and some of its basic concepts have entered our language. These include "imprinting", a specific form of learning which occurs early in life, and which is only possible at a "critical period"; a "fixed action pattern" which is a pre-determined behavioural pattern which is initiated by a specific "innate releasing mechanism"; and "displacement activity", a form of behaviour which appears unrelated to other activity.

It may initially appear paradoxical to seek ethological analogies with regard to suicidal behaviour, but biologists have used such terminology to describe, in a

The International Handbook of Suicide and Attempted Suicide. Edited by K. Hawton and K. van Heeringen.

number of different species, behaviour which is at the very least self-injurious. For example, it has been recorded in macaques, marmosets, squirrel monkeys, leopards, lions, jackals, hyenas, rodents and opossums (Jones, 1982), as well as in dolphins, pink bollworm moths, butterflies, pea aphids, birds and some bacteria (Lester and Goldney, 1997). Therefore, there appears to be a sound basis for examining how an ethological approach could assist our understanding of suicidal behaviour.

THEORETICAL HYPOTHESES

Theoretical hypotheses applying ethological concepts to suicidal behaviour are by no means new. For example, Stengel and Cook (1958), in referring to the then relatively new discipline of ethology, suggested that "the suicidal attempt acts very much as a 'social releaser'", and Stengel (1962) wrote that "the suicidal attempt functions as an alarm system and an appeal for help. It does so almost with the regularity of an 'innate release mechanism'". It is also pertinent that these concepts are embodied well in the title of Farberow and Shneidman's (1961) influential book, *The Cry for Help*, where the suicide attempt results in care being provided, in a manner similar to that described by Henderson (1974), who referred to attempted suicide as "care-eliciting behaviour", and saw it as a developmentally primitive signal for care.

Although the application of ethological principles to man must be pursued with caution, it is increasingly recognized that insights gained from such an approach to behaviour may be of clinical and theoretical relevance. Early examples included those of Bowlby (1958) who utilized such principles in his work on attachment theory and the consequences of maternal deprivation, and the work of Harlow and colleagues (1971) and his successors, such as Kraemer and colleagues (1997), has provided cogent data in regard to depression in primates.

In ethological terms, suicidal behaviour could be interpreted as displacement activity, as an innate releasing mechanism or as a fixed action pattern. With regard to displacement activity, a persuasive theory has been postulated by Jones and Daniels (1996) about the re-direction of aggression towards oneself when either it is not socially appropriate to be angry at others, or there are other powerful barriers to the expression of aggression, for example in institutional populations. Such an hypothesis has some clinical utility.

Suicidal behaviour also acts as a stimulus, which could be interpreted as an innate releasing mechanism, which elicits a response, the fixed action pattern, in other people. Alternatively, it could be interpreted as the fixed action pattern, whereby the behaviour itself is precipitated by external stressors, with the external stressors being the innate releasing mechanism for that suicidal behaviour.

There are also other ethologically-derived concepts (Table 6.1) which appear to have relevance in suicidal behaviour. Experienced clinicians are well aware of the "Janus face" of mixed feelings of wishing to live and die expressed by suici-

Table 6.1 Ethological concepts of potential relevance to suicidal behaviour

Innate release mechanism
Fixed action pattern
Displacement activity
Care eliciting behaviour
Conservation withdrawal
Ritual agonistic behaviour
Yielding behaviour
Social attention holding power
Entrapment
The tipping point

dal subjects, and measures of suicidal intent and lethality confirm this. Often the focus of the distressed person is not so much about living and dying, but rather about the wish to escape from an intolerable situation. This has led to a plethora of synonyms for attempted suicide, including "pseudocide", "parasuicide", "deliberate self-injury", "deliberate self-harm" and even "propetia" (from the Greek, meaning "rashness, headlong haste and containing the idea of falling into something or rushing into it in a reckless manner without previous assessment of the risks"; Seager, 1978).

Such a diversity of suggestions led Goldney (1980) to postulate that the ethological concept of "conservation-withdrawal" of Engel (1962) could render the reasoning behind the perceived need for such terminology to be more apparent than real. Engel noted that there were two opposite patterns of response to increasing external demands: mounting anxiety with the "fight-or-flight reaction, or energy conservation and withdrawal". He stated that conservation withdrawal:

> may lead to behaviour to hold, cling, ingratiate, reward, force or seduce an external object so as to prevent or replace the loss and ensure continued supply . . . it is essentially a conserving of energy and includes heightening of the stimulus barriers to reduce incoming stimuli and a reduction of activity to save energy. It is a holding action until the arrival of external supplies, help in the form of a supporting object (Engel, 1962).

This description appears to provide an ethological link between the external stressors impinging upon susceptible individuals and their subsequent suicidal behaviour. However, it lacks specificity to suicidal behaviour and could equally be utilized in the almost invariably reported wish to escape of those who indulge in illicit drug use. It has also been noted that it does not capture the more active "protest" aspects of some suicidal behaviour (Williams, 1997). However, in addition to having some face validity in regard to the most common form of suicidal behaviour, drug overdose, it also applies in self-cutting, where it has been observed that often there is a feeling of unreality or dissociation, and the cutting brings the person back to reality (Simpson, 1976), often with pain only being felt at the sight of blood. It is of interest that such a form of dissociation has been observed in primates who appear to have a "glazed" visual expression under certain stressful circumstances (Kraemer et al, 1997).

It could be argued that for suicidal behaviour to be considered in an ethological perspective, the appeal component should invariably be evoked. That this is not so is readily observed in the busy emergency room situation, where the responses of professionals to those who engage in suicidal behaviour is often far from empathic and caring (Goldney and Bottrill, 1980). However, that does not negate the ethological analogy. Thus, there is ample evidence that altruistic responses are not invariably elicited in other species. In fact, Trivers (1971) has argued that altruism is "reciprocally altruistic", as natural selection will favour those actions which in the long run benefit the organism performing them, there being a balance between an altruistic response and non-response. In the present context, this depends on the responder's perception of benefit to him/herself and whether or not the suicidal person appears to be "cheating" in his/her behaviour, a balance which is frequently reflected in the ambivalence reported not only by significant others but also by therapists.

Trivers (1971) further discussed various determinants of the degree of altruistic behaviour, and it may be relevant to the preponderance of young women among those who attempt suicide that it appears to be age-dependent. In terms of natural selection, sexually mature young women have greatest reproductive value, and their appeals are more likely to be met altruistically.

A parallel can also be drawn between suicidal behaviour, particularly in young women, and "ritual agonistic behaviour", or the settlement of dispute by exchange of signals, which are often concluded by so-called "yielding behaviour" rather than by physical violence. In this regard, the concept of "resource-holding potential" is pertinent. This implies that the result of ritual encounters between members of the same species depends on the individual's ability to use and conserve attributes such as size, skill and previous success. In essence, this means whether or not individuals consider themselves more powerful than competitors. In humans it has been described as "social attention-holding power", which is "the ability to attract attention and investment from other members of the group" (Stevens and Price, 1996). This has implications in terms of a person's self-esteem and capacity to form social affiliations, be they in the work place or with a partner. Stevens and Price (1996) have stated that:

> A subjective social attention holding power assessment which results in a perception of oneself as being both powerless and unattractive will activate that ancient biological mechanism responsible for the yielding subroutine, with all its depressive and behavioural consequences.

A further dimension to this sequence of events is the concept of "entrapment" described by Williams (1997), in which the individual perceives no other options than to yield. Williams suggested that a sense of entrapment is "central to suicidal behaviour" and that it results in "long-term demobilization, a biological state involving chemical changes".

This appears to indicate that yielding behaviour is disadvantageous. However, that this may not necessarily be the case has been suggested by Sloman and Price (1987), who observed that "acceptance of loss or defeat requires a certain level of developmental maturity". They noted that most people learn both healthy assertion and appropriate yielding in family and group contexts, and that it is normal under certain circumstances to accept defeat or yield during ritual agonistic encounters. It is further pertinent that yielding behaviour is similar to female courtship behaviour, as the female who is able to yield and turn an agonistic encounter with a male into a sexual encounter provides biological advantage to her species. Not uncommonly, such an outcome is observed in suicidal behaviour in young women.

The previous speculations have been based primarily on naturalistic observation of individuals, both human and animal. A broader application of ethological principles, urban ethology, involves a community-wide examination of behaviour. For example, what mechanisms could underline the marked changes in the pattern of suicide for certain groups, such as young males, in some countries over a relatively short period of time? A concept which may be of relevance is that of the "tipping point" (Tittle and Rowe, 1973; Goldney, 1998), which implies that there is a background or base rate of a behaviour, probably as a result of many factors, but that there is a threshold or "tipping point" which, once breached, allows for a dramatic increase in that behaviour. Although this concept is derived from a sociological background, its implications are strikingly similar to a model of suicide based on studies of chaos theory, dynamic systems and self-organization, where it was noted that "in an open system, abrupt changes in the very nature of the structure may take place" (Mishara, 1996).

These concepts are applied to suicidal behaviour in an attempt to understand such behaviour in an overall scientific climate which is becoming increasingly aware that certain processes in nature, although given different names by different disciplines, share many features in common. For example, they are consistent with the "principle of universality", which has been applied to a number of different physical and organizational systems, where it has been observed that a critical point may be reached beyond which sudden changes in many systems occur (Buchanan, 1997). This appears to be particularly germane to suicidal behaviour, as it often emerges in a dramatic and ostensibly unexpected manner as a response to multiple stressors.

RECENT NEUROBIOLOGICAL PERSPECTIVES

In the last 20 years, increasing data have emerged which have clearly demonstrated an association between external stressors, behaviour and neurobiological changes. For example, in his seminal article, "Transduction of psychosocial stress into the neurobiology of recurrent affective disorder", Post (1992) provided a cogent description of the development of depressive conditions after stressors had produced changes in biochemical and neuro-anatomical substrates. This model implies that the experience of depression leaves behind a memory trace that predisposes to further episodes of depression. Consequently, subsequent stressors do not need to be so severe, and a point comes when depression may be spontaneous, without external stressors. In fact, it is as if a critical point or tipping point has been breached.

Such a theory is consistent with the "glucocorticoid cascade" hypothesis, whereby prolonged hypothalamic–pituitary–adrenal axis (HPA) activity produces neuronal, especially hippocampal, damage, with impairment in cognition (O'Brien, 1997). Indeed, that may contribute to what Williams (1996) has described as the "mnemonic interlock" phenomenon, which is a subtle inability of suicidal subjects to recall specific events. It is also consistent with the cognitive science perspective provided by Segal and colleagues (1996), who suggested that the voluntary deployment of attention in order to prevent the escalation of mild depressive states may have an underlying neurobiological basis, which in essence counteracts the development of affective disorders as postulated by Post. Such hypotheses are attractive, as they allow a reconciliation between differing hypothetical paradigms.

ANIMAL STUDIES

There have been a number of recent animal studies that are pertinent. Insel (1997), in a study of the mouse-like mammals, the prairie and montane voles, described "a neurobiological basis of social attachment". Although the prairie and montane voles belong to the same species, they have markedly different social behaviours. Prairie voles are monogamous and highly affiliative, with strong pair bonds, and both males and females participate in parental care. Puberty for the female does not occur at any specific age, but only after exposure to a signal in the urine of an unrelated male, following which she becomes sexually receptive and forms an enduring monogamous bond. By contrast, montane voles are isolated, have little social contact, are not monogamous and females frequently abandon their young.

It is important that there are marked differences in oxytocin and vasopressin receptor distribution in their brains, although after parturition the female montane vole's oxytocin receptor binding changes to resemble that of the more parental prairie vole. Following a series of elegant experiments, Insel and colleagues concluded that:

> Remarkably, the neurohypophyseal neuropeptides oxytocin and vasopressin appear to be important for the formation of social attachments, including pair bonding in monogamous mammals, the initiation of parental care in both males and females, and possibly some aspects of the infant's attachment behavior.

These findings should probably not be considered remarkable, as Liu and colleagues (1997) have demonstrated in rats that early maternal behaviour appeared to programme HPA responses to stress in offspring. They reported that rat pups who received more, rather than less, maternal licking and grooming showed reduced plasma adrenocorticotropic hormone and corticosterone responses to restraint stress. Furthermore, the greater the frequency of maternal licking and grooming during infancy, the lower the HPA response to stress in adulthood.

Kraemer and colleagues (1997) have also investigated changes in HPA activity and brain microstructure in association with isolation and self-injurious behaviour in monkeys, as well as serotonin metabolism, because of the consistent observation that serotonin activity, as measured by cerebrospinal fluid 5-hydroxyindoleacetic acid (CSF 5-HIAA), was low in violent suicide attempters in man (Nordström et al, 1994). In a review of their studies, they described a reduction in dendritic branching of nerve cells in various regions of the brain, including the hippocampal neuronal microstructure, and suggested that the behavioural effects of isolation could be related to the degeneration of brain neurotransmitters and associated denervation hypersensitivity. With regard to serotonin metabolism, it is important that they reported no association between self-injurious behaviour in monkeys reared in isolation and lowered serotonin activity due to pharmacological manipulation. In a series of studies, they explored this further and found that the behavioural effects of the pharmacological manipulation of CSF 5-HIAA was dependent on social rearing factors. Whereas there was no effect with serotonin-lowering drugs on those monkeys who had been reared in isolation, there was an effect in the socially reared monkeys. This led them to postulate a "failure to connect" hypothesis related to early maternal deprivation, with a disruption of the usual relationship between the noradrenaline, dopamine and serotonergic systems, probably due to changes in cellular morphology and synaptic density.

Although not related specifically to suicidality, other researchers have demonstrated an association between measures of sociability and CSF 5-HIAA in rhesus macaques (Mehlman et al, 1995), with CSF 5-HIAA concentration being positively correlated with the total time spent grooming others and being in close proximity with other group members, and with the number of close neighbours. This demonstrates that certain indicators of social competence are related to CSF 5-HIAA in primates, and the findings are consistent with a recent study in non-depressed persons given a selective serotonin re-uptake inhibitor, which reduced negative affect and increased affiliative behaviour (Knutson et al, 1998). Quite clearly, this behavioural change is advantageous in terms of an individual's social attention-holding power, described previously.

The importance of these reports is that they are congruent with molecular and cellular theories of depression in humans, such as those proposed by Post (1992) and more recently by Duman and collaborators (1997). Indeed, the latter stated that "stress can decrease the expression of brain-derived neurotrophic factor and lead to atrophy of these same populations of stress-vulnerable hippocampal neurons". Duman and colleagues (1997) went on to hypothesize, in a manner consistent with the earlier work of Post (1992), and which is entirely compatible with developmental theory, that:

> One possibility is that many individuals who become depressed may have had a prior exposure to stress that causes a small amount of neuronal damage, but not enough to precipitate a behavioural change. If additional damage occurs, either as a result of normal ageing or further stressful stimuli, these effects may then be manifested in the symptoms of a mood disorder.

For obvious reasons, such research is difficult to carry out in man, but it is interesting to reflect on recent findings in other species. In his Presidential Address to the American Psychiatric Association, Hartmann (1992) referred to the work of the neurobiologist, Fernald, and his colleagues, and they have recently published further work which demonstrates that changes in the social state of African teleost fishes are associated with changes in neuronal size (Fox et al, 1997). They demonstrated that how a male fish interacted with other males, with regard to whether it was socially dominant or meek, had an effect on the brain cells regulating the fish's size, colour and capacity to reproduce. The dimensions of those brain cells were seen to be plastic, and if an aggressive fish met a larger and/or more aggressive fish, the hypothalamic neurones of the defeated male rapidly shrank. After the hypothalamic cells had shrunk, the male testes followed suit, decreasing the fish's apparent desire and ability to breed. In the laboratory situation, some male fish were environmentally pushed from dominators to meek types and cellular changes followed. Fernald and his colleagues found that key behavioural changes occurred first and drove the brain changes, and it was quite evident that social changes altered the brain cells.

Such work is consistent with what Edelman (1987) has termed "neural Darwinism", an obvious evolutionary reference to organisms responding to the environment. This has been reviewed further by Gynther and colleagues (1998), who concluded that:

> While the most dramatic examples of neuroplasticity occurred during a critical period of neural development, neuroplasticity can also occur in adult neocortex. Neuroplasticity appears to be activity-dependent: synaptic pathways that are intensively used may become strengthened, and conversely, there may be depression of transmission in infrequently used pathways.

They observed that the most profound examples of activity-dependent plasticity were seen in the first few months following birth, and referred to experiments in newborn kittens deprived of visual input in one eye, where marked changes were observed in the functional organization of their visual cortex.

These findings are similar to those reported by Brainard and Knudsen (1998) in experimental work on young barn owls wearing prisms that displaced their visual field horizontally. The owls were able to adjust to auditory stimuli so that they could correctly orientate themselves to the source of the sound, despite wearing the prisms. That adjustment was mediated by changes in the response properties of neurones in the central auditory pathway, and the phenomenon could be reversed. It is of note that there was a time after which the brains of the owls could not adjust adaptively to prismatic displacement of the visual field, depending on the animals' environment. However, spectacle-reared owls could return to normal after removal of the spectacles during their lifetime, but their capacity to do so depended on the environment. Those mature owls who were able to regain normal sound localization best were those who had been in an enriched environment. In practical terms, those owls that had been caged restrictively could not adapt as well as those who had been free to fly in an open aviary. Thus, where free flight was possible, more neuronal plasticity was observed.

Such findings are reassuring, but probably not unexpected for clinicians. Indeed, as Gynther and colleagues (1998) have stated:

> The finding that neuroplasticity occurs in an activity-dependent fashion should come as no surprise to anyone versed in the bio-psychosocial model. It is probable that such plasticity underlines simple folk law, such as "practice makes perfect" in performing physical or cognitive tasks.

NATURALISTIC LONGITUDINAL COHORT STUDIES

Whilst it is accepted that gross brain damage in humans in the formative years is associated with adult behavioural abnormalities, there has been less focus on the later influence of more subtle brain changes, particularly related specifically to adult suicide. However, recently two naturalistic longitudinal studies have provided persuasive evidence that early adverse developmental factors, presumably both biological and interpersonal, are related to suicide in adult life.

In the first, Barker and collaborators (1995) have demonstrated in two birth cohorts that lower weight gain in infancy was associated with suicide in adult life. They reported that "each kilogram decrease in weight gain between birth and one year was associated with an increased risk of suicide of 45% in men and 31% in women". This finding seemed to have no relationship to social class or method of feeding and there was no evidence of parental neglect being associated with the low-weight-gain infants. However, the authors postulated that there could have been other adverse psychosocial influences which were unrecorded. They also commented on the possible effects of growth hormone, prolactin and abnormalities in the HPA axis, which could influence both growth in infancy and mood in adult life.

In the second, Neeleman and collaborators (1998) described a similar birth cohort study of over 5,000 people which examined correlates of premature causes of death. They found that suicide risk was increased for those with poor childhood and adolescent physical development, noctural enuresis until the age of 4 years, and for those adolescents who had excessive tics, aggression or conduct problems and greater emotional instability. They also reported that similar risk factors were associated with accidental and other causes of premature death, although to a lesser degree, and they suggested there was "an aetiological continuum of self-destruction from subintentional to intentional", a suggestion which is quite consistent with the clinical observation of suicidal subjects. Whilst it is acknowledged that previous research has demonstrated an association between childhood psychiatric illness and future suicidal behaviour, this work clearly delineated temperamental and behavioural variables, which to some extent are biologically determined, and examined their influence prospectively on various causes of death, including suicide.

Whilst these two studies are not confirmatory for either the influence of early brain abnormalities or of external social factors, they are very suggestive of an interaction between early neurobiological changes and adult suicide, and they appear to provide an additional link in the chain of causation of adult suicidal behaviour.

CONCLUSION

It could be argued that the ethological paradigm has been extended beyond its limits in some of the studies referred to. However, there is a logical connection between the early ethological observations and hypotheses, the more recent delineation of biochemical and neurophysiological data associated with developmental issues in other species and in man, and the naturalistic longitudinal cohort observations of factors associated with subsequent suicidal behaviour.

Clinicians can be reassured that as a result of this research derived from ethological principles we are closer to understanding the nexus between early adverse life events and the neurobiology associated with developmental issues. However, we cannot yet draw definite conclusions from such studies. Indeed, as persuasive as some of these hypotheses and analogies may appear, they remain at the level of hypotheses, albeit hypotheses now on a firmer theoretical base then when tentative ethological speculation was made 40 years ago. Importantly, an ethological approach has provided a bridge between sociological and psychological theories on the one hand, and those theories based more on the biological sciences on the other. Even if it were for that reason alone, the value of an ethological approach in the area of suicide and its prevention is assured.

REFERENCES

Barker, D.J.P., Osmond, C., Rodin, I., Fall, C.H.D. and Winter, P.D. (1995) Low weight gain in infancy and suicide in adult life. British Medical Journal, 311: 1203.

Bowlby, J. (1958) The nature of the child's tie to his mother. International Journal of Psycho-analysis, 39: 350–373.

Brainard, M.S. and Knudsen, E.J. (1998) Experience affects brain development. American Journal of Psychiatry, 155: 1000.

Buchanan, M. (1997) One law to rule all. New Scientist, 2107: 30–35.

Duman, R.S., Heninger, G.R. and Mestler, E.J. (1997) A molecular and cellular theory of depression. Archives of General Psychiatry, 54: 597–606.

Edelman, G.M. (1987) Neural Darwinism: The Theory of Neuronal Group Selection. New York: Basic Books.

Engel, G.L. (1962) Anxiety and depression-withdrawal. International Journal of Psychoanalysis, 43: 89–97.
Farberow, N.L. and Shneidman, E.S. (1961) The Cry for Help. New York: McGraw-Hill.
Fox, H.E., White, S.A., Kao, M.H.F. and Fernald, R.D. (1997) Stress and dominance in a social fish. Journal of Neuroscience, 17: 6463–6469.
Goldney, R.D. (1980) Attempted suicide: an ethological perspective. Suicide and Life-Threatening Behavior, 10: 131–141.
Goldney, R.D. (1998) Variation in suicide rates: the "tipping point". Crisis, 19: 136–138.
Goldney, R.D. and Bottrill, A. (1980) Attitudes to patients who attempt suicide. Medical Journal of Australia, 2: 717–720.
Gynther, B.D., Calford, M.B. and Sah, P. (1998) Neuroplasticity and psychiatry. Australian and New Zealand Journal of Psychiatry, 32: 119–128.
Harlow, H.F., Harlow, M.K. and Suomi, S.J. (1971) From thought to therapy: lessons from a primate laboratory. American Science, 59: 538–549.
Hartmann, L. (1992) Presidential address: reflections on humane values and bio-psycho-social integration. American Journal of Psychiatry, 149: 1135–1141.
Henderson, S. (1974) Care-eliciting behavior in man. Journal of Nervous and Mental Disease, 159: 172–181.
Insel, T.R. (1997) A neurobiological basis of social attachment. American Journal of Psychiatry, 154: 726–735.
Jones, I.H. and Daniels, B.A. (1996) An ethological approach to self-injury. British Journal of Psychiatry, 169: 263–267.
Jones, I.H. (1982) Self-injury: toward a biological basis. Perspectives in Biology and Medicine, 26: 137–150.
Knutson, B., Wolkowitz, O.M., Cole, S.W., Chan, T., Moore, E.A., Johnson, R.C., Terpstra, J., Turner, R.A. and Reus, V.I. (1998) Selective alteration of personality and social behavior by serotonergic intervention. American Journal of Psychiatry, 155: 373–379.
Kraemer, G.W., Schmidt, D.E. and Ebert, M.H. (1997) The behavioural neurobiology of self-injurious behavior in Rhesus monkeys. In D.M. Stoff and J.J. Mann (Eds), The Neurobiology of Suicide. Annals of the New York Academy of Sciences, Vol. 836, pp. 12–38. New York: New York Academy of Sciences.
Lester, D. and Goldney, R.D. (1997) An ethological perspective on suicidal behavior. New Ideas in Psychology, 15: 97–103.
Liu, D., Diorio, J., Tannenbaum B., Caldji, C., Francis D., Freedman, A., Sharma, S., Pearson, D., Plotsky, P.M. and Meaney M.J. (1997) Maternal care, hippocampal glucocorticoid receptors, and hypothalamic–pituitary–adrenal responses to stress. Science, 177: 1659–1662.
Mehlman, P.T., Higley, J.D., Fauches, I., Lilly, A.A., Taub, D.M., Vickers, J., Suomi, S.J. and Linnoila, M. (1995) Correlations of CSF-5-HIAA concentration with sociality and the timing of emigration in free-ranging primates. American Journal of Psychiatry, 152: 907–913.
Mishara, B.L. (1996) A dynamic model of suicide. Human Development, 39: 181–194.
Neeleman, J., Wessely, S. and Wadsworth, M. (1998) Predictors of suicide, accidental death, and premature natural death in a general-population birth cohort. Lancet, 351: 93–97.
Nordstrom, P., Samuelsson, M., Asberg, M., Traskman-Bendz, L., Aberg-Wistedt, A., Nordin, C. and Bertilsson, L. (1994) CSF 5-HIAA predicts suicide risk after attempted suicide. Suicide and Life-Threatening Behavior, 24: 1–9.
O'Brien, J.T. (1997) The "glucocorticoid cascade" hypothesis in man. British Journal of Psychiatry, 170: 199–201.
Post, R.M. (1992) Transduction of psychosocial stress into the neurobiology of recurrent affective disorder. American Journal of Psychiatry, 149: 999–1010.
Seager, C.P. (1978) What's in a name? Attempted Suicide. British Journal of Psychiatry, 132: 206–207.

Segal, Z.V., Williams, J.M., Teasdale, J.D. and Gemar, M. (1996) A cognitive science perspective on kindling and episode sensitisation in recurrent affective disorder. Psychological Medicine, 26: 371–380.

Simpson, M.A. (1976) Self-mutilation. In E.S. Shneidman (Ed.), Suicidology. New York: Grune and Stratton.

Sloman, L. and Price, J.S. (1987) Losing behavior (yielding sub-routine) and human depression: proximate and selective mechanisms. Ethology and Sociobiology, 8: 99–109S.

Stengel, E. (1962) Recent research into suicide and attempted suicide. American Journal of Psychiatry, 118: 725–727.

Stengel, E. and Cook, N.G. (1958) Attempted Suicide: Its Social Significance and Effects. Maudsley Monograph Number 4. London: Oxford University Press.

Stevens, A. and Price, J. (1996) Evolutionary Psychiatry: A New Beginning. London: Routledge.

Tittle, C.R. and Rowe, A.R. (1973) Moral appeal, sanction threat and deviance: an experimental test. Social Problems, 20: 488–498.

Trivers, R.L. (1971) The evolution of reciprocal altruism. Quarterly Review of Biology, 46: 35–57.

Williams, J.M.G. (1996) The specificity of autobiographical memory in depression. In D. Rubin (Ed.), Remembering Our Past: Studies in Autobiographical Memory. Cambridge: Cambridge University Press.

Williams, M. (1997) Cry of Pain: Understanding Suicide and Self-harm. London: Penguin.

Chapter 7

Psychiatric Aspects of Suicidal Behaviour: Depression

Jouko K. Lönnqvist
Department of Mental Health and Alcohol Research, National Public Health Institute, Helsinki, Finland

Abstract

Depressive disorders in the general population are common. More than half of clinically depressed persons have suicidal thoughts, and their suicidal ideation is significantly related to the severity of depression. The main cause for the increased mortality in depression is suicide. Suicide risk is elevated in all mental disorders, but particularly so in depressive disorders, with a 20-fold increase for major depression. Findings from psychological autopsy studies conducted over the past 40 years suggest that depression is found in 29–88% of all suicides. Suicide in depression is particularly common among subjects with co-morbid mental and physical disorders. While a large proportion of depressed suicide victims have undergone psychiatric treatment, very few have received adequate therapy for depression. Psychological autopsy studies have shown that 1–5% of all suicides suffered from bipolar disorder. The majority of bipolar suicide victims had a depressive episode just before the suicide, most were co-morbid cases, and compliance problems were reported in almost all cases. It seems evident that lithium treatment in bipolar disorder is associated with a long-sustained reduction of fatal and non-fatal suicidal acts. Attempted suicide is common in the course of depressive disorders. Subjective depressive feelings, hopelessness and suicidal ideation are significantly more marked in suicide attempters than in non-attempters. About two-thirds of attempted suicide patients suffer from a mood disorder. Few depressed suicide attempters receive adequate treatment for depression. Inadequate recognition and treatment of depression and mood disorders has been the focus of professional discussion during the past decade. The best possible treatment for depression is urgently needed for effective suicide prevention.

The International Handbook of Suicide and Attempted Suicide. Edited by K. Hawton and K. van Heeringen.

INTRODUCTION

Depressive disorders in the general population are common—the prevalence of major depression is about 5%, varying around 2–4% in men and 2–6% in women (Regier et al, 1988; Blazer et al, 1994; Meltzer et al, 1995; Ohayon et al, 1999). Overall, depressive symptoms are about five times more frequent than depressive disorders and individuals with depressive symptoms have a four to five times higher risk than others of developing a depressive disorder (Horwath et al, 1992). Depression is usually episodic, and very often relapsing, recurrent and chronic, depending, among other factors, on the quality of treatment received (Melfi et al, 1998). Because the diagnosis of depression is frequently missed, the depressed person often remains untreated or undertreated, which might help to explain why suicide is often the ultimate outcome of a life lived with depression.

The risk of suicidal behaviour has always been connected with depressive disorders. More than half of clinically depressed persons have suicidal thoughts, and their suicidal ideation is significantly related to the severity of depression. The most common predictive depressive symptoms for suicidal ideation in depression are, in addition to depressed mood, hopelessness, feelings of guilt, loss of interest and low self-esteem (van Gastel et al, 1997). Hopelessness uniquely contributes to the prediction of suicidal ideation when the level of depression is statistically controlled for, not only in psychiatric disorders but also in the terminally ill (Chochinov et al, 1998).

Suicidal behaviour is a feature of all forms of depression, not merely its most severe expressions. The risk of suicidal behaviour fluctuates during the course of depressive disorders, depending partly on the type of disorder. The highest risk is often just after hospital treatment.

Because depression is very often a co-morbid but central symptom in many psychiatric disorders (schizophrenia, substance abuse, personality disorders, anxiety disorders) and somatic illnesses (cardiovascular diseases, strokes, cancer, AIDS or any severe and chronic disease), the clinical significance of suicidal behaviour in depression extends far beyond the classic syndrome of pure depression.

Inadequate recognition and treatment of depression and mood disorders has been the focus of lively professional discussion during the past decade. Theory and clinical practice have often been remote from each other. Atypical forms and the high co-morbidity of depression might explain the problems of non-compliance that often arise in the treatment of depressed individuals.

THE RISK OF SUICIDE IN DEPRESSION

Mortality studies suggest that depression substantially increases the risk of death. In the US National Health Interview Survey in 1989 the adjusted hazard rate ratios for all-cause mortality in major depression during the 2.5-year follow-up were 3.1 (95% CI, 2.0–4.9) for white adult males and 1.7 (95% CI, 0.9–3.1) for females (Zheng et al, 1997).

The main single cause for the increased mortality seen in depression is suicide. Based on 25 studies from nine countries, reported between 1966 and 1995, Harris and Barraclough (1998) calculated that the combined causes of death risk for all affective disorders was 1.7 times that expected. Deaths from natural causes were 1.3 times more frequent than expected, accounting for 45% of the excess deaths. The mortality risk for suicide was 20 times and for other violent causes 2.5 times the expected rate in all affective disorders, and 21 and 2.3 times, respectively, in major depression.

Wulsin and colleagues (1999) analysed all relevant English language databases from 1966 to 1996 and found 35 studies that reported rates of suicide as a percentage of deaths among the depressed, ranging from 0% to 64%, with a mean of 10.8%. The suicide rate was independent of the total percentage of all deaths. Among the 23 studies of psychiatric samples, almost exclusively based on former inpatients, suicide accounted for a mean of 16% (0–64%) of all deaths. Among "better studies" with the best strength of evidence, nine also reported the suicide rate, which averaged 7.3%. Three of these studies were psychiatric samples, which had a mean of 19.1%. In the first of these, Norton and Whalley (1984) followed 791 lithium-treated unipolar and bipolar patients for 10 years in Scotland. Twenty-four percent of all deaths (n = 33) were due to suicide. Black and colleagues (1987) studied 1,593 inpatients in Iowa with affective disease and followed their sample for 13 years. Overall mortality in this study was 10% (n = 121), of which 31% were suicides (n = 33). In the third study, Murphy and colleagues (1988) followed 321 depressed patients for 4 years in London. In this sample the total rate of deaths was 34%, but the percentage of suicides was as low as 2.4%. In conclusion, despite the lack of well-controlled studies, the available data show that about every sixth death among people with affective disorder treated as psychiatric patients is caused by suicide. This figure is also consistent with the often quoted rate of 15% of completed suicide among psychiatric patients with severe depressive disorders (Guze and Robins, 1970).

Blair-West and colleagues (1997) argued that the life-time risk of suicide in major depression is lower than 15%. The overestimation may have been due to sampling biases, including the inability to separate heterogeneous types of depression into subclasses with divergent risks of suicide. A majority of studies have been conducted on most severely depressed inpatients who are followed-up during the years of the highest risk of suicide.

The risk of suicide among hospitalized depressed patients is highest in the first weeks following discharge from inpatient treatment (Burgholz-Hansen et al, 1993). In a nationwide Finnish study, where all men aged 35–64 years who were treated in hospital for depression were followed up for 3 years, the risk of suicide was very high for both neurotic depression (relative risk: 30) and affective psychoses (relative risk: 30), and especially high for the first follow-up year (relative risks of 72 and 53, respectively) (Lönnqvist and Koskenvuo, 1988).

Table 7.1 Suicide as outcome of depressive disorders*

Disorder	Observed (*n*)	Expected (*n*)	SMR	95% CI
Major depression	351	17.25	2,035	1,827–2,259
Bipolar disorder	93	6.18	1,505	1,225–1,844
Dysthymia	1,436	118.45	1,212	1,150–1,277
Mood disorders (not otherwise specified)	377	23.41	1,610	1,452–1,781
All functional mental disorders	5,787	478.53	1,209	1,178–1,241

*Adapted from Harris and Barraclough (1997).

The risk of suicide varies markedly across the subclasses of affective disorders. In a recent study, Simon and Von Korff (1998) found the suicide risk to be strongly related to a treatment history of depression. Following up 35,546 individuals treated for depression for 1–3 years (62,159 person-years) from the beginning of their treatment, they found that 36 (4.2%) of all 850 deaths during the period were classified as suicides. The overall suicide rate was 59 per 100,000 person-years, 118 for men and 36 for women, although the risk varied between extremes according to treatment subgroups: from 224 among those treated as psychiatric inpatients to 0 among those treated for depression in primary care without any antidepressants. The risk was 64 per 100,000 for those who received outpatient specialist mental health treatment, and 43 for those treated with antidepressant medication in primary care. These findings confirm that the risk of suicide varies between the subclasses of depression. The risk seems to be related to the intensity of psychiatric treatment, indicating the selection of depressed patients to different levels and location of treatment according to the severity of their suicidal intent.

The comprehensive meta-analysis of studies of suicide risk in all psychiatric disorders by Harris and Barraclough (1997) encompassed the English language medical literature on suicide located on Medline from 1966 to 1993. There were 23 reports on major depression from nine countries, 14 papers from seven countries on bipolar disorder, nine studies from four countries on dysthymia, and 12 publications from seven countries concerning other mood disorders. The risk of suicide was much higher than expected for all mood disorders: 20-fold for major depression, 15-fold for bipolar disorder, 12-fold for dysthymia and 16-fold for all other mood disorders. Suicide risk is elevated in all mental disorders, but particularly so in depressive disorders (Table 7.1).

DEPRESSION AMONG SUICIDES: PSYCHOLOGICAL AUTOPSY STUDIES

The overall aim of a psychological autopsy is to gather enough information about the circumstances of an individual's death to gain an understanding of the reasons

Table 7.2 Depressive disorders in completed suicide in community-based psychological autopsy studies including all age groups

Reference	Country	Study period	Depressive disorders (%)	Mental disorders (%)	Size of sample (*n*)	Males (%)
Robins et al, 1959a	USA	1956–57	45	94	134	77
Dorpat and Ripley, 1960	USA	1957–58	29	100	114*	68
Barraclough et al, 1974	UK	1966–68	70	93	100	53
Beskow, 1979	Sweden	1970–71	45–48	97	271	100
Chynoweth et al, 1980	Australia	1973–74	55	88	135	63
Rich et al, 1986	USA	1981–82	46	95	283	71
Arato et al, 1988	Hungary	1985	58	81	200	64
Åsgård, 1990	Sweden	1982	58	95	104	0
Henriksson et al, 1993	Finland	1987–88	59	93	229	75
Cheng, 1995	Taiwan	1989–91	88	98	116	61
Conwell et al, 1996	USA	1989–92	47	90	141	80
Foster et al, 1997	Northern Ireland	1992–93	36	86	118	79

*Data on psychiatric disorder available in 108 cases.

for the suicide (Hawton et al, 1998). The psychological autopsy studies performed up till now and including all age groups reveal that about half (29–88%) of the suicide victims suffered from depressive disorder, and about half of them had a major depressive episode (Table 7.2). The table does not include studies of very young people who died by suicide.

The very first community-based psychological autopsy study (Robins et al, 1959a,b) highlighted the importance of depression as a predominant mental disorder associated with suicide in the City of St. Louis and St. Louis County in a 1-year period in 1956–1957. Robins and colleagues diagnosed manic-depressive depression as the principal diagnosis, using the criteria of Washington University (very similar to DSM-III diagnoses) in 45% of all 134 consecutive suicides. The percentage was 41 for men and 58 for women. The diagnosis of manic-depressive disease included the diagnoses of involutional melancholia and psychotic depressive reaction. Secondary neurotic depressions did not occur in the sample. Individuals with manic-depressive disease were exclusively in the depressed phase at the time of the suicide. Ninety-two percent of depressed suicide victims were over 40 years of age. Almost three-quarters had received medical care within the past year and half within the month preceding their death. One-third had received treatment by a psychiatrist and one-sixth had been admitted to a psychiatric hospital in their last year. Two-thirds (69%) of the depressed patients had communicated suicidal intentions and 41% had explicitly stated their intent to commit suicide shortly before the final act (Robins et al, 1959b). Robins and co-workers emphasized that all physicians should be aware of the diagnostic features of depression and should ask the patient's family as well as the patient about suicidal communications. In addition, they suggested closed ward hospitalization as the only available effective means of preventing suicide. Further details on the same suicide victims published by Robins (1981) were used in a secondary analysis of the co-morbidity of the male victims (n = 103) by Carlson and colleagues (1991). Of the 45 men who had originally met the criteria for affective disorder, 13 (29%) were reclassified as having co-morbid depression with substance abuse, and of the 29 males with alcoholism as an original diagnosis, eight (28%) also had depressive disorder. Affective disorder was diagnosed alone in 32% and co-morbid with depression in 20% of all male suicides. Affective disorders were strongly associated with middle-aged and elderly victims in this series of suicides. The prevalence of affective disorders was 58% for those older than 40 years, and 32% for those under 40 years. In conclusion, this pioneering psychological autopsy study provided clear evidence of the association between suicide and depression, the co-morbidity of depression and substance abuse among suicide victims, and the central role of depression in suicides of elderly people.

The other early psychological autopsy study was conducted in the Seattle area, and also in the late 1950s (Dorpat and Ripley, 1960). In this study a principal diagnosis of psychotic depression was made for 17% and psychoneurotic depression for 12% of 108 suicide subjects. Psychotic depression was the most frequent diagnosis in those over 60 years. Aside from the principal diagnosis, clinical signs or symptoms of depression were noted in every case where adequate information was available. No psychiatric information was available in six of the total sample of 114 cases studied. Despite the fact that a majority of subjects had been under the care of a physician, the authors suggested that many physicians had overlooked or minimized the depression of their patients.

Depressive illness was the principal diagnosis in 70% of all suicides in the classic study of Barraclough and his colleaques on 100 cases of suicide in West Sussex and Portsmouth, Southern England, in the late 1960s (Barraclough et al, 1974). A depressive illness uncomplicated by other physical or mental disorders was diagnosed in 64 of the suicides: 47% of the males and 53% of the females. In this group, 44% had a past history of psychiatric treatment by a psychiatrist, mainly for depression (41%) or mania (11%). About half of the suicide victims (48%) had a past history of probable previous episodes of depression not treated by a psychiatrist. Only one-third of depressed patients had been prescribed antidepressants, mostly in doses below those recommended. Over half had displayed warnings of suicidal thinking, but the methods of modern psychiatric treatment were not always effectively deployed. Barraclough and Pallis (1975) compared the characteristics of the above-mentioned 64 suicides diagnosed as depressive with 128 living depressives referred for psychiatric treatment. Only three symptoms distinguished the suicides from the living depressives: insomnia, impaired memory, and self-neglect. Other items differentiating the suicide group were: male sex, older age in females, single status, living alone, and a history of suicide attempts.

Beskow (1979) investigated two separate samples (urban and rural) of consecutive male suicides (n = 271) in Sweden during 1970–1971. Depressive disorders were common in both urban and rural areas (45% and 48%), and depressive symptoms even more so. Among the severely depressed suicide victims, depression was mostly untreated or undertreated. Later, Åsgård (1990) published a Swedish study of female suicides (n = 104) in Stockholm in 1982. Major depression was diagnosed using research diagnostic criteria in 35% of suicides, and the overall rate of depression was 59%. The findings of this study also emphasized the undertreatment of depression.

In Brisbane, Australia, Chynoweth and colleagues (1980) investigated all consecutive suicides (n = 135) committed during 12 months in 1973–1974 and found depression in 55%. Again, a minority of depressed people had been properly treated.

In the San Diego Suicide Study, Rich and colleagues (1986) used DSM-III criteria to define depressive disorders, which were found in 46%. Major depressive disorders were diagnosed in only 7% of males and 17% of females. Antidepressants were found at toxicology in only 12% of the depressed suicides.

In their psychological autopsy study, Henriksson and collaborators (1993) used a representative sample of every sixth suicide from a nationwide suicide population consisting of all consecutive suicides (n = 1,397) in Finland during a 12-month period in 1987–1988. In this study, combined depressive disorders (major depression, depressive disorder not otherwise specified, bipolar disorder and dysthymia) were found in 59% of all suicides. The prevalence of major depressive disorder was 31%, 46% for women and 26% for men. One-third of the cases with major depressive disorder had psychotic symptoms. If schizoaffective disorders (depressive types), organic mood disorders and adjustment disorders with depressive mood were included, depressive syndromes were found in two-thirds (66%) of the total sample. The main finding in this study was that the majority of suicide victims with a depressive disorder also suffered from co-morbid mental disorders. In major depression, 28% of the suicide victims had alcohol dependence or abuse, 31% had a personality disorder, 49% suffered from physical illness, and only 15% were without any co-morbidity. Substance use disorders were typically male problems, while personality disorders were more common among younger victims, and physical illnesses among the elderly.

Most suicides victims in the Finnish sample with a depressive disorder had a complicated clinical syndrome (Isometsä et al, 1994a). They were seen in health care facilities, but depression was underdiagnosed and in most cases left untreated or undertreated. This was especially true in the case of milder and non-major depressions, which were often related to recent stressful life events. The treatment situation was much worse among male than among female victims. Antidepressants had been prescribed in only one-third of the suicide victims, and only 3% had received antidepressants in therapeutic doses. Psychotherapy by a trained therapist was also rare. For suicide prevention, the challenge is not so much the lack of services as to improve the quality of treatment (Isometsä and Lönnqvist, 1997).

Cheng (1995) carried out a case-control study of suicide in Taiwan in 1989–1991 among two aboriginal groups and the Han Chinese. Among all suicides (n = 116) the proportion of depressed victims was very high, being 88%. Major depressive disorder alone was diagnosed in 62% of the victims and as a double depression (depressive episode plus dysthymia) in 25%. Half of all depressive disorders were co-morbid with substance abuse. Again, undertreatment of depression was evident, only 4% of all victims having received antidepressive drugs. Cheng (1997) also reported co-morbidity of depression and personality disorders in suicides; personality disorder co-occured in 66% of depressive suicides, while emotionally unstable personality disorder or borderline personality disorder was found alone in 44% of all depressed suicide victims.

Conwell and colleagues (1996) analysed the relationship between age and mental disorders in victims of completed suicide using a psychological autopsy study in Monroe County, New York State, USA. Depressive disorder was found in 47% of the victims and unipolar major depressive disorder in 28%. As in Cheng's study, half of all depressed victims were also substance abusers in this study. In this study older age was clearly associated with the diagnosis of single episode unipolar major depression (57% for those over 75 years, and only 15% for those younger than 55 years). The connection between age and depression in suicide is important because recent studies unexpectedly show that the prevalence of major depression in the general population clearly decreases with age.

Foster and collaborators (1997) studied all suicides in Northern Ireland during 12 months in 1992–1993. Depressive disorder was diagnosed in 36% of suicides, and much more often among females (60%) than males (29%). Major unipolar depression was found as the principal diagnosis in 31% (women 52%, men 26%). Suicides aged 65 years and older were more likely to have suffered from current major unipolar depression than those under 65 years (77% versus 27%). The remaining disorders were dysthymia (1%) and depressive bipolar disorder (3%). Co-morbidity was found in 63% of suicides with major unipolar depression.

In addition to the studies listed in Table 7.2, another study has employed the principles of the psychological autopsy approach in a follow-up investigation. The Lundby Study was a Swedish prospective longitudinal cohort study of 3,563 persons investigated thoroughly in 1947, 1957 and 1972. During the 25-year period 1947–1972, 28 cohort members committed suicide. All suicides were assessed by following the principles of psychological autopsy, using interview data before the suicide and all available data after the death. Fourteen (50%) of the suicide victims (10/23 men and 4/5 women) were diagnosed as having had depression, and in 10 of them the clinical picture was dominated by endogenous features (Hagnell and Rorsman, 1978).

In conclusion, the findings from psychological autopsy studies conducted over the past 40 years suggest that depression is found in 29–88% of all suicides, and moreover that depressive symptoms are connected with almost all these tragic cases. Suicide in depression is particularly common among individuals with co-morbid mental and physical disorders. Diagnostically, most suicides have suffered from unipolar major depression. While a substantial proportion of depressed suicide victims had psychiatric treatment, very few have received adequate therapy for depression. A crucial issue for suicide prevention is the ability of society to establish and foster depression awareness campaigns, and to detect and properly treat depression in all health care settings.

SUICIDAL BEHAVIOUR IN BIPOLAR DISORDER

Bipolar disorder is characterized by the varying consequences of manic and depressive episodes over the course of life, usually from early adulthood, and at least one episode has been mania. Suicide is often connected with bipolar disorder and bipolar families (like Ernest Hemingway's) and is often a sad outcome of this severe disorder. However, the fact is that only a few studies on suicide in bipolar disorder have been conducted in which the latter is a clearly defined diagnostic category in relation to the risk of suicide. Most previous studies have combined all mood disorders without separating bipolar disorder from depressive disorders, thereby using selected samples. Despite all the uncertainties, there seem to be no major differences in life-time risk of suicide between unipolar and bipolar major affective disorders.

Suicidality in bipolar disorder may depend on the severity, course and phase of the disorder. In pure mania suicidality may even be mild, whereas in manic patients with depressive features suicidality is a very common finding. About half of all bipolar patients have attempted suicide in some phase of the disorder, and a suicide attempt is a common reason for psychiatric hospitalization. A family history of suicide and a previous suicide attempt always mean a greater risk of suicide, as does a period following discharge from hospital.

Harris and Barraclough (1997) found 14 studies from seven countries which reported on suicide between 1966 and 1993 in a total bipolar population of 3,700 patients treated between 1900 and 1985. Combining all the studies gave 93 suicides, while the expected number was only six, thus indicating a suicide risk 15 times that expected. The standardized mortality ratio (SMR) was 1,505 and the 95% CI interval 1,225–1,844. This SMR is similar to that in other affective disorders. The largest subsample of bipolar suicides (n = 19) in this meta-analysis was from the province of Alberta in Canada (Newman and Bland, 1991) in 1976–1985, where there was an elevated suicide risk for both manic disorder (9 times) and bipolar affective disorder (23 times).

Sharma and Marker (1994) followed up 472 bipolar patients over 17 years in Edinburgh and found an increased suicide rate: 16% of all deaths were suicides (n = 8), and the suicide risk was 23 times higher than in the general population.

Isometsä and colleagues (1994b) made a careful diagnostic study of all suicides committed in Finland during a 1-year period based on a nationwide psychological autopsy study and found that 3% of all suicides (46/1397) had suffered from bipolar disorder. In three recent psychological autopsy studies using DSM-III-R criteria, the findings are similar: 5% in New Zealand (Joyce et al, 1995), 1% in the USA (Conwell et al, 1996), and 3% in Northern Ireland (Foster et al, 1997). In a nationwide suicide population in Finland, the majority (79%) of the bipolar suicide victims had a depressive episode just before the suicide, and most of these (71%) were co-morbid cases. More than half of the males had become alcohol-dependent. Most cases did not receive adequate treatment for the current episode. The use of lithium or antidepressants at optimal doses and serum levels was rare. Moreover, problems of compliance with treatment were reported in almost all cases.

It seems evident that lithium maintenance treatment in bipolar disorder is associated with a long-sustained reduction of fatal and non-fatal suicidal acts. The rate of suicidal acts with lithium is up to seven times lower than in comparison groups treated without lithium (see Chapter 27 for further discussion of this issue). An abrupt or rapid discontinuation of lithium treatment can increase the risk of suicidal behaviour, especially during the first follow-up year (Baldessarini et al, 1999).

ATTEMPTED SUICIDE AND DEPRESSIVE DISORDER

Attempted suicide is common in the course of depressive disorders. In a sample of consecutive psychiatric hospital patients, subjective depressive feelings, hopelessness and severity of suicidal ideation were all significantly greater in suicide attempters than in non-attempters (Mann et al, 1999). Hopelessness also tends to be greater in suicide attempters than in non-attempters during a depressive episode (Malone et al, 1995), after successful treatment of a major depressive episode (Rifai et al, 1994) and between depressive episodes (Young et al, 1994).

Beautrais and colleagues (1996) compared the prevalence of mood disorders in consecutive subjects who had made medically serious suicide attempts with that in comparison subjects randomly selected from the general population of Canterbury, New Zealand. The prevalence of any mood disorders among attempters was 77% and in comparison subjects 7%, giving an odds ratio of 33 for mood disorders. The prevalence of major depression was 62% and 6%, respectively. Mood disorders were much more strongly related to the risk of a serious suicide attempt for women and older subjects. The central role of mood disorders in attempted suicide is revealed by the fact that eliminating all affective disorders in a statistical procedure reduced the incidence of serious suicide attempts in this population by up to 80%.

In their study of the DSM-III-R diagnoses of consecutive suicide attempters visiting emergency rooms in Finland, Suominen and colleagues (1996) found that 78% of patients had a research diagnosis of depression. The prevalence of major depression in this study was 38%, 44% for females and 30% for males. Half of all depressed patients had co-morbid alcohol abuse or dependence. Other common co-morbid disorders were personality, physical and anxiety disorders. Depressed attempters without alcohol problems had higher suicide intent and lower impulsiveness than attempters having alcohol dependence without major depression (Suominen et al, 1997).

A high frequency of depression has been found in several recent studies on attempted suicide. The co-morbidity of depression has also been stressed, especially in the clinical management of suicidality. Co-morbidity in connection with attempted suicide implies difficulties in the clinical assessment, underdiagnosis in the emergency situation (Suominen et al, 1999) and possibly a higher risk of suicide (Beautrais et al, 1996). Clinical and diagnostic assessment of attempted suicide needs to be improved from the current situation: it is possible to achieve good reliability in the assessment of suicide attempters (van Heeringen et al, 1993).

Major depression and attempted suicide are both risk factors for suicide. In addition, a recent suicide attempt by a person with depression means a particularly high suicide risk (Nordström et al, 1995). Treating suicidal depressed patients actively and intensively might offer an effective way of preventing secondary suicide. It seems that few depressed suicide attempters receive adequate treatment for depression, either prior to or even after their attempts (Suominen et al, 1998). It is not only a large majority of suicide attempters who are undertreated for depression, but all depressed patients—even those who have never attempted suicide are in a similar situation (Oquendo et al, 1999). Fewer than one-third of antidepressant users in general are receiving treatment even minimally consistent with current guidelines (Melfi et al, 1998). Such findings underline the importance of good clinical practice in the assessment and treatment of depressed persons after their suicide attempts.

CONCLUSION

The main cause of the increased mortality in depression is suicide. Depression is a clinically significant factor in more than half of all suicides. Research findings among suicide victims show that depression has generally been co-morbid and complicated, and has caused difficulties in health care. For a variety of reasons, it seems that most suicides have not been properly treated. Similar findings apply to bipolar depression, which might benefit from lithium or other prophylactic maintenance. Depression is also a major clinical disorder in attempted suicides. Non-fatal attempts allow us the opportunity and time to provide the best possible treatment for depression, which is urgently needed for effective suicide prevention.

REFERENCES

Arato, M., Demeter, E., Rihmer, Z. and Somogyi E. (1988) Retrospective psychiatric assessment of 200 suicides in Budapest. Acta Psychiatrica Scandinavica, 77: 454–456.

Åsgård, U. (1990) A psychiatric study of suicide among urban Swedish women. Acta Psychiatrica Scandinavica, 82: 115–124.

Baldessarini, R.J., Tondo, L. and Hennen, J. (1990) Effects of lithium treatment and its discontinuation on suicidal behaviour in bipolar manic-depressive disorders. Journal of Clinical Psychiatry, 60 (Suppl. 2): 57–62.

Barraclough, B.M., Bunch, B., Nelson, B. and Sainsbury, P. (1974) A hundred cases of suicide: clinical aspects. British Journal of Psychiatry, 125: 355–373.

Barraclough, B.M. and Pallis, D.J. (1975) Depression followed by suicide: a comparison of depressed suicides with living depressives. Psychological Medicine, 5: 55–61.

Beautrais, A.L., Joyce, P.R., Mulder, R.T, Ferguson, D.M., Deavoll, B.J. and Nightingale, S.K. (1996) Prevalence and comorbidity of mental disorders in persons making serious suicide attempts: a case-control study. American Journal of Psychiatry, 153: 1009–1014.

Beskow, J. (1979) Suicide and mental disorder in Swedish men. Acta Psychiatrica Scandinavica, 277 (Suppl.): 1–138.

Blair-West, G.W., Mellsop, G.W. and Eyeson-Annan, M.L. (1997) Down-rating lifetime suicide risk in major depression. Acta Psychiatrica Scandinavica, 95: 259–263.

Black, D.W., Winokur, G. and Nasrallah, A. (1987) Is death from natural causes still excessive in psychiatric patients? A follow-up of 1593 patients with major affective disorder. Journal of Mental and Nervous Diseases, 175: 674–680.

Blazer, D.G., Kessler, R.C., McGonagle, K.D. and Swartz, M.S. (1994) The prevalence and distribution of major depression in a national community sample: the National Comorbidity Survey. American Journal of Psychiatry, 151: 979–986.

Buchholtz-Hansen, P.E., Wang, A.G. and Kragh-Sorensen, P. (1993) Mortality in major affective disorder: relationship to subtype of depression. The Danish University Antidepressant Group. Acta Psychiatrica Scandinavica, 87: 329–335.

Carlson, G.A., Rich, C.L., Grayson, P. and Fowler, R.C. (1991) Secular trends in psychiatric diagnoses of suicide victims. Journal of Affective Disorders, 21: 127–132.

Cheng, A.T. (1995) Mental illness and suicide. A case-control study in East Taiwan. Archives of General Psychiatry, 52: 594–603.

Chochinov, H.M., Wilson, K.G., Enns, M. and Lander, S. (1998) Depression, hopelessness, and suicidal ideation in the terminally ill. Psychosomatics, 39: 366–370.

Chynoweth, R., Tonge, J.I. and Armstrong, J. (1980) Suicide in Brisbane: a retrospective psychosocial study. Australian and New Zealand Journal of Psychiatry, 14: 37–45.

Conwell, Y., Duberstein, P.R., Cox, C., Herrman, J.H., Forbes, N.T. and Caine, E.D. (1996) Relationship of age and axis I diagnoses in victims of completed suicide: a psychological autopsy study. American Journal of Psychiatry, 153: 1001–1008.

Coppen, A., Standish-Barry, H., Bailey, J., Houston, G., Silcocks, P. and Hermon, C. (1991) Does lithium reduce the mortality of recurrent mood disorders? Journal of Affective Disorders, 23: 1–7.

Dorpat, T.L. and Ripley, H.S. (1960) A study of suicide in the Seattle area. Comprehensive Psychiatry, 1: 349–359.

Friis, S., Hauff, E., Island, T.K., Lorentzen, S., Melle, I. and Vaglum, P. (1991) The Ulleval acute ward follow-up study: a personal 7-year follow-up of patients with functional psychosis admitted to the acute ward of a catchment area. Psychopathology, 24: 316–327.

Foster, T., Gillespie, K. and McClelland, R. (1997) Mental disorders and suicide in Northern Ireland. British Journal of Psychiatry, 170: 447–452.

Guze, S.B. and Robins, E. (1970) Suicide and primary affective disorders. British Journal of Psychiatry, 117: 437–438.

Hagnell, O. and Rorsman, B. (1978) Suicide and endogenous depression with somatic symptoms in the Lundby study. Neuropsychobiology, 4: 180–187.

Harris, C.E. and Barraclough, B.M. (1997) Suicide as an outcome for mental disorders. British Journal of Psychiatry, 170: 205–228.

Hawton, K., Appleby, L., Platt, S., Foster, T., Cooper, J., Malmberg, A., Simkin, S. (1998) The psychological autopsy approach to studying suicide: a review of methodological issues. Journal of Affective Disorders, 50: 269–276.

Henriksson, M.M., Aro, H.M., Marttunen, M.J., Heikkinen, M.E., Isometsä, E.T., Kuoppasalmi, K.I. and Lönnqvist, J.K. (1993) Mental disorders and co-morbidity in suicide. American Journal of Psychiatry, 150: 935–940.

Horwath, E., Johnson, J., Klerman, G.L. and Weissman, M.M. (1992) Depressive symptoms as relative and attributable risk factors for first-onset major depression. Archives of General Psychiatry, 49: 817–823.

Isometsä, E.T., Henriksson, M.M., Aro, H.M., Heikkinen, M.E., Kuoppasalmi, K.I. and Lönnqvist, J.K. (1994a) Suicide in major depression. American Journal of Psychiatry, 151: 530–536.

Isometsä, E.T., Henriksson, M.M., Aro, H.M. and Lönnqvist, J.K. (1994b) Suicide in bipolar disorder in Finland. American Journal of Psychiatry, 151: 1020–1024.

Isometsä, E.T. and Lönnqvist, J.K. (1997) Suicide in mood disorders. In J.A. Botsis, C.R. Soldatos and C.N. Stefanis (Eds), Suicide: Biopsychosocial Approaches, pp. 33–47. Amsterdam: Elsevier.

Joyce, P., Beautrais, A. and Mulder, R. (1994) The prevalence of mental disorder in individuals who suicide and attempt suicide. In M. Kelleher (Ed.), Divergent Perpectives on Suicidal Behaviour. Cork: Fifth European Symposium on Suicide.

Lönnqvist, J. and Koskenvuo, M. (1988) Mortality in depressive disorders: a 3-year prospective follow-up study in Finland. In T. Helgason and R.J. Daly (Eds), Depressive Illness: Prediction of Course and Outcome. Berlin: Springer-Verlag.

Malone, K.M., Haas, G.L., Sweeney, J.A. and Mann, J.J. (1995) Major depression and the risk of attempted suicide. Journal of Affective Disorders, 34: 173–185.

Mann, J.J., Waternaux, C., Haas, G.L. and Malone, K.M. (1999) Towards a clinical model of suicidal behavior in psychiatric patients. American Journal of Psychiatry, 156: 181–189.

Melfi, C.A., Chawla, J.A., Croghan, T.W., Hanna, M.P., Kennedy, S. and Sredl, K. (1998) The effects of adherence to antidepressant treatment guidelines on relapse and recurrence of depression. Archives of General Psychiatry, 55: 1128–1132.

Meltzer, H., Gill, B., Petticrew, M. and Hinds, K. (1995) The prevalence of psychiatric morbidity among adults living in private households. OPCS Surveys of Psychiatric Morbidity in Great Britain: Report 1. London: HMSO.

Muller-Oerlinghausen, B., Muser-Causemann, B. and Volk, J. (1992) Suicides and parasuicides in a high-risk population on and off lithium long-term medication. Journal of Affective Disorders, 25: 261–270.

Murphy, E., Smith, R., Lindesay, J. and Slattery, J. (1988) Increased mortality rates in late-life depression. British Journal of Psychiatry, 152: 347–353.

Newman, S.C. and Bland, R.C. (1991) Suicide risk varies by subtype of affective disorder. Acta Psychiatrica Scandinavica, 83: 420–426.

Nordström, P., Åsberg, M., Åberg-Wistedt, A. and Nordin, C. (1995) Attempted suicide predicts suicide risk in mood disorders. Acta Psychiatrica Scandinavica, 92: 345–350.

Norton, B. and Whalley, L.J. (1984) Mortality of a lithium-treated population. British Journal of Psychiatry, 145: 277–282.

Ohayon, M.M., Priest, R.G., Guilleminault, C. and Caulet, M. (1999) The prevalence of depressive disorders in the United Kingdom. Biological Psychiatry, 45: 300–307.

Oquendo, M.A., Malone, K.M., Ellis, S.P., Sackeim, H.A. and Mann, J.J. (1999) Inadequacy of antidepressant treatment for patients with major depression who are at risk for suicidal behavior. American Journal of Psychiatry, 156: 190–194.

Regier, D.A., Boyd, J.H., Burke, J.D. Jr, Rae, D.S., Myers, J.K., Kramer, M., Robins, L.N., George, L.K., Karno, M. and Locke, B.Z. (1988) One-month prevalence of mental disorders in the United States: based on five epidemilogic catchment area sites. Archives of General Psychiatry, 45: 977–986.

Rich, C.L., Young, D. and Fowler, R.C. (1986) San Diego Suicide Study I: young vs. old subjects. Archives of General Psychiatry, 43: 577–582.

Rifai, A.H., George, C.J., Stack, J.A., Mann, J.J. and Reynolds, C.F. III (1994) Hopelessness in suicide attempters after acute treatment of major depression in late life. American Journal of Psychiatry, 151: 1687–1690.

Robins, E. (1981) The Final Months. New York: Oxford University Press.

Robins, E., Gassner, S., Kayes, J., Wilkinson, R.H. and Murphy, G.E. (1959a) The communication of suicidal intent: a study of 134 consecutive cases of successful (completed) suicide. American Journal of Psychiatry, 115: 724–733.

Robins, E., Murphy, G.E., Wilkinson, R.H., Gassner, S. and Kayes, J. (1959b) Some clinical considerations in the prevention of suicide based on a study of 134 successful suicides. American Journal of Public Health, 49: 888–899.

Sharma, R. and Markar, H.R. (1994) Mortality in affective disorder. Journal of Affective Disorders, 31: 91–96.

Simon, G.E. and Von Korff, M. (1998) Suicide mortality among patients treated for depression in an insured population. American Journal of Epidemiology, 147: 155–160.

Suominen, K., Henriksson, M., Suokas, J., Isometsä, E., Ostamo, A. and Lönnqvist, J. (1996) Mental disorders and comorbidity in attempted suicide. Acta Psychiatrica Scandinavica, 94: 234–240.

Suominen, K., Isometsä, E., Henriksson, M., Ostamo, A. and Lönnqvist, J. (1997) Hopelessness, impulsiveness and intent among suicide attempters with major depression, alcohol dependence or both. Acta Psychiatrica Scandinavica, 96: 142–149.

Suominen, K., Isometsä, E., Henriksson, M., Ostamo, A. and Lönnqvist, J. (1998) Inadequate treatment for major depression both before and after attempted suicide. American Journal of Psychiatry, 155: 1778–1780.

Suominen, K., Isometsä, E., Henriksson, M., Ostamo, A. and Lönnqvist, J. (1999) Treatment received by alcohol-dependent suicide attempters. Acta Psychiatrica Scandinavica, 99: 214–219.

van Gastel, A., Schotte, C. and Maes, M. (1997) The prediction of suicidal intent in depressed patients. Acta Psychiatrica Scandinavica, 96: 254–259.

van Heeringen, C., Rijckebusch, W., De Schinkel, C. and Jannes, C. (1993) The reliability of the assessment of suicide attempters. Archives of Public Health, 51: 443–456.

Wulsin, L.R., Vaillant, G.E. and Wells, V.E. (1999) A systematic review of the mortality of depression. Psychosomatic Medicine, 61: 6–17.

Zheng, D., Macera, C.A., Croft, J.B., Giles, W.H., Davis, D. and Scott, W.K. (1997) Major depression and all-cause mortality among white adults in the United States. Annals of Epidemiology, 7: 213–218.

Young, M.A., Fogg, L.F., Scheftner, W.A. and Fawcett, J.A. (1994) Interactions of risk factors in predicting suicide. American Journal of Psychiatry, 151: 434–435.

Chapter 8

Psychiatric Aspects of Suicidal Behaviour: Schizophrenia

Marc De Hert
University Centre St. Jozef, Kortenberg, and Psychosocial Centre St. Alexius, Brussels, Belgium,
and
Jozef Peuskens
Catholic University, Louvain, and University Centre St. Jozef, Kortenberg, Belgium

Abstract

Suicide is the most dramatic outcome of schizophrenia. It is estimated that 10% of patients suffering from schizophrenia kill themselves. In this chapter the literature on suicide in schizophrenia is reviewed, together with data from recent studies. The risk of suicide is 40 times higher in the schizophrenic population, compared to the general population. Major risk factors are: male gender, chronic illness with frequent relapse, frequent and short hospitalization, family history of suicide, past suicidal and impulsive behaviour, negative attitude towards treatment, higher IQ, psychosis and depression. Treatment aimed at the prevention of suicide in schizophrenic patients must target the identified risk factors. The effective prevention of suicide in this population requires a comprehensive and systematic approach, with careful assessments and interventions integrated with a general attitude of hope and optimism.

INTRODUCTION

Schizophrenia is a relatively common disorder; 20 million people worldwide are estimated to suffer from it. With its early age of onset and its chronic course, schizophrenia inflicts a great burden on patients, families and society. Schizophrenia is not only a disabling but also a life-shortening disorder. Suicide turns

The International Handbook of Suicide and Attempted Suicide. Edited by K. Hawton and K. van Heeringen.

Table 8.1 Suicide rates and standardized mortality ratios in schizophrenia (De Hert, 1995; De Hert and Peuskens, 1998a)

Author	SR*	SMR all deaths**	SMR suicide**
Tsuang, 1978		1.7–4.2	3.3–6.4
Evenson et al, 1982	147		
Wilkinson, 1982	615		>50
Pokorny, 1983	456	1.6	19.8
Black et al, 1985	524	3.9	31–62
Martin et al, 1985		3.0	
Nyman and Jonsson, 1986	587		25
Allebeck, 1989	395	2.4	9.9–17.5
Cohen et al, 1990	810		
Mortensen and Juel, 1990		1.3	
Newman and Bland, 1991	446	2.6	15.5–20.6
Mortensen and Juel, 1993		3.3	20.7
De Hert, 1995[1]	635	7.8	39.7
Peuskens et al, 1997[1]	896		56
De Hert and Peuskens, 1998b[2]	1,018		58

*SR, suicide rate = *n*/100,000/year; **SMR, standardized mortality ratio, *n* observed: *n* expected; [1] all patients younger than 30 years at inclusion in the study; [2] first-episode patients.

out to be the major cause of premature death. It is estimated that 10% of all schizophrenic patients kill themselves (Barraclough et al, 1974; Tsuang et al, 1980; Wilkinson, 1982; Drake et al, 1985; Allebeck, 1989; Caldwell and Gottesman, 1990, 1992; Newman and Bland, 1991; Modestin et al, 1992; Mortensen and Juel, 1993; De Hert, 1995; Harris and Barraclough, 1997; De Hert and Peuskens, 1998a). The high risk for suicide was acknowledged by the first researchers in schizophrenia: e.g. Kraepelin (1909), "Suicide, especially in the first period of the malady, is not infrequent and occurs, sometimes without any recognizable cause, also in patients who for a long time have been weak-minded and quiet"; and Bleuler (1911), "The most serious of all schizophrenic symptoms is the suicidal drive".

Suicide rates and standardized mortality ratios (SMR) for suicide in different studies are shown in Table 8.1. The suicide rate is 350–650/100,000/year and the risk for suicide is 30–40 times higher than in the overall population (Caldwell and Gottesman, 1992; De Hert, 1995). This chapter will give an overview of older and more recent research on risk factors for suicide in schizophrenic patients.

RISK FACTORS FOR SUICIDE IN SCHIZOPHRENIA

Schizophrenic patients who commit suicide share general risk factors with other suicidal patients (Table 8.2) (Drake et al, 1985; Roy et al, 1986; Caldwell and Gottesman, 1990; Westermeyer et al, 1991). The risk is highest for male patients living in social isolation, without a partner or a job. The risk is further increased

Table 8.2 General risk factors for suicide in schizophrenia

Risk factor	Reference
White	Yarden, 1974; Breier and Astrachan, 1984; Beck et al, 1985; Westermeyer et al, 1991.
Family history of suicide	Roy, 1982; Dingman and McGlashan, 1986.
Male gender	Cohen et al, 1964; Warnes, 1968; Miles, 1977; Tsuang, 1978; Roy, 1982; Pokorny, 1983; Breier and Astrachan, 1984; Drake et al, 1984; Black et al, 1985; Dingman and McGlashan, 1986; Nyman and Jonsson, 1986.
Single	Cohen et al, 1964; Roy, 1982; Breier and Astrachan, 1984; Drake et al, 1984; Allebeck, 1989; Westermeyer et al, 1991; Modestin et al, 1992.
Recent loss	Yarden, 1974; Breier and Astrachan, 1984; Earle et al, 1994.
Social isolation	Lindelius and Kay, 1973; Barraclough et al, 1974; Roy, 1982; Drake et al, 1984; Nyman and Jonsson, 1986.
Past suicidal behaviour	Cohen et al, 1964; Warnes, 1968; Planansky and Johnston, 1973; Barraclough et al, 1974; Shaffer et al, 1974; Virkkunen, 1974; Yarden, 1974; Roy, 1982; Wilkinson, 1982; Breier and Astrachan, 1984; Roy et al, 1984; Dingman and McGlashan, 1986; Allebeck, 1989; Modestin et al, 1992.
Unemployed	Yarden, 1974; Roy, 1982; Drake et al, 1984; Dingman and McGlashan, 1986; Allebeck, 1989; Modestin et al, 1992.

Reproduced by permission from De Hert (1995).

by familial history of suicide, past suicidal behaviour, major life-events, and chronic physical illness. Like other psychiatric patients, they tend to use violent, potentially lethal means to commit suicide (Barraclough et al, 1974; De Hert, 1995).

A specific characteristic of schizophrenic patients is that they commit suicide at a relative young age and early in the course of the disorder (Table 8.3). The risk is highest in the age group 20–35 years and decreases with age (Black et al 1985; Allebeck, 1989; Caldwell and Gottesman, 1990; Newman and Bland, 1991; Peuskens et al, 1997; De Hert and Peuskens, 1998a). The course of illness is characterized by frequent relapse and (mainly short) hospitalizations. The risk for suicide is prominent during hospitalization or shortly after discharge (De Hert, 1995; Peuskens et al, 1997).

Patients with good premorbid functioning, higher IQ and a higher level of education are at greater risk (Dingman and McGlashan, 1986; Roy et al, 1986; Westermeyer et al, 1991; Peuskens et al, 1997). Psychotic episodes and relapses, but especially episodes of depression, increase the risk for suicide (Drake et al, 1985; Drake and Cotton, 1986; Roy et al, 1986; Caldwell and Gottesman, 1990; Peuskens et al, 1997). A small group of patients are believed to commit suicide as a result of command hallucinations (Planansky and Johnston, 1973; Barraclough et al,

Table 8.3 Specific risk factors for suicide in schizophrenia

Risk factor	Reference
Depression and hopelessness	Cohen et al, 1964; Warnes, 1968; Lindelius and Kay, 1973; Yarden, 1974; Virkkunen, 1974; Roy, 1982; Stein, 1982; Pokorny, 1983; Drake et al, 1984; Roy et al, 1984; Dingman and McGlashan, 1986; Drake and Cotton, 1986; Nyman and Jonsson, 1986; Prasad and Kellner, 1988; Roy et al, 1986; Cheng et al, 1990; Roy, 1990.
Frequent exacerbations	Barraclough et al, 1974; Yarden, 1974; Tsuang, 1978; Roy, 1982; Wilkinson, 1982; Breier and Astrachan, 1984; Drake et al, 1984; Nyman and Jonsson, 1986.
Good premorbid level of functioning	Cohen et al, 1964; Roy, 1982; Dingman and McGlashan, 1986; Drake and Cotton, 1986; Nyman and Jonsson, 1986; Westermeyer et al, 1991.
Early in the course of the disorder	Cohen et al, 1964; Warnes, 1968; Barraclough et al, 1974; Shaffer et al, 1974; Virkkunen, 1974; Winokur and Tsuang, 1975; Evenson et al, 1982; Roy, 1982; Pokorny, 1983; Breier and Astrachan, 1984; Drake et al, 1984; Nyman and Jonsson, 1986; Black and Winokur, 1988; Cheng et al, 1989; Westermeyer et al, 1991.
Shortly after discharge	Cohen et al, 1964; Temoche et al, 1964; Yarden, 1974; Roy, 1982; Stein, 1982; Pokorny, 1983; Wilkinson and Bacon, 1984; Earle et al, 1994.
During hospitalization	Levy and Southcombe, 1953; Cohen et al, 1964; Temoche et al, 1964; Warnes, 1968; Barraclough et al, 1974; Roy, 1982; Drake et al, 1984; Allebeck, 1989.

Reproduced by permission from De Hert (1995).

1974; Falloon and Talbot, 1981; Hellerstein et al, 1987). 30–50% of schizophrenic patients make at least one suicide attempt, mainly with a potentially lethal method. These attempts occur at young age and most often during episodes with depressive symptoms (Roy, 1990; De Hert, 1995; Amador et al, 1996; Fenton et al, 1997). Schizophrenic patients with recurrent suicidal thoughts and behaviour are generally more aware of their negative symptoms and delusions than are non-suicidal patients (Amador et al, 1996).

SUICIDE IN SCHIZOPHRENIA: RECENT STUDIES

Several studies have identified risk factors for suicide in schizophrenic patients. However, besides general problems of diagnostic standardization, studies often have the following shortcomings: small number of patients; small number of suicides; different age groups, with mainly older patients; focused on inpatients; no longitudinal perspective; limited numbers of variables; and lack of an adequate control group (Caldwell and Gottesman, 1990; De Hert, 1995; De Hert and Peuskens, 1998a). Recent studies without most of these methodological problems, have, however, reconfirmed the risk factors found in the older studies.

Chesnut Lodge Follow-up Study

Fenton and colleagues (1997) examined the relationship between positive and negative symptoms and suicidal behaviour in a long-term follow-up cohort (total, $n = 322$; schizophrenia, $n = 187$; average duration of follow-up, 19 years). Patients dead from suicide had significantly lower negative symptom severity at index admission. Two positive symptoms (suspiciousness and delusions) were more severe among the suicides. The paranoid subtype was associated with an elevated risk and the deficit subtype was associated with a reduced risk for suicide.

Denmark Nested Case-control Study

The purpose of this large record-linkage study was to identify risk factors for suicide among patients with schizophrenia (Rossau and Mortensen, 1997). Suicide risk was high after admission and discharge, particularly the first 5 days after discharge. Increased risk was associated with multiple admissions during the previous year, previous suicide attempts, previous diagnosis of depression, male gender, and previous admissions to general hospitals for physical disorders. There was some evidence of an excess of suicides during temporary leave from the psychiatric department. "Revolving door" admission patterns were also associated with an increased risk of suicide. The findings suggest that preventive measures could be focused on the first period after discharge, when closer monitoring and better social support may be needed. This may also apply to patients on temporary leave from hospital during a period of admission.

Finnish National Suicide Prevention Project

The aim of this study was to examine the clinical characteristics of suicide victims with schizophrenia in the general population of Finland (Heilä et al, 1997). All suicides over a 12-month period were evaluated and all persons with a diagnosis of schizophrenia were investigated, using the psychological autopsy method. Suicide occurred throughout the course of schizophrenia. Both active illness (78%) and depressive symptoms (64%) were highly prevalent immediately before suicide, and a history of suicide attempts (71%) was also common. About two-thirds of the women but only one-third of the men committed suicide during an acute exacerbation. Nearly one in ten victims suffered from current suicide-commanding hallucinations. Younger male subjects most often used violent suicide methods. At the time of suicide, more than one-quarter of the schizophrenic patients (27%) were receiving inpatient psychiatric care. Another 32% committed suicide shortly after discharge.

Belgian Suicide in Schizophrenia Project

In 1995 we conducted a case-control study on a large cohort (n = 870) of young DSM-III-R (American Psychiatric Association, 1987) schizophrenic patients (De Hert, 1995; De Hert and Peuskens, 1997; Peuskens et al, 1997; De Hert et al, 2000). The high risk of suicide in the schizophrenic population was confirmed in this study. After a mean duration of follow-up of 11.4 years, 63 patients (7.2%) had committed suicide. The annual suicide rate in our sample was 635/100,000 and was twice as high for men as for women. The standardized suicide ratio was 39.7. Our study found similar risk factors to those identified in the older studies. Risk factors and protective factors are shown in Table 8.4.

The case-control design of the investigation allowed the identification of the following risk-factors: male gender; chronic illness with frequent relapse; numerous and short hospitalizations; psychiatric hospitalization and the period shortly after release; history of suicide in the family; impulsive and aggressive behaviour; non-compliance with medication; use of antidepressants; earlier and recent loss situations; negative attitude to treatment; higher IQ and educational level; psychotic episodes; and depression. Protective factors against suicide were: absence of symptoms; ambulatory treatment; participation in a meaningful activity in society; and illness characterized by the early occurrence of cognitive decline and a deficit state. An ongoing 10-year follow-up study of first-episode patients confirmed the identified risk factors and showed that the risk for suicide is particularly high in this specific population (De Hert et al, 1998b). The suicide rate was 1,018 per 100,000 per year (males 1,128 per 100,000 per year, females 759 per 100,000 per year) and the SMR for suicide was 58.

RISK FACTORS AND HYPOTHESES ON SUICIDE IN SCHIZOPHRENIA

Whatever the aetiology of schizophrenia may be, the disorder often runs a chronic course and is usually a personal and social catastrophe. Schizophrenia manifests itself in late adolescence, at a time when matters of fundamental importance to the young person are due to unfold: it is the period of sexual maturation and of crucial developments in social and relational skills, and it is also the time at which studies terminate and a career is chosen. Schizophrenic psychosis inflicts extensive damage on emotional, affective, relational and often cognitive functioning as well. Loss situations in various areas of psychosocial functioning are frequently present after the onset of the illness. That these are

Table 8.4 Risk factors for suicide in schizophrenia compared to controls, and odds ratios

Factor	Case (%)	Control (%)	*p*	Odds ratio (95% confidence interval)
Antecedent variables				
IQ > 100	50	29	0.000	4.3 (1.7–13)
Family history of suicide	27	5	0.001	8.0 (1.9–72)
More than five admissions	56	24	0.000	6.0 (2.1–24)
Impulsivity				
Acting out behaviour	65	22	0.000	6.4 (2.5–21)
Discharge against advice	60	37	0.007	2.5 (1.2–5.8)
Fugues	64	27	0.000	5.6 (2.1–19)
Involuntary commitment	32	6	0.000	17 (2.7–711)
Suicidal behaviour				
Suicide threat	81	35	0.000	5.1 (2.3–14)
Suicide attempt	59	22	0.000	4.8 (2.0–14)
Potentially lethal suicide attempt	40	8	0.000	11 (2.7–137)
Treatment				
Antidepressant index admission	46	30	0.067	2.0 NS
Antidepressant suicide/control	46	25	0.016	2.9 (1.2–8.0)
Non-responder	24	24	NS	
Non-compliance	60	22	0.000	7.0 (2.5–28)
Condition at death or follow-up				
Bad physical health	6	13	NS	
Major loss in previous 6 months	37	5	0.000	7.3 (2.2–38)
Psychiatric admission	48	27	0.017	2.6 (1.1–6.5)
Symptoms at death or follow-up				
Psychotic	60	22	0.000	7.0 (2.5–27.5)
Depressed	60	3	0.000	36 (6.1–1488)
Psychotic and depressed	37	1	0.000	Empty cell
Protective factors				
Ambulatory care	43	64	0.032	2.4 (1.1–6.0)
Useful activity	19	45	0.002	4.2 (1.5–14)
Early defect state	19	44	0.002	6.3 (1.9–33)
Symptom-free	16	76	0.000	20 (5.2–171)

NS, not significant.

intolerable to a substantial group of patients should come as no surprise. Patients who attempt or commit suicide undergo significantly more loss situations early on in the course of their illness: failure at a higher academic level, loss of employment, loss of a partner and loss of a first-degree relative through suicide, most often a parent.

Schizophrenic patients who commit suicide do so at a young age, mostly within 10 years of the onset of their illness. The older the schizophrenic patient, the smaller the risk. This finding is likely to be related to a stabilization of the illness after the first 10 years, as well as to the fact that most loss situations resulting from the disorder occur early on in the course of the disease (Mortensen and

Juel, 1993; Brown, 1997; Harris and Barraclough, 1997). Schizophrenic patients who attempt suicide often choose a way that might be expected to result in death. The choice of a dangerous method seems to express a determination to die, which seems to be confirmed in the use of a potentially lethal method in the not infrequent previous suicide attempts. Along with other people who attempt or commit suicide, schizophrenic patients in this category share the following characteristics: male gender; single; unemployed; solitary living arrangements and social isolation; previous suicide attempts; a history of suicide in the family; and a major loss shortly before the act of suicide.

The history of the illness of patients who commit suicide is marked by a chronic course, punctuated by numerous relapses and frequent hospitalization. The latter is associated with suicidal behaviour in the past, impulsive behaviour and a negative attitude to treatment. This negative attitude may indicate that the patient rejects the illness or treatment, which patients might dislike because of burdensome side-effects. Frequent hospitalizations are highly correlated with discontinuation of pharmacological maintenance treatment, running away from the hospital, repeated acting-out, leaving the hospital against advice, and a history of compulsory commitment to an institution. All variables that reflect an aspect of impulsive behaviour (acting-out, running away, non-compliance, leaving the hospital against advice, and suicidal behaviour) are highly correlated with one another.

The danger of suicide is substantial during a psychiatric hospitalization and in the first months after discharge. Alongside psychotic relapse, suicidal behaviour is also a frequent reason for re-hospitalization. Comparison of hospitalized with non-hospitalized patients shows that hospitalized patients present significantly more psychotic and depressive symptoms. The majority of patients who commit suicide during their stay in hospital do so outside the hospital. Patients who commit suicide are hospitalized significantly more frequently and for shorter periods. The higher incidence of suicide shortly after hospitalization can be explained on the basis of a group of patients who terminate treatment on their own initiative, as well as a group of patients who are released too soon and still need the support of a residential environment.

Psychotic relapse and symptoms are major risk factors. Some patients kill themselves to escape from distressing symptoms. Depression is common in schizophrenic patients (Drake et al, 1985; Roy et al, 1986; Roy, 1990; De Hert, 1995; Peuskens, 1997). The acknowledgement that one is suffering from a severe mental illness with a disabling course is a long and painful process, which often leads to depression, despair and ultimately suicidal behaviour. A course of illness with an early onset of deficit state is not a positive outcome of schizophrenia, but appears to protect patients from suicide. It may be that these patients are less aware or suffer less from the disabling effects of the disorder. Pronounced cognitive deficits impair the mental processes needed to plan and execute a suicide attempt. The other protective factors (being symptom-free, having useful activity in the community, and ambulatory treatment) are highly correlated.

IMPLICATIONS FOR TREATMENT

Suicide is the most dramatic outcome of schizophrenic psychosis. It is generally acknowledged that it is difficult to predict individual suicides. Nevertheless, it is possible to identify predictors of the relative risk of suicidal behaviour (Caldwell and Gottesman, 1990; Fenton et al, 1997). Interventions aimed at reducing the risk for suicide should target the identified risk factors.

Psychotic symptoms should be treated adequately, both pharmacologically and psychotherapeutically (Roy et al, 1986; Rifkin, 1993; Peuskens 1996; Peuskens and De Hert, 1997). Long-term treatment with antipsychotics remains the cornerstone in the prevention of relapse (Kissling, 1991; Peuskens, 1996; Peuskens and De Hert, 1997). Close monitoring of the patient and support of the family are also important in the prevention of relapse. The aim should be as few exacerbations as possible. This may be difficult to achieve in a group of patients with a negative attitude towards their illness and treatment. Treatment with classical neuroleptics is characterized by high rates of motor and cognitive side-effects, which have a negative influence on compliance. They have limited efficacy in the treatment of negative symptoms, they may exacerbate these and may cause depression. Novel antipsychotics induce fewer side-effects and could thus improve compliance in patients who are reluctant to take drugs (Meltzer, 1993; Meltzer and Okayli, 1995; Peuskens, 1995; Peuskens, 1996; Gaebel, 1997; Peuskens and De Hert, 1997; Tollefson et al, 1997). They may also be more effective in the treatment of both negative symptoms and depression in schizophrenia (Azorin, 1995; Keck et al, 1995; Meltzer and Okayli, 1995; Peuskens, 1995; Peuskens, 1997; Peuskens and De Hert, 1997; Tollefson et al, 1997, 1998; Tran et al, 1997; Moore, 1998). In this light, newer antipsychotics may be viewed as the treatment of choice in schizophrenic patients at high risk of suicide (see Chapters 27 and 35).

Depressive symptoms and episodes occur frequently during or after psychotic episodes. Depression in schizophrenic patients should be distinguished from negative symptoms and side-effects, and can be adequately treated with antidepressants (Siris, 1990; Azorin, 1995; De Hert, 1995; Hogarty et al, 1995; Peuskens, 1997). Impulsivity can be controlled with neuroleptics and carbamazepine can be added to the treatment.

People suffering from schizophrenia often have different problems in all domains of psychosocial functioning. Within a comprehensive rehabilitation approach, continuity of care should be offered (De Hert et al, 1996; Peuskens, 1996). The patient should be closely monitored in the period following discharge from the hospital. Psychoeducational programs can help patients to cope better with their illness. Feelings of hopelessness, despair and suicidal ideation should be addressed with the patient (Appelo et al, 1993; De Hert, 1995; Amador et al, 1996; Gaebel, 1997; De Hert and Peuskens, 1998a; De Hert et al, 2000). The suffering, from both acute and chronic symptoms, as well as the unrealized dreams and aspirations of patients, require an approach which is aimed at acceptance of the disorder and disability and which tries to create realistic perspectives for the future (Appelo et al, 1993; De Hert, 1995; De Hert and Peuskens, 1997, 1998a;

De Hert et al, 2000). Through psychoeducation, the patient should be informed about the illness and its treatment (Onyett, 1992; Sellwood et al, 1994; Peuskens and de Hert, 1997; Gaebel, 1997; De Hert and Sperans, 1998). The idea is actively to involve the patient in the treatment and thereby enhance compliance. In individual therapeutic work, any hopeless and depressive feelings must be made amenable to discussion (Billiet et al, 1996). Patients must be helped to work through loss and accept that they suffer from a serious psychiatric disturbance (Appelo et al, 1993; Amador et al, 1996). This must be done in a framework that offers hope and facilitates the elaboration of realistic life prospects. In the long term the objective should be to combat social isolation through appropriate training in social and vocational skills and to organize suitable daily activities and living arrangements (Peuskens et al, 1983; De Hert et al, 1993 and 1996; De Hert and Peuskens, 1997; Peuskens, 1996).

CONCLUSION

Both clinical experience and research indicates that people suffering from schizophrenia are vulnerable to suicide. The risk of suicide is 40 times higher than in the overall population. Studies mainly show the "hard" facts: how many people commit suicide, how they do it and what the risk factors are. Suicide, however, is a matter that reaches us emotionally. For psychiatric caregivers it is virtually the only confrontation with death. It is also a confrontation with the suffering of psychotic patients. For those who treat schizophrenic patients, it is often a matter of losing someone they knew intimately. The pain of this loss is felt just as poignantly by family members as by fellow patients. Treatment aimed at the prevention of suicide in schizophrenic patients must target the identified risk factors. The effective prevention of suicide in this population requires a comprehensive and systematic approach, integrated with careful assessments and interventions, in a general attitude of hope and optimism.

REFERENCES

Allebeck, P. (1989) Schizophrenia: a life-shortening disease. Schizophrenia Bulletin, 15: 81–89.

American Psychiatric Association (1987) DSM-III-R. Washington DC: American Psychiatric Association Press.

Amador, X.F., Friedman, J.H., Kasapis, C., Yale, S.A., Flaum, M. and Gorman, J.M. (1996) Suicidal behavior in schizophrenia and its relationship to awareness of illness. American Journal of Psychiatry, 153: 1185–1188.

Appelo, M.T., Sloof, C.J., Woonings, F.M.J., Carson, J. and Louwerens, J.W. (1993) Grief: its significance for rehabilitation in schizophrenia. Clinical Psychology and Psychotherapy, 1: 53–59.

Azorin, J.M. (1995) Long-term treatment of mood disorders in schizophrenia. Acta Psychiatrica Scandinavica, 91 (Suppl. 388): 20–23.

Barraclough, B., Bunch, J., Nelson, B. and Sainsbury, P. (1974) A hundred cases of suicide: clinical aspects. British Journal of Psychiatry, 125: 355–373.
Beck, A.T., Steer, R.A., Kovacs, M. and Garrison, B. (1985) Hopelessness and eventual suicide: 10-year prospective study of patients hospitalized with suicidal ideation. American Journal of Psychiatry, 142: 559–563.
Billiet, L., De Hert, M. and Peuskens, J. (1996) Psychotherapy with "new chronic" psychotic patients. International Journal of Mental Health, 25: 66–71.
Black, D.W. and Winokur, G. (1988) Age, mortality and chronic schizophrenia. Schizophrenia Research, 1: 267–272.
Black, D.W., Warrack, G. and Winokur, G. (1985) The Iowa record-linking study I. Archives of General Psychiatry, 42: 71–75.
Bleuler, E. (1911) Dementia Praecox oder die Gruppe der Schizophrenien. Leipzig: Deuticke.
Breier, A. and Astrachan, B.M. (1984) Characterization of schizophrenic patients who commit suicide. American Journal of Psychiatry, 141: 206–209.
Brown, S. (1997) Excess mortality of schizophrenia. British Journal of Psychiatry, 171: 502–508.
Caldwell, C.B. and Gottesman, I.I. (1990) Schizophrenics kill themselves too: a review of risk factors for suicide. Schizophrenia Bulletin, 16: 571–589.
Caldwell, C.B. and Gottesman, I.I. (1992) Schizophrenia-a high-risk factor for suicide: clues to risk reduction. Suicide and Life-Threatening Behavior, 22: 479–493.
Cheng, K.K., Leung, C.M., Lo, W.H. and Lam, T.H. (1990) Risk factors of suicide among schizophrenics. Acta Psychiatrica Scandinavica, 81: 220–224.
Cohen, S., Leonard, C.V., Farberow, N.L. and Schneidman, E.S. (1964) Tranquilizers and suicide in the schizophrenic patient. Archives of General Psychiatry, 11: 312–321.
Cohen, L.J., Test, M.A. and Brown, R.L. (1990) Suicide and schizophrenia: data from a prospective community treatment study. American Journal of Psychiatry, 147: 602–607.
De Hert, M. (1995) Suïcide bij jonge schizofrene patiënten. Louvain: University Press.
De Hert, M. and Sperans, F. (1998) In Therapy. Antwerp: EPO.
De Hert, M., Thys, E., Billiet, L., Vercruyssen, V. and Peuskens, J. (1993) Psychosociale rehabilitatie, de zorg voor de chronisch psychiatrische patiënt. Tijdschrift voor Geneeskunde, 49: 1037–1043.
De Hert, M., Thys, E., Vercruyssen, V. and Peuskens, J. (1996) Partial hospitalization at night: the Brussels Nighthospital. Psychiatric Services, 47: 527–528.
De Hert, M. and Peuskens, J. (1997) Suïcide en schizofrenie, risicofactoren en implicaties voor behandeling. Tijdschrift voor Psychiatrie, 39: 462–474.
De Hert, M. and Peuskens, J. (1998a) Suicide in schizophrenia. Acta Psychiatrica Belgica, 98 (Suppl. I): 37–45.
De Hert, M. and Peuskens, J. (1998b) First-episode schizophrenia, a naturalistic 10 year follow-up study. Schizophrenia Research, 29: 143.
De Hert, M., McKenzie, K. and Peuskens, J. (2000) Risk factors for suicide in young patients suffering from schizophrenia. Schizophrenia Research (in press).
Dingman, C.W. and McGlashan, T.H. (1986) Discriminating characteristics of suicides. Acta Psychiatrica Scandinavica, 74: 91–97.
Drake, R.E., Gates, C., Cotton, P.G. and Whitaker, A. (1984) Suicide among schizophrenics: who is at risk? Journal of Nervous and Mental Disease, 172: 613–617.
Drake, R.E., Gates, C., Whitaker, A. and Cotton, P.G. (1985) Suicide among schizophrenics: a review. Comprehensive Psychiatry, 26: 90–100.
Drake, R.E. and Cotton, P.G. (1986) Depression, hopelessness and suicide in chronic schizophrenia. British Journal of Psychiatry, 148: 554–559.
Earle, K.A., Forquer, S.L., Volo, A.M. and McDonnell, P.M. (1994) Characteristics of outpatient suicides. Hospital and Community Psychiatry, 45: 123–126.

Evenson, R.C., Wood, J.B., Nuttall, E.A. and Cho, D.W. (1982) Suicide rates among public mental health patients. Acta Psychiatrica Scandinavica, 66: 254–264.
Falloon, I.R.H. and Talbot, R.E. (1981) Persistent auditory hallucinations: coping mechanisms and implications for management. Psychological Medicine, 11: 329–339.
Fenton, W.S., McGlashan, T.H., Victor, B.J. and Blyler, C.R. (1997) Symptoms, subtype and suicidality in patients with schizophrenia spectrum disorders. American Journal of Psychiatry, 154: 199–204.
Gaebel, W. (1997) Towards improvement of compliance: the significance of psychoeducation and new antipsychotic drugs. International Journal of Clinical Psychopharmacology, 12 (Suppl. 1): 37–42.
Harris, E.C. and Barraclough, B. (1997) Suicide as an outcome for mental disorders. British Journal of Psychiatry, 170: 205–228.
Heilä, H., Isometsä, E.T., Henriksson, M.M., Heikkinen, M.E., Marttunen, M.J. and Lönnqvist, J.K. (1997) Suicide and schizophrenia: a nationwide psychological autopsy study on age- and sex-specific clinical characteristics of 92 suicide victims with schizophrenia. American Journal of Psychiatry, 154: 1235–1242.
Hellerstein, D., Frosch, W. and Koenigsberg, H.W. (1987) The clinical significance of command hallucinations. American Journal of Psychiatry, 144: 219–222.
Hogarty, G.E., McEnvoy, J.P., Ulrich, R.F., DiBarry, A.L., Bartone, P., Cooley, S., Hammill, K., Carter, M., Munetz, M. and Perel, J. (1995) Pharmacotherapy of impaired affect in recovering schizophrenic patients. Archives of General Psychiatry, 52: 29–41.
Keck, P.E., Wilson D.R., Strakowski, S.M., McElroy, S.L., Kizer, D.L., Balistreri, T.M., Holtman, H.M. and DePriest, M. (1995) Clinical predictors of acute risperidone response in schizophrenia, schizoaffective disorder and psychotic mood disorders. Journal of Clinical Psychiatry, 56: 466–470.
Kissling, W. (1991) Guidelines for Neuroleptic Relapse Prevention in Schizophrenia. Berlin: Springer Verlag.
Kraepelin, E. (1909) Psychiatrie, 8th Edn. Leipzig: Barth.
Levy, S. and Southcombe, R.H. (1953) Suicide in a state hospital for the mentally ill. Journal of Nervous and Mental Disease, 117: 504–514.
Lindelius, R. and Kay, D.W.K. (1973) Some changes in the pattern of mortality in schizophrenia, in Sweden. Acta Psychiatrica Scandinavica, 49: 315–323.
Martin, R.L., Cloninger, C.R., Guze, S.B. and Clayton, P.J. (1985) Mortality in a follow-up of 500 psychiatric outpatients. Archives of General Psychiatry, 42: 47–54.
Meltzer, H.Y. (1993) New drugs in the treatment of schizophrenia. Psychiatric Clinics of North America, 16: 365–385.
Meltzer, H.Y. and Okayli, G. (1995) Reduction of suicidality during clozapine treatment of neuroleptic-resistant schizophrenia. American Journal of Psychiatry, 152: 183–190.
Miles, C.P. (1977) Conditions predisposing to suicide: a review. Journal of Nervous and Mental Disease, 164: 231–246.
Modestin, J., Zarro, I. and Waldvogel, D. (1992) A study of suicide in schizophrenic in-patients. British Journal of Psychiatry, 160: 398–401.
Moore, N. (1998) Sudden unexplained deaths in schizophrenic patients: a preliminary report on the possible role of sertindole. Bordeaux Cedex: official report.
Mortensen, P.B. and Juel, K. (1990) Mortality and causes of death in schizophrenic patients in Denmark. Acta Psychiatrica Scandinavica, 81: 372–377.
Mortensen, P.B. and Juel, K. (1993) Mortality and causes of death in first admitted schizophrenic patients. British Journal of Psychiatry, 163: 183–189.
Newman, S.C. and Bland, R.C. (1991) Mortality in a cohort of patients with schizophrenia. Canadian Journal of Psychiatry, 36: 239–245.
Nyman, A.K. and Jonsson, H. (1986) Patterns of self-destructive behaviour in schizophrenia. Acta Psychiatrica Scandinavica, 73: 252–262.
Onyett, S. (1992) Case Management in Mental Health. London: Chapman Hall.

Peuskens, J. (1995) Risperidone in the treatment of patients with chronic schizophrenia. British Journal of Psychiatry, 166: 712–726.

Peuskens, J. (1996) Proper psychosocial rehabilitation for stabilized patients with schizophrenia: the role of new therapies. European Neuropsychopharmacology, 6: 7–12.

Peuskens, J. (1997) The management of depressive symptoms in schizophrenia. In J. Mendlewicz, N. Brunello and L.L. Judd (Eds), New Therapeutic Indications of Antidepressants, pp. 84–95. Basel: Karger.

Peuskens, J. and De Hert, M. (1997) Good Medical Practice Antipsychotics. Copenhagen: Lundbeck.

Peuskens, J., De Hert, M., Cosyns, P., Pieters, G., Theys, P. and Vermote, R. (1997) Suicide in young schizophrenic patients during and after inpatient treatment. International Journal of Mental Health, 25: 39–44.

Peuskens, J., Van Camp, J. and Vermote, R. (1983) Institutionele behandeling van jonge psychotici. In S. Verhaest and R.A. Pierloot (Eds), Vastgelopen jeugd, laatste kans Deventer: Van Loghum Slaterus.

Planansky, K. and Johnston, R. (1973) Clinical setting and motivation in suicidal attempts of schizophrenics. Acta Psychiatrica Scandinavica, 49: 680–690.

Pokorny, A.D. (1983) Prediction of suicide in psychiatric patients. Archives of General Psychiatry, 40: 249–257.

Prasad, A.J. and Kellner, P. (1988) Suicidal behaviour in schizophrenic day patients. Acta Psychiatrica Scandinavica, 77: 488–490.

Rifkin, A. (1993) Pharmacological strategies in the treatment of schizophrenia. Psychiatric Clinics of North America, 16: 351–364.

Rossau, C.D. and Mortensen, P.B. (1997) Risk factors for suicide in patients with schizophrenia: nested case-control study. British Journal of Psychiatry, 171: 355–359.

Roy, A. (1982) Risk factors for suicide in psychiatric patients. Archives of General Psychiatry, 39: 1089–1095.

Roy, A., Schreiber, J., Manzonson, A. and Picknar, D. (1986) Suicidal behavior in chronic schizophrenic patients. Canadian Journal of Psychiatry, 31: 737–740.

Roy, A. (1990) Relationship between depression and suicidal behaviour in schizophrenia. In L.E. Delisi (Ed.), Depression and Schizophrenia. Washington DC: American Psychiatric Press.

Sellwood, B., Haddock, G., Tarrier, N. and Yusupoff, L. (1994) Advances in the psychological management of positive symptoms of schizophrenia. International Review of Psychiatry, 6: 201–215.

Shaffer, J.W., Perlin, S., Schmidt, C.W. and Stephens, J.H. (1974) The prediction of suicide in schizophrenia. Journal of Nervous and Mental Disease, 159: 349–355.

Siris, G.S. (1990) Pharmacological treatment of depression in schizophrenia. In L.E. Delisi (Ed.), Depression in Schizophrenia, pp. 141–162. Washington, DC: American Psychiatric Press.

Stein, G.S. (1982) Dangerous episodes occurring around the time of discharge of four chronic schizophrenics. British Journal of Psychiatry, 141: 586–589.

Temoche, A., Pugh, T.F. and McMahon, B. (1964) Suicide rates among current and former mental institution patients. Journal of Nervous and Mental Disease, 138: 124–130.

Tollefson, G.D., Tran, P.V., Beasley, C.M., Krueger, J.A., Tamura, R.N., Graffeo, K.A. and Thieme, M.E. (1997) Olanzapine versus haloperidol in the treatment of schizophrenia and schizoaffective disorder. American Journal of Psychiatry, 154: 457–465.

Tollefson, G.D., Sanger, T.M. and Thieme, M.E. (1998) Depressive signs and symptoms in schizophrenia, a prospective blinded trial of olanzapine and haloperidol. Archives of General Psychiatry, 55: 250–258.

Tran, P.V., Hamilton, S.H., Kuntz, A.J., Potvin, J.H., Andersen, S.W., Beasley, C.M. and Tollefson, G.D. (1997) Double-blind comparison of olanzapine versus risperidone in the treatment of schizophrenia and other psychotic disorders. Journal of Clinical Psychopharmacology, 17: 407–418.

Tsuang, M.T. (1978) Suicide in schizophrenics, manics, depressives and surgical controls. Archives of General Psychiatry, 35: 153–155.
Tsuang, M.T., Woolson, R.F. and Flemming, J.A. (1980) Premature death in schizophrenia and affective disorder. Archives of General Psychiatry, 37: 979–983.
Virkkunen, M. (1974) Suicides in schizophrenia and paranoid psychoses. Acta Psychiatrica Scandinavica, 250: 305–310.
Warnes, H. (1968) Suicide in schizophrenics. Diseases of the Nervous System, 29: 35–40.
Westermeyer, J.F., Harrow, M. and Marengo, J.T. (1991) Risk for suicide in schizophrenia and other psychotic and non-psychotic disorders. Journal of Nervous and Mental Disease, 179: 259–266.
Wilkinson, D.G. (1982) The suicide rate in schizophrenia. British Journal of Psychiatry, 140: 138–141.
Wilkinson, D.G. and Bacon, N.A. (1984) A clinical and epidemiological survey of parasuicide and suicide in Edinburgh schizophrenics. Psychological Medicine, 14: 889–912.
Winokur, G. and Tsuang, M.T. (1975) The Iowa 500: suicide in mania, depression and schizophrenia. American Journal of Psychiatry, 132: 650–651.
Yarden, P.E. (1974) Observations on suicide and chronic schizophrenia. Comprehensive Psychiatry, 15: 325–333.

Chapter 9

Psychiatric Aspects of Suicidal Behaviour: Substance Abuse

George E. Murphy
Washington University, St. Louis, MO, USA

Abstract

Alcoholism has been recognized for 40 years as a major contributor to suicide (interestingly, Durkheim discounted it). More recently, abuse of other substances has increased alarmingly in the USA and to a considerable degree in the other developed countries of the world. *Pari passu*, it has taken its place beside, and sometimes in lieu of, alcoholism as a precursor to suicide. The spread of drug abuse may be responsible in part for the two- to four-fold increase in youth suicide over the past three decades. Overall, substance abuse (alcoholism included) is found in 25–55% of suicides, a rate far in excess of its prevalence in the adult population. The deliberate dimming of critical consciousness leads to difficulties in making other choices. Social relationships are often damaged, work performance is usually affected, personal care suffers, and with it, health. Impulsivity and risk-taking lower the threshold for suicidal behaviour. Substance-abusing women are less represented than among suicides in general. As troubles mount, so does the danger of suicide. About one-third of suicides in this diagnostic group appear to have been precipitated by loss or disruption of a close personal relationship, most commonly a marital or quasi-marital one. Anticipation of such a loss or of another sort of crisis may also herald self-destruction. An even more important vulnerability factor for suicide in this group is the superimposition of a major depressive episode on the substance abuse. This is found to have occurred in two-thirds or more of substance-abusing individuals who commit suicide. Major depression alone is the leading impetus for ending one's life (see Chapter 7). As a complicating factor in substance abuse it is no less lethal. The most basic step in preventing suicide is successful treatment of the underlying psychiatric illness. This may be hard to achieve with regard to substance abuse. However, successful treatment of depression, whether primary or secondary, is well within our grasp.

The International Handbook of Suicide and Attempted Suicide. Edited by K. Hawton and K. van Heeringen.

THE FACTS

Beyond demographics, our factual knowledge of suicide comes from psychological autopsy studies of consecutive suicides conducted over the past 40 years in at least 10 nations. Over 2,000 individual cases have been studied using this approach, in countries as dispersed as Finland (Henriksson et al, 1993), Australia (Chynoweth et al, 1980), Hungary (Arató et al, 1988), the USA (Robins et al, 1959; Rich et al, 1986) and Taiwan (Cheng, 1995). There is a remarkable uniformity in finding psychiatric illness as an antecedent in 90–100% of cases (Table 9.1). Alcoholism or substance abuse is found second in frequency only to depressive disorders in the roster of psychiatric contributors: it is found in one-fifth to one-half of cases. This has been true both in the early studies that reported only a single diagnosis per case and the later ones identifying more than one diagnosis per subject. Affective disorder has been found to have been present in the terminal phase of two-thirds to three-quarters of alcoholics who had taken their own lives (Murphy et al, 1979; Duberstein et al, 1993; Cheng, 1995). Where the order of onset has been sought, major depression has been seen as a late complication of alcoholism much more often than as its antecedent (Murphy, 1992; Shaffer et al, 1996: but see also Bukstein et al, 1993).

In the early years of the suicide research era, alcohol was the only common substance of abuse. More recently, other substances of abuse have gained prominence, particularly among younger men (Fowler et al, 1986). It is thought likely that the rise in substance abuse has contributed substantially to the alarming increase in suicide among the young—especially in males—in the past three decades in more than a dozen countries (Rich et al, 1986; Brent et al, 1987; Shaffer et al, 1996). But it is not substance abuse alone, but in a co-morbid relationship with affective disorder that it is most lethal in youth (Brent et al, 1993; Bukstein et al, 1993), as it is in adults (Murphy et al, 1992). The role of co-morbidity does not end there. Substance abuse, with or without affective disorder, is found to complicate nearly all of the diagnosed personality disorders identified retrospectively in suicides (Runeson, 1989; Rich et al, 1990; Cheng et al, 1997).

THE LIFETIME RISK OF SUICIDE IN ALCOHOLICS

The proportion of alcoholics expected to end their own lives directly was earlier claimed to be 15% (Miles, 1977). That figure found its way into the suicide literature and is occasionally repeated today. It was based on a dozen small follow-up studies and a large assumption. A close examination of the matter mathematically proved so high a figure to be untenable. Longitudinal studies showed it to be much lower and differing by clinical status (e.g. inpatient treated vs. outpatient, treated vs. untreated alcoholism) as well as by the national suicide rate of the country of origin of the data (Murphy and Wetzel, 1990). For countries with low and intermediate suicide rates, the lifetime risk of

Table 9.1 Selected diagnoses in community samples of suicides studied retrospectively

	(*n*)	Affective disorder (%)	Alcoholism (%)	Schizophrenia (%)	Substance abuse/ dependency (%)	No psychiatriatric diagnoses (%)
Robins et al, 1959**	134	47 (56)*	25 (27)*	2	28*	6
Dorpat and Ripley, 1960	114	30	27	12	31*	0
Barraclough et al, 1974	100	70	15	3	19*	7
Beskow, 1979	270 (males)	28 (45)*	31 (44)*	3	37*	4
Hagnell and Rorsman, 1979	28	50	19	7	39*	7
Chynoweth et al, 1980	135	33 (55)*	22	4	22 (34)*	2
Mitterauer, 1981	94	63*	30*	5	45*	0
Kapamadźija et al, 1982	100	75*	41*	3*	41*	0
Rich et al, 1986	283	44*[#]	54*[#]	3*	56*[+]	5
Arató et al, 1988	200	58*	20*	8*	20*	19
Åsgård, 1990	104 (females)	35 (59)*	7 (16)*	3	23*	<5
Henriksson et al, 1993	229	57*	17 (43)*	10	43	2
Cheng, 1995	116	86*	44*	6*	45*	2
Wolfersdorf, 1993	454	66*	28*	8*	33*	11
Conwell et al, 1996	141	47*[a]	56*	16[b]	63*	10[c]

* Diagnoses inclusive, not hierarchical.
** Diagnoses recalculated, Robins, 1981.
[+] Rich, et al, 1988.
[#] Rich et al, 1989.
[a] "Mood disorders".
[b] Schizophrenia, schizoaffective, delusional disorder, psychotic disorder NOS.
[c] No Axis I disorder.

suicide in alcoholics was found to be about 2.5% for those with lower levels of treatment or none, and about 3.5% for those with a history of inpatient treatment. This difference reflects the fact that those receiving hospitalization are the more severely afflicted. The Scandinavian countries and others with relatively high suicide rates were found to have lifetime suicide risk rates nearly twice as high as those in countries with lower overall rates (Rossow and Amundsen, 1995).

Suicide does not often occur in the early years of alcohol abuse. The mean duration of abuse approached 20 years in one study (Murphy and Wetzel, 1990) and about 18 years in a later one (C.L. Rich, personal communication, 1989). It was shorter for women who, while less frequently abusers, are more severely afflicted by the abuse. The duration of abusive drinking eventuating in suicide was strikingly lower in the small number with onset at age 50 years and over, suggesting a ceiling effect on age at suicide among alcoholics. Comparable data regarding abusers of other substances have not yet become available, but the strong association between such substance abuse and youth among the suicides studied implies that the incubation period is shorter. Whether the illegality of these substances will lead to earlier spontaneous remission of abuse remains to be seen.

The Sex Factor

Despite a higher incidence and prevalence of affective disorder, women have substantially lower suicide rates than men (Murphy, 1998), except in some parts of the orient (Pritchard, 1996; see Chapter 2). They also have lower rates of substance abuse worldwide. The proportion of suicides attributable to substance abuse is accordingly lower (Table 9.2). In the 10 published psychological autopsy studies providing gender-specific data, it is seen that while nearly one-third of suicides in males are identified as alcoholics, the proportion in women is about one in seven for this diagnosis. The mean male:female ratio for suicide overall is 2.3:1, but for alcoholics it is 5.2:1. These differences are even more extreme in adolescence (Shaffer et al, 1996). Clearly, women are under-represented among alcoholic suicides, but those who commit suicide appear to have been more severely afflicted (Murphy, 1992). A history of suicide attempts is much more common, and social isolation, even if in a marriage, is often extreme. Later age of onset and a more fulminating course are often seen. These women appear to have lost the protective factors that often accompany being female (Murphy, 1998).

PREDICTORS OF SUICIDE IN SUBSTANCE ABUSERS

As with the non-substance abusing population, there is no pathognomonic feature—no mark of Cain—that will identify those destined for suicide. Beyond

Table 9.2 Proportions of selected diagnoses in male vs. female suicides and their sex ratios

Study	Males	Females	M/F⁺	Affective Disorder					Alcoholism			
				Males		Females			Males		Females	
				(*n*)	(%)	(*n*)	(%)	M/F⁺	(*n*)	(%)	(*n*)	(%)
Robins et al, 1959 USA	103	31	3.3	42	41	18	58	2.3	27	26	5	16
Barraclough et al, 1974 UK	53	47	1.1	39	57	34	72	1.1	12	23	3	6
Beskow, 1979 Sweden	270	0		28	10				31*	11		
Rich et al, 1988 USA	143	61	2.3	56*	40	32*	53	1.8	60*	43	20*	33
Arató, 1988 Hungary	103	97	1.1	67*	65	49*	51	1.4	11*	11	5*	5
Åsgård, 1990 Sweden	0	104				61	59				7	7
Henriksson et al, 1993 Finland	172	57	3.0	93*	54	38*	67	2.4	82*	48	15*	26
Lesage et al, 1994 Canada	75	0		41*	54				22	29		
Cheng, 1995 Taiwan	72	45	1.6	60*	83	41	91	1.5	40*	56	11	24
Wolfersdorf, 1993 Germany	326	128	2.5	196*	60	104*	81	1.9	117	36	12	9
Totals	1,317	570	2.3	622		377		1.6	402		78	
Principal Diagnosis					47		66			31		14

*Multiple diagnoses.
M/F⁺, male: female ratio.

the presence of psychiatric illness, which is a nearly necessary but insufficient precondition, one must search for features, events or circumstances that bear an unusually close numerical or temporal relationship to the suicide. One such event is loss of a close personal relationship. In the first systematic study of suicide (Robins et al, 1959), roughly one-third of the alcoholics were reported to have experienced such a loss within six weeks or less of their death (Murphy and Robins, 1967). Losses included marital separation, divorce, widowhood, bereavement of a close family member, or other forms of separation. Such events were reported for half of the alcoholics within the year before their deaths, with two-thirds of them occurring within the final six weeks of their lives. This is clearly a non-linear distribution of loss events. Its distinctiveness was heightened by comparison with the suicides suffering primarily from a major depressive disorder. Here, the comparable figures were 15% and 3% for periods of one year and six weeks, respectively. A replication study of 50 alcoholic suicides (Murphy et al, 1979) found 26% to have experienced such loss within six weeks. Threatened and impending losses, not reckoned with those actually occurring, were even more prevalent in both studies (Murphy, 1992).

Later, Rich and colleagues (1988) studied a much larger number of suicides. They compared the loss experiences of substance abusers who were not principally alcoholics, with a roughly equal number who were chiefly alcoholics (abuse of multiple types of substances is common among young abusers.) The two groups had an equally high rate of recent loss (42%) with a somewhat less stringent definition of loss. Again, the loss experience of non-substance abusing depressives was much lower. Duberstein and colleagues (1993) have reported a similar finding. The finding of identical recent loss rates for alcoholics and abusers of other psychoactive substances provides strong confirmation of similar, if not identical, psychodynamics and vulnerability. This is compelling justification for considering all substance abusers together, at least with respect to suicide risk. They are strongly reactive to external events, often consequences of their own behaviour. This has also been found in adolescents who were substance abusers and committed suicide (Gould et al, 1996).

Disruption in the interpersonal realm is not a rare event in the lives of alcoholics. Their relationships are often severely challenged by their erratic, irresponsible and often physically and emotionally abusive behaviour. Why was this particular event followed so closely by the self-destructive act? In nearly all instances it was the last support or meaningful contact that the victim had (Murphy, 1992). In an even greater proportion of cases there was a reported threat of loss. As these were not realized, their impact can only be inferred. Nevertheless, when a disruption is known to be imminent or very recent, increased emotional or physical support for a period of two months may prove protective.

Acute loss is not the only factor in play. A number of associated subacute and chronic variables have been identified as well (Table 9.3). Continued drinking was reported in nearly all of a series of retrospectively studied cases (Murphy et al, 1992). A co-morbid affective disorder was identified in more than two-

Table 9.3 Subacute and chronic risk factors for suicide in 82 alcoholics

Factors	Frequency of occurrence (%)
Current heavy drinking	97
Talk or threat of suicide	86
Major depression	72
Little social support	70
Serious medical problem	54
Unemployed	50
Living alone	38

thirds. It was nearly always a late complication of the alcoholism, rather than the reverse. Its reported duration ranged from one month to five years. Given the known independent role of affective disorder in suicide, its advent in an established substance abuse disorder is clearly an important risk factor.

More that four-fifths of the alcoholic suicides had communicated suicidal thoughts verbally, behaviourly, or by both means. In some it was a new and recent behaviour; in others it was of longer duration or intermittent over many years. Thirty-eight percent were reported to have made a previous suicide attempt. Two-thirds had little or no social support (not limited to those with recent loss). Half were unemployed and half of the remainder did not regularly go to work. Half had significant medical problems. Nearly two-fifths were living alone.

The frequencies of these six sub-acute or chronic antecedent factors, individually and cumulatively, were highly significantly greater in the alcoholic suicides than in those with a primary affective disorder. They were not, however, simply the general case in living alcoholics. Comparisons with a large community sample of living alcoholics and with a larger sample of previously treated alcoholics showed the cumulative frequencies of these six factors to differ far beyond chance (Murphy et al, 1992). With nine of ten alcoholic suicides having at least three of these factors and eight of ten having four or more, it appears that close monitoring of these factors will provide a working estimate of waxing and waning of suicide risk in alcoholics under one's care. Beside this, it is important to ask about thoughts regarding suicide and about access to means for committing suicide. Planning or obtaining means that are potentially lethal is a particularly ominous sign. A non-fatal attempt may represent a practice run and is to be taken seriously. In fact, any history of a previous attempt is a risk factor (see Chapter 13), as is a family history of suicidal behaviour (Mitterauer, 1990).

ATTEMPTED SUICIDE

Substance abuse, especially of alcohol, is a common characteristic of patients who carry out acts of non-fatal deliberate self-harm. Severe abuse ("alcoholism" i.e.

chronic alcoholism and/or physical symptoms of dependence) was identified in 10% of males and 7% of females in a series of 724 deliberate self-harm patients who presented to the general hospital in Oxford, UK, in 1992 (Hawton et al, 1997). These were similar figures to those of 14.6% and 4.2% respectively found in an earlier series during the late 1970s and early 1980s (Hawton et al, 1989). In addition, many patients have problems related to excessive alcohol use. In the recent Oxford study a total of 24% of male patients and 17% of female patients were alcohol misusers reaching either criteria for alcoholism or for problems related to alcohol abuse. Similar prevalence figures were reported for a series of deliberate self-harm patients in Birmingham, UK (Merrill et al, 1992). Alcohol-related problems were more common in a series of male deliberate self-harm patients admitted to the Regional Poisoning Centre in Edinburgh, UK, over a 20-year period during the 1960s to 1980s (41.5%), but similar in females (16.4%) (Platt and Robinson, 1991). The prevalence of alcohol abuse problems appears to be even greater when patients are systematically evaluated with screening schedules rather than just routinely assessed in clinical practice. For example, in a series of suicide attempters of both genders examined carefully after referral to a general hospital in Helsinki, 41.2% met DSM-III-R criteria for alcohol dependence (Suominen et al, 1999), although this high figure might also reflect high rates of alcohol abuse in Finland.

The aetiological link between alcohol abuse and suicidal behaviour was demonstrated elegantly in a 25-year prospective study of Swedish male conscripts (Rossow et al, 1999). Those who abused alcohol, either reported at entry to do so or were known to do so on the basis of an inpatient treatment episode during the follow-up period, had a highly elevated risk of attempted suicide (odds ratio = 27.1). The risk for completed suicide was also elevated (odds ratio = 4.7), but significantly less than for attempted suicide. The risks remained elevated after controlling for psychiatric co-morbidity (attempted suicide odds ratio = 8.8; completed suicide odds ratio = 2.4). The authors related the stronger association with attempted suicide than completed suicide to the possible impact of intoxication and impulsivity on deliberate self-harm behaviour in alcohol abusers.

Rather less information is available on drug misuse in suicide attempters. In a recent series of deliberate self-harm patients assessed in routine clinical practice in Oxford, 12% of males and 6% of females were drug misusers (Hawton et al, 1997). However, these figures are almost certainly an underestimate.

As in completed suicide, alcohol abuse in deliberate self-harm patients very often occurs in the presence of diagnostic co-morbidity, especially with affective disorders and personality disorders (Suominen et al, 1996). This clearly complicates the treatment of alcohol abuse (and other co-morbid conditions) in suicide attempters, although the treatment of the affective disorder is easier than that of substance abuse. Characteristics more common in substance-abusing attempters than in other attempters include male gender and a history of criminal offences. Drug-abusing attempters also tend to be more often unemployed and living alone (Hawton et al, 1997).

A further important feature of substance-abusing suicide attempters is that they have a particularly high rate of repetition of attempts (see Chapter 21). Thus, in a recent study from Oxford there was a history of previous self-harm in 74% of attempters who were drug misusers, 53% of those who were alcohol misusers and 29% of other attempters; 33%, 17% and 11%, respectively, repeated within a year of the study index episode (Hawton et al, 1997). Substance misuse in suicide attempters is usually found to be associated with an increased rate of eventual suicide, particularly if accompanied by other psychiatric disorders (Johnsson Fridell et al, 1996). In 15–24 year-old suicide attempters in Edinburgh, substance abuse was found to be the key diagnostic predictor of eventual suicide (Hawton et al, 1993).

Admission to hospital following an attempt should provide a special opportunity for detection and initiation of treatment for substance-misuse. However, in many cases treatment will already have been received and offers of treatment are frequently rejected (Hawton at al, 1997; Suominen et al, 1999). Nevertheless, general hospital management of attempted suicide patients must include systematic assessment for evidence of alcohol and drug misuse, and close links between self-harm services and clinical services for substance misusers.

PREVENTING SUICIDE

Given the central role of psychiatric illness as an antecedent of suicide, the obvious first step in preventing a suicide is securing remission of the predisposing ailment. The negative consequences of substance abuse appear to play a key role in precipitating suicide in these cases. One can expect a reversal of these consequences with the cessation of such abuse, and thus an amelioration of the motivation for suicide. Unfortunately, we lack the knowledge of how to bring this about with any regularity. Inducing remission of substance abuse is elusive.

Another approach is more promising. Upwards of three-quarters of substance-abusing suicides have been identified as suffering from a co-morbid affective disorder at the time of the fatal act. Here is a target condition we have the means to change. Early studies of antidepressant therapy in alcoholism looked for their effect on alcohol abuse and found little or none. These results were misinterpreted as indicating no effect on the depression. Later work focused on the co-morbid depression and showed considerable promise for pharmacotherapy in improving the affective syndrome in substance abusers (Mason and Kocsis, 1991). Given the central role of depressive disorder in suicide, its conjunction with substance abuse is cause for alarm and calls for vigorous treatment. The newer antidepressants are much less toxic than the older ones. Choice of agent should take toxicity into account in treating any patient at risk of suicide. Given the known lability of substance abusers, it should be given high priority.

Beyond attention to these clinical issues, when risk of suicide is elevated, family members should be strongly advised to remove all firearms from the home (Brent et al, 1987: this is a much more pressing issue in the USA, where private gun ownership is protected by the Constitution). Two months of physical and emotional support for the substance abuser confronted with loss may prove protective. Brief hospitalization is one such measure to be considered. It should be remembered always that a person who has formulated a lethal plan and secured the means for its execution is at extremely high risk and should be treated accordingly. Despite substantial advances in the treatment of depression, in a high proportion of suicides there has been inadequate treatment or no treatment at all, rather more than failure of treatment (Murphy, 1975; Isacsson et al, 1994; Cheng, 1995; Oquendo, 1999).

CONCLUSIONS

Substance abuse, alcohol included, is the second most frequent psychiatric precursor to suicide. The negative consequences of substance abuse accumulate. Social support diminishes; employment and health suffer. Affective disorder supervenes and suicide risk mounts. Help is infrequently sought and poorly utilized. Loss or threatened loss of a close interpersonal relationship can trigger a suicide. Depression and substance abuse together form a lethal combination. Vigorous treatment of depression, whether primary or co-morbid, is our most promising avenue to reducing the toll of suicide.

REFERENCES

Arató, M., Demeter, E., Rihmer, J. and Somogyi, E. (1988) Retrospective psychiatric assessment of 200 suicides in Budapest. Acta Psychiatrica Scandinavica, 77: 454–452.

Åsgård, U. (1990) Suicide among Swedish Women. A Psychiatric and Epidemiologic Study. Stockholm: Kongl Carolinska Medico Chirurgiska Institutet.

Barraclough, B., Bunch, J., Nelson, B. and Sainsbury, P. (1974) A hundred cases of suicide. Clinical aspects. British Journal of Psychiatry, 125: 355–373.

Beskow, J. (1979) Suicide and mental disorder in Swedish men. Acta Psychiatrica Scandinavica, 277 (Suppl.): 1–138.

Brent, D.A., Perper, J.A. and Allman, C. (1987) Alcohol, firearms and suicide among youth: temporal trends in Allegheny County, PA, 1960–1983. Journal of the American Medical Association, 257: 3369–3372.

Brent, D.A., Perper, J.A., Moritz, G., Allman, C., Friend, A., Roth, C., Schweers, J., Balach, L. and Baugher, M. (1993) Psychiatric risk factors for adolescent suicide: a case-control study. Journal of the American Academy of Child and Adolescent Psychiatry, 32: 521–529.

Bukstein, O.G., Brent, D.A., Perper, J.A., Moritz, G., Baugher, M., Schweers, J., Roth, C. and Balach, L. (1993) Risk factors for completed suicide among adolescents with a lifetime history of substance abuse: a case-control study. Acta Psychiatrica Scandinavica, 88: 403–408.

Cheng, A.T.A. (1995) Mental illness and suicide: a case-control study in East Taiwan. Archives of General Psychiatry, 52: 594–603.

Cheng, A.T.A., Mann, A.H. and Chan, K.A. (1997) Personality disorder and suicide. A case-control study. British Journal of Psychiatry, 170: 441–446.

Chynoweth, R., Tonge, J.I. and Armstrong, J. (1980) Suicide in Brisbane. A retrospective psychosocial study. Australian and New Zealand Journal of Psychiatry, 14: 37–45.

Conwell, Y., Duberstein P.R., Cox, C., Herrmann, J.H., Forbes, N.T. and Caine, E.D. (1996) Relationships of age and Axis I diagnoses in victims of completed suicide: a psychological autopsy study. American Journal of Psychiatry, 153: 1001–1008.

Dorpat, T.L. and Ripley, H.S. (1960) A study of suicide in the Seattle area. Comprehensive Psychiatry, 1: 349–359.

Duberstein, P.R., Conwell, Y. and Covine, E.D. (1993) Interpersonal stressors, substance abuse and suicide. Journal of Nervous and Mental Disease, 181: 80–85.

Fowler, R.C., Rich, C.L. and Young, D. (1986) San Diego suicide study, II. Substance abuse in young cases. Archives of General Psychiatry, 43: 962–965.

Gould, M.S., Fisher, P., Parides, M., Flory, M. and Shaffer, D. (1996) Psychosocial risk factors of child and adolescent completed suicide. Archives of General Psychiatry, 53: 1155–1162.

Hagnell, O. and Rorsman, B. (1979) Suicide in the Lundby Study: a comparative investigation of clinical aspects. Neuropsychobiology, 5: 61–73.

Hawton, K., Fagg, J. and McKeown S.P. (1989) Alcoholism, alcohol and attempted suicide. Alcohol and Alcoholism, 24: 3–9.

Hawton, K., Fagg, J., Platt, S. and Hawkins, M. (1993) Factors associated with suicide after parasuicide in young people. British Medical Journal, 306: 1641–1644.

Hawton, K., Simkin, S. and Fagg, J. (1997) Deliberate self-harm in alcohol and substance misusers: patient characteristics and patterns of clinical care. Drug and Alcohol Review, 16: 123–129.

Henriksson, M.M., Aro, H.M., Marttunen, M.J., Heikkinen, M.E., Isometsä, E.T., Kuoppasalmi, K.I. and Lönnqvist, J.K. (1993) Mental disorders and co-morbidity in suicide. American Journal of Psychiatry, 150: 935–940.

Isacsson, G., Bergman, V. and Rich, C.L. (1994) Antidepressants, depression and suicide: an analysis of the San Diego Study. Journal of Affective Disorders, 32: 277–286.

Johnsson Fridell, E., Ojehagen, A. and Träskman-Bendz, L. (1996) A 5-year follow-up study of suicide attempts. Acta Psychiatrica Scandinavica, 93: 151–157.

Kapamadžija, B., Biro, M. and Sovljanski, M. (1982) Socio-psihijatrijska I patomorfoloska analiza 100 izvrsenih samoubistava. Socia Psihijatrijska, 10: 35–56 (Yugoslavia).

Lesage, A.D., Boyer, R., Grunberg, F., Vanier, C., Morissette, R., Ménard-Bateau, C. and Loyer, M. (1994) Suicide and mental disorders: a case-control study of young men. American Journal of Psychiatry, 151: 1063–1068.

Mason, B.J. and Kocsis, J.H. (1991) Desipramine treatment of alcoholism. Psychopharmacology Bulletin, 27: 155–161.

Merrill, J., Milner, G., Owens, J. and Vale, A. (1992) Alcohol and attempted suicide. British Journal of Addiction, 87: 83–89.

Miles, C.P. (1977) Conditions predisposing to suicide: a review. Journal of Nervous and Mental Disease, 164: 231–246.

Mitterauer, B. (1981) Mehrdimensionale Diagnostik von 121 Suiziden im Bundesland Salzburg im Jahre 1978. Wiener Medizinen Wochenschrift, 9: 229–234.

Mitterauer, B. (1990) A contribution to the discussion of the role of the genetic factor in suicide, based on five studies in an epidemiologically defined area (Province of Salzberg, Austria). Comprehensive Psychiatry, 31: 557–565.

Murphy, G.E. (1975) The physician's responsibility for suicide, II. Errors of omission. Annals of Internal Medicine, 82: 305–309.

Murphy, G.E. (1992) *Suicide in Alcoholism*. New York: Oxford University Press, 315pp.

Murphy, G.E. (1998) Why women are less likely than men to commit suicide. Comprehensive Psychiatry, 39: 1–12.

Murphy, G.E., Armstrong, J.W. Jr, Hermele, S.L., Fischer, J.R. and Clendenin, W.W. (1979) Suicide and alcoholism: Interpersonal loss confirmed as a predictor. Archives of General Psychiatry, 36: 65–69.

Murphy, G.E. and Robins, E. (1967) Social factors in suicide. Journal of the American Medical Association, 199: 303–308.

Murphy, G.E. and Wetzel, R.D. (1990) The lifetime risk of suicide in alcoholism. Archives of General Psychiatry, 47: 383–392.
Murphy, G.E., Wetzel, R.D., Robins, E. and McEvoy, L. (1992) Multiple risk factors predict suicide in alcoholism. Archives of General Psychiatry, 49: 459–463.
Oquendo, M.A., Malone, K.M., Ellis, S.P., Sackeim, H.A. and Mann, J.J. (1999) Inadequacy of antidepressant treatment for patients with major depression who are at risk for suicidal behavior. American Journal of Psychiatry, 156: 190–194.
Platt, S. and Robinson, A. (1991) Parasuicide and alcohol: a 20 year survey of admissions to a regional poisoning treatment centre. International Journal of Social Psychiatry, 37: 159–172.
Pritchard, C. (1996) Suicide in the People's Republic of China categorized by age and gender: evidence of the influence of culture on suicide. Acta Psychiatrica Scandinavica, 93: 363–367.
Rich, C.L., Fowler, R.C., Fogarty, L.A. and Young, D. (1988) San Diego Suicide Study: III. Relationship between diagnoses and stressors. Archives of General Psychiatry, 45: 589–592.
Rich, C.L., Sherman, M. and Fowler, R.C. (1990) San Diego Suicide Study: the adolescents. Adolescence, 25: 855–865.
Rich, C.L., Young, D. and Fowler, R.C. (1986) San Diego Suicide Study: I. Young versus old subjects. Archives of General Psychiatry, 43: 577–582.
Robins, E. (1981) The Final Months. A Study of the Lives of 134 Persons who Committed Suicide. New York: Oxford University Press.
Robins, E., Murphy, G.E., Wilkinson, R.H., Gassner, S. and Kayes, J. (1959) Some clinical considerations in the prevention of suicide based on a study of 134 successful suicides. American Journal of Public Health, 49: 888–899.
Rossow, I. and Amundsen, A. (1995) Alcohol abuse and suicide: a forty year prospective study of Norwegian conscripts. Addiction, 90: 685–691.
Rossow, I., Romelsjö, A. and Leifman, H. (1999). Alcohol abuse and suicidal behaviour in young men: differentiating between attempted and completed suicide. Addiction, 94: 1199–1207.
Runeson, B. (1989) Mental disorder in youth suicide: DSM-III-R Axes I and II. Acta Psychiatrica Scandinavica, 79: 490–497.
Shaffer, D., Gould, M.S., Fisher, P., Traufman, P., Moreau, D., Kleinman, M. and Flory, M. (1996) Psychiatric diagnosis in child and adolescent suicide. Archives of General Psychiatry, 53: 339–348.
Suominen, K., Henriksson, M., Suokas, J., Isometsä, E., Ostamo, A. and Lönnqvist, J. (1996) Mental disorders and comorbidity in attempted suicide. Acta Psychiatrica Scandinavica, 94: 234–240.
Suominen, K. Isometsä, E., Henriksson, M., Ostamo, A. and Lonnqvist, J. (1999) Treatment received by alcohol-dependent suicide attempters. Acta Psychiatrica Scandinavica, 99: 214–219.
Wolfersdorf, M., Faust, V., Brehm, M., Moser, K., Hölzer, R. and Hole, G. (1993) Suicide in the Ravensburg area. A study of 508 cases on the basis of criminal investigation data. In K. Böhme, R. Freytag, C. Wächtler and H. Wedler (Eds), *Suicidal Behavior; The State of the Art*. Regensburg: Roederer, pp. 890–895.

Chapter 10

Psychiatric Aspects of Suicidal Behaviour: Personality Disorders

Marsha M. Linehan
Shireen L. Rizvi
Stacy Shaw Welch
and
Benjamin Page*
Behavioral Research and Therapy Clinics, Department of Psychology, University of Washington, Seattle, WA, USA

Abstract

This chapter examines the relationship of personality disorders to suicidal behaviour. The available data were reviewed on the prevalence of personality disorders within individuals who commit suicide; the incidence of suicide within various personality disorders; the relationship between attempted suicide and personality disorders; and risk factors for suicidal behaviours within specific personality disorders. The multiple methodological problems which exist in most current studies on both suicide and personality disorders are discussed. Findings indicate that personality disorders represent a major risk factor for suicidal behaviour, at a level of severity comparable to major depression and schizophrenia. While information is limited, individuals with borderline and antisocial personality disorders seem to represent a group at particularly high risk for suicide. Recommendations for future research are discussed.

* Now at University of Colorado, Boulder, CO, USA.

The International Handbook of Suicide and Attempted Suicide. Edited by K. Hawton and K. van Heeringen.

INTRODUCTION

A dramatic increase in attention to personality disorders as major public health problems, predictors of low quality of life and increased mortality, and as risk factors for the development, exacerbation or intractability of other mental disorders has occurred in the last two decades. This interest has been spurred largely by two factors. First, reliable instruments have been developed to assess Axis II (personality) disorders. Second, accumulating findings indicate that the efficacy of some respected treatments for Axis I disorders is lessened, or even negated, in the presence of a co-morbid Axis II diagnosis. More reliable assessment methodologies, a prerequisite for the scientific study of any phenomenon, is a consequence of the movement over the last 20 years toward less doctrinaire classification systems by the World Health Organization, publishers of the International Classification of Diseases (ICD-8 to ICD-10, World Health Organization, 1967, 1977, 1993), and the American Psychiatric Association, publishers of the Diagnostic and Statistical Manual of Mental Disorders (DSM-III, DSM-III-R, DSM-IV, American Psychiatric Association, 1980, 1987, 1994). The ability to assess these disorders more reliably has also led to a greater examination of the effects of co-morbid Axis II disorders on treatment outcomes.

The prevalence of personality disorders in the general population is estimated to be about 10–15% (Ottoson et al, 1998; Ucok et al, 1998; Lenzenweger et al, 1997; Weissman, 1993). Studies of outpatients in general mental health settings report rates of personality disorders ranging from 12.9% to 62% (Bodlund et al, 1993; Casey and Tyrer, 1990; Fabrega et al, 1993). Among inpatients, personality disorder rates for various disorders have ranged from 11% to 91% (Rounsaville et al, 1998; Cooney et al, 1996; Molinari et al, 1994; DeJong et al, 1993; Oldham and Skodol, 1991). The high rates of personality disorders among individuals with Axis I disorders complicates the analysis of the relationship between presence of Axis I disorders and their course and severity. When examined as a factor in treatment outcome studies, the presence of a personality disorder is generally found to negatively affect response to treatment in obsessive-compulsive disorder (Jenike et al, 1986; Minichiello et al, 1987); alcoholism (Kroll and Ryan, 1983; Poldrugo and Forti, 1988); depression (Pfohl et al, 1984; Pilkonis and Frank, 1988; Shawcross and Tyrer, 1985; Thompson, Gallagher and Czirr, 1988); social anxiety (Turner, 1987); panic disorder (Mavissakalian and Hamann, 1987; Green and Curtis, 1988; Reich, 1988) and bulimia nervosa (Brotman et al, 1988).

The association of Axis II disorders with negative treatment outcomes leads naturally to questions about the relationship of Axis II disorders to fatal outcomes, including suicide. Although non-fatal suicidal behaviour, including suicide attempts, is a criterion for borderline personality disorder, and the prevalence of suicide attempts among individuals meeting criteria for borderline personality disorder is well recognized (Fyer et al, 1988; Snyder et al, 1986; Soloff et al, 1994; Zisook et al, 1994), the association of personality disorders to suicide is not widely documented. The purpose of this chapter is to describe in detail the relationship between personality disorders and suicidal behaviours, particularly suicide. Before summarizing this literature, we first discuss a number of issues surrounding the identification of suicide, attempted suicide and personality disorders. We then summarize available data on the prevalence of personality disorders within individuals who commit suicide, the incidence of suicide within various personality disorders, the association between personality disorders and attempted suicide, and risk factors for suicide behaviours within specific personality disorders. Finally, we discuss the general limitations in current theory and research on suicidal behaviours and recommend future directions. Because Axis II (personality) disorders were not formally diagnosed before 1980, we excluded studies published before that date. We found 14 case control samples and nine longitudinal samples that included data on rates of both completed suicide and personality disorders within the sample.

DESIGNS OF STUDIES EXAMINING SUICIDAL BEHAVIOUR AND PERSONALITY DISORDERS

A number of research designs are used to study the association between suicidal behaviours and personality disorders. Generally, studies can be classified based on three general categories. First is the type of behaviour or event used to select subjects (Axis II disorder, suicidal behaviour, other). A second category involves the temporal relationship between the variables of interest (prospective, retrospective, cross-sectional). The type of control condition represents the third major way that studies can be classified (none, unmatched, matched). We have further organized the studies in this review according to whether they are case-based designs or cohort designs. In case-based studies, subjects are selected for study because they have already committed suicide. If a control condition is included, it consists of subjects who are either alive or who have died by a means other than suicide. Longitudinal studies, sometimes called cohort studies, select subjects because they meet criteria for one or more personality disorders and then follow the subjects over time to determine the rates of suicide within the disorder of interest. If a control condition is included, it consists of subjects who do not have the index personality disorder(s) under investigation. Duberstein and Conwell (1997) have summarized these designs beautifully and the interested reader is referred to their review of personality disorders and completed suicide for a fuller discussion of the strengths and limitations of the different approaches.

The major studies of personality disorders and suicide since 1980 are grouped in Tables 10.1 and 10.2 by the super-ordinate sample investigated. As seen in the tables, several of the studies resulted in multiple publications, each reporting on different subsamples within the larger sample. Tables 10.1 and 10.2 describe the sample, methods of assessment, inclusion–exclusion criteria, and other relevant characteristics of the specific studies and groups of studies investigating completed suicide. We found instances of both retrospective and prospective studies. Within each of these there were some studies with either a matched or unmatched control condition, although many studies, unfortunately, failed to

Table 10.1 Methodological aspects of studies of suicide and personality disorders

Study	Time	Method of sampling	Site of Pt identification	*Inclusion criteria	PD criteria	PD method	PD reliability (kappa)
Selected for suicide							
Finnish National Suicide Prevention Project							
Isometsa et al, 1997; Henriksson et al, 1993, 1995	R	Random	MedExaminer	Suicide	DSM-III-R	PsychAutop	0.58–0.94
Marttunen et al, 1991, 1994				Suicide, age: 13–19	DSM-III-R	CR, S.Int with informant	0.37–0.90
Isometsa et al, 1996				Suicide	DSM-III-R	PsychAutop	0.69–0.78
Western Psychiatric Institute and Clinic (Pittsburgh)							
Brent et al, 1994 (USA)	R	Consecutive	SU = NR, C = census tracts	Age: 13–19, consent of family	DSM-III-R	S.Int with informant	0.89
Brent et al, 1993 (USA)	R	Consecutive	SU = NR, C = census tracts	Age: <19	DSM-III	S.Int with informant	NR
Brent et al, 1988 (USA)	R	Consecutive	SU = NR, C = INPT	Age: <19, C = suicidal ideation with intent to die or suicidal gesture or attempt	DSM-III	S.Int	NR
Brisbane Bridge Jumpers							
Cantor et al, 1989 (Australia)	R	Consecutive	SU = MedExaminer, C = police and hospital records	On bridge	DSM-III-R	CR	NR
Switzerland Suicide Study							
Modestin, 1989 (Switzerland)	R	Consecutive	SU = INPT + MedExaminer, C = INPT	Current psych INPT	ICD 9	CR	NR

Ontario Provincial Hospital Roy and Draper, 1995 (Canada)	R	Consecutive	SU = INPT + MedExaminer, C = INPT	Current psych INPT	ICD (edn not specified)	CR	NR
Iowa Record Linkage Study Black et al, 1985 (USA)	R	Consecutive	SU = INPT + MedExaminer, C = INPT	Prior INPT status, suicide or other death	ICD-9	CR	NR
Vasterbotten County Kullgren et al, 1986 (Sweden)	R	Consecutive	Death Statistics	Within 6 mos of discharge	DSM-III	CR	NR
Greater New York Area Shaffer et al, 1996 (USA)	R	Consecutive	SU = MedExaminer, C = random digit dialing	Age: <20	DSM-III	C.Int with informant	0.58–0.85
Jefferson County, KY Shafii et al, 1985 (USA)	R	Consecutive	SU = MedExaminer, C = friends of suicides	Age: <19, permission of family	NR	C.Int, Q with informant	NR
Gothenburg, Sweden Runeson, 1989; Runeson & Beskow, 1991; Rich et al, 1992 (Sweden)	R	Consecutive	MedExaminer	Classified certain or almost certain suicide, age, 15–29, informant available for interview	DSM-III-R	PsychAutop	NR
San Diego County Rich et al, 1986; Rich et al, 1992 (USA)	R	Consecutive	MedExaminer	Suicide	DSM-III	CR, S.Int with informant	NR
Montreal and Quebec Cities Lesage et al, 1994 (Canada)	R	Random	SU = MedExaminer, C = electoral polls	Age 18–35, male, had available informant; no suicide in prison or hospital	DSM-III-R	C.Int with informant	0.81–0.98

continued overleaf

Table 10.1 *(continued)*

Study	Time	Method of sampling	Site of Pt identification	*Inclusion criteria	PD criteria	PD method	PD reliability (kappa)
Selected for personality disorder							
Long-term follow-up		Follow-up period					
Swedish Conscripts							
Allebeck et al, 1988; Allebeck & Allgulander, 1990 (Sweden)	P	Range 13–14 years	Conscript (compulsory military training)	Male, age 18–20, psychiatric illness	ICD-8	S.Int	NR
Chestnut Lodge							
McGlashan 1984, 1986 (USA)	R	Range 2–32 years, average, 15 years	INPT	Age 16–55, INPT > 90 days, BPD OR schizophreni form psychosis OR unipolar depression	DSM-III (excluding those with MDD)	S.Int, C.Int	0.71
Jewish General Hospital, Montreal							
Paris et al, 1987 (Canada)	P	Average 15 years	INPT CR	BPD based on DIB criteria, INPT	DIB	CR	0.74
PI-500: New York State Psychiatric Institute							
Stone, 1990 (USA)	P	Range 10–23 years	INPT	>3 months stay on the unit age <40 years, IQ > 90	DSM-III	CR	NR
Intermediate-term follow-up							
Psychiatric University Clinic, Berne							
Modestin and Villiger, 1989 (Switzerland)	P	Average 4.6 years	INPT	PD except schizotypal PD	DSM-III	C.Int	0.77 for BPD
McLean Hospital, Belmont, MA							
Pope et al, 1983 (USA)	P	Range 4–7 years	INPT	BPD, score of >6 on DIB, age >18, INPT	DSM-III	S.Int, C.Int	NR

Short-term follow-up							
General Clinic, Memphis, TN							
Akiskal et al, 1985 (USA)	P	Range 6–36 months	OPT	OPT	DSM-III	S.Int	NR
University of Washington, Seattle, WA							
Linehan et al, 1991, 1993 (USA)	P	2 years	OPT	BPD, female, age 18–45, at least two lifetime PA; no current substance dependence, bipolar I, or schizophrenia	DSM-IIIR, DIB	S.Int	NR
Area Hospitals, Hamilton							
Links et al, 1990 (Canada)	P	Average: 20.62 mos	INPT	BPD based on DIB criteria, INPT	DIB	S.Int	1.00

SU = suicide; C = control; NR = not reported; R = retrospective; P = prospective; INPT = inpatient; OPT = outpatient; PD = personality disorder; BPD = borderline personality disorder; PA = parasuicide; S.Int = structured interview; C.Int = clinical interview; CR = chart review; S.Int = structured interview; PsychAutop = psychological autopsy; DIB = Diagnostic Interview for Borderlines.
Method of sampling: if "all" suicides included, it was coded as consecutive.
Psych Autopsy includes both structured psychological autopsies as well as unstructured interviews with informants.
The following studies used a hierarchical diagnosing system which did not allow for multiple diagnoses on Axis I and/or Axis II: Black et al (1985), Cantor et al (1989), Roy & Draper (1995), Kullgren et al (1986), Runeson (1989), Runeson & Beskow (1991).
Brent et al (1994) diagnosis of PD included individuals with one less symptom than DSM-IIIR criteria.
Black et al (1985) grouped PD and sexual disorders together.
Lesage et al (1994) was the only study in which the assessor was blind to suicide status.

Table 10.2 Nature of clinical samples in studies of suicide and attempted suicide

Study	Mean-age (years)	Age range (years)	Female (%)	Total (*n*)	Traced (*n*)	Traced (%)	Assessed (*n*)	Assessed (%)
Selected for suicide								
Finnish National Suicide Prevention Project								
Isometsa et al, 1997; Henriksson et al, 1993, 1995 (Finland)	44.6	13–89	24.9	229	NR	NR	229	100
Marttunen et al, 1991, 1994	17.4	13–19	17	53	NR	NR	53	100
Isometsa et al, 1996	SU = 38.3 C = NR	NR	27.3	134 (SU = 67 C = 67)	SU = 67, C = 115	100	134 (SU = 67 C = 67)	SU = 100 C = 58.4
(Pittsburgh)								
Brent et al, 1994 (USA)	17.5	13–19	14	115 (SU = 56 C = 59)	NR	NR	86 (SU = 43 C = 43)	74.8
Brent et al, 1993 (USA)	17.2	NR	14.9	220 (SU = 91 C = 129)	SU = 82 C = NR	SU = 91.2 C = NR	134 (SU = 67 C = 67	60.9
Brent et al, 1988 (USA)	16.4	<19	45.8	93 (SU = 35 C = 58)	NR	NR	83 (SU = 27 C = 56)	89.2
Brisbane Bridge Jumpers								
Cantor et al, 1989 (Australia)	34.7	17–66	18.4	87 (SU = 47 PA = 16 AbSA = 24)	NR	NR	87	100
Switzerland Suicide Study								
Modestin, 1989 (Switzerland)	38.7	NR	NR	298 (SU = 149 C = 149)	NR	NR	298	100
Ontario Provincial Hospital								
Roy and Draper 1995 (Canada)	37.8	NR	35.1	74 (SU = 37 C = 37)	NR	NR	74	100
Iowa Record Linkage Study								
Black et al, 1985 (USA)	NR	NR	54.2	106	NR	NR	106	100
Vasterbotten County								
Kullgren et al, 1986 (Sweden)	42.8	NR	36.6	145	NR	NR	134	92.4
Greater New York Area								
Shaffer et al, 1996 (USA)	16.7	NR	21	366 (SU = 170 C = 196)	SU = 161 C = NR	SU = 94.7 C = NR	267 (SU = 120 C = 147)	72.9
Jefferson County, KY								
Shafii et al, 1985 (USA)	NR	12–19	SU = 10.0 C = NR	41 (SU = 24 C = 17)	NR	NR	37 (SU = 20 C = 17)	90.2

Gothenburg, Sweden								
Runeson, 1989; Runeson & Beskow, 1991; Rich et al, 1992 (Sweden)	NR	15–29	27.6	58			58	100
San Diego County								
Rich et al, 1986; Rich et al, 1992 (USA)	NR	NR	28.6	283			283	100
Montreal and Quebec Cities								
Lesage et al, 1994 (Canada)	NR	18–35	0	SU = 142 C = NR	SU = 135, C = NR	SU = 96.2 C = NR	150 (SU = 75 C = 75)	SU = 55 C = 40.6
Selected for personality disorder								
Long-term follow-up								
Swedish Conscripts								
Allebeck et al, 1988; Allebeck & Allgulander, 1990 (Sweden)	NR	18–20	0	3,979	NR	NR	NR	NR
Chestnut Lodge								
McGlashan, 1984, 1986 (USA)	NR	NR	53.8	340 (BPD = 94, S = 188, UNI = 58)	NR	NR	288 (BPD = 81, S = 163, UNI = 44)	84.7
Jewish General Hospital, Montreal								
Paris et al, 1987 (Canada)	NR	NR	79.5	322	165	51.2	100	31.1
PI-500: New York State Psychiatric Institute								
Stone, 1990 (USA)	22	13–39	52.6	550	502	91.3	502	91.3
Intermediate-term follow-up								
Psychiatric University Clinic, Berne								
Modestin and Villiger, 1989 (Switzerland)	36.6	NR	42.9	53 (BPD = 26 OPD = 27)	48 (BPD = 22 OPD = 26)	90.6	35 (BPD = 18 OPD = 17)	66
McLean Hospital, Belmont, MA								
Pope et al, 1983 (USA)	25.7	18–42	81.8	33	27	81.8	23	69.7
Short-term follow-up								
General Clinic, Memphis, TN								
Akiskal et al, 1985 (USA)	BPD = 29 C = 30–47	NR	"About 67%"	297 (BPD = 100, Cs = 197)	297	100	297	100
University of Washington, Seattle, WA								
Linehan et al, 1991, 1993 (USA)	NR	NR	100	47	45	95.7	39	83
Area Hospitals, Hamilton								
Links et al, 1990 (Canada)	29	NR	89.9	88	83	94.3	65	73.9

SU = Suicide; C = Control; NR = not reported; PD = personality disorder; BPD = borderline personality disorder; OPD: other personality disorder; PA = parasuicide; AbSA = aborted suicide attempt; S = schizophrenic; UNI = unipolar depression.

include any control condition. The study of suicidal behaviours within Axis II disorders is, regrettably, severely limited by the absence of equal attention to specific disorders. Antisocial personality disorder, borderline personality disorder, and personality disorders as a general category have received by far the most attention. Therefore, there were not enough data to organize the review covering each personality disorder separately.

METHODOLOGICAL ISSUES

Methodological problems in the study of personality disorders and suicidal behaviours exist at almost every level. Research in both suicide and personality disorders is fraught with difficulty. In the study of suicide, for instance, the ethical imperative to prevent suicide precludes experimental analyses of causal factors inducing suicide. Difficulties in generalizing from data collected on individuals who have engaged in one category of suicidal behaviour (e.g. suicide attempts) to those engaging in other categories (e.g. suicide) require that research on suicide focus primarily either on individuals already known to be dead by suicide (case-based studies) or on individuals known to have a high risk for future suicide (cohort studies). In case-based studies, investigation is almost always biased by the absence of blind assessment of the characteristics of the individual who committed suicide. For example, investigators who know that an individual has committed suicide may be more likely to give a post-mortem diagnosis of depression. Control groups are often lacking, and even when present are often unmatched on critical variables. In cohort studies, accurate estimates of suicide rates require follow-up periods extending over the life of individuals in the sample. As can be seen in Table 10.1, however, very few studies follow subjects for even 10 years. Cohort studies also require either very large samples or very precisely picked samples with a high risk of suicide over the follow-up period. Despite decades of research searching for individual attributes associated with later death by suicide, our ability to actually predict suicide is still woefully inadequate. The relative infrequency of suicidal behaviour coupled with the large false-positive rates of current suicide prediction scales requires extremely large research samples to achieve adequate statistical power. Problems with power also dictate that very good subject-tracking procedures must be in place. The feasibility of implementing such procedures, however, is often difficult. In the USA, for example, tracking is much more challenging than in European nations, which have nationalized health services and extensive registries. Even in these nations, however, the aforementioned problems often thwart research efforts.

Variability in Procedures for Identifying Personality Disorders: the Unequal Status of Axis II Disorders

The construct of personality disorder itself is an immediate challenge in the study of the relationship of these disorders to suicidal behaviour. The discrimination of

Axis II disorders from Axis I disorders is based on the idea that so-called "personality" is a characteristic of individuals that is pervasive over time and situation. The system of diagnosis currently in use assumes some underlying "borderline", "antisocial" or "dependent" essence and is based on a *sign* approach to assessment. That is, behaviour is viewed as a sign of some internal or underlying characteristic. In the case of personality disorders, behavioural patterns that constitute the criterion for specific disorders are viewed as signs (or symptoms) of the disordered personality. The disorder is conceptualized as present or absent, measurement is dichotomous, and criterion behaviours are used to measure the disorder in question but are not in themselves the disorder. While reliability in diagnosis has been demonstrated using several measures, such as the Structured Clinical Interview for DSM-IV Axis II Disorders (SCID II) and the International Personality Disorders Examination (IPDE) (based on DSM-IV criteria), there are diverse clusters of behaviour that may be grouped under the same category. According to DSM-IV criteria, for example, there are more than 200 criterion combinations which could qualify as a borderline personality. In the absence of knowing what core problem constitutes particular disorders, it is unclear what characteristics are their direct expression. Furthermore, cut-offs between categories may be fairly arbitrary.

The concept of personality as a causal mechanism underlying individual patterns of behaviour consistent across time and environment, is not without controversy. Mischel (1968), for instance, in his classic review of empirical data underlying this premise, concluded that much of the behaviour attributed to "personality" could better be understood in terms of environmental contingencies. With some additional limits, Mischel's conclusion has withstood the test of intensive critical scrutiny over the years (Mischel, 1990). This view is more compatible with a dimensional conception of personality disorders which, in turn, is based on a conception of behaviour as a *sample* rather than a sign. A given instance of behaviour is regarded as a sample of the individual's repertoire of behaviour in a particular situation. A personality disorder is defined as present when a specified number or set of criterion behavioural patterns is present; the more behaviours present, the more disorder. From this point of view, personality disorders are best represented by dimensional rather than categorical measures. Dimensional approaches may be more appropriate to assess and categorize personality disorders by allowing for (a) an account of phenomena excluded from consideration by diagnostic categories, and (b) dependence on finer measurements than categorical data (suggesting that the phenomenon must be more carefully operationalized and tied to observable behaviour). While a few studies attempt to examine the relationship of personality disorders and suicidal behaviour using a more dimensional approach, the methods used have been haphazard. In the absence of consistent methodology, we are left with information obtained from categorical diagnostic systems. It should be clear, however, that this is not without its pitfalls. As Widiger and Frances (1987) point out, criterion behaviours are at times used as indicators of some underlying pathology (i.e. diagnostically) and at other times as operational criteria of a disorder (i.e. definitionally). Research, in many cases, does not sufficiently distinguish which criteria are definitional and which (if any) diagnostic. Problems with validity and diagnosis are thus, for the categorical classification system, inextricably intertwined.

Another problem in the assessment of personality disorders is varying methodologies among the studies, which makes results extremely difficult to compare. As can be seen in Table 10.1, not only do diagnostic criteria differ among studies, but the manner of arriving at diagnoses also varies. The use of either a hierarchical system for diagnosing all mental illnesses or assessment of only a principal diagnosis poses a serious limitation on the study of personality disorders. In both hierarchical and principal diagnosis systems, Axis II diagnoses are ordinarily given only when an Axis I disorder is absent. The high co-morbidity of Axis I and Axis II disorders, however, ensures a serious underestimate of the prevalence of personality disorders. For example, in the Finnish National Suicide Prevention Project (see Table 10.1), subjects were allowed to have multiple diagnoses and also a principal diagnosis was assigned. Although 31% met criteria for a personality disorder, only 20% were given an Axis II principal diagnosis.

PREVALENCE OF PERSONALITY DISORDERS AMONG INDIVIDUALS WHO COMMIT SUICIDE

The prevalence of personality disorders among suicide completers in the 14 research samples studied since 1980 are listed in Table 10.3. Only two studies investigated a naturalistic, unconstrained sample of suicides: the random sample of 229 suicides in the Finnish National Suicide Prevention Project (Henriksson et al, 1993; Isometsa et al, 1997; Isometsa et al, 1996) and the 204 consecutive suicides in the San Diego study (Rich et al, 1986). The Finnish sample was collected more recently and the diagnostic methods were stronger. In this study, psychological autopsies were conducted to make DSM-III-R diagnoses, reliability coefficients for diagnoses were acceptable, and multiple diagnoses were allowed. Personality disorders were diagnosed in 31% of the sample. In 50% of the sample an Axis II diagnosis was excluded and in the remaining 19% the information was either insufficient or discrepant. In contrast, in the San Diego study only 5% were given a personality disorder diagnosis. Rich and Runeson (1992) make a cogent argument that the low rates of personality disorder in the San Diego sample may have been due to an under-assessment of borderline personality disorder; none were diagnosed in the original sample. In a re-analysis of the youth data from the San Diego sample using a pre-selected set of variables as indicators of borderline personality disorder, the prevalence went from 0% to 41%. This latter finding is more similar to rates of borderline personality disorders found in other comparable suicide samples.

There have been four studies of adolescent and young adult suicides. As can be seen in Table 10.3, personality disorders were diagnosed in 40–53% of these suicides. With the exception of those from the Rich and Runeson study, the results

Table 10.3 Rates of personality disorders within completed suicides

Study	Total (*n*)	PD (%)	PPD (%)	SPD (%)	STPD (%)	ASPD (%)	BPD (%)	HPD (%)	NPD (%)	AVPD (%)	DPD (%)	OCPD (%)	PDNOS (%)	CD (%)	Significant results
Black et al, 1985[1]	68	10.3	–	–	–	–	–	–	–	–	–	–	–	–	NR
Accidental deaths	38	26.3	–	–	–	–	–	–	–	–	–	–	–	–	
Brent et al, 1994	43	41.9	7.0	2.3	0.0	11.6	7.0	2.3	4.7	14.0	7.0	2.3	–	–	PD: SU > C, $p < 0.01$
Matched pair control	43	11.6	0.0	0.0	0.0	2.3	0.0	0.0	0.0	4.7	0.0	2.3	–	–	
Brent et al, 1993	67	–	–	–	–	–	–	–	–	–	–	–	–	28.4	CD: SU > C, $p < 0.0001$
Matched pair control	67	–	–	–	–	–	–	–	–	–	–	–	–	6.0	
Brent et al, 1988	27	–	–	–	–	–	–	–	–	–	–	–	–	22.2	CD: SU = C
Suicidal INPT control	56	–	–	–	–	–	–	–	–	–	–	–	–	30.4	
Cantor et al, 1989[1]	47	12.8	–	–	–	–	–	–	–	–	–	–	–	–	NR
Parasuicide	16	12.5	–	–	–	–	–	–	–	–	–	–	–	–	
Aborted suicide attempters	24	58.3	–	–	–	–	–	–	–	–	–	–	–	–	
Lesage et al, 1994	75	57.3	0.0	6.7	1.3	14.7	28.0	0.0	0.0	0.0	0.0	2.7	16.0	21.3	PD: SU > C, $p < 0.05$
Matched pair control	75	25.3	0.0	8.0	1.3	4.0	4.0	0.0	0.0	0.0	0.0	0.0	9.3	10.7	
Modestin, 1989	149	10.7	–	–	–	–	–	–	–	–	–	–	–	–	PD: C > SU, $p < 0.001$
Matched pair INPT control	149	29.5	–	–	–	–	–	–	–	–	–	–	–	–	
Roy and Draper, 1995[1]	37	2.7	–	–	–	–	–	–	–	–	–	–	–	–	PD: C > SU, $p < 0.003$
Matched pair INPT control	37	27.0	–	–	–	–	–	–	–	–	–	–	–	–	
Shaffer et al, 1996[2]	120	–	–	–	–	–	–	–	–	–	–	–	–	45.8	CD: SU > C, $p < 0.05$ in males only
General population control	147	–	–	–	–	–	–	–	–	–	–	–	–	8.2	

continued overleaf

Table 10.3 *(continued)*

Study	Total (n)	PD (%)	PPD (%)	SPD (%)	STPD (%)	ASPD (%)	BPD (%)	HPD (%)	NPD (%)	AVPD (%)	DPD (%)	OCPD (%)	PDNOS (%)	CD (%)	Significant results
Shaffi et al, 1985[3]	20	–	–	–	–	–	–	–	–	–	–	–	–	70.0	CD: SU > C, $p < 0.003$
Friends—matched pair control	17	–	–	–	–	–	–	–	–	–	–	–	–	23.5	
Kullgren et al, 1986[1]	134	–	–	–	–	–	11.9	–	–	–	–	–	–	–	
Marttunen et al, 1991, 1994	53	39.6	NR	NR	NR	9.4	11.3	NR	3.8	NR	NR	NR	7.5	7.6	
Isometsa et al, 1996, 1997; Henriksson et al, 1993	229	29.3	0.4	0.0	0.0	1.3	7.4	0.0	1.8	1.8	2.2	0.9	13.5	–	
Henriksson et al, 1995[4]	43	11.6	0.0	0.0	0.0	0.0	2.3	0.0	0.0	0.0	0.0	0.0	9.3	–	PD: elderly < non-elderly, $p < 0.05$
Rich and Runeson, 1992[5]	191	40.3	0.0	0.5	0.0	11.0	38.2	0.0	0.0	0.0	0.0	0.0	0.5	–	
Rich et al, 1986[5]	283	NR	NR	NR	NR	5.0	NR	NR	NR	NR	NR	NR	0.4	–	
Runeson, 1989; Runeson and Beskow, 1991[6]	58	34.5	0.0	0.0	0.0	1.7	32.8	0.0	0.0	0.0	0.0	0.0	0.0	–	

PPD = paranoid PD; SPD = schizoid PD; STPD = schizotypal PD; ASPD = antisocial PD; BPD = borderline PD; HPD = histrionic PD; NPD = narcissistic PD; AVPD = avoidant PD; DPD = dependent PD; OCPD = obsessive-compulsive PD; CD = conduct disorder.

[1] Only one diagnosis given per subject (hierarchical).
[2] Control subject information based solely on parent report.
[3] "Antisocial behavior" coded under conduct disorder.
[4] Only elderly suicides (age > 60) included in this table.
[5] "Mixed" personality disorder coded under PDNOS.
[6] Maximum of one Axis I and one Axis II diagnosis given per subject.

are remarkably consistent across studies, indicating high rates of personality disorders among adolescent and young adult suicides when compared to matched-pair community control groups (Brent et al, 1994; Lesage et al, 1994) and to a sample of suicides in those over 30 years of age (Rich et al, 1986). The lower prevalence of personality disorders in individuals who die by suicide after age 30 years may be due to the much lower incidence of personality disorders in those who commit suicide after age 60 years (14% vs. 34% in individuals over and under age 60 years, respectively; Henriksson et al, 1995). The decreasing prevalence of personality disorders among suicides over the life span parallels the decreasing incidence of these disorders with age. Thus, as a risk factor, personality disorders may be constant over time (Ames and Molinari, 1994; Cohen et al, 1994; Molinari and Marmion, 1993).

Although personality disorders are over-represented in the general population of suicides, they appear to be under-represented among suicides by individuals who are current psychiatric inpatients (although, as noted below, previous hospitalization is a risk factor for suicide among individuals with personality disorders). Modestin (1989) conducted the only inpatient study allowing multiple Axis I and Axis II diagnoses and reported an 11% incidence of personality disorders among inpatient suicides. In an almost identical study, Roy and Draper (1995) report a considerably lower rate of 3%. Since Roy and Draper allowed only a principal diagnosis, this is very likely an underestimate of the true prevalence of the disorders. Modestin, as well as Roy and Draper, however, both report similar and higher rates of personality disorders among inpatients who did not commit suicide (30% and 27% for Modestin, and Roy and Draper, respectively). The similarity in diagnoses for non-suicides in the two studies, contrasting with the lower prevalence of personality disorders in completed suicides in the study allowing only a principal diagnosis adds further support to our suggestion that there is a possible bias towards giving an Axis I principal diagnoses when clinical evaluators know that a suicide has occurred. Table 10.4 shows information on prevalence rates of specific Axis I disorders, namely major depressive disorder, any depressive disorder, schizophrenia, and substance use disorder for studies that provided such information. As can be seen in the table, there is wide variability in the rates of both Axis I and Axis II disorders, indicating discrepancies in research design and practices.

The Iowa Record-Linkage study (Black et al, 1985) examined suicides among individuals who had previously been on a psychiatric inpatient unit and compared them to individuals who died by accidental means. Unfortunately, they only gave an Axis II diagnosis when there was no principal Axis I diagnosis and, furthermore, for unclear reasons they combined sexual disorders with personality disorders to arrive at a "personality disorder" prevalence rate of 10%. Among former inpatients who died by accidents, the rates of personality disorders were higher and very similar to the other inpatient studies. Without a breakdown of how many of these had sexual disorders, however, it is hard to estimate the actual prevalence of personality disorders. A final study of inpatients was conducted by Kullgren and colleagues (1986). Applying the Diagnostic Interview for

Table 10.4 Rates of Axis I and II disorders within completed suicides

Study	Total (*n*)	PD (%)	Major depression (%)	Any depression (%)	Schizophrenia (%)	Substance use disorder (%)
Black et al, 1985	68	10.3	NR	32.4	27.9	8.8
Accidental deaths	38	26.3	NR	7.9	15.8	13.2
Brent et al, 1993	67	–	43.3	49.3	NR	26.9
Matched pair control	67	–	4.5	10.5	NR	4.5
Brent et al, 1988	27	–	40.7	63.0	0.0	40.7
Suicidal INPT control	56	–	75.0	82.1	0.0	17.9
Cantor et al, 1989	47	12.8	NR	12.8	44.7	6.4
Parasuicide	16	12.5	NR	25.0	50.0	12.5
Aborted suicide attempters	24	58.3	NR	8.3	8.3	12.5
Lesage et al, 1994	75	57.3	40.0	49.3	6.2	57.3
Matched pair control	75	25.3	5.3	5.3	0.0	16.0
Roy and Draper, 1995	37	2.7	NR	13.5	75.7	43.2
Matched pair INPT control	37	27.0	NR	18.9	32.4	40.5
Shaffer et al, 1996	120	–	31.7	60.8	3.3	35.0
General population control	147	–	0.7	3.4	0.0	4.1
Kullgren et al, 1986	134	–	22.4	NR	13.4	8.2
Marttunen et al, 1991, 1994	53	39.6	22.6	50.9	5.7	30.2
Isometsa et al, 1996, 1997; Henriksson et al, 1993	229	29.3	31.0	53.7	7.0	21.0
Henriksson et al, 1995	43	11.6	44.2	65.1	7.0	30.2
Rich and Runeson, 1992	191	40.3	NR	38.7	NR	64.4
Rich et al, 1986	283	NR	13.4	44.2	3.2	NR
Runeson, 1989; Runeson and Beskow, 1991	58	34.5	24.1	27.6	13.8	27.6

Borderline (Gunderson et al, 1981) criteria to chart reviews, they found that 12% of suicides among individuals on an inpatient unit or within six months of discharge met criteria for borderline personality disorder. It is impossible to know whether the very similar rates of personality disorders in the previous three inpatient studies was due to a heavy representation of borderline personality disorders within those who committed suicide. The methodological problems associated with the various inpatient studies make it extremely difficult to know the relationship between suicide and personality disorders within this subsample of the population. A minority of studies report diagnostic data on specific personality disorders. As can be seen in Table 10.3, the data that we do have suggest that the highest risk for suicide is among individuals meeting criteria for antisocial and borderline personality disorders. Both disorders are associated with impulsivity. Borderline personality disorder, in particular, is associated with very high risk for both non-suicidal self-injury and for suicide attempts. A number of the child and adolescent studies did not diagnose personality disorders, but rather reported rates of conduct disorder (presumably because it is usually considered inappropriate to diagnose personality disorders at a young age). The incidence of antisocial behaviours and conduct disorders is exceptionally high among youth who commit suicide when compared with the incidence of these same patterns among matched-pair controls.

INCIDENCE OF SUICIDE AMONG INDIVIDUALS MEETING CRITERIA FOR AN AXIS II DIAGNOSIS

We could locate only nine studies that followed personality-disordered individuals over time and reported data on the incidence of suicide during the follow-up period. Table 10.5 provides a summary of results. The most striking fact about these studies is the lack of research on disorders other than borderline personality disorder. Allebeck and colleagues (1988, 1990) are the lone investigators who have followed a sample of individuals meeting criteria for personality disorders in general. Other studies generally provide naturalistic follow-ups of individuals following an index hospitalization or outpatient treatment programme.

The nine studies vary from short-term (follow-up 1–3 years after index, on average), to intermediate (4–7 years) or to long-term (14–20 years) analyses of suicide rates within groups selected because they met criteria for a personality disorder at an index point in time. Generally, the index site is a treatment facility for adult treatment seekers and, thus, the index age is some point during adulthood. The different follow-up time periods provide complementary data. While the short-term studies may provide information about the disorder at a point of great severity, they provide no information about the lifetime incidence of suicide. In contrast, the long-term studies provide information about the course of the disorder, but without the short-term studies we generally cannot determine whether suicidal behaviour is an imminent or a long-term risk for individuals with serious personality disorders.

Allebeck and colleagues studied young men conscripted into compulsory military training in Sweden who met criteria for a personality disorder, either at conscription or in hospital care subsequent to conscription. They found an association between suicide among men and personality disorder, regardless of when the diagnosis was made. Those who met criteria for a mental disorder in hospital care later, however, had a three-fold increased risk for suicide. This is an important study because the diagnostic data from both the conscription sample and from hospitalized patients are from the same people. Thus, it is the only study to date that allows a comparison of the effect of making the diagnoses in a general population vs. in a psychiatric inpatient population. The finding of a higher association between diagnosis and suicide within those receiving the diagnoses in an inpatient setting may be due to better assessment at that point or to greater severity or co-morbidity of disorders among inpatients. Some investigators suggest that co-morbidity itself may mediate the relationship between personality disorder and suicide (Goldsmith et al, 1990). The higher suicide risk may also be due to the probability that suicide risk was itself an important factor in leading to hospitalization in the first place.

Among the remaining studies, all examined suicide within borderline personality disorder. In addition, inpatient hospitalization was the index event in six of the eight studies. The two studies selecting individuals from outpatient settings (Akiskal et al, 1985; Linehan et al, 1993) followed patients for only brief periods

Table 10.5 Follow-up studies of samples selected for personality disorder (PD)

	Group	Total (*n*)	Suicide (*n*)	Suicide total (index) (%)	Suicide Traced (%)	Significant differences
Long-term follow-up						
Allebeck et al, 1988[1]	PD	1,366	21	1.6	1.6	
	Schizophrenic psychosis (S)	15	0	0.0	0.0	
	Affective disorder (A)	14	0	0.0	0.0	(PD = N) >
	Neurotic disorder (N)	2,584	28	1.1	1.1	entire cohort
Allebeck et al, 1990[2]	PD	513	27	5.3	5.3	
	Schizophrenic psychosis (S)	304	25	8.2	8.2	
	Unspecified psychosis (UP)	200	13	6.5	6.5	
	Neurotic disorder (N)	895	48	5.4	5.4	
	Alcohol dependence (AD)	1,207	46	3.8	3.8	Each disorder >
	Drug dependence (DD)	584	27	4.6	4.6	entire cohort
McGlashan, 1986	BPD	94	2	2.1	2.5	
	Schizophrenia (S)	188	13	6.9	8.0	
	Unipolar depression (UNI)	58	8	13.8	18.2	BPD = S = UNI
Stone, 1990	BPD	206	17	8.3	8.9	
	Psychotics	227	29	12.2	12.8	
	Neurotics	7	1	14.3	14.3	
	Other	4	0	0.0	0.0	NR
Paris et al, 1987	BPD	322	14[3]	4.4	8.5	

Intermediate-term follow-up						
Modestin and Villiger, 1989	BPD	26	2	7.7	9.1	
	Other PD	27	2	7.4	7.7	BPD = other PD
Pope et al, 1983	BPD	33	2	6.1	7.4	
Short-term follow-up						
Akiskal et al, 1985	BPD	100	4	4.0	4.0	
	Other PD	50	0	0.0	0.0	
	Schizophrenia	57	0	0.0	0.0	
	Bipolar I	50	0	0.0	0.0	
	MDD	40	0	0.0	0.0	NR
Linehan et al, 1993	BPD	47	1	2.1	2.4	
Links et al, 1990	BPD	88	4	4.6	4.8	

[1] Diagnoses at time of conscription into the military.
[2] Diagnoses during subsequent inpatient care during follow-up period after conscription into the military.
[3] Includes 12 "definite suicides" and two "probable suicides".
NR = not reported.
Mehlum and colleagues (1991) also conducted a follow-up study of personality disorders and reported one suicide in their sample of 93. Their study was not included in this table, however, since they did not state in which group the suicide occurred.

of 6 months to 3 years and, thus, it is difficult to compare results with those of the longer-term investigations, which were all follow-up studies of previously hospitalized patients. Summing over studies by time periods and recalculating percentages based on sample sizes, the estimated incidence of suicide in the three studies examining the first three years after the index point was 4.2%. For the five studies estimating suicide rates over 4–7 years (two studies) and 13–20 years (three studies), the rates were 7.5% and 7.7%, respectively. Among the latter three studies, the rates may have been underestimated by inclusion of the McGlashan (1986) study, which excluded from the sample any patient with borderline personality disorder who also met criteria for a depressive disorder. Since the association between the two disorders is high, this exclusion is the best explanation for the relatively low rates of subsequent suicide found in this study. In addition, both McGlashan (1986) and Stone (1990) required that subjects stay at least three months on an inpatient unit. Subjects in both studies were discharged before 1976, however, during a time period when long inpatient stays were much more common than today. Although suicide rates vary widely across studies, these recalculations suggest that most of the suicides occur within a few years of the index assessment. We have very little data on the suicide rates over time in other personality disorders. For example, while Stone's (1989) data suggests that narcissistic personality disorder increases the risk of suicide among borderline personality-disordered patients substantially, we do not know what the rates of suicide are among narcissistic patients without borderline personality disorder. The estimated suicide rate of borderline individuals who have had moderate to extensive mental health care, summing over all eight studies, is 7.8%.

Among longitudinal follow-up studies, difficulty in contacting subjects at follow-up is a common problem. In the two longitudinal studies that attempted to compensate for this problem by comparing variables measured at index for those who did and did not return for follow-up, the authors reported that follow-up subjects generally did not differ from dropouts (Modestin and Villiger, 1989; Paris et al, 1987). The absence of such analyses in other studies, however, greatly limits the interpretation and the ability to generalize their results. Studies also differ in whom they exclude from the subject pool. In addition to excluding individuals with major affective disorder (McGlashan, 1986), subjects meeting criteria for other Axis I diagnoses with demonstrably high co-morbidity with borderline personality disorder, such as a current substance dependence (Linehan et al, 1991, 1993), or schizotypal personality disorder (McGlashan, 1986; Modestin and Villiger, 1989), were also excluded. One investigator excluded males (Linehan et al, 1991, 1993), another females (Allebeck et al, 1988; Allebeck and Allgulander, 1990) and Linehan and her colleagues excluded subjects with no history of parasuicidal behaviour (Linehan et al, 1991, 1993, 1994). It is impossible to determine which variations in findings between studies were due to differences in subjects' behaviours and which were due to variations in methodology. Given the variations in diagnostic methods, method of contacting patients at follow-up, etc., it is hardly surprising that findings varied from study to study. Indeed, given the variability, what is surprising is to see how consistent the studies were in their reporting of suicide rates.

CO-VARIATION OF PERSONALITY DISORDERS AND ATTEMPTED SUICIDE

Due to the methodological problems in defining a "suicide attempt", it is very difficult to make conclusions about the relationship of this phenomenon to personality disorders. Most purported studies on the topic do not measure intent, making it impossible to say whether the behaviour was an actual suicide attempt with intent to die or a self-injurious behaviour with intent to do harm but not to die. In spite of this obvious limitation, research clearly demonstrates that personality disorders and attempts at suicide are highly correlated. Studies that examine personality-disordered individuals have found a history of previous suicide attempts in anywhere from 39% to 90% of the sample (Ahrens and Haug, 1996; Bornstein et al, 1988; Corbitt et al, 1996; Garvey and Spoden, 1980; Modestin et al, 1997). The personality disorder most frequently associated with suicidal behaviours is borderline personality disorder. It is the only personality disorder with suicidal behaviour as a criterion behaviour. Up to 75% of such individuals report at least one previous suicide attempt (Friedman, 1983; Shearer et al, 1988; Soloff et al, 1994; Tucker et al, 1987). Suicide attempts are also quite prevalent in other personality disorders. Sixty percent of individuals meeting criteria for schizotypal disorder (Bornstein et al, 1988) and 72% of individuals meeting criteria for antisocial personality disorder (Garvey and Spoden, 1980) report suicide attempts. The number of studies on disorders other than borderline personality disorder, however, are far fewer and findings have not been extensively replicated. This high rate of suicide attempts among those with personality disorders remains even when specific Axis I disorders, like major depression and panic disorder, are controlled (Corbitt et al, 1996; Friedman et al, 1992). Similarly, Ahrens and Haug (1996) examined differences between inpatients with a primary diagnosis of personality disorder and inpatients with a primary diagnosis of affective disorder. Rates of suicidality did not differ between those with personality disorders (39%) and those with affective disorders (41%).

In studies that examine characteristics of suicide attempters, there is also evidence of high rates of personality disorders. One study of 75 suicide attempters found 68% to meet DSM-IIIR criteria for a personality disorder (Johnson et al, 1996). In this same study it was also found that individuals with a personality disorder were more likely to have repeat suicide attempts during the 5-year follow-up period than those without a personality disorder (88% compared to 56%). Other studies which looked at individuals who have engaged in "parasuicidal acts" (intent to die was not measured or sample was not divided based on intent to die) found rates of personality disorders in more than 55% of the samples (Casey, 1989; Dirks, 1998).

These findings, taken together, indicate that personality disorders are extremely relevant in the study of attempted suicide and may play a crucial role in the assessment of suicide risk. From research to date, however, it is not clear whether suicidal behaviour should be considered as a sample of a wide range of dysfunctional behaviours or as a result (i.e. symptom) of a distinct other disorder. Findings from studies of borderline personality disorder indicating that the tendency to generate any dysfunctional behaviour when confronted with a problem was the best predictor of subsequent parasuicide suggest that suicidal behaviour is perhaps best viewed as a specific example of disordered functioning (Kehrer and Linehan, 1996).

RISK FACTORS FOR SUICIDE AMONG INDIVIDUALS MEETING CRITERIA FOR PERSONALITY DISORDERS

Our current ability to predict suicide risk in the individual case, both for the immediate future and over the long term, is weak at best (see Chapter 33). Ethical problems in even determining whether predictions are accurate, together with the more general problems related to predicting infrequent events, make it unlikely that the state of the art will improve dramatically in the near future. The best that can be done is to describe the characteristics of populations in which rates of suicide are higher than in the population as a whole. Such a description can then be used to determine whether or not a given individual is a member of the population at high risk for suicide. A model for analysing risk factors associated with suicidal behaviours, independent of diagnosis, has been developed by Linehan (1981). An updated version of this model is shown diagrammatically in Figure 10.1. As shown, risk factors are divided into two general but inter-related systems, the environment and the person. Characteristics of the person are further subdivided into those which are organismic and those which are behavioural, and the latter is further subdivided into the cognitive, the physiological and the overt behaviour/action subsystems.

Given the extensive research on factors associated with suicide risk in the general population, the question that we address here is whether risk factors for suicide differ among individuals meeting criteria for a personality disorder. To examine this, we surveyed the available literature for studies comparing individuals with personality disorders who have died by suicide to those with personality disorders who do not commit suicide. Despite a wealth of studies examining differences between personality-disordered individuals who engage in non-fatal suicidal behaviour, we found only six studies examining risk factors for suicide *per se*. All six examined suicide risk for individuals meeting criteria for borderline personality disorder. No risk studies were found for other personality disorders. The studies were all longitudinal follow-up studies. All used chart reviews to estimate diagnosis. None were prospective, rigorously controlled follow-up studies. While results are suggestive, they are certainly not definitive.

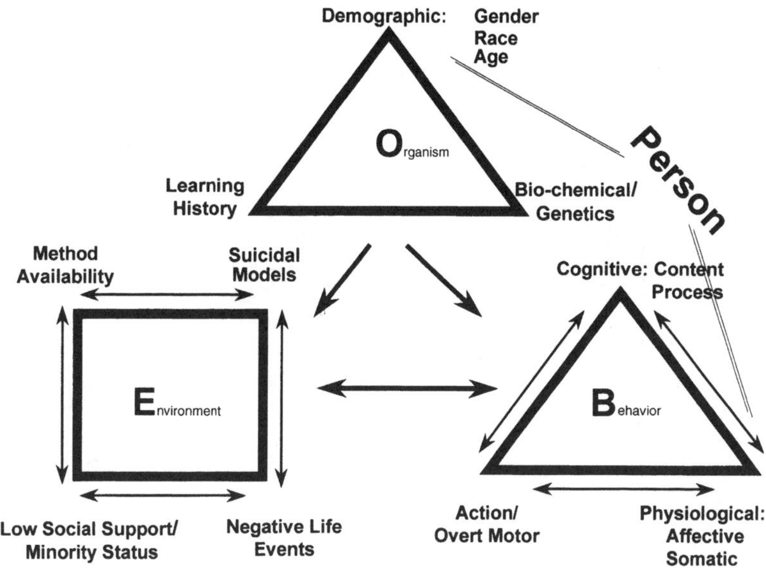

Figure 10.1 Suicide risk factors (independent of psychiatric diagnosis)

In Table 10.6 we list the factors known to be risk factors for the population at large and also those reported as risk factors among individuals with borderline personality disorder. A number of the risk factors are the same, notably: discharge from a psychiatric inpatient unit, previous suicidal ideation and suicide attempts, a history of antisocial behaviours, higher education, and a low probability of asking for or receiving help with problems in living. A number of other factors associated with increased suicide risk in the general population are not associated with greater suicide risk among borderline personality-disordered individuals. Gender, age and marital status, for example, do not appear to predict suicide in persons with borderline personality disorder. The absence of an effect for marital status may be due to low variance; individuals meeting criteria for this diagnosis are less likely to be married. The absence of findings for age may have to do with the follow-up period in the studies reported. None followed elderly individuals meeting criteria for borderline personality disorder. The absence of a gender difference in suicide parallels findings reported by Kreitman (1977) showing similar rates of suicide for males and females with histories of repeated parasuicidal acts, a criterion behaviour for a diagnosis of borderline personality disorder.

CONCLUSIONS

Historically, suicide has been viewed as a symptomatic response to Axis I disorders, primarily depressive disorders or schizophrenia. Studies investigating the

Table 10.6 Factors associated with risk for suicide within personality disorders

	General population: suicide > non-suicide[1]	BPD: suicide > non-suicide	Suicide: PD > non-PD
I. Environmental			
A. Life events	Recent losses		Recent losses[2]
			Recent separations[2]
	Discharge from psychiatric inpatient unit	Threat of or actual unwanted psychiatric inpatient discharge[3,4]	Other life events[2]
B. Social support			
1. Work	Unemployed	Disturbed employment situation[5]	Unemployed[2]
2. Marital rates	Unmarried > married	NS[4,6]	–
3. Interpersonal contact	Low/lives alone		Dependent living situation[5]
C. Models	Family suicide rate higher	–	–
	Widespread suicide publicity	–	–
D. Method availability	Available	–	–
II. Demographic			
A. Gender	Male > female	NS[3,6]	
B. Age	Increases with age	NS[3,6]	
C. Race	White > non-white	–	–
D. Education	Higher > Lower	Higher > Lower[7,8]	

III. Behavioral			
A. Cognitive content	Hopeless	–	–
	Suicide ideation	Suicide ideation[4]	–
B. Physiological/affective			
1. Affective	Depressed	Mixed[9]	Depression NOS[10]
	Indifferent to treatment	No co-morbid anxiety disorder[4]	–
2. Somatic	Poor health	–	Mixed[11]
C. Overt-motor			
1. Interpersonal	Low social involvement		Family, job problems
	Less likely to ask for support or attention	Low contact with a therapist[4]	No contact with health care[10]
2. General behavioral	Substance abuse	NS[7]	Substance abuse[12]
	Previous suicide attempts	Previous suicide attempts [3,4,5,6]	Previous suicide attempts[10]
		Repeated suicide attempts[3,6]	
	Criminal behavior	Antisocial PD	
	Unemployed/retired	–	Unemployed[2]
		High number of lifetime hospitalizations[3]	NS[10]

[1] Adapted from "A social–Behavioral analysis of suicide and parasuicide: implications for clinical assessment and treatment" by M. M. Linehan (1981). In H. Glazer and J. F. Clarkin (Eds), Depression: Behavioral and Directive Intervention Strategies. New York: Garland. Copyright 1981 by Garland Publishing. Adapted by permission. Quoted directly from Cognitive–Behavioral Treatment of Borderline Personality Disorders by M. M. Linehan. New York: Guilford. Copyright © 1993 by Guilford Press. Reproduced by permission.
[2] Heikkinen et al, 1997; within PD in general.
[3] Kullgren, 1988; within BPD.
[4] Kjelsberg et al, 1991; within BPD.
[5] Modestin, 1989; within PD.
[6] Paris et al, 1989.
[7] Paris, 1990; within BPD.
[8] Brodsky, 1997; within BPD.
[9] McGlashan, 1987, found increased risk; Paris et al, 1989, reported no effect.
[10] Isometså et al, 1996; within Cluster B.
[11] Lower in Cluster B, but NS when summed over Clusters A and B; Isometsa et al, 1996.
NS = not significant.

association of suicide with Axis II disorders, as compared to those investigating the role of Axis I disorders, are relatively recent and far fewer in number. However, in a number of the studies included in this review, investigators also reported the corresponding data on suicide in Axis I disorders. Examination of suicide rates across diagnoses within a single study greatly reduces the chances that between-diagnoses differences are due to methodological variability in determining suicide or in diagnosing mental disorders. Generally, the overall findings of the studies suggest that personality disorders are as great a risk factor for suicide and suicide attempts as both major depression and schizophrenia. In the Finnish sample, which was the largest and best designed case-based study, the percentage of suicides with personality disorders (31%) was identical to the percentage with major depression (although it was lower than the 59% with a diagnosis of any depressive disorder and the 43% with an alcohol use disorder). The percentage of suicides with personality disorder was also higher than the 11% with an anxiety disorder and the 7% meeting criteria for schizophrenia. An examination of Table 10.4 indicates that similar ratios between Axis I and Axis II percentage suicides were found across a number of other studies. The two exceptions are the data reported by Henriksson and colleagues (1995) and by Roy and Draper (1995). Subjects in the Henriksson et al (1995) study were in two age categories (elderly and non-elderly), suggesting that the relative risk of suicide among those with personality disorders is less as the population ages, the prevalence of personality disorders is less with age, or the presence of other Axis I disorders overshadows diagnosis of personality disorders more in the elderly than in younger individuals.

Conclusions about the relative role of personality disorders in suicide are complicated greatly by investigators' predetermined beliefs about the importance and primacy of various disorders and their role in suicide. For example, in no studies did the investigator exclude an Axis I diagnosis if an Axis II diagnosis was established. However, as noted above, the exclusion of Axis II diagnoses in the presence of Axis I diagnosis is common, resulting in the loss of potentially important data. Very few individuals who die by suicide meet criteria for only one Axis I disorder. In the Finnish study, 88% of those who committed suicide had at least one other co-morbid disorder. Among those with an Axis I diagnosis of major depression, 31% met criteria for a personality disorder. Furthermore, 42% of those with alcohol dependence and 50% of those with anxiety disorders also met criteria for a personality disorder. We do not have the data on how many of those who died by suicide also had personality traits or behavioural patterns associated with one or more personality disorders. Thus, the role of Axis I disorders vs. the role of multiple problems and stressors in combination with Axis I disorders is not clear.

The scarcity of studies and the methodological limitations of the studies that we conduct pose severe limitations on our ability to interpret findings in the area of personality disorders and suicide. Case-based psychological autopsy studies have potential as a vehicle for studying characteristics associated with suicide.

Unfortunately, very few of the studies conducted to date have adequate control groups—an essential condition for interpreting findings. The potential for bias is so enormous in these investigations that it is impossible to draw clear conclusions until studies are conducted with appropriate control groups, matched on relevant variables. Determination of relevant comparison groups, however, requires that studies be designed to test specific hypotheses about risk variables. The relative absence of theoretically driven research in this area is striking. Without adequate theory and hypotheses to study in future investigations, we are in danger of continuing to amass a mountain of data that is at times contradictory and at other times, uninterpretable.

Eight of the 14 case-based investigations included a control condition, and in four of these, control subjects were matched to the subjects who committed suicide on one or more variables (see Table 10.1). However, only one investigation compared individuals who died by suicide to individuals who had died by a means other than suicide (Black et al, 1985) and no studies have been conducted where the method of death (e.g. gunshot, falling) has been controlled. Without this latter type of study the role of *intent to die*, the defining characteristic of suicide, cannot be adequately studied. Such studies could be conducted, for example, by comparing individuals who kill themselves with a gun to individuals who die by accidental and homicidal shootings. Those who commit suicide by jumping could be compared to those who die by accidental and/or homicidal falling. Fatal intentional self-poisoners could to be compared to those who die by accidental overdoses and homicidal poisonings. Even if methods are not matched, more psychological autopsy studies need to be conducted with controls who have clearly died by accident and/or natural causes, as well as individuals who have clearly died by homicide.

Progress in any science depends on the reliability and validity of its measurements. As noted above, both personality disorder and suicide assessment instruments and procedures have historically been woefully inadequate. While assessment in both areas is improving, more progress is needed. At the very least, computerized assessment instruments need to be designed to control for investigator bias during interviews. The bias of family and friends' reports following a suicide can be investigated by comparing reports of families and friends before and after ambiguous deaths are ruled officially as suicide or not. In both case-based and longitudinal follow-up studies, standardized assessments with adequate documentation of responses are needed both to analyse suicidal behaviours in the present and to create adequate databases which can be re-analysed in light of future questions.

ACKNOWLEDGEMENT

The writing of this chapter was partially supported by Grant MH34486 from the National Institute of Mental Health given to the first author.

REFERENCES

Ahrens, B. and Haug, H-J. (1996) Suicidality in hospitalized patients with a primary diagnosis of personality disorder. Crisis, 17: 59–63.

Akiskal, H.S., Chen, S.E., Davis, G.C., Puzantian, V.R., Kashgarian, M. and Bolinger, J.M. (1985) Borderline: an adjective in search of a noun. Journal of Clinical Psychiatry, 46: 41–48.

Allebeck, P., Allgulander, C. and Fisher, L.D. (1988) Predictors of completed suicide in a cohort of 50,465 young men: role of personality and deviant behaviour. British Medical Journal, 297: 176–178.

Allebeck, P. and Allgulander, C. (1990) Suicide among young men: psychiatric illness, deviant behaviour and substance abuse. Acta Psychiatrica Scandinavica, 81: 565–570.

American Psychiatric Association (1980) Diagnostic and Statistical Manual of Mental Disorders, 3rd Edn. Washington, DC: American Psychiatric Association.

American Psychiatric Association (1987) Diagnostic and Statistical Manual of Mental Disorders: DSM-III-R, 3rd revised Edn. Washington, DC: American Psychiatric Association.

American Psychiatric Association (1994) Diagnostic and Statistical Manual of Mental Disorders: DSM-IV. Washington, DC: American Psychiatric Association.

Ames, A. and Molinari, V. (1994) Prevalence of personality disorders in community-living elderly. Journal of Geriatric Psychiatry and Neurology, 7: 189–194.

Black, D.W., Warrack, G. and Winokur, G. (1985) The Iowa record-linkage study: I. Suicides and accidental deaths among psychiatric patients. Archives of General Psychiatry, 42: 71–75.

Bodlund, O., Ekselius, L. and Lindstroem, E. (1993) Personality traits and disorders among psychiatric outpatients and normal subjects on the basis of the SCID screen questionnaire. Nordic Journal of Psychiatry, 47: 425–433.

Bornstein, R.F., Klein, D.N., Mallon, J.C. and Slater, J.F. (1988) Schizotypal personality disorder in an outpatient population: incidence and clinical characteristics. Journal of Clinical Psychology, 44: 322–325.

Brent, D.A., Perper, J.A., Goldstein, C.E., Kolko, D.J., Allan, M.J., Allman, C.J. and Zelenak, J.P. (1988) Risk factors for adolescent suicide: a comparison of adolescent suicide victims with suicidal inpatients. Archives of General Psychiatry, 45: 581–588.

Brent, D.A., Perper, J.A., Moritz, G., Allman, C., Friend, A., Roth, C., Schweers, J., Balach, L. and Baugher, M. (1993) Psychiatric risk factors for adolescent suicide: a case-control study. Journal of the American Academy of Child and Adolescent Psychiatry, 32: 521–529.

Brent, D.A., Johnson, B.A., Perper, J., Connolly, J., Bridge, J., Bartle, S. and Rather, C. (1994) Personality disorder, personality traits, impulsive violence, and completed suicide in adolescents. Journal of the American Academy of Child and Adolescent Psychiatry, 33: 1080–1086.

Brodsky, B.S. (1997) Characteristics of borderline personality disorder associated with suicidal behavior. American Journal of Psychiatry, 154: 1715–1719.

Brotman, A.W., Herzog, D.B. and Hamburg, P. (1988) Long-term course in 14 bulimic patients treated with psychotherapy. Journal of Clinical Psychiatry, 49: 157–160.

Cantor, C.H., Hill, M.A. and McLachlan, E.K. (1989) Suicide and related behaviour from river bridges. A clinical perspective. British Journal of Psychiatry, 155: 829–835.

Casey, P.R. (1989) Personality disorder and suicide intent. Acta Psychiatrica Scandinavica, 79: 290–295.

Casey, P.R. and Tyrer, P. (1990) Personality disorder and psychiatric illness in general practice. British Journal of Psychiatry, 156: 261–265.

Cohen, B.J., Nestadt, G., Samuels, J.F., Romanoski, A.J., McHugh, P.R. and Rabins, P.V.

(1994) Personality disorder in later life: a community study. British Journal of Psychiatry, 165: 493–499.

Cooney, J.M., Farren, C.K. and Clare, A.W. (1996) Personality disorder among first ever admissions to an Irish public and private hospital. Irish Journal of Psychological Medicine, 13: 6–8.

Corbitt, E.M., Malone, K.M., Haas, G.L. and Mann, J.J. (1996) Suicidal behavior in patients with major depression and comorbid personality disorders. Journal of Affective Disorders, 39: 61–72.

De Jong, C.A., Van den Brink, W., Harteveld, F.M. and Van der Wielen, E.G. (1993) Personality disorders in alcoholics and drug addicts. Comprehensive Psychiatry, 34: 87–94.

Dirks, B.L. (1998) Repetition of parasuicide: ICD-10 personality disorders and adversity. Acta Psychiatrica Scandinavica, 98: 208–213.

Duberstein, P.R. and Conwell, Y. (1997) Personality disorders and completed suicide: a methodological and conceptual review. Clinical Psychology: Science and Practice, 4: 359–376.

Fabrega, H., Ulrich, R., Pilkonis, P. and Mezzich, J.E. (1993) Personality disorders diagnosed at intake at a public psychiatric facility. Hospital and Community Psychiatry, 44: 159–162.

Friedman, R. (1983) History of suicidal behavior in depressed borderline inpatients. American Journal of Psychiatry, 140: 1023–1026.

Friedman, S., Jones, J.C., Chernen, L. and Barlow, D.H. (1992) Suicidal ideation and suicide attempts among patients with panic disorder: a survey of two outpatient clinics. American Journal of Psychiatry, 149: 680–685.

Fyer, M.R., Frances, A.J., Sullivan, T., Hurt, S.W. and Clarkin, J. (1988) Suicide attempts in patients with borderline personality disorder. American Journal of Psychiatry, 145: 737–739.

Garvey, M.J. and Spoden, F. (1980) Suicide attempts in antisocial personality disorder. Comprehensive Psychiatry, 21: 146–149.

Goldsmith, S.J., Fyer, M. and Frances, A. (1990) Personality and suicide. In S.J. Blumenthal and D.J. Kupfer (Eds), Suicide over the Life Cycle: Risk Factors, Assessment, and Treatment of Suicidal Patients, pp. 155–176. Washington, DC: American Psychiatric Press.

Green, M.A. and Curtis, G.C. (1988) Personality disorders in panic patients: response to termination of antipanic medication. Journal of Personality Disorders, 2: 303–314.

Gunderson, J.G., Kolb, J.E. and Austin, V. (1981) The diagnostic interview for borderline patients. American Journal of Psychiatry, 138: 896–903.

Heikkinen, M.E., Henriksson, M.M., Isometså, E.T., Marttunen, M.J., Aro, H.M. and Lönnqvist, J.K. (1997) Recent life events and suicide in personality disorders. Journal of Nervous and Mental Disease, 185: 373–381.

Henriksson, M.M., Aro, H.M., Marttunen, M.J., Heikkinen, M.E., Isometså, E.T., Kuoppasalmi, K.I. and Lönnqvist, J.K. (1993) Mental disorders and comorbidity in suicide. American Journal of Psychiatry, 150: 935–940.

Henriksson, M.M., Marttunen, M.J., Isometså, E.T., Heikkinen, M.E., Aro, H.M., Kuoppasalmi, K.I. and Lönnqvist, J.K. (1995) Mental disorders in elderly suicide. International Psychogeriatrics, 7: 275–286.

Isometså, E., Heikkinen, M., Henriksson, M., Marttunen, M., Aro, H. and Lönnqvist, J. (1997) Differences between urban and rural suicides. Acta Psychiatrica Scandinavica, 95: 297–305.

Isometså, E.T., Henriksson, M.M., Heikkinen, M.E., Aro, H.M., Marttunen, M.J., Kuoppasalmi, K.I. and Lönnqvist, J.K. (1996) Suicide among subjects with personality disorders. American Journal of Psychiatry, 153: 667–673.

Jenike, M.A., Baer, L. and Carey, R.J. (1986) Concomitant obsessive-compulsive disorder and schizotypal personality disorder. American Journal of Psychiatry, 143: 530–532.

Johnsson, F.E., Ojehagen, A. and Träskman-Bendz, L. (1996) A 5-year follow-up study of suicide attempts. Acta Psychiatrica Scandinavica, 93: 151–157.

Kehrer, C.A. and Linehan, M.M. (1996) Interpersonal and emotional problem solving skills in parasuicide among women with borderline personality disorder. Journal of Personality Disorders, 10: 153–163.

Kjelsberg, E., Eikeseth, P.H. and Dahl, A.A. (1991) Suicide in borderline patients—predictive factors. Acta Psychiatrica Scandinavica, 84: 283–287.

Kreitman, N. (1977) Parasuicide. Chichester: Wiley.

Kroll, P. and Ryan, C. (1983) The schizotypal personality on an alcohol treatment unit. Comprehensive Psychiatry, 24: 262–270.

Kullgren, G., Renberg, E. and Jacobsson, L. (1986) An empirical study of borderline personality disorder and psychiatric suicides. Journal of Nervous and Mental Disease, 174: 328–331.

Kullgren, G. (1988) Factors associated with completed suicide in borderline personality disorder. Journal of Nervous and Mental Disease, 176: 40–44.

Lenzenweger, M.F., Loranger, A.W., Korfine, L. and Neff, C. (1997) Detecting personality disorders in a nonclinical population. Application of a two-stage procedure for case identification. Archives of General Psychiatry, 54: 345–351.

Lesage, A.D., Boyer, R., Grunberg, F., Vanier, C., Morissette, R., Menard-Buteau, C. and Loyer, M. (1994). Suicide and mental disorders: a case-control study of young men. American Journal of Psychiatry, 151: 1063–1068.

Linehan, M.M. (1981) A social-behavioral analysis of suicide and parasuicide: implications for clinical assessment and treatment. In H. Glazer and J.F. Clarkin (Eds), Depression, Behavioral and Directive Intervention Strategies, pp. 229–294. New York: Garland.

Linehan, M.M., Armstrong, H.E., Suarez, A., Allmon, D. and Heard, H.L. (1991) Cognitive-behavioral treatment of chronically parasuicidal borderline patients. Archives of General Psychiatry, 48: 1060–1064.

Linehan, M.M., Heard, H.L. and Armstrong, H.E. (1993) Naturalistic follow-up of a behavioral treatment for chronically parasuicidal borderline patients. Archives of General Psychiatry, 50: 971–974.

Linehan, M.M., Tutek, D.A., Heard, H.L. and Armstrong, H.E. (1994) Interpersonal outcome of cognitive behavioral treatment for chronically suicidal borderline patients. American Journal of Psychiatry, 151: 1771–1776.

Links, P.S., Mitton, J.E. and Steiner, M. (1990) Predicting outcome for borderline personality disorder. Comprehensive Psychiatry, 31: 490–498.

Marttunen, M.J., Aro, H.M., Henriksson, M.M. and Lönnqvist, J.K. (1991) Mental disorders in adolescent suicide. DSM-III-R axes I and II diagnoses in suicides among 13- to 19-year-olds in Finland. Archives of General Psychiatry, 48: 834–839.

Marttunen, M.J., Aro, H.M., Henriksson, M.M. and Lönnqvist, J.K. (1994) Antisocial behaviour in adolescent suicide. Acta Psychiatrica Scandinavica, 89: 167–173.

Mavissakalian, M. and Hamann, M.S. (1987) DSM-III personality disorder in agoraphobia: 2. Changes with treatment. Comprehensive Psychiatry, 28: 356–361.

McGlashan, T.H. (1984) The Chestnut Lodge follow-up study. II. Long-term outcome of schizophrenia and the affective disorders. Archives of General Psychiatry, 41: 586–601.

McGlashan, T.H. (1986) The Chestnut Lodge follow-up study. III. Long-term outcome of borderline personalities. Archives of General Psychiatry, 43: 20–30.

McGlashan, T.H. (1987) Borderline personality disorder and unipolar affective disorder. Journal of Nervous and Mental Disease, 175: 467–473.

Mehlum, L., Friis, S., Irion, T., Johns, S., Katterud, S., Vaglum, P. and Vaglum, S. (1991)

Personality disorders 2–5 years after treatment: a prospective follow-up study. Acta Psychiatrica Scandinavica, 84: 72–77.
Minichiello, W.E., Baer, L. and Jenike, M.A. (1987) Schizotypal personality disorder: a poor prognostic indicator for behavior therapy in the treatment of obsessive-compulsive disorder. Journal of Anxiety Disorders, 1: 273–276.
Mischel, W. (1968) Personality and assessment. New York: Wiley.
Mischel, W. (1990) Personality dispositions revisited and revised: a view after three decades. In L. Pervin (Ed.), Handbook of Personality: Theory and Research, pp. 111–134. New York: Guilford.
Modestin, J. (1989) Completed suicide in personality disordered inpatients. Journal of Personality Disorders, 3: 113–121.
Modestin, J., Oberson, B. and Erni, T. (1997) Possible correlates of DSM-III-R personality disorders. Acta Psychiatrica Scandinavica, 96: 424–430.
Modestin, J. and Villiger, C. (1989) Follow-up study on borderline versus nonborderline personality disorders. Comprehensive Psychiatry, 30: 236–244.
Molinari, V. and Marmion, J. (1993) Personality disorders in geropsychiatric outpatients. Psychological Reports, 73: 256–258.
Molinari, V., Ames, A. and Essa, M. (1994) Prevalence of personality disorders in two geropsychiatric inpatient units. Journal of Geriatric Psychiatry and Neurology, 7: 209–215.
Oldham, J.M. and Skodol, A.E. (1991) Personality disorders in the public sector. Hospital and Community Psychiatry, 42: 481–487.
Ottoson, H., Bodlund, O., Ekselius, L., Grann, M., von Knorring, L., Kullgren, G., Lindstroem, E. and Soederberg, S. (1998) DSM-IV and ICD-10 personality disorders: a comparison of a self-report questionnaire (DIP-Q) with a structured interview. European Psychiatry, 13: 246–253.
Paris, J., Brown, R. and Nowlis, D. (1987) Long-term follow-up of borderline patients in a general hospital. Comprehensive Psychiatry, 28: 530–535.
Paris, J., Nowlis, D. and Brown, R. (1989) Predictors of suicide in borderline personality disorder. Canadian Journal of Psychiatry, 34: 8–9.
Paris, J. (1990) Completed suicide in borderline personality disorder. Psychiatric Annals, 20: 19–21.
Pfohl, B., Stangl, D. and Zimmerman, M. (1984) The implications of DSM-III personality disorders for patients with major depression. Journal of Affective Disorders, 7: 309–318.
Pilkonis, P. and Frank, E. (1988) Personality pathology in recurrent depression: nature, prevalence, and relationship to treatment response. American Journal of Psychiatry, 145: 435–441.
Poldrugo, F. and Forti, B. (1988) Personality disorders and alcoholism treatment outcome. Drug and Alcohol Dependence, 21: 171–176.
Pope, H.G., Janas, J.M., Hudson, J.I., Cohen, B.M. and Gunderson, J.G. (1983) The validity of DSM-III borderline personality disorder. Archives of General Psychiatry, 40: 23–30.
Reich, J. (1988) DSM-III personality disorders and the outcome of treated panic disorder. American Journal of Psychiatry, 145: 1149–1152.
Rich, C.L., Young, D. and Fowler, R.C. (1986) San Diego Suicide Study. I. Young vs. old subjects. Archives of General Psychiatry, 43: 577–582.
Rich, C.L. and Runeson, B.S. (1992) Similarities in diagnostic comorbidity between suicide among young people in Sweden and the United States. Acta Psychiatrica Scandinavica, 86: 335–339.
Rounsaville, B.J., Kranzler, H.R., Ball, S., Tennen, H., Poling, J. and Triffleman, E. (1998) Personality disorders in substance abusers: relation to substance use. Journal of Nervous and Mental Disease, 186: 87–95.

Roy, A. and Draper, R. (1995) Suicide among psychiatric hospital in-patients. Psychological Medicine, 25: 199–202.
Runeson, B. (1989) Mental disorder in youth suicide. DSM-III-R Axes I and II. Acta Psychiatrica Scandinavica, 79: 490–497.
Runeson, B. and Beskow, J. (1991) Borderline personality disorder in young Swedish suicides. Journal of Nervous and Mental Disease, 179: 153–156.
Shaffer, D., Gould, M.S., Fisher, P., Trautman, P., Moreau, D., Kleinman, M. and Flory, M. (1996) Psychiatric diagnosis in child and adolescent suicide. Archives of General Psychiatry, 53: 339–348.
Shafii, M., Carrigan, S., Whittinghill, J.R. and Derrick, A. (1985) Psychological autopsy of completed suicide in children and adolescents. American Journal of Psychiatry, 142: 1061–1064.
Shawcross, C.R. and Tyrer, P. (1985) Influence of personality on response to monoamine oxidase inhibitors and tricyclic antidepressants. Journal of Psychiatric Research, 19: 557–562.
Shearer, S.L., Peters, C.P., Quaytman, M.S. and Wadman, B.E. (1988) Intent and lethality of suicide attempts among female borderline inpatients. American Journal of Psychiatry, 145: 1424–1427.
Snyder, S., Pitts, W.M. and Pokorny, A.D. (1986) Selected behavioral features of patients with borderline personality traits. Suicide and Life-Threatening Behavior, 16: 28–39.
Soloff, P.H., Lis, J.A., Kelly, T., Cornelius, J. and Ulrich, R. (1994) Risk factors for suicidal behavior in borderline personality disorder. American Journal of Psychiatry, 151: 1316–1323.
Stone, M.H. (1989) Long-term follow-up of narcissistic/borderline patients. Psychiatric Clinics of North America, 12: 621–641.
Stone, M.H. (1990) The fate of borderline patients: Successful outcome and psychiatric practice. New York: Guilford.
Thompson, L.W., Gallagher, D. and Czirr, R. (1988) Personality disorder and outcome in the treatment of late-life depression. Journal of Geriatric Psychiatry, 21: 133–146.
Tucker, L., Bauer, S.F., Wagner, S., Harlam, D and Sher, I. (1987) Long-term hospitalization of borderline patients: a descriptive outcome study. American Journal of Psychiatry, 144: 1443–1448.
Turner, R.M. (1987) The effects of personality disorder diagnosis on the outcome of social anxiety symptom reduction. Journal of Personality Disorders, 1: 136–143.
Ucok, A., Karaveli, D., Kundakci, T. and Yazici, O. (1998) Comorbidity of personality disorders with bipolar mood disorders. Comprehensive Psychiatry, 39: 72–74.
Weissman, M.M. (1993) The epidemiology of personality disorders: a 1990 update. Journal of Personality Disorders, Suppl., Spring: 44–62.
Widiger, T.A. and Frances, A. (1987) Definitions and diagnoses: a brief response to Morey and McNamara. Journal of Abnormal Psychology, 96: 286–287.
World Health Organization (1967) Manual of the International Statistical Classification of Diseases, Injuries, and Causes of Death. Based on the Recommendations of the Eighth Revision Conference, 1965, and Adopted by the Nineteenth World Health Assembly. Geneva: World Health Organization.
World Health Organization (1977) Manual of the International Statistical Classification of Diseases, Injuries, and Causes of Death. Based on the Recommendations of the Ninth Revision Conference, 1975, and Adopted by the Twenty-ninth World Health Assembly. Geneva: World Health Organization.
World Health Organization (1993) The ICD-10 Classification of Mental and Behavioural Disorders: Diagnostic Criteria for Research. Geneva: World Health Organization.
Zisook, S., Goff, A., Sledge, P. and Shuchter, S.R. (1994) Reported suicidal behavior and current suicidal ideation in a psychiatric outpatient clinic. Annals of Clinical Psychiatry, 6: 27–31.

Chapter 11

Psychiatric Aspects of Suicidal Behaviour: Anxiety Disorders

Christer Allgulander
Karolinska Institutet, Huddinge University Hospital, Huddinge, Sweden

Abstract

Pathological anxiety plays an important role in suicidal behaviour, independently and as a co-morbid symptom. Anxiety increases the risk of suicide in psychiatric disorders, imminently and over the life span. There is a risk for suicidal behaviour in anxiety disorders *per se*, demonstrated in severe cases of anxiety neurosis, panic disorder, social phobia, post-traumatic stress disorder and obsessive-compulsive disorder. Pathological anxiety in all its forms is amenable to treatment. The best our profession can do to prevent suicide is to offer such treatments and continue to improve them. Due to the low base rate of suicide and confounding factors in long-term studies, documenting with a degree of certainty that anxiolytic treatment lowers the risk of completed suicide requires very large case-control studies.

PATHOLOGICAL ANXIETY

Anxiety can be pathognomonic of a primary disorder, it may be a cardinal symptom of depression, substance abuse or psychosis, and it may be the acute response to threat, loss or conflict. It can be measured and classified, it can be part of everyday life, and it may trigger suicide.

In reviewing conditions predisposing to suicide, Miles (1977) pointed to the diagnostic ambiguities in determining a suicide rate in neurotics. He tentatively inferred that "patients diagnosed neurotic are at substantial risk of suicide". Pokorny (1979) wrote that "one of the common oversimplifications about suicide is that it always springs from depressive mental illness". In reviewing the risk for

The International Handbook of Suicide and Attempted Suicide. Edited by K. Hawton and K. van Heeringen.

completed suicide, he noted a minimal emphasis in the literature on its relation to anxiety, and that anxiety neurosis, with or without concurrent substance abuse, conferred a substantially increased risk of suicide in comparison with that of the general population: 100–300 vs. 15–20 per 100,000 per year. The rate was not as high as in affective disorder, alcoholism and schizophrenia. With the shift of cases from the psychoneurosis category into that of affective disorders in DSM-III, he thought it likely that the suicide rate in the residual category of anxiety disorders would be lower in future studies.

Are we in a better position than Miles and Pokorny 20 years ago to assess the suicide risk in anxiety disorders? Yes, if we consider the diagnostic evolution since that time, and the potential of new large and representative study samples. There has been a transition from the ambiguous term "neurotic disorders" into clinically relevant, although overlapping, categories of anxiety disorders that are largely separate from depression, albeit under the influence of maladaptive personality traits. Statistical precision has also been enhanced by the use of exposure time, controlling for age and sex, comparing with matched control samples, and applying computerized analyses which permit multivariate assessment of risk. The efforts to find effective pharmacotherapies and psychotherapies for anxiety disorders have helped to create homogeneous patient groups amenable to treatment and follow-up. The pandemic of anxiety disorders in the general population, documented in American and European surveys, calls for reinforced efforts to assess the consequences of morbidity and the utility of treatment, including the reduction of suicide risk.

This review is structured by the type of study population, and by old and new nosology, to cope with the ambiguity that stems from selection bias and the evolution of classification in clinical samples (Berkson, 1946). It includes relevant studies published until 1998.

MORTALITY STUDIES IN CLINICAL PATIENTS WITH NEUROSIS

In a 10–12-year follow-up study of 259 patients with "*anxiety states*" treated at the Maudsley Hospital in London between 1924 and 1926, three had died by suicide (Harris, 1938). Wheeler and colleagues (1950) reported on 173 cases of *neurocirculatory asthenia* enrolled in a study before 1928. Two had died by suicide. The overall death rate was lower than expected, probably because the cases were screened for the presence of other diseases. Among 126 outpatients with *neurosis* treated in Zurich between 1932 and 1939, there were nine deaths in the follow-up period, of which four were suicides (Ernst, 1959).

In Birmingham, UK, the occurrence of 20 deaths among 166 *neurotic* patients treated in 1959, mostly by suicide, accounted for a mortality rate three times higher than expected (Sims, 1973). The results of another larger study in Birmingham revealed the suicide rate among 1,428 *neurotic* inpatients treated between 1959 and 1968 (excluding substance abusers) to be five times greater than expected (Sims and Prior, 1982, 1985). Most of the deaths occurred within 4 years after hospital admission and among those patients whose condition at the time of discharge had been rated as unsatisfactory (Sims, 1984). In a Scottish study, the number of deaths among first-admitted *neurotic* patients during a 5-year period in the 1960s was twice the expected rate, accounted for by suicides (Innes and Millar, 1970). In Surrey, UK, Rosenberg (1968) reviewed the case histories of 144 inpatients with *anxiety neurosis*, and 144 with *obsessional neurosis*. He found 18 and nine cases of attempted suicide in the two groups, and zero and three cases of suicide over a 1–26 year period. Another study of the outcome of 126 inpatients in Newcastle between 1960 and 1965 with *affective/anxiety disorders* suggested that mortality associated with anxiety alone was greater among men than women (Kerr et al, 1969). In a 4-year study in Sweden, the death rate among 101 patients with *mixed neuroses* treated in 1962 was not higher than expected (Rorsman, 1974). Among 16,147 inpatients identified in Israel in 1978, and followed up for 5 years, the standardized mortality ratio (SMR) for suicide in those with neurosis was 9.26 ($p < 0.001$) (Zilber et al, 1989). Other studies of psychiatric inpatient populations did not find, or did not elucidate, an excessive suicide rate in *neuroses* (Giel et al, 1978; Fegersten Saugstad and Ödegård, 1979; Wood et al, 1985).

In 1966, the case register of Monroe County, New York, recorded 233 deaths among outpatients being treated for *neurosis*, twice the expected mortality rate (Babigian and Odoroff, 1969). In St. Louis, Missouri, Martin and colleagues (1985) found two unnatural deaths after 6–12 years among 60 outpatients with *primary anxiety neurosis* during 1967–1969, compared to an expected number of 0.45 (SMR 4.44), a not statistically significant difference. In Iowa City, Black and colleagues (1985) compared the number of deaths among *neurotic* patients (excluding those with depression) discharged from inpatient care with the number of deaths among control subjects. Of the 348 patients discharged, 14 died within the monitoring period, while the expected death rate was 4.68. Among 54 suicides occurring within 2 years, two had been diagnosed with *neurosis* (Winokur and Black, 1987).

The survival probability and causes of death before the age of 70 years were analysed among 3,302 inpatients with ICD-8 "*pure anxiety neurosis*" in Stockholm, Sweden (Allgulander and Lavori, 1991). There were 21 verified and eight undetermined suicides among the men (expected 8.7 and 3.8), and 26 verified and eight undetermined suicides among the women (expected 11.3 and 3.6), which constituted a significant two-fold excess in both sexes. The suicide risk persisted into old age (71+ years of age) in both sexes (Allgulander and Lavori, 1993). When the suicide risk was compared with the entire cohort of Stockholm psychiatric inpatients, the relative risk for suicide among those with *neurotic disorders* in a saturated proportional hazards general linear model was 1.48 (95% CI, 1.24–1.77) (Allgulander et al, 1992). Having more than one diagnosed psychiatric condition conferred an additional risk of 1.41 compared to the entire patient population ($p < 0.0001$).

Another study of all 9,912 psychiatric inpatients in Sweden between 1973 and 1983 yielded a SMR for suicide before the age of 45 years of 6.7 (95% CI, 4.9–8.4) in men and 4.9 (95% CI, 3.2–6.6) in women with ICD-8 *anxiety neurosis* (Allgulander, 1994). The corresponding SMRs were slightly lower among older men and slightly higher in older women, and overall lower than among patients with depressive neurosis. The risk was substantially increased in the 3 months following discharge from the hospital, but also remained significantly elevated after 8 years of observation.

MORTALITY IN COMMUNITY SAMPLES WITH NEUROSIS OR ANXIETY

Keehn and colleagues (1974) studied the case histories of 9,813 US military inductees who had been disqualified in 1944 because of *psychoneurosis*, 3,407 of whom were classified as anxiety neurosis. In reviewing the causes of 1,140 subsequent deaths among those disqualified, Keehn's group noted that the number of deaths due to circulatory or other natural causes was not greater than expected, but that the overall death rate was 1.2 times greater. Accounting for the higher mortality were alcoholism, suicide, homicide, and trauma. The factors by which expected mortality was exceeded, by cause of death, were alcoholism, 6.5; suicide, 3.2; homicide, 2.6; and trauma, 1.6. In another military study of 15,924 male twins, 2,186 of whom were diagnosed with *neurosis*, there were 24 deaths due to suicide vs. an expected 14.16 (SMR 1.77; $p < 0.005$) (Kendler, 1986). No genetic contribution was found with the small number of suicides.

In a birth cohort of all 50,465 young men conscripted for military service in Sweden in 1969–1970, 895 were subsequently treated in inpatient care with a *neurotic disorder*, among whom there were 48 suicides (5.4%) up to 1983 (Allebeck and Allgulander, 1990a). Controlling for social and behavioural characteristics at the time of conscription, the odds ratio of suicide in those men with neurotic disorders, compared with the rest of the cohort, was 9.3 (95% CI, 6.5–13.4). A lower suicide rate (1.1%) was found among those 895 receiving this diagnosis at the time of conscription, which illustrates that the more severe the condition, the higher the likelihood of suicide (Allebeck and Allgulander, 1990b).

In the Canadian Stirling County study (1952–1968), there were 10 deaths among 42 community subjects with *self-reported anxiety*, i.e. corresponding to the expected rate (Murphy et al, 1987). Another community study in New Haven, Connecticut, found no increase in the death rate of elderly subjects with chronic or recent anxiety disorders (Livingston Bruce and Leaf, 1989). The Swedish Lundby community study found no suicides between 1972 and 1992 among 195 subjects diagnosed with *anxiety disorder* (Gräsbeck et al, 1996).

In a British cohort of 3,591 births in 1946, Neeleman and colleagues (1998) analysed 167 deaths in people between 16 and 50 years of age, among which 11 were regarded as suicide. Self-rated *emotional instability* at age 13 was associated with an odds ratio for suicide of 2.0 (95% CI, 1.2–3.6).

In two random samples of the general Swedish population interviewed about health and social risk factors in 1980 and 1981, there were 23 deaths between 1980 and 1984 among those reporting *severe anxiety* vs. eight expected (95% CI of difference, 5–25) (Allgulander, 1989).

These community samples were interviewed without operationalized diagnostic criteria, and with diagnoses derived by laymen or from medical records. Hidden in the data may be subjects who would qualify for an anxiety syndrome in the ICD-10 or DSM-IV nosologies, as in the case of the Lundby Study by Gräsbeck and colleagues (1996). Very large samples would be required to estimate suicide risk in general population samples, due to the low base rate of suicide.

SUICIDAL BEHAVIOUR AND DSM-III NOSOLOGY IN THE COMMUNITY

In the Munich Follow-up Study, 481 subjects were interviewed in 1981, among whom 53 had *panic attacks* and 66 suffered from *phobias*, according to DSM-III (Bronisch and Wittchen, 1994). Suicide attempts were reported by seven and six of panic and phobic subjects, respectively, compared to six among 316 healthy subjects.

A survey in 1987 of a sample of 825 adults in Reykjavik, Iceland, yielded 3% with thoughts about committing suicide in the past week (Vilhjalmsson et al, 1998). Such thoughts were reported more often (15%) by those scoring at least 4 on a 10-item *anxiety* scale from the SCL-90 checklist, vs. 0.4% among those scoring <4 ($p < 0.001$).

A random sample of 229 of the 1,397 suicides in Finland in 1987 included 25 subjects with a DSM-III-R diagnosis of *anxiety disorder*, of which only two were primary and none was a panic disorder (Henriksson et al, 1993). In a consecutive series of young suicides (median age 23 years) in Gothenburg, Sweden, key informants reported that 31 of 53 had childhood psychiatric symptoms (Runeson, 1998). Anxious symptoms (onychophagia, enuresis nocturna, phobias, nervousness and insomnia) or extreme shyness were reported in 14 cases by the age of 10 years.

The need for more research into suicidality among the young was pointed out in a review by Mattison (1988). A New York random community sample of 1,285 young subjects aged 9–17 years were diagnostically interviewed (Gould et al, 1998). Mood, *anxiety*, and substance abuse independently increased the risk of suicide attempts, after controlling for sociodemographic characteristics. *Panic attacks* and aggressiveness also predicted suicide risk.

Elderly bereaved individuals in Pittsburgh with suicidal ideation were found to have higher symptomatic levels of depression, hopelessness, complicated grief and *anxiety*, as well as lower levels of perceived social support, than those with no suicidal ideation (Szanto et al, 1997). The underlying bereavement appears to have driven these ideations.

A total of 5,995 adult twins in the general population, Australia, were interviewed in 1992–1993 by telephone for DSM-III-R diagnoses and suicidality assessment (Statham et al, 1998). Serious suicide attempts were recalled by 2.0% of women and 1.7% of men. Almost all reported being depressed at the time of the attempt. Two-thirds had a maternal history of depression, and one-third a paternal history of depression and of alcoholism. Controlling for age and gender, the odds ratio (OR) of a serious suicide attempt among those with a history of *panic disorder* was 8.5 (95% CI, 5.0–14.5). The same odds ratio for women with *social phobia* was 15.6 (95% CI, 8.0–30.3) and for men with social phobia 1.4 (95% CI, 0.2–10.7). The ORs remained significantly high for panic disorder in men and women, and for social phobia in women when other psychopathology was controlled for. The estimated heritability of suicidal thoughts and behaviour was 45% (95% CI, 33–51%), unaccounted for by psychiatric, personality and sociodemographic variables.

In a cross-national study of community samples in 1990, the OR of reported suicide attempts in US subjects with *social phobia* as a co-morbid condition was 2.2 (95% CI, 1.4–3.6), compared to subjects with other psychiatric disorders (Weissman et al, 1996). In Edmonton, Canada, the OR was 1.9 (0.7–4.7); in Puerto Rico 2.2 (1.2–4.1); and in Korea 4.1 (1.6–10.1). Among 112 uncomplicated *social phobics* in four urban areas in the USA interviewed between 1980 and 1984 (the NIMH–ECA study), suicide attempts were reported by 0.9% vs. 15.7% in 249 social phobics with co-morbid conditions, and by 1.1% of those with no diagnosed disorder (Schneier et al, 1992). Among all of the 123 social phobics in the study centre in Durham, North Carolina, 12% had attempted suicide, compared to 8.3% of respondents without social phobia (OR 12.8: 95% CI, 7.1–23.1) (Davidson et al, 1993).

Post-traumatic stress disorder was found in 1.3% of the Durham, North Carolina, NIMH–ECA sample of 2,985 community subjects (Davidson et al, 1991). Suicide attempts were reported in 20% of these cases, compared to 0.8% of the healthy respondents (OR 14.9; 95% CI, 5.1–43.7). In a national sample of 1,198 male Vietnam veterans in the USA, suicides attempts were recorded in 44 individuals (3.7%) up to 1988 (Fontana and Rosenheck, 1995). The explanatory variables accounted for only 13% of the variance, among which psychiatric disorders, including post-traumatic stress disorder, were thought to be most likely as a risk factor. Suicide attempts were not predicted by childhood victimization or combat exposure in a study of 177 veteran inpatients with post-traumatic stress disorder (Hiley-Young et al, 1995).

Among the 18,571 respondents in the NIMH–ECA study, 140 were diagnosed with DSM-III *obsessive-compulsive disorder*, and 266 with obsessive-compulsive disorder as a co-morbid condition (mostly other anxiety disorders, alcohol/drug abuse or depression) (Hollander et al, 1997). Uncomplicated obsessive-compulsive disorder increased the risk of suicide attempts to 3.2 (95% CI, 1.3–8.1) compared to healthy respondents. As a co-morbid condition, the OR was 2.2 (95% CI, 1.5–3.2) compared with cases with other psychiatric disorders without obsessive-compulsive disorder. Even after removal of those with major depression or agoraphobia, the OR for suicide attempts in co-morbid obsessive-compulsive disorder was 3.7 (95% CI, 2.1–6.6).

SUICIDAL BEHAVIOUR AND DSM-III NOSOLOGY IN CLINICAL PATIENTS

A consecutive series of 129 cases under 25 years of age, hospitalized for serious suicide attempts in Christchurch, New Zealand, was matched with controls from the general population and were interviewed for DSM-III-R disorders (Beautrais et al, 1998). Current *anxiety disorders* were associated with an OR for suicide attempt of 3.1 (95% CI, 1.3–7.4; $p < 0.01$). However, a multivariate model showed that these anxiety disorders were co-morbid with affective, substance use and antisocial disorders.

Among 116 suicide attempters and 93 with suicidal ideation aged 18–37 years entering an intervention program in Texas, there was a total of 842 current DSM-III-R diagnoses derived by computer-assisted interviews (Rudd et al, 1993). Among these diagnoses were 184 depressive disorders, 90 alcohol abuse, 41 bipolar disorder, eight panic disorder, 79 social phobia, 66 post-traumatic stress disorder, 29 agoraphobia, 14 generalized anxiety disorder, six obsessive-compulsive disorder, and 13 cases with no psychiatric diagnosis. Panic disorder was less influential as a co-morbid diagnosis in suicide attempts than phobias, post-traumatic stress disorder, obsessive-compulsive disorder and generalized anxiety disorder.

Using the Karolinska Scales of Personality, high scores on somatic anxiety, psychic anxiety and muscular tension were found in a sample of 54 patients hospitalized after suicide attempts (Nordström et al, 1996). Five patients committed suicide within 3 years, an act statistically associated with low CSF levels of 5-HIAA, high somatic anxiety and impulsivity, and low socialization.

Adolescents aged 12–19, hospitalized after a suicide attempt in Israel, exhibited higher *trait anxiety*, independent of concurrent depression, than age-matched psychiatric control subjects without suicide attempts (Ohring et al, 1996). *State anxiety* was shown to influence suicide risk by way of depression. *Negative emotions* were similarly found more often among 51 adolescents hospitalized in Israel for suicide attempts than among non-suicidal psychiatric inpatients or community controls (Stein et al, 1998). Multiple attempts appeared to be associated with self-rated anger.

Immigrants to Sweden are over-represented in suicide statistics, and 149 refugees with a history of exposure to severe trauma were referred for psychiatric diagnosis and assessment of suicide risk (Ferrada-Noli et al, 1998). Post-traumatic stress disorder was diagnosed in 117 individuals (79%), among whom 27 reported suicide attempts.

Among 24 women seeking treatment for having been *sexually assaulted* both as children and as adults, 18 were diagnosed with post-traumatic stress disorder,

10 with generalized anxiety disorder, eight with social phobia, and six with panic disorder (Cloitre et al, 1997). Ten women reported a suicide attempt, six of which occurred before the adult assault.

Among 507 outpatients with *alcohol dependence* in France, suicide attempts were reported significantly more often among those with social phobia (33% vs. 18% of non-attempters) and panic disorder (31% vs. 15%), but not with generalized anxiety disorder (49% vs. 52%) (Chignon et al, 1998).

PANIC DISORDER

With the shift towards the DSM-III classification after 1980, based on operationalized criteria, new efforts were made in determining the consequences of pathological anxiety, including the risk of suicide. Several studies in the USA have focused on panic disorder.

Among patients treated for anxiety in Iowa City between 1925 and 1955, 113 were rated by means of a chart review to have suffered from *panic disorder*. These patients were followed up in 1981, by which time 18 had died (from all causes), yielding an SMR of 2.95 among men and 1.84 among women, the excess attributable to unnatural causes and to circulatory system disease in men (Coryell et al, 1982). A second study of 155 outpatients with *anxiety neurosis*, most of whom had panic attacks, replicated this finding (Coryell et al, 1986).

A report of increased suicidal ideation and suicide attempts in 254 subjects with current or past DSM-III panic disorder in the NIMH–ECA study caused controversy (Weissman et al, 1989). Compared with healthy subjects, the OR for suicide attempts in panic disorder was 18 (95% CI, 12.2–26.6). It was not influenced by the co-existence of major depression or substance abuse. Among the panic disorder subjects, however, there was an additional risk of suicide attempts among those with concurrent substance abuse. In a subsequent analysis, uncomplicated panic disorder had an OR for suicide attempt of 5.4 (95% CI, 1.9–15.4), similar to that of uncomplicated major depression, which was 5.1 (95% CI, 3.2–8.3) (Johnson et al, 1990). Beck and colleagues (1991) found no suicide attempt among 73 consecutive outpatients with a SCID (Structural Clinical Interview for DSM-IV)-derived current diagnosis of primary panic disorder without agoraphobia, and only one case among 78 patients with concurrent agoraphobia. Cox and colleagues (1994) found a rate of self-reported suicide attempts similar to that of Weissman and colleagues in a set of 106 outpatients with DSM-III-R panic disorder, 43 of whom had additional diagnoses which did not appear to increase the likelihood of suicide attempts.

Noyes and colleagues (1991), who recorded five suicide attempts and three completed suicides in 74 panic disorder subjects after 7 years, found more severe psychopathology among those with a history of suicidal behaviour. Friedman and colleagues (1992) found, in an outpatient chart review, that 25% of panic disorder subjects with concurrent borderline personality disorder had a history of suicide attempt, compared to 2% of those with only panic disorder. Attempters described their lives as chaotic and/or empty, exhibited other self-destructive behaviour, and showed affective instability. Reviewing the literature on suicide risk in panic disorder, Noyes (1991) proposed that suicide was not triggered by panic attacks *per se*, but by such stressors as interpersonal loss.

Among 100 referrals with DSM-III-R panic disorder to an anxiety clinic in Paris, 42 had attempted suicide, all but four of whom had other lifetime disorders as well, particularly major depression in 30 cases and substance abuse in 19 cases (Lepine et al, 1993). Eleven of the cases attempted suicide before the onset of panic disorder. No patient with singular panic disorder attempted suicide. Suicidal behaviour occurred only among subjects suffering from panic disorder with concurrent depressive disorders in a prospective study in Providence, Rhode Island (Warshaw et al, 1995). Although thoughts about death and dying were more common among 50 "pure" panic disorder subjects with no other psychiatric diagnoses than in matched healthy controls in Maastricht, Holland, there was no increase in suicide attempts or thoughts about suicide (Overbeek et al, 1998).

Panic disorder was found in 108 of 441 (24%) patients with chest pain seeking ambulatory emergency treatment in Montreal, 62 of whom had other affective/anxiety disorders as well, and 47 of whom had a documented history of coronary artery disease (Fleet et al, 1996). In the preceding week, 25% of the patients with panic disorder had suicidal thoughts, as assessed by means of the Beck Depression Inventory, compared to 5% of those without panic disorder. These thoughts were not attributable to concurrent depression. Undiagnosed borderline personality disorder was not a likely confounder, according to the authors. In a subsequent multivariate analysis of risk, the two diagnoses associated with suicidal ideation were panic disorder without co-morbid conditions (OR, 4.3; 95% CI, 2.1–8.8) and dysthymia (OR, 10.0; 95% CI, 4.0–24.8) (Fleet et al, 1997).

CONCLUSIONS

Pathological anxiety plays an important role in suicidal behaviour, independently and as a co-morbid symptom. Anxiety increases the risk of suicide in psychiatric disorders, imminently and over the life span. There is a risk for suicidal behaviour in anxiety disorders *per se*, demonstrated in severe cases of anxiety neurosis, panic disorder, social phobia, post-traumatic stress disorder, and obsessive-compulsive disorder.

Anxiety appears to be a necessary, although not sufficient, prerequisite for suicidal behaviour which is determined by multiple conditions. Pathological anxiety is amenable to treatment. The best our profession can do to prevent suicide is to make such treatments available and continue to improve them.

Fawcett and colleagues (1997) point to the importance of distinguishing acute from chronic suicide risk. Two of their prospective studies showed that anxiety, manifesting itself in severe panic attacks, psychic anxiety, anxious ruminations and agitation, was observed in a almost all depressed patients who subsequently completed suicide (Fawcett et al, 1997). In addition to anhedonia and hopelessness, a pattern of clinically observable dimensions was found which characterized patients at high risk of suicide within weeks and up to a year. He suggested that rapidly acting anxiolytics may reduce this imminent suicide risk.

One can not but agree with his position, although psychopharmacological or psychotherapeutic intervention has not yet been demonstrated to reduce the rate of suicide in any category of patients, with the possible exception of bipolar disorder. This may be beyond the realm of reliable statistical testing, due to the low rate of suicide even in high-risk groups.

To assess the efficacy of anxiolytic treatment in reducing suicidal behaviour would require large prospective long-term studies of well-defined cases, using a common nosology and outcome measures. Such databases exist, e.g. the Harvard/Brown Anxiety Disorders Research Program, the Danish Institute of Psychiatric Demography, and the Kaiser–Permanente health maintenance organization, and several emerging practitioner networks.

A novel means of classification may stem from current efforts to define heritable phenotypes for genetic studies of anxiety (Smoller and Tsuang, 1998). Current knowledge points to defining an anxiety diathesis by selecting cases on the basis of early onset, temperamental extremes (behavioural inhibition, emotionality, harm avoidance), multiple affected family members, concordant and discordant twins and siblings, and experimental provocation of anxiety responses.

REFERENCES

Allebeck, P. and Allgulander, C. (1990a) Suicide among young men: psychiatric illness, deviant behaviour and substance abuse. Acta Psychiatrica Scandinavica, 81: 565–570.

Allebeck, P. and Allgulander, C. (1990b) Psychiatric diagnoses as predictors of suicide. A comparison of diagnoses at conscription and in psychiatric care in a cohort of 50,465 young men. British Journal of Psychiatry, 157: 339–344.

Allgulander, C. (1989) Psychoactive drug use in a general population sample, Sweden: correlates with perceived health, psychiatric diagnoses, and mortality in an automated record-linkage study. American Journal of Public Health, 79: 1006–1010.

Allgulander, C. (1994) Suicide and mortality patterns in anxiety neurosis and depressive neurosis. Archives of General Psychiatry, 51: 708–712.

Allgulander, C., Allebeck, P., Przybeck, T.R. and Rice, J.P. (1992) Risk of suicide by psychiatric diagnosis in Stockholm County. A longitudinal study of 80,970 psychiatric inpatients. European Archives of Psychiatry and Clinical Neuroscience, 241: 323–326.

Allgulander, C. and Lavori, P.W. (1991) Excess mortality among 3,302 patients with "pure" anxiety neurosis. Archives of General Psychiatry, 48: 599–602.

Allgulander, C. and Lavori, P.W. (1993) Causes of death among 936 elderly patients with "pure" anxiety neurosis in Stockholm County, Sweden, and in patients with depressive neurosis or both diagnosis. Comprehensive Psychiatry, 34: 299–302.

Babigian, H.M. and Odoroff, C.L. (1969) The mortality experience of a population with psychiatric illness. American Journal of Psychiatry, 126: 470–480.

Beautrais, A.L., Joyce, P.R. and Mulder, R.T. (1998) Psychiatric illness in a New Zealand sample of young people making serious suicide attempts. New Zealand Medical Journal, 111: 44–48.

Beck, A.T., Steer, R.A., Sanderson, W.C. and Madland Skeie, T. (1991) Panic disorder and suicidal ideation and behavior: discrepant findings in psychiatric outpatients. American Journal of Psychiatry, 148: 1195–1199.

Berkson, J. (1946) Limitations of the application of four-fold table analysis to hospital data. Biometrics, 2: 47–53.

Black, D.W., Warrack, G. and Winokur, G. (1985) The Iowa record-linkage study. III. Excess mortality among patients with "functional" disorders. Archives of General Psychiatry, 42: 82–88.

Bronisch, T. and Wittchen, H.-U. (1994) Suicidal ideation and suicide attempts: comorbidity with depression, anxiety disorders, and substance abuse disorder. European Archives of Psychiatry and Clinical Neuroscience, 244: 93–98.

Chignon, J.M., Cortes, M.J., Martin, P. and Chabannes, J.P. (1998) Tentative de suicide et dépendance alcoolique: résultats d'une enquête épidémiologique. L'Encéphale, 24: 347–354.

Cloitre, M., Scarvalone, P. and Difede, J. (1997) Posttraumatic stress disorder, self- and interpersonal dysfunction among sexually retraumatized women. Journal of Traumatic Stress, 10: 437–452.

Coryell, W., Noyes, R. and Clancy, C. (1982) Excess mortality in panic disorder. Archives of General Psychiatry, 39: 701–703.

Coryell, W., Noyes, R. and House, J.D. (1986) Mortality among outpatients with anxiety disorders. American Journal of Psychiatry, 143: 508–510.

Cox, B.J., Direnfeld, D.M., Swinson, R.P. and Norton, G.R. (1994) Suicidal ideation and suicide attempts in panic disorder and social phobia. American Journal of Psychiatry, 151: 882–887.

Davidson, J.R.T., Hughes, D., Blazer, D.H. and George, L.K. (1991) Post-traumatic stress disorder in the community: an epidemiological study. Psychological Medicine, 21: 713–721.

Davidson, J.R.T., Hughes, D.L., George, L.K. and Blazer, D.G. (1993) The epidemiology of social phobia: findings from the Duke Epidemiological Catchment Area Study. Psychological Medicine, 23: 709–718.

Ernst, K. (1959) Die Prognosen der Neurosen. Monographien aus dem Gesamtgebiete der Neurologie und Psychiatrie. Heidelberg: Springer Verlag.

Fawcett, J., Busch, K.A., Jacobs, D., Kravitz, H.M. and Fogg, L. (1997) Suicide: a four-pathway clinical–biochemical model. Annals of the New York Academy of Sciences, 836: 288–301.

Fegersten Saugstad, L. and Ödegård, Ö. (1979) Mortality in psychiatric hospitals in Norway, 1950–1974. Acta Psychiatrica Scandinavica, 59: 431–447.

Ferrada-Noli, M., Åsberg, M., Ormstad, K., Lundin, T. and Sundbom, E. (1998) Suicidal behavior after severe trauma. Part I: PTSD diagnoses, psychiatric comorbidity, and assessments of suicidal behavior. Journal of Traumatic Stress, 11: 103–111.

Fleet, R.P., Dupuis, G., Marchand, A., Burelle, D., Arsenault, A. and Beitman, B.D. (1996) Panic disorder in emergency department chest pain patients: prevalence, comorbidity, suicidal ideation, and physician recognition. American Journal of Medicine, 101: 371–380.

Fleet, R.P., Dupuis, G., Kaczorowski, J., Marchand, A. and Beitman, B.D. (1997) Suicidal ideation in emergency department chest pain patients: panic disorder a risk factor. American Journal of Emergency Medicine, 15: 345–349.

Fontana, A. and Rosenheck, R. (1995) Attempted suicide among Vietnam veterans: a model of etiology in a community sample. American Journal of Psychiatry, 152: 102–109.

Friedman, S., Jones, J.C., Chernen, L. and Barlow, D.H. (1992) Suicidal ideation and suicide attempts among patients with panic disorder: a survey of two outpatient clinics. American Journal of Psychiatry, 149: 680–685.

Giel, R., Dijk, S. and van Weerden-Dijkstra, J.R. (1978) Mortality in the long-stay

population of all Dutch mental hospitals. Acta Psychiatrica Scandinavica, 57: 361–368.
Gould, M.S., King, R., Greenwald, S., Fisher, P., Schwab-Stone, M., Kramer, R., Flisher, A.J., Goodman, S., Canino, G. and Shaffer, D. (1998) Psychopathology associated with suicidal ideation and attempts among children and adolescents. Journal of the American Academy of Child and Adolescent Psychiatry, 37: 915–923.
Gräsbeck, A., Rorsman, B., Hagnell, O. and Isberg, P.-E. (1996) Mortality of anxiety syndromes in a normal population. Biological Psychiatry, 33: 118–126.
Harris, A. (1938) The prognosis of anxiety states. British Medical Journal, 2: 649–654.
Henriksson, M.M., Aro, H.M., Marttunen, M.J., Heikkinen, M.E., Isometsä, E.T., Kuoppasalmi, K.I. and Lönnqvist, J.K. (1993) Mental disorders and comorbidity in suicide. American Journal of Psychiatry, 150: 935–940.
Hiely-Young, B., David Blake, D., Abueg, F.R., Rozynko, V. and Gusman, F.D. (1995) Warzone violence in Vietnam: an examination of premilitary, military, and postmilitary factors in PTSD inpatients. Journal of Traumatic Stress, 8: 125–139.
Hollander, E., Greenwald, S., Neville, D., Johnson, J., Hornig, C.D. and Weissman, M.M. (1997) Uncomplicated and comorbid obsessive-compulsive disorder in an epidemiologic sample. Depression and Anxiety, 4: 111–119.
Innes, G. and Millar, W.M. (1970) Mortality among psychiatric patients. Scottish Medical Journal, 15: 143–148.
Johnson, J., Weissman, M.M. and Klerman, G.L. (1990) Panic disorder, comorbidity, and suicide attempts. Archives of General Psychiatry, 47: 805–808.
Keehn, R.J., Goldberg, I.D. and Beebe, G.W. (1974) Twenty-four year mortality follow-up of army veterans with disability separations for psychoneurosis in 1944. Psychosomatic Medicine, 36: 27–46.
Kendler, K.S. (1986) A twin study of mortality in schizophrenia and neurosis. Archives of General Psychiatry, 43: 643–649.
Kerr, T.A., Schapira, K. and Roth, M. (1969) The relationship between premature death and affective disorders. British Journal of Psychiatry, 115: 1277–1282.
Lepine, J.P., Chignon, J.M. and Teherani, M. (1993) Suicide attempts in patients with panic disorder. Archives of General Psychiatry, 50: 144–149.
Livingston Bruce, M. and Leaf, P.J. (1989) Psychiatric disorders and 15-month mortality in a community sample of older adults. American Journal of Public Health, 79: 727–730.
Martin, R.L., Cloninger, C.R., Guze, S.B. and Clayton, P.J. (1985) Mortality in a follow-up of 500 psychiatric outpatients. Archives of General Psychiatry, 42: 58–66.
Mattison, R.E. (1988) Suicide and other consequences of childhood and adolescent anxiety disorders. Journal of Clinical Psychiatry, 10 (Suppl.): 9–11.
Miles, C.P. (1977) Conditions predisposing to suicide: a review. Journal of Nervous and Mental Disease, 164: 231–246.
Murphy, J.M., Monson, R.R., Olivier, D.C., Sobol, A.M. and Leighton, A.H. (1987) Affective disorders and mortality. A general population study. Archives of General Psychiatry, 44: 473–480.
Neeleman, J., Wessely, S. and Wadsworth, M. (1998) Predictors of suicide, accidental death, and premature natural death in a general-population birth cohort. The Lancet, 351: 93–97.
Nordström, P., Gustavsson, P., Edman, G. and Åsberg, M. (1996) Temperamental vulnerability and suicide risk after attempted suicide. Suicide and Life-Threatening Behavior, 26: 380–388.
Noyes, R. (1991) Suicidal ideation and panic disorder: a review. Journal of Affective Disorders, 22: 1–11.
Noyes, R., Christiansen, J., Clancy, J., Garvey, M.J., Suelzer, M. and Anderson, D.J. (1991) Predictors of serious suicide attempts among patients with panic disorder. Comprehensive Psychiatry, 32: 261–267.

Ohring, R., Apter, A., Ratzoni, G., Weizman, R., Tyano, S. and Plutchik, R. (1996) State and trait anxiety in adolescent suicide attempters. Journal of the American Academy of Child and Adolescent Psychiatry, 35: 154–157.

Overbeek, T., Rikken, J., Schruers, K. and Griez, E. (1998) Suicidal ideation in panic disorder patients. Journal of Nervous and Mental Disease 186: 577–580.

Pokorny, A.D. (1979) Suicide and Anxiety. In W.E. Fann, I. Karacan, A.D. Pokorny and R.L. Williams (Eds), Phenomenology and Treatment of Anxiety, pp. 79–91. New York: SP Medical and Scientific Books.

Rorsman, B. (1974) Mortality among psychiatric patients. Acta Psychiatrica Scandinavica, 50: 354–375.

Rosenberg, C.M. (1968) Complications of obsessional neurosis. British Journal of Psychiatry, 114: 477–478.

Rudd, M.D., Dahm, P.F. and Rajab, M.H. (1993) Diagnostic comorbidity in persons with suicidal ideation and behavior. American Journal of Psychiatry, 150: 928–934.

Runeson, B.S. (1998) Child psychiatric symptoms in consecutive suicides among young people. Annals of Clinical Psychiatry, 10: 69–73.

Schneier, F.R., Johnson, J., Hornig, C.D., Liebowitz, M.R. and Weissman, M.M. (1992) Social phobia. Comorbidity and morbidity in an epidemiologic sample. Archives of General Psychiatry, 49: 282–288.

Sims, A. (1973) Mortality in neurosis. Lancet, 2: 1072–1075.

Sims, A. (1984) Neurosis and mortality: investigating an association. Journal of Psychosomatic Research, 28: 353–362.

Sims, A. and Prior, P. (1982) Arteriosclerosis related deaths in severe neurosis. Comprehensive Psychiatry, 23: 181–185.

Sims, A. and Prior, P. (1985) The pattern of mortality in severe neurosis. British Journal of Psychiatry, 133: 299–305.

Smoller, J.W. and Tsuang, M.T. (1998) Panic and phobic anxiety: defining phenotypes for genetic studies. American Journal of Psychiatry, 155: 1152–1162.

Statham, D.J., Heath, A.C., Madden, P.A.F., Bucholz, K.K., Bierut, L., Dinwiddie, S.H., Slutske, W.S., Dunne, M.P. and Martin, N.G. (1998) Suicidal behaviour: an epidemiological and genetic study. Psychological Medicine, 28: 2839–2855.

Stein, D., Apter, A., Ratzoni, G., Har-Even, D. and Avidan, G. (1998) Association between multiple suicide attempts and negative affects in adolescents. Journal of the American Academy of Child and Adolescent Psychiatry, 37: 488–494.

Szanto, K., Prigerson, H., Houck, P., Ehrenpreis, L. and Reynolds, C.F. (1997) Suicidal ideation in elderly bereaved: the role of complicated grief. Suicide and Life-Threatening Behavior, 27: 194–204.

Vilhjalmsson, R., Kristjansdottir, G. and Sveinbjarnardottir, E. (1998) Factors associated with suicidal ideation in adults. Social Psychiatry and Psychiatric Epidemiology, 33: 97–103.

Warshaw, M.G., Massion, A.O., Peterson, L.G., Pratt, L.A. and Keller, M.B. (1995) Suicidal behavior in patients with panic disorder: retrospective and prospective data. Journal of Affective Disorders, 34: 235–247.

Weissman, M.M., Klerman, G.L., Markowitz, J.S. and Oullette, R. (1989) Suicidal ideation and suicide attempts in panic disorder and attacks. New England Journal of Medicine, 321: 1209–1214.

Weissman, M.M., Bland, R.C., Canino, G.J., Greenwald, S., Lee, C.-K., Newman, S.C., Rubio-Stipec, M. and Wickramaratne, P.J. (1996) The cross-national epidemiology of social phobia: a preliminary report. International Clinical Psychopharmacology, 11 (Suppl. 3): 9–14.

Wheeler, E.O., White, P.D., Reed, E.W. and Cohen, M.E. (1950) Neurocirculatory asthenia (anxiety neurosis, effort syndrome, neurasthenia). Journal of the American Medical Association, 142: 878–889.

Winokur, G. and Black, D.W. (1987) Psychiatric and medical diagnoses as risk factors for

mortality in psychiatric patients: a case-control study. American Journal of Psychiatry, 144: 208–211.
Wood, J.B., Evenson, R.C., Cho, D.W. and Hagan, B.J. (1985) Mortality variations among public mental health patients. Acta Psychiatrica Scandinavica, 72: 218–229.
Zilber, N., Schufman, N. and Lerner, Y. (1989) Mortality among psychiatric patients—the groups at risk. Acta Psychiatrica Scandinavica, 79: 248–256.

Chapter 12

Sociology and Suicidal Behaviour

Unni Bille-Brahe
Centre for Suicidological Research, Odense, Denmark

ABSTRACT

This chapter describes the essentials of the sociological approach to studies of suicidal behaviour, rather than the many studies carried out since the birth of sociology (Nordström, 1995, found more than 3,000 references to suicide in the Social Sciences Index for 1981–1993 and Stack, 1982, has reviewed some of these). Against the background of the classic works of Émile Durkheim, the meanings of and attitudes towards suicidal behaviour and their impact on the frequencies of suicidal acts, concepts such as social integration, societal stability/instability and spatial and/or age distributions are discussed from various points of view within different schools of sociology.

INTRODUCTION

Sociology can briefly be described as the study of society—or, more comprehensively, as in the *Encyclopaedia Britannica* (1993), as:

> . . . the study of causes and effects in social relations among persons and in communication and interaction among persons and groups. It includes the study of customs, structures, institutions, and the effects on individuals of participation in groups and organizations.

The field of interest is, then, social acts or sociocultural behaviour—a behaviour that is different from the behaviour stemming from inner forces of the individual—and, as far as research is concerned, on another level of abstraction. This does not mean that the sociologist disclaims the existence or importance of

The International Handbook of Suicide and Attempted Suicide. Edited by K. Hawton and K. van Heeringen.

man's individual biological, physical or psychological instincts and needs, but that these individual needs are amplified, reformulated or restricted by the societal forces to which the individual is subjected, *because he/she is living in a society*.

The essence of this approach is that when studying human behaviour as it expresses itself in a society, it is not sufficient to study the individual stimuli and psychological needs: the behaviour of a social group is not simply reducible to a summation of the individual group members' inner drives. In other words, a group is something other than, and more than, an incidental number of members—the group acquires quite its own "supra-individuality". This term is Émile Durkheim's (1895/1966), and it coins something of central importance in the perception of the property of sociology, leading on the one hand to the question of understanding the dynamics of society, and on the other to the understanding of the kind of man society produces.

Social interaction constitutes a massive field of opinions and views, where our behaviour is affected by the presence of others, and where we evaluate the social effect of our own behaviour by trying to interpret and understand the behaviour of the others, i.e. the behaviour of the co-members of our community. This two-sided process is a continuous one that constantly affects social interaction and thereby human behaviour, and it is complicated by the fact that, even if social acts take place concretely at a specific point in time, they are, more or less, both decided by what has taken place in the past and affected by an orientation towards the future. Even the most simple social act, therefore, involves the past, the present and the future. At the same time, the basic ideological foundation for sociological research is in itself abstract and not directly observable. Nevertheless, all sociological analyses take their point of departure in realities, i.e. in concrete human behaviour and what it is that controls this behaviour. The purpose of using abstractions is to develop methods, not in order to "discover" anything, but to improve our understanding of the social realities (e.g. Bille-Brahe, 1998).

THE CLASSICAL SOCIOLOGICAL APPROACH

Within the field of suicidology, the sociological approach has come to be almost synonymous with the theories of Émile Durkheim (1897/1951). No single author within the field of suicidology has been quoted so often and no single book as his *Le Suicide* has so consistently been the favourite target of criticism, ranging from sarcastic comments bordering on ridicule to sober discussions on pros and cons. Reading through, for instance, the latest volume on him, *Émile Durkheim. Le Suicide—100 Years Later* (Lester, 1994), one finds samples of both, and at times it is difficult to understand that the various contributors are talking about the same author and the same book.

Looking at the vast literature on Durkheim, and especially at the critical part of it, it seems, however, that many of his critics have in a certain sense taken Durkheim too literally. Time and again, researchers have wanted to verify his theories by replicating his analysis using modern data, obviously lacking the sense of history that should have told them that the meaning or importance of, for example, divorce or religious affiliation is not the same in secularized, modern, Western societies as it was in Catholic nineteenth-century France. Neither is it particularly productive when today's researchers, with their arsenal of sophisticated software and access to modern information technology, put Durkheim down because of the way he collected and used his data more than 100 years ago.

Years of suicidological research on a micro level have shown that people who have been exposed to diseases, stress, traumatic life events, abuse or other personal problems are at an increased risk of suicidal behaviour. However, only a minority of these various high-risk groups will eventually commit suicide, and so far the existence of individual risk factors has not been able to explain satisfactorily why at times many and at times few in these risk groups kill themselves. This was exactly the starting point for the theories of Durkheim, and he concluded by arguing that the explanation had to be that, while the individual suicide seems to be the result of individual factors and circumstances, the *frequency of suicide* is nevertheless determined by the moral and psychological climate in the society in question. This means that the *variations* in the frequency of suicide can only be explained by the fact that certain societal conditions enhance or discourage the *propensity* to react to problems and pain, not by trying to remove the problems and the pain, but by removing oneself. Frequencies of divorce and the like may or may not coincide with the frequency of suicide; the importance of these social facts is that they create, and at the same time are tokens of, the moral and psychological climate of the society. Being divorced is considered a risk factor at the individual level—but the chance that a divorce in the individual case will lead to suicide depends on this climate and on the prevailing norms and values in the society—or, as expressed by Moksony (1994): "(the emergent phenomenon) . . . is shaped not only by the properties of the actor but also by the characteristics of the social context in which the action takes place".

In the opinion of Durkheim, man is first and foremost *a social being*, who has survived through history by living and collaborating with his fellow human beings. The need to belong in a community is therefore deeply rooted in the individual. This community, be it a smaller group or a more comprehensive society, is, as mentioned above, something other than and above the sum of the number of people being part of the community; the community takes on a particular meaning, a kind of autonomous existence and power. It is this community that provides the framework for existence of the individuals, and it is the task of this community to create and maintain those norms and values that are necessary for making the framework sufficiently firm, distinct and supportive. Man needs to believe in the special and real existence of community and to be part of it, and to have the norms and the rules of the community for support. On the other hand, man also has a need to be himself, for autonomy, and for believing in his own identity and his own vital and unique significance, both as an individual and as part of the community.

In elaborating on Durkheim's theories, some sociologists have mainly been occupied with the question of what is happening when the norm pattern of the community is too rigid and the restrictions placed on the individual too harsh and/or unjustly distributed (e.g. Merton, 1938). Durkheim was more concerned about what would happen in society if the restrictions were insufficient, his point being that man's needs, if left entirely to the individual, are boundless. Unlimited needs are, by definition, insatiable and this insatiability is, as in unquenchable thirst, pure agony. Man therefore needs his wishes and goals to be kept in rein in some way—and in the nature of things, this has to be achieved from outside the individual, namely by the community the individual is part of: the individual must submit to the social control exercised by his community.

Social control is then based on the common set of norms and values laid down as the main framework for the behaviour of individuals. Thus, the individual is—in so far as he/she is a member of the community—both submitted to and executor of this social control. According to Durkheim, this dual role entails feelings of mutuality and confidence (the feeling of belonging) and at the same time the experience of having a voice in the decisions of the community and an influence on what is happening to the individual him/herself and to society. This interplay between the individual and the community is a very central part of the theories of Durkheim: for society to function and develop positively, and for man to be in harmony with himself and his community, there has to be a balance between what we could call "individuality" and "communality".

SOCIAL INTEGRATION

What Durkheim tried to prove was that the frequency of suicide varied in time with this balance, i.e. it is a question of the level of social integration. The level of social integration can be "defined" in two dimensions, one referring to the relation of the individual to his/her community (his/her sense of communality), the other to the relation of the community to the individual (the community's control over the individual). On this basis, Durkheim described four conditions (shown in the following diagram) that may threaten the equilibrium between individuality and collectivity, thereby (again according to Durkheim) increasing in the population the proneness to commit suicide:

	The individual's sense of community	The community's control of the individual
Too strong	Altruism	Fatalism
Too weak	Egoism	Anomie

Besides being described in detail by Durkheim himself, the four states have repeatedly been discussed in the literature, (e.g. Taylor, 1982; Bille-Brahe, 1987; Lester, 1989, 1994); they will therefore only be mentioned very briefly here. Discussions on operational definitions of the various concepts will be omitted, mainly because, as mentioned above, these definitions have to be constructed concretely in accordance with norms, values and attitudes in force at the particular time and in the particular society in question.

The model presented above refers to the various states where the bonds between the individual and his community are either too strong (altruism or fatalism) or too weak (egoism or anomie). The upper part deals with altruism and fatalism, i.e. with situations where the bonds are too strong. Instances of altruistic suicides are individuals sacrificing themselves for the sake of their group, e.g. by suicidal political actions. The counterpart to altruism, where the individual is too absorbed in his community, is fatalism, where the community holds the individual in too firm a grip. Mass suicides may be examples of altruistic and/or fatalistic suicides, while suicide committed in protest against usurpation may be described as fatalistic.

The lower part of the model refers to states in which the bonds between individuals and the community are too weak or non-existent. This can happen in two ways: the individual "I" becoming dominant at the expense of the social "I", which causes the individual to withdraw from the community (egoism)—or the ability of the community to create and maintain norms being inadequate and its power to exercise social control insufficient (anomie).

Neither altruism and fatalism, nor egoism and anomie, necessarily coincide: a person may live in a state of altruism without being exposed to fatalism, and vice versa, and the same goes for egoism and anomie. It does not, however, follow from this that the states are always or totally independent of each other. Social control is exercised via the community, and the better the individual is integrated in his/her community, the more easily the norms and values of the community are internalized. If, for example, ego-orientated attitudes (i.e. cultivation of the individual "I") predominate, as we have seen during this century, then the individual's interest in and feeling of obligation towards the norms and values of the community will weaken—and accordingly, so will the ability of the community to maintain the necessary social control. Likewise, history abounds in instances of altruism and fatalism tending to reinforce each other.

Emphasizing the importance of an equilibrium between individuality and collectivity (i.e. the ideal level of social integration), Durkheim suggested as a "general rule" that the frequency of suicide varies inversely with the degree of integration in the community of which the individual is part. Other researchers have tried to substitute the concept of social integration with terms such as "social network", "social support" or the like, but few have been able to demonstrate on a macro level any link between these parameters and "the moral and psychological climate" in a society—perhaps mainly because the simple counting of heads has been part of the abstract empiricism that for many years was (and to some extent still is) prevailing in sociological research (Mills, 1959).

SUICIDE AS A CULTURAL PHENOMENON

In his recent dissertation on *Some Theoretical, Legal and Historical Views on Suicide and Its Concomitants*, Mäkinen (1997a) questions the existence of any social correlates to suicide and he argues that suicide should be analysed as a predominantly cultural phenomenon, rather than by concentrating on the structural properties of societies, as done by Durkheim. In his study on the impact of the legal view on the rate of suicide, he concludes:

> . . . that the laws concerning suicide, cultural attitudes towards it, and possibly religion . . . are all intertwined in a *cultural-normative* system which generates the (later internalized) patterns of ideas in relation to which the individuals assess their own behaviour and act (present author's italics).

Culture is not, however, just something that happens to occur and is imposed on the individual—it is what emerges when human beings are living together; a conglomeration of ideas, habits, thoughts, traditions, norms and values that manifests itself as the cultural pattern in a specific group of people living together in a community at a specific point in time. According to Parson (1951), as cited by Mäkinen (1997b), we are talking about "systems of symbols", and when

> these are internalized, a cultural motivation forms a "genuine need-disposition" in the individual. *It narrows the range of conceivable alternatives for action, influencing both the motivation of problem-solutions and their practical form* (present author's italics).

An important factor is, however, the process in which the creation and the maintenance of the various elements take place in the said community, and whether they are based on consensus or enforced by rigid social control. Therefore, no cultural pattern can be studied entirely detached from the structural properties of the society: attitudes correlate with the cultural meaning of suicide, and this again will at least to some extent be correlated with the structural properties of the society, such as class, politics, distribution of power, religion, etc.

Views on life and death form one part of the cultural pattern and so do attitudes towards deliberate self-harm. In his discussion of the meaning of suicide as something critical to our understanding of the individual decision-making process, Menno Boldt (1988) argues that:

> Meaning goes beyond the universal psychological criteria for certifying and classifying self-destructive death: it refers to how suicide is conceptualized in terms of cultural normative values. Some examples of particular socio-cultural conceptualizations of suicide are that it is an unforgivable sin, a psychotic act, a human right, a ritual obligation, an unthinkable act, and so on. The meaning of suicide is derived from cultural experiences and encompasses the historical, affective qualities that the act symbolizes for a cultural group.

MEANINGS OF AND ATTITUDES TOWARDS SUICIDE IN A HISTORICAL PERSPECTIVE

Attitudes towards taking one's own life have changed considerably over time and between countries (Bille-Brahe, 1997). During antiquity, attitudes towards self-killing varied, but with an overall tendency towards acceptance and even recommendation. Even though both Socrates and Plato have often been quoted, especially by the fathers of the Roman Church, in support of the condemnation of suicide, Socrates argued that a life without opportunities for critical thinking was not worth living, and his descriptions of the blessings of death came to act as an inspiration for many suicides in the years to come. Also, Plato more or less openly hinted that if life became unbearable, suicide was both a sensible and a justifiable act. A century later, the Greek Stoics saw suicide as the most reasonable and desirable act, and so did the Epicureans. Death was an event far too important to be left to mere chance. The Roman Stoics were even more in favour of "*mors voluntaria*": leading a noble life implied dying a noble death at the appropriate time. It is, however, important to note that the "right" to kill oneself in general was reserved for freeborn citizens (a view also held by the Vikings and the Druids), in that whereas suicide was broadly accepted and practised, it was not tolerated among slaves, serfs, legionnaires and the like.

The general condemnation of self-killing that found its expression in Judaism has had a great impact on the occidental cultures; in the Talmud, the sacredness of life is repeatedly underlined, and taking one's own life is considered a serious offence. In The Old Testament of the Bible, as later in The New Testament, the overall view is that God is the creator of man and the one to decide when man is going to die. However, theologists are not completely in agreement about whether or not suicide was totally condemned in the Bible, several pointing to the fact that when a person faces defeat or dishonour, the biblical attitude to suicide seems to be that it may be both an acceptable and to some extent a recommended act. It is also noted that the merciless condemnation of Judas seems to appear only at a much later date, namely in the eleventh century, when a paragraph was included in the canonical law of the Catholic Church stating that, by hanging himself, Judas had committed a much more serious sin than by betraying Jesus.

Actually, it was not until the middle of the fifth century that the Christian Church took the first step towards condemnation of suicide, and suicide became a crime and an unforgivable sin. In retrospect, we may say that *sin* was then introduced as a preventive tool. With the increasing power of the Catholic Church during the Middle Ages, reprisals against suicides because more and more harsh; their family name was disgraced and their property confiscated (by the Church), their bodies broken and their souls condemned to eternal suffering.

It is worthwhile noting that these very damnatory attitudes towards suicide were not generally questioned until the period of the Enlightenment was well under way, i.e. when views on man and man's universe began to undergo radical changes and the grip of the Church began to loosen. At the same time, there was increasing interest in the reasons why people wanted to kill themselves. Ever since the beginning of the Middle Ages, psychiatric disease had been accepted as an excusable reason for suicide; a person who was not master of himself could not be punished for his suicidal act, and neither could his family. A certificate of insanity was therefore of the greatest importance for the reputation of the deceased and the economy of his family. For years this way out was open only to those who had the right connections or could pay for it, but with the establishment of psychiatry as part of medicine and research, the issue of suicide became anchored more formally at the desk of the psychiatrist.

However, gradually the suicidal act of the individual also came to be seen in relation to societal conditions, and scientists from various disciplines, including the social sciences, began to discuss risk factors stemming from these conditions and the sizes of the so-called "high-risk groups", i.e. groups of people particularly exposed to some factor known or suspected to increase suicidality.

These new views took much of the wind out of the concept of sin as a preventive tool: gradually (and in step with changes in the social structure) the suicidal person has come to be looked upon not as a *sinner*, but as a *victim* of certain conditions in his society, and gradually suicidal behaviour is, at least to some extent, seen more or less as an understandable reaction to traumatic events and pain.

Nevertheless, when the Christian Church decreed suicide a mortal sin, it had a decisive effect on the conception of the meaning of suicide and the attitudes towards killing oneself that prevailed until fairly recently. To this concept of sin was eventually added another essential element of Christianity—the care for one's neighbour. Having established that suicide should be prevented, prevention of suicide became a universal human task. Inadvertently, this introduced the concept of guilt—not the guilt of the sinner, i.e. the person who committed suicide, but the feeling of guilt in those who had not been able to prevent, or perhaps even felt responsible for the sin (the suicide). Attitudes towards suicide were heavily tainted by both the concept of sin and the notion of guilt—together bringing about the taboo that for years has dominated this field.

In recent years, however, there has been an increasing awareness and openness concerning the issue of suicidal behaviour, and an increasing tolerance and even acceptance of suicidal behaviour as a "reasonable" or "rational" way of reacting to problems and pain—a point previously expressed by, for example, Schopenhauer (1951), who stated: ". . . as soon as the terrors of life reach the point at which they outweigh the terrors of death, a man will put an end to his life". Today this attitude is formulated in statements such as, "it is man's privileged right to take his own life if and when he so wants".

Through the eyes of Durkheim, this later development may be seen as an odd kind of combination of fatalistic and egoistic conditions. Through the expansion of the welfare state, at least in the Nordic countries, the public got used to being cared for by the authorities, and the dark side of the welfare picture has been that self-care and the responsibility of individuals for themselves and their near ones have been rendered superfluous; problem solving and pain relief have come to be the task of the community (society). Combined with the individual-orientated attitudes characteristic of the "egoistic" society, man has tended to withdraw from responsibilities and involvement, not wanting to feel any guilt and hence discomfort. In order to escape the feeling af guilt connected with somebody committing suicide, man turns to arguments in favour of the rational suicide: when it was the other person's privileged right to commit suicide, there is no reason whatsoever that one should feel any guilt about it.

So, the *meaning* of suicide has changed from being a proper way to end one's life in antiquity, to being a mortal sin during the Middle Ages, later a psychotic act, and today a rational act or even a human right. Accordingly, *attitudes* towards suicidal behaviour have varied from tolerance and acceptance to the deepest condemnation, scorn and contempt, and later again to increasing tolerance and acceptance. Today some people, especially the young, may even feel they are more or less expected to "act" in this dramatic way to demonstrate the depths of their feelings of pain and despair.

Unfortunately, there are no means by which we can statistically test any correlations between the various attitudes in force during early history from antiquity onwards and the frequencies of suicidal behaviour, but there seems to be some evidence that this correlation exists (e.g. Van Hooff 1990). Also, after studying possible effects of the criminalization of suicide, Mäkinen concludes:

> The relation between the laws on suicide-related acts and the frequency of the act of suicide itself thus exists not because fear of punishment would deter people from committing suicide (a notion which constituted a main line of argument in the debate about the decriminalization of suicide itself), but because of (a) the moral impact of law, and (b) the fact that the law itself already reflects prevailing cultural attitudes towards suicide (Mäkinen 1997a).

SUICIDAL TRANSMISSION AND THE IMPORTANCE OF NORMS, VALUES AND ATTITUDES

In keeping with the increasing tolerance and acceptance of suicidal behaviour, the concept of suicidal transmission is becoming more and more relevant. At the individual level, we see suicidal transmission at work within families or smaller groups; suicidal behaviour is learned as a special kind of communication and means of problem solving, and several studies have shown that if a person has experienced suicidal behaviour in his/her family, this increases the risk of the person eventually him/herself committing suicide or trying to do so. At the macro level, the development of media and information technology has meant increasing possibilities (and markets) for influencing people's attitudes—and also a way of communicating suicidal ideation through a contagious effect (Schmidtke and Häffner, 1988; see Chapter 39). The attitudes inherent in the way the media handles the problem of suicide are of special importance when considering fictional portrayal. If the suicidal act is presented as abject, reckless or despicable, the story will probably not serve as a source of inspiration (although there is some evidence to the contrary), whereas, on the other hand, if it is presented as understandable or appropriate or even heroic, the suicidal act may appear as a reaction worthy of imitation and thereby have an inspirational effect on someone who, for some reason, is in a desperate situation. So, if the suicidal act is depicted as appropriate and acceptable, it may be viewed by an individual as the most suitable solution to his/her own problems.

Thus, increasingly tolerant or accepting attitudes towards suicidal behaviour may have a certain "snowball effect": if this leads to increasing frequencies of suicidal behaviour, it follows that more people will transmit suicidal ideation, and consequently there will be more people prone to react with suicidal behaviour, which in turn will tend to increase the general acceptance, again followed by increasing frequency, and so on. Discussion of the imitation effect of media portrayal of suicidal acts, be they fictional or non-fictional, underlines the importance of norms and values and the fact that attitudes, in which current norms and values express themselves, have an effect on the frequency of suicidal behaviour at the individual level. The development of information technology and the global media world has, however, also had an enormous impact at the macro level. Modern sociologists talk about the "boundlessness of the post-modern societies", a term which is in fact very similar to Durkheim's anomie—or, perhaps, it should rather be seen as an extension of the Durkheimian concept.

Translated literally, the word "anomie" means "normlessness", which, of course, does not make sense in this connection, as it is common norms and values that define a group or a society and bind it together. "Anomie", therefore, refers to situations where changes take place too fast. Norms and values prevailing in a society have, of course, always been subject to continuous change, but in periods of violent processes of change, such as those having taken place in many parts of the world during recent decades, the mechanism of inertia, which normally applies to the setting of norms, will be more or less inactive, so that existing norms are rejected before new norms are generally accepted and internalized. Thus, the process of moulding the norms and values that keep the society together and provide man with the necessary safe and reliable framework for his existence, has been undermined.

In later years another, and perhaps even more serious, aspect of this issue has emerged. Via television and the Internet, the global media world offers an increasing, and therefore diffuse, variety of what are supposed to be valid norms and values. However, this blurred mass of ideas, values and limitless varieties of (apparently commonly accepted) behaviour offers few, if any sustaining patterns of norms that can serve as guidelines for the individual or as a supportive framework for his/her existence. The consequence of this development, which is complicated by the huge amount of commercial interest involved, may be a society which is increasingly normless in the true sense of the word, rather than the situation referred to by the Durkheimian concept of "anomie".

THE SOCIAL ORDER AND SOCIO-ECONOMIC CHANGES

In his interesting paper, "Victims of change or victims of backwardness? Suicide in rural Hungary", presented at the 1996 meeting of the International Academy of Suicide Research, Ferenc Moksony discussed two theories in trying to explain an increase in the frequency of suicide in rural areas. One deals with the spread of modern industrial civilization (e.g. Jarosz, 1985), the other with the changing role of the spatial arrangement of the population (e.g. Wilkinson and Israel, 1984); i.e. the two theories reflect different views on the role played by socio-economic changes. According to the first theory, the profound changes that have taken place in rural areas have been leading to a weakening of social relationships, and the ensuing decline in the level of integration is resulting in a higher suicide risk. In short, it is the changes that have taken place in rural areas, and especially the loss of their traditional characteristics, that are seen as the major triggering factor. The second theory argues that it is precisely because these traditional characteristics persist, i.e. clinging to the past in the changing world of today, that rural areas are more exposed to a high suicidal risk.

Moksony points to the fact that the two theories represent two major paradigms in sociology and two opposing answers to the basic question of what holds societies together. Inherent in the first theory is the widespread belief that the major source of social integration is the *stability* of norms, values and interpersonal relations. The second theory, mostly held by economists and only recently gaining ground in sociology, reflects a totally different concept of social order. According to this view, what binds the ideal society together is precisely the *lack of stability*, since a basic prerequisite for well-being is quick responses to changing circumstances and a constant reallocation of resources, which entails a high level of social and geographical mobility. Moksony also discussed another point where this alternative approach departs from the more traditional one, namely with respect to the question of diversity of goals and interests.

Finally, this new concept of social order also questions the beneficial roles of high network density. Moksony argues that, paradoxical as it may sound, weak ties can be even more powerful than strong relationships in contributing to a higher level of integration, because less strong ties permit bridges between social groups otherwise not in touch with each other. Moksony concludes that the traditional view, stressing the importance of stability, solid social networks and uniformity in needs, has to be seriously revised but that this does not mean that Durkheim's theories on social integration have to be abandoned. The new concept of social order, and theories of suicide based on this concept, fully acknowledge the significance of social integration but they do point to factors other than the usual ones as contributing to a decrease in the level of integration.

As mentioned above, very few sociological theories on suicidal behaviour do not take their point of departure from the theories of Durkheim (or at least from criticisms of his works). One of them is based on the works of the demographer Easterlin (1968, 1978, 1980), who was concerned with the influence of the age composition of the population on the social structure and discussed the impact of the relative size of the individual birth cohort on the frequency of suicide. The philosophy behind Easterlin's theories is that larger birth cohorts require more space than smaller cohorts; as a result, large cohorts are "squeezed in", and will therefore have fewer opportunities and be facing more limited conditions than small birth cohorts. According to these theories, a relatively large cohort size will result in increased psychological stress caused, if not entirely, then first and foremost, by a deterioration in the relative financial situation of the cohort. Interest has therefore been concentrated on the association between changes in the age structure of the population and fluctuations in the "relative income", defined as the ratio between income opportunities and income ambitions or expectations. The general assumption is that small cohorts will have plenty of opportunities to meet their expectations; they will have a high relative income and, as a result, they will not be subjected to any psychological pressure in order to achieve current norms. In contrast, large birth cohorts will have insufficient opportunities and therefore a relatively low income, and will as a result be exposed to strong psychological pressure, which could lead to drug abuse, criminality and suicidal behaviour.

The mechanisms triggered by relative cohort size are enhanced by cyclic variations in the level of expectations. Parents belonging to small cohorts who have had good experiences in the labour market, and therefore a relatively high income, will have relatively many children and these will be brought up with considerable expectations with regard to their future income. However, because of the size of their cohort, these children will have relatively poor prospects. In contrast, parents belonging to large cohorts will have relatively few children, and these children will have low expectations reflecting their parent's poor experiences, yet these children will have relatively good prospects because they are part of a small cohort.

Relative cohort size has mainly been discussed in the literature in relation to suicide among young people, and several studies have shown significant co-variation between the frequency of suicide among young people and their cohort size (Holinger and Offer, 1982; Ahlburg and Schapiro, 1984; Hendin, 1987; Holinger et al 1987). The theories have also been discussed in connection with the increasing number of elderly people in most populations, and an ongoing Danish study on the increasing relative cohort size of elderly people indicates a similar co-variation when considered within the various age groups of the elderly.

A cross-national study carried out by Steven Stack (1987) has, however, qualified the theory by showing that relative cohort size has different effects on suicide rates under different socio-economic conditions. He extrapolated from Parkin's differentiation between three types of political–economical structure, namely capitalism, welfare capitalism, and communism, across which (i.e. from the purely capitalistic through the welfare capitalistic to the communistic systems) there is a continuous progression towards equal distribution of assets (Parkin, 1971). Stack maintains that the policy of distribution in the country in question is of vital importance for the effect of the changes taking place in the age structure of the population. Using data from 12 industrialized countries with various macro-economic structures, Stack demonstrated that relative cohort size is of most importance in capitalistic countries, where the state, to a very limited degree if at all, influences the distribution of income and contributes to social security. In welfare capitalistic societies, as in most Western European countries, the welfare political ideology will, in contrast, be involved in provisions designed to counteract the difficulties resulting from a large cohort size. Thus, when faced by a large birth cohort, provisions are made for when members of the cohort are entering the educational system, require housing, need to find jobs; in other words, attempts are made to alleviate the difficulties resulting from the rising relative cohort size.

CONCLUSIONS

It is interesting to note that the influence of Durkheim is traceable even within the more recent socio-economic frames of reference. This may partly be due to the fact that, as one of the founding fathers of sociology, Durkheim (1895/1966) laid down some of the rules for sociological methods and, accordingly, his works have had a lasting impact on the development of sociology. More important, perhaps, is the fact that the crucial theme in the works of Durkheim is the interdependent relationship between the individual and his/her community, and this is of course still true for the majority of sociologists. Basically, the main difference between the various schools of sociology is, as pointed out by Moksony, between those that are concerned with consensus and stability and those that are concerned with conflicts and instability. However, even between these two "camps" there are obvious commonalities; for instance, the concept of *relative income*, launched by Easterlin and colleagues, bears a definite resemblance to *the balance between the culturally established goals and the institutionalized means*, discussed by Merton, the well-known pupil of Durkheim.

Contrary to many of his negative critics, this author therefore argues that the sociological methods and theories developed by Durkheim may well be adapted to twenty-first century research, provided that they are placed in the proper context and analyses are based on data relevant to a modern community. It is the task of modern sociology and of sociological suicidology to follow the development of society from both a socio-economic and a cultural point of view, and not least to study the impact of the new normlessness described above on the frequency of suicidal behaviour. Maybe the increasing frequency of suicidal behaviour among the young, and also the changes in, for example, regional and urban–rural distributions of suicide rates, can be better understood in the light of this development.

REFERENCES

Ahlburg, D. and Schapiro, M. (1984) Socioeconomic ramifications of changing cohort size. Demography, 21: 97–108.

Bille-Brahe, U. (1987) Suicide and social integration. A pilot study on the integration levels in Norway and Denmark. Acta Psychiatrica Scandinavica, 76 (Suppl. 336): 45–62.

Bille-Brahe, U. (1997) Selfkilling—Selfmurder: attitudes in an historic perspective. Lecture given at the International PhD Seminar on Sanity, Illness and Quality of Life, Rungstedlund.

Bille-Brahe, U. (1998) Sociology, gender differences, and suicidal behaviour. Presented at the 7th European Symposium on Suicide and Suicidal Behaviour, Gent, 1998.

Boldt, M. (1988) The meaning of suicide: implications for research. Crisis, 9: 93–108.

Durkheim, É. (1897/1951) Suicide. New York: Free Press.

Durkheim, É. (1895/1966) The Rules of the Sociological Method. New York: Free Press.

Easterlin, R. (1968) Population, Labor Force and Long Swings in Economic Growth. New York: National Bureau of Economic Growth.

Easterlin, R. (1978) What will 1984 be like? Socioeconomic implications of the recent twist in age structure. Demography, 15: 397–432.

Easterlin, R. (1980) Birth and Fortune: the Impact of Numbers on Personal Welfare. New York: Basic Books.

Encyclopaedia Britannica (1993) The Encyclopaedia Britannica, 15th edn. Micropaedia, Vol. 9, p. 316. Chicago, IL: Encyclopedia Inc.

Hendin, H. (1987) Youth suicide: a psychosocial perspective. Suicide and Life Threatening Behavior 17: 151–165.

Holinger, P.C. and Offer, D. (1982) Prediction of adolescent suicide: a population model. American Journal of Psychiatry, 139: 302–307.

Holinger, P.C., Offer, D. and Ostrov, E. (1987) Suicide and homicide in the United States: an epidemiological study of violent death, population changes, and the potential for prediction. American Journal of Psychiatry; 144: 215–219.

Jarosz, M. (1985) Suicides in Poland as an indicator of social disintegration. Social Indicators Research, 16: 449–464.

Lester, D. (1989) Suicide from a Sociological Perspective. Springfield, IL: Charles C. Thomas.

Lester, D. (Ed.)(1994) Émile Durkheim. Le Suicide—100 Years Later. Philadelphia, PA: Charles Press.

Mäkinen, I.H. (1997a) On Suicide in European Countries. Some Theoretical, Legal and Historical Views on Suicide Mortality and Its Concomitants. Stockholm: Almqvist & Wisell International.

Mäkinen, I.H. (1997b) The Importance of Culture for Suicide Mortality. Stockholm: Almqvist & Wisell International.

Merton, R.K. (1938) Social structure and anomie. American Sociological Review I (3): 672–682.

Mills, C.W. (1959) The Sociological Imagination. London: Oxford University Press.

Moksony, F. (1994) The whole, its parts and the level of analysis: Durkheim and the macrosociological Study on Suicide. In D. Lester (Ed.), Emile Durkheim. Le Suicide—100 Years Later. Philadelphia, PA: Charles Press.

Moksony, F. (1996) Victims of change or victims of backwardness? Suicide in rural Hungary. Paper presented at the Meeting of the International Academy of Suicide Research, St. Louis, MO.

Norström, T. (1995) The impact of alcohol, divorce and unemployment on suicide: A multilevel analysis. Social Force, 74: 293–314.

Parkin, F. (1971) Class Inequality and the Political Order. New York: Prager.

Parson, T. (1951) The Social System. Glencoe: Free Press.
Schmidtke, A. and Häffner, H. (1988) The Werther effect after television films: new evidence for an old hypothesis. Psychological Medicine, 18: 665–676.
Schopenhauer, A. (1951) Essays from the Parerga and Paralipomena. London: George Allan and Unwin.
Stack, S. (1982) Suicide: a decade review of the sociological literature. Deviant Behaviour, 4: 41–66.
Stack, S. (1987) The impact of relative cohort size on national suicide trends, 1950–1980. A comparative analysis. Paper presented at the Annual Meeting of the American Association of Suicidology, San Francisco, CA.
Taylor, S. (1982) Durkheim and the Study of Suicide. New York: St. Martin's Press.
Van Hooff, A.J.L. (1990) From Autothanasia to Suicide: Self Killing in Classical Times. London: Routledge.
Wilkinson, K.P. and Israel, G.D. (1984) Suicide and rurality in urban society. Suicide and Life Threatening Behaviour, 14: 187–200.

Chapter 13

The Genetics of Suicidal Behaviour[1]

Alec Roy
Department of Psychiatry, New Jersey Healthcare Systems, East Orange, NJ, USA
David Nielsen
Laboratory of Neurogenetics, National Institute of Alcohol Abuse and Alcoholism, Bethesda, MD, USA
Gunnar Rylander
Department of Psychiatry, Karolinska Institute, Stockholm, Sweden
and
Marco Sarchiapone
Department of Psychiatry, Catholic University, Rome, Italy

Abstract

In medicine in general, establishing that an illness (or behaviour) has a genetic component requires evidence from clinical, twin, adoption and laboratory molecular genetic studies. Such studies exist in the suicide literature and their data suggest that there is a genetic component to suicidal behaviour. For example, it is now well established that a family history of suicide indicates that an individual is at raised risk for both completed suicide and attempts at suicide. Twin studies have shown that monozygotic twins who share 100% of their genes have a significantly greater concordance for both completed suicide and attempted suicide than dizygotic twins who share ony 50% of their genes. Adoption studies also suggest a genetic component to suicide. Most recently, laboratory molecular genetic studies have shown that a variant in the gene coding for tryptophan hydroxylase, the rate-limiting enzyme in the synthesis of the neurotransmitter serotonin, is associated

[1]This chapter is a modified version of a paper that appeared in the Journal of Clinical Psychiatry (1999), 60 (Suppl. 2): 12–17.

The International Handbook of Suicide and Attempted Suicide. Edited by K. Hawton and K. van Heeringen.

with suicidal behaviour. The evidence now seems incontrovertible that there is a genetic contribution to suicidal behaviour.

INTRODUCTION

Suicide is a multidetermined act. The importance of psychiatric, social and biological factors, psychodynamics and physical illness as determinants of suicide is well established. However, increasing data suggest that genetic factors may also play a part in suicidal behaviour. This paper will examine this possibility by reviewing relevant clinical, twin and adoption studies, as well as recent molecular genetic studies.

CLINICAL STUDIES

A family history of suicide has been noted to be associated with suicidal behaviour at all stages of the life cycle. Clinical studies documenting this in adolescents, adults and the elderly have been extensively reviewed elsewhere (Roy et al, 1997a,b). Studies in psychiatric patients show that a family history of suicide raises the risk of suicidal behaviour (Roy, 1983). For example, among 5,845 consecutively admitted psychiatric patients there were 243 inpatients with a family history of suicide (4.2%). A family history of suicide was found to significantly increase the risk for a suicide attempt in a wide variety of diagnoses. Almost half (48.6%) of those with a family history of suicide had themselves attempted suicide (Roy 1982, 1985a,b).

Similarly, among depressed patients Mitterauer (1990) found that 100 of 342 patients with major depression with a family history of suicide had themselves attempted suicide, compared with only nine of 80 depressed patients without such a history ($p < 0.001$). Also, Malone and colleagues (1995) found that parents of depressed patients who attempted suicide were more likely than parents of non-attempters to have been suicide attempters themselves.

Type of Suicide Attempt

A family history of suicide is often associated with a violent suicide attempt. For example, Roy (1993) reported that a family history of suicide was found significantly more among depressed patients who had made a violent suicide attempt in comparison with either depressed patients who had made a non-violent attempt or in comparison with all patients who had not made a violent attempt.

Linkowski and colleagues (1985) reported similarly. They found that 123 of 713 depressed patients (17%) had a first- or second-degree relative who had committed suicide. A family history of suicide significantly increased the probability of a suicide attempt among the depressed women, especially the risk for a violent suicide attempt. Among the male depressives, a family history of suicide significantly increased the risk only for a violent suicide attempt. The authors concluded that "a positive family history for violent suicide should be considered as a strong predictor of active suicidal attempting behaviour in major depressive illness".

Confounding Factors

However, there are confounding factors in the interpretation of the results of family studies of suicidal behaviour. First, the familial aggregation of suicidal behaviour may involve non-genetic factors, such as exposure to family violence, hostility and discord, low parental involvement, or imitation of suicidal behaviour in a family member (Brent et al, 1996). Second, an increased rate of suicidal behaviour in the families of individuals who have exhibited suicidal behaviour may simply be due to the genetic transmission of the psychiatric disorders associated with suicide, i.e. depression, alcoholism and schizophrenia. This potential confounding effect was addressed in a recent study by Brent and colleagues (1996) in adolescent suicide victims. They found, as expected, that the rate of suicide attempts was increased in the first-degree relatives of suicide probands compared with the relatives of adolescent controls. However, they also found that this significant increase remained even after adjusting for differences in the rates of proband and familial Axis I and II psychiatric disorders. In addition they reported that among suicide probands, higher ratings of aggression were associated with higher familial loading for suicide attempts. They therefore concluded that the liability to suicidal behaviour might be familially transmitted as a trait independent of Axis I and II psychiatric disorders.

The Amish Study

Egeland and Sussex (1985) reported on the 26 suicides over 100 years among the Old Order Amish of Lancaster County, in south-eastern Pennsylvania, USA. Twenty-four of the 26 suicide victims met criteria for a major affective disorder. Almost three-quarters of the 26 suicides were found to cluster in four family pedigrees, each of which contained a heavy loading for affective disorders and suicide. Importantly, the converse was not true, as there were other family pedigrees with heavy loading for affective disorder but without suicides. Thus, a familial loading for affective disorders was not in itself a predictor for suicide. Egeland and Sussex concluded: "Our study replicates findings that indicate an increased suicidal risk for patients with a diagnosis of major affective disorder and a strong family history of suicide".

TWIN STUDIES

Kallman and Anastasio (1947) stated: "If hereditary factors play a decisive role we should find a concordant tendency to suicide more frequently in one-egg than in two-egg pairs regardless of ordinary differences in environment". Recently we reported 176 twin pairs in which one twin had committed suicide (Roy et al, 1991). In nine of these 176 twin pairs, both twins had committed suicide. Seven of these nine twin pairs concordant for suicide were found among the 62 monozygotic (MZ) twin pairs, while only two were found among the 114 dizygotic (DZ) twin pairs. This twin group difference for concordance for suicide (11.3% vs. 1.8%) is statistically significant ($p < 0.01$).

Combining our 176 twin pairs with the other suicide twin pairs in the literature yields 399 twin pairs: 129 MZ twin pairs (17/129, 13.2%, concordant for suicide) and 270 DZ twin (2/270, 0.7%, concordant for suicide) (reviewed in Roy et al, 1991). These combined data demonstrate that MZ twin pairs show significantly greater concordance for suicide, relative to DZ twin pairs ($p < 0.001$).

In a second study we examined attempts at suicide among living co-twins whose twin had committed suicide (Roy et al, 1995). Among 35 twins where one twin had committed suicide, we found that 10 of the 26 living MZ co-twins had themselves attempted suicide compared with 0 of the 9 living DZ co-twins ($p < 0.04$) We have recently replicated this finding (Roy and Segal, 2001). We concluded that, although MZ and DZ twins may have some differing developmental experiences, studies show that MZ twin pairs have significantly greater concordance for both suicide and attempted suicide than DZ twin pairs.

A confounding factor in the interpretation of the results of twin studies of suicidal behaviour is that MZ twins are also more highly concordant for the psychiatric disorders associated with suicide than DZ twins. However, that possible confound was addressed by a recent study of 5,995 Australian twins by Statham and colleagues (1998). These twin pairs were a community sample and not selected on the basis of suicidal behaviour. Nonetheless, controlling for a history of psychopathology in the statistical analysis, a significant association with the co-twins' histories of suicidal thoughts and behaviour remained, with this being stronger in MZ than DZ twin pairs.

Mode of Inheritance

Papadimitriou and colleagues (1991) used the computational model of Slater (1966) to investigate possible modes of transmission of suicidal behaviour, i.e. whether a single dominant gene or polygenic inheritance might be involved. Their sample consisted of 549 depressed patients using a lifetime history of attempting suicide. One relative per subject, whenever possible, was interviewed using a semi-structured interview about suicidal behaviour in their family. Fifteen patients had two or more first- or second-degree relatives who had committed suicide compared with their contrals. However, the results did not show a significant excess of unilateral pairs of suicides in the family, as would be expected in a single-gene dominant transmission. Therefore, the authors concluded that their results were most compatible with polygenic inheritance.

The authors also noted that suicide attempters using violent methods, in comparison with non-violent attempters, had a greater percentage of two or more family members who committed suicide and most of them were on the maternal side. Thus, in this sample it appeared that the choice of violent or non-violent suicide attempt method was associated with a different paternal and maternal loading of suicide in the family.

ADOPTION STUDIES

Adoption studies of suicide were carried out in Denmark by Schulsinger and colleagues (1979). Individuals separated at birth, or shortly afterwards, share their genes, but not subsequent environmental experiences, with their biological relatives. In contrast, adoptees share their environmental experiences through childhood and adolescence with their adopting relatives, but share no genes. Thus, familial aggregation of suicide in adoption studies cannot be attributed to the possible confounding effect of familial non-genetic factors.

The Psykologisk Institut has a register of the 5,483 adoptions in greater Copenhagen between 1924 and 1947. A screening of the register of causes of death revealed that 57 of these adoptees eventually committed suicide. They were matched with adopted controls. Searches of the causes of death revealed that 12 of the 269 biological relatives of these 57 adopted suicides had themselves committed suicide, compared with only two of the 269 biological relatives of the 57 adopted controls ($p < 0.01$). None of the adopting relatives of either the suicide or control group had committed suicide compared with their controls. Schulsinger and colleagues (1979) therefore proposed that there may be a genetic predisposition for suicide independent of, or additive to, the major psychiatric disorders associated with suicide.

Wender and colleagues (1986) went on to study the 71 adoptees identified by the same psychiatric case register as having suffered from an affective disorder. They were matched with 71 control adoptees without affective disorder. Not unexpectedly, and as hypothesized, significantly more of the adoptees with affective disorder had committed suicide compared with, their controls. However, it was particularly adoptee suicide victims with the diagnoses of "affect reaction" who had significantly more biological relatives who had committed suicide than controls. This diagnosis describes an individual who has affective symptoms accompanying a situational crisis, which is often associated with an impulsive suicide attempt. The overall findings led Kety (1986) to suggest that a genetic factor in suicide may be an inability to control impulsive behaviour which has its effect independently of, or additively to, psychiatric disorder.

MOLECULAR GENETIC STUDIES

The evidence from post-mortem studies and studies on cerebrospinal fluid (CSF) that show that reduced serotonergic neurotransmission in the brain is involved in suicidal behaviour is discussed in Chapter 4. Genes make proteins that become the enzymes involved in the synthesis and degradation of serotonin.

Nielsen and colleagues (1994) were the first to report an association between suicidal behaviour and a molecular genetic variant of the serotonin system. Tryptophan hydroxylase (TPH) is the rate-limiting enzyme involved in the biosynthesis of serotonin. It catalyses the oxygenation of tryptophan to 5-hydroxtryptophan, which is decarboxylated to serotonin (Abbar et al, 1995). Nielsen and colleagues had earlier identified a polymorphism in intron 7 of the TPH gene. Two alleles, U and L, were identified.

Nielsen and colleagues studied Finnish violent alcoholic offenders. They took blood, established cell lines and geneotyped for the TPH gene. They found that a history of suicide attempts was associated with the L TPH genotype (Table 13.1). In fact, 34 of the 36 subjects who attempted suicide had either the UL or LL genotype, compared with 24 of the 34 subjects without a history of an attempt. Thus, they concluded that the presence of the L allele was associated with an increased risk of suicide attempts.

When the authors examined multiple suicide attempts they found that such a history was found most in offenders with the LL genotype and to a lesser extent among those with the UL genotype. Thus, they concluded that the L allele was associated with repetitive suicidal behaviour. They also found a significant association between genotype and CSF 5-HIAA. Impulsive alcoholics, who had low CSF 5-HIAA, had more LL and UL genotypes. Overall, Nielsen and colleagues suggested that the presence of one TPH L allele may indicate a reduced capacity to hydroxylate tryptophan to 5-hyroxytryptophan in the synthesis of serotonin, producing low central serotonin turnover and thus low CSF 5-HIAA concentrations. Jonnsson and colleagues (1997) similarly found that TPH genotypes were associated with CSF 5-HIAA concentrations in normal volunteers.

Nielsen and colleagues (1998) went on to carry out further association and sib-

Table 13.1 Population association between tryptophan hydroxylase genotype and history of suicide attempts in alcoholic offenders

	History of suicide attempts		
	With attempt *n* (%)	Without attempt *n* (%)	
Genotype			
UU	2 (17)	10 (29.4)	
UL	19 (53)	17 (50)	$p = 0.016$
LL	15 (65)	7 (20.6)	
Total	36	34	
U allele frequency	0.32	0.54	

Reproduced by permission from Nielsen et al (1994).

pair linkage analyses of this TPH polymorphism in 804 Finnish alcoholic offenders, controls and their relatives, in a sample that included 369 sib-pairs. They replicated their earlier finding of the association of the TPH allele to suicidality in a new group of 122 Finnish offenders. A significant association of TPH genotype to suicidality was observed in the impulsive offenders group (Table 13.2). Genotypes containing the 779C (L allele) were associated with a higher incidence of suicidality in the impulsive group.

The same authors also investigated whether there was a stronger association of TPH genotype with the more medically-damaging, severe suicide attempts (Nielsen et al, 1998). They found that the most highly significant association was indeed with severe suicide attempts, but only in the impulsive group (Table 13.3). In addition, the sib-pair analysis revealed that this TPH allele showed significant linkage to suicidality, alcoholism and socialization score on the Karolinska Scales of Personality.

Nielsen and colleagues concluded that although the linkage and association results reflect an effect of TPH on behaviour, it is unlikely that the effect is due to the polymorphism itself—which is in an intron—but, rather, to another functional variant within the TPH gene, or a nearby gene. For example, the tyrosine hydroxylase and D4 dopamine receptor genes are located near the TPH gene on the short arm of chromosome 11. As suicidality is a multifactorial phenotype, TPH may be one of several genes involved.

Table 13.2 Population association between TPH genotype and history of suicide attempts in the replication group

	History of suicide attempts			
	Impulsive		Non-impulsive	
	With attempt *n* (%)*	Without attempt *n* (%)	With attempt *n* (%)	Without attempt *n* (%)
Genotype				
779A/779A	9 (31)	20 (40)	8 (80)	2 (6.1)
779A/779C	44 (72)	17 (34)	13 (35)	24 (72.7)
779C/779C	19 (59)	13 (26)	9 (56)	7 (21.2)
Total	72	50	30	33
	$p = 0.001$		$p = 0.03$	
Frequency of 779A Allele	0.43	0.57	0.48	0.42

*Number of subjects who attempted suicide. The percentage of suicide attempters among total subjects is given in parentheses.
779A corresponds to the U allele.
Probabilities were calculated using the χ^2 test.
Reproduced by permission from Nielsen et al (1998).

Table 13.3 Population association between TPH genotype and history of severe suicide attempts in the replication group

	History of severe suicide attempters			
	Impulsive		Non-impulsive	
	With attempt *n* (%)*	Without attempt *n* (%)	With attempt *n* (%)	Without attempt *n* (%)
Genotype				
779A/779A	6 (21)	23 (39.7)	8 (80)	2 (5.9)
779A/779C	42 (69)	19 (32.7)	12 (35)	25 (73.5)
779C/779C	16 (50)	16 (27.6)	9 (56)	7 (20.6)
Total	64	58	29	34
	$p = 0.0001$		$p = 0.02$	
Frequency of 779A Allele	0.42	0.56	0.48	0.43

* Number of subjects who attempted suicide. The percentage of suicide attempters away total subjects is given in parentheses.
779A corresponds to the U allele.
Probabilities were calculated with the χ^2 test.
Reproduced by permission from Nielsen et al (1998).

TPH in Surviving Co-twins of MZ Suicide Victims

Among the 17,370 MZ twin pairs in the Swedish Twin Register, there are 36 pairs where one is alive and the other has died from suicide. Access to the register was obtained by one the authors (AR). These twins were contacted and asked whether they would consider participating in a study. Twenty-eight of these twins were interviewed in their homes by one of the authors (GR). Venous blood was sampled from 24 subjects and cell lines established. We found that the surviving co-twins had a significantly higher TPH L allele frequency than 158 demographically sampled general population controls (Roy et al, 2001). This is the first report that the TPH allele is associated with an increased risk of suicide.

TPH Studies in Bipolar and Depressed Patients

Bellivier and colleagues (1998a,b) recently examined the TPH intron 7 A218C polymorphism in DNA samples from 152 patients with bipolar disorder and 94 normal controls. They found that there was a significant association between TPH genotype and bipolar disorder. The authors went on to report an association between TPH genotype and suicidal behaviour in bipolar patients. Mann and colleagues (1997) reported that the less common TPH U allele occurred with significantly greater frequency among depressed patients who had attempted suicide compared with those who had not. Furlong et al (1998) found no significant TPH difference between either unipolar or bipolar patients who had or had not attempted suicide.

TPH Studies in Personality-disordered Patients

It is possible that molecular genetic abnormalities may predispose an individual to suicidal behaviour at times of stress through an effect on personality. For example, the personality traits of impulsivity and aggression are associated with suicidal behaviour (see Chapter 10). Furthermore, as discussed in Chapter 4, impulsivity and/or aggression is associated with decreased central serotonin (low CSF 5-HIAA and reduced prolactin response to challenge with serotonergic agents like fenfluramine or m-CPP).

A first link between the molecular genetics of the serotonergic system and impulsivity and/or aggression was reported by New and colleagues (1998). They measured impulsivity and aggression in 40 personality-disordered patients with the Buss–Durkee Hostility Inventory (BDHI). Male patients with the LL genotype had significantly higher total BDHI scores compared to males with the UL or UU genotype [45.3 (±9.8) vs. 32.9 (±13.5), $p < 0.03$]. They also scored significantly higher on the BDHI irritability subscale. Also, the BDHI assault plus irritability subscales correlated negatively with prolactin responses to fenfluramine ($r = -0.70$, $n = 16$, $p < 0.01$) and patients with the LL genotype had a lower prolactin response, although not significantly so. However, Manuck et al (1999) reported that individuals having any TPH U allele scored significantly higher an aggression and unprovoked anger than individuals hornozygous for the L allele.

Serotonin Transporter Studies

The human platelet serotonin transporter (SERT) is found presynaptically and has attracted renewed interest since Lesch and colleagues (1993) demonstrated that it is identical with the human brain serotonin transporter. Both human brain and platelet serotonin transporten proteins are encoded by the same gene on chromosome 17 (Lesch et al, 1994). Polymorphic regions in the second intron and transcriptional control region have been associated with unipolar depression and neuroticism (Ogilvie et al, 1996; Lesch et al, 1996).

Post-mortem studies of suicide victims have reported changes in the serotonin transporter (Mann et al, 1996) and Mann and colleagues (1992) found that platelet serotonin content was significantly lower in depressed patients who had attempted suicide. Significant differences in human platelet serotonin uptake affinity (K_m) values between different polymorphisms of the human SERT gene have been reported (Rausch et al, 1996). Bellivier and colleagues (1997) found no relationship between an allele of the SERT gene and suicide attempts in bipolar patients and SERT mRNA levels in dorsal and raphe nuclei have been found not to be different between depressed patients committing suicide and controls (Little et al, 1997). Similarly, in our twin study we found no significant difference for SERT alleles between surviving MZ co-twins of suicide victims and controls (Roy et al, 2000b). However, preliminary data have suggested an association between alleles of the SERT gene and clinical measures related to impulsive aggression (New et al, 1996; Sander et al, 1998). This is noteworthy as impulsive-aggression is a heritable personality dimension associated with low CSF 5-HIAA and suicidal behaviour (reviewed in Roy et al, 1988; and Limson et al, 1991).

Monoamine Oxidase Studies

Buchsbaum and colleagues (1976, 1977) found that significantly more college students with low blood platelet monoamine oxidase (MAO) levels had a family history of suicidal behaviour compared with students with high platelet MAO levels. This is relevant as MAO is involved in the metabolism of serotonin. Recently a Dutch family was described whose members exhibited violent behaviour and had a mutation in the gene for MAO A (Brunner et al, 1993).

Serotonin Receptors

Zhang and colleagues (1997) reported an association between a 5-HT_{2A} receptor polymorphism and suicide attempts in depressed patients.

Dopamine Receptors

Recent studies have reported an association between the frequency of the 7 repeat allele of a 48 base pair repeat polymorphism at the dopamine D4 receptor gene and novelty-seeking and risk-taking behaviours (Benjamin et al, 1995; Novick et al, 1995), although this was not replicated by Malhotra and colleagues (1996).

CONCLUSIONS

In summary, a large body of clinical data from family, twin and adoption studies now shows that there is a genetic susceptibility to suicide. However, this susceptibility is only likely to manifest itself in an individual at times of severe stress or when ill with a major psychiatric disorder. The first molecular genetic studies have reported polymorphisms in the TPH gene involved in the synthesis of serotonin. Further replications are needed of this and the other molecular genetic findings reviewed above. It seems likely that further polymorphisms will be found in other genes controlling different parts of the pathways involved in the synthesis and metabolism of serotonin. It is also possible that polymorphisms in other neurotransmitter systems may play a part in the multi-determined act of suicide.

REFERENCES

Abbar, M., Courtet, P., Amadeo, S., Caer, Y., Mallet, J., Baldy Moulinier, M., Castelnau, D. and Malafosse, A. (1995) Tryptophan hydroxylase gene and suicidality. Archives of General Psychiatry, 52: 846–849.

Bellivier, F., Laplanche, J., Leboyer, M., Feingold, J., Bottos, C., Allilaire, J.F. and Launay, J.M. (1997) Serotonin transporter gene and manic depressive illness: an association study, Biological Psychiatry, 41: 750–752.

Bellivier, F., Leboyer, M., Courtet, P., Buresi, C., Beaufils, B., Samolyk, D., Allilaire, J.F., Feingold, J., Mallet, J. and Malafosse, A. (1998a) Association between the tryptophan hydroxylase gene and manic-depressive illness. Archives of General Psychiatry, 55: 33–37.

Bellivier, F., Leboyer, M., Courtet, P., Buresi, C., Samolyk, S., Mallet, J., Allibaire, J., Feingold, J. and Malafosse, A. (1998b) Association between the tryptophan hydroxylase gene and suicidal behavior in bipolar patients. Neuropsychiatric Genetics, 81: 512.

Benjamin, J., Paterson, C., Greenberg, B., Murphy, D. and Hamer, D. (1995) Dopamine D4 receptor gene association with normal personality traits. Psychiatric Genetics, 5: 536.

Brent, D., Bridge, J., Johnson, B. and Connolly, J. (1996) Suicidal behavior runs in families. A controlled family study of adolescent suicide victims. Archives of General Psychiatry, 53: 1145–1149.

Brunner, H., Nelen, M., Breakefield, X., Ropers, H. and van Oost, B. (1993) Abnormal behavior associated with a point mutation in the structured gene of monoamine oxidase A. Science, 262: 578–580.

Buchsbaum, M., Coursey, R. and Murphy, D. (1976) The biochemical high-risk paradigm: Behavioral and familial correlaties of low platelet monoamine oxidase activity. Science, 339–341.

Buchsbaum, M., Haier, R. and Murphy, D. (1997) Suicide attempts, platelet monoamine oxidase and the average evoked response. Acta Psychiatria Scandinavica, 56: 69–79.

Egeland, J. and Sussex, J. (1985) Suicide and family loading for affective disorders. Journal of the American Medical Association, 254: 915–918.

Furlong, R., Ho, L., Rubinsztein, J., Walsh, C., Paykel, E. and Rubinsztein, D. (1998) No association of the tryptoplian hydroxylase gene with bipolar disorder, unipolar affective disorder, or suicidal behavior in major affective disorder. American Journal of Medical Genetics (Neuropsychiatric Genetics), 81: 245–247.

Jonnsson, E., Goldman, D., Spurlock, G., Gustavsson, J., Nielsen, D., Linnoila, M., Owen, M. and Sedvall, G. (1997) Tryptophan hydroxylase and catechol-*O*-methyltransferase gene polymorphisms. Relationship to monoamine metabolite concentrations in CSF of healthy volunteers. European Archives of Psychiatry and Clinical Neurosciences, 247: 297–300.

Kallman, F. and Anastasio, M. (1947) Twin studies on the psychopathology of suicide. Journal of Nervous and Mental Diseases, 105: 40–55.

Kety, S. (1986) Genetic factors in suicide. In A. Roy (Ed.), Suicide. Baltimore, MD: Williams & Wilkins.

Lesch, P., Balling, M., Gross, J., Strauss, K., Wolozin, B., Murphy, D. and Riederer, P. (1994) Organization of the human serotonin transporten gene, Journal of Neural Transmission (Gen. Sect.), 95: 157–162.

Lesch, P., Bengel, D., Heils, A., Sabol, S., Greenberg, B., Petri, S., Benjamin, J., Muller, Hamer, D. and Murphy, D. (1996) Association of anxiety related traits with a polymorphism in the serotonin gene regulatory region. Science, 274: 1522–1531.

Lesch, P., Wolozin, B., Murphy, D. and Riederer, P. (1993) Primary structure of the human platelet serotonin uptake site: identity with the brain serotonin transporter. Journal of Neurochemistry, 60: 2319–2322.

Limson, R., Goldman, D., Roy, A., Lamparski, D., Ravitz, B., Adinoff, B. and Linnoila, M. (1991) Personality and cerebrospinal fluid monamine metabolites in alcoholici and controls. Archives of General Psychiatry, 48: 437–441.

Linkowski, P., De Maertelaer, V. and Mendlewicz, J. (1985) Suicidal behavior in major depressive illness. Acta Psychiatrica Scandinavica, 72: 233–238.

Little, K., McLaughlin, D., Rance, J., Gilmore, J., Lopez, F., Watson, S. Carroll, I. and Butts, J. (1997) Serotonin transporter sites and mRNA levels in depressed persons committing suicide. Biological Psychiatry, 41: 1156–1164.

Malhotra, A., Virkkunen, M., Rooney, W., Eggert, M., Linnoila, M. and Goldman, D. (1996) The association between the dopamine D4 receptor (DRD4) 16 amino acid repeat polymorphisms and novelty seeking. Molecular Psychiatry, 1: 388–391.

Malone, K. Haas, G., Sweeney, J. and Mann, J.J. (1995) Major depression and the risk of attempted suicide. Journal of Affective Disorders, 34: 173–185.

Mann, J.J., Malone, K., Nielsen, D., Goldman, D., Erdos, G. and J. Gelernter, J. (1997) Possible association of a polymorphism of the tryptophan hydroxylase gene with suicidal behavior in depressed patients. American Journal of Psychiatry, 154: 1451–1453.

Mann, J.J., McBride, A., Anderson, G. and Mieczkowski, T. (1992) Platelet and whole blood serotonin content in depressed inpatients: correlations with acute and life-time psychopathology. Biological Psychiatry, 32: 243–257.

Mann, J.J., Underwood, M. and Arango, V. (1996) Postmortem studies of suicide victims. In S. Watson (Ed.), Biology of Schizophrenia and Affective Disease, lst, Edn, pp. 197–220. Washington, DC: American Psychiatric Press.

Manuck, S., Flary, J., Ferrell, R., Dent, K., Mann, J.J. and Muldoon, M. (1999) Aggression and anger-related traits associated with a polymorphism of the tryptophan hydroxylase gene. Biological Psychiatry, 45: 603–614.

Mitterauer, B. (1990) A contribution to the discussion of the role of the genetic factor in suicide, based on five studies in an epidemiologically defined area (province of Salzburg, Austria). Comprehensive Psychiatry, 31: 557–565.

New, A., Gelernter, J., Yovell, Y., Trestman, R., Silverman, J., Mitropolon, V. and Siever, L. (1998) Tryptophan hydroxylase genotype in associated with impulsive aggression measures. American Journal of Medical Genetics (Neuropsychiatric Genetics), 81: 13–17.

New, A., Siever, L., Yovell, Y., Trestman, R., Erdos, J., Mitropoulou, V. and Gelernter, J. (1995) LL genotype of tryptophan hyroxylase and irritable aggression. Poster presented at American College of Neuropsychopharmacology, Puerto Rico.

Nielsen, D., Goldman, D., Virkkunen, M., Tukola, R., Rawlings, R. and Linnoila, M. (1994) Suicidality and 5-hydroxindoleacetic acid concentration associated with a tryptophan hydroxylase polymorphism. Archives of General Psychiatry, 51: 34–38.

Nielsen, D., Virkkunen, M., Lappalainen, J., Eggert, M., Brown, G., Long, J., Goldman, D. and Linnoila, M. (1998) A tryptophan hydroxylase gene marker for suicidality and alcoholism. Archives of General Psychiatry, 55: 593–602.

Novick, O., Ebstein, R., Umansky, R., Priel, B., Osher, Y. and Belmaker, R. (1995) D4 receptor polymorphism associated with personalilty variation in normals. Psychiatric Genetics, 5: 536.

Ogilvie, A., Battersby, S., Bubb, V., Fink, G., Harmar, A., Goodwin, G. and Smith, C. (1996) Polymorphism in serotonin transporten gene associated with susceptibility to major depression. Lancet, 347: 731–733.

Papadimitriou, G., Linkowski, P., Delarbre, C. and Mendlewicz, J. (1991) Suicide on the paternal and maternal sides of depressed patients with a lifetime history of attempted suicide. Acta Psychiatrica Scandinavica, 83: 417–419.

Rausch, J., Fei, Y., Ganapathy, V. and Leibach, F. (1996) 5-HTT gene polymorphism related to differences in 5-HT transport kinetics. Poster presentation at American College of Neuropsychopharmacology Annual Meeting, Puerto Rico.

Roy, A. (1982) Risk factors for suicide in psychiatric patients. Archives of General Psychiatry, 39: 1089–1095.

Roy, A. (1983) Family history of suicide. Archives of General Psychiatry, 40: 971–974.

Roy, A. (1985a) Family history of suicide in manic-depressive patients. Journal of Affective Disorders, 8: 187–189.

Roy, A. (1985b) Family history of suicide in affective disorder patients. Journal of Clinical Psychiatry, 46: 317–319.

Roy, A. (1993) Features associated with suicide attempts in depression: a partial replication. Journal of Affective Disorders, 27: 35–38.

Roy, A., Adinoff, B. and Linnoila, M. (1988) Acting out hostility in normal volunteers: negative correlation with the levels of 5-HIAA in cerebrospinal fluid. Psychiatric Research, 24: 187–194.

Roy. A., Nielsen, D., Rylander, G., Sarchiapone, M. and Segal, A. (1999) Genetics of suicide in depression. Journal of Clinical Psychiatry, 60 (Suppl. 2): 12–17.

Roy, A., Rylander, G. and Sarchiapone, M. (1997a) Genetic studies of suicidal behavior. In J. Mann (Ed.), Psychiatric Clinics of North America: Suicide. Saunders, Philadelphia, 20, 595–611.

Roy, A., Rylander, G. and Sarchiapone, M. (1997b) Genetics of suicide: family studies and molecular genetics. In D. Stoff and J. Mann (Eds), The Neurobiology of Suicide, Annals of the New York Academy of Science, 836: 135–157.

Roy, A., Rylander, G., Forslund, K., Asberg, M., Mazzanti, C.M., Goldman, D. and Nielsen, D.A. (2001) Excess TPH 17 779C allele in surviving co-twins of monozygotic twin suicide victims. Neuropsychobiology, 43: 233–236.

Roy, A., Segal, N., Centerwall, B. and Robinette, D. (1991) Suicide in twins. Archives of General Psychiatry, 48: 29–32

Roy, A., Segal, N. and Sarchiapone, M. (1995) Attempted suicide among living co-twins of twin suicide victims. American Journal of Psychiatry, 152: 1075–1076.

Roy, A. and Segal, N.L. (2001) Suicidal behavior in twins: a replication. Journal of Affective Disorders, 66: 71–64.

Sander, T., Harms, H., Dufeu, P., Kuhn, S., Hoehe, M., Lesch, P., Rommelspacher, H. and Schmidt, L. (1998) Serotonin transporter gene variants in alcohol-dependent subjects with dissocial personality disorder. Biological Psychiatry, 43: 908–912.

Schulsinger, R., Kety, S., Rosenthal, D. and Wender, P. (1979) A family study of suicide. In M. Schou and E. Stromgren (Eds), Origin, Prevention, and Treatment of Affective Disorders, pp. 277–287. New York: Academic Press.

Slater, E. (1966) Expectation of abnormality on paternal and maternal sides: a computational model. Journal of Medical Genetics, 3: 159–166.

Statham, D., Heath, A., Madden, P., Bucholz, K., Dinwiddie, S., Slutake, W., Dunne, M. and Martin, N. (1998) Suicidal behaviour: an epidemiological and genetic study. Psychological Medicine, 28: 839–855.

Wender, P., Kety, S., Rosenthal, D., Schulsinger, F., Ortmann, J. and Lunde, I. (1986) Psychiatric disorders in the biological and adoptive families of adopted individuals with affective disorder. Archives of General Psychiatry, 43: 923–929.

Zhang, H., Ishigaki, T., Tari, K., Chen, K., Shih, J.C., Miyasato, K., Ohara, K. and Ohara, K. (1997) Serotonin-2A receptor gene polymorphism in mood disorders. Biological Psychiatry, 41: 768–773.

Chapter 14

Pathways to Suicide: an Integrative Approach

Kees van Heeringen
Department of Psychiatry, University Hospital, Gent, Belgium
Keith Hawton
Department of Psychiatry, Oxford University, Oxford, UK
and
J. Mark G. Williams
Institute of Medical and Social Care Research, University of Wales, Bangor, UK

Abstract

It may have become apparent from the chapters in Part I of this Handbook that suicidal behaviour is to be regarded as the consequence of a complex interaction between psychological, biological and social characteristics. Recent findings from research in apparently divergent areas such as ethology, psychology, biology and sociology tend to converge to such an extent that earlier questions, like whether suicidal behaviour is primarily a psychologically defined problem or mainly due to biological characteristics, no longer appear to be relevant. A central issue in the development of suicidal behaviour concerns the reciprocal effects of the individual and his/her environment upon each other. These include exposure to specific stressors, which may be in part under genetic control; a sensitivity to such environmental influences, which can be defined in perceptual or cognitive terms; and the behavioural reaction to them. Recent advances in our understanding of the functioning of the brain's prefontal cortex suggest an important role of the latter two phenomena. An important issue in the interpretation of the meaning of findings from the epidemiological, biological, psychological and social areas concerns the specificity of such findings, which influences their power in predicting suicidal behaviour to a great extent. The effect of identified risk factors on the occurrence should therefore be regarded as probabilistic rather than deterministic. Epidemiological research has shown that attempted suicide is the strongest clinical predictor of suicide and indicates that suicide is commonly preceded by a process that may start with fleeting suicidal thoughts, then evolve through more concrete plans and suicide attempts to completed suicide. The biological, psychological and

The International Handbook of Suicide and Attempted Suicide. Edited by K. Hawton and K. van Heeringen.

psychopathological underpinnings of this process are in need of further study, but it has become clear that while in early phases of the process anger and anxiety may be predominant, later stages may be characterized by high levels of depression and especially hopelessness. Findings like these have important implications for our understanding of suicidal behaviour, and for its treatment and prevention. Based on our current knowledge we can thus build a model in which psychological, biological and social characteristics are grouped according to their effects on the development of hopelessness and suicidal behaviour, and according to their risk-increasing or protective properties. Elements of this model will be exemplified in Part II of this Handbook by means of an examination of specific populations and circumstances in which suicidal behaviour may occur. Implications for treatment and prevention will be addressed in Parts III and IV.

INTRODUCTION

Suicidal behaviour is never attributable to one single cause. It is apparent from the contributions in Part I of this Handbook that suicidal behaviour is the consequence of a complex interaction of social, psychological and biological characteristics. These contributions also show that in recent years studies in apparently divergent areas of research, such as biology, genetics, ethology, sociology and psychology, are producing results that are increasingly converging. In Chapter 5 Williams and Pollock described psychology as "the bridge between sociology and biology", and in Chapter 6 Goldney concluded from his overview that ethology is "the bridge between psychology and sociology". The time therefore seems ripe for us to make a serious effort to integrate our current knowledge. Earlier questions, such as whether suicidal behaviour (like mental disorder) is primarily a psychologically defined problem or mainly due to biological influences, no longer appear to be relevant. This has important implications for understanding the suicidal process, assessing risk, developing effective treatment of people at risk, and identifying strategies that may help to prevent suicidal behaviour. In this chapter, the currently available knowledge described in Part I of this Handbook will be integrated in a comprehensive model of suicidal behaviour. Preceding a discussion of this model, several examples of the convergence of recent findings in different areas of research with particular relevance for the study of suicidal behaviour and for the understanding of such a model will be discussed. Elements of this model will be exemplified in Part II of this Handbook by means of examination of specific populations and circumstances in which suicidal behaviour occurs. Implications for treatment and prevention will be addressed in Parts III and IV of the Handbook.

THE INTERACTION BETWEEN THE INDIVIDUAL AND THE ENVIRONMENT

An example of the striking converging character of findings from research in the areas of psychology, biology, ethology and sociology concerns the role of the interaction between the individual and their environment in the development of suicidal behaviour. This interaction concerns the exposure to environmental stressors, the perceived meaning of these stressors, and the behavioural reaction to them.

There is now overwhelming evidence that both genetic and environmental factors impact on the aetiology of emotional and behavioural disorders, and the study of the interaction between these factors now constitutes a major element in the search for understanding these problems. Several plausible models have been developed to describe the interaction between genes and environment, including simple additive effects, genetic control over sensitivity to the environment, and genetic control of exposure to the environment (Kendler and Karkowski-Shuman, 1997). Evidence for the two latter models has been found. The third model might be particularly interesting for suicidology in view of the well-established association between suicidal behaviour and stressful life events of an interpersonal nature. Thus, the question can be posed whether genetic factors act in the development of suicidal behaviour by predisposing individuals to place themselves in stressful situations, which in turn predispose to the development of suicidal behaviour. It has, for instance, been shown that the risk of serious marital difficulties and divorce is partially under genetic control (Kendler et al, 1993), so that the environment can in fact be regarded as the "extended phenotype". Personality traits such as aloofness (Shaffer, 1974; Van Heeringen et al, in press), which are at least in part heritable, may interfere with affiliative capacities to such an extent that they predispose individuals to stressors, such as interpersonal problems, that are indeed commonly found as precipitants of suicidal behaviour.

The important role of sensitivity to environmental influences in the development of suicidal behaviour becomes apparent from the contributions on biological, psychological, ethological and sociological issues in Part I. In Chapter 4, Träskman-Bendz and Mann describe the role of overactivity of the hypothalamic–pituitary–adrenocortical stress system in response to perceived triggering events. Williams and Pollock label these events more specifically in Chapter 5 by stating that suicidal behaviour is the result of the triggering of psychobiological defeat scripts as a consequence of the perception of uncontrollable rejection or loss. With regard to the cognitive component, Goldney describes in Chapter 6 how perception of oneself as being both powerless and unattractive will activate ancient biological mechanisms for the yielding sub-routine, with all its depressive and behavioural consequences. However, the effect of the environment on the occurrence of suicidal behaviour is not limited to exposure to environmental stimuli that may trigger suicidal acts. Based on studies in animals and humans, Goldney highlights the fact that the environment appears to exert its influence even in the antenatal, perinatal and early postnatal periods, and thus affects our ability to deal with stressors at a later age. In this respect, findings from animal studies, showing that early maternal behaviour programmes responses of the hypothalamic–pituitary–adrenocortical axis to stress in offspring and that maternal behaviour during infancy can reduce the rate of neuronal loss and development of deficits in memory in animals as they age, are remarkable.

The substantial increase in suicide among young males in most of the Western World, as described in Chapter 1 by Cantor, may provide a good but tragic example of how social factors influence the occurrence of suicidal behaviour. As this rise in the number of young deaths presumably cannot be attributed to an increased single effect of genetic factors, other factors must be taken into account. In Chapter 12 Bille-Brahe highlights the role of relative cohort size. Thus, where too many people of approximately the same age are seeking access to resources, many will suffer due to the failure to achieve this. At the same time, a period effect may be influential in that these resources (which may include employment prospects, family cohesion and reduced anticipation of long-term roles) diminish. The combined period and cohort effects may thus be influential by shaping the perceived meaning of social stressors, and increasing the risk or level of hopelessness.

It can thus be concluded with regard to the development of suicidal behaviour that individual characteristics (including genetic factors) and the environment do not stand in opposition, but act rather in a reciprocal fashion. The effect of influences such as genetic factors is probabilistic rather than deterministic, and shaped by environmental influences.

AT THE CROSSROADS OF PSYCHOLOGY AND BIOLOGY: THE BRAIN'S PREFRONTAL CORTEX AND ITS MEMORY FUNCTIONS

Biological and psychological theories used to explain suicidal behaviour converge, at least in part, in highlighting the important role of the brain's prefrontal cortex. The prefrontal cortex has, in general, at least three functions: (a) working memory (a short-term component of episodic or autobiographical memory); (b) preparatory set (the priming of sensory and especially motor structures for performance of an act that is contingent on a prior event, and thus on the content of working memory); and (c) inhibitory control (the inhibition of distracting memories or stimuli) (Fuster, 1997). The combination of the first two functions leads to the reconciliation of the past with the future, or of behaviour with goals. As such, the prefrontal cortex plays a major role in cognitive, emotional and motivational aspects of human behaviour, and changes in its functioning lead to changes in the reactivity to external stimuli, and thus in interactions with other people. Adequate functioning of the prefrontal cortex will provide individuals with the capacity to, for example, formulate goals with regard for long-term consequences, generate multiple response alternatives, and initiate goal-directed behaviour (Malloy et al, 1998). In the description of psychological characteristics associated with suicidal behaviour, as provided in the first part of this Handbook, those such as impulsivity and problem-solving deficits seem to be particularly important. The study of the involvement of the prefrontal cortex thus appears very relevant.

With regard to the emotional and motivational aspect of human experience and behaviour, animal studies have shown that lesions in the orbital region of the prefrontal cortex lead to inability to deal with aggression, following which fear and flight gain the upper hand and the animal loses its stand in its community (Fuster, 1997). On the other hand, lesions in the dorsolateral area may influence cognitive functions to such an extent that this may result in an inability to sort out sensory stimuli, to generate multiple-response alternatives and to inhibit the response tendency to flee. Thus, these animal studies demonstrate the role of different areas of the prefrontal cortex in the emotional or motivational and cognitive aspects of the organization of behaviour. It remains to be demonstrated to what extent such findings may be useful in explaining emotional and cognitive aspects, respectively, of human behaviour, and more specifically of suicidal behaviour. Currently available findings come mainly from autopsy studies which, as reported by Träskman-Bendz and Mann in Chapter 4, show an association between suicidal behaviour and changes in the ventral/orbital prefrontal cortex (and not in the dorsolateral areas), which may become apparent through a decrease in cognitive or behavioural inhibition.

It also remains to be demonstrated how the biochemical findings asssociated with suicidal behaviour, as described by Träskmann-Bendz and Mann in Chapter 4, fit into this model. The role of serotonin in the pathogenesis of suicidal behaviour is clear from many studies using different methodologies, among which controlled post-mortem studies have indicated disturbances of the serotonin system in the prefrontal cortex. Thus, the question arises how serotonin may be involved in the functioning of the prefrontal cortex. Animal studies have shown that cortical serotonin is probably mainly involved in the processing of sensory information (Fuster, 1997). Studies in rats have shown an increase of serotonin in the prefrontal cortex (and in the amygdala) following exposure to stress. The post-mortem findings in suicide victims may therefore be due to severe stress or depression. Träskman-Bendz and Mann describe how there is an increase in the number of 5-HT_{1A} receptors in the prefrontal cortex in suicide victims that is independent of psychiatric diagnosis. Moreover, studies in attempted suicide patients have shown a correlation between serotonin levels and measures of aggressiveness, suggesting an involvement of serotonin in the motor-expressive or behavioural component. On the other hand, investigations such as the tryptophan depletion studies have indicated an involvement of serotonin in the regulation of emotional states, especially depression (Delgado et al, 1990). Thus, while there is little doubt about the involvement of serotonin in the pathogenesis of suicidal behaviour, the nature of this involvement still remains unclear. A dissection of the serotonin system in subsystems that serve different functions might be helpful in explaining this. As suggested by Deakin (1996) and described in some more detail later in this chapter, at least two such subsystems need to be considered, namely the 5-HT_1 and 5-HT_2 systems.

It can be expected that diagnostic advances in the area of neuroscience may provide an answer to questions like those raised in the previous paragraphs. First, neuro-imaging techniques, such as functional magnetic resonance imaging (MRI), positron-emission tomography (PET) and single photon-emission tomography (SPECT), can be used to study functional abnormalities *in vivo* in the prefrontal cortex and the subcortical structures, and thus demonstrate functional and biochemical changes associated with suicidal behaviour. A second way to investigate the prefrontal cortex *in vivo* may be provided by neuropsychology. Investigations of attempted suicide patients may provide insight into the involvement of divergent systems in the brain in the pathogenesis of suicidal behaviour, provided that neuropsychological tests are available that may demonstrate abnormalities that are specific to defined areas. With regard to the above-mentioned areas potentially involved in suicidal behaviour, currently available tests include word and figure fluency tasks, the Wisconsin Card Sorting Test and the Stroop Color–Word Test. The role of such tests in the assessment of the risk of suicidal behaviour remains to be demonstrated, the more so as the specificity of these tests to investigation of frontal functions has been questioned (Malloy et al, 1998). In Chapter 5, Williams and Pollock describe the application of an adapted word fluency paradigm to the study of cognitive styles. A recent comparative study indeed showed abnormal scores on the Wisconsin Card Sorting Test in association with borderline psychopathology (including conduct disorder) in children, thus suggesting that this test can be used to demonstrate a trait-dependent vulnerability in children (Paris et al, 1999). The inclusion of neuropsychological assessments in future clinical investigations of individuals who carry out suicidal behaviour should be seriously considered.

THE SPECIFICITY OF FINDINGS

A major problem in the prediction of suicide, as will be described by Goldney in Chapter 33, is the lack of specificity of characteristics that are associated with suicidal behaviour. Studies in the epidemiological, clinical, biological, sociological and psychological areas, as reviewed in the first part of this Handbook, have indicated a role of both environmental (e.g. social characteristics and precipitating life events) and individual (e.g. genetic susceptibility and psychological characteristics) influences on the occurrence of suicidal behaviour. From a theoretical point of view, a specific outcome (i.e. suicidal behaviour) may result from exposure to specific environmental influences in individuals without a particular vulnerability, or from exposure to non-specific environmental influences in individuals with a specific susceptibility. Thus, the question arises to what extent the psychological, social and biological or genetic findings, as described in the first part of this Handbook, are specific to suicidal behaviour. Chapters 4 and 13 have, for example, highlighted the central role of serotonin in the development of suicidal behaviour. However, a similar involvement of the serotonergic system has been described with regard to, for example, eating and anxiety disorders. Similarly, serotonin-mediated characteristics, such as impulsivity or aggressiveness, are not specifically related to suicidal behaviour: the impulse control disorders encompass a wide array of behavioural problems.

A similar question concerns the specificity of the findings in the psychological area, where less comparative research has been performed. As described by Williams and Pollock in Chapter 5, it appears, however, that hopelessness and the occurrence of certain life events are specifically associated with suicidal behaviour. Based on these findings it can be concluded that the development of suicidal behaviour might be associated with the state-inducing exposure to specific life events in aspecifically trait-dependent vulnerable individuals. However, recent research findings have demonstrated that reality is more complicated. First, most studies (e.g. Paykel et al, 1975; Foster et al, 1999) but not all (Mann et al, 1999) show an association between (specific) life events and suicidal behaviour. The reasons for this lack of consistency in research findings are unclear and suggest that suicidal behaviour constitutes a heterogeneous group of acts with regard to the absence or presence of triggering events. This inconsistency can, however, be explained by means of the suicidal process approach. In this approach, which will be discussed in more detail in the next section, suicidal behaviour is regarded as a dynamic process, during which the role of triggering events is evident in the initial stages, but may be become less important during later stages. Secondly, the occurrence of life events appears to be, at least in part, under genetic control, and thus may contribute to a specific vulnerability. As described above, Kendler and colleagues (1999) showed with regard to the onset of depression, seen by Williams and Pollock and others in the field to be the final common pathway to suicidal behaviour, that a substantial causal relationship indeed exists between stressful life events and the onset of episodes of major depression. However, about one-third of the association between such events and the onset of depression is non-causal, since individuals predisposed to major depression select themselves into high-risk environments. In other words, genetically influenced traits predispose to both episodes of major depression and to stressful life events: as noted earlier, the risk for serious marital difficulties and divorce are under partial genetic control. Thirdly, it appears that hopelessness shares trait- and state-dependent characteristics (Mann et al, 1999), and thus may equally contribute to a specific vulnerability. Findings like these underline the need to include specific trait-related characteristics in any model that can be developed in order to explain the occurrence of suicidal behaviour.

THE CONTINUUM OF SUICIDAL BEHAVIOUR AND ASSOCIATED PSYCHOPATHOLOGICAL PHENOMENA

When comparing the epidemiological patterns and trends of suicide and of attempted suicide, as described in Chapters 1–3, more differences than similarities become apparent. From an epidemiological point of view, suicide and attempted suicide therefore apparently constitute two different phenomena.

However, there is compelling evidence (including the strongly increased risk of suicide following attempted suicide, and the co-variance of attempted suicide and suicide rates) to assume that both phenomena are in fact expressions of a continuum of self-harming behaviours. The term "suicidal process" is used to describe the intra-individual process in reaction to a person's environment, starting with feelings of despair, then fleeting suicidal thoughts, and evolving through more concrete plans and suicide attempts, which are often recurrent (as discussed by Sakinofsky in Chapter 21) and may show increasing levels of suicidal intent and lethality of methods used, to completed suicide.

The evolution of psychopathological characteristics during the course of this process is not yet totally clear. As described by Williams and Pollock in Chapter 5, the initial stage of the process is characterized by high levels of "protest", which may become apparent as increased levels of anger and anxiety. Later in the process, when escape potential is eliminated, "despair" gradually gains the upper hand and the patient will show more marked symptoms of depression and especially increased levels of hopelessness. Studies of survivors of medically serious suicide attempts may provide some insight into the psychopathological characteristics of later phases in the process (Beautrais et al, 1996; O'Donnell et al, 1996). These studies show that the prevalence of mental disorders is similarly high for non-fatal serious suicide attempts and completed suicide, and underline the important role of mood disorders: Beautrais and colleagues (1996) showed that elimination of mood disorders would result in a reduction of up to 80% in the risk of a serious suicide attempt.

Goldney's "tipping point" hypothesis (see Chapter 6) remains to be tested in attempted suicide patients. Its potential pathogenetic role in the suicidal process clearly needs further study. The question arises to what extent the repeated exposure to specific stressors gradually undermines the escape potential, possibly through the cytotoxic effects of the corticoid stress hormone on involved memory systems. These effects may gradually diminish the capacity to generate multiple responses to these stressors. As was described above, this capacity is a crucial element in the perception of being entrapped, and may prevent the development of hopelessness and thus mitigate against suicidal behaviour. The suicidal process approach and its psychological and psychopathological underpinnings clearly need further substantive scientific support, as they have important implications for treatment and prevention. The response to psychotherapeutic and pharmacological interventions may well depend on the phase in the process, in a similar way to that suggested by Post (1992) concerning the longitudinal course of affective disorders. For instance, there might be an important role for glucocorticoid antagonists which, if administered during early phases of the process, may well prevent the development of long-lasting damage leading to (repeated) non-fatal suicidal behaviour or suicide. There might be a similar role for psychological interventions. Thus, with regard to prevention, as the suicidal process is in its early stages there are points at which early intervention (biological and, or, psychological) might be beneficial, particularly in terms of preventing a first suicide attempt. Epidemiological data on suicidal behaviour, which are discussed by

Kerkhof in Chapter 3 and elaborated by Sakinofsky in Chapter 21, indeed appear to support Post's hypothesis with regard to affective disorder, that is that having had an episode of depression leaves behind neurobiological and neuropsychological residues that make a person more vulnerable to subsequent episodes (Post, 1992; Segal et al, 1996). Clearly such a vulnerability scar might also have a primarily psychological basis.

It can be concluded that suicidal behaviour occurs at the crossroads of the past—recent with regard to precipitating stressors and more distant with regard to its effects on our resilience against these stressors—and the future, or at least the way it is perceived based on previous experiences. It is remarkable how findings from such divergent scientific approaches as ethology, psychology and biology converge, and point to the central role of memory and learning in explaining suicidal behaviour.

UNDERSTANDING SUICIDAL BEHAVIOUR

From what has been discussed so far it can be concluded that suicidal behaviour results from some degree of state–trait interaction. As was described by Williams and Pollock in Chapter 5, depression is to be regarded as the final common pathway leading to suicide. Lönnqvist showed in Chapter 6, however, that only a limited proportion of patients suffering from a depressive episode will eventually commit suicide, and the question arises which characteristics distinguish depressed non-suicidal from depressed suicidal individuals. From our current knowledge it appears that such characteristics are in the cognitive and behavioural domains of the personality in its social context, which are based on (possibly interrelated) psychological and biological mechanisms. These are often manifest in the problem of co-morbidity of psychiatric disorders (especially depression and substance abuse) and personality disorders (especially borderline and dissocial disorders).

Taking depression as a starting point of the pathway leading to suicide may at first sight be at variance with the statement by Träskman-Bendz and Mann in Chapter 4 that "it is a common misconception that suicide is a complication of depressive syndromes". Suicidal behaviours occur in association with many psychiatric disorders as was described in Chapters 7–11, but the term "depression" is used in this model to describe the emotional status (and not the categorical diagnosis of major depressive episode) that can be described as the final common pathway leading to suicidal behaviour and that may occur in the context of many categorical diagnoses.

Psychological mechanisms predisposing to hopelessness among depressed individuals were described by Williams and Pollock in Chapter 5, and include cognitive rigidity (or an over-general cognitive style) and problem-solving failures, mediated by autobiographical memory deficits. Hopelessness, or the absence of rescue factors such as positive expectancies, thereby may occur independent of depression, or in apparent excess of degree of depression, as has also become clear from clinical studies (Mann et al, 1999). Hypothetical differences in underlying biological mechanisms have been described; indeed, as noted above, Deakin (1996) highlights the differential effects of disturbances in the serotonergic system, depending upon of whether the 5-HT_2 system (associated with hopelessness) and/or the 5-HT_{1A} system (associated with depressive ideation) is involved. The extent to which biological factors contribute to the development of hopelessness clearly needs more study, which is also the case for the influence of environmental factors. Little is known about factors that protect against the development or occurrence of hopelessness in depressed individuals. It can be expected that the identification and adequate treatment of depression will contribute, once hopeless individuals come into contact with health care facilities.

Whether hopelessness leads to suicidal behaviour depends upon the presence or absence of risk and protective factors, which do not simply mirror each other. Identified risk factors include, as described in the first part of this Handbook, impulsivity, a genetic loading of suicide in the family, the availability of means to commit suicide, and (due to their disinhibiting effects) the ingestion of alcohol and/or drugs. Other risk factors will be described in further chapters in the Handbook, and include the presence of role models, either in the individual's social setting or through portrayal by the media (see Chapter 39). Among protective factors, social support has been identified as having an important role.

As described by Träskman-Bendz and Mann in Chapter 4, impulsivity reflects a trait-dependent and serotonin-mediated deficiency in behavioural inhibition, thus defining the risk for self-directed or outwardly directed aggression. In the case of self-destructive behaviour, the degree of impulsivity may correlate positively with suicidal intent and with medical severity of the consequences of this behaviour. However, impulsivity may explain the probability of behaviour, but not the choice of suicidal behaviour, as indicated by Williams and Pollock in Chapter 5, so other factors must influence this choice. Williams and Pollock point to the central role of the perception of being closed in ("entrapment") with no escape potential from a situation in which an individual is placed as a consequence of triggering events. The stronger this perceived entrapment is, the higher the level of hopelessness and the risk of suicidal behaviour.

CONCLUSIONS

In this chapter an attempt has been made to integrate our currently available knowledge of factors that may increase the risk of suicidal behaviour or protect against its development, as they were described in Part I of this Handbook. It could be shown that results from recent research in apparently divergent areas such as ethology, psychology, biology and sociology tend to converge to such an extent that previous distinctions between social, psychological or biological models of suicidal behaviour appear no longer to be valid. Moreover, it is becoming clear that suicidal behaviour is to be regarded as a dynamic phenomenon in the sense that, first, it is commonly the result of the interaction between psychological, social and biological factors, and secondly, that having had an episode of suicidal behaviour may make individuals vulnerable to subsequent epsiodes. As a consequence, suicidal ideation and non-fatal suicidal behaviour are commonly steps in a process that may well lead to suicide.

These findings will be elaborated in Part II of the Handbook in which suicidal behaviour in special circumstances and populations will be described. Implications for the treatment and prevention of suicidal behaviour, and areas for future research, will be discussed in Parts III and IV.

REFERENCES

Beautrais, A.L., Joyce, P.R., Mulder, R.T., Fergusson, D.M., Deavoll, B.J. and Nightingale, S.K. (1996) Prevalence and co-morbidity of mental disorders in persons making serious suicide attempts: a case-control study. American Journal of Psychiatry, 153: 1009–1014.

Deakin, J.F.W. (1996) 5-HT, antidepressant drugs and the psychosocial origins of depression. Journal of Psychopharmacology, 10: 31–38.

Delgado, P.L., Charney, D.S., Price, L.H., Aghajanian, G.K., Landis, H. and Heninger, G.R. (1990) Serotonin function and the mechanism of antidepressant action: reversal of antidepressant-induced remission by rapid depletion of plasma tryptophan. Archives of General Psychiatry, 47: 411–418.

Foster, T., Gillespie, K., McClelland, R. and Patterson, C. (1999) Risk factors for suicide independent of DSM-III-R Axis I disorder. Case-control psychological autopsy study in Northern Ireland. British Journal of Psychiatry, 175: 175–180.

Fuster, J.M. (1997) The Prefrontal Cortex: Anatomy, Physiology, and Neuropsychology of the Frontal Lobe, 3rd Edn. New York: Lippincott-Raven.

Kendler, K.S. and Karkowski-Shuman, L. (1997) Stressful life events and genetic liability to major depression: genetic control of exposure to the environment? Psychological Medicine, 27: 539–547.

Kendler, K.S., Karkowski, L.M. and Prescott, C.A. (1999) Causal relationship between stressful life events and the onset of major depression. American Journal of Psychiatry, 156: 837–841.

Kendler, K.S., Neale, M.C., Kessler, R.C., Heath, A.C. and Eaves, L.J. (1993) A twin study of recent life events and difficulties. Archives of General Psychiatry, 50: 589–596.

Malloy, P.F., Cohen, R.A. and Jenkins, M.A. (1998) Frontal lobe function and dysfunction. In Snyder, P.J. and Nussbaum, P.D. (Eds), Clinical Neuropsychology. Washington, D.C: American Psychological Association.

Mann, J.J., Waternaux, C., Haas, G.L. and Malone, K.M. (1999) Toward a clinical model of suicidal behavior in psychiatric patients. American Journal of Psychiatry, 156: 181–189.

O'Connell, I., Farmer, R. and Catalan, J. (1996) Explaining suicide: the views of survivors of serious suicide attempts. British Journal of Psychiatry, 168: 780–786.

Paris, J., Zelkowitz, P., Guzder, J., Joseph, S. and Feldman, R. (1999) Neuropsychological factors associated with borderline pathology in children. Journal of the American Academy of Child and Adolescent Psychiatry, 38: 770–774.

Paykel, E.S., Prusoff, B.A. and Myers, J.K. (1975) Suicide attempts and recent life events. Archives of General Psychiatry, 32: 327–333.

Post, R.M. (1992) Transduction of psychosocial stress into the neurobiology of recurrent affective disorder. American Journal of Psychiatry, 149: 999–1010.

Segal, Z.V., Williams, J.M.G., Teasdale, J.D. and Gemar, M. (1996) A cognitive science perspective on kindling and episode sensitisation in recurrent affective disorder. Psychological Medicine, 26: 371–380.

Shaffer, D. (1974) Suicide in childhood and early adolescence. Journal of Child Psychology and Psychiatry, 15: 275–291.

Van Heeringen, C., Audenaert, K., Van de Wiele, A. and Verstraete, A. (in press) Cortisol in violent suicidal behaviour: association with personality and monoaminergic activity. Journal of Affective Disorders.

Part II

Suicide and Attempted Suicide in Specific Populations and Circumstances

Chapter 15

Suicidal Behaviour in Children: an Emphasis on Developmental Influences

Cynthia R. Pfeffer
Department of Psychiatry, Weill Medical College of Cornell University, New York Presbyterian Hospital, New York, USA

Abstract

Suicidal behaviour in children aged 5–14 years is an escalating phenomenon and warrants research and clinical attention to prevent this tragic loss of young lives. Although teenage suicide is prevalent in the USA, in 1996 the suicide rate of children and young adolescents increased, while that for adolescents and young adults decreased. Risk factors must be clarified for suicidal behaviour in children and knowledge about this disseminated to clinicians and the general public. Attention should focus on such risk factors as prior suicidal ideation or suicidal acts, mood disorders, family discord and family psychopathology, particularly suicidal behaviour, substance abuse and violent behaviour, as means of reducing suicidal risk in children. Methods of assessing children for risk of suicidal behaviour involve complex issues of direct interviewing of children and their parents. Treatment requires systematic research to identify methods that decrease risk for suicidal behaviour. This chapter addresses these issues by presenting recent material regarding epidemiology, clinical research on risk factors, and treatment of suicidal behaviour in children. Avenues of prevention are suggested that should be systematically studied regarding their effects on reducing suicidal behaviour and risk factors.

INTRODUCTION

There is still a questioning attitude about the occurrence of suicidal behaviour among children, despite the many publications since the mid-1980s about the increasing rates of suicidal behaviour among youth. This chapter will discuss the characteristics of prepubertal suicidal behaviour. Specifically, it will emphasize

The International Handbook of Suicide and Attempted Suicide. Edited by K. Hawton and K. van Heeringen.

factors that influence development and that have a significant impact upon the risk for suicidal behaviour among children. The information discussed is derived principally from empirical investigations and clinical experience, especially when research data are lacking about issues that warrant study but are important to guide hypothesis generation and clinical work.

The following clinical vignette is presented to highlight several features about prepubertal suicidal behaviour that are key issues in characterizing current knowledge about this serious problem among young children.

Patty is a pretty 8 year-old girl who was admitted to a child psychiatric hospital unit within 24 hours of taking an overdose of two of her mother's imipramine tablets. This suicide attempt occurred just before Patty went to sleep and no-one knew about it until the next morning, when Patty did not get up on time to prepare to go to school. Her mother aroused Patty, who complained of a headache, dizziness and tiredness. Patty was tearful and irritable and argued that her mother should "Leave me alone. I want to die". Alarmed, Patty's mother brought Patty to her paediatrician, who examined Patty to determine whether her physical condition was stable and extensively interviewed her regarding her statements about wanting to die. After spending a lengthy time with Patty, the paediatrician recommended that Patty should be hospitalized in a psychiatric unit for evaluation of suicidal behaviour because he was not sure why this had occurred. Patty would not talk to the paediatrician about what was troubling her. He considered that Patty's physical condition was stable, although she should be observed for the sequelae of the overdose of imipramine. He believed that Patty would not be safe at home because she was not able to tell her mother what was upsetting her. Patty insisted that the "best thing would be for me to die".

Patty's mother told the paediatrician that the last 2 months had been very stressful for the family because she and her husband had separated and were planning to divorce. Her mother described feeling very depressed and anxious over the last year, primarily because her husband often came home drunk and would be very hostile to her and threaten her for not being concerned about his problems at work. Patty is a fine student and has many friends but because her mother was not feeling well emotionally, she could not devote time to Patty's needs. Patty's teacher had spoken to Patty's mother about her concern that in the last 2 months Patty was fidgety in class, not able to concentrate and often day-dreamed. Patty's grades had dropped in the last marking period and she often did not complete homework assignments. Unlike Patty's usual involvement with other children, in the last month Patty had preferred to be alone and not join peers in after-school activities. Patty had had several arguments with her best friend.

This clinical vignette illustrates issues to be elaborated upon in this chapter regarding results of empirical research that highlight developmentally relevant factors associated with suicidal behaviour in young children.

DEVELOPMENTAL EPIDEMIOLOGY OF YOUTH SUICIDAL BEHAVIOUR

In the USA, *Vital Statistics Reports* provide data on suicide for the entire population. Therefore, inferences about the developmental specificity of suicide can be made. Despite the lack of national data on suicide attempts, cross-sectional and prospective naturalistic studies provide information about developmental features of non-fatal suicidal behaviour.

Table 15.1 shows a comparative overview of suicide in the USA among children and young adolescents aged 5–14 years and other age groups in 1996 (Peters et al, 1998). In this table, the standard of comparison is the suicide rate for all age groups.

The youngest age group in which suicides are recorded in the USA is 5–14 year-olds (Peters et al, 1998). In contrast to other age groups, this group of children and young adolescents has the lowest number and rate of suicides. Although more males than females commit suicide, the male:female ratio of suicide for 5–14 year-olds is lower (3:1) than for all other age groups (4:1) and for 15–24 year-olds (6:1). In the racially heterogeneous population of the USA, the rate of suicide is higher for whites than non-whites of all ages. Specifically, suicide among Hispanic 5–14 year-olds is ranked as the seventh leading cause of death among this racial group. The rate of suicide is highest for whites (fifth leading cause of death), followed by Hispanics (seventh leading cause of death) and than blacks (eighth leading cause of death) for both genders for the 5–14 year-old group. In general, death rates for Hispanics are lower than for other groups, although this may be an underestimate due to under-reporting of specific causes of death (Peters et al, 1998).

Table 15.1 Comparison of child and young adolescent suicide with suicide in other age groups in the USA in 1996

Group	Rate per 100,000	Number of deaths	Rank order
All races, both sexes, all ages	11.6	30,903	9
All races, both sexes, 5–14 years	0.8	302	6
All races, both sexes, 15–24 years	12.0	4,358	3
All races, male, all ages	19.3	24,998	9
All races, male, 5–14 years	1.1	225	4
All races, male, 15–24 years	20.0	3,724	3
All races, female, all ages	4.4	5,905	>10
All races, female, 5–14 years	0.4	77	7
All races, female, 15–24 years	3.6	634	4
White, both sexes, all ages	12.7	27,856	8
White, both sexes, 5–14 years	1.8	248	5
White, both sexes, 15–24 years	12.6	3,639	2
Black, both sexes, all ages	6.5	2,164	>10
Black, both sexes, 5–14 years	0.6	36	8
Black, both sexes, 15–24 years	9.5	523	3
Hispanic, both sexes, all ages	A	A	>10
Hispanic, both sexes, 5–14 years	0.6	31	7
Hispanic, both sexes, 15–24 years	9.9	490	3

A = Data not listed in reference (Peters et al, 1998).
Rank order reflects the order of cause of death in specific age and/or racial groups.

Use of guns and firearms is the leading cause of suicidal death in the USA for all age groups (Peters et al, 1998). Specifically, the suicide rate for injury by firearms for the 5–14 year-old group is 0.4 per 100,000 compared to 7.5 per 100,000 for 15–24 year-olds. Males aged 5–14 years have a firearm suicide rate of 0.7 per 100,000, compared to 0.2 per 100,000 for similar-aged females. There is a disproportionate gender difference for firearm suicide in the 15–24 year age group, with the male rate being 13.0 per 100,000 compared with the female rate of 1.7 per 100,000.

In the last decade, the rate of suicide among 5–14 year-olds has increased and reflects a trend of escalating suicide rates among youth. In 1998, the rate of suicide for 5–14 year-olds continued to increase, in contrast to a reduced suicide rate for 15–24 year-olds from 1995 to 1996. Various reasons have been offered for the increasing rates of youth suicidal behaviour but a conclusive answer is not apparent. Certainly, social changes may account for the major impact on the rising rate of child, adolescent and young adult suicide. A cohort effect for adolescents and young adults aged 15–24 years and born after World War II has been described, in which these cohorts have higher suicide rates than youth born prior to World War II (Klerman, 1988). Cohort effects for suicide among children and young adolescents, aged 5–14 years, have not been studied, but in recent years increasing suicide rates are documented.

Empirical research on prepubertal suicidal behaviour derived from community and clinical samples suggests that the rates of suicidal ideation are higher for girls and serious suicide attempts are more common among boys (Pfeffer et al, 1986). In addition, racial and social status are not significant risk factors for suicidal ideation or suicide attempts among children (Pfeffer et al, 1986). The incidence of prepubertal suicidal behaviour is suggested by a study of 67 prepubertal children who had no history of suicidal behaviour or psychiatric disorders and who were followed-up for 2 years (Pfeffer et al, 1988). At follow-up, approximately 1% had attempted suicide. Validation of such trends is required using large epidemiological studies of prepubertal children.

FAMILY CORRELATES OF SUICIDAL BEHAVIOUR IN CHILDREN AND YOUNG ADOLESCENTS

Perhaps one of the greatest issues accounting for the increase of suicidal behaviour among children and young adolescents is the risk imparted by familial factors. In 1969, Sabbath described a concept (the "expendable child") that highlighted children's perceptions of themselves relative to their family context. It is an important developmental feature of childhood that children are highly dependent on their caretakers for basic survival, and when this is lacking children exhibit various morbidities. Children's relatively immature cognitive functions are associated with styles of social interactions in which children perceive themselves in egocentric terms relative to their caretakers. Children find it difficult to differentiate their actions and feelings from those of their caretakers. Thus, behaviours and affects experienced within the family circumstances are often conceptualized by children in terms of their own actions and thoughts. It is in this context that the "expendable child" concept is most relevant as fostering guilt, self-blame, poor self-esteem, self-annihilation fantasies, isolation, loneliness, hopelessness and self-destructive behaviour in children. Suicidal children feel that their families will be better if they are no longer present (Sabbath, 1969). With the development of greater cognitive maturity, adolescents are able to utilize abstract concepts in understanding cause-and-effect relationships of events and interactions and their own role in family interactions and problems.

The expendable child concept (Sabbath, 1969) may have a more intense impact within families in which there is severe disorganization, tension and instability. Children may find it impossible to differentiate between their own responses to family stress and concepts of their own culpability for family problems. Such children may respond impulsively to family turmoil, have poor ability to test reality of the circumstances, and may be unable to think of adaptive behaviours under circumstances of family stress. Perceptions suicidal children have of their families include concerns that their families are less cohesive, less expressive, and higher in conflict than children who do not report suicidal tendencies (Asarnow, 1992). In general, suicidal children perceive their families as not providing support for them.

Empirical research suggests that early and chronic life event stresses, particularly within the family context, are associated with prepubertal suicidal behaviour (Pfeffer et al, 1993). Events that lead to family instability, such as moves, death, loss of relatives, illness of significant caretakers, may increase the likelihood for suicidal behaviour among prepubertal children. Pfeffer and colleagues (1993) identified that life event stress in pre-school years increases risk for future suicidal behaviour in children and adolescents. Perhaps early life event stress during critical periods of brain development affects risk for suicidal behaviour. This is an important concept that requires validation in future research.

Results of empirical research suggest that certain factors are associated with suicidal behaviour throughout the life cycle. Specifically, studies of adult suicide victims (Egland and Sussex, 1985), adolescent suicide victims (Brent et al, 1994), adolescents with non-fatal suicidal behaviour (Brent et al, 1988) and prepubertal suicidal children (Pfeffer et al, 1994) point out that suicidal behaviour aggregates in families. Pfeffer and colleagues (1994) found that children children who attempted suicide, in contrast to non-suicidal prepubertal children in a community sample, had a higher prevalence of suicide and suicide attempts among their parents and siblings.

It has been suggested that a constellation of psychopathologies involving parental and sibling substance abuse, violence and antisocial personality disorder are associated with suicide attempts of prepubertal children (Pfeffer et al, 1994). Although symptoms of mood disorders are often prevalent among the parents and siblings of suicidal and non-suicidal children, it has not been empirically demonstrated that symptoms of mood disorders among first-degree relatives of prepubertal suicidal children are associated with the suicide attempts of such children (Pfeffer et al, 1994). This differs from empirical results for adolescent and adult suicide victims or suicide attempters. It is possible that a constellation of psychiatric symptoms, including violence, substance abuse and impulsivity may elevate risk for suicidal behaviour and is related to underlying biological factors. As a corollary to these issues is the strong relationship between physical and sexual abuse and child suicidal behaviour (Wagner, 1997).

PSYCHIATRIC SYMPTOMS AND SUICIDAL BEHAVIOUR IN CHILDREN AND YOUNG ADOLESCENTS

There is ample validation that symptoms of depression are among the strongest correlates of prepubertal suicidal behaviour (Brent, 1987; Pfeffer et al, 1986; Asarnow, 1992; Pfeffer, 1993). This conclusion is also validated for adolescent suicide victims and for adolescent suicide attempters (Brent et al, 1994; Shaffer, 1988). Unlike risk for adolescent suicidal behaviour being associated with alcohol and illicit substance abuse (Brent et al, 1994; Shaffer, 1988), the prevalence of such disorders is low in children and, therefore, has not been identified as a strong correlate of prepubertal suicidal behaviour. Other psychiatric disorders, such as anxiety states, especially post-traumatic stress disorder, have been relatively neglected in empirical research of prepubertal suicidal behaviour and require systematic study. Ample research suggests that child physical and sexual abuse are associated with elevated risk for child and adolescent suicidal behaviour (Dyken et al, 1985). The psychiatric sequelae of such life experiences for childhood suicidal behaviour have been dramatically illustrated in clinical reports of preschool suicidal children who experienced traumatic, abusive family situations (Rosenthal and Rosenthal, 1984; Pfeffer and Trad, 1988). Whether other anxiety states, such as symptoms of panic attacks, are associated with prepubertal suicidal behaviour requires study. However, because of the relatively low prevalence of such symptoms and disorders, current research has not identified them as prominent correlates of prepubertal suicidal behaviour. Similarly, the relation of psychotic disorders, such as schizophrenia, to prepubertal suicidal behaviour has not been widely described, although such psychopathologies are significantly related to suicidal behaviour in adults. These trends suggest that there are distinct developmental differences between the epidemiological trends of psychopathology and risk for suicidal states in children versus other age groups.

COGNITIVE AND SOCIAL ADJUSTMENT PROFILES OF SUICIDAL BEHAVIOUR

Based on studies evaluating varied aspects of cognitive functions in prepubertal children, it can be inferred that suicidal children have aberrant cognitive processes. Studies have suggested that hopelessness, as in studies of adult suicidal individuals (Beck et al, 1985), is associated with prepubertal suicidal behaviour (Kazdin et al, 1983). Suicidal children have poor reality testing, are impulsive, and have problems in emotional and social problem solving (Pfeffer et al, 1995). Whether such characteristics represent trait or state phenomena requires additional investigation. Nevertheless, aberrations in cognitive processes identified for suicidal children impair such children's adaptive functioning, especially when confronted with life event stresses. The combined deficits in cognitive abilities and present life stresses increase vulnerability to suicidal behaviour among children. In fact, compared to suicidal adults, suicidal children have little consistency between their knowledge, fantasies and types of methods that can be used to carry out a suicidal act (Carlson et al, 1987).

Intellectual functioning, estimated by intelligence quotient (IQ), has been little investigated regarding risk for suicidal behaviour. Since developmental processes are associated with risk of suicidal behaviour, as evidenced by increasing rates of suicidal behaviour with age, higher intelligence may be associated with higher suicidal risk. Shaffer (1974) reported, in an uncontrolled early study of suicide in children and young adolescents, that the suicide victims had high IQs. This result has not been validated in other studies. These issues were more recently investigated in a sample of 90 consecutive hospital admissions to a specialty unit for children and adolescents with developmental problems (Walters et al, 1995). Suicidal behaviour was reported among patients with IQs at or above the moderated mental retardation range and was more common among adolescents than among children. A possible important implication of this study is that individuals with higher levels of developmental attainment may be at greater risk. However, such an inference requires extensive validation.

Social adjustment, measured as children's competence in carrying out appropriate social role behaviour, has been shown to be aberrant among children who exhibit suicidal ideation or suicide attempts (Pfeffer et al, 1993). In fact, this is a hallmark of risk for childhood suicidal behaviour and often an important precipitant of suicide attempts in children. For example, loss of a friendship due to arguments, or failure in academic achievement and fear of retribution from parents, are common ingredients for an acute suicidal episode among children. Children may be enveloped by intense family discord, which is a strong correlate for suicide attempts among prepubertal children (Pfeffer et al, 1994). Whether family discord is promoted by a child's problems in social adjustment or an outcome of other family problems, such as parental psychopathology, must be determined on an individual basis in the assessment of suicidal risk of prepubertal children.

BIOLOGICAL CORRELATES OF SUICIDAL BEHAVIOUR IN CHILDREN AND YOUNG ADOLESCENTS

With the development of extensive biological research on suicidal adults, hypotheses have been developed and tested that suggest avenues of research for evaluating the neurodevelopmental features of suicidal behaviour. Numerous studies of adults suggest that impulsivity, violence, substance abuse and suicidal behaviour are associated with dysregulation of serotonergic neurotransmitter functions (Mann and Stanley, 1986; see Chapter 4). Although results of such studies were based on evaluation in adults of post-mortem brains of suicide victims, cerebrospinal fluid assays and peripheral serotonin measures, few studies of children exist, primarily because most of the methodologies used for adults are not possible in children. Recently, Pfeffer and colleagues (1998b) reported that prepubertal children who attempt suicide have distinct peripheral serotonergic profiles. Specifically, this study, one of the few to research serotonin indices in prepubertal children, suggested that the average tryptophan content in blood was significantly lower among prepubertal psychiatric inpatients with a recent suicide attempt than among normal children or child psychiatric inpatients with suicidal ideation. An important implication of this result is that whole blood tryptophan may be a useful marker to identify children at risk for suicidal behaviour. Additional research to validate this inference is needed.

ASSESSMENT OF SUICIDAL BEHAVIOUR IN CHILDREN AND YOUNG ADOLESCENTS

The correlates of prepubertal suicidal behaviour highlighted in this chapter should be an essential part of the assessment of risk for childhood suicidal behaviour. Prospective research of prepubertal suicidal and non-suicidal children suggests that suicidal behaviour imparts significant risk for repeated suicidal behaviour (Pfeffer et al, 1991). In addition, mood disorders and poor social adjustment appear to be among the strongest predictors of future suicidal behaviour (Pfeffer et al, 1993). Other studies that prospectively evaluated prepubertal children who had a diagnosis of major depression suggested that this disorder increases risk for suicidal behaviour in adolescence (Kovacs et al, 1993) and in young adulthood (Rao et al, 1993; Wolk and Weissman, 1996). Such effects appeared to be related to the association between depression in childhood and depression in adulthood, rather than to other factors, such as life events, that are often associated with depressive symptoms. Notably, the rate of suicidal ideation remained relatively constant in children who were followed-up into adolescence, but the rate of suicide attempts increased with time and development (Kovacs et al, 1993). Suicidal and non-suicidal children are at risk for suicide attempts in adolescence when there is a lifetime family history among first-degree relatives of suicidal behaviour, substance abuse, depression and violence (Pfeffer et al, 1998a). Specifically, the risk for adolescent suicidal behaviour is more than seven times higher when mothers have a lifetime history of a suicide attempt and nine times higher when fathers have a lifetime history of substance abuse.

The most important feature of assessment of suicidal behaviour among children is to ask directly about suicidal ideation and suicidal behaviour. Children are capable of describing their suicidal intention, their suicidal fantasies and ideation and their suicidal acts. Speaking about these issues with children does not increase the likelihood that a suicidal state will occur, provided that the interviewer is sensitive in the manner in which questions are posed and observant of a child's discomfort or increasing state of suicidal tendency. Important questions to ask (Jacobsen et al, 1994) are:

1. Did you ever feel so upset that you wished you were not alive or wanted to die?
2. Did you ever hurt yourself or try to kill yourself?
3. Did you tell anyone that you wanted to die or were thinking about killing yourself?
4. Did you do anything to get ready to kill yourself?

Brent (1987) reported that, among suicidal children and adolescents, certain factors, including male sex, presence of mood disorder, high suicidal intent and ingestion of a psychotropic agent, are features that are similar for suicide attempters and suicide victims. Specifically, symptoms and the syndrome of depression are correlated with severity of suicidal behaviour (Brent et al, 1986). Furthermore, severity of suicidal intent and severity of psychopathology were most associated with lethality of suicide attempts in hopeless, dysphoric children and adolescents (Brent, 1987). However, availability of a lethal agent to carry out suicidal intent appeared to be the most important factor for impulsive suicide attempters (Brent, 1987). These issues should be a focus especially when interviewing these subtypes of children at risk for suicidal behaviour.

Interviews with parents are important for risk assessment of childhood suicidal behaviour, since the parent is often able to contribute information not accessible to the child. However, frequently parents lack knowledge about their child's suicidal state or deny the existence of it. Reasons that parents may minimize suicidal states of their children are lack of awareness about their child's suicidal intent or acts, guilt and shame of having a child who is suicidal, and misperceptions of the suicidal state of the child because of parental psychopathology (Jacobsen et al, 1994). In the assessment of suicidal behaviour of children, a clinical consensus is needed that synthesizes all information gathered from multiple sources.

Notably, environmental issues should be assessed. Most important is the identification of the availability of guns and firearms. If present, such weapons should be removed.

Children often express their fantasies and behaviours in drawing, a common pastime in children. Pfeffer and Richman (1991) reported that human figure drawings often reveal suicidal potential, notable in the characteristics of "slash lines" on various body parts. Such indicators do not indicate the severity of suicidal tendency and these indicators may be present when suicidal ideation or behaviour are not present; thereby serving as potential trait markers.

TREATMENT OF SUICIDAL CHILDREN

There are no reported intervention studies highlighting the efficacy of treatment for suicidal prepubertal children. Clinical experience suggests that individual treatment offered to the suicidal child is essential and that co-administered intervention for the child and parents is also required (Pfeffer, 1986). As noted above, prepubertal children are highly dependent upon their caretakers and subject to the effects of the vicissitudes of family life. A treatment approach that enhances family communication, that increases self-esteem of the child, that fosters consistent empathic support from relatives, and that decreases the child's perceptions of blame for family problems, is important. Availability of a therapist during acute crises and when acute suicidal risk is evident is essential. Therapists should be trained in working with suicidal children, be consistent and honest in relating to the suicidal child, be objective in understanding suicidal children's attitudes and life problems, and be optimistic and able to stimulate communication about suicidal children's concerns (Pfeffer, 1990).

Psychopharmacology is now an important feature of intervention for children with psychiatric disturbances. Research on medications to treat suicidal behaviour in prepubertal children is lacking. However, an approach to target symptoms of disorders that increase suicidal risk is a valid approach.

With the development of selective serotonin reuptake inhibitors (SSRIs) to treat depression and with the advent of research to indicate that these types of medications are effective in treating depression in children and adolescents (Emslie et al, 1997), use of SSRIs may decrease acute suicidal behaviour and symptoms of depression. Such medications are relatively safe if taken in overdose.

Intervention should focus on diminishing parental psychopathology and, if needed, parents may be referred for individual psychotherapy or psychopharmacological treatment. Enhancing environmental supports in the child's milieu, such as at school or in recreational situations, is an important adjunctive intervention that can enhance social adjustment. Removal of guns and firearms should be a key element in intervention for suicidal children.

CONCLUSIONS

Suicidal behaviour among children is associated with extensive personal and social morbidity and relatively low mortality. However, suicidal behaviour in children is associated with increased risk for suicidal behaviour and potential mortality in adolescence. Psychiatric symptoms, family discord and family psychopathology are key risk factors for prepubertal suicidal behaviour. The development of new research and clinical techniques may make it more likely that aetiological factors for prepubertal suicidal behaviour will be identified. Developmental distinctions regarding risk for suicidal behaviour are outlined in this chapter and future research may identify underlying parameters that are associated with critical influences on risk for suicidal behaviour of children.

REFERENCES

Asarnow, J.A. (1992) Suicidal ideation and attempts during middle childhood: associations with perceived family stress and depression among child psychiatric inpatients. Journal of Clinical Child Psychology, 21: 35–40.

Beck, A.T., Steer, R.A., Kovacs, M. and Garrison, B. (1985) Hopelessness and eventual suicide: a 10-year prospective study of patients hospitalized with suicidal ideation. American Journal of Psychiatry, 142: 559–563.

Brent, D.A. (1987) Correlates of the medical lethality of suicide attempts in children and adolescents. Journal of the American Academy of Child and Adolescent Psychiatry, 26: 87–91.

Brent, D.A., Kalas, R., Edelbrock, C., Costello, A.J., Dulcan, M.K. and Conover, N. (1986) Psychopathology and its relationship to suicidal ideation in childhood and adolescence. Journal of the American Academy of Child Psychiatry, 25: 666–673.

Brent, D.A., Perper, J.A., Goldstein, C.E., Kolko, D.J., Allan, M.J., Allman, C.J. and Zelenak, J.P. (1988) Risk factors for adolescent suicide: a comparison of adolescent suicide victims with suicidal inpatients. Archives of General Psychiatry, 45: 581–588.

Brent, D.A., Perper, J.A., Moritz, G., Liotus, L., Schweers, J., Balach, L. and Roth, C. (1994) Familial risk factors for adolescent suicide: a case-control study. Acta Psychiatrica Scandinavica, 89: 52–58.

Carlson, G.A., Asarnow, J.R. and Orbach, I. (1987) Developmental aspects of suicidal behavior in children: I. Journal of the American Academy of Child and Adolescent Psychiatry, 26: 186–192.

Dyken, E.Y., Alpert, J.J. and McNamara, J.J. (1985) A pilot study of the effect of exposure to child abuse or neglect on adolescent suicidal behavior. American Journal of Psychiatry, 142: 1299–1303.

Egland J.A. and Sussex J.N. (1985) Suicide and family loading for affective disorders. Journal of the American Medical Association, 254: 915–918.

Emslie, G., Rush, A., Weinberg, W.A., Kowatch, R.A., Hughes, C.W., Carmody, T. and Rintelmann, J. (1997) A double-blind, randomized placebo-controlled trial of fluoxetine in children and adolescents with depression. Archives of General Psychiatry, 54: 1031–1037.

Jacobsen, L.K., Rabinowitz, I., Popper, M.S., Solomon, R.J., Sokol, M.S. and Pfeffer, C.R. (1994) Interviewing prepubertal children about suicidal ideation and behavior. Journal of the American Academy of Child and Adolescent Psychiatry, 33: 439–452.

Kazdin, A.E., French, N.H., Unis, A.S., Esveldt-Dawson, K. and Sherrick, R.B. (1983) Hopelessness, depression, suicidal intent among psychiatrically disturbed inpatient children. Journal of Consulting and Clinical Psychology, 51: 504–510.

Klerman, G.L. (1988) The current age of youthful melancholia: evidence for increase in depression among adolescents and young adults. British Journal of Psychiatry, 152: 4–14.

Kovacs, M., Goldston, D. and Gatsonis, C. (1993) Suicidal behaviors and childhood-onset depressive disorders: a longitudinal investigation. Journal of the American Academy of Child and Adolescent Psychiatry, 32: 8–20.

Mann, J.J. and Stanley, M. (1986) Psychobiology of Suicidal Behavior. Annals of the New York Academy of Sciences, Vol. 487. New York: New York Academy of Sciences.

Peters, K.D., Kochanek, K.D. and Murphy, S.L. (1998) Deaths: Final Data for 1996. National Vital Statistics Reports, Vol. 47, no. 9. Hyattsville, MD: National Center for Health Statistics.

Pfeffer, C.R. (1986) The Suicidal Deed. New York: Guilford.

Pfeffer, C.R. (1990) Clinical perspectives on treatment of suicidal behavior among children and adolescents. Psychiatric Annals, 20: 143–150.

Pfeffer, C.R., Hurt, S.W., Peskin, J.R. and Siefker, C.A. (1995) Suicidal children grow up: ego functions associated with suicide attempts. Journal of the American Academy of Child and Adolescent Psychiatry, 34: 1318–1325.

Pfeffer, C.R., Klerman, G.L., Hurt, S.W., Lesser, M., Peskin, J.R. and Siefker, C.A. (1991) Suicidal children grow up: demographic and clinical risk factors for adolescent suicide attempts. Journal of the American Academy of Child and Adolescent Psychiatry, 30: 609–616.

Pfeffer, C.R., Klerman, G.L., Hurt, S.W., Kakuma, T., Peskin, J.R. and Siefker, C.A. (1993) Suicidal children grow up: rates and psychosocial risk factors for suicide attempts during follow-up. Journal of the American Academy of Child and Adolescent Psychiatry, 32: 106–113.

Pfeffer, C.R., Lipkins, R., Plutchik, R. and Mizruchi, M. (1988) Normal children at risk for suicidal behavior: a two-year follow-up study. Journal of the American Academy of Child and Adolescent Psychiatry, 27: 34–41.

Pfeffer, C.R., McBride, A., Anderson, G.M., Kakuma, T., Fensterheim, L. and Khait, V. (1998a) Peripheral serotonin measures in prepubertal psychiatric inpatients and normal children: associations with suicidal behavior and its risk factors. Biological Psychiatry, 44: 569–577.

Pfeffer, C.R., Normandin, L. and Kakuma, T. (1994) Suicidal children grow up: suicidal behavior and psychiatric disorders among relatives. Journal of the American Academy of Child and Adolescent Psychiatry, 33: 1087–1097.

Pfeffer, C.R., Normandin, L. and Kakuma, T. (1998b) Suicidal children grow up: relations between family psychopathology and adolescents' lifetime suicidal behavior. Journal of Nervous and Mental Disease, 186: 269–275.

Pfeffer, C.R., Plutchik, R., Mizruchi, M.S. and Lipkins, R. (1986) Suicidal behaviour in child psychiatric inpatients and outpatients and in non-patients. American Journal of Psychiatry, 143: 733–738.

Pfeffer, C.R. and Richman, J. (1991) Human figure drawings: an auxiliary diagnostic assessment of childhood suicidal potential. Comprehensive Mental Health Care, 1: 77–90.

Pfeffer, C.R. and Trad, P.V. (1988) The role of parental self-reporting in the treatment of child abuse. American Journal of Psychotherapy, 62: 125–134.

Rao, U., Weissman, M.M., Martin, J.A. and Hammond, R.W. (1993) Childhood depression and risk of suicide: a preliminary report of a longitudinal study. Journal of the American Academy of Child and Adolescent Psychiatry, 32: 21–27.

Rosenthal, P.A. and Rosenthal, S. (1984) Suicidal behavior by preschool children. American Journal of Psychiatry, 141: 520–525.

Sabbath, J.C. (1969) The suicidal adolescent: the expendable child. Journal of the American Academy of Child Psychiatry, 8: 272–289.

Shaffer, D. (1974) Suicide in childhood and adolescence. Journal of Child Psychology and Psychiatry, 15: 275–291.

Shaffer, D. (1988) The epidemiology of teen suicide: an examination of risk factors. Journal of Clinical Psychiatry, 49: 36–41.

Wagner, B.M. (1997) Family risk factors for child and adolescent suicidal behavior. Psychological Bulletin, 121: 246–298.

Walters, A.S., Barrett, R.P., Knapp, L.G. and Borden, M.C. (1995) Suicidal behaviour in children and adolescents with mental retardation. Research in Developmental Disabilities, 16: 85–96.

Wolk, S.I. and Weissman, M.M. (1996) Suicidal behavior in depressed children grown up: preliminary results of a longitudinal study. Psychiatric Annals, 26: 331–335.

Chapter 16

Adolescent Suicidal Behaviour: a General Population Perspective

Erik Jan de Wilde
Department of Clinical and Health Psychology, Leiden University, The Netherlands

Abstract

Most empirical data about adolescent suicidal behaviour are derived from studies with clinical samples. However, the majority of adolescents who perform some sort of suicidal act do not enter a clinical setting because of it. This chapter presents results from studies with these non-clinical adolescent samples. It describes some epidemiological concerns about rates of self-reported suicidal behaviour, correlates of self-reported suicidal behaviour, and preventive efforts. The risk factor characteristics of the "suicidal minority" in the community are very similar to those of inpatient or other clinical samples of adolescents. Although empirical evidence should yet substantiate it, this implies that many adolescents in the general population may actually be in need of help and that perhaps a more outreaching policy by clinicians may be desirable.

INTRODUCTION

The general adolescent population is frequently studied. In the study of suicidal behaviours, however, most empirical data are described in studies that deal with a specific subgroup of the adolescent population: those adolescents who have somehow personally made contact with a clinician. This clinical contact may either have taken place before a first suicidal act (based on a general suspicion of suicidality or perhaps other psychopathology) or after a first suicidal act (when medical attention is usually given to deal with the physical consequences). In

The International Handbook of Suicide and Attempted Suicide. Edited by K. Hawton and K. van Heeringen.

both cases, the clinical setting offers the researcher the opportunity to conduct interviews and administer tests or questionnaires to suicidal persons. It may, therefore, provide valuable, in-depth information about the person's suicidal process.

It is likely, however, that the vast majority of adolescents who perform some sort of suicidal act do not enter this clinical setting at all. It is the purpose of this chapter to examine the characteristics of this majority of non-referred, non-clinical adolescents. It will be limited to data derived from community samples of adolescents.

EPIDEMIOLOGICAL ISSUES

Although ranking as a major cause of death, completed suicide is still a rare event in young people, especially when compared to other age groups. Indeed, several authors state that one of the most basic facts about completed suicide is that its risk increases as a function of age (Diekstra, 1993). It is extremely rare in children under the age of 12 (e.g. see Shaffer and Fisher, 1981; Brooksbank, 1985; Kienhorst et al, 1987; Chapter 15). The highest European national suicide rates in 15–24 year-olds are found in Finland: 8 per 100,000 in females and 45 per 100,000 in young males (Hawton et al, 1998). The observation that completed suicide ranks as a major cause of death is mainly because very few adolescents die from other causes, such as physical diseases.

Although accurate *national* statistics for attempted suicide are unavailable, the number of acts is much higher than that of completed suicides. The data from the *regional* centres in the WHO/EURO Multicentre Study on Parasuicide suggest that in most centres the younger age groups (15–24 years) show the highest rates (Schmidtke et al, 1996). Futhermore, rates of completed suicide and attempted suicide or parasuicide are positively related (Hawton et al, 1998).

Most data on rates of non-fatal suicidal behaviour are based on medical contacts, such as hospital admissions or consultations with general practitioners. They are therefore directly linked to the medical seriousness of the consequences of the suicidal act: adolescents who take too many paracetamol tablets with the expectation of dying, but who end up in the bathroom being sick because of it, are unlikely to seek or get medical attention for this act of self-poisoning. Similarly, adolescents who are on the verge of cutting themselves but decide not do so because, for instance, they suddenly see someone arriving, are unlikely to think that they need medical attention. These cases will not be included in the above-mentioned rates, but are nonetheless of importance for getting a clear picture of the phenomenon under study. To make a more appropriate estimate of the rate of the behaviour in the general population, nationwide screenings may prove to be more accurate.

Because in many countries there is an obligation for youngsters to be at school until the age of 16 years, school seems to provide an adequate entry for collecting such data (of course, adolescents who not attend school often appear to be a

Table 16.1 European community surveys on self-reported suicidal behaviour by adolescents, 1990–1997

Reference	Country	Sample size	"Suicide attempts" (%)	"Suicidal thoughts" (%)
Kienhorst et al, 1990	The Netherlands	9,393	2.2	3.5
Csorba et al, 1994	Hungary	347		2.0–8.2
Rossow and Wichstrom, 1997	Norway	10,839	8.3	
Garnefski et al, 1992	The Netherlands	15,245	5.7	20.2
Essau et al, 1995	Germany	215	5.6	15.9
Buddeberg et al, 1996	Switzerland	1,937	2.3	24.1
Ivarsson and Gillberg, 1997	Sweden	524	3.6	18.6
Rey et al, 1997	Switzerland	9,268	3.0	14.7
De Wilde and Kienhorst, 1998	The Netherlands	19,250	2.6	22.4

special risk group). These school-based studies have been performed many times, predominantly in the USA (e.g. Smith and Crawford, 1986; Andrews and Lewinsohn, 1992; Meehan et al, 1992; Felts et al, 1992; Garrison et al, 1993; Saunders et al, 1994; Vannatta, 1996) and in Western Europe (see Table 16.1 for European studies during the last 10 years).

The results of these studies, where rates are concerned, should be examined with strict caution, because:

1. In most studies a clear description of what actually is meant by "attempted suicide" is not given or does not comply with definitions used, for instance, in the system of the International Classification of Diseases. For interpretation of rates, one then has to rely on the adolescents' own concepts of the behaviour.
2. The extent to which many of the studies include representative samples of adolescents is uncertain.
3. The results vary according to the method of data collection, such as anonymity of the questionnaire (De Wilde and Kienhorst, 1995), wording of the questions on which the results were based, and the time period that was asked about.

Nevertheless, because these self-reported self-harm rates are expressed in terms of *percentages* rather than in terms of *rates per 100,000*, they suggest that the number of self-reported yearly rates is likely to be about 100 times higher than the hospital admission rates.

The same conceptual problems arise when discussing self-report rates of suicidal ideation in the general population. Again, when not using psychometrically sound scales for suicidal ideation, but merely single items, the correct interpretation depends on the adolescents' concepts of the suicidal behaviour (Meehan et al, 1992). It is nevertheless evident that a significant proportion of adolescents report having had thoughts about some sort of self-harm, sometimes up to a point prevalence of 25% (Garnefski et al, 1992; Goldney et al, 1989; Schotte and Clum, 1982; Strang and Orlofsky, 1990; Smith and Crawford, 1986; Swanson et al, 1992).

CONTINUITY OF SUICIDAL PHENOMENA IN THE GENERAL POPULATION

Based upon the rates noted above, it is safe to conclude that at some time during their development many adolescents in the general population will experience some degree of unhappiness, as expressed by self-reports of suicidal thoughts or acts. The question then arises, whether this malaise is specifically "suicidal" during adolescence, or whether other forms of problem behaviour or emotions are also frequent during this developmental period. Using the longitudinal data of the New Zealand Dunedin Multidisciplinairy Health Development Study, Feehan and colleagues (1993) report a 21.5% prevalence rate of DSM-III disorder (as assessed with the Diagnostic Interview Schedule) at age 15 years and a 36% prevalence of DSM-III disorders at age 18 years. The most frequent conditions at age 15 were anxiety disorders (8%), followed by conduct disorders (5%). At age 18 years, the most prevalent disorders were major depressive episode (17%), alcohol dependence (10%) and social phobia (11%). Another New Zealand sample showed that substance use disorders were most prevalent among adolescents aged 14–16 years (Fergusson and Lynskey, 1995).

The next question is whether these problems are incidental, chronic or somewhere in between. Interestingly, in the Dunedin Multidisciplinairy Health Development Study there was considerable continuity of the disorders: 63% of those with a disorder at age 15 years also showed a disorder at age 18 years (Feehan et al, 1993). The issue of continuity of suicidal behaviour in adolescents in the general population is not yet entirely settled. Conceptually, suicidal ideation, attempted suicide and completed suicide are behaviours that are hierarchically related: suicidal thoughts should generally precede suicidal acts, and completed suicides constitute the lethal subgroup of suicide attempts. Although this may not apply for everyone, it is tempting to see these behaviours as successive parts of a continuum of suicidality. In clinical samples, these behaviours are very much interrelated (Brent et al, 1988; Kosky et al, 1990). In a high school sample of 380 pupils, Harkavy and colleagues (1987) suggested that suicidal ideators and suicide attempters represent overlapping groups. In a sample of 1,700 general population adolescents with depressed mood, a report of "having ever had suicidal thoughts" increased the risk of a suicide attempt in the following year 2.5 times (De Wilde and Kienhorst, 1998). A report of "thoughts during the previous month" increased the risk 3.3 times. The conclusion is that in the general population there may very well be a significant relation between the various suicidal phenomena, but more research is needed to establish this empirically and to investigate factors contributing to the continuity.

CORRELATES OF ADOLESCENT SUICIDAL BEHAVIOUR IN GENERAL POPULATION SAMPLES

In this section, the various factors correlated to suicidal behaviour in the general adolescent population will be described in two main clusters: *environmental factors* (influences from outside the adolescent on his/her psychology and suicidal behaviour—subdivided into "external influences" and "exposure to adverse life events"); and *psychological factors* (personality or psychological/psychiatric characteristics that influence suicidal behaviour).

Environmental Factors: External Influences

Adolescents, more than adults, seem particularly susceptible to media influences. Building their own identity, they sometimes seem to be on a permanent lookout for role models to identify with. Total strangers may be idealized on the basis of only their music or looks. This modelling effect may explain why several studies show an increase in suicide rates after exposure to fictional films or television newscasts about suicide (Phillips and Carstensen, 1986; Ostroff et al, 1987; Berman, 1988; see Chapter 39). Furthermore, besides changes in suicide rates, increases have also been found in the use of particular methods of suicide portrayed in the broadcasts (Schmidtke and Häfner, 1988; Ostroff and Boyd, 1987; Berman, 1987; see Chapter 39). However, since these studies are purely correlational, an increase in suicides after exposure to media portrayal of suicide does not demonstrate the existence of imitation. Imitation effects have to be established in controlled experiments. By exposing 116 high school students to different video-simulated conditions, Steede and Range (1989) concluded that adolescents may not be influenced by news about suicide or may just deny such influence. In another experimental study, Range and colleagues (1988) reported that their 142 subjects acknowledged the existence of behavioural contagion after suicide is reported, and that they perceived themselves to be influenced by such information. Of course, it would be rather naive to suggest that people commit suicide solely on the basis of external media influences. In this respect it is surprising that very little is known about the effect of these stimuli on specific subgroups of adolescents, such as suicide ideators.

Models of suicidal behaviour may also occur closer in the vicinity of the adolescent. High school surveys show that adolescents who report having attempted suicide also know more peers or family members who have attempted or committed suicide (Smith and Crawford, 1986; Harkavy et al, 1987). In another North American sample it was found that 40% of the adolescents reported that they knew someone who had committed suicide (Domino and Takahashi, 1991). Of course, modelling is not the only possible explanation for these results. An alternative possibility is that a cause of elevated risk is increased stress of exposure to suicidal behaviour. The possibly direct influence is also displayed in the phenomenon of suicide clusters, which are evidently existent in young populations (Jobes and Cimbolic, 1990; Gould et al, 1989; see Chapter 24).

Environmental Factors: Exposure to Adverse Life Events

The family is a predominant source of influence on the adolescent's suicidal behaviour (Wagner, 1997). Lewinsohn and colleagues (1994) followed a group of 1,500 high school students for 1 year and established that those adolescents who reported having attempted suicide also showed a significantly lower level of family support, even after statistically controlling for depression. In a Dutch cross-sectional study, those reporting suicide attempts had more disturbed relationships with their parents than adolescents who did not report attempts (Kienhorst et al, 1990). These results may be related to the finding that such suicide attempters also report much more physical and/or sexual abuse than non-attempters. This association has been clearly established in studies of a sample of 6,637 Navaho youths (Grossman et al, 1991), 5,730 adolescents in Minnesota (Hernandez et al, 1993), 600 high school students (Riggs et al, 1990) and 1,050 students in grades 7–12 (Wagner et al, 1995). In a Dutch sample (n = 1490) of adolescents who reported having been sexually abused, suicide attempts were five times more common in girls and 20 times more common in boys compared with non-abused adolescents (Garnefski and Arends, 1998).

Psychological Factors

There is a significant relationship between attitude towards suicidal behaviour and suicidal ideation (Stein et al, 1992). So what is the attitude towards suicide in adolescents in the general population? Domino and Takahashi (1991) addressed this question in a high school sample of North American adolescents. His study showed that, in general, adolescents do not have a romanticized, idealistic view of self-inflicted death. The adolescents were able to distinguish between mental illness in general and depression in particular as a significant precursor of suicide. Eighty-nine percent said they agreed with the statement that most people who attempt suicide are lonely or depressed. Eighty-five percent acknowledged that a suicide attempt is often essentially a "cry for help". So, the general attitude seems not unrealistic. However, nearly half of a group of Israeli students did not regard suicide as a shameful act, and approximately two-thirds considered it justifiable under certain conditions. There is also variation with age and gender: older students agree less with different reasons for suicide than younger students. Females sympathize more with reasons for suicide than do males (Stillion et al, 1984).

Psychological factors cannot be seen separately from developmental aspects of the adolescent phase. Adolescence begins with physical growth and maturation and development: the adolescent needs to become familiar with these developments, which may cause confusion and uneasiness. Sexual and erotic feelings need to be incorporated in the personality. Besides physical changes, the adolescent is on course for adulthood. Economic independence and separation from parents are important tasks. Development of a self-concept ("Who am I?", and "What do I want"?) becomes a recurrent theme. In this development, disturbances may occur which are related to suicidal behaviour. Several studies identify low self-esteem scores for adolescents who report having attempted suicide (Overholser et al, 1995). Low self-esteem is also a significant correlate of depression (DeSimone et al, 1994; Brubeck and Beer, 1992; Yanish and Battle, 1985). Depressed mood and depressive disorder are among the highest correlates of adolescent self-reported suicidal behaviour. The occurrence of self-reported depressed mood in the general adolescent population in European samples seems to vary between 10% (Olsson and von Knorring, 1997) and 20% (Madianos et al, 1993). In 529 15–19 year-old UK girls, the estimated 1-year prevalence rate for depression was 18.9% (Monck et al, 1994). It also appeared reasonably stable over a six-month period in young UK adolescents (Charman, 1994).

Other types of problem behaviours also seem to co-vary with the report of suicidal behaviour. In a study of 9,393 Dutch adolescents, Kienhorst and colleagues (1990) found that use of soft drugs was a main predictor of a report of attempted suicide. Investigating other addiction-risk behaviours in a sample of 6,084 16–19 year-olds, Garnefski and De Wilde (1998) established that the percentage of self-reported suicide attempts was linearly related to the number of addiction-risk behaviours. Of the girls who reported four or more addiction-risk behaviours, 45% reported a suicide attempt. In boys the equivalent figure was 14%.

PREVENTION

In the field of primary prevention, the number of curriculum-based programmes introduced into schools in the USA between 1984 and 1989 increased by 200% (Garland et al, 1989) and continues to grow. Briefly, the main goals are: (a) to raise awareness of the problem of adolescent suicide; (b) to train participants to identify adolescents at risk for suicide; and (c) to educate participants about community mental health resources and referral techniques. The programmes are presented by mental health professionals or educators and are most commonly directed to secondary school students, their parents, and educators. The mean duration of the programmes is approximately 2 hours.

Unfortunately, most suicide prevention programmes have fallen short of these requirements. Although many curriculum-based suicide prevention programmes have been operating since 1981 (Garland et al, 1989), there are only a few published evaluation studies, and most of these are poorly designed in that there is no control group. A few exceptions are a suicide awareness program for ninth-graders (Spirito et al, 1988) and the New Jersey study of Shaffer et al (1990). The first study concluded that the programme was minimally effective in imparting knowledge and ineffective in changing attitudes. The latter found few positive effects of three suicide prevention curriculum programmes and some possible negative effects (see Chapter 37 for a further discussion of school-based prevention).

CONCLUSIONS

Separating the results derived from community sample studies from studies in clinical samples gives us more insight in the malaise many adolescents have to cope with. Adolescence is a period of turmoil, demonstrated by fairly high rates of stressful circumstances and psychopathology. Although the majority of adolescents seem to cope well, the risk factor characteristics of the "suicidal minority" in the community are very similar to those of inpatient or other clinical samples of adolescents. While further evidence to substantiate preventive efforts is required, this implies that many adolescents in the general population may actually be in need of help, that a more outreaching prevention policy by clinical services may be more desirable, and that there should be greater access to crisis services (telephone help-lines, walk-in services) that are attractive to, and hence would be used by, adolescents.

REFERENCES

Andrews, J.A. and Lewinsohn, P.M. (1992) Suicidal attempts among older adolescents: prevalence and co-occurrence with psychiatric disorders. Journal of the American Academy of Child and Adolescent Psychiatry, 31: 655–662.

Berman, A. (1988) Fictional depiction of suicide in television films and imitation effects. American Journal of Psychiatry, 145: 982–986.

Berman, A.L. (1987) Adolescent suicide: clinical consultation. Clinical Psychologist, 40: 87–90.

Brent, D., Perper, J., Goldstein, C., Kolko, D., Allan, M., Allman, C. and Zelenak, J. (1988) Risk factors for adolescent suicide. A comparison of adolescent suicide victims with suicidal inpatients. Archives of General Psychiatry, 45: 581–588.

Brooksbank, D. (1985) Suicide and parasuicide in childhood and early adolescence. British Journal of Psychiatry, 146: 459–463.

Brubeck, D. and Beer, J. (1992) Depression, self-esteem, suicide ideation, death anxiety, and GPA in high school students of divorced and non-divorced parents. Psychological Reports, 71: 755–763.

Buddeberg, C., Buddeberg, F.B., Gnam, G., Schmid, J. and Christen, S. (1996) Suicidal behavior in Swiss students: an 18-month follow-up survey. Crisis, 17: 78–86.

Charman, T. (1994) The stability of depressed mood in young adolescents: a school-based survey. Journal of Affective Disorders, 30: 109–116.

Csorba, J., Dinya, E. and Huszar, I. (1994) Suicidal attempt and negative life events in adolescence. Psychiatria Hungarica, 9: 483–493.

De Wilde, E.J. and Kienhorst, C.W.M. (1995) Suicide attempts in adolescence: "self-report" and "other-report". Crisis, 16: 59–65.

De Wilde, E.J. and Kienhorst, C.W.M. (1998) Self-reported suicidal thoughts as predictor of suicide attempts in adolescents with depressed mood. Paper presented at the third conference of Psychology and Health, Kerkrade, The Netherlands.

DeSimone, A., Murray, P. and Lester, D. (1994) Alcohol use, self-esteem, depression, and suicidality in high school students. Adolescence, 29: 939–942.

Diekstra, R.F. (1993) The epidemiology of suicide and parasuicide. Acta Psychiatrica Scandinavica, 371: 9–20.

Domino, G. and Takahashi, Y. (1991) Attitudes toward suicide in Japanese and American medical students. Suicide and Life Threatening Behavior, 21: 345–359.

Essau, C.A., Pevermann, F. and Couradt, J. (1995) Symptomen von Augst und Depression bei Jugendlichen. Praxis der Kinderpsychologie und Kinderpsychiatrie, 44 (8), 322–328.

Feehan, M., McGee, R. and Williams, S. (1993) Mental health disorders from age 15 to age 18 years. Journal of the American Association of Child and Adolescent Psychiatry, 32: 1118–1126.

Felts, W.M., Chenier, T. and Barnes, R. (1992) Drug use and suicide ideation and behavior among North Carolina public school students. American Journal of Public Health, 82: 870–872.

Fergusson, D.M. and Lynskey, M.T. (1995) Childhood circumstances, adolescent adjustment, and suicide attempts in a New Zealand birth cohort. Journal of the American Academy of Child and Adolescent Psychiatry, 34: 612–622.

Garland, A., Shaffer, D. and Whittle, B. (1989) A national survey of school-based, adolescent suicide prevention programs. Journal of the American Academy of Child and Adolescent Psychiatry, 28: 931–934.

Garnefski, N. and Arends, E. (1998) Sexual abuse and adolescent maladjustment: difference between male and female victims. Journal of Adolescence, 21: 99–107.

Garnefski, N. and de Wilde, E.J. (1998) Addiction-risk behaviours and suicide attempts in adolescents. Journal of Adolescence, 21: 135–142.

Garnefski, N., Diekstra, R.F. and de Heus, P. (1992) A population-based survey of the characteristics of high school students with and without a history of suicidal behavior. Acta Psychiatrica Scandinavica, 86: 189–196.

Garrison, C.Z., McKeown, R.E., Valois, R.F. and Vincent, M.L. (1993) Aggression, substance use, and suicidal behaviors in high school students. American Journal of Public Health, 83: 179–184.

Goldney, R.D., Winefield, A.H., Tiggemann, M., Winefield, H.R. and Smith, S. (1989) Suicidal ideation in a young adult population. Acta Psychiatrica Scandinavia, 79: 481–489.

Gould, M.S., Wallenstein, S. and Davidson, L. (1989) Suicide clusters: a critical review. Suicide and Life Threatening Behavior, 19: 17–29.

Grossman, D.C., Milligan, B.C. and Deyo, R.A. (1991) Risk factors for suicide attempts among Navajo adolescents. American Journal of Public Health, 81: 870–874.

Harkavy, F.J., Asnis, G.M., Boeck, M. and DiFiore, J. (1987) Prevalence of specific suicidal behaviors in a high school sample. American Journal of Psychiatry, 144: 1203–1206.

Hawton, K., Arensman, E., Wasserman, D., Hulten, A., Bille-Bratie, U., Bjerke, T., Crepet, P., Deisenhammer, E., Kerkhof, A., De Leo, D., Michel, K., Ostamo, A., Philippe, A., Querejeta, I., Salander, R.E., Schmidtke, A. and Temesvary, B. (1998) Relation between attempted suicide and suicide rates among young people in Europe. Journal of Epidemiology and Community Health, 52: 191–194.

Hernandez, J., Lodico, M. and DiClemente, R. (1993) The effects of child abuse and race on risk-taking in male adolescents. Journal of the National Medical Association, 85: 593–597.

Ivarsson, T. and Gillberg, C. (1997) Depressive symptoms in Swedish adolescents: normative data using the Birleson Depression Self-Rating Scale (DSRS). Journal of Affective Disorders, 42: 59–68.

Jobes, D.A. and Cimbolic, P. (1990) The werther effect and youth suicide clusters. In P. Cimbolic and D.A. Jobes (Eds), Youth Suicide: Issues, Assessment, and Intervention, pp. 103–112. Springfield, IL: Charles C. Thomas.

Kienhorst, C.W., De Wilde, E.J., Van den Bout, J. and Broese-Van-Groenou, M.I. (1990) Self-reported suicidal behavior in Dutch secondary education students. Suicide and Life Threatening Behavior, 20: 101–112.

Kienhorst, C.W., Wolters, W.H., Diekstra, R.F. and Otte, E. (1987) A study of the frequency of suicidal behaviour in children aged 5 to 14. Journal of Child Psychology and Psychiatry, 28: 153–165.

Kosky, R., Silburn, S. and Zubrick, S. (1990) Are children and adolescents who have suicidal thoughts different from those who attempt suicide? Journal of Nervous and Mental Disease, 178: 38–43.

Lewinsohn, P.M., Rohde, P. and Seeley, J.R. (1994) Psychosocial risk factors for future adolescent suicide attempts. Journal of Consulting and Clinical Psychology, 62: 297–305.

Madianos, M.G., Gefou-Madianou, D. and Stefanis, C.N. (1993) Depressive symptoms and suicidal behavior among general population adolescents and young adults across Greece. European Psychiatry, 8: 139–146.

Meehan, P.J., Lamb, J.A., Saltzman, L.E. and O'Carroll, P.W. (1992) Attempted suicide among young adults: progress toward a meaningful estimate of prevalence. American Journal of Psychiatry, 149: 41–44.

Monck, E., Graham, P., Richman, N. and Dobbs, R. (1994) Adolescent girls: II. Background factors in anxiety and depressive states. British Journal of Psychiatry, 165: 770–780.

Olsson, G. and von Knorring, A.L. (1997) Depression among Swedish adolescents measured by the self-rating scale Center for Epidemiology Studies—Depression Child (CES-DC). European Child and Adolescent Psychiatry, 6: 81–87.

Ostroff, R.B. and Boyd, J.H. (1987) Television and suicide. New England Journal of Medicine, 316 (14): 877–879.

Overholser, J.C., Adams, D.M., Lehnert, K.L. and Brinkman, D.C. (1995) Self-esteem deficits and suicidal tendencies among adolescents. Journal of the American Academy of Child and Adolescent Psychiatry, 34: 919–928.

Phillips, D.P. and Carstensen, L.L. (1986) Clustering of teenage suicides after television news stories about suicide. New England Journal of Medicine, 315: 685–689.

Range, L., Goggin, W. and Steede, K. (1988) Perception of behavioral contagion of adolescent suicide. Suicide and Life Threatening Behavior, 18: 334–341.

Rey, C., Michaud, P.A., Narring, F. and Ferron, C. (1997) [Suicidal behavior in adolescents in Switzerland: role of physicians] Les conduites suicidaires chez les adolescents en Suisse: le role des medecins. Archives de Pediatrie, 4: 784–792.

Riggs, S., Alario, A.J. and McHorney, C. (1990) Health risk behaviors and attempted suicide in adolescents who report prior maltreatment. Journal of Pediatrics, 116: 815–821.

Rossow, I. and Wichstrom, L. (1997) [When need is greatest—is help nearest? Help and treatment after attempted suicide among adolescents] Nar noden er storst—er hjelpen naermest? Hjelp og behandling etter selvmordsforsok blant ungdom. Tidsskrift Nor Laegeforen, 117: 1740–1743.

Saunders, S.M., Resnick, M.D., Hoberman, H.M. and Blum, R.W. (1994) Formal help-seeking behavior of adolescents identifying themselves as having mental health problems. Journal of the American Academy of Child and Adolescent Psychiatry, 33: 718–728.

Schmidtke, A., Bille, B.U., DeLeo, D., Kerkhof, A., Bjerke, T., Crepet, P., Haring, C., Hawton, K., Lonnqvist, J., Michel, K., Pommereau, X., Querejeta, I., Phillipe, I., Salander, R.E., Temesvary, B., Wasserman, D., Fricke, S., Weinacker, B. and Sampaio, F.J. (1996) Attempted suicide in Europe: rates, trends and sociodemographic characteristics of suicide attempters during the period 1989–1992. Results of the WHO/EURO Multicentre Study on Parasuicide. Acta Psychiatrica Scandinavica, 93: 327–338.

Schmidtke, A. and Hafner, H. (1988) The Werther effect after television films: new evidence for an old hypothesis. Psychological Medicine, 18: 665–676.

Schotte, D.E. and Clum, G. (1982) Suicide ideation in a college population: a test of a model. Journal of Consulting and Clinical Psychology, 50: 690–696.

Shaffer, D. and Fisher, P. (1981) The epidemiology of suicide in children and young adolescents. Journal of the American Academy of Child Psychiatry, 20: 545–565.

Shaffer, D., Vieland, V., Garland, A., Rojas, M., Underwood, M. and Busner, C. (1990) Adolescent suicide attempters. Journal of the American Medical Association, 264 (24): 3151–3155.

Smith, K. and Crawford, S. (1986) Suicidal behavior among "normal" high school students. Suicide and Life Threatening Behavior, 16: 313–325.

Spirito, A., Overholser, J., Ashworth, S., Morgan, J. and Benedict, D.C. (1988) Evaluation of a suicide awareness curriculum for high school students. Journal of the American Academy of Child and Adolescent Psychiatry, 27: 705–711.

Steede, K.K. and Range, L.K. (1989) Does television induce suicidal contagion with adolescents? Journal of Community Psychology, 17: 166–172.

Stein, D., Witztum, E., Brom, D., DeNour, A.K. and Elizur, A. (1992) The association between adolescents' attitudes toward suicide and their psychosocial background and suicidal tendencies. Adolescence, 27: 949–959.

Stillion, J.M., McDowell, E.E. and May, J.H. (1984) Developmental trends and sex differences in adolescent attitudes toward suicide. Death Education, 8: 81–90.

Strang, S. and Orlofsky, J. (1990) Factors underlying suicidal ideation among college students: a test of Teicher and Jacobs' model. Journal of Adolescence, 13: 39–52.

Swanson, J.W., Linskey, A.O., Quintero, S.R., Pumariega, A.J. and Holzer, C.E. (1992) A binational school survey of depressive symptoms, drug use and suicidal ideation. Journal of the American Academy of Child and Adolescent Psychiatry, 31: 669–678.

Vannatta, R.A. (1996) Risk factors related to suicidal behavior among male and female adolescents. Journal of Youth and Adolescence, 25: 149–160.

Wagner, B.M. (1997) Family risk factors for child and adolescent suicidal behavior. Psychological Bulletin, 121: 246–298.

Wagner, B.M., Cole, R.E. and Schwartzman, P. (1995) Psychosocial correlates of suicide attempts among junior and senior high school youth. Suicide and Life Threatening Behavior, 25: 358–372.

Yanish, D. and Battle, J. (1985) Relationship between self-esteem, depression and alcohol consumption among adolescents. Psychological Reports, 57: 331–334.

Chapter 17

Adolescent Suicidal Behaviour: Psychiatric Populations

Alan Apter
and
Ornit Freudenstein
Department of Child and Adolescent Psychiatry, Tel Aviv University, Tel Aviv, Israel

Abstract

Psychiatrists who treat adolescents with psychiatric disorders are confronted daily with the clinical dilemma of suicidal behaviour. There has been a major increase in the prevalence of suicide among the young in the last few decades. It has been shown that psychiatric disorder and history of psychiatric treatment are major risk factors for all types of suicidality, both non-fatal and fatal. Almost any diagnosable psychiatric disorder, especially affective disorder, is a major risk factor for youth suicide. Psychiatric disorders are particularly dangerous when they occur in combination with other risk factors for suicide and when more than one disorder is present. This chapter reviews theoretical and empirical aspects of the relationship between psychiatric disorders and suicidal behaviour. Several psychiatric disorders, including affective disorders, schizophrenia, substance abuse, conduct disorders, eating disorders, borderline personality disorder and their relationship to suicidality, are described. Many psychiatric disorders seem to occur together and the boundaries between them are often unclear. Thus there may be four co-morbid constellations which have special significance for suicide among adolescents and which require vigorous psychiatric intervention. The first is the combination of schizophrenia, depression and substance abuse. The second is substance abuse, conduct disorder and depression. The third comprises affective disorder, eating disorder and anxiety disorders, and the fourth consists of affective disorder, personality disorder and dissociative disorders.

The International Handbook of Suicide and Attempted Suicide. Edited by K. Hawton and K. van Heeringen.

INTRODUCTION

Adolescent psychiatric populations are of especial interest for the study of suicidal behaviour, as there has been a major increase in the prevalence of suicide among young persons in the last few decades and because it has been shown that psychiatric disorder and history of psychiatric treatment are major risk factors for all types of suicidality, both non-fatal and fatal. Psychological autopsy studies of fatal suicides, as well as examination of adolescents who exhibit suicidal behaviour of various kinds, have found that psychiatric illness is a common feature in these individuals. Most strikingly, adolescents who require hospitalization are frequently admitted for suicidal behaviour and often continue to exhibit this behaviour while in hospital.

It appears that almost any diagnosable psychiatric disorder, especially affective disorder (25–75% of all suicides), is a major risk factor for youth suicide. Some authors also report high incidences of personality disorder, such as borderline personality disorder (25–40% of all suicides; Holinger et al, 1994). Psychiatric illnesses in adolescence are especially dangerous when they occur in combination with other risk factors for suicide and when more than one illness is present. This chapter will deal with the common multi-problem constellations found in clinical practice and will try to suggest rational management strategies.

Four co-morbid constellations can be identified which have special significance for suicide in adolescent populations and which require vigorous psychiatric intervention. The first is the combination of schizophrenia, depression and substance abuse; the second is substance abuse, conduct disorder and depression; the third comprises affective disorder, eating disorder and anxiety disorders; and the fourth consists of affective disorder, personality disorder (cluster A in DSM terminology) and dissociative disorders. The chapter will deal with each of these entities, pointing out where overlap occurs.

OVERVIEW OF SUICIDAL BEHAVIOUR IN PSYCHIATRIC POPULATIONS

There is a paucity of studies that look at serious suicide attempts in adolescents. In a study by Beautrais and colleagues (1996, 1997), almost equal numbers of males and females made serious suicide attempts, and the gender ratio did not differ from controls. The mean age was 19.4 years, with a range of 13–24 years. Twice as many females took overdoses, whereas males more frequently used carbon monoxide poisoning and hanging. Low income and residential mobility were highly associated with a serious attempt. In addition, childhood sexual abuse, low parental care and a poor parental relationship were significant findings. There was also an elevated risk for mood disorder, substance abuse and conduct disorder.

There is also an excess mortality among former adolescent male psychiatric outpatients. Pelkonen and colleagues (1996) looked at a cohort of 156 males and 122 female Finnish adolescents 10 years after having received outpatient psychiatric care. They found that 16 male subjects but no female subjects had died. The mortality for any cause for males was 10.3% and that for suicide was 7.1%. Current suicidal ideation and suicide attempts, poor psychosocial functioning and a recommendation for psychiatric hospitalization during the index treatment were associated with male mortality and suicidality. These findings are similar to those reported in earlier studies, which found that about 10% of male adolescent psychiatric inpatients and about 1% of female inpatients eventually kill themselves.

With regard to inpatients, Stein and colleagues (1998) recently surveyed admissions to our adolescent psychiatric unit over a period of 24 months. Thirty-two patients had made one suicide attempt, 19 had made multiple suicide attempts and 109 were non-suicidal. Most of the suicidal patients were suffering from affective and conduct disorders but others had eating disorders or anxiety disorders.

Thus, the relationship between psychiatric illness and suicidal behaviour is a strong one; clinicians treating suicidal adolescents should be trained to make psychiatric diagnoses, and psychiatrists treating mentally ill adolescents should be on the watch for suicidality.

DEPRESSION

Among teenagers, both attempted and completed suicides are, in the great majority of cases, preceded by depressive symptoms. Comparison of suicide attempters and non-attempters among children and young people who are depressed reveals considerable differences between the two groups. Depressed young people who attempt suicide often come from broken families and have had one or more relatives who have committed or attempted suicide. They have also relatively often run away from home and thus been brought up without favourable role models. Physical and mental abuse, as well as sexual assault, is also more common in this group. Young people who have attempted suicide often have lasting problems at school and also difficulties in achieving workable relationships with their peers, compared with young people who are depressed and have not attempted suicide. Abuse of alcohol and drugs, impulsive behaviour and asocial behaviour are additional risk factors for attempted and completed suicide among depressed young people. Among young people aged 16–17 years in a Swedish study, 3.6% of the boys and 8.8% of the girls stated that they had attempted suicide at some time or another (Von Knorring and Kristiansson, 1995). Sixty percent of boys and 44% of girls who had attempted suicide were currently suffering from moderate or severe depression. These figures may be compared with the findings reported in the same survey that, of those who had not attempted suicide, moderate or severe depression was found in only 2% of the boys and 5% of the girls. Owing to the high incidence of depression among young people who have attempted suicide, it is important to make a diagnosis and provide adequate treatment at an early stage. Studies show that depressive disturbances are more common among children and young people than had previously been believed (Fleming and Offord, 1990). Unfortunately, many young people with depression are not identified, partly because their depressive symptoms are often atypical (American Psychiatric Association, 1994) and partly because adults do not readily recognize depressive symptoms in the young, perhaps because of their wish to see their children as happy and healthy. Since the number of young people with depression appears to have increased after World War II and the age of onset of depressive disturbances has decreased, it is important to detect depressions in order to be able to prevent suicidal behaviour.

Major depression is most easily diagnosed when it appears acutely in a previously healthy child and in these cases the symptoms closely resemble those seen in adults. In many children, however, the onset is insidious and the child may show many other difficulties, such as attention deficit disorder or separation anxiety disorder, before becoming depressed. In addition, mood disorders tend to be chronic when they start at an early age and the children often come from families where there is a high incidence of mood disorders and alcohol abuse. In some cases the depressed adolescent may also be psychotic and have hallucinations and delusions, which are usually mood-congruent. When the psychotic themes are related to suicide, such as in command hallucinations or delusions of guilt, the risk for suicide is very high.

Bipolar disorder was once thought to occur only rarely in youth. However, approximately 20% of all bipolar patients have their first episode during adolescence, with a peak age of onset between 15 and 19 years of age. Developmental variations in presentation, symptomatic overlap with other disorders, and lack of clinician awareness have all led to underdiagnosis or misdiagnosis in children and adolescents. Therefore, clinicians need to be aware of some of the unique clinical characteristics associated with the early-onset form. Similarly, it is important to recognize the various phases and patterns of episodes associated with bipolar disorder. Young people may first present with either manic or depressive episodes. Twenty to thirty percent of young people with major depressions go on to have manic episodes. Risk factors that predict eventual mania include: (a) a depressive episode characterized by rapid onset, psychomotor retardation and psychotic features; (b) a family history of affective disorders, especially bipolar disorder; and (c) a history of mania or hypomania after treatment with antidepressants (Strober and Carlson, 1982). The same risk factors are also noted in the adult literature.

Adolescents with bipolar disorder are at increased risk of completed suicide. Strober and colleagues (1995) found that 20% of their adolescent subjects made at least one medically significant suicide attempt. In the adult literature, a large review of studies examining depressive and manic depressive disorders found the mean rate of completed suicides in bipolar disorder to be 19% (see Chapter 7).

Patients who are male, or who are in the depressed phase of their illness, are at the highest risk.

A major clinical problem for clinicians working in adolescent psychiatric units is that severe depression is common in almost all their patients (Apter et al, 1988), and it can be very difficult to deal with questions of what is primary and what is secondary, especially since co-morbidity is common in referred populations

SCHIZOPHRENIA

Because schizophrenia is a serious disorder with ominous prognosis and social stigma, some clinicians are hesitant to make this diagnosis, even when there is sufficient evidence to do so. This potentially denies the child and family access to appropriate treatment, knowledge about the disorder and specialized support services. Therefore, when the diagnostic criteria are met, the initial diagnosis may be inaccurate, given the overlap in symptoms between schizophrenia, affective disorders with psychotic features and, possibly, personality and dissociative disorders. The patient must then be followed longitudinally, with periodic diagnostic reassessments, to ensure accuracy. Patients and families should be educated about these diagnostic issues.

Many schizophrenic patients are depressed and suicidal, especially when they are young and have not been ill for a very long time. The differentiation between schizophrenia, psychotic depression or mania and schizoaffective disorder is not always easy in adolescence and many conceptual and nosological issues remain to be decided.

Depression in schizophrenia may be related to the fact that the young person feels that he/she is falling apart and becoming mentally ill, and there is indeed evidence that suicidality and depression in these patients is related to good premorbid function, better insight, higher intelligence and preservation of cognitive function (see Chapter 8). Post-psychotic depression and neuroleptic medication may also have a role to play in this condition.

As discussed in Chapter 8, about 10–15% of patients with schizophrenia eventually commit suicide, usually in the initial stages of their illness. Most schizophrenic suicide victims are unmarried men who have made previous suicide attempts. At least two-thirds of the suicides are related to depression and only a small minority to psychotic symptoms such as command hallucinations. The suicide is often shortly after discharge from hospital and thus may be related to lack of social support.

Finally, many adolescents with schizophrenia also abuse drugs and alcohol, thus increasing their risk for suicide (Stone et al, 1989). Sometimes the abuse is an attempt at self-medication. Anticholinergic medications given for the relief of extra-pyramidal symptoms often give the patient a "high" to which they become addicted and the patient may simulate these symptoms in order to obtain these drugs. Child onset and adolescent schizophrenia are often preceded by difficulties of attention and learning, for which stimulant medications are given. Again, in the context of a developing schizophrenic condition there is a potential for abuse and drug-induced depression.

SUBSTANCE ABUSE

The topic of adolescent suicide and drug abuse has recently been extensively reviewed by Kaminer (1996), who noted that many studies have reported an elevated suicide-risk ratio for adolescents diagnosed with psychoactive substance abuse disorder.

Although there has not been extensive research on this subject in adolescence, it is well known that conduct disorders and mood disorders are frequently co-morbid with both substance abuse and suicidal behaviour. Surveys of adolescents with alcoholism show rates of 50% or more for additional psychiatric disorders, especially mood disorders, and 80% of adolescents who abuse alcohol meet criteria for another psychiatric disorder, the combination often leading to psychiatric hospitalization. Clinically it can be difficult to know whether the substance abuse preceded or followed the co-morbid psychiatric disorder. Brent and colleagues (1993) found that odds ratios (OR) for risk factors for adolescent completed suicide were: major depression (OR = 27); bipolar disorder (OR = 9); psychoactive substance use disorder (OR = 8.5) and conduct disorder (OR = 6).

The relationship between suicide, aggression and alcoholism may be especially relevant to subjects with type 2 alcoholism. These persons are characterized by high novelty seeking, low harm avoidance and low reward dependence, and their alcoholism has an early onset and is characterized by a rapid course, severe psychiatric symptoms, fighting, arrests, poor prognosis and multiple suicide attempts. Low levels of serotonin in alcoholism, depression, suicide and aggression have been hypothesized as the biological aetiological correlates of these behaviours.

Surveys have found that suicidal thoughts have been experienced by more than 25% of college students aged 16–19 years (Kaminer, 1996; see Chapter 16). This supports a general non-specificity for adolescent suicidal thoughts. However, students with psychoactive substance use disorder had more frequent and more severe thoughts than average, and also were more likely to have a prolonged desire to be dead. Psychoactive substance use disorder was also found to be associated with more severe medical seriousness of actual suicide attempts.

Studies of completed suicide in adolescents have shown that in Scandinavia, Canada and the USA psychoactive substance use disorder is more common among victims than in the general adolescent population. There is some evidence that alcohol and cocaine may be especially dangerous with regard to suicide, but this has yet to be validated (Kaminer, 1996). Adolescents with psychoactive substance use disorder, especially males, are more likely to commit suicide with guns than are adolescents without this disorder (Brent et al, 1993). Adolescent suicide also seems to be related to more chronic psychoactive substance use disorder in subjects who have not sought treatment. In one study, psychoactive substance use disorder was typically present for at least 9 years before the suicide (Kaminer, 1996).

Many adolescents manifest suicidal behaviour after an acute crisis such as perceived rejection or interpersonal conflict, an acute disciplinary act, sexual assault or immediate loss. Intoxication for the purpose of self-medication, which often follows a crisis, may trigger suicide in an adolescent who feels shame, humiliation or frustration.

For any age group, acute intoxication often precedes suicide attempts. It has been suggested that adolescents may use psychoactive substances to bolster their courage to carry out the suicide attempt. Intoxication may also lead to impaired judgement and decreased inhibition and thus may facilitate suicidal behaviour.

CONDUCT DISORDERS

Aggressive impulsive behaviour is a major risk factor for suicidal behaviour in adolescence. A major concern is the high rate of suicidal behaviours among juvenile delinquents, especially in those who are incarcerated in remand homes or in prisons. Unfortunately, in many countries reform schools often do not have the facilities for adequate mental health treatment, while psychiatric units cannot cope with the violence and aggression displayed by these youths. Many of the risk factors for suicide are also risk factors for conduct disorder. These include broken homes, physical and sexual abuse as children, personal and familial alcoholism and substance abuse, unemployment, poverty and access to firearms (Brent et al, 1988).

In addition, mood disorders are often present in children who have some degree of irritability and aggressive behaviour. It may be quite difficult to make the differential diagnosis between major depressive disorder, bipolar disorder and conduct disorder. There is also a substantial co-morbidity between conduct disorders and affective disorders in adolescents. Again, many factors predisposing to depression also predispose to conduct disorder, including family conflict, negative life events, level of affiliation with delinquent peers and lack of parental involvement.

The relationship between suicide, attempted suicide and aggression has long been recognized by psychoanalysts, and has been best formulated by Menninger (1933), who proposed that a dynamic triad underlies all aggressive behaviour, whether directed inward or outward: the wish to die, the wish to kill, and the wish to be killed. These are all seen to be derivatives of Freud's concept of "thanatos", or the death instinct.

There is now a large biological literature on the relationship between serotonin (5-HT) function, impulsiveness, aggression and suicidal behaviour. This relationship appears to have a genetic basis and is probably most relevant to suicidal behaviour in the young rather than in older people (Apter et al, 1990).

There are many reports in the daily press of murderers who commit suicide. Roughly one in four patients with a history of violent actions has made a suicide attempt (Skodal and Karasu, 1978; Tardiff and Sweillam, 1980). A study on the prevalence of violent and suicidal behaviour in a sample of 51 hospitalized adolescents found that 66.7% had been violent, 43.1% had been suicidal and 27.5% had been both (Inmadar et al, 1982). According to various authors, 7–48% of patients with a history of violent behaviour have also made suicide attempts in the past. This is reported to be true for adults (Skodal and Karasu, 1978) and for pre-pubertal children (Pfeffer et al, 1983). Similar findings have been reported in prisoners (Climent et al, 1977).

Looking at the issue in terms of patients who are predominantly suicidal, Tardiff and Sweillam (1980) found that of a large group of suicidal patients admitted to mental hospitals, 14% of males and 7% of females were assaultive at the time of, or just prior to, admission. Similarly, a "violent depressive type" of patient, who has a long history of suicide attempts as well as a history of violence, has been defined on the basis of detailed studies of psychotic patients (Kermani, 1981). It has likewise been reported that female suicide attempters show more hostility and engage in more arguments and friction with friends and relatives than a comparable group of non-suicidal depressed women. Hospitalized depressed patients with a history of self-destructive acts have been found to have high levels of hostility and violence, as measured by their need for seclusion and restraint (Weissman et al, 1973).

In a large group of adult psychiatric inpatients with mixed diagnoses, about 40% had made a suicide attempt, 42% had engaged in violent behaviour in the past and 23% had histories of both types of behaviour. Almost every one of the 30 variables measured in these patients turned out to be a significant predictor of both suicide risk and violence risk. These results strongly support the idea of a close link between suicide risk and violence risk, regardless of diagnosis (Plutchik et al, 1985).

Another important finding in this regard is that of Shaffer and Fisher (1981), who reported that a combination of depressive symptoms and antisocial behaviour was the most common antecedent of teenage suicide. Assaultiveness and instability of affect, as reflected in borderline personality disorder (Apter et al, 1988), may also be important correlates of adolescent suicidal behaviour, especially in combination with depression. Aggressive or violent behaviour is highly correlated with suicidal behaviour on psychiatric wards (Plutchik and Van Praag 1986) in the histories of psychiatric patients with all kinds of diagnoses and in all age groups (Pfeffer et al, 1988). Psychometric measures of violence risk were highly correlated with measures of suicide risk.

EATING DISORDERS

There has also been recent recognition of a very definite increased risk for suicide in girls with eating disorders (Apter et al, 1995). The relationship between anorexia nervosa and depression is well documented. However, the suicide potential of these adolescents has been neglected in the literature, perhaps because they use denial to a large extent and because it was felt that starvation was a suicidal equivalent, obviating the need for a direct self-attack in these patients. Recently, however, it has been pointed out that suicide is not rare in anorexia nervosa and suicidal behaviour may be an important portent of poor prognosis. Patton (1988) followed up 460 patients with eating disorders and found that the increased standard mortality rate in anorectic patients was mostly due to suicide, with death occurring up to 8 years after the initial assessment. These findings were similar to those of the Copenhagen Anorexia Follow-up Study. Projective testing of anorectic patients also shows a preponderance of suicidal indicators. Furthermore, there seems to be a group of patients with late-onset anorexia in which the loss of weight ultimately comes to express a desire to die.

It is interesting to speculate on the association between depression, suicide and eating disorders. It is possible that for many girls weight loss is a form of self-medication for depression, since in fact many healthy women feel much better when they lose weight. These good feelings are related in many ways to social approval but may also result from the release of endorphins from damaged muscle tissue or from vomiting. In some cases we have seen depression resulting from weight gain, as if the patient was suffering from withdrawal symptoms from her addiction to thinness. However, weight loss may of itself induce quite severe depression and suicidal ideation even in volunteers and in normal dieters. Another very dangerous form of depression occurs in treatment-resistant cases, where the constant battle against gaining weight on the one hand and the constant social pressure to gain weight on the other becomes an intolerable burden. The diary of Ellen West, a famous anorectic patient who eventually killed herself, contained the following passages: "The most horrible thing about my life is that it is filled with continuous fear. Fear of eating but also fear of hunger and fear of fear itself. Only death can liberate me from this dread" and "since I am doing everything from the point of view of whether it makes me thin or fat, all things lose their real value. It has fallen over me like a beast and I am helpless against it" (Bruch, 1973).

Adolescents with bulimia nervosa are also highly prone to suicidal behaviours as part of an impulsive and unstable life-style. Many show self-mutilation and cutting, but often they make serious suicide attempts. In a series of former bulimic adolescent inpatients seen in our unit at Geha Hospital, about 3.5% died from suicide in a 15-year follow-up. This was about 300 times higher than the risk for other former female adolescent psychiatric inpatients. Recently the term "multi-impulsive bulimia" has been coined to describe the increasingly more common association between bulimia, borderline or unstable personality disorder, substance abuse, and depression and conduct disorder. Although most patients with this co-morbid constellation of disorders are women, they are nevertheless at high risk for repeated deliberate self-harm and for suicide.

In "multi-impulsive bulimic" suicide attempters there may be a place for dialectic behaviour therapy (DBT), a form of therapy that has been designed for borderline patients (Linehan, 1993). In anorectic patients, weight gain and refeeding are essential and in many individuals this will restore mood and alleviate suicidal pain. In others, weight gain can cause tremendous disappointment and this may be an incentive for suicide. Open-ended supportive therapy is usually the best way to keep the most severely suicidal eating disorder patients alive in the long run, and where a therapeutic relationship is achieved suicide can be obviated, although the eating disorder usually persists to a greater or lesser degree.

BORDERLINE PERSONALITY DISORDER

Borderline personality disorder is traditionally associated with non-fatal suicide attempts but there is increasing evidence that completed suicide is also common in these patients (see Chapter 10). Intentional self-damaging acts and suicide attempts are the "behavioural specialty" of these patients (Gunderson, 1984). Although "affective instability" is said to be one of the critical symptoms of this disorder, many seem to have a chronic underlying depression and most of the adolescent borderline personality disorder patients who require psychiatric help meet criteria for an affective disorder, most often major depression. In addition, many suffer from chronically stable depression, hopelessness, worthlessness, guilt and helplessness. Another group of suicide-related symptoms are those associated with anger. Many of these patients are very angry and even violent, while others are fearful of losing control of their anger and are unable to express their aggressive feelings. Other frequent co-morbid conditions that increase the likelihood of suicide are conduct disorder, "multi-impulsive" bulimia and substance abuse. An additional co-morbid condition of considerable interest is dissociative disorder, and the common origin of this combination often seems to relate to incest or continuous non-injurious (in the physical sense) sexual abuse. Some authors report even seeing multiple personality disorder developing in these patients, although our group has never seen such a case.

The treatment of the suicidal borderline personality disordered adolescent is challenging and difficult. Hospitalization should be avoided if possible, since it often seems harmful and exacerbates the condition. Of course, when suicidal risk seems very high hospitalization may be unavoidable. The only therapy to have shown results in this group is DBT (Linehan, 1993), although as yet it has not been shown to be effective in adolescents. Several trials are in progress and the results are eagerly awaited. The other form of psychotherapy which is often practised is psychoanalytically-informed supportive psychotherapy (Kernberg, 1976), although no evidence for its efficacy in adolescents exists. It does, however, enable the clinician to "hold" these patients for a considerable length of time until the suicidal crisis resolves.

Many pharmacological interventions are in clinical use. There is some evidence that fluoxetine reduces suicidal behaviour and irritability in these subjects. Many clinicians like to use mood stabilizers, which they feel lessen the mood swings of the young person and reduce the risk of impulsive behaviour. However, they have the disadvantage of being quite toxic in overdose and requiring constant drug monitoring. In addition, most of these patients are female and the most popular mood stabilizer, valproic acid, has been reported to induce polycystic ovaries.

CONCLUSIONS

Psychiatrists who treat adolescents with psychiatric disorders are confronted daily with the problem of suicidal behaviour in all its forms, including the very real danger of a completed suicide. Some of these illnesses have effective treatments but others do not and often "holding" the patient is the only strategy possible. Hospitalization is often unavoidable but is potentially damaging, and so clinical judgement, although often made on shaky grounds, is the only recourse. Many psychiatric illnesses seem to occur together and the boundaries between them are often unclear. However, co-morbidity is of serious portent for suicidal risk and each diagnostic decision must be carefully made. At the present time there are no known effective treatments for suicidal behaviour as such and so treatment of each underlying disorder and its symptoms should hopefully reduce suicide risk. In general the best approach is multi-modal. Psychopharmacological interventions have their place but by themselves are not sufficient. Cognitive-behavioural therapies have a good scientific foundation but are usually not very appropriate for the severely disturbed adolescent. Long-term supportive therapy and intensive casework for both the young person and his/her family, although not well researched, is often the best available choice. Complicated subjects, such as suicidal young people with multi-problems, are not good candidates for rigorous controlled treatment studies, and violent suicidal young people are not attractive to researchers. These teenagers are at high risk to themselves and others, and research into their problems should be the focus of more attention than has hitherto been the case.

REFERENCES

American Psychiatric Association (1994) The Diagnostic and Statistical Manual of Mental Disorders—Fourth Edition, DSM-IV. Washington, DC: American Psychiatric Association.

Apter, A., Bleich, A., Plutchik, R., Mendelsohn, S. and Tyano, S. (1988) Suicidal behavior, depression, and conduct disorder in hospitalized adolescents. Journal of the American Academy of Child and Adolescent Psychiatry, 27: 696–699.

Apter, A., Brown, S., Korn, M. and Van Praag, H.M. (1990) Serotonin and dysregulation of aggression. In S. Brown and H.M. van Praag (Eds), Serotonin in Psychiatry. New York: Bruner Mazel.

Apter, A., Gothelf, D., Orbach, I., Har-Even, D., Weizman, R. and Tyano, S. (1995) Correlation of suicidal and violent behavior in different diagnostic categories in hospitalized adolescent patients. Journal of the American Academy of Child and Adolescent Psychiatry, 34: 912–918.

Beautrais, A.L., Joyce, P.R., Mulder, R.T., Fergusson, D.M., Deavoll, B.J. and Nightingale, S.K. (1996) Prevalence and co-morbidity of mental disorders in persons making

serious suicide attempts: a case-control study. American Journal of Psychiatry, 153: 1009–1014.
Beautrais, A.L., Joyce, P.R. and Mulder, R.T. (1997) Precipitating factors and life events in serious suicide attempts among youth aged 13 through 24 years. Journal of the American Academy of Child and Adolescent Psychiatry, 36: 1543–1551.
Brent, D.A., Perper, J.A. and Goldstein, C.E. (1988) Risk factors for adolescent suicide: a comparison of adolescent suicide victims with suicidal inpatients. Archives of General Psychiatry, 45: 581–588.
Brent, D.A., Perper, J.A., Moritz, G., Allman, C., Roth, C., Schweers, J., Balach, L. and Baugher, M. (1993) Stressful life events, psychopathology, and adolescent suicide: a case control study. Suicide and Life-Threatening Behavior, 23: 179–187.
Bruch, H. (1973) Eating Disorders. New York: Basic Books.
Climent, C., Plutchik, R. and Ervin, F.R. (1977) Parental loss, depression and violence. Acta Psychiatrica Scandinavica, 55: 261–268.
Fleming, J.E. and Offord, D.R. (1990) Epidemiology of childhood depressive disorders: a critical review. Journal of the American Academy of Child and Adolescent Psychiatry, 29: 571–580.
Gunderson, J.G. (1984) Borderline Personality Disorder. Washington, DC: American Psychiatric Press.
Holinger, P.C., Offer, D., Barter, J.T. and Bell, C.C. (1994) Suicide and Homicide among Adolescents. New York: Guilford.
Inmadar, S.E., Lewis, D.O., Siomopolous, G., Shanock, S.S. and Lamella, M. (1982) Violent and suicidal behavior in psychotic adolescents. American Journal of Psychiatry, 139: 932–935.
Kaminer, Y. (1996) Adolescent substance abuse and suicidal behavior. Child and Adolescent Psychiatric Clinics of North America, 5: 59–71.
Kermani, E.J. (1981) Violent psychiatric patients: a study. American Journal of Psychotherapy, 35: 215–255.
Kernberg, O. (1976) Borderline Conditions and Pathological Narcissism. New York: Jason Aronson.
Linehan, M.M. (1993) Cognitive Treatment of Borderline Personality Disorder. New York: Guilford.
Menninger, K. (1933) Man Against Himself. New York: Harcourt Brace.
Patton, G.C. (1988) Mortality in eating disorders. Psychological Medicine, 18: 947–951.
Pelkonen, M., Marttunen, M., Pulkkinen, E., Koivisto, A.M., Laippala, P. and Aro, P. (1996) Excess mortality among former adolescent male outpatients. Acta Psychiatrica Scandinavica, 94: 60–66.
Pfeffer, C.R., Newcorn, J., Kaplan, G., Mizruchi, M.S. and Plutchik, R. (1988) Suicidal behavior in adolescent psychiatric inpatients. Journal of the American Academy of Child and Adolescent Psychiatry, 27: 357–361.
Pfeffer, C.R., Plutchik, R. and Mizruchi, S. (1983) Suicidal and assaultive behavior in children, classification, measurement and interrelation. American Journal of Psychiatry, 140: 154–157.
Plutchik, R., Van Praag, H.M. and Conte, H.R. (1985) Suicide and violence risk in psychiatric patients. In C. Shagass (Eds), Biological Psychiatry. New York: Elsevier.
Plutchik, R. and Van Praag, H.M. (1986) The measurement of suicidality, aggressivity and impulsivity. Clinical Neuropharmacology, 9: 380–382.
Shaffer, D. and Fisher, P. (1981) The epidemiology of suicide in children and young adolescents. Journal of the American Academy of Child and Adolescent Psychiatry, 20: 545–565.
Skodal, A.E. and Karasu, T.B. (1978) Emergency psychiatry: the assault of patients. American Journal of Psychiatry, 135: 202–205.
Stein, D., Apter, A., Ratzoni, G., Har-Even, D. and Avidan, G. (1998) Association between multiple suicide attempts and negative affects in adolescents. Journal of the American Academy of Child and Adolescent Psychiatry, 37: 488–494.

Strober, M. and Carlson, G. (1982) Bipolar illness in adolescents: clinical, genetic and pharmacologic predictors in a three- to four-year prospective follow-up. Archives of General Psychiatry, 39: 549–555.

Strober, M., Schmidt, L.S., Freeman, R., Bower, S., Lampert, C. and De Antonio, M. (1995) Recovery and relapse in adolescents with bipolar affective illness: a five-year, naturalistic, prospective follow-up. Journal of the American Academy of Child and Adolescent Psychiatry, 34: 724–731.

Stone, M.H. (1989) The course of borderline personality disorder. In A. Tasman, R.E. Hales and A.J. Frances (Eds), Review of Psychiatry. Washington, DC: American Psychiatric Press.

Tardiff, K. and Sweillam, A. (1980) Assault, suicide, and mental illness. Archives of General Psychiatry, 37: 164–169.

Von Knorring, A.-L. and Kristiansson, G. (1995) Depression och sjvlvmordsbeteende hos ungdomar (Depression and Suicidal behaviour in young people). In J. Beskow (Ed.), Rvtt till liv lust till liv. Om sjvlvmordsbeteende bland barn och ungdomar. Stockholm: Forskningsruds-nvmnden, Rapport 95, 4: 35–43.

Weissman, M., Fox, K. and Klerman, G.L. (1973) Hostility and depression associated with suicide attempts. American Journal of Psychiatry, 130: 450–455.

Chapter 18

Suicidal Behaviour among the Elderly

Daniel Harwood
University Department of Psychiatry, Warneford Hospital, Oxford, UK,
and
Robin Jacoby
University Department of Psychiatry, Warneford Hospital, Oxford, UK

Abstract

In most countries of the world, the highest rate of suicide is in people over 75 years of age. Suicidal phenomena in older people can be seen as a spectrum, ranging from suicidal thoughts to a completed act of suicide. Indirect suicidal behaviour, such as food refusal and non-adherence to therapy, may be manifestations of suicidality in older physically ill people, particularly in residential homes. Older deliberate self-harm patients have higher levels of depression and higher risk of subsequent suicide than younger patients. Risk factors for deliberate self-harm and suicide in older people overlap and, in addition to depression, include male gender, being divorced or widowed, cognitive impairment and physical illness. Social isolation may be a risk factor but the research evidence is conflicting. The role of personality factors is under-researched, but personality disorder is less frequently associated with suicide in older people than in younger age groups.

INTRODUCTION

With the sole exception of Poland, the highest suicide rates are recorded in the over-75 year age band in all countries submitting data to the World Health Organization (De Leo, 1997) and, as more of the world's population survives into old age, the number of suicides in older people is likely to increase even further.

The International Handbook of Suicide and Attempted Suicide. Edited by K. Hawton and K. van Heeringen.

A few years ago the paucity of research on suicide in older people was often mentioned in research papers. The dramatic increase in suicide rates amongst younger men in Western countries seemed to have shifted research and media attention from the high but more stable rate of suicide in the elderly. However, in recent years the topic has attracted more research interest, resulting in a welcome spate of new publications (De Leo, 1997).

Recent reviews of suicidal behaviour in older people (Bharucha and Satlin, 1997; Conwell, 1997; Shah and De, 1998) have focused mainly on completed suicide. In this chapter we will discuss suicidal behaviour as a spectrum ranging from thoughts of hopelessness to the completed act of suicide. We will discuss the epidemiology of suicidal thinking and the indirect suicidal behaviours, in the belief that an understanding of these issues might illuminate the motives underlying more serious suicidal behaviours.

Readers must bear in mind that most research on suicidal behaviour in older people originates from developed countries, and so the findings may not be completely generalizable to other parts of the world.

COMMUNITY STUDIES OF SUICIDAL IDEATION IN OLDER PEOPLE

Feelings of hopelessness are common in older people but serious suicidal thoughts much rarer. Of a sample of people aged 65 and over in Dublin, 15.5% said they had felt life was not worth living in the month prior to interview but only 3.1% had felt an actual wish to die (Kirby et al, 1997); these results are similar to those of other surveys (Jorm et al, 1995; Linden and Barnow, 1997).

Does the frequency of suicidal thoughts increase with age? Although the very elderly might have a slightly increased frequency of suicidal feelings compared with the younger elderly (Jorm et al, 1995; Forsell et al, 1997), older people in general have a similar frequency of suicidal thoughts to the younger population (Paykel et al, 1974). Most, but not all, studies have shown suicidal feelings to be commoner in older women.

Suicidal ideation is closely linked to psychiatric disorder. Skoog and colleagues (1996) interviewed a sample of Swedish 85-year-olds and found that although only 0.9% of the mentally healthy subjects had thought of suicide, 9.2% of those with mental disorders had these thoughts. Linden and Barnow (1997) argue that, even in the few cases where suicidal thoughts in older people are not associated with a psychiatric diagnosis, significant psychiatric symptoms are nearly always present. In a community survey of the Swedish elderly, Forsell and colleagues (1997) confirmed that depressive symptoms were the main determinant of suicidal thinking, even in those without depression. This study and others have demonstrated an association between suicidal thoughts and dementia. Rao and colleagues (1997) suggested a link between cerebrovascular disease and suicidal thinking, whereas Draper and co-workers (1998) showed the link to be strongest with Alzheimer's disease. Depressive symptoms were present in all suicidal patients with dementia in the latter study. No association was found between suicidal thinking and dementia severity or retention of insight in these studies.

Although psychiatric disorder is the most important contributor towards suicidal thinking in the samples studied, physical disability, pain, visual and hearing impairment, institutionalization, and single marital status are all associated with suicidal thoughts, even when the presence of depression has been controlled for (Forsell et al, 1997; Jorm et al, 1995).

An older person's wish to die may increase the risk of death: a UK study found that an expressed wish to die was a predictor of mortality equal in magnitude to depression (Dewey et al, 1993).

INDIRECT SELF-DESTRUCTIVE BEHAVIOUR

Moving further along the spectrum lie behaviours which, although not direct suicidal acts, still increase the probability of death. Researchers have used various terms to describe these behaviours: "indirect self-destructive behaviour" (Nelson and Farberow, 1980); "intentional life-threatening behaviour" (Osgood et al, 1991); "suicidal erosion" (Miller, 1978); and "silent suicide" (Simon, 1989).

Such behaviours range from acts of clear self-destructive intent, such as food refusal with the aim of starving to death, to behaviours of less direct intent, such as non-adherence to a treatment regime or continuing to smoke against medical advice.

Indirect self-destructive behaviour is commonest in institutional settings. Nelson and Farberow (1980) performed a detailed study in male nursing home patients using a standardized rating scale. They found self-destructive behaviour to be commoner in patients with cognitive impairment, dissatisfaction with life, low religiosity, dissatisfaction with their treatment programme, and significant losses in their lives. The close association of indirect self-destructive behaviour with suicidal thoughts was noted and it was suggested that such behaviours may have been a substitute for more overt suicidal behaviour in a physically ill, relatively immobile population. The researchers argued that, although potentially destructive, such behaviours could also be adaptive in counteracting feelings of powerlessness and low self-esteem in a restrictive institutional setting.

In a questionnaire survey of US nursing homes, Osgood and colleagues (1991) found the prevalence of intentional life-threatening behaviour to be five times greater than the rate of deliberate self-harm. The commonest behaviour of this type was refusal of food, drink or medication. Intentional life-threatening behaviour was more frequent in women (men being more likely to perform overt acts of self-harm) and the very elderly. Nursing homes with high staff turnover and a large number of residents had an increased prevalence of life-threatening behaviours.

Simon (1989) hypothesized that self-injurious behaviour, or "silent suicide" as he called it, was an indicator of depressive illness. This relationship between indirect self-destructive behaviour and psychiatric illness, and its epidemiology in non-institutional settings, remains to be researched.

DELIBERATE SELF-HARM IN OLDER PEOPLE

The boundary between indirect self-destructive behaviours and deliberate self-harm is not distinct. In a study of overdoses taken by older people, Bean (1973) demonstrated overlap in the characteristics of overdoses labelled "deliberate" or "accidental" by the admitting medical team. Bean suggested that the categorization of acts of self-harm may be influenced by factors such as the type of drug ingested, rather than the circumstances of the act itself.

In a thorough review of the topic, Draper (1996) has criticized studies on deliberate self-harm in older people as suffering from selection bias (tending to focus on hospital samples), lack of standardized diagnostic criteria, and neglect of psychosocial precipitants and personality factors.

The frequency of suicidal acts peaks among the young and declines with age, but those over 75 years remain at highest risk of completed suicide (Draper, 1996). The high suicidal intent of most acts of deliberate self-harm in the elderly contrasts with the more heterogeneous nature of attempted suicide in younger age groups, where motivations other than ending life are more likely to underlie the act. Deliberate self-harm in older people can therefore be seen as "failed suicide", and provides a unique opportunity to explore the motivations behind completed suicide in this age group.

Demographic Risk Factors

There is considerable international variation in rates of deliberate self-harm in older people. A recent multi-centre European study revealed rates ranging from 14 per 100,000 in Würzburg, Germany, to 111 per 100,000 in Huddinge, Sweden (De Leo et al, 1994).

Draper (1996) summarizes the demographic risk factors. The *absolute number* of attempted suicides is higher in women, in a 3:2 ratio, but *rates* according to gender are similar because there are fewer men than women in the aged population. This contrasts with completed suicide, where males predominate. Over 45% of older suicide attempters are widowed, and the divorced and separated share a higher risk. Lower socio-economic group and Protestant religion may also be associated with an increased risk of self-harm (Draper, 1996).

Methods of Deliberate Self-harm

Drug overdose is the commonest method. Since the decline of barbiturate prescribing in Western countries, benzodiazepines, analgesics and antidepressants are the usual drugs chosen (Draper, 1996). Self-cutting is the next most frequent mode of self-harm. In Eastern cultures, drug overdose is less often chosen; the commonest method of self-harm in a recent report on the Chinese elderly in Hong Kong was ingestion of a corrosive or detergent (Chiu et al, 1996).

Alcohol use accompanying an attempt is less common than in young suicide attempters, occurring in 13–23% of suicide attempts (Draper, 1996), perhaps reflecting the less impulsive nature of the attempts.

Risk Factors for Deliberate Self-harm

Psychiatric Disorder

More older deliberate self-harm patients have a psychiatric illness than younger patients (Merrill and Owens, 1990). In Draper's (1996) summary of recent studies, 55% of patients suffered "major depression". A high degree of hopelessness persisting after remission of depression in order depressives appears to be associated with a history of suicidal behaviour (Rifai et al, 1994), but other clinical features of depression which might predict self-harm in older people await clarification. The large variation in rates of organic disorders in studies of attempted suicide in older people reflects the varied selection and diagnostic criteria used. Patients with mild cognitive impairment and co-morbid depression may be at particular risk (Draper, 1996). A link between impulsive suicide attempts and frontal lobe dysfunction has been suggested (Draper, 1994). Alcohol abuse occurs in 5–32% of older suicide attempters and other psychiatric diagnoses occur in less than 10%. Only 0–13% have no psychiatric diagnosis (Draper, 1996).

Personality

In a detailed early study, Batchelor and Napier (1953) described 75% of older suicide attempters as "vulnerable personalities", sensitivity, anxiety, obsessionality and dependency being some of the predominant traits. Later studies have been disappointing in their lack of standardized personality assessments, but personality *disorder* seems much rarer than in the younger self-harm population (Draper, 1996).

Physical Illness

The importance of physical illness as a risk factor remains uncertain, as most studies have lacked age-matched control groups. Pierce (1987) found that 63% of his sample suffered "significant physical illness", but in only 18% did he feel that the illness had contributed towards the suicidal act, usually through pain and loss of morale due to physical decline. Terminal illness is rare in older suicide attempters (Draper, 1996). Occasionally, previously unrecognized and treatable disorders can be revealed during the patient's admission (Burston, 1969; Draper, 1994).

Social Factors

Older suicide attempters seem to be more socially isolated than the general population of the same age, with a higher proportion living alone (Nowers, 1993) and a lower proportion having help available at a time of crisis (Lyness et al, 1992).

Unresolved grief, usually following spousal bereavement, was present in 13–44% of subjects in Draper's review of recent studies. The studies that have looked at interpersonal problems associated with self-harm in older people have found rates of around 40% (Draper, 1996).

The threat of nursing home placement may be a precipitant in some older suicide attempters (Draper, 1996). Once in a nursing home, however, the risk of attempted suicide may be lower than the general population (Osgood et al, 1991), perhaps due to reduced availability of methods and consequent use of the more indirect methods of self-harm (see above).

Outcome

A higher proportion of older suicide attempters than younger attempters will receive psychiatric treatment as a result of their presentation, reflecting the higher rates of psychiatric morbidity in older patients (Draper, 1996).

In a 2–5 year follow-up of deliberate self-harm patients over 65 years in Oxford in the UK, Hepple and Quinton (1997) studied their prognosis and the factors associated with repetition of the act. The repetition rate was 5.4% annually, lower than for younger age groups. Repetition was associated with female gender, depression, persistent psychiatric symptoms and psychiatric follow-up. There was an increased mortality from natural causes, as well as a higher rate of suicide (5–7%) than in younger suicide attempters. Risk factors for suicide were male gender, a psychiatric history prior to the index attempt, divorce, and persistent depression being treated by a psychiatric team. Pierce (1996) found that older suicide "repeaters" had lower levels of sociopathic behaviour and substance abuse than younger people repeating suicide.

The study of deliberate self-harm is a unique opportunity to examine risk factors for suicide which are difficult to assess using a psychological autopsy approach. The relation of personality factors, cognitive styles and cognitive impairment to attempted suicide in older people are research challenges waiting to be grasped.

SUICIDE IN OLDER PEOPLE

Data collection techniques used to study suicide include the analysis of suicide notes, coroners' inquest and medical records (e.g. Cattell, 1988; Conwell et al, 1990b; Cattell and Jolley, 1995) and detailed "psychological autopsy" interviews with relatives or friends. Most of the information about the risk factors for suicide in older people is derived from psychological autopsy studies performed in the UK (Barraclough, 1971), Finland (Heikkinen and Lönnqvist, 1995; Henrikkson et al, 1995) and the USA (Carney et al, 1994; Conwell et al, 1996). Shah and De (1998) highlight potential drawbacks of the psychological autopsy study of elderly suicide victims. Young informants may be unable to provide information on early life history, the overlap between physical and psychiatric symptoms in older people can make retrospective psychiatric diagnosis difficult, and socially isolated suicide victims may lack an informant.

Papers reporting the prevalence of risk factors often miss the richness of detail and complex interaction between risk factors captured by a full interview with an informant. Case studies (e.g. Alexopoulos, 1991) can help to bring home the clinical relevance of suicide research, and qualitative research (Moore, 1997) can explore themes not amenable to quantitative analysis.

Epidemiology

Although suicide rates in older people have been declining in many industrialized countries in recent years, in most countries of the world suicide rates are highest in the over-75 age-band (De Leo, 1997; Shah and De, 1998). In England and Wales, the suicide rate for men in the 55–64, 65–74 and 75–84 year-old age-bands have fallen by 30–40% between 1983 and 1995, whilst in men aged 25–34 years the suicide rate had increased by 30% over the same time period (Kelly and Bunting, 1998). In women the rate fell in all age groups, but with more dramatic falls in older age bands. Analysing data from 1974 to 1992, Pritchard (1996) confirmed these declines in the 65–74 year-old age group in most industrialized countries, but interestingly found increases in the suicide rate in the very elderly (those over 75) in men in most of these countries, especially in men.

International Variation in Suicide Rates in Older People

The differences in death registration procedures between countries are not enough to explain the international variations in suicide rate. Table 18.1 summarizes data from the *World Health Organization Statistics Manual 1996* (World Health Organization, 1998). Unfortunately, data are missing from many developing countries, but suicide rates in older people are high in Hungary, Lithuania, Latvia and other Eastern and Central European countries, with relatively low rates in Southern Europe.

Period and Cohort Effects

The best documented period effects on suicide rates in the elderly are World War II and the change-over from toxic coal gas to non-toxic North Sea gas in the UK (Murphy et al, 1986), which were associated with a reduction in the suicide rate.

Table 18.1 International comparison of suicide rates in older people

Country	Rates per 100,000 population			
	65–74 years		75+ years	
	Male	Female	Male	Female
Argentina	29.3	5.3	55.4	8.3
Australia	23.1	4.6	31.7	6.3
Austria	54.6	19.0	121.4	29.0
Belgium	41.5	20.3	83.3	21.0
Canada	19.8	5.6	26.6	3.7
Croatia	69.9	19.8	104.8	26.4
Cuba	61.7	27.3	124.4	30.9
Czech Republic	34.0	15.5	87.5	30.6
Denmark	38.8	22.1	63.7	27.0
Estonia	88.0	25.4	110.5	35.1
Finland	50.4	12.7	54.9	9.7
France	50.0	16.3	97.8	22.1
Germany	35.4	14.4	83.3	23.9
Greece	7.9	2.1	17.4	1.6
Hong Kong	40.5	23.8	64.4	38.9
Hungary	88.0	29.9	168.9	60.0
Ireland	20.0	3.1	12.3	2.9
Israel	20.2	8.4	37.2	22.2
Italy	22.1	8.1	44.6	8.8
Kazakhstan	75.5	19.6	88.0	32.1
Korea	33.8	13.4	47.5	18.9
Kyrgyzstan	44.3	17.1	45.7	11.6
Latvia	103.9	19.2	106.1	38.5
Lithuania	106.3	26.6	135.1	33.0
Mauritius	24.8	12.1	27.8	7.8
Moldova	51.0	18.2	61.7	28.0
The Netherlands	18.2	10.6	25.7	9.9
Norway	18.6	13.6	21.5	5.5
Poland	32.2	8.0	32.4	6.4
Portugal	30.1	6.5	51.6	13.1
Romania	23.8	8.5	31.6	6.7
Russian Federation	89.8	23.0	93.9	34.8
Singapore	36.4	28.7	107.1	53.8
Slovakia	45.9	9.1	54.5	6.3
Slovenia	75.0	19.8	104.7	27.3
Spain	24.0	8.3	44.4	10.0
Sweden	29.3	11.0	42.9	17.2
Thailand	7.2	2.2	9.5	2.0
UK	11.3	4.3	15.7	5.7
USA	27.7	5.4	50.7	5.6
Venezuela	24.8	2.9	28.6	2.0

Derived from 1996 World Health Organization Statistical Manual (World Health Organization, 1998). Most data are from 1994 or 1995.

The data on suicide after gas detoxification suggest that elderly people are less likely than the young to turn to other means of suicide following removal of a popular method, which has implications for suicide prevention (Lindesay, 1986). Nowers and Irish (1988) demonstrated a fall in suicide rates following restrictions placed on barbiturate prescribing in the UK.

Sartorius (1995) described the impact of the recent dramatic political and economic changes in Eastern Europe on suicide rates, and found that although the total population suicide rate has increased in recent years, the rates in those over 75 years old have decreased. This is perhaps because unemployment and job insecurity have less relevance to an older age group, and also older people may have greater resilience to social change, having survived the traumas of World War II.

Cohort effects are more difficult to identify. Lindesay (1991) points out that suicide rates tend to be higher in those age groups constituting larger proportions of the population, and suggests that suicide rates may increase in the UK as the "baby boom generation" ages.

Demographic Factors

Older men have higher suicide rates than older women, although there is variation between countries. In the USA, older male suicides outnumber female by 4:1 (Bharucha and Satlin, 1997). In the USA, UK and Australia, rates for men continue to rise with increasing age, whereas female rates decline after the menopause (Shah and De, 1998). In Sri Lanka, gender differences are more pronounced; men aged 75 years and over have the highest risk, while the highest rates in women occur between 15 and 24 years (Conwell 1993). Similar suicide rates for elderly men and women are found in Hong Kong (Yip et al, 1998).

In most Western countries, suicide rates are highest among the divorced, followed by the widowed, then the single, with lowest rates among the married (Smith et al, 1988), perhaps due to the effects of a supportive social network associated with marriage and the adverse effects of divorce and bereavement. In the USA, divorced men and women are at higher risk of suicide than the married (Smith et al, 1988), but the excess risk of suicide in the widowed depends on gender, with men at much higher risk than women (Li, 1995). However, in Hong Kong the widowed of both genders have lower rates of suicide than the married, with single people at highest risk (Yip et al, 1998).

Suicide rates in older immigrants to Australia and the UK seem largely determined by their country of origin (Raleigh and Balarajan, 1992; Burvill, 1995). In the USA, rates are much higher in older whites than non-whites (Mościcki, 1995). Strong religious beliefs and cohesive family networks in the Muslim Malay elderly in Singapore (Ko and Kua, 1995) and older Jewish people in Israel (Sharlin and Lowenstein, 1997) may explain the low suicide rates in these ethnic groups. Miller (1979) has suggested that membership of the tightly-knit Roman Catholic community in the USA may be protective against suicide.

Characteristics of the Suicidal Act in Older People

The high intent accompanying suicidal acts in older people is manifested in the frequent use of violent methods, particularly by men. Shooting accounts for over 70% of older suicides in the USA (Kaplan et al, 1996; Kaplan et al, 1997) and is also a common method in Australia and Finland. Due to more stringent firearm controls, drug overdose (more common in women), hanging (more common in men), suffocation and jumping from a height are the commonest methods in the UK (Cattell, 1988; Cattell and Jolley, 1995). Analgesics are commonly taken in overdoses (Lindesay, 1991). In England and Wales, the older age groups have the highest rates of suicide from drowining (Kelly and Bunting, 1998). Hanging was the commonest method in a Japanese study (Watanabe et al, 1995). In Sri Lanka, self-poisoning with agricultural organophosphates is a frequent method of suicide in older people (Ganesvaran et al, 1984), and in Hong Kong, where 85% of the population live in high-rise flats, jumping from buildings is the commonest method (Yip et al, 1998).

Cattell and Jolley (1995) found that 43% of older suicides left a note. Most suicides are solitary acts, suicide pacts accounting for only 0.6% of suicides in England and Wales. Of all deaths in pacts, 49% occur in those over 65, and participants tend to be married, female, and of a higher social class (Brown and Barraclough, 1997).

Risk Factors for Suicide in Older People

The neurobiological, psychiatric, personality, physical illness, social and miscellaneous risk factors for suicide in older people will now be discussed.

Neurobiology of Suicide in Older People

Substantial evidence links suicidal behaviour to a reduction in brain 5-HT (see Chapter 4). In one of the few studies of the neurochemistry of suicidal behaviour in older people, Jones and colleagues (1990) demonstrated lower concentrations of CSF 5-hydroxyindoleacetic acid (5-HIAA) and homovanillic acid (HVA) in suicidal depressed patients than in non-suicidal depressed patients. Conwell and colleagues (1995) criticized research in this area for failing to examine the possible changes in the neurobiology of suicide with ageing, particularly as the ageing process alters the brain 5-HT system (Meltzer et al, 1998).

Psychiatric Disorder

Psychiatric illness is present in over 71% of older people who commit suicide (Conwell, 1997). Major depression occurs in 44–87% of elderly suicides (Conwell, 1997; Shah and De, 1998) and is more frequently associated with suicide in older people than in the young (Conwell et al, 1996). Although various depressive symptoms, such as agitation, somatic preoccupation and insomnia, have been suggested as predictive of suicide, this awaits confirmation in controlled studies. Chronic depressive symptoms and a first episode in late life may be associated with increased suicidal risk (Shah and De, 1998). Depression preceding suicide in older people goes untreated, or inadequately treated, in the majority of cases (Caine et al, 1996; Duckworth and McBride, 1996).

The wide variation in reported rates of alcohol and substance misuse in series of older suicide victims may reflect genuine regional differences. Rates of over 20% are reported from the USA (Carney et al, 1994; Conwell et al, 1996), with rates of 10% or lower reported in UK studies (Barraclough, 1971; Cattell, 1988; Cattell and Jolley, 1995). Rates of alcoholism seem higher in the younger elderly, and co-morbidity with depression is common (Conwell et al, 1996).

Schizophrenia and psychotic disorders account for 0–12% of older suicides—lower rates than for younger suicides. Anxiety disorders are rarely associated with suicide in older people. The relationship between dementia and suicide is surprisingly under-researched. Follow-up studies of patients with dementia have not revealed any suicides (Harris and Barraclough, 1997). Henriksson et al (1995) found a rate of 5% of "organic disorders" in their analysis of mental disorder associated with older suicides. The apparently low rates may reflect the fact that patients at risk of suicide may have *mild* cognitive impairment, which is difficult to detect at psychological autopsy. Patients with more severe dementia might lack either the cognitive ability to perform a suicidal act, or have lost suicidal ideas along with their insight. Rohde and colleagues (1995) discuss suicide in Alzheimer's disease in more detail.

Vassilas and Morgan (1994) found that, although over 50% of their series of older suicides had a history of past psychiatric contact, only four out of 22 (18%) had seen a psychiatrist in the month prior to death, which is perhaps indicative of general practitioners' reluctance to refer older patients with depression for psychiatric assessment. Two recent controlled studies, from Switzerland (Modestin, 1989) and Australia (Shah and Ganesvaran, 1997), have investigated suicide in psychogeriatric inpatients and found that, compared with inpatients who had not committed suicide, the suicide group tended to have a long incapacitating illness and higher rates of depression, alcohol misuse and suicidal ideation.

Personality

The few studies of personality factors in old-age suicide have indicated low rates of personality disorder compared with younger suicides. In a recent Finnish study, Henriksson et al (1995) found that 14% of suicides in people aged 60 years and over were associated with an Axis II diagnosis, compared to 34% of those under 60 years.

Given the uncertainty as to whether personality disorder diagnostic criteria are applicable to older people, some researchers feel that a more meaningful approach is the study of personality traits associated with suicide. Duberstein et al (1994) demonstrated a link between suicide in old age and a low "openness to experience" (characterized by methodical, rigid, emotionally restricted personality traits). This contrasts with the impulsive personality traits often associated with younger suicide victims.

Physical Illness

Physical illnesses are the most frequent life events preceding suicide in older people (Heikkinen and Lönnqvist,1995). In 84% of Carney et al's (1994) sample of older suicide victims, physical illness was considered a stressor at the time of death. Terminal illness is not a common factor in older suicides (8% in Cattell's, 1988, series). However, pain is an important factor in around 20% of suicides in older people (Cattell, 1988).

Other factors, such as loss of independence and fear of becoming a burden on relatives, are likely to be important but are under-researched. A study comparing health status prior to death in older people dying from suicide, injury and natural death showed that suicide victims were more likely to have a history of cancer (Grabbe et al, 1997). Conwell and colleagues (1990a) performed a detailed psychological autopsy study on older suicides with cancer, and documented the high levels of associated depressive disorder. Horton-Deutsch et al (1992) showed similar findings in a group of elderly suicides with chronic respiratory disease. Physical illness and suicide is further discussed in Chapter 22.

Over 43% of older suicides have been in contact with their general practitioner within the month preceding death (Conwell, 1997), a higher proportion than for younger suicide victims. Cattell (1988) documented recent hospital discharge and, conversely, the fear of hospitalization, as precipitants to suicide in some older people.

Social Factors and Life Events

Older people who end their lives often live alone, but whether living alone is a risk factor for suicide is uncertain (Shah and De, 1998). Suicide is relatively rare in nursing homes (Osgood et al, 1991), although anticipation of nursing home placement can be a trigger to suicide (Loebel et al, 1991). In only 3% of Conwell et al's (1990b) series was social isolation felt to be a stressor, and Heikkinen and Lönnqvist (1995) found levels of social contact prior to death to be similar in old and young suicide victims. However, Miller (1978) found that older male suicides in Arizona were less likely to have had a confidante before death than a natural death control group.

Loneliness is different from social isolation and more refined research is necessary in order to investigate the possible link between loneliness and suicide. The risk of suicide is greater in the widowed, especially during the first year after bereavement in men (Bunch, 1972). However, bereavement may not be any more common as a precipitant to suicide in the elderly compared to younger age groups (Heikkinen and Lönnqvist, 1995). Retirement can lead to loss of self-esteem, but its precise relationship to suicide in older people has yet to be determined. (Miller, 1978; De Leo and Ormskerk, 1991).

In a study from India, poverty was cited as the most important contributory factor to suicide in the elderly after depression and physical illness (Rao, 1991). Conwell (1995) highlights elder abuse as a probable precipitant to suicidal behaviour in some cases, although research evidence is lacking. Of course, any traumatic event, such as interpersonal conflict, separation or financial problems, may act as a precipitant to suicide in the elderly (Heikkinen and Lönnqvist, 1995).

Miscellaneous Risk Factors

Finnish research has suggested a seasonal excess of suicides in older people in autumn (Hakko et al, 1998). Salib (1997) showed an association between suicide in the elderly and sunny days and low humidity levels. Barraclough (1976) showed that elderly people have an increased risk of committing suicide on their birthday.

Rational Suicide, Physician-assisted Suicide and Euthanasia in Older People

In 1998 an 85 year-old woman with metastatic breast cancer in Oregon, USA, was the first person legally to commit physician-assisted suicide (Josefson, 1998). About 10–20% of suicides in older people are not associated with psychiatric disorder, and undoubtedly some of these are carefully thought-out acts in response to insoluble and unbearable life problems. However, the elderly might be at particular risk if physician-assisted suicide and euthanasia were to become more widely available. Conwell and Caine (1991) are worried that, in light of the strong link between suicidal ideation and depressive illness in older people, the suicidal wishes of older people may erroneously be assumed to be rational, when in fact they are coloured by depression. Post (1997) highlights the vulnerability of people with dementia should physician-assisted suicide or euthanasia become more widely legalized. However, Onwuteaka-Philpsen et al (1997) point out that the rates of euthanasia and physician-assisted suicide amongst older patients performed in The Netherlands are low and there is no evidence that such deaths are increasing. Of course, whether this would be so in countries with different health care systems and socio-economic structures from The Netherlands is open to debate.

CONCLUSIONS

A commonly-held view amongst lay people is that suicide in the elderly is usually a rational act in response to terminal ilness or unbearable physical symptoms, whilst psychiatric professionals have perhaps over-emphasised the importance of depressive illness. In fact, both physical illness and depression are often present in older people who die through suicide. However, both these problems are not infrequent in the older population, and the interesting question is why some people with these problems choose suicide, and some maintain a will to live. To move closer towards an answer will require thorough research using carefully selected control groups, and the exploration of the neglected domains of social and personality variables. In the meantime, there are strategies which could be implemented to improve the well-being of older people and which might possibly reduce the risk of suicide in this group. Suicide prevention in older people is discussed further in Chapter 31.

REFERENCES

Alexopoulos, G.S. (1991) Psychological autopsy of an elderly suicide. International Journal of Geriatric Psychiatry, 6: 45–50.

Barraclough, B.M. (1971) Suicide in the elderly. British Journal of Psychiatry, (Suppl. 6): 87–97.

Barraclough, B.M. (1976) Birthday blues: the association of birthday with self-inflicted death in the elderly. Acta Psychiatrica Scandinavica, 54: 146–149.

Batchelor, I.R.C. and Napier, M.B. (1953) Attempted suicide in old age. British Medical Journal, ii: 1186–1190.

Bean, P. (1973) Accidental and intentional self poisoning in the over-60 age group. Gerontologica Clinica, 15: 259–267.

Bharucha, A.J. and Satlin, A. (1997) Late-life suicide: a review. Harvard Review of Psychiatry, 5: 55–65.

Brown, M. and Barraclough, B. (1997) Epidemiology of suicide pacts in England and Wales, 1988–1992. British Medical Journal, 315: 286–287.

Bunch, J.M. (1972) Recent bereavement in relation to suicide. Journal of Psychosomatic Research, 16: 361–366.

Burston, G.R. (1969) Self-poisoning in elderly patients. Gerontologica Clinica, 11: 279–289.

Burvill, P.W. (1995) Suicide in the multiethnic elderly population of Australia, 1979–1990. International Psychogeriatrics, 7: 319–333.

Caine, E.D., Lyness, J.M. and Conwell, Y. (1996) Diagnosis of late-life depression: preliminary studies in primary care settings. American Journal of Geriatric Psychiatry, 4 (Suppl. 1): 545–550.

Carney, S.S., Rich, C.L., Burke, P.A. and Fowler, R.C. (1994) Suicide over 60: the San Diego study. Journal of the American Geriatrics Society, 42: 174–180.

Cattell, H.R. (1988) Elderly suicide in London: an analysis of coroners' inquests. International Journal of Geriatric Psychiatry, 3: 251–261.

Cattell, H. and Jolley, D.J. (1995) One hundred cases of suicide in elderly people. British Journal of Psychiatry, 166: 451–457.

Chiu, H.F., Lam, L.C., Pang, A.H., Leung, C.M. and Wong, C.K. (1996) Attempted suicide by Chinese elderly in Hong Kong. General Hospital Psychiatry, 18: 444–447.

Conwell, Y. (1993) Suicide in the elderly: cross-cultural issues in late life suicide. Crisis, 14: 152–153.

Conwell, Y. (1995) Elder abuse—a risk factor for suicide? Crisis, 16: 104–105.

Conwell, Y. (1997) Management of suicidal behavior in the elderly. Psychiatric Clinics of North America, 20: 667–683.

Conwell, Y., Caine, E.D. and Olsen, K. (1990a) Suicide and cancer in late life. Hospital and Community Psychiatry, 41: 1334–1339.

Conwell, Y. and Caine, E.D. (1991) Rational suicide and the right to die: reality and myth. New England Journal of Medicine, 325: 1100–1103.

Conwell, Y., Duberstein, P.R., Cox, C., Herrmann, J., Forbes, N.T. and Caine, E.D. (1996) Relationships of age and axis I diagnoses in victims of completed suicide: a psychological autopsy study. American Journal of Psychiatry, 153: 1001–1008.

Conwell, Y., Raby, W.N. and Caine, E.D. (1995) Suicide and aging II: The psychobiological interface. International Psychogeriatrics, 7: 165–181.

Conwell, Y., Rotenberg, M. and Caine, E.D. (1990b) Completed suicide at age 50 and over. Journal of the American Geriatrics Society, 38: 640–644.

De Leo, D. (1997) Suicide in late life at the end of the 1990s: a less neglected topic? Crisis, 18: 51–52.

De Leo, D., Bille-Braha, U., Bjerke, T., Crepet, P., Haring, C., Kerkhof, A., Lönnqvist, J., Michel, K., Pommereau, X., Querejeta, I., Salander-Renberg, E., Schmidtke, A., Temesvary, B., Wasserman, D., Bernadini, M. and Sampaio Faria, J. (1994) Parasuicide in the elderly: results from the WHO/EURO Multicentre Study, 1989–1993. A short report. IPA Bulletin, 11: 15–17.

De Leo, D. and Ormskerk, S.C.R. (1991) Suicide in the elderly: general characteristics. Crisis, 12: 3–17.

Dewey, M.E., Davidson, I.A. and Copeland, J.R.M. (1993) Expressed wish to die and mortality in older people: a community replication. Age and Ageing, 22: 109–113.

Draper, B. (1994) Suicidal behaviour in the elderly. International Journal of Geriatric Psychiatry, 9: 655–661.

Draper, B. (1996) Attempted suicide in old age. International Journal of Geriatric Psychiatry, 11: 577–587.

Draper, B., MacCuspie-Moore, C. and Brodaty, H. (1998) Suicidal ideation and the "wish to die" in dementia patients: the role of depression. Age and Ageing, 27: 503–507.

Duberstein, P.R., Conwell, Y. and Caine, E.D. (1994) Age differences in the personality characteristics of suicide completers: preliminary findings from a psychological autopsy study. Psychiatry, 57: 213–224.

Duckworth, G. and McBride, H. (1996) Suicide in old age: a tragedy of neglect. Canadian Journal of Psychiatry, 41: 217–222.

Forsell, Y., Jorm, A.F. and Winblad, B. (1997) Suicidal thoughts and associated factors in an elderly population. Acta Psychiatrica Scandinavica, 95: 108–811.

Ganesvaran, T., Subramaniam, S. and Mahadevan, K. (1984) Suicide in a northern town in Sri Lanka. Acta Psychiatrica Scandinavica, 69: 420–425.

Grabbe, L., Demi, A., Camann, M.A. and Potter, L. (1997) The health status of elderly persons in the last year of life: a comparison of deaths by suicide, injury, and natural causes. American Journal of Public Health, 87: 434–437.

Hakko, H., Räsänen, P. and Tiihonen, J. (1998) Seasonal variation in suicide occurrence in Finland. Acta Psychiatrica Scandinavica, 98: 92–97.

Harris, E.C. and Barraclough, B.M. (1997) Suicide as outcome for mental disorder: a meta-analysis. British Journal of Psychiatry, 170: 205–228.

Heikkinen, M.E. and Lönnqvist, J.K. (1995) Recent life events in elderly suicide: a nationwide study in Finland. International Psychogeriatrics, 7: 287–300.

Henriksson, M.M., Marttunen, M.J., Isometsä, E.T., Heikkinen, M.E., Aro, H.M., Kuoppasalmi, K.I. and Lönnqvist, J.K. (1995) Mental disorders in elderly suicide. International Psychogeriatrics, 7: 275–286.

Hepple, J. and Quinton, C. (1997) One hundred cases of attempted suicide in the elderly. British Journal of Psychiatry, 171: 42–46.

Horton-Deutsch, S.L., Clark, D.C. and Farran, C.J. (1992) Chronic dyspnea and suicide in elderly men. Hospital and Community Psychiatry, 43: 1198–1203.

Jones, J.S., Stanley, B., Mann, J.J., Frances, A.J., Guido, J.R., Traskman-Bendz, L., Winchel, R., Brown, R.P. and Stanley, M. (1990) CSF 5-HIAA and HVA concentrations in elderly depressed patients who attempted suicide. American Journal of Psychiatry, 147: 1225–1227.

Jorm, A.F., Henderson, A.S., Scott, R., Korten, A.E., Chirstensen, H. and Mackinnon, A.J. (1995) Factors associated with the wish to die in elderly people. Age and Ageing. 24: 389–392.

Josefson, D. (1998) US sees first legal case of physician assisted suicide. British Medical Journal (News), 316: 1037.

Kaplan, M.S., Adamek, M.E. and Geling, O. (1996) Sociodemographic predictors of firearm suicide among older white males. Gerontologist, 36: 530–533.

Kaplan, M.S., Adamek, M.E., Geling, O. and Calderon, A. (1997) Firearm suicide among older women in the US. Social Science and Medicine, 44: 1427–1430.

Kelly, S. and Bunting, J. (1998) Trends in suicide in England and Wales, 1982–1996. Population Trends, 92: 29–41.

Kirby, M., Bruce, I., Radic, A., Coakley, D. and Lawlor, B.A. (1997) Hopelessness and suicidal feelings among the community dwelling elderly in Dublin. Irish Journal of Psychological Medicine, 14: 124–127.

Ko, S.M. and Kua, E.H. (1995) Ethnicity and elderly suicide in Singapore. International Psychogeriatrics, 7: 309–317.

Li, G. (1995) The interaction effect of bereavement and sex on the risk of suicide in the elderly: an historical cohort study. Social Science and Medicine, 40: 825–828.

Linden, M. and Barnow, S. (1997) The wish to die in very old persons near the end of life: a psychiatric problem? Results from the Berlin aging study. International Psychogeriatrics, 9: 291–307.

Lindesay, J. (1986) Trends in self-poisoning in the elderly, 1974–1983. International Journal of Geriatric Psychiatry, 1: 37–43.

Lindesay, J. (1991) Suicide in the Elderly. International Journal of Geriatric Psychiatry, 6: 355–361.

Loebel, J.P., Loebel, J.S., Dager, S.R., Centerwall, B.S. and Reay, D.T. (1991) Anticipation of nursing home placement may be a precipitant of suicide among the elderly. Journal of the American Geriatrics Society, 39: 407–408.

Lyness, J.M., Conwell, Y. and Nelson, J.C. (1992) Suicide attempts in elderly psychiatric inpatients. Journal of the American Geriatrics Society, 40: 320–324.

Meltzer, C.C., Smith, G., DeKosky, S.T., Pollock, B.G., Mathis, C.A., Moore, R.Y., Kupfer, D.J. and Reynolds, C.F. III (1998) Serotonin in aging, late-life depression, and Alzheimer's disease: the emerging role of functional imaging. Neuropsychopharmacology, 18: 407–430.

Merrill, J. and Owens, J. (1990) Age and Attempted Suicide. Acta Psychiatrica Scandinavica, 82: 385–88.

Miller, M. (1979) Suicide After Sixty: the Final Alternative. New York: Springer.

Miller. M. (1978) Geriatric suicide: the Arizona study. Gerontologist, 18: 488–495.

Modestin, J. (1989) Completed suicide in psychogeriatric inpatients. International Journal of Geriatric Psychiatry, 4: 209–214.

Moore, S.L. (1997) A phenomenological study of meaning in life in suicidal older adults. Archives of Psychiatric Nursing, 11: 29–36.

Mościcki, E.K. (1995) Epidemiology of suicide. International Psychogeriatrics, 7: 137–148.

Murphy, E., Lindesay, J. and Grundy, E. (1986) Sixty years of suicide in England and Wales: a cohort study. Archives of General Psychiatry, 43: 969–976.

Nelson, F.L. and Farberow, N.L. (1980) Indirect self-destructive behavior in the elderly nursing home patient. Journal of Gerontology, 35: 949–957.

Nowers, M. (1993) Deliberate self-harm in the elderly: a survey of one London borough. International Journal of Geriatric Psychiatry, 8: 609–614.

Nowers, M. and Irish, M. (1988) Trends in the reported rates of suicide by self-poisoning in the elderly. Journal of the Royal College of General Practitioners, 38: 67–69.

Onwuteaka-Philipsen, B.D., Muller, M.T. and van der Wal, G. (1997) Euthanasia and old age. Age and Ageing, 26: 487–492.

Osgood, N.J., Brant, B.A. and Lipman, A. (1991) Suicide Among the Elderly in Long-term Care Facilities. New York: Greenwood.

Paykel, E.S., Myers, J.K., Lindenthal, J.J. and Tanner, J. (1974) Suicidal feelings in the general population: a prevalance study. British Journal of Psychiatry, 124: 460–469.

Pierce, D. (1987) Deliberate self-harm in the elderly. International Journal of Geriatric Psychiatry, 2: 105–110.

Pierce, D.W. (1996) Repeated deliberate self-harm in the elderly. International Journal of Geriatric Psychiatry, 11: 983–986.

Post, S.G. (1997) Physician-assisted suicide in Alzheimers disease. Journal of the American Geriatrics Society, 45: 647–651.

Pritchard, C. (1996) New patterns of suicide by age and gender in the United Kingdom and the Western World 1974–1992; an indicator of social change? Social Psychiatry and Psychiatric Epidemiology, 31: 227–234.

Raleigh, V.S. and Balarajan, R, (1992) Suicide levels and trends among immigrants in England and Wales. Health Trends, 24: 91–94.

Rao, A.V. (1991) Suicide in the elderly: a report from India. Crisis, 12: 33–39.

Rao, R., Dening, T., Brayne, C. and Huppert, F.A. (1997) Suicidal thinking in community residents over eighty. International Journal of Geriatric Psychiatry, 12: 337–343.

Rifai, A.H., George, C.J., Stack, J.A., Mann, J.J. and Reynolds, C.F. (1994) Hopelessness in suicide attempters after acute treatment of major depression in late life. American Journal of Psychiatry, 151: 1687–1690.

Rohde, K., Peskind, E.R. and Raskind, M.A. (1995) Suicide in two patients with Alzheimer's disease. Journal of the American Geriatrics Society, 43: 187–189.

Salib, E. (1997) Elderly suicide and weather conditions: is there a link? International Journal of Geriatric Psychiatry, 12: 937–941.

Sartorius, N. (1995) Recent changes in suicide rates in selected Eastern European and other European countries. International Psychogeriatrics, 7: 301–308.

Shah, A. and Ganesvaran, T. (1997) Psychogeriatric inpatient suicides in Australia. International Journal of Geriatric Psychiatry, 12: 15–19.

Shah, A. and De, T. (1998) Suicide and the elderly. International Journal of Psychiatry in Clinical Practice, 2: 3–17.

Sharlin, S.A. and Lowenstein, A. (1997) Suicide among the elderly in Israel. Death Studies, 21: 361–375.

Simon, R.I. (1989) Silent suicide in the elderly. Bulletin of the American Academy of Psychiatry and the Law, 17: 83–95.

Skoog, I., Aevarsson, O., Beskow, J., Larsson, L., Palsson, S., Waern, M., Landahl, S. and Östling, S. (1996) Suicidal feelings in a population sample of non-demented 85 year-olds. American Journal of Psychiatry, 153: 1015–1020.

Smith, J.C., Mercy, J.A. and Conn, J.M. (1988) Marital status and the risk of suicide. American Journal of Public Health, 78: 78–80.

Vassilas, C.A. and Morgan, H.G. (1994) Elderly suicides' contact with their general practitioner before death. International Journal of Geriatric Psychiatry, 9: 1008–1009.

Watanabe, N., Hasegawa, K. and Yoshinaga, Y. (1995) Suicide in later life in Japan: urban and rural differences. International Psychogeriatrics, 7: 253–261.

World Health Organization (1998) 1996 World Health Statistics Manual. Geneva: WHO.

Yip, P.S.F., Chi, I. and Yu, K.K. (1998) An epidemiological profile of elderly suicides in Hong Kong. International Journal of Geriatric Psychiatry, 13: 631–637.

Chapter 19

Sexuality, Reproductive Cycle and Suicidal Behaviour

Jose Catalan
*Imperial College of Science, Technology and Medicine, University of London, UK**

Abstract

This chapter brings together a number of topics concerning sexuality and the reproductive cycle. First, the relationship between homosexuality and suicidal behaviour is reviewed, focusing initially on the evidence for an association with completed suicide and then with deliberate self-harm. Methodological problems and issues concerned with the context of research in this socially and politically sensitive topic are discussed. Next, the relationship between pregnancy and suicidal behaviour is considered. Pregnancy and failure to complete it, either voluntarily or otherwise, and the post-partum period are discussed in relation to suicide and deliberate self-harm. Finally, paraphilias, specifically auto-erotic asphyxia and its relationship to suicidal behaviour, are discussed.

INTRODUCTION

Sexual feelings and behaviour and some of their consequences, such as pregnancy, are powerful human experiences which can be both the source of great joy and happiness as well as the cause of much distress and sadness. The links between sexuality and death, including death by suicide, are commonplace in human culture, be it in the arts or in psychological and philosophical thinking. Here, empirical evidence for the association between suicidal behaviour and

* Also at Psychological Medicine Unit, Chelsea and Westminster Hospital Campus, 369 Fulham Road, London SW10, UK.

The International Handbook of Suicide and Attempted Suicide. Edited by K. Hawton and K. van Heeringen.

these human experiences is reviewed. The reproductive cycle is dealt with in a somewhat restricted way, excluding childhood and adolescence as well as old age, as these will be considered elsewhere (see Chapters 15–18).

SEXUAL ORIENTATION AND SUICIDAL BEHAVIOUR

Methodological, Social and Other Issues in Research

Psychiatric research into sexual orientation has focused, until fairly recently, on attempting to describe and understand a behaviour regarded *a priori* as pathological (Danto, 1978; Hartstein, 1996). However, in the last three decades there has been a marked shift in attitudes in Western-style developed countries, among both the general public and the psychological and social sciences community. "Normalization" of homosexual behaviour, in spite of temporary setbacks, as at the beginning of the AIDS crisis in developed countries, has led to a more open acceptance of the homosexual lifestyle as a viable alternative, and to the possibility of more valid psychological and social research.

There are, nevertheless, major obstacles to the study of homosexual behaviour and its correlates. In the case of research into suicidal behaviour and homosexuality, it is not always easy to identify homosexuality amongst people involved in suicide or deliberate self-harm, as homosexual feelings are not self-evident and any prevalence figures must be seen as underestimates. Similarly, even if the prevalence of gay men and lesbians amongst suicides could be determined accurately, establishing the general population prevalence for comparison purposes is an even harder task.

Societies prepared to be open about homosexuality to the extent that research on this topic is carried out may also be those where attitudes are more supportive of homosexual behaviour: researchers are likely to find less of an adverse effect on gay men and lesbians than in a society where homosexuality is a crime or a sin which is heavily punished, and where, by definition, research is impossible to fund and carry out. The research evidence available comes from Western developed countries, and it is therefore not possible to generalize the findings to other societies and cultures.

Finally, politics (in the broadest sense of the term) make it hard to examine the topic dispassionately. What might be called the "victim mentality" would expect gay men and lesbians to have a higher rate of suicidal behaviour, in response to rejection by society and self-attribution of negative attitudes. Such an expectation may be just what those who support a disease model of homosexuality would also assume: failure to develop into a heterosexual as proof of immaturity and associated with increased risk of depression and suicide. On the other hand, finding that gay men and lesbians are at no greater risk of suicidal behaviour than heterosexuals might be seen as weakening calls for greater tolerance and support for an oppressed sexual minority.

Suicide and Sexual Orientation

Self-evident questions to be answered are first, is there an increase in suicide amongst gay men and lesbians?, and second, are there any specific features associated with suicide in homosexual people? Muehrer (1995) has reviewed the literature on suicide and sexual orientation, pointing out the limitations of existing research evidence, including the lack of data on the prevalence of homosexual identity in the general population and problems with the reliability of data on sexual orientation in suicides. Two studies are identified which throw some light on this complex and under-researched area.

Rich and colleagues (1986) carried out a detailed clinical investigation of 133 cases of suicide in men under the age of 30 years and 150 men over this age, identified through the San Diego Coroner's Office between 1981 and 1983. Information about these men was obtained by interviews with relatives, friends and other informants, as well as health and social agencies. Homosexuals were identified, on the basis of the information gathered, if they had regarded themselves as homosexuals and maintained exclusively or predominantly homosexual relationships. A total of 13 (5%) homosexual males were identified, all aged between 21 and 42 years, and they were compared with the rest of the males in this age range (n = 106). As no accurate data exist about the proportion of gay men in the population under study, it is not possible to make confident comparisons, but a proportion of 5% does not suggest an over-representation of gay men amongst suicides. Few differences were found between groups. Gay and heterosexual men did not differ in terms of history of past deliberate self-harm, psychiatric history or legal problems or presence of substance misuse problems, although the diagnosis of schizophrenia was given more often to gay men. Gay men were also significantly more likely to use hanging as the method of suicide. The small sample size raises questions about the reliability of these differences.

A similar "psychological autopsy" investigation was reported by Shaffer and co-workers (1995). A total of 120 consecutive suicides under the age of 20 years, occurring in greater New York City between 1984 and 1986, were included, 95% of whom were male. Comparisons were made with a control stratified random sample drawn from telephone subscribers in the area. Three gay male suicides were identified (3.2% of all males and 2.5% of the total group), and none reported being gay in the control sample, although this difference was not significant. No evidence of stigmatization or lack of support was found in the three suicides.

Against these systematic but still relatively unsatisfactory investigations, there are a number of reports claiming that suicide is more common in homosexuals, in particular amongst young gay men and lesbians, although these statements do not appear to be supported by evidence (for reviews, see Muehrer, 1995; Hartstein, 1996).

A new dimension to the discussion of suicide and homosexuality is its association with HIV infection. While, in worldwide terms, HIV infection is a primarily heterosexual infection, gay and bisexual men represent a majority of cases in many developed countries, and there have been reports from such countries suggesting an increase in the risk of suicide in people with HIV infection (see Chapter 22). The issue remains unresolved, largely because of methodological problems concerned with case identification and accurate matching with control populations (for review, see Catalan et al, 1995a). It is unclear what consequences the development of new and effective treatments for HIV infection has had on the formerly alleged increased risk of suicide, but it seems likely that improvements in health and quality of life in people with HIV has had a beneficial impact on suicide risk (Catalan, 1999).

Deliberate Self-harm and Sexual Orientation

Unsurprisingly, methodological problems also beset research here: case identification is poor amongst people involved in deliberate self-harm, definitions of deliberate self-harm are not universally consistent, and information about the proportion of gay and lesbian individuals in the general population remains unclear (Muehrer, 1995; Hartstein, 1996).

A large-scale study including both men and women, albeit one limited by time, place and sample selection, gives some idea of the relative prevalence of deliberate self-harm in relation to sexual orientation. Under the auspices of the Kinsey Institute for Sex Research, Bell and Weinberg (1978) carried out detailed interviews with 976 gay men and lesbians and 477 heterosexual men and women from the San Francisco Bay Area. Although an element of self-selection is inevitable in this kind of research, the authors made efforts to include as representative a sample as possible. Amongst the wealth of information gathered, a history of deliberate self-harm was found significantly more often in gay men compared with their heterosexual counterparts, usually in association with a relationship break-up or problems in coming to terms with homosexual feelings. Lesbians were no more likely to have made suicide attempts than heterosexual women. Gay men were also more likely to have sought professional help for emotional problems, while only some sub-groups of lesbians were more likely to have done so than heterosexual women.

Two further large-scale surveys of young people have focused on sexual orientation and suicide attempts. Bagley and Tremblay (1997) studied a stratified random sample of 750 men aged 18–27 in Calgary, Canada, between 1991 and 1992, using a computerized questionnaire. A total of 11.1% classified themselves as engaging in homosexual or bisexual behaviour. Sexually active gay and bisexual men reported a greater prevalence of lifetime deliberate self-harm (10%) than sexually active heterosexuals (3%). Interestingly, the highest prevalence was reported by celibate young men, and here again gay men were more likely to report a past history of deliberate self-harm (46%) than heterosexual ones (18%). Faulkner and Cranston (1998) carried out a questionnaire survey of a random sample of more than 3,000 high school students (mean age 16 years) in

Massachusetts in 1993. The results were given for the total sample, without separation by gender, and information was provided about differences amongst sexually experienced participants with same-sex and other-sex experience. Same-sex experienced participants represented 6.4%, and they were more likely to report suicide attempts in the previous 12 months (27.5%) than heterosexual participants (13.4%), as well as more repeated attempts and attempts requiring medical attention. Same-sex participants also reported more episodes of fighting, victimization and substance misuse.

Self-identified samples of gay and bisexual men, sometimes with a control group, have been studied by several authors. Schneider and colleagues (1989), in a survey of 108 gay men aged 16–24 years, found that 20% had a history of deliberate self-harm. In a sample of 137 men aged 14–21 years, Remafedi and colleagues (1991) reported a history of suicide attempts in 30%. Family problems, difficulties in coming to terms with sexual feelings, conflict with peers and relationship difficulties with a partner were the most frequently-cited precipitants. Substance misuse, feminine gender role and younger age of homosexual self-labelling were independently associated with a history of deliberate self-harm. D'Augelli and Hershberger (1993), in their survey of 194 lesbian, gay and bisexual youths aged 15–21, found that 42% had a past history of deliberate self-harm. Male attempters were younger at self-identification and more had experienced greater loss of social supports, had lower self-esteem, and problems in alcohol use. For women, associated factors were loss of social supports and problems with depression and interpersonal sensitivity, amongst other emotional difficulties. van Heeringen and Vincke (in press) studied 404 young persons aged 15–27 in Belgium, the sample including 137 gay or bisexual boys and 82 lesbian or bisexual girls. A history of deliberate self-harm was reported by 12.4% of gay or bisexual boys, against 5.9% by heterosexual boys. The comparable rates reported by lesbian or bisexual and heterosexual girls were 25.0% and 5.4% respectively.

Little is known about the proportion of lesbians, gays and bisexuals presenting for medical care following deliberate self-harm and the nature of their problems. A retrospective study of the case notes of 1,806 people referred to a general hospital psychiatric unit after deliberate self-harm in Oxford, UK, over a 3-year period, identified 29 (1.6%) gay/bisexual or lesbian attempters, representing 3% of men and 0.8% of women attempters (Catalan, 1983). However, questions about sexual orientation were not routinely asked, and so the results give only some indication of issues concerned with conspicuous homosexuality, as opposed to its true prevalence and problems.

HIV has also been linked to deliberate self-harm in gay and bisexual men, and the same methodological problems discussed in relation to suicide and HIV apply here (Catalan et al, 1995a; Catalan, 1999). A case-control investigation of 22 HIV-positive deliberate self-harm patients (21 of whom were gay or bisexual men) found no differences between them and 44 sex- and age-matched controls regarding demographic characteristics, history of deliberate self-harm or alcohol and substance misuse, methods used for self-harm, suicidal intent and reasons given for the act. HIV-infected individuals, however, were more likely to be diagnosed as depressed and to have a history of psychiatric disorder, and less likely to suffer from alcohol misuse. Unsurprisingly, concerns about health were predominant in the HIV group (Catalan et al, 1995b).

Deliberate attempts to become infected with HIV, as an act of suicidal behaviour, have been described (Catalan et al, 1995a) and an increase in risky sexual behaviour following AIDS-related bereavement in gay men has been reported (Mayne et al, 1998).

PREGNANCY AND SUICIDAL BEHAVIOUR

In this section the evidence concerning the association between suicidal behaviour and pregnancy will be reviewed and its significance discussed. For obvious reasons, the literature is confined to the examination of this association in relation to women, although it is clear that the impact of pregnancy is not restricted to the potential or actual mother: the father, other children and the extended family may also be involved in suicidal behaviour, but such events are probably too uncommon to have merited attention in the psychiatric literature. Suicide and non-fatal deliberate self-harm will be reviewed in relation to their occurrence during pregnancy, the postnatal period and in cases of failure to complete pregnancy due to elective termination or other reasons.

Suicide and Pregnancy

Suicide in childbearing women, in particular in comparison with men of the same age, is a rare phenomenon, and there is good evidence to suggest that pregnancy and childbirth may reduce its incidence even further. Failure to complete the pregnancy may not have such a protective effect, and this may well apply to cases where pregnancy is unwanted and elective termination is not available, as in what has been labelled "the Hedda Gabler syndrome", after the heroine of Ibsen's drama (Goodwin and Harris, 1979).

Suicide during Pregnancy

The relatively low frequency of suicide makes it difficult to detect differences compared with the expected prevalence using the typical sample size and the length of follow-up found in most clinical investigations. Maternal mortality investigations, however, have tended to find lower rates of suicide than expected for comparable populations (Barno, 1967; Sachs et al, 1987; and Syverson et al, 1991). Series of female suicides have been studied to determine the proportion of pregnant women amongst them, the results ranging from 0% to 13.5% (for review, see Appleby, 1996).

In a retrospective study based on national population data for England and Wales from 1973 to 1984 (Appleby, 1991, 1996), the suicide rate during pregnancy was found to be one-twentieth of the expected rate (observed: expected mortality ratio, 0.05; 95% CI, 0.029–0.084), but interestingly, the suicide mortality ratio for teenage pregnant women, while still lower than that of non-pregnant ones, was four times greater than for older pregnant women. Marzuk and colleagues (1997), in a similar investigation of autopsy reports of all female suicides of New York City aged 10–44 during 1990–1993, found the age- and race-adjusted risk of suicide among pregnant women to be 0.33 (95% CI, 0.12–0.72), or one-third of the expected risk for non-pregnant women.

Suicide and Failure to Complete Pregnancy

Miscarriage and induced abortion have been reported to be associated with a greater risk of suicide than expected in a comparable population of non-pregnant women or, indeed, of pregnant women who complete their pregnancy. Grissler and colleagues (1996) studied suicide in women of childbearing age in Finland between 1987 and 1994, and found that, against a mean annual suicide rate in this age and sex group of 11.3 per 100,000, women who miscarried (18.1) or had an induced abortion (34.7) showed significantly higher rates. The rate for women who completed their pregnancy was 5.9, significantly lower than expected. Ectopic pregnancy followed by salpingectomy has also been reported to be associated with increased risk of suicide (Farhi et al, 1994).

The association between failure to complete the pregnancy, particularly in the case of induced abortion, leaves open the question of the direction of the association: while it could be argued that suicide was the result of the termination of pregnancy, it is likely that women who had chosen to terminate their pregnancy were already at greater risk of suicide because of other factors, such as depression, low social class, low levels of social support or greater number of adverse life events.

Suicide Following Childbirth

Appleby and co-workers have carried out a number of important studies on the risk of suicide during pregnancy and after childbirth (Appleby, 1991, 1996; Appleby et al, 1998). In the study referred to above, based on population data for England and Wales from 1973 to 1984 (Appleby, 1991, 1996), suicide in the first post-partum year was found to be one-sixth of that expected on the basis of general population rates. Suicide tended to be by violent means and to occur in the first month after childbirth, possibly in association with severe post-partum depressive disorders. Infanticide took place in one in 20 suicides (see Chapter 24). The contribution of severe psychiatric disorder to suicide during the first postnatal year was explored in an investigation of mortality in a sample of 1,567 Danish women admitted to psychiatric hospital after childbirth. In this selected population, suicide in the first postnatal year was found to be 70 times greater than expected (Appleby et al, 1998).

Deliberate Self-harm and Pregnancy

Deliberate Self-harm during Pregnancy

By contrast with suicide, deliberate self-harm is thought to have a similar prevalence in pregnant and non-pregnant women (Whitlock and Edwards, 1968; Rayburn et al, 1984), indicating that suicidal behaviour, when occurring during pregnancy, seldom leads to death. Accidental injury during pregnancy appears to be relatively common, but deliberate self-harm is not a frequent event (Sherer and Schenker, 1989). Reviewing the literature on the proportion of pregnant women found amongst female suicide attempters, Appleby (1996) found that it ranged from 4% to 20%, although most studies reported a figure of less than 10%. A high proportion of 20% was found in Afro-Caribbeans in Birmingham in the UK (Burke, 1976).

Several studies comparing pregnant women admitted to hospital following attempted suicide with non-pregnant attempters have found few or no differences between them, apart from the obvious fact of the pregnancy. Whitlock and Edwards (1968) compared 30 pregnant women admitted to hospital after deliberate self-harm with 453 non-pregnant controls. Pregnant women tended to be younger, but they did not differ in other demographic characteristics, methods used to self-harm or psychiatric diagnosis. The pregnancy was the main reason for the episode of deliberate self-harm in five (17%) and a contributory factor in another eight (27%). In a comparison of 15 consecutive pregnant women and 131 non-pregnant ones, the two groups were found not to differ in measures of depression, hopelessness or suicidal intent, although pregnant women were more likely to report a history of suicide or attempted suicide in a significant person (Lester and Beck, 1988). Common themes were: prior loss of children (due to death, adoption or miscarriage), fear of losing partner, and desire for an abortion.

The timing of deliberate self-harm during pregnancy has been the subject of several investigations. Rayburn and colleagues (1984) found that drug overdoses occurred in the first 3 months of pregnancy in 53% of cases, against 23% in the second and 23% in the final trimester, not entirely comparable to the much-quoted findings of Whitlock and Edwards (1968) (first trimester, 47%; second, 43%; and third, 10%). Interestingly, analysis of the Hungarian data reported below (Czeizel et al, 1984) by Lester (1987) showed an almost reversed pattern: 25% in the first trimester, 43% in the second and 31% in the third. There is one case report involving deliberate self-harm occurring shortly after the start of labour, linked to the woman's fears about the well-being of her baby (Neale, 1976).

As in the case of non-pregnant women, self-poisoning is the most common method of self-harm, but self-injury, including shooting with subsequent death of the fetus, has been reported (Sandy and Koerner, 1989). Detailed information about the substances taken in cases of self-poisoning was obtained by Rayburn and colleagues (1984), who studied 119 pregnant patients referred by telephone to a Poisons Control Centre. Analgesics, including narcotics, were used by 34%; psychotropic medication, including anxiolytics, sedatives, major tranquillizers and antidepresants, were ingested by 26%; followed by nutritional supplements (12%); antibiotics (7%); and antihistamines (6%), amongst others.

Pregnancy Outcome and Health Status of the Offspring of Pregnant Women Who Deliberately Self-harm

Czeizel and co-workers have carried out a number of studies on pregnant women involved in deliberate self-poisoning in Hungary. In the first series they described the outcome of 142 pregnant women who were hospitalized following self-poisoning (Czeizel et al, 1984). Fetal death occurred in 13 (9%), in some instances as a result of the substances ingested, 33 (23%) had a termination of pregnancy, and 96 (68%) of the children survived. In a detailed study of the teratological status of the babies involving a larger sample of 559 women, Czeizel and colleagues (1997) found teratological effects to be no more frequent than expected (9%), although self-poisoning was more likely in the earlier stages of pregnancy (38% in the first and 23% in the second month). Induced abortion was significantly more common than in the control group of pregnant women (40% against less than 1%), and the proportion of live births much lower (35% against 87%). There is a dearth of information about the outcome of self-injury in pregnant women, although there is one report describing the death of the fetus after self-inflicted shooting to the abdomen, with maternal survival (Sandy and Koerner, 1989).

Deliberate Self-harm and Failure to Complete Pregnancy

Suicidal risk has been identified as a factor in a substantial proportion of women undergoing elective termination of pregnancy (Kenyon, 1969; Perera, 1983). An association between termination of pregnancy and subsequent deliberate self-harm has been reported. Gilchrist and co-workers (1995) studied more than 13,100 pregnant women belonging to four groups, those who had: (a) had a termination; (b) had one refused; (c) changed their minds about it; or (d) not wished to have a termination. While women with a past psychiatric history had a greater risk of deliberate self-harm during the 2-year follow-up period, rates in this group were not affected by pregnancy outcome. Amongst women with no previous psychiatric history, however, both those who had their operation refused or those in whom it was carried out had an increased risk of deliberate self-harm. The authors explain these findings in terms of co-existing social and psychological factors, although the possibility of a direct contribution of the termination or its refusal cannot be ruled out. Similar results were reported by Houston and Jacobson (1996), although the significance of this finding has been questioned (Gbolade, 1997). Interestingly, Houston and Jacobson (1996) found that termination of pregnancy was somewhat more likely to *follow* deliberate self-harm, rather than the other way round, highlighting the dangers involved in overhasty assumptions about causality based merely on statistical association. As in the case of suicide following elective abortion (see above), it is likely that both deliberate self-harm and termination of pregnancy share contributing factors.

Deliberate self-harm on the expected date of childbirth in cases of teenage termination of pregnancy have been described as a form of anniversary reaction (Tishler, 1981), although Gilchrist and colleagues (1995) did not find such an anniversary effect. Ectopic pregnancy and salpingectomy have also been reported to be linked to an increase in the risk of deliberate self-harm (Farhi et al, 1994).

Little information is available about the impact of not being able to have a termination when one is wanted. A variety of factors, including legal, religious and financial, will influence access to termination of pregnancy. Early research on the long-term consequences of refusal of elective abortion has failed to find subsequent suicidal behaviour, in spite of the presence of suicidal ideation at the time (Hook, 1963). More recent reports in the literature (Gabinet, 1984; Gilchrist et al, 1995) have found a link between refusal of, or difficulties in obtaining, a termination and subsequent risk of deliberate self-harm.

Deliberate Self-harm Following Childbirth

There is evidence that childbirth has a protective effect against deliberate self-harm during the first year after delivery. Appleby and Turnbull (1995) studied consecutive female attempters aged 15–44 presenting at a general hospital over a 6-month period, under 4% of whom had had a baby in the previous year. The rate of deliberate self-harm was less than half that of non-pregnant women: 1.25 against 2.57 per 1,000 (odds ratio, 0.43; 95% CI, 0.17–0.95), and the authors speculate that, as in the case of completed suicide, the presence of young children may increase the woman's feelings of self-worth, possibly based on her perception of being needed (Appleby and Turnbull, 1995; Appleby, 1996). It is interesting to find such reduction in the risk of deliberate self-harm at a time when the prevalence of psychiatric disorders is known to be increased (Brockington, 1998). An earlier publication (Gabrielson et al, 1970), based on a cohort of teenage mothers aged up to 17 years, suggested an increase in the prevalence of deliberate self-harm after childbirth, but the large majority of episodes of self-harm had occurred over a period of several years, rather than in the first post-partum year, and so comparison with more recent investigations is not possible.

PARAPHILIAS AND SUICIDAL BEHAVIOUR

The association between death and sex is a notorious one in early psychiatric literature, particularly that with a psychoanalytic focus (for review, see Danto, 1978). Systematic investigation of suicidal behaviour and paraphilias is a more recent phenomenon, mostly in relation to fatal or near-fatal auto-erotic episodes of asphyxia. Such behaviours can raise complex forensic, legal and psychiatric issues.

Auto-erotic asphyxial episodes (also known as sexual asphyxia, auto-erotic death and sexual bondage) include evidence of asphyxia produced by hanging or ligature, and where the position of the body or presence of protective measures indicates that death was not intended; evidence of sexual activity (masturbation, erotic materials, cross-dressing); minimal or no evidence of suicidal ideation or behaviour; and evidence of repetitive acts (Walsh et al, 1977).

The true prevalence of auto-erotic asphyxial deaths is unknown, as the stigma associated with suicide is even more apparent in such cases, and efforts may be made by those finding the body to remove evidence linking the death to sexual behaviour. Litman and Swearingen (1972) speculated that about 50 cases per year were occurring in the USA, and others have suggested that they represent a small proportion of death by hanging (Walsh et al, 1977). A few cases of near fatal auto-erotic asphyxia have been described, usually involving serious damage and a need for medical treatment, but the prevalence of behaviour not requiring medical intervention is not known. There are reports of case studies and series which suggest a predominance of males, with a wide age range from adolescence to late middle age. Heterosexual, homosexual and bisexual orientations are represented, and cross-dressing and sado-masochism are not uncommon (Litman and Swearingen, 1972; Walsh et al, 1977; Garza-Leal and Landron, 1991; Byard et al, 1993; Book and Perumal, 1993). Sheehan and Garfinkel (1988) have claimed that auto-erotic deaths represent more than 30% of all deaths by hanging in adolescent males.

Careful investigation of the circumstances of the act and sensitive interviewing of relatives and others will be necessary to establish whether a death by hanging is a suicide or a case of auto-erotic asphyxia.

CONCLUSIONS

Sexual Orientation and Suicidal Behaviour

Research findings need to be qualified, not just by the usual methodological questions but also by the fact that published research is restricted to developed countries with reasonably liberal social attitudes: it is not possible to generalize to less tolerant or simply different societies (Moscicki et al, 1995). Completed suicide does not appear to be more common in gay men and lesbians than in heterosexual persons, although the presence of HIV infection among gay men in some developed countries may well have had some impact on suicide mortality.

The picture is somewhat different in relation to deliberate self-harm. A number of studies have shown that gay men and lesbians have a greater lifetime prevalence of deliberate self-harm than heterosexual men and women, but there is some inconsistency about the relative risks of gay men and lesbians. The contribution of HIV infection to deliberate self-harm in gay men is unclear.

It is clear that further research is needed to clarify fully the relationship between sexual orientation and suicidal behaviour in different societies and cultures, and that such research should pay close attention to matters of definition, case identification and general population rates. However, the limits of current research should not blind those working in the fields of health, social services and education to the needs of young persons discovering their sexuality in what may be perceived by them as a socially excluding and stigmatizing community.

Pregnancy and Suicidal Behaviour

Even allowing for under-reporting, completed suicide during pregnancy is a very rare event, considerably less common than expected for non-pregnant women. By contrast, failure to complete the pregnancy, whether as a result of miscarriage, elective termination or other reasons, is associated with greater risk of suicide. The risk of suicide in the first year after childbirth is also reduced, although this does not apply to women who require psychiatric hospitalization during the postpartum period, who are at much increased risk of suicide.

Deliberate self-harm appears to be no more common during pregnancy than expected, and there are few differences between pregnant and non-pregnant attempters in terms of their mental state and demographic characteristics, although the pregnancy itself is a causal factor in an important proportion of those who make attempts. Most instances of deliberate self-harm involve self-poisoning, and while harm can occur to the fetus as a result, the prevalence of teratological problems does not appear to be higher than expected. Reports are not consistent regarding the timing of the attempt in relation to stage of pregnancy. Elective termination of pregnancy is associated with greater risk of self-harm in women without a previous psychiatric history, as can be difficulty in obtaining access to termination. The rate of deliberate self-harm in the year after childbirth is substantially lower than expected, in spite of a greater prevalence of psychiatric morbidity.

The protective effect of pregnancy towards suicidal behaviour is somewhat counter-intuitive, as pregnancy and childbirth are often associated with psychological morbidity. Explanations for this protective effect have ranged from the purely biological, such as an increase in serotonin during pregnancy leading to reduction in self-destructive behaviour (Marzuk et al, 1997), to improvement in self-esteem and self-worth in the woman in response to caring for the child, actual or future. Whatever the mechanisms, there must be powerful processes at work offering evolutionary advantage to a species able to look after its offspring during gestation and later on, when the baby is at its weakest.

Further research needs to focus on the impact of demographic and social change on reproductive behaviour and suicide risk, in particular in societies experiencing rapid changes. Threats to the old nuclear family may also impact fathers and others affected by reproductive behaviour. At a practical level, further research is needed to improve the identification and management of those at risk of suicidal behaviour in the context of pregnancy.

Paraphilias and Suicidal Behaviour

The true prevalence of auto-erotic asphyxial deaths is not clear, although it may well represent a significant proportion of deaths by hanging in adolescent males. The main issues in relation to suicidal behaviour are forensic and legal.

REFERENCES

Appleby, L. (1991) Suicide during pregnancy and in the first postnatal year. British Medical Journal, 302: 137–140.

Appleby, L. (1996) Suicidal behaviour in childbearing women. International Review of Psychiatry, 8: 107–115.

Appleby, L. and Turnbull, G. (1995) Parasuicide in the first postnatal year. Psychological Medicine, 25: 1087–1090.

Appleby, L., Mortensen, P. and Faragher, E.B. (1998) Suicide and other causes of mortality after post-partum psychiatric admission. British Journal of Psychiatry, 173: 209–211.

Bagley, C. and Tremblay, P. (1997) Suicidal behaviours in homosexual and bisexual males. Crisis, 18: 24–34.

Barno, A. (1967) Criminal abortion deaths, illegitimate pregnancy deaths, and suicides in pregnancy, Minnesota, 1950–1965. American Journal of Obstetrics and Gynecology, 98: 356–367.

Bell, A.P. and Weinberg, M.S. (1978) Homosexualities: a Study Of Diversity Among Men And Women. London: Mitchell Beazley.

Book, R. and Perumal, G. (1993) Sexual asphyxia: a lesser epidemic. Medicine and Law, 12: 687–698.

Brockington, I. (1998) Puerperal disorders. Advances in Psychiatric Research, 4: 312–327.

Burke, A.W. (1976) Socio-cultural determinants of attempted suicide among West Indians in Birmingham: ethnic origin and immigrant status. British Journal of Psychiatry, 129: 261–266.

Byard, R., Hucker, S. and Hazelwood, R. (1993) Fatal and near fatal autoerotic asphyxial episodes in women. The American Journal of Forensic Medicine and Pathology, 14: 70–73.

Catalan, J. (1983) Attempted suicide and homosexuality. British Journal of Sexual Medicine, 1: 11–14.

Catalan, J. (Ed.) (1999) Mental Health and HIV infection. London: University College London Press.

Catalan, J., Burgess, A. and Klimes, I. (1995a) Psychological Medicine of HIV infection. Oxford: Oxford University Press.

Catalan, J., Seijas, D., Lief, T., Pergami, A. and Burgess, A. (1995b) Suicidal behaviour in HIV infection: a case-control study of deliberate self-harm in people with HIV infection. Archives of Suicide Research, 1: 85–96.

Czeizel, A., Szentesi, I., Szkezeres, I., Glauber, A., Bucski, P. and Molnar, C. (1984) Pregnancy outcome and health conditions of offspring of self-poisoned pregnant women. Acta Paediatrica Hungarica, 25: 209–236.

Czeizel, A., Tomcsik, M. and Timar, L. (1997) Teratologic evaluation of 178 infants born to mothers who attempted suicide by drugs during pregnancy. Obstetrics and Gynecology, 90: 195–201.

Danto, B. (1978) Violent sex and suicide. Mental Health and Society, 5: 1–13.

D'Augelli, A. and Hershberger, S. (1993) Lesbian, gay, bisexual youth in community settings: personal challenges and mental health problems. American Journal of Community Psychology, 21: 421–448.

Farhi, J., Ben-Rafael, Z. and Dicker, D. (1994) Suicide after ectopic pregnancy. The New England Journal of Medicine, 330: 714.

Faulkner, A. and Cranston, K. (1998) Correlates of same-sex sexual behaviour in a random sample of Massachusetts high school students. American Journal of Mental Health, 88: 262–266.

Gabinet, L. (1984) Attempted suicide in response to refusal of elective abortion. The Ohio State Medical Journal, 80: 801–803.

Gabrielson, I.H., Klerman, L., Currie, J., Tyler, N. and Jekel, J. (1970) Suicide attempts in a population pregnant as teenagers. American Journal of Public Health, 60: 2289–2301.

Gbolade, B. (1997) Overdose and termination of pregnancy. British Journal of General Practice, 47: 184.

Garza-Leal, J.A. and Landron, F. (1991) Auto-erotic death initially represented as suicide and a review of the literature. Journal of Forensic Medical Pathology, 36: 1753–1759.

Gilchrist, A., Hannaford, P., Frank, P. and Kay, C. (1995) Termination of pregnancy and psychiatric morbidity. British Journal of Psychiatry, 167: 243–248.

Gissler, M., Hemminki, E. and Lönnqvist, J. (1996) Suicides after pregnancy in Finland, 1987–1994: register linkage study. British Medical Journal, 313: 1431–1434.

Goodwin, J. and Harris, D. (1979) Suicide in pregnancy: the Hedda Gabler syndrome. Suicide and Life-Threatening Behavior, 9: 105–115.

Hartstein, N. (1996) Suicide risk in lesbian, gay, and bisexual youth. In R. Cabaj and T. Stein (Eds), Textbook of Homosexuality and Mental Health. Washington, DC: American Psychiatric Press.

Hook, K. (1963) Refused abortion. Acta Psychiatrica Scandinavica, 39: 1–156.

Houston, H. and Jacobson, L. (1996) Overdose and termination of pregnancy. British Journal of General Practice, 46: 737–738.

Kenyon, F.E. (1969) Termination of pregnancy on psychiatric grounds: a comparative study of 61 cases. British Journal of Medical Psychology, 42: 243–254.

Lester, D. (1987) The timing of attempted suicide during pregnancy. Acta Paediatrica Hungarica, 28: 259–260.

Lester, D. and Beck, A.T. (1988) Attempted suicide and pregnancy. American Journal of Obstetrics and Gynecology, 158: 1084–1085.

Litman, R. and Swearingen, C. (1972) Bondage and suicide. Archives of General Psychiatry, 27: 80–85.

Marzuk, P., Tardiff, K., Leon, A., Hirsch, C., Portera, L., Hartwell, N. and Iqbal, M. (1997) Lower risk of suicide during pregnancy. American Journal of Psychiatry, 154: 122–123.

Mayne, T., Acre, M., Chesney, M. and Folkman, S. (1998) HIV sexual risk behaviour following bereavement in gay men. Health Psychology, 17: 403–411.

Moscicki, E., Muehrer, P. and Potter, L. (1995) Recommendations for a research agenda in suicide and sexual orientation. Suicide and Life Threatening Behavior, 25: 82–88.

Muehrer, P. (1995) Suicide and sexual orientaton: a critical summary of recent research and directions for future research. Suicide and Life Threatening Behavior, 25: 72–81.

Neale, R. (1976) Attempted suicide in labour. British Medical Journal, 1: 321–322.

Perera, H. (1983) A review of psychiatric aspects of termination of pregnancy. Ceylon Medical Journal, 28: 42–47.

Rayburn, W., Aronow, R., DeLancey, B. and Hogan, M. (1984) Drug overdose during pregnancy: an overview from a metropolitan poison control center. Obstetrics and Gynecology, 64: 611–614.

Remafedi, G., Farrow, J. and Deisher, R. (1991) Risk factors for attempted suicide in gay and bisexual youth. Pediatrics, 87: 869–875.

Rich, C., Fowler, R., Young, D. and Blenkush, M. (1986) San Diego suicide study: comparison of gay to straight males. Suicide and Life-Threatening Behavior, 16: 448–457.

Sachs, B., Brown, D., Driscoll, S., Schulman, E., Acker, D., Ransil, B. and Jewett, J. (1987) Maternal mortality in Massachusetts: trends and prevention. New England Journal of Medicine, 316: 667–672.

Sandy, E. and Koerner, M. (1989) Self-inflicted gunshot wound to the pregnant abdomen: report of a case and review of the literature. American Journal of Perinatology, 6: 30–31.

Schneider, S., Farberow, N. and Kruks, G. (1989) Suicidal behavior in adolescent and young adult gay men. Suicide and Life Threatening Behavior, 19: 381–394.

Shaffer, D., Fisher, P., Parides, M. and Gould, M. (1995) Sexual orientation in adolescents who commit suicide. Suicide and Life Threatening Behavior, 25: 64–71.

Sheehan, W. and Garfinkel, B. (1988) Adolescent auto-erotic deaths. Journal of the American Academy of Child and Adolescent Psychiatry, 27: 367–370.

Sherer, D.M. and Schenker, J.G. (1989) Accidental injury during pregnancy. Obstetric and Gynecological Survey, 44: 330–338.

Syverson, C., Chavkin, W., Atrash, H., Rochat, R., Sharp, E. and King, G. (1991) Pregnancy-related mortality in New York City, 1980–1984. American Journal of Obstetrics and Gynecology, 164: 603–608.

Tischler, C.L. (1981) Adolescent suicide attempts following elective abortion: a special care of anniversary reaction. Pediatrics, 68: 670–671.

Van Heeringen, K. and Vincke, J. (in press) Suicidal acts and ideation in homosexual and bisexual young people: a study of prevalence and risk factors.

Walsh, F., Stahk, C., Unger, H., Lilienstern, O. and Stephens, R. (1977) Auto-erotic asphyxial deaths: a medico-legal analysis of forty-three cases. In C.H. Wecht (Ed.), Legal Medicine Annual, pp. 157–182. New York: Appleton Century Crofts.

Whitlock, F. and Edwards, J. (1968) Pregnancy and attempted suicide. Comprehensive Psychiatry, 9: 1–12.

Chapter 20

Suicidal Behaviour and the Labour Market

Stephen Platt
Research Unit in Health and Behavioural Change, University of Edinburgh Medical School, Edinburgh, UK
and
Keith Hawton
Department of Psychiatry, Oxford University, Oxford, UK

Abstract

This chapter describes and examines empirical evidence concerning the relationship between suicidal behaviour and the labour market, based on a systematic and structured review of the literature from 1984 onwards. Three aspects of the labour market are distinguished: unemployment; female labour force participation (FLFP); and occupational (class) status and occupational risk. Within suicidal behaviour, completed suicide and deliberate self-harm (attempted suicide or parasuicide) are considered separately. Studies are assigned to one of four types of research design: individual cross-sectional, aggregate cross-sectional, individual longitudinal and aggregate longitudinal. Following a brief overview of the methodological limitations of these designs, we present the main findings in tabular form with a brief accompanying commentary. There is an increased risk of suicide and deliberate self-harm among the unemployed, which may be compatible with both causal and self-selection processes. The review does not find strong evidence to suggest that increased FLFP rates have led to increased suicide rates. On the other hand, data confirming a positive impact of FLFP are equivocal. The risks of suicide and deliberate self-harm are inversely related to social class (the lower the class, the higher the rate), while the occupational groups exhibiting the greatest proportional mortality ratios for suicide are found in classes I and II (e.g. those working in the medical and allied professions). The chapter concludes with a brief consideration of the implications for prevention.

The International Handbook of Suicide and Attempted Suicide. Edited by K. Hawton and K. van Heeringen.

BACKGROUND

It is difficult to grasp all the characteristics and consequences of the major techno-economic revolution which is now being experienced world-wide, but especially in the post-industrial societies of Europe and North America. The accelerating internationalization of finance, investment and trade via the globalization of economic activity is having major consequences, negative and positive, intended and unintended, for the economic, social, psychological, political and cultural environments that shape population health. Nowhere is this new world order more evident than in the changing labour market conditions which have transformed the lives of the economically active (employed as well as unemployed) and fundamentally altered societal attitudes to, and understandings of, economic activity itself.

The restructuring of industry, large-scale corporate re-engineering, privatization and the erosion of the public sector, the abandonment of state commitment to full employment and crises and instability in the world financial and economic markets have combined to increase massively the risk of unemployment. According to the International Labour Organization's *World Employment Report 1998–99*, "the number of unemployed and underemployed workers around the world has never been higher" [International Labour Organization (ILO), 1998]. The ILO estimates that one billion workers, one-third of the world's workforce, is unemployed, that is, seeking or available for work but unable to find it (about 150 million people) or underemployed, that is, working substantially less than full-time but wanting to work longer or earning less than a living wage (between 750 and 900 million people). In the European Union more than 18 million workers are unemployed, without taking into account the "considerable number of 'discouraged' workers who have given up hope of finding work, and involuntary part-time workers". Many advanced countries suffer from permanently high levels of unemployment and, even where unemployment has been falling, the level has remained stubbornly higher than the near-full employment achieved during the periods of economic expansion between the end of the Second World War and the oil shocks of the early 1970s. In addition, the characteristics of those affected by unemployment have changed, so that sectors previously less vulnerable to cyclical economic downturns (e.g. professionals, white-collar workers) have experienced joblessness on a significant scale (although it is important to note that unemployment remains class-related, with the risk being considerably higher in manual occupations).

Another key development over the past 20 years has been the changing composition of the labour force. In Europe the overall labour force participation rate (i.e. total labour force as a percentage of the working population) has tended to increase, although there have been different trends by age and gender. Thus, participation rates have declined among under-25 year-olds, reflecting the growth of tertiary education and training. Participation rates among older workers, particularly males, have fallen, with the steepest decline in Finland, France, The Netherlands and the UK. Participation rates among women, above all in the

25–49 year age group, have increased to a greater extent than among men, so that the gap between male and female participation rates has closed considerably (and almost disappeared in Scandinavia). In general, working hours have been reduced, mainly as a result of the shift in employment from agriculture and manufacturing to services and the growth of female employment. The exceptions to this trend are Ireland and the UK; the latter holds the record for the highest average weekly hours worked by employees in the 12 country (pre-expanded) European Union (43.7 hours in the early 1990s).

The pattern of employment has continued to show movement out of the agricultural and industrial sectors and into service industries. For instance, in Belgium in 1973, 41% of civil employment was in industry and 55% in services; the percentages were 28% and 70%, respectively, in 1992. Overall, in the European Union, the percentage of the employed workforce in service industries increased from 53% in 1980 to 63% in 1993. The decline of manufacturing and the growth of service jobs (many low-paid) has produced some deskilling in the workforce, but technological and organizational change in manufacturing and the demand for IT competence in the service sector have produced an opposite effect.

Probably the most discussed feature of the European labour market has been the drive towards flexibility as a key policy objective, on the grounds of indispensability for economic competition and the reduction of high unemployment rates. While there is little agreement about what is meant by "flexibility", the ability to adapt rapidly to changes in conditions and technology is typically included in most definitions. Adnett (1996) distinguishes between various types of flexibility, of which the most outstanding is the growth of "atypical", "non-standard" or "precarious" employment and the decline of the "standard" full-time, permanent employment contract. Precarious employment includes part-time work, on-call contracts, fixed-term contracts, seasonal work, agency work, homeworking, teleworking, freelancing, self-employment and informal work (Delsen, 1991). Fixed-term and temporary contracts account for 15% of paid employment in the European Union, ranging from 9% in Luxembourg and Austria to 40% in Spain. In the USA in 1995 almost 30% of the workforce were in "flexible" jobs (e.g. part-time, independent or company contract, self-employed, on call, temporary, day labourer). Over half of all part-time (56%) and temporary (63%) employment in the EU occurs in low-skilled occupational groups (service, production and sales workers). In recent years the increase in part-time employment has accelerated, with an average increase of 2.2% during 1991–1995. In all EU member states in 1991 the frequency of part-time employment was about twice as high among female workers as it was for the total working population.

The potential impact of unemployment on the health of the unemployed and the wider population has long been recognized and there is a vast academic literature demonstrating adverse effects on physical and mental health at both individual and aggregate levels. In a recent review, Dooley and colleagues (1996) refer to the inexorable trend away from standard (i.e. full time, permanent) contracts in the USA and speculate that this type of underemployment "could produce adverse effects on health similar to those reported . . . for unemployment". They call for future research to incorporate "these increasingly common statuses that fall between adequate employment and unemployment on the employment continuum". Benach and colleagues (2000) develop this argument, highlighting the need to develop a standardized definition of precarious employment and to generate a multi-level theory of causation that can explain its impact on health.

In this chapter we describe and assess the available empirical evidence concerning the relationship between labour market conditions and suicidal behaviour. The review updates and extends earlier reviews by Platt (1984, 1986a; see also Platt et al, 1992) in two main ways: first, it concentrates on publications published during a more recent time period (1984–1999); and second, it incorporates empirical studies on aspects of the labour market additional to unemployment, which was the sole focus of the earlier review. In the following sections we outline the methods used to identify studies for inclusion in the review and the analytical framework for summarizing the data, prior to presenting the findings and discussing the implications for suicide prevention.

METHODOLOGICAL ISSUES

Literature Search Strategy

The primary method for identifying the literature on labour market conditions and suicidal behaviour was searching electronic bibliographic databases. In view of its sophistication and power, Medline was selected as the starting point for the search and the "gold standard" against which other databases were compared. Following retrieval of all relevant citations from Medline, several other databases (BIDS Embase, BIDS–ISI Social Sciences Citation Index, Psyclit, Sociofile and Cinhal) were searched to generate additional publications falling within the scope of the review. A limited attempt was also made to identify "grey" literature (i.e. publications which cannot be accessed through usual databases or outlets) through the System for Information on Grey Literature in Europe (SIGLE), British reports, Translations and Theses (BRTT), the internet and informal contact with research institutions. References cited in publications identified through the above searching procedures were also pursued. Throughout the search, only literature published after 1983 was considered eligible for inclusion. There was no restriction by country of origin or language, although only publications in English, Spanish and French were obtained in their full, original version.

A preliminary search strategy was generated using keywords, phrases or terms that were identified as being relevant to "labour market conditions" and "suicidal behaviour". Labour market conditions were separated into five "blocks" (labour market participation, restructuring, labour market insecurity, non-employment and changes in work), within which several keywords, etc., were contained. "Suicidal behaviour" was separated into "suicide", "attempted suicide", "parasuicide", "deliberate self-harm", "self-poisoning" and "self-injury" (studies reporting on suicidal thoughts or ideation without any behavioural component were excluded). Although the focus was on original, empirical studies, systematic review articles were also considered eligible for inclusion.

Identification of Relevant Literature

Abstracts of publications generated through the search process were examined in order to assess their prima facie relevance to the review. Any that failed to refer to empirical data or did not appear to offer a relevant overview of (any aspect of) the field were set aside at this stage. The remaining 165 publications were ordered, read and assigned to one of three sets. The largest consisted of empirical studies presenting quantitative data and applying statistical tests to assess the significance of the findings. The quality of these studies was assessed but no minimal threshold was applied: all were included in the review. Methodological and substantive information about each publication was recorded on a standardized data extraction form. These forms were used subsequently to prepare the summaries of each study which can be found in the tables below. The second set comprised review articles that met minimal standards of relevance and showed evidence of having used systematic search procedures. The third set consisted of empirical studies that did not use any statistical tests and failed to present data in a way that permitted such tests to be made post hoc. Studies in this last set are excluded from the review.

Despite the use of over 30 keywords, etc., to identify the relevant labour market literature, examination of the articles reporting empirical data and included in the review shows that most of the analytical categories were empty; that is, no publications were found. The relationship between unemployment and suicidal behaviour continues to be the main preoccupation among researchers, and most of the literature assessed here fall under this heading. Two other aspects of the labour market have generated particular interest: (trends in) female labour force participation rates; and occupational (class) status and occupational risk. The discussion which follows is therefore organized around these three areas. The pleas by Dooley and colleagues (1996) and Benach and colleagues (2000) for consideration of a wider range of labour market conditions and situations have yet to be heeded by researchers in the field of suicidal behaviour.

With respect to suicidal behaviour (defined as a deliberately self-harmful act), we adopt the conventional distinction between behaviour which has a fatal outcome (i.e. suicide) and that which has a non-fatal outcome [variously referred to as "deliberate self-harm" (the term employed in the rest of this chapter), "attempted suicide" and "parasuicide"]. This distinction is relatively easy to make, but the problem of heterogeneity *within* each behaviour remains as a result of variable operational definitions between studies. The key difference in studies of suicide is the adoption of the restricted ICD-9 E950-E959 codes vs. the use of these codes plus E980–E989 ("undetermined whether accidentally or purposely inflicted"). Following Charlton and colleagues' (1992) policy, most British studies now tend to use the latter, broader definition, whereas researchers from other countries, especially the USA, continue to use the former, narrower definition. A further problem, revealed in many of the tables below (especially those concerned with suicide), is the failure to provide any operational definition at all. While there is also variation in the operational definition of deliberate self-harm, in nearly all studies the sample consists of persons admitted to hospital for treatment, and excludes persons treated in other medical facilities or receiving no treatment whatsoever. The sample bias introduced by these selection procedures is unknown. The overall variability in defining suicidal behaviours should be considered when summarizing and interpreting data from the various studies presented in the table below. Uniformity of findings *despite* definitional heterogeneity is likely to strengthen our confidence in their robustness and generalizability, while inconsistent findings may be an artefact of such heterogeneity and therefore conceal real trends or differences (i.e. increase the risk of Type II error).

Categorization of Studies by Research Design

In addition to differentiating studies by labour market condition (unemployment, female labour force participation and occupation) and type of suicidal behaviour (suicide and deliberate self-harm), we also distinguish between four major types of research design. Following the precedent set in the review by Platt (1984), we contrast two orthogonal dimensions: individual vs. aggregate measures; and cross-sectional vs. longitudinal collection of measures. Individual-level studies measure the relationship between the labour market status and suicidal behaviour of individuals, while aggregate-level studies consider the relationship between, for example, the female labour force participation rate and the suicide or deliberate self-harm rate over time (time-series analysis) or over geographical areas (ecological analysis). The temporal design of the research can be either cross-sectional, measuring the relationship between, for example, unemployment and suicide data (individual- or aggregate-level) at one point in time; or longitudinal, where, for example, unemployment in individuals or aggregates is associated with subsequent suicide or deliberate self-harm over two or more points in time. The intersection of these two dimensions results in four types of study: individual cross-sectional, aggregate cross-sectional, individual longitudinal and aggregate longitudinal.

The methodological limitations of each design type have been extensively discussed by Platt (1984) and elsewhere. Cross-sectional studies (individual and aggregate) cannot distinguish between causal and self-selection explanations for any significant association that is discovered. To take an example, an elevated relative risk for suicide among the unemployed may arise because the status of being unemployed somehow determines a suicidal response, either directly (almost certainly only a theoretical possibility) or indirectly [e.g. via the impact of unemployment on psychological, interpersonal and/or financial problems (Jones et al, 1991) which increase the risk of suicidal behaviour]. However, the same elevated relative risk could be explained by virtue of a third factor, e.g. psychiatric illness, which raises the risk of both unemployment and suicidal behaviour. This latter explanation would be compatible with a non-causal or self-selection model of the labour market–suicidal behaviour relationship. Doubts also remain about the ability of the aggregate longitudinal design to settle arguments of causality. The well-known difficulty of inferring cause from simple correlational (ordinary least squares) analysis is found also with more sophisticated time-series analysis.

Aggregate studies (cross-sectional and longitudinal) are prone to the "ecological fallacy", the unwarranted assumption that an association at the aggregate level (e.g. between the unemployment rate and the deliberate self-harm rate) entails a similar association at the individual level. However, to continue with this example, the parasuicidal population may be subsumed entirely within the unemployed population, or only partially, or not at all. This problem has been addressed through empirical investigation of both aggregate- and individual-level data (e.g. Platt and Kreitman, 1985) and by estimating relative risks from aggregate data (Norstrom, 1998).

Two additional methodological issues arise out of the use of the aggregate cross-sectional design. The size of the geographical area used for analysis can lead to problems in interpretation, especially if it is large enough to be characterized by social heterogeneity. Spatial autocorrelation refers to the fact that the presumed independence of units of analysis (i.e. geographical areas) used in calculating measures of association is almost certainly not empirically verifiable: contiguous areas tend to resemble each other in socio-economic and other characteristics. A related limitation of the aggregate longitudinal design is autocorrelated error, which occurs when the residuals from an ordinary least squares regression are not independent. However, more advanced econometric or multiple regression time-series techniques are available and have been applied in order to overcome the problem of autocorrelated error.

The individual longitudinal design, arguably the most powerful of the four types in unravelling temporal sequencing and assessing causal processes, exists in two variants: prospective and retrospective. The prospective cohort design is almost unknown in research on suicidal behaviour, due to its rarity. The retrospective design is considered by some critics (e.g. Dooley and Catalano, 1980) to be as weak as the cross-sectional study in resolving causal vs. self-selection explanations, but there is support (e.g. MacMahon and Pugh, 1970) for the view that prospective and retrospective designs are not conceptually different, neither do they require differences in interpretation of findings.

One final methodological issue which applies to all types of research design should not be overlooked. Despite the almost universal acknowledgement that suicidal behaviour (whether viewed as an individual act or as an emergent property of societal aggregates) is almost certainly the outcome of many differing influences (sociological, economic, psychological and psychiatric, to name but a few), the impact of labour market conditions is often assessed without taking this into account. The result is likely to be omitted variable bias, with unemployment or other indicators of labour market conditions enjoying an over-inflated valuation of their explanatory power due to the close correlation (multi-collinearity) between these indicators and other (omitted) predictors of suicidal behaviour. The Comments column in each table in this chapter draws attention to studies which lack control for such "confounding" variables, and readers are advised to treat their findings more cautiously than findings from "controlled" studies. However, it is also important to be aware of the danger of over-controlling, when mediating or moderator variables are treated as if they were confounders. In general, research in this area suffers badly from the absence of detailed and specified models of suicide and deliberate self-harm, in particular the relationship between labour market and other explanatory variables. The result is the vast array of variables that are thrown into a typical multivariate analysis, making comparison between studies difficult if not impossible.

LABOUR MARKET CONDITIONS AND SUICIDAL BEHAVIOUR: EMPIRICAL EVIDENCE FROM THE LITERATURE

The Relationship between Unemployment and Suicidal Behaviour

Evidence from Individual Cross-sectional Studies

Tables 20.1 and 20.2 summarize findings from individual cross-sectional studies concerning the relationship between unemployment, on the one hand, and suicide and deliberate self-harm, respectively, on the other. Platt and colleagues (1992) found significantly higher suicide risk among the unemployed compared to the employed in Italy [relative risk (RR) = 3.4 among men and 2.2 among women]. Andrian (1996) reported significant, but lower, risks in France (2.3 among men, 1.9 among women); however, the economically inactive were included with the unemployed. Platt and colleagues (1992) also provide estimates of the proportion of the suicide rate statistically attributable to unemployment [population attributable risk (PAR) percent]: this was 9.6% among men and 4.5% among women.

Odds ratios (ORs) or relative risk ratios (RRs) (deliberate self-harm risk among the unemployed compared to the employed) are quoted in 12 of the 19 publications reporting findings from individual cross-sectional studies on deliberate self-harm and unemployment (Table 20.2). Because of overlap between publications, the number of independent studies is approximately seven. The lowest risks are found in a study of medically serious deliberate self-harm (OR = 4.1 for men, 5.1 for women) (Beautrais et al, 1998) and of deliberate self-harm in an ethnic population (RR = 3) (Neeleman et al, 1996). In more unselected hospital deliberate self-harm samples, risks (OR or RR) were found to vary between

Table 20.1 The relationship between unemployment and suicide: individual cross-sectional studies

Study/definition of suicide	Time period/ place	Statistical procedure	Main findings	Comments
Andrian (1996) Not given	1982, 1992, 1989–91 France	RR	In 1992 among men aged 25–59 years the ratio (RR) of suicide among the unemployed and economically inactive (74.9) compared to among the employed (32.3/100,000) was 2.3 (up from 1.8 in 1982). Among women in the same age range the rates were 18.7 and 9.7, respectively, giving a ratio (RR) of 1.9. Analysis by age shows that ratios (RRs) are above average in the 25–49 year age groups among men and 25–29 and 40–49 year age groups among women	No distinction is made between unemployed and economically inactive. No definition of suicide is given
Charlton (1995) ICD-9 E950–E959– and E980–E989 (excluding E988.8)	1990–92 England and Wales	Case control design (control defined as all deaths from natural causes). Standard logistic regression techniques provided ORs of dying from suicide compared to dying from natural causes	The RR of suicide (relative to deaths from natural causes) among men aged 45–64 years was higher in areas with a low level of unemployment: areas with unemployment rates above 5% had lower RRs. For women included aged 16–64 years there was the same trend, but only unemployment rates in excess of 12% were associated with significantly lower RR. Among men aged 16–44 years the local unemployment rate was not associated with RR of suicide	Controls for marital status, country of birth and age-group (five year). Other possible confounders or mediators (e.g. employment status) are not induded
Platt et al (1992) Police/carabinieri data and definition of suicide	1977–87 Italy	RR; PAR percent	Over the period the RR of suicide among the unemployed compared to the employed was 2.2 among women and 3.4 among men. The mean value (range) of the PAR percent (i.e. the proportion of the suicide rate statistically "attributable" to unemployment) was 4.5% (0–13.6%) among women and 9.6% (6.1–16.0%) among men	No controls

Table 20.2 The relationship between unemployment and deliberate self-harm: individual cross-sectional studies

Study/definition of parasuicide	Time period/ place	Statistical procedure	Main findings	Comments
Beautrais et al (1998) Medically serious suicide attempt (SSA) admitted to hospital	1991–1994 Christchurch, New Zealand	OR; PAR percent; conditional logistic regression analysis	Unemployment was associated with serious suicide attempt among both men (OR = 4.1, $p < 0.0001$) and women (OR = 5.1, $p < 0.0001$). However, the PAR percent was only 7.3, suggesting that "exposure to unemployment made only a small contribution to overall rates of serious suicide attempt". After adjusting for age, gender, family, childhood and educational factors the OR was reduced from 4.2 to 2.1 ($p < 0.05$); after adjustment for age, gender and current mental disorders the OR was 1.95 ($p > 0.10$); and after adjustment for all factors combined the OR was 1.7 ($p > 0.10$)	Limitations of the study recognized by the authors are: use of retrospective self-reports of childhood experiences; no information about the temporal sequencing of unemployment periods and episodes of psychiatric morbidity; and uncertain generalizability of findings to other unemployment contexts. The relevance of the findings to the whole range of parasuicidal behaviour is also unclear. But see Jones et al (1991) whose study also raises questions about the causal nature of the unemployment–deliberate self-harm relationship

Fuller et al (1989) Non-fatal deliberate overdose	1984–88 Central London	RR		The rate of unemployment in the sample was higher (60% of males and 40% of females of employable aged) than in the local area (13%). The RR of deliberate self-harm among the unemployed compared to the employed was 11.6	Dearth of technical information (e.g. denominators, definition of economic activity) which would permit evaluation of findings. No control for other possible confounders
Hawton and Rose (1986) Hospital referral following deliberate self-poisoning or self-injury	1979–82 Oxford, UK	RR		Among men, the RR of deliberate self-harm (rate among the unemployed/rate among the employed) was fairly consistent across the period, varying between 12.7 and 15.4. RR varied according to duration of unemployment, with those unemployed over one year having a deliberate self-harm incidence 26–36 times higher than those in work. Unemployed male deliberate self-harm patients reported significantly higher prevalence of psychiatric treatment, alcoholism and repeated deliberate self-harm than their employed counterparts	No control for other possible confounders
Hawton and Fagg (1992) Hospital referral following deliberate self-poisoning or self-injury	1988–89 Oxford, UK	None		Among economically active 16–19 year-old deliberate self-harm patients, 35.1% were unemployed (42.6% of males, 31.5% of females; $p < 0.001$). "Unemployment rates of both male and female (deliberate self-harm patients) were considerably in excess of local unemployment rates for older teenagers"	No control for other possible confounders

continued overleaf

Table 20.2 *(continued)*

Study/definition of parasuicide	Time period/ place	Statistical procedure	Main findings	Comments
Hawton et al (1988) Hospital referral following deliberate self-poisoning or self-injury	1979–82 Oxford, UK	RR	Among women aged 16–59 years, the RR of deliberate self-harm among the unemployed compared to the employed varied between 7.5 and 10.8 (with a declining trend) over the period. RR varied according to duration of unemployment, with those unemployed over one year having a deliberate self-harm incidence 14–33 times higher than those in work. Unemployed female deliberate self-harm patients reported significantly higher prevalence of psychiatric treatment, alcoholism and repeated deliberate self-harm than their employed counterparts	No control for other possible confounders
Hawton et al (1994) Hospital referral following deliberate self-poisoning or self-injury	1989–92 Oxford, UK	RR	Among those aged 16+ years the relative risk of deliberate self-harm among the unemployed compared with the employed was 9.7 for males and 10 for females. (The deliberate self-harm rate for the disabled and permanently sick was higher than that for the economically inactive but RRs were lower than those for the unemployed)	No control for other possible confounders

Jones et al (1991) Hospital referral following deliberate self-poisoning	Not given Newcastle upon Tyne, UK	ORs; logit models	Using a matched case control design ($n = 64$ pairs), the authors tested three alternative model of the relationship between deliberate self-harm and unemployment. Unemployment was significantly higher ($p < 0.01$) among cases. No empirical support was found for the vulnerability or indirect causation models	The authors conclude that "the model that unemployment and self-poisoning are non-causally associated remains a viable hypothesis"
Morton (1993) Hospital-treated non-fatal deliberate self-harm	1984–86 Edinburgh, UK	RR	Male "repeaters" were significantly more likely to be unemployed (73%) than male "first-timers" (51%) ($p < 0.001$)	No control for other possible confounders
Neeleman et al (1996) Intentional overdose admitted to general hospital	1991 Camberwell, London, UK	RR	Among whites unemployment was associated with a nine-fold increased deliberate self-harm rate, while among ethnic minorities the increased risk was three-fold	Small sample size ($n = 105$) and possible sample bias
Nordentoft and Rubin (1993) Hospital admission following deliberate act aimed at self-destruction	1986–87 Copenhagen, Denmark	ORs, stratified for age and sex	In a sample of 100 deliberate self-harm patients aged 14–87 years, the prevalence of non-employment was not significantly different from that expected in the general population	No differentiation between unemployment and economic inactivity

continued overleaf

Table 20.2 *(continued)*

Study/definition of parasuicide	Time period/ place	Statistical procedure	Main findings	Comments
Platt (1986b) Hospital-treated non-fatal deliberate self-harm	1982–83 Edinburgh, UK	Chi-squared test; (conditional) gamma	Male deliberate self-harm patients who were unemployed on admission were significantly more likely to be unmarried, live outside the family, be of lower social class, have a criminal record, be given a diagnosis of abnormal personality and misuse drugs than those who were employed. Within the unemployed group, longer duration of unemployment was associated with personality diagnosis and receipt of psychotropic drug treatment	No controls, apart from age, in the duration of unemployment analysis
Platt and Duffy (1986) Hospital-treated non-fatal deliberate self-harm	1968–71 and 1980–83 Edinburgh, UK	Logistic linear regression analysis	Over both time periods male deliberate self-harm patients who were unemployed on admission were significantly more likely to be unmarried, live outside the family, experienced early separation from mother, have received psychiatric treatment, be given a diagnosis of abnormal personality, have a criminal record, be in serious debt and misuse drugs	It was not possible to demonstrate that the correlates of unemployment in this population were different in times of economic prosperity compared to economic recession

Platt and Dyer (1987) Hospital-treated non-fatal deliberate self-harm	1979 Edinburgh, UK	Chi squared test; *t*-test; co-variance analysis	Among economically active male deliberate self-harm patients, those unemployed on admission were significantly more likely to report depression and hopelessness. After controlling for hopelessness, the relationship between employment status and depression became non-significant; whereas, after controlling for depression, hopelessness and unemployment continued to be significantly associated. Suicidal intent was similar in the two groups	Small sample ($n = 50$ overall), but representative of the wider population from which subjects were taken in respect of age, previous deliberate self-harm, marital status and social class.
Platt and Kreitman (1984) Hospital-treated non-fatal deliberate self-harm	1968–82 Edinburgh, UK	RR; PAR percent	In each year from 1968 to 1982 the rate of deliberate self-harm among unemployed men was higher than the rate among employed men, with RRs ranging from 9.5 to 29.0 (tending to decline until 1976, thereafter remaining fairly stable). Maximum percentage of the overall deliberate self-harm incidence attributable to unemployment varied between 36.6% and 57.8% over the period. Deliberate self-harm risk varied with duration of unemployment, with the highest risk (18.9 in 1982) among those unemployed over 12 months	The excessive risk among the unemployed was evident within each social class. No other controls for confounders are reported

continued overleaf

Table 20.2 *(continued)*

Study/definition of parasuicide	Time period/ place	Statistical procedure	Main findings	Comments
Platt and Kreitman (1985) Hospital-treated non-fatal deliberate self-harm	1970–72 and 1980–82 Edinburgh, UK	Pearson correlation coefficient; RR	Further developing the analysis presented in Platt and Kreitman (1984), it is shown that the unemployment rate was positively associated with the deliberate self-harm rate among the employed across city areas ($r = 0.88$, $p < 0.001$ in 1980–92) and negatively related to the RR ($r = -0.42$, $p < 0.02$ in 1980–82)	No control for possible confounders
Platt and Kreitman (1990) Hospital-treated non-fatal deliberate self-harm	1983–87 Edinburgh, UK	RR	Analysis by duration of unemployment among men shows that, in each of the years under investigation, the highest deliberate self-harm rate was found among those unemployed over 12 months (RR 12–18 compared to the employed). However, the risk for the short-term unemployed (<4 weeks) was also significantly raised (RRs of 3–6 compared to the employed)	No control for possible confounders

Platt et al (1988) Hospital-treated non-fatal deliberate self-harm	1980–82 Edinburgh, and Oxford, UK	RR	In both cities, there was a significant individual-level association between deliberate self-harm and employment status. The RR associated with unemployment was greater among females than males (13.6 and 12.1, respectively, in Edinburgh; 12.8 and 9.4, respectively, in Oxford)	No control for possible confounders
Runeson et al (1996) Hospital treated suicide attempt	1988–89 Stockholm, Sweden	OR; attributable fraction (AF)	In comparison with female controls (matched for nationality and age), female suicide attempters (n = 51) were significantly more likely to report unemployment at some time during the last 5 years (OR = 8.97; AF = 0.42)	Authors note the limitations of the study in respect of small sample size and non-consecutive recruitment. No control for previous deliberate self-harm
Van Heeringen (1994) Referral to A&E department following suicide attempt	1986–90 Gent, The Netherlands	Multivariate logistic regression analysis; OR	In comparison with a control sample of randomly selected city residents aged 15+ years, deliberate self-harm patients were significantly more likely to be unemployed (OR = 5.8). After controlling for marital status and living situation, unemployment was found to be a significant risk factor in males aged 15–34 years (OR = 5.6) and 35–49 years (OR = 11.7) and females aged 35–49 years (OR = 8.1). The risks were higher in males than in females	Limited controls

5.6 and 29.0 among men and between 7.5 and 13.6 among women (see Table 20.2). In studies from Edinburgh and Oxford, evidence about the relationship between duration of unemployment and deliberate self-harm is presented. In both cities, long-term unemployment carried the greatest risk, with RRs of between 19 and 36 among men. In three studies the PAR was calculated. Platt and colleagues (1988) reported a range of PAR percent values based on male deliberate self-harm rates, from 37% to 58%, over a 15 year period, while Runeson and colleagues (1996) estimated 42% over a two-year period for females. A totally dissimilar population attributable fraction (PAF) of 7.3% was quoted by Beautrais and colleagues (1988).

Authors reporting findings from cross-sectional studies on deliberate self-harm and unemployment have recognized that the significantly increased ORs or RRs are compatible with either causal or self-selection explanations. Two studies have attempted to provide data which can go some way towards resolving the issue. Beautrais and colleagues (1998) introduced controls for a range of historical and current factors, thereby reducing the OR to a non-significant value. The authors concluded:

> The implications of these results are clearly that most, or perhaps all, of the association between unemployment and serious suicide attempt risk is explained by: (a) linkages between unemployment and family and childhood factors which are associated with increased risks of serious suicide attempt; and (b) linkages between unemployment and current psychiatric factors which are associated with increased risks of serious suicide attempt.

While this is an important and impressively designed study, the generalizability of the findings to the total deliberate self-harm population remains doubtful. In a second study, based on a small ($n = 64$) but non-selective sample, Jones and colleagues (1991) set out to test alternative indirect causation, vulnerability and self-selection (non-causal) models of the relationship between deliberate self-harm and unemployment. Although unemployment was significantly higher among deliberate self-harm cases than among matched controls, the non-causal model could not be disconfirmed.

These findings, taken together with evidence of considerably higher prevalence of chronic psychopathology and personality disorder among unemployed deliberate self-harm patients, compared to their employed counterparts (see e.g. Hawton and Rose, 1986 and Platt, 1986b), certainly suggest that it would be nonsensical to deny the strength of the case for some element of self-selection in the deliberate self-harm–unemployment relationship (based on individual cross-sectional studies). On the other hand, the extremely high RR and PAR derived from total hospital-treated samples (especially the Edinburgh and Oxford studies) point also to a causal role for unemployment.

Evidence from Aggregate Cross-sectional Studies

Aggregate cross-sectional studies on unemployment and suicidal behaviour are summarised in Tables 20.3 (suicide) and 20.4 (deliberate self-harm). Five of the

Table 20.3 The relationship between unemployment and suicide: aggregate cross-sectional studies

Study/definition of suicide	Time period/ place	Statistical procedure	Main findings	Comments
Agbayewa et al (1998) ICD-9 E950–E959	1981–91 British Columbia, Canada (n = 21 Health Units)	RRs (by means of Poisson regression analyses)	Among males aged 65+ years, the male unemployment rate was significantly associated with the suicide rate (RR = 1.13). Among elderly females no such relationship was found	Controls for year-effect, age group, gender, civil state, female labour market participation, education, migration
Burr et al (1997) Not given	1970, 1980 USA (n = 209 Standard Metropolitan Statistical areas)	Bivariate correlation and ordinary least squares (OLS) multiple regression	After controlling for other factors (see Comments), sex-specific unemployment is unrelated to male or female in both 1970 and 1980	Controls for divorce rate, one-person households, population density, Catholic church membership, female labour force participation, median family income and housing unit change over previous decade. No evidence of multicollinearity or heteroskedasticity
Congdon (1996a) ICD-9 E950–E959, E980–E989	1990–92 London, UK (n = 32 boroughs)	Spearman rank correlation	Unemployment is highly correlated with suicide SMR (all ages: 0.70 among males, 0.54 among females; under 45 years: 0.56 among males, 0.67 among females; over 45 years: 0.54 among males; 0.12 among females)	No control for other possible confounders. More sophisticated analysis undertaken but unemployment combined with other variables to produce material deprivation (Townsend) score

continued overleaf

Table 20.3 *(continued)*

Study/definition of suicide	Time period/ place	Statistical procedure	Main findings	Comments
Congdon (1996b) ICD-9 E950–E959, E980–E989	1990–92 London (NE Thames region) ($n = 253$ wards)	Pearson and Spearman correlation coefficient	Unemployment and suicide were positively correlated ($r = 0.20$ for ages 15+ and 15–59 years; $r = 0.055$ for ages 60+ years)	No control for other possible confounders. No significance testing. No test for spatial autocorrelation
Gessner (1997) ICD-9 E950–E959	1979–93 Alaska, USA ($n = 25$ census areas)	Multiple linear regression analysis	Among 14–19 year-olds the average yearly suicide rate was related directly to the unemployment rate. After controlling for several variables (see Comments), however, this relationship became statistically non-significant	Controls for percentage of family households with married couples, percentage of population that is Alaska Native, percentage of population aged 14–19 years, percentage of people over 24 years who are high school graduates, per capita income. Authors point out several methodological limitations
Krupinski et al (1994) Not given	1983–89 Victoria, Australia ($n =$ 11 labour force regions)	Pearson correlation coefficient	There was a significant correlation between the unemployment rate and the suicide rate among males aged 15–19 years (0.67, $p < 0.05$) and 20–24 years (0.76, $p < 0.01$). No such association was found among females	No control for other possible confounders. Relationship between unemployment and suicide among men may be confounded by the relationship between unemployment and metropolitanism

Lester (1992) Not given	1975 USA ($n = 23$ metropolitan areas)	Pearson correlation coefficient	Male unemployment was not associated with the (?total) suicide rate (0.09, $p > 0.10$)	No control for other possible confounders
Norstrom (1995) Not given	1963–65 Sweden ($n = 24$ counties and Stockholm)	Regression analysis (semi-logarithmic model)	The zero-order correlation between the age-standardized suicide rate among men and unemployment was significantly *negative* ($r = -0.54$, $p < 0.01$). On removal of an outlier this correlation was reduced and became non-significant. After controlling for several variables (see Coments), the male suicide rate was unrelated ($p > 0.10$) to unemployment (analysis excluding the outlier)	Use of Box–Jenkins method which removes linear trends by means of differencing the data. Controls for alcohol consumption, divorce rate and real wages. The removal of an outlier affects the findings to a considerable degree
Platt et al (1992) Police/carabinieri data and definition of suicide	1977–87 Italy ($n = 18$ regions)	Spearman rank correlation coefficient	The correlation between the mean annual suicide rate and the mean annual unemployment rate over the period was significantly negative for both women ($r_s = -0.60$, $p < 0.01$) and men ($r_s = -0.53$, $p < 0.05$). The relationship between the regional unemployment rate, on the one hand, and suicide rates among the employed and unemployed and the RR, on the other, were all negative	No control for possible spatial autocorrelation. No control for other possible confounders

continued overleaf

Table 20.3 *(continued)*

Study/definition of suicide	Time period/ place	Statistical procedure	Main findings	Comments
Saunderson et al (1998) ICD-9 E950–E959, E980–E989	1989–92 England and Wales (local authority districts; *n* not given)	Multiple regression analysis (ordinary least squares estimates based directly on SMRs)	After controlling for several variables (see Comments column), the male unemployment rate was not significantly associated with suicide or combined suicide and undetermined rates among males or females	Controls for percentage of single non-pension households, percentage of working population in social classes IV and V; percentage of working population in agricultural employment; percentage of population of Asian ethnic origin. No consideration of spatial autocorrelation
Trovato and Vos (1992) Not given	1971 and 1981 Canada (*n* = 9 provinces)	Log-linear analysis	After controlling for several variables (see Comments column), unemployment and suicide rates were unrelated among men (both time periods) and among women in 1981. In 1971, however, unemployment was positively and significantly related to female suicide risk	Controls for age, gender, time period, divorce rate, percentage with no religious affiliation and married female labour force participation rate

Yang and Lester (1988) Not given	1980 USA ($n = 48$ states)	Multiple regression analysis	Controlling for several other variables (see Comments), the unemployment rate was not significantly related to the male or female suicide rates	Controls for median family income, percentage of population that is white, birth rate, urbanization, persons aged 65+ years, personal per capita income, female labour force participation, divorce rate and migration. No test for spatial autocorrelation
Zimmerman (1995) Not given	1960, 1970, 1980, 1985, 1990 USA ($n = 50$ states)	Multiple regression analysis	After controlling for other variables (see comments), unemployment was unrelated to suicide in any year, regardless of whether the suicide variable was lagged or unlagged	Controls for divorce rate, population density, percentage white, percentage population change, public welfare expenditures, males per 100 females. No test for spatial autocorrelation

13 publications on suicide failed to consider possible confounders (Table 20.3). Two inter-related studies (Congdon 1996a, b) found positive associations among males and females, while Krupinski and colleagues (1994) reported a positive correlation among males aged 15–24 years but no association among women in this age group, Lester (1992) failed to discover any association, and Platt and colleagues (1992) uncovered significant negative associations for both men and women. Among the eight studies which controlled for possible confounders, Trovato and Vos (1992) reported a positive and significant association (but only in one out of four gender by year tests of association), Agbayewa and colleagues (1998) pointed to a significant association in males aged 65+ years (but not in older women), and six found no association at all.

Table 20.4 presents findings from five relevant studies on deliberate self-harm. Four of these studies examined intra-country variation and all reported positive zero-order correlations. The introduction of controls for social deprivation did not reduce the strength of the association between unemployment and deliberate self-harm in one study (Kelleher et al, 1996), whereas poverty appeared to be the mediating variable ("unemployment causes deliberate self-harm via its impact on standards of living") in Platt and Kreitman (1984). The one study of inter-country variation (Bille-Brahe et al, 1996) produced a negative, non-significant ecological correlation between unemployment and the total deliberate self-harm rate. On the basis of the findings presented in Tables 20.3 and 20.4, we conclude that, with regard to the aggregate cross-sectional design, there is scant evidence to refute the null hypothesis of no relationship between unemployment and suicide and limited evidence to suggest an association between unemployment and deliberate self-harm within the same country.

Evidence from Individual Longitudinal Studies

Findings on the association between suicidal behaviour and unemployment based on individual longitudinal studies are summarized in Tables 20.5 (suicide) and 20.6 (deliberate self-harm). Significantly higher ORs, RRs or standardized mortality rates (SMRs) for suicide among the unemployed are consistently reported, even after the introduction of control variables (Table 20.5). The most rigorous analyses were those based on the England and Wales Longitudinal Study. Lewis and Sloggett (1998) calculated an OR of 2.6 for suicide over a 20 year follow-up period among those unemployed at baseline, after controlling for a range of socio-demographic variables. Their findings support the conclusion reached by Moser and colleagues (1984, 1986, 1987), based on a shorter follow-up period and controlling only for social class, but also demonstrating a significant effect on the wives of unemployed men, that there is "a direct effect of unemployment on mortality among those most directly affected by the experience". Based on the findings reported in Table 20.5, the OR or RR for suicide among the unemployed over the medium–long term appears to be in the region of 2–3. It is interesting to note that, in a study of a high-risk suicide group (young people aged 15–24 years with a history of previous deliberate self-harm), unemployment at baseline

Table 20.4 The relationship between unemployment and deliberate self-harm: aggregate cross-sectional studies

Study/definition of parasuicide	Time period/ place	Statistical procedure	Main findings	Comments
Bille-Brahe et al (1996) Not given	Around 1990 15 Centres in 13 European countries	Spearman rank correlation coefficient	Across 12 centres the correlation between the unemployment rate and the deliberate self-harm rate was −0.26 ($p > 0.4$) for men and for women	No control for other possible confounders. Problems of ensuring comparable unemployment data
Congdon (1996b) Hospital admission following self-injury or self-poisoning	1990–92 London (NE Thames region) ($n = 253$ wards)	Pearson and Spearman correlation coefficient	Unemployment and deliberate self-harm were positively correlated ($r = 0.48$ for ages 15+ years; $r = 0.36$ for ages 15–29 years; $r = 0.44$ for ages 30–59 years; $r = 0.28$ for ages 60+ years). Correlations were somewhat higher among males ($r = 0.45$) than among females ($r = 0.37$)	No control for other possible confounders. No significance testing. No test for spatial autocorrelation
Kelleher et al (1996) Hospital admission following deliberate self-poisoning	1988 Cork, Ireland ($n = 34$ city wards)	Spearman rank correlation coefficient; partial correlation analysis; regression analysis	Across the city wards, there was a significant ($p < 0.001$) correlation between the deliberate self-harm rate and the percentage of labour force unemployed (0.71). After controlling for other measures of social deprivation (see Comments), unemployment and deliberate self-harm remained significantly correlated (0.70, $p < 0.001$). Unemployment rate was the first variable to be included in the regression equation, explaining 51% of variation in deliberate self-harm	Controls for social distress calls, percentage educated to 16 years or less, population density, family size, overcrowding, over 44 years of age. The authors point out that the multiple regression equation suffers from multicollinearity

continued overleaf

Table 20.4 *(continued)*

Study/definition of parasuicide	Time period/ place	Statistical procedure	Main findings	Comments
Platt and Kreitman (1984) Hospital-treated deliberate non-fatal self-harm	1970–72 and 1980–82 Edinburgh, UK Scotland [23 city wards (1970–72) and 31 regional electoral divisions (1980–82)]	Pearson correlation coefficient	The association between male unemployment rates and male deliberate self-harm rates across different areas of the city were significant in both time periods: $r = 0.76$ in 1970–72 ($p < 0.001$) and $r = 0.95$ in 1980–82 ($p < 0.001$). Partialling out social class composition differences reduced the correlations but both remained significant. Partialling out differences in poverty reduced the correlation to a non-significant level	No control for spatial autocorrelation. The authors speculate that "unemployment causes deliberate self-harm via its impact on standards of living"
Smith (1995) Hospital-treated self-inflicted injury or poisoning	1991–93 Tayside, UK ($n = 72$ general practices)	None	The hospital deliberate self-harm admission rate increased in line with the prevailing rate of unemployment in the postcode sector where the practice was located (from 1.1/1,000 patients located where the unemployment rate was under 5% to 4.6 in areas where the unemployment rate was over 15%)	No statistical significance tests. No control variables. No consideration of spatial autocorrelation

Table 20.5 The relationship between unemployment and suicide: individual longitudinal studies

Study/ definition of suicide	Time period/ place	Statistical procedure	Main findings	Comments
Costa et al (1989) ICD-9 E950–E959	1981–85 Turin, Italy	SMR	Among men aged 15–59 who were unemployed and seeking work at baseline there was a significantly high suicide SMR (285). Those employed in both 1976 and 1981 had a significantly lower suicide SMR, while those unemployed in 1981 (whether employed or unemployed in 1976) had a significantly higher suicide SMR	Based on a small number of deaths. Control for social class was attempted by comparing suicide SMRs among the unemployed in own home and rented home groups. Both showed significantly raised suicide SMRs
Hawton et al (1993) ICD-9 E950–E959, E850–E859	1968–85 Edinburgh, UK	Conditional logistic regression; OR	In a case-control study intended to identify factors predictive of future suicide among patients aged 15–24 years when admitted to hospital following deliberate self-poisoning or self-injury, unemployment was found to discriminate between cases and controls (OR = 2.8). Unemployment was not identified, however, as a significant factor in the multivariate analysis	Controls for social class, previous inpatient psychiatric treatment, substance misuse, personality disorder and previous deliberate self-harm
Iversen et al (1987) ICD-9 E950–E959	1970–80 Denmark	Multiplicative hazard regression models	Among unemployed men aged 20–64 years and "normally in the labour force" on 9 November 1970, suicide rates were 192% higher over the period 1970–75, 113% higher during 1975–80 and 151% higher over the whole 10 year follow-up period. Among women the excess suicide mortality was 146% (1970–75), 144% (1975–80) and 145% (1970–80)	The authors themselves raise questions about the appropriateness or otherwise of the statistical techniques employed to analyse their data

continued overleaf

Table 20.5 *(continued)*

Study/ definition of suicide	Time period/ place	Statistical procedure	Main findings	Comments
Johansson and Sundquist (1997) ICD-8/9 E950–E959 and E980–E989	1979–93 Sweden	RR (proportional hazard model)	An 11-year follow-up of a cross-sectional sample of over 37,000 Swedish people aged 20–64 years revealed that the RR for suicide among those receiving unemployment/sickness pension at baseline was 3.86. After controlling for other variables (see Comments column), the RR was reduced to 1.93 (still statistically significant)	Controls for sex, age, marital status, housing tenure and perceived health status. Definition of unemployment to include those receiving sickness pension appears to confuse economic activity/ inactivity distinction
Lewis and Sloggett (1998) ICD-9 E950–E959, E980–E989	1971–92 England and Wales	Logistic regression; OR; PAF	Over a 20 year follow-up period suicide mortality among a randomly selected population sample was strongly associated with unemployment status at baseline after controlling for several variables (OR = 2.58, $p < 0.001$ compared to employed reference group) (see Comments). Compared to those employed in both 1971 and 1981, those unemployed on both occasions had an adjusted OR for suicide 1983–92 of 3.30 ($p < 0.001$), while those employed in 1971 and unemployed in 1981 had an adjusted OR of 2.39 ($p < 0.001$). The PAF for unemployment was 7.4% overall, increasing to 11.4% for the population aged 15–54 years and 12.6% for the population aged 15–44 years	Controls for age, time period, sex, marital status/living alone, social class, education level, access to car and housing tenure

Moser et al (1984) "Suicide etc." ICD-8 850–877, 942, E950–E959, E980–E989	1971–81 England and Wales	SMR	Over a 10-year period suicide (etc.) mortality among men aged 15–64 at death, who were seeking work in 1971, was raised (SMR-241), even after standardization for social class (SMR-169). Suicide (etc.) mortality of women whose husbands were seeking work in 1971 was also higher than expected (SMR-160), but the finding was not statistically significant because of small *n*	The authors propose a test of the health-related selection hypothesis by comparing SMRs in 1971–75 with SMRs in 1976–81. The evidence (no change in SMRs over time) neither confirms nor refutes the hypothesis
Moser et al (1986) "Suicide etc." ICD-8 850–877, 942, E950–E959, E980–E989	1971–81 England and Wales	SMR	Over a 10 year period suicide (etc.) mortality among men aged 15–64 at death, who were seeking work in 1971, was raised in the north and west region (SMR-333) and, to a lesser extent, in the central region (286). These were the regions with the highest level of unemployment and the longest duration of unemployment. The suicide (etc.) SMR among women in households containing an unemployed man (not her husband) was also elevated (143) but the finding was not statistically significant because of small *n*	The authors conclude: "Taken together these new findings strengthen the argument for a direct or indirect effect of unemployment on mortality among those most directly affected by the experience"

continued overleaf

Table 20.5 *(continued)*

Study/ definition of suicide	Time period/ place	Statistical procedure	Main findings	Comments
Moser et al (1987) "Suicide etc." ICD-8 850–877, 942, E950–E959, E980–E989	1981–83 England and Wales	SMR	Over a 3 year period suicide (etc.) mortality among men aged 15–64 at death, who were seeking work in 1981, was raised (SMR-241), although the finding was not statistically significant because of small *n*	No control for other possible confounders
Norstrom (1988) ICD-9 E950–E959	1960–70 Sweden	Age-standardized RR	Among men aged 20–69 who were unemployed for at least 4 months in 1960 the RR of suicide over the period 1961–65 (using the rest of the male population aged 20–69 as the reference category) was significantly elevated at 3.04. During the period 1996–70 the RR was somewhat reduced (but again significantly high) at 2.41. The associated attributable fraction (AF) for the whole period was 0.028, ie about 3% of male suicides could be directly attributable to unemployment	The author casts doubt on whether the reduced RR in the second follow-up period provides evidence (as proposed by Fox et al, 1985) for rejecting the selection hypothesis

Table 20.6 The relationship between unemployment and deliberate self-harm: individual longitudinal studies

Study/definition of deliberate self-harm	Time period/ place	Statistical procedure	Main findings	Comments
Fergusson et al (1997) Not given	ca 1993–95 Christchurch, New Zealand	Mantel-Haenzel test of linear trend. Multiple logistic regression	Duration of unemployment was significantly associated with suicide attempt between ages 16 and 18 (from 2.5% among those never unemployed to 9.9% among those unemployed over 6 months). However, following adjustment for co-variates (see Comments), the prevalence of suicide attempts did not differ significantly between duration of unemployment subgroups	Controls for psychiatric disorder, measures of family social background, measures of family functioning, individual factors, measures of parental and peer relationships, and measures of prior history of psychiatric disorder and substance use (n = 13 co-variates)
Morton (1993) Hospital-treated non-fatal deliberate self-harm	1984–86 Edinburgh, UK	RR	Male deliberate self-harm patients who were unemployed on admission were more likely to repeat deliberate self-harm over the next 1–2 years (17.5%) than those who were employed (8.4%) ($p < 0.05$). The association between unemployment and deliberate self-harm repetition was particularly strong for the long-term (> 1 year) unemployed. When the population was stratified by age, social class and presence/absence of a past psychiatric history, the association between unemployment and deliberate self-harm repetition remained in at least one of the two follow-up years	The relationship between unemployment and repeat self-harm disappeared after controlling for presence/ absence of personality disorder and by previous admission (or not) to Regional Poisoning Treatment Centre

continued overleaf

Table 20.6 *(continued)*

Study/definition of deliberate self-harm	Time period/ place	Statistical procedure	Main findings	Comments
Nordentoft and Rubin (1993) Hospital admission following deliberate act aimed at self-destruction	1986/87–1990 Copenhagen, Denmark	Log-rank test	Over a follow-up period of 3–5 years seven out of 100 deliberate self-harm patients (aged 14–87 years) died by suicide. Patients who were not employed at the time of their index attempt were over-represented among those who committed suicide ($p < 0.01$)	No differentiation between unemployment and economic inactivity
Owens et al (1994) "Overdose" or "self-poisoning"	1985–86 Nottingham, UK	Chi-squared test	Those repeating deliberate self-harm within one year were significantly less likely to be in paid employment at index admission than non-repeaters	No control for other possible confounders
Platt and Kreitman (1985) Hospital-treated non-fatal deliberate self-harm	1968–82 Edinburgh, UK	Pearson correlation coefficient; RR	Further developing the analysis presented in Platt and Kreitman (1984), it is shown that increasing unemployment rates in the general population were associated over time with a decrease in deliberate self-harm among the unemployed ($r = -0.82$, $p < 0.001$), and a declining RR ($r = -0.69$, $p < 0.01$)	No controls for confounders. No controls for serial autocorrelation
Platt and Kreitman (1990) Hospital-treated non-fatal deliberate self-harm	1968–87 Edinburgh, UK	Pearson correlation coefficient; RR	Over the period 1968–87 the deliberate self-harm rate among the unemployed was always higher than the rate among the employed, but the former tended to decline over time. The RR also fell until 1979 since when it has fluctuated at about 10. Both the deliberate self-harm rate among the unemployed and the RR were significantly negatively associated with unemployment ($r = -0.94$, $p < 0.001$ and $r = -0.75$, $p < 0.01$, respectively, for males; the correlations among women were almost identical)	No controls for confounders. No controls for serial autocorrelation

did not discriminate between cases (future suicides) and controls (survivors), after adjusting for other variables (Hawton et al, 1993).

Individual longitudinal studies on unemployment and deliberate self-harm do not present a coherent picture. Three studies showed that risk of future suicide (Nordentoft and Rubin, 1993) and repeat deliberate self-harm (Owens et al, 1994; Morton, 1993) in deliberate self-harm populations was elevated among those who were not in paid employment at baseline. However, only in the paper by Morton (1993) was the risk associated with unemployment separated from that linked to economic inactivity. Fergusson and colleagues (1997) showed that, after adjustment for co-variates, deliberate self-harm prevalence was not significantly associated with duration of unemployment. Finally, Platt and Kreitman (1985, 1990) demonstrated a negative association between the unemployment rate, on the one hand, and the deliberate self-harm rate among the unemployed and the RR, on the other. It is difficult to reach any definite conclusions on the basis of these studies.

Evidence from Aggregate Longitudinal Studies

Fifty studies using an aggregate longitudinal design and exploring the relationship between suicide and unemployment have been published since 1984. The findings from these studies are summarised in Table 20.7. The publications are highly heterogeneous, covering a range of countries and time periods, using a variety of methods, and adopting differing definitions of suicide and outcome variables (e.g. total, male and female suicide rates; suicide rates by age group and ethnicity). Findings of significant positive, significant negative and non-significant associations have been reported, with differences to be found within as well as between studies. Crudely summarizing these findings, we find that of the 29 studies looking at the male suicide rate as the outcome variable, 22 reported positive associations (sometimes only for specific socio-demographic subgroups), two reported negative findings and 15 non-significant findings (the numbers add up to more than 50 because several studies reported multiple and differing associations, arising from the disaggregation of the data). Of the 21 studies which examined the association with the female suicide rate, positive associations were found in 10, negative associations in two and non-significant findings in 15.

The evidence of a positive association is certainly stronger in relation to men, but even here the weight of anomalous findings should be taken into account. The two studies by Crombie (1989, 1990) certainly give pause for thought. In the first study he showed how, despite a significant overall correlation between suicide and unemployment rates among men aged 25–64 years in Scotland (1971–1986), no association was found between trends in regional unemployment during 1971–1981 and suicide rates for the period before a rapid increase in suicide (1974–1977) and after the increase (1983–1986). In the second study Crombie found a poor fit between actual suicide rates across 16 countries and the predicted suicide rate, estimated on the basis of a model he had developed. His observation that "an increase in suicide is not an inevitable consequence of

Table 20.7 The relationship between unemployment and suicide: aggregate longitudinal studies

Study/definition of suicide	Time period/ place	Statistical procedure	Main findings	Comments
Agbayewa et al (1998) ICD-9 E950–E959	1981–91 British Columbia, Canada	RRs (by means of Poisson regression analyses)	Among those aged 65+ years, the unemployment rate was not significantly associated with the suicide rate	Controls for year-effect, age group, gender, geographical area, civil state, female labour market participation, education, migration
Brenner (1987) Not given	1950–80 Sweden	Multiple regression time series analysis	The unemployment rate lagged 6–10 years was significantly associated with the suicide rate. However, the peak lag for male suicide was 1–2 years	Methodological criticism of Brenner's work has included incorrect variable specification, inappropriate estimation techniques and lack of attention to aggregation problems
Caces and Harford (1998) Not given	1934–87 USA	Time series analysis (detrended)	The overall unemployment rate was significantly associated with the total suicide rate ($p < 0.01$), the female suicide rate ($p < 0.01$), and the suicide rate among those aged under 60 years ($p < 0.01$) and over 60 years ($p < 0.05$). However, the association between unemployment and suicide among men was not statistically significant	Controls for alcohol consumption, divorce, per capita income and World War II

Charlton et al (1987) Not given	1975–83 (quarterly) England and Wales	Regression analysis of suicide trends using the actual rate of change in each Family Practitioner Committee (FPC) area. Trends in age-specific suicide rates were examined separately for men and women by means of logistic regression	FPCs with the smallest increases in long-term (>6 months) unemployment (July 1980–July 1981, ages 25–44) had the lowest male suicide mortality rates for the period ($p < 0.05$). Areas that experienced the largest increases in unemployment had relatively greater increases in suicide, but differences in trends were not statistically significant. Trends for female suicide mortality were downwards and unrelated to unemployment experience	The authors claim that their "results do not confirm Brenner's predictions that a rise in unemployment leads to a rise in mortality"
Chuang and Huang (1996) Not given	1952–92 USA and Taiwan	Time series regression analysis	In both the USA and Taiwan the overall unemployment rate was significantly associated ($p < 0.001$) with the overall suicide rate	Controls for GNP, GNP growth, female labour force participation and divorce. Findings partially replicate Yang et al (1992a)
Cormier and Klerman (1985) Not given	1966–81 Quebec, Canada	Time-series regression analysis	Statistically significant positive association between the total unemployment rate and both male and female suicide rates across age groups from 10–14 to 65+ years (except males 55–64 years)	No control for other possible confounders. R squares mistakenly presented as regression coefficients

continued overleaf

Table 20.7 *(continued)*

Study/definition of suicide	Time period/ place	Statistical procedure	Main findings	Comments
Crombie (1989) ICD-9 E950–E959	1971–86 Scotland, UK	Spearman rank correlation coefficient	Suicide and unemployment rates among men aged 25–64 years were highly correlated (0.81, $p < 0.01$). However, when trends in regional unemployment for men during 1971–81 were compared with suicide rates for the period before the increase in suicide (1974–7) and the period after the rapid increase (1983–6), no association was found between suicide and unemployment trends across the 13 health boards or aggregated sets of local government districts	No control for other possible confounders
Crombie (1990) Not given	1973–83 Australia, USA, Canada, Japan and 12 European countries	Actual increases in suicide rates were compared with predicted increases, estimated using model developed by author	Among men the predicted suicide rate in 1982–84 was lower in all countries than the observed rate. Predictions for women were extremely poor. In nine countries there was a fall in suicide when the upward unemployment trend would have predicted a rise. The argument that increases in suicide could have resulted from a more general economic effect (not only on the unemployed) is undermined by the inconsistencies between countries	The author concludes that "an increase in suicide rates is not an inevitable consequence of increased unemployment", thus underlining the importance of multifactorial models in explaining suicide trends

Dooley et al (1989) Not given	1975–82 (monthly) Los Angeles, USA	Time series analysis (Box–Jenkins method)	Although there was a simple correlation ($r = 0.25$) between unemployment rate and total suicides, after the introduction of statistical controls (see Comments section) unemployment was unrelated to suicide in any demographic subgroup (age, gender, race) or in the total population	Controls for change in total employment, change in service sector employment and mean temperature
Gruenewald et al (1995) Not given	1970–89 USA	Time series analysis (least squares dummy variable regression)	In two separate analyses (1976–89 over 38 states and 1970–89 over 50 states) unemployment rates were significantly ($p < 0.03$; one-tailed test) related to suicide rates	Controls for age, gender, race, per capita land area, metropolitanism, income, divorce, religious preference
Hassan and Tan (1989) Not given	1901–85 Australia	Time series analysis (ordinary least squares)	After adjustment for other factors (see Comments section), the unemployment rate was only weakly ($p < 0.10$) associated with male suicide rates in one equation (and not significantly ($p > 0.10$) in three other equations). Among females there were no significant associations ($p > 0.10$ in all four equations). Unemployment was, however, significantly associated with the male–female suicide ratio in three of the four equations ($p < 0.05$ in two; $p < 0.10$ in one)	Controls for female labour market participation, urbanization, divorce–marriage ratio, war, time trend

continued overleaf

Table 20.7 *(continued)*

Study/definition of suicide	Time period/ place	Statistical procedure	Main findings	Comments
Hutchinson and Simeon (1997) Death certificates by the attending medical officer	1978–92 Trinidad and Tobago	Spearman rank correlation coefficient significance level set at $p < 0.01$)	Male unemployment was significantly associated with both male (0.78) and female (0.73) suicide rates. Male unemployment lagged one year was also significantly associated with male (0.72), but not female (0.68), suicide rates. Female unemployment, synchronous or lagged, was not significantly associated with male or female suicide rates	No control for other possible confounders
Kreitman and Platt (1984) Not given	1955–80 England, Wales and Scotland (UK)	Pearson correlation coefficient	Over the period 1955–80 male unemployment was significantly negatively correlated with the total male suicide rate ($r = -0.73$, $p < 0.01$) but significantly positively correlated with suicide by non-carbon monoxide methods ($r = 0.88$, $p < 0.01$)	No consideration of the possibility of serial autocorrelation
Leenaars and Lester (1995) Not given	1965–85 Canada and USA	Pearson correlation coefficient; time-series regression analysis	In Canada unemployment was correlated significantly ($p < 0.05$) with unemployment among males aged 15–44 years and 75+ years, and among females aged 75+ years only. In the USA the correlations were significant for both genders and all ages, except males aged 75+ years and females aged 25–34 years. The regression analysis shows that, after controlling for other variables (see Comments column), unemployment was unrelated to suicide (both genders, all age groups) in Canada and significantly related only among men aged 35–54 years in the USA	Controls for divorce, marriage and birth rates. Time-series analysis corrected for serial autocorrelation

Leenaars and Lester (1998) Not given	1960–85 Canada	Pearson correlation coefficient; time-series regression analysis	The regression analysis shows that, after controlling for other variables (see Comments column), unemployment was unrelated to male or female suicide	Controls for divorce, marriage and birth rates. Time-series analysis corrected for serial autocorrelation
Leenaars et al (1993) Not given	1950–85 Canada and USA	Pearson correlation coefficient; time-series regression analysis	In both Canada and the USA the unemployment rate was correlated significantly with the suicide rate (0.73, $p < 0.001$ and 0.49, $p < 0.01$, respectively). However, after controlling for other variables (see Comments column), unemployment and suicide trends were unrelated	Controls for divorce, marriage and birth rates. Time-series analysis corrected for serial autocorrelation
Lester (1993) Not given	1967–86 USA	Time-series regression analysis	After controlling for relative income, the ratio of African–American to white unemployment rates was not correlated with either African–American or white suicide rates (males and females)	Time-series analysis corrected for serial autocorrelation
Lester (1994) Not given	1957–86 (monthly) USA	Time-series regression analysis	After controlling for marriage rates, unemployment was positively associated with suicide in 10 out of 12 analyses (for each of the 12 months separately over the 30 year period). In only two analyses was the association statistically significant	Time-series analysis corrected for serial autocorrelation. The authors claim that the findings replicate those of Yang and Lester (1992), thus ruling out a seasonality effect
Lester (1995) Not given	1958–86 New Mexico, USA	Pearson correlation coefficient; time-series regression analysis	The average suicide rate of American Indians in New Mexico for three tribes was positively associated with the overall New Mexico unemployment rate ($r = 0.63$)	Time-series analysis corrected for serial autocorrelation. No control for other possible confounders

continued overleaf

Table 20.7 *(continued)*

Study/definition of suicide	Time period/ place	Statistical procedure	Main findings	Comments
Lester (1996) Not given	1955–87 USA (American Indian reservation states)	Pearson correlation coefficient; time-series regression analysis	The American Indian suicide rate was not associated with the national unemployment rate ($r = 0.05$)	Time-series analysis corrected for serial autocorrelation. No control for other possible confounders
Lester (1997) Not given	1960–85 Canada (10 provinces)	Time-series regression analysis	After controlling for other variables (see Comments column), the unemployment rate was not significantly associated with the suicide rate in any of the 10 provinces	Controls for divorce, marriage and birth rates. Time-series analysis corrected for serial autocorrelation
Lester and Yang (1991) Not given	1946–84 Australia and USA	Time-series regression analysis	Controlling for other variables (see Comments column), male, female and total suicide rates were unrelated to unemployment rates in Australia. In the USA the male suicide rate was positively associated with unemployment rate. In both countries the male/female ratio of suicide rates was positively related to the unemployment rate. The findings were similar regardless of the inclusion or exclusion of a time trend	Analysis conducted with and without time trend component. Controls for female labour market participation and divorce/ marriage ratio
Lester et al (1992) Not given	1953–82 Japan and USA	Pearson correlation coefficient; time-series regression analysis	Controlling for other variables (see Comments column) total and male suicide rates were positively and significantly ($p < 0.05$) associated with the suicide rate in Japan, whereas suicide rates were unrelated to unemployment in the USA	Controls for change in GNP, female labour force participation and divorce. Time-series analysis corrected for serial autocorrelation

Lester et al (1997) Not given	1960–90 England and Wales, Northern Ireland, Scotland and Ireland, UK	Multiple regression analysis	Controlling for other variables (see Comments column), the male suicide rate was positively and significantly associated with the unemployment rate in Northern Ireland and Scotland, while the female suicide rate was correlated negatively and significantly with the unemployment rate in England and Wales and Scotland	Controls for marriage and birth rates. No mention of correction for serial autocorrelation
McCall and Land (1994) Not given	1946–88 USA	Pearson correlation coefficient; time-series regression analysis (ordinary/generalized least squares)	After controlling for other variables (see Comments column), the unemployment rate among males aged 16–19 years was not significantly related to the white male suicide rate in the 15–19 age group. Unemployment was also unrelated to suicide among white males aged 20–29 years. However, the unemployment rate among males over 65 years was positively and significantly ($p < 0.05$; one-tailed test) associated with the suicide rate in the 65–74 age group	Check for autocorrelated errors. Controls for relative cohort size and family structure index
Makela (1996) Not given	1950–91 Finland	Time-series regression analysis	After controlling for other variables (see Comments column), the unemployment rate was unrelated to the suicide rate for the total population aged 15+ years and for all age groups except 50–69 years where the association was of borderline significance ($p = 0.06$)	Controls for divorce rate, alcohol consumption and real wages. Test for serial autocorrelation
Morrell et al (1993) Not given	1907–90 Australia	Time-series regression analysis	Among males aged 15–24 years increases in the suicide and unemployment rates were highly associated ($R^2 = 68\%$) over the period 1966–87	Time-series analysis corrected for serial autocorrelation

continued overleaf

Table 20.7 *(continued)*

Study/definition of suicide	Time period/ place	Statistical procedure	Main findings	Comments
Motohashi (1991) Not given	1953–86 Japan	Multiple regression analysis	During the period 1953–72, after controlling for several variables (see Comments column), the unemployment rate was significantly associated with male (but not the female) suicide rate. During 1973–86 unemployment was unrelated to either male or female suicide rates	Check for serial autocorrelation. Controls for GNP, change in private sector investment, price inflation, percent employed in primary, secondary and tertiary industry, male and female labour force participation, divorce rate
Norstrom (1988) ICD-9 E950–E959	1920–68 Sweden	Time-series regression analysis	The unemployment rate was significantly associated with the age-standardized suicide rate among males aged 20–69 years, after controlling for alcohol consumption. The RR of suicide among the unemployed (compared to the employed), based on the findings from the time series analysis, was 4.65	Use of Box–Jenkins method which removes linear trends by means of differencing the data
Norstrom (1995) Not given	1930–69 Sweden	Time-series regression analysis	After controlling for several variables (see Comments column), the age-standardized suicide rate among men was significantly ($p < 0.001$) associated with unemployment	Use of Box–Jenkins method which removes linear trends by means of differencing the data. Controls for alcohol consumption, divorce rate and real wages

Platt et al (1992) Police/carabinieri data and definition of suicide	1977–87 Italy	Spearman rank correlation coefficient	The temporal relationship between suicide and unemployment was non-significantly negative among women ($r_s = -0.53$, $p > 0.05$) but positively and significantly correlated among men ($r_s = 0.80$, $p < 0.01$). However, among both women and men changes in unemployment and suicide (1987/7 compared to 1977/8) across 18 regions were not significantly correlated	No control for possible serial autocorrelation
Pritchard (1988) Not given	1974–85 Nine European countries	Spearman rank correlation coefficient	There was a significant association between unemployment rates in 1984 and the level of change in the suicide rate 1974–85 among males ($r_s = 0.73$, <0.05) and females ($r_s = 0.85$, <0.01)	No control for possible serial autocorrelation
Pritchard (1990) Not given	1964–86 18 European countries, plus USA, Canada, New Zealand, Australia and Japan	Spearman rank correlation coefficient	There was no association between unemployment rates in 1972 and the level of change in the suicide rate 1964–73 among males or females. However, there was a significant relationship between unemployment rates in 1985 and the level of change in the suicide rate 1974–86 among both males ($r_s = 0.51$, $p < 0.01$) and females ($r_s = 0.46$, $p < 0.05$)	No control for possible serial autocorrelation

continued overleaf

Table 20.7 *(continued)*

Study/definition of suicide	Time period/ place	Statistical procedure	Main findings	Comments
Pritchard (1992) Not given	1974–88 12 European countries	Spearman rank correlation coefficient	In 9/12 countries the adult (15+ years) male suicide rate was significantly ($p < 0.01$) correlated with the unemployment rate lagged one year. The relationship between the young adult (15–24 years) suicide rate and the young adult unemployment rate (18–24 years) was significantly positive in 7/12 countries and significantly negative in one. In general the male suicide–unemployment association was stronger in the total population than in the 15–24 year age group	No control for possible serial autocorrelation
Snyder (1992) Not given	1961–79 Northern Ireland	Pearson correlation coefficient	Among males suicide and unemployment rates were significantly positively correlated ($r = 0.49$, $p < 0.05$) among those aged 15–24 years and significantly negatively correlated ($r = -0.51$, $p < 0.05$) among those aged 45–54 years. In other male age groups and all female age groups the correlation between unemployment and suicide rates was not significant	No control for possible serial autocorrelation
Stack (1987) Not given	1948–83 USA	Time-series regression analysis	After controlling for other variables (see Comments column), the unemployment rate was significantly ($p < 0.05$) related to total, male and female suicide rates (age 20–39 years) during the period 1948–63. However, all these associations remained positive, but none was statistically significant, over the years 1964–80	Test for serial autocorrelation. Controls for lagged suicide rate, divorce rate and female labour force participation rate

Stack (1993) Not given	1968–80 USA	Time-series regression analysis	After controlling for other variables (see Comments column), the unemployment rate was positively and significantly ($p < 0.05$) associated with the suicide rate	Test for serial autocorrelation. Controls for lagged suicide rate, publicized suicide story and war
Stack and Haas (1984) Not given	1948–78 USA	Time-series regression analysis	After controlling for the divorce rate and female labour market participation, the average duration of unemployment was positively and significantly associated with total, male and female suicide rates	Test for serial autocorrelation
Starrin et al (1990) Not given	1963–83 Sweden	Stepwise regression analysis	After controlling for other variables (see Comments column), neither unemployment rate nor length of unemployment was significantly ($p < 0.05$) associated with male or female suicide rates in the 45–64-year age group. On the other hand, overtime work was positively and significantly associated with male and female suicide in this age group, while the level of employment for women was negatively and significantly associated with female suicide	Test for serial autocorrelation. Controls for job applicants, level of employment, overtime work, geographical mobility, percentage on public welfare and sale of alcohol and tobacco
Travis (1990) Not given	1970–84 Alaska, USA	Logistic regression analysis	In a series of analyses controlling for several other variables (see Comments), there was little evidence of a significant association between unemployment and suicide	Controls for gender, age, marital status and interactions. No test for serial autocorrelation

continued overleaf

Table 20.7 *(continued)*

Study/definition of suicide	Time period/ place	Statistical procedure	Main findings	Comments
Trovato (1986) Not given	1950–82 Canada	Time-series regression analysis	Controlling for the immigration rate and age composition, the unemployment rate was negatively associated with both male and female suicide ($p < 0.01$ among females). In the 15–34 year age group, unemployment was positively associated with both male and female suicide ($p < 0.05$ among males)	Control for serial autocorrelation
Viren (1996) Not given	1878–1884 Finland	Time-series regression analysis	Controlling for several variables (see Comments column), unemployment (defined as the number of unemployed persons) was positively related to the suicide rate	Controls for GDP, bankruptcies and average age of the population. Test for serial autocorrelation
Wasserman (1984) Not given	1964–77 (monthly) USA	Time-series regression analysis	Controlling for several other variables (see Comments column), the unemployment rate lagged 9 months was positively and significantly ($p < 0.01$) associated with the suicide rate	Controls for serial autocorrelation and lagged effects. Controls for seasonal effects, war and divorce rate (lagged 9 months)
Weyerer and Wiedenmann (1995) Not given	1881–1989 Germany	Pearson correlation coefficient	Unemployment and suicide rates were positively and significantly ($p < 0.01$) correlated during the period 1881–1939, but negatively and significantly correlated during 1949–1989. Annual changes in rates were correlated positively, but non-significantly, in both periods	No control for other possible confounders. No test for serial autocorrelation

Yang (1992) Not given	1940–84 USA	Time-series regression analysis	Controlling for other variables (see Comments column), the unemployment rate was positively and significantly ($p < 0.05$) associated with the total and white male suicide rates (not with the rates for females or non-white males)	Controls for war, GNP, female labour force participation rate, divorce rate and Roman Catholic church membership. Test for serial autocorrelation
Yang and Lester (1990) Not given	1940–84 USA	Time-series regression analysis	Controlling for several other variables (see Comments column), unemployment and suicide rates (actual and year-to-year changes) were positively and significantly ($p < 0.05$) correlated	Controls for GNP, female labour force participation rate and divorce rate. Test for serial autocorrelation
Yang and Lester (1992) Not given	1957–86 (annual and monthly) USA	Time-series regression analysis	Controlling for marriage rate, annual unemployment rates were unrelated to annual suicide rates, but monthly unemployment rates were positively and significantly ($p < 0.05$) related to monthly suicide rates	Test for serial autocorrelation
Yang and Lester (1995) Not given	1950–85 Nine European countries, Japan, Taiwan and the USA	Time-series regression analysis	Suicide and unemployment rates were significantly (*$p < 0.05$ or **$p < 0.01$) associated in Japan*, The Netherlands**, Taiwan** and the USA*. The association between percentage changes in suicide and unemployment was statistically significant only for the the USA*	Test for serial autocorrelation
Yang et al (1992a) Not given	1952–84 USA and Taiwan	Time series regression analysis	Controlling for other variables, the unemployment and suicide rates were positively and significantly ($p < 0.001$) associated in the USA but unrelated in Taiwan	Controls for GNP/GDP, female labour force participation rate and divorce rate. Test for serial autocorrelation
Yang et al (1992b) Not given	1940–84 USA	Time series regression analysis	Whether using smoothed predictor variables against a smoothed suicide rate or fluctuations in the predictor variables against fluctuations in the suicide rate, unemployment was positively and significantly ($p < 0.01$) associated with suicide	Controls for GP, divorce rate, female labour force participation rate and divorce. Test for serial autocorrelation

increased unemployment" is confirmed by findings from other studies. Although unemployment is likely to have significant explanatory power in certain countries under certain conditions, other independent variables (particularly those measuring major socio-demographic change, e.g. divorce) need to be included in multi-factorial models which are intended to explain and predict a significant proportion of the variance in suicide trends. Proof of this contention is provided by the findings of several studies reported in Table 20.7: when appropriate controls were introduced, the association between suicide and unemployment was attenuated or else disappeared altogether (see especially Leenaars and Lester, 1995). All uncontrolled studies reporting a significant bivariate relationship between unemployment and suicide should be treated with considerable caution because of the risk of this type of (omitted variable) bias.

Table 20.8 summarizes findings from aggregate longitudinal studies of the association between deliberate self-harm and unemployment. In Oxford, Hawton and Rose (1986) and Hawton and colleagues (1988) found a weak association between the male and female unemployment rates in the general population and the proportion of economically active men or women, respectively, who were unemployed at the time of deliberate self-harm. However, the relationship between annual deliberate self-harm and unemployment rates among women aged 16–59 years were non-significant and negative over a 10-year period. In Edinburgh, Platt and Kreitman (1984, 1990) found a significant and positive correlation between unemployment and deliberate self-harm rates (for men and women separately) in the first half of the period under review (1969–1977), but negative correlations (significant for men) in the second half (1977–1987). Finally, in Leeds, multiple significance testing of the association between quarterly trends in unemployment and deliberate self-harm yielded only three significant findings, of which two were in a negative direction. None of the studies controlled for possible confounders or serial autocorrelation. On the basis of these (somewhat methodologically limited) studies, we can conclude that the British evidence over the 1970s and 1980s does not provide evidence of a positive temporal association between unemployment and deliberate self-harm.

The Relationship between Female Labour Force Participation (FLFP) and Suicidal Behaviour

We were unable to identify any studies which examined deliberate self-harm as an outcome (dependent) variable or employed an individual longitudinal design.

Evidence from Individual Cross-sectional Studies

In the only relevant study using this type of design (see Table 20.9), Stack (1996/97) reported that the suicide rate among women aged 25–65 years tended to be higher for the economically inactive than for those in the labour force, regardless of marital status (the exception to this finding was a reversed

Table 20.8 The relationship between unemployment and deliberate self-harm: aggregate longitudinal studies

Study definition of deliberate self-harm	Time period/ place	Statistical procedure	Main findings	Comments
Furness et al (1985) Patients admitted to hospital aged 16+ years with diagnosis ICD-9 N960-N989	1974–83 Hartlepool, UK	Pearson correlation coefficient	The level of unemployment quadrupled during the period under review but the deliberate self-harm rate remained fairly constant. The association between deliberate self-harm and unemployment was not statistically significant ($r = 0.23$, $p > 0.05$)	No control for other possible confounders
Hawton and Rose (1986) Hospital referral following deliberate self-poisoning or self-injury	1976–82 Oxford, UK	Correlation coefficient (undefined)	There was a weak correlation (0.68, $p < 0.10$) between the male unemployment rate in the general population and the proportion of economically active men who were unemployed at the time of deliberate self-harm	No control for other possible confounders
Hawton et al (1988) Hospital referral following deliberate self-poisoning or self-injury	1976–85 Oxford, UK	Rank-order correlation	There was a weak association (0.58, $p < 0.10$) between the female unemployment rate in the general population and the proportion of economically active women aged 16–59 years who were unemployed at the time of deliberate self-harm. Annual unemployment rates were negatively (–0.41, ns) correlated with female deliberate self-harm rates (16–59 year olds)	No control for other possible confounders

continued overleaf

Table 20.8 *(continued)*

Study definition of deliberate self-harm	Time period/ place	Statistical procedure	Main findings	Comments
Platt and Kreitman (1984) Hospital-treated non-fatal deliberate self-harm	1968–82 Edinburgh, UK	Pearson correlation coefficient	The correlation between male deliberate self-harm rates and male unemployment rates was significantly high ($r = 0.77$, $p < 0.001$) over the period. The proportion of economically active men who were unemployed on admission was also significantly associated with trends in male unemployment ($r = 0.82$, $p < 0.001$)	No control for serial autocorrelation. No control for possible confounders
Platt and Kreitman (1990) Hospital-treated non-fatal deliberate self-harm	1968–87 Edinburgh, UK	Pearson correlation coefficient	Over the whole period the correlation between unemployment and deliberate self-harm was not was not significant: $r = 0.33$ for males, $r = -0.22$ for females. Contrasting patterns were evident in earlier and later years: significantly positive correlations for men and women over the years 1969–77, and negative correlations (significant for men) in 1977–87	No control for serial autocorrelation. No control for possible confounders
Standish-Barry et al (1989) Hospital-treated non-fatal deliberate self-harm	1978–82 (quarterly) Leeds, UK	Pearson and Spearman correlation coefficient	An examination of trends in unemployment and deliberate self-harm rates revealed significant associations among men only in the 44–49 (positive) and 55–59 (negative) year age groups, while among women the overall relationship was significantly negative ($r = -0.46$, $p < 0.05$)	No control for serial autocorrelation. No control for possible confounders. No data about sample sizes

Table 20.9 The relationship between female labour force participation and suicide: individual cross-sectional study

Study/ definition of suicide	Time period/ place	Statistical procedure	Main findings	Comments
Stack (1996/97) ICD-9 E950–E959	1985 USA (16 states)	None	In the 25–65 year age group, regardless of marital status, the suicide rate among not employed women is higher than the rate among employed women (with only one exception: the rate is higher among the employed for single women aged 45–64 years). In the 65+ years age group suicide rates are consistently and markedly higher among the employed compared to the not employed	No statistical tests are presented. Controls for age and marital status

association among single women aged 45–64 years). In the 65+ year age group, the economically active had a higher suicide risk than the economically inactive.

Evidence from Aggregate Cross-sectional Studies

Five studies have presented findings on the association between FLFP and suicide (Table 20.10) using an aggregate cross-sectional design. Significantly negative, significantly positive and non-significant associations were reported across the same time periods and among males and females separately. Two studies which examined changes in the association between suicide and FLFP over approximately the same 10 year period (1970–1971 to 1980–1981) (Burr et al, 1997; Trovato and Vos, 1992) uncovered different patterns: consistently negative associations among men in the former study, positive then negative associations among men in the latter; non-significant then negative associations among women in the former study, positive then negative associations among women in the latter. The one definite finding relating to the most recent time period was the absence of any positive association between FLFP and suicide among women. This constitutes some evidence in support of the role expansion/accumulation, rather than role conflict, model of the FLFP–suicide relationship. In other words, the greater involvement of women in the labour market has tended to lead to enhanced opportunities for self-fulfilment and improved psychological well-being (thus reducing suicide risk), rather than to a higher degree of

Table 20.10 The relationship between female labour force participation and suicide: aggregate cross-sectional studies

Study/definition of suicide	Time period/place	Statistical procedure	Main findings	Comments
Agbayewa et al (1998) ICD-9 E950-E959	1981–91 British columbia, Canada (n = 21 health units)	RR (by means of Poisson regression analyses)	Among males aged 65+ years, the female labour force participation rate was significantly associated with the suicide rate (RR = 1.04). Among elderly females no such relationship was found	Controls for year-effect, age group, gender, civil state, unemployment, education, migration
Burr et al (1997) Not given	1970 and 1980 USA (n = 209 Standard Metropolitan Statistical areas)	Bivariate correlation and ordinary least squares (OLS) multiple regression	After controlling for other factors (see Comments column), female labour force participation (FLFP), defined as number of married females (husband present) with children under 6 years old as a proportion of the total female civilian labour orce, was unrelated to female suicide but negatively related to male suicide in 1970. In 1980 FLFP was significantly negatively related to both male and female suicide	Controls for divorce rate, one-person households, population density, Catholic church membership, unemployment, median family income and housing unit change over previous decade. According to the authors, there was no evidence of multicollinearity or heteroskedasticity

Stack (1998) Not given	1980 53 Nations (representing "all levels of socio-economic development")	Multiple regression analysis	Female labour force participation (FLFP) rate was positively and significantly ($p < 0.05$) associated with both male and female suicide rates, after controlling for industrialization level and rate of economic growth. In countries with high FLFP rates FLFP was not significantly associated with the female suicide rate	Tests for multicollinearity revealed no problem
Trovato and Vos (1992) Not given	1971 and 1981 Canada ($n = 9$ provinces)	Log-linear analysis	After controlling for several variables (see Comments column), married female labour force participation (FLFP) rate was significantly associated with both male and female suicide risk: positively in 1971 and negatively in 1981	Controls for age, gender, time period, divorce rate, percentage with no religious affiliation and unemployment rate
Yang and Lester (1988) Not given	1980 USA ($n = 48$ continental states)	Multiple regression analysis	The overall female labour force participation (FLFP) rate was unrelated to the male suicide rate but positively and significantly ($p < 0.05$) related to the female suicide rate. Controlling for several other variables (see Comments), the rate of married women working was negatively and significantly associated with the male suicide rate, but FLFP was not related to the female suicide rate	Controls for median family income, percentage of population that is white, birth rate, urbanization, persons aged 65+ years, personal per capita income, unemployment, divorce rate and migration. No test for spatial autocorrelation

irreconcilable demands at home and work and greater psychological distress (which would exacerbate suicide risk).

Evidence from Aggregate Longitudinal Studies

Table 20.11 summarizes findings from the 11 studies that have used an aggregate longitudinal design to investigate the relationship between FLFP and suicide. In seven publications, data from the USA are presented, covering the period from the Second World War. Findings include significant negative associations, significant positive associations and absence of association. Inconsistent results have been produced in studies by different authors covering approximately the same time period (e.g. Lester et al, 1992, vs. Stack and Haas, 1984), within the same study through use or non-use of detrending (Lester and Yang, 1991) and across different time periods within the same country (Lester et al, 1992; Motohashi (1991) in respect of Japan). Given also the wide variety of controls employed in the various studies, we conclude that it is not possible to reach a definitive conclusion about the FLFP–suicide relationship based on studies using an aggregate longitudinal design.

The Relationship between Occupational Status, Occupation and Suicidal Behaviour

Evidence from Individual Cross-sectional Studies

The findings from nine relevant publications are summarized in Table 20.12. Two have provided data on variation in suicide by social class in Great Britain (Kreitman et al, 1991; Drever et al, 1997). Both reported lower suicide SMRs in the non-manual social classes (I, II, IINM) and among skilled manual workers (IIIM) and significantly elevated suicide SMRs in the semi-skilled and unskilled manual classes (IV and V). Kreitman and colleagues (1991) confirmed the finding of higher SMRs for social classes IV and V in England and Wales around 1981, for Scotland at about the same time, and for all three countries around 1971. In a subsequent analysis, Drever and colleagues (1997) reported the same inverse relationship between social class and suicide in England and Wales for the period 1991–1993. One other important finding reported by Kreitman and colleagues (1991) was that of a significant interaction between age and social class, with particularly high suicide rates among those aged 25–44 years in social class V (unskilled).

Analysis of variation in suicide risk by occupational group has been reported in three publications relating to England and Wales (Charlton et al, 1992; Kelly et al, 1995; Kelly and Bunting, 1998). The statistic used in these studies is the proportional mortality ratio (PMR), which is the number of observed suicide deaths divided by the number of expected suicide deaths, expressed as a percentage.

Table 20.11 The relationship between female labour force participation and suicide: aggregate longitudinal studies

Study/definition of suicide	Time period/ place	Statistical procedure	Main findings	Comments
Agbayewa et al (1998) ICD-9 E950–E959	1981–91 British Columbia, Canada	RR (by means of Poisson regression analyses)	Among those aged 65+ years, the female labour force participation rate was significantly associated with the suicide rate (RR = 1.04)	Controls for year-effect, age group, gender, civil state, unemployment, education, migration
Chuang and Huang (1996) Not given	1952–92 USA and Taiwan	Time series regression analysis	In both the USA and Taiwan the female labour force participation rate was significantly negatively associated ($p < 0.001$ and $p < 0.01$, respectively) with the overall suicide rate	Controls for GNP, GNP growth, unemployment and divorce. Findings partially replicate Yang et al (1992a)
Hassan and Tan (1989) Not given	1901–85 Australia	Time series analysis (ordinary least squares)	After adjustment for other factors (see Comments), the female labour force participation (FLFP) rate not associated with male or female suicide rates, but was significantly associated with the male-female suicide ratio ($p < 0.05$)	Controls for unemployment, urbanization, divorce–marriage ratio, war, time trend
Lester and Yang (1991) Not given	1946–84 Australia and USA	Time-series regression analysis	Controlling for other variables (see Comments column), male, female and total suicide rates and the male/female ratio of suicide rates were positively and significantly ($p < 0.05$) related to female labour force participation (FLFP) rates in Australia when a time trend was excluded. After inclusion of a time trend only male suicide was significantly related to FLFP, but in a negative direction. In the USA the total and the male suicide rates were positively associated with FLFP rate when a time trend was excluded. After inclusion of a time trend the only significant finding was a positive association between male/female ratio of suicide rates and the FLFP rate	Analysis conducted with and without time trend component. Controls for unemployment and divorce/marriage ratio

continued overleaf

Table 20.11 *(continued)*

Study/definition of suicide	Time period/ place	Statistical procedure	Main findings	Comments
Lester et al (1992) Not given	1953–82 Japan and USA	Pearson correlation coefficient; time-series regression analysis	Controlling for other variables (see Comments column) total and male suicide rates were positively and significantly ($p < 0.05$) associated with the female labour force participation (FLFP) rate in Japan, whereas suicide rates were unrelated to the FLFP rate in the USA	Controls for change in GNP, unemployment and divorce. Time-series analysis corrected for serial autocorrelation
Motohashi (1991) Not given	1953–86 Japan	Multiple regression analysis	During the period 1953–72, after controlling for several variables (see Comments column), the male labour force participation (MLFP) rate was significantly associated with male and female suicide rates. The female labour force participation (FLFP) rate was also significantly associated with the female suicide rate. During 1973–86 neither MLFP nor FLFP rates were related to male or female suicide rates	Check for serial autocorrelation. Controls for GNP, change in private sector investment, price inflation, percent employed in primary, secondary and tertiary industry, unemployment, divorce rate
Stack (1987) Not given	1948–83 USA	Time-series regression analysis	After controlling for other variables (see Comments column), the female labour force participation (FLFP) rate was positively and significantly ($p < 0.05$) related to total, male and female suicide rates (ages 20–39 years) during the period 1948–63. However, over the years 1964–80, while increases in FLFP rates are associated with increases in total and male suicide rates, the FLFP–suicide relationship disappears for women	Test for serial autocorrelation. Controls for lagged suicide rate, divorce rate and unemployment

Stack and Haas (1984) Not given	1948–78 USA	Time-series regression analysis	After controlling for the divorce rate and average unemployment duration, the female labour market participation rate was negatively and significantly associated with the male suicide rate but not with the female or total suicide rates	Test for serial autocorrelation
Yang (1992) Not given	1940–84 USA	Multiple regression analysis	Controlling for other variables (see Comments column), the female labour force participation rate was negatively and significantly ($p < 0.05$) associated with the total, white female and non-white female suicide rates; and positively and significantly with the non-white male suicide rate (and not related to the rate for white males)	Controls for war, GNP, unemployment rate, divorce rate and Roman Catholic church membership. Test for serial autocorrelation
Yang et al (1992a) Not given	1952–84 USA and Taiwan	Time series regression analysis	Controlling for other variables, the female labour force participation and suicide rates were negatively and significantly ($p < 0.001$) associated in both the USA and Taiwan	Controls for GNP/GDP, unemployment rate and divorce rate test for serial autocorrelation
Yang et al (1992b) Not given	1940–84 USA	Time series regression analysis	Whether using smoothed predictor variables against a smoothed suicide rate or fluctuations in the predictor variables against fluctuations in the suicide rate, the female labour force participation rate was negatively and significantly ($p < 0.5$) associated with the suicide rate	Controls for GNP, divorce rate, unemployment rate and divorce. Test for serial autocorrelation

Table 20.12 The relationship between occupation/social class and suicide: individual cross-sectional studies

Study/definition of suicide	Time period/ place	Statistical procedure	Main findings	Comments
Andrian (1996) Not given	1989–91 France	None	Among men aged 25–59 years there were variations in the suicide rate by occupational group, from 13.6/ 100,000 in the higher grades of the professions to rates of 52.2 among salaried agricultural workers and 52.3 among service sector workers	No definition of suicide is given. No controls for other variables known/likely to affect suicide (e.g. marital status)
Burnley (1994) ICD-9 E950–E959	1980–85, 1986–89 New South Wales, Australia	Testing for statistically significant high and low suicide mortality (indirectly standardized rates) in major occupational groups using the Poisson probability distribution	Among males aged 25–39 years in 1986–89 suicide rates were significantly low in the professional, administrative, service and clerical groups and among miners/quarrymen; and significantly high among farmers, transport/communications, tradesmen/ production process workers/labourers, and those not in the workforce. Similar findings were reported for males aged 40–64 years and in the earlier time period	Authors did not believe that the omission of "undetermined" deaths prejudices the findings of the study, since there was evidence that this category was used only sparingly in New South Wales

Charlton (1995) ICD-9 E950–E959 and E980–E989 (excluding E988.8)	1990–92 England and Wales	Case control design (control defined as all deaths from natural causes). Standard logistic regression techniques provided ORs of dying from suicide compared to dying from natural causes	Among men aged 16–44 years, veterinarians had 361% increased suicide relative to natural causes deaths but no other occupational groups had significantly increased suicide risk. Among men aged 45–64 years, however, veterinarians (462%), dentists (419%), pharmacists (315%), medical practitioners (122%) and farmers (93%) showed an increased suicide risk. Among women aged 16–64 veterinarians (662%), doctors (354%) and nurses (51%) were at significantly greater relative risk of suicide	Controls for marital status, country of birth and age-group (five-year). Other possible confounders or mediators (e.g. employment status) are not included
Charlton et al (1992)	1979–90	PMR	Among men aged 16–64 years at death, significantly high PMRs were found in the medical and associated professions	See comment in Kelly and Bunting (1998) about problems in interpreting PMRs
Drever et al (1997) ICD-9 E950–E959, E980–E989	1991–93 England and Wales	SMR	Among men aged 20–64 years there was a strong inverse association between suicide and social class, with significantly low SMRs in classes I–IIINM and significantly high SMRs in class IV (SMR 107) and class V (SMR 215)	A further analysis controlling for age (see Drever and Bunting, 1997) showed that class V males had excessively high suicide mortality in all age groups, but particularly in 20–44 year-olds

continued overleaf

Table 20.12 *(continued)*

Study/definition of suicide	Time period/ place	Statistical procedure	Main findings	Comments
Kelly et al (1995) ICD-9 E950–E959 and E980–E989	1982–87 and 1998–92 England and Wales	PMR	Among men aged 16–64 years and women aged 16–59 years at death, significantly high PMRs were found across both time periods in the medical and associated professions. Among men only PMRs were also consistently high for farmers, forestry workers and chemical scientists and engineers. Among women only PMRs were also consistently high for government inspectors, ambulancewomen and nurses	See comment in Kelly and Bunting (1998) about problems in interpreting PMRs. The number of suicides in some occupational groups was as low as 5 across all 11 years. The authors conclude: "The occupations at greatest risk for suicide, for both men and women, are mostly in Social Classes I and II. . . ."
Kelly and Bunting (1998) ICD-9 E950–E959 and E980–E989	1982–87 and 1991–96 England and Wales	PMR	Among men and women aged 20–64 years, significantly high PMRs were found across both time periods in the medical and associated professions. Among men PMRs were also consistently high for farmers, horticulturists, farm managers; sales representatives; shop salesmen and assistants; and gardeners and groundsmen. Among women PMRs were also consistently high for nurses and nurse administrators; and students	"PMRs should be interpreted with care because the proportion of deaths from the cause of interest is affected by the relative frequency of other causes of death. . . . [A]n observed excess may represent a true difference, but may also simply represent a deficit of deaths from other causes"

Kreitman et al (1991) ICD-9 E950–E959, E980–E989	1969–73, 1979–83 England and Wales, Scotland	Chi-square, log-linear analysis	Data for males aged 16–64 years in England and Wales around 1979 show no clear trend in SMRs across the top three social classes (92 in SCI, 83 in SCII, 99 in IIINM, 88 in SCIIIM), followed by a substantial rise to 116 in SCIV and 200 in SCV. There was a significant interaction between age and social class, with particularly high suicide rates among those aged 25–44 years in social class V. Findings were similar in respect of "undetermined" deaths. The findings of higher SMRs for SCIV and SCV, and the interaction between age and social class were confirmed for Scotland around 1981 and all countries around 1971	No controls
Yip (1997) ICD-9 E950–E959	1981–94 Hong Kong	None	Across a range of occupational groupings (including professionals, service workers, agricultural workers, production workers and labourers) the average crude suicide rate over the period varied between 4 and per 100,000, with an average of 5 for economically active persons. Among economically inactive persons, however, the average crude suicide rate was 20, ranging from 12 for "homemakers" aged 15–64, through 35 for "homemakers" aged 65+ years to 44 for the retired	No controls (age a major confounder)

"The expected deaths are computed by applying the proportion of total deaths due to suicide in the comparison . . . population (. . . all men aged 20–64 years or all women aged 20–59 years) to the total deaths in the occupation group of interest" (Kelly and Bunting, 1998). This statistic is used where the total number of individuals in an occupational group and their age distribution is not known, so that the SMR cannot be computed. It should be noted, however, that the PMR for suicide in a particular group can be misleading, since it depends not only on the number of deaths from suicide in the group but also on the number of deaths from other causes. Thus, an elevated suicide PMR may represent a true difference, but can also reflect a relative deficit of deaths from other causes.

Tables 20.13 and 20.14 show the occupational groups in England and Wales which, on the basis of PMRs, appear to have had a high risk of suicide in males and females, respectively, during the 1980s (1979–1990 for men and 1982–1987 for women) and 1991–1996. Among males, medical and allied occupations and farming appear to carry the highest suicide risk, while among females additional groups with elevated PMRs are nurses, professionals in education, health and welfare and those in personal service employment. Kelly and Bunting (1998) drew attention to the discrepancy between the *PMR-based* findings, with high suicide risk occupations coming predominantly from social classes I and II (see Tables 20.12–20.14) and *SMR-based* findings, which show much lower suicide rates in the same social classes. They speculate that "the high PMRs found for

Table 20.13 High-risk occupational groups for suicide (suicide and open verdicts), male deaths, England and Wales, 1979–90 (16–64 years) and 1991–96 (20–64 years)

	PMR	Number of individuals (*n*)
1979–1990[1]		
Veterinary surgeons	364	(35)
Pharmacists	217	(51)
Dentists	204	(38)
Farmers	187	(526)
Medical practitioners	184	(152)
1991–1996[2]		
Veterinary surgeons	324	(9)
Dental practitioners	249	(25)
Pharmacists	171	(25)
Garage proprietors	155	(43)
Sales representatives	151	(97)
Medical practitioners	147	(71)
Farmers, horticulturists, farm managers	144	(190)

Sources: [1]Charlton et al (1992); [2]Kelly and Bunting (1998).

Table 20.14 High risk occupational groups for suicide (suicide and open verdicts), female deaths, England and Wales, 1982–87 and 1991–96 (20–59 years)

	PMR	Number of individuals (*n*)
1982–1987		
Ambulancewomen	396	(4)
Medical practitioners	355	(28)
Pharmacists	274	(10)
Therapists (not elsewhere classified)	269	(14)
Physiotherapists	256	(9)
Domestic housekeepers	210	(15)
Waitresses	148	(32)
Nurse administrators, nurses	146	(276)
1991–1996		
Veterinarians	500	(4)
Medical practitioners	285	(25)
Domestic housekeepers	247	(16)
Waitresses	187	(37)
Professional and related in education, welfare and health	183	(26)
Students	139	(132)
Cleaners, window cleaners, road sweepers	138	(95)
Nurse administrators, nurses	137	(240)
Hospital ward orderlies	130	(139)

Source: Kelly and Bunting (1998).

doctors, vets and dentists reflect the fact that their overall mortality is low and therefore the proportion of deaths from suicide is high relative to other causes". Empirical support for this suggestion can be found in the report by Charlton and colleagues (1992). Nevertheless, there is also evidence from other data and other countries that at least some of the occupational groups shown in Tables 20.13 and 20.14 are generally at increased risk of suicide. Thus, a systematic review of suicide mortality in medical doctors (Lindeman et al, 1996) estimated RRs of 1.1–3.4 in male doctors, and 2.5–5.7 in female doctors, compared to the general population, and 1.5–3.8 in males and 3.7–4.5 in females, compared to other professionals. It is notable that in several of the studies reviewed the risk of suicide in female doctors was as high as that in male doctors, which is very different from the gender-specific risk in the general population. Hawton and Vislisel (1999), reviewing the literature on suicide in nurses, noted that findings from the majority of studies confirm a "substantially elevated" RR of suicide in female nurses. Finally, high rates of suicide in farmers have been reported in several, but not all, studies from North America, France and Australia (reviewed by Hawton et al, 1998; see also Andrian, 1996 and Burnley, 1994).

The identification of occupational groups in the UK at apparent high risk of suicide has prompted research into the particular problems that may contribute to this risk. This work has initially focused on farmers. Using the psychological approach (Hawton et al, 1998; Malmberg et al, 1999) it was shown that farmers in England and Wales who died by suicide had high rates of mental illness, especially depression, which was often unrecognized, or if detected was in several cases treated inadequately. Previous suicide threats, but not attempts, were common, suggesting that most acts of deliberate self-harm by farmers are fatal. The majority of the farmers were facing occupational and/or financial problems. Physical illness was also common and in several cases was limiting the individual's ability to carry out his/her farm work (it is striking that in a longitudinal study of a large sample of Finnish farmers, the occurrence of suicide was strongly associated with back pain at entry to the study; Penttinen, 1995). There was often a background of relationship difficulties within the family. Compared with a general sample of farmers, significantly more of the farmers who died by suicide were living alone, lacked close friends and had no confidant. This work resulted in a series of recommendations, several of which were intended to improve the mental health of farmers and to ensure that those with mental or physical health problems can receive adequate care (Hawton et al, 1998).

We have located only one study using the individual cross-sectional research design which addresses the relationship between social class and deliberate self-harm (see Table 20.15). Platt and colleagues (1988) demonstrated a marked gradient in male deliberate self-harm rates by social class in both Edinburgh and Oxford in 1980–1982: the higher the social class, the lower the deliberate self-harm rate.

Table 20.15 The relationship between occupation/social class and deliberate self-harm: individual cross-sectional study

Study/ definition of suicide	Time period/ place	Statistical procedure	Main findings	Comments
Platt et al (1988) Hospital-treated non-fatal deliberate self-harm	1980–82 Edinburgh and Oxford, UK	RR	In both cities, there was a significant individual-level inverse relationship between male deliberate self-harm and social class. The RR for deliberate self-harm in class V compared to classes I and II was 12.2 in Edinburgh and 8.7 in Oxford	No control for other possible confounders

Evidence from Aggregate Cross-sectional Studies

In three publications reporting findings from aggregate cross-sectional studies, a positive association between area-level (lower) social class composition and suicide rates has been reported (Table 20.16): the greater the proportion of the working population in the semi-skilled and unskilled occupational groups (IV and V), the higher the suicide rate. However, in the only study to differentiate suicide by gender (Saunderson et al, 1998), the association was found only among males. Congdon (1996b) also found a weak negative correlation among those aged 60+ years (the correlations among 15+ and 15–59 year-olds being positive). In the only study of this type which considered deliberate self-harm as the outcome variable, Congdon (1996b) reported positive associations with the proportion of the working population in classes IV and V in all age groups (including those aged 60+ years) (Table 20.17). The correlations for deliberate self-harm were markedly higher than those obtained for suicide.

The evidence here points to a positive correlation between the social class composition of an area and its rate of suicidal behaviour. However, it is important to note that only the study by Saunderson and colleagues (1998) attempted to control for confounders and no study has tested for spatial autocorrelation.

Evidence from Individual Longitudinal Studies

Two studies have used an individual longitudinal design to explore the relationship between social class and suicide (Table 20.18). Lewis and Sloggett (1998) failed to find any association between social class at baseline and suicide risk over a 20-year period in a randomly selected population sample, after controlling for several socio-economic confounders. In a follow-up study of Australian National Service conscripts who served in Vietnam (O'Toole and Cantor, 1995), occupational class prior to the draft did not predict suicide risk, after controlling for post-school education. These studies do not, therefore, provide evidence of a social class–suicide association.

SUMMARY OF MAIN FINDINGS

The main findings of this review can now be briefly summarized. In relation to the literature on unemployment, we will comment on any major differences compared with the findings of the review relating to the period up to 1983 (Platt, 1984); the absence of comment signifies similar findings.

Unemployment and Suicidal Behaviour

Individual cross-sectional studies reveal an increased rate of suicide and deliberate self-harm among the unemployed. Although the micro risk estimates [relative risk (RR) ratio and population attributable risk (PAR) percent] are high,

Table 20.16 The relationship between occupation/social class and suicide: aggregate cross-sectional studies

Study/definition of suicide	Time period/place	Statistical procedure	Main findings	Comments
Congdon (1996a) ICD-9 E950–E959, E980–E989	1989–91 England ($n = 90$ Family Health Service Authorities) 1990–92	Quasi-likelihood negative binomial model	The proportion of the working population in classes IV and V was associated with excess suicide incidence	Controlled for change of address in last year, previous suicide SMR, metropolitan (vs. not), North (vs. South)
Congdon (1996b) ICD-9 E950–E959, E980–E989	1990–92 London (NE Thames region) ($n = 253$ wards)	Pearson and Spearman correlation coefficient	The proportion of the working population in classes IV and V was positively (but weakly) associated with suicide mortality among all aged 15+ years ($r = 0.06$) and those aged 15–59 years ($r = 0.10$), and negatively (but weakly) associated with suicide among those aged 60+ years ($r = -0.05$)	No control for other possible confounders. No significance testing. No test for spatial autocorrelation
Saunderson et al (1998) ICD-9 E950–E959, E980–E989	1989–92 England and Wales (local authority districts; *n* not given)	Multiple regression analysis (ordinary least squares estimates based directly on SMRs)	After controlling for several variables (see Comments column), the percentage of working population in social classes IV and V was significantly associated with suicide and combined suicide and undetermined (S + U) rates among males. There were no such associations among females. The percentage of working population in agricultural employment was also significantly related to suicide and combined S + U rates among males only	Controlled for percentage analysis single non-pension households, percentage working age males unemployed; percentage population of Asian ethnic origin. No consideration of spatial autocorrelation

Table 20.17 The relationship between occupation/social class and deliberate self-harm: aggregate cross-sectional study

Study/ definition of suicide	Time period/ place	Statistical procedure	Main findings	Comments
Congdon (1996b) Hospital admission following self-injury or self-poisoning	1990–92 London (NE Thames region) ($n = 253$ wards)	Pearson and Spearman correlation coefficient	The proportion of the working population in classes IV and V was positively associated with the deliberate self-harm rate ($r = 0.45$ among all aged 15 + years; $r = 0.38$ among those aged 15–29 years; $r = 0.38$ among those aged 30–59 years; and $r = 0.22$ among those aged 60+ years)	No control for other possible confounders. No significance testing. No test for spatial autocorrelation

Table 20.18 The relationship between occupation/social class and suicide: individual longitudinal studies

Study/ definition of suicide	Time period/ place	Statistical procedure	Main findings	Comments
Lewis and Sloggett (1998) ICD-9 E950–E959, E980–E989	1971–92 England and Wales	Logistic regression; OR	Over a 20 year follow-up period suicide mortality among a randomly selected population sample was not associated with social class at baseline after controlling for several variables (see Comments column)	Controls for age, time period, sex, marital status/living alone, economic activity, education level, access to car and housing tenure
O'Toole and Cantor (1995) ICD-8 plus review committee decision	1965–82 Australia	Chi squared test; multiple regression analysis	Among male Australian National Service conscripts who spent at least 12 months in the army and served in the Vietnam theatre, subsequent suicides ($n = 91$ over a 11–16 year follow-up period) were significantly less likely to have had a white-collar or skilled blue-collar job ($p < 0.005$) between school and being drafted (veteran than survivors). In a subsequent regression analysis occupation was not significant when added to a model which contained post-school course	

particularly with respect to deliberate self-harm, suggesting a causal impact of unemployment, the evidence from several studies highlights a possible role for self-selection in accounting for the relationship between unemployment and deliberate self-harm. While aggregate cross-sectional studies do not present convincing evidence of an association between unemployment and suicide, rates of unemployment and deliberate self-harm across geographical areas within the same country do appear to be more closely associated. Findings from individual longitudinal studies point to a significantly raised (two- to three-fold) risk of suicide among the unemployed, but the literature relating to unemployment and deliberate self-harm using this type of design generates inconsistent evidence (in the earlier review, only one study of unemployment and deliberate self-harm based on an individual longitudinal design was identified). Finally, aggregate longitudinal analyses of unemployment and suicide produce heterogeneous findings, although the weight of evidence for a positive association is more convincing for men than for women. Limitations of study design and methodology preclude a more definitive assessment. With respect to unemployment and deliberate self-harm, findings from Great Britain point to instability in the temporal association, with a positive relationship in the 1970s followed by a negative or non-significant relationship in the 1980s (the earlier review was published before this change in the unemployment–deliberate self-harm relationship was fully evident).

Female Labour Force Participation and Suicidal Behaviour

Most of the evidence is derived from aggregate-level studies with suicide as the sole outcome. Cross-sectional analyses have failed to uncover a positive relationship between female labour force participation (FLFP) and female suicide rates, thus lending some support to the view that labour market changes have not had a seriously damaging effect on women's mental health. However, there is little evidence that higher levels of FLFP are mental health-promoting. Longitudinal analyses produce inconsistent results which do not permit any definitive conclusion.

Occupational Status, Occupation and Suicidal Behaviour

Studies using an individual cross-sectional design clearly show an excess suicide risk in lower social class groups and a reduced suicide and deliberate self-harm risk in higher social class groups. Occupational groups with high proportional mortality ratios (PMRs) for suicide are those working in medical and allied occupations (men and women); farmers (males only); and nurses, health, education and welfare professionals and personal service workers. The apparent incompatibility of these findings with respect to upper occupational groups may be partly explained by the use of different population risk statistics. Aggregate cross-sectional analyses point to an association between the social class composition of an area and its suicide and, even more markedly, deliberate self-harm rate, with a greater proportion of class IV and V linked to a higher rate of suicidal behaviour. Evidence from individual longitudinal studies does not, however, suggest an association between suicide and social class.

IMPLICATIONS FOR PREVENTION

When considering strategic approaches to preventing suicide (e.g. Lewis et al, 1997; Gunnell and Frankel, 1994) it is conventional to distinguish between high-risk and population-based strategies. Among the former would be the high-risk occupational groups, such as doctors, nurses and farmers, identified through their high PMRs. Lewis and colleagues (1997) estimate the impact of a hypothetical intervention that would reduce the suicide rate in the targeted group by 25% and also calculate the "number needed to treat" (NNT) to prevent one suicide. In the case of doctors, the NNT is 25,000, while in the case of farmers it is 33,000. These figures are dauntingly high (and therefore likely to lead to inefficient use of resources), not least when easy access to lethal methods (medication, guns) is taken into account. In view of the overwhelming evidence of an association between suicide prevalence and availability of means (Gunnell and Frankel, 1994), the prevention of suicide presents a particular challenge in these occupational groups. Health promotion initiatives targeted at the farming and medical communities, designed to reduce organizational stressors and provide enhanced personal and inter-personal skills for managing stress, would constitute a combined high-risk and population-based approach to enhancing mental health and reducing suicide risk. Both occupational groups, but particularly the medical profession, also need help in recognizing mental health problems in themselves and seeking help before the problems become chronic and suicidogenic. How to inhibit access to lethal means should be a prime consideration in any professional response to an individual from these occupational groups at a time of high risk. An enhanced presence of The Samaritans in rural areas might also be worth evaluating.

Among population-based public health strategies, the reduction of the overall unemployment rate has been considered as a possible suicide prevention measure. Assuming an unemployment rate of 6% and a RR of 3, Lewis and colleagues (1997) calculate that the population attributable fraction (PAF) is 10.9%. If the suicide rate were to be reduced by the PAF, it is assumed that the relationship between unemployment and suicide is causal and that an intervention will reduce the suicide risk among the unemployed to that of the employed. Lewis and colleagues (1997) note that, while the unemployment–suicide relationship may be confounded by psychiatric disorder, high levels of unemployment may lead to increased feelings of insecurity even among those in work. "Economic policies that reduce unemployment may therefore also reduce the population suicide rate". Although full employment is not a central plank of public policy in most post-industrial societies, governments are increasingly stressing the undesirability of "benefit dependence" and seeking to promote employment opportunities through supply-side mechanisms. On the other hand, the growth of precarious employment and labour market insecurity is likely to alter the meaning of work and possibly its beneficial impact on health (compared to unemployment). The implications of these and other labour market changes for suicide risk among the economically active population is difficult to predict at the present time.

CONCLUSIONS

Although the voluminous literature on labour markets and suicidal behaviour continues to expand at an ever-increasing rate (compare the quantity of studies covered in this chapter with that included in the previous review by Platt, 1984), several research needs remain unfulfilled. In the first place, quantitative empirical work in this area would benefit from a more rigorous methodology and a firmer theoretical foundation. Too many studies suffer from a failure to apply state-of-the-art statistical techniques and/or a reluctance to specify the elements of a comprehensive model of suicidal behaviour which can serve to guide the choice of variables and data-analytic procedures. There are, of course, exceptions to this generalization, for example sociological approaches to investigating the possible influence of female labour force participation (see Table 20.11), but it will not be possible to reduce the amount of uncertainty about how to interpret findings derived from the literature until standards of empirical research are improved.

Second, qualitative researchers should be encouraged to engage with this research area, so that we can supplement quantitative approaches to identifying contextual (macro) effects and expand our understanding of subjective experience and lay meaning systems as they apply to the relationship between labour markets and suicidal behaviour (micro aspects). Although our search strategy did not place any constraints on the types of research approach that could be used in an empirical study, we were unable to locate publications which relied exclusively or mainly on qualitative methods. While we cannot rule out the possibility of bias in the bibliographic databases which we consulted, it should be noted that these covered a wide disciplinary spectrum. It is more likely that there is simply a dearth of relevant qualitative studies. We believe that this is detrimental to the development of new ideas and insights in this research area, and urge funders of research and researchers themselves to take remedial action.

One final research priority is the expansion of the existing rather narrow focus on the topics considered in this review to incorporate wider aspects of labour market conditions and situations and their impact on suicide and attempted suicide. We noted earlier that there is an urgent need to explore how increasing labour market insecurity affects population health. In view of what has already been established about the impact of unemployment, there is a strong likelihood that suicidal behaviour will be elevated in individuals, groups, organizations and communities that are exposed to the risk of precarious employment. We should start from the assumption that vulnerability to the impact of labour market insecurity will not be confined to those who are unemployed, but is also likely to be encountered among the employed and the economically inactive. This has major consequences for the way in which we frame our research questions and design our empirical investigations.

REFERENCES

Agbayewa, M.O., Marion., S.A. and Wiggins, S. (1998) Socio-economic factors associated with suicide in elderly populations in British Colombia: an 11-year review. Canadian Journal of Psychiatry, 43: 829–836.

Adnett, N. (1996) European Labour Markets: Analysis and Policy. London: Longman.

Andrian, J. (1996) Le suicide en pleine force de l'age: quelques donnees recentes (Recent data on adult suicide in France). Cahiers de Sociologie et de Demographie Medicales, 36: 171–200.

Beautrais, A.L., Joyce, P.R. and Mulder, R.T. (1998) Unemployment and serious suicide attempts. Psychological Medicine, 28: 209–218.

Benach, J., Benavides, F.G., Platt, S., Diez-Roux, A.V. and Muntaner, C. (1999) The potential for new types of flexible employment to damage health: a challenge for public health researchers. American Journal of Public Health (in press).

Bille-Brahe, U., Andersen, K., Wasserman, D., Schmidtke, A., Bjerke, T., Crepet, P., De Leo, D., Haring, C., Hawton, K., Kerhof, A., Lönnqvist, J., Michael, K., Phillippe, A., Querejeta, I., Salander-Renberg, E. and Temesváry, B. (1996) The WHO–EURO Multicentre Study: risk of parasuicide and the comparability of the areas under study. Crisis, 17: 32–42.

Brenner, M.H. (1987) Relation of economic change to Swedish health and social well-being, 1950–1980. Social Science and Medicine, 25: 183–195.

Burnley, I.H. (1994) Differential and spatial aspects of suicide mortality in New South Wales and Sydney, 1980 to 1991. Australian Journal of Public Health, 18: 293–304.

Burr, J.A., McCall, P.L. and Powell-Griner, E. (1997) Female labor force participation and suicide. Social Science and Medicine, 44: 1847–1859.

Caces, F.E. and Harford, T. (1998) Time series analysis of alcohol consumption and suicide mortality in the United States, 1934–1987. Journal of Studies on Alcohol, 59: 455–461.

Charlton, J. (1995) Trends and patterns in suicide in England and Wales. International Journal of Epidemiology, 24 (Suppl. 1): S45–S52.

Charlton, J.R., Bauer, R., Thakhore, A., Silver, R. and Aristidou, M. (1987) Unemployment and mortality: a small area analysis. Journal of Epidemiology and Community Health, 41: 107–113.

Charlton, J., Kelly, S., Dunnell, K., Evans, B. and Jenkins, R. (1992) Suicide deaths in England and Wales: trends in factors associated with suicide deaths. Population Trends, 71: 34–42.

Chuang, H.L. and Huang, W.C. (1996) A reexamination of "Sociological and economic theories of suicide: a comparison of the USA and Taiwan". Social Science and Medicine, 43: 421–423.

Congdon, P. (1996a) The epidemiology of suicide in London. Journal of the Royal Statistical Society Series A, 159: 515–533.

Congdon, P. (1996b) Suicide and parasuicide in London: a small-area study. Urban Studies, 33: 137–158.

Cormier, H.J. and Klerman, G.L. (1985) Unemployment and male–female labor force participation as determinants of changing suicide rates of males and females in Quebec. Social Psychiatry, 20: 109–114.

Costa, G., Crepet, P. and Florenzano, F. (1989) Unemployment and mortality in Italy: the Turin Longitudinal study. In: S. Platt and N. Kreitman (Eds), Current Research in Suicide and Parasuicide. Edinburgh: Edinburgh University Press, pp. 40–46.

Crombie, I.K. (1989) Trends in suicide and unemployment in Scotland, 1976–86. British Medical Journal, 298: 782–784.

Crombie, I.K. (1990) Can changes in the unemployment rates explain the recent changes in suicide rates in developed countries? International Journal of Epidemiology, 19: 412–416.

Delsen, L. (1991) Atypical employment relations and government policy in Europe. Labour, 5: 123–149.

Dooley, D. and Catalano, R. (1980) Economic change as a cause of behavioral disorder. Psychological Bulletin, 87: 450–468.

Dooley, D., Catalano, R., Rook, K. and Serxner, S. (1989) Economic stress and suicide: multilevel analyses. Part 1: Aggregate time-series analyses of economic stress and suicide. Suicide and Life-Threatening Behavior, 19: 321–336.

Dooley, D., Fielding, J. and Levi, L. (1996) Health and unemployment. Annual Review of Public Health, 17: 449–465.

Drever, F., Bunting, J. and Harding, D. (1997) Male mortality from major causes of death. In F. Drever and M. Whitehead (Eds), Health Inequalities. London: The Stationery Office, pp. 122–142.

Drever, F. and Bunting, J. (1997) Patterns and trends in male mortality. In F. Drever and M. Whitehead (Eds), Health Inequalities. London: The Stationery Office, pp. 95–107.

Fergusson, D.M., Horwood, L.J. and Lynskey, M.T. (1997) The effects of unemployment on psychiatric illness during young adulthood. Psychological Medicine, 27: 371–381.

Fox, A.J., Goldblatt, P.O. and Jones, A.R. (1985) Social elase differentials: artefact, selection or life circumstances? Journal of Epidemiology and Community Health, 39: 1–8.

Fuller, G.N., Rea, A.J., Payne, J.F. and Lant, A.F. (1989) Parasuicide in central London 1984–1988. Journal of the Royal Society of Medicine, 82: 653–656.

Furness, J.A., Khan, M.C. and Pickens, P.T. (1985) Unemployment and parasuicide in Hartlepool 1974–83. Health Trends, 17: 21–24.

Gessner, B.D. (1997) Temporal trends and geographic patterns of teen suicide in Alaska, 1979–1993. Suicide and Life-Threatening Behavior, 27: 264–273.

Gruenewald, P.J., Ponicki, W.R. and Mitchell, P.R. (1995) Suicide rates and alcohol consumption in the United States, 1970–89. Addiction, 90: 1063–1075.

Gunnel, D. and Frankel, S. (1994) Prevention of suicide: aspirations and evidence. British Medical Journal, 308: 1227–1233.

Hassan, R. and Tan, G. (1989) Suicide trends in Australia, 1901–1985: an analysis of sex differentials. Suicide and Life-Threatening Behavior, 19: 362–380.

Hawton, K. and Rose, N. (1986) Unemployment and attempted suicide among men in Oxford. Health Trends, 18: 29–32.

Hawton, K. and Fagg, J. (1992) Deliberate self-poisoning and self-injury in adolescents. A study of characteristics and trends in Oxford, 1976–89. British Journal of Psychiatry, 161: 816–823.

Hawton, K. and Vislisel, L. (1999) Suicide in nurses. Suicide and Life-Threatening Behavior, 29: 86–95.

Hawton, K., Fagg, J. and Simkin, S. (1988) Female unemployment and attempted suicide. British Journal of Psychiatry, 152: 632–637.

Hawton, K., Fagg, J., Platt, S. and Hawkins, M. (1993) Factors associated with suicide after parasuicide in young people. British Medical Journal, 306: 1641–1644.

Hawton, K., Fagg, J., Simkin, S. and Mills, J. (1994) The epidemiology of attempted suicide in the Oxford area, England (1989–1992). Crisis, 15: 123–135.

Hawton, K., Simkin, S., Malmberg, A., Fagg, J. and Harriss, L. (1998) Suicide and Stress in Farmers. London: The Stationery Office.

Hutchinson, G.A. and Simeon, D.T. (1997) Suicide in Trinidad and Tobago: associations with measures of social distress. International Journal of Social Psychiatry, 43: 269–275.

International Labour Organization (ILO) (1998) World Employment 1998–1999: Employability in the Global Economy—How Training Matters. Geneva: International Labour Organization.

Iversen, L., Andersen, O., Andersen, P.K., Christoffersen, K. and Keiding, N. (1987) Unemployment and mortality in Denmark, 1970–80. British Medical Journal, 295: 879–884.

Johansson, S.E. and Sundquist, J. (1997) Unemployment is an important risk factor for suicide in contemporary Sweden: an 11-year follow-up study of a cross-sectional sample of 37,789 people. Public Health, 111: 41–45.

Jones, S.C., Forster, D.P. and Hassanyeh, F. (1991) The role of unemployment in para-suicide. Psychological Medicine, 21: 169–176.

Kelleher, M.J., Kelleher, M.J.A., Corcoran, P., Daly, M., Daly, F., Crowley, M.J. and Keeley, H. (1996) Deliberate self-poisoning, unemployment, and public health. Suicide and Life-Threatening Behavior, 26: 365–373.

Kelly, S. and Bunting, J. (1998) Trends in suicide in England and Wales, 1982–96. Population trends, 92: 29–41.

Kelly, S., Charlton, J. and Jenkins, R. (1995) Suicide deaths in England and Wales, 1982–92: the contribution of occupation and geography. Population Trends, 80: 16–25.

Kreitman, N. and Platt, S. (1984) Suicide, unemployment, and domestic gas detoxification in Great Britain. Journal of Epidemiology and Community Health, 38: 1–6.

Kreitman, N., Carstairs, V. and Duffy, J. (1991) Association of age and social class with suicide among men in Great Britain. Journal of Epidemiology and Community Health, 45: 195–202.

Krupinski, J., Tiller, J.W.G., Burrows, G.D. and Hallenstein, H. (1994) Youth suicide in Victoria: a retrospective study. Medical Journal of Australia, 160: 113–116.

Leenaars, A.A. and Lester, D. (1995) The changing suicide pattern in Canadian adolescents and youth, compared to their American counterparts. Adolescence, 30: 539–547.

Leenaars, A.A. and Lester, D. (1998) Social factors and mortality from NASH in Canada. Crisis, 19: 73–77.

Leenaars, A.A., Yang, B. and Lester, D. (1993) The effect of domestic and economic stress on suicide rates in Canada and the United States. Journal of Clinical Psychology, 49: 918–921.

Lester, D. (1992) Unemployment, suicide and homicide in metropolitan areas. Psychological Reports, 71: 558.

Lester, D. (1993) Economic status of African–Americans and suicide rates. Perceptual and Motor Skills, 77: 1150.

Lester, D. (1994) Suicide and unemployment: a monthly analysis. Psychological Reports, 75: 602.

Lester, D. (1995) American Indian suicide rates and the economy. Psychological Reports, 77: 994.

Lester, D. (1996) American Indian suicide and homicide rates and unemployment. Perceptual and Motor Skills, 83: 1170.

Lester, D. (1997) Domestic integration and suicide rates in the provinces of Canada. Psychological Reports, 81: 1114.

Lester, D. and Yang, B. (1991) The relationship between divorce, unemployment and female participation in the labour force and suicide rates in Australia and America. Australian and New Zealand Journal of Psychiatry, 25: 519–523.

Lester, D., Motohashi, Y. and Yang, B. (1992) The impact of the economy on suicide and homicide rates in Japan and the United States. International Journal of Social Psychiatry, 38: 314–317.

Lester, D., Cantor, C.H. and Leenaars, A.A. (1997) Suicide in the United Kingdom and Ireland. European Psychiatry, 12: 300–304.
Lewis, G., Hawton, K. and Jones, P. (1997) Strategies for preventing suicide. British Journal of Psychiatry, 171: 351–354.
Lewis, G. and Sloggett, A. (1998) Suicide, deprivation, and unemployment: record linkage study. British Medical Journal, 317: 1283–1286.
Lindeman, S., Laara, E., Hakko, H. and Lönnqvist, J. (1996) A systematic review on gender-specific suicide mortality in medical doctors. British Journal of Psychiatry, 168: 274–279.
McCall, P.L. and Land, K.C. (1994) Trends in white male adolescent, young-adult, and elderly suicide: are there common underlying structural factors? Social Science Research, 23: 57–81.
MacMahon, B. and Pugh, T.F. (1970) Epidemiology: Principles and Methods. Boston, MA: Little, Brown.
Malmberg, A., Simkin, S. and Hawton, K. (1999) Suicide in farmers. British Journal of Psychiatry, 175: 103–105.
Makela, P. (1996) Alcohol consumption and suicide mortality by age among Finnish men, 1950–1991. Addiction, 91: 101–112.
Morrell, S., Taylor, R., Quine, S. and Kerr, C. (1993) Suicide and unemployment in Australia 1907–1990. Social Science and Medicine, 36: 749–756.
Morton, M.J. (1993) Prediction of repetition of parasuicide: with special reference to unemployment. International Journal of Social Psychiatry, 39: 87–99.
Moser, K.A., Fox, A.J. and Jones, D.R. (1984) Unemployment and mortality in the OPCS longitudinal study. Lancet, ii: 1324–1329.
Moser, K.A., Fox, A.J., Jones, D.R. and Goldblatt, P.O. (1986) Unemployment and mortality: further evidence from the OPCS longitudinal study 1971–81. Lancet i: 365–367.
Moser, K.A., Goldblatt, P.O., Fox, A.J. and Jones, D.R. (1987) Unemployment and mortality: comparison of the 1971 and 1981 longitudinal study census samples. British Medical Journal, 294: 86–90.
Motohashi, Y. (1991) Effects of socio economic factors on secular trends in suicide in Japan, 1953–86. Journal of Biosocial Science, 23: 221–227.
Neeleman, J., Jones, P., Van Os, J. and Murray, R.M. (1996) Parasuicide in Camberwell—ethnic differences. Social Psychiatry and Psychiatric Epidemiology, 31: 284–287.
Nordentoft, M. and Rubin, P. (1993) Mental illness and social integration among suicide attempters in Copenhagen. Comparison with the general population and a four-year follow-up study of 100 patients. Acta Psychiatrica Scandinavica, 88: 278–285.
Norstrom, T. (1988) Deriving relative risks from aggregate data. 2. An application to the relationship between unemployment and suicide. Journal of Epidemiology and Community Health, 42: 336–340.
Norstrom, T. (1995) The impact of alcohol, divorce, and unemployment on suicide: a multilevel analysis. Social Forces, 74: 293–314.
O'Toole, B.I. and Cantor, C. (1995) Suicide risk factors among Australian Vietnam era draftees. Suicide and Life-Threatening Behavior, 25: 475–488.
Owens, D., Dennis, M., Read, S. and Davis, N. (1994) Outcome of deliberate self-poisoning. An examination of risk factors for repetition. British Journal of Psychiatry, 165: 797–801.
Penttinen, J. (1995) Back pain and the risk of suicide among Finish farmers. American Journal of Public Health, 85: 1452–1453.
Platt, S. (1984) Unemployment and suicidal behaviour: a review of the literature. Social Science and Medicine, 19: 93–115.
Platt, S. (1986a) Parasuicide and unemployment. British Journal of Psychiatry, 149: 401–405.
Platt, S. (1986b) Clinical and social characteristics of male parasuicides: variation by

employment status and duration of unemployment. Acta Psychiatrica Scandnavica, 74: 24–31.

Platt, S. and Duffy, J.C. (1986) Social and clinical correlates of unemployment in two cohorts of male parasuicides. Social Psychiatry, 21: 17–24.

Platt, S. and Dyer, J.A.T. (1987) Psychological correlates of unemployment among male parasuicides in Edinburgh. British Journal of Psychiatry, 151: 27–32.

Platt, S. and Kreitman, N. (1984) Trends in parasuicide and unemployment among men in Edinburgh, 1968–82. British Medical Journal, 289: 1029–1032.

Platt, S. and Kreitman, N. (1985) Parasuicide and unemployment among men in Edinburgh 1968–82. Psychological Medicine, 15: 113–123.

Platt, S. and Kreitman, N. (1990) Long-term trends in parasuicide and unemployment in Edinburgh, 1968–87. Social Psychiatry and Psychiatric Epidemiology, 25: 56–61.

Platt, S., Hawton, K., Kreitman, N., Fagg, J. and Foster, J. (1988) Recent clinical and epidemiological trends in parasuicide in Edinburgh and Oxford: a tale of two cities. Psychological Medicine, 18: 405–418.

Platt, S., Micciolo, R. and Tansella, M. (1992) Suicide and unemployment in Italy: description, analysis and interpretation of recent trends. Social Science and Medicine, 34: 1191–1201.

Pritchard, C. (1988) Suicide, unemployment and gender in the British Isles and European Economic Community (1974–1985). A hidden epidemic? Social Psychiatry and Psychiatric Epidemiology, 23: 85–89.

Pritchard, C. (1990) Suicide, unemployment and gender variations in the Western world 1964–1986. Are women in Anglophone countries protected from suicide? Social Psychiatry and Psychiatric Epidemiology, 25: 73–80.

Pritchard, C. (1992) Is there a link between suicide in young men and unemployment? A comparison of the UK with other European Community countries. British Journal of Psychiatry, 160: 750–756.

Runeson, B., Eklund, G. and Wasserman, D. (1996) Living conditions of female suicide attempters: a case-control study. Acta Psychiatrica Scandinavica, 94: 125–132.

Saunderson, T., Haynes, R. and Langford, I.H. (1998) Urban–rural variations in suicides and undetermined deaths in England and Wales. Journal of Public Health Medicine, 20: 261–267.

Smith, T. (1995) Differences between general practices in hospital admission rates for self-inflicted injury and self-poisoning: influence of socio-economic factors. British Journal of General Practice, 45: 458–462.

Snyder, M.L. (1992) Unemployment and suicide in Northern Ireland. Psychological Reports, 70: 1116–1118.

Stack, S. (1987) The effect of female participation in the labor force on suicide: a time series analysis, 1948–1980. Sociological Forum, 2: 257–277.

Stack, S. (1993) The media and suicide: a non-additive model, 1968–1980. Suicide and Life-Threatening Behavior, 23: 63–66.

Stack, S. (1996/97) The effect of labor force participation on female suicide rates: an analysis of individual data from 16 states. Omega—Journal of Death and Dying, 34: 163–169.

Stack, S. (1998) The relationship of female labor force participation to suicide: a comparative analysis. Archives of Suicide Research, 4: 249–261.

Stack, S. and Haas, A. (1984) The effect of unemployment duration on national suicide rates: a time series analysis, 1948–1982. Sociological Focus, 17: 17–29.

Standish-Barry, H.M., Clayden, A. and Sims, A.C.P. (1989) Age, unemployment and parasuicide in Leeds. International Journal of Social Psychiatry, 35: 303–312.

Starrin, B., Larsson, G., Brener, S.-O., Levi, L. and Petterson, I.-L. (1990) Structural changes, ill health, and mortality in Sweden, 1963–83: a macroaggregated study. International Journal of Health Services, 20: 27–42.

Travis, R. (1990) Halbwachs and Durkheim: a test of two theories of suicide. British Journal of Sociology, 41: 225–243.

Trovato, F. (1986) A time series analysis of international immigration and suicide mortality in Canada. International Journal of Social Psychiatry, 32: 38–46.
Trovato, F. and Vos, R. (1992) Married female labor force participation and suicide in Canada, 1971 and 1981. Sociological Forum, 7: 661–677.
van Heeringen, K. (1994) Epidemiological aspects of attempted suicide—a case-control study in Gent, Belgium. Crisis, 15: 116–122.
Viren, M. (1996) Suicide and business cycles: Finnish evidence. Applied Economics Letters, 3: 737–738.
Wasserman, I.M. (1984) A longitudinal analysis of the linkage between suicide, unemployment, and marital dissolution. Journal of Marriage and the Family, 46: 853–859.
Weyerer, S. and Wiedenmann, A. (1995) Economic factors and the rates of suicide in Germany between 1881 and 1989. Psychological Reports, 76: 1331–1341.
Yang, B. (1992) The economy and suicide: a time-series study of the USA. American Journal of Economics and Sociology, 51: 87–99.
Yang, B. and Lester, D. (1988) The participation of females in the labor force and rates of personal violence (suicide and homicide). Suicide and Life-Threatening Behavior, 18: 270–278.
Yang, B. and Lester, D. (1990) Time-series analyses of the American suicide rate. Social Psychiatry and Psychiatric Epidemiology, 25: 274–275.
Yang, B. and Lester, D. (1992) Suicide, homicide and unemployment: a methodological note. Psychological Reports, 71: 844–846.
Yang, B. and Lester, D. (1995) Suicide, homicide and unemployment. Applied Economics Letters, 2: 278–279.
Yang, B., Lester, D. and Yang, C.-H. (1992a) Sociological and economic theories of suicide: a comparison of the USA and Taiwan. Social Science and Medicine, 34: 333–334.
Yang, B., Stack, S. and Lester, D. (1992b) Suicide and unemployment: predicting the smoothed trend and yearly fluctuations. Journal of Socio-Economics, 21: 39–41.
Yip, P.S.F. (1997) Suicides in Hong Kong, 1981–1994. Social Psychiatry and Psychiatric Epidemiology, 32: 243–250.
Zimmerman, S.L. (1995) Psychache in context. States' spending for public welfare and their suicide rates. Journal of Nervous and Mental Disease, 183: 425–434.

Chapter 21

Repetition of Suicidal Behaviour

Isaac Sakinofsky
Clarke Division, Centre for Addiction and Mental Health, Toronto, Ontario, Canada

Abstract

Samples of individuals who repeat suicidal behaviour include a wide diversity of patients with differing degrees of suicide intent. This makes it difficult to evaluate the prevalence of subsequent suicide in prospective studies of "suicide attempters". At one end of this spectrum are the minor self-mutilators, whose behaviour is personal, private, and of little or no suicide intent. At the other extreme are those who have been frustrated in their genuine attempts to end their lives. However, one-third of self-mutilators also make serious suicide attempts at some time and many serious attempters never go on to take their lives. Recurrent deliberate self-harmers or suicide attempters are a heterogeneous population whose suicidal behaviour is in constant flux. This, together with the relative rarity of suicide, makes the prediction of suicide or non-fatal deliberate self-harm following attempted suicide difficult and inaccurate. To prevent suicide we need to treat the underlying high-risk groups, including those of persons who make a current suicide attempt. Nonetheless, some studies have provided helpful pointers for clinicians evaluating suicidal behaviour, such as the degree of precautions taken to prevent discovery during the act, and the presence of substance abuse (particularly in young people). As many as two-thirds of suicides have a history of a prior suicide attempt, yet at least half have had no contact with a mental health professional in their final year of life. Obviously, there is a gap in aftercare here that needs to be filled. The risk of a fatal repetition of a suicide attempt is highest in the period immediately following the act. In prospective studies of suicide attempters, 1–3% will die by suicide within 1 year, up to 9% within 5 years, and in longer studies, up to 11%. About half the suicide attempters seen for the first time by a clinician have carried out at least one previous act of deliberate self-harm. Many demographic and psychosocial variables have been associated with repetition of suicidal behaviour, reflecting the diversity of the population and the interests of researchers. The cognitive component, generating the idea of self-harm or suicide, and perpetuating it, is universal among repeaters, and indeed in all persons with suicidality. The cognitive component is essential for suicidal behaviour, although depression and hopelessness are not.

The International Handbook of Suicide and Attempted Suicide. Edited by K. Hawton and K. van Heeringen.

Repeated suicidal behaviour seems often to be the product of maladaptive learning during personality development, possibly out of a sense of powerlessness, frustrated anger, and learned deviant thinking, and may be associated with childhood trauma and abuse. Biological researchers have found lower levels of CSF 5-HIAA in suicide attempters who later committed suicide, particularly among those who made violent attempts, and there have been other studies also implicating dysfunctional serotonergic neurotransmission.

INTRODUCTION: THE SPECTRUM OF REPETITIVE DELIBERATE SELF-HARM AND ITS RELATIONSHIP TO SUICIDE

Repeated attempts at suicide are often synonymously included under the rubric of deliberate self-harm or "parasuicide"—a practice understandably confusing to the uninitiated reader, because the latter terms were invented to highlight the fact that many acts of deliberate self-harm are not intended to bring about death, but to achieve other aims compatible with life (Stengel and Cook, 1958; Shneidman, 1963; Kessel, 1966; Kreitman et al, 1969). In the WHO/EU Study on Parasuicide (see Chapter 3), for instance, "all intentional self-destructive behaviours are included, as long as these behaviours apparently are intended to bring about changes in the present situation through the actual or intended harm or unconsciousness inflicted upon the body" (Bille-Brahe et al, 1994). Even though its findings were published in a book entitled *Attempted Suicide in Europe*, the main inclusion criterion of this important study gave primacy to the intention to harm oneself, over the intention to kill oneself. The overlap between the two categories was, of course, recognized.

Because of the confusion engendered by conventional nomenclature, something must be said in this chapter about the phenomenon of minor self-mutilation, which is a form of deliberate self-harm that is almost always repetitive and chronic, and in non-psychotic, non-mentally retarded individuals seldom leads to suicide. Major self-mutilation, confined to psychotics acting out their delusions, is uncommon, but can lead to serious bodily trauma, as in enucleation of an eye or self-castration. Minor self-mutilation is far more common and usually begins in early adolescence in young females, who chance upon the discovery that anger, tension or dissociative numbness may be relieved by cutting an arm, thigh; breast or torso with a razor blade, burning the hand with a cigarette, or banging the head against a wall. The skin of habitual self-mutilators characteristically displays a complex grid of vertical and horizontal scars in various stages of healing. When cutting (often painless) occurs, the behaviour is self-terminated by relief of tension following the sight of blood welling up in the wound (Brain et al, 1998). Self-mutilators describe experiencing this sensation as pleasurable, almost eroticized. The meaning of self-mutilation thus appears to be strictly personal, an often private, self-gratifying behaviour that is concealed from others. Unlike misuse of illicit substances, it is seldom practised in a group, but the author has known a case where a mutually self-mutilating couple tasted each other's blood. The cuts are not usually placed over a major blood vessel, unless the self-mutilator deliberately crosses the boundary between self-mutilation and attempted suicide and slashes a wrist, when tendon, nerve or vessel damage may result.

In contrast to most deliberate self-harm, which may be conceptualized as self-harm for the purpose of influencing *others* to ameliorate one's predicament, self-mutilation "may best be thought of as a purposeful, if morbid, act of *self*-help" (Favazza, 1989a). However, more than half of self-mutilators also take drug overdoses, a quarter of them repeatedly, and one-third expect to be dead within 5 years (Favazza, 1989b). Although many self-mutilators are diagnosed in DSM as borderline or antisocial personalities, axis I substance abuse, intermittent explosive disorder, and post-traumatic stress disorders are also independently correlated with self-mutilative behaviour (Zlotnick et al, 1999).

Methodological limitations make it difficult to evaluate prevalence reports of suicide mortality across different samples of deliberate self-harm patients, because authors of studies frequently do not define their inclusion/exclusion criteria clearly, or adequately describe the intended lethality of their subjects' acts (suicide intent). When self-mutilation is carried out in a manner that does not simulate or mimic suicide, such patients should not properly be included in attempted suicide samples, but they are likely to be included inadvertently in several of the studies reviewed in this chapter that combine several methods of self-harm.

THE IMPORTANCE OF REPEATED SUICIDE ATTEMPTS IN MORTALITY FROM SUICIDE

Although a large proportion of suicides die in their first attempt, psychological autopsy studies report that from one-third (Clark and Horton-Deutsch, 1992) to two-thirds (Beskow, 1979; Roy, 1982; Rich et al, 1986; Asgard, 1990; Runeson et al, 1996; Heilä et al, 1998; Isometsä and Lönnqvist, 1998; Appleby et al, 1999b) attempted at least once before. A history of self-harm was independently associated with suicide within 5 years (odds ratio of 3) in a case-control study of discharged inpatients (Appleby et al, 1999a). Further, even though they might have visited a general practitioner, half to three-quarters of suicides had no contact with a specialized mental health professional during their final year (Clark and Horton-Deutsch, 1992; Lesage et al, 1994; Pirkis and Burgess, 1998; Appleby et al, 1999b). Given that 88–100% of suicides suffered at least one psychiatric condition as detected at psychological autopsy, these findings indicate two targets for suicide prevention: the first would be to identify and treat potential suicides who have never been treated (primary prevention); and the second, to prevent the one-third or more of potential suicides with a history of previous attempts from repeating (secondary prevention).

Achieving the first target is exceedingly difficult because the population-at-risk is huge and indefinable, notwithstanding the known high-risk groups (see Chapter 34). Suicide attempters constitute one of these high-risk groups, but efforts at intervention must begin directly, because the risk of fatal repetition is highest in the attempt succeeding the initial one. In a Chicago psychological autopsy study, 70% died during their first attempt. In their second attempt a further 14% succumbed, but thereafter the proportions tailed off sharply with each succeeding act of self-harm (Maris, 1992). In the psychological autopsy component of the Finnish National Suicide Prevention Project, half the 1397 suicides died in their first attempt, a further one-fifth in the second, one-tenth in the third, and the remainder in subsequent acts (Isometsä and Lönnqvist, 1998).

Tables 21.1–21.3 present data on prospective follow-up studies of attempted suicide in the literature that report suicide mortality. Since there are no community-based studies, the investigations relate to treated attempters identified at index acts of self-harm when they presented to hospitals. The tables are separated into short-term (1 year or less), medium-term (>1 year <5 years) and long-term (5 years or greater) follow-up. In the first year of follow-up, somewhere between 1% and 3% will complete suicide (however, an older group, composed of attempters with chronic physical illness, had a 10% toll, and one of adolescents, none). In the medium term, the cumulative proportion increases within a range of 0–9%, significantly higher among elderly samples (5–9%), and low for adolescent samples. In the group of long-term studies there is wide variation, ranging from 2.2% to 10.9% according to the age, gender composition and geographic location of the sample, with Scandinavian studies and older age samples generally reporting higher suicide mortality.

In a survival analysis of suicide risk in a cohort of 1,573 suicide attempters, followed for 5 years by Nordström and colleagues (1995) the suicide mortality was 6%, almost twice as prevalent among the males as females. Although males of all ages were at risk, older women were also more at risk than younger women. Risk for all was highest during the first year.

REPETITION PREVALENCE AT INDEX CONTACT

Only a few of the studies cited in Tables 21.1–21.3 stated the proportion of attempters seen during index episodes with previous histories of non-fatal suicidal behaviour (35–55%). Kreitman and Casey (1988) cited the proportion of "first-evers" reported in the UK over 20 years as 40–60%, implying that half the admissions were repetitions. However, in studies comparing persons with events, the ratio of repeaters to first-evers could be spuriously inflated by a small number of multiple repeaters who repeat during the timespan of the studies. They advised that unduplicated counts of individuals are preferable, and should be classified as "first-evers" (no previous history of attempted suicide), "minor" repeaters (lifetime history of two to four attempts), and "major" or "grand" repeaters, with five attempts or more. In three large Edinburgh cohorts (total n = 3,166), each separated by 5 years, they found 48% of males to be first-evers, 36% minor and

Table 21.1 Prospective follow-up studies of suicide in suicide attempters: short-term (up to 1 year)

Reference	Country	*n*	Special details	Duration	Repeated (%)	Suicides (%)
Spirito et al, 1992	USA	130	Median age 15. 35% attempted before	3 months	10.0	0
Kessel and McCulloch, 1966	Scotland	511	Edinburgh RPTC‡. All ages >15. 39% attempted before	1 year	19.0	1.6
Rosen, 1970	Scotland	886	Edinburgh RPTC. Medically serious attempts 2.3 times risk non-serious attempts	1 year		0.9
Rygnestad, 1982	Norway	229/257	Ages 13–88. Medical admissions	1 year		2.6†
Stenager et al, 1994	Denmark	72	Physical illness (mean age 46, 52% of sample) Deaths tended to be older	1 year	42.0	9.7
Sakinofsky, 1998	Canada	228	Mean age 30 (13–84). 55% previous attempts	1 year	28.5	1.8

† Females 1.4%, Males 3.9%.
‡ Edinburgh Regional Poisoning Treatment Centre.

Table 21.2 Prospective follow-up studies of suicide in suicide attempters: medium-term (> 1 < 5 years)

Reference	Country	*n*	Details	Average duration (years)	Repeated (%)	Suicide (%)
Hengeveld et al, 1991	The Netherlands	227	Females only (>19 years). No difference between responders and non-responders	1.2		4.6
Hassanyeh et al, 1989	England	71	Mean age 34 (14–82). Females, 57%	1.5	30.0	2.8
Suleiman et al, 1989	Kuwait	92	Mean age 23. Females, 86%	2.0	19.6	1.1
Bille-Brahe and Jessen, 1994	Denmark	773	47% attempted before	2.0	30.0	3.0
Goldacre and Hawton, 1985	England	2,492	Age 12–20. Record linkage study	2.8	9.5	0.2†
Van Aalst et al, 1992	USA	118	Mean age 35, 87% male. Trauma admissions with serious, violent attempts	2.8	6.7	0
Hepple and Quinton, 1997	England	95	Age >65, mean 76. 65% women	3.5	20.0	7.4
Lönnqvist and Achte, 1985	Finland	55	Excludes non-admissions. Age >65. 65% females	4.0		9.1‡
Pierce, 1996	Wales	39	Repeaters aged 60–87 (mean 68). Females 72%	4.2		5.1

† Probable suicides: 0.7% of males and 0.1% of females (conservative estimate).
‡ All suicides completed during first year of follow-up.

Table 21.3 Prospective follow-up studies of suicide in suicide attempters: long-term (5 years or greater)

Reference	Country	*n*	Details	Average duration (years)	Repeated (%)	Suicide (%)
Rygnestad, 1988	Norway	253	Age 13–88, medical admissions. Females 60%	5.0		8.3[†]
Ekeberg et al, 1991	Norway	934	All self-poisoning admissions. 64% males and 34% females were substance abusers	5.0		4.0
Kotila, 1992	Finland	362	Age 15–19. Females 68%	5.0		2.2
Johnsson Fridell et al, 1996	Sweden	75	Females 59%. 48% attempted previously. Suicides older	5.0	42.5	13.3
Nordström et al, 1995	Sweden	1,573	All Karolinska ER referrals. Mean age, males 38, females 37	5.0		6
Hawton and Fagg, 1988	England	1,959	Females 67%. Age 10–60, mostly 20–29. Suicides older	8.3		2.2
Nordentoft et al, 1993	Denmark	974	Poisoning Centre, admitted cases. Females 58%	10.0		10.6[‡]
Ekeberg et al, 1994	Norway	926	"Cries for help" excluded. Unselected self-poisonings	10.0		5
O'Donnell et al, 1994	England	94	Subway train attempters. Mean age 41. Males 52%	10.0		10
Rygnestad, 1997	Norway	587	Poisoning unit. Index years 1978 and 1987. Females 58%	10.0		7.0
Zonda, 1991	Hungary	577	Psychiatric ward admissions. Females 68%	11.6	1.4	3.0
Hall et al, 1998	Scotland	8,304	Linkage study. Females 60%. Median age 30 (10–96)	13.0	31.6	2.6
Mehlum, 1994	Norway	51	Male military conscripts, mean age 20 (18–25)	20.0		3.9
Dahlgren, 1977	Sweden	229	Medical and psychiatric admissions. Females 59%	35.0		10.9

[†] 6% Females, 12% males.
[‡] 9.8% Females, 11.7% males.

16% grand repeaters. The proportions for females were similar: 53% first-evers, 35% minor, and 12% grand repeaters. In some categories a higher proportion were repeaters than were first-evers, the most obvious finding being the relationship of frequency of episodes with lower socio-economic class. Bancroft and Marsack (1977) noted that repeaters could be divided into three groups: chronic, habitual repeaters; those who enact a flurry of self-harm events within a short time-frame and are then quiescent for a lengthy period; and those who repeat only very occasionally.

The most comprehensive effort to date in measuring the prevalence of repetition is the current WHO/EU Multicentre Study on Parasuicide (Kerkhof et al, 1994). The Repetition-Prediction component comprises structured interview data from suicide attempters aged 15 years and older, drawn from a number of Western European centres. Once again, about half (54%) had attempted at least once before. In the prospective follow-up at 1 year (eight centres reporting) 30% had repeated at least once, and 17% had repeated two or more times (Kerkhof et al, 1998).

PREDICTION OF NON-FATAL REPETITION

The predictive validity of scales developed to predict which individual will repeat a non-fatal suicidal act is unsatisfactory, sometimes yielding too high a proportion of false positives for targeting of health care resources. Kreitman and Foster (1991) developed an 11-item scale, designed to be used unweighted clinically but weighted for research, to identify those at low, intermediate and high risk for further parasuicide episodes. The items comprised:

- Previous parasuicide.
- Personality disorder.
- Alcohol misuse.
- Previous psychiatric treatment.
- Unemployment.
- Social class V (Registrar General's criteria).
- Drug abuse.
- Criminal record.
- Physical violence.
- Age 25–54 years.
- Civil status single, divorced, or separated.

When validated on two Edinburgh cohorts the scale proved cautiously "efficient" (a ratio of the actual repetition rate of the high-risk group divided by that of the low risk group). However, individual items (such as use of alcohol) were less useful prospectively than as retrospective discriminators, suggesting that different predictors of repetition apply at different stages in the progression of the problem. Hawton and Fagg (1995) evaluated the new scale on two Oxford cohorts totalling 465 males and 715 females. It performed acceptably when using an attempt-based method of evaluation but not as well with a person-based method, and was not superior to the earlier, simpler six-item Edinburgh scale (Buglass and Horton, 1974; Siani et al, 1979). Both scales were limited by being based on demographic and clinical factors (Hawton and Fagg, 1995) and could be improved by taking into account personality variables such as impulsivity, aggression and problem-coping skills (e.g. Sakinofsky and Roberts, 1990). Corcoran and colleagues (1997) developed a model including the following 11 items:

- Age.
- Sex.
- Alcohol taken at time of act.
- Method of parasuicide.
- Drugs taken at time of act.
- Previous parasuicide.
- Change in domestic situation.
- Abuse of street drugs.
- Civil state.
- Level of education.
- Presence of harm caused by alcohol use.

They tested this model on 212 Cork attempted suicide patients over a 6 month period, and were able to identify 96% of the 23% who repeated and 86% of those who did not. This clearly needs replication in different samples.

In the WHO/EU Multicentre Study on Parasuicide, the number of previous parasuicide events, an appeal motive and higher age emerged as prospective predictors of repetition in a stepwise multiple regression analysis (Kerkhof et al, 1998). A non-linear principal components analysis identified two components. The first loaded highest on previous psychiatric treatment, score on the Beck Depression Inventory, maltreatment in childhood, and maltreatment by a partner, but negatively on suicide intent. The second component loaded highly on the Beck Depression Inventory score, state anger, hopelessness and maltreatment by a partner. Clearly, there is much overlap between these principal components, but they suggest the possibility of different types of suicidal behaviour calling for different predictive models.

Table 21.4 lists many of the variables that univariate and multivariate studies in the literature have suggested as predictors of repeated suicidal behaviour. In many ways the items reflect the intuitive preferences of various investigators. Even in sophisticated multivariate analyses, such as logistic regression, the selection of predictors is determined by which variables are included in the equation or are omitted, including potential confounders. There are undoubtedly potentially relevant personality, genetic and biochemical predictors of repetition (e.g. results of fenfluramine challenges, or cognitive-evoked changes visualized by special imaging techniques like positron emission tomography) that have not so far been included in prospective studies of repetition, for practical reasons. Measurement of other predictors requiring invasive techniques (such as CSF estimations) cannot yet be applied outside particular research institutes.

Table 21.4 Predictors of repetition of suicide attempts

Predictor item	Sources
Age	Sakinofsky and Roberts, 1990; Corcoran et al, 1997; Kreitman and Foster, 1991; Buglass and Horton, 1974; Kreitman and Casey, 1988
Alcohol abuse	Kreitman and Foster, 1991; Hjelmeland, 1996; Kerkhof et al, 1998
Civil status unmarried	Bagley and Greer, 1971; Kreitman and Foster, 1991
CNS disease	Bagley and Greer, 1971; Allgulander and Fisher, 1990
Criminality	Kreitman and Foster, 1991
Depression and hopelessness	Scott et al, 1997; Kerkhof et al, 1998
Hostility	Sakinofsky and Roberts, 1990; Kerkhof et al, 1998
No confidante	Scott et al, 1997
Normlessness	Sakinofsky and Roberts, 1990
Not living with relative	Buglass and Horton, 1974
Poor socio-economic status	Kotila and Lönnqvist, 1987; Kreitman and Foster, 1991
Poor problem-solving	Scott et al, 1997
Poor relationship with mother	Sakinofsky, 1998
Powerlessness	Sakinofsky and Roberts, 1990
Previous attempt low lethality	Sakinofsky and Roberts, 1990
Previous attempts	Bagley and Greer, 1971; Buglass and Horton, 1974; Allgulander and Fisher, 1990; Kreitman and Foster, 1991; Sakinofsky, 1998
Problems seem overwhelming	Sakinofsky, 1998
Psychiatric history	Buglass and Horton, 1974; Kreitman and Foster, 1991; Hjelmeland, 1996; Dirks, 1998; Kerkhof et al, 1998
Reduced serotonin	Nordström et al, 1996; Verkes et al, 1997
Separation from parents	Buglass and Horton, 1974; Kurz et al, 1982
Sexual abuse	Hjelmeland, 1996
Short prodrome (impulsive)	Sakinofsky and Roberts, 1990
Sociopathy	Bagley and Greer, 1971; Buglass and Horton, 1974; Siani et al, 1979; Kreitman and Casey, 1988; Kreitman and Foster, 1991; Dirks, 1998
Suicide intent (inversely)	Pierce, 1984; Hjelmeland et al, 1998; Kerkhof et al, 1998
Unemployment	Kreitman and Foster, 1991; Dirks, 1998
Unstable address	Siani et al, 1979
Unstable relationships	Kurz et al, 1982
Younger at first act	Sakinofsky and Roberts, 1990; Sakinofsky, 1998

PREDICTION OF FATAL REPETITION

Multivariate analysis of samples of persons considered to be at high risk for suicide (for instance, psychiatric patients with affective disorders, among them persons with suicidal ideation, threats and/or attempts) have identified some of the characteristics that may be predictive for such samples (Motto et al, 1985; Fawcett et al, 1990; Goldstein et al, 1991; Pokorny, 1993), but suicide is notoriously difficult to predict at the level of the individual. When models derived from predictive research attempt to identify actual suicides in validation (replication) samples, or are put to use in the clinic, their predictive accuracy is woefully inadequate. In clinical practice most people who commit suicide are unrecognized as such at their final service contact (Appleby et al, 1999b). These inherent problems apply equally to predicting future suicides among current attempters (Nielsen, 1997).

The main problem is the low base rate (relative rarity) of suicide, yielding large numbers of false-positives and poor predictive power overall. Kreitman (1982) identified additional theoretical, practical and ethical problems, not the least important being that deliberate self-harm patients change over time (because of treatment or altered protective factors) in their degree of vulnerability to suicide; the original predictive factors may no longer apply. Rather than endeavouring to identify the individual suicides, suicide prevention may be accomplished more practically by treating those whom we know to be members of high-risk groups, such as those who have made current, especially serious attempts at suicide (Murphy, 1984; Nordentoft et al, 1993).

One of the more successful efforts to devise predictive scales for fatal repetition was made by Pallis and colleagues (1982). In a 2-year follow-up of 1,263 attempted suicides (a validation sample), 10 of 12 suicides that occurred were found to have scored in the top quartile of a short scale obtained from a discriminant function analysis of suicides and attempted suicides (Pallis et al, 1984). These items were: age over 45, communication of suicidal intent, currently retired, higher socio-economic status (Registrar-General's Social Class I or II), currently unemployed, male, and living alone. The performance of the shorter scale, as well as an 18-item, longer version, were further enhanced by rating intent to die during the index suicide attempt. Pierce (1981) studied the predictive validity of a modified version of Beck's Suicidal Intent Scale in 500 suicide attempters followed for 5 years. At the end of this time there were seven definite and six suspected suicides. Although differences were not statistically significant, there was a trend to higher scores among the future suicides. Particularly important was the finding that individuals who repeated self-injuring behaviour a number of times before committing suicide had a significantly higher score for the penultimate episode than those in the total group of attempted suicide patients. Beck and Steer (1989) carried out a 5–10 year prospective study of 10 potential clinical and demographic indicators of suicide in a sample of suicide attempters. Instruments included were the Beck Depression Inventory, Beck Hopelessness Scale and Beck Suicidal Intent Scale. Multiple logistic regression implicated alcoholism as predictive of eventual suicide (adjusted odds ratio of 6.5). The Precautions subscale of the Beck Suicidal Intent Scale also predicted eventual suicide (adjusted odds ratio of 1.7), the eventual suicides having taken more precautions to prevent discovery at the time of the index suicide attempt. This would seem an important point to apply in clinical practice.

Hawton and colleagues (1993) studied a young (aged 15–24 years) sample of deliberate self-harm patients admitted to the Regional Poisoning Centre in

Edinburgh, who eventually committed suicide between 1968 and 1985, each case being matched with two surviving attempters. Low socio-economic class, unemployment, previous inpatient psychiatric treatment, substance misuse, personality disorder, and previous attempted suicide were identified in univariate analyses as risk factors for suicide. Multivariate analysis selected substance misuse (alcohol and/or drugs) and previous inpatient psychiatric treatment as suicide predictors (both with adjusted odds ratios approaching 4). These results underline the importance of treatment programmes for substance abuse, particularly in young people, and mirror the findings of psychological autopsy studies of younger suicides (Rich et al, 1986; Lesage et al, 1994; Runeson et al, 1996).

Common sense suggests that those who demonstrate their readiness to make a dangerous attempt (high medical lethality) would be at particular risk in any subsequent suicide attempts. Rosen (1976) conducted a 5 year follow-up study of 886 people who had previously attempted suicide. Of the one-fifth with medically serious attempts, 6.5% committed suicide compared with 3% of the less serious attempters (note that this example demonstrates a prevalence of 93.5% false-positives, even among those who had been selected for demonstrated high lethality). Other known risk factors for suicide among suicide attempters that have been referred to elsewhere in this chapter include older age, male gender, and the presence of an Axis I psychosis, mood disorder or schizophrenia, particularly if compounded by concomitant substance abuse disorder or medical illness (Johnsson Fridell et al, 1996). Nordström and colleagues (1994, 1996) identified low CSF 5-HIAA combined with temperamental vulnerability (anxiety proneness, impulsivity and low socialization) as vulnerability factors for future suicide in suicide attempters.

CAUSES OF REPETITION

From the lists of identified predictors in Table 21.4 and the previous section, we may well conclude that the antecedents of repetition are extremely heterogeneous. It may be that the only collective factor uniting repeaters as a group is a propensity to repeat acts of deliberate self-harm under the influence of a wide variety of non-specific stresses. By definition, suicide attempts, deliberate self-harm, parasuicide and its other synonyms are assumed to have a degree of conscious intention. Therefore, there is a cognitive component that precedes and is concomitant with the action. The set of cognitions may comprise suicidal ideation (thinking about committing suicide) or self-harm ideation (thinking about hurting oneself without killing oneself) or a blurred overlap between the two. When "reasons" for the action are formally explored by independent "judges", they appear to fall into four categories: communicating hostility, influencing others, relieving a state of mind, and suicidal intent (Bancroft et al, 1979). The repeated acts will vary in their degree of threat to life (lethality), seriousness of motivation (suicidal intent), and length of prodrome (from impulsive-reflexive to considered and unhurried weighing of choices). On theoretical grounds we can expect some degree of depression and hopelessness to be present immediately before the act, but it is not necessarily serious or of lasting duration. In acutely reactive individuals, the dysphoric mood may be evanescent, so that Beck Depression scores fall precipitously in a few days, signalling the passing of a crisis rather than the presence of an affective illness (Ennis et al, 1989). Sometimes acts of self-harm come in clusters in the life of an individual during a period under duress, with subsequent long remissions or even permanent cessation (Bancroft and Marsack, 1977). Goldney and colleagues (1991) found that 40% of school-leavers could not recall suicidal ideation 4 years after revealing it, suggesting repression of recall of the difficult periods in a young person's life.

Although a cognitive component is the only immediate and necessary (but not sufficient) precondition shared by all non-fatal and fatal suicidal acts, it is poorly understood. Previous studies suggested a narrow and inflexible cognitive style that restricted choices (Neuringer, 1967; Levenson and Neuringer, 1971; Patsiokas et al, 1979; McLeavey et al, 1987) or preferences (Wilson et al, 1995) for problem-solving. Rich and Bonner (1987) collected self-report data from 202 college students and explained 56% of the variance in self-assessed probability of future suicide by a linear combination of current suicidal ideation, hopelessness, dysfunctional cognitions, and few reasons for living. Parker (1981) explored by repertory grid analysis the meaning of the acts of deliberate self-poisoners of low and high suicidal intent. The low-suicidal-intent group perceived the overdose as much closer to "being alone and crying" or "getting drunk" than to "killing myself". Their overdoses were temporary, desperate escapes from tension. The high-intent group, on the other hand, perceived their overdoses as closer to suicide, conceptualized as an expression of feelings and needs, as well as an escape, without necessarily confronting the prospect of death. There were other differences as well between the two groups: the low-suicidal-intent group viewed the possibility of resolution of conflict by discussion with key persons positively, but the higher-intent group was negatively disposed to this strategy. This finding has implications in suicide preventive work: suicidal ideators who have higher suicidal intent may be more resistive to therapeutic collaboration, and may conceal the extent of their suicidality from the mental health professional.

Deliberate self-harm, particularly when repeated, may thus be viewed as a form of maladaptive coping behaviour; a means of escaping from one's predicament, with or without communication of one's pain to significant others. Death may be central or merely peripheral to the core intention, which is to escape from problems as well as to express angst or anger about having to resort to extreme measures. Inherent in the act is either the need to portray oneself as an object for compassion or to express reproach to significant others who have wronged or abandoned one. Although the attempters may have alienated themselves from others, the interpersonal and familial contexts remain strongly operative (Keitner et al, 1990).

Even when their problems have been resolved, a minority of attempters go on to repeat this behaviour within a short time (Sakinofsky et al, 1990). This minority is distinguished from the non-repeaters by perceiving their problems as more insuperable, and themselves as relatively powerless over their lives, possibly resulting from a negative attributional style (Joiner and Rudd, 1995). They score higher on scales measuring "normlessness" (socially deviant attitudes and beliefs) (Dean, 1961) and hostility, directed both externally and inwardly (Brittlebank et al, 1990; Farmer and Creed, 1989), but external hostility appears greater in males (Romanov et al, 1994). They lack self-esteem, are more sensitive to criticism, and are more poorly adjusted socially. The findings that they were significantly younger at their first attempts, had a greater number of prior episodes, and their index attempts were of lower lethality supports the notion of a learned maladaptive behaviour, or of some other vulnerability manifesting early in life, including a genetic (Statham et al, 1998) or biochemical mechanism (Nordström et al, 1996). The maladaptive learning may be accentuated by informal labelling (Wenz, 1978) and possibly by iatrogenic labelling. However, modelling on the examples of others is not as apparent as might be expected (Platt, 1993). Using mathematical modelling techniques, Clark and colleagues (1989) showed that vulnerability (or predisposition) of some kind is more likely to be the perpetuator than the result of the initial suicide attempt itself. Vulnerability may kindle further suicidal activity soon afterwards or much later on; flurries of non-lethal attempts may be succeeded by other non-lethal flurries.

The seeds of this maladaptive learning may originate in childhood trauma (van der Kolk et al, 1991). Krarup and colleagues (1991) found that repeaters, although growing up with both parents more often than first-evers, experienced more of an unhappy childhood. In the context of childhood, sexual and physical abuse are recognized risk factors for suicidal ideation (Webster and Sakinofsky, 1995) and repeated self-harm (Brown and Anderson, 1991; Yeo and Yeo, 1993; Taylor et al, 1994). In children prospectively followed over 6–8 years, Pfeffer and colleagues (1995) related ego functioning (impulsivity, poor reality testing, and defence mechanisms) to suicide attempts.

Biological vulnerability mechanisms that may conceivably facilitate maladaptive learning and expression of suicidal behaviour have been linked with serotonergic neurotransmission in the brain. Träskman and colleagues (1981) found lower concentrations of 5-HIAA (a metabolite of serotonin) in the cerebrospinal fluid of suicide attempters than healthy volunteers, particularly those who had made violent attempts, irrespective of the presence of depression. HVA (a metabolite of dopamine) was lower only in depressed suicide attempters. Those who had 5-HIAA levels below the mean were more likely to commit suicide within a year (Träskman-Bendz et al, 1992; Nordström et al, 1994). Verkes and colleagues (1997) undertook repeated measurements of platelet serotonin and monoamine oxidase at 6, 12, 24, 36 and 52 weeks after the index suicide attempts of 106 patients (females 61%; mean age 36 years, range 18–70 years; patients with a DSM-III-R Axis I diagnosis or on antidepressants excluded). Higher levels of platelet serotonin at baseline significantly predicted recurrence of the attempt within a year, suggesting a trait relationship, and a higher affinity constant of platelet [3H]paroxetine binding was related to recurrence within a much shorter period, suggesting a state relationship.

CONCLUSIONS

Repeated acts of deliberate self-harm or attempted suicide constitute a heterogeneous aggregate of morbid behaviours that are ordered along intersecting dimensions of suicidal intent, medical seriousness of the act, motivation to influence significant others in their social field, underlying psychiatric diagnosis, and several others. This being so, there is an onus to construct more homogeneously defined cohorts in research, and we ought to specify more closely the characteristics of the population samples we are describing; the findings of such research may not apply to other samples.

Up to two-thirds of suicides have a history of at least one previous suicide attempt, but little has been prospectively documented about these attempts, and their relationship to the eventual suicide is poorly understood. Were they indeed failed suicide attempts, or were they acts of deliberate self-harm independent of the final event? No matter, because of the high prevalence of prior attempts among suicide we may hope to prevent many suicides if we can treat suicide attempters and their underlying psychiatric and social conditions more effectively. However, we will rarely be rewarded with the certainty that the suicide would otherwise have occurred.

Repeaters of deliberate self-harm, who may never have killed themselves with or without our intervention, are needy consumers of mental health and social services. The quality of their lives is experienced by them as stressful and fraught with crisis; and their habitual acts of repetition are for coping purposes. We are able to bring to them the repertoire of treatments (described elsewhere in this Handbook), some of which show encouraging results, and newer ones still to come. Given the problems in predicting suicide following acts of deliberate self-harm, we have no right to deny such patients our best help on the basis of cost-effectiveness in suicide prevention. Habitual repeaters of deliberate self-harm, whether their underlying psychiatric diagnosis is a major Axis I illness, or an Axis II personality disorder, are notoriously resistant to treatment. Although this resistance also signals treatment-resistance of the underlying illness or personality disorder, future research should focus more on the cognitive element that is common to all suicide ideators and attempters, its causes (biological as well as psychological), and perpetuating and protective factors.

REFERENCES

Allgulander, C. and Fisher, L.D. (1990) Clinical predictors of completed suicide and repeated self-poisoning in 8895 self-poisoning patients. European Archives of Psychiatry and Neurological Sciences, 239: 270–276.

Appleby, L., Dennehy, J., Thomas, C., Faragher, E. and Lewis, G. (1999a) Aftercare and clinical characteristics of people with mental illness who commit suicide: a case-control study. Lancet, 353: 1397–1400.

Appleby, L., Shaw, J., Amos, T., McDonnell, R., Harris, C., McCann, K., Kiernan, K., Davies,

S., Bickley, H. and Parsons, R. (1999b) Suicide within 12 months of contact with mental health services: national clinical survey. British Medical Journal, 318: 1235–1239.
Asgard, U. (1990) A psychiatric study of suicide among urban Swedish women. Acta Psychiatrica Scandinavica, 82: 115–124.
Bagley, C. and Greer, S. (1971) Clinical and social predictors of repeated attempted suicide: a multivariate analysis. British Journal of Psychiatry, 119: 515–521.
Bancroft, J., Hawton, K., Simkin, S., Kingston, B., Cumming, C. and Whitwell, D. (1979) The reasons people give for taking overdoses: a further inquiry. British Journal of Medical Psychology, 52: 353–365.
Bancroft, J. and Marsack, P. (1977) The repetitiveness of self-poisoning and self-injury. British Journal of Psychiatry, 131: 394–399.
Beck, A.T. and Steer, R.A. (1989) Clinical predictors of eventual suicide: a 5 to 10-year prospective study of suicide attempters. Journal of Affective Disorders, 17: 203–209.
Beskow, J. (1979) Suicide and mental disorder in Swedish men. Acta Psychiatrica Scandinavica, 277 (Suppl.): 1–138.
Bille-Brahe, U. and Jessen, G. (1994) Repeated suicidal behavior: a two-year follow-up. Crisis, 15: 77–82.
Bille-Brahe, U., Schmidtke, A., Kerkhof, A.J.F. M., De Leo, D., Lönnqvist, J. and Platt, S. (1994) Background and introduction to the study. In A.J.F.M. Kerkhof, A. Schmidtke, U. Bille-Brahe, D. De Leo and J. Lönnqvist (Eds), Attempted Suicide in Europe: Findings from the Multicentre Study on Parasuicide by the WHO Regional Office for Europe, pp. 3–17. Leiden: DSWO Press.
Brain, K.L., Haines, J. and Williams, C.L. (1998) The psychophysiology of self-mutilation: evidence of tension reduction. Archives of Suicide Research, 4: 227–242.
Brittlebank, A.D., Cole, A., Hassanyeh, F., Kenny, M., Simpson, D. and Scott, J. (1990) Hostility, hopelessness and deliberate self-harm: a prospective follow-up study. Acta Psychiatrica Scandinavica, 81: 280–283.
Brown, G.R. and Anderson, B. (1991) Psychiatric morbidity in adult inpatients with childhood histories of sexual and physical abuse. American Journal of Psychiatry, 148: 55–61.
Buglass, D. and Horton, H.J. (1974) A scale for predicting subsequent suicidal behaviour. British Journal of Psychiatry, 124: 573–578.
Clark, D.C., Gibbons, R.D., Fawcett, J. and Scheftner, W.A. (1989) What is the mechanism by which suicide attempts predispose to later suicide attempts? A mathematical model. Journal of Abnormal Psychology, 98: 42–49.
Clark, D.C. and Horton-Deutsch, S.L. (1992) Assessment in absentia: the value of the psychological autopsy method for studying antecedents of suicide and predicting future suicides. In R.W. Maris, A.L. Berman, J.T. Maltsberger and R.I. Yufit (Eds), Assessment and Prediction of Suicide. New York: Guilford.
Corcoran, P., Kelleher, M.J., Keeley, K.S., Byrne, S., Burke, U. and Williamson, E. (1997) A preliminary statistical model for identifying repeaters of parasuicide. Archives of Suicide Research, 3: 65–74.
Dahlgren, K.G. (1977) Attempted suicides: 35 years afterwards. Suicide and Life-Threatening Behavior, 7: 75–79.
Dean, D.G. (1961) Alienation: its meaning and measurement. American Sociological Review, 26: 753–758.
Dirks, B.L. (1998) Repetition of parasuicide—ICD-10 personality disorders and adversity. Acta Psychiatrica Scandinavica, 98: 208–213.
Ekeberg, O., Ellingsen, O. and Jacobsen, D. (1991) Suicide and other causes of death in a five-year follow-up of patients treated for self-poisoning in Oslo. Acta Psychiatrica Scandinavica, 83: 432–437.
Ekeberg, O., Ellingsen, O. and Jacobsen, D. (1994) Mortality and causes of death in a 10-year follow-up of patients treated for self-poisonings in Oslo. Suicide and Life-Threatening Behavior, 24: 398–405.

Ennis, J., Barnes, R.A., Kennedy, S. and Trachtenberg, D.D. (1989) Depression in self-harm patients. British Journal of Psychiatry, 154: 41–47.

Farmer, R. and Creed, F. (1989) Life events and hostility in self-poisoning. British Journal of Psychiatry, 154: 390–395.

Favazza, A. (1989a) Why patients mutilate themselves. Hospital and Community Psychiatry, 40: 137–145.

Favazza, A. (1989b) Suicide gestures and self-mutilation. American Journal of Psychiatry, 146: 408–409.

Fawcett, J., Scheftner, W.A., Fogg, L., Clark, D.C., Young, M.A., Hedeker, D. and Gibbons, R. (1990) Time-related predictors of suicide in major affective disorder. American Journal of Psychiatry, 147: 1189–1194.

Goldacre, M. and Hawton, K. (1985) Repetition of self-poisoning and subsequent death in adolescents who take overdoses. British Journal of Psychiatry, 146: 395–398.

Goldney, R.D., Smith, S., Winefield, A.H., Tiggeman, M. and Winefield, H.R. (1991) Suicidal ideation: its enduring nature and associated morbidity. Acta Psychiatrica Scandinavica, 83: 115–120.

Goldstein, R.B., Black, D.W., Nasrallah, A. and Winokur, G. (1991) The prediction of suicide. Archives of General Psychiatry, 48: 418–422.

Hall, D.J., OBrien, F., Stark, C., Pelosi, A. and Smith, H. (1998) Thirteen-year follow-up of deliberate self-harm, using linked data. British Journal of Psychiatry, 172: 239–242.

Hassanyeh, F., O'Brien, G., Holton, A.R., Hurren, K. and Watt, L. (1989) Repeat self-harm: an 18-month follow-up. Acta Psychiatrica Scandinavica, 79: 265–267.

Hawton, K. and Fagg, J. (1988) Suicide, and other causes of death, following attempted suicide. British Journal of Psychiatry, 152: 359–366.

Hawton, K. and Fagg, J. (1995) Repetition of attempted suicide: the performance of the Edinburgh predictive scales in patients in Oxford. Archives of Suicide Research, 1: 261–272.

Hawton, K., Fagg, J., Platt, S. and Hawkins, M. (1993) Factors associated with suicide after parasuicide in young people. British Medical Journal, 306: 1641–1644.

Heila, H., Isometsä, E.T., Henriksson, M.M., Heikinnen, M.E., Marttunen, M.J. and Lönnqvist, J.K. (1998) Antecedents of suicide in people with schizophrenia. British Journal of Psychiatry, 173: 330–333.

Hengeveld, M.W., van Egmond, M., Bouwmans, P.M. and van Rooyen, L. (1991) Suicide risk in female suicide attempters not responding to a follow-up study. Acta Psychiatrica Scandinavica, 83: 142–144.

Hepple, J. and Quinton, C. (1997) One hundred cases of attempted suicide in the elderly. British Journal of Psychiatry, 171: 42–46.

Hjelmeland, H. (1996) Repetition of parasuicide: a predictive study. Suicide and Life-Threatening Behavior, 26: 395–404.

Hjelmeland, H., Stiles, T.C., Bille-Brahe, U., Ostamo, A., Renberg, E.S. and Wasserman, D. (1998) Parasuicide: the value of suicidal intent and various motives as predictors of future suicidal behaviour. Archives of Suicide Research, 4: 209–225.

Isometsä, E.T. and Lönnqvist, J.K. (1998) Suicide attempts preceding completed suicide. British Journal of Psychiatry, 173: 531–535.

Johnsson Fridell, E., Ojehagen, A. and Träskman-Bendz, L. (1996) A 5-year follow-up study of suicide attempts. Acta Psychiatrica Scandinavica, 93: 151–157.

Joiner, T.E. Jr and Rudd, M.D. (1995) Negative attributional style for interpersonal events and the occurrence of severe interpersonal disruptions as predictors of self-reported suicidal ideation. Suicide and Life-Threatening Behavior, 25: 297–304.

Keitner, G.I., Ryan, C.E., Miller, I.W., Epstein, N.B., Bishop, D.S. and Norman, W.H. (1990) Family functioning, social adjustment, and recurrence of suicidality. Psychiatry, 53: 17–30.

Kerkhof, A.J.F.M., Schmidtke, A., Bille-Brahe, U., De Leo, D. and Lönnqvist, J. (1994) Attempted Suicide in Europe. Leiden: WHO/DSWO Press.

Kerkhof, A.J.F.M., Arensman, E., Bille-Brahe, U., Crepet, P., De Leo, D., Hjelmeland, H., Lönnqvist, J., Michel, K., Platt, S., Salander-Renberg, E., Schmidtke, A. and Wasserman, D. (1998) Repetition of attempted suicide: results from the WHO/EU Multicentre Study on Parasuicide, repetition-prediction part. 7th European Symposium on Suicide, Gent.

Kessel, N. (1966) The respectability of self-poisoning and the fashion of survival. Journal of Psychosomatic Research, 10: 29–36.

Kessel, N. and McCulloch, W. (1966) Repeated acts of self-poisoning and self-injury. Proceedings of the Royal Society of Medicine, 59: 89–92.

Kotila, L. (1992) The outcome of attempted suicide in adolescence. Journal of Adolescent Health, 13: 415–417.

Kotila, L. and Lönnqvist, J. (1987) Adolescents who make suicide attempts repeatedly. Acta Psychiatrica Scandinavica, 76: 386–393.

Krarup, G., Nielsen, B., Rask, P. and Petersen, P. (1991) Childhood experiences and repeated suicidal behavior. Acta Psychiatrica Scandinavica, 83: 16–19.

Kreitman, N. (1982) How useful is the prediction of suicide after parasuicide? Bibliotheca Psychiatrica, 162: 77–84.

Kreitman, N. and Casey, P. (1988) Repetition of parasuicide: an epidemiological and clinical study. British Journal of Psychiatry, 153: 792–800.

Kreitman, N. and Foster, J. (1991) The construction and selection of predictive scales, with special reference to parasuicide. British Journal of Psychiatry, 159: 185–192.

Kreitman, N., Philip, A.E., Greer, S. and Bagley, C.R. (1969) Parasuicide. British Journal of Psychiatry, 115: 746–747.

Kurz, A., Torhorst, A., Wachtler, C. and Möller, H.J. (1982) Comparative study of 295 patients with singular and repeated suicide attempts. Archiv für Psychiatrie und Nervenkrankheiten, 232: 427–438.

Lesage, A.D., Boyer, R., Grunberg, F., Vanier, C., Morissette, R., Menard-Buteau, C. and Loyer, M. (1994) Suicide and mental disorders: a case-control study of young men. American Journal of Psychiatry, 151: 1063–1068.

Levenson, M. and Neuringer, C. (1971) Problem-solving behavior in suicidal adolescents. Journal of Consulting and Clinical Psychology, 37: 433–436.

Lönnqvist, J. and Achte, K. (1985) Follow-up study on attempted suicides among the elderly in Helsinki in 1973–1979. Crisis, 6: 10–18.

Maris, R.W. (1992) The relationship of non-fatal suicide attempts to completed suicides. In R.W. Maris, A.L. Berman, J.T. Maltsberger and R.I. Yufit (Eds), Assessment and Prediction of Suicide. New York: Guilford.

McLeavey, B.C., Daly, R.J., Murray, C.M., O'Riordan, J. and Taylor, M. (1987) Interpersonal problem-solving deficits in self-poisoning patients. Suicide and Life-Threatening Behavior, 17: 33–49.

Mehlum, L. (1994) Young male suicide attempters 20 years later: the suicide mortality rate. Military Medicine, 159: 138–141.

Motto, J.A., Heilbron, D.C. and Juster, R.P. (1985) Development of a clinical instrument to estimate suicide risk. American Journal of Psychiatry, 142: 680–686.

Murphy, G. (1984) The prediction of suicide: why is it so difficult? American Journal of Psychotherapy, 38: 341–349.

Neuringer, C. (1967) The cognitive organization of meaning in suicidal individuals. Journal of General Psychology, 76: 91–100.

Nielsen, B. (1997) Can suicide be predicted? Nordic Journal of Psychiatry, 51 (Suppl. 38): 15–19.

Nordentoft, M., Breum, L., Munck, L.K., Nordestgaard, A.G., Hunding, A., Laursen and Bjaeldager, P.A. (1993) High mortality by natural and unnatural causes: a 10 year follow-up study of patients admitted to a poisoning treatment centre after suicide attempts. British Medical Journal, 306: 1637–1641.

Nordström, P., Gustavsson, P., Edman, G. and Åsberg, M. (1996) Temperamental vulnerability and suicide risk after attempted suicide. Suicide and Life-Threatening Behavior, 26: 380–394.

Nordström, P., Samuelsson, M. and Åsberg, M. (1995) Survival analysis of suicide risk after attempted suicide. Acta Psychiatrica Scandinavica, 91: 336–340.

Nordström, P., Samuelsson, M., Åsberg, M., Träskman-Bendz, L., Aberg-Wistedt, A, Nordin, C. and Bertilsson, L. (1994) CSF 5-HIAA predicts suicide risk after attempted suicide. Suicide and Life-Threatening Behavior, 24: 1–9.

O'Donnell, I., Arthur, A.J. and Farmer, R.D. (1994) A follow-up study of attempted railway suicides. Social Science in Medicine, 38: 437–442.

Pallis, D.J., Barraclough, B.M., Levey, A.B., Jenkins, J.S. and Sainsbury, P. (1982) Estimating suicide risk among attempted suicides. I. The development of new clinical scales. British Journal of Psychiatry, 141, 37–44.

Pallis, D.J., Gibbons, J.S. and Pierce, D.W. (1984) Estimating suicide risk among attempted suicides. II. Efficiency of predictive scales after the attempt. British Journal of Psychiatry, 144: 139–148.

Parker, A. (1981) The meaning of attempted suicide to young parasuicides: a repertory grid study. British Journal of Psychiatry, 139: 306–312.

Patsiokas, A.T., Clum, G.A. and Luscomb, R.L. (1979) Cognitive characteristics of suicide attempters. Journal of Consulting and Clinical Psychology, 47: 478–484.

Pfeffer, C.R., Hurt, S.W., Peskin, J.R. and Siefker, C.A. (1995) Suicidal children grow up: ego functions associated with suicide attempts. Journal of the American Academy of Child and Adolescent Psychiatry, 34: 1318–1325.

Pierce, D.W. (1981) The predictive validity of a suicide intent scale: a five-year follow-up. British Journal of Psychiatry, 139: 391–396.

Pierce, D.W. (1984) Suicidal intent and repeated self-harm. Psychological Medicine, 14: 655–655.

Pierce, D.W. (1996) Repeated deliberate self-harm in the elderly. International Journal of Geriatric Psychiatry, 11: 983–986.

Pirkis, J. and Burgess, P. (1998) Suicide and recency of health care contacts. A systematic review. British Journal of Psychiatry, 173: 461–474.

Platt, S. (1993) The social transmission of parasuicide: is there a modeling effect? Crisis, 14: 23–31.

Pokorny, A.D. (1993) Suicide prediction revisited. Suicide and Life-Threatening Behavior, 23: 1–10.

Rich, A.R. and Bonner, R.L. (1987) Concurrent validity of a stress-vulnerability model of suicidal ideation and behavior: a follow-up study. Suicide and Life-Threatening Behavior, 17: 265–270.

Rich, C.L., Young, D. and Fowler, R.C. (1986) San Diego Suicide Study. 1. Young vs. old subjects. Archives of General Psychiatry, 43: 577–582.

Romanov, K., Hatakka, M., Keskinen, E., Laaksonen, H., Kaprio, J., Rose, R.J. and Koskenvuo, M. (1994) Self-reported hostility and suicidal acts, accidents, and accidental deaths: a prospective study of 21,443 adults aged 25 to 59. Psychosomatic Medicine, 56: 328–336.

Rosen, D.H. (1970) The serious suicide attempt: epidemiological and follow-up study of 886 patients. American Journal of Psychiatry, 127: 764–770.

Rosen, D.H. (1976) The serious suicide attempt. Five-year follow-up study of 886 patients. JAMA, 235: 2105–2109.

Roy, A. (1982) Risk factors for suicide in psychiatric patients. Archives of General Psychiatry, 39: 1089–1095.

Runeson, B.S., Beskow, J. and Waern, M. (1996) The suicidal process in suicides among young people. Acta Psychiatrica Scandinavica, 93: 35–42.

Rygnestad, T. (1988) A prospective 5-year follow-up study of self-poisoned patients. Acta Psychiatrica Scandinavica, 77: 328–331.

Rygnestad, T. (1997) Mortality after deliberate self-poisoning—a prospective follow-up study of 587 persons observed for 5,279 person-years: risk factors and causes of death. Social Psychiatry and Psychiatric Epidemiology, 32: 443–450.

Rygnestad, T.K. (1982) Prospective study of social and psychiatric aspects in self-poisoned patients. Acta Psychiatrica Scandinavica, 66: 139–153.

Sakinofsky, I. (1998) Persistent non-fatal suicidality. Paper presented at the 7th European Symposium on Suicide and Suicidal Behaviour, Gent.

Sakinofsky, I. and Roberts, R.S. (1990) Why parasuicides repeat despite problem resolution. British Journal of Psychiatry, 156: 399–405.

Sakinofsky, I., Roberts, R.S., Brown, Y., Cumming, C. and James, P. (1990) Problem resolution and repetition of parasuicide. A prospective study. British Journal of Psychiatry, 156: 395–399.

Scott, J., House, R., Yates, M. and Harrington, J. (1997) Individual risk factors for early repetition of deliberate self-harm. British Journal of Medical Psychology, 70: 387–393.

Shneidman, E.S. (1963) Orientations toward death: a vital aspect of the study of lives. In R.W. White (Ed.), The Study of Lives. New York: Atherton Press.

Siani, R., Garzotto, N., Zimmerman Tansella, C. and Tansella, M. (1979) Predictive scales for parasuicide repetition: further results. Acta Psychiatrica Scandinavica, 59: 17–23.

Spirito, A., Plummer, B., Gispert, M., Levy, S., Kurkjian, J., Lewander, W., Hagberg, S. and Devost, L. (1992) Adolescent suicide attempts: outcomes at follow-up. American Journal of Orthopsychiatry, 62: 464–468.

Statham, D.J., Heath, A.C., Madden, P.A.F., Bucholz, K.K., Bierut, L., Dinwiddie, S.H., Slutske, W.S., Dunne, M.P. and Martin, N.G. (1998) Suicidal behaviour: an epidemiological and genetic study. Psychological Medicine, 28: 839–855.

Stenager, E.N., Stenager, E. and Jensen, K. (1994) Attempted suicide, depression and physical diseases: a 1-year follow-up study. Psychotherapy and Psychosomatics, 61: 65–73.

Suleiman, M.A., Moussa, M.A. and El-Islam, M.F. (1989) The profile of parasuicide repeaters in Kuwait. International Journal of Social Psychiatry, 35: 146–155.

Taylor, C.J., Kent, G.G. and Huws, R.W. (1994) A comparison of the backgrounds of first time and repeated overdose patients. Journal of Accident and Emergency Medicine, 11: 238–242.

Träskman-Bendz, L., Alling, C., Oreland, L., Regnell, G., Vinge, E. and Ohman, R. (1992) Prediction of suicidal behavior from biologic tests. Journal of Clinical Psychopharmacology, 12: 21–26S.

Träskman, L., Asberg, M., Bertilsson, L. and Sjostrand, L. (1981) Monoamine metabolites in CSF and suicidal behavior. Archives of General Psychiatry, 38: 631–636.

Van Aalst, J.A., Shotts, S.D., Vitsky, J.L., Bass, S.M., Miller, R.S., Meador, K.G. and Morris, J.A. Jr (1992) Long-term follow-up of unsuccessful violent suicide attempts: risk factors for subsequent attempts. Journal of Trauma, 33: 457–464.

Van der Kolk, B.A., Perry, J.C. and Herman, J.L. (1991) Childhood origins of self-destructive behavior. American Journal of Psychiatry, 148: 1665–1671.

Verkes, R.J., Fekkes, D., Zwinderman, A.H., Hengeveld, M.W., Van der Mast, R.C., Tuyl, J.P., Kerkhof, A.J.F.M. and Van Kempen, G.M.J. (1997) Platelet serotonin and [3H] paroxetine binding correlate with recurrence of suicidal behavior. Psychopharmacology, 132: 89–94.

Webster, G. and Sakinofsky, I. (1995) Impact of childhood sexual abuse on sex differences in lifetime attempted suicide. Canadian Academy of Psychiatric Epidemiology Annual Meeting, Victoria, BC.

Wenz, F.V. (1978) Multiple suicide attempts and informal labeling: an exploratory study. Suicide and Life-Threatening Behavior, 8: 3–13.

Wilson, K.G., Stelzer, J., Bergman, J.N., Kral, M.J., Inayatullah, M. and Elliott, C.A. (1995) Problem solving, stress, and coping in adolescent suicide attempts. Suicide and Life-Threatening Behavior, 25: 241–252.

Yeo, H.M. and Yeo, W.W. (1993) Repeat deliberate self-harm: a link with childhood sexual abuse? Archives of Emergency Medicine, 10: 161–166.
Zlotnick, C., Mattia, J.I. and Zimmerman, M. (1999) Clinical correlations of self-mutilation in a sample of general psychiatric patients. Journal of Nervous and Mental Disease, 187: 296–301.
Zonda, T. (1991) A longitudinal follow-up study of 583 attempted suicides, based on Hungarian material. Crisis, 12: 48–57.

Chapter 22

Physical Illness and Suicidal Behaviour

Elsebeth Nylev Stenager
Odense Municipality and Institute of Public Health, Odense University, Denmark
Egon Stenager
Esbjerg Centralsygehus, Esbjerg and The Danish Multiple Sclerosis Registry, Rigshospitalet, Copenhagen, Denmark

Abstract

In this chapter, the psychosocial problems associated with chronic somatic disorders and the methodological problems associated with studies on the risk of suicidal behaviour in patients with physical illnesses are reviewed. It is recommended that studies include well-defined groups of patients and employ clear diagnostic criteria. The background population should be used as controls and it is recommended that age and sex-adjusted standard mortality ratios (SMRs) are calculated. The literature on physical illness and suicidal behaviour is reviewed. Cancer is associated with an increased risk of suicide, especially in the first year after diagnosis. An increased risk of suicide is also found in a number of neurological diseases, such as multiple sclerosis, stroke, spinal cord lesions and epilepsy. Studies on the risk of suicide in common disorders, such as heart and lung diseases and rheumatological diseases, are problematic due to old and methodologically inadequate studies. The results are therefore inconclusive, and new, well-conducted studies are needed. The change in the risk of suicide in AIDS patients is reviewed, from high suicide risk in the 1980s to a marginally increased risk in the 1990s. Studies on the risk of suicide in patients suffering from kidney failure have not been able to demonstrate any difference between patients who have received a kidney transplant and those who have not. The implication of this finding is discussed in relation to the emergence of new but complicated treatment possibilities. Studies on suicide attempters have shown that physical symptoms and disorders are common. Some studies indicate that physical illness could be a risk factor for suicide in suicide attempters. Suicidal behaviour can result from psychiatric, psy-

The International Handbook of Suicide and Attempted Suicide. Edited by K. Hawton and K. van Heeringen.

chological, physical and social problems. Initiatives to prevent suicidal behaviour should include patients with somatic disorders as well as those with other problems, and should involve all relevant professional groups in health and social care.

INTRODUCTION

The association between chronic somatic disorders and the risk of suicidal behaviour has been investigated in many studies (Dorpat and Ripley, 1960; Farberow et al, 1971; Shapiro and Waltzer, 1980; Whitlock, 1985; Hjortsjö, 1987; Stenssmann and Sundqvist-Stenssmann, 1988; Wolfersdorf, 1988; Allgulander and Fischer, 1990; Stenager and Stenager, 1992, 1997; and reviewed by Harris and Barraclough, 1994). The studies have shown wide variation in quality and choice of methods.

Two important factors have to be taken into account when designing studies on suicidal risk in somatic disorders. First, the somatic disorder should be characterized by well-defined diagnostic criteria, and, second, the influence of the course of the somatic disorder should be examined. In disorders with a chronic progressive course, like multiple sclerosis, the risk during the entire course is of interest, while in life-threatening disorders like some cancers, the risk during the acute phase is usually of most interest. Also, some hereditary disorders, like Huntington's chorea, can be predicted before onset. How does this affect the risk of suicide? In this chapter, we first discuss psychosocial aspects of chronic disorders; second, we examine methods of studying suicidal behaviour in somatic disorders and their validity; and third, we review the present knowledge about suicidal behaviour in selected disorders.

Psychosocial Consequences of Somatic Disorders

Being afflicted by an illness is associated with many problems in physical, psychological and social terms. A somatic disorder may be accompanied by pain, disability, worries whether about or not the disease is life-threatening, complicating psychiatric disorders, limitations in social behaviour, loss of ability to work, and pressure from social welfare authorities.

Some of the following periods during the course of the disease may be critical. The period before the diagnosis has been made—*the prediagnostic period*—can be associated with disbelief (am I really ill?), worry (what is the diagnosis?) and periods of waiting for examinations and tests. Such conditions can provoke a crisis reaction. After the diagnosis has been made—*the diagnostic period*—new worries arise: what is the prognosis?; what are the treatment possibilites? There may be expectations regarding a cure and compensation from social welfare in terms of insurance, economic compensation during illness, and disability pension. Typically, a crisis reaction may be provoked, involving primarily denial, followed by resistance, acceptance and finally integration. In the subsequent period, where the patient has to adapt to a chronic disorder—*the post-diagnostic period*—new problems may arise, such as reduced self-esteem due to both visible and invisible impairments, worsening of the disease, lack of success of treatments, and social problems such as lack of full compensation for loss of income.

Thus, a large number of circumstances related to illness may result in disillusionment at various stages during the course of the disease. Additionally, complicating psychiatric disorders may arise, such as depression, cognitive deficits, anxiety, abuse of medication in disorders causing pain, psychosis, and organic psychosyndromes. It is reasonable to assume that physical disorders particularly associated with an increased risk of psychiatric disorders will also have an increased risk of suicide.

STUDY METHODS

There are several methods for investigating whether or not an increased risk of suicide exists in certain disorders. Three aspects of the quality of the study are particularly important. First, how is the study population selected in comparison to the whole patient population? Has the selected group an expected high or low risk of suicide? Second, how is the death registered as a suicide, and who decides whether or not it is a suicide? In some countries, forensic examiners (e.g. coroners) decide whether or not the death is a suicide on the basis of police and pathology reports. In other countries, police or legally trained persons make the decision. Obviously, it is of importance how such differences influence the validity of suicide statistics. In people with somatic disorders it is more likely that sudden unexpected deaths will be attributed to somatic causes. Third, how has the control group been selected?

Many early studies were based on patients who committed suicide and were examined in a forensic department, i.e. *autopsy studies*. These studies encompass several problems:

1. A control group is difficult to define and select.
2. The groups are not representative because the selection is biased.
3. When the risk of suicide is estimated in the study population and in the background population, a comparison of dead and living persons is made.
4. Problems regarding sex- and age-standardization are common.

Another type of investigation is the *follow-up study*. Patients with a defined disorder are followed for a defined period of time and compared with a control group regarding the risk of suicidal behaviour. This method is frequently used in mortality studies. The problems with this type of study include:

1. Clear defined diagnostic criteria for somatic disorders have often not been used.

2. The selection of patients may be biased. For example, only hospital-admitted patients might be included.
3. Variable follow-up periods are used.
4. There may be problems concerning the choice of an appropriate control group.
5. There may also be problems concerning the use of optimal statistical procedures.

From a methodological point of view, the best method of investigating possible associations between somatic disorders and suicidal behaviour is through register studies, i.e. a regional or nationwide registration of all patients with a disorder with well-defined diagnostic criteria, compared to a background population. This makes it possible to compare causes of death, such as suicide, based on sex- and age-standardized mortality ratios. The advantages are as follows:

1. Comparisons of causes of death (e.g. suicide) are made between a well-defined group of patients in a region or country in a defined period and the background population as the control group.
2. Standardized mortality ratios (SMRs) adjusted for age and sex can be made, comparing patients with control groups.

Thus, when studies on the risk of suicide are performed, the following criteria regarding design should be fulfilled:

1. A well-defined disorder with clear diagnostic criteria.
2. A large population (suicide is not a frequent cause of death).
3. The groups should be representative (no selection bias).
4. Validated registration of causes of death.
5. The background population from the region or country should be used as a control group.
6. Statistics including SMRs or survival analysis should be used.

In many disorders, it is not possible to fulfil these requirements, but they are important to have in mind when results are evaluated.

SUICIDE IN PHYSICAL ILLNESS

Cancer

The diagnosis of cancer is frequently connected with ideas of unpleasant treatments, pain, uncertain prognosis and economic consequences, and frequently results in depression and a crisis reaction. Often the disease is lethal. Thus, it may not be surprising that the diagnosis of cancer is associated with an increased risk of suicide. This has been investigated in many studies. The methods have included both autopsy and register studies (Whitlock, 1978; Marshall et al, 1983; Bolund, 1985a, 1985b; Breitbart, 1990; Stenager et al, 1991). Good-quality register studies based on a large population have been conducted in Scandinavia, Switzerland and the USA (see Table 22.1; Campbell, 1966; Louhivouri and Hakama, 1979; Fox et al, 1982; Allebeck et al, 1989; Levi et al, 1991; Storm et al, 1992). These studies have demonstrated that cancer patients have an increased risk of suicide compared to the background populations. The SMRs for women varied between 0.9 and 2.2, and for men between 1.3 and 3.6. The results of the best studies from a statistical point of view appear to be consistent in the extent of the risk in men (1.9–2.8), but inconsistent about whether or not women have an increased risk. The risk is particularly increased in the period after the diagnosis has been made (Allebeck et al, 1989).

Neurological Disorders

Neurological disorders have received most attention after cancer, and the best studies have probably been performed in this area (Whitlock, 1982; Stenager and Stenager, 1992). This is understandable, given the fact that several neurological disorders are associated with an increased risk of psychiatric disorders, such as depression. The findings support the hypothesis that neurological disorders may be associated with an increased risk of suicide.

Multiple Sclerosis

The largest and, from a methodological point of view, probably the most correctly conducted study included approximately 5,000 patients with multiple sclerosis who were on the Danish Multiple Sclerosis Register (Stenager et al, 1992). In patients diagnosed with multiple sclerosis before the age of 40 years, the SMR in men was 3.12 and in women 2.12. Patients diagnosed after the age of 40 years did not have an increased risk of suicide. The risk was highest within the first 5 years after the diagnosis was made. The accumulated risk of suicide was approximately twice the risk of the background population. An American study found a substantially higher risk of suicide, namely 7.5 (Sadovnik et al, 1985). However, this study did not estimate the SMR. Sex standardization was not performed which, due to a skewed sex distribution in this disorder, resulted in a considerable bias. Thus, multiple sclerosis appears to be associated with a moderately increased risk of suicide, but only in younger patients.

Huntington's Chorea

This an autosomal dominant disorder which can be diagnosed before symptom onset. How this affects the risk of suicide has not been sufficiently evaluated (Schoenfeld et al, 1984). Most studies have shown an increased risk of suicide, but all have severe bias, making it impossible to reach a conclusion on the extent of the risk (Farrer, 1986).

Table 22.1 Suicide and cancer epidemiological studies

Study	Study period	Gender	Number of suicides	Relative risk	SMR	Comments
Campbell (1966), USA	1959–1966	Male	<55 years, 2	3.6		Suicide risk increased; small sample
		Male	>55 years, 15	2.2		
		Female	<55 years, 0			
		Female	>55 years, 2	1.2		
		Total	19	3.8		
Louhivouri and Hakama (1979), Finland	1960–1966	Male	49	1.3		Suicide risk increased; correct statistical method
		Female	19	1.9		
Fox et al (1982), USA	1940–1969	Male	160		2.3	Suicide risk increased; correct statistical method
		Female	32		0.9	
		Total	192			
Allebeck et al (1989), Sweden	1962–1979	Male	645		1.9	Suicide risk increased; correct statistical method
		Female	318		1.6	
	One year after diagnosis	Male	138		16.0	
		Female	44		15.4	
Storm et al (1992), Denmark	1971–1986	Male	352	1.5		Correct statistical method
		Female	216	1.3		
	One year after diagnosis	Male	115	2.0		
		Female	48	1.4		
Levi et al (1991), Switzerland	1976–1987	Male	39	2.76		Correct statistical method
		Female	16	2.22		
	One year after diagnosis	Both genders	25	3.95		

Spinal Cord Lesions

These are frequently the result of accidents, especially in young men, who may be confined to a wheel chair for the rest of their lives. Several studies have estimated the risk of suicide, but most have considerable methodological problems (DeVivo et al, 1991; Le and Price, 1992). One good-quality study identified a 4.9-fold increased risk of suicide (DeVivo et al, 1991).

Epilepsy

Many studies have been conducted on the risk of suicide in people with epilepsy. In a follow-up study, 2,000 patients receiving anticonvulsant medication who were admitted to hospital between 1931 and 1971 and followed up until 1977, were compared to the background population (White et al, 1979). Sex and age standardization was performed, and period at risk was taken into account. This study found a 5.4-fold increased risk of suicide in epilepsy. Based on a review of the existing literature, Barraclough (1987) found that patients with temporal lobe epilepsy had a five-fold increased risk of suicide, and patients with treatment-resistant epilepsy a 25-fold increased risk. However, patients from a large number of non-representative patient groups from different countries were used in the calculations, which makes the study open to criticism. New studies on the risk of suicide in epilepsy are needed in order to decide whether or not improved treatment possibilities regarding both medication and social care have reduced the risk of suicide.

Brain Lesions

Studies on the risk of suicide in patients with brain lesions are old and primarily based on veterans from World War II (Achté et al, 1971; Lewin et al, 1979). They are methodologically inadequate. However, they identified an increased risk of suicide. New studies are needed.

Brain Tumours

The studies of risk of suicide in cancer have not shown any difference between patients with brain tumours compared to patients with other kinds of cancers (Stenager et al, 1991). Patients with the most malignant brain tumours only survive for a short period of time, and may also be cognitively impaired. Because of this, their risk of suicide is thought to be low, and consequently difficult to measure.

Parkinson's Disease

Only one study of suicide in Parkinson's disease exists, comprising 485 patients in a neurological department, with a follow-up period of almost 20 years

(Stenager et al, 1994a). Compared to the background population, the risk of suicide in men was lower and in women at the same level. The low risk of suicide in patients with Parkinson's disease could be explained by the relatively old age at onset, and reasonably good treatment possibilities. However, the number of patients in the study was small, and therefore the results should be interpreted with caution.

Stroke

A recent Danish study of 37,869 patients with stroke admitted to hospitals during a period of 17 years showed that the risk of suicide in women below 60 years of age was increased 13 times, and in men in the same age group approximately six times (Stenager et al, 1998). Patients older than 60 years of age had a moderately increased risk of suicide, of the order of 1.5–2 times that of the background population. In women with stroke, an increased risk of depression has been demonstrated, and may in part explain these results.

Amyotrophic Lateral Sclerosis/Motor Neurone Disease

One study has been performed on the risk of suicide in patients with amyotrophic lateral sclerosis/motor neurone disease (Bak et al, 1994). This Danish study did not find an increased risk of suicide. However, the disease is rare, and thus only 116 patients were included in the study.

Other Somatic Disorders

A number of authors have discussed suicide in other somatic disorders. Primarily, they are based on forensic studies. Among people in general committing suicide, the proportions with somatic disorders have varied widely, 18–70% having had a physical disorder (Dorpat and Ripley, 1960; Stennsmann and Sundqvist-Stenssmann, 1988; Whitlock, 1985; Wolfersdorf, 1988; Wedler, 1991). The studies have had methodological problems, but indicate that several other somatic disorders are associated with an increased risk of suicide.

Heart and Lung Diseases

Only a few methodologically problematic studies have examined the risk of suicide in patients with cardiac and pulmonary disorders (Farberow et al, 1966; Whitlock, 1985; Sawyer et al, 1983). No association has been found. By contrast, studies have been conducted on the risk of suicide and other violent deaths in patients who use cholesterol-reducing medication. In one study, 35,000 men were followed-up for 12 years (Neaton et al, 1992) and the risk of suicide was increased 1.6 times in men with reduced cholesterol levels. A separate meta-analysis found that patients with low cholesterol levels had an increased risk of dying from other disorders than heart diseases, including suicide (Jacobs et al, 1992). Much uncertainty surrounds such studies, especially the fact that a number of important risk factors cannot be included. Thus, we do not have a conclusive answer to the question of whether or not cholesterol-reducing medication increases the risk of suicide.

Gastro-intestinal Disease

Some of the gastro-intestinal disorders, such as Crohn's disease and ulcerative colitis, frequently affect young people and often result in pain and surgery. Crohn's disease is associated with an increased risk of depression and in one study an increased risk of suicide was found (Cooke et al, 1980). Several studies have demonstrated an increased risk of suicide in patients with peptic ulcers (Berglund, 1986; Viskum, 1975). The full understanding of this result illustrates the difficulty of evaluating studies in somatic disorders. Peptic ulcers may have been associated with alcohol abuse, which is also a recognized risk factor for suicide (see Chapter 9). Therefore, it is difficult to estimate whether it is the ulcer, the alcohol abuse or both that result in the increased risk of suicide. In recent years, treatment possibilities for peptic ulcer have increased considerably, especially with the advent of effective non-surgical treatments. However, there are no recent studies showing whether or not these advances have had a positive effect on risk of suicide.

Liver Transplantation

This is one of the new medical advances. It is a very demanding treatment for patients, often requiring considerable financial resources and access to suitable organs. The candidates for transplantation are likely to have an increased risk of depression, anxiety, metabolic encephalopathy and also uncertainty concerning the future. The clinical impression, however, is that suicide is a rare occurrence among liver-transplanted patients. A case report by Riether and Mahler (1994) challenged this impression by describing suicide and suicide attempts in patients, as well as lack of compliance with medication. They recommend assessment for possible psychiatric problems in intended recipients. The number of liver transplants is small, therefore it is difficult to be certain whether or not there is an increased risk of suicide in transplant patients.

Renal Disorders

Patients with kidney failure have an increased risk of suicide. The size of the risk is uncertain because of methodological problems in the available studies (Abram et al, 1971; Burton et al, 1986). Recipients of kidney transplants have been compared to patients who have not received a transplant (Haenel et al, 1980). No difference concerning the risk of suicide was found. A possible explanation is that the treatment involves life-long medication, on-going need for electrolyte control and risk of rejection of the kidney. Careful psychosocial assessment before transplantation is recommended (Washer et al, 1983).

Endocrine Disorders

Among studies conducted in patients with *diabetes*, only one study has used an adequate method (Kyvik et al, 1994). In this study of 1,682 men with insulin-dependent diabetes, 12 committed suicide, giving a SMR of 2.98 for the age group 20–24 years. For the whole group the SMR was 1.6. The number of suicides may have been underestimated, because a number of patients died of unknown causes (e.g. hypoglycemia).

Cushing's syndrome and *thyrotoxicosis* are associated with an increased risk of psychotic symptoms, but only case reports exist on the risk of suicide.

Rheumatological and Related Disorders

Studies in this area have almost exclusively dealt with the risk of suicide in arthritis and among amputees from World War II (Bakalim, 1969; Hrubec and Ryder, 1979; Shukla et al, 1982). Whitlock (1985) did not find an increased risk of suicide in patients with arthritis, while a two- to three-fold increased risk was found in a psychological autopsy study (Dorpat and Ripley, 1960). Other studies have been conducted, but with inconclusive results.

Tinnitus

One study found that the life-time prevalence of depression was 62% in patients with tinnitus, compared to 21% in controls (Harrop-Griffith et al, 1987). In another study of 20 suicides in patients with tinnitus, the patients committing suicide tended to be male, elderly and socially isolated (Lewis et al, 1994). Almost all had psychiatric disorders, including 70% with depression. Five had previously attempted suicide. Forty percent committed suicide within the first year and half within the first two years after onset of the tinnitus. Thus, tinnitus may be a risk factor for suicide. An attempt was made to compare these results with the risk of suicide in the background population. As previously discussed, such comparisons result in considerable bias.

AIDS

Initially, AIDS was characterized as being lethal, having an epidemic spread and being without treatment possibilities. Therefore, it is not surprising that from the start it was considered likely that there would be an association with an increased risk of suicide. A study by Marzuk and colleagues in 1988 from the USA found a 36-fold increased risk of suicide in men with AIDS. Another study, based on death certificates, supported this finding by reporting a 21-fold increased risk in men aged 20–39 years (Kizer et al, 1988). Since then, there have been several therapeutic advances, resulting in prolonged survival and reduced social stigmatization. In keeping with this, a study reported in 1992 found that the risk of suicide was increased only 7.4 times. During the study period, the risk declined (Coté et al, 1992). A study from 1991 to 1993 found a number of other risk factors beyond the risk of suicide, such as drug abuse, and concluded that the risk of suicide was now limited (Marzuk et al, 1997). Finally, a study has shown that suicidal thoughts occurred in the diagnostic period, but disappeared during the 2-month period after the diagnosis was made (Perry et al, 1990).

ATTEMPTED SUICIDE AND PHYSICAL ILLNESS

Compared to suicide, suicide attempts in somatic disorders have received less attention and consequently the present knowledge is sparse. Three types of studies have been conducted:

1. Studies in suicide attempters in which types and incidence of somatic disorders have been registered.
2. Follow-up studies of suicide attempters in which the risk of repeated suicidal behaviour in those with somatic disorders has been estimated.
3. Studies on the frequency of suicide attempters in defined groups of patients, in which the risk of attempts has been compared to controls.

Studies and follow-up studies of suicide attempters have found somatic disorders in 27–50% of individuals, the figures depending on whether all patients, including emergency room patients, were included, as well as on how somatic disorders were defined (Hawton and Fagg, 1988; Kontaxakis et al, 1988; Nielsen et al, 1990; Dietzfelbinger et al, 1991; Öjehagen et al, 1991; Stenager et al, 1994). Between 13% and 21% of patients in such studies have complained of pain. A recent study reported that 50% of attempters with somatic disorders had rheumatological disorders, 22% neurological disorders, 15% heart diseases and 19% gastro-intestinal diseases. Several patients had more than one disease. Symptoms included headache (50%), joint pain (31%), muscle pain (38%), lumbar pain (31%), and gastric pain (14%) (Stenager et al, 1994b). In a follow-up study of patients repeating suicide attempts, it was found that those with somatic disorders had an increased risk of suicide (Nielsen et al, 1990).

Studies in the third category above have involved a number of disorders. The risk of suicide attempts in patients with *migraine* with aura was found to be increased three-fold compared to a control group of individuals without migraine (Breslau et al, 1991).

Mackay (1979), during 1972–1976, studied 130 *epilepsy* patients who made a total of 171 suicide attempts by self-poisoning. Compared to the incidence of epilepsy in the general population, self-poisoning among epilepsy patients occurred seven times more often than expected, and 18.5% repeated the self-poisoning, compared to 7% of the attempters who did not have epilepsy. Alcohol consumption occurred less frequently in the epilepsy patients, but they were more often given a diagnosis of psychopathy. In a two-year period, Hawton and colleagues (1980) studied the frequency of epilepsy among patients who were admitted following a suicide attempt. Compared to the background population, the frequency of suicide attempts was increased five-fold. Patients with epilepsy had more frequently received psychiatric treatment and had more often made repeat attempts compared with the controls. In another study in which suicide attempters with and without epilepsy were compared, Mendez and colleagues (1989) concluded that patients with epilepsy more frequently had borderline personality disorders, psychotic disorders and previous suicide attempts.

In a study employing a self-rating questionnaire to measure the frequency of suicidal thoughts in 1,217 patients admitted to hospital with *psoriasis*, almost 10% expressed death wishes and 5.5% reported suicidal thoughts at the time of the study (Guptaa et al, 1993). Unfortunately, since no controls were included in the study, it is impossible to decide whether or not an increased risk of suicidal ideation occurs in patients with psoriasis.

The frequency of suicide attempts in *diabetes* has frequently been discussed. Insulin-dependent patients have a potent method available for expressing self-destructive behaviour. In a review of the literature on the misuse of insulin, 17 cases of suicide and 80 cases of attempted suicide were found (Kaminer and Robbins, 1989). Another study found that four out of 204 episodes of insulin overdose were suicide attempts (Gale, 1980). Several other studies have supported the supposition that suicide attempts and suicide are not uncommon in diabetes (Arem and Zogbi, 1985). A two-year prospective study on self-poisoning in 386 diabetic patients found that 64 used hypoglycaemic drugs, while the rest took various other drugs in overdose (Jeffereys and Volans, 1983). Thus, suicide attempts undoubtedly occur in people with diabetes, but there has so far been no study on the frequency of attempts compared to that in the background population.

PAIN AND SUICIDE

This review of suicidal behaviour in people with somatic disorders has demonstrated that many conditions involving pain, such as cancer and mutiple sclerosis, also have an increased risk of suicide (Bolund, 1985b; Breitbart, 1990; Stenager and Stenager, 1992). When the possible association between pain and suicide is subjected to further study, several methodological problems arise. For example, how is the diagnois of depression defined and validated, especially in severely ill persons? How is pain defined and validated? How should patients be selected for such studies? Which groups would be suitable controls? These and other problems make it very complicated to conduct proper studies on this association. Only single case-reports exist and it is thus an important area for further research (Fishbain et al, 1992).

CONCLUSION

This review has shown that a wide variety of disorders are associated with an increased risk of suicide and suicide attempts. An increased risk of suicide in a number of neurological disorders and cancer has been convincingly documented, while in other more common disorders, such as heart and rheumatological diseases, only older studies or single case reports are available. Thus, it is not possible to demonstrate whether or not new treatment advances in these disorders may have reduced this ultimate measure of quality of life.

It is interesting that no difference was found regarding the risk of suicide in patients with kidney failure, whether or not they had received kidney transplantations. Some of the new treatments now available may be so awkward that life still becomes unbearable in spite of a succesful transplant. Furthermore, medication and follow-up could be demanding and expectations may not be fulfilled. This aspect is important when future recipients of new, sophisticated, expensive and complicated treatments are selected. It has generally been accepted that illness is a biological, psychological and social process. It is surprising, therefore, that the interest in psychosocial aspects of somatic disorders has not led to an increased interest in studying suicidal behaviour in patients suffering from various physical conditions. Suicidal behaviour is usually only viewed in a psychiatric context. This is too simplistic. Health personnel should be aware of the risk of suicidal behaviour because it may occur in a range of disorders. Indicators of a risk of suicidal behaviour in the physically ill would be depression, anxiety, previous suicide attempts, suicidal thoughts, hopelessness, pain, crisis reaction, abuse problems, social problems in terms of family, work and finance, and various periods of stress during the course of the illness.

REFERENCES

Abram, H.S., Moore, G. and Vestervelt, F.B. (1971) Suicidal behaviour in chronic dialysis patients. American Journal of Psychiatry, 127: 1199–1204.

Achté, K.A., Lönnqvist, J. and Hillbomi, E. (1971) Suicides following war brain-injuries. Acta Psychiatrica Scandinavica (Suppl. 225): 3–92.

Allebeck, P., Bolund, C. and Ringbäck, G. (1989) Increased suicide rate in cancer patients. Journal of Clinical Epidemiology, 42: 611–616.

Allgulander, C. and Fisher, L.D. (1990) Clinical predictors of completed suicide and repeated self-poisoning in 8,895 self-poisoning patients. European Archives of Psychiatrical and Neurological Science, 239: 270–276.

Arem, R. and Zogbi, W. (1985) Insulin overdose in eight patients: insulin pharmacokinetics and review of the literature. Medicine, 64: 323–332.

Bak, S., Stenager, E.N., Stenager E., Boldsen, J. and Smith, S.A. (1994) Suicide in patients with motor neurone disease. Behavioural Neurology, 7: 181–184.

Barraclough, B.M. (1987) The suicide rate of epilepsy. Acta Psychiatrica Scandinavica, 76: 339–345.

Bakalim, G. (1969) Causes of death in a series of 4,738 Finnish war amputees. Artificial Limbs, 13: 27–36.

Berglund, M. (1986) Suicide in male alcoholics with peptic ulcers. Alcoholism 10: 631–634.
Bolund, C. (1985a) Suicide and cancer: II. Demographic and social characteristics of cancer patients who committed suicide in Sweden, 1973–1976. Journal of Psychosocial Oncology, 3: 17–30.
Bolund, C. (1985b) Suicide and cancer: II. Medical and care in suicides by patients in Sweden, 1973–1976. Journal of Psychosocial Oncology, 3: 31–52.
Breitbart, W. (1990) Cancer, pain and suicide. Advances in Pain Research and Therapy, 16: 399–412.
Breslau, N., Davis, G.C. and Andreski, P. (1991) Migraine, psychiatric disorders, and suïcide attempts: an epidemiological study of young adults. Psychiatry Research 37: 11–23, 14.
Burton, H.J., Kline, S.A., Lindsay, R.M. and Heidenheim, A.P. (1986) The relationship of depression to survival in chronic renal failure. Psychosomatic Medicine, 48: 261–269.
Campbell, P.C. (1966) Suicide among cancer patients. Health Bulletin, 80: 207–212.
Cooke, W.T., Mallas, E., Prior, P. and Allan, R.N. (1980) Crohn's disease: course, treatment, and long-term prognosis. Quarterly Journal of Medicine 49: 363–384.
Coté, T.R., Biggar, R.J. and Dannenberg, A.L. (1992) Risk of suicide among persons with AIDS. A national assessment. JAMA, 268: 2066–2068.
DeVivo, M.J., Black, K.J., Scott Richards, J. and Stover, S.L. (1991) Suicide following spinal cord injury. Paraplegia, 29: 620–627.
Dietzfelbinger, T., Kurz, A., Torhorst, A. and Möller, H.J. (1991) Körperliche ind seelishe Krankheit als Hintergrund parsuizidalens Verhaltens. In H. Wedler and H.J. Möller (Eds), Körperliche Krankheit und Suizid, pp. 101–115. Regensburg: Roderer Verlag.
Dorpat, T.L. and Ripley, H.S. (1960) A study of suicide in the Seattle area. Comprehensive Psychiatry, l: 349–359.
Farberow, N.L., Ganzler, S., Cutter, E. and Reynolds, D. (1971) An 8-year survey of hospital suicides. Life Threatening Behavior, 1: 184–202.
Farberow, N.L., McKelligott, J.W., Cohen, S. and Darbonne, A. (1966) Suicide among patients with cardiorespiratory illnesses. JAMA, 195: 128–134.
Farrer, L.A. (1986) Suicide and attempted suicide in Huntington's Disease. Implications for preclinical testing of persons at risk. American Journal of Medical Genetics, 24: 305–311.
Fishbain, D.A., Goldberg, M., Meagher, R.B., Steele, R. and Rosomoff, H. (1992) Male and female chronic pain patients categorized by DSM-III psychiatric diagnostic criteria. Pain, 26: 181–197.
Fox, B.H., Stanek, E.J., Boyd, S.C. and Flannery, J.T. (1982) Suicide rates among cancer patients in Connecticut. Journal of Chronic Diseases, 35: 89–100.
Gale, E. (1980) Hypoglycaemia. Clinics in Endocrinology and Metabolism, 9: 461–475.
Guptaa, M.A., Schork, N.J., Gupta, A.K., Kirkby, S. and Ellis, C.N. (1993) Suicidal ideation in psoriasis. International Journal of Dermatology, 32: 188–190.
Haenel, T.H., Brunner, F. and Battegay, R. (1980) Renal dialysis and suicide: occurrence in Switzerland and in Europe. Comprehensive Psychiatry, 21: 140–145.
Harris, E.C. and Barraclough, B.M. (1994) Suicide as an outcome for medical disorders. Medicine, 73: 281–296.
Harrop-Griffith, J., Katon, W., Bobie, R., Sakai, C. and Russo, J. (1987) Chronic tinnitus: association with psychiatric diagnosis. Journal of Psychosomatic Research, 31: 613–621.
Hawton, K. and Fagg, J. (1988) Suicide and other causes of death following attempted suicide. British Journal of Psychiatry, 152: 259–266.
Hawton, K., Fagg, J. and Marsack, P. (1980) Association between epilepsy and attempted suicide. Journal of Neurology, Neurosurgery and Psychiatry, 43: 168–170.
Hjortsjö, T. (1987) Suicide in relation to somatic illness and complications. Crisis, 8: 125–137.

Hrubec, Z. and Ryder, R.A. (1979) Report to the Veteran's Administration Department of Medicine and Surgery on service connected traumatic limb amputations and subsequent mortality from cardiovascular disease and other causes of death. Bulletin of Prosthetics Research, 16: 29–53.

Jacobs, D., Blackbum, H., Higgins, M., Reed, D., Iso, H., McMillan, G., Neaton, J., Nelson, J., Potter, J., Ritkind, B., Rossouw, J., Shekelle, R. and Yusuf, S. (1992) Report of the conference on low blood cholesterol mortality associations. Circulation, 86: 1046–1060.

Jeffereys, D.B. and Volans, G.N. (1983) Self-poisoning in diabetic patients. Human Toxicology, 2: 345–483.

Kaminer, Y. and Robbins, D.R. (1989) Insulin misuse: a review of an overlooked psychiatric problem. Psychosomatics, 30: 19–24.

Kizer, K.W., Green, M., Perkins, C.L., Doebbert, G. and Hughes, M.J. (1988) AIDS and suicide in California. Journal of the American Medical Association, 260: 1881.

Kontaxakis, V.P., Christodolou, G.N., Mavreas, V.G. and Havaki-Kontaxaki, B.J. (1988) Attempted suicide in psychiatric outpatients with concurrent physical illness. Psychotherapy and Psychosomatics, 50: 201–206.

Kyvik, K., Stenager, E.N., Green, A. and Svendsen, A. (1994) Suicides in men with IDDM. Diabetes Care, 17: 210–212.

Le, C.T. and Price, M. (1992) Survival from spinal cord injury. Journal of Chronic Diseases, 35: 487–492.

Lewis, J.E., Stephens, S.D.G. and McKenna, L. (1994) Tinnitus and suicide. Clinical Otolaryngology, 19: 50–54.

Louhivouri, K.A. and Hakama, M. (1979) Risk of suicide among cancer patients. American Journal of Epidemiology, 109: 59–64.

Levi, F., Builliard, J.L. and La Vecchia, C. (1991) Suicide risk among incident cases of cancer in the Swiss Canton Vaud. Oncology, 48: 44–47.

Lewin, W., Marshall, T. F. De. C. and Roberts, A.H. (1979) Long-term outcome after severe head injury. British Medical Journal, 2: 1533–1538.

Mackay, A. (1979) Self-poisoning: a complication of epilepsy. Br. J. Psychiatry, 134: 277–282.

Marshall, J.R., Bumett, W. and Brasure, J. (1983) On precipitating factors: cancer as a cause of suicide. Suicide and Life Threatening Behavior, 13: 15–27.

Marzuk, P.M., Tiemey, H., Tardiff, K., Gross, E.M., Morgan, E.B., Hsu, M.A. and Mann, J.J. (1988) Increased suicide risk of suicide in persons with AIDS. Journal of the American Medical Association, 259: 1333–1337.

Marzuk, P.M., Tardiff, K., Leon, A.C., Hirsch, C.S., Hartwell. N., Portera, L. and Iqbal, M.L. (1997) HIV seroprevalence among suicide victims in New York City, 1991–1993. American Journal of Psychiatry, 154: 1720–1725.

Mendez, M.F., Lanska, D.J., Manon-Espaillat, R. and Bumstine, T.H. (1989) Causative factors for suicide attempts by overdose in epileptics. Archives of Neurology, 46: 1065–1068.

Neaton, J.D., Blackbum, H., Jacobs, D., Kuller, L., Lee, D.J., Sherwin, R., Shih, J., Stamler, J. and Wentworth, D. (1992) Serum cholesterol level and mortality findings for men screened in the Multiple Risk Factor Intervention Trial. Archives of International Medicine, 152: 1490–1500.

Nielsen, B., Wang, A.G. and Bille-Brahe, U. (1990) Attempted suicide in Denmark, IV: a five-year follow-up. Acta Psychiatrica Scandinavica, 81: 250–254.

Öjehagen, A., Regnell, G. and Träskman-Bendz, L. (1991) Deliberate self-poisoning: repeaters and non-repeaters admitted to an intensive care unit. Acta Psychiatrica Scandinavica, 84: 266–271.

Perry, S., Jacobsberg, L. and Fishman, B. (1990) Suicidal ideation and HIV testing. JAMA, 263: 679–682.

Riether, A.M. and Mahler, E. (1994) Suicide in liver transplant patients. Psychosomatics, 35: 574–577.

Sadovnick, A.B., Ebers, G.C., Paty, D.W. and Eisen, K. (1985) Causes of death in multiple sclerosis. Canadian Journal of Neurological Science, 12: 189.

Sawyer, J.D., Adams, K.M., Conway, W.L., Reeves, J. and Kvale, P.A. (1983) Suicide in cases of chronic obstructive pulmonary disease. Journal of Psychiatric Treatment and Evaluation, 5: 281–283.

Schoenfeld, M., Myers, R.H., Cupples, L.A., Berkman, B., Sax, D.S. and Clark, E. (1984) Increased rate of suicide among patients with Huntington's disease. Journal of Neurology, Neurosurgery and Psychiatry, 47: 1283–1287.

Shapiro, S. and Waltzer, H. (1980) Successful suicides and serious attempts in a general hospital over a 15 year period. General Hospital Psychiatry 2: 118–126.

Shukla, G.D., Sahu, S.C., Triapathi, R.P. and Gupta, D.K. (1982) A psychiatrie study of amputees. British Journal of Psychiatry, 141: 50–53.

Stenager, E.N. and Stenager, E. (1992) Suicide in patients with neurological diseases. Methodological problems. Literature review. Archives of Neurology, 49: 1296–1303.

Stenager, E.N. and Stenager, E. (1997) Disease, Pain and Suicidal Behaviour. New York: Haworth.

Stenager, E.N., Bille-Brahe, U. and Jensen, K. (1991) Kraeft og selvmord: En litteraturoversigt. Ugeskrift for Laeger, 153: 764–769.

Stenager, E.N., Wermuth, L., Stenager, E. and Boldsen, J. (1994a) Suicide in patients with Parkinson's disease. Acta Psychiatrica Scandinavica, 90: 70–72.

Stenager, E.N., Stenager, E. and Jensen, K. (1994b) Depression, pain and somatic diseases. A one year follow-up study. Psychotherapy and Psychosomatics, 61: 65–74.

Stenager, E.N., Stenager, E., Koch-Henriksen, N., Bronnum-Hansen, H., Hyllested, K., Jensen, K. and Bille-Brahe, U. (1992) Multiple sclerosis and suicide. An epidemiological study. Journal of Neurology, Neurosurgery and Psychiatry, 55: 542–545.

Stenager, E.N., Madsen, C., Stenager, E. and Boldsen, J. (1998) Suicide in stroke patients. An epidemiological study. British Medical Journal, 316: 1206.

Stennsmann, R. and Sundqvist-Stennsman, U.B. (1988) Physical disease and disability among 416 cases in Sweden. Scandinavian Journal of Social Medicine, 16: 149–153.

Storm, H.H., Christensen, C. and Jensen, O.M. (1992) Suicide, violent death, and cancer. Cancer, 69: 1507–1512.

Viskum, K. (1975) Ulcer, attempted suicide, and suicide. Acta Psychiatrica Scandinavica, 51: 221–227.

Washer, G.F., Schröter, G.P.J., Starzl, T.E. and Weill, R. (1983) Causes of death after kidney transplantation. JAMA, 250: 49–54.

Wedler, H. (1991) Körperliche Krankheiten bei Suizidpatienten einer internistischen Abteilung. In H. Wedler and H.J. Möller (Eds), Körperliche Krankheit und Suizid, pp. 87–101. Regensburg: Roderer Verlag.

White, S.J., McLean, A.E.M. and Howland, C. (1979) Anticonvulsant drugs and cancer. Lancet ii: 458–461.

Whitlock, F.A. (1978) Suicide, cancer, and depression. British Journal of Psychiatry, 132: 269–274.

Whitlock, F.A. (1982) The neurology of affective disorders and suicide. Australian and New Zealand Journal of Psychiatry, 16: 1–12.

Whitlock, F.A. (1985) Suicide and physical illness. In A. Roy (Eds), Suicide, pp. 151–170. Baltimore: Williams & Wilkins.

Wolfersdorf, V.M. (1988) Depression und suizid bei körperlichen Krankheiten. Fortschritt in Medicine, 106: 269–274.

Chapter 23

Ethical and Legal Issues

Antoon Leenaars*
University of Leiden, The Netherlands
Christopher H. Cantor
Australian Institute for Suicide Research and Prevention, Griffith University, Australia
John Connolly
St Mary's Hospital, Castlebar, Ireland
Marlene EchoHawk
Alcohol & Substance Abuse Program, Indian Health Service, Albuquerque, NM, USA
Danute Gailiene
University of Vilnius, 2004 Vilnius, Lithuania
Zhao Xiong He
Guangxi Academy of Social Sciences, Nanning, Guangxi, People's Republic of China
Natalia Kokorina *and* **Andrew Lopatin**
Kemorovo State Medical Academy, Kemerovo, Russia
David Lester
Center for the Study of Suicide, Blackwood, NJ, USA
Mario Rodriguez
Ciudad Habana, Cuba
Lourens Schlebusch
Faculty of Medicine, University of Natal, Durban, South Africa
Yoshitomo Takahashi
Tokyo Institute of Psychiatry, Tokyo, Japan
and
Lakshmi Vijayakumar
Madras, India

* Correspondence to: Antoon Leenaars, 880 Ouellette Avenue, Suite 7-806, Windsor, Ontario, Canada N9A 1C7.

The International Handbook of Suicide and Attempted Suicide. Edited by K. Hawton and K. van Heeringen.

Abstract

Ethical and legal issues in suicidology are complex, indeed so complex that they extend the knowledge of one person. To discuss such issues from only one perspective would thus be myopic. Therefore this chapter is written by authors from 12 countries, each of whom have been able to reflect on the issues in their own nations and cultures. The countries are: Australia, China, Cuba, Ireland, India, Japan, Lithuania, Russia, South Africa, The Netherlands, Turtle Island and the USA. The issues in the field are multitudinous. To narrow the topics, the following issues were addressed: suicide and attempted suicide, assisted suicide and euthanasia, standards of reasonable and prudent care, responsibility for care, failure in care, liability and malpractice. It is noted that the legal positions on suicide, euthanasia and assisted suicide, as well as application for assisting death, vary considerably worldwide. It is a myth that there is a uniform legal position on euthanasia and assisted suicide. Furthermore, no one standard of care applies in all countries, although the United Nations has outlined some universal principles. For example, it has stated, "All persons with mental illness, or who are being treated as such persons, should be treated with humanity and respect for the inherent dignity of the human person" (United Nations, 1991). Legal and ethical standards are defined according to, first, the standards of community practices and, second, the resources available and hence what reasonably can be expected. Finally, it is concluded that there is need for ongoing research and discussion of these complex issues globally.

INTRODUCTION

Ethics and legal issues in this field are complex, varying greatly from country to country. Therefore this chapter is written by authors from 12 regions, each of whom have been able to reflect on these issues in their own nations and cultures. These are: Australia, China, Cuba, Ireland, India, Japan, Lithuania, Russia, South Africa, The Netherlands, Turtle Island and the USA. We recognize that we do not represent the world or even our own nations. Yet, we hope that our perspectives will cast a wider net over these issues than one view in isolation. To discuss such issues from, say, only the American viewpoint, which is the most prolific perspective on the topic, would be myopic.

Ethical and legal issues are multitudinous. This is as true in the area of suicidology as it is in any area. To narrow the possible topics, the following issues have been addressed, knowing full well that many issues would not be addressed: suicide and attempted suicide, assisted suicide and euthanasia, standards of reasonable and prudent care, responsibility for care, failure in care, liability and malpractice.

Legal issues are of course, complex across the globe and often not even uniform within a country. In the USA, for example, legal issues are complicated by at least two facts. First, the USA comprises 50 states, and each state has a certain degree of autonomy in setting its own legal rules and requirements. On occasion, local laws and rulings may be appealed to higher courts at the federal level, the results of which modify the ruling of the lower court. However, even here, the country is divided into several federal districts, each of which may rule differently. Only when the US Supreme Court rules on an issue does some means of unity develop.

A second factor in the USA is that civil suits play a major role in determining the standards for the nation, but again, these suits begin at the local level, and only if and when they are reviewed at the federal level does a uniform standard develop. Of course, from a global perspective each country or culture has its own standards. The USA is given only as an example of the complexity of the issues addressed here.

SUICIDE AND ATTEMPTED SUICIDE

Suicide constitutes a serious public and mental health problem worldwide. In many countries suicide ranks among the top ten causes of death. The World Health Organization has estimated that by the year 2000 almost one million people will commit suicide worldwide yearly. In addition, at least 10 times as many persons engage in non-fatal suicidal behaviour. The sheer number makes suicide and attempted suicide a public and mental health problem of prime importance.

Historically, suicide has been viewed differently in various regions. Confucianism and Taoism in China, which are reflected in the Chinese traditional medical classic *Huang Di Nei Jing*, valued life as more precious than to be measured by gold. The *Old Testament* of the West does not directly forbid suicide, but in Jewish law suicide is wrong. During the early Christian years there was excessive martyrdom through suicide, resulting in considerable concern on the part of the Church Fathers. St Augustine (AD 354–430) categorically rejected suicide. Suicide was considered a sin because it violated the Sixth Commandment, "Thou shalt not kill". By AD 693, the Church of the Council of Toledo proclaimed that individuals who attempted suicide should be excommunicated.

The Dharmashastras (book on the codes of living in ancient India) are explicit in their condemnation of suicide. For instance, Yama Smriti (600 BC) says that the bodies of those who die by suicide should be defiled. If a person survived an attempt, he/she should pay a fine and if the person killed him/herself, the sons or friends should pay the fine (Thakur, 1963). Although suicide was condemned in *The Dharmashastras*, there is also a chapter on allowed suicides. Scriptures, such as by Manu and Kautilya, were against suicide. These sentiments were echoed for ages in India. Even today, attempted suicide is a crime under the Indian Penal Code, although the neighbouring country of Sri Lanka has removed attempted suicide as a punishable offence. Assisting and abetting suicide is also a punishable offence in India.

In the USA, which is only part of Turtle Island (renamed by colonialists as North America), there are over 500 federally recognized tribes and each tribe has its own culture and traditions. Yet, despite the diversity, it would be safe to say that suicide is viewed as a taboo. The Native people of Turtle Island view life as a precious gift, which is to be cherished and protected. There is also the philosophy that to fully enjoy the "gift of life" one must live in balance in terms of the mental, physical, social and spiritual aspects of the whole person. When there is a person who is "out of balance" or "out of harmony", then negative events can happen, such as suicide.

Today there is a wide array of legal positions on suicide and attempted suicide. In the USA, completed suicide is not against the law in any state (Victoroff, 1983). However, there are some local variations and six states have current penalties for attempting suicide. Neither suicide nor attempted suicide are illegal at present in Japan. Throughout the history of Japan there has been no period when suicide was prohibited by law, except in the early eighteenth century, when a cluster of lover suicide pacts (Joshi) was triggered by Chikamatsu Monzaemon's dramas (Takahashi, 1997). In The Netherlands the principle that all punishment for crime ends with death was introduced in 1809 and was applied to suicide and attempted suicide. In the former Soviet Union, "suicide" was omitted from legal discussion because it was dictated that such a problem could not possibly exist in a socialistic society; yet, by the mid-1980s the problem was beginning to be acknowledged and addressed from a medical-legal viewpoint. Suicide and attempted suicide are not illegal in Australia. In South Africa, suicide is not a crime, although it is considered to be against public policy. There are also no laws against suicide in Cuba and Lithuania. Ireland was the last European country to decriminalize suicide, which it did in 1993 by the Criminal Law (Suicide) Act, where we read, "Suicide shall cease to be a crime". Thus it can be concluded that not only in the past but also in the present and probably in the future, there will be great diversity about the laws governing suicide and attempted suicide.

EUTHANASIA AND ASSISTED SUICIDE

The "right-to-die" concept is one of the most controversial and elusive legal and ethical issues facing suicidology around the world. The increased control that has been gained over biological life because of progress in medical treatment will force a confrontation with the subject (Diekstra, 1992). Before these perspectives are addressed, we need to clarify our terms, mainly because there is considerable confusion about the terms "euthanasia" and "assisted suicide". Euthanasia literally means an easy or good death. It refers to the practice of allowing a person to die with assistance, often by a medical doctor. Assisted suicide is not performed by another person; rather, the means are provided by which the person can end his/her own life. These distinctions are critical, especially if one looks at the diversity of views around the globe.

The Netherlands can be chosen to illustrate the right-to-die debate. Euthanasia in The Netherlands is relatively tolerated, probably more than in any other area of the world. Yet the Northern Territory Government of Australia had come even closer to legalizing assisted suicide and euthanasia in a way that would be much more overt than in The Netherlands. There have been numerous appeals and counter-appeals in the territory, although at this time both assisted suicide and euthanasia continue to be illegal.

For those familiar with the right-to-die debate, the Dutch case of Nico Speijer is important (Leenaars and Diekstra, 1997). Nico Speijer was The Netherlands's leading suicidologist; Dr Speijer completed assisted suicide, after suffering from incurable terminal illness. He did so after he wrote the rules and regulations for assisted death, entitled *Assisted Suicide: A Study of the Problems Related to Self-chosen Death* (Speijer and Diekstra, 1980). In this book, which was the first to address exclusively the issue of assisted death from ethical, legal and professional perspectives, the authors outlined a set of criteria for health care professionals who assist self-chosen death in cases of unbearable physical illness without reasonable prospects for improvement or for recovery of an acceptable quality of life (see Table 23.1).

The book initially received little attention, but the death of Speijer brought a drastic change in this respect. In fact, Speijer had followed the rules of conduct in the book for his own demise. Three months after the event, in December 1981, the Court of the City of Rotterdam convicted a female lay volunteer who had helped an elderly chronic terminally ill patient to die by feeding her, at her request, with a chocolate pudding in which barbiturates had been mixed. The court gave the volunteer a suspended prison sentence, stating that in providing assistance at the request of the deceased she had not (as she could not have, because of the simple fact that she was a volunteer) acted carefully, which was then operationalized by reference to the rules of conduct as formulated in *Assisted Suicide*. By implication, the court asserted that had the assistance been carried out in accordance with those rules, the volunteer may have gone unpunished. Since then, jurisprudence throughout the country has complied with the verdict of the Rotterdam Court. No health care professional who has been known to have assisted with death and who carefully observed the rules of conduct has been prosecuted or been put on trial. This is not to say that there are no problems in The Netherlands. Issues of reporting, of following the guidelines, and of consent have all been raised (van der Maas et al, 1992). There are questions such

Table 23.1 Criteria and rules of conduct for assisted suicide (Speijer and Diekstra, 1980)

1. Request made voluntarily and directly by actor
2. Actor *compos mentis* (mentally competent) at time of request
3. Wish to end life is longstanding
4. Presence of unbearable suffering (subjective)
5. No reasonable perspective of improvement (objective)
6. Remaining treatment alternatives uncertain/only palliative (offered but rejected)
7. Helper is acknowledged professional
8. Helper has used intercollegial consultation (1–6) (actor has been seen and examined by colleague(s))
9. Avoidance of preventable harm/damage to others
10. Decision-making process and steps taken documented for professional and legal evaluation

as: How is "unbearable suffering" defined? Does "unbearable suffering" refer to terminal illness, depression, etc? In 1991, H. Bosscher, a depressed, physically healthy 55 year-old female was assisted in her death by Dr Boudewijn Chabot because the depression was "unbearable". Dr Chabot was charged and found guilty of unlawful assisted suicide because he did not use intercollegial consultation, although the court left open the possibility that mental illness may be "unbearable suffering" (Burgess and Hawton, 1998). There are further questions. Does a patient have a right to refuse treatment? Is there a slippery slope?

Regardless of one's view, the developments in The Netherlands have sparked considerable attention and debate. One should, of course, be cautious about transposing the Dutch perspective to other cultures (Lester and Leenaars, 1996). Indeed, views in The Netherlands are themselves not uniform.

No legislation on euthanasia exists in China. Historically, at times of low production and lack of surplus products, people abandoned the old and sick when they moved to another habitat, as in almost all regions of the world historically. As late as in the seventh century, the famous Chinese monk named Xuan Zang (602–664 AD) witnessed a seeing-off ceremony, in which a person was drowned in the River Ganges because of poverty. The people on both sides of the river bid farewell to the euthanasic with drum and gong. In India, drownings occurred in the Holy Ganges because of religious beliefs. There is a place called Sangaman, where three rivers unite and the belief is that if one dies there one can escape the cycle of births and deaths. In India today, there are, however, no specific laws to deal with assisted suicide and euthanasia.

In Japan, assisted suicide and euthanasia are illegal under the penal code. There are nevertheless cases of assisted suicide and euthanasia, some of which are well known. The famous Yamanouchi case in 1960 is an example (Japanese Association for Dignified Death, 1990). In that case, a son killed his father, who was suffering from apoplexy, upon the latter's request by giving him milk containing pesticide. The Nagoya High Court's judgement on the Yamanouchi case in 1961 has often been cited. According to this judgement, euthanasia should be permitted under strict conditions that meet the six criteria that are listed in Table 23.2.

Table 23.2 Criteria for euthanasia (Japanese Association for Dignified Death, 1990)

1. The patient is suffering from incurable illness according to the most up-to-date medical knowledge and technology, and the death is impending in the near future
2. His or her agony is so severe that no one can bear to see him or her suffering
3. The purpose of terminating the patient's life is to palliate his or her agony
4. In the situation that the patient's consciousness is clear, he or she should state his or her wish clearly that his or her life should be terminated by someone else
5. The physician should terminate the patient's life. If someone else terminates the patient's life, there should be most reasonable circumstances for the act
6. The method of terminating the patient's life should be ethically acceptable (for example, the use of medical drugs instead of pesticides)

Any act should fulfil these six criteria to be considered as euthanasia, which can then be acquitted under Japan's penal code (in fact a vast majority of cases do not fully meet the criteria). In the Yamanouchi case, the defendant was judged not to have met criteria (5) and (6). He was found guilty of murder at the victim's request and sentenced to 1 year's imprisonment with 3 years' suspension of sentence.

In Russia, euthanasia is considered to be a medical issue, which means that there is no possibility that assisted suicide and euthanasia can be legalized. Therefore, both acts are prohibited by Russian law. Medical personnel are not allowed to assist in the death of a patient, whether active or passive, even at the patient's request. Yet, there have been strong supporters, notably the late Professor Sergey Dolsky, who was strongly in favour of "merciful" death. To date, however, a person who assists or prompts a patient's death in Russia is subject to criminal responsibility.

In Ireland, euthanasia and assisted suicide are illegal. In recent years, however, as in much of the rest of the world, these topics have been given a great deal of public airing. The celebrated case of Dr Paddy Leahy is well known. Dr Leahy had publicly admitted to euthanasia with no legal prosecution. More recently, being terminally ill himself, he promoted the idea of assisted suicide for the terminally ill. Yet, there is little support for Dr Leahy's ideas. The Medical Council of Ireland's *Guide to Ethical Conduct* (1994) explicitly states that euthanasia is professional misconduct.

In the USA, assisted suicide has received wide and varied attention from Jack Kevorkian's practice, advocating no debate (". . . all of these (issues) have been well debated in the past and there is nothing new to learn"; Kevorkian, 1988), to Derek Humphry's 1991 book, *Final Exit*, which reached the best-seller list in the *New York Times*, and to Herbert Hendin's (1997) extreme opposite perspective in *Seduced by Death*. In 1997 the US Supreme Court decided that there was no constitutional right for physician-assisted suicide (that is, the American Constitution did not address the issue), leaving the matter of legislating physician-assisted suicide to the individual state. Despite the debate, at the present time only Oregon has passed a law permitting physician-assisted suicide. Following passages of this law, between November 1997 and July 1998 there were eight doctor-assisted suicides in Oregon. However, several lawsuits have been placed to block the Oregon initiative and the federal government has expressed reservations.

Euthanasia is not often considered an issue at this time for the Native American population on Turtle Island. The most vulnerable time for suicide for Native people is youth, and most attention is directed to this phenomenon (EchoHawk, 1997). There are, of course, laws against causing death that have application to the issues of euthanasia and assisted suicide. The Zuni tribe of New Mexico, for example, have a tribal code regarding "Causing a Suicide". There are strong sanctions against such practices.

In Cuba there exists an article of the Penal Code, "The one who brings help or induces another to suicide, incurs a sanction of prevention of liberty for two to five years". Euthanasia and assisted suicide are forbidden in South Africa (although there is growing debate), Australia (except for a few months in the Northern Territory) and Lithuania. Despite the differences across regions, the debate about these issues will be essential in the future, especially as we move towards a global world community.

STANDARDS OF REASONABLE AND PRUDENT CARE

Care for the suicidal person should be reasonable and prudent. But what is "reasonable" and "prudent"? The yardstick is typically defined by the community, since there is no universal standard care. Most commentaries about standards emanate from the USA. The writings of Thomas Gutheil, one of the most prolific authors on this topic, himself an American, espouses the community-based perspective. He defines "community standard" as what any reasonable similarly qualified practitioners would have done (Gutheil, 1992; Gutheil et al, 1983). In some countries, such as the USA, external circumstances (e.g. available resources) may be taken into account. This would be equally true in countries like Lithuania, India, Cuba and so on, especially since these countries lack resources. However, in some countries, such as Australia, the lack of resources does not itself offer protection, if standards of care are not practised (Cantor and McDermott, 1994).

In Japan the standards of reasonable and prudent care are also set by the community. Ireland, The Netherlands, Turtle Island and South Africa also follow the rules of standards of care. In Cuba a similar yardstick is applied, yet there is less clarity of definition. In Russia the Ministry of Health acknowledged such a standard and in May of 1998 issued an act, "On specialized aid to citizens with crisis states and suicidal behaviour". The standards were based on the community practice of the Moscow Institute of Psychiatry, established in the beginning of the 1970s by Professor Aina Ambrumova. India and China follow a similar rule, though the overall lack of services is immense because of the large populations in these nations.

Lithuania provides an interesting point of observation because a reform in the health care system is in progress. In 1995, the Parliament of the Republic of Lithuania adopted the Law of Mental Health Care, creating mental health centres in municipalities. Special postgraduate training is offered to family physicians. Yet, there are few psychiatric care services for certain populations; for example, mental health care for children and teenagers is almost non-existent except in the largest cities. People who attempt suicide in Lithuania receive emergency care, in which only the patient's immediate physical condition is assessed and treated. Most attempters leave the hospital immediately, after the emergency care, except for those suffering from serious mental illnesses. Eight psychiatric hospitals provide psychiatric care, and qualified psychological and psychotherapeutic care are rare but developing in larger cities. In smaller communities, where twice as many suicides occur as in the cities, mental health care is lacking. The very first special crisis centres are just being established. Telephone crisis services are now available in all cities. The economic situation is still unstable and the reforms in the health service system are proceeding, but very slowly. Thus the standards of care are changing and what the community labels as standard care is evolving.

Standards of reasonable and prudent care in some countries or cultures are developing, some are changing, and some are well defined. In conclusion, the standards in *each* community continue to define what is reasonable and prudent care.

RESPONSIBILITY OF CARE

Suicide has been viewed in different ways historically and this continues to be so across the globe. As nations moved away from legislating suicide and suicide attempts as illegal and a mental health perspective was adopted (see Shneidman and Farberow, 1957), responsibility for care was placed with the health professional. Yet there is no universal perspective on responsibility. Litman (1988, 1994) and, more recently, Bongar (1991; Bongar and Greaney, 1994) have written extensively on the topic. Litman (1994), for example, offers the hospital setting as a prime example of care. Hospitals in all countries are the forefront situation for care of suicidal people. Litman asks, "How do we evaluate care?" Patients in hospitals have a right to receive "reasonable care"; yet, as Litman notes, the standards are unclear. Once more, the prevailing standard in the community should be our guide.

The responsibility for care in all nations or cultures is with the primary caregivers (e.g. doctors, psychiatrists, psychologists, nurses, social workers). Some regions of the world have set laws. In Japan, for example, according to Japan's Mental Health and Welfare Law, at least two psychiatrists with qualified mental health examiner's licenses should interview a patient, and if they agree that the patient is suffering from mental illness and is an imminent danger to others or self, then the patient should be admitted for treatment even if it is against the patient's wish (Takahashi, 1992). In less severe cases, if a psychiatrist recognizes a patient's imminent suicidal risk while treating him/her at an outpatient clinic, and evaluates that the patient needs hospitalization, the psychiatrist is responsible for explaining his/her evaluation to both the patient and the family and for referring the patient to a hospital. The psychiatrist is responsible until the patient is hospitalized safely. The responsibility of other service providers such as psychologists, social workers, and nurses in such situations remains obscure.

In other regions, such as Cuba, it is difficult to establish responsibility of care. Institutions, hospitals, specific services or professionals, at different levels of the community, are often responsible. Yet there seems to exist a belief in Cuba that when people kill themselves, only they are responsible for the death. In Russia, new legislation has been adopted on responsibility of care, such as, "The

Principles of the legislation of the Russian Federation on the health protection of citizens", adopted in 1993. There is also a new 1997 criminal code that deals partly with responsibility (e.g. failure to help a patient, improper treatment). However, these changes do not address responsibility as far as suicide risk is concerned. The person him/herself is central in responsibility on Turtle Island. Traditionally, after an individual has reached puberty, the main person responsible for his/her life is that person him/herself. Other people are not allowed to interfere with what an individual is experiencing, and unless that person requests help or communicates his/her needs in some way to another person, or a traditional healer, the chances are that the individual will be left alone.

Responsibility for care varies; yet, from a global view, there may be international guidelines that apply to everyone (see Cantor and McDermott, 1994). The United Nations Working Group on the Principles for the Protection of Persons with Mental Illness and for the Improvement of Mental Health Care (United Nations, 1991) has, for example, offered some principles. Its first principle on basic rights has as its second clause: "All persons with mental illness, or who are being treated as such persons, shall be treated with humanity and respect for the inherent dignity of the human person". Responsibility for care implies humanity and respect in care, otherwise it is not responsibility.

The United Nations' report describes standards of care as: "1. Every patient shall have the right to receive such health and social care as appropriate to his or her health needs . . ." and "2. Every patient shall be protected from harm, including unjustified medication, abuse by other patients, staff or others or other acts causing mental distress or physical discomfort". There may well be universal principles concerning responsibility of care.

FAILURE IN CARE

Once a person is taken into care, there are issues of failure of care. These issues vary from India, with its limited available services, to Lithuania, with its developing services, to the USA, with its extensive services. Gutheil (1992) and Bongar (1991; Bongar and Greaney, 1994) have written extensively on the topic, although their perspectives are limited to the USA and may not apply even to similar countries such as The Netherlands. Once again, it is the community that defines "failure". The most common failure issues identified in the literature to date (Robertson, 1988) are as follows:

1. Failure to predict or diagnose the suicide.
2. Failure to control, supervise or restrain.
3. Failure to conduct proper tests and evaluations of the patient to establish suicidal intent.
4. Failure to medicate properly.
5. Failure to observe the patient continuously or on a sufficiently frequent basis.
6. Failure to take an adequate history.

7. Inadequate supervision and failure to remove belts or other dangerous objects.
8. Failure to place the patient in a secure room.

Although various proposals have been advanced for the above failures, typically the results of civil law suits in the USA determine the final version of the standard. In *Bell vs. New York City Health and Hospital Corporation (1982)*, a psychiatrist was found liable for premature release of an inpatient who committed suicide because the psychiatrist's examination of the patient prior to release was judged to be inadequate. He failed, for example, to request previous treatment records or enquire about the patient's psychotic symptoms. Thus, he failed in the community's standards of care. In contrast, in *Dillman vs. Hellman (1973)*, the psychiatrist was cleared after a psychiatric inpatient jumped to her death when transferred to a less secure ward because the psychiatrist had based his decision on a well-documented and clear assessment. The court ruled that psychiatrists cannot ensure results or be held liable for honest errors of judgment. Negligence on the part of staff, however, provides clear grounds for liability, and is an issue beyond failure. For example, in *Wilson vs. State (1961)*, an attendant forgot to lock a laundry chute, and a psychiatric inpatient jumped to her death through it. The attendant was clearly negligent in his supervision. We shall address these issues in more detail in the liability and malpractice section below.

Failure in care is an issue in all nations. In Japan, the judiciary now has a consensus that even suicidal patients should be treated in an open atmosphere as long as the treating staff record the patient's condition in detail, evaluate suicidal risk repeatedly for changes in the clinical course, and frequently discuss risk–benefit analysis about the patient's condition and treatment. If these matters are considered but suicide occurs, the suicide is often regarded as unpredictable. Otherwise the treating staff are judged to have failed in providing proper patient care. In Russia, failure in care is rarely discussed or analysed publicly (e.g. in textbooks, or manuals for students). The issue is addressed by the following approach: a doctor is trained to cure properly and this is considered a guarantee against possible mistakes. In other nations with limited resources (e.g. India, Cuba) or developing resources (e.g. Lithuania), there is no consensus on these issues and things are even less clear. However, issues identified by Bongar and Greaney (1994), such as calculated risk taking, adequate protection measures, early release, failure to commit, abandonment, are likely to be confronted in the future, even if not now.

Calculated risk taking (see Maltsberger, 1994) is an essential element of care today, even in the USA with the recent move to limited "managed" care, but it should be calculated, and not flippantly or dictated by economic factors such as a patient's insurance coverage. Calculated risk must often be taken about hospitalization, discharge and so on, as hospitalization, especially if long-term, may promote regression (Cantor and McDermott, 1994). Adequate prevention means that one must take reasonable care to safeguard the patient's environment, especially in hospital settings. The issue of abandonment of patients is frequently discussed; in short, abandonment is not prudent behaviour. It is clear that there is a duty of care to a patient, and if for some reason or another one needs to transfer a patient, the therapist should take full responsibility for ensuring that the transition to another therapist is successful. In the USA, furthermore, it is regarded as failure in care to abandon a patient if his/her insurance fees run out. Failure to admit and premature discharge are some other issues relevant to failure in care.

LIABILITY AND MALPRACTICE

What constitutes wrong-doing? What is malpractice? When are mental health workers liable? Gutheil (1992) suggested that there are fundamentals of malpractice related to the following: the existing clinician–patient relationship; negligence or the breach of duty (although negligence itself does not necessarily equate with liability); the negligence results in specific danger or harm; and the fact that the clinician was negligent, resulting in the patient committing suicide, if the element of causation is determinable. Demonstrating causation is often difficult; the following metaphorical example, presented by Gutheil (1992), illuminates the issue well:

> Consider a camel with serious osteoporosis of the spine, whose back is laden with straw. A final piece of straw (the proverbial "last straw") is placed on the back, and the camel's back breaks. In utilizing a clinical analysis of the situation, the clinician would consider the pre-existing condition of the camel and its back, the burden posed by the pre-existing straw, and the final straw leading to the condition of clinical compensation.

The legal viewpoint, at least in the USA, focuses on the last straw, which is called the "proximate cause". The important question is a "but for", and we quote Gutheil again, "But for this last straw, the camel's back would not have been broken". In suicide, of course, the causal relationship is often more complicated; yet the metaphor still applies. The question is, did the failure in care (or the negligence) cause the suicide? The answer lies in the statement, "Dereliction of a duty directly causing dangers" (Gutheil, 1992). Of course, the concept of dereliction can be applied to in-hospital suicide, suicide after release, outpatient suicide, and, especially, misuse or non-use of medication, and so on.

Diverse malpractice and liability issues exist across the world, and even if they resemble those in the USA, as is the case in Australia, Ireland and The Netherlands, for example, there are differences between countries. For example, in the USA, negligence, as defined by the American Learned Hand rule of 1947, refers to failure to invest resources up to a level commensurate with anticipated saving in dangers (Gutheil et al, 1983). However, this differs from Australia's approach, regarding negligence as a breach of duty of care rather than being based on a cost–benefit analysis (Cantor and McDermott, 1994). Thus, even if laws appear to be the same, they are often based on markedly different foundations. Once more, caution is in order in extrapolating from one country or culture to another. There are variations, even within the USA. American laws cover people working with Native people in America; yet there are traditional tribal practices that may result in complexities in malpractice issues.

Most countries and cultures have laws against causing suicide. These issues were addressed to some extent earlier when euthanasia and assisted suicide were considered, but we will provide a few further examples here. In Cuba there are two groups of sanctions applying to medical and mental health workers. These sanctions are gathered in the Work Code and in a Judicial Decree. Negligence (affecting the life of a person) constitutes one of the most severely sanctioned behaviours. According to Judicial Decrees, any person "Acting with manifest negligence or indolence in the fulfillment of his/her work contents and orders, implying serious alteration of health services due to the production of heavy irreversible lesions or death to the patient" may be excluded from the National Health System. There are less severe sanctions for other behaviours, such as "the unfulfillment of medical indications or the delegation of technical function to unauthorized personnel" or "the unfulfillment of the obligation established for the performance of his/her function, or of the internal disposition of the center". In such cases the person may be moved temporarily or indefinitely from his/her place of work. However, in many cases it is difficult to establish responsibility and there is a belief in Cuba that when a suicidal person dies, only he/she is responsible for the death. Similar principles apply in most regions. In Russia, for example, a doctor is assumed not to be responsible because his/her training is regarded as a guarantee of competent and prudent behaviour. In Japan, although increasing attention has been paid to malpractice suits regarding suicides by patients, the number of malpractice suits because of suicide are still far lower than those of malpractice suits for improper treatments or operations for physical illnesses.

Let us return, in conclusion, to the advice of Gutheil (1992), as it may be applicable globally to some degree. He suggests that the approach to liability prevention involves responsible and prudent assessment, responsible and prudent intervention, durable documentation and consultation. Regardless of one's culture or nation, maintaining a reasonable standard of care prevails, although the standard should be defined by each community.

CONCLUSION

Ethical and legal issues surrounding suicide are complex. To present only one view to an international audience would be myopic, whether discussing euthanasia and assisted suicide from The Netherlands or discussing reasonable and prudent care from the USA, and so forth. The legal positions on suicide, euthanasia and assisted suicide, as well as applications for assisting death, vary considerably worldwide. It is a myth that there is a uniform legal position on euthanasia and assisted suicide. There is, however, a uniform position on murder. For example, on March 26 1999, Jack Kevorkian was found guilty of homicide in the death of Thomas Youk, a 52-year old male with Lou Gehrig's disease. Kevorkian was also found guilty of illegally delivering a controlled substance. As stated before (Leenaars and Diekstra, 1997), these issues must proceed with research and debate.

No one standard of care applies in all countries. The issues are multitudinous and include the following: standards of reasonable and prudent care, responsibility for care, failure in care, liability and malpractice. Legal and ethical standards are defined according, first, to the standards of community practices and, second, to the resources available and hence what can reasonably be expected. Finally, we do not wish to suggest that we have presented all the global perspectives, or even represented all views within our communities. Yet, we hope that we have cast a wider net over some of the ethical and legal issues facing suicidology today. We have omitted some topics, for example failure to diagnose properly, means restriction, and postvention. We have not presented the diversity of cases that confront clinicians in the application of the ethical and legal issues that have been discussed (Burgess and Hawton, 1998). In fact, the limitations of this chapter reflect the need for ongoing discussion of these complex issues at a global level.

REFERENCES

Bongar, B. (1991) The Suicidal Patient: Clinical and Legal Standards of Care. Washington, DC: American Psychological Association.

Bongar, B. and Greaney, S. (1994) Essential clinical and legal issues when working with the suicidal patient. In A. Leenaars, J. Maltsberger and R. Neimeyer (Eds), Treatment of Suicidal People. Washington, DC: Taylor & Francis.

Burgess, S. and Hawton, K. (1998) Suicide, euthanasia, and the psychiatrist. Philosophy, Psychiatry and Psychology, 5: 113–126.

Cantor, C. and McDermott, P. (1994) Suicide litigation: from legal to clinical wisdom. Australia and New Zealand Journal of Psychiatry, 28: 431–437.

Diekstra, R. (1992) Suicide and euthanasia. Italian Journal of Suicidology, 2: 71–78.

EchoHawk, M. (1997) Suicide: the scourge of Native American people. In A. Leenaars, R. Maris, and Y. Takahashi (Eds), Suicide: Individual, Cultural, International Perspectives. New York: Guilford.

Gutheil, T. (1992) Suicide and suit: liability after self-destruction. In D. Jacobs (Ed.), Suicide and Clinical Practice. Washington, DC: American Psychiatric Press.

Gutheil, T., Bursztajn, H., Hamm, R. and Brodsky, A. (1983) Subjective data and suicide assessment in light of recent legal developments. Part 1: Malpractice prevention and the use of subjective data. International Journal of Law and Psychiatry, 6: 317–329.

Hendin, H. (1997) Seduced by Death: Doctors, Patients and the Dutch Cure. New York: Norton.

Humphry, D. (1991) Final Exit. Eugene, OR: Hemlock Society.

Japanese Association for Dignified Death (Eds.) (1990) Dignified Death. Tokyo: Kodonsea.

Kevorkian, J. (1988) The least fearsome taboo: medical aspects of planned death. Medicine & Law, 7: 1–14.

Leenaars, A. and Diekstra, R. (1997) The will to die: an international perspective. In

A. Botsis, C. Soldatos and C. Stefanis (Eds), Suicide: Biopsychosocial Approaches. Amsterdam: Elsevier Science.

Lester, D. and Leenaars, A. (1996) The ethics of suicide and suicide prevention. Death Studies, 20: 162–184.

Litman, R. (1988) Psychological autopsies, mental illness and intention in suicide. In J. Nolan (Ed.), The Suicide Case: Investigation and Trial of Insurance Claims. Chicago, IL: American Bar Association.

Litman, R. (1994) Responsibility and liability for suicide. In E. Shneidman, N. Farberow and R. Litman (Eds), The Psychology of Suicide. Northvale, NJ: Aronson.

Maltsberger, J. (1994) Calculated risk-taking in the treatment of suicidal patients: ethical and legal problems. In A. Leenaars, J. Maltsberger and R. Neimeyer (Eds), Treatment of Suicidal People. Washington, DC: Taylor & Francis.

Robertson, J. (1988) Psychiatric Malpractice. New York: Wiley.

Shneidman, E. and Farberow, N. (Eds) (1957) Clues to suicide. New York: McGraw-Hill.

Speijer, N. and Diekstra, R. (1980) Assisted suicide: A Study of the Problems Related to Self-chosen Death. Deventer: van Loghum Slaterus.

Takahashi, Y. (1992) Clinical Evaluation of Suicide Risk and Crisis Intervention. Tokyo: Kongo-Shuppan.

Takahashi, Y. (1997) Psychology of Suicide. Tokyo: Kodansha.

Thakur, U. (1963) History of Suicide in India. Munshi: Ram Manohar Lal.

The Medical Council of Ireland (1994) Guide to Ethical Conduct. Cork: Medical Council of Ireland.

United Nations, (1991) Human Rights and Scientific and Technological Developments. Report of the working group on the principles for the protection of persons with mental illness and for the improvement of mental health care. Resolution 98B. New York: United Nations.

van der Maas, P., Van Delden, J. and Pijnenborg, L. (1992) Euthanasia and Other Medical Decisions Concerning End of Life. Amsterdam: Elsevier Science.

Victoroff, V. (1983) The Suicidal Patient. Oradell, NJ: Medical Economics Books.

Chapter 24

Suicide and Violence

Matthew K. Nock
Department of Psychology, Yale University, New Haven, CT, USA
and
Peter M. Marzuk
Weill Medical College of Cornell University and New York Presbyterian Hospital, New York, USA

Abstract

Suicidal and violent behaviours are major mental health problems around the world. These phenomena have been studied separately for decades, and have long been thought to be mutually exclusive. In recent years, however, researchers have reported similarities among individuals who display suicidal and violent behaviour, and have reported cases in which both behaviours are observed in the same person. In this chapter we briefly discuss social, psychiatric and neurobiological factors that may contribute to the link between suicide and violence. We propose that suicide and violence do not have an inverse relationship, but are instead overlapping endpoints on a continuum of aggressive behaviour. We also explore different clinical phenomena that provide evidence for such a link and inform clinicians and researchers of settings and circumstances in which an individual who is both suicidal and violent may be encountered. These include suicidal psychiatric patients who display violent behaviour; jail and prison suicide; murder–suicide; and suicide pacts—in which a person who is suicidal typically coerces another person (or persons) into consenting to be killed. The epidemiology, phenomenology and aetiology of these phenomena, as well as clinical management and prevention, are discussed.

INTRODUCTION

The relationship between suicide and violence has puzzled scholars for many years. Nearly a century ago, Freud postulated that suicide is an expression of anger toward a love object that the individual turns back on himself (Freud, 1915). Menninger (1938) later described suicide as the gratification of self-

The International Handbook of Suicide and Attempted Suicide. Edited by K. Hawton and K. van Heeringen.

destructive tendencies, which include “a wish to kill, a wish to be killed, and a wish to die”.

In later years, suicide and homicide were thought to have an inverse relationship. For example, Henry and Short (1954) proposed that homicide was the response of the lower social class to “external constraints” placed on them, while suicide was thought to be the upper social class’s self-blaming reaction to its frustrations. However, evidence for this inverse socio-economic relationship within countries is lacking. Although subsequent studies have shown that homicide is more prevalent in lower socio-economic groups (Smith and Parker, 1980), suicide is seen in all socio-economic groups and seems to be more directly related to loss of social status and downward mobility (Breed, 1963; Maris, 1975). In addition, some countries, such as the USA, have a high rate of both suicide and homicide. In other countries, such as Norway or Ireland, the rate of both suicide and homicide are quite low (van Praag et al, 1990).

Although suicide and violence have each been studied as independent behaviours by psychiatric researchers for decades, the two are rarely considered to be linked. Only recently have researchers and clinicians come to view these behaviours as overlapping phenomena. Of course, most suicidal individuals will never be violent and most violent individuals will never be suicidal. However, studies of psychiatric and forensic populations have reported that nearly 30% of those who are violent have a history of self-destructive behaviour, and 10–20% of those who are suicidal have a history of violence (van Praag et al, 1990).

THE LINK BETWEEN SUICIDE AND VIOLENCE

Suicide and violence are both multidetermined acts that are influenced by environmental factors, psychiatric diagnosis and biological predispositions. Some environmental factors have been shown to underlie both behaviours, including the early loss of one’s parents, violence in the home (Botsis et al, 1995), a deviant family environment (Plutchik, 1995), unemployment (Platt, 1984), overcrowding (Cox et al, 1984), the accessibility of lethal means, and the availability of alcohol and other drugs (Fagan, 1993; Hendin, 1995).

It is well known that 90–95% of those who commit suicide have a diagnosable psychiatric illness at the time of their death (Robins et al, 1959; Barraclough et al, 1974; Rich et al, 1986). In recent years, a number of studies have also offered convincing evidence linking psychiatric illness and violent behaviour (Swanson et al, 1990; Hodgins, 1992; Link et al, 1992; Hodgins et al, 1996; Eronen et al, 1996). Thus, it is possible that suicide and violence are often observed in the same individual because they are shared features of an underlying psychiatric illness.

The psychiatric illnesses most often associated with increased suicidal behaviour are mood disorders, alcohol and substance abuse, schizophrenia and personality disorders—particularly antisocial personality disorder and borderline personality disorder (all are discussed in detail in Part I of this book). The same diagnoses have been linked to violent behaviour. The psychiatric illness most commonly observed in those who exhibit violent behaviour is alcohol and substance abuse (Hodgins, 1992; Hodgins et al, 1996; Steadman et al, 1998). Steadman et al (1998) reported that alcohol and drug abuse significantly raised the prevalence of violence in both patient and community samples. Another study found that risks of suicide and violence were significantly and positively correlated in a sample of alcoholic inpatients, demonstrating an overlap of the two behaviours in such a population (Greenwald et al, 1994). Psychotic disorders such as schizophrenia have also been associated with increased risk of violence (Swanson et al, 1990; Link et al, 1992; Eronen et al, 1996). One study (Link et al, 1992) reported that the difference in rates of violence between those with mental illness and never-treated community residents is largely explained by the level of psychotic symptoms present, not by the label of "mental patient". Personality disorders, particularly antisocial and borderline personality disorders, are also commonly diagnosed in those who are violent (Eronen et al, 1996; Volavka, 1995). In fact, anger, aggressiveness and impulsiveness are among the criteria used for diagnosing such disorders (DSM-IV; American Psychiatric Association, 1994). Mood disorders have also been reported in violent individuals (Rosenbaum and Bennet, 1986; Malmquist, 1995). The Epidemiological Catchment Area survey reported that the prevalence of mood disorders was approximately three times higher among the violent respondents than the non-violent respondents (Swanson et al, 1990).

The "common thread" underlying violence and suicide in all of the aforementioned disorders appears to be symptoms of increased impulsiveness, affective lability, disinhibition, and problems with reasoning and decision-making. These symptoms could lead to an overall increase in aggressiveness, which is common in both suicidal and violent behaviour. It is probably this increased aggressiveness, rather than the diagnostic label itself, that is important in the prediction of suicide and violence (Marzuk, in press).

Violent and suicidal behaviour may also be linked through an underlying biological or genetic predisposition. The neurobiology of suicide is discussed in detail by Träskman-Bendz and Mann in Chapter 4. The most impressive finding to date in this area is the association between low cerebrospinal fluid (CSF) levels of the neurotransmitter serotonin and impulsive, aggressive behaviour. Åsberg and colleagues (1976), the first to report this link, found low CSF levels of the serotonin metabolite 5-hydroxyindoleacetic acid (5-HIAA) in depressed suicide attempters, compared with depressed non-attempters and normal controls. It was later shown that CSF 5-HIAA was lower in impulsive suicide attempters than in suicide attempters who had planned the act (Träskman et al, 1981). This negative correlation between serotonin levels and violent behaviour led investigators to discover that low CSF 5-HIAA levels are also present in those who commit other impulsive, aggressive acts, such as arson (Virkkunen et al, 1987), unpremeditated homicide (Linnoila et al, 1983), murder–suicide (Lidberg et al, 1992), cruelty towards animals (Kruesi, 1989) and aggressive behaviour in children (Kruesi et al, 1992).

Violence and Suicide in Psychiatric Populations

Epidemiology, Phenomenology and Aetiology

Much of the evidence for the link between suicide and violence has come from observing violent behaviour in people who are mentally ill, and in some cases suicidal, and from observing suicidal behaviour among violent criminals who have been arrested (discussed in the next section). These studies are limited in scope because individuals have already been labelled as "mentally ill" or "criminal" and do not represent community-based samples. Moreover, whether one is classified as "mentally ill" vs. "criminal" is often simply a product of what system one encounters first, the psychiatric or the legal. Nonetheless, these studies provide useful data from a wide variety of patient settings and demonstrate the overlap between suicide and violence.

In a comprehensive study of 9,365 patients admitted to public hospitals in New York, Tardiff and Sweillam (1980a) found that 15.1% of male patients who displayed assaultive behaviour also had a history of suicidal behaviour, compared with only 8.7% of male patients without assaultive behaviour. Among females, 18.4% of the assaultive patients had a history of suicidal behaviour, compared with 15.2% of those without assaultive behaviour—a non-significant difference. In another study, Tardiff and Sweillam (1980b) examined factors related to the risk of assaultive behaviour in suicidal patients. They found that 14% of the suicidal males and 7% of the suicidal females admitted to psychiatric hospitals during the study period were assaultive just prior to admission. Interestingly, there was no difference between assaultive and non-assaultive suicidal patients in regard to frequency of depressive symptoms. However, for both sexes, assaultive suicidal patients were more likely to have delusions, hallucinations, feelings of suspicion or persecution, as well as anger, belligerence, agitation and antisocial behaviour. In a similar study, Plutchik and colleagues (1986) reported that in a sample of psychiatric inpatients, 40% reported a history of suicidal behaviour, 42% had a history of violent behaviour, and 23% of the total sample reported a history of both behaviours. In an emergency room setting, Skodol and Karasu (1978) reported that 17% of all patients over a 2-week period had suicidal tendencies without "other-directed aggression", and 17% were outwardly violent. Of those who were violent, almost 30% displayed suicidal tendencies in addition to their violent behaviour.

Weissman and colleagues (1973) compared a group of 29 acutely depressed female outpatients with matched suicide attempters who came into a hospital emergency room, and found that overt hostility, even after controlling for severity of depression, was an important distinguishing characteristic of the suicide attempters.

Clinical Management and Prevention

Perhaps most importantly, the clinician should consider violent patients to be potentially suicidal and suicidal patients to be potentially violent. The management of suicidal inpatients has been discussed elsewhere in this book (Chapters 29, 32 and 35). A similar set of procedures should be followed when managing the care of violent psychiatric patients (see Tardiff, 1996). All patients should be assessed for violence risk upon admission. The assessment of violence risk is analogous to that for suicide, and should include an exploration of past violence (time of onset, frequency, magnitude and target) and current violent ideation (severity, intensity, frequency, presence of specific plan, specific target and intent to injure). The clinician should also assess for presence of current mental disorder, current alcohol or substance use, and access to lethal means. Those not at immediate risk of violent behaviour, but potentially violent during hospitalization, should be continuously observed, allowing staff to quickly intervene should a violent situation occur. Many patients who display violent behaviour are amenable to verbal intervention, while others, such as those with functional psychosis or organic mental disorder, are difficult to influence through verbal means. If a patient puts himself or others in "imminent" danger, and is not responsive to verbal intervention, hospital staff should consider the use of more restrictive methods for controlling violent behaviour, such as emergency medication to treat the underlying disorder and sedation of the patient, or seclusion and restraint to ensure the safety of the patients and hospital staff (Tardiff, 1996).

Jail and Prison Suicide

Epidemiology, Phenomenology and Aetiology

For the purposes of both devising improved suicide prevention strategies and understanding better the link between suicide and violence, some investigators have studied suicide in *police lock-ups* (<24-hour facilities), *jails* (for persons awaiting trial or sentenced to <1 year's imprisonment), and *prisons* (for those sentenced to >1 year's imprisonment). The rates of suicide and the characteristics of those inmates who are suicidal vary, depending on the type of correctional facility (Lester and Danto, 1993).

Suicide is the leading cause of death in US jails, with a rate approximately nine times greater than that of the general US population (Hayes and Kajdan, 1981; Hayes and Rowan, 1988). Moreover, the number of actual suicides in US jails is probably greatly understated (Hayes and Kajdan, 1981; Hardyman, 1983).

The only two national studies in the USA to date, conducted by the National Center for Institutions and Alternatives (NCIA), reported that most of those who commit suicide in police lock-ups and jails are single (52–54%), white (67–72%), males (94–96%), aged 18–27 years (43–54%), who commit suicide by hanging (94–97%), while in isolation (67–68%) within the first 24 hours of incarceration (51–52%); many (27–29%) within the first 3 hours (Hayes and Kajdan, 1981; Hayes and Rowan, 1988). Those who commit suicide within the first 24 hours of confinement tend to be charged with minor, non-violent, alcohol and/or drug-related offences (Danto, 1989; Hayes and Kajdan, 1981; Hayes and Rowan, 1988). Many of these victims were acutely intoxicated and may have had disinhibited behaviour, impaired decision-making abilities, or increased emotional lability.

Although prison suicide has been less studied than jail suicide, suicide is also the leading cause of death among those in prisons in a number of countries (Topp, 1979; Hayes, 1983; Dooley, 1990; Joukamaa, 1997), with a rate that is several times higher than demographically similar general population rates (Joukamaa, 1997; Kerkhof and Bernasco, 1990; Burtch, 1979; Hoff, 1973). Most longer-term jail inmates and prisoners who commit suicide have been charged with violent crimes against others, not minor drug or alcohol offences (Du Rand et al, 1995; Marcus and Alcabes, 1993; Esparza, 1973; Frost and Hanzlick, 1988; Salive et al, 1989). In a study of all suicides in a large urban jail in the USA during 1967–1992, Du Rand and colleagues (1995) reported that inmates charged with murder or manslaughter comprised 39% of all suicides and only 2% of the jail population, and were thus 19 times more likely to commit suicide than were inmates charged with other offences. Similarly, in a study of 44 jail and prison suicides and 198 attempted suicides in The Netherlands during 1973–1984, Kerkhof and Bernasco (1990) found that 40% of all suicide victims and 18% of suicide attempters had been charged with murder/manslaughter, compared with only 7% and 4% of controls, respectively. Length of sentence may have been a confounding variable, since 61% of all suicides and 37% of attempters had been given a sentence of 1 year or more (compared with 12% and 12% of controls). Nevertheless, being charged with murder/manslaughter seems to be an important risk factor for suicide.

The reason for high rates of suicide in jail and prison inmates is largely unknown. However, it is likely that many jail inmates have psychiatric illnesses. Teplin (1990) compared the rate of mental disorders in a random sample of 728 male, urban, jail detainees in one county in the USA with that obtained from the five-city Epidemiologic Catchment Area Program, and found that the prevalence of severe mental disorders (major depressive episode, manic episode, and schizophrenia) in jails is two to three times higher than in the general population. The observed ratio of *current* jail rates of mental illness to current population rates was substantially higher than the comparable ratio of *lifetime* rates, suggesting that the arrests occurred during a period of acute mental illness. Furthermore, Novick and Remmlinger (1978) reported that over 75% of correctional facility inmates who committed suicide in New York City during 1971–1976 had psychiatric problems. Marcus and Alcabes (1993) reported that 46% of New York City jail inmates who completed suicide had a history of previous inpatient or outpatient psychiatric care, and 63% had a history of suicidality, ranging from threats to gestures to previous attempts. Seventy-three percent of suicide completers in that sample had been referred for mental health evaluations in the jail, 91% of whom had been seen by mental health staff in the jail. In a study of all prison suicides in Finland during 1969–1992, Joukamaa (1997) reported that more than half of prison suicide victims had a "psychiatric disturbance", and half of all suicides had sought help from prison health services for their psychiatric problem within 1 week of their suicide. Kerkhof and Bernasco (1990) also reported that half of the jail and prison suicide victims in their Dutch study had gone to health services within the week before their deaths.

Despite Teplin's (1990) finding of a higher prevalence of severe mental disorders in inmates than in the general population, the percentage of jail and prison suicide victims with a mental illness has been lower than the percentage of suicide victims with a mental illness in psychological autopsy studies in the general population. One explanation is ascertainment bias. Had jail and prison studies of suicide screened adequately for mental illness, rates of mental illness among inmate suicides might have been similar to rates found in suicide victims in the general population. Another possibility is that stressful events or environmental factors assume relatively more importance than psychiatric diagnosis *per se* in a forensic population compared to a community sample. Among these factors are the humiliation, guilt and shame associated with being arrested, and the isolation, interpersonal violence, hopelessness and entrapment experienced in confinement. Kerkhof and Bernasco (1990) interviewed 25 inmates who had made non-lethal suicide attempts and found that the main stressors that precipitated the attempts were problems with relatives, staff, other inmates, trial-related matters or substance abuse. Overcrowding has also been associated with an increased suicide rate in some facilities (Cox et al, 1984; Innes, 1987).

Clinical Management and Prevention

A number of authors have suggested strategies for the clinical management of potentially suicidal jail and prison inmates (Smialek and Spitz, 1978; Hayes, 1983; Jordan et al, 1987; Kerkhof and Bernasco, 1990; Marcus and Alcabes, 1993; Lester and Danto, 1993; Farmer et al, 1996; Joukamaa, 1997; Hayes, 1997). Most have focused on the increased recognition and treatment of mental illness and on greater efforts towards physical prevention of suicide attempts. Some suggested strategies for the prevention of jail and prison suicides are listed in Table 24.1.

Although many inmates may feign suicidal ideation and make low-lethality attempts in order to be removed from their cells and placed in more desirable sur-

Table 24.1 Suggested strategies for the prevention of jail and prison suicides

- Immediate screening of all new inmates for suicidality, mental illness, and alcohol and drug use
- Close observation, including the installation of video surveillance cameras, in holding cells
- Removal of lethal means (e.g. belts, laces, sharp objects, etc.)
- Installation of plexiglass covers over bars of holding cells to prevent hangings
- Removal of all other structures (e.g. hooks, pipes) which might be used for hanging
- Housing with other cell mates/avoidance of solitary cells
- Training of all staff to recognize signs of suicidality, mental illness, and drug and alcohol abuse
- Continued observation and assessment of high-risk inmates

roundings, Haycock (1989) reported that the presence of manipulation in suicide attempters provides no guide to the medical lethality of subsequent suicidal behaviour. Therefore, even though many attempters may not have death as their primary goal, all attempts should be treated seriously and receive proper medical attention. Many facilities that have adopted programmes to improve suicide prevention efforts have reduced the incidence of both completed and attempted suicide in their settings (Lester and Danto, 1993; Hayes, 1997; Farmer et al, 1996).

Murder–Suicide

Epidemiology, Phenomenology, and Aetiology

Perhaps the most extreme manifestation of the link between violent and suicidal behaviours is murder–suicide, a dramatic phenomenon in which an individual kills one or more persons, and shortly thereafter kills himself. Murder–suicide provides the unique opportunity to observe violent and suicidal behaviour in one individual nearly simultaneously. Nock and Marzuk (1999) provide a comprehensive review of the epidemiology, phenomenology, and aetiology of murder–suicide elsewhere; however, some of the key issues related to this phenomenon are summarized below. Marzuk and colleagues (1992) defined murder–suicide as an event in which, "on the basis of medical examiner review, a person has committed a homicide and subsequently commits suicide within one week of the homicide" (p. 3179). The defining aspect is the intrinsic linkage of the homicide and the suicide (Nock and Marzuk, 1999). If more than 1 week has elapsed between acts, or if both behaviours are not unitary in the motivation of the perpetrator (as is often the case in jail and prison suicide, in which a murderer often commits suicide after an extended period of time), then they should be considered separate events and not murder–suicides.

Although we will discuss only the phenomenon known as murder–suicide, the reader should be aware that similar phenomena exist in various cultures, such as *amok* in Malaysia, *wihtiko psychosis* among the Cree Indians, *jumping Frenchman* in Canada, and *imu* in Japan (Cooper, 1934). Amok, perhaps the most well-known variation of murder–suicide, is "an acute outburst of unrestrained violence associated with homicidal attacks, preceded by a period of brooding, and ending with exhaustion and amnesia" (Yap, 1951). These impulsive outbursts typically end when the perpetrator is either safely captured and imprisoned, is killed by others while attempting to stop him, or commits suicide.

Most countries record annual statistics for homicide and suicide separately; none to our knowledge have a national surveillance system for tracking murder–suicides. Thus, the annual incidence of these events is difficult to determine. In a review of 17 studies from 10 nations, Coid (1983) concluded that murder–suicide occurred at a remarkably constant rate, averaging 0.20–0.30 per 100,000, although the countries studied showed marked variation in their overall simple homicide and simple suicide rates (Coid, 1983). Thus, murder–suicide as a percentage of all homicides and suicides differs markedly among countries.

For example, Philadelphia, Pennsylvania, USA, had an extremely high homicide rate during 1948–1952 and Denmark had a remarkably low homicide rate during 1958–1960; however, both had virtually identical murder–suicide rates (0.21 and 0.22 per 100,000, respectively). During this period, only 3.6% of all murderers in Philadelphia subsequently committed suicide, whereas 42% of those in Denmark who committed murder later committed suicide (Wolfgang, 1958; West, 1967). According to this rate, it is likely that roughly 1.5% of all suicides and 5% of all homicides in the USA occur in the context of murder–suicide.

In a review of studies of murder–suicide in the USA, Marzuk and colleagues (1992) reported that the average age of perpetrators was 39.6 years; that 93–97% of perpetrators were male; 50–86% were white; and over 85% of all victims were female. Furthermore, perpetrators and victims were usually of the same race, and almost 90% of all murder–suicide incidents involved only one victim. They also found that the principal method of both homicide and suicide was firearms, which were used in 80–94% of all cases. The demographic characteristics of perpetrators and victims are different in other countries. For example, in the USA, parent–child murder–suicides account for only 6–16% of all murder–suicide incidents (Palmer and Humphrey, 1980; Allen, 1983; Hanzlick and Koponen, 1994), whereas they account for 40% of murder–suicides in Sweden (Lindqvist, 1986), 48% in England (West, 1967), and 70% in Japan (Sakuta, 1995).

Although demographics differ across nations, most murder–suicides involve family members. Marzuk and colleagues (1992) proposed a classification system that categorizes murder–suicide by type of victim–offender relationship and by class of common precipitants or motives (see Table 24.2).

Murder–suicide between spouses or lovers represents one-half to three-quarters of all murder–suicides in the USA (Dorpat, 1966; Palmer and Humphrey, 1980; Allen, 1983; Currens et al, 1991). Marzuk and colleagues (1992) termed this the spousal–amorous jealousy type. It is most frequently the result of a chaotic, abusive relationship marked by amorous jealousy, which is also referred to in the literature as psychotic or morbid jealousy (Shepherd, 1961; Selkin, 1976; Berman, 1979). The suspected infidelity may be real or imagined and thus ranges from ruminative or obsessional to psychotic (Nock and Marzuk, 1999). The murder–suicide typically occurs after a prolonged, bitter conflict, marked by verbal abuse and sublethal violence (Dorpat, 1966; Berman, 1979; Allen, 1983). The event is often precipitated by the victim's attempt to separate from her spouse or lover.

In another type, termed spousal–declining health by Marzuk and colleagues (1992), the typical perpetrator is an elderly man who either has an ailing spouse or is medically ill himself, who kills his partner and then commits suicide (West, 1967; Currens et al, 1991; Fishbain et al, 1989). The murder–suicide is typically precipitated by an increased burden on the caretaker (Copeland, 1985), such as financial problems or worsening medical or psychiatric conditions in his spouse or himself. Murder–suicide of this type seems to fit the "extended suicide" model (Berman, 1979; Palermo, 1994), in which the primary motive for murder is the "altruistic" desire to "protect" the victim from life without the caretaker. Such events are similar in many ways to suicide pacts, which are described below.

Filicide–suicide involves the killing of one's child followed by suicide. Between

Table 24.2 Proposed clinical classification of murder–suicide based on victim–offender relationship (type) and principal motive or precipitant (class)

Type of relationship

I. Spousal or Consortial[a]
   Perpetrator
   1. Spouse
   2. Consort

   Type of Homicide
   i. Uxoncidal (spouse-killing)
   ii. Consortial (murder of lover)

II. Familial[b]
   Perpetrator
   1. Mother
   2. Father
   3. Child (under 16 years)
   4. Other adult family member (over 16 years)

   Type of Homicide
   i. Neonaticide (child <24 hours)
   ii. Infanticide (child >1 day, <1 year)
   iii. Pedicide (child 1–16 years)
   iv. Adult family member (>16 years)

III. Extrafamilial[c]

Class

A. Amorous jealousy
B. "Mercy killing" (because of declining health of victim or offender)
C. "Altruistic or extended suicides" (includes salvation fantasies of rescue and escape from problems)
D. Family financial or social stressors
E. Retaliation
F. Other
G. Unspecified

Note: Classification of murder–suicides is specified by type (Roman numeral) with subtype of perpetrator (number) and subtype of homicide (lower case Roman numeral), as well as by letters to denote principal motives or precipitants. This classification can include mixed types of victims and multiple motives of offenders. Examples using the typology, including a "mixed type", are as follows: (1) A husband who killed his wife out of suspicions of infidelity would be coded type I(1)i-A. (2) A mother who killed her 2-year-old son (maternal filicide) to "rescue" him from a perceived ruinous world would be coded type II(1)iii-C. (3) An adult who kills his adult brother for unknown motives would be coded type II(4)iv-G. (4) A man who kills his wife and 6-year-old son and 2-year-old daughter because he suspects his wife of infidelity and is under severe financial pressures represents a mixed category and would be coded type I(1)i/II(2)ii,iii/A,D.

[a] Principal victim–offender relationship is spouse or lover.

[b] Principal victim–offender relationship is consanguineal (blood relative) or other familial, non-marital relationship.

[c] Principal victim–offender relationship is not marital, consortial, or familial and includes friends, acquaintances and strangers.

16% and 29% of mothers and 40–60% of fathers who kill their children subsequently commit suicide (Adelson, 1991; Myers, 1970; Rodenberg, 1971; Wilkey et al, 1982; d'Orbán, 1979). In most cases the child is between 1 and 16 years of age. Maternal perpetrators of filicide–suicide tend to use less violent methods to kill their children, such as drowning, gassing or suffocating them, and less frequently, beating and defenestration. Paternal perpetrators, however, use more violent methods, such as beating, stabbing, kicking and firearms (Adelson, 1991; Myers, 1970; Resnick, 1969; Rodenberg, 1971; Marks and Kumar, 1995). Filicide–suicide in the first 6 months of a child's life is usually associated with post-partum depression and psychosis in the maternal perpetrator (Resnick, 1969; Marks and Lovestone, 1995). Schizophrenia has also been associated with filicide–suicide and often involves delusions of salvation (West, 1967; Resnick, 1969; Browne and Palmer, 1975). Case studies of mothers who committed filicide–suicide described motives that were often referred to as "altruistic"—"there would be no-one to care for the children"; and delusional—"to save them from a violent world" (Resnick, 1969; d'Orban, 1979).

Familicide–suicide occurs when one member of the family kills all other members of the household, including spouse, children, parents, other relatives and even pets, and subsequently commits suicide. It is much less common than either spousal type or filicide–suicide, but seems to combine elements of all of them. This type of perpetrator closely resembles what Dietz called the "family annihilator", who is typically "the senior man of the house who is depressed, paranoid, intoxicated, or a combination of the three" (Dietz, 1986). Notes left by familicide–suicide perpetrators describe themselves as "altruistically" delivering their family from continued hardships or from shame and humiliation (Selkin, 1976; Daly and Wilson, 1988). There is often a history of depression in the perpetrator, as well as health problems with a family member, financial problems, and marital difficulties. Some familicide–suicides have a phenomenological analogue in the suicide pact phenomenon, which is described below.

It is rare that a murder–suicide victim is unknown or even unrelated to the perpetrator. In *extrafamilial murder–suicide*, perpetrators often kill employees, physicians, police or government workers before committing suicide. The perpetrators resemble Dietz's "pseudocommando" type, who are "preoccupied by firearms and commit their raids after long deliberation" (Deitz, 1986). The event is often precipitated by a perceived rejection or humiliation, and the violence is seen as a form of vindication from those who have "wronged" them, as well as anyone else who may be present at the time.

The aetiology of murder–suicide is not known. Some researchers have suggested that murder–suicide derives from suicidal intent which is extended to others, while others have postulated that the drive for murder–suicide comes from murderous impulses turned against the self. We believe both ideas are correct, and the intent of perpetrators of murder–suicide spans a spectrum, which varies by the types described above, from predominantly suicidal to predominantly homicidal (Nock and Marzuk, 1999). Whatever the principal motive, in every incident of murder–suicide there undoubtedly exists a simultaneous desire to murder as well as a desire to commit suicide. Nock and Marzuk (1999) proposed that an underlying theme seen in each of these typologies is the perpetrator's over-valued attachment to a relationship which, plagued with problems and threatened by dissolution, leads him to destroy the relationship.

Mental illness should undoubtedly feature prominently in any explanation of murder–suicide. Investigators who reviewed medical and legal records following murder–suicides have reported that 30–75% of murder–suicide perpetrators have a diagnosable mental illness at the time of the event (West, 1967; Rosenbaum, 1990; Cooper and Eaves, 1996; Lindqvist, 1986), which falls between similar figures for simple suicide and simple homicide. As we have mentioned above, mood disorders and psychotic disorders, especially schizophrenia, have been cited as diagnostic motivational factors leading to murder–suicide (Rosenbaum, 1983; Selkin, 1976; Browne and Palmer, 1975). The use of alcohol and drugs should also be considered a risk factor for murder–suicide. Although it may not directly cause the event, alcohol and substance use can act to disinhibit behaviour, impair judgement, induce paranoia or exacerbate existing depression (Marzuk and Mann, 1988).

Most of these suicides occur *immediately* after the homicides. Furthermore, Wolfgang (1958) reported that murder–suicide perpetrators use significantly more acts of violence than simple murderers to kill their victims (e.g. shooting five times instead of one). This suggests that murder–suicide events may be the result of the perpetrators' uncontrollable impulses. It is possible that this could be the result of a deficit in serotonergic functioning. Lidberg and colleagues (1992) reported a case of low CSF 5-HIAA in a murder–suicide perpetrator who killed his two sons, attempted to kill his lover and later committed suicide.

Clinical Management and Prevention

The assessment and intervention of those at risk for murder–suicide is discussed in depth elsewhere (Nock and Marzuk, 1999). However, a few main points should be highlighted. The prediction of murder–suicide is extremely difficult, as many families and couples have troubled relationships, and most such families do not end in murder–suicide. Nevertheless, clinicians should assess patients for risk whenever their presentation resembles one of the aforementioned typologies. This includes chaotic, violent relationships where amorous jealousy is present; older couples with declining health; depressed mothers with young children, especially when displaying over-possessiveness or "altruistic" delusions; depressed fathers whose families are experiencing difficult or humiliating circumstances; and employees who are disgruntled, especially when voicing threats of violence. Assessment of a potential perpetrator of murder–suicide should include a diagnostic interview, an exploration of motives, and an evaluation of risk for suicide and violence. If a person is thought to be at risk of committing murder–suicide, intervention should include intensive treatment of any underlying mental illness, diffusion of the intensity of the victim–perpetrator relationship, removal of lethal means, and provision of social support.

Suicide Pacts

Epidemiology, Phenomenology and Aetiology

Although suicide is most often conceptualized as a personal, isolated act, it sometimes involves pairs of victims and even large groups. A "suicide pact" is a mutual arrangement, usually between two people, to kill themselves at the same time, usually in the same place (Cohen, 1961). In one type of dyadic suicide pact, death is mutually agreed upon and both parties act independently; in another, one person in the pair coerces the other into being killed, or to kill the instigator first and then him/herself. This latter type may actually constitute the majority of pacts (West, 1967; Hemphill and Thornley, 1969; Rosen, 1981; Fishbain et al, 1984). Thus, suicide pacts are often like murder–suicides, and contain the element of aggression in one of the parties.

Suicide pacts are difficult to study, as they are very rare events. In most instances, the couple has been isolated from family and friends for some time, which makes psychological autopsy studies extremely difficult. The limited data available come from death certificate studies, in which rates of suicide pacts are compared to single suicide rates in the same population, some psychological autopsy studies of families and friends who may have had contact with the pact participants prior to the event, and studies that involve interviews with those who survive unsuccessful or aborted attempts.

In England and the USA suicide pacts account for 0.28–1.00% of all suicides (Cohen, 1961; Hemphill and Thornley, 1969; Fishbain et al, 1984; Brown and Barraclough, 1997); whereas in India and Japan 0.77–3.1% of all suicides involve pacts (Vijayakumar and Thilothammal, 1993; Sathyavathi, 1975; O'Hara, 1963). The high percentage of suicide pacts in Eastern cultures seems to be the result of the especially high number of *lover pacts* seen in those countries, as well as the inclusion of murder–suicides in the "suicide pact" classification in some Eastern countries (Fishbain and Aldrich, 1985). The characteristics of suicide pact participants differ between the East and West. Therefore, separate descriptions of the two groups seem warranted.

Cohen's (1961) seminal work on 58 suicide pacts in England during 1955–1958 reported that most who die in suicide pacts are not impulsive young lovers, *vis-à-vis* Romeo and Juliet, but co-dependent couples over the age of 50. Subsequent studies, which together examined 101 suicide pacts, have supported Cohen's original findings (Rosenbaum, 1983; Young et al, 1984; Fishbain et al, 1984; Brown et al, 1995; Brown and Barraclough, 1997). An analysis of the six studies reveals that 0–20% of pacts included young lovers whose death was the result of a perceived insurmountable obstacle to marriage. In contrast, 72–100% of pact participants were married, with an average age of 58 years. The motivation for the suicide pact in most cases was failing health and social isolation, and the pact participants tended to use less violent methods (e.g. auto-exhaust, drug overdose, etc.) in their suicides than those used in single suicides. Three of the studies reviewed case reports of pact participants and diagnosed a psychiatric illness in

61–100% of them (Rosenbaum, 1983; Young et al, 1984; Brown et al, 1995). Three of the studies reported that a number of the pairs contained at least one person who had made a previous suicide attempt (Cohen, 1961; Rosenbaum, 1983; Brown et al, 1995).

In contrast to the findings of these Western studies, most who died in suicide pacts in the East were young lovers under the age of 30. Three studies of suicide pacts in Japan (O'Hara, 1963) and India (Sathyavathi, 1975; Vijayakumar and Thilothammal, 1993) reported that 19–74% of suicide pacts in those countries involve lovers, while only 13–57% involve married couples. These studies also reported a higher percentage of friend (9–19%) and family suicide pacts, but many of these may be murder–suicides by Western classification standards. As in the West, most suicide pact participants die by non-violent methods—typically poisoning (O'Hara, 1963; Sathyavathi, 1975; Vijayakumar and Thilothammal, 1993). These studies most often cite inability of the participants to marry each other, rather than declining health, as a precipitant; however, none of them reported the prevalence of psychiatric illness in the subjects.

Although the precipitants of suicide pacts can vary, all suicide pacts seem to share certain characteristics. Hemphill and Thornley (1969) were the first to describe in detail the union between those involved in suicide pacts, which they termed "the encapsulated unit". Members of this "unit" become isolated from society, and communicate only with their spouse/lover. If this interdependent unit is threatened by dissolution (due to illness, marriage to another person, etc.), the members agree to die together rather than be separated (Fishbain et al, 1984; Noyes et al, 1977).

Perhaps the most important element in the pact dynamic is the influence of the "domineering member" over the "submissive member". Most studies have suggested that one of the pact participants is clearly the instigator who coerces the other person into participating in the pact. Furthermore, interviews with pact survivors typically describe an aggressive, depressed man, often with a history of suicidal behaviour, who convinces his female partner to commit suicide with him (Rosenbaum, 1983; Rosen, 1981). Rosenbaum (1983) compared five suicide pact instigators with 148 murderers, and 148 perpetrators of murder–suicide. The perpetrators in each of the three groups were most likely to be men with psychiatric illnesses, typically depression, and 100%, 15%, and 32%, respectively, had made a previous suicide attempt. In four of the five cases of suicide pacts Rosenbaum investigated, the cooperators survived. However, none of them continued to display suicidal behaviour after the event.

Although suicide pacts typically involve couples, there have been reports of suicides of entire families or groups, which usually occur in the context of an external threat to the existence of the family or group. Similar dynamics seem to be present, such as social isolation and the coercion of submissive cooperators by a domineering, suicidal instigator. *Family suicide pacts* reported in the literature have described motivations that include the escape of the family from extreme poverty (Venkoba Rao, 1975) or domination by a foreign power (e.g. Nazi invasion) (Noomen, 1975). Such cases are similar to familicide–suicide, and many may actually be cases of murder–suicide, as voluntary consent from all participating members is uncertain.

Mass suicides, although rare, have been documented throughout history—from the 960 Jews who committed suicide at Masada in AD 73, to the 913 followers of the People's Temple Cult in Jonestown, Guyana, in 1978, and most recently the 39 members of the Heaven's Gate Cult in southern California in 1997. Investigations of cult suicide suggest that charismatic group leaders, who are sometimes delusional, often use manipulation and coercion to effect the suicides of their group members. Although most of their members are verbally persuaded to commit suicide, in some cases there is resistance, and many persons (reports suggest half of those who died at Jonestown) are murdered by other group members, who subsequently commit suicide themselves (Hendin and Nock, in press).

Clinical Management and Prevention

The prevention of suicide pacts is difficult. The chance of rescue is diminished because those involved have often been socially isolated for a long period of time, and rarely warn others of their suicidal intent. Furthermore, there is typically premeditation and cooperation between the participants, and plans are so thorough that few pact members survive (Cohen, 1961; Hemphill and Thornley, 1969; Fishbain et al, 1984; Brown and Barraclough, 1997). The physician or therapist is rarely informed in advance of the occurrence. Therefore, attempts at intervention should focus on identifying those at demographic risk for suicide pacts. In Western countries this includes couples over the age of 50, where one or both persons are threatened by declining health, psychiatric illness or other threats to the relationship (e.g. one member being sent to a nursing home). In Eastern cultures the focus should be on young lovers facing barriers to marriage. Those matching such profiles should be carefully screened for risk of both suicide and homicide.

CONCLUSION

Suicide and violence are not opposite and unrelated acts. They appear instead to be overlapping endpoints on a continuum of aggressive behaviour. This observation is evident from studies showing an increased risk of violence in suicidal psychiatric patients, and an increased risk of suicidal behaviour in those known to be violent. Murder–suicide and suicide pact events, in which both suicidal and violent behaviours are observed almost simultaneously, provide additional examples of the overlap between the two behaviours. The field continues to await a testable, coherent explanation of why the link between violence and suicide exists. Both behaviours seem to stem from a predisposition to impulsive, aggressive behaviour, which probably results from a combination of environmental, psychiatric and neurobiological factors. The relative importance of factors governing the "vector" of aggression (i.e. inward vs. outward) remains to be established. Some researchers, for example Plutchik and colleagues (1989), have developed models to address these issues. The data accumulating about the link between suicide and violence forces us to see suicide for what it really is, an act of aggression. Future research focusing on aggression, which we propose is the key element underlying both behaviours, will lead to better understanding, prediction and prevention of these destructive behaviours.

REFERENCES

Adelson, L. (1991) Pedicide revisited: the slaughter continues. American Journal of Forensic Medicine and Pathology, 12: 16–26.

Allen, N.H. (1983) Homicide followed by suicide: Los Angeles, 1970–1979. Suicide and Life-Threatening Behavior, 13: 155–165.

American Psychiatric Association (1994) Diagnostic and Statistical Manual of Mental Disorders, 4th edn. Washington, DC: American Psychiatric Association.

Åsberg, M., Träskman, L. and Thorén, P. (1976) 5-HIAA in the cerebrospinal fluid. A biochemical suicide predictor? Archives of General Psychiatry, 33: 1193–1197.

Barraclough, B., Bunch, J., Nelson, B. and Sainsbury, P. (1974) A hundred cases of suicide: clinical aspects. British Journal of Psychiatry, 125: 355–373.

Berman, A. (1979) Dyadic death: murder–suicide. Suicide and Life-Threatening Behavior, 9: 15–23.

Botsis, A.J., Plutchik, R., Kotter, M. and van Praag, H.M. (1995) Parental loss and family violence as correlates of suicide and violence. Suicide and Life-Threatening Behavior, 25: 253–260.

Breed, W. (1963) Occupational mobility and suicide among white males. American Sociological Review, 28: 179–188.

Brown, M., King, E. and Barraclough, B. (1995) Nine suicide pacts. A clinical study of a consecutive series, 1974–93. British Journal of Psychiatry, 167: 448–451.

Brown, M. and Barraclough, B. (1997) Epidemiology of suicide pacts in England and Wales, 1988–92. British Medical Journal, 315: 286–287.

Browne, W.J. and Palmer, A.J. (1975) A preliminary study of schizophrenic women who murdered their children. Hospital and Community Psychiatry, 26: 71–75.

Burtch, B.E. (1979) Prisoner suicide reconsidered. International Journal of Psychiatry and the Law, 2: 407–413.

Cohen, J. (1961) A study of suicide pacts. Medico-Legal Journal, 29: 144–151.

Coid, J. (1983) The epidemiology of abnormal homicide and murder followed by suicide. Psychological Medicine, 13: 855–860.

Cooper, J.M. (1934) Mental disease situations in certain cultures: a new field for research. Journal of Abnormal Social Psychology, 29: 10–17.

Cooper, M. and Eaves, D. (1996) Suicide following homicide in the family. Violence and Victims, 11: 99–112.

Copeland, A.R. (1985) Dyadic death—revisited. Journal of the Forensic Science Society, 25: 181–188.

Cox, J.F., Paulus, P.B. and McCain, G. (1984) Prison overcrowding research. American Psychologist, 39: 1148–1160.

Currens, S., Fritsch, T., Jones, D., Busch, G., Vance, J., Frederich, K., Adkins, M., Bothe, J., Murphy, G., Webb, C. and Finger, R. (1991) Homicide followed by suicide—Kentucky, 1985–1990. Morbidity and Mortality Weekly Report, 40: 652–653, 659.

d'Orbán, P.T. (1979) Women who kill their children. British Journal of Psychiatry, 134: 560–571.

Daly, M. and Wilson, M. (1988) Homicide. New York: Aldine DeGruyter.
Danto, B.L. (1989) The role of the forensic psychiatrist in jail and prison suicide litigation. In R. Rosner and R.B. Harmon (Eds), Correctional Psychiatry. New York: Plenum.
Dietz, P.E. (1986) Mass, serial and sensational homicides. Bulletin of the New York Academy of Medicine, 62: 477–491.
Dooley, E. (1990) Prison suicide in England and Wales, 1972–87. British Journal of Psychiatry, 156: 40–45.
Dorpat, T.L. (1966) Suicide in murderers. Psychiatry Digest, 27: 51–55.
Du Rand, C.J., Burtka, G.J., Federman, E.J., Haycox, J.A. and Smith J.W. (1995) A quarter century of suicide in a major urban jail: implications for community psychiatry. American Journal of Psychiatry, 152: 1077–1080.
Eronen, M., Hakola, P. and Tiihonen, J. (1996) Mental disorders and homicidal behaviour in Finland. Archives of General Psychiatry, 53: 497–501.
Esparza, R. (1973) Attempted and committed suicide in county jails. In B.L. Danto (Ed.), Jailhouse Blues. Orchard Lake, MI: Epic.
Fagan, J. (1993) Interactions among drugs, alcohol, and violence. Health Affairs, 12: 65–79.
Farmer, K.A., Felthous, A.R. and Holzer, C.E. (1996) Medically serious suicide attempts in a jail with a suicide prevention program. Journal of Forensic Sciences, 41: 240–246.
Fishbain, D.A., D'Achille, L. Barsky, S. and Aldrich, T.E. (1984) A controlled study of suicide pacts. Journal of Clinical Psychiatry, 45: 154–157.
Fishbain, D.A. and Aldrich, T.E. (1985) Suicide pacts: international comparisons. Journal of Clinical Psychiatry, 46: 11–15.
Fishbain, D.A., Goldberg, M., Rosomoff, R.S. and Rosomoff, H.L. (1989) Homicide–suicide and chronic pain. Clinical Journal of Pain, 5: 275–277.
Freud, S. (1915/1917/1957) Mourning and melancholia. In J. Strachey (Trans. and Ed.), The Standard Edition of the Complete Psychological Works of Sigmund Freud, pp. 243–258. London: Hogarth.
Frost, R. and Hanzlick, R. (1988) Death in custody. Atlanta Jail and Fulton County Jail, 1974–1985. American Journal of Forensic Medicine and Pathology, 9: 207–211.
Greenwald, D.J., Reznikoff, M. and Plutchik, R. (1994) Suicide risk and violence risk in alcoholics. Journal of Nervous and Mental Disorders, 182: 3–8.
Hanzlick, R. and Koponen, M. (1994) Murder–suicide in Fulton County, Georgia, 1988–1991. American Journal of Forensic Medicine and Pathology, 15: 168–173.
Hardyman, P.L. (1983) The Ultimate Escape: Suicide in Ohio's Jails and Temporary Detention Facilities, 1980–1981. Columbus, OH: Ohio Bureau of Adult Detention Facilities and Services.
Haycock, J. (1989) Manipulation and suicide attempts in jails and prisons. Psychiatric Quarterly, 60: 85–98.
Hayes, L.M. and Kajdan, B. (1981) And Darkness Closes. In: A National Study of Jail Suicides. Washington, DC: National Center on Institutions and Alternatives.
Hayes, L.M. (1983) And darkness closes in . . . a national study of jail suicides. Criminal Justice and Behaviour, 10: 461–484.
Hayes, L.M. and Rowan, J.R. (1988) National Study of Jail Suicides: Seven Years Later. Alexandria, VA: National Center on Institutions and Alternatives.
Hayes, L.M. (1997) From chaos to calm: one jail system's struggle with suicide prevention. Behavioural Sciences and the Law, 15: 399–413.
Hemphill, R.E. and Thornley, F.I. (1969) Suicide pacts. South African Medical Journal, 1335–1338.
Hendin, H. (1995) Suicide in America. New York: W.W. Norton.
Hendin, H. and Nock, M.K. (in press) Suicide. In R. Gottesman and M. Mazón (Eds), Violence in America: an Encyclopedia. New York: Charles Scribner's Sons.
Henry, A. and Short, J. (1954) Suicide and Homicide: Some Economic, Sociological, and Psychological Aspects of Aggression. Glencoe, IL: Free Press.

Hodgins, S. (1992) Mental disorder, intellectual deficiency, and crime: evidence from a birth cohort. Archives of General Psychiatry, 49: 476–483.

Hodgins, S., Mednick, S.A., Brennan, P.A., Schulsinger, F. and Engberg, M. (1996) Mental disorder and crime: evidence from a Danish birth cohort. Archives of General Psychiatry, 53: 489–496.

Hoff, H. (1973) Prevention of suicide among prisoners. In B. Danto (Ed.), Jailhouse Blues. Orchard Lake, MI: Epic.

Innes, C.A. (1987) The effects of prison density on prisoners. Criminal Justice Archive and Information Network, 1: 3.

Jordan, F.B., Schmeckpeper, K. and Strope, M. (1987) Jail suicides by hanging: an epidemiological review and recommendations for prevention. American Journal of Forensic Medicine and Pathology, 8: 27–31.

Joukamaa, M. (1997) Prison suicide in Finland, 1969–1992. Forensic Science International, 89: 167–174.

Kerkhof, J.F.M. and Bernasco, W. (1990) Suicidal behaviour in jails and prisons in The Netherlands: incidence, characteristics, and prevention. Suicide and Life-Threatening Behavior, 20: 123–137.

Kruesi, M.J. (1989) Cruelty to animals and CSF 5-HIAA. Psychiatry Research, 28: 115–116.

Kruesi, M.J., Hibbs, E.D., Zahn, T.P., Keysor, C.S., Hamburger, S.D., Bartko, J.J. and Rapoport, J.L. (1992) A 2-year prospective follow-up study of children and adolescents with disruptive behaviour disorders. Prediction by cerebrospinal fluid 5-hydroxyindoleacetic acid, homovanillic acid, and autonomic measures? Archives of General Psychiatry, 49: 429–435.

Lester, D. and Danto, B. (1993) Suicide Behind Bars: Prediction and Prevention. Philadelphia, PA: Charles.

Lidberg, L., Winborg, I.M. and Åsberg, M. (1992) Low cerebrospinal fluid levels of 5-hydroxyindoleacetic acid and murder–suicide. Nordic Journal of Psychiatry, 49: 17–24.

Lindqvist, P. (1986) Criminal homicide in northern Sweden 1970–1981: alcohol intoxication, alcohol abuse, and mental disease. International Journal of Law and Psychiatry, 8: 19–37.

Link, B.G., Andrews, H. and Cullen, F.T. (1992) The violent and illegal behaviour of mental patients reconsidered. American Sociological Review, 57: 275–292.

Linnoila, M., Virkkunen, M., Scheinin, M., Nuutila, A., Rimon, R. and Goodwin, F.K. (1983) Low cerebrospinal fluid 5-hydroxyindoleacetic acid concentration differentiates impulsive from non-impulsive violent behaviour. Life Sciences, 33: 2609–2614.

Malmquist, C.P. (1995) Depression and homicidal violence. International Journal of Law and Psychiatry, 18: 145–162.

Marcus, P. and Alcabes, P. (1993) Characteristics of suicides by inmates in an urban jail. Hospital and Community Psychiatry, 44: 256–261.

Maris, R.W. (1975) Sociology. In S. Perlin (Ed.), A Handbook for the Study of Suicide. New York: Oxford University Press.

Marks, M.N. and Kumar, R. (1995) Infanticide in Scotland. Medicine, Science, and the Law, 36: 299–305.

Marks, M. and Lovestone, S. (1995) The role of the father in parental postnatal mental health. British Journal of Medical Psychology, 68: 157–168.

Marzuk, P.M. (in press) Violence and suicidal behaviour: what is the link? In K. Tardiff (Ed.), Medical Management of the Violent Patient. New York: Marcel Dekker.

Marzuk, P.M. and Mann, J.J. (1988) Suicide and substance abuse. Psychiatric Annals, 18: 639–645.

Marzuk, P.M., Tardiff, K. and Hirsch, C.S. (1992) The epidemiology of murder–suicide. Journal of the American Medical Association, 267: 3179–3183.

Menninger, K. (1938) Man Against Himself. New York: Harvest.

Myers, S.A. (1970) Maternal filicide. American Journal of Diseases of Children, 120: 534–536.
Nock, M.K. and Marzuk, P.M. (1999) Murder–suicide: phenomenology and clinical implications. In D.G. Jacobs (Ed.), Harvard Medical School Guide to Suicide Assessment and Intervention. Cambridge, MA: Simon and Schuster.
Noomen, P. (1975) Suicide in The Netherlands. In N.H. Farberas (Ed.), Suicide in Different Cultures, Baltimore, MD: University Park Press.
Novick, L.F. and Remmlinger, E. (1978) A study of 128 deaths in New York City correctional facilities, 1971–1976. Medical Care, 16: 749–756.
Noyes, R., Freye, S. and Hartford, C.E. (1977) Conjugal suicide pact. Journal of Nervous and Mental Disorders, 165: 72–75.
O'Hara, K. (1963) Characteristics of suicide in Japan, especially of parent–child double suicide. American Journal of Psychiatry, 120: 382–385.
Palermo, G.B. (1994) Murder–suicide—an extended suicide. International Journal of Offender Therapy, 38: 205–216.
Palmer, S. and Humphrey, J.A. (1980) Offender–victim relationships in criminal homicide followed by offender's suicide, North Carolina, 1972–1977. Suicide and Life-Threatening Behavior, 10: 106–118.
Platt, S. (1984) Unemployment and suicidal behaviour: a review of the literature. Social Science and Medicine, 19: 93–115.
Plutchik, R. (1995) Outward and inward directed aggressiveness: the interaction between violence and suicidality. Pharmacopsychiatry, 28: 47–57.
Plutchik, R., van Praag, H.M. and Conte, H.R. (1986) Suicide and violence risk in psychiatric patients. In C. Shagass (Ed.), Biological Psychiatry. New York: Elsevier.
Plutchik, R., van Praag, H.M. and Conte, H.R. (1989) Correlates of suicide and violence risk: III. A two-stage model of countervailing forces. Psychiatric Research, 28: 215–225.
Resnick, P.J. (1969) Child murder by parents: a psychiatric review of filicide. American Journal of Psychiatry, 126: 325–334.
Rich, C.L., Young, D. and Fowler, R.C. (1986) San Diego suicide study, I: young vs. old subjects. Archives of General Psychiatry, 43: 577–582.
Robins, E., Murphy, G.E., Wilkinson, R.H. Jr, Gassner, S. and Kayes, J. (1959) Some clinical considerations in the prevention of suicide based on a study of 134 successful suicides. American Journal of Public Health, 49: 888–889.
Rodenburg, M. (1971) Child murder by depressed parents. Canadian Psychiatric Association Journal, 16: 41–48.
Rosen, B.K. (1981) Suicide pacts: a review. Psychological Medicine, 11: 525–533.
Rosenbaum, M. (1983) Crime and punishment—the suicide pact. Archives of General Psychiatry, 40: 979–982.
Rosenbaum, M. (1990) The role of depression in couples involved in murder–suicide and homicide. American Journal of Psychiatry, 147: 1036–1039.
Rosenbaum, M. and Bennet, B. (1986) Homicide and depression. American Journal of Psychiatry, 143: 367–370.
Sakuta, T. (1995) A study of murder followed by suicide. Medicine and the Law, 14: 141–153.
Salive, M.E., Smith, G.S. and Brewer, T.F. (1989) Suicide mortality in the Maryland state prison system 1979–1987. Journal of the American Medical Association, 262: 365–369.
Sathyavathi, K. (1975) Usual and unusual suicide pact in Bangalore: a report. Indian Journal of Social Work, 36: 173–180.
Selkin, J. (1976) Rescue fantasies in homicide–suicides. Suicide and Life Threatening Behavior, 6: 79–85.
Shepherd, M. (1961) Morbid jealousy: some clinical and social aspects of a psychiatric syndrome. Journal of Mental Science, 107: 687–753.
Skodol, A.E. and Karasu, T.B. (1978) Emergency psychiatry and the assaultive patient. American Journal of Psychiatry, 135: 202–205.

Smialek, J.E. and Spitz, W.U. (1978) Death behind bars. Journal of the Amarican Medical Association, 240: 2563–2564.

Smith, M.D. and Parker, R.N. (1980) Type of homicide and variation in regional rates. Social Forces, 59: 136–147.

Steadman, H.J., Mulvey, E.P., Monahan, J., Robbins, P.C., Appelbaum, P.S., Grisso, T., Roth, L.H. and Silver, E. (1998) Violence by people discharged from acute psychiatric inpatient facilities and others in the same neighborhoods. Archives of General Psychiatry, 55: 393–401.

Swanson, J.W., Holzer, C.E., Ganju, V.K. and Jano, R.T. (1990) Violence and psychiatric disorders in the community: evidence from the Epidemiologic Catchment Area survey. Hospital and Community Psychiatry, 41: 761–770.

Tardiff, K. (1996) Assessment and Management of Violent Patients. Washington, DC: American Psychiatric Press.

Tardiff, K. and Sweillam, A. (1980a) Assault, suicide, and mental illness. Archives of General Psychiatry, 37: 164–169.

Tardiff, K. and Sweillam, A. (1980b) Factors related to the increased risk of assaultive behaviour in suicidal patients. Acta Psychiatrica Scandinavica, 62: 63–68.

Teplin, L.A. (1990) The prevalence of severe mental disorders among male urban jail detainees: comparison with the Epidemiologic Catchment Area Program. American Journal of Public Health, 80: 663–669.

Topp, D.O. (1979) Suicide in prison. British Journal of Psychiatry, 134: 24–27.

Träskman, L., Åsberg, M., Bertilsson, L. and Sjostrand, L. (1981) Monoamine metabolites in CSF and suicidal behaviour. Archives of General Psychiatry, 38: 631–636.

van Praag, H.M., Plutchik, R. and Apter, A. (Eds) (1990) Violence and Suicidality: Perspectives in Clinical and Psychobiological Research. New York: Brunner Mazel.

Venkoba Rao, A. (1975) Suicide in India. In N.H. Farberow (Ed.), Suicide in Different Cultures. Baltimore, MD: University Park Press.

Vijayakumar, L. and Thilothammal, N. (1993) Suicide pacts. Crisis, 14: 43–46.

Virkkunen, M., Nuutila, A., Goodwin, F.K. and Linnoila, M. (1987) Cerebrospinal fluid monoamine metabolite levels in male arsonists. Archives of General Psychiatry, 44: 241–247.

Volavka, J. (1995) Neurobiology of Violence. Washington, DC: American Psychiatric Press.

Weissman, M., Fox, K. and Klerman, G.L. (1973) Hostility and depression associated with suicide attempts. American Journal of Psychiatry, 130: 450–455.

West, D.J. (1967) Murder Followed by Suicide. Cambridge, MA: Harvard University Press.

Wilkey, I., Pearn, J., Petric, G. and Nixon, J. (1982) Neonaticide, infanticide, and child homicide. Medicine, Science, and the Law, 22: 31–34.

Wolfgang, M.E. (1958) Patterns in Criminal Homicide. Oxford: Oxford University Press.

Yap, P.M. (1951) Mental diseases peculiar to certain cultures: a survey of comparative psychiatry. Journal of Mental Science, 97: 313–327.

Young, D., Rich, C.L. and Fowler, R.C. (1984) Double suicides: four modal cases. Journal of Clinical Psychiatry, 45: 470–472.

Chapter 25

Suicide among Psychiatric Inpatients

Manfred Wolfersdorf
Department of Psychiatry and Psychotherapy, Bezirkskrankenhaus Bayreuth, Germany

Abstract

Suicides in psychiatric hospital inpatients have been described in the clinical and scientific literature for more than 100 years. In the first part of this chapter an overview is provided of reports of this problem in various psychiatric hospitals worldwide, specifically the apparent increase in inpatient suicides which has been observed during the last three or four decades. In the second part of the chapter the characteristics of inpatient suicides are reviewed and recommendations made for suicide prevention according to different diagnostic groups.

INTRODUCTION

The increased rate of suicide among mentally ill people is well documented (see Chapters 7–11). However, there is hardly any information on the number of mentally ill people who commit suicide while in inpatient psychiatric treatment. Estimates regarding the proportion of inpatient suicides relative to the total number of suicides in the general population vary between 4% and 7% (Goldney et al, 1985; Wolfersdorf, 1989, 1992; National Confidential Inquiry into Suicide and Homicide by People with Mental Illness, 1999).

The prevention of suicidal behaviour is traditionally a goal of outpatient and inpatient psychiatry and psychotherapy. Reduction in suicidality is always an important component in the treatment of mentally ill people. Acute suicide risk is a frequent cause of emergency admission to psychiatric clinics; statistics in the relevant literature vary between 15% and 60% admissions being because of

The International Handbook of Suicide and Attempted Suicide. Edited by K. Hawton and K. van Heeringen.

suicide risk. The so-called "basic suicidality" in a psychiatric hospital, i.e. the proportion of patients at acute risk of committing suicide, is thought to be approximately 30% (Ritzel and Kornek, 1983).

Suicide has always been a characteristic of patients in psychiatric clinics and under conditions of inpatient psychiatric and psychotherapeutic treatment, and there have been reports on this in the literature for more than 100 years (Damerow, 1865; Edel, 1891; Copas and Robin, 1982; Morgan and Priest, 1991; Morgan and Stanton, 1997; Wolfersdorf et al, 1997). In the 1960s and 1970s suspicion was expressed, first in American psychiatry and then in Germany, that there had been an increase in the number of people committing suicide in psychiatric institutions. The first indications in this respect were reported, for example, by Farberow and colleagues (1971; Farberow and MacKinnon, 1975; Farberow and Williams, 1982) on the basis of the suicide statistics for the psychiatric departments of the Veterans' Administration Hospitals in the USA.

THE CURRENT STATE OF RESEARCH

Table 25.1 provides an overview of suicide statistics in psychiatric hospitals in various countries (for more detailed overviews, see Ernst and Kern, 1974;

Table 25.1 Suicide rates in psychiatric hospitals—selected examples (see Wolfersdorf, 1989, 1991; Wolfersdorf et al, 1997)

Authors, year of report, psychiatric hospital, country	Period covered	Suicide rates, comments
Damerow (1865) Heil- und Pflegeanstalt Halle, Germany	1845–63	617 per 100,000 inpatients calculated
Edel (1891) Psychiatrische Anstalt, Charlottenburg, Berlin, Germany	1885–89	338 per 100,000 inpatients calculated
Schlosser and Strehle-Jung (1982) Psychiatrische Klinik, Hannover, Germany	1972–78	425 per 100,000 admissions increase after change of treatment approach
Ritzel and Kornek (1983) Psychiatr. Krankenhaus, Hildesheim, Germany	1974–81	83 per 100,000 admissions, increase
Heydt and Bort (1987) Psychiatr. Klinik, Stuttgart, Germany	1971–85	167 per 100,000 admissions, increase
Foerster and Gill (1987) Psychiatr. Universitäts-klinik, Tübingen, Germany	1965–85	285 per 100,000 admissions, increase
Koester and Engels (1970) 6 Rhein. Landeskrankenhäuser, Germany	1962–68	57.4 per 100,000 inpatients per year
Gorenc-Krause (1980) 10 Bayer. Bezirkskrankenhäuser, Germany	1950–59/ 1967–76	First period 49.6, second period 65.8 per 100,000 inpatients per year, increase

Table 25.1 *(continued)*

Authors, year of report, psychiatric hospital, country	Period covered	Suicide rates, comments
Wolfersdorf et al (1997) Five psychiatric hospitals, Germany (Keller & Wolfersdorf 1995)	1970–93	Suicide rates between 76.9 to 414.5 per 100,000 admissions per year; increase 1970–80, plateau since 1980
Wolfersdorf and Keller (2000) Twelve psychiatric hospitals, Germany	1970–97	Different suicide rates between 0 and 668 per 100,000 admissions per year, increase 1970–80, different course since 1980 (increase and decrease)
Modestin (1982) Psychiatric University Hospital, Bern, Switzerland	1961–80	88–343 per 100,000 treated patients per year, increase
Ernst (1979) Psychiatric University Hospital, Zürich, Switzerland	1900–77	180 per 100,000 discharged patients, increase
Mitterauer (1981) Psychiatric hospital, Salzburg, Austria	1969–79	79 per 100,000 admissions
Hessö (1997) Psychiatric hospital in Sweden, Norway, Finland	1930–59	Sweden: 67–132 per 100,000 inpatients per year, increase
	1950–69	Finland: 118–208 per 100,000 inpatients per year, increase
	1930–74	Norway: 32–277 per 100,000 inpatients per year, increase
Lönnqvist et al (1974) Psychiatric University Hospital, Helsinki, Finland	1841–1971	134.1 per 100,000 patients per year
Farberow et al (1971) Veteran Administration Hospitals, Psychiatric Clinics, USA	1959–66	72 per 100,000 inpatients per year, increase 1950–58, 56.8; 1959–66, 81.1
Farberow and McKinnon (1975) VA Psychiatric Hospitals, USA	1950–72	145 per 100,000 inpatients per year, increase
Farberow and Williams (1982) VA Psychiatric Hospitals, USA	1950–80	49.7 (1950–52) increase to 326.8 (1979–80)
James and Levin (1964) Psychiatric hospital, Perth, Australia	1955–61	119 per 100,000 inpatients
Goldney et al (1985) Glenside Hospital, Adelaide, Australia	1972–82	222 per 100,000 patients (in- and outpatients)
Retterstöl (1979) Psychiatric hospitals, England and Wales, UK	1920–22/ 1945–47	First period 49, second period 51 per 100,000 inpatients
Walk (1967) Psychiatric hospital, West Sussex, UK	1954–62	202 per 100,000 patients
Sayil and Ceyhun (1981) Four psychiatric hospitals, Ankara, Turkey	1965–80	100 (1965–70) decrease to 40 (1976–80)
Lerer and Avni (1976) Psychiatric hospital, Hassah University, Israel	1965–74	450 per 100,000 inpatients per year

Wolfersdorf, 1989; Blain and Donaldson, 1995). The rate of suicide among inpatients in all countries is considerably higher than the rate in the general population. This is hardly surprising because, as already noted, acute risk of suicide is an important indication for inpatient psychiatric hospital treatment. One of the problems regarding calculation of inpatient suicide rates is the different methods used, including calculation according to admissions per year, to discharges per year, or to patient-years at risk. During the last two decades most of the European studies have reported rates based on admissions per year.

According to today's state of knowledge, however, the numbers of inpatients committing suicide have increased worldwide. It was demonstrated that this increase was not due to an artefact (Ernst et al, 1980; Modestin, 1987; Keller and Wolfersdorf, 1995). By using trend analyses, Wolfersdorf (1989) showed an increase in the rate of suicide among patients in various German, Swiss, Norwegian and American psychiatric hospitals; other authors (e.g. Goldney et al, 1985) have produced similar findings on the basis of the development of suicide mortality in the psychiatric hospitals which they examined.

The causes of this increase (see Table 25.2; Wolfersdorf, 1991) are difficult to determine. They can only be described as "clinical hypotheses" which cannot be verified and for which there is currently no scientific confirmation, as they cannot be tested due to ethical and methodological problems. Possible explanations for the increase include:

- Structural changes in psychiatric hospitals in the last few decades.
- A lack of internal structure in mixed psychiatric wards.
- Changes in patient groups which are felt to be increasingly difficult to manage, and are more demanding and suicidal.
- Changes in societal attitudes towards mental illness and chronic illness with an increased acceptance of suicidal behaviour.
- Depression induced by the traditional or typical neuroleptic drugs.
- So-called forced rehabilitation.
- The lack of protection as a result of the increased reduction in the amount of time spent in care.
- Greater liberty in respect of the freedom and holiday time permitted to patients.

Suicide among inpatients occurs particularly often in schizophrenic patients, because depressives were always considered to be a group with a higher rate of mortality due to suicide. Risk factors for suicide in schizophrenic inpatients (Roy, 1982a,b, 1983, 1986; Fernando and Storm, 1984; Langley and Bayatti, 1984; Goldney et al, 1985; Modestin, 1987; Wolfersdorf, 1989, 1996a,b; Roy and Draper, 1995) include:

- Male sex.
- Three or more hospitalizations in a short period of time.
- Paranoid-hallucinatory schizophrenia.
- Schizo-affective psychosis.

Table 25.2 Various factors discussed in the literature as influencing the risk of inpatient suicide (see Wolfersdorf, 1991)

General and patient-related factors

- Changed inpatient clientele (more depressives; increase in suicidal patients; increase in young schizophrenic patients; more difficult and more suicidal inpatients, etc.)
- Unrecognized or underestimated influences on the part of primary relational figures (overestimation of security of therapeutic relationships)
- Changed attitudes to suicide in the general population ("suicide as personal choice"; so-called "rational suicide")
- Increase in suicidality in general population (and hence in inpatients)
- Social and political pressure on therapeutic measures and psychiatric institutions (stigmatization of inpatient treatment in psychiatric hospitals, e.g. electroconvulsive therapy; security and control measures, etc.)
- Increasing problems of resocialization (unemployment; isolation of mental patients in the family; loss of families, etc.)

Ward- and treatment-related factors

- Poor ward atmosphere, insufficient integration of patients
- Isolation and loneliness, especially among long-term patients
- Negative prognoses ("therapeutic hopelessness"), such as transfer into long-term ward (loss of hope and chances for new orientation)
- Premature or insufficiently prepared vacations, premature free outings
- Too short a duration of inpatient treatment, insufficiently prepared aftercare, unresolved social situation
- Rehabilitation pressure (overactivation); so-called "forced rehabilitation"
- Loss of "right of domicile"; too early discharge
- Frequent change of treatment strategies
- Inadequate pharmacotherapeutic and psychotherapeutic measures (false diagnoses, misindications)
- "Pharmacogenic depression" caused by antipsychotic (neuroleptic) medication
- Diagnostic errors, especially in the diagnosis of suicidality

Factors in education and hospital organization

- Deficits in education and continuing education of staff, particularly involving estimation of suicidality and in handling of suicidal patients
- Lack of, or insufficient, therapeutic supervision and lack of support from hospital management (inadequate policies for management of suicidal patients)
- Lack of medical staff leadership or turnover in leadership positions (transitional periods)
- Frequent staff turnover (loss of personal relationships, particularly in long-term wards; exposure traumas and instability)
- Oversized or undersized treatment wards (excessive emotional pressure or lack of emotional security)
- Insufficiently prepared renovation and change of wards (hospital instability; change of social relationships; compulsion to reorientation)
- Insufficient safeguarding strategies (organizational, mechanical, human—i.e. safeguarding through "relationship")
- Poor architectural design (such as unsafe shafts and stairwells, windows which can be easily opened, access to pipes and similar structures, etc.)
- Careless handling in wards of instruments and objects potentially usable in suicide; opportunities for access to such objects

Table 25.3 Psychopathological risk factors for inpatient suicide during psychiatric hospital treatment

- Depressed mood
- Hopelessness
- Ideas of worthlessness
- Depressive delusions (especially of guilt or sin)
- Depressive thinking of being a burden to others (e.g. family)
- Paranoid ideas of persecution, ego-destruction
- Auditory hallucinations (imperative voices urging suicide)
- Restlessness, agitation and akathisia
- Sleeping disturbances over a longer period
- Suicide attempt prior to the index episode
- Suicidal behaviour or ideation during inpatient stay
- Course of illness characterized by rapid deterioration of psychological functioning
- Hopelessness and resignation due to the course of illness
- Short period (weeks to months) between last discharge and re-admission

A number of psychopathological characteristics have been found associated with inpatient suicide (see Table 25.3). The description of these risk factors is based on clinical experience, as only a few studies have been published (Copas and Robin, 1982; Goldney et al, 1985; Modestin and Kopp, 1988; Wolfersdorf, 1989; Roy and Draper, 1995; Proulx et al, 1997). On the one hand, there are well-known psychopathological phenomena such as depression, hopelessness, symptoms of delusion and auditory hallucinations in the form of imperative voices which urge the patient to commit suicide. On the other hand, there are psychomotor phenomena, such as inner restlessness, agitation and akathisia due to neuroleptic drugs. Rapid progress of the illness and impairment in occupational potential and interpersonal relationships have also been found to be associated with inpatient suicide among schizophrenic patients.

Recent studies show that following a rise in the occurrence of suicide in German psychiatric hospitals between the 1970s and the first half of the 1990s, rates of inpatient suicide are decreasing (Wolfersdorf and Keller, 2000). It is unclear whether this is connected with increased awareness of the suicide-related problems of psychiatric inpatients or with improved treatment opportunities.

RECOMMENDATIONS FOR THE PREVENTION OF INPATIENT SUICIDE

The prevention of suicide in psychiatric hospitals primarily concerns the following groups:

1. Patients with severe depressive illnesses who are admitted to hospital because of—among other reasons—suicidality.
2. Patients with acute schizophrenic illness who have to be re-admitted due to a paranoid-hallucinatory episode or as a result of a chronic residual course,

Table 25.4 Recommendation for suicide prevention in a psychiatric hospital

- Each newly admitted patient must be assessed according to his/her suicidal potential, including different forms of suicidal behaviour such as suicide ideation, death wishes and hopelessness, concrete suicide plans, including psychopathology which leads to a higher suicide risk
- Establish a close relationship (therapeutic, nursing care) between suicidal inpatients and staff
- Allow close control and communication with the patient (the best control is close communication)
- Repeated assessment and documentation of suicidality, especially in crises
- Adequate psychopharmacotherapy and psychotherapy of the underlying mental illness, including use of sedatives and hypnotics if neccessary
- Generate a positive short- and long-term treatment plan, including prevention of repetition of suicidal behaviour
- Careful check for environmental risk factors (e.g. open waterpipes, hooks on walls or doors, heights)

and patients with symptoms of depression and anxiety within the context of a schizo-affective illness.

3. People who have become suicidal due to occupational or social relationship problems (e.g. chronic unemployment, being uprooted) or a crisis in a relationship (e.g. loss of a partner).
4. People who have become suicidal in connection with a physical illness (e.g. cancer, other illnesses which restrict the quality of life).

One group of inpatients at particular risk of suicidal behaviour are younger, male patients with schizophrenia who either become suicidal within the context of a paranoid-hallucinatory psychosis or an exacerbation of a known and long-term illness with increasing psychosocial dysfunctioning, and especially those with an increasing awareness of the long-term consequences regarding the course of the illness (Retterstöl, 1987). Depressed patients at increased risk of suicide are especially those with acute high-risk psychopathology (particularly hopelessness, delusions), or those who are facing a current conflict or other crisis within a relationship or other psychosocial situation. Patients with addiction disorders who are particularly at risk are those who are dependent on alcohol and undergoing acute withdrawal treatment or detoxification, perhaps as an anti-suicidal measure. Many alcohol-dependent patients are only suicidal when intoxicated or under the influence of drugs. In the absence of co-morbidity with depression or personality disorder (see Chapter 9), the risk is usually reduced following withdrawal treatment.

A number of recommendations for the prevention of inpatient suicide can be formulated (see Table 25.4). In the psychiatric hospital, suicide prevention includes a comprehensive assessment of the acute risk of suicidal behaviour (patient is suicidal—yes/no; type of suicidality—death wishes, ideas of committing suicide, concrete and declared intentions to commit suicide; previous suicidal actions, etc.) as well as of the primary mental illness and psychopathology which are associated with suicide risk (Blain and Donaldson, 1995; Hawton, 1987; Appleby, 1992). In addition to intensive psychotherapeutic care by psychological and nursing staff, there must also be adequate psychopharmacotherapeutic treatment of the primary illness as well as accompanying medical treatment of suicidality. The pharmacotherapy of suicidal ideation and behaviour is discussed in Chapter 27.

Prevention may be enhanced by trying to improve the relationships between staff and patients, such as by ensuring that each patient has one or two named nurses who are his/her key workers. In addition, there must be attention to enironmental factors, including structures from which patients might hang themselves, access to places from which to jump, and access to local sites for suicide (e.g. railway lines, rivers).

It must be emphasized, however, that even within the best therapeutic, nursing and safety-controlled context it is impossible to be absolutely safe and always successful in the prevention of suicide. Approximately 40% of all patients who commit suicide in hospital show no signs of, or give any indications of, their acute risk of suicide, or the medical and nursing team does not observe any indications of an increase in the acute risk of suicide or of an acute intention of committing suicide. Thus, it is important to accept that there are limitations in the extent to which suicide can be prevented in the context of inpatient treatment. There is no absolutely certain way of preventing suicide in a psychiatric hospital; there can only be well-meaning efforts to avert suicidality in patients as far as is reasonably possible.

CONCLUSIONS

Suicide during psychiatric and psychotherapeutic inpatient treatment has been identified as a problem in psychiatric hospitals for more than 100 years. This is hardly surprising because suicide risk is one of the most important indications for inpatient psychiatric treatment. During the last three decades, psychiatrists have been concerned about an increase in suicides in psychiatric hospital inpatients, which has been observed worldwide. In this chapter some of the possible reasons for this increase have been discussed and the characteristics of inpatients who die by suicide reported in various studies were described. Today, our attention to preventing inpatient suicides should focus especially on patients with severe depression (for example, depressed people with delusions) and patients with acute schizophrenia, especially young and male patients who have developed awareness of the possible long-term consequences of their illness.

REFERENCES

Applebly, L. (1992) Suicide in psychiatric patients: risk and prevention. British Journal of Psychiatry, 161: 749–758.

Blain, P.A. and Donaldson, L.J. (1995) The reporting of inpatient suicides: identifying the problem. Public Health, 109: 293–301.

Copas, J.B. and Robin, A. (1982) Suicide in psychiatric inpatients. British Journal of Psychiatry, 141: 503–511.

Damerow (1865) Zur Statistik der Provinzial-Irren-Heil- und Pflege Anstalt bei Halle vom 1. November 1844 bis Ende December 1863, nebst besonderen Mittheilungen und Ansichten über Selbsttödtungen. Allgemeine Zeitzchrift für Psychiatrie, 22: 219–251.

Edel (1891) Das Suicidium in Irrenanstalten und § 222 d. StGB. Allgemeine Zeitschrift für Psychiatrie, 41: 422–429.

Ernst, K. (1979) Die Zunahme der suizide in den Psychiatrischen Kliniken. Tatsachen, Ursachen, Prävention. Sozial-und Präventiomedizin 24: 34–37.

Ernst, K. and Kern, R. (1974) Suizidstatistik und freiheitliche Klinikbehandlung 1900–1972. Archiv für Psychiatrie und Nervenkrankheiten, 219: 255–263.

Ernst, K., Moser, U. and Ernst, C. (1980) Zunehmende Suizide psychiatrischer Klinikpatienten: Realität oder Artefakt. Archiv für Psychiatrie und Nervenkrankheiten, 228: 351–363.

Farberow, N.L. and MacKinnon, D. (1975) Status of suicide in the Veterans Administration. Report III–Revised. Los Angeles, CA: Central Research Unit V.A., Wadsworth Hospital Center (unpublished paper)

Farberow, N.L. and Williams, J.L. (1982) Status of suicide in Veterans Administration Hospitals, Report VI. Los Angeles, CA: Veterans Administration Central Research Unit, Wadsworth Medical Center (unpublished paper).

Farberow, N.L., Ganzler, S., Cutter, F. and Reynolds, D. (1971) An eight-year survey of hospital suicides. Suicide and Life-Threatening Behavior, 1: 184–202.

Fernando, S. and Storm, V. (1984) Suicide among psychiatric patients of a district general hospital. Psychological Medicine, 14: 661–672.

Foerster, K. and Gill, A. (1987) Die Suicide während stationärer Therapie an der Psychiatrischen Universitätsklinik Tübingen 1965–1985. In M. Wolfersdorf and R. Vogel (Eds), Suizidalität bei Stationären Psychiatrischen Patienten pp. 229–239. Weinsberg: Weissenhof-Verlag Dr Jens Kunow.

Goldney, R.D., Positano, S., Spence, N.D. and Rosemann, S.J. (1985) Suicide in association with psychiatric hospitalisation. Australian and New Zealand Journal of Psychiatry, 19: 177–183.

Gorenc-Krause, K.D. (1980) Der Suizid in den bayrischen Bezirkskrankenhäusern. Medical Dissertation, München: LM-Universität.

Hawton, K. (1987) Assessment of suicide risk. British Journal of Psychiatry, 150: 145–153.

Hessö, R. (1977) Suicide in Norwegian, Finnish and Swedish psychiatric hospitals. Archiv für Psychiatrie und Nervenkrankheiten, 224: 119–127.

Heydt, G. and Bort, G. (1986) Suizide in den psychiatrischen Kliniken. Suizidprophylaxe, 13: 313–344.

James, J.P. and Levin, S. (1964) Suicide following discharge from psychiatric hospital. Archives of General Psychiatry, 10: 43–46.

Keller, F. and Wolfersdorf, M. (1995) Changes of suicide numbers in psychiatric hospitals: analysis using log-linear models. Social Psychiatry and Psychiatric Epidemiology, 30: 169–273.

Koester, H. and Engels, G. (1970) Gelungene Suizide im Psychiatrischen Krankenhaus. Zeitschrift für Präventiomedizin, 15: 19–26.

Langley, G.E. and Bayatti, N.N. (1984) Suicides in Exe Vale Hospital, 1972–1981. British Journal of Psychiatry, 145: 463–467.

Lerer, B. and Auni, J. (1976) Suicide in a General Hospital Psychiatric Department. Psychiatria Clinica, 9: 106–111.

Lönnqvist, J., Niskanen, P., Rinta-Mänty, R., Achte, K. and Kärhä, E. (1974) Suicides in psychiatric hospitals in different therapeutic eras. Psychiatria Fennica, 265–274.

Miles, C. (1977) Conditions predisposing to suicide: a review. Journal of Nervous and Mental Disease, 164: 231–246.

Mitterauer, B. (1981) Können Selbstmorde in einem Psychiatrischen Krankenhaus verhindert werden? Psychiatrische Praxis, 8: 25–30.

Modestin, J. (1982) Suizid in der Psychiatrischen Institution. Die Nervenarzt, 53: 254–261.
Modestin, J. (1987) Suizide in der Psychiatrischen Klinik. Stuttgart: Enke.
Modestin, J. and Kopp, W. (1988) Study of suicide in depressed inpatients. Journal of Affective Disorders, 15: 157–162.
Morgan, H.G. and Priest, P. (1991) Suicide and other unexpected deaths among psychiatric inpatients: the Bristol Confidential Inquiry. British Journal of Psychiatry, 158: 368–374.
Morgan, H.G. and Stanton, R. (1997) Suicide among psychiatric inpatients in a changing clinical scene. British Journal of Psychiatry, 171: 561–563.
National Confidential Inquiry into Suicide and Homicide by People with Mental Illness (1999) Safer Services, p. 36. London: Department of Health.
Proulx, F., Lesage, A.D. and Grunberg, F. (1997) One hundred inpatient suicides. British Journal of Psychiatry, 171: 247–250.
Retterstöl, N. (1987) Schizophrenie—Verlauf und Prognose. In K.P. Kisker, H. Lauter, J.-E. Meyer, C. Müller and E. Strömgren (Eds), Psychiatrie der Gegenwart 4, pp. 71–115. Berlin: Springer.
Ritzel, G. and Kornek, G. (1983) Fördern freizügige und individuelle Therapie und Klinikführung den Suizid? Psycho, 9: 7–80.
Roy, A. (1982a) Risk factors for suicide in psychiatric patients. Archives of General Psychiatry, 39: 1089–1095.
Roy, A. (1982b) Suicide in chronic schizophrenia. British Journal of Psychiatry, 141: 171–177.
Roy, A. (1983) Suicide in depressives. Comprehensive Psychiatry, 24: 487–491.
Roy, A. (1986) Suicide in schizophrenia. In A. Roy (Ed.), Suicide, pp. 97–112. Baltimore, MD: Williams & Wilkins.
Roy, A. and Draper, R. (1995) Suicide among psychiatric hospital inpatients. Psychological Medicine, 25: 199–202.
Sayil, J. and Ceyhun, B. (1981) A study on successful suicide. In J.P. Soubrier and J. Vedrinne (Eds), Depression and Suicide. Proceedings of the XIth Congress of the International Association for Suicide Prevention, Paris, July 5–8. Paris: Pergamon. pp. 496–501.
Schlosser, J. and Strehle-Jung, G. (1982) Suizide während Psychiatrischer Klinikbehandlung. Psychiatrische Praxis, 9: 20–26.
Walk, D. (1967) Suicide and community care. British Journal of Psychiatry, 113: 1381–1391.
Wolfersdorf, M. (1989) Suizid bei Stationären Psychiatrischen Patienten. Regensburg: Roderer.
Wolfersdorf, M. (1996a) Patientensuizid im psychiatrischen Krankenhaus: Ausgewählte Ergebnisse der Kliniksuizid-Verbundstudie (KSV) I/II 1970–1992 der AG "Suizidalität und psychiatrisches Krankenhaus". Psychiatrische Praxis, 23: 84–89.
Wolfersdorf, M. (1996b) Suizidalität im psychiatrischen Krankenhaus. Nervenheilkunde, 15: 507–514.
Wolfersdorf, M. (1992) Suizid als Ausgang psychischer Erkrankung. Zum Suizid psychisch Kranker während und nach stationärer psychiatrischer behandlung. In B. Steiner, F. Keller and M. Wolfersdorf (Eds), Katamnese-Studien in der Psychiatrie, pp. 133–157. Göttingen: Hogrefe Verlag für Psychologie.
Wolfersdorf, M. (1991) Hospital suicide in psychiatric institution. In A. Seva (Ed.), The Europe Handbook of Psychiatry and Mental Health, pp. 1804–1815. Barcelona: Antrophos, Editorial del Hombre.
Wolfersdorf, M., Keller, F. and Kaschka, W.P. (1997) Suicide of psychiatric inpatients 1970–1993 in Baden-Württemberg (Germany). Archives of Suicide Research, 3: 303–311.
Wolfersdorf, M. and Keller, F. (2000) Patientensuizide während stationärer psychiatrischen Therapie. Neue Entwicklungen Psychiatrische Praxis, 27: 1–5.

Chapter 26

The Impact of Suicide on Relatives and Friends

Sheila E. Clark
Department of General Practice, University of Adelaide, Australia,
and
Robert D. Goldney
Department of Psychiatry, University of Adelaide, Australia

Abstract

This chapter examines current beliefs about suicide bereavement from research and clinical perspectives. An overview of comparative studies looks at the effects of mode of death and predictors of bereavement outcome on the process of adjustment, and places the discussion in a historical perspective. The difficulties of bereavement research are discussed and recommendations for study designs are reviewed. The effects of a suicide death on family and friends, the community and the treating therapist are described. Clinical aspects of postvention are discussed and include immediate intervention at the site of a suicide, counselling issues and general bereavement care. Recent evaluations of postvention programmes are reviewed.

INTRODUCTION

About one million people worldwide commit suicide annually and, for every death, it has been estimated that six people suffer intense grief (Shneidman, 1969). Therefore as many as six million people are bereaved each year through suicide. The death of a close family member is one of the greatest of life's stresses (Holmes and Rahe, 1967). Considering that the process of normal adjustment to the loss of a close relationship can be as long as 4 years (Zisook and Shuchter, 1986), and even longer-term sequelae may be observed in clinical practice, the

The International Handbook of Suicide and Attempted Suicide. Edited by K. Hawton and K. van Heeringen.

collective morbidity resulting from completed suicide is clearly deserving of attention.

HISTORICAL PERSPECTIVE

Traditionally, suicide has been regarded as being associated with a particularly difficult grief process, and early case studies described major pathology among relatives and friends (Cain and Fast, 1972; Whitis, 1972). However, the use of more rigorous methodologies, including control groups of those bereaved through accidental death, has modified this opinion. In 1982 Calhoun and colleagues drew attention to shortcomings in the design of earlier studies, many of which had taken the form of interviews and had lacked comparison groups. Subsequent reviewers have concluded that the previously held belief that suicide bereavement was more severe could not be supported (McIntosh, 1993; Ness and Pfeffer, 1990; Van der Wal, 1989).

Rigorous studies have used comparison groups, larger group sizes and more sophisticated data analysis, including control for sociodemographic variables (Barrett and Scott, 1990; Cleiren, 1993; Cleiren et al, 1996; Demi, 1984; Farberow et al, 1987; Farberow et al, 1992a; Grad and Zavasnik, 1996; Séguin et al, 1995a). Also, standardized and task-specific bereavement outcome instruments have been used to measure the intensity of grief reactions, psychological and physical health, and social adjustment. For example, the work of Farberow and colleagues (1987, 1992a) was significant in tracking changes over 30 months in large groups of persons bereaved through suicide and natural death, and comparing them to non-bereaved controls. The Leiden Bereavement Study (Cleiren, 1993) was also important in elucidating the effects of various demographic and psychosocial variables, along with mode of death, on the outcome of bereavement. Subsequent research continued to increase understanding of the psychosocial factors influencing the outcome of suicide bereavement (Cleiren et al, 1996; Séguin et al, 1995a, 1995b).

The intimate nature of grief and the lack of clarity in defining and measuring bereavement outcomes have resulted in ethical and methodological difficulties. These include obtaining and retaining true study and control groups, and defining and measuring relevant morbidity outcomes. Therefore, the application of results of any one study to that of the general population, let alone to different cultures, must be approached with caution.

Recommendations have been made for improving study designs (Cleiren, 1993; McIntosh, 1993; Ness and Pfeffer, 1990; Woof and Carter, 1997). These include: recruiting subjects from the general bereaved population, rather than using self-selected or clinical groups; using a control group of non-bereaved as well as comparison mode of death groups; standardizing for age, gender, kinship and culture; using longitudinal design (ideally prospective); clearly defining morbidity outcomes; using standardized instruments and developing appropriate new grief measures; measuring at several definitive time intervals; and measuring and controlling for personality, psychological, family, social, cultural and economic factors.

THE PRESENT POSITION

The general consensus is that bereavement causes major effects in terms of grief and poor mental health functioning over a number of years, compared to non-bereaved controls. There are more similarities than differences in morbidity between those bereaved through suicide and through other causes, and the specific mode of death itself creates few if any quantitative differences in bereavement outcome, although recovery may be slower in the first 2 years after a suicide (Farberow et al, 1992a). However, differences in the themes of grief are common findings, but so far results are not consistent, and differences detected may not be exclusive to suicide. Demographic and psychosocial factors (see below) have more effect on outcome than the mode of death, but when these are controlled for, differences in morbidity no longer hold true. This led Cleiren and colleagues (1994) to conclude that:

> The mode of death plays only a marginal role in adaption to bereavement. The "crisis atmosphere" which some authors in the field continue to create around suicide bereavement may be more stigmatizing to suicide survivors than anything else.

Recent studies (Cleiren, 1993; Cleiren et al, 1996; Séguin et al, 1995a, 1995b) have found that better predictors of bereavement outcome than mode of death include: age of deceased; kinship lost; age, gender and culture of the bereaved; their attitude to the loss; and the quality of their relationship with the deceased. Other examples are: pre-loss stress; expectancy of the loss; support received after the death; and the severity of grief in the early months. For example, Cleiren's (1993) study found grief recovery to be more difficult for mothers of young deceased adults. There is a higher prevalence of some of the major predictors of poor bereavement outcome among those bereaved through suicide compared to those bereaved through natural death. For example, there are proportionately more people grieving the death of a young person, and more bereaved parents and females among those bereaved through suicide than among those bereaved through natural death. It is interesting to note that in those bereaved through accidental death there is an even higher prevalence of these factors than for suicide. Many psychosocial predictors of poor bereavement outcome are over-represented in the suicide group and include: higher prevalence of psychiatric illness in the family; more disturbed family dynamics; higher rate of adult and childhood loss; more conflictual or dependent relationships with the deceased; and, in most studies, lack of support in bereavement. Most of these are on-going functions within families, so the suicide is added to an already problem-laden background. In addition, these behaviours may be perpetuated and have intergenerational effects. Therefore, it is not unexpected that some families bereaved through suicide may experience extreme difficulty.

Evidence for this intergenerational effect also comes from recent evidence that, contrary to certain earlier views, suicidal behaviour does run in some families (Brent et al, 1996). Furthermore, as many as one-third of requests for help at a suicide prevention centre were reported to come from those who had experienced a suicide (Colt, 1987). Therefore those bereaved by suicide may be an "at-risk" group, not so much because of the mode of death but because suicide identifies the vulnerable.

GRIEF THEMES

Although an individual's grief is as unique as his/her fingerprint, there are commonalities to the emotional experiences following suicide. An understanding of these themes has come from qualitative studies that use interview and field methodologies. For clinical practice, it is pertinent to address some of these themes which are characteristic, but not necessarily unique, to suicide bereavement. The following paragraphs highlight some important aspects of the experience from a number of sources (Clark and Goldney, 1995; Van Dongen, 1991; Dunn and Morrish-Vidners, 1987; McIntosh, 1987; Van der Wal, 1989; Valente and Saunders, 1993). These are summarized in Table 26.1.

Shock

Themes relating to the shock of discovering the body may be recurring and long-lasting. The bereaved may relive the visual image of discovering it, or feelings and smells associated with cleaning up residue of the deceased. It might be thought that post-traumatic stress disorder would be more prevalent in those bereaved through suicide, but so far this has not been reported.

Relief vs. Family Disaster

Grief phenomena are affected by the context of the suicide and in this respect the concept of polarization of outcome can be useful. For some families, the suicide becomes a means of resolving existing problems and threats, whereas for others it is clearly a disaster (Séguin et al, 1995a). Families who struggle for years with a depressed individual and suicidal threats may experience relief after suicide, as their family life has an opportunity to return to normal. Comparative studies indicate that detachment from the deceased is easier for them generally than for those bereaved though traffic accidents. This is probably related to the

Table 26.1 Grief themes

Shock	—of discovering the body —that the person killed him/herself
Relief	—that the threat of suicide is over —that life can resume normality —that the deceased is out of his/her distress
Disbelief	—that the person is dead —that suicide is the cause of death
Horror	—about the emotional distress of the deceased —about the suffering in the dying process
How?	—what method and substances were used
Why?	—the events and relationships leading to the death —the state of mind of the deceased before death
Guilt	—for contributing to the suicide —for not preventing the suicide —for poor parenting, the breakdown of the relationship, or for sibling rivalry with the deceased before death —for not identifying the suicidal behaviour before the death —using the guilt to punish oneself for the suicide —about a death wish —at the sense of relief after the death —from the content of the suicide note
Blame	—towards other people for their contribution
Rejection	—feeling deserted or betrayed
Shame	—about mental illness, the suicide, blame, guilt
Loss of trust	—difficulty in maintaining old or forming new relationships —loneliness and social isolation
Wasted life	—remorse at unfulfilled talents and opportunities
Crisis of values	—fall of self-esteem —confusion in personal and existential values and beliefs
Suicidal thoughts	—to join the deceased —from loss of meaning and purpose in life, clinical depression
Fear of another suicide	—over-protection of family members
Unfinished business	—wishing the deceased had known how much he/she was appreciated —about past disputes
Anger	—at the deceased for the emotional pain and added responsibilities, at being cheated out of the relationship, at not being able to retaliate —at the system, self, press, therapist, God
Grief recovery	—reasoning that the deceased is out of emotional pain —discerning a peaceful expression on the deceased's face after death —fulfilment of the deceased's wish —the strength of the deceased —relief that the suicide is over —recognizing there may be few answers —developing a new spiritual relationship with the deceased —finding meaning from the loss

expectancy of the death and to less satisfactory pre-death relationships with the deceased in the suicide bereaved group (Cleiren et al, 1994). Indeed the family may regard suicide to be inevitable as they watch the deterioration in the mental state of the distressed person. By the time the suicide occurs they may have accepted mental illness as the cause of death, and by so doing, feelings of guilt, shame and rejection tend to be reduced. They may also be comforted that the deceased is out of distress, even though they regret the means.

On the other hand, for some families the suicide creates disaster. This includes families in which the suicide is totally unexpected and which had previously regarded themselves as functioning normally. Also, for already problem-laden families, which are ineffectual in resolving difficulties, the suicide adds to these problems and may increase the dysfunction.

Disbelief

After a totally unexpected suicide, disbelief at the cause of death may be paramount and the bereaved may cling to other explanations. Such convictions may be reinforced by feelings of shame, so that false information of the cause of death may be given. This can create further complications later. For example, children may lose trust in their parents when subsequently they discover they had been deceived. If denial persists long enough, the result of the post mortem or inquest may come as a shock.

Horror

Particular themes of horror encountered may include the realization of the extreme depth of distress the deceased must have been in. The bereaved may fantasize about the suffering of the dying process and, if it was slow, whether the deceased had changed his/her mind, but too late to act.

How?

The family may wish to know precisely how the person died, whether drugs or medications were ingested, and the effects of those substances physically and mentally. Information from a medical practitioner and the post mortem report may assist.

Why?

A quest for a reason for the suicide is a common theme. The bereaved examine the events and relationships leading to the death, and explore the state of mind of the deceased. Particular questions may arise, such as what external pressures were acting on the deceased, and why there was a breakdown in communication, such that they were not approached for help.

Guilt and Blame

Particular guilt issues commonly arise from the quest for "why?". The bereaved may feel they contributed to the suicide and blame themselves for not having prevented it. They may feel they should have been totally in control of the deceased to the extent of being overly responsible for him/her. They may blame themselves for the poor relationship and be unaware of the normal difficulties of communicating with someone suffering a mental illness. Parents may feel there was something suspect in their parenting. They may feel that as the closest in kinship to their child, they should have been the ones to see the signs of hopelessness and to have acted as their child's confidante. "If only . . ." is a common phrase used to describe acts which might have helped to prevent the suicide. They may not be aware that the source of much of their guilt is imagined and unrealistic. Some bereaved seem unconsciously to use their guilt to punish themselves. Particular difficulties may arise if there had been any overt or covert death-wish on the deceased resulting from disturbed family dynamics. Some families feel they did all they could, whereas others, even if they had participated in the deceased's care, may have unrealistic feelings of remorse. Guilt may also be felt at the sense of relief created by the death.

The suicide note may influence the bereaved into assuming responsibility and guilt. Through a simulated study, Rudestam and Agnelli (1987) found the recipients of notes that blamed the bereaved acted defensively, but notes in which the deceased blamed him/herself generated increased remorse. Analysis of notes has consistently found them to contain disturbed thinking. Nevertheless, the bereaved regard the original note as important and may react angrily if it is taken away for forensic purposes.

Blame from others may be experienced. In-laws may blame the surviving partner, particularly where the relationship was disapproved of, unconventional or socially stigmatized. In contrast to the support normally expected from in-laws after the death of a spouse, the partner may find him/herself criticized or even condemned by them. This may reinforce perceived feelings of rejection.

Rejection

Suicide is sometimes seen as a reasoned choice made by the deceased and felt as a conscious rejection of the family in favour of death. The bereaved may feel betrayed by the secrecy of the act. Further, following difficult relationships they may interpret the death as a malicious act with no opportunity for redress.

Stigma, Loss of Trust and Social Isolation

Feelings of stigma associated with the death vary between studies and appear to be culturally-based. Even where stigma is absent, feelings of shame may arise due to guilt, blame, rejection, being the subject of gossip, and the associations of suicide with mental illness. Some families feel there is a tainting of the family tree or come to hold superstitious beliefs that the suicide was caused by evil in the family. Séguin and colleagues (1995a) found a significant increase in shame in those bereaved through suicide as compared to accident.

There are many anecdotal reports of social isolation, which are supported by comparative studies. Séguin and colleagues (1995a) describe shame as playing an important role in constraining interpersonal relationships and postulates that the bereaved may create their own social isolation. Another factor which may contribute to this is the loss of trust in others that some people experience after being let down by the suicide of someone in whom they had previously trusted.

Social support, an important protective factor in bereavement, is multifaceted and measured by different parameters. Some comparative studies find no differences in many parameters of social support across modes of death (Cleiren, 1993; Range and Niss, 1990), but results from various research methodologies point, in particular, to a lack of emotional support for those bereaved through suicide (Cleiren et al, 1996; Farberow et al, 1992b; McNeil et al, 1988). Community studies indicate a mismatch in knowledge and attitudes between the bereaved and professional or community groups (Goldney et al, 1987; Thornton et al, 1989). After a suicide the bereaved may have an additional burden of educating their friends about the causes and nature of suicide and about how to behave toward them.

Wasted Life

Remorse at the waste of a life and at the unfulfillable opportunities for the deceased person and for the members of the bereaved family is a common theme.

Crisis of Values

These negative themes may contribute to a "crisis of values". Van der Wal (1989) used this term to describe the intense decline in self-esteem and confusion in existential and personal values. Some become distraught that their previous beliefs in God and the afterlife are in turmoil, with particular reference to their own future and the spiritual state of the deceased.

Suicidal Thoughts and Fear of Another Suicide

As is usual in bereavement, suicidal thoughts are common and may be in part a longing to rejoin the deceased and to complete unfinished business, or it can be caused by depression. Added fears about a repeat family suicide may cause complications. For example, families may become over-protective; in particular, parents may worry about the risk to younger siblings when they reach the age at which the older child took his/her life. Adolescents may have difficulty dealing with the boundaries between themselves and a role model who took his/her life, or even feel fated to die. Acquaintances may worry about contagion, which may cause them to withdraw support.

Unfinished Business

Unfinished business may be considerable, and results not just from the suddenness of the death, but also because of difficulties in communicating with the deceased beforehand. Particular fears relate to wishing the deceased had known how much he/she was loved, and that he/she died feeling unloved.

Anger

Anger at the deceased may result from the emotional pain experienced, particularly if the bereaved person holds the opinion the deceased chose to die, or if he/she were blamed in the suicide note. When a partner suicides, there may be anger at being cheated out of the relationship or at being left to carry the full burden of the family's responsibilities. Anger may also be expressed towards the health care team, God or the therapist him/herself. There may be anger at the press for inaccurate, exaggerated or sensational reports, and for the loss of privacy at the time of family tragedy.

Grief Recovery

Some themes may be particularly helpful to recovery. Reasoning that the deceased is out of emotional pain, and discerning a peaceful expression on the face of the deceased after death, may be comforting. Other comforting factors include the deceased's wish being fulfilled and his/her strength to carry out the act. Families who experience relief that the impending crisis is over may resume better functioning more quickly.

Eventually, most bereaved settle for the uncertainty of never finding a complete answer to many of the questions and issues raised by the suicide. As they progress through the fears of moving away from their physical relationship with the deceased, many find a new emotional or spiritual relationship with them comforting. In addition, deriving meaning in terms of finding something positive to emerge from the experience may change priorities and create a new purpose in life.

OUTCOME

The level of grief may remain high for several years. Studies of bereaved spouses have found significant grief still at 2.5 years following bereavement (Farberow et al, 1992a), and at 4 years, 20% rated their adjustment as only "fair" or "poor" (Zissook and Shuchter, 1986). Grief commonly intensifies at the anniversary and other significant dates such as birthdays, Christmas and Mothers' Day and may resurge with subsequent unrelated losses.

Comparative studies show no differences between modes of death. Reports of strengthening of the family unit after suicide vary between 33% and 100% of families (Séguin et al, 1995a; Van Dongen, 1991). Demi (1984) found the social functioning of widows, following the suicide of their spouse, to be better than those following other modes of death, and reasoned that their husband's mental illness had accustomed them to this role before the death. On the other hand, complications may arise, such as depression, substance abuse and relationship breakdown and some families clearly remain dysfunctional.

PRACTICAL ISSUES AND BEREAVEMENT CARE

Empathic support, although important, is not sufficient (Parkes, 1988). To provide appropriate assistance, an individual's grief needs to be understood not only in terms of mode of death but also in the context of the known predictive factors. An outline of some of the main postvention issues, derived from several sources (Clark, 1995; Dunne and Morrish-Vidners, 1987; Wertheimer, 1991), is summarized here in Table 26.2.

A physician certifying death at the site of suicide can allay initial confusion and provide explanation about such matters as why resuscitation was stopped, or not begun, and the need for the police, medical examiner and coroner's investigation at a time of personal tragedy. Opportunity can also be made for the family to spend time with the body, as this helps them accept the reality of the death, and assists in resolving unfinished business. Families may become distraught if the body is taken away too soon.

There are three matters which need to be raised with the family immediately after the death to prevent complications in the grieving process. First, telling the truth from the outset about the cause of death will prevent difficulties in trying to maintain future deceptions. Details of the method used are not necessary and not always appropriate. Second, opportunity should be offered to view the body, but if it is mutilated the alternative of maintaining vigil over the covered body

Table 26.2 Bereavement interventions

At the site of suicide	
Instruct the family that, for forensic purposes, nothing should be touched	
Explain resuscitation and official procedures	
Arrange opportunity for the family to spend time with the body, preferably alone, after the investigation	
Debrief the resuscitation team	
Arrange professional cleaning services	
Debrief with a colleague	
First 24 hours	
Information:	
Tell others the true cause of death, including children	
Viewing or photographs of the body	
Public funeral	
Follow-up	
Information	
Models of suicide, including the neurotransmitter model	
Causes of mental illness and risk for survivors	
Limitations of prediction of suicide	
Lifestyle education and grief survival strategies	
Counselling	
Assess mental state	
Rationalize unrealistic negative feelings	
The 'why' may never be solved	
Mark achievements	
Raise self-esteem	
Specific agencies	
Medical practitioners	Information on the dying process
	Interpretation of the post mortem report
	Mental state and psychosocial assessment
	Physical review, e.g. blood pressure check
	Medical certificates
Coroner's office	Return of suicide notes
	Information on how the death occurred
	Post mortem report
Support group	
Minister of religion	
Review	
Three months	
At issue of post mortem report	
Anniversaries	

may be preferred. Families may be angry if this opportunity is denied. If a decision is taken not to view the body, negotiations should be made with a family member or the funeral director to take photographs of the body in case of future need. These may be useful later to alleviate fantasies of misidentification or trauma in the dying process. Third, if a public funeral is not held, regrets about not giving adequate tribute to the deceased may arise. In addition, the opportunity is denied for other significant mourners, such as school friends or work colleagues, to commence their grieving. If the funeral is private or if there is no funeral at all, the bereaved may also deprive themselves of the usual demonstrations of support. They are often comforted that a large attendance at the funeral signified that their loved one meant so much to so many.

An explanation of various models of suicide, particularly the neurotransmitter model (see Chapter 4), may be particularly helpful in understanding why the person took his/her life, and such a no-blame model may alleviate feelings of guilt, rejection and shame. Similarly, neurophysiological explanations of the causes of mental illness and its treatment can help rationalize fear about risk to others and reduce stigma. Any apparent social stress or other environmental causes of the suicide must, of course, be acknowledged. Also, discussion of the limitations of the prediction of suicide by professionals may help to reduce feelings of guilt.

Counselling may be helpful to assist a bereaved person to rationalize unrealistic feelings, particularly guilt, rejection and those arising from the suicide note. The quest for why the suicide occurred may become all-consuming, and directing the bereaved to turn their attention to other grief issues may be more productive. An issue in which a minister of religion may be helpful is the often-raised question of the location of the soul of the deceased after death.

A gentle exploration of feelings, on the basis that the introjection of such feelings contributes to emotional distress, is usually therapeutic, although the timing of such intervention needs skilled judgement. The bereaved need to be encouraged to progress along the course of resolution of bereavement, for example by attention to suitable memorials and the appropriate disposition of ashes. A cognitive–behavioural approach, encouraging the view that all societies have such rituals and that they can be negotiated successfully, often proves helpful. In addition, skills in thought stoppage, a daily grief time, keeping a record of feelings and memories, and time for recreation, may prove valuable survival strategies.

The mental state of bereaved individuals should be regularly assessed and a challenge is whether or not antidepressant medication should be utilized. If severe symptoms of depression persist, this should raise the possibility that it may be of value. Often bereaved persons are reluctant to take medication, and it can be offered as a trial and as one component of successfully negotiating the grief and mourning process. The principles of using antidepressants are the same as for other clinical situations, with the added emphasis that safe antidepressants should be utilized to minimize the risk of suicidal behaviour in this vulnerable group, and that such medication is adjunct to the psychological grief work, rather than a replacement for it.

Chronic tiredness may make the grief process more difficult. Education about specific strategies, such as avoiding caffeine, taking daily physical exercise, and establishing a relaxing pre-sleep routine, may assist in overcoming insomnia.

Hypnotics can be a useful addition in the short term to re-establish sleep patterns, although requests for them may indicate the need for further exploration of problems. In addition to the risk of addiction, a danger is that they may blur the reality of the funeral, which may impede the grieving process.

Pre-existing medical conditions may be more difficult to control following the death and new symptoms may arise, so a medical check-up, particularly for blood pressure, may be pertinent.

In the course of bereavement counselling, it is not uncommon for previously hidden issues, such as depression and sexual abuse, to be unveiled. This provides opportunity for appropriate intervention.

As those bereaved through suicide are a group at risk of poor bereavement outcome, psychosocial problems and suicidal behaviour, it is pertinent to ask what postvention programmes exist. Farberow (1998), in reviewing the 52 member countries of the International Association of Suicide Prevention, found only 27% reported any such programmes. Mostly these were support groups provided by non-government and non-professional sources. In reviewing support groups in the USA, it was found that access is mainly by word of mouth and that there is a paucity of services for certain groups, such as children, adolescents and ethnic groups (Campbell, 1997; Rubey and McIntosh, 1996). Support groups have developed in response to community need for assistance. They are valuable in assisting the bereaved person to recognize that his/her feelings of intense emotional pain are normal, and to provide experiential expertise and role models of survival. Other important functions are those of advocacy within the community and destigmatization. Accounts of the structure and function of groups include those of Billow (1987), Clark et al (1993), Farberow (1992) and Wrobleski (1984).

ISSUES FOR THE TREATING THERAPIST

The therapist's own response to suicide has recently received much-needed attention, and sequelae have been described in a wide range of professionals and volunteers (Grad, 1996; Hodgkinson 1987; Michel et al, 1997). These are feelings of personal loss, including shock, sadness, relief (that intolerable suffering is over, that the stress of professional vigilance has ended), feelings of professional failure, fear for one's reputation, and anger at the deceased for the disruption he/she caused. Lasting personal sequelae, such as physical sickness, depression, irrational fears and deterioration in interpersonal and professional relationships, may occur.

Other sequelae include depersonalization and distancing from patients and colleagues, or the opposite of over-involvement in the professional role, absenteeism, fear of anger from the family and of malpractice suits, and even change of career. Female therapists have a greater tendency to feel more shame and guilt, to doubt their professional expertise and to seek consolation. No differences have been found according to years of experience or profession (Grad et al, 1997). Some accounts include a personal resolution of these issues, with the therapist seeing the suicide as a medium for expanding his/her own personal or professional horizons by learning from the experience. Repression of feelings learnt through professional training may contribute to non-resolution of the therapist's grief, which may prevent him/her from fulfilling his/her immediate professional responsibilities. Therapists may find themselves in the dilemma of dealing with their own emotions at the same time as being required to provide objective support to the bereaved family, fellow-patients of the suicide victim, and team members. This needs to be resolved quickly, as early contact with these groups is likely to minimize misunderstandings.

In a retrospective study, Grad and Zavasnik (1998) confirmed many of these themes but found little difference between general practitioners' reactions after a suicide compared with the aftermath of other types of death. Therapists' reactions, like those of the bereaved, may not be so different as originally thought and prospective longitudinal studies are necessary to elucidate this.

The suicide of a patient or client is a professional hazard for those who work with the suicidal. For example, a full-time general practitioner may experience the suicide of a patient every 4–5 years (Lewis et al, 1997). There exist few accounts of preparation of the therapist or institution for a suicide. Recommendations include training to deal with the personal and professional issues of the aftermath, a contingency plan and review protocol for the institution, and the availability of professional support for the individual therapist.

ISSUES FOR THE COMMUNITY

Groups ranging from the resuscitation team to the deceased's school, club or workplace may be affected. In fact, adolescent peers may fare worse than siblings in terms of depression (Brent et al, 1994). Institutions need a prepared crisis plan to facilitate appropriate grieving and to assist their members to return to productivity (Lamb and Dunne-Maxim, 1987). This may include allowing members to share in the public family rituals, but care needs to be taken to prevent heroism and romanticism of the suicide, which may lead to secondary gain and suicide contagion.

Sensitive media reporting can play an important role in preventing contagion and in educating the community in relation to suicide, thereby fostering appropriate attitudes and assistance for the bereaved. In many countries, health officials and media are working to form a set of recommendations regarding the reporting of suicide (see Chapter 39).

EVALUATION OF BEREAVEMENT INTERVENTIONS

Evaluation of bereavement interventions, including those of support groups and in schools, carries all the methodological difficulties mentioned previously. Early reports produced anecdotal claims that the bereaved had been helped. Goldney and Berman (1996), in reviewing postvention programmes, point out that although they may seem desirable to alleviate emotional pain, little hard evidence from controlled studies exists of their effectiveness. However, Woof and Carter (1997) reviewed 11 controlled trials (although it is not clear whether these were randomized) of general and suicide bereavement support groups and found that in seven trials the subjects showed significant improvements on one or more measures, compared to controls. A recent randomized controlled study showed that although participants rated a 10-week group progamme to be beneficial, outcome scores on mental health and grief measures did not altogether support this (Murphy et al, 1998). Changes in scores indicated that, compared to controls, highly distressed mothers benefited most, whereas those less distressed, and fathers, generally appeared worse off. This clearly has implications for further research and for managers of postvention programmes. As McIntosh (1996) points out in his comprehensive literature review, there are still many gaps in our knowledge.

CONCLUSION

Worldwide, at least six million people are bereaved through suicide annually. Findings from rigorous comparative studies show that bereavement through suicide is no more difficult than bereavement following other modes of death. However, it is more likely that families bereaved through suicide are also struggling with pre-existing problems, which may complicate the grieving process. Therefore Shneidman's assertion (1969) that "postvention is prevention for the next decade and for the next generation" still holds true, but for reasons that were not originally fully appreciated. The bereaved are left with difficult emotional themes and questions which are different in many respects from those resulting from other modes of death, and which are important for professionals and carers to understand so that appropriate bereavement care can be provided. Because of such large numbers of bereaved persons, this clearly presents a challenge to the capacity of professional and volunteer organizations, particularly in this era of diminished funding. Therefore, the elucidation of the optimum form of intervention, for whom it should be provided and its timing, are priorities for future research.

REFERENCES

Barrett, T.W. and Scott, T.B. (1990) Suicide bereavement and recovery patterns compared with non-suicide bereavement patterns. Suicide and Life Threatening Behavior, 20 (1): 1–15.

Billow, C.J. (1987) A multiple family support group for survivors of suicide. In E.J. Dunne, J.L. McIntosh and K. Dunne-Maxim (Eds), Suicide and Its Aftermath. Understanding and Counseling the Survivors. New York: W.W. Norton.

Brent, D.A., Bridge, J., Johnson, B.A. and Connolly, J. (1996) Suicidal behavior runs in families. A controlled family study of adolescent suicide victims. Archives of General Psychiatry, 53: 1146–1152.

Brent, D.A., Perper, J.A., Moritz, G., Liotus, L., Schweers, J. and Canobbio, R. (1994) Major depression or uncomplicated bereavement? A follow-up of youth exposed to suicide. Journal of the American Academy of Child and Adolescent Psychiatry, 33: 231–239.

Cain, A.C. and Fast, I. (1972) The legacy of suicide: observations of the pathogenic impact of suicide upon marital partners. In A.C. Cain (Ed.), Survivors of Suicide. Springfield, IL: Charles C. Thomas.

Calhoun, L.G., Selby, J.W. and Selby, L.E. (1982) The psychological aftermath of suicide: an analysis of current evidence. Clinical Psychology Review, 2: 409–420.

Campbell, F.R. (1997) Changing the legacy of suicide. Suicide and Life Threatening Behavior, 27 (4): 329–338.

Clark, S.E. (1995) After Suicide: Help for the Bereaved. Melbourne: Hill of Content.

Clark, S.E., Jones, H.E., Quinn, K., Goldney, R.D. and Cooling, P. (1993) A support group of people bereaved through suicide. Crisis, 14 (4): 161–166.

Clark, S.E. and Goldney, R.D. (1995) Grief reactions and recovery in a support group for people bereaved by suicide. Crisis, 16 (1): 27–33.

Cleiren, M.P.H.D. (1993) Bereavement and Adaption. A Comparative Study of the Aftermath of Death. Washington, DC: Hemisphere.

Cleiren, M.P.H.D., Diekstra, R.F.W., Kerkhof, A.J.F.M. and Van der Wal, J. (1994) Mode of death and kinship in bereavement: focusing on the "who" rather than "how". Crisis, 15: 22–36.

Cleiren, M.P.H.D., Grad, O., Zavasnik, A. and Diekstra, R.F.W. (1996) Psychosocial impact of bereavement after suicide and fatal traffic accident: a comparative two-country study. Acta Psychiatrica Scandinavica. 94: 37–44.

Colt, G.H. (1987) The history of the suicide survivor: the mark of Cain. In E.J. Dunne, J.L. McIntosh and K. Dunne-Maxim (Eds), Suicide and Its Aftermath: Understanding and Counselling the Survivors. New York: W.W. Norton.

Demi, A.S. (1984) Social adjustment of widows after a suicide death: suicide and non-suicide survivors compared. Death Education, 8: 91–111.

Dunn, R.G. and Morrish-Vidners, D. (1987) The psychological and social experiences of suicide survivors. Omega, 18 (3): 175–215.

Farberow, N. (1992) The Los Angeles Survivors-After-Suicide program. Crisis, 13 (1): 23–34.

Farberow, N. (1998) Suicide survivor programs in IASP member countries: a survey. In R.J. Kosky, H.S. Eshkevari, R.D. Goldney and R. Hassan (Eds), Suicide Prevention: The Global Context. New York: Plenum.

Farberow, N., Gallagher, D.E., Gilewski, M. and Thompson, L. (1987) An examination of the early impact of psychological distress in survivors of suicide. The Gerontologist, 27 (5): 592–589.

Farberow, N., Gallagher-Thompson, D.E., Gilewski, M. and Thompson, L. (1992a) Changes in grief and mental health of bereaved spouses of older suicides. Journal of Gerontology, 47 (6): 357–366.

Farberow, N., Gallagher-Thompson, D.E., Gilewski, M. and Thompson, L. (1992b) The role of social supports in the bereavement process of surviving spouses of suicide and natural death. Suicide and Life Threatening Behavior, 22 (1): 107–124.

Goldney, R. and Berman, L. (1996) Postvention in schools: affective or effective? Crisis, 17 (3): 98–99.

Goldney, R., Spence, N. and Moffit, P. (1987) The aftermath of suicide: attitudes of those bereaved by suicide, of social workers, and of a community sample. Journal of Community Psychology, 15: 141–148.

Grad, O.T. (1996) Suicide: how to survive as a survivor?. Crisis, 17 (3): 136–142.

Grad, O.T. and Zavasnik, A. (1996) Similarities and differences in the process of bereavement after suicide and after traffic fatalities in Slovenia, Omega, 33(3): 245–251.

Grad, O.T. and Zavasnik, A. (1998) The caregivers' reactions after suicide of a patient. In R.J. Kosky, H.S. Eshkevari, R.D. Goldney and R. Hassan (Eds), Suicide Prevention: the Global Context. New York: Plenum.

Grad, O.T., Zavasnik, A. and Groleger, U. (1997) Suicide of a patient: gender differences in bereavement reactions of therapists. Suicide and Life Threatening Behavior, 27 (4): 379–386.

Hodgkinson, P. (1987) Responding to in-patient suicide. British Journal of Medical Psychology, 60: 387–392.

Holmes, T.H. and Rahe, R.H. (1967) The social readjustment rating scale. Journal of Psychosomatic Research, 11: 213–218.

Lamb, F. and Dunne-Maxim, K. (1987) Postvention in schools: policy and process. In E.J. Dunne, J.L. McIntosh and K. Dunne-Maxim (Eds), Suicide and Its Aftermath: Understanding and Counselling the Survivors. New York: W.W. Norton.

Lewis, G., Hawton, K. and Jones, P. (1997) Strategies for preventing suicide. British Journal of Psychiatry, 171: 351–354.

Michel, K., Armson, S., Fleming, G., Rosenbauer, C. and Takahashi, Y. (1997) After suicide: who counsels the therapist? Report from the workshop of the 29th Congress of the IASP. Crisis, 18 (3): 128–139.

McIntosh, J.L. (1987) Survivor family relationships: literature review. In E.J. Dunne, J.L. McIntosh and K. Dunne-Maxim (Eds), Suicide and Its Aftermath. Understanding and Counselling the Survivors. New York: W.W. Norton.

McIntosh, J.L. (1993) Control group studies of suicide survivors: a review and critique. Suicide and Life Threatening Behavior, 23: 146–161.

McIntosh, J.L. (1996) Survivors of suicide: a comprehensive bibliography update, 1986–1995. Omega, 33 (2): 147–175.

McNeil, D.E., Hatcher, C. and Reubin, R. (1988) Family survivors of suicide and accidental death: consequences for widows. Suicide and Life Threatening Behavior, 18 (2): 137–148.

Murphy, S.A., Johnson, C., Cain, K., Gupta, A.D., Dimond, M. and Lohan, J. (1998) Broad spectrum group treatment for parents bereaved by violent deaths of their 12–28 year-old children: a randomized controlled trial. Death Studies, 22: 209–235.

Ness, D.E. and Pfeffer, C.R. (1990) Sequelae of bereavement resulting from suicide. American Journal of Psychiatry, 143 (3): 279–285.

Parkes, C.M. (1988) Bereavement as a psychosocial transition: processes of adaption to change. Journal of Social Issues, 44 (3): 53–65.

Range, L.M. and Niss, N.M. (1990) Long-term bereavement from suicide, homicide accidents and natural deaths. Death Studies, 14: 423–433.

Rubey, C.T. and McIntosh, J.L. (1996) Suicide survivors groups: results of a survey. Suicide and Life Threatening Behavior, 26 (4): 351–358.

Rudestam, K.E. and Agnelli, P. (1987) The effect of the content of suicide note on grief reactions. Journal of Clinical Psychology, 43 (2): 211–218.

Séguin, M., Lesage, A. and Kiely, M.C. (1995a) Parental bereavement after suicide and accident: a comparative study. Suicide and Life Threatening Behavior. 25 (4): 489–498.

Séguin, M., Lesage, A. and Kiely, M.C. (1995b) History of early loss among a group of suicide survivors. Crisis, 16 (3): 121–125.

Shneidman, E.S. (1969) Prologue. In E.S. Schneidman (Ed.), On the Nature of Suicide. San Francisco, CA: Jossey-Bass.

Thornton, G., Whittemore, K.D. and Robertson, D.U. (1989) Evaluation of people bereaved through suicide. Death Studies, 13: 119–126.

Valente, S.M. and Saunders, J.M. (1993) Adolescent grief after suicide. Crisis, 14 (1): 16–46.

Van Dongen, C.J. (1991) Experiences of family members after a suicide. Journal of Family Practice, 33 (4): 375–380.

Van der Wal, J. (1989) The aftermath of suicide: a review of empirical evidence. Omega, 20 (2): 149–171.

Wertheimer, A. (1991) A Special Scar: The Experiences of People Bereaved through Suicide. London: Routledge.
Whitis, P.R. (1972) The legacy of a child's suicide. In A.C. Cain (Ed.), Survivors of Suicide. Springfield, IL: Charles C. Thomas.
Woof, W.R. and Carter, Y.H. (1997) The grieving adult and the general practitioner: a literature review in two parts (part 2). British Journal of General Practice, 47: 509–514.
Wrobleski, A. (1984) The suicide survivors' grief group. Omega, 15 (2): 173–184.
Zisook, S. and Shuchter, S.R. (1986) The first four years of widowhood. Psychiatric Annals, 16: 288–294.

Part III

The Treatment of Suicidal Behaviour

Chapter 27

Pharmacotherapy of Suicidal Ideation and Behaviour

Robbert J. Verkes
Department of Psychiatry, Nijmegen University Hospital, Nijmegen, The Netherlands,
and
Philip J. Cowen
Psychopharmacology Research Unit, University of Oxford, Warneford Hospital, Oxford, UK

Abstract

Virtually all psychiatric disorders, but particularly recurrent mood disorders and schizophrenia, are associated with increased rates of suicide. The use of psychotropic drug treatment for the prevention of suicide is based on the principle that successful therapy of an underlying psychiatric disorder will decrease the risk of suicidal ideation and behaviour. While this has been difficult to establish from prospective trials, epidemiological studies suggest that rates of suicide are significantly lower in patients treated with antidepressants drugs and mood stabilizers. However, this effect could presumably be attributed to the fact that those who seek treatment are less likely to exhibit suicidal behaviour than those who do not. In addition, lower suicide rates of those in treatment may not be due to the specific effects of drug therapy. To some extent these caveats are offset by the fact that drug treatments appear to have differential effects on suicidal behaviour. For example, lithium may be more effective than carbamazepine in lowering suicide rates in patients with recurrent mood disorders. Similarly, the atypical antipsychotic drug, clozapine, is probably more effective than conventional antipsychotic agents in decreasing suicidal behaviour in patients with schizophrenia. While treatment with selective serotonin re-uptake inhibitors may decrease impulsivity and suicide attempts in patients with personality disorders, benzodiazepines can produce the opposite effect. Whatever the precise mechanisms involved, current evidence suggests that the appropriate use of psychotropic medication in patients with recurrent or chronic psychiatric disorders can make a useful contribution to the reduction of suicide rates.

The International Handbook of Suicide and Attempted Suicide. Edited by K. Hawton and K. van Heeringen.

INTRODUCTION

Psychiatric disorders such as mood disorders, schizophrenia, anxiety disorders and personality disorders carry an increased mortality from suicide. Pharmacotherapy is often required for the management of these disorders and it is usually assumed that effective treatment lessens the risk of suicide. It has, however, proved difficult to demonstrate this unequivocally.

Another question is the postulated existence of a suicidality syndrome independent of specific major psychiatric disorder. Hopelessness, low self-esteem, social isolation and inadequate control of aggressive impulses may be core symptoms of such a syndrome (Ahrens and Linden, 1996). There has been much speculation concerning the role of decreased brain serotonin function in this syndrome, as indications of lowered serotonin function have been found in patients manifesting suicidal behaviour across boundaries of specific psychiatric disorders (see Chapter 4). This suggests that drugs which potentiate brain serotonin function may have a particular role in lowering suicidal behaviour, even in subjects without a specific Axis I disorder. Equally, it is possible that some drugs might actually exacerbate the risk of suicidal behaviour, even if they produce symptomatic improvement in other psychological domains.

Controlled studies on the effect of pharmacological treatment on suicidality itself are scarce. Available information from prospective controlled trials is mostly derived from treatment studies in patients with a particular major psychiatric disorder. However, in such trials, patients with serious suicidal ideation are often excluded.

Another source of information comes from epidemiological studies. Suicide rates of patients taking drug treatment, compared with those who are not, can be estimated in various ways. The problem with this approach is the fact that subjects in such studies have not been randomly allocated to treatment, and apparent differences in suicidal behaviour may be linked to help-seeking behaviour rather than any specific effects of drug treatment.

In this chapter we will review the effects on suicidality of the main classes of psychopharmacological agents, including findings from epidemiological investigations and controlled trials. Suicide is fortunately a rare event and it is therefore common for investigators to assess effects of drug treatment on proxy markers, such as attempted suicide or suicidal ideation. While the former is definitely linked to completed suicide, the relationship of the latter to suicidal behaviour is more complex. Persons who exhibit aggressive, impulsive behaviour towards others are also more prone to impulsive, auto-aggressive, i.e. suicidal, behaviour. Therefore, the effect of pharmacological treatment on aggressive behaviour may be relevant to suicidal behaviour, and will be addressed where data are available.

ANTIDEPRESSANTS

Depressive Disorders

Antidepressant drugs are clearly effective in the treatment of major depression and prospective random allocation studies demonstrate their efficacy in lowering suicidal ideation (Beasley et al, 1991). Prospective data showing that this leads to reduction in attempted and completed suicide are more sparse. However, a meta-analysis of trials of short-term treatment with paroxetine suggests a trend towards such an effect, compared to placebo treatment (Montgomery et al, 1995).

In their epidemiological study, Isacsson and colleagues (1996) calculated that each year about 1,000 people with major depression commit suicide in Sweden. From autopsy data, these authors estimated that the risk of suicide in subjects taking antidepressants was about 1.8 times less than in those who were not. This suggests that antidepressant drug treatment is associated with lower suicide rates but cannot, of course, imply a causal mechanism.

Such studies treat antidepressants as an homogeneous group, but potentially important pharmacological differences exist between them which could influence their effects on suicidality. For example, over the course of a 1 year trial of prophylactic treatment for depression the antidepressant drug maprotiline was associated with significantly more suicide attempts than placebo. Of the 331 patients on placebo, only one committed suicide, whereas of the 661 patients on maprotiline, eight patients attempted suicide and a further six committed suicide (Rouillon et al, 1989). Nevertheless, maprotiline was superior to placebo in its effect on depression. These findings suggest that maprotiline may provoke suicidal behaviour, despite its antidepressant effects.

Maprotiline is predominantly a noradrenaline re-uptake inhibitor, lacking significant serotonin re-uptake inhibition. It therefore potentiates the effect of noradrenaline but not that of serotonin. As noted above, there are theoretical reasons for supposing that antidepressants which potently enhance the activity of serotonin, such as the selective serotonin re-uptake inhibitors (SSRIs), may be particularly useful in the treatment and prevention of suicidal behaviour. Indeed, in the meta-analysis of paroxetine mentioned above, this SSRI produced an earlier improvement in suicidal ideation than the comparator antidepressant, imipramine, a conventional tricyclic antidepressant (Montgomery et al, 1995). Similar data exist for another SSRI, namely fluvoxamine (Ottevanger, 1991).

These findings suggest that SSRIs may be effective in the treatment of suicidal ideation in depressed patients. Nevertheless, patients have been described who experience intense suicidal ideation or sudden self-harm after starting or increasing the dose of the SSRI fluoxetine (see Power and Cowen, 1992). It must be noted, however, that antidepressants from all classes, and even ECT and light therapy in seasonal affective disorder, have occasionally and anecdotally been associated with worsening or emergence of suicidal ideation or behaviour (Mann and Kapur, 1991; Praschak-Rieder et al, 1997). Furthermore, analyses of pooled, double-blind drug studies in patients with major depression, indicated less frequent emergence or worsening of substantial suicidal ideation with SSRIs than with tricyclics or placebo (Beasley et al, 1991; Montgomery et al, 1995; Letizia et al, 1996).

These data raise the question of whether SSRIs may decrease suicidal behaviour in patients with depressive disorders, even when the underlying mood disturbance continues. However, in patients with brief recurrent depression, fluoxetine (120 mg per week, administered bi-weekly), in comparison to placebo, failed to prevent both depressive episodes and suicidal behaviour during a 6-month follow-up period (Montgomery et al, 1994). This suggests that the effect of SSRIs to decrease suicidal ideation and behaviour in depressive states may be dependent on concomitant improvement in the underlying mood disorder.

Anxiety Disorders

The suicide risk in patients with primary anxiety disorders is about five times higher than in the general population (Allgulander, 1994; see Chapter 11), and in particular the combination with depressive disorder increases this risk considerably. In a prospective study in 954 patients with major depression, the 13 patients who committed suicide within 1 year of follow-up were characterized by severe anxiety and the presence of panic attacks (Fawcett et al, 1990). There is no doubt that prompt and adequate treatment of anxiety and agitation is sometimes needed to avoid an immediate risk of suicide (Fawcett, 1995).

Antidepressant drugs are increasingly used in the treatment of anxiety disorders (Cowen, 1996), but the impact of pharmacotherapy on suicidal ideation and behaviour in patients with anxiety syndromes has been little studied. There are, however, data to show that the SSRI fluoxetine was superior to placebo in the reduction of suicidality in obsessive-compulsive disorder (Beasley et al, 1992), anxiety disorders (Warshaw and Keller, 1996) and bulimia nervosa (Wheadon et al, 1992).

Personality Disorder

Recurrent suicide threats are characteristic for certain patients with personality disorder, particularly those meeting criteria for the borderline type. In patients with borderline personality disorder, several small open trials with the SSRI fluoxetine, 5–80 mg/day (Norden, 1989; Markovitz et al, 1991), and sertraline, 50–200 mg/day (Kavoussi et al, 1994), have demonstrated improvement in suicidality, self-injury and impulsive aggression. In a double-blind, placebo-controlled study, a decrease in anger was shown with fluoxetine, 20–60 mg/day (Salzman et al, 1995). More recently, Coccaro and Kavousi (1997) studied the effect of fluoxetine (20–60 mg/day) in 40 non-depressed subjects with personality disorders. Compared with placebo, fluoxetine produced a sustained improvement in self-report measures of irritability and aggression. These effects were not mediated through changes in depression, anxiety or alcohol use.

In a randomized placebo-controlled trial in 91 recurrent suicide attempters without a major psychiatric DSM-IV Axis I disorder, and with predominantly borderline personality features, the SSRI paroxetine, 40 mg/day, showed an effect in the reduction of the suicide attempt rate during the 1-year duration of the study (Verkes et al, 1998). All patients received supportive psychotherapy on a weekly to fortnightly basis. In the group as a whole, paroxetine failed to show a significant effect on suicidal behaviour compared to placebo, but in the subgroup of patients with less than five previous suicide attempts, the attempt rate decreased from 36% in the placebo group (n = 33) to 17% in the paroxetine group (n = 30) (see Figure 27.1). In the subgroup of patients meeting less than 15 criteria for cluster B personality disorders, there was a 70% lower rate of repetition in those prescribed paroxetine compared to those on placebo. However, major repeaters and patients more severely compromised by cluster B criteria had little or no benefit from treatment with paroxetine. In this study, paroxetine was, overall, not significantly different from placebo in its effect on depressive mood and hopelessness, and showed only a temporary effect in reducing anger. This effect on anger appeared in the first 2 weeks of treatment. This rapid onset is in accordance with reports by others on the effects of SSRIs in borderline

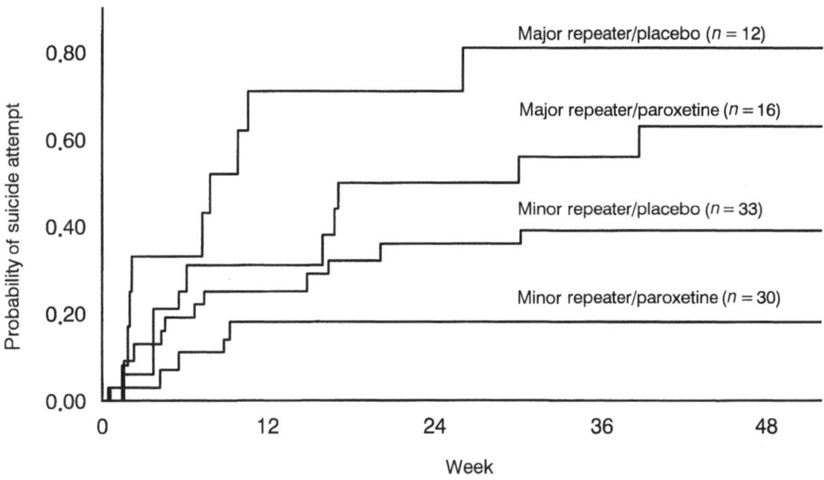

Figure 27.1 Results of a trial of paroxetine versus placebo in recurrent suicide attempters. Kaplan–Meier curves for the probability of another suicide attempt for double-blind randomized treatment groups stratified for minor, i.e. patients with two to four previous suicide attempts, vs. major repeaters, i.e. patients with five or more previous suicide attempts. There was a significant difference between treatment between treatment groups (stratified logrank test, $\chi^2 = 4.9$, df = 1, $p = 0.03$). Reproduced by permission from Verkes et al (1998), copyright © 1998, The American Psychiatric Association

patients (Norden, 1989; Kavoussi et al, 1994) and a mixed group of patients experiencing intense anger (Rubey et al, 1996).

Trials of other antidepressants in patients with personality disorders have shown a less favourable outcome. Montgomery and colleagues (1983) performed a placebo-controlled randomized trial with mianserin, 30 mg/day in a group of 38 patients with at least two documented acts of deliberate self-harm prior to the "index" suicide attempt, who were not suffering from schizophrenia or depression. Thirty patients fulfilled the criteria for a borderline personality disorder. During the 6 months of the study, 47% of the mianserin-treated patients vs. 57% of the placebo-treated patients attempted suicide again, which was a non-significance difference. Hirsch and colleagues (1983) also failed to find that either mianserin or nomifensine were effective in the prevention of recurrent suicidal behaviour in patients with personality disorder.

The effect of the tricyclic antidepressant amitriptyline was assessed by Soloff and colleagues (1986, 1989) in a controlled, double-blind trial in 90 patients with borderline personality disorder, some of whom had major depression. Amitriptyline was compared to haloperidol and placebo. The 29 patients on amitriptyline did, on average, only marginally better than those on placebo on some depression scores, irrespective of the presence of a co-morbid diagnosis of major depression. Comparing responders and non-responders to amitriptyline and placebo, it appeared that more extreme outcomes were found for those on amitriptyline. Thus, compared to placebo non-responders, the 13 amitriptyline non-responders showed an increase in suicidal threats and impulsive behaviour, with poorer global functioning.

Conventional monoamine oxidase inhibitors (MAOIs) may be more useful than amitriptyline in decreasing hostility in patients with borderline personality disorder. Soloff and colleagues (1993) found that 38 patients receiving phenelzine (average dose 60 mg/day) did better in terms of anger and hostility than the 34 patients receiving placebo.

Overdose Toxicity

The issue of toxicity in overdose is important when assessing the role of antidepressant treatment in the prevention of suicide, in view of the fact that even fairly modest overdoses (<1 g) of tricyclic antidepressants can lead to cardiovascular complications, seizures, coma and death. In contrast, newer antidepressants (SSRIs, trazodone, venlafaxine, nefazodone, mirtazapine) are safer in overdose because they appear to lack direct cardiotoxicity.

It would be relevant to know the frequency with which a particular drug causes a fatal overdose. One approach is to calculate a fatal toxicity index (FTI), which is the ratio of the number of cases in which a particular drug is involved in a fatal overdose in a circumscribed region (the numerator) and the number of prescriptions of the drug in that region (the denominator) (Henry, 1997). The validity of this FTI is based on the assumption that once a particular drug is prescribed, the chance to be taken in overdose is the same as any other drug in the group to be compared. This assumption does not hold for the group of antidepressants as a whole, for a number of reasons. For example, patients regarded as being at high risk of suicide are more likely to be prescribed non-toxic drugs. In addition, newer antidepressants, because of their lack of autonomic effects, are more likely to be prescribed to older depressed patients, who are known to have a higher risk of suicide. These factors presumably increase the risk of newer antidepressants being involved in an overdose (Henry, 1997).

Even with these limitations, FTIs may provide information about the relative chance of individual antidepressants being associated with fatal overdoses. In the last 10 years, a number of studies have calculated FTIs on nationwide data. These studies have provided consistent findings that conventional tricyclic antidepressants (TCAs), particularly desipramine and dothiepin, have substantially higher FTIs than newer antidepressants such as SSRIs.

These findings have given rise to the argument that antidepressants such as TCAs should no longer be prescribed for the treatment of depression. However, the proportion of patients who kill themselves by taking tricyclic antidepressants is rather small. In the UK, for example, of about 5,000 annual suicides, around 300 are due to tricyclic overdose. Jick and colleagues (1995) studied 143 people who had killed themselves while taking antidepressants. Overall, more of these subjects were taking fluoxetine than would be expected, but this was probably due to selective prescribing of a less toxic agent to those perceived to be at greater risk of self-harm. Overall, however, these data suggest that replacement of conventional tricyclics by SSRIs and other newer antidepressants would not make a large impact on suicide rates. It is likely that more benefit would accrue simply by treating greater numbers of depressed patients with effective antidepressant drugs in adequate doses for sufficient time.

MOOD STABILIZERS

Bipolar Disorder

Lithium treatment has established efficacy in the prophylaxis of bipolar disorder and recurrent major depression. Epidemiological studies have indicated that patients with recurrent mood disorders taking lithium have a substantially lowered mortality compared to those who are not. For example, Coppen and colleagues (1991) reported an 11-year follow-up of 103 patients attending a lithium clinic, none of whom died from suicide, and Tondo and colleagues (1998) found a seven-fold decrease in suicide attempt rate in bipolar patients treated with lithium compared to those without lithium. A review of 27 studies, involving over 17,000 patients, showed an overall risk of suicide attempts of 0.37% in the lithium-treated patients compared to 3.39% in patients not receiving lithium (Tondo et al, 1997).

Therefore, it seems well established that patients receiving lithium, usually in the setting of a lithium clinic, have a substantially reduced risk of suicide and suicidal behaviour compared to other patients with recurrent mood disorders. However, this of course may not be due solely, or even to a major extent, specifically to lithium treatment. In these studies, lithium treatment is not randomly allocated and it is quite plausible that patients who are compliant with lithium and attend for regular follow-up are a selected group who, for other reasons, are less likely to exhibit suicidal behaviour.

These objections can only be answered by random allocation studies, which are few in number. However, Thies-Flechtner and colleagues (1996) prospectively studied 378 patients suffering from recurrent mood disorders or schizoaffective disorder who were randomly allocated to lithium or carbamazepine for a 2-year follow-up period. During the study, no patients in the lithium-treated group exhibited suicidal behaviour. In contrast, five patients taking carbamazepine attempted suicide and a further four committed suicide.

This study provides good evidence that lithium prophylaxis indeed confers protective effects against suicidal behaviour, relative to other treatments. Is this because lithium is more effective as a mood stabilizer and patients who are less symptomatic patients have a decreased likelihood of suicidal behaviour? While this may be part of the explanation, Müller-Oerlinghausen and colleagues (1992) found that, compared to pre-treatment measures, rates of suicidal behaviour were significantly decreased in patients with recurrent mood disorders taking lithium, even when mood-stabilization had not occurred. This suggests that lithium may exert antisuicidal effects independent of its mood-stabilizing properties.

Personality Disorder

In a 3-week double-blind, placebo-controlled, crossover trial of lithium and desipramine in 15 patients with borderline personality disorder, anger and suicidal symptoms improved in 8/11 patients on lithium vs. 4/11 on desipramine and 5/11 on placebo (Links et al, 1990). These findings are consistent with those from an early study by Sheard and colleagues (1976), who examined the effect of lithium in 66 male prisoners with a history of chronic aggressive behaviour. In comparison to placebo, lithium produced a significant reduction in aggressive behaviour, as measured by a decrease in violent incidents. During crossover to placebo, there was a return of impulsive, aggressive behaviour.

In their 6-week double-blind crossover trial among patients with borderline personality disorder, Cowdry and Gardner (1988) found that while receiving placebo, 8/13 (62%) patients had episodes of moderate to severe behavioural dyscontrol vs. 1/15 (7%) while receiving carbamazepine (600 mg/day in three doses). However, one subject developed psychotic depression and four showed allergic skin reactions while receiving carbamazepine.

Valproate was studied in an open trial in 11 patients with borderline personality disorder. Eight patients completed the 8-week study period, and four of these showed improvement (Stein et al, 1995). In another open study, in 35 patients with a variety of psychiatric disorders, valproate reduced agitation in the 10 borderline disordered patients (Wilcox, 1995).

ANTIPSYCHOTIC DRUGS

Schizophrenia

Although patients with schizophrenia are at risk for suicide throughout all stages of the illness, the risk is highest in the period following the first admission (see Chapter 8). Some believe that the introduction of antipsychotics has increased the suicide rate in patients suffering from schizophrenia (see Modestin and Schwarzenbach, 1992), but this has not been proved. It does appear, however, that the suicide rate in patients taking conventional antipsychotic drugs is similar in patients who respond clinically, compared to those who do not (see Meltzer, 1997). Suicide in patients with schizophrenia is strongly associated with depressive symptoms (Jones et al, 1994). While the use of antidepressant drugs during episodes of acute psychosis is not helpful in the resolution of either mood disturbance or psychosis, the benefit of antidepressants in post-psychotic depression is established by controlled trials (Siris et al, 1991). Whether this results in less frequent suicidal behaviour is unclear.

Newer atypical antipsychotic drugs, such as olanzapine, appear to have greater antidepressant activity than conventional agents such as haloperidol (Tollefson et al, 1998) and could theoretically decrease the risk of suicidal behaviour. In a 28-week double-blind randomized trial in patients with schizophrenia and other primary psychotic disorders, olanzapine was compared to risperidone (Tran et al, 1997). Patients treated with olanzapine showed significantly fewer suicide attempts (1/172, 0.6%) than those treated with risperidone (7/167, 4.2%). Olanzapine also showed a better overall response rate.

In addition, there is epidemiological evidence that the atypical antipsychotic drug, clozapine, lowers the risk of suicidal behaviour. For example, Meltzer and Okayli (1995) found that in 184 patients with schizophrenia who were resistant to treatment with conventional agents, treatment with clozapine improved depression and lowered the rate of suicide attempts from 25% to 3%. In a retrospective study of 67,072 patients receiving clozapine over a 2.5-year period, there was a dramatic reduction in the mortality of current users of clozapine compared to previous users (relative rate 0.17) (Walker et al, 1997). Most of this reduction was due to a lowered suicide rate.

It is unclear whether this striking effect is due to the beneficial effects of clozapine on intractable psychotic symptoms or to a more specific effect on suicidality. Another factor may be the decreased risk of akathisia with drugs such as clozapine compared to conventional agents. Akathisia has been associated with suicidal ideation and behaviour (Power and Cowen, 1992) and therefore patients receiving drugs less likely to cause it may be at decreased risk of suicidal behaviour.

Borderline Personality Disorder

Depot flupenthixol (20 mg every 4 weeks) has been shown to decrease suicidal behaviour compared to placebo in 30 patients with personality disorder and a history of at least three documented suicide attempts (see Montgomery and Montgomery, 1982). Flupenthixol (3 mg/day) was also effective in a prospective study in 13 adolescents with a rigorous diagnosis of borderline personality disorder. During this 8-week study, the patients improved on measures of impulsivity, degression/dysphoria and global functioning (Kutcher et al, 1995). However, therapeutic effects of antipsychotic drugs in borderline personality may not be maintained with continued treatment. For example, Soloff and colleagues (1993) found that the beneficial effects of haloperidol (up to 6 mg/day) during 16 weeks of maintenance treatment were apparent only for ratings of irritability. There was also a high drop-out rate (64%).

BENZODIAZEPINES

The efficacy of benzodiazepines in the treatment of anxiety disorders, including generalized anxiety disorder and panic disorder, has been established by numerous placebo-controlled trials. Anxiety and problems with sleep are often present in patients with suicidal ideation and behaviour. Therefore, benzodiazepines may be effective in preventing suicidal behaviour in such patients. However, there is little experimental evidence for this idea, and in addition some evidence to the contrary.

For example, in a follow-up study of 13,708 women interviewed between 1975 and 1981, by 1985, 1.1% (n = 4) of the 345 regular hypnotic-using women had died by suicide vs. 0.1% (n = 13) of the non-using women (adjusted multivariate odds ratio = 2.6) (Allgulander and Näsman, 1991). Neutel and Patten (1997) compared a population of 225,796 persons with prescriptions for benzodiazepines with 97,862 individuals who did not receive benzodiazepines. There was a positive relationship between benzodiazepine use and suicide attempts, especially in young males not using antidepressants.

What do these findings imply? Are benzodiazepines prescribed to persons at risk of suicidal behaviour, and would there be even higher suicide attempt rates without benzodiazepines? Are benzodiazepines prescribed to patients who would in fact require treatment with antidepressants? Or, do benzodiazepines provoke suicide attempts? At present it is difficult to give a definitive answer, but there is some evidence from prospective studies that benzodiazepines can in fact have disinhibitory effects on behaviour in some individuals (see below).

Anxiety Disorder

In a placebo-controlled study in 154 patients with panic disorder and agoraphobia, patients receiving alprazolam showed increased irritability during the 8-week study period. Serious disinhibition was observed 14% of the patients on alprazolam vs. 0% on placebo (O'Sullivan et al, 1994). There is also evidence for increased aggression in patients with panic disorder taking alprazolam (Bond et al, 1995).

Depressive Disorder

Benzodiazepines are considered not to have a specific antidepressive effect, although alprazolam has efficacy in the treatment of mild to moderate depressive illness (Jonas and Hearron, 1996). As mentioned above, in depressed patients the treatment of symptoms of anxiety and agitation may be important to decrease suicide risk. The prescription of an antidepressant in combination with a benzodiazepine is often suggested as a strategy for this. In major depressive disorder, the combination of an antidepressant with a benzodiazepine has been claimed to ameliorate the anxiety and sleep disturbances more rapidly than an antidepressant alone. There is, however, sparse support from clinical trials to support this strategy. For example, the combination of fluvoxamine and the benzodiazepine prazepam was not clinically superior to treatment with fluvoxamine alone with respect to anxiety in depressive patients (Nutt, 1997).

The effects of alprazolam on suicidality in depressed patients were evaluated in a meta-analysis of well-controlled studies in depressive disorder (Jonas and Hearron, 1996). Pooled data were available from 22 placebo- and/or active drug-controlled studies, comprising 3,217 patients. Although alprazolam did not differ from placebo in the risk of worsening suicidal ideation (19% vs. 22%), it worsened suicidal ideation significantly more than imipramine (13%) and amitriptyline (11%). In addition, while alprazolam significantly improved suicidal ideation compared to placebo (72% vs. 58%), its effects were significantly less than that of amitriptyline (82%). The same trend, with rather more worsening of suicidal ideation, was seen with a small number of depressed patients treated with diazepam alone (Jonas and Hearron, 1996).

Personality Disorder

In their crossover trial of patients with borderline personality disorder, Cowdry and Gardner (1988) found that severe behavioural dyscontrol emerged in seven out of 12 patients receiving alprazolam, compared with two out of 13 receiving placebo. The dyscontrol disappeared after discontinuation of alprazolam. The authors report that, while the physicians evaluated the alprazolam negatively because of the increase in dyscontrol, some patients themselves evaluated the alprazolam effect positively, as they experienced improved mood.

In a naturalistic follow-up study of 95 recurrent suicide attempters with predominantly borderline personality disorder characteristics, subjects using and not-using benzodiazepines at base-line were compared (Verkes et al, 1997). The risk of repeated suicidal behaviour was significantly higher in those using ben-

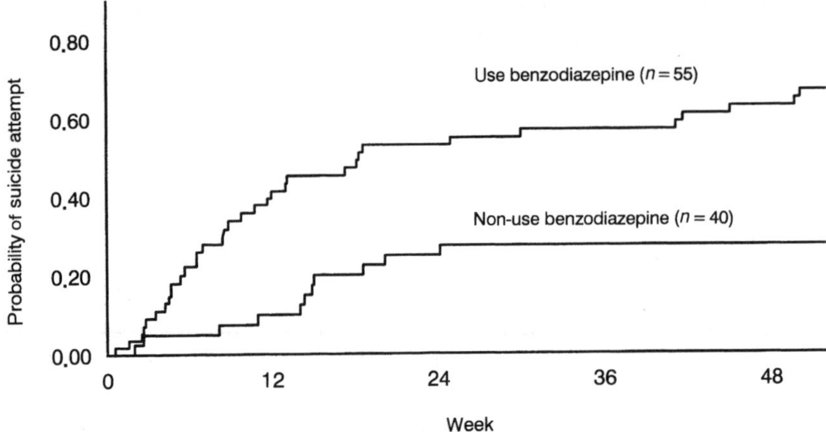

Figure 27.2 Outcome of attempted suicide patients receiving benzodiazepines versus those who were not. Kaplan–Meier curves for the probability of another suicide attempt for patients prospectively followed after an "index" suicide attempt, with and without use of benzodiazepines at baseline (logrank test, $\chi^2 = 14.5$, df = 1, $p < 0.001$)

zodiazepines (Figure 27.2). Prescription bias may explain only some part of this increased risk, as the risk remained elevated after correction for other factors that did predict repeated suicidal behaviour, i.e. the number of previous suicide attempts, hopelessness, suicidal ideation and depressive mood.

CONCLUSIONS (see Table 27.1)

There is reasonable evidence that drug treatment can lower suicide rates and suicidal behaviour in patients with major mood disorders. While it is not yet possible to conclude with certainty that the lower mortality of drug-treated patients is due exclusively to the pharmacological effects of treatment, from the practical point of view it appears that, for patients with major depression and bipolar disorder, compliance with drug treatment programmes is associated with a lower suicide rate. This is particularly the case for the use of lithium in patients with recurrent mood disorders, but it is uncertain whether this benefit extends to other mood-stabilizing drugs. For major depression, it appears that antidepressant drugs that potentiate serotonin function appear to have the best demonstrated effects on lowering suicidal ideation, but whether this will result in a greater impact on suicidal behaviour is unclear.

For patients with schizophrenia, the use of the atypical antipsychotic drug clozapine appears to be associated with lower suicide rates. It will obviously be important to determine whether similar effects occur with other atypical agents, such as olanzapine and risperidone. The role of pharmacotherapy in patients

Table 27.1 Psychotropic drugs and suicidal behaviour

Drug	Effect on suicidal behaviour
Tricyclic antidepressants, selective serotonin re-uptake inhibitors	Decrease suicidal ideation in patients with major depression
Selective serotonin re-uptake inhibitor (paroxetine)	Decreases suicide attempts in subgroup of repeat attempters
Flupenthixol	Decreases suicide attempts in repeat attempters
Lithium carbonate	Decreases suicide and suicide attempts in patients with recurrent mood disorders
Clozapine	Decreases suicide rate in patients with refractory schizophrenia
Benzodiazepines	May increase risk of suicidal behaviour in repeat attempters

who make repeated suicide attempts in the context of personality disorder is unclear. However, they may obtain benefit from selective serotonin re-uptake inhibitors and, perhaps, low-dose antipsychotic drug treatment. The latter possibility also needs to be investigated using newer and better-tolerated antipsychotic drugs.

Finally, it appears that the use of benzodiazepines is associated with increased risk of self-harm in some groups of subjects, and these drugs should therefore be used with caution, particularly as a single drug therapy, in subjects at risk of suicidal behaviour.

REFERENCES

Ahrens, B. and Linden, M. (1996) Is there a suicidality syndrome independent of specific major psychiatric disorder? Results of a split-half multiple regression analysis. Acta Psychiatrica Scandinavica, 94: 79–86.

Allgulander, C. (1994) Suicide and mortality patterns in anxiety neurosis and depressive neurosis. Archives of General Psychiatry, 51: 708–712.

Allgulander, C. and Näsman, P. (1991) Regular hypnotic drug treatment in a sample of 32,679 Swedes: associations with somatic and mental health, inpatient psychiatric diagnoses and suicide, derived with automatic record-linkage. Psychosomatic Medicine, 53: 101–108.

Beasley, C.M., Dornseif, B.E., Bosomworth, J.C., Sayer, M.E., Rampey, A.H., Heiligenstein, J.H., Thompson, V.L., Murphy, D.J. and Masica, D.N. (1991) Fluoxetine and suicide: a meta-analysis of controlled trials of treatment for depression. British Medical Journal, 303: 685–692.

Beasley, C.M., Potvin, J.H., Masica, D.N., Wheadon, D.E., Dornseif, B.E. and Genduso, L.A. (1992) Fluoxetine: no association with suicidality in obsessive-compulsive disorder. Journal of Affective Disorders, 24: 1–10.

Bond, A.J., Curran, H.V., Bruce, M.S., O'Sullivan, G. and Shine, P. (1995) Behavioral aggression in panic disorder after 8 weeks' treatment with alprazolam. Journal of Affective Disorders, 35: 117–123.

Coccaro, E.F. and Kavoussi, R.J. (1997) Fluoxetine and impulsive aggressive behavior in personality-disordered subjects. Archives of General Psychiatry, 54: 1081–1088.

Coppen, A., Standish-Barry, H., Bailey, J., Houston, G., Silcocks, P. and Hermon, C. (1991) Does lithium reduce mortality of recurrent mood disorders? Journal of Affective Disorders, 23: 1–7.

Cowdry, R.W. and Gardner, D.L. (1998) Alprazolam, carbamazepine, trifluoperazine, and tranylcypromine. Archives of General Psychiatry, 45: 111–119.

Cowen, P.J. (1996) Pharmacotherapy for anxiety disorders: drugs available. Advances in Psychiatric Treatment, 3: 66–71.

Fawcett, J., Scheftner, W.A., Fogg, L., Clark, D.C., Young, M.A., Hedeker, D. and Gibbons, R. (1990) Time-related predictors of suicide in major affective disorder. American Journal of Psychiatry, 151: 1189–1194.

Fawcett, J. (1995) The detection and consequences of anxiety in clinical depression. Journal of Clinical Psychiatry, 58 (Suppl. 8): 35–40.

Henry, J.A. (1997) Epidemiology and relative toxicity of antidepressant drugs in overdose. Drug Safety, 16: 374–390.

Hirsch, S.R., Walsh, C. and Draper, R. (1983) The concept and efficacy of the treatment of parasuicide. British Journal of Clinical Pharmacology, 15: 189–194S.

Isacsson, G., Bergman, U. and Rich, C.L. (1996) Epidemiological data suggest antidepressants reduce suicide risk among depressives. Journal of Affective Disorders, 41: 1–8.

Jick, S.S., Dean, A.D. and Jick, H. (1995) Antidepressants and suicide. British Medical Journal, 310: 215–218.

Jonas, J.M. and Hearron, A.E. (1996) Alprazolam and suicidal ideation: a meta-analysis of controlled trials in the treatment of depression. Journal of Clinical Psychopharmacology, 16: 208–211.

Jones, J.S., Stein, D.J., Stanley, B., Guido, J.R., Winchel, R. and Stanley, M. (1994) Negative and depressive symptoms in suicidal schizophrenics. Acta Psychiatrica Scandinavica, 89: 81–87.

Kavoussi, R.J., Liu, J. and Coccaro, E.F. (1994) An open trial of sertraline in personality disordered patients with impulsive aggression. Journal of Clinical Psychiatry, 55: 137–141.

Kutcher, S., Papatheodorou, G., Reiter, S. and Gardner, D. (1995) The successful pharmacological treatment of adolescents and young adults with borderline personality disorder: a preliminary open trial of flupenthixol. Journal of Psychiatry and Neuroscience, 20: 113–118.

Letizia, C., Kapik, B. and Flanders, W.D. (1996) Suicidal risk during controlled clinical investigations of fluvoxamine. Journal of Clinical Psychiatry, 57: 415–421.

Links, P.S., Steiner, M., Boiago,I. and Irwin D. (1990) Lithium therapy for borderline patients: preliminary findings. Journal of Personality Disorder, 4: 173–181.

Mann, J.J. and Kapur, S. (1991) The emergence of suicidal ideation and behavior during antidepressant pharmacotherapy. Archives of General Psychiatry, 48: 1027–1033.

Markovitz, P.J., Calabrese, J.R., Schultz, S.C. and Meltzer, H.Y. (1991) Fluoxetine in the treatment of borderline and schizotypal presonality disorders. American Journal of Psychiatry, 148: 1064–1067.

Meltzer, H.Y. (1997) Treatment-resistant schizophrenia—the role of clozapine. Current Medical Research Opinion, 14: 1–20.

Meltzer, H.Y. and Okayli, G. (1995) Reduction of suicidality during clozapine treatment of neuroleptic-resistant schizophrenia: impact on risk–benefit assessment. American Journal of Psychiatry, 152: 183–190.

Modestin, J. and Schwarzenbach, F. (1992) Effect of psychopharmacotherapy on suicide risk in discharged psychiatric inpatients. Acta Psychiatrica Scandinavica, 85: 173–175.

Montgomery, D.B., Roberts, A., Green, M., Bullock, T., Baldwin, D. and Montgomery, S.A.

(1994) Lack of efficacy of fluoxetine in recurrent brief depression and suicidal attempts. European Archives of Psychiatry and Clinical Neurological Sciences, 244: 211–215.

Montgomery, S.A. and Montgomery, D.B. (1982) Pharmacological prevention of suicidal behaviour. Journal of Affective Disorders, 4: 291–298.

Montgomery, S.A., Roy, D. and Montgomery, D.B. (1983) The prevention of recurrent suicidal acts. British Journal of Clinical Pharmacology, 15: 183–188S.

Montgomery, S.A., Dunner, D.L. and Dunbar, G.C. (1995) Reduction of suicidal thoughts with paroxetine in comparison with reference antidepressants and placebo. European Neuropsychopharmocology, 5: 5–13.

Müller-Oerlinghausen, B., Müser-Causemann, B. and Volk, J. (1992) Suicides and parasuicides in a high-risk patient group on and off lithium long-term medication. Journal of Affective Disorders, 25, 261–270.

Neutel, C.I. and Patten, S.B. (1997) Risk of suicide attempts after benzodiazepine and/or antidepressant use. Annals of Epidemiology, 7: 568–574.

Norden, M.J. (1989) Fluoxetine in borderline personality disorder. Progress in Neuropsychopharmacology and Biological Psychiatry, 13: 885–893.

Nutt, D. (1997) Management of patients with depression associated with anxiety symptoms. Journal of Clinical Psychiatry, 58 (Suppl. 8): 11–16.

O'Sullivan, G.H., Noshirvani, H., Basoglu, M., Marks, I., Swinson, R., Kuch, K. and Kirby, M. (1994) Safety and side-effects of alprazolam: controlled study in agoraphobia with panic disorder. British Journal of Psychiatry, 165: 79–86.

Ottevanger, E.A. (1991) Fluvoxamine activity profile with special emphasis on the effect on suicidal ideation. European Journal of Clinical Research, 1: 47–54.

Power, A.C. and Cowen, P.J. (1992) Fluoxetine and suicidal behaviour: some clinical and theoretical aspects of a controversy. British Journal of Psychiatry, 161: 735–741.

Praschak-Rieder, N., Neumeister, A., Hesselmann, B., Willeit, M., Barnas, C. and Kasper, S. (1997) Suicidal tendencies as a complication of light therapy for seasonal affective disorder: a report of three cases. Journal of Clinical Psychiatry, 58: 389–392.

Rouillon, F., Phillips, R., Serrurier, D., Ansart, E. and Gerard, M.J. (1989) Prophylactic efficacy of maprotiline on relapses of unipolar depression. Encephale (Paris), 15: 527–534.

Rubey, R.N., Johnson, M.R., Emmanuel, N., Lydiard, R.B. (1996) Fluoxetine in the treatment of anger: an open clinical trial. Journal of Clinical Psychiatry, 57: 398–401.

Salzman, C., Wolfson, A.N., Schatzberg, A., Looper, J., Henke, R., Albanese, M., Swartz, J. and Miyawaki, E. (1995) Effect of fluoxetine on anger in symptomatic volunteers with borderline personality disorder. Journal of Clinical Psychopharmacology, 15: 23–29.

Sheard, M.H., Marini, J.L., Bridges, C.I. and Wagner, E. (1976) The effect of lithium on impulsive aggressive behavior in man. American Journal of Psychiatry, 133: 1409–1413.

Siris, S.G., Bermanzohn, P.C., Gonzalez, A., Mason, S.E., White, C.V. and Shuwall, M.A. (1991) Use of antidepressants for negative symptoms in a subset of schizophrenic patients. Psychopharmacology Bulletin, 27: 331–335.

Soloff, P.H., George, A., Nathan, R.S., Schulz, P.M. and Perel, J.M. (1986) Paradoxical effects of amitriptyline on borderline patients. American Journal of Psychiatry, 143: 1603–1605.

Soloff, P.H., George, A., Nathan, R.S., Schulz, P.M., Cornelius, J.R., Herring, J. and Perel, J.M. (1989) Amitriptyline versus haloperidol in borderlines: final outcomes and predictors of response. Journal of Clinical Psychopharmacology, 9: 246.

Soloff, P.H., Cornelius, J., George, A., Nathan, S., Perel, J.M. and Ulrich, R.F. (1993) Efficacy of phenelzine and haloperidol in borderline personality disorder. Archives of General Psychiatry, 50: 377–385.

Stein, D.J., Simeon, D., Frenkel, M., Islam, M.N. and Hollander, E. (1995) An open trial of valproate in borderline personality disorder. Journal of Clinical Psychiatry, 56: 506–510.

Thies-Flechtner, K., Müller-Oerlinghausen, B., Seibert, W., Walther, A. and Greil, W. (1996) Effect of prophylactic treatment on suicide risk in patients with major affective disorders. Pharmacopsychiatry, 29: 103–107.

Tollefson, G.D., Sanger, T.M., Lu, Y. and Thieme, M.E. (1998) Depressive signs and symptoms in schizophrenia—a prospective blinded trial of olanzepine versus haloperidol. Archives of General Psychiatry, 55: 250–258.

Tondo, L., Jamison, K.R. and Baldessarini, R.J. (1997) Effect of lithium maintenance on suicidal behavior in major mood disorders. Annals of New York Academy of Science, 836: 340–351.

Tondo, L., Baldessarini, R.J., Hennen, J., Floris, G., Silvetti, F. and Tohen, M. (1998) Lithium treatment and risk of suicidal behavior in bipolar disorder patients. Journal of Clinical Psychiatry, 59: 405–414.

Tran, P.V., Hamilton, S.H., Kuntz, A.J., Potvin, J.H., Andersen, S.W., Beasley, C. and Tollefson, G.D. (1997) Double-blind comparison of olanzapine versus risperidone in the treatment of schizophrenia and other psychotic disorders. Journal of Clinical Psychopharmacology, 17: 407–418.

Verkes, R.J., Fekkes, D., Zwinderman, A.H., Hengeveld, M.W., Van der Mast, R.C., Tuyl, J.P., Kerkhof, A.J.F.M. and Van Kempen, G.M.J. (1997) Platelet serotonin and [3H]paroxetine binding correlate with recurrence of suicidal behavior. Psychopharmacology, 132: 89–94.

Verkes, R.J., Van der Mast, R.C., Hengeveld, M.W., Tuyl, J.P., Zwinderman, A.H. and Van Kempen, G.M.J. (1998) Reduction by paroxetine of suicidal behavior in patients with repeated suicide attempts but not major depression. American Journal of Psychiatry, 155: 543–547.

Walker, A.M., Lanza, L.L., Arellano, F. and Rothman, K.J. (1997) Mortality in current and former users of clozapine. Epidemiology, 8: 1181–1185.

Warshaw, M.G. and Keller, M.B. (1996) The relationship between fluoxetine use and suicidal behavior in 654 subjects with anxiety disorders. Journal of Clinical Psychiatry, 57: 158–166.

Wheadon, D.E., Rampey, A.H., Thompson, V.L., Potvin, J.H., Masica, D.N., Beasley, C.M. (1992) Lack of association between fluoxetine and suicidality in bulimia nervosa. Journal of Clinical Psychiatry, 53: 235–241.

Wilcox, J.A. (1995) Divalproex sodium as a treatment for borderline personality disorder. Annals of Clinical Psychiatry, 7: 33–37.

Chapter 28

Psychotherapeutic Approaches to Suicidal Ideation and Behaviour

Heidi L. Heard
Department of Psychology, University of Washington, Seattle, Washington, USA

Abstract

The aim of this chapter is to review the current psychotherapeutic approaches in the treatment of suicidal ideation and behaviours. The chapter first describes those psychotherapeutic approaches to suicidal behaviours which have been developed to the point of examination in randomized controlled trials. Only two types of psychotherapeutic approaches, cognitive-behavioural therapies (including problem-solving therapies and cognitive therapies) and outreach and intensive therapies (therapies that add outreach components to or intensify standard psychotherapies), have received such examination. Next, the chapter addresses general issues in the delivery of psychotherapy to suicidal patients, including poor treatment compliance, the impact of diagnosis and the cost of the treatment. Treatment compliance has consistently been identified as one of the greatest obstacles to treating suicidal behaviours with psychotherapy. A review of the data, however, suggests that psychotherapies can successfully develop or modify interventions to increase compliance. The existence of psychiatric disorders can have an important impact on both the content and the course of treatment. It is suggested that directly targeting suicidal behaviours may prove a more efficient way to decrease suicidal behaviour rather than indirectly treating them by targeting associated psychiatric disorders. Lastly, in view of the limited resources for health care, those developing and delivering psychotherapies must now also concern themselves with the financial cost, as well as the clinical success, of their therapeutic approach. Finally, outcomes of randomized, controlled psychotherapy trials, focusing on patients with a history of deliberate self-harm behaviour, are reviewed. Unfortunately, very few of the studies report significantly better

The International Handbook of Suicide and Attempted Suicide. Edited by K. Hawton and K. van Heeringen.

results for either treatment condition in terms of repetition of deliberate self-harm. Grouping studies by type of experimental intervention added some further but limited information. The interpretation of the results is hindered by the small sample sizes in many of the studies and substantial variation in the research designs used. Suggestions for future research include conducting multicentre research projects which would allow researchers to increase their sample size and the homogeneity of study designs.

INTRODUCTION

Within the context of psychotherapy, suicidal individuals consistently provide therapists with some of their greatest challenges. The intensity of suffering and high risk of imminent death with which suicidal patients often present certainly contribute to the distress experienced by therapists, but many therapists are equally distressed by the seeming inefficacy of their psychotherapeutic interventions. While this ineffectiveness may reflect a problem with the dissemination or delivery of developed therapies, we must first consider whether the field has actually developed efficacious psychotherapies for suicidal behaviours. This chapter, therefore, aims to review the current psychotherapeutic approaches in the treatment of suicidal behaviours. For the purposes of this chapter, the term "psychotherapeutic approaches" refers to any psychosocial intervention that involves repeated face-to-face contact with a mental health professional. The chapter first examines the most developed psychotherapeutic approaches to suicidal behaviours. Next, general issues in the delivery of psychotherapy to suicidal patients are addressed. Finally, outcomes of randomized, controlled psychotherapy trials are reviewed.

OVERVIEW OF PSYCHOTHERAPEUTIC APPROACHES

Although a substantial amount of literature on psychotherapy for suicidal patients exists, a review of this literature reveals the absence of a solid empirical base, particularly in the form of controlled treatment trials. Despite a paucity of such trials, psychotherapeutic interventions for suicidal behaviours are widely available to therapists and delivered to patients. Perhaps one reason why therapists so frequently experience apparently unsuccessful treatments with suicidal patients is because the front line has become the testing ground. To emphasize the need for empirical support, this overview includes only those psychotherapeutic approaches for suicidal behaviour that have been developed to the point of being evaluated in controlled clinical trials.

Cognitive-behavioural Therapies

Cognitive-behavioural therapies include a range of approaches which share several principles and practices. In terms of their development, these psychotherapies emphasize the need for a theoretical foundation, attention to empirical data and the development of a treatment manual. Similarities also appear with respect to the therapeutic structure and process. The therapies are generally time-limited and focus on the here-and-now (i.e. current problems in the patient's life). Therapists play a very active and direct role in helping patients to change, as well as understand, their behaviour.

Problem-solving Therapy

Of the psychotherapeutic approaches examined in this overview, only the problem-solving therapies have both developed treatment manuals which allow wide dissemination and demonstrated some evidence of clinical efficacy. For this reason, more attention is paid here to this approach. Also, problem-solving therapy is reasonably easily taught to clinicians (Hawton and Kirk, 1989). The approach includes both traditional problem-solving therapies (e.g. Bancroft, 1986; Hawton and Catalan, 1987; McLeavey and Daly, 1988) and dialectical behavioural therapy (Linehan, 1993a,b), in which problem-solving strategies form the core.

Problem-solving therapy postulates that maladaptive behaviour occurs when individuals lack the psychological resources to resolve their problem in any other way. In their chapter on the psychology of suicidal behaviour, Williams and Pollock review several studies that indicate that suicidal patients experience significant difficulties with solving problems (see Chapter 5). Among other factors, these studies suggest that suicidal patients tend to attempt to solve problems passively. Problem-solving therapies counteract this style by requiring patients to take a very active role in identifying and understanding their problems and in generating and implementing adaptive solutions.

In therapy, problem solving can be roughly divided into two phases: first analysing the problem, followed by analysing solutions. In the first phase, the therapist helps the patient to orientate to and define the problem and then to assess and understand the variables that contribute to the problem. To understand these variables, the therapist may conduct a behavioural analysis in which every event, thought, emotion and behaviour leading to a recent maladaptive behaviour are identified. This procedure, which requires patients to recall past events with great specificity, may have a positive impact on the problems that suicidal patients tend to have with overgeneral autobiographical memories, as described by Williams and Pollock in Chapter 5.

During the second phase, the therapist helps the patient to generate solutions to the problem, to evaluate those solutions and then to implement the chosen solutions. Williams and Pollock note that suicidal patients have difficulty in generating alternative solutions, a factor that may be related to the cognitive rigidity and frequently depressed mood of these patients. Problem-solving therapies address this problem by encouraging patients to "brainstorm" when generating alternative solutions, i.e. to think of as many potential solutions as possible, even odd or extreme ones, before evaluating any of them. After generating potential solutions, the therapist helps the patient to evaluate and choose the most effective solutions. They may discuss the pros and cons of alternative solutions but, as the Williams and Pollock chapter suggests, suicidal patients may tend to emphasize the potential negative outcomes of alternative solutions. This emphasis on negative outcomes may result from: (a) lack of skills related to the solution; (b) cognitive distortions; (c) anticipation or experience of extreme affect, such as fear; or (d) environments that punish or at least do not reward adaptive solutions. To overcome this bias, the therapist might, respectively: (a) teach patients new skills; (b) challenge the patient's thoughts or style of thinking; (c) expose the patient to the cues that elicit the fear, or other emotions; and (d) help the patient to obtain rewards for implementing solutions. Finally, the therapist coaches the patient in implementing solutions. Either during or following the process of selecting solutions, the patient should rehearse the solutions, either behaviourally or cognitively, during the session. This rehearsal allows the therapist and patient to identify and solve problems that might interfere with the successful implementation of the solution. Also, Williams and Pollock cite evidence that suicidal patients may be more likely to anticipate negative events because they cannot think of how they could prevent them. Cognitive or behavioural rehearsal of solutions leading to successful outcomes may help to change this cognitive pattern.

Cognitive Therapy

Although cognitive therapy for suicidal behaviour shares many of its techniques with problem-solving therapy, it differs in terms of its theoretical model and case conceptualization. Cognitive therapy for suicidal behaviour (e.g. Freeman and Reinecke, 1993) is primarily derived from the cognitive therapies developed to treat depression (e.g. Beck et al, 1979; Ellis, 1984). Cognitive therapy postulates that the way individuals interpret events and experiences affects their subsequent affect and behaviour. Over time, individuals tend to develop particular automatic patterns of interpretation that may be distortions of reality. Such cognitive distortions may then activate maladaptive coping behaviours, including suicidal behaviour. Dichotomous thinking, which was discussed in Chapter 5 by Williams and Pollock, is one type of cognitive distortion closely associated with suicidal behaviour. These distortions are maintained by the individual's basic underlying assumptions or "schemata" about the self and the world. These underlying assumptions influence both cognitive content and processes.

The cognitive therapist aims to change the patient's suicidal behaviour and associated affect primarily by focusing on changing the patient's cognitive content and processes. The specific techniques used to change the patient's thinking are very similar to the cognitive techniques used in problem-solving therapy. Cognitive therapy often employs some behavioural techniques as well.

Outreach and Intensive Therapies

This group of psychotherapeutic approaches includes those psychotherapy programmes that add outreach components to, or intensify, standard outpatient psychotherapies. The primary functions of such modifications would appear to be to intervene in crises before they lead to severe suicidal behaviour and to enhance treatment compliance, at which suicidal patients are notoriously poor (for review, see van Heeringen, 1992). These modifications, however, seldom have a substantial theoretical foundation and are generally just added to the therapy, rather than integrated into the theoretical approach of the therapist.

Outreach and intensive therapies employ a variety of interventions. To increase the intensity of the treatment, therapies may increase the duration or frequency of therapy sessions, or they may add extra modalities to a treatment programme (e.g. individual therapy plus family therapy). Outreach is usually provided by telephone calls, letters or home visits, with many therapies providing 24-hour access to some form of intervention. The potential effect of outreach strategies was demonstrated in two recent non-psychotherapy studies that provided deliberate self-harm patients in the experimental conditions with "green cards" in addition to standard care (Cotgrove et al, 1995; Morgan et al, 1993). These cards enabled patients to obtain immediate psychiatric attention on demand. Compared to control patients, who received only standard care (which did not necessarily include psychotherapy), experimental patients were approximately half as likely to repeat deliberate self-harm, although in neither study were the findings statistically significant (see Chapter 29 for further discussion of this approach).

ISSUES IN THE DELIVERY OF PSYCHOTHERAPY

Problems with Treatment Compliance

Clinicians developing treatments and researchers examining outcomes consistently identify poor treatment compliance, and particularly poor attendance, as one of the greatest obstacles to treating suicidal behaviours. Poor compliance has frequently been blamed on poor motivation for improvement, but the data fail to support this hypothesis. Correlational studies have reported either a complete absence of an association between patient motivation and treatment compliance (reported in Moller, 1989) or a positive but non-significant correlation (Hawton et al, 1987). One experimental study (Torhorst et al, 1987) reported that the addition of a motivational interview failed to enhance attendance. An alternative hypothesis is that practical or psychological obstacles or a combination of the two may interfere with compliance. For example, arranging therapy appointments around child-care or employment can present practical difficulties for clients, but these practical difficulties are often complicated by psychological factors, such as depression, which could decrease the likelihood that the client will make the necessary arrangements for an appointment or remember to attend the appointment. Other potential psychological obstacles include severely depressed mood or agoraphobia that make leaving home difficult, social phobia that makes group therapy more challenging, fears about the process of therapy, anger at the therapist and hopeless thoughts about the success of the treatment. The majority of studies described here attempt to reduce such obstacles.

The first challenge for any intervention is getting the patient to the initial therapy session. Interventions that have significantly increased first session attendance include: (a) simply scheduling a fixed initial aftercare appointment at the time of referral (Moller, 1989); (b) following-up patients who failed to respond to an outpatient referral with up to three home visits (van Heeringen et al, 1995); and (c) continuation of care with the same therapist, as opposed to changing therapist, when patients move from inpatient (general hospital after the attempt) to outpatient settings (Torhorst et al, 1988). Of note, in a study comparing short-term weekly and long-term monthly psychotherapy, attendance did not differ for the first session but was substantially lower in the monthly treatment by the second session (Torhorst et al, 1987).

Although fewer studies have examined rates of treatment completion, the pattern of results appears the same. Hawton and colleagues (1981) found that delivering a brief problem-solving intervention in the patient's home, rather than in an outpatient clinic, significantly increased the rate of treatment completion from 42% to 83%. Similarly, Linehan and colleagues (1991) found that dialectical behavioural therapy, as opposed to standard outpatient care, significantly increased the proportion of patients who remained in treatment with a single therapist, also from 42 to 83%. Dialectical behavioural therapy identifies poor attendance as a primary treatment target and uses telephone calls and other types of outreach to contact patients who have missed an appointment. In summary, the data suggest that it is possible to successfully develop or modify psychotherapeutic interventions to increase compliance.

Role of Psychiatric Disorders

The existence of a psychiatric disorder can play a major role in the treatment of suicidal behaviours. It can have an impact on both the content and the course of treatment. The impact of a psychiatric disorder on the content of psychotherapy depends largely on whether suicidal behaviour is in itself viewed as a proper focus for therapy, or whether it is simply a "symptom" of a "primary disorder", such as a psychiatric condition, on which the treatment should focus instead. While proponents of the former approach target the behaviour directly, proponents of the latter assert that the behaviour will dissipate in association with the successful treatment of the primary disorder, and therefore target the behaviour indirectly. The emphasis on treating the psychiatric disorder receives support from the strong associations between the presence of certain psychiatric disorders and suicidal behaviours (Freeman and Reinecke, 1993; see Chapters 7–11). However, a recent review by Linehan (1998) of the links between the treatment of depression (commonly associated with suicidal behaviours) and decreases in suicide or deliberate self-harm behaviour reveals that the successful treatment of one does not always directly relate to the successful treatment of the other. Linehan suggests, therefore, that directly targeting suicidal phenomena, which would include suicidal ideation, may prove more efficient.

Certain psychiatric disorders also may influence the treatment of suicidal behaviours by their impact on the course of treatment. Unfortunately, few studies have assessed this possibility. Two studies have reported an association between lower treatment compliance and either a general history of psychiatric problems (Allard et al, 1992) or "personality problems" specifically (Hawton et al, 1987). Allard and colleagues found that the presence of borderline personality disorder or drug abuse predicted poorer treatment results, while Chowdhury and colleagues (1973) found that alcohol problems, depression plus a personality disorder, or a "psychopathic personality" predicted poorer results. If these correlations reflect any causal associations, attention to such associations could prove important in the development of effective treatments. For example, if certain behaviours associated with these diagnoses interfere with patients receiving the treatment, an effective treatment would need to develop additional interventions for these behaviours. However, of the psychotherapies described above, only one (dialectical behavioural therapy for borderline personality disorder; Linehan, 1993a) directly attends to the impact of a particular diagnosis on the course of treatment.

Cost of Treatment Delivery

In addition to concerns about the efficacy of an intervention, those developing treatments must now also concern themselves with the cost. The move from inpatient treatments to outpatient treatments has occurred partly in response to concerns about cost. Attention to who delivers the treatment may provide additional opportunities to reduce the cost of the treatment without affecting its content. For example, Hawton and colleagues (1981) found no major outcome differences between medical and non-medical therapists delivering two variations of a brief problem-solving intervention. Although the previous training of these therapists varied, they all received special training in the problem-solving approach. Thus, training background may not be as important as the amount of training in (or adherence to) a particular psychotherapeutic approach. Also of note, an intensive psychotherapy may appear expensive due to greater direct costs (e.g. telephone contact, home visits) but may actually prove to be relatively cheap if it can reduce other health costs (e.g. accident and emergency department visits, hospitalizations). For example, Linehan and Heard (1999) found that while the direct costs of dialectical behavioural therapy (which includes concurrent individual and group therapy) were higher than treatment-as-usual, the total health care costs were significantly lower, primarily due to patients spending fewer days in hospital.

REVIEW OF TREATMENT OUTCOMES

Although patients with a variety of suicidal phenomena, ranging from suicidal ideation to suicide attempts, are treated with psychotherapy, this review of treatment outcomes will focus on patients with a history of deliberate self-harm behaviour. This review focuses on deliberate self-harm both because of the strong association between a history of deliberate self-harm behaviour and eventual suicide and the potential negative consequences of the behaviour itself. This emphasis on deliberate self-harm behaviour is also consistent with two recently published reviews of psychosocial and pharmacological treatment approaches to suicidal behaviour (Hawton et al, 1998; Linehan, 1998).

The outcome studies of psychotherapeutic approaches to deliberate self-harm behaviour reviewed here were collected from literature searches using the databases Medline and Psyclit up to 1998. For inclusion in the review, the study must have met the following criteria: (a) subjects must have had a recent history of deliberate self-harm; (b) subjects must have been randomly assigned to either the experimental or control conditions; and (c) at least one of the conditions must have involved a psychotherapeutic approach. Table 28.1 describes the 15 studies that met these criteria. To facilitate review, the studies are organized according to the type of experimental intervention. The organization here is similar to the one employed by Hawton and colleagues (1998) in their review.

Treatment Efficacy

Alarmingly few of the studies reported significantly better results for either treatment condition in terms of repetition of deliberate self-harm. A search for a pattern of findings based on type of experimental intervention provides little insight. Neither of the problem-solving only studies produced significant results, but one study (McLeavey et al, 1994) used different styles of problem-solving approaches for both conditions, thus perhaps minimizing the probability of finding a significant treatment effect. Neither of the inpatient cognitive-behavioural therapy studies produced significant results, but both studies had very small sample sizes. The standard treatment plus intensive care/outreach studies produced mixed results that cannot be explained by any obvious differences in design. Similarly, the problem-solving plus outreach studies also produced mixed results, with no obvious pattern. Linehan and colleagues (Linehan et al, 1991, 1993) reported significant results for dialectical behavioural therapy versus routine care, but these results need replication. The only common treatment factor among all of the studies in which the experimental condition produced statistically significant, or near-significant, results was the addition or integration of some form of intensive care and/or outreach either to a standard psychotherapy (studies 2 and 4 in Table 28.1) or to a specialist cognitive-behavioural therapy (studies 9 and 11). A possible interpretation of the data is that the

Table 28.1 Summary of randomized controlled trials of psychotherapeutic approaches to suicidal behaviours

Study	Sample	Interventions	Follow-up	Results
Standard therapy plus intensive care and/or outreach				
1. Chowdhury et al, 1973[1,2]	Admitted to poison centre for parasuicide, all repeaters	E (n = 71): regular and frequent outpatient appointments, home visits to patients who fail to keep appointments or in response to emergency calls, 24-hour emergency phone service. Service provided by psychiatrist and SW. C (n = 84): standard referral to outpatient clinic	6 Months	Parasuicide[3] rate: E = 23.9%, C = 22.6%, n.s.
2. Welu, 1977[1,2]	>16 Years, admitted to A&E for suicide attempt, 60% repeaters	E (n = 63): contact by nurse, SW or mental health worker following discharge, home visit if possible, weekly or bi-weekly therapy or monitoring of therapy for 4 months. C (n = 57): standard service leading to immediate hospitalization and/ or a community health center referral	4 Months	Suicide attempt rate: E = 4.8%, C = 15.8%, $p < 0.05$
3. Allard et al, 1992[1,2]	Admitted to A&E for suicide attempt, 50% repeaters	E (n = 76): standard therapy appointments tapering from weekly to monthly over a year, at least one home visit by a SW, written or telephone reminders or home visits if appointment missed. Project team were psychiatrists and a SW. C (n =74): referral to other hospital personnel for treatment	24 Months	Suicide rate: E = 4.8%, C = 1.6%, n.s. Suicide attempt rate: E = 34.9%, C = 30.2%, n.s.
4. van Heeringen et al, 1995[1,2]	≥15 Years, admitted to A&E for suicide attempt, 30% repeaters	E (n = 258): up to three home visits by a community nurse to resolve compliance problems if patient failed to attend an outpatient referral. C (n = 258): standard referral only—90.3% to outpatient mental health providers	12 Months	Suicide rate: E = 3.1%, C = 3.6%, n.s. Suicide attempt rate: E = 7.7%, C = 13.9%, $p = 0.07$[3] Suicide or suicide attempt: E = 10.7%, C= 17.4%, $p = 0.056$

continued overleaf

Table 28.1 *(continued)*

Study	Sample	Interventions	Follow-up	Results
Problem-solving therapy				
5. Hawton et al, 1987[1,2]	>16 Years, admitted to hospital after deliberate self-poisoning, 31% repeaters	E ($n = 41$): brief outpatient problem-orientated counselling by non-medical therapists at a clinic. C ($n = 39$): referral to and advice given to GP	12 Months	Suicide rate: E = 2.4%, C = 0%, n.s. Self-poisoning rate: E = 7.3%, C = 15.4%, n.s.
6. McLeavey et al, 1994[1]	15–45 Years, admitted to A&E after deliberate self-poisoning, 35.6% repeaters	E ($n = 19$): up to six weekly sessions of interpersonal problem-solving skills training. C ($n = 20$): brief problem-orientated therapy. E and C both conducted by clinical psychologists and registrars in psychiatry	12 Months	Self-poisoning rate: E = 10.5%, C = 25%, n.s.[3]
Problem-solving therapy plus intensive care and/or outreach				
7. Gibbons et al, 1978[1,2]	>17 Years, presented at A&E after deliberate self-poisoning, mix of first episode and repeaters	E ($n = 200$): up to 3 months task-centered casework by SW at home. C ($n = 200$): standard referral—54% to GP, 33% to psychiatric	12 Months	Self-poisoning rate: E = 13.5%, C = 14.5%, n.s.
8. Hawton et al, 1981[1,2]	≥16 Years, admitted to hospital after deliberate self-poisoning, 32% repeaters	E ($n = 48$): up to 3 months of problem-orientated counselling by therapist at home plus telephone access. C ($n = 48$): brief problem orientated counselling by therapist at clinic. E and C both conducted by junior psychiatrists, a psychiatric nurse and a SW	12 Months	Self-poisoning rate: E = 10.4%, C = 14.6%, n.s. Suicidal ideation: E = C
9. Salkovskis et al, 1990[1,2]	16–65 Years admitted to A&E after antidepressant self-poisoning, all repeaters	E ($n = 12$): brief (five sessions over 1 month) problem-solving counselling by a CPN either at home or beginning on inpatient and finished at home. C ($n = 8$): treatment as usual, referral to GP	12 Months	Suicide attempt rate: 6 month—E = 0%, C = 37.5%, $p < 0.05$; 18 month—E = 25%, C = 50%, n.s. Suicide ideation over 1 year: Beck's SIS Scale 1—E = C; Scale 2—E < C, $p < 0.05$

10.	van der Sande et al, 1997[1]	≥16 Years admitted to hospital after suicide attempt, 73% repeaters	E (n = 140): brief psychiatric inpatient treatment followed by weekly outpatient problem-solving treatment with a CPN plus 24-hour access to the inpatient unit. C (n = 134): standard care—25% admitted to an inpatient unit and 65% referred to an outpatient clinic	12 Months	Suicide rate: E = 0.01, C = 0.01, n.s. Suicide attempt rate: E = 17.1%, C = 14.9%, n.s.
Dialectical behaviour therapy					
11.	Linehan et al, 1991, 1993a,b[1,2]	18–45 Year-old females with a recent parasuicide and a diagnosis of borderline personality disorder, all repeaters	E (n = 24): 1 year of dialectical behavioural therapy which included weekly individual therapy, weekly skills training and phone consultation as needed. Individual therapists included psychologists and a psychiatrist, group therapists included psychologists and Master's level therapists. C (n = 23): referral to standard psychotherapy	24 Months	Suicide rate: 2 years—E = 4.6%, C = 0%, n.s. Parasuicide rate: 1 year—E = 59.1%, C = 95.5%, $p < 0.01$; 1–2 year—E = 26.3%, C = 60%, $p < 0.01$ Medical severity of parasuicide: 1 year—E < C, $p < 0.05$ Suicidal ideation at 1 year: E = C
Inpatient CBT					
12.	Liberman and Eckman, 1981[1,2]	18–47 Years, referred to an inpatient programlye, all repeaters	E (n = 12): inpatient behavioural therapy provided by a psychologist. C (n = 12): inpatient insight-orientated therapy by psychologists and SWs. E & C both received 4 hours of therapy per day for 8 days on an inpatient unit plus aftercare upon discharge	24 Months	Suicide attempt rate: E = 16.7%, C = 25%, n.s. Suicide ideation: E = 41.7%, C = 75%, n.s. Suicidal plans: E = 0%, C = 33.3%, $p < 0.05$

continued overleaf

Table 28.1 *(continued)*

Study	Sample	Interventions	Follow-up	Results
13. Patsiokas and Clum, 1985[2]	Admitted to psychiatric inpatient unit for suicide attempts, proportion of repeaters not reported	E1 ($n = 5$) cognitive restructuring therapy. E2 ($n = 5$) problem-solving therapy. C ($n = 5$) non-directive therapy. Each intervention consisted of 10 sessions over a 3-week period conducted in an inpatient unit by a clinical psychology graduate student	3 Weeks	Suicidal ideation: E1 = E2 = C
Other				
14. Moller, 1989; Torhorst et al, 1987[1,2]	Admitted to hospital for attempted suicide by self-poisoning, 26% repeaters	E ($n = 68$) continuity of care—referral for up to 12 weekly therapy sessions with psychiatrist who had conducted the inpatient intervention. C ($n = 73$) change of care—referral to a specialist suicide prevention centre	24 Months	Suicide rate: E = 4.6%, C = 2.9%, n.s. Suicide attempt rate: 13.6% versus 4.3%, $p < 0.05$ Suicide or suicide attempt: 18.2% versus 7.1%, $p < 0.05$
15. Torhorst et al, 1988[1]	Attempted suicide by intoxication, all repeaters	E ($n = 40$) long term therapy consisting of monthly sessions for 1 year. C ($n = 40$) short term crisis-orientated therapy consisting of weekly sessions for 12 weeks	12 Months	Parasuicide rate: E = 22.5%, C = 22.5%, n.s.

[1] Study reviewed by Hawton et al, 1998.
[2] Study reviewed by Linehan, 1998.
[3] For those studies that published the suicide and parasuicide rates but did not publish significance levels, significance levels were calculated using a two-tailed Fisher's exact test or a chi-square test corrected for continuity depending on sample size. A&E = accident and emergency/emergency room; C = control condition; CPN = community psychiatric nurse; GP = general practionner/family doctor; SW = social worker; n.s. = not significant.

inclusion of intensive care or outreach interventions may be essential but not always sufficient.

To summarize the efficacy of the psychotherapeutic approaches evaluated by multiple studies, Hawton and colleagues (1998) calculated a summary odds ratio (OR) for each type of experimental condition that had more than one study. The evaluation of intensive care plus outreach included studies numbered 1–4, 8 and 10 in Table 28.1. These studies reported mixed results with respect the direction of effect, resulting in a summary OR of 0.86 (95% confidence interval 0.60–1.23). The evaluation of problem-solving vs. standard aftercare included studies 5–7 and 9. All of these studies reported lower rates of self-harm in the experimental condition, but they still resulted in a non-significant summary OR of 0.73 (0.45–1.18). These summary analyses may offer stronger support for a problem-solving approach, but this position currently remains rather weak. The main problem was the relatively small size of the studies for detecting clinically significant results, even when the trials are combined in a meta-analysis.

Although the variations in study design complicate the interpretations of the results, these variations may also help to explain the mixed results. In her review, Linehan (1998) noted that the best predictor of statistically significant clinical results was the inclusion of subjects at high risk for suicide or deliberate self-harm. She identified studies 2, 4, 9 and 11–13 in Table 28.1 as including high-risk subjects, and studies 1, 5, 7, 8 and 14 as excluding them. According to Linehan's criteria, study 10 also included high-risk subjects, while studies 6 and 15 did not. Notably, not a single study that excluded high-risk patients obtained significantly better results for the experimental condition. One explanation could clearly be that much larger numbers of subjects are needed in studies of lower-risk patients to detect clinically significant effects.

Although disappointing, these treatment outcome results do suggest several directions for future research. First, multicentre research projects would allow researchers to increase their sample size and the homogeneity of study designs. Second, researchers may want to include subjects at high risk of suicide or repeated deliberate self-harm, as these subjects may be more responsive to specialized psychotherapies or more likely to demonstrate clinical change at a statistically significant level. Third, researchers may want to avoid using unproven control conditions that closely resemble the experimental condition, particularly when the sample sizes are small.

Compliance and Efficacy

Although research has consistently demonstrated that certain interventions can enhance rates of treatment attendance and completion, the association between enhanced compliance and the reduction of deliberate self-harm behaviour remains to be demonstrated. Comparing treatment completers with non-completers, one study found no differences in the frequency of repeated suicide attempts (Hawton et al, 1981), while another study reported significantly higher rates for treatment completers (Allard et al, 1992). Two studies measuring varying degrees of compliance suggested that the least compliant subjects have the worst outcomes, followed by the most compliant, with those in between having the best outcome (Torhorst et al, 1987; van Heeringen et al, 1995). Five studies described experimental conditions that lead to significantly higher rates of compliance. Only two of these studies, however, reported significantly lower (Linehan et al, 1991) or near-significantly reduced (van Heeringen et al, 1995) rates of repeated deliberate self-harm as well. Of the remaining studies, two (Hawton et al, 1981; Torhorst et al, 1988) reported no significant treatment effects and one (Torhorst et al, 1987) reported a better outcome for the control condition. Interestingly, the first two studies included just subjects at high risk of repetition, while in the latter studies there were mixed populations of patients.

CONCLUSION

It is surprising how, at present, there is so little in the form of evidence-based (i.e. fully evaluated) psychotherapeutic approaches to assist the clinician in delivering psychotherapy to suicidal patients. To date, only psychotherapeutic approaches involving intensive care or outreach and cognitive-behavioural therapies have been developed to the point of examination in randomized, controlled trials. A number of issues confront these treatments, including the impact of diagnosis, poor treatment compliance and the cost of the treatment. The most important issue, however, is demonstrating that the treatment can reduce suicidal behaviour. Unfortunately, few trials in which treatments have been evaluated have produced significant results. A major methodological problem with such trials is that nearly all have included insufficient number of patients to detect possible clinically significant differences in efficacy at a level of statistical significance. Currently, psychotherapeutic approaches involving a manualized problem-solving component combined with some intensive care or outreach, especially for patients with difficulties in attending hospital clinic-based treatment, may offer the best opportunity for disseminating and delivering an efficacious treatment.

REFERENCES

Allard, R., Marshall, M. and Plante, M.C. (1992) Intensive follow-up does not decrease the risk of repeat suicide attempts. Suicide and Life-Threatening Behavior, 22: 303–314.

Bancroft, J. (1986) Crisis intervention. In S. Bloch (Ed.), An Introduction to Psychotherapies, 2nd Edn. Oxford: Oxford University Press.

Beck, A.T., Rush, A.J., Shaw, B.F. and Emery, F.G. (1979) Cognitive Therapy of Depression. New York: Guilford.

Chowdhury, N., Hicks, R.C. and Kreitman, N. (1973) Evaluation of an after-care service for parasuicide (attempted suicide) patients. Social Psychiatry, 8: 67–81.

Cotgrove, A.J., Zirinsky, L., Black, D. and Weston, D. (1995) Secondary prevention of attempted suicide in adolescence. Journal of Adolescence, 18: 569–577.
Ellis, A. (1984) Rational-emotive Therapy and Cognitive Behaviour Therapy. New York: Springer.
Freeman, A. and Reinecke, M.A. (1993) Cognitive Therapy of Suicidal Behaviour. New York: Springer.
Gibbons, J.S., Butler, J., Urwin, P. and Gibbons, J.L. (1978) Evaluation of a social work service for self-poisoning patients. British Journal of Psychiatry, 133: 111–118.
Hawton, K., Arensman, E., Townsend, E., Bremner, S., Feldman, E., Goldney, R., Gunnell, D., Hazell, P., van Heeringen, K., House, A., Owens, D., Sakinofsky, I. and Träskman-Bendz, L. (1998) Deliberate self-harm: systematic review of efficacy of psychosocial and pharmacological treatments in preventing repetition. British Medical Journal, 317: 441–447.
Hawton, K., Bancroft, J., Catalan, J., Kingston, B., Stedeford, A. and Welch, N. (1981) Domiciliary and out-patient treatment of self-poisoning patients by medical and non-medical staff. Psychological Medicine, 11: 169–177.
Hawton, K. and Catalan, J. (1987) Attempted Suicide: A Practical Guide to its Nature and Management, 2nd Edn. Oxford: Oxford University Press.
Hawton, K., McKeown, S., Day, A., Martin, P., O'Connor, M. and Yule, J. (1987) Evaluation of out-patient counseling compared with general practitioner care following overdoses. Psychological Medicine, 17: 751–761.
Hawton, K. and Kirk, J. (1989) In K. Hawton, P.M. Salvkovskis, J. Kirk and D.B. Clark (Eds), Cognitive Behaviour Therapy for Psychiatric Problems: A Practical Guide, pp. 406–427. Oxford: Oxford University Press.
Liberman, R.P. and Eckman, T. (1981) Behaviour therapy vs. insight-oriented therapy for repeated suicide attempters. Archives of General Psychiatry, 38: 1126–1130.
Linehan, M.M. (1993a) Cognitive Behavioral Therapy of Borderline Personality Disorder. New York: Guilford.
Linehan, M.M. (1993b) Skills Training Manual for Treating Borderline Personality Disorder. New York: Guilford.
Linehan, M.M. (1998) Behavioral treatments of suicidal behaviours: definitional obfuscation and treatment outcomes. Annals of the New York Academy of Science, 302–328.
Linehan, M.M., Armstrong, H.E., Suarez, A., Allmon, D. and Heard, H. (1991) Cognitive-behavioral treatment of chronically parasuicidal borderline patients. Archives of General Psychiatry, 48: 1060–1064.
Linehan, M.M. and Heard, H.L. (1999) Borderline personality disorder: costs, course, and treatment outcomes. In N. Miller (Ed.), The Cost-effectiveness of Psychotherapy: A Guide for Practitioners, Researchers and Policy-makers (pp. 291–305). New York: Oxford University Press.
Linehan, M.M., Heard, H.L. and Armstrong, H.E. (1993) Naturalistic follow-up of a behavioural treatment for chronically parasuicidal borderline patients. Archives of General Psychiatry, 50: 971–974.
McLeavey, B.C. and Daly, R.J. (1988) Manual for interpersonal problem-solving training. Cork: University College, unpublished manuscript.
McLeavey, B.C., Daly, R.J., Ludgate, J.W. and Murray, C.M. (1994) Interpersonal problem-solving skills training in the treatment of self-poisoning patients. Suicide and Life Threatening Behavior, 24: 382–394.
Moller, H.J. (1989) Efficacy of different strategies of aftercare for patients who have attempted suicide. Journal of the Royal Society of Medicine, 82: 643–647.
Morgan, H.G., Jones, E.M. and Owen, J.H. (1993) Secondary prevention of non-fatal deliberate self-harm: the green card study. British Journal of Psychiatry, 163: 111–112.
Patsiokas, A. and Clum, G.A. (1985) Effects of psychotherapeutic strategies in the treatment of suicide attempters. Psychotherapy, 22: 281–290.

Salkovskis, P.M., Atha, C. and Storer, D. (1990) Cognitive-behavioural problem solving in the treatment of patients who repeatedly attempt suicide: a controlled trial. British Journal of Psychiatry, 157: 871–876.

Torhorst, A., Moller, H.J., Burk, F., Kurz, A., Wachtler, C. and Lauter, H. (1987) The psychiatric management of parasuicide patients: a controlled clinical study comparing different strategies of outpatient treatment. Crisis, 8: 53–61.

Torhorst, A., Moller, H.J., Kurz, A., Schmid-Bode, K.W. and Lauter, H. (1988) Comparing a 3-month and a 12-month outpatient aftercare program for parasuicide repeaters. In H.J. Moller, A. Schmidtke and R. Welz (Eds), Current Issues of Suicidology, pp. 419–424. Berlin: Springer-Verlag.

van der Sande, R., van Rooijen, E., Buskens, E., Allart, E., Hawton, K., van der Graaf, Y. and van Engeland, H. (1997) Intensive in-patient and community intervention versus routine care after attempted suicide: a randomised controlled intervention. British Journal of Psychiatry, 171: 35–41.

van Heeringen, C. (1992) The management of non-compliance with outpatient aftercare in suicide attempters: a review. Italian Journal of Suicidology, 2: 79–83.

van Heeringen, C., Jannes, S. Buylaert, W., Henderick, H., de Bacquer, S. and van Remoortel, J. (1995) The management of non-compliance with referral to out-patient aftercare among attempted suicide patients: a controlled intervention study. Psychological Medicine, 25: 963–970.

Welu, T.C. (1977) A follow-up program for suicide attempters: evaluation of effectiveness. Suicide and Life-Threatening Behavior, 7: 17–30.

Chapter 29

General Hospital Management of Suicide Attempters

Keith Hawton
Department of Psychiatry, Oxford University, Oxford, UK

Abstract

Most patients who receive treatment following deliberate self-harm first come to attention after presentation to a general hospital because of the effects of deliberate self-poisoning or self-injury. This chapter describes the important aspects of the clinical care of these patients in the general hospital, including management in the accident and emergency department, medical care and psychiatric assessment, and attention to the risk of further suicidal behaviour in the general hospital. A structured assessment procedure is presented which incorporates attention not just to the problems that patients are facing, but also to the risk of further suicidal behaviour. The issue of multidisciplinary staffing of services for deliberate self-harm patients is addressed and a model for a service presented. Arrangements for aftercare are usually made by staff working in the general hospital, and while treatments are described in detail in other chapters some aspects are presented here, particularly in relation to the role of general hospital staff. General hospital provisions for very young and elderly attempters are discussed, as are aftercare possibilities for frequent repeaters of self-harm and substance abusers. Overall it is concluded that provision of good quality general hospital services for suicide attempters must be a key element in any local or national suicide prevention policy.

INTRODUCTION

This chapter focuses on the management of suicide attempters in the general hospital following presentation because of deliberate self-poisoning or self-injury ("attempted suicide"). Many such acts do not lead to general hospital presenta-

The International Handbook of Suicide and Attempted Suicide. Edited by K. Hawton and K. van Heeringen.

tion (see Chapter 16); the nature of the act will be an important determinant of whether this occurs (e.g. because of loss of consciousness, threat to life, etc.). Whether or not a person receives psychiatric treatment following an attempt will often depend on their being assessed in hospital by a member of a psychiatric service. Those patients that leave hospital prematurely or are otherwise not seen may receive no help. Most registration of attempted suicides is also based on hospital-referred cases, but often provides artificially low figures due to only those seen by the hospital psychiatric service being included.

Whether or not a person survives a suicide attempt after reaching hospital will not only depend on the method used in the act but also on the facilities available in the hospital. It will also depend on the location of other hospitals which can provide highly specialized treatment (e.g. for liver failure), should this be required. This can be a particular problem in less developed countries.

Decisions about possible psychiatric aftercare are ideally made while the patient is in the general hospital. This should be based on the findings of a thorough assessment. A structured approach to assessing patients is desirable, particularly for less experienced clinical staff. This should include not only consideration of psychiatric diagnosis but also assessment of risk of repetition of an attempt, including of completed suicide. Such assessments are, however, beset by problems associated with low specificity of predictive measures, especially for suicide. In order to formulate a comprehensive treatment plan, the patient's problems should be identified, including those in social, psychiatric, personality, socioeconomic and physical health domains.

At present there are few substantive findings on which to base treatment strategies for when a patient leaves hospital but there are some pointers to potentially useful approaches. Treatment plans must largely be guided by each patient's individual needs. Establishment of coordinated and readily available hospital services staffed with experienced clinical personnel is essential in ensuring that deliberate self-harm patients receive adequate care.

ARRIVAL OF PATIENTS AT THE GENERAL HOSPITAL

Attention to the general hospital care of deliberate self-harm patients should include ensuring that appropriate procedures are in place for patients on arrival at the general hospital. In addition to the immediate assessment of medical consequences of self-poisoning or self-injury, accident and emergency department staff should be capable of conducting a brief assessment of patients' psychiatric status and risk. In particular they need to determine whether a patient has a serious psychiatric disorder (e.g. psychosis or severe depression) and is actively suicidal, such that urgent attention by the psychiatric service is required. Dangerous tablets or other potential methods of self-harm should be removed. Staff should be aware that in many hospitals a large number of patients leave accident and emergency departments before a psychiatric assessment can be conducted. Such patients often have substance abuse disorders and a history of previous attempts, and may show behavioural disturbance in the department. Many have features associated with suicide risk and tend to present to hospital with further repeat attempts more often than patients who are assessed in the accident and emergency department (Crawford and Wessely 1998; Hickey et al, 2001). These facts highlight the need for accident and emergency staff to have basic skills in assessment and for them to be able to readily obtain urgent psychiatric assessment when they judge it to be necessary.

MEDICAL CARE

Management of medical complications of suicide attempts is not a major focus of this chapter but requires some comment in relation to suicidal phenomena. The physical consequences of attempts will often depend on the availability of specific treatments. For overdoses of some substances, a patient's survival can depend on whether appropriate antidotes or other treatments can be administered sufficiently quickly. To take the example of paracetamol (tylenol) overdose, administration of the antidote *N*-acetyl cysteine, which protects against liver damage, should take place within 24 hours of an overdose (and preferably much sooner) to be effective. Similarly, effective management of overdoses of respiratory depressants, such as the dextropropxyphene which is included in some paracetamol compounds, requires fairly immediate treatment using respiratory support. Overdoses of drugs that can cause cardiac arrythmias, such as tricyclic antidepressants, will often necessitate cardiac monitoring in an intensive care unit and urgent treatment of any arrythmias that are detected.

Treatment of dangerous self-poisoning in remote areas may be a particular problem, especially in developing countries. An example is the use of seeds of the yellow oleander plant (*Thevetia peruviana*) for self-poisoning in Sri Lanka. This often causes potentially lethal cardiac irregularities. These can usually be treated effectively in sophisticated central hospitals, but the absence of effective treatment facilities in rural hospitals and the time taken for transfer to major hospitals mean that a significant proportion of patients die before they can receive treatment (Eddleston et al, 1998).

The majority of the cost of general hospital management of deliberate self-harm patients is incurred in their physical care, rather than in psychiatric psychiatric management. Costs are greatly increased where admission to a specialized unit, such as an intensive care unit, is necessary. It has been shown, for example, that tricyclic antidepressant overdoses result in significantly greater hospital costs than do overdoses of specific serotonin re-uptake inhibitors because of the frequent necessity for cardiac monitoring, usually in an intensive care unit (Ramchandani et al, 2000).

PSYCHIATRIC ASSESSMENT

Psychiatric assessment should not usually take place until a patient has recovered from any neurotoxic effects of an attempt, because otherwise assessment of

Table 29.1 Factors that should be covered in assessment of attempted suicide patients

- Life events that preceded the attempt
- Motives for the act, including suicidal intent and other reasons
- Problems faced by the patient
- Psychiatric disorder
- Personality traits and disorder
- Alcohol and drug misuse
- Family and personal history
- Current circumstances, such as:
  Social (e.g. extent of social relationships)
  Domestic (e.g. living alone or with others)
  Occupation (e.g. whether employed)
- Psychiatric history, including previous suicide attempts
- Risk of a further attempt
- Risk of suicide
- Coping resources and supports
- What treatment is appropriate to the patient's needs
- Motivation of patient (and significant others where appropriate) to engage in treatment

mental state is difficult and the patient may manifest distorted or impaired recall of events. Clearly, more urgent assessment is indicated if the patient is severely disturbed or regarded as being at acute risk.

A semi-structured assessment procedure is recommended, possibly supplemented by the use of questionnaires. The nature of such a procedure will only be summarized here. For fuller details the reader is referred to Hawton and Catalan (1987).

The main factors that should be covered are listed in Table 29.1. A useful way of assessing the events and patient's problems that preceded the act, the nature of the attempt, possible motivation and suicidal intent, is to obtain a very detailed account of the few days leading up to the act. Whenever possible the patient's account should be supplemented by enquiry of other informants, such as a partner, relatives and friends. Information should also be sought from professionals and others involved in the patient's care, including the general practitioner.

Suicidal intent (i.e. the extent to which the patient wished to die at the time of the attempt) can usefully be assessed by means of the Beck Suicidal Intent Scale (Beck et al, 1974), which includes the items listed in Table 29.2. It is extremely important to recognize that the apparent physical danger of an overdose is a poor and potentially misleading measure of the extent to which a patient may have wanted to die (Beck et al, 1975). Many patients are extremely ignorant of the relative dangers of substances taken in overdose, although increasing attention to suicidal behaviour by the media may be changing this (O'Connor et al, 1999). Thus, a small overdose of a benzodiazepine hypnotic or even an antibiotic may represent a serious attempt at suicide for some patients, whereas a large overdose of a highly dangerous paracetamol–dextropropoxyphene

Table 29.2 Factors that suggest high suicidal intent

- Act carried out in isolation
- Act timed so that intervention unlikely
- Precautions taken to avoid discovery
- Preparations made in anticipation of death (e.g. making will, organizing insurance)
- Preparations made for the act (e.g. purchasing means, saving up tablets)
- Communicating intent to others beforehand
- Extensive premeditation
- Leaving a note
- Not alerting potential helpers after the act
- Admission of suicidal intent

Table 29.3 Motives or reasons for deliberate self-harm

- To die
- To escape from unbearable anguish
- To get relief
- To escape from a situation
- To show desperation to others
- To change the behaviour of others
- To get back at other people/make them feel guilty
- To get help

analgesic combination might be taken with low intent by other patients. People in the medical and allied professions of course represent an exception, and usually the danger of their acts is a good measure of intent. In many cases the methods used will be related to their special access to medication and other substances, such as anaesthetic agents (Hawton et al, 2000).

Very dangerous self-injuries are often associated with high suicidal intent, but this is not always so. In a study of individuals admitted to hospital in Australia following non-fatal self-inflicted gunshot injuries, for example, many of the cases appeared to have been highly impulsive, occurred in the midst of an interpersonal dispute and were subsequently regretted (de Moore et al, 1994). These characteristics are not dissimilar to what is found in many cases of overdose in settings where guns are less available.

Assessment of motives for deliberate self-harm should be based on the precedents, circumstances of the act, the patient's account, that of other informants, and deduction by the clinician. The list of motivational reasons shown in Table 29.3, which was developed on the basis of research conducted during the 1970s (Birtchnell and Alarcon 1971; Bancroft et al, 1979; Hawton et al, 1982b), has proved to be useful in clinical practice and also in further research investigations (Hjelmeland 1995).

Estimation of the risk of repetition and of suicide following attempted suicide, both short-term and long-term, is a very important part of the assessment. Factors which should be considered in relation to this are discussed in Chapter 21 and summarized in Tables 29.4 and 29.5. It is essential, however, to recognize that such predictive measures are notoriously imprecise. For repetition, this is because the predictive factors are relatively crude, and while those patients who score high on the scales that have been developed have a high risk of repeating (e.g. Buglass and Horton, 1974; Kreitman and Foster, 1991), a substantial proportion of repeaters, possibly more than half, do not score highly (Hawton and Fagg 1995; Kapur and House, 1998). It is unclear whether this is because we are as yet unaware of some important predictive factors or simply because prediction of human behaviour is difficult, particularly in the absence of information about likely future life events. The main point is that assessment must not rely solely on a score derived from a scale but also include attention to the individual patient's unique characteristics and circumstances. Prediction of suicide risk in deliberate self-harm patients is even more difficult, a major reason being that suicide is relatively uncommon even in such a high-risk group (see Chapter 21). Factors associated with suicide risk are well known but have a very high false positive rate (Hawton 1987).

Assessment of coping resources and supports should be based on past behaviour under stress and the patient's account of to whom they can turn for support.

Table 29.4 Factors associated with risk of repetition of attempted suicide

- Previous attempt(s)
- Personality disorder
- Alcohol or drug abuse
- Previous psychiatric treatment
- Unemployment
- Lower social class
- Criminal record
- History of violence
- Age 25–54 years
- Single, divorced or separated

Table 29.5 Factors associated with risk of suicide after attempted suicide

- Older age (females only)
- Male gender
- Unemployed or retired
- Separated, divorced or widowed
- Living alone
- Poor physical health
- Psychiatric disorder (particularly depression, alcoholism, schizophrenia and "sociopathic" personality disorder)
- High suicidal intent in current episode
- Violent method involved in current attempt (e.g. attempted hanging, jumping)
- Leaving a suicide note
- Previous attempt(s)

It is particularly important to assess whether the patient has specific deficits in problem solving (see Chapter 5), as these will be an important target for psychosocial therapy (see Chapter 28). The best evidence for these will be methods of problem solving used in the past. It is important, however, to determine whether any apparent difficulties in problem solving are in fact due to depression (Kinsbury et al, 1999) or other psychiatric disorders.

Deliberate self-harm patients are frequently ambivalent about accepting help, or even frankly dismissive of it. However, this may be understandable in the context of acts that often represent interpersonal communications or have other functions unconnected with help seeking. Also, many deliberate self-harm patients come from socio-economic backgrounds in which help seeking for emotional problems is rarely considered. Therefore, clinicians may have to work hard in some cases to explain to patients how treatment might be of benefit. These factors also mean that a brief intervention, such as problem solving (see Chapter 28), is likely to be more acceptable to a sizeable proportion of patients than more lengthy therapeutic approaches.

The assessment procedure can itself be highly therapeutic. Patients may be provided with their first opportunity to discuss their difficulties with a clinician. Joint interviews with family members can help highlight issues that need addressing and assist with communication problems. This emphasizes the need for clinicians staffing general hospital services for deliberate self-harm patients to have good clinical skills.

WHO SHOULD ASSESS DELIBERATE SELF-HARM PATIENTS?

At one time the assessment of deliberate self-harm patients was regarded as primarily the responsibility of psychiatrists. In the UK, therefore, official guidelines in the 1960s specified that all such patients should be assessed by psychiatrists (Ministry of Health, 1961). Increases in the clinical responsibilities of non-medical clinical staff and the findings of research (see Chapter 32) have resulted in a major change in the pattern of services in many places. In the UK it has been demonstrated that nurses, social workers and other clinicians can assess these patients reliably, make effective aftercare arrangements and provide effective therapy (Gardner et al, 1978; Newson-Smith and Hirsch, 1979; Catalan et al, 1980; Hawton et al, 1981). This has resulted in new official guidelines that reflect these findings (Department of Health and Social Security, 1984; Royal College of Psychiatrists, 1994).

It is imperative that staff of whatever discipline who are involved in this work have reasonable background experience and skills in the management of patients with emotional and psychiatric disorders and be properly trained in assessment and treatment of deliberate self-harm patients. They must also have support from senior psychiatrists, especially for patients with severe psychiatric disorders and where compulsory admission to hospital may be required. They must also be highly motivated and have good support systems in place, as working with deliberate self-harm patients can be extremely demanding.

GENERAL HOSPITAL SERVICES FOR DELIBERATE SELF-HARM PATIENTS

The specific components of general hospital services for deliberate self-harm patients will depend on local patterns of the problem of self-harm and available resources. It is well-recognized, however, that services vary widely in quality and that very often they are inadequate, especially in the light of the needs of this patient population and the risks of further suicidal behaviour, including fatal acts. Development of high quality general hospital services for deliberate self-harm patients should be a major element in any national or local suicide prevention strategy (see Chapters 34 and 36). The Royal College of Psychiatrists in the UK has published recommended standards for good quality services (Royal College of Psychiatrists 1994). Surveys of available services have shown that most fall well below these standards (Ebbage et al, 1994; Hawton and James, 1995; Hughes et al, 1998), although there are now major efforts in many centres in the UK to remedy this situation.

The ideal level of staffing of a service for a general population of, for example, 400,000–500,000 in the UK might be as follows:

- 3–5 Experienced psychiatric nursing staff.
- 2 Junior psychiatrists (plus emergency cover by other juniors).
- 1 Social worker.
- 1 Clinical psychologist.
- 1 Consultant psychiatrist, with back-up from other senior colleagues.

Such a service was developed as a model prototype in Oxford in the 1970s (Hawton et al, 1979) and has been followed in several other centres. Clearly, the numbers of staff in particular professional groups might vary.

The functioning of a service can be improved if deliberate self-harm patients who do not require physical treatment in specialized settings (e.g. an intensive care unit) can be admitted to one short-stay medical ward rather than to a large number of wards. The attitudes of general medical and nursing staff to deliberate self-harm patients are often negative, especially those of doctors towards patients whose acts they perceive as having low suicidal intent (Ramon et al, 1975; see Chapter 6). Clinical experience shows that attitudes are far more favourable when admission to a single ward is possible. General medical and nursing staff in such wards develop more experience of managing these patients. Closer working relationships with members of the deliberate self-harm service can also be developed.

One important problem is how to provide an adequate 24-hour service, seven days per week. Most services are fully available during the working day but depend on on-call psychiatric services at night, which may of course limit the speed of availability of clinical assessments. In an emergency, ideally an assessment should be available within an hour of it being requested, especially for patients judged to be at particular risk by accident and emergency department staff. Similar limitations may apply to weekends, although clearly there is no clinical reason why a service should be less adequate at these times than during weekdays, especially as self-harm is just as frequent at this time (Jessen et al, 1999).

Ideally, the service should include some means of monitoring all self-harm presentations to the hospital and the activity of the clinical service. This can serve a useful audit function and can also provide an important basis for research. The national and international value of such monitoring is exemplified by the World Health Organization/European Union Multicentre Study on Parasuicide, as discussed in Chapter 3.

While the costs of such a clinical service are clearly substantial, they are justified in terms of the provision of a high-quality service for needy patients, the reduction in demands on general hospital medical staff, and the speed with which medical beds can be cleared (Hawton et al, 1979). There is also the potential for reducing subsequent suicidal behaviour.

It is advisable for a planning group for the service to be established. This will obviously include some members of the service, but should also include representatives of accident and emergency department staff, general medical and nursing staff, research staff and a hospital manager. This group can assess local needs, identify the necessary level of staffing of the service, review its functioning, attend to links and relationships with other services, investigate problems that may arise and plan future projects and developments.

While what has been discussed in this section represents the components of an ideal service, clearly such a provision will not be feasible in many centres, especially in developing countries. It may even not be necessary where rates of deliberate self-harm are relatively low, such as in some countries in Southern Europe (see Chapter 3). However, it is strongly recommended that there be some level of specific service, with particular staff available to provide high-quality clinical assessments, rather than reliance being totally on an on-call local general psychiatric service.

Specific Subgroups of Patients

The Very Young

While older adolescent self-harm patients can usually be managed by the general deliberate self-harm service, children and very young adolescents will require specialist attention from child and adolescent psychiatry services (Royal College of Psychiatrists, 1998). Where there are relatively large numbers of such patients, a clinician from the child and adolescent services might work in the overall deliberate self-harm service, or at least act as the liaison person between the services. Restrictions on resources, however, mean that these patients are usually managed by staff from local child and adolescent psychiatry services who attend the general hospital when necessary.

Very young patients are usually admitted to a paediatric ward when this is available in the general hospital. It is advisable for all very young attempters to be admitted, rather than dealt with in the accident and emergency department, as they require particularly careful and often prolonged assessment, including interviewing of families and possible involvement of community statutory services (e.g. social services). Fuller details of the management of young attempters are provided in Chapter 30.

The Elderly

As indicated in Chapter 18, while deliberate self-harm in the elderly is less common than in younger people, it very often involves higher suicidal intent (Pierce, 1987). Routine admission to a medical bed is therefore also recommended for this group. Close links should be established with the local psychogeriatric service (if one exists) so that clinicians from the service can provide assessment and make arrangements for aftercare.

Patients Who Refuse Treatment

There are two groups of patients who refuse treatment who pose particular problems for clinicians. The first group comprises those who refuse potentially life-saving treatment for the physical consequences of deliberate self-harm and the second those patients who are assessed as being of high suicide risk but who refuse admission for psychiatric treatment.

Patients who refuse medical treatments are the most difficult group. The dilemma for the clinician is whether to instigate potentially life-saving treatment against a patient's will. Studies in the UK have shown that clinicians very often disagree on the best course of action (Hardie et al, 1995; Hassan et al, 1999). The issue is whether patients always have a right to refuse physical treatments or whether there are circumstances under which their wishes can be overruled. This dilemma not uncommonly presents with self-poisoning, such as large overdoses of paracetamol, in which early treatment can prevent development of potentially fatal liver damage. In the UK the issue primarily comes down to one of mental capacity (Hassan et al, 1999). To show that they have the capacity to refuse treatment, patients:

- Must be able to understand and retain information on the treatment proposed, its indications and its main benefits, as well as possible risks and the consequences of non-treatment.
- Must be shown to believe that information.

- Must be capable of weighing up the information in order to arrive at a conclusion.

If a clinician instigates treatment against a patient's wishes in spite of the patient appearing to have capacity to refuse, then they are at risk of being accused of battery. Where the patient is judged as lacking capacity, essential treatment can either be instigated (a) directly by a physician, or (b) after the patient has been placed on a mental health order because of the degree of mental illness, in which case the treatment for the physical condition is given because the overdose is judged to be the result of mental illness. In situations of dire emergency, most clinicians would instigate essential treatment to save the patient's life and then try to sort out the legal issues afterwards. Such understandable action is unlikely to lead to successful litigation if the clinician acted in a way that they judged at the time to be in the patient's best interest.

The question of how to manage the patient who refuses psychiatric treatment when this is judged to be essential is usually more straightforward. It comes down to a judgement of whether the patient is suffering, or likely to be suffering, from a mental illness which necessitates hospital assessment and/or treatment. The regulations for dealing with such circumstances vary greatly between countries (see Chapter 23). In most countries, if a patient thought to be at serious risk and/or mentally ill has presented to a general hospital following deliberate self-harm but is refusing to stay for a psychiatric assessment, accident and emergency department staff would be judged to be acting reasonably if they restrained the patient under "common law" until a psychiatric opinion can be obtained.

RISK OF SUICIDAL BEHAVIOUR IN THE GENERAL HOSPITAL

While rare, suicidal acts do occur in the general hospital (White et al, 1995). This fact should be borne in mind by clinical staff, especially when assessment reveals ongoing suicidal ideation. It should also be considered in the planning of specialized units for deliberate self-harm patients, be they in general medical or psychiatric wards. Jumping from windows or balconies and down internal drops is probably the most common means (White et al, 1995). Where units are based above ground level, the degree to which windows open and access to other sites for jumping should therefore be restricted.

AFTERCARE ON DISCHARGE FROM THE GENERAL HOSPITAL

The following is an overview of the types of aftercare that may be organized for patients by general hospital staff. The range of possible aftercare provisions is very wide and will be determined by patient needs and local availability of resources.

Psychiatric Inpatient Treatment

This is necessary for patients with current severe psychiatric disorders, especially where there is a major risk of further suicidal behaviour. It may also be necessary to allow a fuller psychiatric assessment. Brief admission can be helpful for patients at risk who are in a state of crisis. The proportion of deliberate self-harm patients who require admission to a psychiatric unit will depend on several factors. These include:

1. The general characteristics of the self-harm population—more patients usually require admission if the age distribution tends to include more middle-aged and older patients, rather than a very high proportion of teenagers and very young adults. This is because the prevalence of serious psychiatric disorders and of patients at high risk of suicide is likely to be greater.
2. The availability of local support services and resources—fewer patients will require admission if there is a good quality and readily available aftercare service.
3. The experience and knowledge of members of the general hospital psychiatric service—fewer patients seem to be admitted to inpatient psychiatric care if the clinicians who conduct assessments in the general hospital are very experienced. We have shown this to be the case in Oxford, a significantly lower proportion of patients being admitted during times when very experienced nursing staff were manning the service, compared with the times when junior and relatively inexperienced psychiatric trainees were doing the front-line work (unpublished findings).

Outpatient and Community-based Care

Aftercare for the majority of deliberate self-harm patients can be provided in outpatient and community-based (e.g. home-based treatment) settings. The types of treatment and evidence for efficacy are discussed fully in Chapter 28 and therefore will only be briefly considered here. When a patient is suffering from a major psychiatric condition it is, of course, essential that it is adequately treated, wether by pharmacological (see Chapter 27) and/or, psychological (Hawton et al, 1989) means.

The most pragmatic general approach to treatment of deliberate self-harm patients is probably brief problem-solving therapy. This is because, first, these patients face a wide range of problems (Bancroft et al, 1977; Hawton et al, 1982a); second, there is evidence for impaired problem solving in many cases (see

Chapter 5); and third, this approach is acceptable to many patients. There is, however, only limited evidence from controlled clinical trials that problem-solving therapy is effective in this patient population, probably because all the trials conducted so far have been too small to demonstrate clinically significant effects in terms of reduction of repetition of self-harm at a statistically significant level (Hawton et al, 1998). There is, however, more substantial evidence that problem resolution is more likely when this approach is used rather than "treatment as usual", the latter tending to consist of routine psychiatric outpatient or general practitioner care (Hawton et al, 1987; Salkovskis et al, 1990). There is a major need for evaluation of this approach in a large randomized controlled clinical trial.

Continuity of care can be an important factor in determining compliance with aftercare. Thus, Torhorst and colleagues (1987) demonstrated that when deliberate self-harm patients in Germany were offered aftercare with the same clinicians who assessed them in hospital after their attempts, the rate of attendance at the first treatment session was significantly higher than when the aftercare was with a different clinician. This clearly has relevance to the design and staffing of clinical services.

Attendance at treatment sessions is also better if patients are seen in their own homes (Hawton et al, 1981). This approach is, however, costly and therefore might best be reserved for patients who are likely to have problems in attending clinic-based treatment, because of either motivational problems or difficulty of access. The finding by Van Heeringen and colleagues (1995), that home visiting by a nurse who worked on the motivation of patients who failed to attend initial clinic-based treatment sessions significantly increased the number who subsequently attended, suggests another way to improve compliance with therapy.

In settings where patients live a substantial distance from hospitals or where transport is a major problem there will be a much greater need for community-based aftercare. This will be particularly necessary in developing countries, especially for patients from rural areas. In Sri Lanka, for example, there have been major efforts to provide care in rural villages through community support programmes (Ratnayeke, 1998)

Open Access to Services

In some centres, after discharge from hospital patients are given the opportunity to gain emergency access to clinical services, mostly by telephone. This is usually through patients being given a card that provides details of an access telephone number. The results of two initial randomized controlled clinical trials of this approach were encouraging in terms of prevention of repetition of self-harm. One, involving adult patients who had made their first attempts, was conducted in Bristol in the UK (Morgan et al, 1993) and the other involved very young adolescents and was conducted in London (Cotgrove et al, 1995). However, both trials were too small for the apparent reduction in repetition to reach statistical significance (Hawton et al, 1998). A more recent, much larger, trial from Bristol, which included both repeaters of self-harm as well as first-time attempters, did not result in an overall reduction in repetition of self-harm, but there were some interesting sub-group differences (Evans et al, 1999). There was a non-significant trend towards first-time attempters who were given the emergency card having a lower subsequent repetition rate, whereas repeaters (especially males) given the card had a significantly higher repetition rate than those not given it. Unfortunately, this sub-group comparison was not based on stratified randomization and hence the findings are not easy to interpret and suggest that further trials are required. The findings also suggest that at present clinicians should think carefully about which patients might benefit from the provision of emergency direct access, especially as it requires establishment of a 24-hour back-up service to receive calls. Also it can prove stressful for clinical staff, particularly when faced with calls from drunk and abusive patients.

Patients with Specific Problems and Disorders

Frequent Repeaters of Self-harm

Patients who frequently repeat self-harm present a major therapeutic challenge (see Chapter 21). Those with borderline personality disorders comprise an important subgroup of this population (see Chapter 10). There have been some recent advances in the treatment options for repeaters. As discussed in Chapter 28, a treatment programme consisting of intensive individual and group therapy ("dialectical behaviour therapy") produced promising results in a clinical trial in Seattle, USA, in female patients with borderline personality disorders. The patients who received this treatment showed reduced repetition of self-harm and also other positive outcomes, such as less time spent in inpatient psychiatric care and more time in employment (Linehan et al, 1991, 1993). This requires further evaluation and also investigation in male patients. In terms of pharmacological therapy, there is also evidence from one trial that depot neuroleptic medication (flupenthixol) may reduce repetition of self-harm in frequent repeaters (Montgomery et al, 1979; see Chapter 27). Further evaluation of this approach, including use of oral neuroleptics, is also required. Results of a recent trial of treatment with the specific serotonergic re-uptake inhibitor antidepressant, paroxetine, suggests that it may reduce repetition of self-harm in those patients with a history of two to four attempts (Verkes et al, 1998; see Chapter 27). However, this result must be treated with caution, since if was based on findings from a subgroup not stratified in the initial randomization of patients to treatment conditions (paroxetine or placebo). There is also limited evidence that mood stabilizers, such as lithium and carbamazepine, may be helpful in reducing behavioural problems in personality disordered patients (see Chapter 27) and hence possibly suicidal behaviour.

Adequate treatment of frequent repeaters will depend not just on specific therapies but also on the establishment of carefully planned and coordinated service provision. This might include allocation of a key clinician to coordinate care and good communication between staff in the general hospital and in the community who are likely to be involved in clinical care. In particular, inpatient psychiatric care should be kept to a minimum because of the deterioration in behaviour which often results and the potential spread of self-harming behaviour to other vulnerable inpatients (Hawton, 1978). For some patients, carefully coordinated long-term support is the most pragmatic approach.

Substance Abusers

The strong association between suicidal behaviour and substance abuse, especially abuse of alcohol, was discussed in detail in Chapter 9. Not only is alcohol abuse a risk factor for suicidal behaviour in the first place, it is also associated with increased risk of repetition of attempts and of eventual suicide (see Chapters 9 and 21). In adolescents and very young adults, substance abuse is a particularly important risk factor for suicide after deliberate self-harm that has resulted in general hospital referral (Hawton et al, 1993). Therefore, not only is treatment of substance abuse an important potential factor in reducing suicidal behaviour, but admission to the general hospital following an attempt may provide an opportunity for detection (and hence treatment) of previously undiagnosed substance abuse (Hawton et al, 1997). Therefore, there should be close association between general hospital services for suicide attempters and services for substance abusers, preferably with ready availability of substance abuse service staff to provide assessments and initiate treatment while patients are still in the general hospital.

CONCLUSIONS

Most suicide attempters who enter psychiatric care have initially presented to the general hospital following their acts of self-poisoning or self-injury. The provision of general hospital services of good quality for these patients is therefore highly important, both as part of a comprehensive psychiatric service and of a general suicide prevention strategy. However, services are known to often fall below the level of recommended standards. In designing a service, attention should be paid to the reception of patients to the hospital, especially management in the accident and emergency department. The staffing and availability of a deliberate self-harm service needs careful consideration. It is essential that assessment in the general hospital is closely linked with the provision of appropriate treatment selected from a range of possible aftercare interventions. As elsewhere in this book, the paucity of evidence for efficacy of treatment interventions is acknowledged, but potential strategies for which there is some supportive evidence have been highlighted. Specific provisions should be made wherever possible for very young and elderly self-harm patients, with close links with local services for these two groups. General hospital management also requires particular attention to the needs and treatment of frequent repeaters of self-harm and abusers of alcohol and drugs.

Provision of high quality general hospital and aftercare services for suicide attempters must be a major element in comprehensive local or national suicide prevention strategies.

REFERENCES

Bancroft, J., Hawton, K., Simkin, S., Kingston, B., Cumming, C. and Whitwell, D. (1979) The reasons people give for taking overdoses: a further inquiry. British Journal of Medical Psychology, 52: 353–365.

Bancroft, J., Skrimshire, A., Casson, J., Harvard-Watts, O. and Reynolds, F. (1977) People who deliberately poison or injure themselves: their problems and their contacts with helping agencies. Psychological Medicine, 7: 289–303.

Beck, A.T., Schuyler, D. and Herman, I. (1974) Development of Suicidal Intent Scales. In The Prediction of Suicide pp. 45–56. A.T. Beck, H.L.P. Resnik and D.J. Lettieri (Eds), Philadelphia, PA: Charles Press.

Beck, A.T., Beck, R. and Kovacs, M. (1975) Classification of suicidal behaviors: I. Quantifying intent and medical lethality. American Journal of Psychiatry, 132: 285–287.

Birtchnell, J. and Alarcon, J. (1971) The motivation and emotional state of 91 cases of attempted suicide. British Journal of Medical Psychology, 44: 45–52.

Buglass, D. and Horton, J. (1974) A scale for predicting subsequent suicidal behaviour. British Journal of Psychiatry, 124: 573–578.

Catalan, J., Marsack, P., Hawton, K.E., Whitwell, D., Fagg, J. and Bancroft, J. (1980) Comparison of doctors and nurses in the assessment of deliberate self-poisoning patients. Psychological Medicine, 10: 483–491.

Cotgrove, A.J., Zirinsky, L., Black, D. and Weston, D. (1995) Secondary prevention of attempted suicide in adolescence. Journal of Adolescence, 18: 569–577.

Crawford, M.J. and Wessely, S. (1998) Does initial management affect the rate of repetition of deliberate self harm? Cohort study. British Medical Journal, 317: 985.

De Moore, G.M., Plew, J.D., Bray, K.M. and Snars, J.N. (1994) Survivors of self-inflicted firearm injury. A liaison psychiatry perspective. Medical Journal of Australia, 160: 421–425.

Department of Health and Social Security (1984) The Management of Deliberate Self-Harm. HN (84) 25. London: Department of Health and Social Security.

Ebbage, J., Farr, C., Skinner, D.V. and White, P.D. (1994) The psychosocial assessment of patients discharged from accident and emergency departments after deliberate self-poisoning. Journal of the Royal Society of Medicine, 87: 515–516.

Eddleston, K., Resvi Sheriff, M.H. and Hawton, K. (1998) Deliberate self-harm in Sri Lanka—an overlooked tragedy in the developing world. British Medical Journal, 317: 133–135.

Evans, M.O., Morgan, H.G., Hayward, A. and Gunnell, D.J. (1999) Crisis telephone consultation for deliberate self-harm patients: effects on repetition. British Journal of Psychiatry, 175: 23–27.

Gardner, R., Hanka, R., Evison, B., Mountford, P.M., O'Brien, V.C. and Roberts, S.J. (1978) Consultation–liaison scheme for self-poisoned patients in a general hospital. British Medical Journal, ii: 1392–1394.

Hardie, T., Bhui, K. and Brown, P. (1995) The emergency treatment of overdose: a problem of consent to treatment. Psychiatric Bulletin, 19: 7–9.

Hassan, T.B., MacNamara, A.F., Davy, A., Bing, A. and Bodiwala, G.G. (1999) Managing patients with deliberate self-harm who refuse treatment in the accident and emergency department. British Medical Journal, 319: 107–109.
Hawton, K. (1978) Deliberate self-poisoning and self-injury in the psychiatric hospital. British Journal of Medical Psychology, 51: 253–259.
Hawton, K., Gath, D. and Smith, E. (1979) Management of attempted suicide in Oxford. British Medical Journal, 2: 1040–1042.
Hawton, K., Bancroft, J., Catalan, J., Kingston, B., Stedeford, A. and Welch, N. (1981) Domiciliary and out-patient treatment of self-poisoning patients by medical and non-medical staff. Psychological Medicine, 11: 169–177.
Hawton, K., O'Grady, J., Osborn, M. and Cole, D. (1982a) Adolescents who take overdoses: their characteristics, problems and contacts with helping agencies. British Journal of Psychiatry, 140: 118–123.
Hawton, K., Cole, D., O'Grady, J. and Osborn, M. (1982b) Motivational aspects of deliberate self-poisoning in adolescents. British Journal of Psychiatry, 141: 286–291.
Hawton, K. (1987) Assessment of suicide risk. British Journal of Psychiatry, 150: 145–153.
Hawton, K. and Catalan, J. (1987) Attempted Suicide: A Practical Guide to its Nature and Management. Second Edition. Oxford: Oxford University Press.
Hawton, K., McKeown, S., Day, A., Martin, P., O'Connor, M. and Yule, J. (1987) Evaluation of outpatient counselling compared with general practitioner care following overdoses. Psychological Medicine, 17: 751–761.
Hawton, K., Salkovskis, P.M., Kirk, J. and Clark, D.M. (1989) Cognitive Behaviour Therapy for Psychiatric Problems: A Practical Guide. Oxford: Oxford University Press.
Hawton, K., Fagg, J., Platt, S. and Hawkins, M. (1993) Factors associated with suicide after parasuicide in young people. British Medical Journal, 306: 1641–1644.
Hawton, K. and Fagg, J. (1995) Repetition of attempted suicide: the performance of the Edinburgh predictive scales in patients in Oxford. Archives of Suicide Research, 1: 261–272.
Hawton, K. and James, R. (1995) General hospital services for attempted suicide patients: a survey in one region. Health Trends, 27: 18–21.
Hawton, K., Simkin, S. and Fagg, J. (1997) Deliberate self-harm in alcohol and drug misusers: patient characteristics and patterns of clinical care. Drug and Alcohol Review, 16: 123–129.
Hawton, K., Arensman, E., Townsend, E., Bremner, S., Feldman, E., Goldney, R., Gunnell, D., Hazell, P., Van Heeringen, C., House, A., Owens, D., Sakinofsky, I. and Träskman-Bendz, L. (1998) Deliberate self-harm: a systematic review of the efficacy of psychosocial and pharmacological treatments in preventing repetition. British Medical Journal, 317: 441–447.
Hawton, K., Clements, A., Simkin, S. and Malmberg, A. (2000) Doctors who kill themselves: a study of the methods used for suicide. Quarterly Journal of Medicine, 93: 351–357.
Hickey, L., Hawton, K., Fagg, J. and Weitzel, H. (2001) Deliberate self-harm patients who leave the accident and emergency department without a psychiatric assessment: a neglected population at risk of suicide. Journal of Psychosomatic Research, 50: 87–93.
Hjelmeland, H. (1995) Verbally expressed intentions of parasuicide: I. Characteristics of patients with various intentions. Crisis, 16: 176–181.
Hughes, T., Hampshaw, S., Renvoize, E. and Storer, D. (1998) General hospital services for those who carry out deliberate self-harm. Psychiatric Bulletin, 22: 88–91.
Jessen, G., Andersen, K., Arensman, E., Bille-Brahe, U., Crepet, P., de Leo, D., Hawton, K., Haring, C., Hjelmeland, H., Ostamo, A., Salander-Renberg, E., Schmidtke, A., Temesvary, B. and Wasserman, D. (1999) Temporal fluctuations and seasonality in attempted suicide in Europe: findings from the WHO/EURO multicentre study on parasuicide. Archives of Suicide Research, 5: 57–69.

Kapur, N. and House, A. (1998) Against a high-risk strategy in the prevention of suicide. Psychiatric Bulletin, 22: 534–536.

Kingsbury, S., Hawton, K., Steinhardt, K. and James, A. (1999) The psychological characteristics of adolescents who take overdoses: comparison with community and psychiatric controls. Journal of the American Academy of Child and Adolescent Psychiatry, 38: 1125–1131.

Kreitman, N. and Foster, J. (1991) Construction and selection of predictive scales, with special reference to parasuicide. British Journal of Psychiatry, 159: 185–192.

Linehan, M.M., Armstrong, H.E., Suarez, A., Allmon, D. and Heard, H.L. (1991) Cognitive-behavioral treatment of chronically parasuicidal borderline. Archives of General Psychiatry, 48: 1060–1064.

Linehan, M.M., Heard, H.L. and Armstrong, H.E. (1993) Naturalistic follow-up of a behavioral treatment for chronically parasuicidal borderline patients. Archives of General Psychiatry, 50: 971–974.

Ministry of Health (1961) HM Circular (61), 94. London: Ministry of Health.

Montgomery, S.A., Montgomery, D.B., Jayanthi-Rani, S., Roy, D.H., Shaw, P.J. and McAuley, R. (1979) Maintenance therapy in repeat suicidal behaviour: a placebo controlled trial. Proceedings of the 10th International Congress for Suicide Prevention & Crisis Intervention, pp. 227–229.

Morgan, H.G., Jones, E.M. and Owen, J.H. (1993) Secondary prevention of non-fatal deliberate self-harm. The green card study. British Journal of Psychiatry, 163: 111–112.

Newson-Smith, J.G.B. and Hirsch, S.R. (1979) A comparison of social workers and psychiatrists in evaluating parasuicide. British Journal of Psychiatry, 134: 335–342.

O'Connor, S., Deeks, J.J., Hawton, K., Simkin, S., Keen, A., Altman, D.G., Philo, G. and Bulstrode, C. (1999) Television portrayal of self-poisoning increases knowledge of specific dangers of paracetamol: population-based surveys. British Medical Journal, 318: 978–979.

Pierce, D. (1987) Deliberate self-harm in the elderly. International Journal of Geriatric Psychiatry, 2: 105–110.

Ramon, S., Bancroft, J.H.J. and Skrimshire, A.M. (1975) Attitudes towards self-poisoning patients among physicians and nurses in a general hospital. British Journal of Psychiatry, 127: 257–264.

Ranchandani, P., Murray, B., Hawton, K. and House, A. (2000) Deliberate self-poisoning with antidepressant drugs: a comparison of the relative hospital costs of cases of overdose of tricyclics with those of selective-serotonin re-uptake inhibitors. Journal of Affective Disorders, 60: 97–100.

Ratnayeke, L. (1998). Suicide in Sri Lanka. In: R.J. Kosky, H.S. Eshkevari, R.D. Goldney and R. Hassan (Eds), Suicide Prevention: The Global Context, pp. 139–142. New York: Plenum.

Royal College of Psychiatrists (1994) The General Hospital Management of Adult Deliberate Self-Harm. Council Report CR32. London: Royal College of Psychiatrists.

Royal College of Psychiatrists (1998) Managing Deliberate Self-harm in Young People. Council Report CR63. London: Royal College of Psychiatrists.

Salkovskis, P.M., Atha, C. and Storer, D. (1990) Cognitive-behavioural problem solving in the treatment of patients who repeatedly attempt suicide. A controlled trial. British Journal of Psychiatry, 157: 871–876.

Torhorst, A., Möller, H.J., Burk, F., Kurz, A., Wachtler, C. and Lauter, H. (1987) The psychiatric management of parasuicide patients: a controlled clinical study comparing different strategies of outpatient treatment. Crisis, 8: 53–61.

Van Heeringen, C., Jannes, S., Buylaert, W., Henderick, H., De Bacquer, D. and Van Remoortel, J. (1995) The management of non-compliance with referral to outpatient after-care among attempted suicide patients: a controlled intervention study. Psychological Medicine, 25: 963–970.

Verkes, R.J., Van der Mast, R.C., Hengeveld, M.W., Tuyl, J.P., Zwinderman, A.H. and Van Kempen, G.M.J. (1998) Reduction by paroxetine of suicidal behavior in patients with repeated suicide attempts but not major depression. American Journal of Psychiatry, 155: 543–547.

White, R.T., Gribble, R.J., Corr, M.J. and Large, M.M. (1995) Jumping from a general hospital. General Hospital Psychiatry, 17: 208–215.

Chapter 30

Treatment Strategies for Adolescent Suicide Attempters

Philip Hazell
University of Newcastle, New South Wales, Australia

Abstract

This chapter outlines standard approaches to the therapeutic management of the adolescent suicide attempter and reviews the evidence for the efficacy of experimental treatments directed to reducing repetition rates. Based on existing data about the characteristics of adolescent suicide attempts, other potential treatment strategies are considered. The therapeutic care of the adolescent suicide attempter requires a competent assessment of the risk of further suicidal behaviour, the precipitants and context of the suicide attempt, the presence of coexisting psychopathology, and the availability of supports for the patient. The decision of whether to hospitalize the patient will depend on the availability of a suitable treatment unit, the acuity of the problem and the level of protection against further suicidal behaviour that is available at the place of residence. Attendance at outpatient follow-up tends to be poor, but there are useful strategies that may be adopted to improve compliance with follow-up treatment. There is little empirical evidence available as yet to inform the treatment of the adolescent suicide attempter. Individual treatment strategies with the most promise include cognitive therapy and a variant, problem-solving therapy. Given that family conflict is a common precipitant to suicidal behaviour in adolescents, treatment directed to communication, conflict resolution and affect regulation within the family should be of benefit. Intensive intervention with home visiting does not appear to offer any advantage over office-based treatment. Offering automatic readmission to hospital if the adolescent experiences another suicidal crisis seems to reduce the rate of re-attempting, even though the option of hospitalization is rarely exercised. There is a need for systematic evaluation of treatments directed to adolescent suicide attempters. Attention needs also to be given to the style of services available to adolescents. Most suicide crises occur outside office hours, which suggests the need for extended-hours services available to adolescents.

The International Handbook of Suicide and Attempted Suicide. Edited by K. Hawton and K. van Heeringen.

INTRODUCTION

Lifetime estimates of suicidal behaviour among adolescents are in the range 1.3–3.8% for males and 1.5–10.1% for females (Brent, 1997; see Chapter 16). Only a small proportion of these attempters (about 1 in 10) reach settings where treatment directed to the suicidality may be instituted (Silburn et al, 1991). A smaller proportion again are successfully engaged in treatment (Piacentini et al, 1995), yet based on estimates of risk, treatment directed to adolescent suicide attempters should offer one of the more promising preventive strategies against completed suicide (Patton and Burns, 1996). Although adolescents make up a significant proportion of total suicide attempters, there have been few intervention studies directed specifically to this age group. Results from all-age or adult-specific studies may not generalize to the adolescent population, for several reasons. First, the outcome for adolescent suicide attempters is somewhat different from older attempters, with a lower rate of subsequent suicide completion in the short to medium term (Safer, 1997). Second, adolescents may not respond to treatment strategies that have demonstrated efficacy in adults (Hazell et al, 1995). Traditional approaches to the management of adolescent suicide attempters may have overemphasized the assessment of the risk of repetition at the expense of engaging the adolescent in a treatment alliance.

"STANDARD AFTERCARE"

The standard by which novel treatment strategies directed against repetition of suicidal behaviour are measured is "standard aftercare". Such treatment is usually developed through clinical wisdom and adopted by consensus, but is rarely supported by empirical evidence. Much of the everyday management of adolescent suicide attempters, however, may not be amenable to systematic evaluation. An examination of the literature suggests there is considerable heterogeneity in the standard aftercare of adolescent suicide attempters, determined by factors such as the availability of treatment resources, financing of medical services, and defence against litigation. Adolescents in the USA, for example, are three times more likely to receive psychiatric hospitalization following a suicide attempt than their counterparts in western Europe (Safer, 1996), and will be offered up to four times as many outpatient follow-up visits as adolescents in the UK (Brent, 1997). Many health authorities have produced guidelines for the assessment and management of young suicide attempters. Table 30.1 is a list of generic principles that may be adapted according to local circumstances.

Assessment

The objectives of the mental health assessment of the adolescent suicide attempter are summarized in Table 30.2.

Table 30.1 Generic clinical pathway guidelines for the assessment and management of adolescent suicide attempters. Specific details may be added to suit local circumstances

- Date: . . . .
- Date for Review: . . . .
- Prepared by: . . . . (names of participating agencies or professionals)
- General Principles
  - Pathways accepted and endorsed by the local clinical community
  - Pathways promote, wherever possible, continuity of care
- Inflow to emergency assessment and treatment setting, e.g. hospital emergency department
  - 24-hour free call number for advice and triage
  - When suicidal adolescent known to community treatment agency, active encouragement for key person from that agency to attend emergency assessment with the patient
- Triage
  - Triage nurse identifies patient as having engaged in deliberate self-harm
  - Triage nurse activates protocol for management of deliberate self-harm, which may include provisions for close observation, monitoring of vital signs, nursing in specified area of the emergency department, establishing priority for medical review, and early notification of the mental health team
- Mental health assessment
  - Assessment of immediate danger of repetition
  - Attend to access to lethal means
  - Diagnostic assessment
  - Social assessment, including degree of support from family or other sources
  - Plan of action, which may include further inpatient observation, transfer to a psychiatric unit, or discharge with follow-up arrangements
  - Discharge planning should be conducted in cooperation with likely aftercare services
- Aftercare
  - Active booking of follow-up appointment to occur within *x* days of discharge
  - Written communication to aftercare agency summarizing circumstances of presentation, results of assessment, and treatment
  - Reminder call to patient *x* days before appointment
  - Telephone call or home visit if patient defaults on follow-up appointment
- Other considerations
  - Effective method of recording all self-harm presentations
  - Intermittent audit of cases
  - Intermittent review of procedures

Table 30.2 Objectives of the mental health assessment of the adolescent suicide attempter

- Assessment of the immediate risk of repetition or suicide completion
- Assessment and resolution of contextual crises that may have precipitated the suicidal behaviour
- Assessment and mobilization of any support systems that may be available to the patient
- Recognition and treatment, where indicated of coexisting pyschopathology

In most countries, mental health assessment will first be undertaken in the same setting in which medical resuscitation may have occurred, usually the emergency department of a general hospital. Sometimes an adolescent may come to clinical attention in other settings several days after the suicide attempt, when medical management is no longer relevant. The approach to mental health assessment, however, is much the same. Only a few emergency departments will have specific facilities available for paediatric patients, so it is highly probable that the adolescent will have been managed among adult medical and surgical emergencies. Emergency department staff can hold ambivalent or even antagonistic attitudes toward the adolescent suicide attempter. At the point of first mental health assessment, therefore, the adolescent suicide attempter may be traumatized by both the events preceding the attempt and the events that have followed. An approach to the initial assessment is summarized in Table 30.3.

The most common stresses preceding adolescent suicidal behaviour are conflict with a parent, conflict with others, disciplinary crises and school problems (Beautrais et al, 1997; Negron et al, 1997). The nature of the stress does not seem to differentiate ideators from attempters (Negron et al, 1997) and similar stresses are also seen in adolescent suicide completers (Groholt et al, 1998). Perception of the stress, however, may be a marker of cognitive distortion in the adolescent, and provide a focus for treatment. Stresses involving other family members may suggest that the family be engaged in the therapeutic intervention.

Acute Management

An early consideration in the management of the suicide attempter is whether further hospitalization is required. The decision is affected by local factors, such as the availability of inpatient resources and the availability of intensive community care. Factors that influenced the decision of clinicians in the USA to recommend the hospitalization of suicidal adolescents, based on hypothetical cases, included problems with family support, the presence of depression, conduct disorder or substance abuse, a history of previous attempts, and the presence of suicidal behaviour in a relative (Morrissey et al, 1995). Experienced clinicians were less likely to recommend hospitalization than were less experienced clinicians. Some clinicians use the unwillingness of an adolescent to enter into a "no-suicide" contract as a marker of imminent danger, and therefore a determinant of hospitalization (Rotheram-Borus and Bradley, 1990). Successful contracting against suicide may also represent the beginnings of a workable treatment alliance (Brent, 1997). Such a strategy needs to be supported by adequate 24-hour clinical back-up. Contracting as a means of preventing the repetition of suicidal behaviour has not been evaluated directly.

If the adolescent is to be hospitalized, it is important that the unit is sensitive to the developmental needs of young people, and has clear protocols for the monitoring and maintenance of the safety of suicidal individuals. The admitting physician should ensure that there are clearly written instructions regarding the

Table 30.3 Approach to assessment

- Attend to the adolescent's immediate discomfort and distress (may include strategies such as advocating to move the patient to a quieter area of the emergency department, and even arranging for fluids or a snack when there are no medical contra-indications)
- Whenever possible, first speak with the adolescent alone (promotes therapeutic alliance)
- Obtain corroborative information about the circumstances of the suicide attempt from accompanying relatives or friends after interviewing the adolescent, preferably with the adolescent's consent
- Assess determinants of further suicide risk:
    - Level of suicidal intent
    - Lethality of the attempt as perceived by the adolescent (may be inaccurate)
    - Intensity of the precipitating crisis
    - Motivation
    - Previous suicidal behaviour
    - Concurrent mental disorder or substance abuse
    - Access to lethal means (especially firearms)
- Screen for psychopathology, with specific attention to:
    - Depression
    - Conduct problems
    - Personality disorder
    - Substance abuse
    - Anxiety
    - Less common conditions with a high risk of suicide, such as psychosis and bipolar disorder
- Mental state assessment, with specific attention to continued intoxication and delirium (if either is suspected, the clinician should delay decisions about disposition until the patient's sensorium is clear)
- Degree of hopelessness, impulsivity and aggression desplayed by the patient, since all have been associated with increased suicide risk
- Assess stresses preceding adolescent suicidal behaviour
- Assess the motivation parents may have to assist the teenager in attending follow-up appointments
- Assess other support systems available to the adolescent (may include members of the extended family, peers, school welfare staff, and community youth support workers)

intensity of nursing supervision, and the frequency of psychiatric review. Provision should be made for clear "handover" of important clinical information at the change of nursing and of medical shifts. Mental health legislation generally requires that the inpatient environment is the least restrictive necessary to manage the patient's condition, but steps should be taken to minimize access to means of further self-harm. These may include ensuring that the patient does not have unsupervised access to balconies, stairwells or rooftops from which he/she could jump, or access to objects such as shower fittings from which the patient may attempt to hang. It is unusual for involuntary treatment to be required for this age group.

Case Example

Rachel, aged 16 years, had presented many times to the general hospital with self-harm behaviour, usually involving wrist cutting and/or overdose with over-the-counter analgesic medication. The precipitant was most often conflict with her adoptive mother, who was at a loss to know how to manage her. Rachel met diagnostic criteria for borderline personality disorder, complicated by substance misuse and dysthymia. She had not attended school for 2 years. Once in hospital Rachel would often cut herself again using a razor blade hidden in her belongings. Recognizing that there was a pattern to Rachel's behaviour, the consultant psychiatrist providing outpatient treatment organized for Rachel to always be admitted to the same medical ward, where a very experienced nursing sister supervised her care. Her belongings were routinely searched for blades. Clear orders were written regarding the level of nursing supervision required. If necessary, Rachel would receive 1:1 nursing from a "special". Contrary to the belief that individuals such as Rachel crave extra attention, the frequency of her presentations to hospital decreased and eventually stopped, although she continued with her outpatient treatment.

Aftercare

Following mental health assessment in the emergency department, most adolescent suicide attempters are discharged to the care of their parents or guardians, or in some circumstances to welfare agencies. A follow-up appointment is usually arranged in an outpatient or community clinic, but the experience of many centres is that the appointment is not kept. Factors in the adolescent that may contribute to treatment non-adherence include a desire to minimize the suicide attempt, to dissociate themselves from the event, and to avoid further family conflict. Older adolescents are less likely to attend follow-up than are younger patients (Piacentini et al, 1995). Factors thought to adversely affect treatment adherence by the family include a temporary reduction in family conflict caused by the suicide crisis, false beliefs about psychotherapy, cultural differences between the family and the treatment providers, and unpleasant experiences in the emergency department (Rotheram-Borus et al, 1996). Various strategies have been recommended to promote treatment adherence. These are summarized in Table 30.4.

There is no consensus regarding the optimum therapeutic modality to use once an adolescent suicide attempter does attend follow-up. Typically, the adolescent may receive multiple modes of treatment. Individual psychotherapy based on *cognitive-behavioural therapy* principles may focus on erroneous assumptions and beliefs that occur in the suicidal adolescent. A typical false logic that can arise in an egocentric teenager is, "He argued with me, therefore he does not love me, therefore nobody must love me, therefore I am unlovable". The therapist may gently challenge these assumptions and assist the adolescent to recognize that he/she is overgeneralizing from a specific incident. Other cognitive distortions identified in suicidal adolescents that may be a focus of intervention include selective abstraction or arbitrary inference (drawing conclusions from minimal

Table 30.4 Strategies to improve treatment adherence in the aftercare of adolescent suicide attempters

- Positive regard shown towards adolescent at time of triage
- Arrange a definite time for the follow-up appointment at the time of initial assessment
- Prompt follow-up (within days)
- Reminder telephone calls
- 24-hour clinical back-up for emergencies
- Vigorous attempts to contact non-attenders
- Explicit contracting about the nature of treatment to be provided
- Involvement of family members and significant other people in the treatment
- Continuity of clinician from hospital assessment to aftercare

or even absent evidence), over- or underestimating the significance of events, dichotomous thinking (seeing things as "black or white") and catastrophizing (Hartford, 1990). Some adolescents are inclined to project all the blame for an event on to others, or alternatively to take personal responsibility for events that have multiple causes (Spirito, 1997). A useful cognitive technique therefore involves reattribution of blame for the suicide precipitant. The suicidal adolescent may be invited to generate a list of alternative actions that may be taken in response to a suicide precipitant. Suicide may be included as an option, but the aim of the exercise is to teach the adolescent that suicide is only one of many possible options, and is hopefully also seen as one of the least desirable (Spirito, 1997). One version of cognitive therapy has been shown to be superior to standard aftercare in reducing repetition of suicidal behaviour among a specially selected group of young adult female suicide attempters (Linehan et al, 1991; see Chapter 28), but the strategy has yet to be trialled with adolescents.

Some suicidal adolescents have difficulty in generating a range of solutions to problems and in evaluating their effectiveness (Sadowski and Kelley, 1993). *Problem-solving therapy*, which is a specific form of cognitive therapy, addresses these deficiencies, and may be especially appropriate for the impulsive suicide attempter (Brent, 1997). An important component of problem solving is the progression though a specific sequence of steps. One such sequence for suicidal adolescents and their families involves problem definition, followed by brainstorming of alternative solutions. Rules for brainstorming include allowing as many solutions as possible without criticism, fostering creativity, and a requirement that participants offer to change one of their own behaviours (Spirito, 1997). This strategy has much in common with the principles of conflict mapping used in corporate management. In one non-randomized clinical control trial, Donaldson et al (1997) found fewer re-attempts among adolescents treated with telephone-administered problem-solving therapy, compared with subjects receiving standard aftercare (0/23 vs. 7/78), but the results were not statistically significant. Four randomized control studies involving older patients have also shown a statistically non-significant trend favouring problem-solving therapy over standard aftercare (Hawton et al, 1998).

One construct for understanding suicidal behaviour is that it represents a maladaptive form of communication. *Social skills training* teaches the adolescent how to communicate more effectively with those with whom he/she has disagreement, often through role play. A related strategy involves the *recognition and regulation of anger* before it escalates to suicidal behaviour. The adolescent and family members are coached to recognize the signs of increasing tension, and also the "point of no-return" beyond which there is likely to be some disruptive behaviour. These points are mapped on a "feeling thermometer", which provides an indicator of when the adolescent and family need to employ strategies such as temporary disengagement to defuse difficult situations (Rotheram, 1987). Several other approaches to *family therapy* are currently being evaluated (Brent, 1997), but no outcomes have yet been reported. Some centres adopt a family psychoeducational approach, while others focus on communication skills and conflict resolution. One study has found that compliance with family-based treatment was markedly less than for individual psychotherapy or for pharmacotherapy (King et al, 1997). Persistent disengagement of the parents from the suicidal adolescent may represent a significant risk for repetition. Clinicians and welfare professionals sometimes despair that they have greater concerns for the welfare of a suicidal adolescent than do the family.

Treatment of Coexisting Problems

Attention needs also to be given to the treatment of coexisting psychopathology. Depression may be targeted with cognitive-behavioural therapy or pharmacotherapy. Cognitive therapy has been demonstrated to be superior to either family therapy or supportive psychotherapy in the treatment of adolescent depression (Brent et al, 1997), and is considered by some to be the first line of treatment for depression in this age group, owing to its safety relative to pharmacotherapy. Caution must be applied in prescribing medication, since this may offer to the adolescent a potential means of suicide. The odds of a young person overdosing on prescribed psychotropic medication are substantially higher than that for the elderly (Buckley et al, 1996). It is wise to withhold prescribing until an outpatient treatment alliance is satisfactorily established, since the adolescent's mood may lift once the immediate crisis has passed. Evidence for the efficacy of antidepressant medication in this age group lags well behind that for adults. Tricyclic drugs offer no advantage over placebo in adolescents (Hazell et al, 1995) and, given their toxicological profile, should arguably never be used in this population when there is a risk of suicide. There is encouraging evidence supporting the efficacy of at least one selective serotonin reuptake inhibitor (Emslie et al, 1997), but the response rate is not as high as for adults. Other new-generation antidepressant medications have yet to be evaluated in randomized controlled trials in children and adolescents.

There is a range of treatment modalities available to manage substance abuse problems in adolescents, with none having been demonstrated to have superior efficacy over another (American Academy of Child and Adolescent Psychiatry, 1997). Choice of treatment will be guided by local availability, and the severity of the substance abuse and co-morbid psychiatric problems. Management options include individual psychotherapies, self-help groups, family therapy, community-based interventions, and diversionary programmes such as "wilderness camps".

Monitoring Safety

It is important that the clinician providing aftercare to the suicidal adolescent remains responsive to cues of continuing or emerging suicidality. The clinician has a responsibility to monitor access to lethal means of suicide. It is clinically wise, for example, to advocate the removal of firearms from the household for at least the period of follow-up treatment (Brent, 1997), although it remains uncertain whether this is an effective suicide prevention measure (Beautrais et al, 1996; Hintikka et al, 1997).

There is no consensus concerning the optimum length of treatment and follow-up of adolescent suicide attempters. A sensible approach involves a period of intense intervention followed by intermittent low-intensity contact. The therapeutic strategy of asking the adolescent to decide whether or not it is necessary to continue appointments is highly questionable. Even the adolescent at high risk is likely to interpret this to mean "You don't need to come", and some could feel that they are being rejected by the clinician.

EXPERIMENTAL TREATMENTS

Systematic evaluation of treatments directed to a reduction in repeat suicide attempts among adolescent suicide attempters are few, and generally involve replication of strategies that have been applied to adults. One randomized (Harrington et al, 1998), and one non-randomized (Deykin et al, 1986) clinical controlled trial demonstrated no benefit of intensive intervention with home visiting compared with standard aftercare for adolescent suicide attempters. These data are consistent with a meta-analysis of similar studies in adults (Hawton et al, 1998). Home visiting sometimes improves other aspects of functioning in suicide attempters, but this was not demonstrated in the study by Harrington et al (1998), despite a sample size that provided sufficient power to detect modest clinical effects. Consistent with a study in adults, an emergency card that provides the suicide attempter with guaranteed access to 24-hour clinical follow-up demonstrated a trend towards a reduction in the experimental group compared with a group given standard aftercare, but the difference was not statistically significant (Cotgrove et al, 1995). Given the simplicity and potentially widespread application of the strategy, the study warrants replication in a larger sample, perhaps recruited through a multicentre trial.

In a controlled clinical trial, Rotheram-Borus et al (1996) have evaluated the effect of a programme introduced to a hospital emergency department that consisted of staff education, a psychoeducational video directed to adolescent suicide attempters and their families that promoted the importance of follow-up, and one emergency family therapy session. The experimental group and controls were then offered the same standardized aftercare, consisting of cognitive-behavioural therapy and family therapy. Unfortunately, rates of repetition were not reported, but adolescents exposed to the emergency department programme reported significantly lower depression and suicidal ideation scores on standard checklists at follow-up. However, adherence with aftercare, the primary focus of intervention, was not significantly different between the experimental and control groups of adolescents or their parents.

OTHER STRATEGIES

As outlined in Chapter 16, various methods have been adopted to characterize populations of adolescent suicide attempters, including the mandatory reporting of self-harm behaviour, as occurs in Oregon (Centers for Disease Control, 1995), self-report surveys of suicidal ideation and behaviour among community samples, and comparisons of suicide attempters presenting to hospital with suicide completers, non-suicidal psychiatric controls, and normal controls. In addition, some studies have compared hospitalized with non-hospitalized attempters, or drawn a distinction between medically serious and medically trivial attempts. Another approach to characterizing suicide attempters is through individual case studies. Theoretical frameworks for understanding suicidal behaviour in adolescents include psychopathological, cognitive psychological, sociological, and public health perspectives. Much attention has been given to the universal aspects of suicide attempting, possibly to the detriment of understanding factors that may have a specific influence in particular groups. At the risk of perpetuating this imbalance, the following generalizations may be made about what we think we have learned about adolescent suicidal behaviour:

Adolescent self-harm behaviour occurs on a continuum of medical seriousness and a related, but not identical, continuum of intent to die. As few as 0.2% of adolescents reporting self-harm behaviour may have true intent to die (Patton et al, 1997), but the estimate is almost certainly affected by the way in which one frames the question. As intent and medical seriousness increase, there is a trend toward greater psychiatric disability and less intercurrent stress (approximating to older concepts of endogenous vs. reactive problems) and an inverse relationship with help-seeking behaviour prior to the attempt (Tiller et al, 1997). However, suicide attempters as a group do come into contact with psychiatric services far more than do normal controls, and a proportion will use telephone counselling or help-line services (Beautrais et al, 1998). Most adolescent suicide attempts occur in the evening (see Figure 30.1; Silburn et al, 1991) at the place of residence (see Figure 30.2; Centers for Disease Control, 1995) and are precipitated by conflict with parents or significant others (Beautrais et al, 1997;

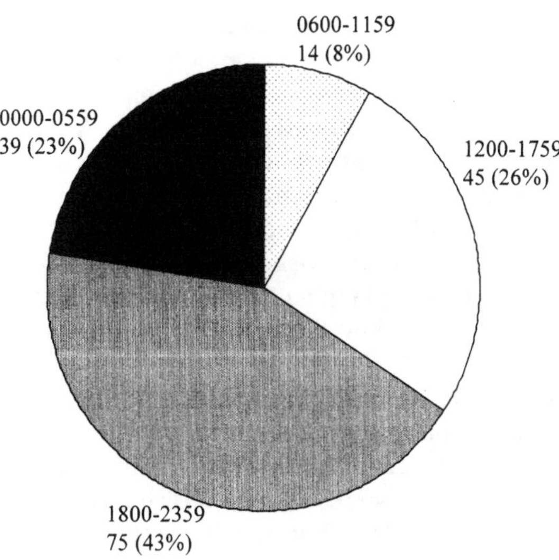

Figure 30.1 Time of arrival of adolescent suicide attempters at emergency department in Perth, Western Australia. Adapted by permission from Silburn et al (1991)

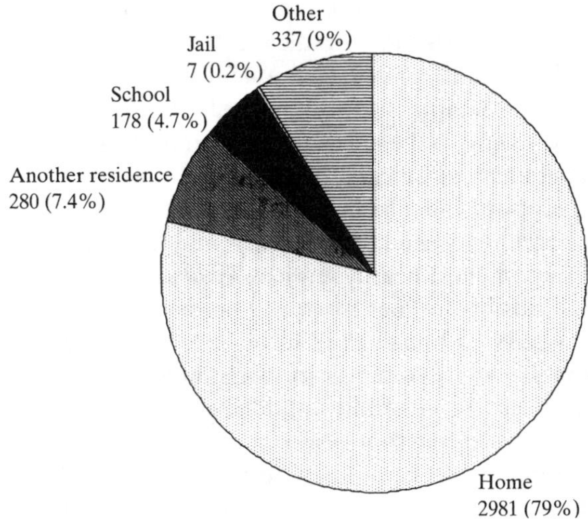

Figure 30.2 Location of suicide attempts made by adolescents aged 17 years and under in Oregon, 1988–1993

Silburn et al, 1991) suggesting that adolescent attempted suicide is predominantly a domestic problem.

While family and clinicians often attribute the motivation of suicidal behaviour to manipulation of interpersonal relationships, suicide attempters are more likely to describe their behaviour as an attempt to relieve distress (Hawton et al,

1982; Williams and Pollock, 1993). Contagion, in which the behaviour of one individual influences the behaviour of others (see Chapter 37), has been implicated as a precipitating factor in completed suicide, but may in fact be a more potent factor in attempted suicide (Hazell and Lewin, 1993). Adolescents are poor at attending appointments for psychiatric aftercare, but their parents are possibly even worse. The vicissitudes of treatment adherence may mask a degree of self-selection on the part of adolescent suicide attempters. Spirito et al (1994) have reported that adolescents who carry risk factors for repetition, such as a history of previous attempts, greater planning of the attempt, and substance misuse, are actually more likely to follow through with treatment than their low-risk counterparts.

Most adolescent suicide attempts occur outside normal office hours, at a time when most mental health professionals are off-duty. This demands some rethinking of traditional models of mental health service delivery to adolescents. Twenty-four-hour community-based response teams directed to youth in distress have been developed in some centres, but require systematic evaluation of their acceptability and effectiveness. Flexible working arrangements to extend the hours of existing adolescent mental health services should also be explored. Effort should be given to making access to adolescent mental health services "user-friendly". The community management of suicidal adolescents is gaining support in many regions, led by the innovative work of Rotheram-Borus and colleagues (Rotheram-Borus and Bradley, 1990). In this model, the emergency department may be seen as just one component of a network of services directed to adolescent suicide attempters and adolescents at risk. The strategy may be very resource-intensive, owing to the need to train community personnel in the recognition and management of suicidality and, most importantly, to provide them with continuing support and supervision. The advantage is that services may be adapted to local conditions and, if necessary, may operate in rural areas where there are no tertiary mental health services. Evaluation data are needed.

Hot-lines or 24-hour help-lines for young people have the advantage of accessibility and anonymity, although they have been criticized for failing to reach young males, who are at greatest risk for completed suicide (Berman and Jobes, 1995). Such help-lines are generally established to *prevent* suicide acts, but an additional role may be to function as a contact point for young people who have made an attempt and are seeking access to medical and psychiatric treatment. It is essential that telephone counsellors have sufficient skill and experience to be able to engage the young person in crisis. Counsellors must also have full knowledge of the means of accessing local treatment resources. A conflict of purpose may occur in this situation, because although organizations that provide help-lines generally emphasize the importance of anonymity, ascertaining the location of an adolescent who has made a suicide attempt may make the difference between a successful retrieval and death.

Family conflict plays an important role in adolescent suicidal behaviour. The nature of the conflict can include disciplinary crisis, arguments about suitable friendships, and the testing of limits to acceptable behaviour. Parents, intimidated by the intensity of an adolescent suicide attempt, may retreat to a position of minimal limit setting, or seek to transfer responsibility for the supervision of their child to an external agency. Family intervention could seek to orientate the parents toward limit setting in a non-coercive way that is sensitive to the developmental needs of the adolescent but still provides him/her with containment. Such a strategy probably holds more promise as a primary preventive measure directed to families with younger children, however, than it does as a secondary preventive measure directed to families where an adolescent has already made a suicide attempt.

Attention should also be given to factors that may promote the contagion of suicide attempting among adolescents (see Chapter 37). While much emphasis has been given to external factors, such as media reporting of suicide, contagion of attempting is as likely to be transmitted directly through adolescent friendship networks, or through intermediate exposure in the milieu such as schools and correctional facilities (Hazell, 1993). There may be a place for developing novel strategies that target the peer group of adolescent suicide attempters, both as a primary prevention measure for the peers, and a secondary prevention measure for the attempter.

CONCLUSIONS

Adolescent suicidal behaviour exists on continua of both suicidal intent and medical lethality. We are most likely to see clinically those who have harmed themselves sufficiently to warrant treatment in a hospital emergency department, or those in the community who have drawn attention to their behaviour. Possibly most adolescent suicide attempts do not come to clinical attention. However, suicide attempts among adolescents are a sufficiently common clinical problem that the skills necessary to conduct a competent triage assessment and formulate and deliver aftercare treatment should be considered generic rather than specialized. Clinicians may find that their own health authorities have developed practice guidelines for the acute management of adolescent suicide attempters, but the guidelines will generally not be evidence-based. There is less information available to guide the choice of aftercare treatment, most of which will be conducted by outpatient or community clinics. Adherence to aftercare can be poor, but there is preliminary evidence that, through self-selection, adolescents with the greatest need are also the most likely to be exposed to treatment. Standard treatments directed to adolescent suicide attempters include cognitive-behavioural therapy, problem-solving skills, social skills training, affect management, family psychoeducation and conflict resolution within the family. Systematic evaluation of treatment is needed to better inform practice.

To date, experimental treatments that involve more intensive aftercare have not proved to be more successful than standard care in reducing repetition rates among adolescent suicide attempters, demonstrating that more is not necessarily better. Given the cost implications of intensive treatments, more attention should be given to developing and evaluating low-cost strategies. The emergency card project developed by Morgan and adapted for use among adolescents by Cotgrove and colleagues is one such example. There is a need to reorientate the way in which adolescent mental health services are delivered, to provide better access for young people at the times they most need it.

REFERENCES

American Academy of Child and Adolescent Psychiatry (1997) Practice parameters for the assessment and treatment of children and adolescents with substance use disorders. Journal of the American Academy of Child and Adolescent Psychiatry, 36 (Suppl.): 140–156S.

Beautrais, A.L., Joyce, P.R. and Mulder, R.T. (1996) Access to firearms and the risk of suicide: a case control study. Australian and New Zealand Journal of Psychiatry, 30: 741–748.

Beautrais, A.L., Joyce, P.R. and Mulder, R.T. (1997) Precipitating factors and life events in serious suicide attempts among youths aged 13 through 24 years. Journal of the American Academy of Child and Adolescent Psychiatry, 36: 1543–1551.

Beautrais, A.L., Joyce, P.R. and Mulder, R.T. (1998) Psychiatric contacts among youths aged 13 through 24 years who have made serious suicide attempts. Journal of the American Academy of Child and Adolescent Psychiatry, 37: 504–511.

Berman, A.L. and Jobes, D.A. (1995) Suicide prevention in adolescents (age 12–18). Suicide and Life-Threatening Behavior, 25: 143–154.

Brent, D.A. (1997) Practitioner review: the aftercare of adolescents with deliberate self-harm. Journal of Child Psychology and Psychiatry, 38: 277–286.

Brent, D.A., Holder, D., Kolko, D., Birmaher, B., Baugher, M., Roth, C., Iyengar, S. and Johnson, B.A. (1997) A clinical psychotherapy trial for adolescent depression comparing cognitive, family, and supportive therapy. Archives of General Psychiatry, 54: 877–885.

Buckley, N.A., Dawson, A.H., Whyte, I.M., Hazell, P.L., Meza, A. and Britt, H. (1996) An analysis of age and gender influences on the relative risk for suicide and psychotropic drug self-poisoning. Acta Psychiatrica Scandinavica, 93: 168–171.

Centers for Disease Control (1995) Leads from the Morbidity and Mortality Weekly Report, Atlanta, GA: fatal and non-fatal suicide attempts among adolescents—Oregon, 1988–1993. Journal of the American Medical Association, 274: 452–453.

Cotgrove, A.J., Zirinsky, L., Black, D. and Weston, D. (1995) Secondary prevention of attempted suicide in adolescence. Journal of Adolescence, 18: 569–577.

Deykin, E.Y., Hsieh, C.C., Joshi, N. and McNamarra, J.J. (1986) Adolescent suicidal and self-destructive behaviour. Results of an intervention study. Journal of Adolescent Health Care, 7: 88–95.

Donaldson, D., Spirito, A., Arigan, M. and Aspel, J.W. (1997) Structured disposition planning for adolescent suicide attempters in a general hospital: preliminary findings on short-term outcome. Archives of Suicide Research, 3: 271–282.

Emslie, G.J., Rush, J.A., Weinberg, W.A., Kowatch, R.A., Hughes, C.W., Carmody, T. and Rintelmann, J. (1997) A double-blind, randomized, placebo-controlled trial of fluoxetine in children and adolescents with depression. Archives of General Psychiatry, 54: 1031–1037.

Groholt, B., Ekeberg, O., Wichstrom, L. and Haldorsen, T. (1998) Suicide among children and younger and older adolescents in Norway: a comparative study. Journal of the American Academy of Child and Adolescent Psychiatry, 37: 473–481.

Harrington, R., Kerfoot, M., Dyer, E., McNiven, F., Gill, J., Harrington, V., Woodham, A.

and Byford, S. (1998) Randomized trial of a home-based family intervention for children who have deliberately poisoned themselves. Journal of the American Academy of Child and Adolescent Psychiatry, 37: 512–518.

Hartford, J.E. (1990) Cognitive behavioural group treatment. In M.J. Rotheram-Borus, J. Bradley and N. Obolensky (Eds), Planning to Live. Evaluating and Treating Suicidal Teens in Community Settings. Tulsa, OK: National Resource Centre for Youth Services, pp 211–250.

Hawton, K., Cole, D., O'Grady, J. and Osborn, M. (1982) Motivational aspects of deliberate self-poisoning in adolescents. British Journal of Psychiatry, 141: 286–291.

Hawton, K., Arensman, E., Townsend, E., Bremner, S., Feldman, E., Goldney, R., Gunnell, D., Hazell, P., van Heeringen, K., House, A., Owens, D., Sakinofsky, I. and Träskman-Bendz, L. (1998) Deliberate self-harm: a systematic review of the efficacy of psychosocial and pharmacological treatments in preventing repetition. British Medical Journal, 317: 441–447.

Hazell, P.L. (1993) Adolescent suicide clusters: evidence, mechanisms and prevention. Australian and New Zealand Journal of Psychiatry, 27: 653–665.

Hazell, P.L. and Lewin, T.J. (1993) Friends of adolescent suicide attempters and completers. Journal of the American Academy of Child and Adolescent Psychiatry, 32: 76–81.

Hazell, P.L., O'Connell, D., Heathcote, D., Robertson, J. and Henry, D. (1995) Efficacy of tricyclic drugs in treating child and adolescent depression: a meta-analysis. British Medical Journal, 310: 897–901.

Hintikka, J., Lehtonen, J. and Vinamaki, H. (1997) Hunting guns in homes and suicides in 15–24 year-old males in Eastern Finland. Australian and New Zealand Journal of Psychiatry, 31: 858–861.

King, C.A, Hovey, J.D., Brand, E., Wilson, R. and Ghaziuddin, N. (1997) Suicidal adolescents after hospitalization: parent and family impacts on treatment follow-through. Journal of the American Academy of Child and Adolescent Psychiatry, 36: 85–93.

Linehan, M.M., Armstrong, H.E., Suarez, A., Allmon, D. and Heard, H.L. (1991) Cognitive-behavioural treatment of chronically parasuicidal borderline patients. Archives of General Psychiatry, 48: 1060–1064.

Morrissey, R.F., Dicker, R., Abikoff, H., Alvir, J.M.J., DeMarco, A. and Koplewicz, H.S. (1995) Hospitalizing the suicidal adolescent: an empirical investigation of decision-making criteria. Journal of the American Academy of Child and Adolescent Psychiatry, 34: 902–911.

Negron, R., Piacentini, J., Graae, F., Davies, M. and Shaffer, D. (1997) Microanalysis of adolescent suicide attempters and ideators during the acute suicidal episode. Journal of the American Academy of Child and Adolescent Psychiatry, 36: 1512–1519.

Patton, G. and Burns, J. (1996) Scope for Preventive Intervention in Youth Suicide: A Risk Factor Based Approach. Report to the National Health and Medical Research Council of Australia. Melbourne: Centre for Adolescent Health.

Patton, G.C., Harris, R., Carlin, J.B., Hibbert, M.E., Coffey, C., Schwartz, M. and Bowes, G. (1997) Adolescent suicidal behaviours: a population-based study of risk. Psychological Medicine, 27: 715–724.

Piacentini, J., Rotheram-Borus, M.J., Gillis, J.R., Graae, F., Trautman, P., Cantwell, C., Garcia-Leeds, C. and Shaffer, D. (1995) Demographic predictors of treatment attendance among suicide attempters. Journal of Consulting and Clinical Psychology, 63: 469–473.

Rotheram, M.J. (1987) Evaluation of imminent danger for suicide among youth. American Journal of Orthopsychiatry, 57: 102–110.

Rotheram-Borus, M.J. and Bradley, J. (1990) Evaluation of suicide risk. In M.J. Rotheram-Borus, J. Bradley and N. Obolensky (Eds), Planning to Live. Evaluating and Treating Suicidal Teens in Community Settings. Tulsa, OK: National Resource Centre for Youth Services pp. 109–136.

Rotheram-Borus, M.J., Piacentini, J., Miller, S., Graae, F., Dunne, E. and Cantwell, C. (1996) Toward improving treatment adherence among adolescent suicide attempters. Clinical Child Psychology and Psychiatry, 1: 99–108.

Sadowski, C. and Kelley, M.L. (1993) Social problem solving in suicidal adolescents. Journal of Consulting and Clinical Psychology, 61: 121–127.

Safer, D. (1996) A comparison of studies from the United States and western Europe on psychiatric hospitalization referrals for youths exhibiting suicidal behaviour. Annals of Clinical Psychiatry, 8: 161–168.

Safer, D. (1997) Adolescent/adult differences in suicidal behaviour and outcome. Annals of Clinical Psychiatry, 9: 61–66.

Silburn, S., Zubrick, S., Hayward, L. and Reidpath, D. (1991) Attempted Suicide Among Perth Youth. Perth: Health Department of Western Australia.

Spirito, A. (1997) Individual therapy techniques with adolescent suicide attempters. Crisis, 18: 62–64.

Spirito, A., Lewander, W.J., Levy, S., Kurkjian, J. and Fritz, G. (1994) Emergency department assessment of adolescent suicide attempters: factors related to short-term follow-up outcome. Pediatric Emergency Care, 10: 6–12.

Tiller, J., Krupinski, J., Burrows, G., Mackenzie, A., Hallenstein, H. and Johnstone, G. (1997) A Prospective Study of Completed and Attempted Youth Suicides in Victoria. Melbourne: University of Melbourne.

Williams, J.M.G. and Pollock, L.R. (1993) Factors mediating suicidal behaviour: their utility in primary and secondary prevention. Journal of Mental Health, 2: 3–26.

Chapter 31

Treatment and Prevention of Suicidal Behaviour in the Elderly

Diego De Leo
Psychogeriatric Service, University of Padua, and IRCCS, Centro S. Giovanni di Dio, Brescia, Italy; and Australian Institute for Suicide Research and Prevention, Griffith University, Brisbane, Australia
and
Paolo Scocco
Psychogeriatric Service, University of Padua, and Department of Mental Health, ULSS 12 Mestre, Venice, Italy

Abstract

Elderly suicide prevention programmes envisage intervention at primary, secondary and tertiary levels. The targets for each intervention level are, respectively, protective factors, the suicidal crisis and survivors. While further studies on outcome are warranted, various intervention activities do appear to be needed. In the area of primary prevention, the focus is on general health and more incisive retirement and social support network planning. Secondary prevention promotes the use of mental health services and treatment of depression and the psychological consequences of physical illness, seeks to improve strategies for detecting suicidal phenomena and activates community support programmes and helplines. Tertiary prevention or postvention is orientated around support of survivors and includes crisis intervention, more structured, prolonged psychotherapy and pharmacotherapy and the establishment of self-help groups.

INTRODUCTION

Suicide is perhaps the most dramatic epilogue of human existence. It seems to assume different connotations in the public mind according to the age of the

The International Handbook of Suicide and Attempted Suicide. Edited by K. Hawton and K. van Heeringen.

Table 31.1 Male old/young ratios (75+/15–24 years) of suicide rates (Gulbinat, 1995)

Continent	Suicide rate (median)	
	1960–1964	1985–1989
Australia	4.1	1.7
Americas	3.3	2.9
Europe	5.1	4.4
Asia	3.2	6.4

Data from WHO suicide databank.

person involved. Epidemiological data, however, indicate that almost everywhere in the world, suicide rates are higher in the elderly, particularly in older males, than in any other age group (Pearson and Conwell, 1995). A recent update of the World Health Organization (WHO, 1993) suicide data bank indicated that suicide in the over-75s, a phenomenon observed in all reporting countries, is up to seven times higher than adolescent suicide (medians for four continents) and the order of magnitude of these indices is stable over a time period of approximately 30 years (see Table 31.1).

An increase in suicide rates among the elderly population, in contrast to a decrease in rates among 15–24 year-olds, has also been observed in a study considering a time period of over a century in Italy (De Leo et al, 1997). By contrast, however, Deavoll and associates (1993) observed different trends in a similar study conducted in New Zealand. In males, the peak observed in the final stage of the study (1971–1988) was due largely to the rise in rates among the under-45s, particularly among 15–24 year-olds, rather than in elderly males. In females aged over 65, rates began to increase steadily towards the 1980s, while the 15–24 year-old rate was consistently low up to the final 20-year period, when a steady rise occurred.

One phenomenon which has not yet received sufficient attention is the proportional increase in suicide rates in old age, particularly in Latin countries, with an almost parallel decrease in Anglo-Saxon countries (Cantor et al, 1999). A similar trend has been observed in South American countries (Diekstra and Gulbinat, 1993). The explanation for this is probably related to the differences existing between these two cultural poles, which highlights above all the less favourable position of elderly people in Latin countries (De Leo, 1998). This is most likely due, in recent decades, to a breakdown in family structure, particularly in Latin countries. Consequently, there has been a significant decline in "spontaneous" social support accompanied by an absence of replacement by "formal" support or education on coping with aging (De Leo, 1998). Another hypothesis is that the fruition of more comprehensive retirement plans (with improved social security benefits), enjoyed above all by Anglo-Saxon citizens (particularly in the UK and the USA), has further widened the gap between them and citizens in Latin countries, which are on the whole rather backward in old-age-related socio-economic policy.

The number of elderly suicides is destined to rise because elderly people constitute the fastest-growing segment of the population in terms of both increase in longevity and the "cohort effect", or rather the ageing of the "baby boom generation" (Conwell, 1992). It is indeed worth questioning whether the high risk of suicide in baby boomers is an American phenomenon only, or whether it holds true for other countries (Bille-Brahe et al, 1994). Current mean life expectancy at 65 years is approximately 19 years for females and 15 years for males. This falls to 9 and 7 years, respectively, if we consider "disability-free" years, followed by 10 and 8 years in the presence of disability (Trabucchi, 1994). Present forecasts do not envisage a change in life expectancy ratios, with or without disability, over the next few years, which may maintain suicide rates at current levels. Increasing socio-economic pressure, combined with a progressive decline in the proportion of the active population, may nevertheless worsen the quality of life of inactive subjects, particularly the elderly (and more so the old-old), with an increase in the incidence of suicides (Conwell, 1992). While the above data seem rather pessimistic, they do not consider that, at least in more advanced countries, the "cohort effect" may be accompanied by changes "for the better", giving rise to "new older adults". Newly developing attitudes and social attributes are beginning to modify traditional cultural stereotypes. For example, there has been a rise in elderly travellers, sportsmen and women, and older migrants.

The incidence of suicide and deliberate self-harm exhibit opposite tendencies with respect to age. The ratio between attempted suicide and suicide in older adults has been estimated at approximately 4:1, versus a ratio of between 8:1 and 15:1 in the general population and 200:1 in the young (McIntosh, 1992). According to findings emerging from the WHO/EU Multicentre Study on Parasuicide, based on data collected over the period 1989–1993 by 16 centres from 13 European countries, the population aged 65 and over showed a mean suicide rate of 29.3 per 100,000 and a mean parasuicide rate of 61.4 per 100,000 for the total sample. The parasuicide: suicide ratio was 2.09 (De Leo et al, 2000). Marked differences in suicidal behaviours also emerged from the above study between the various centres participating in the project.

Of the phenomena which can be located along the suicidality continuum, suicidal ideation is the most difficult to examine. There are the difficulties in studying a phenomenon which, unlike suicide and deliberate self-harm, cannot be objectively examined since it is reported by the subject. Also, there have been considerable differences in the methods adopted in studies conducted to date on suicidal ideation in the elderly. The frequency of recent feelings of dissatisfation with life, thoughts of death, or self-destructive or frankly suicidal thoughts among the elderly ranges between 2.3% and 17% (Jorm et al, 1995; Skoog et al, 1996; Forsell et al, 1997; Rao et al, 1997; Scocco et al, 2000).

PREVENTION AND TREATMENT

As in other areas of prevention, there are traditionally three levels of prevention with regard to suicidal behaviour: primary, secondary and tertiary. Primary prevention is targeted at healthy subjects and seeks to avoid the appearance of the disease by strengthening factors which aid health and remove or correct causal factors. Secondary prevention is adopted for subjects who are already ill, albeit in the early stages. Tertiary prevention envisages the clinical–therapeutic control of diseases, maintaining chronic ones in acceptable clinical equilibrium. More narrowly, secondary and tertiary prevention are diagnostic–therapeutic types of intervention.

Effective preventive intervention is hindered chiefly by the lack of knowledge regarding risk (and protective) factors distinguishing suicidal from non-suicidal individuals. Another difficulty concerns the assessment of the outcome of these preventive interventions. Gunnell and Frankel (1994) examined the evidence on available intervention and points of access to the general population at risk. They concluded that the greatest potential seemed to lie in limiting the availability of methods. The authors did not, however, consider the elderly among the groups at recognized increased risk of suicide.

Suicidal behaviours may be located along a continuum including suicidal ideation, attempted suicide and, lastly, completed suicide. The relationship between these manifestations is not linear, or rather, not all patients who take their lives have a history of deliberate self-harm. The same applies to suicidal ideation. Older adults who commit suicide are less likely than younger ones to have a past history of suicidal behaviour, even though attempted suicide in advanced age is a predictive factor for subsequent completed suicide (Hawton and Fagg, 1988; Nordentoft et al, 1993). Elderly attempters tend to have relatively high suicidal intent scores (Pierce, 1977), the act is less impulsive, methods tend to be violent and there is less opportunity for rescue.

Elderly attempters exhibit high mortality from both completed suicide and death from other causes following attempted suicide (Hepple and Quinton, 1997). Between 2.8% and 7% of aged suicide attempters killed themselves in the 2–12 years following an index attempt (Kreitman, 1976; Pierce, 1987; Hepple and Quinton, 1997). Observations that the elderly suicidal career (suicidal ideation > suicide attempt > suicide) is often not typical, or rather that most suicides are not previous attempters, may have practical implications, indicating that preventive strategies must differ from those targeted at younger people. Suicide prevention schemes orientated towards elderly attempters run the risk of acting on a proportionately smaller part of the risk population than is the case in younger age groups. Hence, preventive intervention for the elderly should emphasize identification and management of subjects with suicidal ideation, although this target may not be easy to pursue.

A preventive programme aimed at reducing suicide rates, developed along the three levels described above, should have the following intervention targets (Table 31.2):

- Primary prevention: protective factors.
- Secondary prevention: the suicidal crisis.
- Tertiary prevention (or postvention): the survivors.

Table 31.2 Stages and targets for suicide prevention in the elderly

Primary prevention
Economic issues and welfare
General health care
Retirement planning
Social support networks
Secondary prevention
Detection of suicidal feelings
Care of elderly suicide attempters
Help-lines
Community support programmes
Access to mental health services
Educational programmes, including health professionals
Treatment of depression
Treatment of psychological and psychiatric consequences of physical illness
Tertiary prevention
Crisis intervention
Educational programmes, including health professionals
Individual and group psychotherapy
Self-help resocialization groups

PRIMARY PREVENTION

Primary level prevention should focus on subjects who are currently not feeling or manifesting any suicidal tendency, with a view to decreasing the risk that such a tendency will afflict them in the future. Protective factors are not simply the mirror image of risk factors; rather, they are circumstances which, in the presence of considerable risk, act preventively without altering the risk factors themselves (Appleby, 1992). Few studies have sought to study these factors and virtually none of them have focused on such factors in the elderly.

Economic Issues and Welfare

Of the macro-protective factors, variations in older adults' economic status appear to be associated with suicide rates. Farber (1965) suggested that introduction of the social security programme (Old Age Pensioner Program) in the USA has reduced the likelihood of suicide among the elderly by relieving economic distress. Improved income status is negatively correlated with suicide rates for elderly white males (Marshall, 1978). Using a time series regression model to determine the extent of the association between social factors (impoverishment, government expenditure and health care availability) and age-, race- and sex-specific suicide rates, McCall (1991) suggested that the elderly white male population has benefited from growing societal affluence, represented as the reduction in the percentage of elderly persons living below the poverty line, improved health care availability (medicare enrolment and doctors per capita), and increased financial security afforded by social security.

General Health Care

The general improvement in elderly health conditions and the lengthening of average longevity are giving way to a series of rather significant social and behavioural changes. First and foremost, the senescence threshold is gradually shifting from 65 years, as at the beginning of the 1980s, towards 75 years, the age previously considered to mark the divide between "young-old" and "old-old". Consequently, there is a growing tendency for 65–74 year-olds to refuse to be called "elderly" or even "young-old" and to prefer the term "older adults". Many epidemiologists do in fact tend to report suicide mortality data for the 75 years and over band, considering this category more homogeneous than the broader 65 years and over group (Gulbinat, 1995; Pearson and Conwell, 1995). In the demographically "rejuvenated" 65–74 year-old population (who undoubtedly have better overall physical health than previous generations but still have to cope with the usual psychosocial problems of old age), distress-related phenomena typical of younger people are beginning to emerge, such as "cry-for-help" or frankly manipulative suicidal behaviour. These phenomena, referred to as "elderly adolescentism", seem to be associated (at least in Italy) with an increase in deliberate self-harm, in contrast to the stabilization or decline in fatal acts (De Leo, 1998). Improving prevention, detection and care of physical health problems will continue to be an important factor in the prevention of suicidal behaviour in the elderly.

Retirement Planning

Since the increased longevity of the population is largely the result of generally improved health conditions, individuals are presumably less prepared to exit from the productive world at a retirement age conceived many years previously as the ceiling for an acceptable performance level. While, from a gerontological point of view, increasing emphasis is being laid on the timeliness of developing "second careers", very few countries have made the retirement age more flexible. These include the above Anglo-Saxon nations which, as stated above, are also the ones that generally offer the best retirement schemes (pioneering and paradigmatic in this field was the British Old Age Pensioner Programme of the 1960s).

Social Support Networks

Another phenomenon correlated with the above is the increasingly marked differential between subjects aged 65–74 years and 75 years and over. The latter group have higher suicide rates, presumably owing to the concentration (at a more advanced age) of more unfavourable life circumstances, including a decline in physical health, lower degree of autonomy and more frequent losses. The relationship between a rapid transformation in the organization of society and the change in suicide rates makes Durkheim's observations on social integration still appropriate. Watanabe and colleagues (1995), for example, suggested that the rapid change in family organization, from the traditional three-generational family to the nuclear unit in a rural region of Higashikubiki in Japan, might account for the disproportionate suicide rates between the above region and Kawasaki. Greater opportunities for relations with peers and better access to recreational facilities may provide support for urban elderly people and facilitate role transitions typical of old age, including retirement and the exit of children from the home (Watanabe et al, 1995).

By its very nature, which is generally structural, primary prevention involves large-scale intervention and requires a long time, since it demands changes in society or behavioural models for broad population bands. These considerations may also indirectly attract more attention to aspects such as correct socio-economic planning for retirement (confirmed by the fact that unexpected changes in such plans often have devastating effects on the individual), systematic monitoring of physical health (especially with advancing age) and reinforcement of the social support network.

SECONDARY PREVENTION

This second level of prevention presupposes that the various factors which influence suicidal behaviour can be identified and treated.

Detection of Suicidal Ideas

We know that non-fatal suicidal behaviour among the elderly is commonly associated with suicidal intent and the use of violent methods, while suicide is less frequently preceded by attempted suicide (De Leo and Diekstra, 1990). Identifying suicidal ideation in the elderly is therefore a preventive goal of fundamental importance, bearing in mind that:

> . . . every communication of suicidal ideation or intent should be regarded as evidence of serious pathology, although not necessarily of suicidal risk. Among seriously suicidal persons, communication is usually by more than one means and to more than one person. It occurs more than once and is frequently of recent onset (Murphy and Robins, 1994).

Spontaneously reported suicidal feelings may be an indication of high, although not specific, suicide risk and is a principal determinant in the management of emergency psychiatric service users (Hawley et al, 1991). The elderly may not communicate suicidal intention or it may be masked, allusive or in any event underestimated. The fact that communications of intent may have consequences (i.e. people tend to act upon the inferred intent) does not imply that they should be understood as "messages" (Kovacs et al, 1976). However, only a proportion of suicidal elderly inform anyone directly about their intentions; old people at risk of suicide seem unable to apprehend their need or seek out appropriate help (Scott, 1996).

Care of Elderly Suicide Attempters

Suicide attempters, including the elderly, are a population at high suicide risk, whose care represents a preventive priority. Intervention with suicide attempters may be diagnostic or therapeutic, somatic or psychosocial–psychotherapeutic, or combined. The choice of intervention depends on the period elapsing from self-harm to the time of observation, which may be between the suicidal crisis (crisis intervention) and the patient's return home (long-term treatment). Diagnostic–therapeutic intervention varies according to the seriousness of the self-destructive act, with somatic intervention having priority where the patient's life is endangered by outcome. From a study conducted in the emergency rooms of two hospitals in Padova and Stockholm, however, it emerged that the approach to suicidal crisis management differed in some aspects and was probably influenced by organizational variables or the resources available to the health unit providing care, rather than by the characteristics of the patient or of the self-destructive act (Runeson et al, 2000).

Immediate assessment of the somatic outcome is followed by assessment of the psychic conditions, including any residual presence of suicidal ideation. Various types of pharmacological, psychosociotherapeutic and electroconvulsive treatment (ECT) are used to treat conditions that have influenced these behaviours (psychiatric pathologies, physical illnesses, isolation, etc.). Drug prescription in the elderly must take account of the pharmacokinetic and pharmacodynamic properties of the preparations used, which must guarantee a certain degree of safety, even in the case of overdose. Hence, preference should undoubtedly be given to those preparations that are "safe, simple, specific, scientific and superfast in action" (the five Ss; Linehan, 1999).

Unfortunately, psychiatric and gerontopsychological clinical research has paid little attention to the treatment of suicidal elders. Although a variety of therapeutic approaches have been reported to be helpful, substantially more controlled research needs to be initiated on the effectiveness of these approaches across different geriatric patients with suicidal ideation and intent, including outpatients with and without depressive symptoms, nursing home residents, and the chronically medically ill and frail elders (Pearson and Conwell, 1995).

Help-lines and Community Support Programmes

Only a small proportion of callers to agencies such as the Samaritans are elderly and the aged are under-represented in the clientele of suicide prevention programmes and general mental health facilities (McIntosh et al, 1994). The reasons for such low utilization of existing services by the elderly are numerous, and range from poor information about their existence and conviction that they are not meant for the elderly or are costly, to the low credit typically given by latterday older adults to all types of agencies or institutions (McIntosh et al, 1994). Irrespective of the potential that isolation and poor social support, so common among the elderly, can have in inducing suicidal ideation, these factors also lower the opportunity for expressing or communicating any suicidal intention. Therefore, strategies that facilitate communication of feelings and intentions are warranted. Telecommunications, on which most crisis services are based, are a popular form of human contact among the younger generations, but not necessarily among the elderly. An attempt to overcome elderly people's reticence to contact centres for collecting alarm signals has been through the use of "centripetous" recruitment programmes. One such experience is the "Tele-Help/Tele-Check Service" established in the Veneto region of Italy (De Leo et al, 1995). Tele-Help is a portable device that lets users send alarm signals activating a pre-established network of assistance and help. In Tele-Check, trained staff members at a centre contact each client on an average of twice a week to monitor the client's condition through a short, informal interview and to offer emotional support. The client may also contact a centre at any time for any need. Clients are enrolled in the service at the request of social workers or general practitioners in the local health service, who single out elderly individuals needing additional home help. Since many of the traditional risk factors for suicide were identified in the elderly subjects studied, this service appears to provide support of relevance for the prevention of suicide in the elderly. Thus, 10 years after the introduction of the service to a population of 20,000 elderly people living at home, it has been associated with a statistically significant fall in the number of deaths by suicide compared to the expected number (De Leo and Dello Buono, 2000).

The increase in the use of crisis intervention centres should probably lead to adjustment of intervention methods adopted by these agencies and increased awareness of the phenomenon among professionals and the general public. Law (1997) suggested that face-to-face befriending seemed to be a more appropriate form of contact with the elderly, especially the physically weak and isolated, through visits to their home, recreational centres for the elderly and hospitals.

Other experiences adapting existing services to potential elderly users are the "Center for Elderly Suicide Prevention and Grief Related Service" and the "Gatekeepers Program and Elderly Service" recently established in the USA. The former consists of a Friendship Line providing 24-hour crisis intervention, as well as referral and information for elders who call or for those calling on their behalf, in addition to ongoing home visits and telephone contact with isolated or homebound elderly (McIntosh et al, 1994). One particularly interesting aspect of the approach to elderly suicide adopted by the Gatekeepers Program is collaboration with businesses and other organizations, whose employees are in frequent contact with older adults, especially isolated ones. These employees are given special training in the recognition of signs and symptoms associated with a need for help and refer cases to elderly services (McIntosh et al, 1994).

Improved Access to Mental Health Services

Another strategy is to help older adults to contact facilities able to deal with their problems. Since we have seen how the elderly tend to make less use of mental health care providers, one preventive goal might be to encourage use of mental health services by elderly people, considering that such intervention seems to have a positive effect on suicide mortality (De Leo and Diekstra, 1990). Walk (1967), for example, showed a decline in suicide rates among the elderly after the introduction in 1958 of a community psychiatric service in the UK. Developing awareneness of the problem may target the general population, thereby including the elderly as well as their families, friends and family doctors. This could be achieved by publicity campaigns which may teach the audience to listen more carefully to signs communicated by older people (suicidal ideation, depressive symptoms), be attentive to their behaviour, and act when necessary (Kerkhof et al, 1991). The public should be informed of the existence of facilities or schemes through which to receive further information, support and treatment. The imitative effect consequent to messages provided by the mass media, known as the "Werther effect" (see Chapter 39), has not been sufficiently studied in the elderly population, but should be borne in mind. Another aspect rather neglected by research is the "modelling" impact of the suicide of an elderly person on younger members of the general population, whether or not they have family ties.

Educational Programmes

Educational programmes targeted at more narrow populations, such as professionals who come into contact with the elderly in a whole variety of settings, should consider the importance of:

- Altering mistaken myths which develop around suicidal behaviours.
- Providing information on risk factors.
- Providing training on the recognition of signs indicating suicidal intention.
- Illustrating locally available resources to contact where necessary.
- Increasing knowledge on the various types of self-destructive behaviour, including the ones that characterize the suicidal process (McIntosh, 1995; De Leo and Diekstra, 1990).

It has been extensively reported that most suicidal subjects contact their general practitioners in the weeks prior to their death (Barraclough, 1971; De Leo and Diekstra, 1990). Educational programmes addressed towards general practitioners should therefore cover all the above aspects, with the focus on psychiatric and somatic risk factors. The impact of physical disorders and the possibility of influencing suicidal behaviour through treatment of depressive pathologies is discussed in Chapters 22 and 27.

Improved Treatment of Depression

The predominant role of mood disorders in increasing the risk of a serious suicide attempt suggests that elimination of affective disorders might substantially reduce the incidence of serious suicide attempts by up to 80%, particularly among older adults (60 years and over), among whom the association between mood disorder and suicide attempts appears to be particulary strong (Beautrais et al, 1996). Haskell and colleagues (1975) observed that depressed outpatients receiving antidepressant therapy exhibited a marked reduction in suicidal thoughts in the first 2 weeks of treatment. Based on a forensic toxicological screening study of 3,400 suicides, an antidepressant was found to be present in less than 16% of cases. This suggests that most depressed patients who commit suicide have not taken antidepressants prior to death (Isacsson et al, 1994). Waern and colleagues (1996), however, reached a different conclusion by showing how, in a group of 75 elderly suicides, the proportion of subjects receiving antidepressant treatment was surprisingly high. According to the authors, therefore, the problem does not seem to concern identifying depression as much as its treatment, which in this study was clearly often inadequate in terms of dosage and/or duration over time. Suicide risk in untreated depressive patients is almost twice as high as in treated depressives, despite the fact that inclusion of inadequately treated, non-compliant patients in the treated group tends to reduce the apparent effect of adequate treatment on suicide risk (Isacsson et al, 1996). In a study assessing regional distribution of suicide rates, the rate of diagnosed depression and the prevalence of working physicians in Hungary, it emerged that the more physicians per 100,000 inhabitants, the better the recognition of depression and the lower the suicide rate in the given region (Rihmer et al, 1993). However, the effectiveness of programmes for educating general practitioners in the diagnosis and treatment of depression assessed on Gotland, a Swedish island, indicated a decline in suicide rates and other measures of psychiatric morbidity in the year after intervention, but two years after the programme suicide rates rose again (Rutz et al, 1992; see Chapter 38). It may therefore be necessary to repeat such programmes every few years. Long-term lithium has been found to reduce the risk of suicide among those attending lithium clinics, compared with matched non-attenders with similar diagnoses (Coppen et al, 1990). Such compliant patients may differ from those who do not take the drug and clinic attendance may be beneficial *per se* rather than the effects of the prescribed medicine (Gunnell and Frankel, 1994; see Chapter 27). Some non-pharmacological approaches to the treatment of senile depression may also be considered, both alone and in combination with drugs, particularly cognitive therapy (Effective Health Care, 1993; Gallagher-Thompson and Thompson, 1996) and interpersonal psychotherapy (Reynolds et al, 1994, 1999; Scocco et al, 2000).

Treatment of the Psychosocial Consequences of Physical Illness

The presence of a physical illness, whether or not accompanied by pain, must receive the attention of physicians owing to its direct or mediated association with suicidal behaviour (see Chapter 22). It is important to discuss the disease with the patient in order to get an impression of the patient's reaction to the disorder and to establish their resources and supportive network (Stenager and Stenager, 1998). Exploring thoughts about death and loss of the desire to live, and confronting the wish to die to the point of uncovering detailed suicidal plans, may enable patients to discuss topics which they were unable previously to share with anyone, or at least take counsel with a therapist who is adequately trained, both emotionally and professionally, who can treat them or help them to identify alternative coping strategies. The frequent association of depression with physical disorders often entails the need for antidepressant treatment, even though medication is not always the answer in reactive conditions.

Discussion and counselling, as well as explanation of symptoms, problems and doubts should always be offered by competent clinicians (Stenager and Stenager, 1998). According to Gunnell and Frankel (1994), no single intervention has been demonstrated, in a well-conducted randomized controlled trial, to reduce suicide. It may therefore be that this multidetermined phenomenon can only be managed through a multidisciplinary approach; hence the complexity of causes necessitates a complexity of cures (Diekstra, 1992). Most patients who share the demographic and clinical characteristics of the high-risk group will in fact not attempt suicide, raising the question as to the practicality of treatment for a large number of "false-positives". From a clinical point of view, however, the problem of false positives in this case is irrelevant because these people require treatment in any event and such treatment may prevent some suicides (Murphy, 1971).

TERTIARY PREVENTION OR POSTVENTION

Tertiary prevention consists of management of survivors, that is family members and others who have suffered a loss by suicide (see Chapter 26). Individuals affected by the suicide of a relative experience emotional stress requiring special attention, as they too are at high risk for suicide (Dunne et al, 1987). Since each suicide involves at least six survivors (Shneidman, 1969), the extent of the problem is clearly vast.

Survivors of elderly suicides can be divided into two groups:

- Adults, children and associated kin, including daughters-, brothers- and sisters-in-law and grandchildren. These often belong to another family unit and are therefore involved in affective, social and other relations which might exert a protective effect in working through the grief process and its consequences.
- Spouse, siblings and friends. These are often age peers and therefore more

vulnerable to the consequences and changes entailed by the bereavement, including solitude, financial difficulties, life changes, adjustment and adaptation to a new life style.

Supportive intervention provided by tertiary prevention facilities should therefore pay special attention to the elderly, be they survivors of peer suicides or younger individuals, bearing in mind, as stressed above, that older adults rarely take advantage of formal crisis intervention and support facilities. These interventions may range from simple assessment to crisis intervention, or even more structured, prolonged psychotherapy and pharmacotherapy, not forgetting inclusion in self-help or resocialization groups.

General practitioners have a particularly important role in identifying needs and organizing the feasibility of such interventions since they are often the only contact elderly people actively seek or request of health and social services.

CONCLUSION

Unfortunately, in the care of the elderly competing political priorities and new financial arrangements very often result in abdication of public health responsibilities. This is accompanied by a generally low tolerance for problems related to the elderly, based on a rather negative attitude to them. One of the most harmful consequences of this is the lack of knowledge on geriatric matters. Hence, alteration of these culturally-rooted attitudes is the fundamental necessity of any important preventive measure. As emphasized by Shah and De (1998), the development of geriatric psychiatry as a medical speciality (as in the UK) and in the form of specialized clinical care, may considerably motivate any move to overcome this cultural impasse.

It is undoubtedly true, however, that research into and prevention of suicidal behaviour is based on theoretical speculation supported by very little or no empirical evidence as to the efficacy of instruments and programmes. It is therefore essential to be able to assess the outcomes of preventive strategies, despite the difficulties inherently linked to the rarity of the suicidal phenomenon, its multicausal nature and the difficulties in avoiding non-controllable "contamination" from other interventions.

Accurate prospective assessment of outcome therefore requires samples to be so large as to make surveys very difficult to accomplish. The lack of information and certainty is even more serious in the field of geriatric suicidology. Nevertheless, in our opinion, this may be an extremely interesting field of preventive work.

The elderly, having almost come to the end of their life cycle "unscathed" (from a suicidological viewpoint), may be considered a select sample and, in epidemiological terms, more homogeneous and responsive to preventive intervention.

The preponderance of depressive pathology in elderly suicide compared to other age groups may undoubtedly represent a strong point in all preventive strategies involving elderly populations, notwithstanding the risk of running into dangerous simplifications by attributing what remains a complex reality to a sole pathology.

REFERENCES

Appleby, L. (1992) Suicide in psychiatric patients: risk and prevention. British Journal of Psychiatry, 161: 749–758.

Barraclough, B.M. (1971) Suicide in the elderly. In D.W.K. Kay and A. Walk (Eds), Recent Developments in Psychogeriatrics. Ashford, Kent: Headley.

Beautrais, A.L., Joyce, P.R., Mulder, R.T., Fergusson, D.M., Deavoll, B.J. and Nightingale, S.K. (1996) Prevalence and comorbidity of mental disorders in persons making serious attempts: a case-control study. American Journal of Psychiatry, 153: 1009–1014.

Bille-Brahe, U., Jensen, B. and Jessen, G. (1994) Suicide among the Danish elderly: now and in years to come. Crisis, 15: 37–43.

Cantor, C.H., Neulinger, K. and De Leo, D. (1999) Australian suicide trends, 1964–1997. Youth and beyond? Medical Journal of Australia, 171: 137–141.

Conwell, Y. (1992) Suicide in the elderly. Crisis, 13: 6–8.

Coppen, A., Standish-Barry, H., Bailey, J., Houston, G., Silcocks, P. and Hermon, C. (1990) Long-term lithium and mortality. Lancet, 335: 1347.

Deavoll, B.J., Mulder, R.T., Beautrais, A.L. and Joyce, P.R. (1993) One hundred years of suicide in New Zealand. Acta Psychiatrica Scandinavica, 87: 81–85.

De Leo, D. (1998) Is suicide prediction in old age really easier? Crisis, 19: 60–61.

De Leo, D. and Diekstra, R.F.W. (1990) Depression and Suicide in Late Life. Toronto: Hogrefe & Huber.

De Leo, D., Carollo, G. and Dello Buono, M. (1995) Lower suicide rates associated with a Tele-Help/Tele-Check service for the elderly at home. American Journal of Psychiatry, 152: 632–634.

De Leo, D., Conforti, D. and Carollo, G. (1997) A century of suicide in Italy: a comparison between the old and the young. Suicide and Life-Threatening Behavior, 27: 239–249.

De Leo, D., Padoani, W., Scocco, P., Bille-Brahe, U., Arensman, E., Bjerke, T., Crepet, P., Haring, C., Hawton, K., Lonnqvist, J., Michel, K., Pommereau, X., Querejeta, I., Phillipe, J., Salander-Renberg, E., Schmidtke, A., Fricke, S., Weinacker, B., Temesvary, B., Wasserman, D. and Sampaio-Faria J.G., J. (2000) Elderly suicidal behaviour: results from the WHO/EURO Multicentre Study on Parasuicide (submitted for publication).

De Leo, D. and Dello Buono, M. (2000) Prevention of suicide in the elderly: Ten-year experience with TeleHelp/TeleCheck (submitted for publication).

Diekstra, R.F.W. (1992) Epidemiology of suicide: aspects of definition, classification and preventive policies. In P. Crepet, G. Ferrari, S. Platt and M. Bellini (Eds), Suicidal Behaviour in Europe. Recent Research Findings, pp. 15–45. Rome: John Libey CIC.

Diekstra, R.F.W. and Gulbinat, W. (1993) The epidemiology of suicidal behaviour: a review of three continents. WHO Statistical Quarterly, 46: 52–68.

Dunne, E.J., McIntosh, J.L. and Dunne-Maxim, K. (1987) Suicide and Its Aftermath: Understanding and Counseling the Survivors. New York: Norton.

Effective Health Care (1993) The Treatment of Depression in Primary Care, pp. 1, 12. Leeds: University of Leeds.

Farber, M.L. (1965) Suicide and Welfare State. Mental Hygiene, 49: 371–373.

Forsell, Y., Jorm, A.F. and Winblad, B. (1997) Suicidal thoughts and associated factors in an elderly population. Acta Psychiatrica Scandinavica, 95: 108–111.

Gallagher-Thompson, D. and Thompson, L.W. (1996) Applying cognitive-behavioral therapy to the psychological problems of later life. In S.H. Zarit and B.G. Knight (Eds), A Guide to Psychotherapy and Aging: Effective Clinical Intervention in a Life-stage Context. Washington, DC: American Psychological Association.

Gulbinat, W. (1995) The epidemiology of suicide in old age. In R.F.W. Diekstra, W. Gulbinat, I. Kienhorst and D. De Leo (Eds), Preventive Strategies on Suicide. Leiden: E.J. Brill.

Gunnell, D. and Frankel, S. (1994) Prevention of suicide: aspirations and evidence. British Medical Journal, 308: 1227–1233.

Haskell, D., DiMascio, A. and Prusoff, B. (1975) Rapidity of symptom reduction in depression treated with amitriptyline. Journal of Nervous and Mental Disease, 160 (1): 24–33.

Hawton, K. and Fagg, J. (1988) Suicide and other causes of death following attempted suicide. British Journal of Psychiatry, 152: 359–366.

Hawley, C.J., James, D.V., Birkett, P.L., Baldwin, D.S., De Ruiter, M.J. and Priest, R.G. (1991) Suicidal ideation as a presenting complaint: associated diagnoses and characteristics in a casualty population. British Journal of Psychiatry, 159: 232–238.

Hepple, J. and Quinton, C. (1997) One hundred cases of attempted suicide in the elderly. British Journal of Psychiatry, 171: 42–46.

Isacsson, G., Bergman, U. and Rich, C.L. (1996) Epidemiological data suggest antidepressant reduce suicide risk among depressives. Journal of Affective Disorders, 41: 1–8.

Isacsson, G., Holmgren, P., Wasserman, D. and Bergman, U. (1994) Use of antidepressants among people committing suicide in Sweden. British Medical Journal, 308: 506–509.

Jorm, A.F., Henderson, A.S., Scott, R., Korten, A.E., Christensen, H. and Mackinnon, A.J. (1995) Factors associated with the wish to die in elderly people. Age and Ageing, 24: 389–392.

Kerkhof, A.J.F.M., Visser, A., Diekstra, R.F.W. and Hirschhorn, P.M. (1991) The prevention of suicide among older people in The Netherlands: intervention in community mental health care. Crisis, 12: 59–72.

Kreitman, N. (1976) Age and parasuicide (attempted suicide). Psychological Medicine, 6: 113–121.

Kovacs, M., Beck, A.T. and Weissman, A. (1976) The communication of suicidal intent: a re-examination. Archives of General Psychiatry, 33: 198–201.

Law, F.Y.W. (1997) Elderly suicides in Hong Kong: the role of volunteer befrienders. Crisis, 18: 55–56.

Linehan, M.M. (1999) Combining psychopharmacology with the dialectical behaviour therapy of BPD. Abstract from 152nd Annual Meeting of American Psychiatric Association: The Clinician. Washington, DC, May 15–20 1999.

Marshall, J.R. (1978) Changes in aged white male suicide. Journal of Gerontology, 33: 763–768.

McCall, P.L. (1991) Adolescent and elderly white male suicide trends: evidence of changing well-being? Journal of Gerontology, 46: S43–51.

McIntosh, J.L. (1992) Suicide of elderly. In Bongar, B. (Ed.), Suicide: Guidelines for Assessment, Management and Treatment, pp. 106–127. New York: Oxford University Press.

McIntosh, J.L., Santos, J.F., Hubbard, R.W. and Overholser, J.C. (1994) Elder Suicide Research, Theory and Treatment. Washington, DC: American Psychological Association.

McIntosh, J.L. (1995) Suicide prevention in the elderly (age 65–99). Suicide and Life-Threatening Behavior, 25: 180–192.

Murphy, G.E. (1971) Clinical identification of suicidal risk. Archives of General Psychiatry, 27: 356–359.

Murphy, G.E. and Robins, E. (1994) The communication of suicidal ideas. In H.L.P. Resnik (Ed.), Suicidal Behaviours, Diagnosis and Management. New Jersey: Jason Aronson.

Nordentoft, M., Breum, L., Munck, L.K., Nordestgaard, A.G., Hunding, A. and Laursen-Bjaeldager, P.A. (1993) High mortality by natural and unnatural causes: a ten year follow-up study of patients admitted to a poisoning treatment centre after suicide attempts. British Medical Journal, 306: 1637–1640.

Pearson, J. and Conwell, Y. (1995) Suicide in late life: challenges and opportunities for research. International Psychogeriatrics, 7: 131–136.

Pierce, D.W. (1977) Suicidal intent in self-injury. British Journal of Psychiatry, 130: 377–385.

Pierce, D.W. (1987) Deliberate self-harm in the elderly. International Journal of Geriatric Psychiatry, 2: 105–110.

Rao, R., Dening, T., Brayne, C. and Huppert, F.A. (1997) Suicidal thinking in community residents over eighty. International Journal of Geriatric Psychiatry, 12: 337–343.

Reynolds, C.F., Frank, E., Perel, J.M., Miller, M.D., Cornes, C., Rifai, H., Pollock, B.G., Mazumdar, S., George, C.J., Houck, P.R. and Kupfer, D.J. (1994) Treatment of consecutive episodes of major depression in the elderly. American Journal of Psychiatry, 151: 1740–1743.

Reynolds, C.F., Frank, E., Perel, J.M., Imber, S.D., Cornes, C., Miller, M.D., Mazumdar, S., Houck, P.R., Dew, M.A., Stack, J.A., Pollock, B.G. and Kupfer, D.J. (1999) Nortriptyline and interpersonal psychotherapy as maintenance therapies for recurrent major depression. Journal American Medical Association, 281: 39–45.

Rihmer, Z., Rutz, W. and Barsi, J. (1993) Suicide rate, prevalence of diagnosed depression and prevalence of working physicians in Hungary. Acta Psychiatrica Scandinavica, 8: 391–394.

Runeson, B., Scocco, P., DeLeo, D., Meneghel, G. and Wasserman, D. (2000) Management of suicide attempts in Italy and Sweden: a comparison of the services offered to consecutive samples of suicide attempters (submitted for publication).

Rutz, W., Von Knorring, L. and Walinder, J. (1992) Long-term effect of an educational program for general practitioner given by the Swedish Committee for the Prevention and Treatment of Depression. Acta Psychiatrica Scandinavica, 85: 83–88.

Scocco, P., Meneghel, G., Dello Buono, M. and De Leo, D. (2000) Suicidal ideation and its correlates: survey of an over-65-year-old population (submitted for publication).

Scocco, P., de Girolamo, G. and Frank, E. (2000) Psicoterapia interpersonale. In P. Scocco, D. De Leo and L. Pavan (Eds), Manuale di Psicoterapia dell'Anziano (Handbook of Psychotherapy in Old Age). Torino: Bollati Boringhieri.

Scott, V. (1996) Reaching the suicidal: the volunteer's role in preventing suicide. Crisis, 17: 102–104.

Shah, A. and De, T. (1998) Suicide and the elderly. International Journal of Psychiatry in Clinical Practice, 2: 3–17.

Shneidman, E.S. (1969) Prologue: fifty-eight years. In E.S. Shneidman (Ed.), On the Nature of Suicide. San Francisco, CA: Jossey-Bass.

Skoog, I., Aevarsson, O., Beskow, J., Larsson, L., Palsson, S., Waern, M., Landahl, S. and Ostling, S. (1996) Suicidal feelings in a population sample of nondemented 85-years-olds. American Journal of Psychiatry, 153: 1015–1020.

Stenager, E.N. and Stenager, E. (1998) Disease, Pain, and Suicidal Behaviour. New York: Haworth Medical Press.

Trabucchi, M. (1994) L'invecchiamento tra demografia e democrazia. In D. De Leo and A. Stella (Eds), Manuale di Psichiatria dell'Anziano (Handbook of Psychiatry in Old Age). Padova: Piccin.

Waern, M., Beskow, J., Runeson, B. and Skoog, I. (1996) High rate of antidepressant treatment in elderly people who commit suicide. British Medical Journal, 313: 1118.

Walk, D. (1967) Suicide and community care. British Journal of Psychiatry, 113: 1381–1391.

Watanabe, N., Hasegawa, K. and Yoshinaga, Y. (1995) Suicide in later life in Japan: urban and rural differences. International Psychogeriatrics, 7: 253–261.

WHO (1993) Guidelines for the primary prevention of mental, neurological and psychosocial disorders. 4: Suicide. Technical Report, Division of Mental Health. Geneva: World Health Organization.

Chapter 32

Multidisciplinary Approaches to the Management of Suicidal Behaviour

Kees van Heeringen
Department of Psychiatry, University Hospital, Gent, Belgium

Abstract

This chapter provides an overview of approaches to the management of attempted suicide patients in which psychiatrists are not directly involved, but in which nurses, social workers or general medical teams carry out the assessment and/or treatment of these patients. These approaches were developed as alternatives to management by psychiatrists for two reasons. First, the substantial amount of referrals following attempted suicide puts considerable strains on scarce psychiatric resources. Second, as suicidal behaviour is commonly precipitated by social and interpersonal problems, the management of these patients might benefit from the involvement of social workers and other non-psychiatrists in assessment and treatment. A number of controlled studies have been conducted in which the efficacy of these alternatives has been assessed. Although these studies were mainly conducted on selected samples of patients, namely those at relatively low risk of suicide and not suffering from major psychopathology, the results show, first, that nurses, general medical teams and social workers can reliably assess deliberate self-harm patients if adequate training and supervision is provided. Second, community psychiatric nurses and social workers can play an important role in the management of these patients in increasing compliance with after-care by means of outreach strategies, and in their treatment by means of a brief problem-orientated approach.

INTRODUCTION

As described in Chapter 3, deliberate self-harm constitutes a major public health problem. In many countries the official policy is to refer deliberate self-harm

The International Handbook of Suicide and Attempted Suicide. Edited by K. Hawton and K. van Heeringen.

patients to general hospitals, following which a thorough psychosocial and psychiatric assessment is strongly recommended as good clinical practice (e.g. Royal College of Psychiatrists, 1994, 1995). Due to the increased demands on psychiatrists' time, among other reasons, the official policy is commonly disregarded, and minimal standards of care are often not met (Ebbage et al, 1994). Even within countries, substantial differences exist between hospitals in the management of deliberate self-poisoning with respect to rates of discharge from accident and emergency departments and the proportions of patients receiving specialist psychosocial assessment (Kapur et al, 1998). Studies in several countries have shown that only approximately half of deliberate self-harm patients referred to a general hospital have such a psychosocial assessment before discharge from the emergency department (Suokas, 1991; Kapur et al, 1998). Observational studies suggest that the introduction of liaison psychiatric nurses leads to an increase in the proportion of deliberate self-harm patients receiving adequate psychosocial assessment before leaving the emergency department (Williams et al, 1998). The question has even been raised whether the routine assessment of self-harming patients by psychiatrists should be encouraged, as a majority of these patients may benefit more from social than from psychiatric intervention, so that such an assessment actually means a waste of already scarce resources.

There might be a second motive for the development of multidisiciplinary approaches to the management of suicidal behaviour. As described in Chapter 14, suicidal behaviour is a multifaceted problem resulting from complex interactions between social, biological and psychological factors. Therefore, the management of suicidality can be expected to benefit from such a multidisciplinary approach. As social and interpersonal problems are common precipitants of suicidal behaviour, the threshold for seeking help may be lower for attempted suicide patients if this help is provided by, for example, social workers.

Controlled studies have provided evidence on the efficacy of management approaches by non-psychiatric or non-medical staff following referral to a general hospital of deliberate self-harm patients, including their assessment, decisions regarding admission to hospital or discharge to home, and their treatment. This chapter will review such studies, in which approaches to the management of suicidal behaviour involving different disciplines in mental health care have been examined. The chapter will focus particularly on the role of nurses, general medical staff and social workers in the management of suicidal behaviour. The role of other disciplines, such as general practitioners, involved in the management of suicidal ideation and behaviour is discussed in other chapters.

ASSESSMENT OF DELIBERATE SELF-HARM PATIENTS

Accurate clinical assessment of attempted suicide patients in emergency departments is becoming increasingly important, as the proportion of patients discharged home directly from these departments is increasing. This is due to the continuing reduction in numbers of hospital beds, the increasing rates of deliberate self-harm, and the rise in the number of presentations for other reasons. However, as described above, the management of attempted suicide patients puts considerable strain on services, and on psychiatrists in particular, and referral to psychiatrists for assessment may therefore not always be possible, so that other disciplines in emergency departments should be able to manage these patients efficaciously. The extent to which this actually is the case has been the focus of several studies involving nurses, general medical teams and social workers.

Nurses

By means of a controlled clinical trial in Oxford, UK, Catalan and colleagues (1980) compared doctors (i.e. psychiatric or general practitioner trainees) and psychiatrically trained nurses in the assessment of deliberate self-poisoning patients following referral to a general hospital. Prior to the study, all assessors were trained in the use of an assessment manual. Outcome measures included blind assessment of the adequacy of the interviews with patients (judged by senior psychiatrists with regard to a range of factors, including detection of severe psychiatric illness and suicidal risk) and management plans. The two groups were also compared with regard to patients' compliance with treatment, consumers' views (the patients' evaluation of the rapport with the assessors, and general practitioners' satisfaction with the assessors' involvement) and repetition of deliberate self-harm during a 6-month follow-up period. No important differences were found between the assessments of the doctors and nurses, and those differences that were found did not consistently favour either group of assessors. Thus, the findings support the idea that nurses can provide a reliable and adequate alternative to doctors in the assessment of self-poisoning patients, provided that they have adequate training and supervision. The study demonstrated further that team meetings involving a senior psychiatrist can provide an effective back-up to the initial assessment.

Medical Teams

In a controlled clinical trial in Cambridge, UK, Gardner and colleagues (1978) compared differences in initial psychiatric assessment and decisions about disposal (aftercare) of deliberate self-harm patients between medical teams (consisting of junior doctors and nurses) and psychiatrists in a general hospital. The initial assessment included questions about the nature of the self-poisoning (accidental versus deliberate), medical and suicidal risk, psychiatric diagnosis, and necessity of further psychiatric treatment. Unfortunately, no results of statistical analysis were provided, but the authors report no substantial differences between the two groups of assessors. Thus, it is concluded that the medical teams' initial psychiatric assessments are clinically sound, as similar proportions of psychiatric diagnoses and similar numbers of patients requiring further psychiatric treatment were identified. Based on their experience, the authors stressed the need for the training of junior doctors and nurses in the psychiatric, psychological and social evaluation of self-poisoning patients in addition to formal medical education.

This need was further studied by Black and Creed (1988) in Manchester, UK. They examined the case notes of patients presenting to a hospital following deliberate self-poisoning to see whether episodes of self-poisoning were being adequately assessed by junior medical staff, and whether such assessments were most thorough in those whose attitude to self-poisoning was the most sympathetic. Quality of assessment was determined by comparing the case notes to the reports of the psychiatrist who examined the patient following referral by the physician. The results showed that assessments by junior medical staff were inadequate with regard to important issues, such as documentation of depressed mood and suicidal status. The results of this study further suggested that the poor quality of assessment was not due to unfavourable attitudes towards self-poisoning patients, as no correlation was found between the doctors' attitudes and the amount of information recorded in the notes. Inadequate assessment may therefore reflect a lack of education rather than of motivation. Thus, this study also indicated the need for further education of medical staff in order to assess deliberate self-harm patients adequately.

In an intervention study in London, Crawford and colleagues (1998) examined the impact of such training for accident and emergency staff on the quality of psychosocial assessment of deliberate self-harm patients. By examining case notes, the psychosocial assessments by nurses and junior doctors of an accident and emergency department were compared before and after a 1-hour teaching session. Staff knowledge of and attitudes to deliberate self harm were assessed by means of a questionnaire. The results of this study clearly showed a beneficial effect of the training on the quality of psychosocial assessments, on the liaison between accident and emergency staff and the hospital's deliberate self-harm team, and on the numbers of staff who reported that they felt they had the necessary skills to play their part in the assessment of deliberate self-harm patients.

Burn and colleagues (1990), in Southampton, UK, studied the impact of the use of a short and easy-to-administer questionnaire on the quality of the assessment of self-poisoning patients by house physicians in a university hospital. In order to study the effect of the questionnaire, house physicians were randomly divided into a group who used this questionaire (without any further training) and another group who asked whatever questions they thought appropriate. Following the house physicians' assessment, the patients were interviewed by a research assistant (i.e. a psychiatric trainee with a special knowledge of self-poisoning and back-up by a consultant) and the two assessments for each patient were then compared. The clinical questionnaire included items used in established standardized structured interviews and scales, including the Present State Examination (Wing et al, 1974), the CAGE alcoholism screening instrument (Mayfield et al, 1974) and a modified form of the Beck Suicidal Intent scale (Beck et al, 1974). It could be administered in 10–15 minutes. Following the interview, the house physician and the research assistant were required to carry out independent assessments of severity of depression, purpose of the suicide attempt, suicidal intent, whether the attempt was impulsive or contemplated, life events preceding the overdose, psychiatric diagnosis, risk of repetition, and future management. The study clearly showed greater agreement between the research assistant and the house physicians who used the questionnaire than in those who interviewed patients in an unstructured way, with respect to severity of depression, purpose of the act, suicidal intent, diagnosis and, perhaps most importantly, decisions regarding future management. With respect to the latter item, it appeared that whenever there were differences between the house physician and the research assistant, the house physicians were more cautious by more frequently requesting an urgent psychiatric opinion before discharging the patients.

Social Workers

In a study in London by Newson-Smith and Hirsch (1979), attempted suicide patients who were consecutively admitted to medical wards were assessed by social workers prior to routine assessment by junior psychiatrists. Both disciplines completed a scale to rate the presence of mental or physical illness and suicidal intent, and described the patients' personal and situational characteristics. The social workers' and psychiatrists' rating schedule responses were compared, and their decisions were examined against further information obtained by a research psychiatrist, which included standardized mental state assessment. It appeared that social workers more commonly rated mental illness as present by defining patients with a moderate number of depressive or neurotic symptoms as being mentally ill. Social workers also rated suicidal intent of some degree more frequently, and noted the presence of physical illness more correctly than psychiatrists. Furthermore, social workers attached greater significance to situational factors, including relationship problems, family problems and forced separation preceding the attempt. However, significant agreement between both disciplines was found for the assessment of the need and urgency for a psychiatric opinion and for the decision regarding immediate management (including compulsory detention). Overall, the results showed that social workers can safely and reliably assess attempted suicide patients, and that they are more cautious than psychiatrists. Based on these findings, the authors suggest that social workers can deal with some or all referred attempted suicide patients, provided that psychiatrists are available for consultations about urgent problems and for regular (perhaps weekly) meetings with the social workers.

Bateson and colleagues (1989) in Manchester in the UK conducted a controlled but non-randomized clinical trial in which the impact of psychiatric social work on repetition rates, types of help offered, patient satisfaction, social circumstances and general health was examined by comparing patients who were assessed by a psychiatrist alone to those who were assessed by both a psychiatrist and a psychiatric social worker. It appeared that while no differences were found with regard to rates of subsequent repetition of suicidal behaviour, the joint approach was superior to the assessment by the psychiatrist only in that more patients were offered follow-up, that follow-up was received sooner, and that more patients received domiciliary (home-based) care. Moreover, patients reported greater satisfaction and also impact of the service on their situation, particularly in terms of improved family relationships. Finally, the joint service appeared to reduce the general level of somatic illness. An important finding was the impact on subsequent help-seeking behaviour at times of stress. While patients in both groups did not see psychiatrists as the professionals to contact at times of stress, more patients who were jointly assessed sought help at times of stress than those who were assessed by a psychiatrist only.

TREATMENT OF ATTEMPTED SUICIDE PATIENTS

Nurses

Community psychiatric nurses have been involved in a number of studies in which the efficacy of an experimental treatment condition has been assessed (e.g. Salkovskis et al, 1990; van der Sande et al, 1997). The design of these studies, however, does not allow any conclusions about the specific contribution of these nurses, as they may have also been involved in the "treatment-as-usual" control conditions. However, in one study conducted in Gent in Belgium the experimental condition differed from the control condition in that the contribution of the nurse was limited to the experimental condition. This randomised controlled trial in deliberate self-harm patients examined the effects of home visits by a community nurse on rates of non-compliance with outpatient aftercare and on rates of repetition of suicidal behaviour (van Heeringen et al, 1995). In the experimental condition, patients were visited at home up to three times by the community nurse if they were non-compliant with referral to outpatient aftercare following a suicide attempt. During these home visits, reasons for non-compliance and needs for help were assessed, following which the community nurse tried to match these needs with aftercare services. When compared to treatment-as-usual, the experimental condition resulted in a statistically significant increase in the proportion of patients that attended outpatient appointments, and a near-significant reduction in subsequent non-fatal suicidal behaviour during the 1-year follow-up period.

Social Workers

The involvement of social workers in the management and treatment of deliberate self-harm patients has been evaluated in a number of studies. Chowdhury and colleagues (1973) studied the effectiveness of a "medico-social" aftercare service for patients in Edinburgh who had repeatedly attempted suicide. They compared repetition of attempted suicide during a 6-month follow-up period and improvement in psychiatric and social state in patients alternately allocated to the experimental aftercare service condition and to conventional care, in terms of repetition of self-harm and improvement in social adjustment. The experimental service was conducted by a psychiatrist and psychiatric social workers, and its special features were domiciliary visits in case of non-attendance of outpatient appointments and a 24-hour emergency call service, in addition to outpatient clinics. Follow-up assessments demonstrated that patients treated by the experimental service showed significant improvement with regard to social problems related to housing, finance and employment. However, no effect on psychiatric and behavioural problems could be demonstrated, and rates of repetition of attempted suicide did not differ between treatment groups.

The potential benefits of a social work service for self-poisoning patients were studied further by Gibbons and colleagues (1978) in a randomized controlled clinical trial in Southampton, UK. Patients were excluded from the trial if they suffered from psychiatric illness requiring immediate treatment; if they were judged to be at immediate risk of suicide; or if they were in continuing treatment with a psychiatrist or social worker. Core characteristics of the experimental service were the systematic and explicitly time-limited approach, which was immediately available and offered at each patients' home. Patients in the control group received routine care. When assessed after a 4-month follow-up period, the patients in the experimental condition reported significantly greater improvement in social problems than those in the control group. However, no significant differences were found for rates of repetition of attempted suicide and for severity of depressive symptoms.

In the USA, Deykin and colleagues (1986) in Boston developed an intervention aiming at reducing suicidal and self-destructive behaviour among high-risk adolescents aged 13–17 years. The intervention consisted of, first, a community-based and outreaching direct service to identify at-risk adolescents by a trained social worker, and, second, a programme of community education. The direct service aimed, among other things, to provide support and to act as an advocate for adolescents, to provide a liaison between adolescents and hospital or community services, and to ensure that adolescents kept follow-up and referral appointments to specialty clinics. The community education programme consisted of day-long workshops for service providers, teachers and court of justice personnel, which were designed to increase participants' knowledge of adolescent depression and suicidal behaviour and to inform them of relevant community resources. Workshops were also organized for peer leaders in high and middle schools in order to teach them how to respond to classmates expressing suicidal thoughts, including listening, organizing a referral and dealing with confidentiality. The efficacy of the direct service and community education intervention was assessed by means of a non-randomised trial in suicidal, self-destructive adolescents who were identified at the emergency room. Outcome measures included repetition of suicidal behaviour and compliance with follow-up visits or referrals to speciality clinics. The study showed that, although health problems were commonly found, many young people find it difficult to accept a medical regimen that produces slow improvement, and the greatest impact of the intervention programme was on increasing compliance with medical recommendations. A slight, but not statistically significant, reduction in admissions following suicidal and life-threatening acts was found. There was, however, a simultaneous increase in emergency room admissions involving adolescents with recurrent suicidal thoughts without self-inflicted injuries, which appeared to be attributable to the community education programme, as most were referred by workshop participants. Thus, this study showed that a direct outreach service by social workers increased compliance with after-care, and that the educational programme enhanced primary prevention through early identification and referral. The lack of effect on repetition, however, suggests that adolescents at risk of repeated suicidal behaviour may refuse this direct service, or that the intervention was not effective in preventing repetition.

In their randomized controlled trial of the efficacy of domiciliary versus outpatient treatment, Hawton and colleagues (1981) also assessed the relative effectiveness of management by medical (i.e. junior psychiatrists) and non-medical (i.e. psychiatric nurse and social worker) therapists. All therapists underwent special additional training in assessment and management procedures, and a treatment manual was available. The treatment consisted of a brief problem-orientated approach (which was briefer than the task-centred casework method used by Gibbons and colleagues, 1978, as described above), and averaged 3 hours of therapist–patient contact. Patients were excluded from the trial if they were in current psychiatric treatment, in need of treatment for alcoholism or drug addiction, or in need of inpatient or day-patient care because of psychiatric illness or serious suicide risk. Outcome measures included repetition of self-poisoning, mood, target problems, suicidal ideation and social adjustment post-treatment and after 6 months, and repetition of self-poisoning after 1 year. With regard to the comparison of the medical and non-medical therapists, the study showed no differences in the mean duration of treatment, the proportions of their patients whose treatment sessions included other people, and the proportions of their patients who completed treatment. For the patients who completed treatment, however, the medical therapists held more treatment sessions than did the non-medical therapists. There were no major differences in outcome in terms of repetition of self-poisoning, social adjustment, outcome on target problems and suicidal ideation. However, patients allocated to non-medical therapists tended to have better scores on the mood scale at the post-treatment assessment for "anxiety" and "fatigue", and at the 6-month assessment for "fatigue".

CONCLUSIONS

This overview of controlled studies of approaches to the assessment and treatment of deliberate self-harm patients shows that nurses, social workers or general medical personnel can safely assess and/or treat these patients, albeit under certain conditions. A number of methodological issues should, however, be taken into account when interpreting the results of these investigations. First, all of them were conducted on selected groups of deliberate self-harm patients. In all the studies, patients with major psychiatric disorders and with a high risk of suicide were excluded from participation. The results of these studies should, therefore, not be considered applicable to deliberate self-harm patients in general. However, in view of the fact that our ability to predict suicidal behaviour accurately is currently limited (see Chapter 33), it could be argued that it is not reasonable to exclude the so-called high risk groups. Perhaps the only way to demonstrate the efficacy and effectiveness of interventions, as described in this and other chapters, is to include these alleged high-risk groups.

Second, with the exception of the investigations that included outreaching components, all the studies were performed in general hospitals. Thus, it is not yet clear whether disciplines other than psychiatrists can contribute to the management of patients with suicidal risk and behaviour outside general hospitals. More research is needed on the management of deliberate self-harm patients in other settings, such as community mental health services, particularly in view of the increasing emphasis on community mental health care in many countries.

While keeping these methodological limitations in mind, this overview clearly indicates the benefits of a multidisciplinary approach to the assessment of suicidal behaviour if adequate training, an interview questionnaire and psychiatric supervision (e.g. by means of regular team meetings) are provided. With regard to the involvement of non-psychiatric staff in the treatment of deliberate self-harm patients, several studies reviewed in this chapter demonstrate a positive effect of outreach programmes by a community psychiatric nurse or social worker on compliance with treatment. One study even showed a near-significant effect of such an outreaching strategy on repetition of suicidal behaviour. These positive effects may, at least partly, be due to the fact that, as reported in several studies, deliberate self-harm patients do not tend to view their problems in medical or psychiatric terms. The finding that deliberate self-harm patients do not usually regard psychiatrists as the professionals to contact at times of stress further indicates the important role of other disciplines in the prevention of repetition of suicidal behaviour. It therefore appears that the benefits of a multidisciplinary approach outweigh any additional costs involved, especially as it was shown in one study that the costs of hospital treatment of one suicide attempter equal two months' salary of a community psychiatric nurse (van Heeringen, 1993).

The finding that, in the treatment studies which were reviewed, no significant effect of the experimental condition could be demonstrated on repetition rates is almost certainly not due to the involvement of non-medical therapists. As described in Chapter 28, there is surprisingly little evidence for the efficacy of psychotherapeutic approaches to suicidal patients, the small size of most trials being a major factor limiting the detection at a statistically significant level of any differences. From an overview of treatment studies, it was concluded that psychotherapeutic approaches involving a manualised problem-solving component, combined with some intensive care or outreach, may offer the best opportunity for delivering an efficacious treatment. This chapter has described the important role of psychiatric nurses and social workers in achieving this goal.

REFERENCES

Bateson, M., Oliver, J.P.J. and Goldberg, D.P. (1989) A comparative study of the management of cases of deliberate self-harm in a district general hospital. British Journal of Social Work, 19: 461–477.

Beck, R.W., Morris, J.B. and Beck, A.T. (1974) Cross-validation of the Suicidal Intent Scale. Psychological Reports, 34: 445–446.

Black, D. and Creed, F. (1988) Assessment of self-poisoning patients by psychiatrists and junior medical staff. Journal of the Royal Society of Medicine, 81: 97–99.

Burn, W.K., Edwards, J.G. and Machin, D. (1990) Improving house physicians' assessments of self-poisoning. British Journal of Psychiatry, 157: 95–100.

Catalan, J., Marsack, P., Hawton, K., Whitwell, D., Fagg, J. and Bancroft, J.H.J. (1980) Comparison of doctors and nurses in the assessment of deliberate self-poisoning patients. Psychological Medicine, 10: 483–491.

Chowdhury, N.L., Hicks, R.G. and Kreitman, N. (1973) Evaluation of an aftercare service for parasuicide (attempted suicide) patients. Social Psychiatry, 8: 67–81.

Crawford, M.J., Turnbull, G. and Wessely, S. (1998) Deliberate self-harm assessment by accident and emergency staff—an intervention study. Journal of Accident and Emergency Medicine, 15: 18–22.

Deykin, E.Y., Hsieh, C.C., Joshi, N. and McNamarra, J.J. (1986) Adolescent suicidal and self-destructive behavior: results of an intervention study. Journal of Adolescent Health Care, 7: 88–95.

Ebbage, J., Farr, C., Skinner, D.V. and White, P.D. (1994) The psychosocial assessment of patients discharged from accident and emergency departments after deliberate self-poisoning. Journal of the Royal Society of Medicine, 87: 515–516.

Gardner, R., Hanka, R., Evison, B., Mountford, P.M., O'Brien, V.C. and Roberts, S.J. (1978) Consultation-liaison scheme for self-poisoned patients in a general hospital. British Medical Journal, 2: 1392–1394.

Gibbons, J.S., Butler, J., Urwin, P. and Gibbons, J.L. (1978) Evaluation of a social work service for self-poisoning patients. British Journal of Psychiatry, 133: 111–118.

Hawton, K., Bancroft, J.H.J., Catalan, J., Stedeford, A. and Welch, N. (1981) Domiciliary and outpatient treatment of self-poisoning patients by medical and non-medical staff. Psychological Medicine, 11: 169–177.

Kapur, N., House, A., Creed, F., Feldman, E., Friedman, T. and Guthrie, E. (1998) Management of deliberate self-poisoning in adults in four teaching hospitals: descriptive study. British Medical Journal, 316: 831–832.

Mayfield, D., McLeod, G. and Hall, P. (1974) The CAGE questionnaire: validation of a new alcoholism screening instrument. American Journal of Psychiatry, 131: 1121–1123.

Newson-Smith, J.G.B. and Hirsch, S.R. (1979) A comparison of social workers and psychiatrists in evaluating parasuicide. British Journal of Psychiatry, 134: 335–342.

Royal College of Psychiatrists (1994) Guidance on the management of deliberate self-harm. Psychiatric Bulletin, 7: 210–212.

Royal College of Psychiatrists (1995) The Psychological Care of Medical Patients: Recognition of Need and Service Provision. London: Royal College of Psychiatrists.

Salkovskis, P.M., Atha, C. and Storer, D. (1990) Cognitive-behavioural problem solving in the treatment of patients who repeatedly attempt suicide: a controlled trial. British Journal of Psychiatry, 15: 871–876.

Suokas, J. (1991) Selection of patients who attempted suicide for psychiatric consultation. Acta Psychiatrica Scandinavica, 83: 179–182.
van der Sande, R., van Rooyen, L., Buskens, E., Allart, E., Hawton, K., van der Graaf, Y. and van Engeland, H. (1997) Intensive in-patient and community intervention versus routine care after attempted suicide: a randomised controlled intervention study. British Journal of Psychiatry, 171: 35–41.
van Heeringen, C. (1993) Epidemiological Aspects of Attempted Suicide. Unpublished doctoral thesis, University of Gent.
van Heeringen, C., Jannes, S., Buylaert, W., Henderick, H., De Bacquer, D. and van Remoortel, J. (1995) The management of non-compliance with referral to outpatient aftercare among attempted suicide patients: a controlled intervention study. Psychological Medicine, 25: 963–970.
Williams, E., Mitchell, C., Preston, J., Augarde, K., Barber, R., Catalan, J. and Jones, B. (1998) Management of deliberate self-poisoning: liaison psychiatric nurses can be used to increase psychosocial assessments. British Medical Journal, 317: 415–416 (letter).
Wing, J.K., Cooper, J.E. and Sartorius, N. (1974) The Description and Classification of Psychiatric Symptomatology. An Introduction Manual for the PSE and CATEGO System. London: Cambridge University Press.

Part IV

The Prevention of Suicide and Attempted Suicide

Chapter 33

Prediction of Suicide and Attempted Suicide

Robert D. Goldney
Department of Psychiatry, University of Adelaide, South Australia

Abstract

A limiting factor in our ability to prevent suicide is that we are unable to predict suicidal behaviour in those individuals among the many who are suicidal. This has been known for over 40 years, and repeated attempts to refine prediction to the extent that it would be of clinical value have failed. This chapter focuses mainly on those studies designed to predict suicide, although it also addresses the prediction of repeated attempted suicide. In doing so it emphasizes the statistical limitations, in terms of experimental design, that are imposed upon those pursuing research examining the effectiveness of programmes designed to prevent suicide or repeated attempted suicide. It is suggested that the ideal research design of randomized controlled trials may not be feasible in confirming the efficacy of such programmes, and that alternative studies utilizing innovative methodologies may be more appropriate. Such studies may provide persuasive evidence for the clinician that, despite our inability to predict suicidal behaviour in any individual, there are treatments with demonstrated effectiveness.

INTRODUCTION

Suicide is a dramatic event which has the almost inevitable effect of evoking thoughts about how specific interventions might have prevented that suicide. However, the sobering reality is that there has not been any research which has indicated that suicide can be predicted or prevented in any individual. The result of this is that programmes designed specifically to prevent suicide, even those which purport to focus upon so-called high-risk groups, have not yet demonstrated a reduction in suicide rates. Not unexpectedly, this has led to pessimistic

The International Handbook of Suicide and Attempted Suicide. Edited by K. Hawton and K. van Heeringen.

conclusions, such as: "The reality is that there is no convincing evidence that education, improved social conditions and support, or better training play a substantive part in preventing suicide" (Wilkinson, 1994). However, such acerbic assertions need to be considered in the perspective that suicide, for all its drama and the clarity with which retrospective analyses provide, has a low base rate, with the attendant clinical limitations that this imposes.

PREDICTION OF SUICIDE

The challenge of detecting those who will go on to commit suicide has been well recognized for over 40 years. Rosen (1954) was probably the first to draw attention to the limitations of the prediction of infrequent events in suicidal subjects, with a cogent description of the interaction between the low incidence of suicide itself and the large number of false positives that are predicted on the basis of those subjects possessing the conventional risk factors associated with suicide.

That early work appears to have been overlooked for 20 years until Farberow and MacKinnon (1975) reported on 54 patients who had committed suicide and a control group who were compared on the Neuropsychiatric Hospital Suicide Potential Scale. They observed that their statistical analysis allowed the accuracy of prediction to be increased five-fold over the base rate, but because of the low base rate of suicide they concluded that "the level of prediction of suicide is still too minimal to permit individual clinical application".

Probably the most influential work in this area has been that of Pokorny (1983), who identified 67 suicides in a study of 4,800 American veterans, giving a suicide rate of 279 per 100,000 per year, which is obviously a population at high risk. A number of items were found by discriminate function analyses to be significantly associated with suicide, including the diagnoses of depression or schizophrenia; a history of suicide attempts or having been placed on suicide precautions; overt evidence of depression on the basis of a clinical examination; and the complaint of insomnia and the presence of guilt feelings. In addition there were 45 other items, although their predictive value was not as great.

Using a statistical method of calculating the power of individual predictors and then using the 20 best predictors, it was possible to identify 35 of the 67 subjects who had committed suicide. However, that prediction of a little over a half of those who committed suicide was a clear indication of the lack of specificity of the predictors, a fact borne out by there being 1,206 false-positive identifications.

This led Pokorny to conclude that "We do not possess any item of information or any combination of items that permits us to identify to a useful degree the particular persons who will commit suicide". Pokorny (1993) re-visited his data 10 years later, but even with further sophisticated re-analysis, including in one test removing a number of the non-suicide cases to increase the base rate, his results still fell far short of any clinical utility.

Such limitations were also illustrated in Australian data, where patients who committed suicide after having had contact with a psychiatric hospital were compared with control subjects (Goldney and Spence, 1987). Ten clinical features distinguished the two groups, including the presence of a schizophrenic or depressive illness; a history of previous admissions, substance abuse and attempted suicide; and a history of them having been involuntarily treated. Using discriminant function analysis, focusing on those subjects who had six or more of the 10 high-risk features, 24 of the 37 suicides for whom complete data were available were correctly identified. However, that prediction was on the premise of a base rate of suicide of 1 in 2, with there being 37 suicides out of the total of 74 suicide and control group subjects. When the true base rate for suicide of patients in psychiatric hospitals in Australia, that of 220 per 100,000 admissions, was factored into the statistical analysis, the predictive ability of the six or more of the 10 clinical features was no greater than that which could have been obtained by tossing a coin.

A further attempt to predict suicide in a high-risk group was reported by Goldstein et al (1991), who examined 1,906 patients with affective disorders admitted to a tertiary care hospital. The usual risk factors of the number of prior suicide attempts, the degree of suicidal ideation on admission, the presence of a bipolar disorder, gender, and outcome at discharge were identified, but the model failed to identify those who committed suicide and the authors concluded that "the results appear to support the contention that, based on present knowledge, it is not possible to predict suicide, even among a high-risk group of patients".

Another illustration of our inability to predict suicide in individual subjects was provided by Furst and Huffine (1991), who gave four comprehensive case histories with demographic and clinical data to 300 members of the American Association of Suicidology. Two of the four subjects had committed suicide and members of the Association were asked to delineate on a five-point scale, from very vulnerable to not at all vulnerable, the risk of suicide of those subjects. Contrary to expectation, Association members assigned a higher degree of vulnerability to the two subjects who did not commit suicide, and the degree of vulnerability assigned to those who did commit suicide was actually lower than that expected by chance. Factors associated with accurate prediction of suicide were female gender and the presence of a family member having committed suicide, whereas negative correlates of accurate prediction included the degree of education and the number of years and time spent in research. These results could be interpreted as indicating that those with an increasing familiarity with the subject of suicidal behaviour appreciate the problems of prediction, and therefore underestimate the potential for suicide.

Not unexpectedly, in view of the foregoing, the one meta-analytic study of work in this area also reached a negative conclusion. Following a review of 81 articles examining differences between those with varying degrees of suicidal ideation and behaviour, those who committed suicide and non-suicidal subjects, van Egmond and Diekstra (1990) stated that "suicide prediction research has made little headway over the past 25 years".

In contrast to the previous studies, it is possible that biological tests could prove of value in the prediction of those who commit suicide. This has arisen from the observation that for those who attempt suicide in a violent manner, there is more likelihood that they will go on to commit suicide if they have a relatively low cerebrospinal fluid (CSF) level of 5-hydroxyindoleacetic acid (5-HIAA) (Nordstrom et al, 1994). As described in Chapter 4, this is a metabolite of serotonin, which appears to be of importance in aggression and suicidality. Although there are accumulating data about the importance of this, its use remains experimental and it is unrealistic to anticipate that examination of CSF would ever be part of the standard assessment of those who are suicidal.

Despite our inability to predict accurately who will commit suicide, the fact remains that there are a number of clinical features that are, at the very least, statistically associated with subsequent suicide. For example, Beck et al (1989) reported that a high degree of hopelessness was associated with future suicide for psychiatric patients, and other clinical features include the expression of suicidal ideation; the presence of psychiatric illness, particularly depression and schizophrenia; alcohol and other substance abuse; physical illness; social isolation; and the availability of the means of suicide (Appleby, 1992).

Such clinical findings have been well validated, for example in recent work emphasizing the importance of previous attempted suicide in those with mood disorders (Nordstrom et al, 1995) and substance abuse in young persons (Hawton et al, 1993). Furthermore, the fact that some clinical findings are "time-related predictors" has been emphasized by Fawcett et al (1990), where suicide within a year of presentation with a major depressive disorder was predicted by panic attacks, severe psychic anxiety, diminished concentration, global insomnia, moderate alcohol abuse and anhedonia, whereas suicide more than a year after assessment was associated more with severe hopelessness, suicidal ideation and a history of previous suicide attempts.

Experienced clinicians are also aware of issues more proximal to suicide, which appear to be of importance, and these have been well summarized by Morgan and Priest (1991) in the concept of "terminal malignant alienation", which "refers to a series of events, often related to recurrent relapse and failure to respond to treatment, in which such patients experience profound loss of sympathy, even antipathy, from staff and probably relatives alike, who commonly invoke deliberate manipulation, assumption of symptoms, or over-dependency". It is also of interest that Hulten and Wasserman (1998) have recently reported on the importance of the lack of continuity of clinical care in young people who committed suicide. It may well be that such issues, although challenging and sensitive to research, offer more hope in terms of them being proximate predictors of suicide.

Notwithstanding the heuristic value of such clinical findings, the dilemma remains that their lack of specificity and the low base rate of suicide preclude them from being of any particular value in any one patient in the clinical situation. Furthermore, those same reasons prove to be a virtually insurmountable obstacle in designing research projects to demonstrate the effectiveness of any intervention to prevent suicide.

The latter is illustrated well by examining the estimated sample sizes that would be required for the evaluation of an intervention targeted at particular population groups, in order to demonstrate the effectiveness of an intervention to prevent suicide. Gunnell and Frankel (1994) have calculated these, and to demonstrate a 15% reduction in those discharged from psychiatric hospitals, where there is a 0.9% chance of committing suicide in the subsequent year, over 140,000 patients would be required in the sample. Similarly, to demonstrate a 15% reduction in suicide for those who have attempted suicide, where there is a 2.8% chance of committing suicide in the subsequent 8 years, it would require a sample size of almost 45,000 subjects.

Lewis and colleagues (1997) developed this theme further and provided a mathematical model for deriving the numbers needed to treat to prevent suicide in high-risk populations. Examples were given for both medical practitioners and farmers in the UK, two groups with a demonstrated greater degree of mortality due to suicide. There were about 187,000 doctors on the General Medical Council list and about 172,000 farmers in England and the numbers needed to treat for an intervention that would reduce the suicide rates in doctors and farmers by 25 per cent would be 25,000 and 33,000 respectively. Not unexpectedly, the authors expressed reservations about the feasibility and affordability of studies to demonstrate such effectiveness.

The magnitude of such research can also be illustrated by considering the feasibility of the establishment of a hypothetical project to prevent youth suicide in schools, an admirable aim and one which has much appeal for the community and politicians. Assume that there is a population of 1 million in the particular area being targeted, and that there are 100,000 persons aged between 15 and 19 years. Let us focus resources on the 50,000 young males, as their suicide rate is appreciably higher than that in young females, and as it is a rigorous research project, we could have an intervention group of 25,000 and compare them to a control group of the other 25,000. Let us assume that there are 100 schools, 50 of which, each with 500 young males, are in the intervention group. Now, if we assume that there is a suicide rate of 20 per 100,000, a hypothetical figure which is higher than in most countries for that age group, we could expect 5 out of the 25,000 each year to commit suicide. That is, there would on average be one suicide in every 10 schools per year; or, put another way, 1 suicide every 10 years in each school.

When one considers the uncritical enthusiasm with which some researchers and clinicians approach suicide prevention in areas such as individual schools or school regions, it is quite evident that there is a lack of understanding of the limitations of the low base rate of suicide and the impossibility of ever demonstrating scientifically that the intervention would be effective.

PREDICTION OF ATTEMPTED SUICIDE

The work reviewed so far has applied to suicide rather than attempted suicide, but the same principles apply, albeit to a lesser degree. Thus again, although attempted suicide also has a profound impact upon others, and notwithstanding the fact that its prevalence is approximately 10–30 times greater than suicide, it is still a relatively infrequent phenomenon. Furthermore, there are many intervening variables determining not only its occurrence, but also an individual subject's compliance with intervention programmes. Not unexpectedly, these factors impose significant constraints on the follow-up research process.

Instruments to predict repeated attempted suicide have been devised, such as the Edinburgh Risk of Repetition Scale (Kreitman and Foster, 1991). However, using that instrument in a replication study in a different setting, Hawton and Fagg (1995) found only a modest ability to predict repetition of suicide attempts over a period of a year in two different samples, and only a minority of repeaters were from the highest risk group. They concluded that such a scale could only provide adjunctive information to a full clinical assessment, and that even if the sensitivity of the instrument were increased, it would result only in a "disproportionately larger number of non-repeaters" being identified, exactly the same problem which arises in regard to the prediction of completed suicide.

In an innovative attempt to enhance the prediction of repeated suicidal behaviour, Erdman et al (1987) devised a computerized interview. This was reported to be significantly better at predicting suicide attempters, whereas clinicians were significantly better at predicting non-attempters. However, the overall receiver operating characteristic curves demonstrated that the difference was non-significant. Nevertheless, it is of interest that the better clinician prediction of non-attempters was probably related to the fact that clinicians appreciate the problems of prediction and therefore underestimate the potential for suicidal behaviour, as noted previously in relation to the study of the predictive ability of members of the American Association of Suicidology (Furst and Huffine, 1991).

A recent statistical model for identifying repeat suicide attempters has been developed by Corcoran and colleagues (1997). It is of particular interest as, in order that the data could be collected by non-clinical hospital personnel, information related to psychiatric diagnosis and use of treatment services was not considered. Instead, 11 demographic and sociological variables were chosen as the potential predictors. These included age; gender; civil status; level of education; whether there had been a previous act of parasuicide; the main method of parasuicide; whether drugs or alcohol had been taken at the time of the act; whether there had been abuse of street drugs in the past or present; whether there was a history of social, physical or psychological harm due to alcohol; and whether there had been a change in the person's domestic situation near the time of the act. Logistic regression analysis produced an estimate that an individual would repeat his/her suicide attempt within 6 months, and this predicted 96% of the repeaters and 81% of the non-repeaters. The programme is designed to upgrade potential predictors with ongoing data collection, but the authors emphasized that the demographic and sociological data which predict repeaters in their research setting would not necessarily do so in other centres, and the programme would need to be modified for use elsewhere.

Despite the constraints on pursuing such research, there have been many studies purporting to assess the effectiveness of psychosocial or pharmacological treatments in reducing repeated attempted suicide. However, in a comprehensive review, only 20 studies were considered to have fulfilled randomized controlled trial research criteria (Hawton et al, 1998). There is tentative evidence that certain interventions in carefully selected subjects may be effective, but it must be acknowledged that overall the results are disappointing. However, the studies analysed had the constraints delineated previously in regard to suicide. Thus, there were too few subjects to detect statistical and clinically meaningful differences in repeat suicide attempts between experimental and control groups. Hawton et al (1998) observed that:

> The number needed is a function of both the expected rate of repetition (i.e. that in the control group) and the size of the difference. If the predicted rate were 10% in the experimental group vs. 15% in the control, with α set at 0.05 and β set at 0.2, a total of 687 subjects would be required in each treatment group, while if the rates were 20% and 30%, 293 subjects would be required in each group. Even when the results from similar trials are synthesized using meta-analytical techniques, there are insufficient numbers of patients to detect such differences.

The importance of this for future research has been further emphasized by Hawton (1998), who has gone so far as to state that unless sufficient numbers are utilized, it "is a waste of scientific time and funding, and could be deemed unethical in terms of patient participation".

It is possible that multicentred collaborative trials could be utilized to fulfil the need for sufficient numbers to demonstrate the effectiveness of intervention programmes in preventing repeated attempted suicide. For example, in the World Health Organization/European Union follow-up study of those who had attempted suicide, 2,159 subjects in eight centres were asked to participate (Kerkhof et al, 1998). Of those, 1,098 (50%) completed a first interview within 1 week or as soon as possible after medical treatment for their suicide attempt, and 601 (55%) were re-examined after 1 year. This represents an excellent follow-up rate for a study personally examining subjects over a 1-year period, as opposed to a case note review, and such results are not unexpected in work coming from centres investigating suicidal behaviour. Nevertheless, when one combines this retention rate after 1 year with the need for randomization of treatment and control subjects in future studies, the challenge in designing outcome research in this area is quite evident, even with highly motivated researchers in dedicated centres such as in this study.

THE CHALLENGE

Bearing in mind the above research on the prediction of suicide and attempted suicide, it is not unexpected that it has been stated that "No single intervention has been shown in a well-conducted randomized control trial to reduce suicide"

(Gunnell and Frankel, 1994). Whilst such a statement is technically correct, and whilst one must acknowledge the importance of evidence-based medicine, the question must be posed as to whether or not there could ever be a randomized control trial of sufficient magnitude to demonstrate the efficacy of any particular suicide prevention strategy.

Whilst that may not be possible, it is more likely that a multi-centre trial could demonstrate the effectiveness of interventions designed to prevent repeated attempted suicide. For example, a randomized controlled treatment programme focusing on young males 18–30 years of age, with a mood disorder, substance abuse and previous suicidal behaviour, could be feasible. However, mounting such a trial would provide a considerable administrative, financial and, not the least, ethical challenge.

With regard to demonstrating the effectiveness of suicide prevention *per se*, it appears to be more pragmatic to resort to alternative research methodologies. Thus, the measurement of the effect of broad population interventions or changes in treatment practices upon the natural history of certain conditions, such as depression or schizophrenia, and relating those changes to variations in suicide rates, may be the most parsimonious method of circumventing the low base rate of suicide and the lack of specificity of the predictors. Indeed, by utilizing such research methodology, there are grounds for optimism in suicide prevention (Goldney, 1998). For example, consistent use of lithium for bipolar disorders results in appreciably lower suicide rates than those reported for the natural history of untreated illness (Coppen, 1994). Also the introduction of antidepressants in Sweden has been associated with a reduction in suicide and, on the basis of research examining prescribing patterns and the recognition and treatment of depression, it has been calculated that there would be a further reduction in suicide with better management of depression (Isacsson et al, 1996). Moreover, a reduction in suicidality in schizophrenia has been reported with the introduction of clozapine treatment (Meltzer and Okayli, 1995).

It is also reassuring to note that, although we are unable to predict and prevent suicide with any clinical utility in any one individual, a public health model of adopting broad community measures, which could well defy individual measurement, and which would not conform to conventional randomized controlled trials, may influence suicide rates favourably. Rose (1993) has contrasted such an approach with the clinical high-risk strategy of treating populations who are considered to be at risk as the "iceberg phenomenon". By that he means that treating the high-risk population is like sending warships to control icebergs by shooting off their visible portions, when in fact nothing is being done to address other diverse risk factors. He noted that whilst the high-risk intervention did help some individuals, its weakness lay in our inability to predict which individuals would, in our specific case, commit suicide. He went on to state that "it is a matter of simple arithmetic: a large number of people exposed to a small risk commonly generated many more cases than a small number exposed to a high risk". Elsewhere, Rose (1992) referred to the public health "prevention paradox" where a "preventive measure that brings large benefits to the community offers little to each participating individual", with the clear implication that, although individuals may not obtain benefit that could be measured either individually or in groups of subjects with relatively small numbers, the overall community impact could be quite significant.

CONCLUSION

It could be argued that experienced clinicians are aware of subtle nuances of patient presentation that may herald suicidal behaviour. However, the task remains to quantify such phenomena in order to provide more accurate prediction, a task which is limited severely because of the constraint of the low base rate and the lack of specificity of those factors associated with suicide and attempted suicide, notwithstanding the emotional impact that such behaviour evokes.

From the strictly scientific point of view, it is unlikely that there will ever be randomized controlled trials of broad treatment programmes to prevent suicide, although there could be focused treatments upon clearly delineated groups of patients in multicentered trials to prevent repetition of suicidal behaviour.

From the community point of view, it must be acknowledged that there may be political and social imperatives to be seen to be doing something about suicidal behaviour, despite the limitations in our ability to predict and delineate just who should be the recipients of what intervention programme. Scientists need not necessarily be pessimistic about such programmes, even though they may not meet the rigorous criteria essential for scientific research. Whilst shortcomings about what could be anticipated from data analysis should be pointed out, thereby preventing the unnecessary expenditure of valuable resources in examining the outcome of interventions which could not demonstrate statistically significant results, the possibility that such programmes could influence community attitudes, perceptions and actions in the direction of there being some impact on the overall rate of suicidal behaviour must be acknowledged. Indeed, that is consistent with the public health perspective and the "prevention paradox" model provided by Rose (1992), where an imperceptible effect on an individual may in fact result in a measurable change at the population level.

From the individual clinician's point of view, the constraints of our predictive ability should be conceded, but not with a sense of pessimism. Thus, there are studies, several of which have been referred to, which, although not meeting the criteria of randomized controlled trials, do provide persuasive evidence that certain interventions are effective in preventing suicide (Goldney, 1998). Furthermore, clinicians routinely make judgements about suicide risk, often in situations where it would probably be unethical to allocate patients to a randomized controlled trial. Whilst, on a statistical basis, the majority of those who are treated would not have committed suicide, the dilemma is that there is no way of knowing when a suicide has actually been prevented. Therefore, clinicians can heed no better advice than that of Murphy (1983), who, after acknowledging our limitations in the prediction and prevention of suicide, stated that "our efforts must be designed to relieve the substrate of despair that is the proximate basis for most suicides".

REFERENCES

Appleby, L. (1992) Suicide in psychiatric patients: risk and prevention. British Journal of Psychiatry, 161: 749–758.

Beck, A.T., Brown, G. and Steer, R.A. (1989) Prediction of eventual suicide in psychiatric in-patients by clinical ratings of hopelessness. Journal of Consulting and Clinical Psychology, 57: 309–310.

Coppen, A. (1994) Depression as a lethal disease: prevention strategies. Journal of Clinical Psychiatry, 55 (Suppl. 4): 37–45.

Corcoran, P., Kelleher, M.J., Keeley, H.S., Byrne, S., Burke, U. and Williamson, E. (1997) A statistical model for identifying repeaters of parasuicide. Archives of Suicide Research, 3: 65–74.

Erdman, H.P., Greist, J.H., Gustafson, D.H., Taves, J.E. and Klein, M.H. (1987) Suicide risk prediction by computer interview: a prospective study. Journal of Clinical Psychiatry, 48: 464–467.

Farberow, N.L. and MacKinnon, D. (1975) Prediction of suicide: a replication study. Journal of Personality Assessment, 39: 497–501.

Fawcett, J., Scheftner, W.A., Fogg, L., Clark, D.C., Young, M.A., Hedeker, D. and Gibbons, R. (1990) Time-related predictors of suicide in major affective disorder. American Journal of Psychiatry, 147: 1189–1194.

Furst, J. and Huffine, C.L. (1991) Assessing vulnerability to suicide. Suicide and Life Threatening Behavior, 21: 329–344.

Goldney, R.D. (1998) Suicide prevention is possible: a review of recent studies. Archives of Suicide Research, 4: 329–339.

Goldney, R.D. and Spence, N.D. (1987) Is suicide predictable? Australian and New Zealand Journal of Psychiatry, 21: 3–4.

Goldstein, R.B., Black, D.W., Nasrallah, A. and Winokur, G. (1991) The prediction of suicide. Sensitivity, specificity, and predictive value of a multi-variate model applied to suicide among 1,906 patients with affective disorders. Archives of General Psychiatry, 48: 418–422.

Gunnell, D. and Frankel, S. (1994) Prevention of suicide: aspirations and evidence. British Medical Journal, 308: 1227–1233.

Hawton, K. (1998) Treatment studies of deliberate self-harm patients: recommended standards of the design of randomised controlled trials. Paper presented at International Academy for Suicide Research, Gent, 9 September.

Hawton, K., Fagg, J., Platt, S. and Hawkins, M. (1993) Factors associated with suicide after parasuicide in young people. British Medical Journal, 306: 1641–1644.

Hawton, K., Arensman, E., Townsend, E., Bremner, S., Feldman, E., Goldney, R., Gunnell, D., Hazell, P., van Heeringen, K., House, A., Owens, D., Sakinofsky, I. and Traskman-Bendz, L. (1998) Deliberate self-harm: the efficacy of psycho-social and pharmacological treatments. British Medical Journal, 317: 441–447.

Hawton, K. and Fagg, J. (1995) Repetition of attempted suicide: the performance of the Edinburgh Predictive Scales in patients in Oxford. Archives of Suicide Research, 1: 261–272.

Hulten, A. and Wasserman, D. (1998) Lack of continuity—a problem in the care of young suicides. Acta Psychiatrica Scandinavica, 97: 326–333.

Isacsson, G., Bergman, U. and Rich, C.L. (1996) Epidemiological data suggest antidepressants reduce suicide risk among depressives. Journal of Affective Disorders, 41: 1–8.

Kerkhof, A.J.F.M., Arensman, E., Bille-Brahe, U., Crepet, P., de Leo, D., Hjelmeland, H., Lonnqvist, J., Michel, K., Salander-Renberg, E., Schmidtke, A. and Wasserman, D. (1998) Epidemiology of suicidal processes in Europe: findings of the WHO/EU study on parasuicide. Paper presented at the Seventh European Symposium on Suicide and Suicidal Behaviour, Gent, 9–12 September.

Kreitman, N. and Foster, J. (1991) Construction and selection of predictive scales, with special reference to parasuicide. British Journal of Psychiatry, 159: 185–192.

Lewis, G., Hawton, K. and Jones, P. (1997) Strategies for preventing suicides. British Journal of Psychiatry, 171: 351–354.

Meltzer, H.Y. and Okayli, G. (1995) Reduction of suicidality during clozapine treatment of neuroleptic-resistant schizophrenia: impact on risk benefit assessment. American Journal of Psychiatry, 152: 183–190.

Morgan, H.G. and Priest, P. (1991) Suicide and other unexpected deaths among psychiatric in-patients. British Journal of Psychiatry, 158: 368–374.

Murphy, G.E. (1983) On suicide prediction and prevention. Archives of General Psychiatry, 40: 343–344.

Nordstrom, P., Samuelsson, M., Asberg, M., Traskman-Bendz, L., Aberg-Wistedt, A., Nordin, C. and Bertilsson, L. (1994) CSF 5-HIAA predicts suicide risk after attempted suicide. Suicide and Life-Threatening Behavior, 24: 1–9.

Nordstrom, P., Asberg, M., Aberg-Wistedt, A. and Nordin, C. (1995) Attempted suicide predicts suicide risk in mood disorders. Acta Psychiatrica Scandinavica, 92: 345–350.

Pokorny, A.D. (1983) Prediction of suicide in psychiatric patients. Archives of General Psychiatry, 40: 249–257.

Pokorny, A.D. (1993) Suicide prediction revisited. Suicide and Life-Threatening Behavior, 23: 1–10.

Rose, G. (1992) The Strategy of Preventive Medicine. Oxford: Oxford University Press.

Rose, G. (1993) Mental disorder and the strategies of prevention. Psychological Medicine, 23: 553–555.

Rosen, A. (1954) Detection of suicidal patients: an example of some limitations in the prediction of infrequent events. Journal of Consulting Psychology, 18: 397–403.

van Egmond, M. and Diekstra, R.F. (1990) The predictability of suicidal behaviour: the results of a meta-analysis of published studies. Crisis, 11: 57–84.

Wilkinson, G. (1994) Can suicide be prevented? British Medical Journal, 309: 860–862.

Chapter 34

General Population Strategies of Suicide Prevention

Rachel Jenkins
WHO Collaborating Centre, Institute of Psychiatry, London, UK
and
Bruce Singh
Department of Psychiatry, University of Melbourne, Melbourne, Australia

Abstract

This chapter is concerned with strategies which can be applied to whole populations to attempt to reduce suicide rates. By necessity many such strategies (but by no means all) involve government intervention. Such involvement by government in an act which has been seen as intensely personal has received encouragement from recent statements by the World Health Organization and more recently the United Nations. These principles are described and the Finnish model for implementing them highlighted. The efforts being made by a number of other nations receive particular attention. Methods for which success has been demonstrated or for which evidence is accumulating are described as are some which are still controversial.

INTRODUCTION

The potential for applying general population strategies to suicide prevention has been apparent for more than 100 years, since Durkheim observed that the frequency of suicide varied inversely with social integration (Durkheim, 1952). Whilst it may be facile to suggest that measures to improve social cohesion would make suicide less likely, we should not discount the possibility that approaches to a whole community might well have some impact on suicide rates. This might

The International Handbook of Suicide and Attempted Suicide. Edited by K. Hawton and K. van Heeringen.

particularly be the case when those approaches are supplemented by interventions aimed at those sections of the community which appear to be, at different times and for varying reasons, particularly at risk (e.g. currently young people aged 18–25 years in much of the Western World; see Chapter 1).

Over the century, as the art and science of prevention in psychiatry has developed, new models of both implementing and evaluating prevention strategies have emerged. One approach is the now traditional primary, secondary and tertiary prevention model first articulated by Gerald Caplan (1964). Alternative but overlapping approaches include those proposed by the Irish Department of Health and Children (1998), which divides measures into three levels:

- General public health measures.
- Early and timely interventions for mental illnesses which predispose to suicide.
- Comprehensive community care to provide services to those stricken with mental illness.

The Swedish national programme to develop suicide prevention suggests a similar three-level involvement (The National Council for Suicide Prevention, 1996):

- General suicide prevention, which involves measures for increasing resilience.
- Indirect suicide prevention, intended to reduce suicidal acts by changing background factors, including the availability of means of suicide.
- Direct suicide prevention, directed at individuals experiencing suicidal thoughts and urges.

These approaches demonstrate the distinction between those aimed at influencing a population and those involved with influencing the individual. This chapter is concerned with population strategies. Such strategies may be conceptualized and implemented by a variety of societal organizations. These include professional bodies (e.g. medical and pharmacist bodies) and community organizations e.g. Schizophrenia, and National Emergency (SANE) and The Samaritans, religious groups or political parties. Such groups might be involved in education, information dissemination, articulation of principles and advice to the community. They depend for their authority on their status, history, prestige, knowledge and expertise to fulfil this role. Notwithstanding their efforts and exhortations to the community, it eventually falls to governments to become involved in setting and implementing policy. This position was put clearly by the United Nations when it stated that national governments should be encouraged to set policies for the prevention of suicide which could be complemented by their own institutional structures responsible for individual, family and community well-being (United Nations, 1996).

Government health policies usually aim to protect, promote and improve health and to reduce premature avoidable mortality. Premature death from suicide is a significant cause of mortality around the globe–official suicides alone are equivalent in magnitude to deaths from road traffic accidents or to deaths from malaria. Furthermore, we know that in all countries there is a greater or lesser degree of stigma that attaches to suicide and so not all actual suicide numbers are recorded as such. Epidemiological and autopsy studies in a number of countries suggest that the magnitude of unofficial suicide numbers is also very great. Premature death from suicide has many adverse consequences. Over and above the direct loss of life there is the consequence for the family of the loss of a breadwinner and parent, the long-lasting psychological trauma of children, friends and relatives, and the loss of economic productivity for the nation. It is therefore long overdue that governments should take steps to reduce the mortality from suicide.

It is sometimes argued that suicide is a personal decision in which governments have no justification in trying to interfere. However, there is strong evidence that nearly all suicides occur in the context of some degree of mental disorder (see Chapters 7–11), and so they are just as much an appropriate issue for governments to tackle as road traffic accidents or deaths from infectious diseases. Taking road traffic accidents as an example, various ministries in individual governments are usually involved in trying to reduce deaths. Transport and environment ministries influence safety standards on roads and in vehicles, insisting on structural modifications to vehicles, safety barriers on motorways and seatbelts in the front and rear of cars. Health ministries work to improve standards for managing accidents, including ambulance procedures, and developments in surgical and intensive care techniques. The ministry for education influences education in road safety in schools. A similar approach can be taken to suicide.

This chapter sets out some of the methods which can be used at national population level by governments to reduce suicide and discusses the extent to which governments are putting them into practice.

RATIONALE

The World Health Organization has identified suicide as an increasingly important area for public health action, and has issued guidelines to member states in order to develop and implement coordinated comprehensive national and international strategies. In 1989, the World Health Organization recommended that member states should develop national preventive programmes, where possible linked to other public health policies, and establish national coordinating committees. Its approach was based on identification of groups at risk and restricting access to means of suicide (World Health Organization, 1990).

The United Nations has also identified suicide as a major priority. In a report published in 1996 based on a meeting involving 14 countries, it acknowledged that suicide was a global tragedy involving at least a half million victims per year, that there was a significant problem of under-reporting, and that the trend was upward, particularly amongst younger age groups. One consequence of this development has been that in the majority of countries suicide now ranks amongst the top ten causes of death for individuals of all ages and amongst the three leading causes of death for adolescents and young adults (Murray and Lopez, 1996). In some countries, suicide is the leading cause of death for those aged in their late 20s, and in many centres is higher than deaths from motor vehicle accidents. The United Nations report proposed that most cases of suicide are preventable and that a national focus on both the behaviour and its antecedents was called for. It noted that comprehensive national strategies existed in only a few countries and proposed that such national strategies were necessary to achieve change. It also proposed that implementation and evaluation of such strategies require the establishment of a national coordinating body. Importantly, the report advocated the development of a conceptual framework that allowed easy identification of intervention targets. It suggested that one such framework was the traditional public health model of attention to host, environment and agent. "Host" referred to potential suicide victims who could be readily identified, e.g. at-risk populations and suicide attempters. At the environmental level, factors such as social support, homelessness, poverty, unemployment, legal sanctions, community attitudes including stigma, which contributes to increase vulnerability of "host" groups can be targeted. At the "agent" level, the prime methods of intervention are education about suicide and restriction of the means of suicide.

APPROACHES

Our knowledge about suicide allows the construction of a model of the pathway to suicide which helps to identify the different points at which action is possible.

In the traditional model of primary, secondary and tertiary forms of intervention, primary prevention would try to minimize the risks of resorting to self-injury. This would involve adequate and early treatment of all at risk, predominantly those with established mental illness. Secondary prevention would involve appropriate treatment of those who have attempted self-injury by adequate training of all front-line mental health and emergency professionals. Tertiary prevention would be aimed as those who are affected by the death of others, including family, friends and survivors.

An alternative approach is one illustrated in Table 34.1 and Figure 34.1. Here the crescendo to completed suicide is illustrated and the general population strategies that may minimize or ameliorate the progression to the next stage are described. It is this approach which we will take in the remainder of this chapter. This view of intervention is underpinned by the now irrefutable evidence that suicide is only rarely a choice made unclouded by depression or other temporary or more enduring abnormal mental states. Psychological autopsy studies confirm that in nine out of ten cases a diagnosable and potentially treatable mental illness or abnormal mental state was present at the time (see Chapters 2 and 7–9). In addition, the acute disinhibiting effects or more chronic consequences of alcohol or use of other mind-influencing drugs cannot be underestimated—abuse which is also potentially reversible.

Table 34.1 General population strategies in minimizing progress to suicide

Steps in pathway to suicide	Specific actions to prevent suicide
Factors causing depression	Policy on employment, education, social welfare, housing, child abuse, children in care and leaving care, and substance abuse Media guidance, public education School mental health promotion (coping strategies, social support, bullying) Workplace mental health promotion Action on alcohol and drugs Action on physical illness and disability
Depressive illness and other illnesses with depressive thoughts Suicidal ideation Suicidal plans	Support of high-risk groups detection, Professional training about prompt assessment, diagnosis and treatment Good risk management in primary care Building safety into routine assessments Taboo enhancement Good practice guidelines on looking after suicidal people in primary and secondary care
Gaining access to means of suicide	Controlling access to means of suicide
Use of means of suicide	Prompt intervention Good assessment and follow-up of suicide attempters
Aftermath	Audit and learn lessons for prevention Responsible media policy

GOVERNMENT ATTENTION TO SUICIDE REDUCTION

In response to World Health Organization and United Nations endorsement of the role of governments in introducing general population strategies and, independently, because of their concern for their populations, a number of countries have set up processes to develop such strategies. Some have gone so far as to implement some or all of them. As would be expected, reports from different countries share many common themes, as detailed in Table 34.2 (Taylor et al, 1997).

The strategy being implemented in Finland is particularly well developed and is put forward in the United Nations document as a model which could fruitfully be followed by other countries (National Research and Development Centre for Welfare and Health, 1993). It has four stages and commenced with a research project evaluating the 1397 suicides which had occurred in a single year. Target

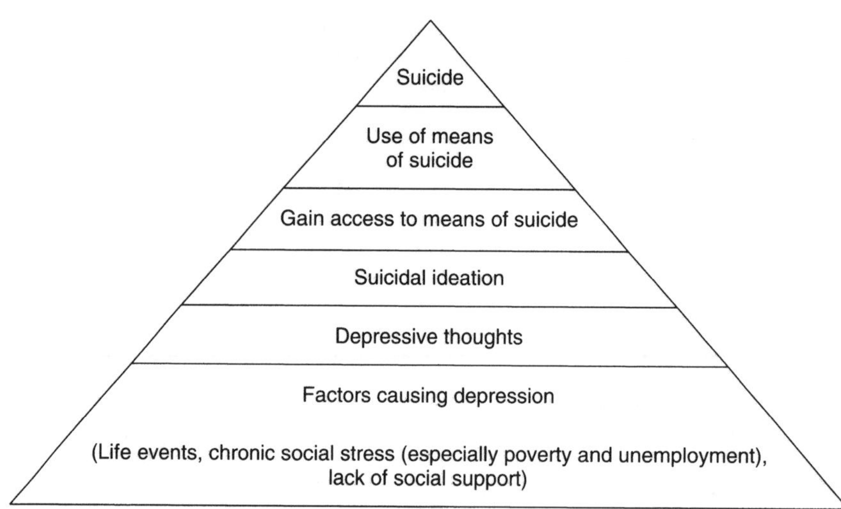

Figure 34.1 Pathway to suicide

Table 34.2 Common themes of intervention

Public education
Responsible media reporting
School-based programmes
Detection and treatment of depression and other mental disorders
Attention to those abusing alcohol and drugs
Attention to those suffering somatic illness
Enhanced access to mental health services
Improvement in assessment of attempted suicide
Postvention
Crisis intervention
Work and unemployment policy
Training of health professionals
Reduced access to lethal methods

areas, interventions and those responsible were identified. Implementation of local sub-projects involved local decision making—incorporating local information about suicide in the area. This merging of overarching policy at a national level with local implementation is a particular strength of the Finnish experiment. The significant decrease in suicide mortality over the present decade in Finland may well be attributable to this strategy (Ohberg and Lönnqvist, 1997).

Other countries, such as England, have used the approach of setting specific targets to be achieved in regard to suicide rates. As part of the Health of the Nation Strategy, two of the three targets specified for mental illness were related to suicide reduction. These were to reduce the overall suicide rates by at least

15% by the year 2000 (from 11.00 per 100,000 population in 1990 to no more than 9.4) and to reduce the suicide rate of severely mentally ill people by at least 33% by the year 2000 (from 15% in 1990 to no more than 10%). The Health of the Nation strategy set out a framework for achieving the targets in *The Health of the Nation Key Area Handbook* (Department of Health, 1994). The target to reduce the overall suicide rate has been reinforced in the new Labour government's strategy, "*Saving Lives: Our Healthier Nation*" (Department of Health, 1999).

Evidence up to this point suggests that such an approach has been successful, as judged by falling rates, but more importantly by the focus that it puts on suicide as a preventable outcome which warrants a national approach. However, the strategy is not, of course, without its critics, who contend that setting such specific, and in their view unrealistic, goals leads to a culture of blame and recrimination if such targets cannot be achieved. Progress so far on overall suicide reduction in England shows striking progress towards the target (see Figure 34.2).

Australia too has taken such an approach. In 1994 the Commonwealth Department of Health committed itself to achieving targets in four areas—cardiovascular health, cancer control, injury control and mental health. One of the two goals specified for mental health was a reduction in the rate of suicide in people with mental disorders. Targets specified were a reduction of 15% in overall

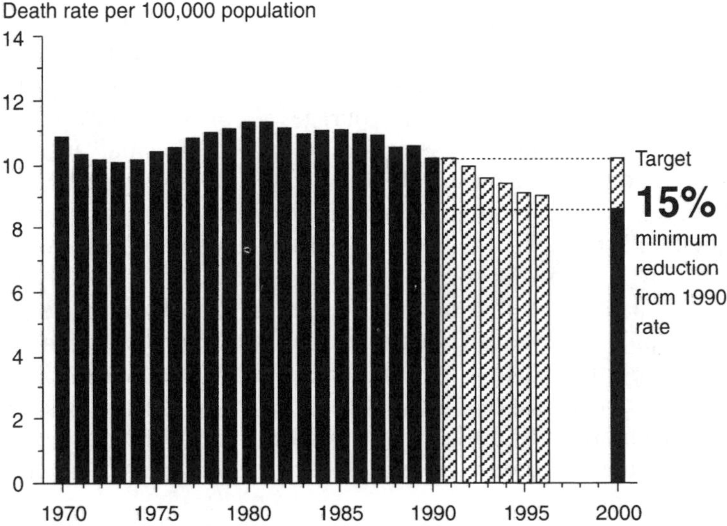

Figure 34.2 Death rates for suicide and undetermined injury, England 1969–1997 and target for the year 2000—all persons. Rates are calculated using the European Standard Population to take account of differences in age structure. Three-year average rates are shown. The rates for 1993 onwards have been re-coded by ONS so that they should be broadly comparable to those for 1992 (and earlier years). Data from the Office for National Statistics (ONS) ICD E950-E959, plus E980-E989, excluding E988.8 (inquest adjoumed)

Australian suicide rates and a 25% reduction in rates of suicide in those with schizophrenia over the next 10 years (Commonwealth of Australia, 1994).

The effect of a government setting targets is several-fold. It influences priorities within the Ministry of Health itself, in terms of time, resources, and emphases. It also influences priorities within and across other government departments. For example, England had a Health of the Nation Cabinet Committee to achieve and support such coordination. However, the effect on the government itself is only a part of the process. It also affects priorities, funding and management emphases within the health service, and influences training, continuing education and clinical management amongst professionals. Thirdly, it influences the shaping of priorities and the contributions made by voluntary bodies, charitable organizations and by business companies shaping their health policies. In other words, it very explicitly sets a framework in which the responsibility for the achievement of the targets does not rest with the individual clinicians alone but with all sectors of the nation.

NATIONAL PREVENTION STRATEGIES

Public Education and the Issue of Stigma

Public education is an important component of all strategies, and necessarily confronts the vexed question of the stigma of suicide as well as the stigma of psychiatric illness. The stigma surrounding psychiatric illness discourages people from seeking and accepting help, limits treatment and support when they need it and reduces the resources available to deliver that help and support. The additional stigma surrounding suicide discourages people from seeking help when they are suicidal, and discourages accurate reporting of actual suicides. It also limits the attention focused on suicide prevention at local, regional and national levels. However, the stigma surrounding suicide also helps reduce the ease with which people will actually contemplate suicide when under duress (Shaffer et al, 1998). Therefore, tackling the stigma of suicide is a complex task that, first, needs to be carefully handled so that suicide is regarded as an appropriate and legitimate area for public preventive action; second, suicidal people feel able to seek and obtain help; but third, they are not encouraged to feel that suicide is a reasonable course of action. It may be best to focus on the general issue of stigma surrounding mental illness, rather than to focus specifically on the stigma of suicide, in case it inadvertently increases the ease with which individuals will contemplate suicide.

National Strategies and Public Education

Public education is incorporated into all existing national strategies. Norway has proposed education programmes on television and radio in order to reduce the stigma of suicide (Retterstol, 1995). In the UK The Royal College of Psychiatrists is running a national campaign to reduce the stigma surrounding mental illness. Also, for several years there was a Government-backed public information strategy in England about mental health, incorporating television and radio programmes and educational materials for distribution to the general public via primary care and health promotion professionals. Australia has also had this as part of its National Mental Health policy. Finland is running a well coordinated public education campaign to enhance people's personal resources and coping abilities, to educate the public about the importance of good parenting and the effects of different parenting styles, and to support activities preparing for retirement.

Public education programmes have also been used to address alcohol misuse and child abuse, bereavement, bullying in schools, and HIV. However, often these programmes are not well integrated with each other, leading to inefficiencies in cost and effectiveness.

School-based Educational Programmes

School-based programmes are of two types—those that aim to promote awareness of suicide and thus promote peer case finding, and those that promote awareness of depression and promote peer support. There is evidence suggesting that promoting awareness of suicides may be counterproductive in that although such programmes succeed in their primary objective of increasing awareness of suicide, they may have the unfortunate consequence of making it more acceptable for youngsters to contemplate suicide. Clearly, if this is the case it could potentially lead to an overall increase rather than decrease in the overall suicide rate in schoolchildren who receive the programme (Shaffer et al, 1998; see Chapter 37). Those that promote awareness of depression seem to work well. Some countries, such as New Zealand, have incorporated these recommendations into guidelines for schools (Ministry of Education (New Zealand) 1997).

PREVENTION, DETECTION AND TREATMENT OF DEPRESSION

The ubiquity of depression in the community and its clear association as a major contributor to suicide makes it a natural focus for general population measures to attempt to reduce its prevalence in the community and its effects on individuals. It is no surprise, therefore, that the most advanced of community education programmes have been developed in the area of depression. With the aim of raising community awareness of the disorder, its consequences and its treatability, depression awareness projects are now conducted in the USA, Canada, the UK and Australia.

In the USA the first campaign was initiated by the National Institute of Mental Health in 1986. Whilst it was initially aimed at mental health professionals and primary care practitioners, it was then broadened to a more community focus, using a media campaign supplemented by partnerships with other community organizations to drive the message home. Since 1991 a national depression screening day has been held in both the USA and Canada in October as part of Mental Health Awareness Week (Jacobs, 1995). The campaign has been strongly supported by the Eli Lilly Foundation, the pharmaceutical company which manufactures fluoxetine (Prozac), an association which has not been lost on the critics of the campaign, whose main concern is the "medicalization and pathologization of everyday life". The Canadian effort has taken a similar form and received similar pharmaceutical support.

In the UK the depression awareness project has been led by the Royal College of Psychiatrists in collaboration with the Royal College of General Practitioners. The campaign was supported by a variety of organizations, including the Department of Health, business companies and pharmaceutical companies. One of the outcomes of the project has been a 13% reduction in the number of people who think antidepressants are addictive (Priest et al, 1995). The campaign in the UK was aimed at changing attitudes, primarily of the profession but also of the community, that medical intervention for depression was appropriate, necessary and effective (Priest et al, 1995). A key component of the strategy was the development of guidelines for the management of depression in general practice, where the majority of such cases are seen. The two colleges produced a consensus statement on good practice guidelines, and an evaluation of the effect of training using these guidelines on the behaviour of general practitioners is currently under way (Paykel et al, 1992).

The outcome of these campaigns appears to be some modification in community and professional attitudes in the direction sought. Whether this change translates into greater recognition and more effective treatment has yet to be conclusively shown, and the same applies to evidence that these changes have an impact on the suicide rate. Given the evidence from both the UK and Australia, which has recently become available, on the extent of public illiteracy about mental illness and their prevailing lack of knowledge of the availability of effective treatments, even in a well-educated society (Jorm et al, 1997), such approaches would appear to be both logical and potentially beneficial.

IMPROVEMENT OF ACCESS TO MENTAL HEALTH SERVICES

The moulding of a purely asylum-based mental health service into a responsive, locally accessible, community-based service is a transition being undertaken in a number of countries. Measures to provide early intervention and improve the support and supervision of patients, with severe mental illness in the community are key components of such a strategy. Increased freedom for psychiatric patients, with consequent increased access to drugs and alcohol and to the means of suicide, without assertive outreach and case management in the community might otherwise have the potential for increasing suicide rates. In the UK, innovations have been put in place in response to growing disquiet about the success of community care. One of these is the Care Programme Approach, which is a good practice framework comprising four elements:

1. A health and social care needs assessment.
2. A care plan to meet those health and social needs.
3. Regular review as appropriate.
4. The concept of the key worker, who is the main point of contact for the patient and family.

Another innovation is the development of effective information systems to "track" patients as they move through different components of the service.

Equally important are clear channels of communication between accident and emergency departments, where the majority of people who commit "deliberate self-harm" are assessed, and specialist mental health teams who need to carry out the follow-up. Similarly, the periods of transition of patients between services or between primary care and specialist services have been identified as times when patients are at particular risk of suicidal behaviour, since they may be overlooked by both services at these times. In some countries, such as Australia, the establishment of National Mental Health Policies and Plans have raised the profile of the mental health services and forced confrontation with these challenging issues in service development for a new era of care.

IMPROVED ASSESSMENT OF DELIBERATE SELF-HARM

One of the trends in suicide research in the past few decades is understanding that the previous dichotomy drawn between suicide and deliberate self-harm is false and that considerable overlap exists between the two populations. In addition, there is increasing awareness of the high prevalence of a range of deliberate self-harm and risk-taking behaviours other than overdose, particularly by young people. These are coming to be seen as precursors to formal suicide attempts. Surprising figures have also emerged as to the extent of suicidal ideation in this group (see Chapter 16). (The peak incidence of these behaviours and experiences in the 15–24 year age group is mirrored by the increasing rate of suicide in this age group in recent years in many developed countries.) Such young people must be considered a high-risk group and in addition to general measures aimed at mental health promotion may well require targeting for more specific intervention. Rather than the brief crisis counselling that follows a first attempt, more sustained involvement, either with individuals or groups of patients, may be necessary, particularly in light of the fact that the risk for repeat attempts is as high as 33% and that the risk of completed suicide is increased

100-fold in the 12 months following a suicide attempt (see Chapter 21). It is therefore essential to improve assessment and follow-up of attempted suicide patients. A number of countries now provide explicit guidelines for the management of self-harm in accident and emergency departments (e.g. Royal College of Psychiatrists, 1994).

SUPPORT TO HIGH-RISK GROUPS

Occupation

General population approaches need to be complemented by specific interventions with both non-malleable characteristics, such as age and sex, as well as those that are malleable to a greater or lesser extent. The workplace is a particular setting in which general suicide prevention methods may be helpful—such as reduction in stress in working environments, restrictions on hours of work and minimizing shift work. Some occupational groups appear to be particularly at risk. Data from the UK, for example, in the period 1979–1990, showed the highest rates for males in "medical" professional groups (veterinary surgeons, pharmacists, dentists and doctors) and farmers. The easy access to means of suicide may be a factor in all these groups—health professionals to drugs and farmers to firearms, although other factors such as stressful occupations, a strong culture of having to cope, an unwillingness to seek help and familiarity with death and dying could also be operating (Charlton et al, 1993).

In the UK in the 1990s, ministers met with the leaders of the above occupational groups to discuss ways in which better support systems might be developed to reduce suicide rates in these occupations. The Samaritans, the Citizens' Advice Bureau and the National Farmers' Union combined forces to provide support to farmers and ran a leaflet campaign partly funded by the Department of Health. The Department of Health also set up, at the request of the Royal College of Practitioners, a fellowship to examine ways of reducing stress for general practitioners.

REDUCTION OF DISINHIBITING AND FACILITATING FACTORS SUCH AS ALCOHOL

The relationship between alcohol and other drug misuse and suicide is well established (see Chapter 9). They share similar risk factors and a high proportion of those who commit suicide are alcoholics. Alcohol may also be used frequently both immediately before and during suicide attempts and may make successful suicide more likely. It might be expected, then, that efforts to reduce alcohol consumption in a population, which are known to have an effect on the prevalence of alcohol abuse in populations (the Lederer effect), might also influence suicide rates in a favourable way. Finland has incorporated clear recommendations for restricting alcohol abuse as part of its suicide prevention strategy.

Interesting data supporting this approach have come from a study of changes in suicide rates in the former USSR. Rates fell in all 15 Republics of the USSR during the period 1984–1990. Some authors have contended that this was due to a strict anti-alcohol policy implemented by President Gorbachev as part of *Perestroika*. This policy included strict limitation of alcohol sales and punishment for over-imbibing. The rate of violent deaths, including suicide, fell, as did death from alcohol poisoning. However, as with other prohibition eras in other countries, home distillation of alcohol has increased (Värnik, 1998).

THE ROLE OF THE MEDIA

It is self-evident that in considering general population strategies for suicide reduction the role of the media is critical, in terms of both its potential to influence reduction in the rate or to increase it (see Chapter 39). High rates of literacy and ownership of television and radio in developed countries, as well as the growth and penetration of the media to all levels of society throughout the world, increase its potency as a vehicle for communication within and between societies. The role of the media in contributing to copycat suicides and suicide clustering appears clear in relation to suicidal behaviour amongst young people (see Chapter 37) but nebulous in regard to adults. Hassan (1995) and others have provided evidence that media presentation of youth suicide in newspapers or in musical products have led to measurable increases in suicidal behaviour. Some studies have noted that the presentation of a particular means of suicide in the media can lead to an increase in suicide by that method (Schmidtke and Häfner, 1988; see Chapter 39). A focus on the hopelessness of the young person's situation, failure to indicate that accessible and non-stigmatizing help is available, and covert and sometimes overt endorsement of the behaviours as attractive and acceptable appear to increase the effect of contagion.

Most responsible groups, such as the Centers for Disease Control (1992) and the United Nations (1996), support the development and acceptance by the media of responsible codes of conduct for media reporting and programme content as a potentially valuable approach to reducing the likelihood of "copycat" suicidal behaviour. These include avoiding glamourizing the victim, and avoiding giving details of the method employed, as well as providing comments by youth workers that help is available and depression is treatable. More generally, the media can play an important role in promoting positive self-image for both young men and women, and in influencing youth culture. They may even go so far as to advocate for primary prevention programmes and spread information about available support. Whilst such means may be helpful, it is impossible to deny that widespread information as to the means of suicide continue to proliferate, particularly on the Internet, where it appears to be immune to "censorship".

AUDIT OF SUICIDES TO LEARN THE LESSONS FOR PREVENTION

Many clinicians have always audited suicides of patients in their care as simple good practice in order to learn the lessons for prevention. Researchers in Finland conducted a detailed psychological autopsy study of every suicide in the country in 1986, and the data has provided a wealth of material with which to inform Finland's prevention strategy.

In the UK, a confidential inquiry has been established by the Royal College of Psychiatrists, funded by the Department of Health. This has followed the format of other confidential inquiries in the UK (e.g. into surgical deaths and obstetric deaths). The Confidential Inquiry into Suicide is now run from Manchester University, and has extended its coverage to include all suicides. It has produced a series of helpful reports. The perceived low risk that professionals had assigned to many patients with mental illness who subsequently completed suicide has been highlighted, as has the fact that many patients who died were non-compliant with treatment (Appleby et al, 1999). It is important that individual local suicide audits are seen as helpful and supportive to a service seeking to reduce suicide rates and do not simply become vehicles of assigning blame or finding scapegoats, which will simply demoralize a service rather than supporting it to achieve better practice.

CHANGING AVAILABILITY OF MEANS

One area of activity in which there is a consensus that government may have a role in a population-based approach is through developing policy on the means of suicide. Governments have to a greater or lesser degree accepted a responsibility to minimize or lower the risk of morbidity and mortality associated with the introduction of new technologies or products which may have a detrimental impact on their citizens. The introduction of the motorcar has been an enormous boon to civilization, but with its increasing use came increasing accidents, leading to an increasing incidence of brain damage and death. As these trends became apparent, governments moved first to educate, and eventually to legislate to reduce the possibility of these consequences (e.g. speed restrictions, introduction of seatbelts and drink–driving legislation). Whilst the details of such legislation may vary across countries (e.g. levels of blood alcohol considered unsafe for safe driving), its introduction has nonetheless reduced the toll of road traffic fatalities dramatically by highlighting to the community the seriousness with which government regards the issue.

The United Nations guidelines for the formulation of national strategies contains a series of recommendations developed in Finland, including emphasis on changing the availability of means of suicide. Recommendation 4 states: "Discussion, supervision and restriction are necessary to ensure that typical instruments of suicide are not easily accessible, especially to those at risk". It then specifies guns, prescription and non-prescription drugs with toxic properties, physical defects in health care units, and car exhaust gas, as worthy of particular attention. To this list might be added the availability of pesticides toxic to humans, particularly in the developing world.

Rationale

The reasons for a concerted population-based approach to means of suicide is based on the existence at the time of the suicidal act of a strong, sometimes overwhelming and irresistable, wish for escape from life. Shneidman (1985) put it as follows, "Given that the omnipresent action in committed suicide is to leave the scene (egression) then it follows that where possible the means of exit should be blocked". A practical application of this view is to "get the gun" in a suicidal situation where it is known that the individual intends to shoot himself and has a weapon. Such a course of action would only be logical if the urge to commit suicidal acts varied in intensity in individuals over time and in different circumstances. This is known to be the case.

Psychological autopsy studies of those who have completed suicide and intensive study of those "near misses" who have made determined efforts to end their lives but survived reveal, almost uniformly, that urges to commit suicide fluctuate considerably in intensity and almost always exist at the same time as urges to continue living. Even in those who make long-term plans and preparations to attempt suicide, the eventual action often occurs impulsively and in the presence of the means. If, therefore, availability of the means were reduced at those critical moments, the potential lethality of the act could be influenced. It would follow that whatever can be done to make the means of suicide less accessible when individuals are in what might be described as a suicidal state of mind should achieve reduction in the suicide rate (Heim and Lester, 1991). The reduction in suicide rates that followed the substitution of North Sea gas for coal gas provides persuasive support for such an approach (Kreitman, 1976).

While some have suggested that when one means is removed another will take its place, this has been disputed by experts such as Kreitman. In any case, if such a shift occurs, it does so over time and may not necessarily be of relevance to a particular individual taking his/her life. We shall examine each of the means in greater detail.

Guns

The issue of firearms legislation to minimize both homicide and suicide is contentious around the world. While it is recognized that death by firearms is the most common means of suicide by men in many countries, attempts to impose firearms legislation are determined by broader political social and cultural attitudes to the rights of individuals to "bear arms" for self-protection. It is a fact that suicide rates are higher in countries where legislation controlling fire-arms availability is lax (Lester and Murrell, 1980). In all countries, however, there should be careful scrutiny of applications for licences, and in any event information on the safe storage of guns and ammunition at home to minimize access by the young and intoxicated individuals. This is particularly so in rural settings, where the use and acceptability of firearms is more common.

Prescription Medication with Toxic Properties

This is an area of suicide prevention in which the pendulum is swinging between education of those who prescribe and the public, through self-directed attempts by pharmaceutical manufacturers, and prescribers and dispensers to reduce access to unrestricted quantities of these medications, and government regulation to achieve the same ends. A case in point is the response of the manufacturers and the medical profession to the epidemiological data demonstrating high rates of successful suicide utilizing tricyclic antidepressants. Guidelines were produced by the medical profession alerting doctors to the toxicity of these drugs and the need to reduce supplies to patients. Manufacturers responded by packaging the drugs in individual blister packets to decrease the possibility of an individual opening large amounts easily.

In Australia, restrictive legislation on the availability of barbiturates was associated with a temporary decline in the method-specific and total suicide rates (Oliver and Hetzel, 1973).

The situation in regard to over-the-counter medication, such as paracetamol, which has been available in the United Kingdom in unrestricted quantities, is more complex. Paracetamol is highly toxic above a certain threshold dose and is a fairly common cause of successful suicide, particularly in women (Gunnell et al, 1997). As a result, the UK Government recently introduced legislation to restrict the number of tablets that can be sold to individual customers.

Environmental Toxins

Two common but differing causes of suicide in the developed and developing world are car exhaust fumes (carbon monoxide) and pesticides, respectively. They both provide opportunities for population-based approaches.

Suicide by inhaling car exhaust fumes has been a common means for many years. In response to this information, manufacturers are making attempts to modify exhaust outlets to make it more difficult to attach hoses to these outlets. In addition, as a result of changes in technology, catalytic converters have been incorporated into petrol- and diesel-powered engines which have reduced the toxicity of the exhaust gas. Although this intervention was incorporated to reduce the overall toxicity of car fumes for the environment, its introduction has influenced the suicide rate by this means (Tarbuck and O'Brien, 1992). In the developing world, the use of pesticides is ubiquitous to improve agricultural productivity and enable countries to provide for their essential food needs. It has been estimated that two million cases a year are hospitalized following suicide attempts utilizing these agents, most commonly organophosphates and paraquat (Meredith, 1993).

These cases occur predominantly in rural communities and in many instances comprise the majority of suicides in the counties involved. Although less toxic alternatives may be available, these compounds are more expensive and less effective, so debate continues to rage about the economics of substitution. Reticence to provide substitutes is a characteristic of the multinational chemical companies who manufacture these agents, as is the reluctance of farmers to buy more expensive agents. In many countries a stand-off has thus occurred between the wish of a Ministry of Health to restrict availability and the economic needs of the country for adequate food production. It is, of course, possible that the increasing demand for organic food production may eventually contribute to the solution of the problem. The Finnish example of restrictions on the use of parathion dramatically changing its use as an agent for suicide (although the effect on the total suicide rate was modest) may encourage both groups involved in this debate (Ohberg et al, 1995).

CONCLUSIONS

The role of general population strategies to affect reduction of suicide has considerable face validity and there is some evidence to support their efficacy, particularly in regard to availability of means. Whilst it might be considered a government role to set the policy for the general population strategies and evaluate their effectiveness, with or without the explicit step of setting targets, it is up to multiple other agencies and organizations in the community to implement the programmes. These include other government departments, local authorities, the professions, the media, employers, educational institutions and religious and voluntary organizations, to name but a few.

Research has provided the basis for some coherent strategies but such work as has been done is often fragmentary and isolated and provides only part of the picture. Generic strategies, as has been suggested in this chapter, can and should be implemented but need to be enriched by local knowledge and data. The process and methods of implementation need to be culturally appropriate and sensitive, and targeted to the level of understanding of those to whom the messages are directed. This is as important within a society as between societies.

The potential for reducing suicide rates or preventing their increase is considerable. There is now much more attention to this area of human behaviour than was ever the case. The debate is moving from a pessimistic acceptance of the inevitability of suicide to what can be done at a national level. The endorsement by both the World Health Organization and the United Nations of the framing of national strategies has put particular onus on governments to respond in an area of health in which they traditionally have had little interest. Although progress across the world in development of such policies is uneven, there is now virtually no country which is not mounting some effort, however limited. This is a substantial change in the past two decades and augurs well for continuing progress in trying to prevent one of the most tragic events in the life of a family and a community.

REFERENCES

Appleby, L., Shaw, J. and Amos, T. (1997) National Confidential Inquiry into Suicide and Homicide by People with Mental Illness. British Journal of Psychiatry, 170: 181–182.

Appleby, L., Shaw, J., Amos, T., McDonnell, R., Harris, C., McCann, K., Kiernan, K., Davies, S., Bickley, H. and Parsons, R. (1999) Suicide within 12 months of contact with mental health services: national clinical survey. British Medical Journal, 318: 1235–1239.

Caplan, G. (1964) Principles of Preventive Psychiatry. New York: Basic Books.

Charlton, J., Kelly, S., Dunnel, K., Evans, B. and Jenkins, R. (1993) Suicide deaths in England and Wales: Part 2. Trends in factors associated with suicide. Population Trends, 71: 34–42.

Commonwealth of Australia (1994) Better Health Outcomes for Australians—National Goals, Targets and Strategies for Better Health Outcomes into the Next Century. Canberra: Commonwealth of Australia.

Centers for Disease Control (1992) Youth Suicide Prevention Program: A Resource Guide. Atlanta, GA: Center for Disease Control.

Department of Health (1994) Health of the Nation Key Area Handbook. London: The Stationery Office.

Department of Health (1999) Saving Lives: Our Healthier Nation: A Contract for Health. Cm4386. London: The Stationery Office.

Department of Health and Children (1998) Report of the National Task Force on Suicide. Dublin: The Stationery Office.

Durkheim, E. (1952) Suicide. London: Routledge and Kegan Paul.

Gunnell, D., Hawton, K., Murray, V., Garner, R., Bismuth, C., Fagg, J. and Simkin, S. (1997) Use of paracetamol for suicide and non-fatal poisoning in the UK and France: are restrictions on availability justified? Journal of Epidemiology and Community Health, 51: 175–179.

Hassan, R. (1995) Suicide Explained: The Australian Experience. Melbourne: Melbourne University Press.

Heim, N. and Lester, D. (1991) Factors affecting choice of method for suicide. European Journal of Psychiatry, 5: 161–165.

Jacobs, D.G. (1995) National Depression Screening Day: Educating the public, reaching those in need of treatment and broadening professional understanding. Harvard Review of Psychiatry, 3: 156–159.

Jorm, A.F., Korten, A.E., Jacomb, P.A., Christensen, H., Rodgers, B. and Pollitt, P. (1997) Mental health literacy. Medical Journal of Australia, 166: 182–186.

Kreitman, N. (1976) The coal gas story. UK suicide rates 1960–71. British Journal of Preventative and Social Medicine, 30: 86–93.

Ministry of Education (New Zealand) (1997) The prevention, recognition and management of young people and risk of suicide—development of guidelines for schools. New Zealand: National Health Committee.

Lester, D. and Murrel, M.E. (1980) The influence of gun control laws on suicidal behaviour. American Journal of Psychiatry, 137: 121–122.

Meredith, T.J. (1993) Epidemiology of poisoning. Pharmacology and Therapeutics, 59: 351–356.

Murray, C. and Lopez, A. (1996) The Global Burden of Disease. USA: World Bank and Oxford University Press.
The National Council for Suicide Prevention (1996) Support in Suicidal Crises. Stockholm: National Board of Health and Welfare.
National Research and Development Centre for Welfare and Health (1993) Suicide can be prevented: a target and action plan for suicide prevention. Helsinki: Painatuskoskus Oy.
Ohberg, A. and Lönnqvist, J. (1997) Suicide trends in Finland 1980–1995. Psychiatria Fennica, 28: 11–23.
Ohberg, A., Lönnqvist, J., Sarna, S., Vuori, E. and Pentila, A. (1995) Trends and availability of suicide methods in Finland: proposals for restrictive measures. British Journal of Psychiatry, 166: 35–43.
Oliver, R.G. and Hetzel, B.S. (1973) An analysis of recent trends in suicide rates in Australia. International Journal of Epidemiology, 3: 91–101.
Paykel, E.S. and Priest, R.G. (1992) Recognition and management of depression among general practitioners: a consensus statement. British Medical Journal, 305: 1198–1202.
Priest, R.G., Paykel, E.S., Hart, D., Baldwin, D.S., Roberts, A. and Vize, C. (1995) Progress in defeating depression. Psychiatric Bulletin, 19: 491–495.
Retterstol, N. (1995) National Plan for Suicide Prevention in Norway. Italian Journal of Suicidology, 5: 19–24.
Royal College of Psychiatrists (1994) The General Hospital Management of Adult Deliberate Self-harm. Council Report No 32. London: Royal College of Psychiatrists.
Schmidke, A. and Häfner, H. (1988) The Werther effect after television films: new evidence for an old hypothesis. Psychological Medicine, 18: 665–676.
Shaffer, D., Garland, A., Gould, M., Fisher, P. and Trautman, P. (1988) Preventing teenage suicide—a critical review. Journal of the American Academy of Child and Adolescent Psychiatry, 27: 675–687.
Shneidman, E.S. (1985) Definition of Suicide. Chichester: Wiley.
Tarbruck, A.F. and O'Brien, J.T. (1992) Suicide and vehicle exhaust and emissions. British Medical Journal, 304: 1374.
Taylor, S.J., Kingdon, D. and Jenkins, R. (1997) How are nations trying to prevent suicide? An analysis of national suicide prevention strategies. Acta Psychiatrica Scandinavica, 95: 457–463.
United Nations (1996) Prevention of Suicide Guidelines for the Formulation and Implementation of National Strategies. New York: United Nations.
Värnik, A. (1998) Suicide in the former republics of the USSR. Psychiatria Fennica, 29: 150–162.
World Health Organization (1990) Consultation on Strategies for Reducing Suicidal Behaviour in the European Region. Summary Report. Geneva: World Health Organization.

Chapter 35

Prevention of Suicide in Psychiatric Patients

Louis Appleby
School of Psychiatry and Behavioural Sciences, University of Manchester, Withington Hospital, Manchester, UK

Abstract

Approximately half of all suicides have had contact with psychiatric services at some time, around one-quarter in the year before death. This chapter deals with suicide prevention in psychiatric patients and considers the possible benefits of three approaches: population strategies, reduced access to means of suicide and, in particular, the activities of mental health services. Population measures, e.g. to reduce unemployment or substance misuse, are an important component of a broad suicide prevention strategy. However, there is a risk that people with severe mental illness would benefit less than other groups and specific initiatives for the mentally ill might be required. Reducing access to, or lethality of, important means of suicide can reduce suicide by these methods and, in some cases, overall suicide rates. The principal methods of suicide in patient populations are hanging and overdose with psychotropic drugs. The use of drugs which are less toxic in overdose and a restriction on the duration of prescriptions available to people at high risk would be beneficial. If mental health services are to improve suicide prevention, three steps are essential. First, high-risk groups of patients, identified by key risk factors, should be the main target of preventive measures. Second, services should increase the intensity of their activities at high-risk periods such as the first 3 months following hospital discharge. Third, specific aspects of services which would be expected to reduce risk should be strengthened—these include good risk assessment based on training, and measures to improve compliance.

INTRODUCTION

Suicide is strongly associated with mental disorder. Estimates of risk in major psychiatric disorders such as schizophrenia or severe depression suggest a 5–15-

The International Handbook of Suicide and Attempted Suicide. Edited by K. Hawton and K. van Heeringen.

fold increase in comparison to the general population and risk of the same order has also been found in alcohol dependence and personality disorder (Pokorny, 1966; Allebeck and Wistedt, 1986; Harris and Barraclough, 1997: see Chapters 9 and 10). In a recent meta-analysis (Harris and Barraclough, 1997), the highest risks, increased over 20-fold, were calculated for anorexia nervosa, affective disorder and substance misuse, but risk was high in all disorders with the exception of dementia and learning disability. Conversely, studies of suicide victims have reported evidence of mental disorder in most cases (Barraclough et al, 1974; Foster et al, 1997).

However, many people who die by suicide are not current psychiatric patients. Most studies of contact with mental health services have found the rate of lifetime contact with specialist services to be of the order of 50% (King and Barraclough, 1990), while in a large English sample, contact with mental health services in the year before death was found in 24% (Appleby et al, 1999). Even this figure includes those who have lost contact with services by the time of death and those whose contact has been brief. This chapter is concerned with suicide prevention in current and recent psychiatric patients, i.e. those individuals who suffer from mental disorder and are under the care of mental health services. Suicide prevention in other settings is addressed in other chapters.

There has been no intervention study in people with mental illness in which suicide has been the primary outcome, largely because such a study would require a prohibitively large subject sample, even if it were to focus on patients at high risk. Consequently, most of what is known about suicide prevention in psychiatric patients is based on observational studies in which the characteristics of suicides have been examined. This chapter discusses whether three approaches to the prevention of suicide would benefit the mentally ill. The three approaches are: (a) population strategies; (b) reducing access to lethal means; and (c) clinical strategies. Most emphasis is placed on the third of these, i.e. how the evidence on suicide by people with mental illness can be used to improve suicide prevention by mental health services.

POPULATION STRATEGIES

Population strategies for suicide prevention are described in Chapter 34. They are based on the strong association between population suicide rates and certain social and behavioural characteristics of the population as a whole. These characteristics tend to be indicators of social adversity, such as unemployment, or "risk behaviours", such as alcohol or substance misuse. Reducing the prevalence of such risk factors is expected to reduce the outcome, suicide, with which they are linked.

To what extent could such an approach reduce suicide among psychiatric patients? This depends on three factors: the effectiveness of population-based intervention strategies in general, whether the targeted population risk factors are also linked to suicide in the mentally ill, and whether any reduction in the population rate of a targeted risk factor would also occur in the mentally ill.

The evidence on the effectiveness of population or public health interventions remains unclear despite the obvious potential of this approach (Lewis et al, 1997). For example, up to 10% of suicides may be related to unemployment and measures to improve employment and other social circumstances could be expected to reduce suicide rates. However, such changes are probably beyond the scope of a health strategy. Similarly, health education or promotion initiatives directed at consumption of alcohol or drugs, although of great potential impact, are so far of uncertain benefit (Gunnell and Frankel, 1994). The Defeat Depression campaign in the UK, a broadly-based public health initiative to improve public and professional awareness of depression and so reduce untreated depression, is currently under evaluation (Paykel et al, 1997).

It is also uncertain to what extent the rate of suicide in the mentally ill is related to rates of population risk factors. The individual characteristics of general population suicides, which broadly reflect ecological risk factors such as unemployment or substance misuse, tend also to be found in mentally ill suicides. Most studies report high rates of unemployment, living alone and alcohol misuse in samples of suicides in general (Barraclough et al, 1974; Heikkinen et al, 1995) and among patient populations (Allebeck et al, 1987; Roy, 1982a). However, there is also evidence that social risk factors are less predictive of suicide in the mentally ill, in whom clinical factors such as features of mental state and previous self-harm may be more important (Dennehy et al, 1996).

Assuming that population strategies could be effective and that the risk factors they address are related to suicide in the mentally ill, it is still possible that any impact on suicide by psychiatric patients would be less than that achieved for the population as a whole, because social adversity affects the mentally ill disproportionately. Reducing overall unemployment rates, for example, is likely to give greatest benefit to the most easily employed people, and specific initiatives would be required to provide jobs for the mentally ill.

ACCESS TO LETHAL MEANS

There is good evidence that the use of a particular method of suicide is related to its availability (Farmer and Rohde, 1980; Marzuk et al, 1992); e.g. there is a high rate of suicide by jumping from buildings in Hong Kong (Yip, 1997), while the use of firearms by suicides across the USA is proportionate to rates of gun ownership (Kaplan and Geling, 1998). There is also evidence that reducing the availability of a particular method can reduce its use. For example, a fall in suicide by barbiturate overdose was observed in Sweden after prescription of this class of drug was restricted (Carlston et al, 1996); the introduction of legal restrictions on gun ownership in the UK has been followed by a fall in suicides by farmers (Hawton et al, 1998). It is less clear, however, that overall rates of suicide can be reliably lowered by restricting the availability or the lethality of individual methods, because of substitution of other methods, although there are studies in which this has been clearly demonstrated (Kreitman, 1976; Marzuk et al, 1992).

If restricted availability of lethal means were to be used to prevent suicide in psychiatric patients, the most important methods to target would differ from those for the general population, because the frequencies with which certain methods are used by people with mental illness differ in three main ways. Firstly, there is a lower rate of self-asphyxiation with car exhaust fumes. This method is one of the most commonly used in the UK and some other developed countries, where it is particularly associated with young men (McClure, 1984; Department of Health, 1992). As a result, detoxification of car exhaust emissions may have contributed to a fall in UK suicide rates in the early 1990s (Kelly and Bunting, 1998) in a way analogous to the effect of switching to natural gas in British homes three decades ago (Kreitman, 1976). But in England the proportion of suicides among current and recent psychiatric patients that result from car exhaust poisoning is 11% (Appleby et al, 1997), compared to a general population figure of 19% (Office for National Statistics, 1997), presumably the result, at least in part, of lower rates of car ownership among the mentally ill.

Secondly, there is greater use of violent methods such as hanging or jumping from a height (Appleby, 1992). Thirdly, overdoses are most likely to be of psychotropic drugs; only 3% of suicides (13% of fatal overdoses) by psychiatric patients involve paracetamol (Appleby et al, 1997), the method which, in the UK for example, has most attracted preventive measures in the form of restricted over-the-counter sales.

The methods of suicide employed by psychiatric patients are shown in Figure 35.1 (Appleby et al, 1999). Of the main methods listed, overdose with psy-

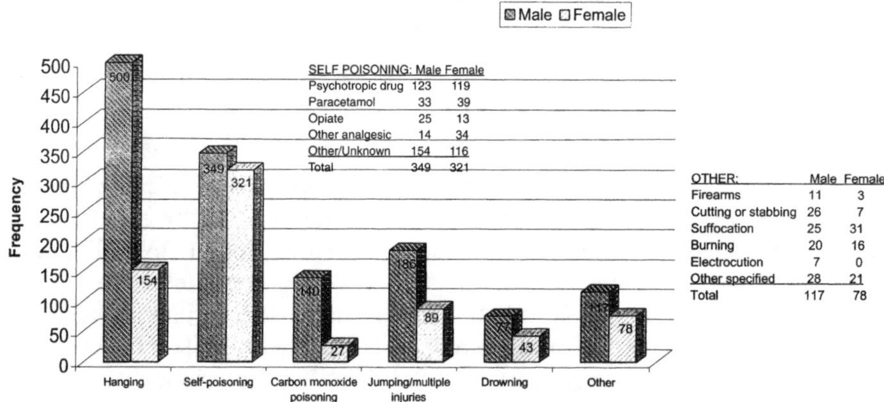

Figure 35.1 Cause of death and gender in a 2-year UK national sample of suicides in contact with mental health services in the previous year. Reproduced by permission from Appleby et al (1999)

chotropic drugs appears the one most open to restrictions on availability. The possible approaches are to reduce either the toxicity of the drugs or the quantity that a patient can easily obtain.

In the case of antidepressant drugs, toxicity varies widely from the older tricyclic compounds to the newer neurotransmitter re-uptake inhibitors (e.g. selective setotonin re-uptake inhibitors—SSRIs). The number of fatal overdoses per million prescriptions has been found to be highest for tricyclic drugs, and the majority of deaths from antidepressant overdose are due to amitriptyline and dothiepin, tricyclic compounds which are known to cause ECG abnormalities and arrhythmias (Henry et al, 1995). However, these calculations of deaths per million prescriptions do not take account of prescription practice; the most depressed patients, those who are most likely to commit suicide, may be prescribed the older, more familiar drugs because their doctors feel more confident that these will be effective. In fact, there is little evidence that any of the main types of antidepressant is more effective than the others, with the possible exception of clomipramine (Cowen, 1996), so that the choice of antidepressant should be made according to other criteria, such as cost (which favours tricyclics), compliance, side-effects and safety (all of which favour SSRIs and similar drugs) (Anderson and Tomenson, 1995; Henry et al, 1995). In psychiatric practice, therefore, it makes clinical sense to balance these criteria and prescribe SSRIs rather than tricyclics for patients at high risk. Whichever class of drug is used, it should be possible to dispense small quantities frequently rather than single long-term supplies.

The same principles apply to the use of other psychotropic drugs such as antipsychotic agents. The more cardiotoxic compounds, such as chlorpromazine and thioridazine, should not be prescribed to patients at high risk, for whom drugs such as haloperidol, trifluoperazine and the "atypical" drugs are safer (Royal College of Psychiatrists Psychotherapy Subgroup, 1997). With both antipsychotic drugs and mood-stabilizing agents, short-term prescriptions are preferable, particularly for people at risk. How these at risk patients might be identified is dealt with in the next section.

Most of the other suicide methods among psychiatric patients are not readily open to specific interventions designed to reduce availability or lethality, except when they are used by inpatients. Hanging is the method of suicide in 25% of suicides in the whole population, 31% of suicides by current and recent patients, and around 40% of inpatients (Appleby et al, 1997; Proulx et al, 1997). Although only one-third of inpatient suicides occur on the ward itself—the others occur in patients who are off the ward, with or without leave—over 50% of ward suicides are by hanging. To reduce inpatient suicides it is vital, therefore, to use specific measures to reduce access to the means of hanging, such as collapsible curtain rails. Similarly, ward design and location should make it difficult for suicidal patients to jump from a height or in front of a moving vehicle. Wards should, where possible, be on the ground or first floor, staircases should not have open balconies, and windows should open to only a limited degree (Farberow et al, 1971). Wards should not be located next to a railway line or fast road; if they are, barriers should be erected at likely (or previous) points of access (Langley and Bayatti, 1984). Regular review of such physical features of ward structure and location should be undertaken (Farberow et al, 1971).

CLINICAL SERVICES

The absence of evidence on the clinical effectiveness of any service intervention in preventing suicide has led some commentators to doubt the importance of clinical measures.

However, the results of observational studies suggest that suicide might be prevented in mental health services by addressing the following questions:

- Who is at risk?
- When are they at risk?
- Which aspects of services are associated with higher or lower risk?

Which Psychiatric Patients Are at Risk?

Recognition of the highest risk groups would allow services to target their preventive strategies. The majority of suicides in psychiatric patients have a primary diagnosis of major affective disorder, schizophrenia, alcohol dependence or misuse or personality disorder (Appleby et al, 1997). Overall, however, diagnosis itself is of limited value in identifying a suitable target group because the main high-risk conditions embrace a large proportion of people under mental health care. Further characteristics of high risk are required to refine the priority patient group.

Additional risk is conferred by co-morbidity (Henriksson et al, 1993; Lesage et al, 1994; Beautrais et al, 1996). Usually this refers to a secondary "behavioural" diagnosis, such as alcohol or substance misuse or personality disorder (Berglund, 1984; Cheng, 1995; Isometsä et al, 1996) occurring with a primary diagnosis of major mental illness, but it also includes patients with schizophrenia who have a concurrent affective disorder or a history of one (Roy, 1982b; Cohen et al, 1990; Heila et al, 1997). Increased risk is also indicated by features of clinical history, such as previous self-harm and frequent relapse or admission. Recent or current clinical characteristics that increase risk are low mood, suicidal ideas or self-harm, and hopelessness (Roy, 1982a; Cheng, 1995; Dennehy et al, 1996; Beck et al, 1985). Some indicators of risk may be diagnosis-specific, e.g. insomnia in depressive illness (Fawcett et al, 1990)

The difficulty in planning preventive services based on risk factors is their low specificity. For example, although previous self-harm is strongly associated with suicide, the majority of patients who harm themselves do not commit suicide. This means that targeting suicide prevention measures on patients with a history of self-harm could be seen as wasteful of resources. One of the priorities for research is therefore to improve prediction of suicide, and one way of achieving this is by understanding how risk factors interact. Services may also have to accept the need to intensify their treatment of many non-suicides in order to prevent a comparatively small number of suicides. However, as most likely suicide prevention measures, e.g. closer supervision, are aspects of good general care, there would be many benefits to the most needy psychiatric patients as a whole.

When Are Psychiatric Patients at Highest Risk?

Although a high risk of suicide appears to persist from the time of first onset of illness, it is not uniform throughout the subsequent course. Risk is highest in the first 1–5 years (Flood and Seager, 1968; Roy, 1982a) following onset or first contact, although this pattern is most evident in serious mental illness and may not apply to patients with alcohol dependence and other chronic conditions, in whom suicide appears to be associated with long-term illness (Inskip et al, 1998; see Chapter 9).

There is clear evidence that suicides cluster around the time of acute episodes of illness, both at onset and during resolution (Copas et al, 1971). As a result, suicide is associated with inpatient admission and the period following discharge from inpatient care. Approximately 16% of suicides in people under mental health care, or 4% of all suicides, are current psychiatric inpatients. Around one-third of these occur in the first week of admission, while another one-third occur during the period of planning discharge (Appleby et al, 1999).

Some of the highest estimates of risk relate to the first 1–12 months following inpatient discharge, the highest risk being found in those most recently discharged. Increases in risk greater than 100-fold in comparison to the general population have been reported in the first month after discharge (Goldacre et al, 1993; Geddes and Juszczak, 1995), while the risk in the first 6–12 months is increased 30–60-fold (Goldacre et al, 1993; Temoche et al, 1964). During the first 3 months post-discharge, around one-quarter of suicides by people under mental health care occur (Dennehy et al, 1996; Appleby et al, 1999). There are several possible reasons why risk is highest at a time of apparent recovery. Recovery may be incomplete and mental state may deteriorate; the return of insight may lead to a depressing awareness of the consequences of the illness; the abrupt withdrawal of inpatient care may enhance vulnerability; discharge may re-expose patients to the stresses which precipitated admission; and on leaving hospital they may have easier access to the means of suicide.

For services, the implication is that improved integration of inpatient and community-based care would reduce risk at this critical transition. This would require early follow-up following hospital discharge, close supervision, regular assessment of risk and specific measures to address major stressors.

Which Aspects of Services Are Related to Risk?

Service Organization

There is little reliable evidence that the changes in service provision that have increased the provision of care in the community in many countries in the last three decades have either improved or impaired suicide prevention in psychiatric patients. In Italy in the 1970s, rapid de-institutionalization allowed an examination of regional suicide rates before and after community-based provision, and there was no consistent trend (Williams et al, 1986). However, changes in rates have sometimes been reported as services have been re-organised; for example, in Chichester in the UK, where a fall in suicide occurred in the elderly population after services became community-based (Walk, 1967). No difference in numbers of suicides was found in a comparison of two forms of community care in the USA (Cohen et al, 1990) or in a comparison of intensive community care with hospital-based care (Marks et al, 1994), although in both cases the statistical power of the studies was insufficient to examine differences in suicide rates.

However, one feature of community care which may be related to suicide risk is short duration of hospital admission. A Scottish study of post-discharge suicide rates over a 20-year period reported an increase in the risk of suicides in the month after discharge, and a simultaneous decrease in the average duration of admission (Geddes and Juszczak, 1995). In Sweden, a rise in suicide in the first month after inpatient discharge was attributed to a reduction in length of hospital stay (Perris et al, 1980). In England, suicides in the first 3 months post-discharge had a high rate of admissions lasting less than 7 days, compared to suicides occurring later (Appleby et al, 1997). It is not possible to say the relationship is causal, i.e. that short admissions increase risk, but the evidence suggests the need to avoid early discharge and/or to ensure immediate follow-up in high-risk individuals.

One further aspect of service organization that is highlighted by reports into individual suicides and homicides by psychiatric patients in the UK, is communication between professionals. Failure to pass on information relevant to risk is often found between health services and other agencies, most often those responsible for social care, and between services in different districts in which patients have been resident. In the UK, the Care Programme Approach (Department of Health, 1990) was introduced nationally in the early 1990s to improve the quality and co-ordination of care for the most needy patients, those with severe and enduring mental illness, but subsequent studies of suicide have found that only around one-third of psychiatric patients who commit suicide are subject to the more intensive clinical management that it can provide (Dennehy et al, 1996).

Features of Services

Although there is little conclusive evidence for the effectiveness of specific treatments in reducing suicide, the clustering of suicides in acute episodes of illness strongly supports the need for early, effective treatment and measures to ensure compliance. In the Finnish national psychological autopsy study, only half the suicides with depression were receiving psychiatric treatment, only 3% were receiving adequate doses of antidepressants and none of the psychotic depressives were receiving adequate pharmacotherapy (Isometsä et al, 1994). Similar findings from a Hungarian study have linked suicide to lack of recognition of depression and therefore of treatment (Rihmer et al, 1990). The suicide rate in treated depression has been shown to be lower than in untreated cases (Isacsson et al, 1996), although the influence of personality and other suicide risk factors in influencing the taking of treatment cannot be ruled out.

In the National Confidential Inquiry into Suicide and Homicide by People with Mental Illness in the UK, around one-quarter of psychiatric patients who died by suicide were not compliant with treatment. Measures to improve compliance include motivational interviewing, the use of drugs with fewer side-effects, such as SSRIs for depression and atypical antipsychotics for schizophrenia, and closer supervision.

In general, individual compounds within a particular class of drugs are of equivalent effectiveness, but when treatment failures occur in high-risk individuals, alternative or combination treatments are needed, including ECT in severe depression and individual or family psychosocial therapies in both depression and schizophrenia. The rate of suicide in schizophrenic patients whose clinical care includes clozapine has been found to be substantially lower than that for all patients with schizophrenia (Meltzer and Okayli, 1995; Reid et al, 1998), although the significance of this finding is uncertain, as patients were not randomized to treatment groups. Several studies have reported a reduction in suicide in patients with bipolar disorder during lithium prophylaxis and, although this has not been subject to a satisfactory trial, the evidence is convincing that compliance with lithium treatment reduces risk, at least once illness prophylaxis is established (Isometsä et al, 1992; Müller Oerlinghausen et al, 1994; Tondo et al, 1998).

Satisfactory supervision, allowing direct observation and regular monitoring of mental state, is an important aspect of the care of patients who are at risk of suicide. Mental health teams who gave information on suicides to the National Confidential Inquiry in the UK, when asked what would have lowered risk in each case, most commonly referred to closer supervision and better treatment compliance. Family members can assist in the supervision of patients in the community but to be effective they also need a point of access to the service to allow them to report their concerns promptly. On inpatient wards, observation policies are usually designed to provide supervision commensurate with degree of risk. However, observation protocols have not been subject to satisfactory evaluation and, although suicides are rare in patients undergoing constant, close, individual ("one-to-one") observation, it is not certain that intermediate levels of observation are sufficient to prevent suicide in patients at moderate or fluctuating risk. Clearly, ward structure and design should ensure good supervision, and "intensive care" facilities, in which the staff-to-patient ratio is optimal, should be available for the highest risk patients (Crammer, 1994).

Service measures to manage risk assume that risk is firstly recognized and accurately assessed. While there is no reason to assume that risk recognition and assessment are generally poor in clinical practice, it is nevertheless a common finding that risk has been underestimated prior to suicide (Morgan and Priest, 1991), despite in many cases the communication of suicidal ideas (Morgan and Priest, 1984). In the National Confidential Inquiry cases, most suicides had been judged to be at no or low immediate risk at the last contact with services, which in around 50% of cases occurred within a week of death. Similarly, most suicides were under routine care at the time of death. This implies the need for regular training on risk recognition, while also raising doubts about understanding of risk (see below).

One further aspect of mental health care which has regularly been linked to individual suicides concerns the relationship between patients and staff. Suicides are frequently reported to occur when the therapeutic alliance breaks down, in a vicious cycle in which staff lose hope for the patient's improvement and the patient drifts out of care, eliciting hostile attitudes in the staff, a process known as "malignant alienation" (Morgan and Priest, 1991). Poor relationships between staff members and low staff morale are also said to increase risk.

MODELS OF RISK

There is considerable evidence that risk recognition is difficult in clinical practice, despite the fact that the risk factors for suicide are widely known. There are at least four reasons for this. The first two listed below have already been discussed. The third and fourth reasons indicate the need for more complex models of risk.

First, risk factors in the population may not be applicable to groups such as people with mental illness. Second, key risk factors are often of low specificity. Third, assessment of suicide risk in the individual patient tends to be based on the number of risk factors; it may be more accurate to regard risk as a balance between risk factors and protective factors, such as the aspects of care discussed above. According to the risk/protective factor model, a person with numerous risk factors may not be at high risk if each is counterbalanced. Similarly, a patient whose clinical condition is stable may become high-risk because the care he/she receives is reduced—as may be the case in post-discharge suicides.

Fourth, the conventional risk factor approach treats suicide as an event, when in reality it is the end-point of a sequence of events. For example, a patient leaves hospital, stops his medication, becomes depressed and starts drinking; his wife leaves him and he kills himself. Marital break-up is the terminal event but there may have been evidence of increasing risk for weeks or months. Identifying such models of cumulative risk, each with different opportunities for prevention, may improve prediction and prevention.

Table 35.1 Components of risk management by mental health services

Reduced access to the main methods of suicide
- Restriction on duration of drug prescriptions
- Removal of structures on wards from which hanging would be possible

Identification of high-risk groups
- Diagnoses of affective disorder, schizophrenia, alcohol or drug dependence, personality disorder
- Co-morbidity
- History of self-harm
- Frequent relapse or admission

More intensive service activity at times of high risk
- First year of illness
- During inpatient admission
- In the first 3 months following discharge from inpatient care

Specific service measures
- Early effective treatment of relapse
- Maintenance of prophylactic therapy
- Measures to improve compliance with treatment
- Early follow-up of hospital discharges
- Adequate observation of inpatients
- Close supervision of high-risk patients in the community
- Routine risk assessment
- Training in risk assessment

CONCLUSION

In summary, the main components of a suicide prevention strategy for psychiatric patients are: reduced access to the main methods of suicide; identification of high-risk groups to whom services should give priority; more intensive service activity at times of high risk, recognizing the long-term nature of risk in some; specific measures to ensure effective and acceptable treatment, adequate supervision and satisfactory risk assessment.

These elements of risk management are presented in more detail in Table 35.1.

REFERENCES

Allebeck, P., Varla, A., Kristjansson E. and Wistedt, B. (1987) Risk factors for suicide among patients with schizophrenia. Acta Psychiatrica Scandinavica, 76: 414–419.

Allebeck, P. and Wistedt, B. (1986) Mortality in schizophrenia. Archives of General Psychiatry, 43: 650–653.

Anderson, I.M. and Tomenson, B.M. (1995) Treatment discontinuation with selective serotonin reuptake inhibitors compared with tricyclic antidepressants: a meta-analysis. British Medical Journal, 310: 1433–1438.

Appleby, L., Shaw J., Amos T., McDonnell, R., Davies, S., Harris, C., McCann, K., Firth, C. and Douglas, A. (1997) The National Confidential Inquiry into Suicide and Homicide by People with Mental Illness. Progress Report 1997. London: Department of Health.

Appleby, L. (1992) Suicide in psychiatric patients: risk and prevention. British Journal of Psychiatry, 161: 749–758.
Appleby, L., Shaw, J., Amos, T., McDonnell, R., Kiernan, K., Davies, S., Harris, C., McCann, K., Bickley, H. and Parsons, R. (1999) Safer services. Report of the National Confidential Inquiry into Suicide and Homicide by People with Mental Illness. London: Department of Health.
Appleby, L., Shaw, J., Amos, T., McDonnell, R., Harris, C., McCann, K., Kiernan, K., Davies, S., Bickley, H. and Parsons, R. (1999) Suicide within 12 months of contact with mental health services: national clinical survey. British Medical Journal (in press).
Barraclough, B., Bunch, J., Nelson, B. and Sainsbury, P. (1974) A hundred cases of suicide: clinical aspects. British Journal of Psychiatry, 125: 355–373.
Beautrais, A.L., Joyce, P.R., Mulder, R.T., Fergusson, D.M., Deavoll, B.J. and Nightingale, S.K. (1996) Prevalence and comorbidity of mental disorders in persons making serious suicide attempts: a case-control study. American Journal of Psychiatry, 153: 1009–1014.
Beck, A.T., Steer, R.A., Kovacs, M. and Garrison, B. (1985) Hopelessness and eventual suicide: A 10-year prospective study of patients hospitalized with suicidal ideation. American Journal of Psychiatry, 142: 559–563.
Berglund, M. (1984) Suicide in alcoholism. A prospective study of 88 suicides: I. The multidimensional diagnosis at first admission. Archives of General Psychiatry, 41: 888–891.
Carlsten, A., Allebeck, P. and Brandt, L. (1996) Are suicide rates in Sweden associated with changes in the prescribing of medicines? Acta Psychiatrica Scandinavica, 94: 94–100.
Cheng, A. (1995) Mental illness and suicide. A case-control study in East Taiwan. Archives of General Psychiatry, 52: 594–603.
Cohen, L.J., Test, M.A. and Brown, R.L. (1990) Suicide and schizophrenia: data from a prospective community treatment study. American Journal of Psychiatry, 147: 602–607.
Copas, J.B., Freeman-Browne, D.L. and Robin, A.A. (1971) Danger periods for suicide in patients under treatment. Psychological Medicine, 1: 400–404.
Cowen, P.J. (1996) Advances in psychopharmacology: mood disorders and dementia. British Medical Bulletin, 52: 539–555.
Crammer, J.L. (1994) The special characteristics of suicide in hospital in-patients. British Journal of Psychiatry, 145: 460–476.
Dennehy, J.A., Appleby, L., Thomas, C.S. and Faragher, E.B. (1996) Case-control study of suicide by discharged psychiatric patients. British Medical Journal, 312: 1580.
Department of Health. (1990) The Care Programme Approach for People with a Mental Illness Referred to the Specialist Psychiatric Services. Circular HC(90)23/ LASSL(90)11. London: Department of Health.
Department of Health (1992) The Health of the Nation. Strategy for Health in England. London: HMSO.
Farberow, N.L., Ganzler, S., Cutter, F. and Reynolds, D. (1971) An eight-year survey of hospital suicides. Life Threatening Behavior, 1: 184–202.
Farmer, R. and Rohde, J. (1980) Effect of availability and acceptability of lethal instruments on suicide mortality. Acta Psychiatrica Scandinavica, 62: 436–446.
Fawcett, J., Scheftner, W.A., Fogg, L., Clark, D.C., Young, M.A., Hedeker, D. and Gibbons, R. (1990) Time-related predictors of suicide in major affective disorder. American Journal of Psychiatry, 147: 1189–1194.
Flood, R.A. and Seager, C.P. (1968) A retrospective examination of psychiatric case records of patients who subsequently committed suicide. British Journal of Psychiatry, 114: 443–450.
Foster, T., Gillespie, K. and McClelland, R. (1997) Mental disorders and suicide in Northern Ireland. British Journal of Psychiatry, 170: 447–452.

Geddes, J.R. and Juszczak, E. (1995) Period trends in rate of suicide in first 28 days after discharge from psychiatric hospital in Scotland, 1968–92. British Medical Journal, 311: 357–360.

Goldacre, M., Seagroatt, V. and Hawton, K. (1993) Suicide after discharge from psychiatric inpatient care. Lancet, 342: 283–286.

Gunnell, D. and Frankel, S. (1994) Prevention of suicide aspirations and evidence. British Medical Journal, 308: 1227–1233.

Harris, E.C. and Barraclough, B. (1997) Suicide as an outcome for mental disorders. British Journal of Psychiatry, 170: 205–228.

Hawton, K., Fagg, J., Simkin, S., Harriss, L. and Malmberg, A. (1998) Methods used for suicide in farmers in England and Wales. The contribution of availability and its relevance to prevention. British Journal of Psychiatry, 173: 320–324.

Heikkinen, M.E., Isometsä, E.T., Aro, H.M., Sarna, S.J. and Lönnqvist, J.K. (1995) Age-related variation in recent life events preceding suicide. Journal of Nervous and Mental Disease, 183: 325–331.

Heilä, H., Isometsä, E.T., Henriksson, M.M., Keikkinen, M.E., Marttunen, M.J. and Lönnqvist, J. (1997) Suicide and schizophrenia: a nationwide psychological autopsy study on age- and sex-specific clinical characteristics of 92 suicide victims with schizophrenia. American Journal of Psychiatry, 154: 1235–1242.

Henriksson, M.M., Aro, H.M., Marttunen, M.J., Heikkinen, M.E., Isometsä, E.T., Kuoppasalmi, K.I. and Lönnqvist, J. (1993) Mental disorders and comorbidity in suicide. American Journal of Psychiatry, 150: 935–940.

Henry, J.A., Alexander, C.A. and Sener, E.K. (1995) Relative mortality from overdose of antidepressants. British Medical Journal, 310: 221–224.

Inskip, H.M., Harris, E.C. and Barraclough, B. (1998) Lifetime risk of suicide for affective disorder, alcoholism and schizophrenia. British Journal of Psychiatry, 172: 35–37.

Isacsson, G., Bergman, U. and Rich, C.L. (1996) Epidemiological data suggest antidepressants reduce suicide risk among depressives. Journal of Affective Disorder, 41: 1–8.

Isometsä, E., Henriksson, M. and Lönnqvist, J. (1992) Completed suicide and recent lithium treatment. Journal of Affective Disorders, 26: 101–103.

Isometsä, E.T., Aro, H.M., Henriksson, M.M., Heikkinen, M.E. and Lönnqvist, J.K. (1994) Suicide in major depression in different treatment settings. Journal of Clinical Psychiatry, 55: 523–527.

Isometsä, E.T., Henriksoon, M.M., Keikkinen, M.E., Aro, H.M. and Marttunen, M.J. (1996) Suicide among subjects with personality disorder. American Journal of Psychiatry, 153: 667–673.

Kaplan, M.S. and Geling, O. (1998) Firearm suicides and homicides in the United States: regional variations and patterns of gun ownership. Social Science and Medicine, 46: 1227–1233.

Kelly, S. and Bunting, J. (1998) Trends in suicide in England and Wales, 1982–96. Population Trends, 92: 29–41.

King, E. and Barraclough, B. (1990) Violent death and mental illness. A study of a single catchment area over eight years. British Journal of Psychiatry, 156: 714–720.

Kreitman, N. (1976) The coal gas story. United Kingdom suicide rates, 1960–71. British Journal of Preventive Social Medicine, 30: 86–93.

Langley, G.E. and Bayatti, N.N. (1984) Suicides in Exe Vale Hospital, 1972–1981. British Journal of Psychiatry, 145: 463–467.

Lesage, A.D., Boyer, R., Grunberg, F., Vanier, C., Morissette R., Ménard-Buteau, C. and Loyer, M. (1994) Suicide and mental disorders: a case-control study of young men. American Journal of Psychiatry, 151: 1063–1068.

Lewis, G., Hawton, K. and Jones, P. (1997) Strategies for preventing suicide. British Journal of Psychiatry, 171: 351–354.

Marks, I.M., Connolly, J., Muijen, M., Audini, B., McNamee, G. and Lawrence, R.F. (1994)

Home-based versus hospital-based care for people with serious mental illness. British Journal of Psychiatry, 164: 179–194.

Marzuk, P.M., Leon, A.C., Tardiff, K., Morgan, E.B., Stajic, M. and Mann, J. (1992) The effect of access to lethal methods of injury on suicide rates. Archives of General Psychiatry, 49: 451–458.

McClure, G.M.G. (1984) Trends in suicide rate for England and Wales, 1975–80. British Journal of Psychiatry, 144: 199–126.

Meltzer, H.Y. and Okayli, G. (1995) Reduction of suicidality during clozapine treatment of neuroleptic-resistant schizophrenia: impact on risk–benefit assessment. American Journal of Psychiatry, 152: 183–190.

Morgan, H.G. and Priest, P. (1984) Assessment of suicide risk in psychiatric in-patients. Symposium on suicide in hospital. British Journal of Psychiatry, 145: 467–469.

Morgan, H.G. and Priest, P. (1991) Suicide and other unexpected deaths among psychiatric in-patients. The Bristol Confidential Inquiry. British Journal of Psychiatry, 158: 368–374.

Office for National Statistics (1997) Mortality Cause 1995. Office for National Statistics. London: HMSO.

Müller Oerlinghausen, B., Wolf, T., Ahren, B., Schou, M., Grof, E., Grof, P., Lenz, G., Simhandl, C., Thau, K. and Wolf, R. (1994) Mortality during initial and during later lithium treatment. A collaborative study by the International Group for the Study of Lithium-treated Patients. Acta Psychiatrica Scandinavica, 90: 295–297.

Paykel, E.S., Tylee, A., Wright, A., Priest, R.G., Rix, S. and Hart, D. (1997) The Defeat Depression Campaign: psychiatry in the public arena. American Journal of Psychiatry, 154: 59–65.

Perris, C., Beskow, J. and Jacobson, L. (1980) Some remarks on the incidence of successful suicide in psychiatric care. Social Psychiatry, 15: 161–166.

Porkorny, A.D. (1966) A follow-up study of 618 suicidal patients. American Journal of Psychiatry, 122: 1109–1116.

Proulx, F., Lesage, A.D. and Grunberg, F. (1997) One hundred in-patient suicides. British Journal of Psychiatry, 171: 247–250.

Reid, W.H., Mason, M. and Hogan, T. (1998) Suicide prevention effects associated with clozapine therapy in schizophrenia and schizoaffective disorder. Psychiatric Services, 49: 1029–1033.

Rihmer, Z., Barsi, J., Veg, K. and Katona, C.L.E. (1990) Suicide rates in Hungary correlate negatively with reported rates of depression. Journal of Affective Disorders, 20: 87–91.

Roy, A. (1982a) Risk factors for suicide in psychiatric patients. Archives of General Psychiatry, 39: 1089–1095.

Roy A. (1982b) Suicide in chronic schizophrenia. British Journal of Psychiatry, 141: 171–177.

Royal College of Psychiatrists Psychopharmacology Subgroup (1997) Report of the Working Group on the Association between Antipsychotic Drugs and Sudden Death. London: Royal College of Psychiatrists.

Temoche, A., Pugh, T.F. and McMahon, B. (1964) Suicide rates among current and former mental institution patients. Journal of Nervous and Mental Disease, 138: 124–130.

Tondo, L., Baldessarini, R.J., Hennen, J., Floris, G., Silvetti, F. and Tohen, M. (1998) Lithium treatment and risk of suicidal behavior in bipolar disorder patients. Journal of Clinical Psychiatry, 59: 405–414.

Walk, D. (1967) Suicide and community care. British Journal of Psychiatry, 113: 1381–1391.

Williams, P., De Salvia, D. and Tansella, M. (1986) Suicide, psychiatric reform, and the provision of psychiatric services in Italy. Social Psychiatry, 21: 89–95.

Yip, P.S. (1997) Suicides in Hong Kong, 1991–1994. Social Psychiatry and Psychiatric Epidemiology, 32: 243–250.

Chapter 36

Approaches to Suicide Prevention in Asia and the Far East

R. Srinivasa Murthy
Department of Psychiatry, National Institute of Mental Health and Neurosciences, Bangalore, India

Abstract

Asia and the Far East represent a major part of the world population, both in numbers and in the variations in religion, ethnicity, socio-economic status and types of health care and mental health care. This variety offers a rich source for understanding suicide and approaches to suicide prevention. Suicide is viewed very differently by different cultural groups. This overview examines: (a) the ways suicide is viewed in different major religions of the region; (b) differences in rates across countries; (c) developments in suicide prevention in some of the countries of the region; (d) international developments relevant to the region; and (e) an approach relevant to suicide prevention in the region. Suicide is condemned in Islam. The Buddhist stance on suicide is ambiguous. Some have condemned it, but others have approved it. The Japanese attitude toward death is enormously complex, with differences among individuals. The ideal death to many is daiojo-death in ripe old age after life has taken its course, when one's body peacefully leaves the world. In Hinduism the aim of the idealized ascetic, to attain release and end the cycle of rebirth, provided an acceptable rationale for suicide in highly selected circumstances. Suicide rates among the immigrants from Asia and Far East have been studied in Australia and America. These studies have found that the rates of suicide of immigrants are more closely aligned with rates in the country of origin than with rates in the adopted country. Generally, suicide rates among immigrants appear higher than in the countries of origin, and methods of suicide are closely linked to the methods used traditionally in the original culture. The review of developments in the area of suicide prevention from the point of view of crisis intervention programmes, legal status and professional apathy presents a pessimistic picture. This contrasts with the excellent analysis of the needs by different professionals from different countries. There is a mismatch between perceptions

The International Handbook of Suicide and Attempted Suicide. Edited by K. Hawton and K. van Heeringen.

and actions and there needs to be a *realistic* plan of action rather than an *ideal* plan of action. The most important aspect of prevention is recognition that suicide is a social problem. As a result, interventions have to involve many domains, most importantly: (a) the legal status of attempted suicide and suicide; (b) the family as a social unit; (c) public awareness of suicidal feelings as legitimate; (d) informal carers and initiatives from non-governmental organizations; (e) formal carers in medical and mental health professionals; and (f) social policies. In the final analysis, progress in this area will come from social action and not only from professional action. The earlier we can move suicide into the social and public arena, the better the issue can be addressed.

INTRODUCTION

Asia and the Far East represent a major part of the world population, both in numbers and in the variations in religions, ethnicity, socio-economic status and types of physical and mental health care. This variety offers a rich source for understanding suicide and approaches to suicide prevention. It is well documented that suicide is viewed very differently by different cultural groups (Farberow, 1975). It is recognized that community education and awareness programmes would need to take into account these different values and attitudes towards suicide and be presented in ways that are culturally and linguistically appropriate (McDonald and Steel, 1997). This overview examines: (a) the ways suicide is viewed in different major religions in Asia and the Far East; (b) differences in suicide rates across countries; (c) developments in suicide prevention in some of these countries; (d) relevant international developments; and (e) approaches relevant to suicide prevention in this region.

SUICIDE IN DIFFERENT RELIGIONS

Some of the major religions of the world are represented in Asia and the Far East and their attitudes to suicide differ markedly. Suicide is condemned in Islam. The Holy Koran says, "Do not cast yourself into perdition". It is God who has given life and is alone entitled to take it. The Hadith explicitly forbids a Muslim from praying for death (Rahman, 1989). The Buddhist stance on suicide is ambiguous. Some groups have condemned it, but others have approved of it. The ambiguity was evident most conspicuously during the war in Vietnam, when some monks committed suicide by setting fire to themselves. Suicide is expressly forbidden in the scriptures but there are some exceptions that in fact became an honoured path in China and other far-eastern countries, namely self-immolation or self-sacrifice based on religious motivations (Kitagawa, 1989).

The Japanese attitude toward death is extremely complex, with many different views among individuals. The ideal death to many is daiojo-death, that is, death at a ripe old age after life has taken its course, when one's body peacefully leaves the world. Yet some types of suicide are not only culturally sanctioned but also romanticized and beautified. To take one's own life, as long as it is, culturally speaking, for a good reason, can manifest utmost self-control, a taking in hand not merely of life's affairs but of one's own destiny (Tierney, 1989).

In Hinduism the aim of the idealized ascetic, to attain release and end the cycle of rebirth, provided an acceptable rationale for suicide in highly selected circumstances. The Dharmasastra literature, which outlines the Hindu code of conduct, also refers to another form of religious suicide, the "great journey", justified by incurable disease or great misfortune. Questions about these carefully reasoned suicides, usually sanctioned only for the elderly, were framed in religious rather than medical contexts. Weiss (1994) contrasts the views in the West and in India as follows:

> Suicide in the West typically raises questions about deviance and mental disorder. Concerns for victims are framed in clinical terms, with a focus on prevention and cure of psychopathology associated with suicidal impulses. Hindu traditions that consider suicide are concerned with a different set of questions, which focus not on deviance but on cultural values.

DIFFERENCES ACROSS COUNTRIES

Suicide rates among immigrants from Asia and the Far East have been studied (Tousignant and Mishara, 1981) in Australia (McDonald and Steel, 1997), England (Burke, 1976; Raleigh, 1996) and America (Patel and Gaw, 1996). These studies have found that suicide rates among immigrants are more closely aligned to rates in the country of origin than to the rates in the country of adoption. Generally, suicide rates among immigrants are higher than in the country of origin, and studies have shown that the methods of suicide are closely linked to those used traditionally in the culture of origin. For example, in a 5-year period it was found that suicide by burning was nearly 10 times more common in females from the Indian subcontinent than in the overall female population in England and Wales (Raleigh and Balarajan, 1992).

Bangladesh

The information available from Bangladesh is limited. Mental health care is at a very early phase of development. For a population of 123 million inhabitants, only one psychiatric hospital (400 beds) and about 40 psychiatrists are available. There is no crisis centre in the whole country (Ahsan et al, 1994; Faureun and Blanchet, 1989).

China and Hong Kong

The characteristics of suicide and attempted suicide in China and Hong Kong are well documented (Zhang and Jin, 1998) and there are studies covering the different historical periods. The striking aspect of suicide in China is the high incidence of suicide among young women in rural areas. The effectiveness of crisis help, both in the community and through emergency services, has been described (Cheng, 1995; Jianlin, 1995; Ho, 1996; Pritchard, 1996; Xie et al, 1996; Cheng et al, 1997; Law, 1997; Wang et al, 1997; Chi et al, 1998; Zhang and Jin, 1998).

Malaysia

With a population of 21 million, Malaysia has a reported suicide rate of 10 per 100,000. The population consists of 55% Malays, 34% Chinese and 9% from the Indian subcontinent. There are differences between the suicide rates of the ethnic groups, and higher rates are reported from people of South Indian origin. The rate is also higher among Hindus as compared to Malay Muslims. The most common method of suicide is deliberate self-poisoning with pesticides among Indians and by drug overdose among other groups. There are four Befrienders counselling centres in the country (Deva, personal communication; Maniam, 1988; Zam, 1991; Habil et al, 1992).

Pakistan

Suicidal behaviour is an understudied subject in Pakistan. Recent reports have provided new information. Javed (1996) found that 45% of depressed patients showed suicidal psychopathology. Suicidal ideation was more common in females and significant associations were found between the severity and duration of depressive illness and suicidal thoughts. Khan and Reza (1998) reported that most suicide attempters in Karachi were young adults, with married women representing the single largest group. Self-poisoning with medication was the most common method, and benzodiazepines the drug most frequently taken in overdose. Interpersonal conflict with the opposite sex was the most common precipitating cause and marital problems were identified as a significant stress factor. Khan and Reza (1998) found that three-quarters of suicidal persons were under the age of 30 years. Compared to male attempters, the women were younger and more often married. Both women and men tended to use benzodiazepines in overdoses, but more women used organophosphate insecticides. The authors concluded that legal, social and economic discrimination predispose women in Pakistan to psychological distress and subsequent suicidal behaviour. The protective effect of religion seems not to operate among the younger generation.

Sri Lanka

Suicide and attempted suicide have become a public health priority in Sri Lanka (see Chapter 2). The two decade-old ethnic conflict has contributed to the problem, resulting in a very high suicide rate. The suicide rate rose from 18.2 per

100,000 in 1971, to 36.3 per 100,000 in 1983, and 40 per 100,000 in 1996. What is striking is that there are marked differences in the different regions, with variations in rates from 20 (Jaffna) to 90 per 100,000 (Pollineyeru). Acute pesticide poisoning is a major public health problem (Eddleston et al, 1998). Most of the cases are intentional and occur among adults (Senanayake and Peiras, 1995; Van der Hock et al, 1998). The mortality due to poisoning has increased from 11.8 to 43 per 1,000 deaths in the last 20 years. In addition, this increase has been most marked in rural areas, where it has risen from 8 per 100,000 to 70 per 100,000. An interesting finding has been the marked drop in the suicide rate during the war in the Jaffna area, especially among males and young people of both genders (Somasundaram and Rajadurai, 1995). Interpersonal disputes involving domestic problems and love affairs are the main precipitating causes for suicidal behaviour. Improving family relations may help in the prevention of self-poisoning (Hethamachchi and Kodituwakku, 1980).

In a recent study, Eddleston and colleagues (1998) found that poisoning was the main reason for general hospital admission, and far in excess of all other causes. In interviews in general wards with 85 self-poisoning patients, more than 90% stated that they knew someone who had harmed him/herself. It was also noted that the young have few support systems and are unable to cope with societal and cultural demands. The authors emphasized the need for improvement in the medical management of acute poisonings. Another measure is to decrease access to poisons. A further measure is to aim for widespread education in life skills and increased availability of help through counselling. The Befrienders approach to counselling is now available in a number of centres in Sri Lanka (Ellawala, 1994; Ratnayeke, 1996).

India

Suicide rates in India have shown a gradually increasing trend. The rate in 1996 was 9 per 100,000. The striking aspect of Indian data is the large variation in different parts of India. States and cities with rapid social change are associated with higher suicide rates, such as the states of Kerala and Goa, and cities like Pondicherry and Bangalore. The other important association is alcohol dependence as a direct or indirect cause of suicide (Adityanjee, 1986; Gupta and Srinivasan, 1988; Veluri and Green, 1990; Chaddha et al, 1991; Agarwal, 1993; Jayaram et al, 1993; Vijayakumar, 1993, 1994; Siwach and Gupta, 1995; Latha, 1996; Etzersdorfer et al, 1998; Latha and Narendra, 1998; Singh et al, 1998; Tousignant et al, 1998).

The Indian experience is considered more fully in terms of: (a) crisis intervention centres; (b) the mental health care programme; and (c) judicial initiatives concerning suicide. The setting up of *crisis centres* is of recent origin. The important initiatives are the Medico-Pastoral Association, Bangalore; Sanjivini, Delhi; Sumaitri, Delhi; Helpline, Bombay; Sneha, Madras; Sahaya, Hyderabad; Viswas, Bangalore; and Helpline, Bangalore. Other centres are in Calcutta, Goa,

Pondicherry and Trivandrum. All of these centres use volunteers as care providers. There are a number of aspects that are common to all the centres. First, development of most of the centres has resulted from the personal efforts of individuals. The centres are based around leaders, who are usually charismatic individuals. Second, overall growth in the last two decades has been far from satisfactory in that it has not really taken on a national character in terms of recognition and activities. To illustrate this point, even in Bangalore, with a population of 5 million people, the current level of activity is far from adequate. Third, there has been very limited documentation of the work and analysis of the experiences at the centres. Fourth, networking is very problematical, especially in rural areas. Fifth, crisis intervention work is separate from the mainstream mental health services. No psychiatric centre (psychiatric hospital or psychiatric department) has a crisis facility, such as a committed telephone line or a confidential centre where people can drop in for help, other than the medical emergency services which are too "medical" to encourage help-seeking by persons with suicidal feelings.

Another aspect of the role of crisis centres relates to the help seekers themselves. Crisis intervention work in India takes place against a background of extremely limited mental health services. As a result, those seeking help from the crisis centres represent a complex and heterogeneous group of distressed persons. These include not only those needing befriending, as is likely to be the case in Western countries, where other people in need of formal mental health care can usually have access to such care, but also severely mentally ill people. In India it is vital that volunteers working in crisis centres are sensitive to the possibility that severely ill persons may approach them for help. Not every person who talks about suicide is reacting to a life crisis—some of them are seriously depressed and in need of urgent psychiatric help. Therefore, the training of the volunteers has to be more extensive than just the provision of listening skills. Another issue relates to the matching between the help seeker and help provider. In India, the general public does not clearly differentiate the different care providers offer based on their professional training. In a hospital, everyone who provides help, whether a doctor, social worker, psychologist or priest, is regarded as a "doctor". Therefore, many help seekers are not expecting just "limited" care from the crisis centres but may expect "real" care for their total needs. Furthermore, help providing occurs not just in a one-to-one situation, as the family and community aspects often predominate in a crisis situation such as a disturbed heterosexual relationship, failure in studies, adolescent problems, marital problems, etc. This means a fine balance has to be struck between encouraging autonomy and increasing social support and family involvement as the goal in crisis situations. This could also mean bringing other important person(s) into the help-giving situation at appropriate times. Lastly, the volunteers themselves lead a double life. In the crisis centre they are all-accepting and available to callers, but in their own real-life situations such a stance is not possible. This aspect of volunteering needs greater attention during training and supervision. In terms of planning for the future, one of the urgent needs is to bring together all the crisis centres to share their experiences and to identify areas for networking as well as joint action.

The mental health care programme in India is limited. With a population of nearly a 1,000 million there are only 5,000 mental health professionals and about 35,000 psychiatric beds. In order to meet the wide gap between needs and resources, innovative approaches to mental health care have been adopted. The chief measure is the integration of mental health care with primary health care. This has meant priority setting, focused training, simplification of information and interventions, and support of professionals. This method of decentralized and de-professionalized mental health care has relevance to suicide prevention programmes (Srinivasa Murthy, 1996).

The judicial initiatives can be important, as seen from the rapid changes in the legal status of attempted suicide. Until 1994, attempted suicide was a punishable act. In 1994 this provision was considered unconstitutional. However, threats from euthanasia groups and problems relating to dowry deaths have restored the penal status of attempted suicide. Legal provisions can hamper intervention programmes.

INTERNATIONAL DEVELOPMENTS RELEVANT TO ASIA AND THE FAR EAST

Another important development is the recognition of the multiple causes of suicide. It is evident that sociological variables have little predictive power. Similarly, psychiatric variables represent only a small part of the relevant psychological factors that contribute to the risk of suicidal acts. It is suggested that the study of suicide is an aspect of the more general study of aggression and violence, and the common base lies in the realm of interpersonal relations.

The publication of the book *World Mental Health* (Desjarlais et al, 1995) by the Harvard Medical School has focused world attention on mental health problems and priorities in low-income countries. Suicide is one of the nine areas selected by this report. The major conclusions about suicide concern: (a) recognition of the wide variation in suicide rates across countries and rural–urban areas; (b) determinants of suicide, with a focus on social factors; (c) means of completing suicide; and (d) emphasis on an interdisciplinary approach to suicide. The salient conclusions are:

1. The extent that suicide can be explained as treatable psychopathology underscores the need for mental health professionals to formulate programmes for prevention and treatment.
2. Crisis management and suicide prevention should be part of "essential clinical services".
3. Effective health education messages need to be developed and disseminated through the mass media to advise people of available services and of the transient nature of many self-destructive impulses.

4. Regional centres of suicide research need to be established for the study of the variations in the contexts of suicide.
5. There should be changes in social policies to restrict access to handguns, pesticides and other readily available means of suicide.
6. Media coverage of suicides should be limited to reduce the number of imitative suicides.
7. There should be active dialogue and continuous interaction between ethicists, policy makers, clinicians, the judiciary and related disciplines towards social policy formulation.

FUTURE AREAS OF ACTION

Against the background of the wide variety of social, political, economic and religious aspects of the countries of Asia and the Far East, suicide prevention programmes have to be rooted in the broader local situations. No one method will be adequate.

In the following section, the various aspects and areas of intervention are considered. They are grouped into 10 categories (see Table 36.1).

1. Acceptance of "Normalcy" of Suicidal Feelings

The situation in India, where attempted suicide is a criminal act, leads to secrecy and a lack of willingness to seek help. It is important for the mass media to present the experience of suicidal feelings as a common human experience.

2. Life Skills to Cope with Stress

Adolescents and young adults in the developing countries are experiencing high levels of stress from various forces operating in schools, homes and the

Table 36.1 The prevention of suicide: levels of intervention

1. Acceptance of "normalcy" of suicidal feelings
2. Life skills to cope with stress
3. Enrichment of family life
4. Community institutions for crises
5. Crisis help
6. Care of people with chronic physical illnesses
7. Early treatment of mental disorders
8. Help for suicide attempters
9. Support for families
10. Social policies

fast-expanding media. At the same time there is loss of the protective function of the joint family and the community. It is important for schools to provide life skills to all children as part of the educational experience (World Health Organization, 1994). In India this has been taken up as a measure in about two dozen centres.

3. Enrichment of Family Life

One of the common associations with suicide is family and interpersonal stress, especially in women. Traditionally, family life was regulated and guided by social norms. However, urbanization, women entering the working world and globalization have put an end to traditional values. There is a need for a redefinition of family life, particularly to reduce intergenerational conflicts. Religion has an important role to play in this process. As noted earlier, it is members of the younger generation, even in Islamic countries, who most commonly attempt suicide, while the older generation, who hold more firm religious values, are more able to cope with social changes. Religion has the potential to provide a framework for understanding the vicissitudes of life, especially in a situation of "moral vacuum".

4. Community Institutions for Crisis Resolution

Although the causes of suicidal behaviour are largely universal, solutions have to be local and rooted in local practices and institutions. Traditionally, crisis situations were resolved by elders in the family, community leaders and religious leaders. There is a need to rebuild community life through common cultural, social and recreational activities to provide opportunities for group commitment to values and norms of behaviour. In addition, small homogenous communities can build places for young people to meet, play and resolve their growth-related problems. Religious centres like temples, churches and mosques can play a vital part by responding to the needs of the younger generation.

5. Crisis Help

This has come to be a very important institutional mechanism for suicide prevention. There are both telephone hotlines and places for people in distress to drop in. The limitations have been considered in the earlier section on the Indian experience. There are many issues that need fuller understanding. However, crisis help must be a component of suicide prevention, especially in urban areas.

6. Care of Persons with Chronic Physical Illnesses

In many developing countries, people with chronic physical illnesses attempt suicide as a way of solving their distress. Adequate healthcare, formation of self-help groups, and supportive home help can decrease the helplessness of people with chronic illnesses.

7. Early Treatment of Mental Disorders

A significant proportion of individuals who attempt suicide have mental disorders. Developing measures such as decentralized mental health care and integration of mental health with primary health care can lead to early identification of mentally ill persons. This approach also encourages regular follow-up and reintegration of the individuals into society. In developing countries, innovative approaches to mental health care are an important measure for suicide prevention.

8. Help for Suicide Attempters

In the majority of situations, an individual who has attempted suicide is not provided with adequate help to understand his/her life situation, adopt alternative methods of coping and avoid repeat attempts. Help should be available for all suicide attempters, including psychiatric assessment, emotional support at the individual and group levels, and work with the families of attempters. It is hoped that this approach can limit the rate of repeat suicide attempts.

9. Support for Families

The families of people who have attempted or completed suicide experience intense emotional turmoil and distress (see Chapter 26). Feelings of guilt, shame and failure are all part of this process. In some families the grieving of family members occurs in isolation from each other. Organizing support groups, periodic home visits and adequate follow-up for about 3–6 months would be beneficial. Religion and religious rituals could also be utilized to make sense of the loss and to come to accept it. These initiatives should be culture-sensitive and locally organized, with the full utilization of local beliefs and practices.

10. Social Policies

The larger social policies relating to alcohol use, urbanization, pesticide use, family laws and displacement of people all have an important contribution to suicide rates. In this area, the important factors are to sensitize planners and policy makers to these issues, continuously monitor the effects of policies on suicide rates, and develop innovative methods of meeting the emotional needs of the people affected by these policies. Decriminalization of attempted suicide would be an important measure.

CONCLUSIONS

In the final analysis, progress in this area will come from social action in addition to professional action. The earlier suicide moves into the social and public arena, the more likely we will be to address the issue. Suicide prevention in Asia and the Far East overlaps with approaches proposed in Western countries, but the very wide variety of religious and cultural values means that policies must be developed in accordance with local customs and beliefs. There is a particular need for social policies in addition to those relating to psychiatric services. Increasing rates of suicide in several countries in the region highlight the urgency for preventive action.

REFERENCES

Adityanjee, D.R. (1986) Suicide attempts and suicides in India: cross-cultural aspects. International Journal of Social Psychiatry, 32: 64–73.

Agarwal, S.B. (1993) A clinical, biochemical, neurobehavioural, and sociopsychological study of 190 patients admitted to hospital as a result of acute organophosphorus poisoning. Environmental Research 62: 63–70.

Ahsan, G.A.S., Chowdhury, M.A., Azhar, M.A. and Rafiqueddin, A.K. (1994) Copper sulphate poisoning. Tropical Doctor, 24: 52–53.

Burke, A.W. (1976) Attempted suicide among Asian immigrants from Birmingham. British Journal of Psychiatry, 128: 528–533.

Chadda, R.K., Shome, S. and Bhatia, M.S. (1991) Suicide in Indian women. British Journal of Psychiatry, 158–434.

Cheng, A.T., Mann, A.H. and Chan, K.A. (1997) Personality disorder and suicide: a case-control study. British Journal of Psychiatry, 170: 441–446.

Cheng, A.T. (1995) Mental illness and suicide: a case-control study in East Taiwan. Archives of General Psychiatry, 52: 594–603.

Chi, I., Yip, P.S., Yu, G.K. and Halliday, P. (1998) A study of elderly suicides in Hong Kong. Crisis, 19: 35–46.

Desjarlais, R., Eisenberg, L., Good, B. and Kleinman, A. (1995) World Mental Health—Problems and Priorities in Low-income Countries. Oxford: Oxford University Press.

Eddleston, M., Sheriff, M.H.R. and Hawton, K. (1998) Deliberate self-harm in Sri Lanka: an overlooked tragedy in the developing world. British Medical Journal, 317: 133–135.

Ellawala, N. (1994) The Sumithrayo strategy for the reduction of suicide in Sri Lanka. Crisis, 15: 53–54.

Etzersdorfer, E., Vijayakumar, L., Schony, W., Grausgruber, A. and Sonneck, G. (1998) Attitudes towards suicide among medical students: comparison between Madras (India) and Vienna (Austria). Social Psychiatry and Psychiatric Epidemiology, 33: 104–110.

Farberow, N.L. (Ed.) (1975) Suicide in Different Cultures. Baltimore, MD: University Park Press.

Faurean, V. and Blanchet, J. (1989) Deaths from injuries and induced abortion among rural Bangladeshi women. Social Science and Medicine, 29: 1121–1127.

Gupta, R.K. and Srinivasan, A.K. (1998) Study of fatal burns cases in Kanpur (India). Forensic Science International, 37: 81–89.

Habil, M.H., Ganesvaran, T. and Agres, L.S. (1992) Attempted suicide in Kuala Lumpur. Asia and Pacific Journal of Public Health, 6: 5–7.

Hethamachchi, J. and Kodituwakku, G.C. (1980) Self-poisoning in Sri Lanka: motivational aspects International Journal of Social Psychiatry, 35: 204–208.

Ho, T.P. (1996) Changing patterns of suicide in Hong Kong. Social Psychiatry and Psychiatric Epidemiology, 31: 235–240.

Javed, M.A. (1996) Suicidal symptoms in depressed Pakistani patients. Journal of the Pakistan Medical Association, 46: 69–70.

Jayaram, V., Ramakrishna, K.M. and Davies, M.R. (1993) Burns in Madras, India: an analysis of 1,368 patients in 1 year. Burns, 19: 339–344.

Jianlin, J. (1995) Hotline for mental health in Shanghai, China. Crisis, 16: 116–120.

Khan, M.M. and Reza, H. (1998) Gender differences in non-fatal suicidal behaviour in Pakistan. Significance of sociocultural differences. Suicide and Life-Threatening Behavior, 28: 62–68.

Kitagawa, J.M. (1989) Buddhist medical history. In Sullivan, L.E. (Ed.), Healing and Restoring—Health and Medicine in the World's Religious Traditions. New York: Macmillan.

Latha, K.S. and Narendra, R. (1998) Dowry death: implications of law. Medicine, Science and the Law, 38: 153–156.

Latha, K.S. (1996) Suicide pact survivors: some observations. Medicine, Science and the Law, 36: 295–298.

Law, F.Y. (1997) Elderly suicides in Hong Kong: the role of volunteer befrienders. Crisis, 18: 55–56.

Maniam, J. (1988) Suicide and parasuicide in a hill resort in Malaysia. British Journal of Psychiatry, 153: 222–225.

McDonald, B. and Steel, Z. (1997) Immigrants and Mental Health—An Epidemiological Analysis. Sydney: Transcultural Mental Health Centre.

Patel, S.P. and Gaw, A.C. (1996) Suicide among immigrants from the Indian subcontinent: a review. Psychiatric Services, 47: 517–521.

Pritchard, C. (1996) Suicide in the People's Republic of China categorized by age and gender: evidence of the influence of culture on suicide. Acta Psychiatrica Scandinavica, 93: 362–367.

Rahman, F. (1989) Islam and Health/medicine: a historical perspective. In L.E. Sullivan (Ed.), Healing and Restoring—Health and Medicine in the World's Religious Traditions. New York: Macmillan.

Raleigh, V.S. (1996) Suicide patterns and trends in people of Indian subcontinent and Caribbean origin in England and Wales. Ethnic Health, 1: 55–63.

Raleigh, V.S. and Balarajan, R. (1992) Suicide and self-burning among Indians and West Indians in England and Wales. British Journal of Psychiatry, 161: 365–368.

Ratnayeke, L. (1996) Suicide and crisis intervention in rural communities in Sri Lanka. Crisis, 17: 149–151.

Senanayake, N. and Peiris, N. (1995) Mortality due to poisoning in a developing agricultural country: trends over 20 years. Human Experimental Toxicology, 14: 808–811.

Singh, S.P., Santosh, P.J., Avasthi, A. and Kulhara, P. (1998) A psychosocial study of self-immolation in India. Acta Psychiatrica Scandinavica, 97: 71–75.

Siwach, S.B. and Gupta, A. (1995) The profile of acute poisonings in Haryana—Rohtak study. Journal of the Association of Physicians in India, 43: 756–759.

Somasundaram, D.J. and Rajadura, S. (1995) War and suicide in northern Sri Lanka. Acta Psychiatrica Scandinavica, 91: 1–4.
Srinivasa Murthy, R. (1996) Economics of mental health care in developing countries. In F. Lie Mak and C. Nadelson (Eds), International Review of Psychiatry, Vol. 2. Washington, DC: American Psychiatric Press.
Tierney, E.O. (1989) Health care in contemporary Japanese religions. In L.E. Sullivan (Ed.), Healing and Restoring—Health and Medicine in the World's Religious Traditions. New York: Macmillan.
Tousignant, M., Seshadri, S. and Raj, S. (1998) Gender and suicide in India: a multiperspective approach. Suicide and Life-Threatening Behavior, 28: 50–61.
Tousignant, M. and Mishara, B.L. (1981) Suicide and culture. A review of the literature (1969–1980). Transcultural Psychiatric Review, 18: 5–31.
Van der Hock, W., Konradsen, F., Athukorala, K. and Wanigadewa, T. (1998) Pesticide poisoning: a major health problem in Sri Lanka. Social Science and Medicine, 56: 495–504.
Veluri, R. and Green, V.T. (1990) Suicide in Hindu women. British Journal of Psychiatry, 157: 149–150.
Vijayakumar, L. (1993) Thilothammal: suicide pacts. Crisis, 14: 43–46.
Vijayakumar, L. (1994) Befriending the suicidal in India—a column from Befrienders International. Crisis, 15: 99–100.
Wang, C.S. et al: (1997) An analysis of unnatural deaths between 1990 and 1994 in A-Lein, Taiwan. Injury, 28: 203–208.
Weiss, M. (1994) Hinduism. In W.T. Reich (Ed.), Encyclopaedia of Bioethics, Vol. 2. New York: Macmillan.
World Health Organization (1994) Life Skills Education in Schools. WHO/MNH/PSF/93. 7A Rev 2. Geneva: World Health Organization.
Xie, X., Weinstein, L. and Meredith, W. (1996) Hotline in China: one way to help Chinese people. Psychological Reports, 78: 90.
Zam, A.M. (1991) Profile of inpatient suicides in two hospitals in Malaysia. Medical Journal of Malaysia, 46: 171–176.
Zhang, J. and Jin, S. (1998) Interpersonal relations and suicide ideation in China. Genetics Society General Psychology Monograph, 124: 79–94.

Chapter 37

Suicide Prevention in Schools

David Shaffer
and
Madelyn Gould
Columbia University College of Physicians and Surgeons and School of Public Health, New York, NY, USA

Abstract

School-based suicide-prevention programmes most commonly take the form of some type of didactic curriculum. The educational goals are usually: (a) to promote help-seeking behaviour or make it more effective through, for example, destigmatization and providing information on resources; (b) to encourage and help students identify others at risk for suicide, by describing "warning signs" and giving instructions on how to contact a responsible adult; and (c) to counteract permissive and positive attitudes about suicide that are common among suicidal youth. Regrettably, there is no evidence that these excellent goals can be met by the programmes that have been described and tested in the literature. There is also some very limited evidence of potentially harmful effects. Because so little research has been done on educational strategies, it is quite possible that there are specific content elements or styles of presentation that could improve help seeking and counter the attitudes that facilitate suicidal behaviour. In the absence of such research, educational strategies directed to students only should be viewed with caution. A school environment is also well suited to provide relevant information to mature adults such as parents, school psychologists, counsellors and other people. Such programmes can be carried out safely and without incurring the risk that may be present in direct presentations of suicide to students. A quite different but effective and less controversial prevention activity is to systematically screen students for the mental disorders that predispose to suicide. Screening is not without its difficulties: it inevitably results in many false-positives and it requires extensive and expensive back-up to ensure that affected teenagers can receive appropriate treatment. However, given the magnitude of the public health problem of youth suicide, it is an approach that should be encouraged. Although schools are well placed to provide group interventions, there is no empirical evidence that effective coping skills can be taught in groups in a functionally useful way. Similarly, there is no evidence that group interventions are useful in the management of adolescent mood disorder, which is the condition that, above all others, predisposes to suicide. The processes

The International Handbook of Suicide and Attempted Suicide. Edited by K. Hawton and K. van Heeringen.

that occur within a school community after the suicide of a student are only starting to be uncovered, and an empirically-based approach to postvention needs to wait until more is known. At this point in time it seems likely that help needs to be targeted to at-risk pupils at an individual level, rather than in a generic way.

INTRODUCTION

Some type of school-based suicide-prevention programme has been estimated to reach about 1% of the teen population in the USA (Garland et al, 1989). Nineteen states have legislated policies on youth suicide; many require or recommend a suicide prevention curriculum presented either independently or as part of a health education programme (Metha et al, 1998). Most programmes use a psycho-educational approach, but there has also been experience with other methods, such as screening pupils directly for suicide risk, providing some active treatment or preventive intervention, or intervening with students after the suicide of a peer (postvention) (for reviews, see Shaffer et al, 1988; Berman and Jobes, 1991).

General Considerations

There are a number of reasons why a school-based approach to teen-suicide prevention is appealing:

1. Suicidal ideation and attempts are common during high-school years.
2. The great majority of adolescent suicides will have experienced a psychiatric disorder for some time *before* their death (Marttunen et al, 1991; Brent et al, 1993a; Shaffer et al, 1996b). Had these disorders been identified and treated, death might have been avoided.
3. Adolescents gather conveniently in schools, so that evaluations can be carried out or interventions provided in a cost-effective manner.
4. Schools are a good place for treatment; teenagers attend school-based clinics more regularly than they do hospital-based clinics (Adelman and Taylor, 1991), and the school environment is often supportive and conducive to frank disclosures and discussion.

However, there are also reasons for caution:

1. Suicidality is usually nested in complex psychodynamic and psychosocial influences that do not lend themselves to simple didactic explanations.
2. Talking openly with an adolescent on the topic of suicide is not necessarily a benign or even neutral process. It may be distressing to some, it may produce attitudes towards suicide that are unhelpful (Shaffer et al, 1990), and it may induce a negative mood state (Overholser et al, 1989).
3. Some of the best indicators of suicide risk (e.g. suicidal ideation, feelings of hopelessness, etc.) may not be apparent in everyday activities or conversa-

tions. This limits the value of an approach that depends on training teachers or pupils to observe "warning signs".

4. There is no evidence that mood disorder—the condition most commonly associated with suicide—can be altered by any didactic approach or prevented by group training in coping or social skills, methods that are often advocated as appropriate primary prevention techniques.
5. About half of teen suicides occur among 18- and 19-year-olds, a group that in most countries has already left high school.
6. Many adolescents who commit suicide are isolated and have either dropped out or do not attend school regularly and so are beyond the reach of school-based programmes (Shaffer, 1974; Hawton, 1986; Gould et al, 1996).

Types of Programme

School-based suicide-prevention programmes can be conveniently grouped into one of the following four categories:

1. *Psycho-educational or curriculum-based programmes.* These are the most common and the type of programme best accepted by school personnel (Miller et al, 1999). They are most often designed to enhance awareness of the problem, encourage the identification of students at risk (*case-finding*), promote help-seeking behaviour, and reduce the stigma attached to obtaining help for mental disorders. They work to find "cases" either "directly", by encouraging suicidal students to seek help themselves, or "indirectly", by instructing teachers and/or other students to identify adolescents who are at risk for suicide, giving guidance on how to confront the suicidal student and encourage him/her to obtain professional help.
2. *Direct case-finding or screening programmes.* These apply some form of screening instrument to all or selected students to identify those with important risk factors for suicide, such as recurrent suicidal ideation, symptoms of depressed mood, and a history of suicide attempts. Programmes that screen for high risk will usually include some mechanism for providing or facilitating appropriate treatment.
3. *Preventive or therapeutic interventions* include educating professional staff in a school-based mental health clinic or school counsellors on how best to treat suicidal teens, establishing a school-based suicide hotline, or establishing groups to promote coping skills.
4. *Postvention* provides an intervention after a suicide by one or more pupils. Postvention activities may include screening for risk, reducing distress among friends and faculty who were close to the deceased, and preventing post-traumatic stress among any students who witnessed the act or discovered the body. In principle, postventions could be designed to reduce the risk of copycat suicides, but as the mechanisms of imitation are not currently known, this remains only a hypothetical possibility (see below).

PSYCHO-EDUCATIONAL PROGRAMMES

Target Audience

In-service educational programmes target teachers and school counsellors and may also include parents (Miller and duPaul, 1996; Sandoval and Brock, 1996; Davidson and Range, 1999). Other programmes are directed to the student body itself (Miller et al, 1999; Poland, 1989), because of the evidence that suicidal teens—if they disclose their intention to anyone—are most likely to do so to their friends (Shaffer et al, 1991; Zimmerman, 1994). In-service training programmes have generally been met with enthusiasm and little concern, but there has been considerable debate over the value of programmes targeted at students (Hazell and King, 1996; Shaffer et al, 1991).

Models of Suicide

Most programmes provide an explicit or implicit model for suicide. The most common model (Garland et al, 1989) explains suicide as an understandable but misinformed *response to stress*, and downplays, or may explicitly contradict, a model that views suicide as a symptom of an underlying mental illness. Many programmes include video-taped material with a teenager who had previously attempted suicide. The teenager will typically describe his/her earlier suicide attempt, most often indicating that it was triggered by some external stressor rather than by a mood change. He/she will then detail positive aspects of his/her current status, making the point that no matter how overwhelming a problem might seem at one moment, it may not remain that way. Training materials like this have not been systematically tested, but one concern is that, if a teenager selected for a demonstration video is attractive and articulate and his/her mood at the time of interview is assertive and confident, it could add status and desirability to the behaviour. It is also possible that a model that downplays the importance of mental illness could encourage students to see suicide as a potential solution to their own problems (Garland and Zigler, 1993). The appeal of this approach to programme designers is probably based on the unsupported view that presenting suicide as a response to external circumstances is less stigmatizing than presenting it as a fatal complication of a mental illness, even though the evidence supports the latter.

A novel approach to linking suicide to mental illness has been described by Ciffone (1993), who developed a teaching tape in which a suicide attempt was labelled as manipulative and unheroic and a suicide completer was shown as clearly mentally ill, taking his life after experiencing a stress with which most adolescents could cope. The impact of this programme in a small controlled study was promising (see below).

Identification of "Warning Signs"

Warning signs are clinical behaviours, noticeable by others, such as sadness, irritability, social withdrawal, explicit statements of suicidal intent, or giving away possessions. Most warning signs lack specificity—that is, they are common in non-suicidal teens. Yet others, such as giving away possessions, are relatively rare precursors of a suicide and are often absent in suicidal teens, or, like sadness or irritability, may require clinical experience or training to perceive. Another concern is that linking the clinical features of depression with suicidality could lead a depressed teenager to regard suicide as a "normal" accompaniment to depression, whereas it is actually a somewhat unusual and highly specific feature (Johnson and Hunt, 1979; Roy-Byrne et al, 1988; King et al, 1997).

Teaching How to Respond to the Suicidal Students

A minority of programmes provide opportunities for peers and teachers to rehearse how to suggest to the student that they get help from an appropriate adult, how to set up a "no-suicide" agreement (Davidson and Range, 1997), and how to report what the student told them to an authoritative adult (Garland et al, 1989). But judging whether a student is suicidal is difficult for a clinician and much more so for a lay person (Malley et al, 1994). It calls for the adoption of unusual and unfamiliar roles and may require the "helping" student or teacher to violate confidential elements of a relationship by disclosing what they may have learned in private. These may be some of the reasons why, at least in brief programmes, most students do not heed the advice they receive about how to deal with a distressed friend (Vieland et al, 1991).

Destigmatization and Encouraging Help-seeking

Almost all programmes promote help-seeking in one way or another. Given the many barriers faced by children in obtaining mental-health services (Tuma, 1989), the reported relationship between reluctance to seek help and depression (Garland and Zigler, 1994), and the importance of confidentiality to teenagers (Ford et al, 1997), this is an area of great importance. However, a large controlled study of the effects of a brief stress-based model (Vieland et al, 1991) found that teenagers who participated in the programme were significantly *less* likely to seek help for themselves or recommend it to others than those who did not. This was especially likely in students who had made a previous suicide attempt—that is, the students who were most in need of treatment. Other methods used to promote help-seeking include giving students details of available resources, and making use of traditional case management procedures (Shivack and Sullivan, 1991). Barriers to help-seeking may include cost, location and convenience of clinics, the attitude of helping professionals, and any "resistence" felt by patients.

Overcoming these barriers to psychiatric care requires more than a good "attitude". Szapocznik and colleagues (1988) and McKay and colleagues (1996) have proposed the use of telephone-based therapies as a solution to the logistic component of compliance problems.

Some programmes attempt to destigmatize suicide by introducing the concept that suicidal ideation or behaviour after a stress or loss is understandable and not indicative of an underlying psychiatric disturbance. Shaffer and colleagues (1990) found that even very brief programmes with this "normalization" approach can be disturbingly effective in changing adolescent views. Students who, before participation in a programme, had held that thinking about or committing suicide in response to an outside stressor was abnormal, were significantly more likely to regard suicide as a normal or expected response after attending the programme. This was not obviously helpful, because the change in beliefs was not associated with a greater preparedness to seek or recommend help and might have reduced any protective taboo on the subject.

Although not yet replicated, Ciffone's (1993) programme, which emphasized mental illness, did result in significant changes of attitude among students who had previously said that they would not break a suicidal confidence, would not take another student's talk of suicide seriously, would not talk to others about their own suicidal thoughts, and did not believe that suicidal ideas were associated with mental illness. The emphasis on linking suicide to mental illness did not appear to reduce the students' willingness to seek help from a mental health professional. Esters and colleagues (1998) described significant and sustained improvements in *attitudes* towards seeking psychiatric treatment in a programme that emphasized educating the students about mental illness and the role of different mental health professionals. However, it requires more research to learn whether that change in attitude translates into changed behaviour. In summary, attempting to destigmatize suicide by directly divorcing it from the "stigma" of mental illness is not only untrue but does not help achieve the goal of prevention.

What would be the impact of the very successful approach to destigmatization used by various patient advocacy groups that emphasize the biological origins of mental illness and the similarity between physical and mental illness? Their message that mental illness is not a sign of a weak or inadequate personality or temperament might be especially powerful among adolescents.

Some alternative educational strategies to prevent suicide that have been suggested in the popular press, but which have not, to our knowledge, been tested, include the use of scare tactics—for example, showing bodies of completed suicides in the mortuary or focusing on the grief felt by survivors.

Impact of Psycho-educational Programmes

The efficacy of curriculum-based programmes has been reviewed (Range, 1993; Ploeg et al, 1996). Because of the absence of careful programmatic research, there is little agreement about the most appropriate content for educational programmes or any widely accepted measure of effectiveness (Ciffone, 1993). None of the controlled studies have found either an increase or a decrease in suicidal ideation or behaviour (Shaffer et al, 1991; Garland and Zigler, 1993; Miller and duPaul, 1996) following participation in such a programme. Most have found some increase in knowledge, more often among girls than boys (Kalafat and Elias, 1994, 1995), but a substantial number of students who held unusual or possibly dangerous ideas experienced no change (Spirito et al, 1988; Overholser et al, 1989; Shaffer et al, 1991; Metha et al, 1998). Two studies reported negative effects. One (Shaffer et al, 1990, 1991; Vieland et al, 1991) found that participants who had made a previous suicide attempt were significantly more likely to regard the class as disturbing and were less likely to endorse it as being valuable or helpful for others. Another group (Overholser et al, 1989) found an *increase* in expressed hopelessness and maladaptive coping responses in boys *after* participation in the educational programmes.

Finally, given the well-established phenomenon of suicide contagion (Bollen and Phillips, 1982; Gould and Shaffer, 1986; Coleman, 1987; Schmidtke and Hafner, 1988; Velting and Gould, 1997; see Chapter 39), it cannot be assumed that a didactic programme on suicide will have only beneficial or neutral effects. It is likely that there will be significant variation in the responses of different students and that these will relate systematically to their mental state and prior experience.

DIRECT CASE-FINDING OR SCREENING

Only a minority of adolescents who commit suicide have ever been evaluated by a mental health professional (Brent et al, 1988; Shaffer et al, 1996b). This may be because the symptoms of depression often go unnoticed in teenagers. Given this degree of under-identification, there is a strong case for developing programmes that proactively identify suicidality by a technique other than a purely educational one. Direct screening (Shaffer et al, 1988; Reynolds, 1991) is such an alternative, even though screening programmes are significantly less acceptable to principals and other school officials than psycho-educational programmes (Miller et al, 1999), possibly because of a lack of familiarity or possibly because of concerns about legal responsibility (Bongar et al, 1992).

In direct screening, students are asked, directly and often with an assurance that information will not be disclosed to the teaching staff, whether they are experiencing any symptoms of depression, have suicidal ideation or have ever made a suicide attempt and/or have an alcohol- or substance-abuse problem. Their replies, usually on a standardized instrument such as the Suicidal Ideation Questionnaire (SIQ) (Reynolds, 1987) or the Columbia Teen Screen (which elicits information on mood and substance-abuse disorders as well as suicidal ideation and behaviour) (Shaffer et al, 1996c), are examined and, if abnormal, the student is referred for clinical care (Reynolds, 1991; Shaffer et al, 1996c; Shaffer and Craft, 1999). Although this approach to suicide prevention takes place in a school setting, it has no educational component. It does not involve suicide awareness lectures, with their attendant risks, or charge students and teachers with the task of acting like mental health professionals.

Direct screening may involve a single-stage, a two-stage or a three-stage procedure. In the first stage of a three-stage procedure, students complete a brief, self-report questionnaire with high sensitivity and low specificity that, although it will miss very few suicidal teens, will inevitably identify many false-positives. Students who score above a given threshold advance to the second phase of the process and are further assessed on a self-administered, computerized, diagnostic interview, such as the Diagnostic Interview Schedule for Children (DISC) (Shaffer et al, 1996a). The purpose of this second stage is to reduce the burden of false-positive students to be seen by a clinician at the third stage, and to assist the clinician who carries out the evaluations. With the DISC information, the clinician who sees the student in the third and final stage can interview the student personally for a shorter time and at less cost. The clinician's task is to determine whether the student needs to be referred for treatment or further evaluation. Under optimal conditions, the clinician is assisted by a case manager who contacts the student's parents and establishes links with a clinic to optimize treatment compliance.

An examination of the Teen Screen among 2,004 teenagers from eight New York metropolitan area high schools (Shaffer and Craft, 1999) illustrates this process. Twenty-seven percent of the total number screened scored positively on the initial screen (the Columbia Teen Screen), meeting at least one of the positive-screening criteria for depression, dysthymia or substance/alcohol abuse, coupled with either recurrent suicide ideation or a previous attempt. The sensitivity of the initial screen was approximately 88% and specificity was 76%. While only three cases went undetected by the Columbia Teen Screen (false-negatives), there were 257 false-positive screens. This indicates the importance of implementing a second phase to exclude those who carry a lesser risk for suicide. This study also revealed that most of the adolescents who were at high risk for suicide were not known to others, and very few had ever received treatment. Rather similar findings were reported by Reynolds using a threshold of 40 on the Suicide Ideation Questionnaire (SIQ) (Reynolds, 1991).

Identifying high school students who are depressed, thinking often about suicide or have made a suicide attempt is likely to result in a benefit that extends well beyond the high school years. In a six-year follow-up of suicide attempters, suicide ideators, non-suicidal depressives, and "normals" identified during a school screening exercise, two-thirds of those who would attempt suicide or become depressed in the six years after the screen were drawn from the initial high-risk group (Restifo et al, 1998).

ACTIVE INTERVENTIONS

School-based clinics provide treatment in a familiar setting. They avoid the costs of transportation for the patient and may reduce other barriers to treatment

(Weist et al, 1996). The selection and training of the staff at such clinics is likely to influence the management of previously suicidal teens who are seen there. To this end, Eggert and colleagues (1995) focused their training programme on teachers and counsellors who had already been identified as "natural help-givers" by students and other adults.

A number of preventive interventions have been designed for use in schools. Most provide training in "coping skills" over several meetings. Klingman and Hochdorf (1993) developed a cognitive-behavioural therapy (CBT)—based programme that was designed to improve teenagers' ability to cope with their own stress and to identify and respond better to the stress of their peers. It used common cognitive approaches, such as the rational examination of thoughts, transforming self-defeating talk into active coping, empathy training, help-seeking behaviour (modelled and reinforced with role-playing), refuting irrational beliefs, modifying cognitive processes such as automatic thoughts, and techniques for developing or strengthening a social-support network. The intervention led to improved awareness of coping responses and (according to a postvention questionnaire assessment) a lessened intent to commit suicide in boys. Further research would be needed to determine whether these changes in attitude are translated into actual behaviour.

Orbach and Bar-Joseph (1993) devised an intervention for eleventh graders in which feelings, inner experiences and life difficulties were discussed in small groups for seven weekly two-hour sessions. Coping skills were taught for dealing with family problems, feelings of helplessness, failure, stress, depression and suicidal urges. Students' personal problems were the starting point for discussion. Students taking the course showed improved coping skills and believed that the programme improved their problem-solving. Some teens with a conduct disorder showed improvements on the research measurements, but were embarrassed by the personal revelation required by the programme. The impact of the programmes on suicidal or depressed mood has not been evaluated.

Eggert and colleagues (1995) targeted a population of chronic truants and drop-outs, groups that are at high risk for suicidal behaviour (Thompson et al, 1994; Gould et al, 1996). After a two-stage screening procedure, one randomly selected group of students deemed at risk for suicide were introduced to a school case manager who knew the particulars of each student's case and informed a parent of the student's status. The other students at risk for suicide received this same introduction and communication, but were also placed in an intervention class, meeting daily in small groups. Students in the class were trained in anger and stress management and taught a cognitive approach to correct depression, heighten self-esteem, improve communication and decision-making skills, and acquire and use available social networks. Although students emerged from the class with a reduction in several at-risk behaviours (including suicidal behaviour, depression, hopelessness and anger), the change was similar to that in the assessment-only group, leading Eggert to conclude that the assessment provided might have worked as an effective intervention. Perceived ability to handle problems and effect positive outcomes *was* improved in twice as many of the students who received skills training, leading to the hypothesis that long-term coping skills are a protective factor that might not be measured in the short-term assessment of risk factors.

There is some evidence that counsellor-led programmes that use a generic approach to increasing self-esteem (Lavoritano and Segal, 1992) have minimal impact on self-worth. Programmes designed to enhance social competence are commonly viewed as having an antisuicide potential, but there is no documented evidence of this (Weissberg and Elias, 1993).

INTERVENTION AFTER A SUICIDE—POSTVENTION/CRISIS INTERVENTION

A broad range of psychological sequelae is likely to occur among individuals in the aftermath of a suicide (see Chapter 26). These deleterious effects can include suicidality (Gould et al, 1990a, 1990b, 1994), the onset or exacerbation of psychiatric disorders (e.g. post-traumatic stress disorder, major depressive disorder, etc.) and other symptoms related to pathological bereavement (Brent et al, 1993b, 1993c, 1994). The underlying rationale for postvention/crisis intervention is that a timely response to these outcomes among the surviving friends and fellow students is likely to reduce subsequent morbidity and mortality. The major goals of postvention programmes are to assist survivors in the grief process; identify and refer those individuals who may be at risk following the suicide; provide accurate information about suicide, while attempting to minimize suicide contagion; and implement a structure for ongoing prevention efforts (Hazell, 1993; Underwood and Dunne-Maxim, 1997).

The first task of most crisis-intervention programmes is to identify who will be in a leadership role (usually the school superintendent or school principal) as well as the members of a "crisis management team". The crisis management team often includes the school psychologist, guidance counsellors, school social workers, and the school nurse, as well as outside resources, such as mental-health professionals and clergy. The crisis management team is responsible for determining the location and number of "crisis stations" in the school; assigning crisis station counsellors; identifying students thought to be at risk and contacting them and their families; selecting a counsellor to follow the schedule of the deceased and sit in those classes throughout the day following the death; contacting the family of the deceased to express condolences, obtain information about the funeral, and provide the family with information about local mental health services; and assigning a single media spokesperson. As soon as the crisis management team has been mobilized and the overview of the response plan is set, a statement about the death is released to faculty and students. Announcements are usually given to the faculty at a meeting on the first day following the death. Faculty will then in turn read the announcement to their students later in class. At the faculty meeting, factors of the case are reviewed; procedures for handling parental inquiries are reviewed; support available for students, faculty and staff are presented; and the faculty is asked to be involved in identifying additional students who may be at risk. To address parental concerns, letters are sent home to inform them of the facts of the death and about the school's postvention activities. Small parent groups are often assembled, facilitated by crisis-team staff, within a few days of the death.

One of the critical challenges of most postvention programmes is the identification of vulnerable students. At-risk students are usually identified among the following groups: close friends of the deceased; students on the same teams or other school clubs with the deceased; friends of siblings of the deceased; students with known drug or alcohol problems, emotional problems or previous suicidal ideation or attempts; students identified by peers, faculty or parents; and students who self-identify (Underwood and Dunne-Maxim, 1997). Regrettably, the identification process is conducted in a somewhat "hit-or-miss", haphazard fashion by existing crisis-intervention programmes. Many high-risk students may not self-identify or be recognized by school personnel. Furthermore, this set of vulnerable students is not exhaustive. For example, preliminary results from an ongoing study on youth suicide clusters in the USA indicate that the majority of school-aged victims in a cluster were not best or close friends (Gould, 1999a). Systematic assessment procedures, such as school-wide screenings, would complement the efforts of existing crisis intervention programmes to identify at-risk students.

The number of postvention programmes has shown a substantial increase in recent years (Hill, 1984; Shaffer et al, 1988; Siehl, 1990; Catone and Schatz, 1991; Hazell, 1991; Wenckstern and Leenars, 1991), often from public concern over suicide clusters. However, there is little systematic research in this area (Shaffer et al, 1988). The existing research on school-based postvention programmes is very limited (Hill, 1984; Shaffer et al, 1988). The only evaluation research in this area was a study by Hazell and Lewin (1993) examining a postvention programme implemented in two schools after a student's suicide. Hazell and Lewin (1993) examined the efficacy of 90-minute group counselling sessions offered to groups of 20–30 students seven days following the suicide. The students had been selected by school staff predominantly on the basis of a close friendship with the deceased student. The evaluation was conducted eight months after the suicide occurred. No differences in outcome were found between counselled subjects and matched controls in the schools. It was unclear whether this was due to inappropriateness of the criteria for student selection for postvention counselling, the intervention itself, the duration of the distress, or whether there may have been a differential short-term effect that was not evident at eight months after the death. It is imperative that school-based interventions be better planned and evaluated. Otherwise, they are liable not to address the needs of the survivors, be a waste of resources, and may have the potential for exacerbating the problem through the induction of imitation. An aim of an ongoing project funded by the National Institute of Mental Health (Gould et al, 1999b) is to develop research-based administrative guidelines and intervention programmes to be implemented in the schools, in order to facilitate a timely and efficacious crisis response.

In summary, the underlying rationale of postvention/crisis intervention is strong, reflecting several empirical studies that have examined the sequelae to suicide exposure; however, few evaluation studies have been conducted, and the efficacy of this prevention/intervention strategy has not yet been demonstrated. A limitation of many postvention/crisis-intervention programmes is that high-risk students are not necessarily identified without a systematic screening. Lastly, a response plan needs to be in place prior to a crisis; yet the motivation for development often occurs after a crisis.

CONCLUSION

Schools offer an excellent setting in which to identify children and adolescents who are at high risk for suicide and, when appropriate, provide them with treatment. However, there is no evidence that a purely educational, or didactic, approach effectively leads depressed or suicidal teens to reveal their ideation or seek treatment, neither do they significantly alter the permissive and positive attitudes toward suicide that are held by disturbed youth. However, it is likely that important and helpful information about the features of adolescent mood disorders and suicidality can be provided to parents and appropriate school personnel in a school setting, and that this can be done without incurring the risk attendant on talking directly to students on the subject of suicide. The procedure that appears to be most effective and least controversial is the systematic screening for unidentified and untreated mental disorders that predispose to suicide. This is appealing in its simplicity, but, in practice, requires extensive and expensive back-up to ensure that identified teenagers are directed towards, and can receive, appropriate treatment. Although schools are well suited to provide group interventions, there is no empirical evidence that coping skills can be taught in a functionally useful way, or that group interventions are useful in the management of mood disorders, the condition that above all others predisposes to suicide.

The processes that occur within a school community after the suicide of a student are only starting to be uncovered, and an empirically-based approach to postvention needs to wait until more is known. At this point in time, it seems likely that individualized help needs to be targeted to at-risk individuals at an individual level, rather than in some generic fashion.

REFERENCES

Adelman, H.S. and Taylor, L. (1991) Early school adjustment problems: some perspectives and a project report. American Journal of Orthopsychiatry, 61: 468–474.

Berman, A.L. and Jobes, D.A. (1991) Adolescent Suicide: Assessment and Intervention. Washington, DC: American Psychological Association.

Bollen, K.A. and Phillips D.P. (1982) Imitative suicides: a national study of the effects of television news stories. American Sociological Review, 47: 802–809.

Bongar, B., Maris, R.W., Berman, A.L. and Litman, R.E. (1992) Outpatient standards of care and the suicidal patient. Suicide and Life-Threatening Behavior, 22: 453–477.

Brent, D.A., Perper, J.A., Goldstein, C.E., Kolko, D.J., Allan, M.J., Allman, C.J. and Zelenak, J.P. (1988) Risk factors for adolescent suicide. A comparison of adolescent suicide victims with suicidal inpatients. Archives of General Psychiatry, 45: 581–588.

Brent, D.A., Perper, J.A., Moritz, G., Allman, C., Friend, A., Roth, C., Schweers, J., Balach, L. and Baugher, M. (1993a) Psychiatric risk factors for adolescent suicide: a case-control study. Journal of the American Academy of Child and Adolescent Psychiatry, 32: 521–529.

Brent, D.A., Perper, J.A., Moritz, G.M., Allman, C., Liotus, L., Schweers, J., Roth, C., Balach, L. and Canobbio, R. (1993b) Bereavement or depression? The impact of the loss of a friend to suicide. Journal of the American Academy of Child and Adolescent Psychiatry, 32: 1189–1197.

Brent, D.A., Perper, J.A., Moritz, G.M., Friend, A., Schweers, J., Allman, C., McQuiston, L., Boylan, M.B., Roth, C. and Balach, L. (1993c) Adolescent witness to a peer suicide. Journal of the American Academy of Child and Adolescent Psychiatry, 32: 1184–1188.

Brent, D.A., Perper, J.A., Moritz, G.M., Liotus, L., Schweers, J. and Canobbio, R. (1994) Major depression or uncomplicated bereavement? A follow-up of youth exposed to suicide. Journal of the American Academy of Child and Adolescent Psychiatry, 33: 231–239.

Catone, W.V. and Schatz, M.T. (1991) The crisis moment: a school's response to the event of suicide. School Psychology International, 12(11–2): 17–23.

Ciffone, J. (1993) Suicide prevention: a classroom presentation to adolescents. Social Work, 38: 197–203.

Coleman, L. (1987) Suicide Clusters. Boston: Faber and Faber.

Davidson, M.W. and Range, L.M. (1999) Are teachers of children and young adolescents responsive to suicide-prevention training modules? Yes. Death Studies, 23: 61–71.

Davidson, M. and Range, L.M. (1997) Practice teachers' responses to a suicidal student. Journal of Social Psychology, 137: 530–532.

Eggert, L.L., Thompson, E.A., Herting, J.R. and Nicholas, L.J. (1995) Reducing suicide potential among high-risk youth: tests of a school-based prevention program. Suicide and Life-Threatening Behavior, 25: 276–296.

Esters, I.G., Cooker, P.G. and Ittenbach, R.F. (1998) Effects of a unit of instruction in mental health on rural adolescents' conceptions of mental illness and attitudes about seeking help. Adolescence, 33: 469–476.

Ford, C.A., Millstein, S.G., Halpern-Felsher, B.L. and Irwin, C.E.J. (1997) Influence of physician-confidentiality assurances on adolescents' willingness to disclose information and seek future health care. A randomized controlled trial [see comments]. Journal of the American Medical Association, 278: 1029–1034.

Garland, A., Shaffer, D. and Whittle, B. (1989) A national survey of school-based, adolescent-suicide-prevention programs. Journal of the American Academy of Child and Adolescent Psychiatry, 28: 931–934.

Garland, A.F. and Zigler, E. (1993) Adolescent-suicide prevention. Current research and social policy implications. American Psychologist, 48: 169–182.

Garland, A.F. and Zigler, E.F. (1994) Psychological correlates of help-seeking attitudes among children and adolescents. American Journal of Orthopsychiatry, 64: 586–593.

Gould, M.S. (1999a) Psychological autopsy of cluster suicides in adolescents. National Institute of Mental Health, Grant R01 MH47559-04S2.

Gould, M.S. (1999b) Epidemiologic sequelae of suicide in schools. National Institute of Mental Health, Grant R01 MH52827-04.

Gould, M.S., Fisher, P., Parides, M., Flory, M. and Shaffer, D. (1996) Psychosocial risk factors of child and adolescent completed suicide. Archives of General Psychiatry, 53: 1155–1162.

Gould, M.S. and Shaffer, D. (1986) The impact of suicide in television movies: evidence of imitation. New England Journal of Medicine, 315: 690–694.

Gould, M.S., Petrie, K., Kleinman, M. and Wallenstein, S. (1994) Clustering of attempted suicide: New Zealand national data. International Journal of Epidemiology, 23: 1185–1189.

Gould, M.S., Wallenstein S., Kleinman, M.H., O'Carroll, P. and Mercy, J. (1990a) Suicide clusters: an examination of age-specific effects. American Journal of Public Health, 80: 211–212.

Gould, M.S., Wallenstein, S. and Kleinman, M. (1990b) Time-space clustering of teenage suicide. American Journal of Epidemiology, 131: 71–78.

Hawton, K. (1986) Suicide and Attempted Suicide Among Children and Adolescents. Beverly Hills, CA: Sage.

Hazell, P. (1991) Postvention after teenage suicide: an Australian experience. Journal of Adolescence, 14: 335–342.

Hazell, P. (1993) Adolescent-suicide clusters: evidence, mechanisms, and prevention. Australian and New Zealand Journal of Psychiatry, 27: 653–665.

Hazell, P. and King, R. (1996) Arguments for and against teaching suicide prevention in schools. Australian and New Zealand Journal of Psychiatry, 30: 633–642.

Hazell, P. and Lewin, T. (1993) An evaluation of postvention following adolescent suicide. Suicide and Life-Threatening Behavior, 23: 101–109.

Hill, W.H. (1984) Intervention and postvention in schools. In H.S. Sudak, A.B. Ford and N.B. Rushforth (Eds), Suicide in the Young, pp. 407–416. Boston: John Wright.

Johnson, G.F. and Hunt, G. (1979) Suicidal behavior in bipolar manic-depressive patients and their families. Comprehensive Psychiatry, 20: 159–164.

Kalafat, J. and Elias, M. (1994) An evaluation of a school-based suicide awareness intervention. Suicide and Life-Threatening Behavior, 24: 224–233.

Kalafat, J. and Elias, M.J. (1995) Suicide prevention in an educational context: broad and narrow foci. Suicide and Life-Threatening Behavior, 25: 123–133.

King, C.A., Hovey, J.D., Brand, E., Wilson, R. and Ghaziuddin, N. (1997) Suicidal adolescents after hospitalization: parent and family impacts on treatment follow-through. Journal of the American Academy of Child and Adolescent Psychiatry, 36: 85–93.

Klingman, A. and Hochdorf, Z. (1993) Coping with distress and self-harm: the impact of a primary prevention program among adolescents. Journal of Adolescence, 16: 121–140.

Lavoritano, J. and Segal, P.B. (1992) Evaluating the efficacy of a school counseling program. Psychology in the Schools, 29: 61–70.

Malley, P.B., Kush, F. and Bogo, R.J. (1994) School-based adolescent-suicide-prevention and intervention programs: a survey. The School Counselor, 42: 130–136.

Marttunen, M.J., Aro, H.M., Henriksson, M.M. and Lönnqvist, J.K. (1991) Mental disorders in adolescent suicide. DSM-III-R axes I and II diagnoses in suicides among 13–19 year-olds in Finland. Archives of General Psychiatry, 48: 834–839.

McKay, M.M., McCadam, K. and Gonzales, J.J. (1996) Addressing the barriers to mental health services for inner-city children and their caretakers. Community Mental Health Journal, 32: 353–361.

Metha, A., Weber, B. and Webb, L.D. (1998) Youth-suicide prevention: a survey and analysis of policies and efforts in the 50 states. Suicide and Life-Threatening Behavior, 28: 150–164.

Miller, D.N. and DuPaul, G.J. (1996) School-based prevention of adolescent suicide: issues, obstacles, and recommendations for practice. Journal of Emotional and Behavioral Disorders, 4: 221–230.

Miller, D.N., Eckert, T.L., DuPaul, G.J. and White, G.P. (1999) Adolescent-suicide prevention: acceptability of school-based programs among secondary-school principals. Suicide and Life-Threatening Behavior, 29: 72–85.

Orbach, I. and Bar-Joseph, H. (1993) The impact of a suicide-prevention program for adolescents on suicidal tendencies, hopelessness, ego identity, and coping. Suicide and Life-Threatening Behavior, 23: 120–129.

Overholser, J.C., Hemstreet, A.H., Spirito, A. and Vyse, S. (1989) Suicide-awareness programs in the schools: effects of gender and personal experience. Journal of the American Academy of Child and Adolescent Psychiatry, 28: 925–930.

Ploeg, J., Ciliska, D., Dobbins, M., Hayward, S., Thomas, H. and Underwood, J. (1996) A systematic overview of adolescent-suicide-prevention programs. Canadian Journal of Public Health, 87: 319–324.

Poland, S. (1989) Suicide Intervention in the Schools. New York: Guilford.

Range, L.M. (1993) Suicide prevention: guidelines for schools. Educational Psychology Review, 5: 135–154.

Restifo, K., Shaffer, D., Garfinkel, R., Munfakh, J.L., Fisher, P., Busner, C. and Calderon, G. (1998) Five-year follow-up of adolescent suicide attempters screened in high school. Poster presented at the Anaheim AACAP meeting, Anaheim, CA.

Reynolds, W.M. (1987) Adult Suicidal Ideation Questionnaire. Odessa, FL: Psychological Assessment Resources.

Reynolds, W.M. (1991) A school-based procedure for the identification of adolescents at risk for suicidal behaviors. Family Community Health, 14: 64–75.

Roy-Byrne, P.P., Post, R.M., Hambrick, D.D., Leverich, G.S. and Rosoff, A.S. (1988) Suicide and course of illness in major affective disorder. Journal of Affective Disorders, 15: 1–8.

Sandoval, J. and Brock, S.E. (1996) The school psychologist's role in suicide prevention. School Psychology Quarterly, 11: 169–185.

Schmidtke, A. and Hafner, H. (1988) The Werther effect after television films: new evidence for an old hypothesis. Psychological Medicine, 18: 665–676.

Shaffer, D. (1974) Suicide in childhood and early adolescence. Journal of Child Psychology and Psychiatry and Allied Disciplines, 15: 275–291.

Shaffer, D. and Craft, L. (1999) Methods of adolescent-suicide prevention. Journal of Clinical Psychiatry, 60: 70–74.

Shaffer, D., Fisher, P., Dulcan, M.K., Davies, M., Piacentini, J., Schwab-Stone, M.E., Lahey, B.B., Bourdon, K., Jensen, P.S., Bird, H.R., Canino, G. and Regier, D.A. (1996a) The NIMH Diagnostic Interview Schedule for Children, Version 2.3 (DISC-2.3): description, acceptability, prevalence rates, and performance in the MECA Study (Methods for the Epidemiology of Child and Adolescent Mental Disorders Study). Journal of the American Academy of Child and Adolescent Psychiatry, 35: 865–877.

Shaffer, D., Garland, M., Gould, M., Fisher, P. and Trautman, P. (1988) Preventing teenage suicide: a critical review. Journal of the American Academy of Child and Adolescent Psychiatry, 27(6): 675–689.

Shaffer, D., Garland, A., Vieland, V., Underwood, M. and Busner, C. (1991) The impact of curriculum-based suicide-prevention programs for teenagers. Journal of the American Academy of Child and Adolescent Psychiatry, 30: 588–596.

Shaffer, D., Gould, M.S., Fisher, P., Trautman, P., Moreau, D., Kleinman, M. and Flory, M. (1996b) Psychiatric diagnosis in child and adolescent suicide. Archives of General Psychiatry, 53: 339–348.

Shaffer, D., Vieland, V., Garland, A., Rojas, M., Underwood, M. and Busner, C. (1990) Adolescent suicide attempters. Response to suicide-prevention programs. Journal of the American Medical Association, 264: 3151–3155.

Shaffer, D., Wilcox, H., Lucas, C., Hicks, R., Busner, C. and Parides, M. (1996c), The development of a screening instrument for teens at risk for suicide. Poster presented at the 1996 meeting of the Academy of Child and Adolescent Psychiatry, New York.

Shivack, N. and Sullivan, T. (1991) Use of telephone prompts at an inner-city outpatient clinic. Hospital and Community Psychiatry, 40: 851–853.

Siehl, P.M. (1990) Suicide postvention: a new disaster plan. What a school should do when faced with a suicide. School Counselor, 38: 52–57.

Spirito, A., Overholser, J., Ashworth, S., Morgan, J. and Benedict-Drew, C. (1988) Evaluation of a suicide-awareness curriculum for high school students. Journal of the American Academy of Child and Adolescent Psychiatry, 27: 705–711.

Szapocznik, J., Perez-Vidal, A., Brickman, A.L., Foote, F.H., Santesteban, D., Hervis, O. and Kurtines, W.M. (1988) Engaging adolescent drug abusers and their families in treatment: a strategic structural-systems approach. Journal of Consulting and Clinical Psychology, 56: 552–557.

Thompson, E.A., Moody, K.A. and Eggert, L.L. (1994) Discriminating suicide ideation among high-risk youth. Journal of School Health, 64: 361–367.

Tuma, J.M. (1989) Mental-health services for children. American Psychologist, 44: 188–199.

Underwood, M.M. and Dunne-Maxim, K. (1997) Managing sudden traumatic loss in the schools. In University of Medicine and Dentistry of New Jersey: New Jersey Adolescent Suicide Prevention Project, pp. 1–134.

Velting, D.M. and Gould, M.S. (1997) Suicide contagion. In R.W. Maris, M.M. Silverman and M.S. Gould (Eds), Review of Suicidology, pp. 96–137. New York: Guilford.

Vieland, V., Whittle, B., Garland, A., Hicks, R. and Shaffer, D. (1991) The impact of curriculum-based suicide-prevention programs for teenagers: an 18-month follow-up. Journal of the American Academy of Child and Adolescent Psychiatry, 30: 811–815.

Weissberg, R. and Elias, M. (1993) Enhancing young people's social competence and health behavior: an important challenge for educators, scientists, policymakers, and funders. Applied and Preventive Psychology, 2: 179–190.

Weist, M.D., Paskewitz, D.A., Warner, B.S. and Flaherty, L.T. (1996) Treatment outcome of school-based mental-health services for urban teenagers. Community Mental Health Journal, 32: 149–157.

Wenckstern, S. and Leenars, A. (1991) Suicide postvention: a case illustration in a secondary school. In A. Leenars and S. Wenckstern (Eds), Suicide Prevention in Schools. New York: Hemisphere.

Zimmerman, J.K. (1994) Gallup survey of adolescent suicidality. Newslink, 20: 6–7.

Chapter 38

Suicide Prevention and Primary Care

Konrad Michel
Medical School, University of Bern and Psychiatric Outpatient Clinic, University Hospital, Bern, Switzerland

Abstract

In this chapter it is argued that the primary care physician has an important role in the prevention of suicide. Suicide prevention should not only be understood as the detection of the high-risk patient with an acute risk of suicide, but should start "at the bottom of the iceberg", i.e. early in the development of serious emotional problems which might eventually lead to a suicidal crisis. Yet there are a number of problems. Successful communication between suicidal patients and health professionals is not an easy task. In order to make communication meaningful, physicians must have a model to understand the patients and their motives that lead to suicide or attempted suicide, and they must have an understanding of their role in suicide prevention. Suicide as such is an act and therefore does not readily fit into the traditional causal disease model. A further problem lies in the difficulty in detecting psychiatric disorders, particularly depression. Many patients, particularly men, do not present with obvious signs of depression. Adequate and often life-saving antidepressant treatment can only be prescribed when the diagnosis has been established. Training programmes for primary care physicians are needed, but they should address knowledge as well as attitudes. In summary, primary care physicians need a thorough knowledge of the main risk factors and the skills to understand the patient as an individual human being. Only the integration of both aspects will allow the physician to decide on the adequate management of the suicidal patient.

In a seminar, a general practitioner from a rural practice related the following story. On a busy Saturday practice morning a 45 year-old teacher whom he has not seen for 2 years presents with a strained left ankle. The patient tells him that it happened a couple of days ago when he went for a walk in the forest. The general practitioner cannot find anything remarkable, and he discharges the patient with an ointment

The International Handbook of Suicide and Attempted Suicide. Edited by K. Hawton and K. van Heeringen.

and an elastic bandage. Two hours later the patient's wife calls to ask if her husband is still with him, as he has not returned yet. She calls again an hour later, reporting that her husband has been found dead in the forest. He had shot himself through the head.

THE COMMUNICATION OF INTENT

The story illustrates a typical problem in suicide prevention—suicidal persons often are under medical care, but they rarely talk about their intentions. Fifty percent or more of those committing suicide have seen a general practitioner or a medical specialist within a month before their death (Murphy, 1975; Michel, 1986). In a psychological autopsy study of 571 suicides in Finland, in which a health care professional had been contacted prior to the suicide, Isometsä and colleagues (1995b) found that at the occasion of the last visit the issue of suicide had been discussed in 22% of the cases (in psychiatric outpatients 39%, in general practice 11% and in other specialties 6%). An increase in the frequency of visits to general practitioners prior to suicide and attempted suicide has been demonstrated (Appleby et al, 1996; Michel et al, 1997), which suggests that the reasons for the visits to the primary care physician are related to the development of a suicidal crisis. In fact, as in the introductory example, it is not at all rare that patients visit their doctor even a few hours before committing suicide. In the Finnish study, 18 percent of those who had contacted a physician had done so on the day of committing suicide, yet even then the issue of suicide was discussed in only 21% of these cases.

One possible explanation for this apparent lack of communication of suicidal intent is that the patient's declared reason for the visit usually is not the suicidal ideation itself, but rather physical health problems. When asked in retrospect about the reason for the last visit before attempting suicide, about 50% of the patients from patient samples in Bern as well as in Stockholm indicated physical reasons only (Michel et al, 1997). Patients generally find it difficult to talk to their physicians about emotional problems because they may be ashamed, or out of fear of stigmatization, and may therefore choose to stay on safe ground by presenting physical problems only. Rutz and colleagues (1997) recently pointed out that this is predominantly so with male patients, suggesting that there might be a specific male depressive syndrome, with more acting-out and little obvious depressive mood or apathy.

SUICIDE RISK FACTORS

The classical retrospective investigations by Barraclough and colleagues (1974), Robins (1981), and others (e.g. Isometsä et al, 1995b; Conwell et al, 1996) confirmed that the vast majority, in fact over 90%, of adults who commit suicide fulfil the criteria of a psychiatric diagnosis. The same applies to persons making serious suicide attempts (Beautrais et al, 1996). The most frequent diagnosis found in retrospective studies of consecutive cases of suicide is major depression (between 40% and 60% of the cases). The proportion of patients who are under medical care may even be higher than in unselected suicides. In the Finnish study mentioned above, depression was reported to have been present in 75% of those patients who had seen a physician within the 4 weeks prior to committing suicide.

Unfortunately, symptoms of depression too often remain unrecognized (Freeling et al, 1985) and consequently patients do not receive adequate (and life-saving) antidepressant treatment (Barraclough et al, 1974; Murphy, 1975). Despite major efforts in training, the problem remains largely unchanged (Isometsä et al, 1994), and recent studies confirmed earlier reports of alarmingly low rates of prescriptions for antidepressants amongst people committing suicide (Isacsson et al, 1994; Marzuk et al, 1995). One reason for the underdiagnosis of depression appears to be that often the signs of depression are not obvious. Freeling and colleagues (1985) found that depressed patients unrecognized by general practitioners showed less evidence of overt depressed mood than those whose depression was recognized. They also showed a greater lack of insight into being ill or depressed. Physical complaints may cover the typical symptoms of depression: pain, autonomic symptoms and gastrointestinal symptoms are common in depressed patients (Lin et al, 1989). A further problem lies in the classification of depressive disorders, i.e. in the traditional dichotomy into reactive and endogenous depression. Murphy (1975) noted that too often "a psychological explanation for the patient's emotional state appears to have served in lieu of diagnosis and treatment". In Bern, general practitioners who were contacted after the suicide of one of their patients had a tendency to associate a depression which appeared to be reactive to situational events with a non-serious and self-limiting condition of psychological origin, and therefore saw no indication for antidepressant medication (Michel, 1986). The problem was cogently summarized by Fawcett (1972): "The presence of a reason for depression does not constitute a reason for ignoring its presence". The new diagnostic systems (ICD-10, DSM-IV), which are based on phenomenological descriptions and which classify depressive states by the severity of symptomatology (and not by the presumed aetiology), should help practitioners to avoid this diagnostic trap.

Short-term risk of suicide is particularly high in depression associated with agitation, anxiety or panic attacks (Fawcett et al, 1990). On a psychological level, depressive cognitions, hopelessness or negative expectations about one's future have been shown to correlate with an increased risk of suicide (Beck et al, 1990). Of special relevance for the primary care physician is that recent discharge from inpatient psychiatric care is associated with an increased risk of suicide (Goldacre et al, 1993; see Chapter 35). Discharged patients may not be able to cope with the realities of a difficult life situation after discharge, and may again fall into a state of hopelessness and suicidal despair. It would be a mistake if the primary care physician assumed that psychiatric in-patient treatment "cures" the risk of suicide.

Other clinical aspects associated with an increased risk of suicide include substance abuse (20–40%), schizophrenia (10%) and severe borderline personality disorder (5–30%). It should be noted that the percentages of these diagnoses in actual practice are likely to be higher, because most retrospective assessments based on information from psychological autopsies do not allow multiple diagnoses, although in practice co-morbidity (e.g. major depression and substance abuse) is common (Conwell et al, 1996).

Careful history taking may reveal past suicide attempts—a long-term risk factor. Between 30% and 50% of patients who kill themselves have made previous suicide attempts (Foster et al, 1997). Depression and a history of a past suicide attempt increases the risk (Nordström et al, 1995) and so does a history of multiple attempts (Hawton and Fagg, 1988, Nordentoft et al, 1993). These findings indicate how important it is to ask patients routinely about past emotional and suicidal crises and to gather more detailed information about the severity of past deliberate self-harm, as well as about treatment.

In spite of a large literature on risk factors, it remains difficult to determine which individual patients require strict supervision and intensive medical care to prevent deliberate self-harm or self-destruction. Generally, factors predictive of infrequent behaviour lead to large numbers of false-positive and false-negative cases and may give the wrong impression of scientific predictability (Murphy, 1984; Pokorny, 1983; see Chapter 33). Identifying the rare acute high-risk patient seems rather like searching for a needle in a haystack, particularly considering that the average general practitioner has one suicide of a patient every 3–5 years. In a recent meta-analysis, Harris and Barraclough (1997) found that virtually all psychiatric diagnoses have an increased risk of suicide. Therefore, for clinical practice, risk factors can be said to be necessary, but not sufficient for, the recognition of an acute risk of suicide. The second necessary prerequisite for the evaluation of the risk of suicide lies in a good and trusting patient–doctor relationship. Only then can the communication of intent be expected or the doctor's enquiry about suicidal thoughts become possible.

In the training of physicians, a model that considers completed suicide as the tip of an iceberg may be useful. In this model, the visible part above the waterline includes the cases of completed suicide and those of attempted suicide that come to medical attention (possibly only one-quarter of all cases of deliberate self-harm), while the major part under water, i.e. largely invisible to the physician, represents crises with suicidal ideation, and, even lower, the "common" emotional crises. The important point is that suicide prevention does not only deal with the tip of the iceberg but starts by recognizing the (often covert) signs of emotional problems. When physicians initiate discussion of the possible psychosocial reasons for a patient's complaints, they not only signal to the patient that they are there to listen and try to understand the patient as a human being, but this also gives the patient a model which integrates psychosocial aspects of health problems. To start with, the doctor may ask simple questions such as "How are you getting on with life?", "How do you feel about the future?", "Could it be that something is burdening you?", etc., and, if necessary, it will then be easy to continue and ask, "Have you ever thought that life is not worth living, that you would like to put an end to it all?", etc. There is universal agreement that asking questions about suicidal ideation does not trigger suicidal behaviour and that encouraging the patient to confide in another person is of therapeutic value. Times of crises and emotional problems wax and wane in the course of life, and so do thoughts about suicide as a solution. General practitioners in Bern who attended seminars on suicide prevention later reported that they were surprised how many patients, when actually questioned, reported that recently they had indeed thought about suicide as a possible solution (Michel, unpublished data).

In summary, primary care physicians need a thorough knowledge of the main risk factors and the ability to accept the patient as an individual human being. In order to do this they need an understanding of the motives related to suicidal behaviour. Only the integration of both aspects will allow the physician to decide on the most appropriate form of treatment.

MODELS TO UNDERSTAND SUICIDAL BEHAVIOUR

Although suicide is associated with medical conditions, it is more than just a medical issue. Psychological, biographical, situational, interpersonal and even cultural aspects of suicidal behaviour must also be considered. The antithetical position to the physician's endeavours to prevent a patient from killing himself maintains that suicide is the freedom and basic right of every human being and that nobody, not even a medical professional, has the right to interfere. It is obvious that a physician's model determines the way he/she is going to manage the case, yet, unfortunately, this aspect is rarely addressed in training. The traditional biomedical model is a causal model and assumes that pathology is a result of a "fault in the system"—therefore, the physician tries to find the cause of an illness or a symptom and decides on a way to treat it. However, suicidal persons do not readily fit into this model. Suicide or attempted suicide *per se* is not an illness but a behaviour, or an action, which can best be understood within a psychosocial frame.

Bancroft and colleagues (1979) found a most striking disagreement between patients' explanations and those of psychiatrists for patients' overdoses: the two reasons chosen most frequently by the psychiatrists ("communicating hostility"; "aiming to influence other people") were both rarely chosen by the patients; on the other hand, "escape" and "loss of control", both commonly chosen by the patients, were seldomly chosen by the psychiatrists.

Actions may be understood as goal-directed, determined by conscious or unconscious plans and motives (Michel and Valach, 1997). In fact, when patients are asked specifically about their motives for attempting suicide, the most frequent answers are "to escape from an unbearable situation or state of mind" (Bancroft et al, 1976; Michel et al, 1994). It appears that the typical mental state immediately before the initiation of deliberate self-harm is characterized by an acute state of anxious emotional perturbation, which the individual experiences as unbearable and which has to be distinguished from the underlying and often long-lasting problems (often interpersonal) a person faces. This is consistent with Shneidman's cubic model of suicide (Shneidman, 1987), which distinguishes three forces, called "pain", "perturbation" and "press". Shneidman (1993) stressed the importance of unbearable mental pain ("psychache") and of the thought that the cessation of consciousness is the solution for this unbearable condition. Thus, the suicidal act should primarily be understood as an act aimed at obtaining relief from an unbearable mental state.

A psychosocial developmental model interprets actions in terms of short- and long-term aspects of a person's life career. In this view, suicidal behaviour is seen as part of a person's life story, emerging as a possible solution in times of crisis due to unsolvable difficulties, failures or conflicts. Rich and colleagues (1991) found that the most frequent stressors were interpersonal conflicts, separation and rejection, and less frequently economic problems and medical illness. The frequencies of these stressors differed according to the life cycles in adult development. When questioned, most people who have attempted suicide say that in past difficult life-periods they had repeatedly thought of suicide as a possibility. It is in this context that Maris (1981) used the concept of a suicide career, or development towards suicide. This model stresses that repeated painful experiences lead to an increasing feeling of unhappiness, or clinical depression, both resulting in a more internalized interpretation of life difficulties.

In practice, it may be best to use a model which integrates biomedical as well as psychosocial aspects, and to understand suicidal thoughts as a possible solution to a difficult life situation or an unbearable state of mind, against the background of a person's present life situation and individual biography.

KNOWLEDGE AND ATTITUDES

Not surprisingly, health professionals have been found to have difficulties in accepting and understanding suicide attempters, especially in the absence of psychiatric illness (Patel, 1975; Reimer and Arantewicz, 1986). Physicians have been found to have a more favourable attitude towards patients whose motives were interpreted as "wanting to die" than those whose behaviour was seen as manipulative (Ramon et al, 1975; Hawton et al, 1981). Suicidal patients often do not consider contacting their general practitioner or psychiatrist when in a suicidal crisis because they perceive doctors as unhelpful (Hawton and Blackstock, 1976; Wolk-Wasserman, 1987). Suicidal adolescents are particularly reluctant to seek help (Choquet and Menke, 1989). When a suicidal person expects that the physician will label an act of deliberate self-harm as pathological or irrational, he/she is likely to keep suicidal thoughts to him/herself.

As seen above, there is a tendency for physicians and psychiatrists to interpret suicidal behaviour as manipulative, whereas the patients themselves less often mention interpersonal reasons for attempting suicide. Not surprisingly, professional helpers who have a better knowledge about suicidal behaviour less often interpret a suicide attempt as manipulative, and recognize a greater number of signs of suicide (Domino and Swain, 1985).

Murphy (1975) found that only two-fifths of physicians were aware that their patients had a history of attempted suicide. In Bern, nearly 50% of general practitioners were surprised by the suicide or suicide attempt of their patients (Michel, 1986). Furthermore, in 67% of cases of attempted suicide, general practitioners were not aware of past episodes of deliberate self-harm. One-third of them said that in future, in a similar situation, they would ask the patient directly about suicidal thoughts and prescribe antidepressants earlier or in a higher dosage. The majority expressed a wish for more training.

Rutz and colleagues (1989) in the Gotland Study took up the challenge and offered a structured educational programme in the recognition and treatment of depressive disorders to general practitioners on the Swedish island of Gotland, while monitoring several variables, such as referrals to psychiatry, sick leave for depressive states, inpatient care for depressive states, suicides and the use of antidepressants and benzodiazepines. The training sessions were held in the form of interactive seminars, combining lessons, group work and sharing of personal experiences. One primary goal of the training programme was to give the general practitioners more responsibility in the treatment of depressive disorders. The authors actually feared that this might lead to an increase in the suicide rate. However, when comparing the number of suicides each year with the 4 preceding years, they found a significant decrease after the training (although it should be mentioned that the analysis of the data became the subject of a subsequent debate; MacDonald, 1993; Williams and Goldney, 1994; MacDonald, 1995). Referrals to psychiatry for depression decreased by 50%. Sick leave because of depressive states decreased by over 50%, and inpatient care for depression by about 75%. The number of prescriptions for antidepressants increased, but decreased for benzodiazepines. There appears to have been a subsequent fading out of these effects, probably because about half of the general practitioners who had participated in the course left their positions in the following years (Rutz et al, 1992).

Written information about recognition and treatment of depression is not enough to change attitudes and knowledge. Michel and Valach (1992) offered training in the recognition and treatment of suicide risk to general practitioners, either by written text alone or combined with interactive seminars. They found that in the seminar group, knowledge and attitudes changed significantly, while those doctors receiving written material only—although mailed on order only—had similar results to those who had received no written or verbal teaching. The authors concluded that the training should be based on a "working relationship" between mental health professionals and primary care physicians, including didactic elements such as discussion of attitudes towards suicide, the role of the primary care physician in suicide prevention, the sharing of personal experiences, role plays, etc.

In summary, the recognition of depression and a risk of suicide is associated with knowledge about and attitudes towards suicide and the role of the physician in suicide prevention. A better understanding of suicidal behaviour is likely to improve the communication and the therapeutic relationship with the suicidal patient.

AVAILABILITY AND CONTINUITY

A common problem in the aftercare of suicidal patients is that attendance rates are generally poor. In comparing different aftercare strategies for suicide attempters, Kurz and colleagues (1988) found that when patients were given appointments with the doctor who had seen them first in hospital, attendance at aftercare was better, but even then, non-compliance for the first outpatient appointment was 50%. Hawton and colleagues (1981) compared a home-based treatment programme with weekly hospital-based outpatient appointments. Patients in the first group showed far better compliance, but there were no major differences in terms of repetition of attempts between the two groups. This raises the question of what kind of aftercare is beneficial for people who attempt suicide.

Hawton and colleagues (1998) recently reviewed different treatment strategies for suicide attempters. Of relevance for the primary care physician is that, to date, no form of treatment has been shown to be clearly effective in reducing the risk of repetition. Not surprisingly, the perception of the amount of help received after attempted suicide, as reported by patients, was associated with such staff attributes as sympathy and listening behaviour (Treolar et al, 1993). Furthermore, for follow-up, patients requested the possibility of emergency contacts and follow-up by social workers and nurses. In a study by Van Heeringen and colleagues (1995), a community nurse visited at home suicide attempters who did not keep their follow-up appointments, which increased outpatient attendance and resulted in a near-significant reduction in the occurrence of further suicide attempts. Morgan and colleagues (1993) in the Green Card Study used a minimal intervention approach. Patients who had attempted suicide were given an emergency card ("green card"), which indicated that a health professional was available at all times should further problems arise. In the experimental group a reduction of actual or seriously threatened deliberate self-harm was found, although the difference compared to the control group did not reach statistical significance.

From these results it appears that continuity of care, availability in times of crisis and, if necessary, actively seeking contact with the patient at risk, are important aspects of prevention of suicide in primary care. These are all aspects of medical care that can be provided by the primary care physician. The advantage of the primary care physician is that he/she is usually known to the patient and is one of the first sources of help in times of emotional crisis. There can hardly be any doubt that a trusting and consistent relationship with a health professional is of eminent importance. This may partly depend on the characteristics of the health care system. In a comparison between Bern and Stockholm, it was found that in Bern more patients had seen their general practitioners regularly, more had talked about their suicidal thoughts and fewer had been prescribed psychotropic medication at the last visit before attempting suicide (Michel et al, 1997).

THE USE OF MEDICATION IN PRIMARY CARE

It has been pointed out that depression is usually underdiagnosed, and that the Gotland study has indicated that there is a direct association between competence in the recognition of depression and the use of antidepressants.

There are three main aspects to be taken into consideration. The first and most important is that the medication must be effective in reducing the symptoms of depression. Use of inadequate doses of tricyclic antidepressants has been identified as a reason for ineffective antidepressant treatment in primary care (Isometsä et al, 1998). Therefore, the physician must closely monitor the severity of symptoms in the course of treatment, and adjust the dose of antidepressants accordingly. It should be expected that with any antidepressant drug a certain proportion of patients will not respond, and that in a proportion of cases it will be necessary to switch to another drug.

In the initial phase of antidepressant treatment, acute states of suicidal anxiety and agitation, which the patient experiences as unbearable states of mind, may continue to occur. In this case, the administration of a short-acting anxiolytic drug reduces the imminent risk of suicide or attempted suicide.

The second aspect concerns the fact that suicidal patients often use the prescribed medication in an overdose (Hawton and Blackstock, 1976). This is particularly important when antidepressant drugs are prescribed, because of their potential toxicity in deliberate self-poisoning. However, it is generally accepted that the toxicity of the antidepressants prescribed is of secondary importance, because in the prevention of suicide the first priority must lie in the efficacy of the antidepressant treatment, i.e. in the quality of the management of the suicidal patient. The issue of whether less toxic antidepressants (e.g. SSRIs) should be used in preference to older, more toxic antidepressants is discussed in Chapter 27. If tricyclic antidepressants are prescribed in the treatment of a severe depression, they (as well as all other drugs) should be dispensed in small amounts of tablets at each visit, and frequent appointments are necessary until the condition of the patient has improved markedly. When psychotropic drugs are prescribed, it should also be kept in mind that patients often take drug cocktails in overdose, including tranquillizers, and that a combination of alcohol and less toxic drugs may be lethal (Michel et al, 1994).

The third aspect is compliance. Hopelessness may stop patients complying with the prescription, especially as at the beginning of treatment they may not feel any effect of the medication or, worse, only side-effects. Isacsson and colleagues' (1994) finding that only in 16% of 3,400 cases of suicide antidepressants were found in toxicological screening may not be due only to a failure to recognize and adequately treat depression, but may also be the expression of poor compliance. Patients may stop taking medication because of side-effects or because of the delayed response. It is therefore crucial to be supportive and skilful in explaining to patients what effect of the drug treatment can be expected and what side-effects might possibly occur.

The use of medication in the treatment and prevention of suicide is discussed in more detail in Chapter 27 of this book.

HIGH-RISK PATIENTS MAY NEED ADMISSION

Patients at high risk for suicide usually need inpatient care. In the individual case, however, it may be difficult to decide if or when the patient should be referred for psychiatric care. In such cases it is advisable to address the risk of suicide openly with the patient and the relatives and discuss options of treatment and prevention. For instance, it may be advisable, with the agreement of the patient, to remove possible means of suicide, such as drugs, firearms or the car key, and to keep admission open as an option. The question of admission to inpatient treatment should be carefully discussed with the patient. Many patients have a fear of stigmatization due to psychiatric treatment, and the decision should best be a joint decision between physician and patient. However, it should be kept in mind that depressed patients are often unable to make up their minds, or that rejection of treatment may sometimes be a sign of a presuicidal state.

If a physician, in spite of the patient's denials or promises, still suspects a high risk of suicide and the patient rejects inpatient treatment, involuntary admission may become necessary. Depending on health care resources, a psychiatrist's opinion may be sought, but it may become necessary to admit the patient without delay. The patient should then be admitted directly from the practice or, in the case of a domiciliary visit, from home, and the physician or a nurse should stay with the patient until safe transport has been arranged. However, it should be noted that admission does not automatically prevent suicide. In fact, inpatient suicide is not uncommon, as is discussed in Chapter 25.

The legal aspects of the treatment of suicidal patients have been discussed by Fawcett and colleagues (1993) and are considered further in Chapter 23.

CONCLUSIONS

The main aspects of suicide prevention in primary care can be summarized in the following guidelines for clinical practice:

1. *Model of suicide* Suicidal tendencies are best understood using a model which integrates biomedical as well as individual psychosocial and biographical aspects.

2. *Patient–doctor relationship* The patient should feel that the physician wants to understand him/her as an individual with an unique history and life situation. Continuity and availability of care are probable protective factors.
3. *Iceberg paradigm* Suicide prevention in primary care should not only concentrate on the recognition of the (rare) acute high-risk patient but should be applied on a broader level, by opening up communication about emotional problems.
4. *Communication* Many patients do not talk openly about their problems or spontaneously mention past or present suicidal ideas. The physician should therefore actively enquire about suicidal thoughts and past episodes of self-harm.
5. *Risk factors* Signs of major psychiatric disorder, above all depressive illness, alcoholism and/or drug abuse, must be screened for by asking specific questions. In patients with past episodes of depression, special care should be paid to the early detection and adequate treatment of recurrent depressive symptomatology.
6. *Medication* Any medication should be dispensed in small portions, because of the risk of overdose. The effect of antidepressant treatment must be closely monitored and medication reviewed if the response is unsatisfactory.
7. *Further management of patients at risk* In this case further steps must be considered. Treatment options should be discussed with the patient and the patient's family. In case of acute danger, admission to inpatient care must be discussed. If in such cases a working relationship cannot be established, involuntary admission may be necessary.

REFERENCES

Appleby, L., Amos, T., Doyle, U., Tommenson, B. and Woodman, M. (1996) General practitioners and young suicides. British Journal of Psychiatry, 168: 330–333.

Bancroft, J., Hawton, K., Simkin, S., Kingston, B., Cumming, C. and Whitwell, D. (1979) The reasons people give for taking overdoses: a further enquiry. British Journal of Medical Psychology, 52: 353–365.

Bancroft, J., Skrimshire, A. and Simkin, S. (1976) The reasons people give for taking overdoses. British Journal of Psychiatry, 128: 583–588.

Barraclough, B., Bunch, J., Nelson, B. and Sainsbury, P. (1974) One hundred cases of suicide. British Journal of Psychiatry, 125: 355–373.

Beautrais, A.L., Joyce, P.R., Mulder, R.T., Fergusson, D.M., Deavoll, B.J. and Nightingale, S.K. (1996) Prevalence and comorbidity of mental disorders in persons making serious suicide attempts: a case-control study. American Journal of Psychiatry, 153: 1009–1014.

Beck, A.T., Brown, G., Berchick, R.J., Stewart, B.L. and Steer, R.A. (1990) Relationship between hopelessness and ultimate suicide: a replication with psychiatric outpatients. American Journal of Psychiatry, 147: 190–195.

Choquet, M. and Menke, H. (1989) Suicidal thoughts during early adolescence: prevalence, associated troubles and help-seeking behaviour. Acta Psychiatrica Scandinavica, 81: 170–177.

Conwell, Y., Duberstain, P.R., Cox, C., Herrmann, J.H., Forbes, N.T. and Caine, E.D. (1996)

Relationship of age and axis I diagnoses in victims of completed suicide: a psychological autopsy study. American Journal of Psychiatry, 153: 1001–1009.

Domino, G. and Swain, B.J. (1985) Recognition of suicide lethality and attitudes toward suicide in mental health professionals. OMEGA, 16: 301–308.

Fawcett, J. (1972) Suicidal depression and physical illness. JAMA, 219: 1303–1306.

Fawcett, J., Clark, D.C. and Busch, K.E. (1993) Assessing and treating the patient at risk for suicide. Psychiatric Annals, 23: 244–255.

Fawcett, J., Scheftner, W.A., Fogg, L., Clark, D.C., Young, M.A., Hedeker, D. and Gibbons, R. (1990) Time-related predictors of suicide in major affective disorder. American Journal of Psychiatry, 147: 1189–1194.

Foster, T., Gillespie, K. and McClelland, R. (1997) Mental disorders and suicide in Northern Ireland. British Journal of Psychiatry, 170: 447–452.

Freeling, P., Rao, B.M. and Paykel, E.S. (1985) Unrecognized depression in general practice. British Medical Journal, 290: 1880–1883.

Goldacre, M., Seagroatt, V. and Hawton, K. (1993) Suicide after discharge from psychiatric inpatient care. Lancet, 342: 283–286.

Harris, E.C. and Barraclough, B. (1997) Suicide as an outcome for mental disorders. A meta-analysis. British Journal of Psychiatry, 170: 205–228.

Hawton, K. and Fagg, J. (1988) Suicide and other causes of death, following attempted suicide. British Journal of Psychiatry, 152: 259–266.

Hawton, K., Arensman, E., Townsend, E., Bremner, S., Feldman, E., Goldney, R., Gunnell, D., Hazell, P., van Heeringen, K., House, A., Owens, D., Sakinofsky, I. and Träskman-Bendz, L. (1998) Deliberate self-harm: systematic review of efficacy of psychosocial and pharmacological treatments in preventing repetition. British Medical Journal, 317: 441–447.

Hawton, K., Bancroft, J., Catalan, J., Kingston, B., Stedeford, A. and Welch, N. (1981) Domiciliary and out-patient treatment of self-poisoning patients by medical and non-medical staff. Psychological Medicine, 11: 169–177.

Hawton, K. and Blackstock, E. (1976) General practice aspects of self-poisoning and self-injury. Psychological Medicine, 6: 571–575.

Hawton, K. and Fagg, J. (1988) Suicide and other causes of death, following attempted suicide. British Journal of Psychiatry, 152: 751–761.

Hawton, K., Marsack, B. and Fagg, J. (1981) The attitudes of psychiatrists to deliberate self-poisoning: comparison with physicians and nurses. British Journal of Medical Psychology, 54: 341–347.

Isacsson, G., Holmgren, P., Wasserman, D. and Bergman, U. (1994) Use of antidepressants among people committing suicide in Sweden. British Medical Journal, 308: 506–509.

Isometsä, E.T., Heikkinen, M.E., Marttunen, M.J., Henriksson, M.M., Aro, H.M. and Lönnqvist, J.K. (1995a) The last appointment before suicide: is suicide intent communicated? American Journal of Psychiatry, 152: 919–922.

Isometsä, E., Henriksson, M., Marttunen, M., Heikkinen, M., Aro, H., Kuoppasalmi, K. and Lönnqvist, J. (1995b) Mental disorders in young and middle aged men who commit suicide. British Medical Journal, 310: 1366–1367.

Isometsä, E.T., Henriksson, M.M., Aro, H.M. and Lönnqvist, J.K. (1994) Suicide in bipolar disorder in Finland. American Journal of Psychiatry, 151: 1020–1024.

Isometsä, E., Seppälä, I., Henriksson, M., Kekki, P. and Lönnqvist, J. (1998) Inadequate dosaging in general practice of tricyclic vs. other antidepressants for depression. Acta Psychiatrica Scandinavica, 6: 451–454.

Kurz, A., Möller, H.J., Bürk, F., Torhorst, A., Wächtler, C. and Lauter, H. (1988) Evaluation of two different aftercare strategies of an outpatient aftercare program for suicide attempters in a general hospital. In H.J. Möller, A. Schmidtke and R. Welz (Eds), Current Issues in Suicidology, pp. 414–418. Berlin: Springer.

Lin, E.H.B., von Korff, M. and Wagner, E.H. (1989) Identifying suicide potential in primary care. Journal of General and Internal Medicine, 4: 1–6.

MacDonald, A. (1993) The myth of suicide prevention by general practitioners. British Journal of Psychiatry, 163: 260.

MacDonald, A.J.D. (1995) Suicide prevention in Gotland. British Journal of Psychiatry, 166: 402.

Maris, R. (1981) Pathways to Suicide: a Survey of Self-destructive Behaviors. Baltimore, MD: Johns Hopkins University Press.

Marzuk, P.M., Tardiff, K., Leon, A.C., Hirsch, C.S., Stajic, M., Hartwell, N. and Portera, L. (1995) Use of prescription of psychotropic drugs among suicide victims in New York City. American Journal of Psychiatry, 152: 1520–1522.

Michel, K. (1986) Suizide und Suizidversuche: Könnte der Arzt mehr tun? Schweizerische medizinische Wochenschrift, 116: 770–774.

Michel, K., Arestegui, G. and Spuhler, T. (1994) Suicide with psychotropic drugs in Switzerland. Pharmacopsychiatry, 27: 114–118.

Michel, K., Runeson, B., Valach, L. and Wasserman, D. (1997) Contacts of suicide attempters with GPs prior to the event: a comparison between Stockholm and Bern. Acta Psychiatrica Scandinavica, 95: 94–99.

Michel, K., Valach, L. and Waeber, V. (1994) Understanding deliberate self-harm: the patients' views. Crisis, 15: 172–178.

Michel, K. and Valach, L. (1997) Suicide as goal-directed behaviour. Archives of Suicide Research, 3: 213–221.

Michel, K. and Valach, L. (1992) Suicide prevention: spreading the gospel to general practitioners. British Journal of Psychiatry, 160: 757–760.

Morgan, H.G., Jones, E.M. and Owen, J.H. (1993) Secondary prevention of non-fatal deliberate self-harm; the Green Card Study. British Journal of Psychiatry, 163: 111–112.

Murphy, G.E. (1975) The physician's responsibility for suicide. II. Errors of omission. Annals of Internal Medicine, 82: 305–309.

Murphy, G.E. (1984) The prediction of suicide: why is it so difficult? American Journal of Psychotherapy, 38: 341–349.

Nordentoft, M., Breum, L., Munck, L.K., Nordestgaard, A.G., Hunding, A. and Bjældager, P.A.L. (1993) High mortality by natural and unnatural causes: a 10-year follow-up study of patients admitted to a poisoning treatment centre after suicide attempts. British Medical Journal, 306: 1637–1641.

Nordström, P., Åsberg, M., Åberg-Wistedt, A. and Nordin, C. (1995) Attempted suicide predicts suicide risk in mood disorders. Acta Psychiatrica Scandinavica, 92: 345–350.

Patel, A. (1975) Attitudes towards self-poisoning. British Medical Journal, ii: 426–430.

Pokorny, A.D. (1983) Predicition of suicide in psychiatric patients: report of a prospective study. Archives of General Psychiatry, 40: 249–257.

Ramon, S., Bancroft, J. and Skrimshire, A. (1975) Attitudes towards self-poisoning among physicians and nurses in a general hospital. British Journal of Psychiatry, 127: 257–264.

Reimer, Ch. and Arantewicz, G. (1986) Physician's attitudes toward suicide and their influence on suicide prevention. Crisis, 7: 80–83.

Rich, C.L., Warsadt, G.M., Nemiroff, R.A., Fowler, R.C. and Young, D. (1991) Suicide, stressors, and life cycle. American Journal of Psychiatry, 148: 524–527.

Robins, E. (1981) The Final Months. A Study of the Lives of 134 Persons who Committed Suicide. New York: Oxford University Press.

Rutz, W., von Knorring, L. and Walinder, J. (1992) Long-term effects of an educational program for general practitioners given by the Swedish Commitee for the Prevention and Treatment of Depression. Acta Psychiatrica Scandinavica, 85: 83–88.

Rutz, W., Walinder, J., von Knorring, L., Rihmer, Z. and Philgren, H. (1997) Prevention of depression and suicide by education and medication: impact on male suicidality. An update from the Gotland study. International Journal of Psychiatry in Clinical Practice, 1: 39–46.

Rutz, W., von Knorring, L. and Walinder, J. (1989) Frequency of suicide on Gotland after systematic postgraduate education of general practitioners. Acta Psychiatrica Scandinavica, 80: 151–154.

Shneidman, E.S. (1987) A psychological approach to suicide. In G.R. Van den Bos and B.K. Bryant (Eds), Cataclysms, Crises, and Catastrophes. Washington, DC: American Psychological Association.

Shneidman, E.S. (1993) Suicide as a psychache. Journal of Nervous and Mental Disease, 181 (3): 145–147.

Treolar, A.J. and Pinfold, T.J. (1993) Deliberate self-harm: an assessment of patients' attitudes to the care they receive. Crisis, 14: 83–89.

Van Heeringen, C., Jannes, S., Buylaert, H., Henderick, H., de Bacquer, D. and van Remoortel, J. (1995) The management of non-compliance with referral to out-patient after-care among attempted suicide patients: a controlled intervention study. Psychological Medicine, 25: 963–970.

Williams, J.M.G. and Goldney, R.D. (1994) Suicide prevention in Gotland. British Journal of Psychiatry, 165: 692.

Wolk-Wasserman, D. (1987) Contacts of suicidal neurotic and prepsychotic/psychotic patients and their significant others with public care institutions before the suicide attempt. Acta Psychiatrica Scandinavica, 75: 358–372.

Chapter 39

The Role of Mass Media in Suicide Prevention

Armin Schmidtke
and
Sylvia Schaller
Universitäts-Nervenklinik, Würzburg, Germany

Abstract

This chapter provides an overview of studies on imitation effects of mass media portrayal of suicidal behaviour, and shows that many findings remain controversial. However, when various types of analysis and the varying nature of models are taken into account, theoretical justifications can be found for the diversity of findings. To study imitative and preventive effects it is necessary to understand the conceptual framework of learning by modelling or imitation, which should be distinguished from effects due to contagion. Moreover, various methodological problems should be taken into account, such as the fact that exposure to models may be age- and gender-specific and depend on size of coverage and audience or readership. Currently available knowledge provides substantial evidence for an imitative effect but also indicates that imitation effects may depend on a number of factors, including characteristics of the model and the extent to which model behaviour is reinforced. The frequency and manner of presentation are important, as are characteristics of the observer, such as age, gender, self-esteem and personality variables that moderate the probability of exhibiting the learned behaviour. In view of the evidence in favour of imitation effects, the portrayal of suicidal behaviour in the mass media on can be regarded as a natural advertisement for suicide, which may increase the risk of suicidal behaviour in the short term but may also sow the seeds of suicide in the distant future. Far less evidence is available on the potential preventive effects of mass media portrayal of suicidal behaviour. Currently available knowledge indicates that changing media coverage of suicidal behaviour in the context of suicide prevention strategies should mainly focus on toning down the portrayal of suicidal behaviour by the mass media.

The International Handbook of Suicide and Attempted Suicide. Edited by K. Hawton and K. van Heeringen.

INTRODUCTION

It is well recognized that the exposure to models of suicidal behaviour can be a risk factor for suicidal behaviour (see Chapter 14). It appears that suicidal behaviour can be learnt by imitation, especially among children, adolescents and young adults (Kreitman et al, 1970; Schmidtke, 1988, 1998; Schmidtke and Schaller, 1998; Diekstra, 1974; Steede and Range, 1989; Platt, 1993; Velting and Gould, 1997). Explanations for the temporal clustering of the use of particular methods for suicide, such as special herbicides (Dahm and Händel, 1970), asphyxiation (Church and Phillips, 1984; Kirch and Lester, 1986a) or burning (Henseler, 1975; Grosby et al, 1977; Ashton and Donnan, 1981), or the use of special locations like bridges (e.g. the Golden Gate Bridge; Seiden and Spence, 1982, 1983; Kirch and Lester, 1986b), must also include the social transmission of suicidal behaviour.

The effects of the mass media as a transmitter of models for imitation must be included in hypotheses about imitation of suicidal behaviour. However, media influences have also been a particular source of controversy. The discussion of this topic has mainly focused on two questions (Schmidtke and Häfner, 1989). The first is whether the specific presentation of suicide themes (and changes in these) merely reflect existing attitudes and opinions. The second is whether the reporting of suicidal acts and/or the mode of presentation of such acts by the media influences attitudes towards this behaviour and, as a consequence, the occurrence of subsequent suicidal behaviour. Most importantly, can the mass media be used in the prevention of suicidal behaviour?

In this chapter an overview will be presented of findings from research on the effects of modelling following mass media portrayal of suicidal behaviour in books, music, stage plays, newspapers, television and films, and the Internet. Secondly, results of meta-analyses of imitation effects will be reviewed. Following this, methodological problems in the study of modelling effects will be discussed. Finally, the potential role of the mass media in the prevention of suicidal behaviour will be described.

AN OVERVIEW OF RESEARCH FINDINGS ON MODELLING EFFECTS FOLLOWING MASS MEDIA PORTRAYAL OF SUICIDAL BEHAVIOUR

Early examples of such modelling can be found in historical accounts of suicide epidemics (e.g. the mass suicide of the Milesian virgins; Singer 1980, 1984). In the early scientific literature there are also references to suicidal behaviour being caused by imitation (Farr, 1841, cited in Pell and Watters, 1982; Mathews, 1891, cited in Phelps, 1911; Strahan, 1893; Phelps, 1911). "Epidemics of suicides or of suicidal behaviour" were reported by Popow as early as 1911. There have been similar frequent references to the suggestive power of mass media or similar media (including rumours) in influencing suicidal behaviour.

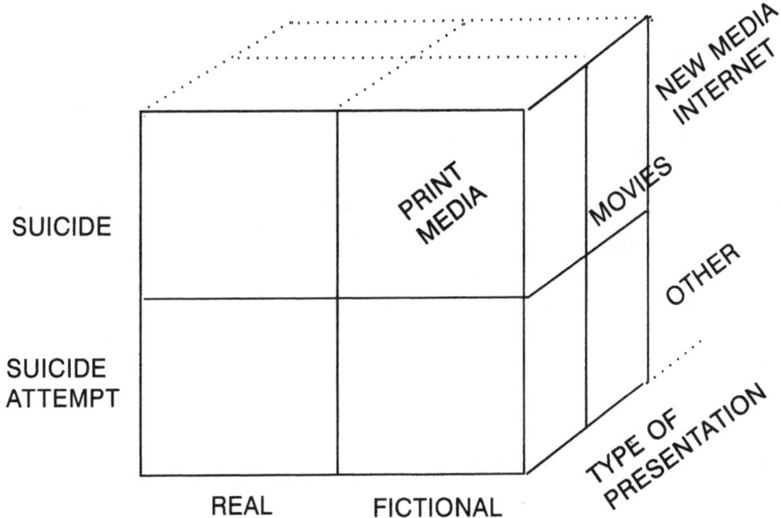

Figure 39.1 Classification of model behaviour and presentation

As shown in Figure 39.1, the findings from more recent research can be classified according to several characteristics. In order to evaluate the modelling effects and the preventive potential of the mass media, the behaviour and the method of presentation have to be classified and differentiated. With regard to suicidal behaviour, the characteristics of the model behaviour and the model can be differentiated according to the type of suicidal behaviour, the type of model, and the type of presentation. The model can be real or fictional, and the suicidal behaviour can be suicidal ideas, a suicide attempt or an actual suicide. The type of presentation can be in print media (literature and press), music, broadcasting, films, TV, theatre and, more recently, electronic media (e.g. the Internet).

Real and Fictional Suicidal Behaviour in Books

In 1774, Johann Wolfgang von Goethe published his novel *The Sorrows of Young Werther*, in which the hero finally shoots himself after a sentimental and hopeless love affair. The story has been reported to have had imitation effects in two ways, namely the "Werther's dress" (blue tailcoat, yellow waistcoat, yellow trousers and brown bucket-topped boots) and suicidal behaviour by young men who shot themselves with pistols. The extent of this imitation effect has been a matter of debate, but the "Werther Effect" has often been cited as the earliest recorded evidence of imitative effects on the occurrence of suicide being produced by literature.

More recently, there have been many reports about imitation effects of books (e.g. in Hungary: Fekete and Schmidtke, 1995, 1996a,b). Stack (1999) found the most direct evidence for a copycat effect in the publication of the book *Final Exit*. This book recommended asphyxiation as a method of committing suicide. In the year of publication of the book, suicides using this method increased in New York City by 313%. In 27.3% of the cases a copy of the book was found at the scene of the suicide (Marzuk et al, 1993, 1994; Stack, 1999).

However, the study of the imitative effects of suicidal behaviour in literature is complicated by potential time-period effects. Thus, it is difficult to determine the time of "learning" of the model behaviour, and also to control for the period of time between exposure and the imitation act. Conversely, it is difficult to prove that books have any preventive effect on suicide. Therefore, it is not surprising that no study exists which shows such an effect of books, either fictional or non-fictional.

Fictional Suicidal Behaviour in Music

The same methodological problems arise when one tries to examine imitative effects of suicidal behaviour in music. Numerous operas contain suicides and suicidal behaviour. There are also some hypotheses about the imitative effect of popular songs, for example, the effect of the song *Gloomy Sunday* on suicides in Hungary (Fekete and Schmidtke, 1995). There was a legal suit against the producer of the rock band Judas Priest because parents believed that a song by this group prompted two young boys to commit suicide. However, due to the time period problems noted above and the difficulty of controlling for concomitant variables, it is difficult to take this anecdotal evidence as proof for effects through imitation. Thus, there is also no study on potential effects on the prevention of suicide.

Fictional Suicidal Behaviour in Stage Plays

In a controlled experiment, Jackson and Potkay (1974) examined the effects on undergraduates of a one-act stage play about suicide and the possibly different effect(s) resulting from its presentation by other media. They did not find any increase in the occurrence of suicidal ideas.

Real Suicidal Behaviour in Newspapers

Motto hypothesized that during newspaper strikes the absence of models should cause a decrease in suicides by possible imitators. The results of the first study (Motto, 1967) and those of replications by others (Motto, 1970; Blumenthal and Bergner, 1973) were contradictory.

The results of the studies by Phillips are more convincing (Figure 39.2). He found that the more publicity a suicide case was given, especially on the front pages of newspapers, the more suicides were found in the period following pub-

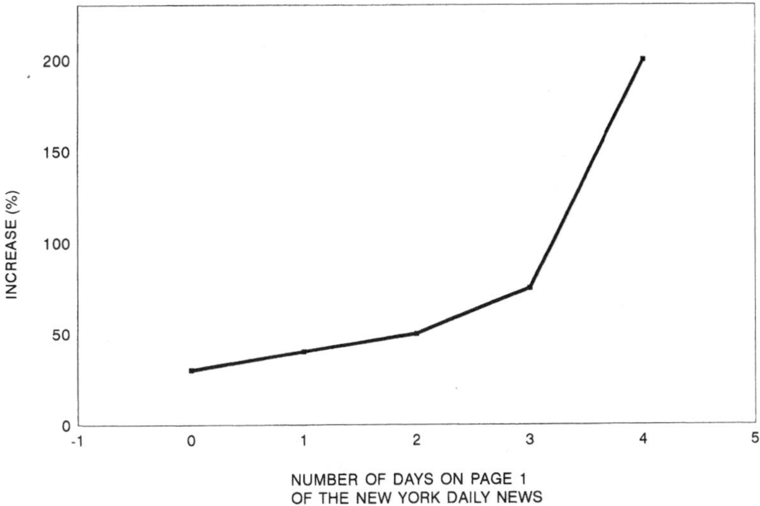

Figure 39.2 Increase in suicides by degree of publicity of a suicide story. Data from Phillips (1974, 1982)

lication (Phillips, 1974). Many other studies have shown a significant relationship between the reporting of real suicide(s) and the occurrence of subsequent suicides (Stack, 1987a, 1996; Phillips and Carstensen, 1988; Gundlach and Stack, 1990; Ishii, 1991; Etzersdorfer et al, 1992; Sonneck et al, 1993; Hassan, 1995; Hills, 1995). This effect has also been found for car accidents (Phillips, 1977, 1979), airplane fatalities (Phillips, 1978), and mass homicides and suicides (Cantor and Sheehan, 1996). However, there are also some contradictory findings which question a copycat effect (Altheide, 1981; Baron and Reiss, 1985a,b; Horton and Stack, 1984; Kessler and Stipp, 1984; Kessler et al, 1988; Jonas, 1992; Wasserman, 1993).

The problem with a number of these studies is that often contradictory findings are reported from the same study (e.g. Jonas, 1992; Platt, 1987, 1988, 1993). The reason for the contradictory nature of findings may be that there are differential imitation effects. Stack (1996), for example, investigated imitation effects in Japan. The increase in the occurrence of suicide following exposure to portrayal of suicide in newspapers was similar in magnitude to that reported in the context of the American culture; however, the imitative effect was restricted to Japanese victims. A more recent study by Hassan (1995) in Australia also showed a significant increase in the average daily suicide rate after the publication of suicide stories in some Australian media. However, the rise tended to be limited to an increase in male suicides.

Real Suicidal Behaviour in Television and Films

The effects of portrayal of real suicidal behaviour on television are less clear. Bollen and Phillips (1982) found an increase in suicide rates up to 10 days after television news reports about suicide. The effects remained significant after controlling for holidays and unequal variability (Phillips and Bollen, 1985). Similar findings were reported by Phillips and Carstensen (1986). Equivocal findings have been reported concerning the possible effects of reporting of suicidal behaviour on the subsequent occurrence of accidents (Phillips, 1980).

Martin (1996) examined the influence of television suicides in a general adolescent population. Fourteen year-old students claiming more than two exposures to suicidal behaviour shown on television took more risks and were more prone to substance abuse, knew more suicides in real life, had higher depression scores, and more commonly had a history of deliberate self-harm, when compared to age peers without such exposure. In those who reported knowing someone who had died from suicide, frequent exposure to suicide on television appeared to contribute to the variance in the occurrence of suicide attempts. However, the exposure contributed little to the occurrence of depression or suicidal thoughts. There are some methodological weaknesses in this study, as it is not clear whether the television suicides were real or fictional. Moreover, when the knowledge of someone who committed suicide was controlled for, the association between reports of suicide on television and the occurrence of deliberate self-harm no longer remained significant.

The results of a study by Horton and Stack (1984) did not support the hypothesis of imitation. They investigated co-variation between the monthly suicide rate and the amount of time (in seconds) given to the coverage of suicide-related stories on the evening national news in the USA. The results indicated the absence of any relationship between the length of news coverage and the monthly suicide rate after controlling for seasonal factors and for rates of unemployment and divorce.

So far there have been no studies examining the effects of the portrayal of a real suicide in films, either on television or in the cinema.

Fictional Suicidal Behaviour on Television and in Films

In 1986 Ellis and Walsh reported that during the week after an episode of the English television soap opera *Eastenders*, in which a leading female character took an overdose, an increased number of patients were admitted to hospital after having taken overdoses. Similar effects were reported in two other English cities (Fowler, 1986; Sandler et al, 1986), while no effects could be found in a fourth city (Daniels, 1986). Platt (1987, 1988) extended the investigation to 63 English hospitals. Although a significant increase in the number of suicide attempts for the total female population was found compared to the corresponding rates in the same period in the year before, no significant effect in the group closest to the "assumed" age of the "model" could be demonstrated. A further study in two accident and emergency departments also failed to reveal any convincing association (Williams et al, 1987).

Evidence for an imitation effect was found with regard to the film *The Deer*

Hunter. Following the release of this film, in which Russian roulette was shown in a scene and in which a leading character of the film later committed suicide by this method, 43 young men in the USA committed suicide using the same method (Coleman, 1987). This method of suicide is usually so uncommon that one can assume imitation effects.

Wilson and Hunter (1983) reported a similar increase in the occurrence of suicide in the USA after the broadcast of the television series *Death of a Student* (see below), but they did not provide any statistical analysis. In a similar anecdotal style, Ostroff and colleagues (1985) reported an increase in the number of suicide attempts among adolescents after the broadcasting of a television film showing the suicide of a young couple and its effect on their parents.

Phillips (1982) investigated the effect of suicides in "soap operas" on American television networks in 1977. The effect was measured among white Americans because most of the suicide models were white. In the second half of the week after such broadcasts, the number of suicides among white Americans significantly increased in comparison to the expected number. The number of road accidents involving people who were killed or seriously injured (the latter group could only be monitored in California) increased correspondingly. However, in a re-analysis of Phillips' findings, Kessler and Stipp (1984) attempted to correct false assumptions about the timing of some of the suicides as well as the model behaviour in some cases. They could not find any evidence of a linkage between suicidal behaviour in soap-operas and subsequent real-life fatalities.

The results reported by Gould and Shaffer (1986) also provoked discussion. They examined variations in the number of suicides and suicide attempts in the greater New York area before and after the broadcasting of four television films dealing with the theme "suicide" during the autumn and winter of 1984–1985. In the two weeks following these broadcasts the mean number of suicide attempts was significantly higher than the mean number observed before. After three of these films a significant increase in the number of suicides was observed when compared to the average number prior to the broadcasts. This study was repeated in some other states in the USA. However, most of these studies failed to confirm Gould and Shaffer's results (Berman, 1988; Wasserman, 1993).

Schmidtke and Häfner (1988a,b) used a "natural single-case-experiment" design with replication to prove an imitation effect. The second German television channel broadcasted a six-episode TV series entitled *Death of a Student* in 1981 (Figure 39.3). The lethal outcome of a railway suicide of a 19 year-old male student was repeatedly shown at the start of each episode, and the beginning of the suicidal act was shown in episodes 2–6. The series was shown on television again in 1982. An increase in railway suicides was found, most markedly among groups whose age and sex closely resembled those of the fictional model, namely young men. Among 15–29 year-old males, 62 suicides occurred during the observation period of 70 days after the first broadcasting of the series, indicating an increase of 86% when compared to the means for previous years. Among females of the same age, 14 suicides occurred, representing an increase of 75%, which was considerably lower than the increase among males. A striking finding was that

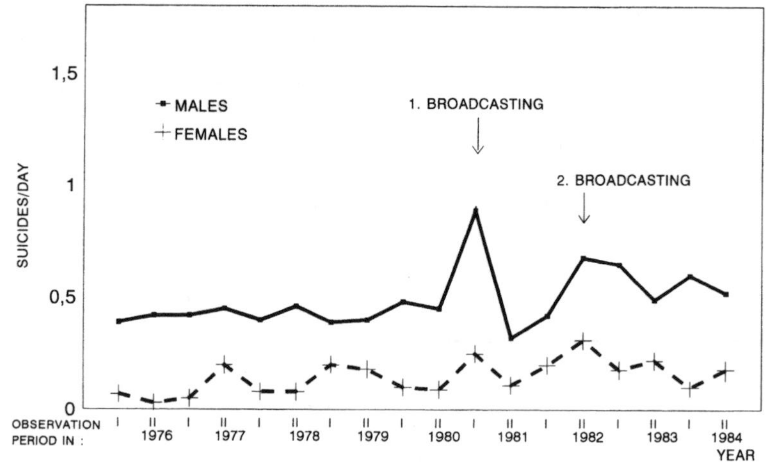

Figure 39.3 Suicides of 15–29 year-old males and females during and after first and second period of broadcasting of the TV serial *Death of a Student* (male, 19 years old). Data from Schmidtke and Hafner (1988b)

the frequency of suicides remained elevated for a longer period of time following the broadcasting of the model than indicated in Phillips' studies. The numbers of suicides in 15–19 year-old males was elevated for 16 weeks. In 20–24 year-old males the number of suicides ceased to show any excess after the tenth week. The effects of the second broadcast were less marked. The extent of the increases in the number of railway suicides among 15–29 year-old males during and after the first and second broadcasts corresponded to the audience viewing figures in this age group.

With regard to the depiction of suicidal behaviour in stories on voluntary or scientific organizations, it is not always clear whether this behaviour should be classified as real or fictional. For example, Holding (1974, 1975) studied the effects of an 11-episode television series entitled *The Befrienders*, about the work of The Samaritans. Each episode showed a predicament leading to a suicidal situation. One episode ended with a suicide. There was a subsequent substantial increase in the number of contacts with The Samaritans but no changes in the number of patients admitted to hospital after suicide attempts.

Real and Fictional Suicidal Behaviour on the Internet

Despite the fact that new media, such as the Internet, increasingly deal with suicide themes (Baume et al, 1997; Conwell, 1998) there has so far been no study on the potential imitative effects of this, for example, with regard to provision of instructions on how to commit suicide. However, there have been a limited number of studies regarding the Internet showing that it may have a considerable influence on individuals who wish to share their suicidal ideation with others (Baume et al, 1997), and that the influence of such information on vulnerable, suicidal people may be the same as information provided in the printed media (Conwell, 1998).

META-ANALYSES OF STUDIES

There have been some meta-analyses of studies on imitation of suicidal behaviour. These analyses include "comprehensive narrative" or literature research reviews (Phillips, 1989; Stack, 1982, 1990a; Häfner and Schmidtke, 1986; Schmidtke and Häfner, 1989; Lester, 1992; Phillips et al, 1992; Fekete and Schmidtke, 1996b; Velting and Gould, 1997), background-orientated evaluations (Schmidtke, 1996; Schmidtke and Schaller, 1998) and methodology-orientated meta-analyses in a stricter sense (Stack, 1999).

Interestingly, based on their meta-analyses, Schmidtke (1996) and Schmidtke and Schaller (1998) noted that findings were more in favour of the imitation hypothesis when the background of the researcher(s) was more clinically orientated (e.g. Gould and Shaffer, 1986; Schmidtke and Häfner, 1988a,b), although the studies by Phillips are an exception. For example, Velting and Gould (1997) wrote in their summary that, in general, the evidence to date suggested that suicide contagion is a real effect, albeit of a smaller effect size than other psychiatric and psychosocial risk factors for suicide. In contrast, even when the results were more or less in favour of the imitation hypothesis, most of the authors with a more sociological background (e.g. Platt, 1987, 1988, 1993; Jonas, 1992) were very critical and even contradictory in their own reports, although even Durkheim (1897) had mentioned imitation processes. Additionally, research performed by persons with connections with or belonging to the research divisions of broadcasting networks has tended to find little evidence supporting copycat effects (e.g. Kessler and Stipp, 1984; Kessler et al, 1988; see also Stack, 1999). The methodology-orientated study by Stack (1999), in which 293 findings from 42 studies were analysed, showed that the characteristics of the stories were key predictors of finding a copycat effect. Studies measuring the effect of the suicide of an entertainer or a political celebrity were 14.3 times more likely to find a copycat effect than studies that did not. Studies based on real stories as opposed to fictional stories were 4.03 times more likely to identify an imitation effect. The medium of coverage was also a significant predictor of copycat effects. Stories on television were 82% less likely to affect suicide imitation than newspaper-based stories. Some evidence was also found for period effects and stories were linked more often to the incidence of suicide attempts than completed suicides.

METHODOLOGICAL PROBLEMS

Most of the findings discussed so far have been based on "natural observations" or "field experiments". The validity of such designs is limited, especially since it is not possible to rule out competing hypotheses. These methodological problems are the reason why the "Werther Effect" has been associated with so much controversy. On the one hand, it is argued that the effect is derived from aggregated data, which can create the problem of "ecological fallacy" (which means that aggregated data show an effect that, in reality, is due to other characteristics). On the other hand, it has been stated that some studies have not been subject to experimental rigour.

The first prerequisite when interpreting an association between a publicized model and an increase in the occurrence of suicide (or a preventive effect) as causal is a clearly defined type of model behaviour, which can also be identified precisely *at the level of imitation*. Taking basic research findings into account, it is supposed that learning by modelling depends on certain characteristics of the model, including age, gender and social status, on the corresponding characteristics of the observer, and on mood variables. The imitation effects also seem to depend on the frequency and degree with which the model is presented.

If a significant increase in the behaviour shown by the model is found, the hypothesis of learning by modelling gains plausibility, provided it can also be shown that the extent of imitation depends on the degree of concordance between certain characteristics of the model and imitator and the length and scope of presentation. If no attention is paid, for example, to age and gender or to the type of suicidal behaviour, it will be impossible to detect the imitative effect of a specific type of model behaviour. A true modelling or preventive effect might not be observed, either because it is too small or because the increases in the occurrence of imitated behaviours in certain age (or other) groups are balanced by decreasing trends in others. Official statistics for causes of death, which were used in the majority of the studies cited above, do not provide a suitable basis for the assessment of time-related modelling effects. In these statistics the classification of suicide methods and the determination of the time of death are usually imprecise, and the date and time of a suicidal act are often unknown, at least when "softer" methods of deliberate self-harm, such as self-poisoning, are used. Suicide attempts, which account for an essential part of the imitation effect of suicide models, are not included in official statistics and are, in many cases, difficult to assess reliably from other sources. To rule out alternative hypotheses, such as seasonal influences or long-term trends, it is also necessary to use adequate methods of analysing the data, such as time series analyses, whether or not using transfer models (see e.g. Box and Jenkins 1979; Schlittgen and Streitberg, 1997). Transfer models are statistical models to evaluate effects in time series analyses. Based on previous data and their internal data dependencies, new sections of the time series are forecasted and analysed to assess whether external variables have influenced changes in the level or trends of the data. An adequate number of measurements and sufficiently long control periods are needed for these statistical approaches.

However, in a limited number of studies such methodological problems have been solved. Schmidtke and Häfner (1998a,b) were able to use a natural single case design (ABAB) to overcome the potential objection that the results were due to chance. It is also often pointed out that it is unknown whether or not suicide victims have really read or watched the model presentation and, therefore, whether the model could really have influenced their decision. However, there are also some results indicating that there are "real" imitation effects. In the year of the publication of the book *Final Exit*, in which asphyxiation was recommended as a method of committing suicide, a copy of the book was found at the scene of the suicide in 27.3% of the cases using this method in New York City (Marzuk et al, 1993, 1994; Stack, 1999). More recently, a study by Hawton and co-workers (1999) was the first that used a more experimental design to solve this methodological problem. The showing of an episode of a popular weekly television drama, in which an RAF pilot took an overdose of paracetamol and suffered potentially fatal liver damage, presented the opportunity to study an interrupted time series analysis of presentations at emergency departments during the three weeks both prior to and following the broadcast. Data on presentations were collected in 49 accident and emergency departments and psychiatric services. Additionally, in 23 centres the patients were questioned about various factors related to imitation. Presentations for self-poisoning increased by 17% in the week after the broadcast and 9% in the second week. Increases in the method used by the model (paracetamol overdose) were more marked than increases in non-paracetamol overdoses. Twenty percent of the interviewed patients reported that the model had influenced their behaviour, and 17% said that it had influenced their choice of drug. The most compelling evidence of modelling from this study was that use of the specific drug for overdose doubled after the episode among overdose patients who were viewers compared with overdose patients prior to the index broadcast who were viewers of previous episodes.

SUICIDE PREVENTION BY MASS MEDIA

There appears to be an association in different countries between how mass media report suicide and attitudes towards suicide and suicide prevention. European, American and Asian countries differ significantly with regard to the number and content of newspaper headlines with suicide themes (Fekete et al, 1994, 1998a). The varying ways in which the consequences and characteristics of suicidal behaviour are described in the headlines indicate that there are rather more accepting attitudes toward suicide in some countries than in others. The content of the press reports (and headlines) also varies with national suicide rates. Up to the time of the fall of the Iron Curtain, there were almost no newspaper reports of suicide in Eastern European countries. The rate of suicide reports of "positive" prominent celebrities is highest in Hungary. Also, reports indicating positive consequences of suicide are highest in Hungary and Lithuania, while reports of suicides by "negative" celebrities and reports of negative consequences are significantly more frequent in German and Austrian newspaper headlines. American headlines label suicide in a more criminalizing way, while suicidal behaviour is portrayed more commonly as a tragedy and political protest in Hungarian headlines (Fekete et al, 1994; Fekete and Schmidtke, 1996a,b; Schmidtke and Fekete, 1996; Fekete et al, 1998a,b). One can hypothesize that the divergent ways suicide is labelled in the media reflect different attitudes towards suicide. According to these findings, the portrayal of positive consequences of suicidal behaviour increases the possibility of identification with a suicide model and more imitation, while the portrayal of negative consequences decreases this possibility (Schmidtke and Fekete, 1996). Consequently, Diekstra and Garnefski (1995) have suggested that the more frequent presentation of positive suicide models may be a reason for the increase of suicidal behaviour among adolescents.

There are very early examples of possible more direct preventive effects of "mass media". Stories about the mass suicide of the Milesian virgins mention prevention. Thus, it is said that the rumour, spread by a joker, that the next dead virgin would be carried naked through the market place, immediately stopped the epidemic behaviour. In more recent times, the aftermath of the "Werther Effect" is often cited as the earliest example (Phillips, 1974, 1985). The impression at the time of an imitation effect was so strong that it has been reported that authorities in Denmark, Saxony and Milan banned the book to prevent further suicides (Phillips, 1974, 1985).

More recently, Motto demonstrated a possible preventive effect of the absence of media reports of suicide. The association between newspaper strikes and a decrease in suicides (Motto, 1967, 1970; Blumenthal and Bergner, 1973) suggested a preventive effect because of absence of reporting of models. As a consequence of the results of the study by Schmidtke & Häfner (1988b) on the effects of the television series *Death of a Student*, which were described above, German Television subsequently portrayed the suicide victim in the series as less heroic.

Some studies also show more directly that suicide prevention measures involving the media may be effective. The study by Sonneck and co-workers (1993) in Vienna (Figure 39.4) provides a good example of this. Since its opening in 1978, the Viennese subway system has often been used as a method of attempting or committing suicide. The number of deaths was very low in early years, but from 1984 onwards suicides and suicide attempts became more common. This trend was due neither to an extension of the length of the Viennese subway system nor to an increase in the number of passengers. However, the major Austrian newspapers portrayed these suicides in a very sensational and dramatic way. Therefore, in June 1987, the Austrian Association for Suicide Prevention issued media guidelines and requested the press to follow them. Following publication of these guidelines, the characteristics of reporting changed markedly. Instead of printing sensational articles, the newspapers printed either short reports, rarely on the front page, or did not report the suicides at all. The number of suicides in the subway significantly decreased from the first to the second half of 1987, and the rates remained low, as shown in Figure 39.4 (Sonneck et al, 1994). A similar effort was made in Switzerland. In the context of the Swiss national suicide prevention programme, the Swiss Association for Suicide Prevention tried to persuade the

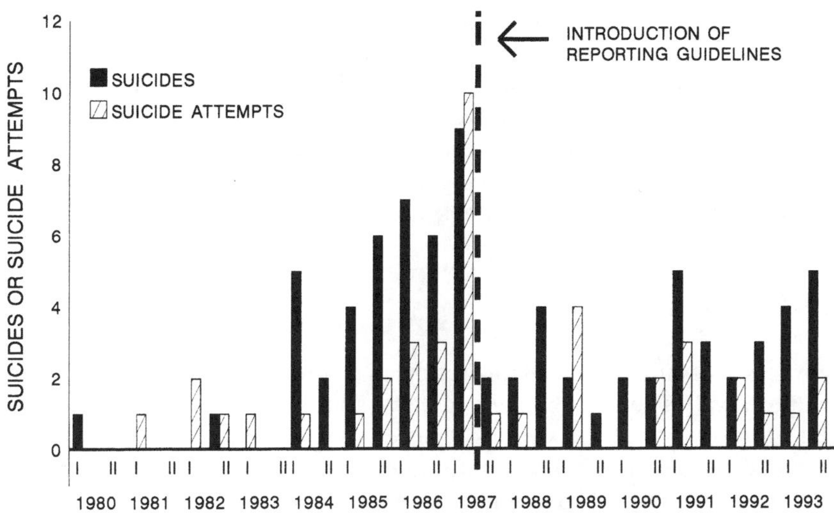

Figure 39.4 Suicides and suicide attempts in the Vienna subway system, 1980–1993. Reproduced by permission from Sonneck et al (1994)

press not to report suicides in a sensational fashion. Following this intervention, a change in the nature of reporting suicide rates was found (space devoted to the reports, degree of sensationalism) (Michel et al, 1998).

In spite of anecdotal reports of imitation effects of the suicide of the singer Kurt Cobain, it has been hypothesized that the depiction of his suicide in the media as an unreasonable act and a useless way of problem solving, especially in an interview with his widow Courtney Love, prevented copycat suicides (Kienhorst, 1994; Berman et al, 1997; Jobes et al, 1996).

The association between changes in the style of reporting by the print media and changes in the number of suicides supports the hypothesis that reports and portrayal of real and fictional suicidal behaviour, especially in particular ways, may trigger additional suicides and lead to imitation of suicide methods. Changes in the style of reporting, on the other hand, may well have a preventive effect.

Potentially beneficial effects of the media portrayal of suicidal behaviour were shown by O'Connor and colleagues (1999), using responses to a questionnaire sent to members of the BBC Viewing Panel. They found that one week after the broadcast of the episode of deliberate self-poisoning with paracetamol which was described above, more viewers (85%) than non-viewers (45%) correctly identified paracetamol as having hepatotoxic effects. Nevertheless, Hawton and colleagues (1999) concluded that the benefits of media portrayal of suicidal behaviour can be seriously questioned in view of the increase in overdoses, especially of paracetamol, which they demonstrated after the broadcast of the same television episode. Thus, such an approach to prevention might have both positive and negative effects. Whether the new media, such as the Internet, may offer possibilities to prevent suicide remains to be demonstrated. Conwell (1998) found that the great majority of sites on the Internet that deal with suicidal behaviour are thoughtfully designed and may provide a wealth of helpful information. Perhaps via this medium preventive efforts can be widely distributed at low cost to people in need. However, the Internet may equally have harmful effects by, for example, showing or recommending dangerous methods of suicide, thus lowering the threshold for suicidal behaviour in vulnerable individuals who might otherwise have benefited from some kind of treatment.

CONCLUSIONS

This overview of currently available results of studies on imitation effects of mass media portrayal of suicidal behaviour shows that many findings remain controversial. However, when the various types of analyses and the varying nature of models and behaviour are taken into account, theoretical justifications can be found for the diversity of the findings (see e.g. Groebel, 1986).

To study imitative and preventive effects it is necessary to understand the conceptual framework of learning by modelling or imitation. Imitative effects should be distinguished from contagious effects on suicidal behaviour, which are also commonly mentioned in the literature (see e.g. Resnik, 1969; Taylor, 1984; Phillips, 1985; Walsh and Rosen, 1985; Steede and Range, 1989). However, from a psychological point of view the theory of imitation should be preferred, as this theoretical framework makes it easier to explain some of the findings with regard to imitative behaviour in the field of suicidology, including some that appear contradictory. In contrast to imitation, contagion implies a kind of infectious disease, not allowing the "infected" person to act and to choose for him/herself. Learning by modelling refers to the acquisition of new patterns of behaviour through the observation of the behaviour of one or more models. Therefore, imitation is not limited to learning from real-life models.

Currently available knowledge indicates that the imitation effects of reported or portrayed suicidal behaviour depend on a number of factors. These include the characteristics of the model (e.g. age, gender, race and social status) and the extent to which the behaviour of the model is reinforced (i.e. appears to be positive or approved). Moreover, the frequency and manner of presentation of the model appear to be important, including the size and number of headlines, and the number of repetitions of a story, television programme or film. Finally, characteristics of the model, and perhaps also of the method shown, and those of the observer, appear to play a role. These include, first, age, as younger people are more suggestible and thus more prone to imitate their peers than older persons. However, the elderly may also be more receptive to copycat effects, whereas middle-aged people may be relatively protected, since they are more highly integrated in society (Stack, 1999). Second, gender is thought to play a role, as females in general are, for example, more field-dependent. Other important characteristics include self-esteem, self-efficacy—which, according to Bandura (1976, 1977), is one of the most important variables in social learning—and extroversion, impulsiveness, and mood congruence (i.e. when model and observer are in the same mood condition). Similarities between specific characteristics of the model and those of the observer thus play an important role, even in learning from symbolic models. Consequently, newspaper or television reports and films have been shown to disproportionately influence young people, especially when the models are young (Phillips, 1974, 1977; Bollen and Phillips, 1982; Phillips and Cartensen, 1986; Schmidtke and Häfner, 1988a,b). If a story is about an elderly suicide victim, the increase in copycat suicides is also very high (Stack, 1999). Ethnic "model preferences" apparently also exist, as suicides of foreigners do not trigger copycat suicides among native individuals (Stack, 1987a, 1996). The influence of race was clearly demonstrated by Molock et al (1994) and Stack (1996). As suicidal behaviour in the USA is commonly viewed by African–Americans as a problem afflicting white Americans, the former may be less likely to engage in imitative behaviour when exposed to white models. In the study of Stack (1996) in Japan, the imitation effect was restricted to Japanese victims. According to Meichenbaum (1971), it is also important whether a coping model (that means a model that demonstrates to a potential imitator how to cope, e.g. how not to use suicidal behaviour as a problem-solving strategy) or a master model (a model of an expert showing how to solve a problem) is available for imitation learning. The latter type of model often is not accepted when the differences between the master model and the potential imitator are too great.

Thus, learning by modelling can be regarded as a function of certain characteristics of both the model and the observer. Personality characteristics of the observer may also moderate the probability of exhibiting the learned behaviour. Stimulating events or motivating processes determine whether responses acquired by observation are actually performed at a specific point in time. Therefore, a behavioural strategy learned by observation may be used a considerable amount of time after the observation has taken place, and even contrary behaviour may occur. As a consequence, films aimed at preventing suicide may cause imitative behaviour (see e.g. Gould and Shaffer, 1986). Therefore, it is also not surprising that extremely publicized mass suicides, such as those in Jonestown, Waco or San Diego, and the mass suicides of the Order of the Solar Temple in Canada, France and Switzerland, were apparently not followed by imitation effects. This can perhaps, at least in part, also be explained by the involuntary nature of the suicides (e.g. Stack, 1983; Kroth, 1984) and the "non-attractiveness" of some of the group leaders. Also, when the models are particular celebrities who are unknown to a large audience or to vulnerable sub-groups such as youngsters or the elderly, as in the study of Jonas (1992), an imitation effect is unlikely because the model characteristics are not relevant for those potentially most likely to imitate.

The overview of research findings presented in this chapter demonstrates that there is substantial evidence for an imitative effect. More particularly, the studies by Phillips (in spite of some methodological drawbacks), Ellis and Walsh (1986), Gould and Shaffer (1986), Schmidtke and Häfner (1988a,b) and Hawton and colleagues (1999), provide firm evidence in favour of the imitation hypothesis for the portrayal of both real and fictional suicidal behaviour. These studies not only demonstrate effects on general rates of suicide or attempted suicide, but also age- and gender-specific modelling effects with regard to suicidal behaviour, particularly the methods used. The study by Schmidtke and Häfner (1987, 1988a) showed that the repeated broadcasting of a clearly defined type of model behaviour, involving a specific method of suicide and defined model variables, resulted in an increase in the use of a specific method to commit suicide (i.e. railway suicides). The effect was most marked in groups whose age and gender most closely resembled those of the model. Similar results showing imitation in the use of a specific portrayed method (i.e. deliberate self-poisoning using paracetamol) were clearly shown in the study by Hawton and colleagues (1999).

Various methodological problems have to be taken into account in evaluating the studies on imitation and preventive effects. Exposure to models in newspapers and television programmes may be age- or gender-specific. For example, when studying the effects of "celebrity" suicides, the extent of popularity of these individuals in different age groups has to be determined. Pop stars are often not very well known among elderly people, while famous international authors (especially modern authors) are not very well known among youngsters. The number of quotations in journals is not an adequate measure and their use may lead to insignificant results. This methodological problem is probably one of the reasons for the non-significant results of the study of Jonas (1992). The readership of journals varies, as pop magazines are not read by the elderly, and the Internet will not be commonly used by this age group. The choice of journals, magazines and television programmes is also influenced by gender. Hassan (1995) sees one of the reasons for his finding of an increase in male suicides following media reports of suicides in the fact that some Australian journals have a greater male than female readership. Also, as Stack (1999) has noted, the size of coverage and audience or readership has to be taken into account. Stack (1999) stressed that when a large number of less publicized suicide stories are included in a study, copycat effects are not likely to be found. The different size of the effects found by Schmidtke and Häfner (1987, 1988a,b) in terms of the two showings of the programme they were studying were correlated significantly with the size of the audience: the first six episodes were broadcast on Monday evenings, whereas the second broadcast took place on Sunday afternoons, with consequently smaller audience viewing figures. An additional methodological problem in interpreting findings is caused by the echoing of suicide stories first published in one medium (e.g. press, books) in other media (e.g. radio, television, other channels; Stack, 1990b, 1999).

This review further shows that multiprogramme and highly publicized stories have the greatest impact by affecting more youth or other vulnerable groups (Phillips and Carstensen, 1986, 1988; Phillips et al, 1992). Phillips and colleagues (1992), therefore, stated that media portrayal of "model" suicides creates "natural advertisements for suicide". A similar conclusion can be made from the study by Hawton and co-workers (1999).

A second hypothesis may explain the divergent nature of the findings between the studies of Phillips (1989) and of Schmidtke and Häfner (1988a). The media presentation of fictional suicide models may well influence the occurrence of suicidal behaviour in a population in two ways, namely in the short term and in the long term. There may also be different types of responders. "Early" responders may be more impulsive and may have already contemplated suicide. In particular, among young people undergoing a crisis resembling that of the model, the broadcasting or reporting may precipitate a suicidal act (e.g. Eisenberg, 1986). In contrast, "late" responders may exhibit a less impulsive, more considered response to a model. Thus, the media may help to "sow the seeds of suicide in the distant future" (Barraclough et al, 1977). As Littmann (1985) suggested, the publication or broadcasting of suicide-related issues and suicidal modelling behaviour may lead to the view that this form of behaviour is "a common and understandable way" of problem solving, thus increasing the likelihood that a person will choose suicidal behaviour as a problem-solving strategy in a stressful situation. Therefore, suicide models may be especially effective in combination with factors such as stress, depression and social isolation, because these models might impact upon already existing problems or they may induce in the recipient (or viewer) a "morbid rationale" which they believe will solve their problems.

In view of the evidence cited above, it is no surprise that for some time groups of professionals engaged in suicide prevention have been addressing this theme. As early as 1910, during the historical symposium of the Viennese Psychoanalytical Association in Vienna which dealt with the problem of suicides among young students, a special section was devoted to the question of whether newspaper reports on suicide caused suicides among school children (Oppenheimer, 1910; Unus Multorum, 1910).

Phelps had already suggested in 1911 that reports on suicides and the discussion of this subject in the literature could induce suicidal events through imitation. In the same year, a committee of the American Academy of Medicine and the American Medical Association considered the problem of the modelling effect of press reports on suicide. This committee also quoted examples of increases in the rate of suicide by similar methods (albeit in a rather anecdotal form) when the press gave detailed reports of cases of suicide and the accompanying circumstances (Hemenway, 1911). The influence of newspaper stories was also emphasized by Rost (1912), who was both a famous German journalist and an expert in suicidal behaviour. Since that time, discussion about imitative and preventive effects of mass media in relation to suicidal behaviour has been a constant theme (see Häfner and Schmidtke, 1986).

More recently, based on these findings and hypotheses, the World Health Organization has listed "toning down press reports" as a means to change press reports about suicidal behaviour among the six most important basic steps for suicide prevention (World Health Organization, 1993). The proposed measures are: avoiding sensational reporting; no front-page stories; no photographs; no mentioning of suicidal behaviour as an understandable way of problem solving; and publishing of addresses and phone numbers of helping agencies such as hot-lines and The Samaritans. These proposals are now widely accepted and have been published by various suicide prevention organizations, including the International Association for Suicide Prevention, the American Association for Suicidology and the Associations for Suicide Prevention in Germany, Austria and Switzerland.

REFERENCES

Altheide, D.L. (1981) Airplane accidents, murder, and the mass media: comment on Phillips. Social Forces, 60: 593–596.

Ashton, J.R. and Donnan, S. (1981) Suicide by burning as an epidemic phenomenon: an analyses of 82 deaths and inquests in England and Wales in 1978–9. Psychological Medicine, 11: 735–739.

Bandura, A. (1976) Lernen am Modell. Klett: Stuttgart.

Bandura, A. (1977) Self-efficacy: towards a unifying theory of behavioural change. Psychological Review, 84: 191–215.

Baron, J.N. and Reiss, P.C. (1985a) Same time, next year: aggregate analyses of the mass media and violent behavior. American Sociological Review, 50: 347–363.

Baron, J.N. and Reiss, P.C. (1985b) Reply to Phillips and Bollen. American Sociological Review, 50: 372–376.

Barraclough, B., Shepherd, D. and Jennings, C. (1977) Do newspaper reports of coroner's inquests incite people to commit suicide? British Journal of Psychiatry, 131: 528–532.

Baume, P., Cantor, C. and Rolfe, A. (1997) Cybersuicide: the role of interactive suicide notes on the Internet. Crisis, 18: 73–79.

Berman, A. (1988) Fictional depiction of suicide in television films and imitation effects. American Journal of Psychiatry, 145: 982–986.

Berman, A., Jobes, D.A. and O'Carroll, P. (1997) The aftermath of Kurt Cobain's suicide. In D. De Leo, A. Schmidtke and R.F.W. Diekstra, Suicide Prevention: a Holistic Approach, pp. 139–143. Dordrecht: Kluwer.

Blumenthal, S. and Bergner, L. (1973) Suicide and newspapers: a replicated study. American Journal of Psychiatry, 130: 468–471.

Bollen, K.A. and Phillips, D.P. (1981) Suicidal motor vehicle fatalities in Detroit: a replication. American Journal of Sociology, 87: 404–412.

Bollen, K.A. and Phillips, D.P. (1982) Imitative suicides: a national study of effects of television news stories. American Sociological Review, 47: 802–809.

Box, G.E.P. and Jenkins, G.M. (1979) Time Series Analysis Forecasting and Control. San Francisco, CA: Holden-Day.

Cantor, C. and Sheehan, P. (1996) Violence and media reports—a connection with Hungerford. Archives of Suicide Research, 2: 225–266.

Church, I.C. and Phillips, J.P.N. (1984) Suggestion and suicide by plastic bag asphyxia. British Journal of Psychiatry, 144: 100–101.

Coleman, L. (1987) Suicide Clusters. Winchester: Faber & Faber.

Conwell, Y. (1998) Suicide and the Internet. Newslink of the American Association of Suicidology, 8.

Dahm, K. and Händel, K. (1970) Untersuchungen über Selbstmorde und Selbstmordversuche in einem ländlichen Bevölkerungsgebiet. Materia Medica Nordmark, 63.

Daniels, R.G. (1986) Emotional crises imitating television (letter). Lancet, i: 856.

Diekstra, R.F.W. (1974) A social learning approach to the prediction of suicidal behaviour. In N. Speyer, R.F.W. Diekstra and K.J.M. van de Loo (Eds), Proceedings of the 7th International Conference for Suicide Prevention, Amsterdam, August 27–30, 1973. Amsterdam: Swets & Zeitlinger.

Diekstra, R.F.W. and Garnefski, N. (1995) On the nature, magnitude, and causality of suicidal behaviors: an international perspective. Suicide and Life-Threatening Behavior, 25: 36–57.
Durkheim, E. (1897) Le Suicide: Etude de Sociologie. Paris: Alcan.
Eisenberg, L. (1986) Does bad news about suicide beget bad news? New England Journal of Medicine, 315: 705–707.
Ellis, S.J. and Walsh, S. (1986) Soap may seriously damage your health. Lancet, March, 686.
Etzersdorfer, E., Sonneck, G. and Nagel-Kuess, S. (1992) Newspaper reports and suicide. New England Journal of Medicine, 327: 502–503.
Fekete, S. and Schmidtke, A. (1995) Suicidium—Modellkövetés—Család. Psychiatria Hungarica, 10: 131–145.
Fekete, S. and Schmidtke, A. (1996a) Attitudes toward suicide in the mass media. In J.L. McIntosh (Ed.), Suicide: Individual, Cultural, International Perspectives. Proceedings of 29th Annual Conference American Association for Suicidology. Washington, DC: American Association of Suicidology.
Fekete, S. and Schmidtke, A. (1996b) The impact of mass media reports on suicide and attitudes towards self-destruction: previous studies and some new data from Hungary and Germany. In B. Mishara (Ed.), The Impact of Suicide. New York: Springer.
Fekete, S., Domino, G., Schmidtke, A. and Takahashi, Y. (1998a) Attitudes toward suicide—a cross-cultural study. Paper presented at the 31st Conference of the American Association of Suicidology (AAS), Washington, DC (Abstract Book, 29).
Fekete, S., Schmidtke, A., Etzersdorfer, E. and Gailiene, D. (1998b) Media reports in Hungary, Austria, Germany and Lithuania in 1981 and 1991. Reflection, mediation and changes of sociocultural attitudes towards suicide in the mass media. In D. DeLeo, A. Schmidtke and R.F.W. Diekstra (Eds), Suicide Prevention—A Holistic Approach. Dordrecht: Kluwer.
Fekete, S., Schmidtke, A., Marton, K. and Kózczán, G. (1994) Az öngylkossággal kapcsolatos attitúdök a médiában. Német-magyar összehasonlító vizsgálat (Attitudes towards suicidal behavior in the mass media. A comparative study in Germany and Hungary). Psychiatrica Hungarica, 9: 117–127.
Fowler, B.P. (1986) Emotional crisis imitating television (letter). Lancet, i: 1036–1037.
Gould, M.S. and Shaffer, D. (1986) The impact of suicide in television movies. New England Journal of Medicine, 315: 690–694.
Groebel, J. (1986) International research on television violence: synopsis and critique. In L.R. Huesman and L.D. Eron (Eds), Television and the Aggressive Child: A Cross-national Comparison. Hillsdale, NJ: Erlbaum.
Grosby, K., Rhoe, J.D. and Holland, J. (1977) Suicide by fire: a contemporary method of political protest. International Journal of Social Psychiatry, 23: 60–69.
Gundlach, J. and Stack, S. (1990) The impact of hyper media coverage on suicide: New York City, 1910–1920. Social Science Quarterly, 71: 619–627.
Häfner, H. and Schmidtke, A. (1986) Effects of the mass media on suicidal behaviour and deliberate self-harm. Paper presented at the WHO Conference on Preventive Practices in Suicide and Attempted Suicide, York, 1986. Copenhagen: World Health Organization Document ICP/PSF 017/10.
Hassan, R. (1995) Effects of newspaper stories on the incidence of suicide in Australia: a research note. Australian and New Zealand Journal of Psychiatry, 29: 480–483.
Hawton, K., Simkin, S., Deeks, J.J., O'Connor, S., Keen, A., Altman, D.G., Philo, G. and Bulstrode, C. (1999) Effects of a drug overdose in a television drama on presentations to hospital for self-poisoning: time series and questionnaire study. British Medical Journal, 318: 972–977.
Hemenway, H. (1911) To what extent are suicide and other crimes against the person due to suggestion from the press? Bulletin of the American Academy of Medicine, 12: 253–263.

Henseler, H. (1975) Zu H. Wedler: Fragen über Fernsehsendungen zum Selbstmordproblem. Suizidprophylaxe, 2: 139–140.
Hills, N.F. (1995) Newspaper stories and the incidence of suicide. Australian and New Zealand Journal of Psychiatry, 29: 699.
Holding, T.A. (1974) The BBC *Befrienders* series and its effects. British Journal of Psychiatry, 124: 470–472.
Holding, T.A. (1975) Suicide and *The Befrienders*. British Medical Journal, 3: 751–752.
Horton, H. and Stack, S. (1984) The effect of television on national suicide rates. Journal of Suicide Psychology, 123: 141–142.
Ishii, K. (1991) Measuring mutual causation: effects of suicide news in Japan. Social Science Research, 20: 188–195.
Jackson, E.D. and Potkay, C.R. (1974) Audience reactions to the suicide play *Quiet Cries*. Journal of Community Psychology, 2: 16–17.
Jonas, K. (1992) Modelling and suicide. A test of the Werther effect. British Journal of Social Psychology, 31: 295–306.
Kessler, R., Downey, G. and Stipp, H. (1988) Clustering of teenage suicides after television news stories about suicide: a reconsideration. American Journal of Psychiatry, 145: 1379–1883.
Kessler, R.C. and Stipp, H. (1984) The impact of fictional television suicide stories on US fatalities: a replication. American Journal of Sociology, 90: 151–167.
Kienhorst, I. (1994) Kurt Cobain. Crisis, 15: 62–63.
Kirsch, M.R. and Lester, D. (1986a) Clusters of suicide. Psychological Reports, 59: 1126.
Kirsch, M.R. and Lester, D. (1986b) Suicide from the Golden Gate Bridge: do they cluster over time? Psychological Reports, 59: 1314.
Kreitman, N., Smith, P. and Tan, E.S. (1969) Attempted suicide in social networks. British Journal of Preventive and Social Medicine, 23: 116–123.
Kreitman, N., Smith, P. and Tan, E.S. (1970) Attempted suicide as language: an empirical study. British Journal of Psychiatry, 116: 465–473.
Kroth, J. (1984) Recapitulating Jonestown. Journal of Psychhistory, 11: 383–393.
Lester, D. (1987) Living in the Shadow: An Example of the Social Learning Theory of Suicide. Paper presented at the Meeting of the American Association of Suicidology and the International Association for Suicide Prevention, San Francisco, CA, 1987.
Lester, D. (1992) Why People Kill Themselves. Springfield, IL: Thomas.
Littmann, S.K. (1985) Suicide epidemics and newspaper reporting. Suicide and Life-Threatening Behavior, 15: 43–50.
Marks, A. (1987) Television and suicide. New England Journal of Medicine, 316: 877.
Martin, G. (1996) The influence of television suicide in a normal adolescent population. Archives of Suicide Research, 2: 103–117.
Marzuk, P.M., Tardiff, K., Hirsch, C.S., Leon, A.C., Stajic, M., Hartwell, N. and Portera, L. (1993) Increase in suicide by asphyxiation in New York City after the Publication of *Final Exit*. New England Journal of Medicine, 329: 1508–1510.
Marzuk, P.M., Tardiff, K., Hirsch, C.S., Leon, A.C., Stajic, M., Hartwell, N. and Portera, L. (1994) Increase in suicide by asphyxiation in New York City after the Publication of *Final Exit*. Publishing Research Quarterly, 10: 62–68.
Mastroianni, G.R. (1987) Television and suicide. New England Journal of Medicine, 316: 877.
Meichenbaum, D. (1971) Examination of model characteristics in reducing avoidance behavior. Journal of Personality and Social Psychology, 17: 298–307.
Michel, K., Frey, C. and Valach, L. (1998) Suicide reporting in print media: an evaluation of the effect of guidelines issued to editors and journalists. Presented at the 7th European Symposium on Suicide and Suicidal Behaviour, Gent, Belgium, September.
Milavsky, J.R., Kessler, R.C. and Stipp, H.H. (1987) Do television news reports of suicide cause suicide? Paper presented at the meeting of the American Association of Suicidology/International Association of Suicide Prevention, San Francisco, CA.

Molock, S.D., Williams, S., Lacy, M. and Kimborough, R. (1994) Werther effects in a black college sample. Paper presented at the 27th Annual Congress of the American Association of Suicidology, New York.

Motto, J.A. (1967) Suicide and suggestibility—the role of the press. American Journal of Psychiatry, 124: 252–256.

Motto, J.A. (1970) Newspaper influence on suicide. Archives of General Psychiatry, 23: 143–148.

O'Connor, S., Deeks, J.J., Hawton, K., Simkin, S., Keen, A., Altman, D.G., Philo, G. and Bulstrode, C. (1999) Effects of a drug overdose in a television drama on knowledge of specific dangers of self-poisoning: population based surveys. British Medical Jourual, 318: 978–979.

Oppenheimer, D.E. (1910) In P. Friedman (Ed.) (1967) On Suicide. With Particular Reference to Suicide among Young Students. New York: International Universities Press.

Ostroff, R.B. and Boyd, J.H. (1987) Television and suicide. New England Journal of Medicine, 316: 876–977.

Ostroff, R.B., Behrends, R.W., Kinson, L. and Oliphant, J. (1985) Adolescent suicides modelled after television movie. American Journal of Psychiatry, 142: 989.

Pell, B. and Watters, D. (1982) Newspaper policies on suicide stories. Canada's Mental Health, 30: 8–9.

Phelps, E. (1911) Neurotic books and newspapers as factors in the mortality of suicide and crime. Journal of Sociological Medicine, 12: 264–306.

Phillips, D.P. (1974) The influence of suggestion on suicide: substantive and theoretical implications of the Werther effect. American Sociological Review, 39: 340–354.

Phillips, D.P. (1977) Motor vehicle fatalities increase just after publicized suicide stories. Science, 196: 1464–1465.

Phillips, D.P. (1978) Airplane accident fatalities increase just after newspaper stories about murder and suicide. Science, 201: 748–749.

Phillips, D.P. (1979) Suicide, motor-vehicle fatalities and the mass-media: evidence towards a theory of suggestion. American Journal of Sociology, 84: 1150–1174.

Phillips, D.P. (1980) Airplane accidents, murder, and the mass media: towards a theory of imitation and suggestion. Social Forces, 58: 1001–1024.

Phillips, D.P. (1982) The impact of fictional television stories on US adult fatalities: new evidence on the effect of the mass media on violence. American Journal of Sociology, 87: 1340–1359.

Phillips, D.P. (1983) The impact of mass media violence on US homicides. American Sociological Review, 48: 560–568.

Phillips, D.P. (1985) The Werther effect. Suicide, and other forms of violence, are contagious. Sciences, 25: 32–39.

Phillips, D.P. (1989) Recent advances in suicidology: the study of imitative suicide. In R.F.W. Diekstra, R. Maris, S. Platt, A. Schmidtke and G. Sonneck (Eds), Suicide and Its Prevention—the Role of Attitude and Imitation, pp. 299–312. Leiden: Brill.

Phillips, D.P. and Carstensen, L.L. (1986) Clustering of teenage suicides after television news stories about suicide. New England Journal of Medicine, 315: 685–689.

Phillips, D.P. and Carstensen, L.L. (1987) Television and suicide. New England Journal of Medicine, 316: 877–878.

Phillips, D.P. and Carstensen, L.L. (1988) The effect of suicide stories on various demographic groups, 1968–85. Suicide and Life-Threatening Behavior, 18: 100–114.

Phillips, D.P. and Bollen, K.A. (1985) Same time, last year: selective data dredging for negative findings. American Sociological Review, 50: 364–371.

Phillips, D.P., Lesyna, M.A. and Paight, D.J. (1992) Suicide and the media. In: R.W. Maris, A.L. Berman, J.T. Maltsberger and R.I. Yufit (Eds), Assessment and Prediction of Suicide. New York: Guilford.

Platt, S. (1987) The aftermath of Angie's overdose: is soap (opera) damaging to your health? British Medical Journal, 294: 954–957.

Platt, S. (1988) The consequences of a televized soap opera drug overdose: is there a mass media imitation effect? In R.F.W. Diekstra, R.W. Maris, S.D. Platt, A. Schmidtke and G. Sonneck (Eds), Attitudinal Factors in Suicidal Behaviour and its Prevention. Amsterdam: Swets & Zeitlinger.

Platt, S. (1993) The social transmission of parasuicide: is there a modelling effect? Crisis, 14: 23–31.

Popow, N.M. (1911) The present epidemic of school suicides in Russia. Newrol. Vestnik, 18: 312–317.

Resnik, H. (1969) The neglected research for the suicidococcus contagiosa. Archives of Environmental Health, 19: 307–308.

Rost, H. (1912) Der Selbstmord in den Deutschen Städten. Paderborn: Schöning.

Sandler, D.A., Connell, P.A. and Welsh, K. (1986) Emotional crises imitating television (letter). Lancet 1986, i: 856.

Schlittgen, R. and Streitbery, B.H.J. (1997) Zeitreihenanalyse. Munich: Oldenbourg.

Schmidtke, A. (1988) Verhaltenstheoretisches Erklärungimodell Suizidalen Verhaltens. Regensburg: Roderer.

Schmidtke, A. (1996) Mass media: their impact on suicide among adolescents. Paper presented at the International Conference, "Suicide: Biopsychosocial Approaches", Athens.

Schmidtke, A. and Fekete, S. (1996) The International Study on Newspaper Headlines about suicidal behavior: design and preliminary results. Paper presented at the Meeting of the International Academy for Suicide Research (IASR), St. Louis, MO.

Schmidtke, A. and Häfner, H. (1987) Public attitudes towards and effects of the mass media on suicidal and deliberate self-harm behaviour. In R.F.W. Diekstra, S.D. Maris, S.D. Platt, A. Schmidtke and G. Sonneck (Eds), Attitudinal Factors in Suicidal Behaviour and its Prevention. Amsterdam: Swets & Zeitlinger/Brill.

Schmidtke, A. and Häfner, H. (1988a) Imitation effects after fictional television suicides. In H.J. Möller, A. Schmidtke and R. Welz (Eds), Current Issues of Suicidology, pp. 341–348. Heidelberg: Springer.

Schmidtke, A. and Häfner, H. (1988b) The Werther effect after television films—evidence for an old hypothesis. Psychological Medicine, 18: 665–676.

Schmidtke, A. and Häfner, H. (1989) Public attitudes towards and effects of the mass media on suicidal and deliberate self-harm behaviour. In R.F.W. Diekstra, R. Maris, S. Platt, A. Schmidtke and G. Sonneck (Eds), Suicide and its Prevention—The Role of Attitude and Imitation, pp. 313–330. Leiden: Brill.

Schmidtke, A. and Schaller, S. (1998) What do we know about media effects on imitation of suicidal behaviour: state of the art. In D. DeLeo, A. Schmidtke and R.F.W. Diekstra (Eds), Suicide Prevention—A Holistic Approach. Dordrecht: Kluwer, pp. 121–137.

Schmidtke, A. and Schaller, S. (1991) The Werther effect: imitation effects after fictional television suicides. Paper presented at the congress "Psychology and promotion of health", Lausanne.

Seiden, R.H. and Spence, M.C. (1982) A tale of two bridges: comparative suicide incidence on the Golden Gate and San Francisco Oakland Bay Bridges. Crisis, 3: 32–40.

Seiden, R.H. and Spence, M. (1983) A tale of two bridges: a comparative suicide incidence on the Golden Gate and San Francisco Oakland Bay Bridges. Omega, 14: 201–209.

Singer, U. (1980) Massenselbstmord. Stuttgart: Hippokrates.

Singer, U. (1984) Der Massensuizid von Massada bis Guayana. In V. Faust and M. Wolfersdorf (Eds), Suizidgefahr. Stuttgart: Hippokrates.

Sonneck, G., Etzersdorfer, E. and Nagel-Kuess, S. (1994) Imitative suicide on the Viennese subway. Social Science and Medicine, 38: 453–457.

Stack, S. (1982) Suicide: a decade interview of the sociological literature. Deviant Behavior, 4: 41–66.
Stack, S. (1983) The effect of the Jonestown suicides on American suicides rates. Journal of Social Psychology, 119: 145–146.
Stack, S. (1987a) Celebrities and suicide: a taxonomy and analysis, 1948–1983. American Sociological Review, 52: 401–412.
Stack, S. (1987b) Suicide: media impacts in war and peace, 1910–1920: a research note. Paper presented at the Combined Meeting of the American Association of Suicidology and the International Association for Suicide Prevention, San Francisco, CA.
Stack, S. (1990a) Media impact on suicide. In D. Lester (Ed.), Current Concepts in Suicide. Bowie: Charles.
Stack, S. (1990b) Audience receptiveness, the media and aged suicide. Journal of Ageing Studies, 4: 195–209.
Stack, S. (1996) The effect of the media on suicide: evidence from Japan. Suicide and Life-Threatening Behavior, 26: 405–414.
Stack, S. (1999) Media impacts on suicide: a quantitative review of 293 findings. Paper presented at the Annual Meeting of the American Association of Suicidology, Houston, TX.
Steede, K.K. and Range, L.M. (1989) Does television induce suicidal contagion with adolescents? Journal of Community Psychology, 17: 166–172.
Strahan, S.A. (1893) Suicide and Insanity. London: Swan Sonnenschein.
Taylor, P. (1984) Cluster phenomenon of young suicides raises "contagion" theory. Washington Post, March 11, A 3.
Unus Multorum (1910) Kapitel I. In Vereinsleitung des Wiener psychoanalytschen Vereins (Ed.), Über den Selbstmord insbesondere den Schülerselbstmord. Wiesbaden: Bergmann.
Velting, D.M. and Gould, M.S. (1977) Suicide contagion. In R.W. Maris, M.M. Silverman and S.S. Canetto (Eds), Review of Suicidology, pp. 96–137. New York: Guilford.
Walsh, B.W. and Rosen, P. (1985) Self-mutilation and contagion: an empirical test. American Journal of Psychiatry, 142: 119–231.
Wasserman, I.M. (1984) Imitation and suicide: a re-examination of the Werther effect. American Sociological Review, 49: 427–436.
Wasserman, I.M. (1993) Comment on hyper media coverage of suicide in New York City. Social Science Quarterly, 74: 216–218.
Williams, J.M.G., Lawton, C., Ellis, S.J., Walsh, S. and Reed, J. (1987) Copycat suicide attempts. Lancet, II: 102–103.
Wilson, W. and Hunter, R. (1983) Movie-inspired violence. Psychological Reports, 53: 435–441.
Winter, K. (1986) Medicine and the Media. British Medical Journal, 292: 1073.
World Health Organization (1993) Guidelines for the primary prevention of mental, neurological and psychosocial disorders. 4. Suicide. Geneva: World Health Organization (WHO/MNH/MND/93.24).

Chapter 40

Volunteers and Suicide Prevention

Vanda Scott
Befrienders International, London, UK
and
Simon Armson
The Samaritans, Slough, UK

Abstract

This chapter considers the role of the volunteer and approaches this from a number of viewpoints. It recognizes that the lay volunteer brings the fundamental qualities of a human being, such as empathy, awareness and humanity, unfettered by the need for the acquiring of clinical knowledge and experience. There is arguably, therefore, a greater motivational interest in volunteers in contrast to that of the highly trained specialist. However, it will be clear that the roles of the volunteer and professionals are entirely complementary and will result in a better overall service for those who need intervention of this nature. Selection, training and supervision are prerequisites for an effective volunteer workforce and therefore the potential for most communities across the cultures to establish a suicide prevention programme is discussed. The need for collaboration, locally, nationally and internationally, in order for a preventive strategy to be effective in reducing the rate of suicide, is a theme throughout this chapter. It draws on the international experience of the authors, who work professionally in the voluntary sector in suicide prevention as well as being volunteers in suicide prevention agencies.

INTRODUCTION

People volunteer for a myriad of reasons, for a wide selection of activities and in a great variety of ways. Therefore, when considering the utilization of a human resource in the broadly-based field of volunteerism which, in general, crosses all

The International Handbook of Suicide and Attempted Suicide. Edited by K. Hawton and K. van Heeringen.

professional, cultural and social boundaries, there is no one common motivation, purpose or system of service provision. However, there are identifiable common factors evident in volunteers involved in suicide prevention activities; these are the human qualities of compassion, empathy and warmth.

In the Aves Memorial lecture in the UK, the Chief Charity Commissioner, talking of the volunteer, said: "The capacity to give, or to choose to give, something beyond the basic obligations of human life, is as important to the individual as it is to the society to which he is contributing" (Guthrie, 1986).

For the basis of this chapter, the working definition for "volunteer" will be that used in the health and social services:

> A person who voluntarily provides an unpaid direct service for one or more other persons to whom the volunteer is not related. The volunteer normally provides his or her service through some kind of formal scheme, rather than through an informal neighbourly arrangement (Darvill and Mundy, 1984).

This chapter will identify the issues surrounding the recruitment and deployment of volunteers as a composite part of an overall strategy for the prevention of suicide. It will refer to the literature on volunteerism and the experiences of both authors in establishing volunteer-resourced suicide prevention services in different parts of the world.

VOLUNTEERING—AN OVERVIEW

Volunteerism is a deeply entrenched part of the culture and religions of many countries and is strongly influenced by the socio-economic and political boundaries that exist in a community. In times of religious and political unrest, volunteer action clearly reflects the changing climate and economic pressures. In the USA the trends in volunteerism have been regarded as an indicator of social responsibility, showing clearly that at times of economic growth volunteer activity is at its peak. Conversely, at times of recession and greatest social deprivation, when health and social services are in greater demand, volunteer resources are at their weakest.

The availability of volunteers should be considered in context. It is necessary to look at the limited surveys that have been produced over the past years. Methods of measuring the extent of volunteering worldwide appear to be ill-defined, with unreliable data. There is also confusion between voluntary agency membership and active volunteer participation.

An extensive study on volunteers in Europe emphasized the complexity and diversity of volunteering throughout the Continent and draws out a few key factors about volunteers:

- Most are employed.
- They have relatively high educational and occupational status, income and social grade.

- There are equal numbers of men and women.
- They span the age range, with a slight concentration in the middle age group.
- In the past year, 23% of the population had volunteered.
- Each volunteer averages 120 hours annually.

The authors note that an increasingly high profile for voluntary services has evolved in Europe as a result of "the retraction and restructuring of the welfare state, due to economic and political pressures" (Gaskin and Davis Smith, 1997). This is also being experienced in the former communist countries, in which the economic pressures and removal of state controls has led to an increase in non-governmental organizations.

Internationally the variations in volunteer commitment are immense. In Australia, for example, a recent survey of four states (Victoria, Queensland, New South Wales and South Australia) suggests an overall decline in volunteering in the past 15 years which has not kept pace with the growth in population. Even so, it is noted that there has been an increase in personal commitment (especially among women) by those directly involved in voluntary activity (Lyons and Fabiansson, 1998). In Israel, by contrast, a high level of commitment is evident, where nearly 20% of the adult population give time to volunteering. Sixty percent of these are active in health and social service provision, thus supplying a significant service to their communities (Gidron, 1997).

The complexity of volunteer motivation is well recognized, but a theory taking account of the intricacies of the sector has yet to be provided. This chapter considers the role of the volunteer and approaches this from a number of viewpoints. Volunteers characteristically have reflective dispositions. When compared with the rest of the population, they have a higher degree of religious or moral conviction, are less materialistic and have a higher measure of psychological well-being. Furthermore, they frequently have an active interest in politics and place importance on personal experience (Gerard, 1983).

The social and political structures have significant bearing on the attitude and culture of volunteer activity. Although there was a growth of volunteerism in Japan during the 1990s, it still represented only 10% of that of the USA (Hotta, 1997). Volunteering in Japan is not considered to be a totally acceptable activity by the public. This is clearly reflected in the low numbers of businessmen participating in the voluntary sector. The strong work ethic that underpins the social and economic fabric of society creates an atmosphere in which being seen to have free time to volunteer is not considered to be compatible with a commitment to the employer and to economic growth. In the rural areas there is an extension to this reasoning which is predicated by a strong reluctance to receive help from volunteers, as families and not strangers are regarded to be the source of help and support.

However, the Great Hanshin Earthquake may have signalled a lasting change in the volunteer support system in Japan, when over 1 million volunteers engaged in the rescue operation in the disaster area. Voluntary agencies collaborated with government services in bringing relief to the victims of the earthquake. During the following months, volunteers from the suicide prevention centre in Osaka made regular visits to the bereaved, homeless and distraught people of Kobi, where they gave emotional support and listened for hours, often in silence, to the sobbing and confused despair. It will be interesting to monitor whether this upsurge in volunteering is manifested in an on-going willingness of people to volunteer in other fields.

Essentially, the effectiveness of a service being provided by volunteers requires a clear understanding of the motivational factors of the work force. However, to compare volunteer motivation with work motivation has its limitations; volunteers are not like employees, in that their main thrust is concern for others and rewards cannot be compared (Van Til, 1989; Handy, 1988). A link between the degree of formality in volunteering and the needs of the individual can be identified (Scott, 1989), as can the motivational need of people who are attracted to volunteer work as an alternative interest to that of their work place. External social and economic factors have an influence, as seen in the growth of the feminist movement in the USA, which changed attitudes towards volunteering from the social acceptability of wanting to help, to seeking tangible rewards of work skills and a career potential. Conversely, it is also debated that the ideology of giving might hide the real motives of self-interest. Although it is a misused concept, altruism was traditionally believed to be the sole motivating factor in volunteerism (Van Til, 1989). Furthermore, it continues to be regarded as a critical force in volunteer motivation. In fact, people are motivated by a combination of altruism, self-interest and sociability: the humanitarian need to help others and to feel useful is undoubtedly a significant factor.

ROLE OF VOLUNTEERS IN SUICIDE PREVENTION

Suicide is frequently regarded as the ultimate expression of distress. That is the point when there is no vision of a future, when it seems that every aspect of life has become so futile or so overwhelming that there is no possibility of coping, and the only option is of complete and final self-destruction.

What do people in distress need? They need someone who:

- Can be trusted to be available.
- Will not "take over".
- Will patiently support and try to understand.
- Will have the strength to withstand the pressures and demands of another's crisis.

In addition, the person in distress often needs to be allowed to be anonymous. T. S. Eliot eloquently stated:

The luxury of an intimate disclosure to a stranger

That stranger in many communities could be a volunteer.

A medical practitioner referred a patient to a suicide prevention centre in Asia after she had made two almost fatal attempts on her life. The patient was not only in the medical profession but also was married to a well-known doctor in the community. Over a number of months the patient attended regular consultations with a psychiatrist but found she was unable to express her anxieties and could only respond to routine questions. Initially, reticent to put her energies into seeking other help, especially from volunteers, the patient in desperation called the suicide prevention centre. She talked about her suicidal feelings freely, for the first time in her life, to someone who responded on an equal level and who listened with unconditional, uncritical acceptance and respect. As the lady became more stable the need to talk receded, her deep distress declined and consequently her visits to the centre decreased. Ordinary lay persons who were, by the nature of the service, available any time of the day or night had enabled this to happen.

Volunteers befriend the caller and "befriending" is a listening therapy. It is one therapeutic model in the multi-faceted approach to suicide prevention—it is the response to an immediate emotional crisis by lay volunteers who are given professional support by appointed medical and psychiatric consultants. Using the model utilized by many of volunteer based suicide organizations worldwide, volunteers are carefully selected, trained, monitored, supervised and thoroughly prepared to respond to callers' emotional crises. As the work in itself is so often emotionally demanding, they are also given structured support.

In contrast to this approach of intervention, it is relevant to consider here the way in which other approaches might tackle the same issues. In particular, consider the clinical approach, using the traditional medical model. Here, the aetiology of suicide will be assessed with reference to sociological, psychological and biological factors, having accounted for those that will predispose towards, precipitate and perpetuate the likelihood of suicide in this way. It is likely that the conventional aetiological matrix will be employed. Compared with this, the risk assessment undertaken by volunteers, in relating to those who are potentially suicidal, may be seen to be rather more simplistic. Here factors such as current mood state, family background, the evidence of any previous psychological illness, together with relevant social factors (e.g. employment, housing, debt, substance abuse, etc.), will be taken into account. Whilst this approach will not have the same depth of that of the medical model, it is nevertheless relevant to note that the volunteer engaged in suicide prevention is essentially concerned with making an effective intervention at the moment of crisis. Consequently, factors relating to the immediate seem to be more relevant and important than past history or consideration of the future.

That said, the fundamental emotions of hopelessness, helplessness and worthlessness will be as eagerly sought after by clinicians and volunteers alike. As discussed elsewhere in this chapter, the skill of the well-trained and well-supported volunteer is to reach towards the pain of the individual in distress and to enable that to be expressed and supported.

While volunteers actively listen to callers' stories, most importantly they help callers explore their deep feelings of despair by enabling them to ventilate their anger and talk about their distress and frustration. Not only does skilled active listening assist volunteers in steering towards a caller's pain but it significantly helps with the exploration of suicidal feelings. Volunteers come from all walks of life; some may be health professionals, but the significant majority have no medical or specific mental health qualifications; they are selected for their ability to care and listen. In this way therefore, volunteers offer emotional support to those for whom life may be getting too much to bear and who may be in danger of taking their own lives.

Volunteers may be ordinary people, chosen for their qualities rather than their qualifications, but they are extraordinary ordinary people. Not only are they carefully selected for their ability to listen actively and supportively, but also for:

- Their ability to communicate warmth.
- Seeing "people" not problems.
- Caring about "feelings" not facts.
- Being enablers rather than doers.
- Their tolerance, humility, patience and, metaphorically speaking, their willingness to stand alongside someone who is on the edge of the precipice of his/her life.

The selection process never stops. At any time a volunteer can be asked to leave if the quality of their befriending in any way diminishes. The ability to remain a volunteer, despite the harrowing and emotionally draining nature of befriending, comes from the strong and secure structure of support. Volunteers work within a code of practice that governs the way they respond to callers, and includes the promise of complete confidentiality, and respect for the right of those who contact us to make their own decisions, even if that decision is to die.

Through preparation and training, volunteers are helped to discover and make available that part of themselves that will provide the caller with emotional support that will help develop the foundation of a relationship of trust, on which a future can be built. Volunteers find a place beside the caller in the abyss of despair but do so without losing their own grasp on reality, safety and support. Most of the locally-based suicide prevention services have between 50 and 200 volunteers at any one time. One international voluntary organization has a total of 40,000 volunteers. The same organization estimates that nearly a million volunteers have been trained since its inception in 1953, a number which represents a significant contribution to society.

It is important at this point to consider any differences that might exist between the volunteer-based services that are exclusively focused on suicide prevention and those many others that exist to address a wide range of different social problems. Those agencies that exist to address such issues as relationship problems, drug and substance abuse, AIDS/HIV, homelessness, etc. will receive contact from those seeking specific interventions for which the agency exists, some of whom will be suffering from a degree of emotional distress with the possible outcome being suicide. Agencies, which are therefore cause-specific, will be likely to recruit their volunteer workers with particular regard to their knowledge and experience to the issue for which the agency exists.

Consequently, the ability of these workers to relate to clients whose emotional state is such as to bring suicide into sharp focus may be limited. This compares with those agencies (of which this chapter is the subject) which exist explicitly for those for whom suicide could be a real option. As discussed elsewhere, volunteers in suicide prevention agencies have at the very heart of their involvement the concept of the reality of suicide, together with risk assessment and intervention techniques.

One of the fundamental concerns in using volunteers in any service, particularly in one that is concerned in suicide prevention, where the stakes are so high, is that of the need to ensure consistent high standards of service provision. This carries with it the need for such agencies to invest time, energy and other resources into selection, training and supervision. There need to be clear unequivocal standards against which volunteers are constantly assessed. The absence of such standards and such assessments will create a high rate of failure, with a consequent likelihood of the user of the service suffering at the hands of the incompetent and inexperienced.

EFFECTIVENESS OF VOLUNTEERISM

Voluntary agencies have the reputation of being in the forefront of service development. Having established the areas of priority for initiating volunteer services, through the implementation of feasibility studies in which data is collated and influencing factors are explored, a full programme of service provision can be implemented. Such assessment is made on the basis of a community identifying a local need for provision of support for people in distress.

To deliver a service more effectively, it is increasingly important to define the parameters within which volunteers are required to focus their attention and it is essential to be as specific as possible in identifying particular groups where the risk of suicide appears to be high. Suicide has tended to be addressed in a narrow research focus and in terms of programme implementation. The findings are often of limited use. An example is the need for research that explores contemporary cultural perceptions of suicide in a specific context. By focusing on a specific community, within a specific social context, for example a rural community, it is hoped that a clear understanding will be found on the causes of suicide within the group. In drawing out such information, education initiatives can be effectively targeted, and the provision of care can be developed along more socially appropriate and culturally sensitive lines.

There are significant features that underpin the effectiveness of voluntary agencies in responding to community needs:

Availability

A response to a suicidal person alone and in despair in the middle of the night cannot necessarily be provided by a psychiatrist, especially in countries such as India, China, Brazil and other South American countries, where there is a shortage of mental health support. Suicidal urges can be impulsive and will not necessarily wait for appointments. The approach of the volunteer is to put feelings first, before appointments and schedules. The latter can be alien to the chaotic, sometimes illogical, nature of people who are emotionally needy. So often what is immediately required is someone to talk to, whether that someone is in the medical profession, the church or in the community as with lay people. Time is critical, both in terms of their cry for help and also in the immediacy of the risk to life: time to listen; time to support and time to help the painful feelings to be articulated gradually and with care; time that is available whenever it is needed, 24 hours a day, 365 days a year.

In, for example, the UK, the USA, Australia and Singapore, or in urban environments or ones in which telephones are the popular means of communication, this is frequently possible. In contrast, for a number of reasons, daytime availability is the only viable option in many developing countries because public transport closes down at night, cutting off access to both volunteer and the suicidal caller. Also, in many Asian and African countries it is not always thought suitable for females, whether callers or volunteers, to be out of the home after sunset.

Accessibility

In many developing countries, telephones are not widely available or not an accepted means of communication. In high-density towns in Brazil and Zimbabwe, remote rural areas of India and Southern Africa, among the elderly population in Hong Kong, who represent a high-risk group, private telephone facilities are limited. Therefore, essential direct face-to-face contact with volunteers has proved to be the most appropriate working model.

The suicide rate in the rural areas in Sri Lanka is particularly high: 118 per 100,000 recorded for 1994 in the North Central Province, where agriculture is principally paddy cultivation and cash crops (Keir and Whiting, 1996). Access to these remote areas is difficult and social conditions are bleak: geographical and psychological isolation is prevalent; psychiatric support is minimal and agricultural pesticides are readily available. For this reason, drop-in centres were established in remote villages and on tea plantations which can be reached by callers, who often travel long distances to talk of their distress and suicidal feelings to a volunteer. During an 18-month period of civil unrest in the early 1990s, when public transport was not available, the commitment of these volunteers was amply demonstrated, as they walked many kilometres to the centres in order to maintain the service.

The immediacy of help is made possible by the voluntary nature of the service, together with the sheer numbers of people who give their time in this way. In India and Sri Lanka, where there is a predominance of women volunteering, many suicide prevention centres (Hyderabad, Chennai, Cochin and Colombo) have no shortage of suitable recruits. In the Western world the social, political and economic factors impact significantly on the availability of both financial and human resources.

Acceptability

Provision of volunteer help to those in crisis has been an issue in countries where political and military constraints are apparent. Confidentiality and voluntary provision of help as an alternative to state mental health and social service provision are commonly alien and furthermore can be considered mutually exclusive. Under the Soviet regime, suicide was not recognized as a problem. It was maintained that the state provided adequately for its people, leaving them no cause for despair. With the fall of communism, however, the need for the provision of emotional support has become more openly recognizable and telephone helplines have proliferated.

Consideration must also be given to making the service acceptable to those who have no tradition of seeking emotional support from strangers. This is an issue in Africa, where historically help has been sought from the extended family. However, with the breakdown of such traditional support systems, the need for confidential befriending services provided from outside the family network is steadily increasing. Political developments and emerging societal trends in South Africa, for example, accentuate the need for evolving models of practice that are relevant, appropriate and comprehensive to the community that is served (Heslop, 1998). Although the process of urbanization required adaptation by all sections of the population, changes were often most traumatic for the black population. For example, the latter frequently have to cope with the physical transition of moving from rural to urban areas, large-scale contact with other population groups, as well as housing problems, adjustment to the market economy and, in particular, deterioration of the traditional support systems and systems of authority.

Adaptability

Because of the nature of the voluntary sector, with a strong emphasis on adaptability, flexibility and innovation, there is common drive among volunteers to identify local needs as seen by the community and not by the external policy advisors. Being adaptable to community needs is an essential requirement in providing valid suicide prevention services in changing societies, environments and geographical boundaries. The ability to identify specific high-risk groups has been obfuscated by changes in national boundaries and the movement of people. In the former Yugoslav Federation, a number of national suicide prevention initiatives were disrupted at the outbreak of war, but recently independent programmes have been activated in several of the newly formed countries. A crisis line, focusing on the needs of these high-risk groups, was established by a group of university professors. The volunteers, who were medical and psychology students, were trained and the centres are now active in the wider community.

In adapting to the changing needs of society, the voluntary sector has the potential to be particularly innovative when reaching out to those individuals who appear to be at highest risk, and who may be in the greatest need of the support that can be offered. Befriending schemes in prisons, and for people living in rural and isolated environments, are some examples. Befriending schemes are also being provided for certain occupational and age groups, those living in multicultural groups, those who have suffered the effects of unemployment, those who are homeless, and those who have already been diagnosed as mentally ill and are known to be at risk of suicide.

In response to concerns about the high rate of suicide of young men, an e-mail befriending service was established in the UK to look at alternative ways of increasing accessibility through the use of a medium acceptable to this group. As computers seem to be a medium many young people are comfortable with, communication by e-mail via the Internet seemed a possibility. Over 80% of the contacts made through this scheme acknowledged that they had suicidal feelings. E-mail is proving to be an effective way of reaching a group who are at greatest risk of suicide, who are notoriously difficult to reach, and who are often reluctant to talk about their feelings; it is a unique service that crosses all cultural, emotional and geographical boundaries.

THE ROLE OF VOLUNTARY AGENCIES IN SETTING THE PUBLIC AGENDA

In a study on suicide prevention activities within the European Union, it was found that volunteer-resourced suicide prevention agencies provided effective national coverage in only three countries: Germany, Ireland and the UK. However, the study also stated that other more generalist help-lines and services were available at a national level in a further two countries: France and Italy. It also drew attention to the lack of cohesive networks and the duplication of programmes (Befrienders International, 1995). In North America there are over 600 suicide prevention centres. Worldwide, a total of possibly 2,000 suicide prevention centres are serviced by volunteers. This does not take into account the thousands of telephone help-lines that are serving the specific needs of people, some of whom will be distressed and potentially suicidal.

Voluntary agencies have played a significant role by contributing to a national forum on suicide and its prevention. It was only in the 1990s that suicide, international volunteerism, programme design and activities were freely discussed in the People's Republic of China. Statistics on suicide have only recently become available. These indicate extremely high rates of suicide in young people, especially women, in rural areas (see Chapter 2). However, within the political climate during this period, the authorities have only allowed volunteer hot-lines to exist in the major cities.

As previously discussed, the recent breakdown of the Russian Federation has resulted in a more open approach to suicide prevention in some of the now independent countries. However, it is too early to assess the effect this will have in gaining a clearer perspective on the issues of suicide in this complex region. Volunteer activity has been difficult, due to the economic pressure, and yet a number of agencies have been operative for some time. In one old Eastern bloc country, where volunteer activity is illegal, a crisis hot-line for young people has been functioning successfully in areas where there are very few mental health professionals. Additionally, in conjunction with psychiatrists, a joint project in Estonia has been established and resourced by an international voluntary agency in order to facilitate research and initiate new targeted prevention programmes in specific communities.

Volunteers are invited into educational institutions, prisons, factories and commercial companies to provide sophisticated training programmes in listening skills and coping strategies. In recent years, greater proactivity in the community through the marketing of awareness programmes has resulted in specially designed awareness training being provided for the emergency services, such as the fire brigade, police and the nursing profession.

EVALUATING VOLUNTEER RESOURCED SUICIDE PREVENTION CENTRES

Studies have been conducted in several countries on the effectiveness of crisis intervention hot-lines in reducing suicide, the majority of which have produced conflicting results. The methodological complexity of such studies have been well recognized (Goldney, 1998) and the social and economic variables necessary to establish an accurate assessment has been clearly described (Barraclough et al, 1977). Gunnell and Frankel (1994) have outlined the requirement for a large population sample to allow effective assessment of the impact of any one suicide prevention initiative or strategy.

A number of studies have looked at the effectiveness of suicide prevention centres in reducing the rate of suicide in a community by comparing with areas where no such service is available. The results have been inconclusive if not conflicting, as was evident in the studies on the effectiveness of The Samaritans in the UK (Bagley, 1968; Barraclough et al, 1977; Lester, 1994). Over a period of 2 years (1997–1998) in Sri Lanka, a well-documented programme of trained volunteers regularly visited a village of 100 families, offering emotional support to people at risk and to families bereaved through suicide. The initial study of the data indicated (in direct comparison with a comparable neighbouring village without such services) a significant drop in attempted and completed suicide (Ratnayeke and Maracek, 1998). The initial findings of this volunteer programme concurred with the results of the study in Italy of the Tele-Check progamme for elderly persons at home, in which regular contact was made with elderly persons, resulting in a lower suicide rate among this vulnerable group (De Leo et al, 1995; see Chapter 31).

One aim of most suicide prevention centres will be that of raising awareness of suicide in the community, which by the nature of the activity could have a long-term impact that would be difficult to evaluate. Market research was undertaken in the UK to assess current public perception of a crisis intervention service. The study determined that there is (in the adult population) a 97% prompted awareness of The Samaritans (Ogilvy and Mather, 1998). Advertising as a service to which people in emotional crisis may call, this one organization receives more than 4 million calls annually.

CONCLUSION

The role of voluntary organizations is to act in conjunction with other community-based activities and to complement similar services. It is to provide a significant part of the service: alternative help, which neither duplicates nor competes in service provision. The relationships are based on strict guidelines for good practice, a willingness to collaborate and trust. Therefore, there continues to be a need for national suicide prevention strategies, which incorporate the volunteer networks and promote greater coordination of activities across the sectors. This in turn would result in the sharing of knowledge, information and the better use of resources. Increasing awareness of suicide would evolve from these strategies, encouraging those communities and countries that are enveloped in the stigma and legal implications of suicide to address the high rate of suicide among their people.

The key feature of an effective partnership in suicide prevention strategy is an understanding of the boundaries of the sectors, a clear role definition and trust. While resources continue to be limited, for whatever reason, the unnecessary repetition and duplication of services provided for those in crisis is unacceptable. In today's world, the constant cry from the consumer, user, patient or client is, "Why are we not asked what we need in order to survive"? A combination of medical, psychological and emotional support can be a successful recipe for a complex situation.

Collaboration is, therefore, a major component in suicide prevention if it is to be effective. It is important to recognize that preventing suicide is everybody's responsibility and therefore there is an onus on all of humanity to help shoulder this burden. Society cannot just rely on psychiatrists in particular or the medical profession in general, neither can responsibility be left to those simply labelled "psychologist" or "therapist" and the voluntary sector. If this premise is accepted, then logically it can be deduced that everybody has a responsibility to help promote the growth of volunteer work, to enable local communities to understand that distressed people will benefit from emotional support offered by other human beings. There needs to be a motivated collaborative effort to work together in reducing suicide worldwide.

REFERENCES

Bagley, C. (1968) The evaluation of a suicide prevention scheme by an ecological method. Social Science and Medicine, 2: 1–14.

Barraclough B.M., Jennings C. and Moss J.R. (1977) Suicide prevention by The Samaritans: a controlled study of effectiveness. Lancet, ii: 237–239.

Befrienders International (1995) Study of Suicide Prevention within the European Community, pp. 8–19. London: European Commission/Befrienders International.

Darvill, G. and Munday B. (1984) Volunteers in the Personal Social Services, pp. 17–25. London: Tavistock.

De Leo, D., Carrollo, G. and Dello Bueno, M. (1995) Lower suicide rates associated with a Tele-Help/Tele-Check service for the elderly at home. American Journal of Psychiatry, 152: 632–634.

Gaskin, K. and Davis Smith, J. (1997) A New Civic Europe? A Study of the Extent and Role of Volunteering, pp. 28–31. London: Volunteer Centre.

Gerard, D. (1983) Charities in Britain: Conservation and Change. London: Bedford Square Press.

Gidron, B. (1997) Patterns of Giving and Volunteering in the Israeli Public: Preliminary Results, pp. 24–25. Tel Aviv: Israeli Centre for Research of Non-profit Organizations at Ben-Gurion University.

Gunnell, D. and Frankel, S. (1994) Prevention of suicide: aspirations and evidence. British Medical Journal, 308: 1227–1233.

Guthrie, R. (1986) Aves Memorial Lecture 1986. London: Volunteer Centre.

Handy, C. (1988) Understanding Voluntary Organisations. London: Penguin.

Heslop, A.P. (1998) Models of volunteering in black townships: attitudes to suicide and prevention. London: Befrienders International.

Hotta, T. (1997)Volunteers in Japan. Tokyo: unpublished Foreign Press Center paper.

Keir, N. and Whiting, N. (1996) Study of Pesticide Related Suicide. London: Befrienders International.

Lester, D. (1994) Evaluating the effectiveness of The Samaritans in England and Wales. International Journal of Health Sciences, 5: 73–74.

Lyons, M. and Fabiansson, C. (1998) Is volunteering declining in Australia? Australian Journal of Volunteering, 3: 15–20.

Ogilvy and Mather, Plc (1998) Quantative Research Findings on Brand Awareness, Image and Usage. London: NOP Omnibus Survey.

Ratnayeke, L. and Marecek, J. (1998) Suicide prevention initiative in the rural community. Colombo, Sri Lanka: unpublished Sumithrayo paper.

Scott, V.M. (1989) Retaining Volunteers: a Significant Resource. London: London School of Economics, unpublished MSc thesis.

Van Til, J. (1989) Mapping the Third Sector: Voluntarism in a Changing Social Economy. London: Volunteer Centre.

Chapter 41

Future Perspectives

Keith Hawton
Department of Psychiatry, Oxford University, Oxford, UK
and
Kees van Heeringen
Department of Psychiatry, University Hospital, Gent, Belgium

Abstract

This Handbook has covered the major areas in the field of suicide and attempted suicide. In this chapter we take the opportunity to look into the future in terms of areas of need and likely fruitful developments. We consider, first, how knowledge of causes of suicidal behaviour might be advanced. There are many challenging areas for future research. These particularly include investigation of how biological, psychological and social factors interact during the process of the development of suicidal ideation and its translation into suicidal acts. It is argued that the limitations of the standard psychological autopsy approach, especially for the investigation of psychological, social, biological and genetic factors, necessitate more of a focus on survivors of serious suicide attempts defined in terms of physical danger and/or suicidal intent associated with their acts. Genetics research should probably focus on the genetic basis of personality risk factors for suicidal behaviour, such as aggression and impulsivity. Current brain imaging techniques should allow substantial steps to be taken to investigate the morphological and functional substrates that may be relevant to suicidal behaviour. The reasons why co-morbidity is so important in suicide and attempted suicide require elucidation, particularly the chronological sequence of development of disorders and the extent to which they have a common biological or psychological basis. It is clear that there are several important subgroups of people at high risk of suicidal behaviour which require further close examination. We highlight developments that are needed with regard to treatment of suicide attempters and other people at risk, especially investigation of pragmatic therapies in studies with sufficient statistical power to advance our knowledge of what psychosocial and pharmacological approaches are truly effective. We go on to make a plea for improved care of those who have suffered the impact of suicidal behaviour in someone close to them. Finally, we examine key aspects of programmes for the prevention of suicide and attempted suicide, particularly the impor-

The International Handbook of Suicide and Attempted Suicide. Edited by K. Hawton and K. van Heeringen.

tance of integration of population-based strategies with strategies targeted towards high-risk groups.

RESEARCH NEEDS CONCERNING THE CAUSES OF SUICIDAL BEHAVIOUR

The Relationship between Biological, Psychological and Sociological Factors in the Aetiology of Suicidal Behaviour

It has become very apparent in the past decade or two that the causes of suicide and attempted suicide are multifactorial and that we particularly need more information on the relationships and interactions between biological, psychological and sociological factors. The design of research investigations should take this into account. Much is likely to be gained from multidisciplinary investigations in which the skills of researchers from different backgrounds are integrated, such that studies are designed in ways that can explore and clarify these interrelationships. A clearly fruitful area is the impact of stress, especially that which leads to a sense of entrapment, first on development of suicidal ideation and feelings of hopelessness, and second on biological substrates thought to be important in suicidal behaviour. As Träskmann-Bendz and Mann have made clear in Chapter 4, these biological mechanisms should, of course, include the serotonergic system, but other related systems also ought to be examined. These particularly include any systems likely to be affected by altered activity of the hypothalamic–pituitary–adrenocortical axis.

There are several reasons to include personality traits or temperament styles in future research. As described in Chapter 14, suicidal behaviour is to be regarded as the result of some degree of state–trait interaction. As such traits or temperamental styles are, at least in part, heritable and stable over time, their identification may well lead to early recognition of individuals at risk. The study of temperament may also have clinical applications. Temperamental characteristics may be useful for the classification of attempted suicide patients who form heterogeneous groups with regard to clinical features and outcome. As will be discussed later in this chapter, the delineation and more detailed study of subgroups of suicides or attempted suicide may contribute substantially to our understanding of suicidal behaviour. Moreover, temperament is currently the strongest predictor of response to antidepressant treatment in depressed patients. In view of the limited effect of currently available treatments on the repetition of suicidal behaviour, the extent to which temperament also predicts the response to treatments of suicidal ideation and behaviour can be considered a research priority.

A key question about suicide risk is why and how individuals with risk factors, especially those relating to personality or temperamental styles, become suicidal in relation to stressful events. In other words, how do events impact on mental mechanisms to initiate the psychological and biological stages of the suicidal process? There is a need to conduct more laboratory-style studies in which vulnerable individuals can be exposed to stressful stimuli that simulate those faced in real life. Such studies might focus on problem solving and factors that lead to frustration and development of a sense of entrapment and hopelessness. There is a particular need to relate such developments to general styles of coping in ways that can indicate potential therapeutic strategies that might modify this process.

The role of depression in influencing psychological processes is clearly crucial to understanding how suicidal thoughts develop and requires further exploration. One approach might be the use of mood induction procedures, particularly in individuals susceptible to major shifts in mood and suicidal ideation, in order to examine how cognitive mechanisms related to suicidality change with mood. Because of questions about the extent to which induced mood changes truly mirror naturally occurring shifts in mood, one might instead examine patients who show frequent major mood changes. Another approach might be the use of tryptophan depletion to induce mood changes in patients who have suffered from depression (Smith et al, 1997).

Beyond the Psychological Autopsy Approach

Much of our knowledge about risk factors for suicide has come from psychological autopsy studies (Shneidman, 1981; Hawton et al, 1998a; see Chapters 7–11). There are several reasons, however, why the extent and quality of information that can be gained from this approach is severely limited. One is the refusal of some potential informants to be interviewed; this is often more of a problem in the recruitment of informants for controls than in recruiting relatives and friends as informants for suicide victims, but either way it can clearly lead to biased and possibly misleading findings. Probably more important are the severe limitations on the range of factors that can be examined in psychological autopsy studies. This approach can be reasonably informative about psychiatric and personality disorders, and life events and problems, that are associated with suicide—although even these items have their limitations—but the approach cannot tell us much about the psychological mechanisms that are so fundamental to the suicidal process. Also, there are severe limitations on the extent to which biological factors can be investigated. In future, therefore, it is likely that there will be much more emphasis on investigations of survivors of serious suicide attempts, who can be viewed as living would-be suicide victims. This approach is highly attractive, especially as such individuals can be followed-up and, for example, the process of development of future suicidal thinking examined. It will allow full investigation of biological, psychological, psychiatric, social and genetic factors. One serious methodological problem inherent in this approach, however, is how to define what constitutes a "severe attempt" and ideally one that is truly a "failed suicide". Definition of such cases should incorporate not just the physical danger of an act of self-harm (e.g. attempted hanging, survivor of car exhaust poisoning, antidepressant overdose which causes cardiac arrythmia) but also serious suicidal intent. This is because of the considerable ignorance many people have about the physical dangers of certain methods, especially self-poisoning. However, it is feasible to overcome this problem, and perhaps to develop standard criteria for identification of individuals who should be included, so as to allow informative comparison between the findings of different studies.

Epidemiological Research

The field of epidemiological investigation of suicidal behaviour has advanced considerably in recent years, developments in case control designs and in multivariate statistical procedures being key features in this. Further developments could accrue from standardization of case identification for both suicide and deliberate self-harm. The former will continue to be limited while there remain such vast differences between the official procedures used to define suicides in different countries. Standardization of approaches would be a highly significant step forward but one that at present looks unlikely. It would perhaps be most likely to come about by development of research criteria for causes of death in the ICD and DSM diagnostic systems. Standardization of criteria for identification of deliberate self-harm, including subcategories of types of acts, would be another important step that could lead to improved data for use in epidemiological and other research approaches.

The need for more large-scale longitudinal investigations is very clear. Much reliance has been placed on identification of risk factors for suicidal behaviour from cross-sectional studies. However, the longitudinal design is a much more powerful and informative approach. This was demonstrated clearly in a birth cohort longitudinal study in New Zealand, in which it was possible to examine the relationship between childhood and early factors and adolescent suicide attempts that had occurred in the sample by the age of 16 years (Fergusson and Lynskey, 1995). Because of the relative rarity of suicidal acts (especially suicide), even in high-risk groups, such studies are much more likely to be productive if they are large. This is especially so when the interactions between risk factors are to be examined. Also, the study period may have to be prolonged.

Many investigations to date have, understandably, focused on risk factors. We will gain further valuable information relevant to treatment and prevention investigations from in-depth examination of individuals or broader epidemiological approaches if they also focus on factors that protect against the development of suicidal thinking and translation of such thoughts into suicidal acts. It is also likely to be informative to try to determine why and how events and experiences tip the scales such that the influence of protective factors is nullified and the option of a suicidal act becomes more attractive.

Genetics Research

The field of genetics in general, especially molecular genetics, is advancing at a rapid rate. As Roy and colleagues have described in Chapter 13, there is clearly a significant genetic contribution to suicide risk but at present we are largely ignorant of the mechanisms underlying this. It seems inherently unlikely that suicidal behaviour itself has a specific genetic basis, but it is entirely credible that genetic factors may influence attributes that enhance suicide risk. At present the most fruitful area appears to be that of genetic subtypes or polymorphisms of monoamine receptors or transporter systems, with the serotonergic system being that which might repay particular attention. Several aspects of investigations in this area require refinement. These include, as noted earlier, standardization of case definition, plus use of sufficiently large samples to increase the chance of detection of reliable findings and careful screening of control populations. Again, such investigations might usefully be conducted on survivors of "serious suicide attempts". These studies might also include examination of the relationship of genetic factors to other risk factors, including personality and temperamental variables (e.g. impulsivity, aggression).

Structural and Functional Brain Imaging

The technique of neuro-imaging as a powerful research method in neuroscience is also advancing rapidly. Imaging techniques make it possible to study *in vivo* structures and functions of the central nervous system which, until only very recently, could only be studied post-mortem, with inherent methodological shortcomings, as described by Träskman-Bendz and Mann in Chapter 4. A number of structural imaging studies using magnetic resonance imaging (MRI) have been conducted in patients with mood disorders (for an overview, see Soares and Mann, 1997). For example, quantitative volumetric analyses in depressed patients have shown reductions in size of the frontal lobe, basal ganglia and hippocampus, and enlargement of the pituitary gland. Many of these findings appear to support the model of suicidal behaviour as described in Chapter 14 of this Handbook. However, no studies to date have focused specifically on correlates of suicidal behaviour among depressed patients. Moreover, the clinical utility of such findings is severely limited, as no norms are yet available and considerable within-group variations have been found. There is an equally great need for comparative functional neuro-imaging studies in individuals who have shown suicidal behaviour, using functional magnetic resonance imaging (MRI), positron-emission tomography (PET) or single photon-emission tomography (SPET). Such techniques offer a unique possibility to study the neurobiological and biochemical substrates of suicidal behaviour. Particularly interesting will be the functional study of potentially involved brain structures by means of biochemical or (neuro-) psychological challenge techniques. This approach will offer the opportunity to study the central nervous system equivalent of the blunted neuroendocrine responses seen in depressed patients, particularly those who have attempted suicide (see Chapter 4). Longitudinal designs will make it possible to study the trait- or state-dependent character of identified risk factors, such as hypoactivity of the serotonergic system.

The Importance of Co-morbidity

As discussed in several chapters in this Handbook, studies of both suicides and suicide attempters have shown that co-morbidity of psychiatric and personality disorders, especially depression, alcohol abuse disorders and personality disorders, makes an extremely important contribution to risk of suicidal behaviour. This is found across the age span, although most predominantly in younger people who engage in suicidal behaviour. We need to know more about the nature of co-morbidity, including its origins and exactly how it contributes to suicide risk. For example, what is the chronological pattern of the development of disorders, particularly in relation to the development of suicidality? An important contribution in this direction has been the finding by Shaffer and colleagues (1996) that in those adolescents who died by suicide in New York who had co-morbid diagnoses of conduct disorder, substance abuse and depression, the sequence in which these developed was usually, first, conduct disorder, then substance abuse, and finally depression leading to hopelessness and suicide. It would also be valuable to determine whether there is a common substrate to co-morbidity, be this biological, psychological, or both. Such information could increase our knowledge of how this lethal combination is best treated.

Investigation of Subgroups

There has been an understandable move towards delineation and investigation of subgroups of suicides and suicide attempters. These include, for example, groups defined according to the nature of psychiatric or personality disorders, and also groups defined by age group. Such an approach has helped to identify specific risk factors for suicidal behaviour in, for example, individuals with depression (see Chapter 7), schizophrenia (see Chapter 8) and alcohol abuse disorders (see Chapter 9). It has also facilitated awareness of risk factors that are specific to the very young (see Chapter 17) and the very elderly (see Chapter 18). This will continue to be a valuable direction for research, although the limitations inherent in the search for risk factors for suicidal behaviour, which were identified by Goldney in Chapter 33, must always temper the extent of our expectations. However, this avenue of research should increase our awareness of specific treatment approaches and prevention strategies for subgroups of individuals.

TREATMENT

Potential Developments in Treatment

In this Handbook the current status of treatments for suicide attempters and people with suicidal ideation has been reviewed in detail (Chapters 27, 28 29 and 32). It is clear that there is much room for further developments. The following are some of the needs, each including a requirement for proper evaluation:

1. It is essential that pragmatic brief therapies suitable for a sizeable proportion of suicide attempters be developed. These should utilize knowledge about psychological mechanisms and vulnerability factors that lead to attempted suicide and are associated with its repetition.
2. There would appear to be a place for the development of a stepped-care approach to treatment of suicide attempters, in which the intensity of treatment depends on the response to initial brief therapy (e.g. problem solving). Thus, if this initial approach appears ineffective for some patients, they could then be offered more prolonged or intensive therapy, perhaps based on the principles of a full programme of cognitive-behavioural therapy as developed and shown to be effective for a range of psychiatric disorders (Hawton et al, 1989).
3. Specific treatments may be necessary for subgroups of attempters, especially those classified according to psychiatric diagnoses. For example, patients with alcohol abuse may benefit from an approach that combines specific treatment for the substance abuse, with psychological treatment aimed at helping with the vulnerability many such individuals appear to have in coping with loss experiences and which seems to be a specific risk factor for suicide in this group (see Chapter 9).
4. There is clearly a major need for the development of effective treatments for individuals with those personality disorders that are particularly associated with risk of suicidal behaviour. These include borderline and dissocial disorders (see Chapter 10). The innovative work of Linehan and colleagues (1991; see Chapter 28) in relation to female patients with borderline personality disorders represents an important step forward that must help overcome the therapeutic nihilism which many clinicians experience when faced by patients with personality disorders, especially those who have engaged in suicidal behaviour. Further developments may also result from initiatives in which psychological therapies are combined with pharmacological treatments.
5. Very little progress has been made in the treatment of repetitive self-cutting. Often this is a symptom of a personality disorder but, nevertheless, initiatives are required to find techniques to modify the sequence of feelings and thoughts that culminate in this behaviour (see e.g. Hawton, 1990).
6. There is much room for investigation of a range of potential pharmacological treatments for suicidal behaviour and ideation. One example is further

evaluation of the potential for neuroleptics to reduce repetitive self-harm (Montgomery et al, 1979; see Chapter 27). This might include investigation of the potential effectiveness of the newer generation atypical neuroleptics in this role. Another example is investigation of whether antidepressants differ in the speed and extent to which they reduce suicidal ideation. Given the very strong association between depressive disorders and suicidal behaviour, there is a major need to determine whether long-term maintenance with antidepressants after recovery from depression in people with particular risk factors (e.g. recurrent depressive episodes and a history of attempted suicide) prevents future suicidal acts.

Methodological Aspects of Treatment Research

The gold standard for the evaluation of treatments is the randomized controlled trial. Review of the worldwide literature on studies of treatments of suicide attempters indicates that most investigations conducted so far have had serious methodological flaws (Hawton et al, 1998b; see Chapters 28 and 29). These include patient samples far too small to allow detection of clinically significant differences (e.g. in repetition of self-harm) at a statistically significant level, poor description of the content of treatments (especially of control treatments), and paucity of outcome variables. Because of these problems, especially too-small sample sizes, we lack a sound scientific basis on which to shape clinical services for suicide attempters. It is strongly recommended that, except in pilot studies, future evaluations of treatment should be designed to have sufficient statistical power to detect differences between outcomes of clinical importance at a statistically significant level. This will inevitably involve relatively large samples of subjects, often far greater than those which can be assembled in one centre within a reasonable time period. Thus, future treatment studies will often need to be carried out in multiple centres, possibly in more than one country. In addition to the greater likelihood of getting definitive answers from such studies, carrying them out in several centres is more likely to indicate the potential generalizability of the findings.

Treatment studies, be they primarily psychosocial or pharmacological investigations, should include more attention to the process of change. Verification of prior hypotheses about *how* treatments are thought to work will add to the confidence in the findings of studies and is likely to enhance the development of future treatments that include similar approaches. Treatment process research usually necessitates costly extra assessments, but these can often be conducted on a subsample of the overall patient population, as differentiation between process measures for different treatment approaches does not usually necessitate the sort of sample sizes necessary for evaluation of outcome of treatments.

There is also a need to identify important prognostic factors that can be used in clinical practice to distinguish between patients likely to respond to treatment and those who are less likely to benefit. Investigation of prognostic factors usually requires fairly large samples of patients.

PROVISION OF HELP FOR PEOPLE WHO HAVE EXPERIENCED SUICIDAL ACTS IN PEOPLE CLOSE TO THEM

Clark and Goldney (Chapter 26) have very clearly described the nature and extent of problems that are experienced by most people who have suffered the loss of someone close to them because of suicide. Yet in most countries there is an alarming paucity of services to which they can turn for help. It is usually fortuitous if those who wish for help can find effective support. This has probably been highlighted further with the increase in suicide rates in young people that has occurred in many countries and the long-lasting consequences such suicides usually have on parents, siblings and friends. The rapidly growing "survivors" groups that have developed in several countries are testimony to the extent of need. A good case can be made for the development of support programmes, be they established by survivors' groups or by statutory agencies, that might be offered pro-actively through agencies such as coroners' offices.

Most attention in the literature has been paid to the impact of completed suicide. We know very little about the impact that suicide attempts can have on other people. Yet this may also be substantial and therefore merits clinical investigation in order to determine what help might usefully be incorporated within broader treatment approaches for suicide attempters and those close to them.

PREVENTION OF SUICIDAL BEHAVIOUR

Population and High-risk Group Strategies

Attention is being paid by increasing numbers of governments throughout the world to prevention of suicide and attempted suicide. These programmes need to include integration of a variety of approaches. Prevention programmes should be based as far as possible on sound evidence rather than idealistic thinking. Careful consideration is required to determine which strategies are likely to have the greatest impact. In particular, planners need to give careful thought to the potential role of population-based and high-risk group strategies (Lewis et al, 1997; see Chapter 34). The former are generally likely to have a greater impact than the latter (Rose, 1992), yet most attention tends to be focused on strategies targeted at high-risk groups. It should be remembered that, for example, a quarter or less of people who die by suicide have been in contact with psychiatric services during the year before their deaths (Appleby et al, 1999) and thus potentially accessible to preventive efforts by these services. Therefore, most impact is likely to result from a combination of prevention strategies. These should be directed partly at the factors that increase the risk of suicidal behaviour in a population (e.g. availability of dangerous means for suicidal acts, knowledge and attitudes of the population concerning the prevalence, nature and treatability of mental disorders, and media portrayal of suicidal behaviour) and partly at recognized high-risk groups (e.g. people with recurrent depressive disorders, suicide attempters, and people with certain co-morbid mental and personality disorders).

Evaluation of Prevention Strategies

Evaluation of preventive measures is extremely problematic (Gunnel and Frankel, 1994), mainly because of the relative rarity of suicidal acts and therefore the difficulty of demonstrating the impact of strategies. Also, it is unusual for only a single measure to be applied at one time so that it can be difficult to determine which specific strategy has been effective. Nevertheless, efforts should be made to evaluate prevention programmes, including their specific elements. Careful evaluation can not only indicate whether or not a specific strategy should be continued but can also be informative for planners in other countries.

The Role of Suicide Prevention Targets

Some countries have also introduced suicide prevention targets. In the UK, for example, there was a target to reduce the overall suicide rate by 15% between 1992 and 2000 (Department of Health, 1992). This has been replaced by a new target, namely to reduce the suicide rate by 20% by 2010 (Department of Health, 1999). Are such targets helpful? Overall they probably are, provided they are not seen as targets solely for the attention of clinical services but to encourage a broad-based approach. The main usefulness of a target is probably not so much whether or not it is achieved (in fact, as shown in Chapter 34, considerable progress has been made to achieving the previous UK target). Rather, it the its role of a target as a guiding beacon that can lead to the problem of suicidal behaviour being taken more seriously and galvanize more active planning of national policy to improve mental health and mental health care.

Voluntary Agencies

Lastly, it is important to emphasize the role of voluntary agencies within national suicide prevention policy. Voluntary agencies such as The Samaritans are accessed by many people who do not have contact with either statutory health care or social agencies. This potential has been enhanced by innovative developments, such as outreach programmes to provide support to people in rural areas and in prisons, and through the introduction of e-mail counselling.

While evaluation of the effectiveness of voluntary agencies is extremely difficult, particularly because of the necessary confidentiality of the interactions of volunteers with people who contact them, it is nonetheless important that their role within a national prevention programme is acknowledged and supported.

CONCLUSIONS

In this chapter we have considered just some of the important directions in which we think our field should be moving during the early years of this new millenium. It has by no means been a comprehensive perspective. Readers will no doubt have their own ideas about other needs that can be added to the list. It is hoped, however, that some of the directions we have suggested will stimulate new clinical developments, research initiatives and prevention planning efforts. The last millenium ended with an increasingly strong momentum in many countries of the world to tackle their problems of suicide and attempted suicide seriously. We hope that this Handbook will contribute to sustaining this progress and that yet more countries will begin to address these ultimate indicators of personal pain and distress.

REFERENCES

Appleby, L., Shaw, J., Amos, T., McDonnell, R., Harris, C., McCann, K., Kiernan, K., Davies, S., Bickley, H. and Parsons, R. (1999) Suicide within 12 months of contact with mental health services: national clinical survey. British Medical Journal, 318: 1235–1239.

Department of Health (1992) The Health of the Nation. London: HMSO.

Department of Health (1999) Saving Lives: Our Healthier Nation: A Contract for Health. Cm4386. London: The Stationery Office.

Fergusson, D.M. and Lynskey, M.T. (1995) Childhood circumstances, adolescent adjustment, and suicide attempts in a New Zealand birth cohort. Journal of the American Academy of Child and Adolescent Psychiatry, 34: 612–622.

Gunnell, D. and Frankel, S. (1994) Prevention of suicide: aspirations and evidence. British Medical Journal, 308: 1227–1233.

Hawton, K. (1990) Self-cutting: can it be prevented? In K. Hawton and P. Cowen (Eds), Dilemmas and Difficulties in the Management of Psychiatric Patients, pp. 91–103. Oxford: Oxford University Press.

Hawton, K., Salkovskis, P.M., Kirk, J. and Clark, D.M. (1989) Cognitive Behaviour Therapy for Psychiatric Problems: A Practical Guide. Oxford: Oxford University Press.

Hawton, K., Appleby, L., Platt, S., Foster, T., Cooper, J., Malmberg, A. and Simkin, S. (1998a) The psychological autopsy approach to studying suicide: a review of methodological issues. Journal of Affective Disorders, 50: 271–278.

Hawton, K., Arensman, E., Townsend, E., Bremner, S., Feldman, E., Goldney, R., Gunnell, D., Hazell, P., van Heeringen, K., House, A., Owens, D., Sakinofsky, I. and Träskman-

Bendz, L. (1998b) Deliberate self-harm: a systematic review of the efficacy of psychosocial and pharmacological treatments in preventing repetition. British Medical Journal, 317: 441–447.

Linehan, M.M., Armstrong, H.E., Suarez, A., Allmon, D. and Heard, H. (1991) Cognitive-behavioral treatment of chronically parasuicidal borderline patients. Archives of General Psychiatry, 48: 1060–1064.

Lewis, G., Hawton, K. and Jones, P. (1997) Strategies for preventing suicide. British Journal of Psychiatry, 171: 351–354.

Montgomery, S.A., Montgomery, D.B., Jayanthi-Rani, S., Roy, D.H., Shaw, P.J. and McAuley, R. (1979) Maintenance therapy in repeat suicidal behaviour: a placebo controlled trial. Proceedings of the 10th International Congress for Suicide Prevention and Crisis Intervention, pp. 227–229.

Rose, G. (1992) The Strategy of Preventive Medicine. Oxford: Oxford University Press.

Shaffer, D., Gould, M., Fisher, P., Trautman, P., Moreau, D., Kleinman, M. and Flory, M. (1996) Psychiatric diagnosis in child and adolescent suicide. Archives of General Psychiatry, 53: 339–348.

Shneidman, E.S. (1981) The psychological autopsy. Suicide and Life-Threatening Behavior, 11: 325–340.

Smith, K.A., Fairburn, C.G. and Cowen, P.J. (1997) Relapse of depression after rapid depletion of tryptophan. Lancet, 349: 915–919.

Soares, J.C. and Mann, J.J. (1997) The anatomy of mood disorders: review of structural neuro-imaging studies. Biological Psychiatry, 41: 86–106.

Author Index

Subject Index